Basic Medical Microbiology

FIFTH EDITION

Robert F. Boyd, Ph.D.

Little, Brown and Company
Boston New York Toronto London

Fifth Edition

Library of Congress Cataloging-in-Publication Data

Boyd, Robert F.
Basic medical microbiology / Robert F. Boyd.—5th ed.
p. cm.
Includes bibliographical references and index.
ISBN 0-316-10445-0
1. Medical microbiology.
[DNLM: 1. Microbiology. QW 4 B789b 1995]
QR46.B65 1995
616.01—dc20
DNLM/DLC
for Library of Congress 94-24134
CIP

Printed in the United States of America

KP

Editorial: Evan R. Schnittman, Kristin Odmark
Production Editor: Anne Holm
Copyeditor: Mary Babcock
Indexer: Robert F. Boyd
Production Supervisor: Louis C. Bruno, Jr.
Designer: William T. Donnelly
Cover Designer: Hannus Design Associates
Cover Illustration: Peg Gerrity

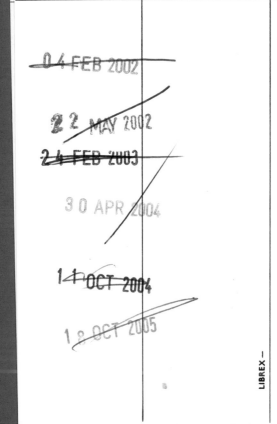

Basic Medical Microbiology

To the memory of Bryan Hoerl, friend, colleague, and coauthor of previous editions. His dedication to excellence in the teaching of infectious diseases made this book possible, and he will be sorely missed.

Contents

Under the Microscope xiii

Preface xv

PART I
General Bacteriology 1

CHAPTER 1
Scope and History of Microbiology 3
Scope, 4
History, 4
Modern Microbiology, 9

CHAPTER 2
Characteristics of Bacteria 11
Classification and Nomenclature, 12
Bacterial Structure and Function, 14
Cytoplasmic Membrane, 16
Cell Wall, 18
Extracellular Polymeric Substances (Capsules and Slime Layers), 22
Flagella and Other Structures Associated with Movement, 22
Pili (Fimbriae), 23
Structures Within the Cytoplasm, 24

CHAPTER 3
Microbial Metabolism 29
Enzymes: Biological Catalysts, 30
How Microbial Cells Produce Energy, 34
Metabolic Processes That Generate Energy, 35
Biosynthesis: A Process That Utilizes Energy, 41
Control of Metabolic Activity, 42

CHAPTER 4
Microbial Growth 46
Growth of Bacterial Cells, 47
Chemical Requirements for Growth, 48
Physical Requirements for Growth, 51
Cultivation of Microbial Species, 52
Techniques for Isolating Bacteria, 54
Preservation of Isolated Microorganisms, 56
Laboratory Measurement of Microbial Growth, 56

CHAPTER 5
Microbial Genetics 61
Nucleic Acids: The Basis of Heredity, 62
DNA Structure and Replication, 63
DNA Transcription, 66
Translation of the Genetic Code: Protein Synthesis, 66
Control of Protein Synthesis, 67
Mutation, 69
DNA Transfer Other Than in Cell Division, 74
Plasmids, 78
DNA Transfer and Infectious Disease, 79

CHAPTER 6
Biotechnology and Medicine 82
Genetic Engineering and Recombinant DNA, 83
Overview of Events in Producing Recombinant DNA, 83
Polymerase Chain Reaction, 86
Medical Applications of Genetic Engineering, 89

PART II
Control of Microorganisms 91

CHAPTER 7
Sterilization and Disinfection 93
Terminology, 94
General Considerations, 95
Physical Methods, 95
Chemical Methods, 98
Disinfection of Critical Instruments, 102
Disinfection of Semicritical Instruments, 102
Disinfection of Noncritical Items, 102
Practical Recommendations, 103

CHAPTER 8
Chemotherapy 104
General Characteristics of Chemotherapeutic Agents, 105
Chemotherapeutic Agents, 106

PART III
Immunology 127

CHAPTER 9
Nonspecific Host Resistance 129
Nonspecific vs. Specific Immunity, 130
Cellular Mechanism of Antimicrobial Defense, 130
Noncellular Mechanisms of Defense, 139

CHAPTER 10
Antigens and Antibodies 143
Antigens, 144
Immunoglobulins (Antibodies), 145
Antibody Diversity, 150
Immunoglobulins as Antigens, 152
Antigens and Antibodies in Immunodiagnosis, 153

CHAPTER 11
Cells and Tissues of the Immune System 155
Primary Lymphoid Organs and Tissues, 156
Secondary Lymphoid Organs and Tissues, 156
Major Histocompatibility Complex, 157
Cytokines, 158
Lymphoid Cells, 160
Non-T, Non-B Lymphocytes, 165
Mononuclear and Polymorphonuclear Phagocytes, 165

CHAPTER 12
The Immune Response (Humoral vs. Cell-Mediated Immunity) 168
Chemical Regulators of the Immune Response, 169
Nonspecific Defenses Against Microorganisms, 172
Specific Defenses Against Microorganisms, 173
Immunity Through Vaccination, 177

CHAPTER 13
Immunological Disorders 183
Immunodeficiency Diseases, 184
Hypersensitivities, or Allergies, 185
Autoimmune Diseases, 193
Graft Rejection and Transplantation Immunology, 194
Tumor Immunology (Cancer and the Immune System), 196

PART IV
Host-Parasite Interaction 201

CHAPTER 14
Microorganisms as Commensals and Parasites 203
Microorganisms as Commensals and Parasites, 204
Terminology Associated with the Infectious Disease Process, 205
Host Factors Affecting the Disease Process, 206
Microbial Factors and the Disease Process, 211

CHAPTER 15
Epidemiology 220
Clinical Stages of Disease in the Host, 221
Reservoirs and Sources of Disease, 222
Transmission of Infectious Microorganisms, 225
Patterns of Disease in the Community, 230
Laboratory Techniques in Epidemiology, 232

PART V
Bacteria That Cause Infectious Disease 237

CHAPTER 16
Clinical Microbiology 239
Specimen Collection, 240
Laboratory Identification, 240
Antimicrobial Susceptibility Testing, 243
Computers in the Clinical Laboratory, 243
Laboratory Safety, 243
Terminology, 244

CHAPTER 17
The Gram-Positive Cocci 246
The Staphylococci, 247
Staphylococcus aureus, 247
The Micrococci, 252
The Streptococci, 252

CHAPTER 18
Gram-Negative Diplococci: The *Neisseria* and Related Genera 263
Neisseria, 264
Neisseria meningitidis—The Meningococcus, 264
Neisseria gonorrhoeae—The Gonococcus, 267
Other Members of the Neisseriaceae, 270

CHAPTER 19
The Gram-Positive Sporeformers: The Bacilli and Clostridia 272
Bacillus, 273
Clostridium, 275

CHAPTER 20
***Corynebacterium diphtheriae* and Related Bacteria** **284**
Corynebacterium diphtheriae, 285
Other Corynebacteria, *Listeria,* and *Erysipelothrix rhusiopathiae,* 288

CHAPTER 21
Gram-Negative Enteric Bacteria **292**
Characteristics of the Enterobacteriaceae, 293
Isolation of the Enterobacteriaceae, 294
Screening and Identification of the Enterobacteriaceae, 295
Escherichia coli, 296
Salmonella, 298
Shigella, 302
Yersinia, 305
Opportunistic Enteric Bacilli, 308

CHAPTER 22
***Pseudomonas* and Related Organisms** **310**
Pseudomonas aeruginosa, 311
Other *Pseudomonas* Species and Related Bacilli, 313

CHAPTER 23
Vibrionaceae **315**
Vibrio, 316
Aeromonas, 318
Plesiomonas, 319

CHAPTER 24
Gram-Negative Coccobacillary Aerobic Bacteria **321**
Hemophilus, 322
Bordetella, 324
Brucella, 326
Francisella, 327

CHAPTER 25
Mycobacteria **330**
Mycobacterium tuberculosis, 331
Nontuberculous Mycobacterioses, 336
Mycobacterium leprae, 337

CHAPTER 26
Spirochetes and Spiral and Curved Rods **340**
The Spirochetes, 341
Spiral and Curved Rods, 349

CHAPTER 27
Mycoplasmas and L-forms **354**
General Characteristics of the Mycoplasmas, 355
General Characteristics of L-forms, 355
Pathogenesis, 356
Laboratory Diagnosis, 356
Treatment and Prevention, 357

CHAPTER 28
Rickettsiae and Chlamydiae **358**
The Rickettsiae, 359
The Chlamydiae, 363

CHAPTER 29
Actinomycetes **368**
Actinomycosis, 369
Nocardiosis and Actinomycetoma, 371
Caries, Periodontal Disease, and Actinomycetes, 372

CHAPTER 30
Miscellaneous Pathogens **374**
Legionella, 376

PART VI
Virology 379

CHAPTER 31
Viruses **381**
Animal Viruses, 382
Bacterial Viruses, 403

CHAPTER 32
Viral Diseases **407**
DNA Viruses and Associated Diseases, 409
RNA Viruses and Associated Diseases, 421

PART VII
Medical Mycology 463

CHAPTER 33
The Pathogenic Fungi **465**
Characteristics of the Fungi, 466
Fungal Diseases, 474

PART VIII
Medical Parasitology 497

CHAPTER 34
Protozoa, Helminths, and Arthropods **499**
General Characteristics of Parasites and Parasitic Infections, 500
The Protozoa, 503
The Nemathelminthes, 517
The Platyhelminthes, 523
The Arthropoda, 527

PART IX
Hospital Infections 531

CHAPTER 35
Hospital-Acquired Diseases **533**
Epidemiology, 534
Factors Important in Nosocomial Infections, 536
Prevention and Control of Nosocomial Infections, 543

Appendices

APPENDIX A
Observation of Microorganisms: Microscopy and Staining **549**

APPENDIX B
Immunological Tests **560**

APPENDIX C
Tables of Infectious Disease Based on Body Site **575**

APPENDIX D
Tables of Human Microflora **585**

APPENDIX E
Vaccines, Toxoids, and Immune Globulins 588

APPENDIX F
Table of Infectious Diseases Reportable to the Centers for Disease Control 590

Glossary 592

Additional Readings 606

Index 619

Under the Microscope

1. Dr. Ehrlich's "Magic Bullets" ... 9
2. Sulfur and Enzymatic Activity ... 32
3. Gene Probes ... 87
4. Amphotericin B and Liposomes ... 110
5. Defensins: Natural Peptide Antibiotics Produced by Humans and Animals ... 132
6. Tumor Necrosis Factor, Endotoxin, and Gram-Negative Septicemia ... 160
7. Treatment for SCID Patients Who Are ADA-Deficient ... 185
8. The Imported Fire Ant and Anaphylactic Reactions ... 187
9. Avoiding Iron Overload ... 211
10. Biofilms and Adhesion ... 213
11. Adenyl Cyclase and Bacterial Virulence ... 216
12. Superantigens ... 250
13. Changing Streptococcal Epidemiology ... 255
14. Plasmid-Mediated Antimicrobial Resistance in *Neisseria gonorrhoeae* ... 269
15. Fish Botulism ... 277
16. Botulinal Toxin for Human Treatment ... 278
17. Acne and *Propionibacterium acnes* ... 288
18. Typhoid Mary ... 300
19. *Salmonella* as Vaccine Vectors ... 302
20. *Shigella* and the Genetics of Virulence ... 303
21. Slime Exopolysaccharide and Hospital-Associated Infections ... 313
22. Biological False-Negatives and Syphilis ... 346
23. Guillain-Barré Syndrome and *Campylobacter* ... 351
24. Laboratory Diagnosis: *Campylobacter* ... 351
25. Bacterial Vaginosis ... 376
26. Epstein-Barr Virus and Nasopharyngeal Carcinoma ... 394
27. Human Retrovirus Evolution ... 395
28. The Genetics of Carcinogenesis ... 396

29. The Legacy of Henrietta Lacks 397
30. Congenital Cytomegalovirus Disease: A Major Health Problem 411
31. Cytomegalovirus and AIDS 412
32. B Viruses: A Simian Counterpart to Herpes Simplex Virus 415
33. Influenza Viruses: Evolution and Variation 429
34. Rhinovirus Structure and Drug Design 433
35. Hantavirus Infection—United States 439
36. Ice and the Norwalk Virus 443
37. HIV and Latency: Maybe Not 445
38. Hepatitis A Among Drug Abusers 453
39. Hepatitis B: A Disease Not Taken Seriously Even Among Health Care Workers 457
40. Prions and Slow Infections 457
41. *Candida* Virulence: High-Frequency Switching 472
42. Multistate Outbreak of Sporotrichosis in Seedling Handlers, 1988 480
43. Nonimmune Defense Breakdown and Fungal Infection 484
44. Heroin, Lemon Juice, and *Candida* Infections 487
45. *Fusarium:* Infectious Agent 492
46. Pathogenic vs. Nonpathogenic *Entamoeba histolytica* 506
47. *Acanthamoeba* Keratitis in Soft Contact Lens Wearers 508
48. Malaria Relapse and the Hypnozoite 515
49. Coccidia and *Isospora belli* 517
50. Scabies 527
51. Povidone-Iodine Solution Contamination 534
52. A New Hospital Technique—Lithotripsy 543
53. HIV Infection in Health Care Workers 545
54. The Gram Stain: Important to the Microbiologist and the Physician 559

Preface

Students preparing to enter the health care professions clearly need a solid foundation of basic scientific knowledge. Faced with a growing body of scientific information, however, most students now demand from the very beginning of their education that the science they learn be directly relevant to what they will be doing in their future professional lives. Textbooks that are user-friendly in pedagogy and design and manageable in size are also increasingly important in helping students learn the seemingly overwhelming amount of information they must absorb.

From its inception, *Basic Medical Microbiology* has met the needs of students of the health sciences by focusing on those aspects of general microbiology and immunology that pertain to infectious diseases in humans. This new edition includes all the student-friendly features that were introduced in the fourth edition—chapter outlines and objectives; end-of-chapter summaries and self-test questions; and brief, clinically interesting supplemental essays, called Under the Microscope (many of which are new to this edition)—and utilizes a brand-new design that harmoniously brings all these features together. The result is a shorter, more visually appealing book that students will find easy and enjoyable to use.

In addition, the following changes have been made in the book's content for the fifth edition.

1. A concerted effort has been made throughout to simplify the style of presentation and eliminate speculative material, thus ensuring that the key points in each discussion are more easily accessible to the reader than ever before.
2. A separate chapter on biotechnology in medicine has been added, covering the basics of recombinant DNA technology.
3. A new appendix listing the diseases that are reportable to the Centers for Disease Control has been included.
4. The immunology section has been completely reorganized and updated to reflect contemporary concepts and methodology. Abundant new illustrations and tables enhance the revised immunology section.
5. More information on collection techniques and specimen analysis is included in many chapters. For example:

   A discussion of the disinfection of critical and semicritical instruments and noncritical items has been added to Chapter 7.

   The new class of beta-lactams called carbapenems, as well as the E test for microbial sensitivity, is discussed in Chapter 8.

   Specific guidelines for specimen collection, as well as discussions of molecular techniques in laboratory identification of organisms and the use of computers in the laboratory, are included in Chapter 16.

   Laboratory safety is also covered in Chapter 16, and universal precautions for the HIV and hepatitis viruses are discussed in Chapter 32.

   New laboratory diagnostic techniques in medical mycology appear in Chapter 33.

6. New and updated disease discussions include
   Escherichia coli and hemolytic uremic syndrome;
   Rochalimaea infections such as cat-scratch disease and bacillary angiomatosis;
   HIV and AIDS, including pediatric AIDS;
   Hepatitis, particularly hepatitis C, D, and E;
   The roundworms associated with filariasis and the tapeworms associated with echinococcosis and taeniasis;
   Catheter-associated infections, including both urinary and vascular catheters.
7. A new appendix listing the available vaccines, toxoids, and immune globulins has been included.

I would like to thank the many individuals who provided feedback and advice for the fifth edition; if this edition succeeds, it is because of their energies. Special thanks go to Dr. James Barrett and Dr. Gerry Silverman for their meticulous review of the immunology chapters. I would like to thank Ruth Steinberger for her patience and outstanding work in providing the line drawings for this and previous editions. I would also like to thank my editor at Little, Brown, Evan Schnittman, as well as Kristin Odmark, the developmental editor for this edition, for the time she spent editing the book and for providing me with the materials to keep the fifth edition on schedule.

R. F. B.

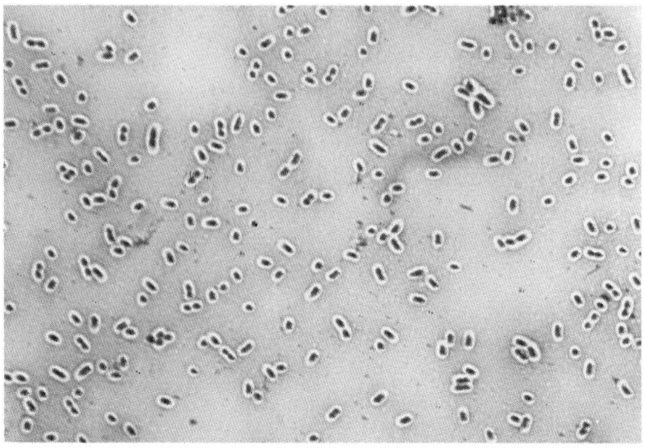

PLATE 1 Capsule stain. Capsule appears as white halo in a blue background that has been stained by a dye. Bacterial cells were counterstained with a red dye. ($\times$1250.) (From R. E. Corstvet et al., *J. Clin. Microbiol.* 16:1123, 1982.)

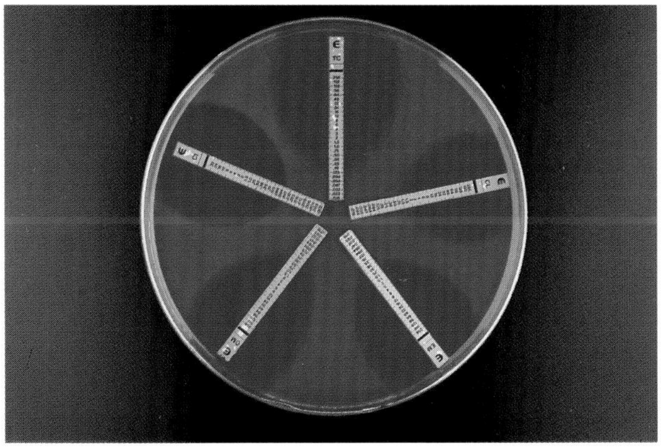

PLATE 2 The E test for antimicrobial sensitivity. Five strips containing continuous gradients of antibiotics (underside of the strips) are placed on Mueller-Hinton agar that has been streaked with a specific isolate. The point at which the zone of inhibition intersects the antimicrobial strip is the minimal inhibitory concentration (MIC). The MIC scale is printed on the upper surface of the strips. (From C. N. Baker, S. A. Stocker, D. H. Culver, and C. Thornsberry, *J. Clin. Microbiol.* 29:533, 1991.)

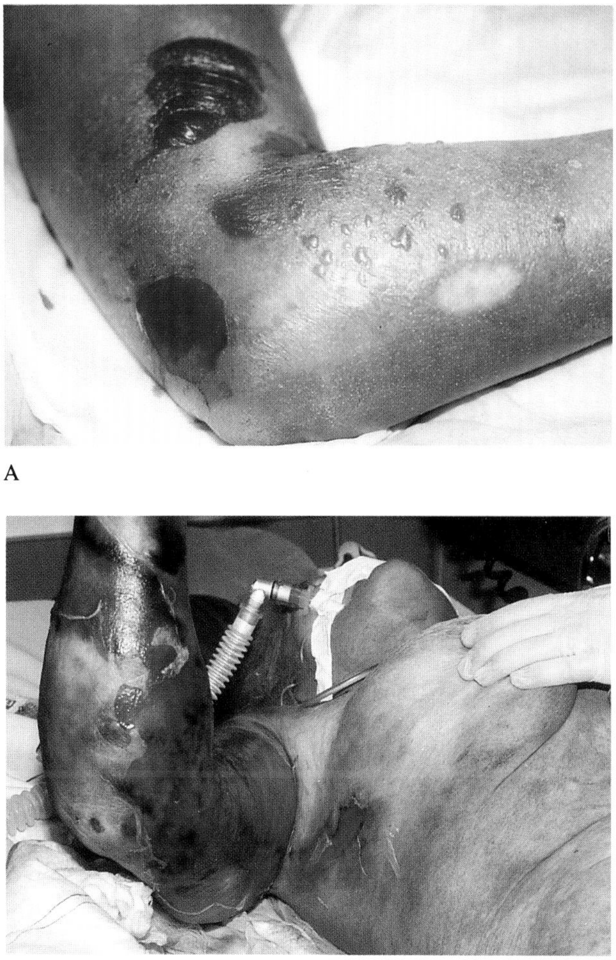

A

B

PLATE 3 Manifestations of severe group A streptococcal infection. A. Necrotizing fasciitis of arm with multiple intact bullae, some of which are filled with hemorrhagic fluid. There is sloughing of skin over lesion on elbow. B. Necrotizing fasciitis of right arm, axilla, and chest wall with myocutaneous gangrene necessitating forequarter amputation and debridement. (From B. Demers, A. E. Simor, H. Vellend, et al., *Clin. Infect. Dis.* 16:792, 1992.)

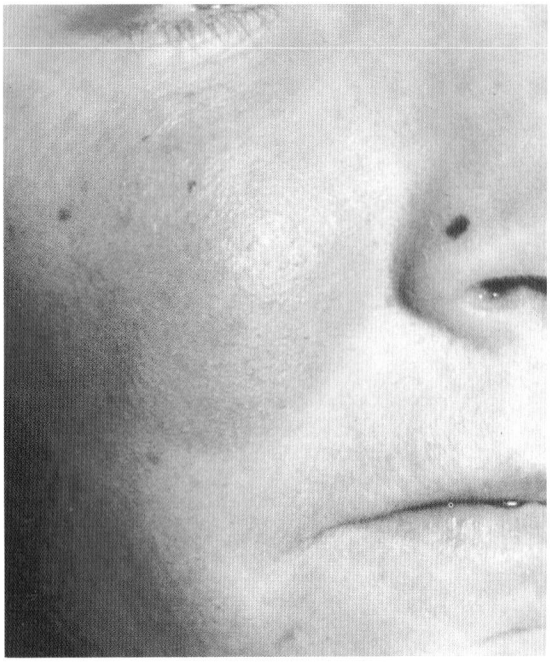

PLATE 4 Erysipelas. (From J. H. Stein, ed., *Internal Medicine*, 3rd ed. Boston: Little, Brown, 1990.)

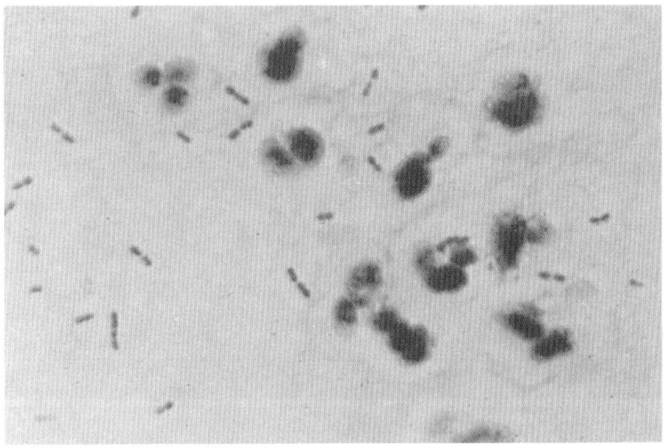

PLATE 5 Gram-positive diplococci (*Streptococcus pneumoniae*) as seen in high power. (×1000.) (From J. H. Stein, ed., *Internal Medicine*, 3rd ed. Boston: Little, Brown, 1990.)

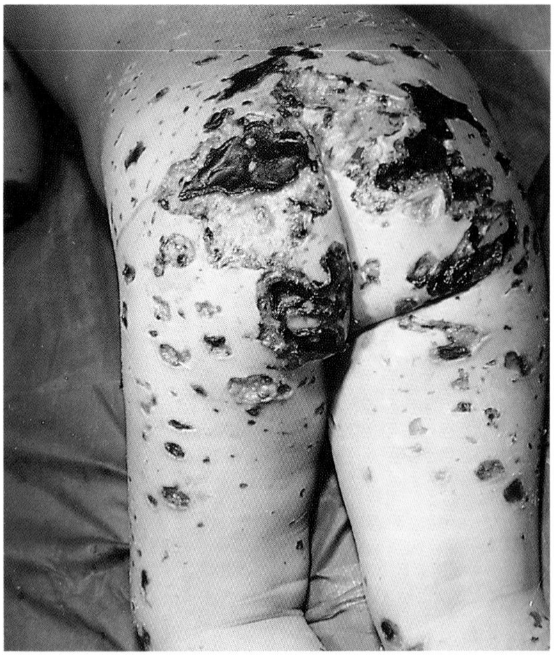

PLATE 6 Massive cutaneous hemorrhage from meningococcal disease. (From H. Peltola and I. Simula, *Rev. Infect. Dis.* 5:71, 1983.)

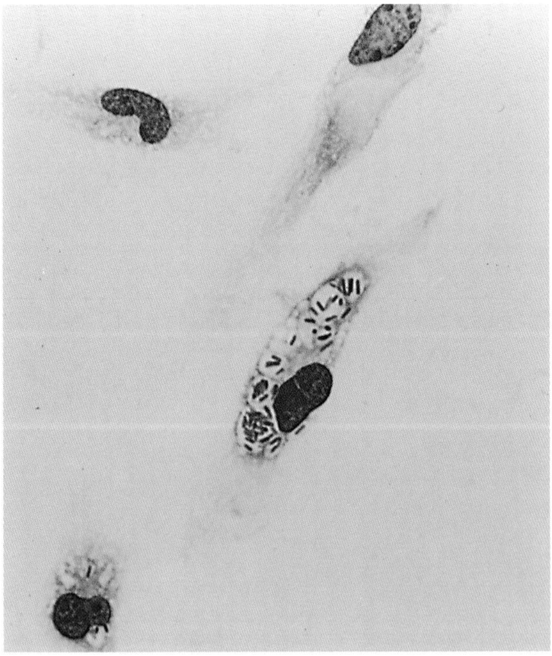

PLATE 7 Peritoneal macrophage with intracellular *Salmonella typhimurium* bacilli. (×2000.) (From J. V. DeSiderio and S. Campbell, *J. Infect. Dis.* 148:563, 1983.)

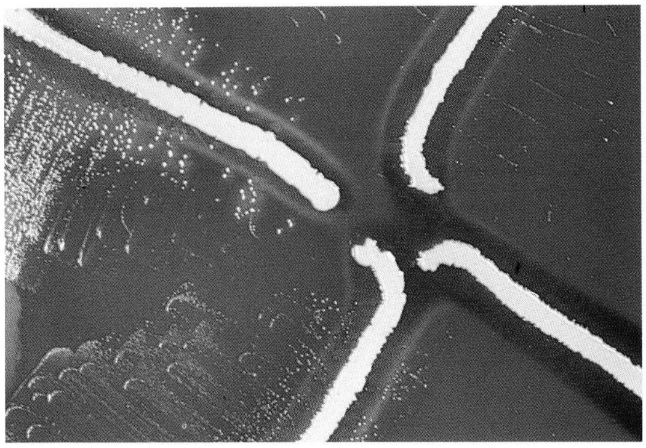

PLATE 8 Satellite phenomenon. Small colonies of *Hemophilus influenzae* are observed in the vicinity of large streaks of *Staphylococcus aureus.*

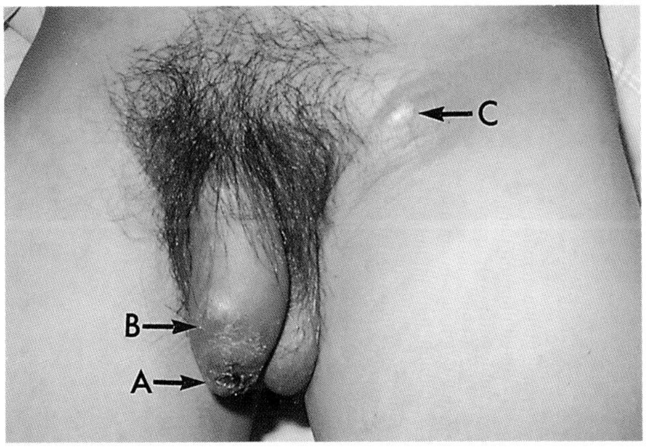

PLATE 9 Chancroid. A. Ulceration of prepuce. B. Lymphadenopathy. C. Inguinal buboe about to rupture. (From G. W. Hammond, *Rev. Infect. Dis.* 2:867, 1980.)

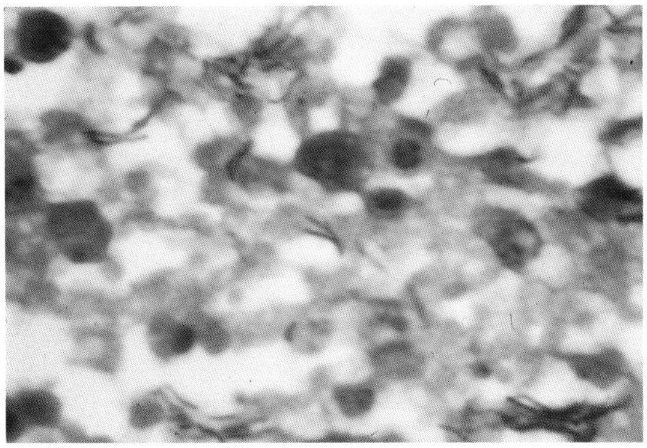

PLATE 10 Ziehl-Neelsen acid-fast stain of *Mycobacteria.* (From H. M. Sommers. In E. H. Lennette, ed., *Manual of Clinical Microbiology,* 4th ed. Washington, D.C.: American Society for Microbiology, 1985.)

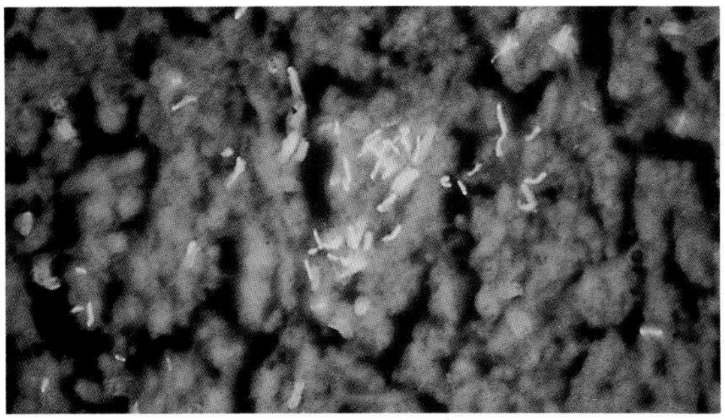

PLATE 11 Yellow fluorescing *Mycobacterium tuberculosis.* (From H. M. Sommers. In E. H. Lennette, ed., *Manual of Clinical Microbiology,* 4th ed. Washington, D.C.: American Society for Microbiology, 1985.)

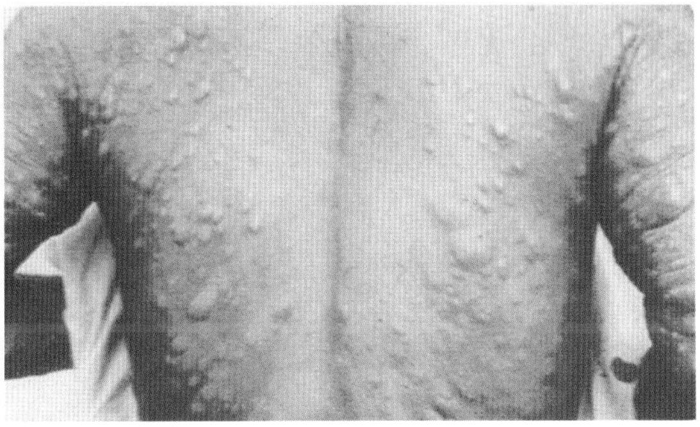

PLATE 12 Lepromatous leprosy. (From J. H. Stein ed., *Internal Medicine,* 3rd ed. Boston: Little, Brown, 1990.)

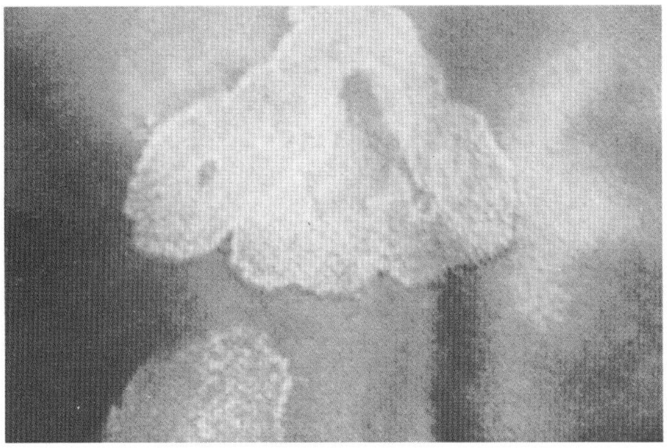

PLATE 13 Tuberculoid leprosy. (From J. H. Stein, ed., *Internal Medicine,* 3rd ed. Boston: Little, Brown, 1990.)

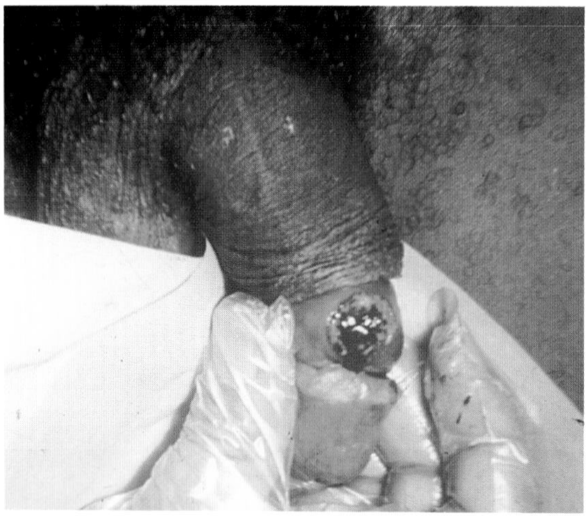

PLATE 14 Hard chancre. (Courtesy of Centers for Disease Control, Atlanta, GA.)

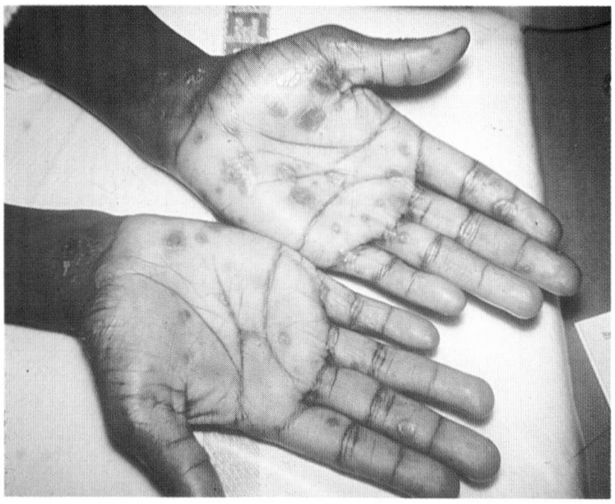

PLATE 15 Secondary syphilis. (Courtesy of Centers for Disease Control, Atlanta, GA.)

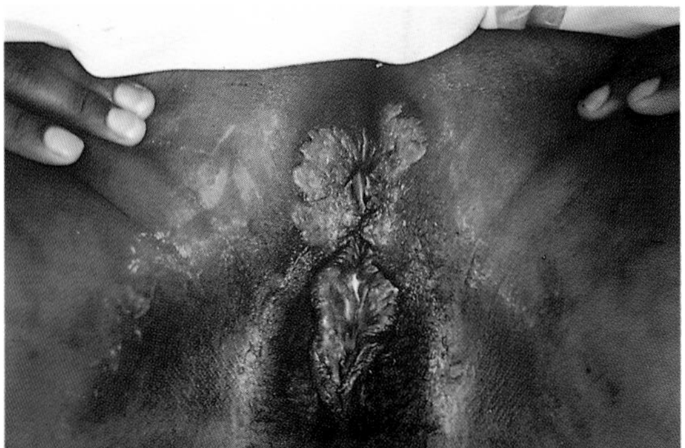

PLATE 16 Condylomata lata during secondary stage of syphilis. (From P. S. Friedman, *Br. J. Vener. Dis.* 53:276, 1977.)

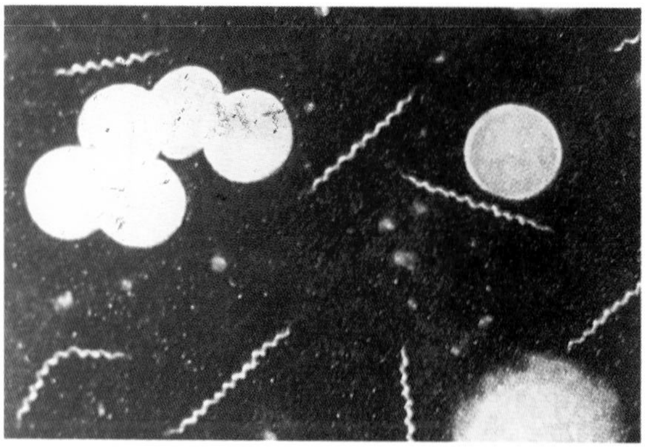

PLATE 17 Dark-field microscopy of spirochetes (spiral-shaped organisms). (Courtesy of Centers for Disease Control, Atlanta, GA.)

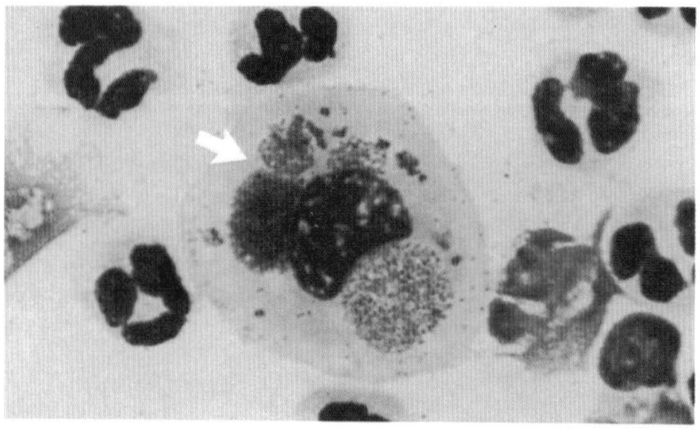

PLATE 18 Giemsa stain of conjunctiva scraping showing typical cytoplasmic inclusion of *Chlamydia trachomatis.* (From J. H. Stein, ed., *Internal Medicine,* 3rd ed. Boston: Little, Brown, 1990.)

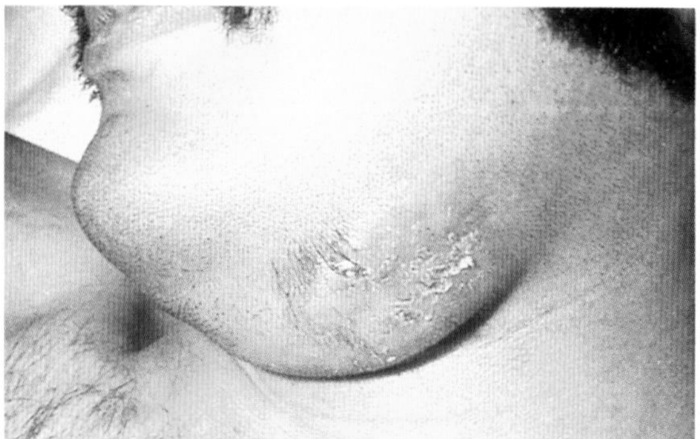

PLATE 19 Actinomycosis. (From J. H. Stein, ed., *Internal Medicine,* 3rd ed. Boston: Little, Brown, 1990.)

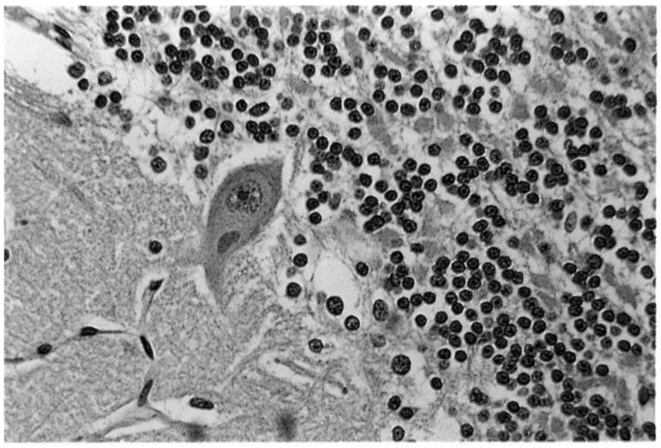

PLATE 20 Negri body in human rabies. In the center is a well defined cell with nucleus and Negri body. (Courtesy of F. A. Murphy.)

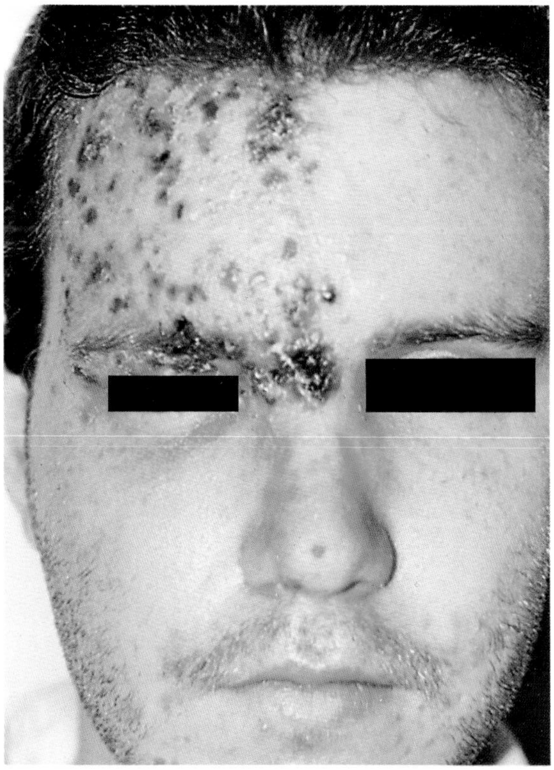

PLATE 21 Herpes zoster of the face. (Courtesy of H. E. Kaufman, M.D.)

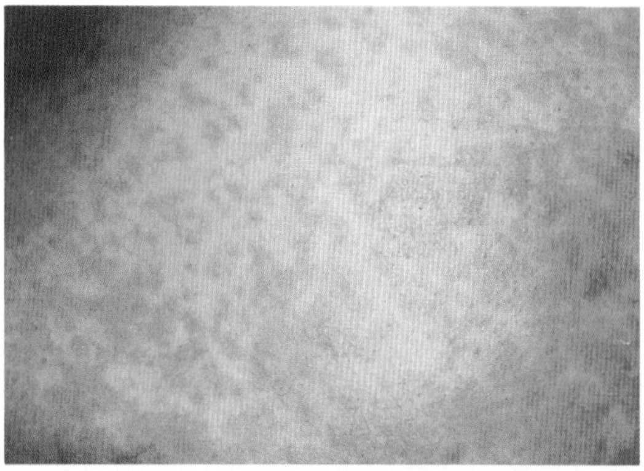

PLATE 22 Typical maculopapular rash of measles. (From J. H. Stein, ed., *Internal Medicine,* 3rd ed. Boston: Little, Brown, 1990.)

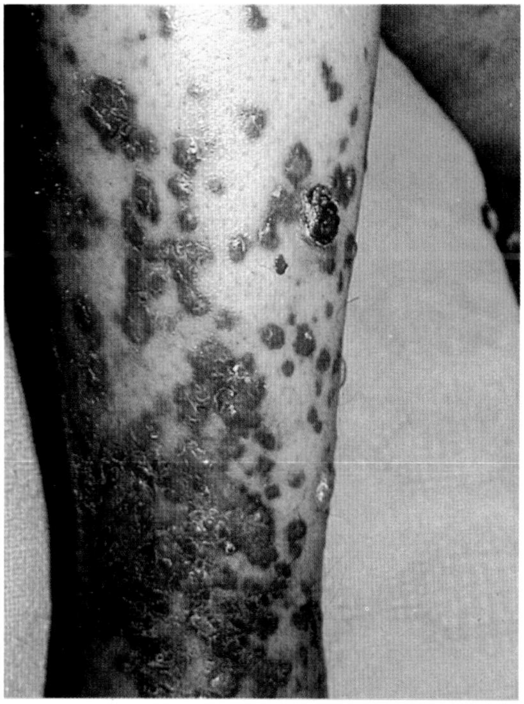

PLATE 23 Kaposi's sarcoma. (From J. H. Stein, ed., *Internal Medicine,* 3rd ed. Boston: Little, Brown, 1990.)

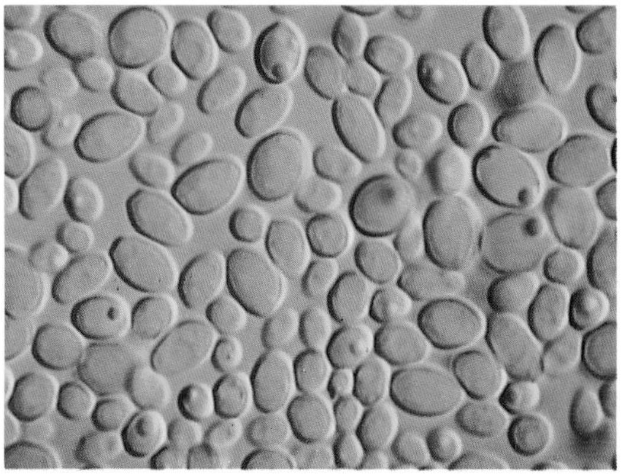

PLATE 24 Oval yeast cells as seen by Nomarski interference microscopy. (×1000.) (From M. Ogawa et al., *Appl. Environ. Microbiol.* 46:912, 1983.)

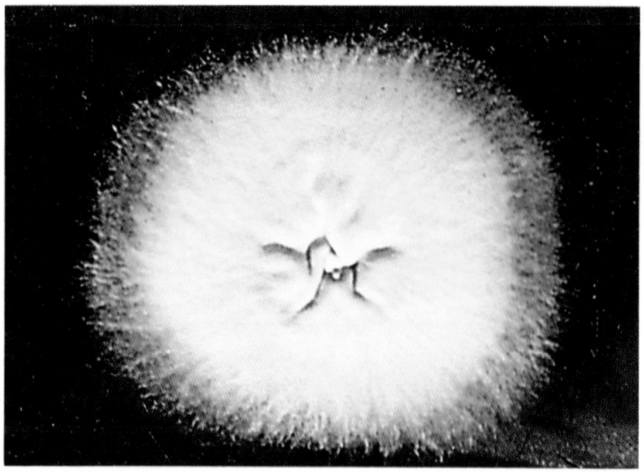

PLATE 25 Typical "mold" colony showing cottony appearance.

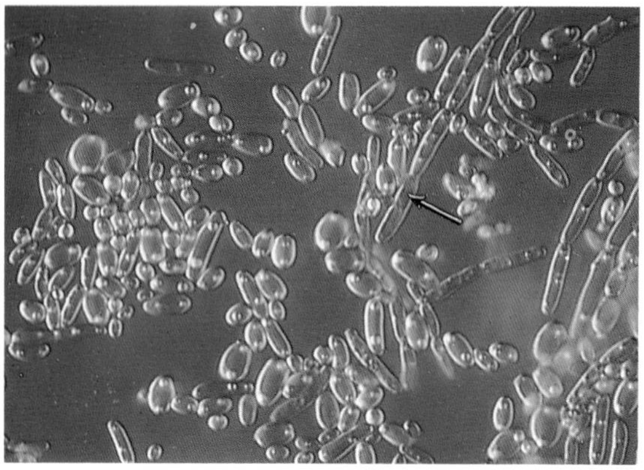

PLATE 26 Pseudohyphae *(arrow)* formation in *Candida* as seen by Nomarski interference microscopy. (×400.) (From M. Ogawa et al., *Appl. Environ. Microbiol.* 46:912, 1983.)

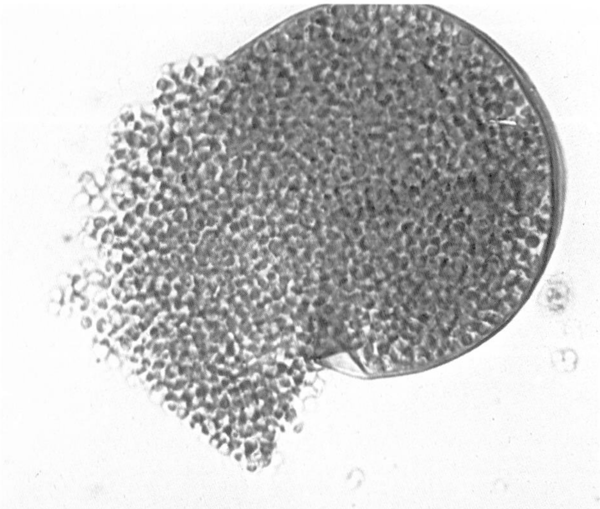

PLATE 27 Spherule of *Coccidioides immitis* showing endospores. (From S. M. Finegold and E. J. Baron. In *Bailey and Scott's Diagnostic Microbiology,* 7th ed. St. Louis: Mosby, 1987.)

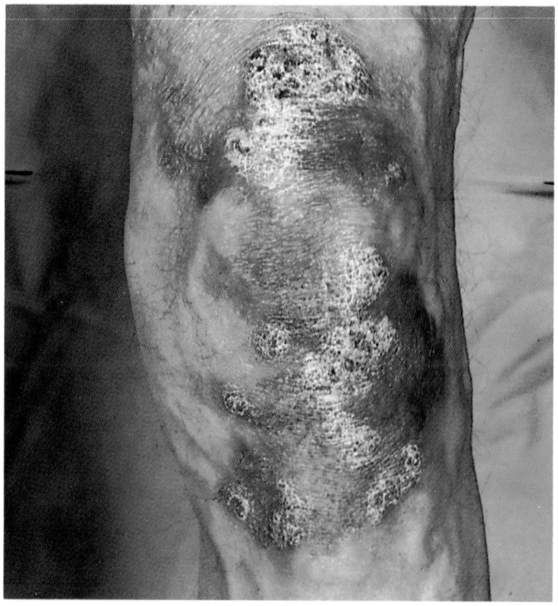

PLATE 28 Cutaneous blastomycosis. (Courtesy of John Utz, M.D.)

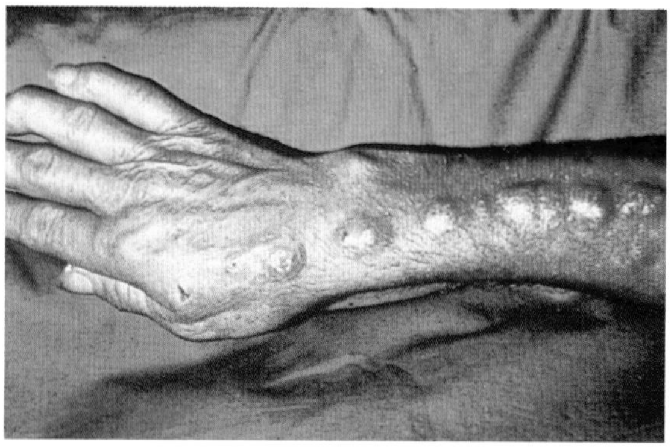

PLATE 29 Sporotrichosis. (From J. H. Stein, ed., *Internal Medicine,* 3rd ed. Boston: Little, Brown, 1990.)

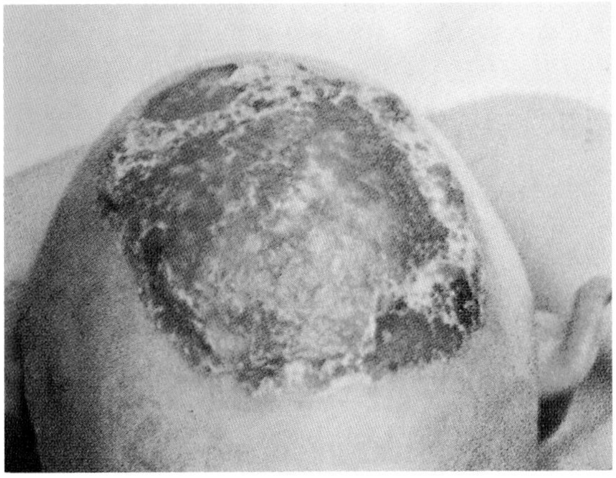

A

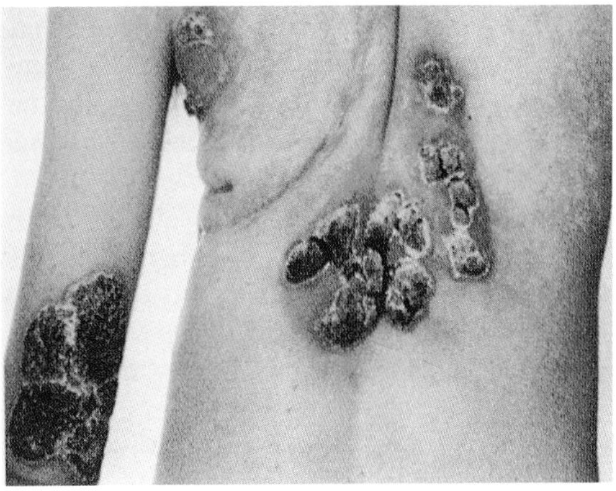

B

PLATE 30 Chronic mucocutaneous candidiasis involving head (A) and back (B). (From P. Phillips et al., *Rev. Infect. Dis.* 9[Suppl. I]:87, 1987.)

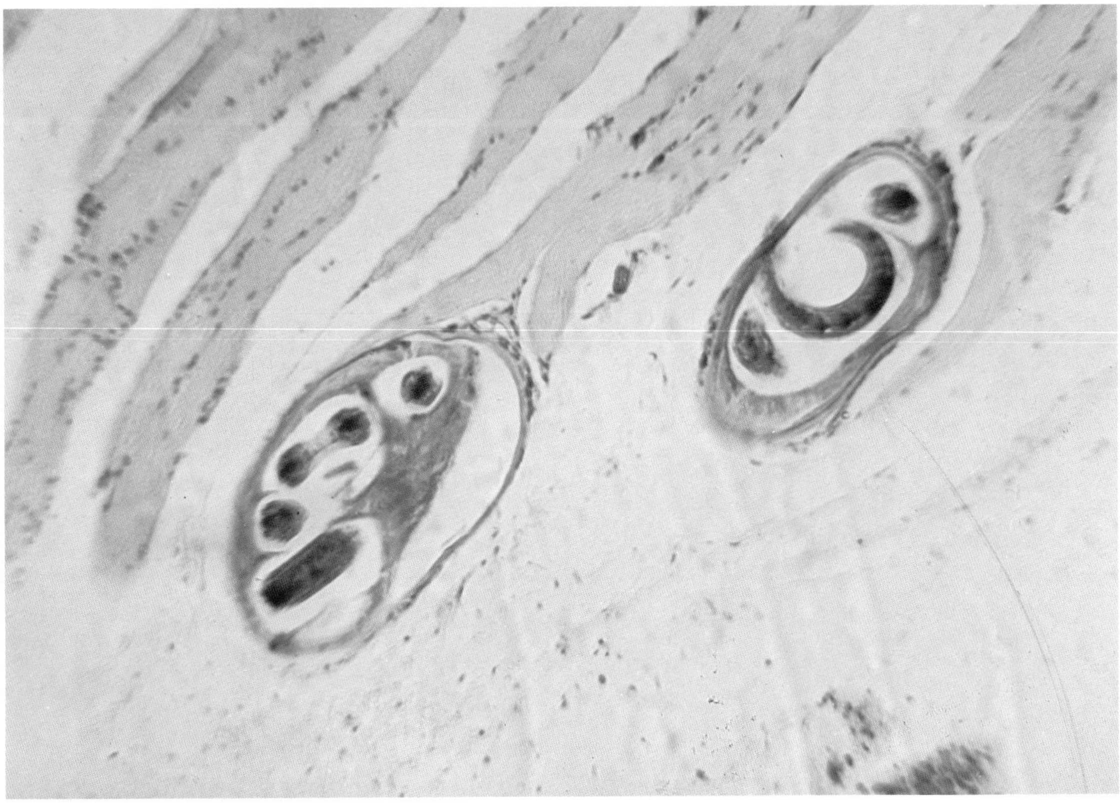

PLATE 31 *Trichinella* larvae encysted in muscle. (From S. M. Finegold and E. J. Baron. In *Bailey and Scott's Diagnostic Microbiology*, 7th ed. St. Louis: C. V. Mosby, 1987.)

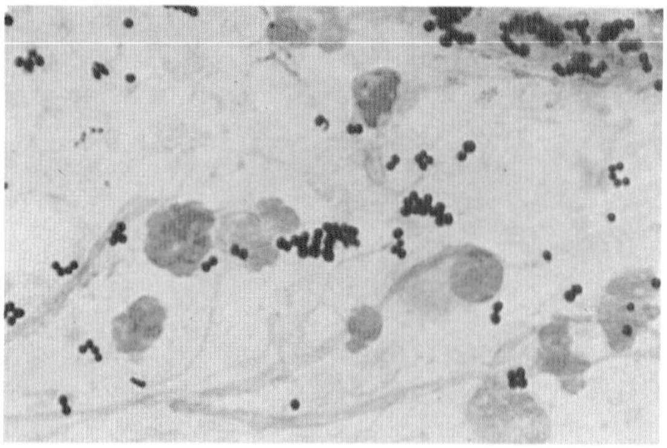

PLATE 32 Gram stain of gram-positive staphylococci (purple, clustered spherical cells). (From J. H. Stein, ed., *Internal Medicine,* 3rd ed. Boston: Little, Brown, 1990.)

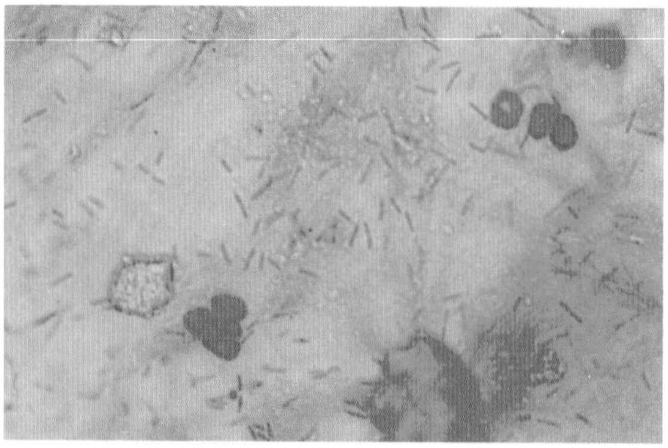

PLATE 33 Gram stain of gram-negative *Klebsiella pneumoniae.* The red-stained bacterial cells are short, thin rods in the photomicrograph. (From J. H. Stein, ed., *Internal Medicine,* 3rd ed. Boston: Little, Brown, 1990.)

PART I
General Bacteriology

NOTICE

CHAPTER 1

Scope and History of Microbiology

OBJECTIVES

To understand the importance of microbiology to medicine as well as to applied areas of science

To describe the contributions of the following scientists to microbiology: Leeuwenhoek, Pasteur, Koch, Lister, Jenner, and Ehrlich

To explain what is meant by the theory of spontaneous generation and how the theory was refuted

To list the steps that are required to identify the causative agent of an infectious disease

OUTLINE

SCOPE

HISTORY
- Early Concepts of Disease
- First Observations of Microorganisms
- Spontaneous Generation
- Germ Theory of Disease
- The Golden Age of Microbiology (1870–1890)
  - Isolation Techniques
  - Staining
  - Immunology
- Virology
- Chemotherapy

MODERN MICROBIOLOGY

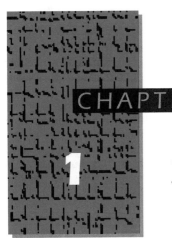

Scope

Microbiology is a science that is primarily concerned with the study of of microorganisms. Included within the family of microorganisms are bacteria, fungi, certain algae, protozoa, and viruses. Even though viruses are often referred to as microorganisms, they do not exhibit cellular characteristics. In fact, viruses are totally dependent on the presence of a living cell for replication. Algae are not ordinarily associated with disease in humans and are not discussed in this book.

There are many divisions of microbiology, each of which may require different skills. Medical microbiology is a specialty that deals with microorganisms that cause infectious disease. Individuals studying medical microbiology should have some understanding of the chemical and physical properties of all potentially harmful microbial agents. To comprehend fully medical microbiology, one should also have a clear understanding of the etiology (causation), disease manifestations, laboratory diagnosis, treatment, and prevention of infectious disease. Even though the nurse may be more interested in prevention, the medical technologist in laboratory diagnosis, and the epidemiologist in the causation of disease, a basic understanding of all aspects of medical microbiology leads to better decision making by all groups.

Modern medical microbiology now includes an area of study referred to as **immunology.** Immunology deals specifically with the study of the relationship of antigens or foreign substances to antibody production in the host. The study of immunology will provide you with a perception of the concepts associated with resistance to infectious disease. In addition, immunological techniques provide us with new tools that aid in the classification and identification of infectious as well as noninfectious microorganisms.

Genetic engineering also is included within the scope of medical microbiology. Our understanding of the relationship of DNA structure to function was initiated in 1953. In that year, **Watson** and **Crick** discovered the structure of the DNA molecule. From that time until the present, the science of genetics has contributed immensely to advancements in medical microbiology as well as other biological sciences. We now have within our grasps the potential to conquer, or at the very least temper, the infectious and noninfectious diseases that plague humankind. Discoveries in medical microbiology are emerging each day. We hope that the importance of these discoveries will become evident as you read the chapters of this book.

History

EARLY CONCEPTS OF DISEASE

Microbiology had its origins in the concepts that were first formulated to explain disease. In some ancient civilizations, disease was believed to be a punishment sent from the gods for human wrongdoing. Many of the philosophers during these early periods in history, however, were of the belief that disease was transmitted by invisible "animals." Since the animals could not be seen, the theory remained just that, a theory. The Italian physician **Fracastorius** (1486–1553) later postulated that disease was transmitted from one person to another or from contact with the clothing or utensils of the infected. This theory was not widely disseminated or even considered valid by many scientists who knew of it. Two hundred years elapsed before a detailed description of microorganisms was made.

FIRST OBSERVATIONS OF MICROORGANISMS

Anton van Leeuwenhoek (c. 1685), who took up microbiology as a hobby, was an amateur microscope builder. Leeuwenhoek's curiosity led him to discover microscopic organisms in pond water, in debris surrounding teeth, and in hay infusions (Fig. 1-1). The microscope used by this scientist was a little over 2 inches in length and capable of magnifications approaching 160 to 200 times (Fig. 1-2).

SPONTANEOUS GENERATION

Even though his descriptions of microorganisms were among the first to be recognized, Leeuwenhoek's peers either ignored or denied the existence of microorganisms. Instead, most scientists accepted the theory of **spontaneous generation,** that is, that life can only arise from dead or organic matter. For example, the scientific community was convinced that blowflies could arise spontaneously from rotted meat. Scientists such as **Francisco Redi** (1668) and **Spallanzani** (1776) performed experiments that showed that organic matter, when protected from contamination by boiling it and by eliminating the presence of air, did *not* give rise to new life. However, the proponents of spontaneous generation suggested that air was the **vital force** required for generating life.

The spontaneous generation theory prevailed until the early nineteenth century. The experiments of **Louis Pasteur** (Fig. 1-3) in the mid 1900s provided enough scientific evidence to discredit the proponents of the spontaneous generation theory. Using swan-necked flasks (Fig. 1-4), Pasteur boiled organic solutions to destroy any microorganisms that might be present. There was no barrier to the passage of air in these flasks. The flasks could sit for days with no visible turbidity—a condition that would indicate the absence of multiplying microorganisms. The experiment showed that air outside the flask could diffuse freely into the organic broth. In addition, if any microorganisms were present in the air, they could go no further than the walls of the flask's neck, where they would settle out. When the liquid in the flask was allowed to come in contact with the microorganisms in the neck (by tilting the flask and then returning the contaminated fluid by tilting the flask back again), the broth became turbid after 24 hours.

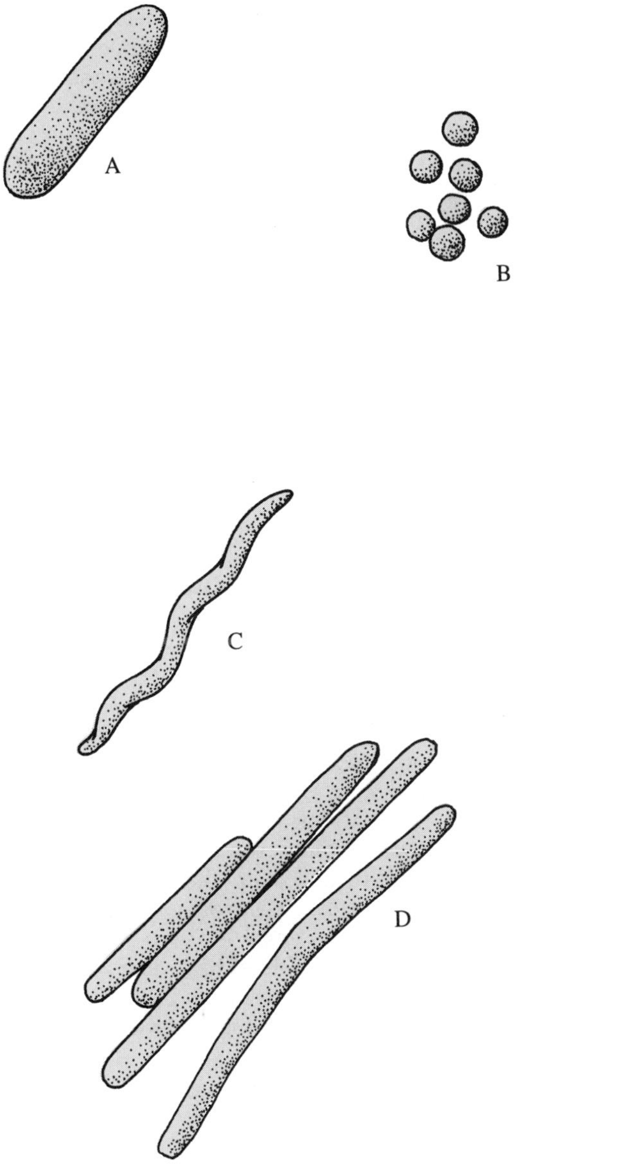

FIGURE 1-1
Shapes of microorganisms observed by Leeuwenhoek in samples taken from the human mouth. A. Rod-shaped (bacillus). B. Spherical (cocci). C. Spiral-shaped (spirochete). D. Cigar-shaped rods.

Pasteur made many important contributions to microbiology and related sciences (Table 1-1). For this reason Pasteur has been called the **Father of Microbiology.**

GERM THEORY OF DISEASE

The theoretical explanations of infectious disease, as proposed by Fracastorius in 1546, were not supported by experimental proof until the 1800s. **Semmelweis** in Austria and **Oliver Wendell Holmes** in the United States demonstrated that handwashing prevented the transmission of infectious disease, in particular **puerperal (childbed) fever.** The majority of physicians refused to believe that

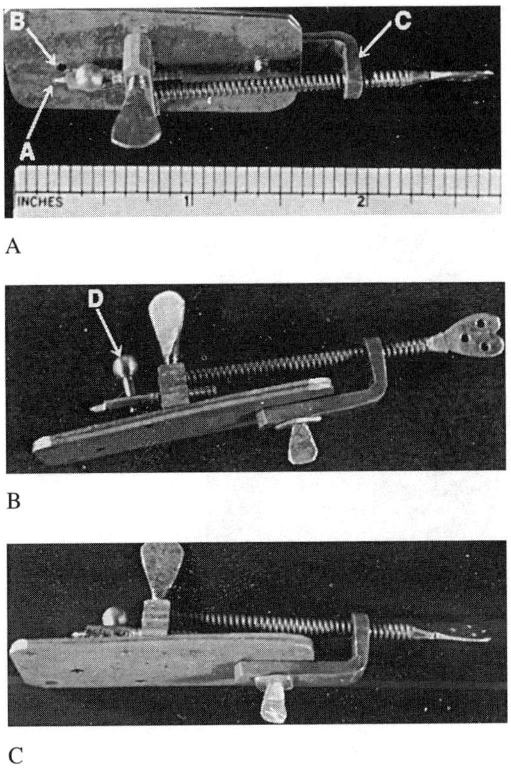

FIGURE 1-2
Actual-size replica of Leeuwenhoek microscope from Leyden, Holland, showing various views (A–C) of the instrument. *A,* pin on which the object is placed for viewing; *B,* lens; *C,* screw for coarse adjustment; *D,* screw for fine adjustment. (From D. A. Anderson and R. J. Sobieski, *Instruction to Microbiology,* 2nd ed. St. Louis: Mosby, 1980.)

microorganisms, or the diseases they were supposed to cause, could be transmitted by unclean hands.

In 1857 Pasteur theorized that microorganisms could cause disease by producing specific types of molecules, as certain yeasts cause "diseases" of wine and other fermented beverages—that is, bad-tasting beverages. In England at this time the surgeon **Joseph Lister** recognized

TABLE 1-1
Contributions of Louis Pasteur to Microbiology and Related Sciences

Development of attenuated vaccines for anthrax and chicken cholera
Immunization against rabies
Relationship of crystal structure to optical rotation
Study of diseases of swine and silkworms
Discovery of technique for selective destruction of microorganisms by heat (pasteurization)
Refutation of theory of spontaneous generation
Discovery of microorganisms that live in the absence of air (anaerobes)
Contributions to understanding the causes of fermentation

FIGURE 1-3
Louis Pasteur (1822–1895). (From P. L. Carpenter, *Microbiology*, 4th ed. Copyright © 1977 by W. B. Saunders Company. Reprinted by permission of CBS College Publishing.)

the importance of Pasteur's experiments. Lister proposed that infections of open wounds were due to microorganisms present in the air around the patient. It soon became Lister's policy to spray the air around each patient with phenol before surgical operations. This procedure of destroying or removing viable microorganisms from an environment is called **aseptic technique.** Although Lister's procedures dramatically decreased the number of deaths from surgical wound infections, his results were not totally accepted in the scientific community.

In the late 1800s a German physician named **Robert Koch** (Fig. 1-5) demonstrated the relationship between microorganisms and the infectious disease process. Koch studied anthrax, a disease of cattle that can be transmitted to humans. He isolated the organisms from infected cattle in **pure culture** (the cultivation of a single species of microorganism) and then injected a small amount of the pure culture into healthy animals. The injected animals became infected and anthrax developed. The infectious agent was then isolated from this second group of animals. This sequence of isolation, reinfection, and recovery of the infective agent is called **Koch's postulates.** By following Koch's postulates, it was now possible to establish the causative agent of many infectious diseases. Although numerous scientists at that time were busily engaged in isolating and characterizing microorganisms, scientists like Koch and Pasteur were also interested in developing techniques that would be effective in destroying bacteria and thus reduce human misery.

THE GOLDEN AGE OF MICROBIOLOGY (1870–1890)

Isolation Techniques

During the Golden Age of Microbiology, many of the bacterial agents responsible for so many of the fatal diseases of that time were isolated (Table 1-2). Viruses had not yet been discovered and little was known about fungi and animal parasites as infectious agents.

Perhaps one of the most important technical advances during this period was the discovery that **agar-agar** could be used with microbiological media for isolating microorganisms in pure culture. Agar-agar is a carbohydrate isolated from seaweed that is stable to heat, enzyme-stable, solid, transparent, and easily sterilized. **Frau Hesse,** the wife of a physician interested in the bacteriology of air,

TABLE 1-2
Disease-Producing Bacteria Discovered During the Golden Age of Microbiology (1870–1890)

Year	Disease	Causative agent	Researcher(s)
1872	Anthrax	*Bacillus anthracis*	Rayer and Devaine, Pasteur and Koch
1873	Relapsing fever	*Borrelia recurrentis*	Obermeier
1874	Leprosy	*Mycobacterium leprae*	Hansen
1879	Gonorrhea	*Neisseria gonorrhoeae*	Neisser
1880	Pneumonia	*Diplococcus pneumoniae*	Pasteur, Sternberg
1880	Abscesses	*Staphylococcus aureus*	Pasteur, Ogston, Rosenbach
1882	Tuberculosis	*Mycobacterium tuberculosis*	Koch
1883	Cholera	*Vibrio cholerae*	Koch
1884	Diphtheria	*Corynebacterium diphtheriae*	Klebs, Loeffler
1884	Tetanus	*Clostridium tetani*	Nicolaier, Kitasato
1885	Foodborne illness, paratyphoid	*Salmonella choleraesuis* and related species	Salmon and Smith, Gärtner, Schottmüller
1887	Epidemic meningitis	*Neisseria meningitidis*	Weichselbaum
1887	Brucellosis	*Brucella melitensis* and other species	Bruce, Bang

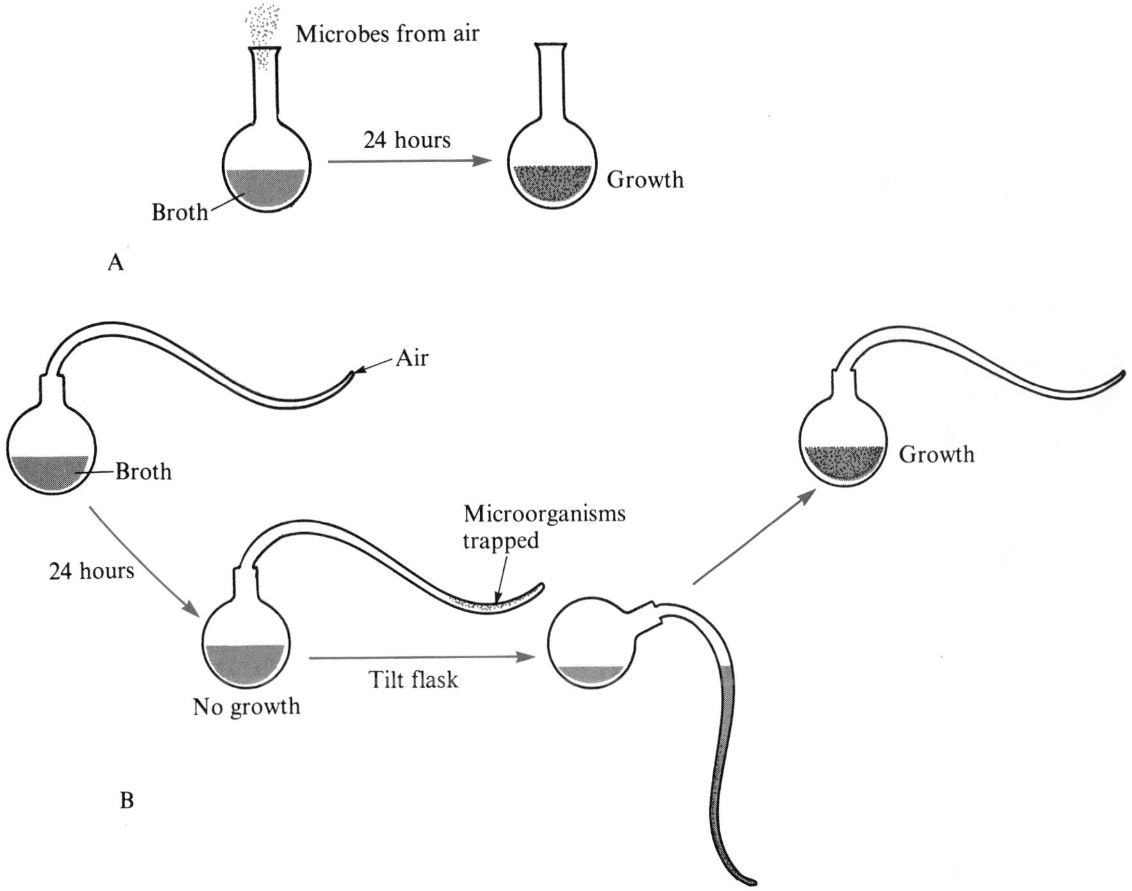

FIGURE 1-4
Swan-necked flasks were used by Pasteur to disprove spontaneous generation. Flask A, which is not swan-necked, contains sterile broth that is directly exposed to the air and becomes turbid after 16 to 24 hours. Microorganisms in the air settle into the broth, where they reproduce and make the broth turbid. Flask B, which is swan-necked, also contains sterile broth. Because of its shape, air, but not microorganisms, can enter the space above the broth. The broth in the swan-necked flask shows no turbidity even several days after exposure to air unless the flask is tilted and the broth makes contact with microorganisms.

had been using agar-agar in her kitchen to prepare fruits and jellies. She suggested that agar-agar might be used in culture media. Dr. Hesse mentioned his wife's suggestion to **Robert Koch,** who adapted the new medium in his laboratory. The use of agar-agar in media made possible the isolation of single colonies on a solid medium, a technique that could not be accomplished with liquid media. This discovery, coupled with the design of the **Petri dish** (Fig. 1-6) in 1887 by J. R. Petri as a container for media, provided bacteriologists with a new tool for isolating bacteria in pure culture.

Other microbiologists, using Koch's postulates and aided by the new isolation techniques, would make many contributions to an understanding of the microbial agents causing disease.

Staining

Visualization of microorganisms was enhanced by the discovery of various staining agents. **Weigert,** in 1878, was the first to stain bacteria using various aniline dyes. Further refinement in staining led to Gram's stain (1884), which can be used for most bacterial species, and the Ziehl-Neelsen stain, used to stain the organism causing tuberculosis. **Loeffler** utilized methylene blue to identify the organism causing diphtheria.

Immunology

Society had recognized for more than 200 years that individuals who recovered from disease could not "catch" the disease a second time. In 1796 **Edward Jenner** discovered that milkmaids infected with the mild variety of pox called **cowpox** were immune to the more severe form of the disease, **smallpox.** Jenner inoculated fluid from a cowpox pustule into a healthy boy and later infected the same boy with smallpox. The boy did not contract smallpox.

In 1879 **Pasteur** noted that if chicken cholera bacteria were left on laboratory media for periods of time, they

FIGURE 1-5
Robert Koch (1843–1910). (From K. L. Burdon and R. P. Williams, *Microbiology*, 6th ed. New York: Macmillan, 1968. Copyright © 1968 by Macmillan Publishing Company.)

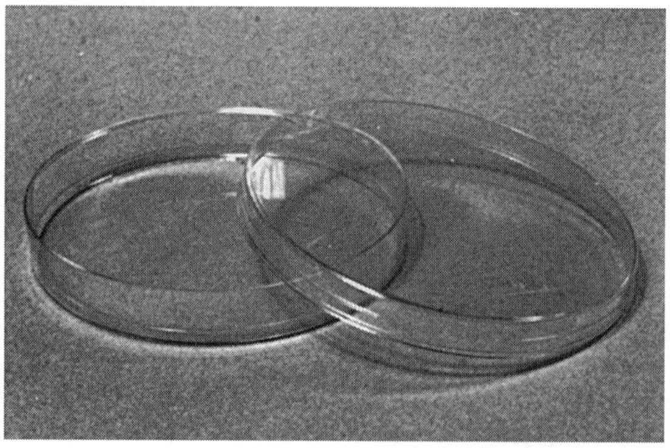

FIGURE 1-6
Petri dish. The bottom portion of the dish *(left)* can be partially filled with a solid medium. The covering plate fits over the bottom portion. Petri dishes can be obtained presterilized and filled with sterilized media, or they may be unsterilized and filled with unsterilized media and then sterilized by autoclaving (steam under pressure).

lost their virulence (they became **attenuated**). When injected into healthy chickens, the attenuated bacteria not only did not cause cholera but also protected them from infection by fresh virulent strains. These experiments eventually lead to our present-day vaccination techniques and methods of immunization. Today all of us are aware of vaccination procedures used against such disease as tetanus, diphtheria, polio, and whooping cough.

VIROLOGY

Viral diseases such as smallpox, rabies, polio, and others had been known for centuries. The nature of the infectious agent involved, however, did not become apparent until the late 1890s. **Iwanowsky** took the fluids pressed from tobacco plants afflicted with tobacco mosaic disease and filtered them through porcelain filters to remove bacteria. The fluid still caused disease in new plants, and thus the infectious agent was recognized as a filterable material that did not contain bacteria. **Loeffler** and **Frosch** (1898) were the first to demonstrate a filterable agent as the cause of an animal disease called **foot-and-mouth disease.** During the twentieth century, viruses that could infect all types of cells including bacteria were discovered.

In the past 30 years there have been many advances in virology. Most of the viral agents associated with human disease have been isolated and identified. In addition, many human vaccines have been successfully developed to prevent disease. Our understanding of the molecular biology and genetics of viruses has led to important discoveries in mammalian genetics and the malignant process caused by certain viruses.

CHEMOTHERAPY

In the late 1800s, **Paul Ehrlich,** the German chemist, noted that dyes were selectively absorbed in some cell types and not in others. His observations led him to believe that certain chemicals taken into the body could selectively destroy bacteria and not affect normal body cells. He called this process **chemotherapy.** An arsenical compound, which Ehrlich called **606,** was found to be effective in the treatment of syphilis (see Under the Microscope 1). Until the discovery of penicillin, 606 (salvarsan) remained the major chemotherapeutic agent in the treatment of syphilis.

Following Ehrlich's success, many scientists began to test thousands of chemicals for antibacterial activity. In 1932, **Gerhard Domagk,** a German chemist, prepared and tested many dyes. He discovered that the red dye **Prontosil** was highly effective in the treatment of numerous bacterial diseases. It was later discovered that in the body Prontosil is converted to an active colorless derivative called **sulfanilamide.**

It had been known for several years before the turn of the century that certain bacteria and molds were capable of producing substances that killed or inhibited the growth of various types of microorganisms. In 1928 **Sir Alexander Fleming** discovered that a particular culture of *Staphylococcus* on an agar plate had become contaminated with mold from the air. Some of the bacterial colonies around one mold had stopped growing. The mold, later found to be *Penicillium notatum,* produced an antibacterial substance called **penicillin.** In 1940 **Chain** and other scientists in **Florey's** laboratory in Oxford purified penicillin from culture fluids and demonstrated its potency. In 1942 penicillin was ready for injection into human subjects.

The work of Fleming, Chain, Florey, and others provided some important experimental procedures that led to the discovery of other antimicrobials. After World War II, a wider range of antibiotics including tetracycline, chloramphenicol, and erythromycin was discovered.

UNDER THE MICROSCOPE 1

Dr. Ehrlich's "Magic Bullets"

One of the most important contributions to the healing art of medicine was made by Paul Ehrlich, the father of modern chemotherapy. Ehrlich was born in Silesia, Germany, in 1854. He was primarily a chemist and his earliest work was in the field of histology and specifically in the staining of tissues. He proposed that certain dyes stain specific areas of the cell because of the chemical affinity between molecules in the tissue and molecules in the dye. He suggested that by changing the constitution of the chemical compound, one could also change its effects.

Ehrlich proposed a theory that would be the guiding light in his later quest for chemotherapeutic agents. He stated that if a dye can stain just one type of tissue, there must be one that does not stain tissue but stains and kills only the microorganism attacking the tissue. Ehrlich called these compounds, with affinity for microbes but not for tissue, **"magic bullets."**

One of the compounds used by Ehrlich was called atoxyl, an organic molecule containing arsenic. Atoxyl had been used to treat human sleeping sickness, based on results with laboratory mice. The drug was so toxic to humans that it caused blindness before the patient had time to die of the disease. Chemists of the day said that atoxyl could not be chemically altered to decrease its toxicity and should not be used to treat human infections. Ehrlich, however, believed that atoxyl could be changed. For two years Ehrlich and his colleagues developed different derivatives of atoxyl. After 606 trials a derivative that killed only parasites and did not adversely affect laboratory mice was found. Later, the drug, now called **606** or **salvarsan,** was used to treat syphilis, and the results were miraculous. Yet, despite saving thousands of lives, salvarsan adversely affected some patients. Ehrlich could not foresee that "magic bullets" can be two-edged swords.

Modern Microbiology

Microbiology is now in the forefront of biological science. Many of the discoveries in microbiology have led to research interest and important discoveries in higher organisms. Much of the new interest has resulted from the development of gene-splicing techniques. Gene splicing **(recombinant DNA** or **genetic engineering)** is based on the ability of scientists to use DNA or genes from different sources and insert them into microbial DNA. The inserted DNA can then be expressed in the microbial cell. Gene splicing has already been used to produce various mammalian products in bacterial cells. Insulin, mammalian growth hormone, and interferon are just some of the mammalian products produced by bacterial cells. "Superbugs" or microorganisms containing foreign genes that code for highly degradative enzymes also have been developed. They are being used to break down products such as petroleum compounds, herbicides, and pesticides that are environmental pollutants and are relatively resistant to microbial attack in soil or water.

Despite our ability to isolate, identify, and control most of the microorganisms that cause disease in humans, we are still confronted with new infectious agents. Diseases such as legionnaires' disease, Lyme disease, and acquired immunodeficiency syndrome (AIDS) make us realize that nature has found new ways to plague humankind. In addition, many of the drugs used to treat "old" infectious diseases are no longer effective. Thus, the medical community is challenged to develop new solutions to old problems. Infectious disease is still a major problem in developing countries and a nagging problem in developed countries such as the United States. The solution to these problems will require the combined efforts of both medical and allied health personnel.

Summary

1. Microbiology is a science that is concerned with the study of microorganisms such as bacteria, fungi, algae, and protozoa as well as noncellular viruses. Medical microbiology is concerned with the study of infectious disease.

2. For many centuries disease was believed to be a divine punishment. In the sixteenth century, Fracastorius theorized that microorganisms were transmitted from human to human to cause disease. Leeuwenhoek, in the seventeenth century, was the first to observe microorganisms. Until the late nineteenth century, many believed that microorganisms arose spontaneously from organic matter.

3. Many scientists, including Redi, Spallanzani, and others, designed experiments to disprove spontaneous generation. Pasteur, in the late 1800s, was the first to lay the theory to rest. He demonstrated that microorganisms are carried in the air and can contaminate objects and solutions. Pasteur, because of his many discoveries, is considered the Father of Microbiology.

4. Robert Koch was one of the first to show the relationship of microorganisms to infectious disease. He demonstrated the pure culture technique and formulated what we now know as Koch's postulates. In the period between 1870 and 1890, the Golden Age of Microbiology, the bacte-

rial agents causing many infectious diseases were isolated and identified. These isolations and identifications were greatly enhanced by other developments including techniques for staining bacteria and the discovery of agar-agar.

5. In 1796, Edward Jenner recognized the importance of immunity in resistance to infection. Pasteur later developed immunization practices in the form of vaccines.

6. The nature of viruses was first recognized by Iwanowsky, who showed that they were filterable agents; that is, they were smaller than bacteria. The relationship of virus to animal disease was demonstrated in 1898 by Loeffler and Frosch, who showed that foot-and-mouth disease was caused by a filterable agent.

7. The use of natural compounds to cure disease has been known for centuries. Ehrlich, however, was the first to propose that drugs can selectively destroy infectious microorganisms without causing undue harm to the host. Fleming, in 1928, was the first to recognize that microorganisms can produce and release chemicals (antibiotics) that inhibit the activity of other microorganisms. From this discovery, penicillin was isolated and purified by Florey, Chain, and others in 1940.

8. Medical microbiology in the modern era still relies on the basic practices of isolation, identification, and treatment of infectious agents. These practices have been aided by experiments in genetics and the development of the field of genetic engineering.

Questions for Study

1. How do you reconcile the theory of spontaneous generation with the theory of evolution?
2. What was the importance of Frau Hesse's suggestion for the use of agar-agar in microbiology?
3. Can you give some reasons why viruses are not considered "living"?
4. Describe the major contributions of the following to microbiology: Pasteur, Koch, Ehrlich, Iwanowsky, and Jenner.
5. Make a list of the various fields in microbiology and describe how they might be affiliated with medical microbiology.

CHAPTER

2 Characteristics of Bacteria

OBJECTIVES

To describe the characteristics that differentiate prokaryotes from eukaryotes

To differentiate the terms genus, species, and strain

To explain the basis of bacterial taxonomy and what procedures are used to classify a bacterium

To list the components of a bacterial cell and their chemical composition

To describe the functions of the cytoplasmic membrane

To describe the ways in which solute can pass into and out of the cell

To describe the chemical similarities and differences in the cell wall of gram-positive and gram-negative bacteria

To describe the functions of the capsule and slime layer of bacteria

To illustrate the importance of flagella and pili to the bacterial cell

To describe the process of sporulation and its importance to bacteria

To define the terms taxonomy, coccus, bacillus, pleomorphism, mesosome, peptidoglycan, periplasm, porin, endotoxin, osmosis, protoplast, spheroplast, capsule, slime layer, flagellum, chemotaxis, nucleoid, ribosome, endospore, and vegetative cell

OUTLINE

CLASSIFICATION AND NOMENCLATURE
- Taxonomic Methods

BACTERIAL STRUCTURE AND FUNCTION
- Size and Morphology
- Pleomorphism

CYTOPLASMIC MEMBRANE
- Functions of Membrane Proteins
  - Nutrient Transport
  - Respiration
- Other Functions Associated with the Cytoplasmic Membrane
  - Cell Wall Biosynthesis
  - Site of DNA Synthesis

CELL WALL
- Gram-Positive Bacteria
- Gram-Negative Bacteria
- Osmosis and Cells Without Cell Walls

EXTRACELLULAR POLYMERIC SUBSTANCES (CAPSULES AND SLIME LAYERS)

FLAGELLA AND OTHER STRUCTURES ASSOCIATED WITH MOVEMENT

PILI (FIMBRIAE)

STRUCTURES WITHIN THE CYTOPLASM
- Nucleoids
- Ribosomes
- Inclusion Bodies (Intracellular Inclusions)
- Endospores
  - The Sporulation Process
  - The Germination Process

Each day new microbial properties are revealed by our advances in microscopy, biochemistry, and molecular biology. These advances not only have given us greater insight into microbial life and the factors that affect it, but also have given us insight into the properties of higher forms of life. The results obtained from the study of metabolic, physiological, and genetic characteristics in microbial models have provided us with a better understanding of many human functions.

In this chapter we examine the chemistry and function of the various structures that make up the anatomy of the microbial cell. An understanding of microbial anatomy is important because the ability of chemical and physical agents to inhibit the growth of, or kill, infectious microorganisms is related to the presence or absence of specific microbial components. First, however, we briefly discuss how microorganisms are classified.

Classification and Nomenclature

Classification is one branch of a science called **taxonomy.** The purpose of classification is to arrange organisms into specific groups, called **taxa,** based on a similarity of characteristics. Until the discovery of microorganisms, the biological world was divided into two major groups: plants and animals. Bacteria were originally classified as plants. Unicellular microorganisms possess characteristics that are neither plant nor animal, and for this reason some authorities preferred to place them in a separate group called the **Protista.** Even among the unicellular microorganisms, however, there was one important feature that showed that the term Protista was not practical. This unique feature was the presence or absence of a nuclear membrane (the membrane surrounding the hereditary information of the cell). Organisms devoid of a nuclear membrane were called **prokaryotes** (from the Greek *protos,* primitive and *karyon,* nucleus) while organisms possessing a nuclear membrane were called **eukaryotes** (Greek *eu,* true, and *karyon,* nucleus). Other characteristics also separate these two divisions and are outlined in Table 2-1. Bacteria represent the largest number of species that are infectious for humans and their classification will be discussed in more detail. This classification scheme is appropriate for medically important microorganisms but we should point out that because of the work of Carl Woese and others, there has been a reassessment of the divisions of all life forms. All life forms are now divided into three domains (formerly kingdoms): **Archea, Bacteria,** and **Eucarya.** The domain Archea represents a group of bacteria

TABLE 2-1
Important Characteristics Distinguishing Prokaryotes from Eukaryotes[a]

Characteristic or structure	Eukaryote	Prokaryote	Virus
Size (average based on unicellular species)	5–10 μm	1–3 μm	0.025–0.200 μm
Cell wall	Present in fungi and algae	Present except in *Mycoplasma*	Absent
Cytoplasmic membrane	Membrane possesses sterols	Membrane contains no sterols except in *Mycoplasma*	Absent, but a lipid membrane surrounds some viruses
Nuclear membrane	Present	Absent	Absent
Nucleolus	Present	Absent	Absent
Hereditary information	DNA; more than one chromosome in nucleus; proteins associated with chromosomes	DNA; single chromosome; no associated proteins	DNA or RNA and may be single- or double-stranded; some have enzymes associated with them
Ribosomes	Larger than prokaryotes (sedimentation constant of 80S[b])	Smaller than eukaryotes (sedimentation constant of 70S[b])	Absent
Respiration	Associated with mitochondrion	Associated with particles in cytoplasmic membrane	Absent
Reproduction	Sexual and asexual	Asexual (binary fission)	Asexual
Habitat	Found almost exclusively in environments containing oxygen; does not require an intracellular habitat in which to reproduce	Can be found equally in environments that may or may not contain oxygen; some (e.g., *Rickettsia*) require a living host in order to reproduce	Can reproduce only within the environment of a living host

[a] We have also included the acellular viruses to make the comparison of microorganisms more complete.
[b] S refers to Svedberg, which is a relative size unit derived from sedimentation studies.

(Archaeobacteria) that possess characteristics that are both prokaryotic and eukaryotic. They are found in extreme environments that might contain high salt concentrations or hot acids or that might produce methane in the absence of oxygen. The domain Bacteria contains typical bacterial species including the medically important ones. The domain Eucarya represents the remaining life forms (eukaryotes) including the medically important microorganisms such as fungi, protozoa, and helminths (worms).

Nomenclature is the assignment of names to a taxonomic group that has been defined by similarities in certain characteristics. The scientific naming is based on the taxonomic group, which incorporates two names **(binomial nomenclature)** called **genus** and **species.** The bacterial species, which is the basic taxonomic group, signifies a distinct member of a group of microorganisms that possess similar characteristics but differ in important ways from related groups of bacteria in other independent characteristics. The genus (plural, genera) name is capitalized, while the species name is not. Both words are italicized, for example, *Pseudonomas aeruginosa*. Much can be learned from the genus and species names. The genus name of bacteria often indicates the morphology of the species, for example, *Streptococcus* (chain of spherical cells), *Bacillus* (rod-shaped), *Spirochaeta* (spiral-shaped), but it can also indicate the organism's discoverer, for example, *Escherichia* (Theodor Escherich), as well as various other characteristics. The species name frequently indicates a metabolic feature, biochemical characteristic, or disease association, for example, *Staphylococcus aureus,* in which *aureus* refers to a golden pigment produced by the species, or *Klebsiella pneumoniae,* in which *pneumoniae* refers to the type of disease caused by the species. The term **strain** will be seen in this book. A species may be composed of a group of related strains. For example, *K. pneumoniae* may consist of strains each of which is attacked by a different group of related bacterial viruses. *K. pneumoniae* could therefore be described as *K. pneumoniae* A1, A2, A3, A4. Letters or numbers or their combinations are used after the species name to indicate a strain that has properties distinct from other strains of the species.

The classification of bacteria is based on the wide variety of characteristics, or properties, associated with the organism. Related genera of bacteria are grouped into families, related families into orders, and so on up to kingdoms or superkingdoms. There is no official classification of bacteria and artificial classification schemes have appeared from time to time. The most widely accepted is *Bergey's Manual of Determinative Bacteriology,* which is in its ninth edition. The current edition has classified prokaryotes into the Kingdom Procaryotae, under which there are various *sections.* Each section represents a specific group of bacteria that has been separated on the basis of one or more features, such as staining characteristics, morphology, oxygen requirements, physiological responses, spore formation, and other characteristics. Each section, which can be further subdivided into families and orders, contains a number of genera. A breakdown of the various sections and some of their characteristics appears in Table 2-2.

TAXONOMIC METHODS

The arrangement of organisms into various taxonomic groups is based on their degree of relatedness. Classification of bacteria based on natural relationships, that is, a fossil record, is called **phylogenetic classification.** Unlike higher forms of life, which have a fossil record in which certain characteristics can be compared, the fossil record of bacteria is virtually absent. Even the few fossil records of bacteria that have been discovered reveal only age and little else. Morphological, biochemical, and physiological characteristics as well as staining properties are used most frequently to differentiate bacteria. The use of such characteristics in taxonomy, however, represents an artificial scheme. Morphological traits are usually stable characteristics that are not influenced by environmental factors. Physiological traits, however, are subject to some variation. The temperature and pH requirements for growth or the fermentation products released by bacteria can be influenced by the environment. The kind of trait that can be used to separate or classify certain groups of bacteria may vary from one group to another. By evaluating various morphological or nonmorphological characteristics, bacteria can be arranged into certain taxonomic groups. Unfortunately, not all scientists agree on which microbial characteristics are most important. Some microbial properties are given more weight than others by one investigator, while another investigator may suggest that these properties should not be considered for classification. A technique called **numerical taxonomy** gives equal weight to all the characteristics examined. All the characteristics of the organism are evaluated by a computer. A percentage of the total number of traits held in common between the organisms is expressed as a similarity profile. Those organisms showing similarity in 80 percent or more of specific characteristics are considered part of the same species.

There are techniques for determining phylogenetic relatedness between microorganisms, and this is based on analysis of large molecules such as DNA, RNA, and protein. These large molecules (called macromolecules) are made up of many smaller subunits and their sequence in the macromolecule is an evolutionary profile. Thus, these molecules represent a fossil record of the bacterium. Methods are now available for measuring relatedness between the DNA molecules of two organisms. The DNA can be cleaved into fragments and the amount of DNA sequences that are common between two organisms determines the degree of relatedness.

The proper classification or organisms should consist of

1. Measuring and comparing specific biochemical reactions (and other significant characteristics) of the microorganisms.
2. Testing the DNA relatedness of the organisms that have been grouped together based on tests described in 1.
3. Reexamination of the biochemical characteristics of each DNA-related group in order to define the biochemical boundaries of each species.

TABLE 2-2
Outline of The Taxonomic Divisions Found in *Bergey's Manual of Determinative Bacteriology* That Contain the Major Human Pathogens

Section	Section description	Important genera	Disease
1	The Spirochetes	*Treponema, Borrelia, Leptospira*	Syphilis (*Treponema*), undulant fever (*Borrelia*)
2	Aerobic/Microaerophilic, Motile, Helical/Vibroid, Gram-Negative Bacteria	*Spirillum, Campylobacter*	Rat-bite fever (*Spirillum*), intestinal disease (*Campylobacter*)
4	Gram-Negative Aerobic Rods and Cocci	*Pseudomonas, Legionella, Neisseria, Brucella, Bordetella, Francisella*	Opportunistic* (*Pseudomonas*), legionnaires' disease (*Legionella*), meningitis and gonorrhea (*Neisseria*), brucellosis (*Brucella*), whooping cough (*Bordetella*), tularemia (*Francisella*)
5	Facultatively Anerobic Gram-Negative Rods	*Escherichia, Shigella, Salmonella, Klebsiella, Yersinia, Proteus, Vibrio, Hemophilus*	Intestinal disease (*Escherichia*), opportunistic* (*Escherichia, Klebsiella,* and *Proteus*) plague (*Yersinia*), cholera (*Vibrio*), meningitis (*Hemophilus*)
6	Anaerobic Gram-Negative, Straight, Curved and Helical Rods	*Bacteroides, Fusobacterium, Leptotrichia*	Infections of oral cavity, opportunistic*
9	The Rickettsias and Chlamydias	*Rickettsia, Chlamydia, Coxiella*	Typhus and Rocky Mountain spotted fever (*Rickettsia*), psittacosis and genitourinary tract disease (*Chlamydia*), Q fever (*Coxiella*)
10	The Mycoplasma	*Mycoplasma, Ureaplasma*	Pneumonia (*Mycoplasma*), genitourinary tract disease (*Ureaplasma* and *Mycoplasma*)
12	Gram-Positive Cocci	*Staphylococcus, Streptococcus*	Skin infections (*Staphylococcus*), rheumatic fever (*Streptococcus*), opportunistic* (*Staphylococcus*)
13	Endospore-Forming Gram-Positive Rods and Cocci	*Bacillus, Clostridium*	Anthrax (*Bacillus*); tetanus, botulism, and gas gangrene (*Clostridium*)
15	Irregular, Nonsporing, Gram-Positive Rods	*Corynebacterium, Actinomyces*	Diphtheria (*Corynebacterium*), lesions of face and lungs (*Actinomyces*)
16	Mycobacteria	*Mycobacterium*	Tuberculosis and leprosy
17	Nocardioforms	*Nocardia*	Lesions of skin

* Opportunistic pathogens are organisms that cause disease in individuals compromised by some underlying illness or condition. Most opportunistic infections occur in the hospital.
SOURCE: From J. G. Holt, ed. *Bergey's Manual of Determinative Bacteriology,* 9th ed. Baltimore: Williams & Wilkins, 1984.

Bacterial Structure and Function

SIZE AND MORPHOLOGY

Bacteria show considerable variation in size, from cells barely visible with the compound light microscope (0.2 μm) to spiral organisms that may reach lengths up to 60 μm. Most bacteria infectious for humans have average lengths of 1 to 3 μm and can be observed with the compound light microscope. Some of the basic structures that can be observed microscopically in a typical bacterial cell are illustrated in Figure 2-1.

Bacteria have four basic shapes: spherical, rod, spiral, and square (Fig. 2-2). Spherical cells are called **cocci** (singular, coccus) and may exist in different arrangements. When cocci divide, they usually remain attached to one another, and the arrangement that follows is based on the plane of cell division (Fig. 2-3). Cocci that divide along the same axis may form chains of cocci varying in length from 2 to 20 cocci. A pair of cocci are called **diplococci,** while chains of 4 to 20 are called **streptococci.** Cocci that divide in two planes form a **tetrad.** Division in three planes results in the formation of a group of eight called **sarcina** or large clusters of cocci called **staphylococci.** Rod-shaped bacteria are called **bacilli** (singular, bacillus). They divide in one plane and are sometimes observed to be in short chains, but usually they appear singly (see Fig. 2-2). The term bacillus, which signifies a type of morphology, should not be confused with the taxonomic genus called *Bacillus.* Spiral-shaped microorganisms, which appear in a helical or corkscrew shape, divide in one plane and separate at cell division. The square-shaped bacteria are a recently discovered group found in areas of high salt content (Great Salt Lake, for example). Square bacteria

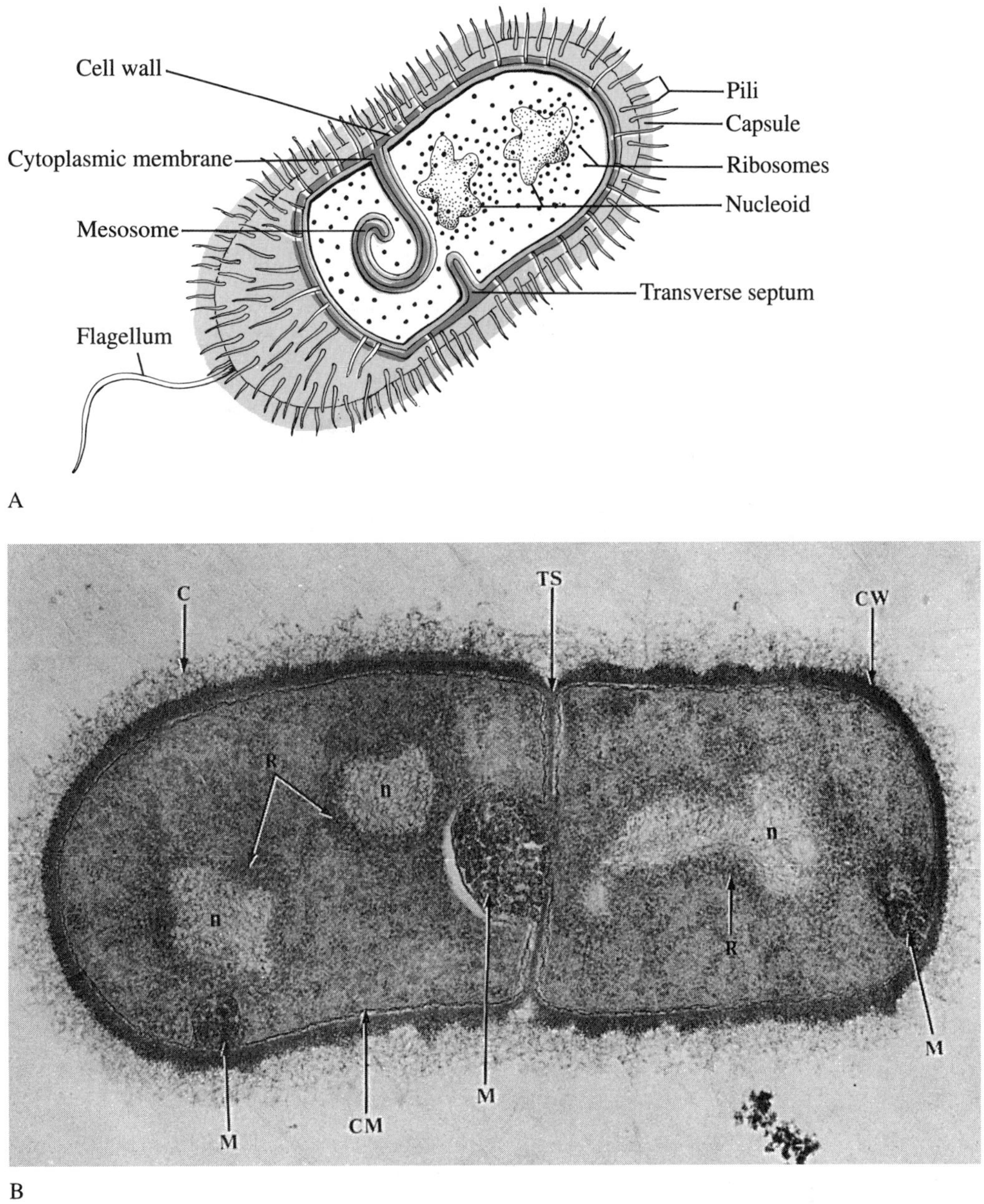

FIGURE 2-1
A. Basic morphology of a bacterial cell. Some of the features, for example, flagella and extracellular polymeric substances (capsule), may not be present in all bacterial cells. B. Electron micrograph of a rod-shaped bacterium illustrating its basic morphology. C = capsule; TS = transverse septum; CW = cell wall; M = mesosome; CM = cytoplasmic membrane; n = nuclear area or nucleoid; R = ribosome. The transverse septum is the site of cell division. (From D. J. Ellar, D. J. Lundgren, and R. A. Slepecky, *J. Bacteriol.* 94:1189, 1967.)

are not known to be infectious and therefore not discussed further in this text.

PLEOMORPHISM

Pleomorphism is defined as the existence of different morphological forms of the same species or strain. Pleomorphism usually refers to changes in microbial shape within the organism's natural environment. In the natural environment of some microorganisms there is a differentiation process in which a change of shape is normal. Some bacteria (usually not infectious for humans) under the influence of nutrient starvation, for example, change their morphology from ovoid to filamentous. Under adverse conditions in the laboratory (old cultures, for example) most bacteria show variations in shape (ballooning, bulging, branching, and so on), but this is not the normal state.

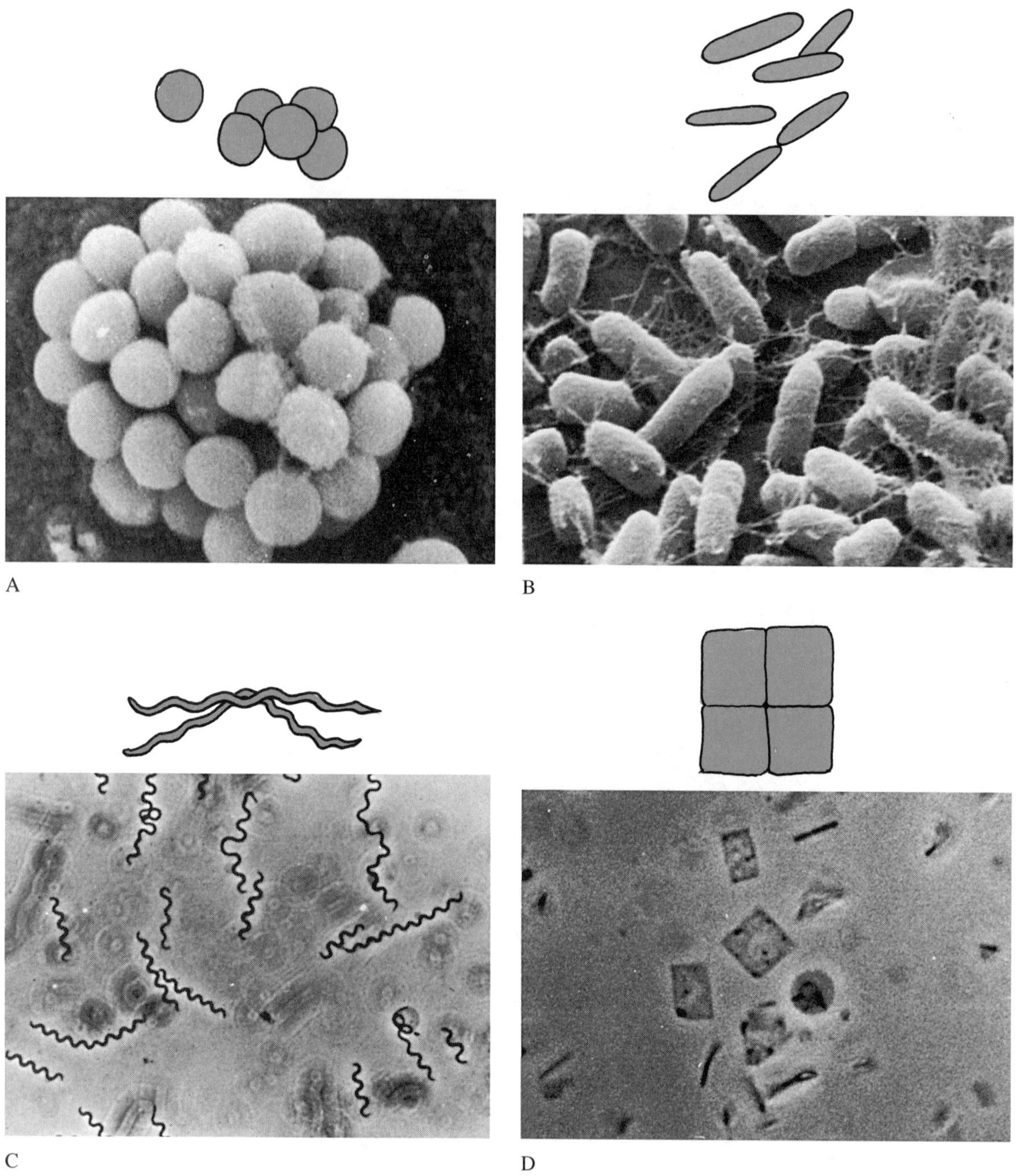

FIGURE 2-2
Shapes of bacteria. A. Spherical (coccus). Scanning electron micrograph of staphylococci (× 14,000). (Courtesy of Z. Yoshii.) B. Rod (bacillus). Scanning electron micrograph of bacilli. (From T. J. Kerr et al., *Appl. Environ. Microbiol.* 46:1201, 1983.) C. Spiral. Micrograph of rumen treponemes. (From A. Ziolecki, *Appl. Environ. Microbiol.* 37:131, 1979.) D. Square. Micrograph is phase contrast (× 1600 before 20 percent reduction). (From D. Stoeckenius, *J. Bacteriol.* 148:352, 1981.)

Cytoplasmic Membrane

The cytoplasm of the cell is surrounded by a membrane referred to as the **cytoplasmic** or **plasma membrane.** The cytoplasmic membrane is a dynamic, flexible structure that is actively and passively engaged in several cellular functions. Many of these functions are directly related to the structure of the cytoplasmic membrane.

The cytoplasmic membrane is made up of a phospholipid matrix into which are embedded various proteins. The phospholipid can be described as a molecule consisting of three units. One unit, called the head, contains a phosphate (PO_4) group, while the other two units are

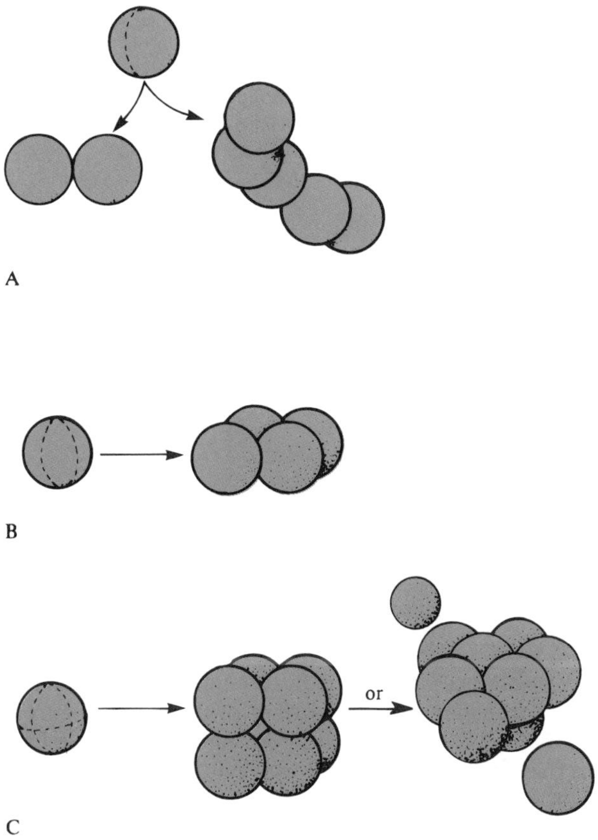

FIGURE 2-3
The arrangement of cocci is based on the plane of cell division. A. Division in one plane produces diplococci or streptococci. B. Division in two planes produces a tetrad. C. Division in three planes produces a group of eight (sarcina) or clusters (staphylococci).

long-chain fatty acids that can be described as tails (Fig. 2-4). When phospholipids are placed in water, the phosphate heads are attracted to water **(hydrophilic)** but the fatty acid tails avoid water **(hydrophobic)** and huddle together. This results in a double layer (bilayer) of phospholipid (Fig. 2-5). The proteins that are superimposed onto the lipid bilayer are of two general types, those that span the membrane and those that do not. These proteins perform specific functions, which are now discussed.

FUNCTIONS OF MEMBRANE PROTEINS

Nutrient Transport

The cytoplasmic membrane acts as a barrier to some molecules (for example, large ones such as proteins) but permits the entry of other molecules into the cytoplasm of the cell. Some molecules, such as oxygen and water, can move passively across the cytoplasmic membrane. The direction of this passive movement depends on the concentration of the dissolved molecules (solute) on either side of the cytoplasmic membrane. Solute will move from an area where its concentration is high to an area where its concentration is low (Fig. 2-6A) until the concentration of solute on either side of the membrane is the same. This type of solute transport mechanism is called **passive diffusion.**

Some solutes can be transported into the cytoplasm by exploiting carriers. The **carriers** are proteins located in the cytoplasmic membrane (Fig. 2-6B). They pick up solutes on one side of the cytoplasmic membrane and transport them, chemically unchanged, to the opposite side of the cytoplasmic membrane. This transport process is called **facilitated diffusion.***

The most important transport mechanism is called **active transport.** Microorganisms live primarily in environments where most nutrients are at a lower concentration outside the cell. Nutrients can, however, be transported into the cell against this concentration gradient through the use of carriers and by an expenditure of energy, that is, active transport. Carrier proteins transport the solute through channels produced by other proteins that span the cytoplasmic membrane (Fig. 2-6C). The transported solute is not chemically changed during this transport process.

* Facilitated diffusion, like passive diffusion, is involved in the movement of solutes from an area of high concentration to an area of low solute concentration.

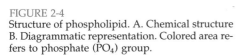

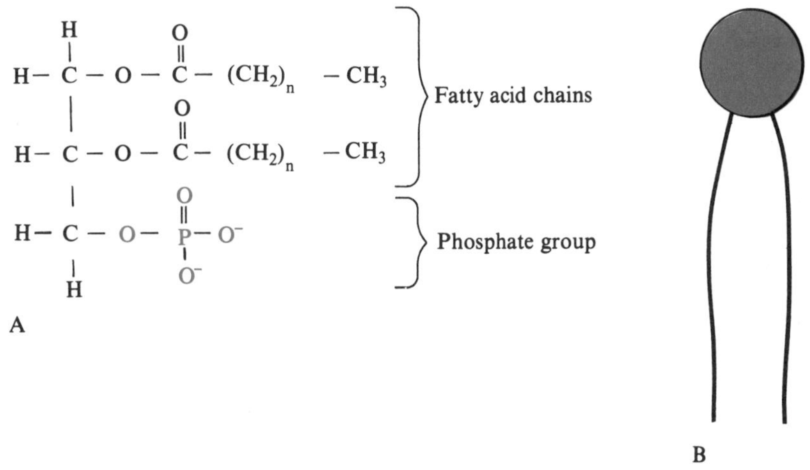

FIGURE 2-4
Structure of phospholipid. A. Chemical structure B. Diagrammatic representation. Colored area refers to phosphate (PO_4) group.

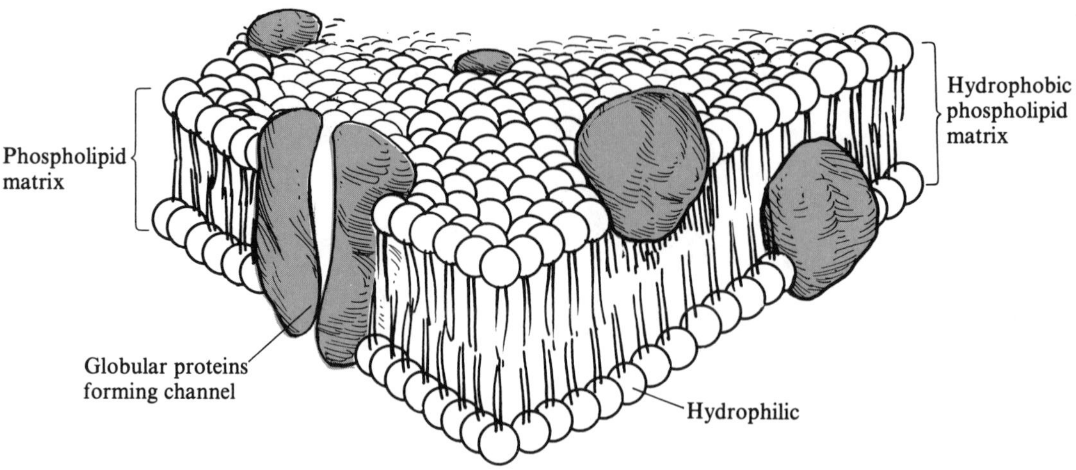

FIGURE 2-5
Model of cytoplasmic membrane. Globular proteins are embedded in a phospholipid matrix. (Adapted from S. J. Singer and G. I. Nicolson, *Science* 175:720, 1972.)

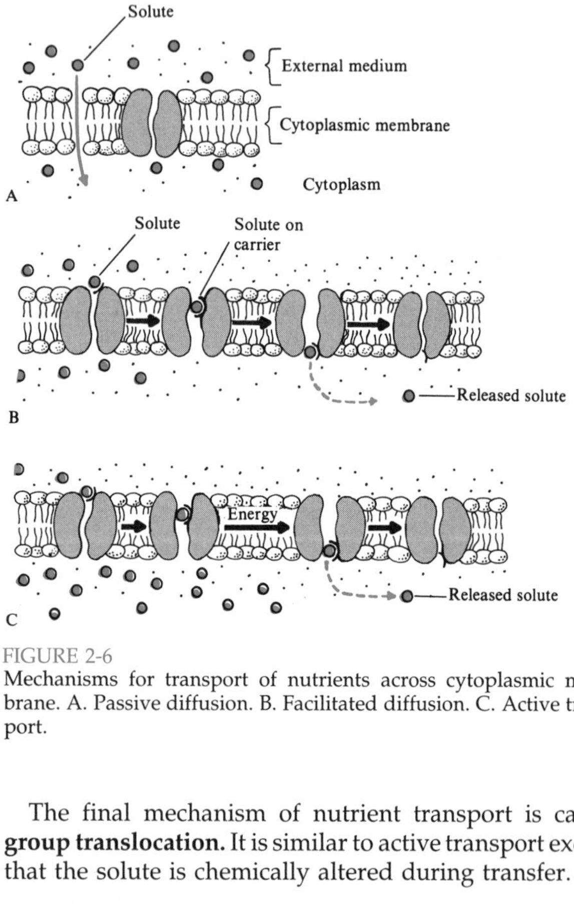

FIGURE 2-6
Mechanisms for transport of nutrients across cytoplasmic membrane. A. Passive diffusion. B. Facilitated diffusion. C. Active transport.

The final mechanism of nutrient transport is called **group translocation.** It is similar to active transport except that the solute is chemically altered during transfer.

Respiration

Several proteins associated with respiration, that is, electron transport and energy formation, are located in the cytoplasmic membrane. In eukaryotes these respiratory activities are associated with organelles called mitochondria. Respiration is discussed at more length in Chapter 3.

OTHER FUNCTIONS ASSOCIATED WITH THE CYTOPLASMIC MEMBRANE

Many substances produced in the cytoplasm of the cell must be transferred to the surface of the cell or to structures that are external to the cytoplasmic membrane. Proteins that are required for cell wall synthesis, for example, are produced in the cytoplasm. Various toxins that are produced by microorganisms, and may be involved in human disease or inhibit other bacteria, are also produced in the cytoplasm and must be transported to the exterior. In addition, many bacteria produce enzymes that are secreted outside the cell to break down macromolecules into smaller units so they can be transported across the cytoplasmic membrane.

Cell Wall Biosynthesis

The enzymes involved in the assembly of cell wall components are located in the cytoplasmic membrane.

Site of DNA Synthesis

During the replication of the DNA molecule in the cell, the cytoplasmic membrane is believed to be an anchoring site for the ends of the DNA molecule. These membrane attachment sites are believed to be invaginated areas of the cytoplasmic membrane called **mesosomes.** They are usually associated with the site of division of bacteria **(septum)** but can be found elsewhere in the cell (see Fig. 2-1).

Cell Wall

The bacterial cell wall is a thick and relatively rigid layer that lies outside the cytoplasmic membrane. The wall protects the fragile cytoplasmic membrane and the contents it encloses. The wall is also responsible for maintaining the shape of the bacterium.

The bacterial world, with few exceptions, is divided into two basic cell wall types, **gram-positive** and **gram-**

negative, on the basis of a staining procedure called the Gram's stain (see Appendix A). Division into gram-positive and gram-negative is based on marked differences in the physical and chemical makeup of the cell wall. A cell is gram-positive if it resists decolorization by alcohol after the application of a primary stain and gram-negative if it is decolorized by alcohol after primary staining. The backbone material of both cell types is the **peptidoglycan** layer. The peptidoglycan is composed of layers of polysaccharide chains that are linked by short peptides (peptides are chains of amino acids of varying length). The peptidoglycan is composed of two alternating sugars, **N-acetylmuramic acid** (abbreviated NAM) and **N-acetylglucosamine** (abbreviated NAG). Let us compare the composition and structure of the two cell wall types.

GRAM-POSITIVE BACTERIA

The peptidoglycan layer of gram-positive bacteria is very thick compared to the gram-negative peptidoglycan layer and consists of layer upon layer of molecules. The peptidoglycan layer of gram-positive bacteria therefore accounts for 50 to 60 percent of the total dry weight of the cell wall. Much of the remaining cell wall material is a special polysaccharide called **teichoic acid** (Fig. 2-7A). The peptidoglycan of *S. aureus,* a gram-positive bacterium, is illustrated in Figure 2-8. The degree of cross-linking of polysaccharide chains via peptides in the peptidoglycan of gram-positive bacteria is very high and this results in a very rigid cell wall. Teichoic acids not only permeate the peptidoglycan but also appear on the surface of the cell wall. Their function to the cell is not fully understood.

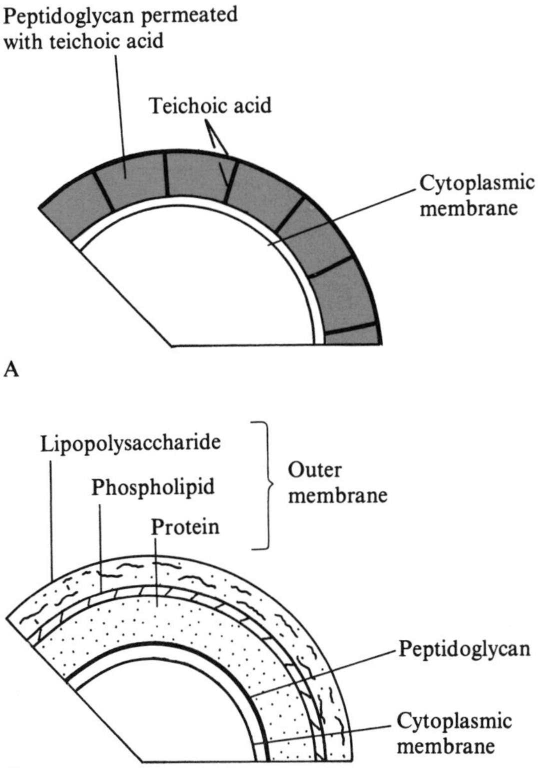

FIGURE 2-7
Relative composition and structure of the bacterial cell wall. A. Gram-positive cell wall. Peptidoglycan is very thick and is permeated by teichoic acids that also cover the surface. B. Gram-negative cell wall. The wall is multilayered, with the peptidoglycan layer much thinner than in the gram-positive cell. Figure shows only the relative composition. More details of the precise location of cell wall components can be found in Figures 2-8 and 2-9.

GRAM-NEGATIVE BACTERIA

The gram-negative cell wall, unlike the gram-positive wall, is multilayered (Fig. 2-7B). The peptidoglycan layer of the gram-negative bacterium is only one or two molecules thick and accounts for only 5 to 10 percent of the total dry weight of the cell wall. External to the peptidoglycan is a complex cell wall layer called the **outer membrane.** The outer membrane is attached to the peptidoglycan by means of lipoprotein molecules (Fig. 2-9). The outer membrane is made up of phospholipid (20–30 percent), lipopolysaccharide (30 percent), and protein (40–50 percent). The phospholipid of the outer membrane resembles the bilayer arrangement seen in the cytoplasmic membrane. Located in the phospholipid are protein channels, called **porins,** that are involved in transport. Nutrients transported through porins must first enter the **periplasmic space,** an area between the cytoplasmic membrane and the outer membrane.

A summary of outer membrane functions is outlined in Table 2-3. The periplasmic space contains several types of molecules, including enzymes that process molecules before they enter the cytoplasm. The periplasmic space also contains protein molecules that act as carriers of nutrients and are similar to the carriers in the cytoplasmic

TABLE 2-3
Functions of the Outer Membrane

Function	Molecules or components affected
Export	Proteins (toxins), periplasm proteins
Restriction	Hydrophobic molecules (some antibiotics), large hydrophilic molecules (enzymes, polysaccharides)
Selective permeability	Porins, which select small hydrophilic molecules for entry into cell
Export	Building blocks of capsules, protein enzymes, toxins, periplasmic proteins
Anchor cell components	Flagella, pili, capsules
Immunological	Antibodies
Receptors	Bacterial viruses, bacteriocins, sex pili, various surfaces (cells, polymers, metals, etc.)

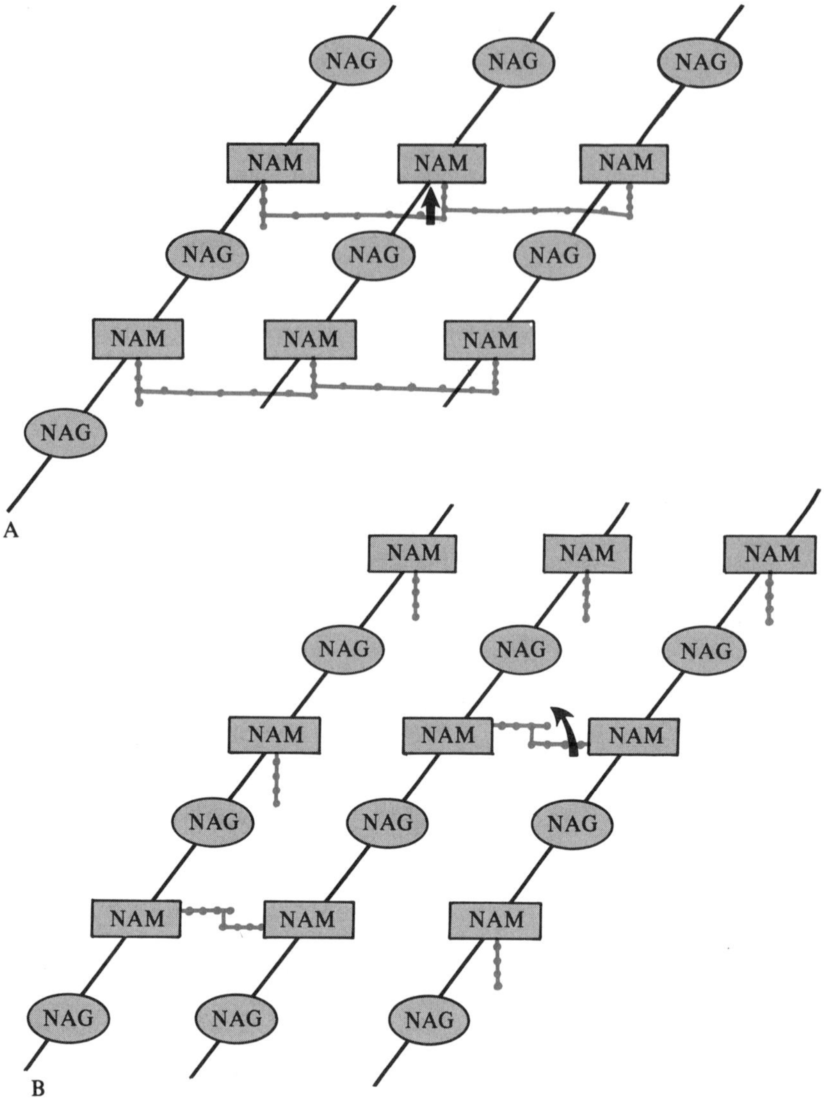

FIGURE 2-8
Comparative peptidoglycan structure in gram-positive (A) and gram-negative bacteria (B). Arrows indicate the sites where penicillin prevents linkage of adjacent strands. NAM = N-acetylmuramic acid; NAG = N-acetylglucosamine.

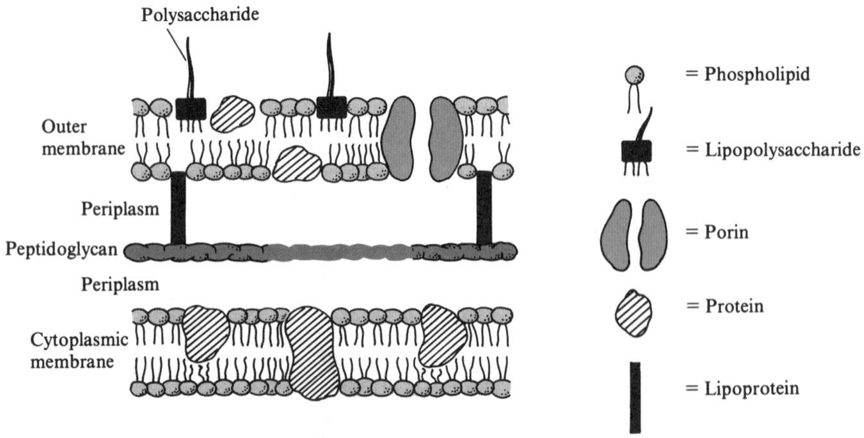

FIGURE 2-9
More detailed illustration of the outer membrane of the gram-negative cell wall and its relationship to peptidoglycan. Note that this figure is not drawn to scale.

membrane. Other molecules located in the periplasmic space that are of special interest are a group of enzymes that are capable of inactivating drugs such as antibiotics. These antibiotic-inactivating enzymes render the microorganism resistant to the affected antibiotic.

The lipid component of the lipopolysaccharide is embedded in the phospholipid while the polysaccharide portion projects from the surface of the cell (Fig. 2-9). Only the lipid component of the lipopolysaccharide, called lipid A, is toxic, but since the two molecules are released as a single unit, the lipopolysaccharide is referred to as **endotoxin.** Endotoxin causes fever and can result in lysis of red blood cells. The polysaccharide portion of the lipopolysaccharide that projects from the surface of the cell is made of various sugars that vary from species to species. These sugars serve as markers that enable microbiologists to differentiate species in the laboratory.

OSMOSIS AND CELLS WITHOUT CELL WALLS

The cell wall is not a totally rigid structure but is capable of expanding and contracting. The solute concentration in the cell is usually greater than that outside the cell. In other words, the cytoplasm of the cell is **hypertonic,** while the environment or medium is **hypotonic.** In a hypotonic medium water moves from the solution outside the cell into the cell cytoplasm to establish an equilibrium—a process called **osmosis** (Fig. 2-10). The cell contents swell but do not burst because of the rigidity of the cell wall. Without the cell wall the cytoplasmic membrane would expand and burst.

Sometimes in research it is necessary to remove the cell wall and produce a cellular unit that possesses an intact cytoplasmic membrane. This can be accomplished through the use of the enzyme **lysozyme,** which cleaves specific bonds in the peptidoglycan, and by placing the cells in a hypertonic medium. Once the wall has been digested, one of two types of intact cell membrane unit is produced: a **protoplast** or a **spheroplast.** Protoplasts possess no cell wall material and are produced from gram-positive cells but spheroplasts possess some cell wall remnants and are produced from gram-negative bacteria. In a hypertonic medium the protoplast or spheroplast does not burst because a hypertonic medium contains a high concentration of solutes. These solutes exert enough pressure outside the cell to counterbalance the pressure from the solutes inside the cell that push against the cytoplasmic membrane.

One genus of bacteria called *Mycoplasma* lacks a cell wall. These bacteria can survive without walls because their cytoplasmic membranes are fortified by the inclusion of large molecules called sterols. These organisms grow very slowly and require special media for laboratory cultivation.

FIGURE 2-10
Osmosis. A. Microbial cell in hypotonic medium takes water into the cell but does not burst. B. Microbial cell in hypotonic medium containing lysozyme. As lysozyme degrades the cell wall, water is taken into the cell, which causes the cytoplasmic membrane to expand then eventually burst.

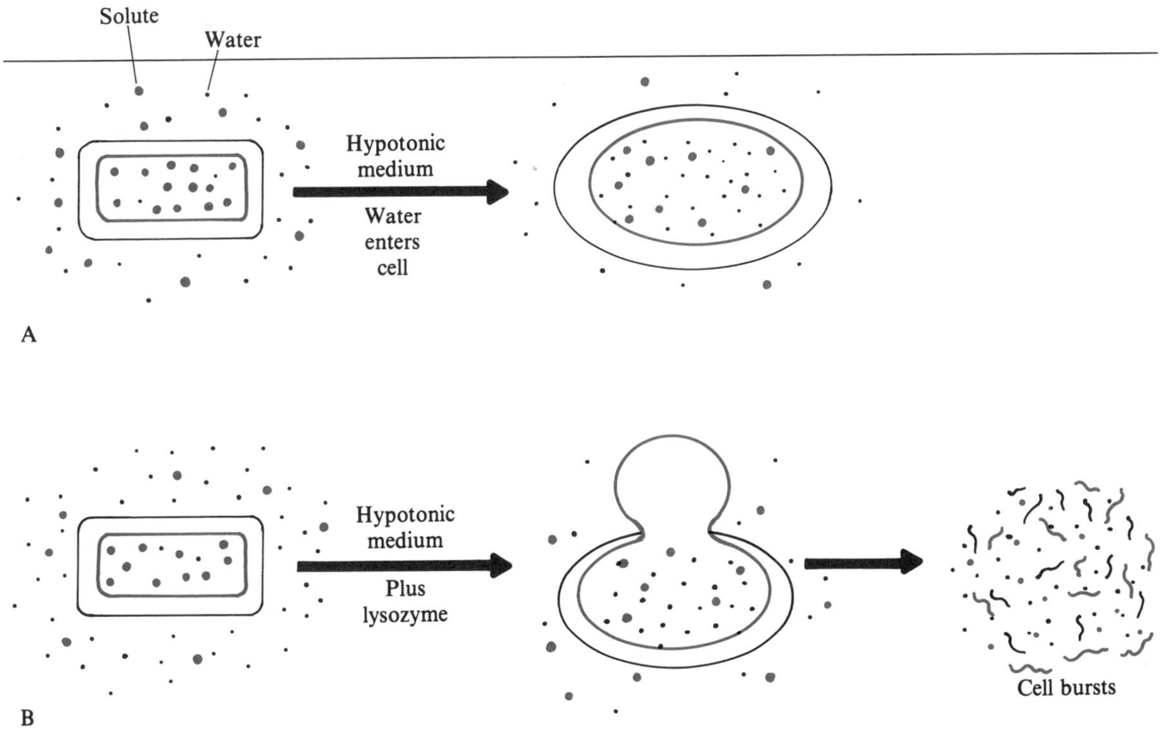

Extracellular Polymeric Substances (Capsules and Slime Layers)

The bacterial cell may possess polymeric substances that are attached externally to the cell wall. These extracellular polymeric substances (EPS) are composed primarily of polysaccharides, but a few bacteria, such as *Bacillus anthracis,* have polypeptide EPS. EPS are considered **capsules** if they exhibit some organization and adhere strongly to the cell wall. Loosely organized EPS that are not strongly attached to the cell wall are called **slime layers.** The EPS do not take up ordinary stains; therefore, they can be demonstrated by suspending the bacteria in a solution containing colloidal particles such as India ink or by using stains that "stain" the background (Plate 1). The particles cannot penetrate the EPS; therefore, the cell appears to have a halo. EPS are not necessary for the survival of the cell, and continued cultivation of an organism in the laboratory may result in the eventual loss of EPS. The capsule can perform some functions that may play a role in disease:

1. Adherence. Microorganisms can use the capsule for adherence to other members of their species to form colonies or to adhere to various surfaces. Adherence to human cells via EPS appears to be necessary for oral microorganisms such as *Streptococcus mutans,* the organism associated with the formation of cavities in teeth (caries). This organism synthesizes EPS that are polymers of glucose (glucans) as well as fructose (fructans). These polymers bind to the tooth surface and enable other bacteria to bind. Eventually a film called **plaque** covers the tooth surface.
2. Inhibition of phagocytosis. Phagocytosis is a process, carried out by certain blood or tissue cells, in which foreign objects, such as bacteria, are ingested. Ingested bacteria are usually destroyed by the phagocytic cells. Phagocytosis is, therefore, a defense measure on the part of the host's immune system. Some bacteria can resist phagocytosis because they possess extracellular molecules in the form of capsules or slime layers. *Streptococcus pneumoniae,* for example, can resist phagocytosis only if the strains of that species produce a capsule. The capsules and slime layers of some bacteria do not prevent phagocytosis. In addition, some of the encapsulated bacteria that are not ingested by phagocytes do not necessarily cause disease.
3. Antigenic activity. The term **antigen** refers to molecules, such as proteins and polysaccharides, that stimulate the formation of antibodies when injected into a mammalian host. Antibodies in effect can neutralize the activity of the antigen, which may be a molecule or a whole cell. The EPS of infectious microorganisms such as *S. pneumoniae* and *Hemophilus influenzae* are antigenic and have been purified and used as vaccines to prevent disease caused by these microorganisms. Antigenicity is also used in the identification of specific EPS-producing bacteria. Antibodies to a specific EPS can be applied to a culture of unknown bacterial cells. If the bacteria have an EPS that is the same as that of the EPS used to induce antibody formation, the antibodies will cause the EPS to swell. This swelling is referred to as the **quellung reaction.** (See Chapter 17.)

Flagella and Other Structures Associated with Movement

Bacteria suspended in a solution can be observed microscopically to be moving in a random fashion. This random movement is called **brownian movement** and is due to bombardment by water molecules on the surface of the cell. Many bacteria, however, are capable of independent and directed movement that is directly related to the presence of protein appendages called **flagella.** A bacterial cell may have a single flagellum or more than one, depending on the species (Fig. 2-11). The flagellum, which consists of a filament, hook, and basal body, may be 20 μm in length (Fig. 2-12). The rings observed in the basal body differ between gram-positive and gram-negative bacteria, but their function remains the same—anchoring the flagellum to the cytoplasmic membrane and in some instances to the cell wall as well.

Flagella-like filaments called **axial filaments** are found in the group of bacteria called spirochetes. Axial filaments are chemically and structurally similar to flagella, but they do not emanate from the surface of the cell. Axial filaments are located beneath the outer surface of the bacterial cell. They appear to originate at the poles of the organism and then wrap themselves about the body of the spirochete (Fig. 2-13). Axial filaments are, therefore, not exposed to the external environment as are the flagella of other bacteria. Axial filaments are not hindered by the viscosity of the medium; thus, spirochetes can move more rapidly through viscous media than can flagellated bacteria.

Flagella are not an essential requirement for survival of the cell, but they do provide certain advantages. The involuntary movement of an organism in response to stimuli is called **taxis,** or a tactic response. Tactic responses are absolutely dependent on the possession of motility. Taxes result in the accumulation of bacteria in physiologically favorable environments; they may also prevent accumulation in unfavorable environments. Stimulants of taxes include nutrients **(chemotaxis),** air **(aerotaxis),** or light **(phototaxis).** Flagella may also help the bacterial cell to attach to surfaces including epithelial cells.

Rotation of flagella provides the cell with movement and is a consequence of the activity of the basal body. Flagellar rotation occurs in a direction opposite to that of the body of the cell (Fig. 2-14). When flagellar rotation is counterclockwise, the bacterium swims smoothly toward an attractant. In the presence of a repellent the flagellar rotation is clockwise and the cell demonstrates a tumbling effect (Fig. 2-14B) to get away from the repellent.

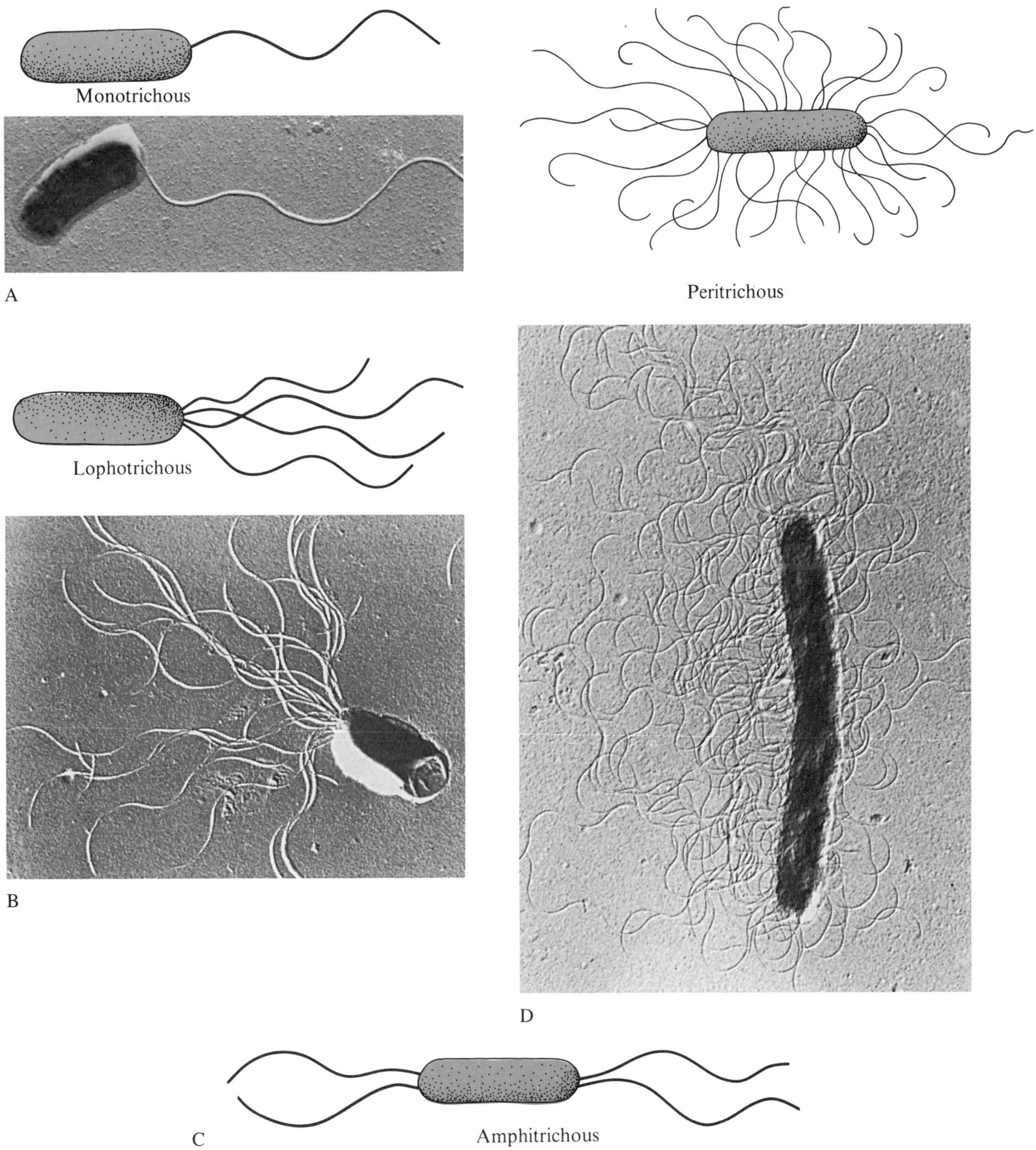

FIGURE 2-11
Flagellar arrangement. A. Monotrichous. Electron micrograph (× 24,000 before 50 percent reduction). B. Lophotrichous. Electron micrograph (× 30,000 before 59 percent reduction). C. Amphitrichous. D. Peritrichous. Electron micrograph (× 24,000 before 44 percent reduction). (Electron micrographs courtesy of W. Hodgkiss.)

Pili (Fimbriae)

Pili (singular, pilus) are protein appendages that project from the surface of the cell but are shorter than flagella (Fig. 2-15). Pili range in length from 0.3 to 0.20 μm. The term **fimbriae** frequently is used synonymously with pili by some in the scientific community. We consider pili to be of two types, **sex pili** and **attachment** or **common pili.** Sex pili are found primarily on gram-negative bacteria. They are few in number (one to three) and are involved in the transport of DNA between the donor and recipient cell in the process called conjugation (see Chapter 5). Attachment or common pili, which are found in great num-

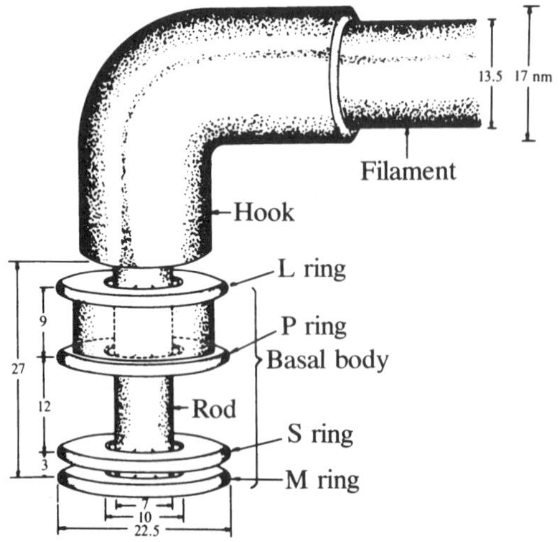

FIGURE 2-12
Prokaryotic flagellar structure. Flagellum consists of a filament, hook, and basal body. In gram-negative cells, the L and P rings are anchored to the outer membrane of the cell wall, and the S and M rings are attached to the cytoplasmic membrane. In gram-positive cells, the flagellum has only S and M rings. (From M. L. DePamphilus and J. Adler, *J. Bacteriol.* 105:384, 1971.)

bers on the surface of the cell, are used for adhesion to various surfaces including plant and animal cells. Adherence to plant and animal cells is often an important factor in the infectious disease process (see Chapter 15). Attachment pili are found primarily in gram-negative bacteria, but some species of gram-positive bacteria, such as *Corynebacterium renale* and *Actinomyces naeslundii,* also possess them.

Structures Within the Cytoplasm

NUCLEOIDS

Bacteria possess no nuclear membrane but do have areas of DNA concentration, called **nucleoids** (Fig. 2-16). The

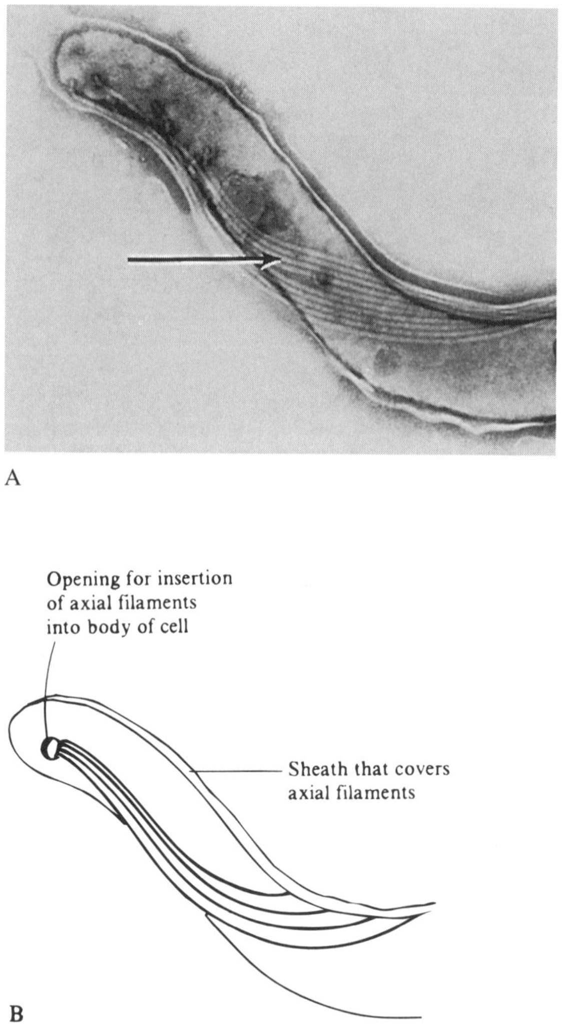

FIGURE 2-13
Axial filaments. A. Electron micrograph of axial filaments *(arrow)* as they appear to wind around the body of the spirochete. B. A diagrammatic representation of the micrograph. (From M. A. Listgarten and S. S. Socransky, *J. Bacteriol.* 88:1087, 1964.)

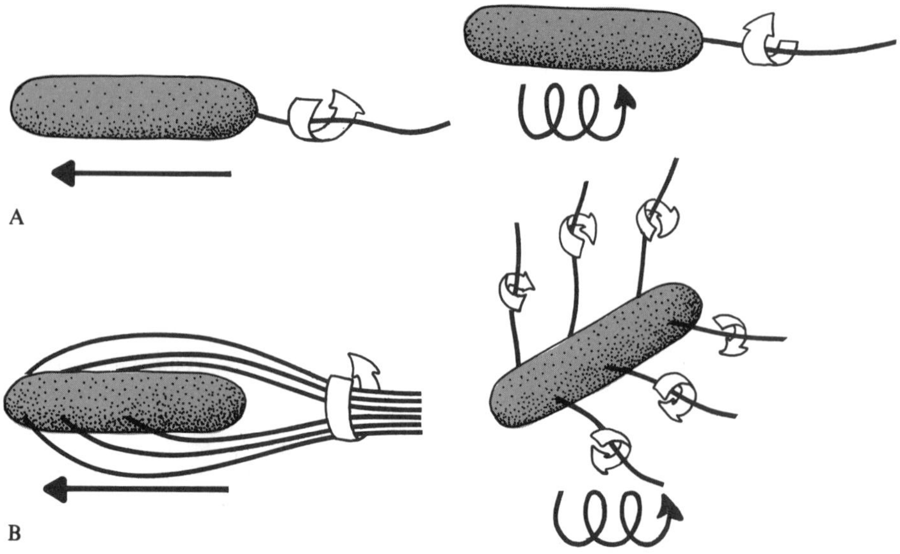

FIGURE 2-14
Flagellar rotation. A. Rotation of a polar flagellum counterclockwise *(left)* results in smooth swimming, with the flagellum trailing the cell. Clockwise rotation *(right)* causes the cell to tumble, with the flagellum ahead of the cell. B. In a peritrichously flagellated cell, counterclockwise rotation causes the flagella to form a bundle and the cell swims smoothly. When the flagella rotate clockwise, the flagella fly apart and the cell tumbles.

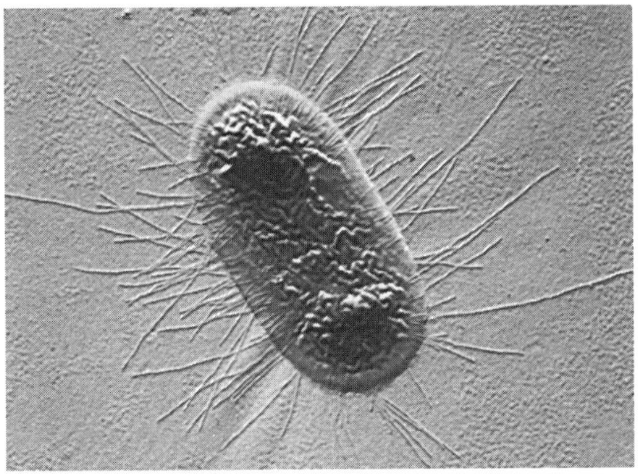

FIGURE 2-15
Negatively stained electron micrograph of pili (fimbriae) covering the surface of *Escherichia coli*. (From S. Knutton et al., *Infect. Immun.* 44:514, 1984.)

bacterial DNA molecule is circular and is not associated with proteins, as is eukaryotic DNA. The DNA in bacterial cells such as *Escherichia coli* can be carefully removed from the cell and when spread out is 1100 to 1400 μm long. DNA, therefore, is considerably condensed in the cell. Before bacterial cells divide, DNA is replicated while still attached to membranous areas called mesosomes (see Fig. 2-1). Since each cell will receive a copy of DNA, it is not surprising that the nuclear material can be observed at the center of the cell and site of cell division (septum). The number of nucleoids seen in the cell is usually dependent on the growth rate. When bacteria are dividing very rapidly, as many as four nucleoids can be observed in each bacterial cell, but only one nucleoid may be observed if the bacteria are dividing very slowly.

RIBOSOMES

Ribosomes are structures involved in protein synthesis in the cell. They are composed of approximately 60 percent RNA and 40 percent protein. When thin sections of bacteria are observed microscopically, ribosomes can be seen to fill the cytoplasm (see Fig. 2-16). They may make up as much as 50 percent of the dry weight of the cell when it is growing very rapidly.

INCLUSION BODIES (INTRACELLULAR INCLUSIONS)

Bacterial growth under certain conditions can result in the accumulation of particles within the cytoplasm of the cell. These particles may or may not be covered with a membrane. Many of these inclusion bodies are observed in microorganisms found in the soil and water, where nutrient deprivation often occurs. These organisms are, however, not infectious for humans. **Gas vacuoles** in aquatic bacteria, **polyhedral bodies** in organisms that use carbon dioxide (CO_2) as a carbon source, and **sulfur granules** in bacteria that oxidize hydrogen sulfide are examples of inclusions in bacteria that do not cause disease in humans.

FIGURE 2-16
Electron micrograph of *E. coli* demonstrating nucleoids and ribosomes. The dark-like areas around the nucleoids (N) are ribosomes (R). CW = cell wall; CM = cytoplasmic membrane. (Courtesy of A. Ryter, Institute of Pasteur.)

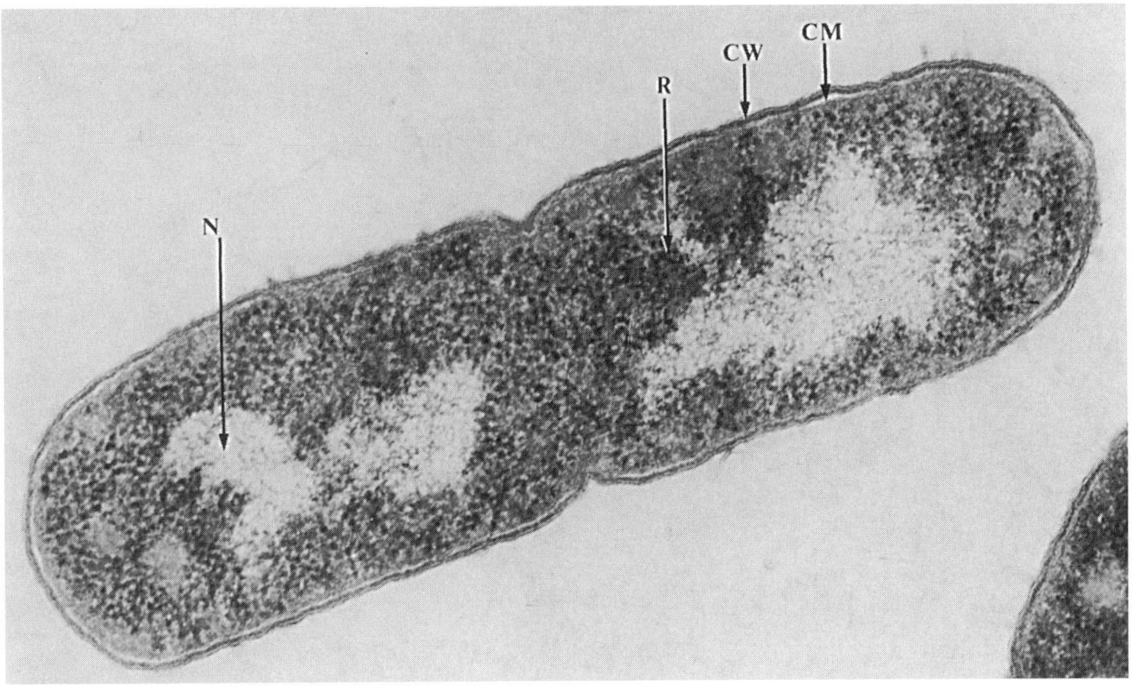

Inclusions found in bacteria that infect humans are **glycogen, lipid,** and **polyphosphate granules.** Glycogen is a polymer of glucose that can be used as a source of energy or carbon or both by the bacterial cell. Lipid storage in the cell often takes the form of polyhydroxybutyrate granules. Inorganic phosphate is stored by the bacterial cell in the form of polyphosphate granules. These granules are also called volutin or **metachromatic granules.**

ENDOSPORES

Cells that are engaged in active growth and reproduction are referred to as **vegetative cells** or as being in the vegetative state of growth. There are several groups of microorganisms, including bacteria, that under environmental stress (nutrient depletion or oxygen depletion, for example) are capable of ceasing vegetative growth and producing intracellular bodies called **endospores.** Endospores are produced by gram-positive bacteria. The two most important genera of bacteria causing disease and also producing endospores are *Bacillus* and *Clostridium. Bacillus anthracis,* for example, is the cause of anthrax, an invariably fatal disease in cattle that may also affect humans, while *Bacillus cereus* is a cause of food poisoning in humans. *Clostridium* species such as *C. botulinum, C. tetani,* and *C. perfringens* are the cause of human diseases such as botulism, tetanus, and gas gangrene, respectively. A knowledge of endospore-forming bacteria is important to allied health personnel because the spore is resistant to high temperatures, chemicals, and radiation that would normally kill non-sporeforming bacteria. The endospore is a highly refractile body that is difficult to stain but it can be observed easily in the unstained condition (Fig. 2-17). Once environmental conditions are suitable for growth, the endospore can be induced to return to the vegetative state. The endospore represents the bacterial cell's mechanism for surviving under unsuitable conditions.

The Sporulation Process

During endospore formation the following events occur (Fig. 2-18). The DNA material is extended along the entire length of the cell. The cell membrane invaginates, the DNA becomes compartmentalized, and a second membrane is formed around the unit, which can now be called a **forespore.** A peptidoglycan is synthesized and laid down between the two membranes of the forespore. This peptidoglycan layer, called the **cortex,** differs chemically from the peptidoglycan of the vegetative cell. Within the area surrounded by the cortex is a compound called **calcium dipicolinate,** which is found only in endospores. Thick coats of peptides that are impermeable to water are laid down around the cortex. Completion of the spore coats signals the end of endospore formation. The spore may be located at the poles or at other various positions in the cell. The spore is released into the environment as soon as the vegetative portion of the cell disintegrates.

The mechanisms for resistance of spores to chemical and physical agents are not completely understood. For example, the degree of dehydration (loss of free water) is believed to be an important mechanism for resistance to heat. The greater the degree of dehydration, the greater the resistance to heat. Vegetative bacterial cells are usually killed at temperatures of 70 C and higher, but spores can resist boiling temperatures for several hours. Only temperatures of 121 C for at least 15 minutes at 15 pounds of pressure per square inch will ensure destruction of the most heat-resistant endospores. Preventing spores from contaminating food, wounds, dressings, and so on, and various medical objects that come into contact with the human body is of obvious importance to medical personnel. Once the spore germinates, the vegetative cell may reproduce and cause disease.

The Germination Process

A spore may remain dormant for hundreds of years before becoming transformed into a vegetative cell. The

FIGURE 2-17
Electron micrograph (× 76,250 before 23 percent reduction) of ultrathin section of sporulating *Clostridium bifermentans.* The spore is the white refractile body in the cell. (From P. D. Walker, *J. Appl. Microbiol.* 33:1, 1970.)

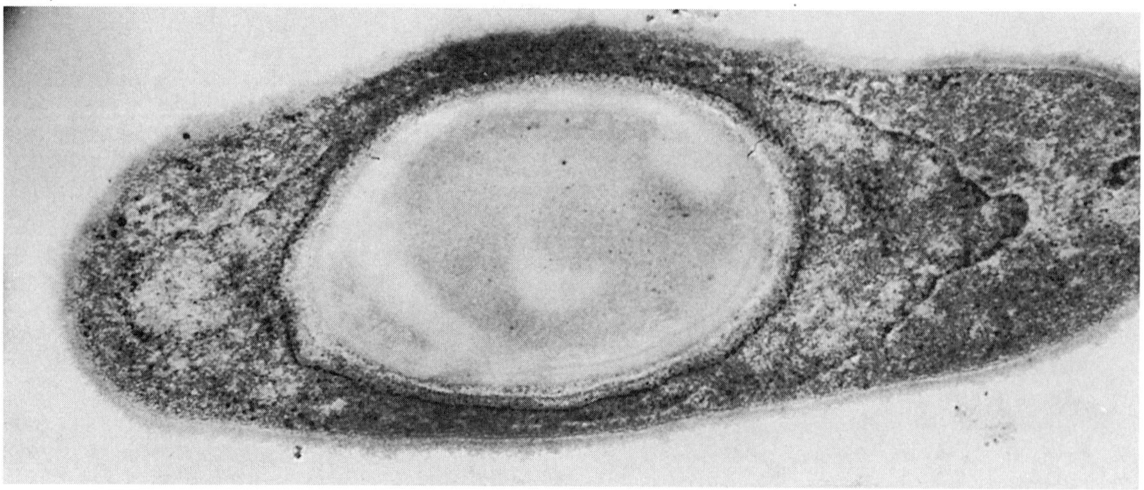

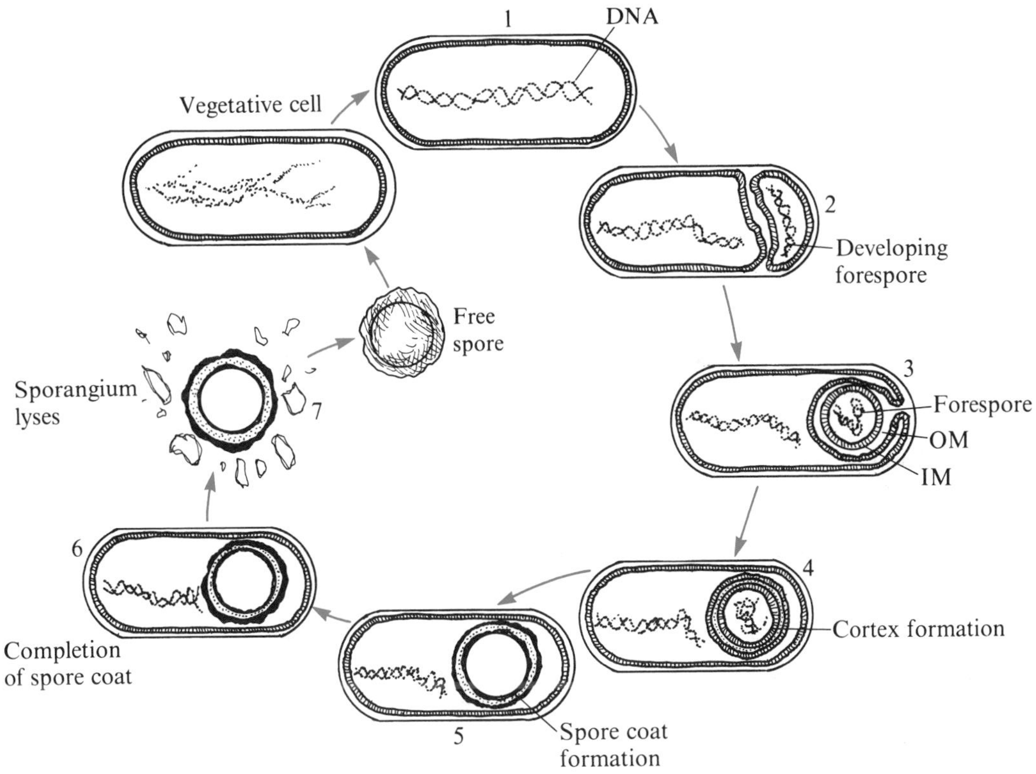

FIGURE 2-18
Events in the sporulation process. See text for details. OM = outer membrane; IM = inner membrane.

transformation is related not to the age of the spore but to the need for certain environmental conditions. Before germination takes place, the spore must first be activated—for example, by heat in the presence of water, although other agents or conditions may also initiate activation. Once activated, the spore enters the stage of germination, in which portions of the spore coats become degraded. In the presence of growth-supporting nutrients the germinating spore swells and enters a period of biosynthetic activity in which vegetative cellular components are produced. This period ends with release of the spore coat and the initiation of vegetative growth.

Summary

1. The basic distinction between prokaryotes or bacteria and all other organisms is the nuclear membrane—present in eukaryotes and absent in prokaryotes. Other characteristics separating prokaryotes from eukaryotes are outlined in Table 2-1.

2. Bacteria are given names (nomenclature) based on certain criteria. They are given Latin or Greek names that usually describe an important characteristic of the organism. Bacteria, like other organisms, are classified into various units, called taxa, based on the species, the fundamental unit of classification. The main purpose of classification is to distinguish one group of organisms from another, while nomenclature provides a convenient system of communication to define an organism without having to list all the characteristics of the species.

3. The most widely accepted scheme of bacterial classification is *Bergey's Manual of Determinative Bacteriology*. The various taxonomic groups have been arrived at on the basis of identification of specific characteristics, such as biochemical properties and physiological traits. Biochemical similarities and differences can be tested by determining DNA relatedness between two organisms.

4. Bacteria range in size from 0.20 to 60 μm in length, but the bacteria infectious for humans are usually 1.0 to 3.0 μm in length. There are four basic shapes of bacteria: spherical (coccus), rod-shaped (bacillus), spiral, and square.

5. Bacterial morphology, even in a single species, may vary depending on the growth conditions. Such morphological variation is referred to as pleomorphism, and this prevents taxonomists from using size as a criterion in classification.

6. All bacteria, except *Mycoplasma,* have cell walls and are divided into two basic groups: gram-positive and gram-negative. This separation is based on the chemical composition of the cell wall and its response to specific reagents during the Gram-staining procedure. In addition to the cell wall, other structures found in bacteria and their function are outlined in Table 2-4.

TABLE 2-4
Summary of Prokaryotic Structure and Function

Structure	Chemical composition	Function
Cell wall		Cell shape and protection of cytoplasmic contents
Gram-positive	Mainly peptidoglycan plus teichoic acid	—
Gram-negative	Very little peptidoglycan: outer membrane multilayered, containing phospholipid, lipopolysaccharide, and protein	—
Cytoplasmic membrane	Phospholipid bilayer containing globular proteins	Controls movement of solutes into cell; site of respiratory enzymes; secretes cytoplasmic products; contains enzymes for cell wall synthesis; site of DNA synthesis
Extracellular polymeric substances	Single polysaccharides; mixed polysaccharides, or proteins	Adherence to substrates; inhibition of phagocytosis
Flagella	Protein	Movement
Pili	Protein	Conjugation in gram-negative bacteria; adherence to inanimate and animate surfaces
Nucleoid	DNA	Carries hereditary information
Ribosomes	RNA and protein	Protein synthesis
Inclusion bodies		
Glycogen	Polysaccharide (glucose)	Storage form of energy
Polyhydroxybutyrate	Lipid	Storage form of energy
Volutin (metachromatic granules)	Polyphosphate	?
Endospores	Complex peptidoglycan unit containing calcium dipicolinate; a dehydrated form of the vegetative cell	Protection from environmental stresses of a chemical or physical nature

Questions for Study

1. Outline the characteristics that distinguish eukaryotes from prokaryotes.
2. Indicate the structures or molecular components that may be associated with the infectious disease process.
3. Describe the makeup of the outer membrane of gram-negative bacteria. What are the function and role the outer membrane plays in medical microbiology?
4. What are the distinctions between active transport and passive transport of molecules across the cytoplasmic membrane? Can you give any common everyday examples of either type?
5. In what way(s) are the cytoplasmic membrane and outer membrane of gram-negative bacteria similar? In what way(s) are they different?
6. Is it true that because the gram-negative cell has a very small amount of peptidoglycan, it is more susceptible to penicillin than gram-positive cells? Explain.
7. What would be the osmotic effect on a bacterial cell culture if alcohol were added to the solution? (See also Chapter 7.)
8. What does water have to do with the sporulation or germination process?

CHAPTER

3 Microbial Metabolism

OBJECTIVES

- To explain how enzymes are able to speed up chemical reactions
- To discuss the factors affecting enzyme activity
- To explain the difference between substrate level phosphorylation and electron transport phosphorylation
- To explain the relationship between electron transport, energy, and ATP formation
- To explain the differences and similarities, if any, between fermentation and respiration
- To explain the specific functions of the glycolytic pathway, Krebs cycle, and electron transport chain in aerobic respiration
- To explain what cellular conditions are needed for biosynthesis to be initiated in the cell
- To explain how allosteric enzymes control metabolic activity
- To define the terms coenzyme, energy of activation, denaturation, dehydrogenation, beta oxidation, and feedback inhibition

OUTLINE

- ENZYMES: BIOLOGICAL CATALYSTS
  - General Characteristics
  - How Enzymes Speed Up Chemical Reactions
  - Factors Affecting Enzyme Activity
    - Hydrogen Ion Activity
    - Temperature
    - Substrate Concentration
    - Inhibitors
  - Classification of Enzymes
    - Based on Chemical Reaction
    - Based on Biological Activity
  - Enzymes: Infectious Disease Implications
- HOW MICROBIAL CELLS PRODUCE ENERGY
  - Electrons, Oxidation, and Energy
  - Adenosine Triphosphate: The Energy Molecule of the Cell
- METABOLIC PROCESSES THAT GENERATE ENERGY
  - Fermentation
    - Glycolysis
    - Other Pathways of Glucose Oxidation
    - Molecules Other Than Sugars Can Be Fermented
  - Respiration
    - Aerobic Respiration
      - Energy Profile for Aerobic Respiration
    - Anaerobic Respiration
    - Sources of Electrons Other Than Carbohydrates
- BIOSYNTHESIS: A PROCESS THAT UTILIZES ENERGY
  - The Need for Carbon Skeletons
    - Glycolysis
    - Pentose Phosphate Pathway
    - Krebs Cycle
  - The Need for Reducing Power
- CONTROL OF METABOLIC ACTIVITY
  - Allosteric Enzymes and Metabolic Control
    - Feedback Inhibition

The primary function of all living material is to grow and reproduce. Both growth and reproduction rely on the outcome of chemical reactions in the cell. The sum of all cellular chemical reactions is referred to as **metabolism.** The metabolic process that involves the degradation of chemical components is called **catabolism,** while the synthesis of chemical components is called **anabolism** or **biosynthesis.** Catabolic processes are important because they result in the formation of molecules, such as adenosine triphosphate (ATP), which are immediate sources of energy. Energy is used to synthesize the necessary molecules that will become important components of the cell. In this chapter we discuss the importance of enzymes in metabolic processes and then describe some of the more important metabolic processes that occur in the microbial cell.

Enzymes: Biological Catalysts

GENERAL CHARACTERISTICS

Most metabolic processes in the cell would take forever if it were not for enzymes. Enzymes are proteins that have molecular weights ranging from 600 to 12,000. Their function is to speed up the various chemical reactions that occur in the cell. Molecules that speed up chemical reactions are called **catalysts.** Enzymes often cannot function alone and require additional molecules, called **cofactors,** to enhance activity. Some cofactors are organic molecules, such as vitamins, and are referred to as **coenzymes.** Inorganic cofactors are metal ions such as calcium, zinc, and magnesium. How cofactors enhance enzyme activity is discussed shortly.

HOW ENZYMES SPEED UP CHEMICAL REACTIONS

In every cellular chemical reaction there is a molecule or molecules, called **substrates** (S), that interact with enzymes (E) and are converted to products (P). The reaction can be written:

$$S + E \rightleftharpoons ES \rightarrow P + E$$
$$\text{E-S complex}$$

Chemical reactions involve the making and breaking of bonds, and this requires energy, also called the **energy of activation.** In the example below, an amino acid such as alanine can have its amino group (NH_2) removed (deamination), resulting in the formation of a product called pyruvic acid:

$$\underset{\text{Alanine}}{H-\overset{\overset{\displaystyle H}{|}}{\underset{\underset{\displaystyle H}{|}}{C}}-\overset{\overset{\displaystyle NH_2}{|}}{\underset{\underset{\displaystyle H}{|}}{C}}-COOH} \rightarrow \underset{\text{Pyruvic acid}}{H-\overset{\overset{\displaystyle H}{|}}{\underset{\underset{\displaystyle H}{|}}{C}}-\overset{\overset{\displaystyle O}{\|}}{C}-COOH} + NH_2$$

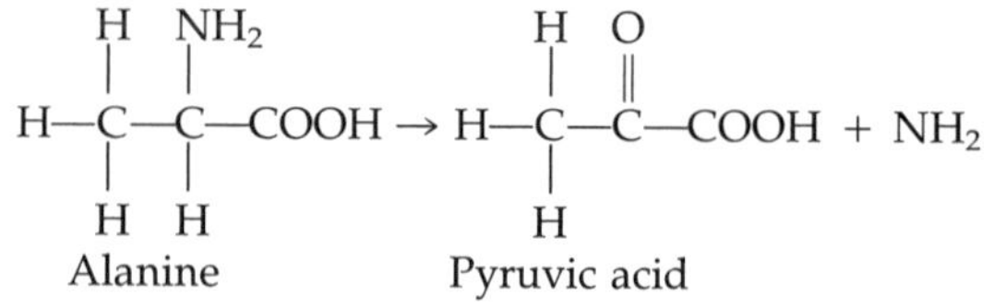

The bond holding NH_2 to the remainder of the molecule must be broken for this reaction to occur, and this requires a certain amount of energy. The activation energy could be supplied in the form of heat, but the amount of heat required would literally burn up the cell. The cell, however, is endowed with enzymes that act as substitutes for heat energy. Enzymes lower the energy of activation. The question is, how do enzymes do this?

Enzymes, because they are proteins, are made up of a chain or chains of amino acids (also called polypeptide chain) that are folded in such a way as to resemble a globular shape. This folding produces specific arrangements in which certain amino acids are brought into close contact. For example, an amino acid at one end of the chain can be brought into close proximity to the amino acid at the opposite end of the chain by the way the enzyme is folded (Fig. 3-1). The folding of the protein and the arrangement of various amino acids in the enzyme produce a specific conformational site, called the **active site,** where the substrates of a chemical reaction can bind (Fig. 3-1). Thus, there is a conformational specificity between substrate and enzyme—a lock-and-key relationship. There are about 1000 different enzymes in a micro-

FIGURE 3-1
How the polypeptide chain of a protein is folded to produce a globular shape. Each sphere in the chain represents an amino acid. A. Linear arrangement of amino acids in the polypeptide chain. B. Folding of the polypeptide chain produces a globular shape and close contact between amino acids B and X. The folding of the polypeptide produces a site where substrate (colored S) can bind by contact with amino acids S, V, and Y.

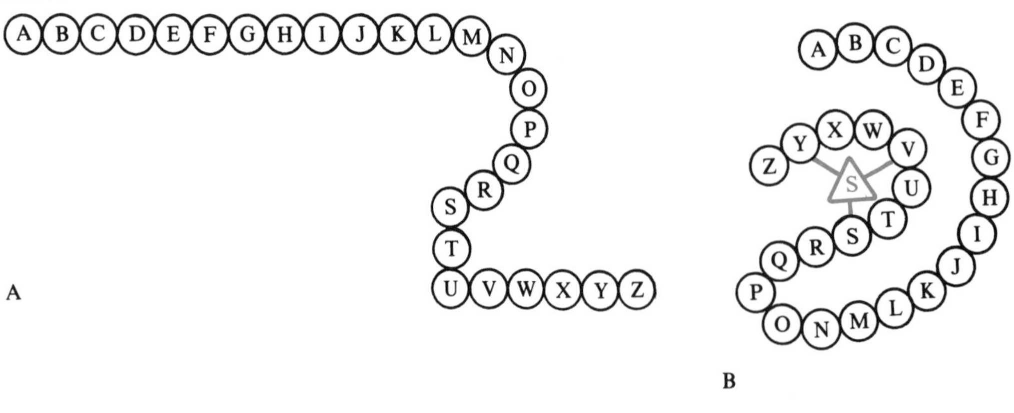

TABLE 3-1
Vitamins and Their Function in Microbial Metabolism

Vitamin	Function
Thiamine	A coenzyme involved in decarboxylation reactions
Riboflavin	As part of the flavin adenine dinucleotide molecule is a coenzyme involved in electron transport
Niacin	As part of the nicotinamide adenine dinucleotide (NAD) or NADP molecule is a coenzyme involved in electron transport
Pantothenic acid	As part of coenzyme A (CoA) molecule functions as carrier of acyl groups
Pyridoxal	Functions as coenzyme; important in amino acid metabolism, particularly in group transfer reactions involving the amino (NH_2) group
Biotin	Coenzyme important as carrier of CO_2
Folic acid	Acts as a carrier of formyl (HCHO) group. Very important in purine biosynthesis
Vitamin B_{12}	Coenzyme functioning as a carrier of alkyl groups

bial cell, and since the sequence of amino acids in each of them is different, the locks and keys are also different. The active site usually possesses amino acids that have a positively or negatively charged group, for example, an NH_3^+ or COO^- group. These charged groups help to bind substrate but it is the conformation of the active site that is the major determinant of specificity with a substrate. To simplify our discussion about how the active site is involved in bond breaking or bond making, we use the following example. Suppose a substrate consists of a long chain of repeating units that we wish to cleave into smaller fragments. The fragments could be produced by heating the substrate in a test tube containing water. The heating process causes the molecules of water to collide with the substrate and bonds are broken—sometimes the broken bonds are the ones we want, and sometimes they are not. Enzymes can also break bonds, but with lower energy requirements, because they bring the substrate, and the specific bonds to be broken, to the active site. The active site possesses amino acids with charged groups that take part in bond breaking. Inorganic factors, such as calcium, carry positive charges, which are believed to aid in the binding of substrate to active site, while many vitamins (Table 3-1) act as carriers of small chemical groups that are part of the enzymatic reaction. Since the enzyme itself is not altered in the chemical reaction, it is free to engage other substrate molecules once the product is released from the enzyme.

FACTORS AFFECTING ENZYME ACTIVITY

Enzymes are proteins subject to the same chemical and physical factors that affect other proteins. Conditions such as hydrogen ion concentration and temperature that alter the shape of the protein also affect its catalytic activity.

Hydrogen Ion Activity

The hydrogen ion concentration, or pH, greatly influences the activity of enzymes. The amino acids in enzymes can take up hydrogen ions (H^+) in acid solution and release them in alkaline (OH^-) solutions. For example, the COO^- group and the NH_2 group on an amino acid such as alanine take up H^+ in acid solution and become positively charged:

$$H-\underset{\underset{H}{|}}{\overset{\overset{H}{|}}{C}}-\underset{\underset{H}{|}}{\overset{\overset{NH_2}{|}}{C}}-COO^- + 2H^+ \rightarrow H-\underset{\underset{H}{|}}{\overset{\overset{H}{|}}{C}}-\underset{\underset{H}{|}}{\overset{\overset{NH_3^+}{|}}{C}}-COOH$$

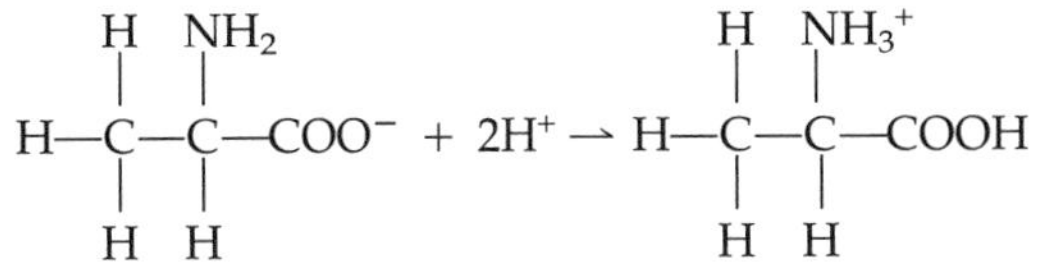

but release hydrogen ions in alkaline solution and become negatively charged:

$$H-\underset{\underset{H}{|}}{\overset{\overset{H}{|}}{C}}-\underset{\underset{H}{|}}{\overset{\overset{NH_3^+}{|}}{C}}-COOH + OH^- \rightarrow H-\underset{\underset{H}{|}}{\overset{\overset{H}{|}}{C}}-\underset{\underset{H}{|}}{\overset{\overset{NH_2}{|}}{C}}-COO^- + HOH$$

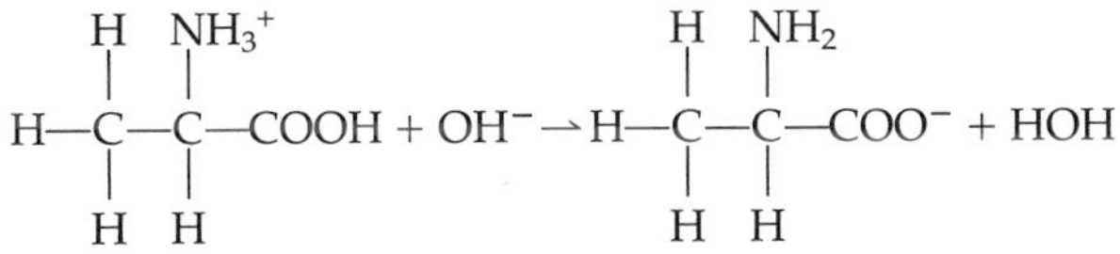

In addition, sulfur-sulfur (S-S) bonds in proteins can also take on hydrogen ions to become sulfhydryl (SH) groups. (See Under the Microscope 2.) Most enzymes in the cell are active at pHs between 5 and 8 (Fig. 3-2).

Temperature

The most favorable temperature for enzyme activity in most biological systems is 37°C. In measuring enzyme activity as a function of temperature, there is a doubling of activity for every 10°C increase in temperature. As the temperature increases, however, there is a point where the enzyme molecule begins to unfold and activity drops off very quickly. This unfolding process is called **denaturation** (Fig. 3-3). As you will see later, heating is a technique for killing microorganisms.

FIGURE 3-2
Effect of hydrogen ion (pH) concentration on enzyme activity.

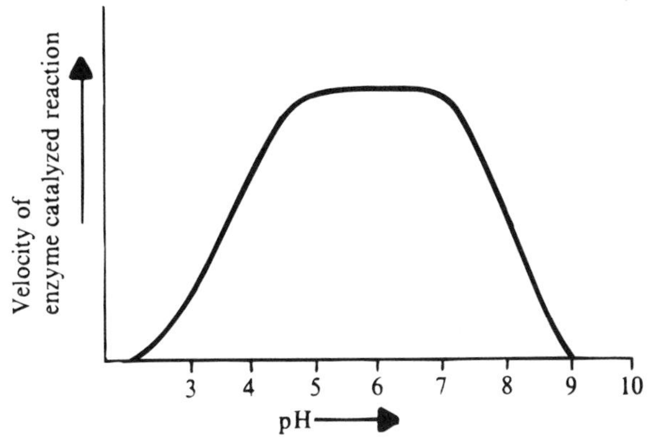

UNDER THE MICROSCOPE 2

Sulfur and Enzymatic Activity

Sulfur is an element required by all living cells. It is a component of the amino acid cysteine, in which it can exist as a **sulfhydryl (SH)** group, that is,

$$SH-CH_2-\overset{\displaystyle H}{\underset{\displaystyle NH_3^+}{C}}-COO^-$$

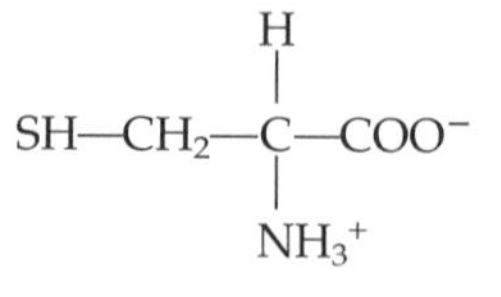

Cysteine

Cysteine plays a particularly important role in protein structure because the sulfur of one cysteine can bond with the sulfur of another cysteine residue in the protein to form a disulfide (S-S) bond. For example, some enzymes have 8 cysteine residues that produce 4 disulfide bonds. When these disulfide bonds are formed, the enzyme assumes a particular configuration. The activity of enzymes relies on specific configurations and if these configurations are disturbed, enzyme activity is decreased or lost completely. Cysteine can exist in either a reduced or an oxidized form. In the oxidized form (loss of hydrogen) the sulfurs of cysteines in the protein molecule are devoid of their hydrogens and they can form disulfide bonds. In a reduced form the sulfur of cysteine exists as a sulfhydryl (SH) group and disulfide bonds cannot form in the protein. For example, if an enzyme in its natural configuration contains 4 disulfide bonds, we can add a reducing agent that will break the disulfide bonds and the protein will assume a different configuration:

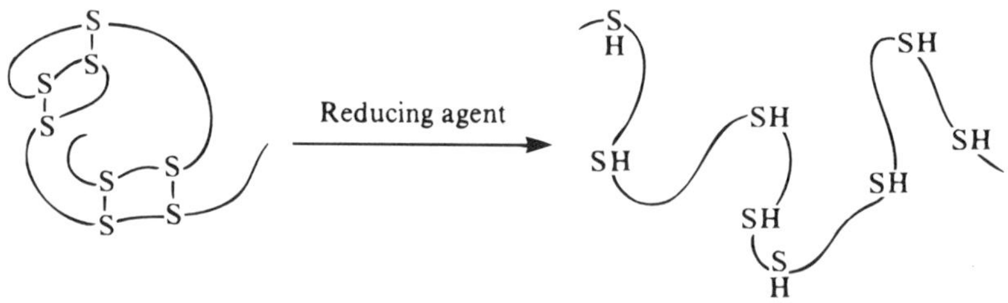

Active enzyme with
4 disulfide bonds

Inactive enzyme (disulfide
bonds broken and sulfhydryl
groups produced)

FIGURE 3-3
Effect of temperature on enzyme activity.

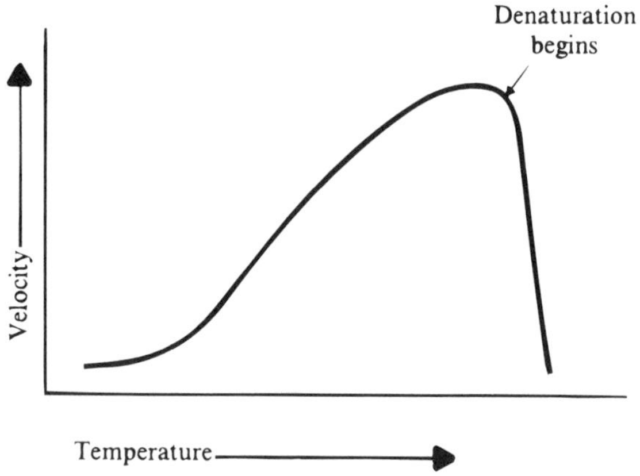

Substrate Concentration

When substantial amounts of enzyme are present, the rate of the catalyzed reaction is directly proportional to the substrate concentration, provided all other factors, such as pH and temperature, have been standardized. As the substrate concentration is increased, a point is reached at which all of the enzyme is in the form of an enzyme-substrate complex and the velocity of the reaction is at a maximum (Fig. 3-4) and independent of substrate concentration. Further increases in substrate concentration produce no further increase in activity, and only by adding more enzyme can the maximum velocity be increased.

Inhibitors

In medicine the control of some infectious diseases is generally based on the control of microorganisms. Agents that affect enzyme activity also affect the growth of microorganisms. Scientists are continually looking for chemical

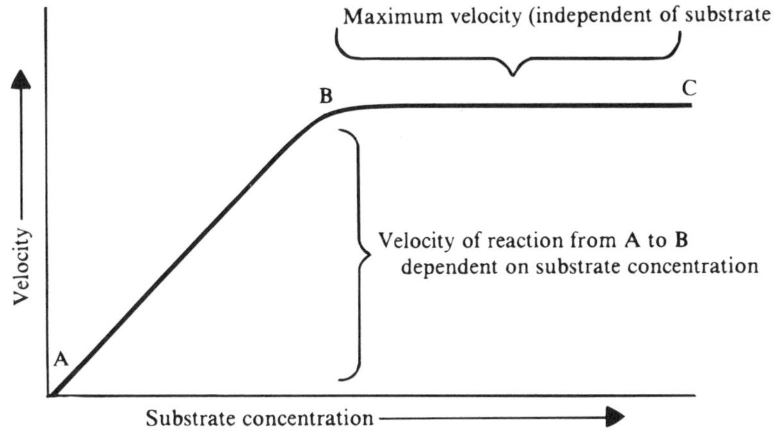

FIGURE 3-4
Effect of substrate concentration on enzyme activity.

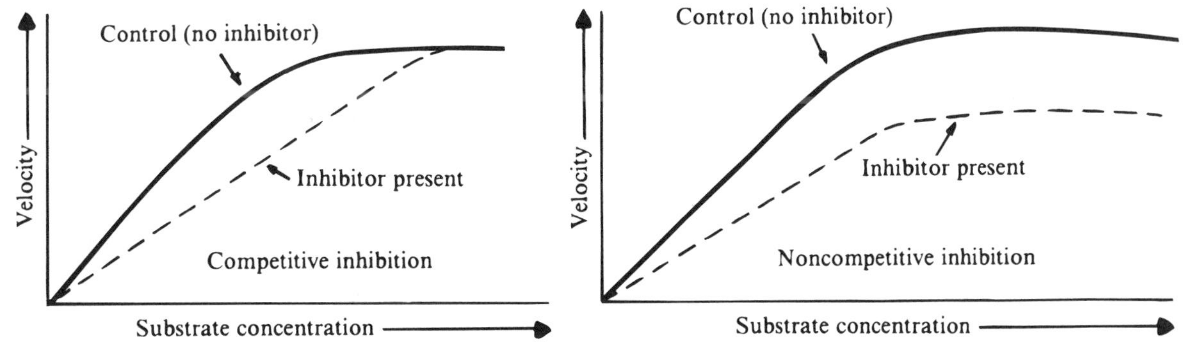

A B

FIGURE 3-5
Effect of inhibitors on enzyme activity. A. Competitive inhibitors. B. Noncompetitive inhibitors.

agents that selectively inhibit microbial enzymes without affecting host enzymes. Most of the chemical agents that show this selective inhibition are antibiotics, which are discussed in Chapter 8. Inhibitors of enzyme activity are of two types: **competitive inhibitors** and **noncompetitive inhibitors.** Competitive inhibitors compete with the normal substrate for the active site on the enzyme molecule. The competitive inhibitor has a structure similar to the natural substrate, which enables it to bind to the enzyme, but is different enough that it is not converted to the normal product. The inhibitor forms an enzyme-substrate complex just like the normal substrate. In competitive inhibition the velocity of the reaction is slowed, but the maximum velocity that is characteristic of the reaction in the absence of inhibitors can be obtained if the substrate concentration is increased (Fig. 3-5A). Noncompetitive inhibitors do not bind to the active site but at another site. The noncompetitive inhibitor affects the binding of substrate to the active site, probably by inducing some conformational change in the enzyme. Even if the substrate binds to the active site in the presence of inhibitor, a product may be formed very slowly or not at all. Increasing the substrate concentration will have no effect on enzyme activity in the presence of noncompetitive inhibitors, as it would for competitive inhibitors (Fig. 3-5B).

CLASSIFICATION OF ENZYMES

Based on Chemical Reaction

Except for enzymes such as pepsin and chymotrypsin, which were identified and named many years ago, enzymes end in the suffix *-ase,* for example, protease. The first part of the name usually indicates the type of substrate, chemical group, or type of chemical reaction that is catalyzed by the enzyme. Current nomenclature divides all enzyme-catalyzed reactions into the following groups:

1. **Oxidoreductases** are involved in electron (hydrogen) transfer reactions.
2. **Transferases** transfer specific groups such as aldehydes or phosphates from one substrate to another.
3. **Hydrolases** add water across chemical bonds to be cleaved or hydrolyzed.

4. **Lyases** remove chemical groups from substrates, forming double bonds, or add chemical groups to double bonds.
5. **Isomerases** rearrange certain compounds to produce molecules having the same groups of atoms, but in different arrangements.
6. **Ligases** produce bonds accompanied by the cleavage of ATP.

Based on Biological Activity

Some enzymes synthesized by the cell remain within the cell to carry out specific reactions and are called **endoenzymes,** while others are released from the cell into the surrounding environment and are called **exoenzymes.** Many microbial cells release exoenzymes that attack macromolecules and convert them into smaller units that can be selectively absorbed by the cell, for example, the conversion of the polysaccharide cellulose into units of glucose.

The prefixes *endo-* and *exo-* have also been used to describe the site of enzyme activity on macromolecules. Exoenzymes, for example, catalyze reactions involving the terminal residues on a macromolecule, while endoenzymes catalyze reactions involving residues found in the interior of the molecule.

ENZYMES: INFECTIOUS DISEASE IMPLICATIONS

Whether one is a nurse, physician, medical technician, or microbiology researcher, there will be a time when enzymes are used or identified as part of occupational tasks. Let us outline some of these tasks and indicate areas in the textbook where they are discussed in more detail.

1. Identification of bacteria. Some bacteria release enzymes whose presence is indicative of the microbe's involvement in disease. **Catalase,** for example, is produced by the agents of gonorrhea (see Chapter 18) and tuberculosis (see Chapter 25). **Coagulase** is produced by *Staphylococcus aureus* (see Chapter 17). **Cytochrome oxidase** is produced by the agent of gonorrhea (see Chapter 18). Several enzymes are produced by *Escherichia coli* (see Chapter 21). Bacteria and other microbial agents whose presence is minimal in disease can also be identified using the reaction called **polymerase chain reaction.** The enzyme used is called **DNA polymerase** (see Chapter 6).
2. Identification of specific antibodies. Some enzymes can be conjugated with antibodies in tests such as **enzyme immunoassays.** The identified antibodies may be associated with a certain disease (see Appendix A).
3. Genetic engineering. Enzymes such as **restriction enzymes** are used to cut out specific genes from any type of DNA. The isolated DNA can then be inserted into totally unrelated DNA molecules. This type of process has been used in the area of **gene therapy** (see Chapter 7). In addition, restriction enzymes have been used by the epidemiologist to isolate specific sequences of microbial DNA that can later be used to differentiate specific strains of bacteria.
4. Treatment. The enzyme **streptokinase** is a proteolytic enzyme produced by species of *Streptococcus*. The enzyme has been produced commercially and used in the clinical setting to dissolve fibrin clots. The enzyme converts blood plasminogen to active plasmin, the proteolytic component that breaks down fibrin molecules. Streptokinase is used in the treatment of deep venous thrombosis and massive pulmonary embolisms, conditions that ordinarily require surgical removal of vascular clots.

How Microbial Cells Produce Energy

Some microorganisms use sunlight as a source of energy and convert this energy into chemical energy. These organisms are photosynthetic and are not infectious. Some bacteria found in the soil use inorganic elements such as sulfur and iron as sources of energy, and they too are not infectious. Microorganisms that infect humans must be able to utilize energy sources in a manner similar to that of their hosts. Infectious microorganisms obtain their energy from the degradation of organic molecules. Much of the time, these organic sources of energy also provide the microbial cell with the necessary carbon skeletons it needs to synthesize organic molecules. For example, glucose (Fig. 3-6) is used as an energy source and during its degradation the carbons are used by the cell to produce other organic molecules.

ELECTRONS, OXIDATION, AND ENERGY

The release of energy from the degradation of organic molecules is associated with the release of electrons and their subsequent capture by other molecules in the cell.

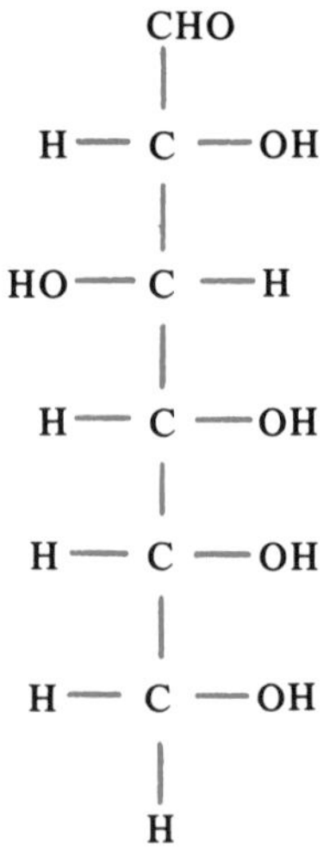

FIGURE 3-6
Structure of glucose.

In chemistry the removal of electrons from a substance is called **oxidation,** while the gain of electrons by a substance is called **reduction.** Oxidation of organic molecules usually means the loss of an electron and proton together that is a hydrogen atom (H). In the reaction below:

$$AH_2 + B \rightharpoondown BH_2 + A$$

AH_2 represents a compound (A) that contains hydrogen atoms (H_2) and in the reaction it loses them; that is, A is oxidized. B in the reaction becomes reduced to BH_2 by accepting the hydrogen atoms. In the reaction, AH_2 is considered the electron donor and B the electron acceptor. Oxidations in which H atoms are lost are called **dehydrogenations.**

Electron donors are molecules that release energy, while molecules that accept electrons are not sources of energy. If you observe the structure of glucose (see Fig. 3-6), a common source of energy for microorganisms, you see that it possesses many hydrogen atoms and is therefore a source of electrons; that is, it is an **electron donor.** Electrons released as part of hydrogen atoms are first transferred to carrier molecules. One of the most important carrier molecules is called **nicotinamide adenine dinucleotide,** or **NAD.** NAD takes the electrons, which are at a high energy level, and transfers them to a chain of molecules located in the cytoplasmic membrane called the **electron transport chain.** The electrons are transferred in the chain in a manner similar to running water that falls over a series of water wheels. The energy of the water at the top of the cascade (comparable to the energy in the electrons carried by NAD) is released in small increments as it tumbles over each wheel (comparable to the electron transport components). The last wheel might be considered the **final electron acceptor.** What happens to the energy generated during electron transfer?

ADENOSINE TRIPHOSPHATE: THE ENERGY MOLECULE OF THE CELL

The energy released during the transfer of electrons in the electron transport chain is conserved in the cell in the form of ATP. The energy trapped in ATP is used to perform specific tasks, such as movement, nutrient transport, and biosynthesis. ATP is formed by the addition of phosphate to a molecule of adenosine diphosphate (ADP), a process called **phosphorylation.** Most of the energy in the ATP molecule is actually part of the last two phosphates and is represented as a squiggle (~), that is A-P ~ P ~ P. The reaction can be represented as:

$$\underset{\text{(ADP)}}{\text{A-P}{\sim}\text{P}} + PO_4 + \text{energy} \rightharpoondown \underset{\text{(ATP)}}{\text{A-P}{\sim}\text{P}{\sim}\text{P}}$$

while the reverse reaction releases energy:

$$\text{A-P} \sim \text{P} \sim \text{P} \rightarrow \text{A-P} \sim \text{P} + PO_4 + \text{energy}$$

ATP is not the only high-energy molecule used by the cell, but it is the most important one. Other high-energy molecules include acetyl phosphate, phosphoenol pyruvate, and acetylcoenzyme A (acetyl-CoA). Later in the chapter we discuss how energy is trapped in the molecule during the transfer of electrons.

Phosphorylation reactions in which ATP is produced can be divided into two types as they relate to infectious microorganisms: **substrate phosphorylation** and **electron transport phosphorylation** (also called **oxidative phosphorylation**). Substrate phosphorylation is a process in which the phosphate to be added to ADP is a high-energy phosphate that is part of a carbon compound in the cell:

$$C \sim PO_4{}^* + ADP \rightarrow ATP + C$$

* Carbon compound containing high-energy phosphate

Electron transport phosphorylation is a process in which energy released from electron transfer is trapped during the addition of phosphate to ADP. The term oxidative phosphorylation implies that the final electron acceptor is oxygen, but this is not always the case. We will see how substrate and electron transport phosphorylation operate when we discuss fermentation and respiration, metabolic processes that generate energy.

Metabolic Processes That Generate Energy

FERMENTATION

Fermentation is an oxidation process in which an organic electron donor gives up its electrons to an organic electron acceptor. Oxygen is not involved in fermentation; that is, it is an anaerobic process. A special fermentation process that occurs in most living cells is called **glycolysis,** which is also called the **Embden-Meyerhoff-Parnas (EMP) pathway.**

Glycolysis

Glycolysis is a metabolic process in which the electron donor is glucose, a 6-carbon sugar. Glycolysis can be divided into two groups of reactions (Fig. 3-7). In the first group of reactions glucose is cleaved, rearranged, and phosphorylated. The net result of this set of reactions is the formation of two 3-carbon molecules, dihydroxyacetone phosphate and glyceraldehyde 3-phosphate, and the consumption of two molecules of ATP. In the second set of reactions two molecules of glyceraldehyde 3-phosphate (dihydroxyacetone phosphate is converted to glyceraldehyde 3-phosphate) are rearranged to form two molecules of pyruvic acid. During the glycolytic oxidation, four molecules of ATP are produced by substrate phosphorylation and electrons are captured by the carrier NAD to form $NADH_2$. The final electron acceptor in glycolysis is **pyruvic acid,** which is converted to lactic acid:

Glucose (6 C)

2 ATP
2 ADP
2 ATP consumed

Dihydroxyacetone phosphate (3C)
Glyceraldehyde 3-phosphate (3 C)

2 NAD
2 NADH$_2$
2 ADP
2 ATP
2 ATP generated
2 NADH$_2$ generated

2-Phosphoenol pyruvate (3 C)

2 ADP
2 ATP
2 ATP generated

2-Pyruvic acid (3 C)

2-Lactic acid (3 C) + 2 NAD (to be reused in glycolysis)

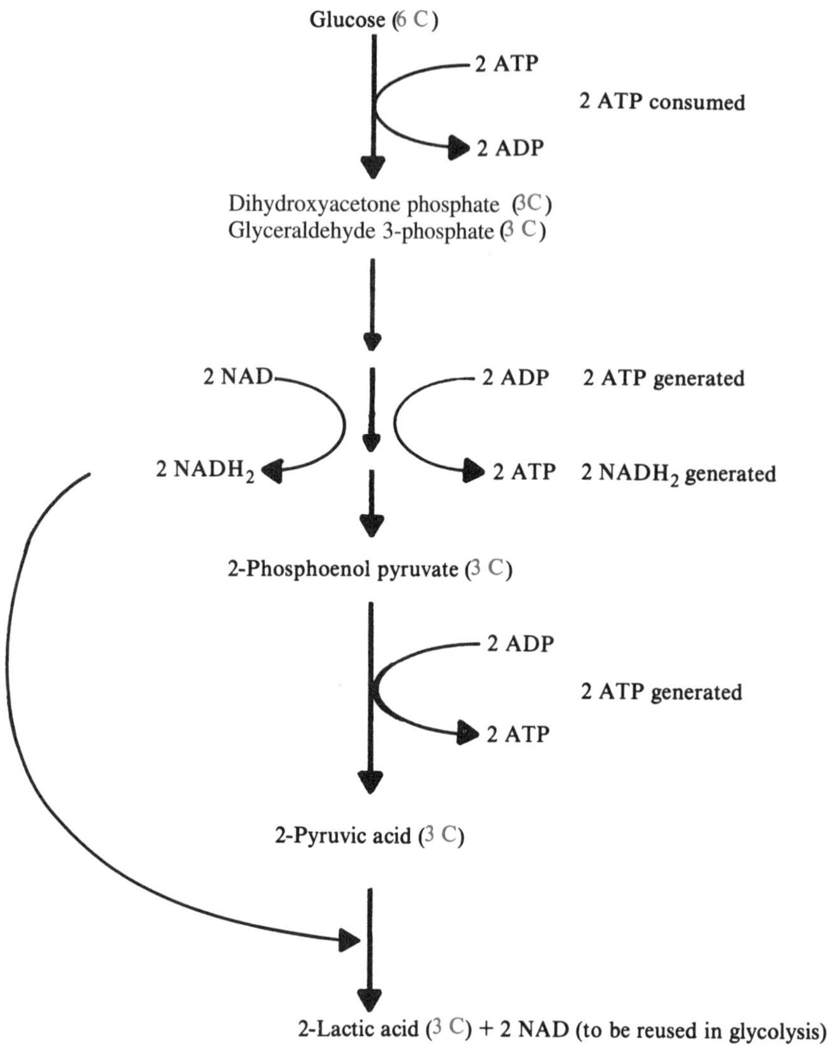

FIGURE 3-7
Simplified scheme for glycolysis in which a molecule of glucose is converted to two molecules of pyruvic acid. The number of carbon atoms is indicated in parentheses. Note that dihydroxyacetone phosphate is converted to a molecule of glyceraldehyde 3-phosphate; thus, actually two molecules of glyceraldehyde 3-phosphate are oxidized. NAD is regenerated during the reduction of pyruvic acid to lactic acid by NADH$_2$.

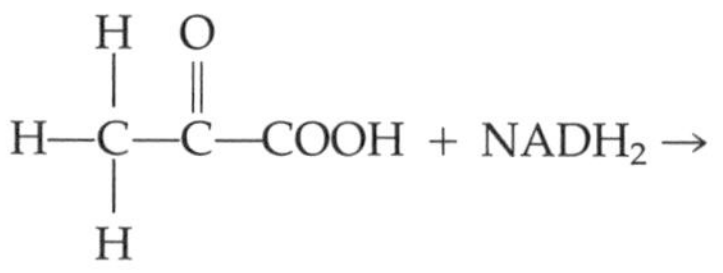

$$H-\overset{\overset{\displaystyle H}{|}}{\underset{\underset{\displaystyle H}{|}}{C}}-\overset{\overset{\displaystyle O}{\|}}{C}-COOH + NADH_2 \rightarrow$$

Pyruvic acid

$$H-\overset{\overset{\displaystyle H}{|}}{\underset{\underset{\displaystyle H}{|}}{C}}-\overset{\overset{\displaystyle OH}{|}}{\underset{\underset{\displaystyle H}{|}}{C}}-COOH + NAD$$

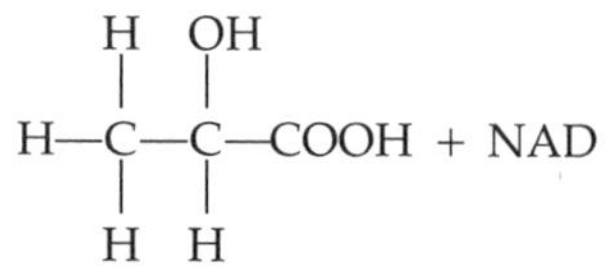

Lactic acid

Lactic acid may be a major end product of fermentation for some microorganisms, such as the lactic acid bacteria. Other microorganisms, however, can produce a variety of products from the metabolism of pyruvic acid (Fig. 3-8). Pyruvate or lactate, as well as some of the other products of pyruvic acid metabolism, is incompletely oxidized and as a consequence some of the potential energy it possesses is lost. The products of fermentation are excreted by the cell. In order to extract all the potential energy from a molecule such as glucose, it must be completely oxidized to carbon dioxide (CO_2) and water—a process we will discuss shortly.

In the overall process of glycolysis two molecules of ATP are consumed and four molecules of ATP are produced, leaving a net gain of two molecules of ATP for every molecule of glucose fermented. Let us look at what happens when glucose is made available to **obligate aerobes, facultative anaerobes,** and **obligate anaerobes:**

1. Obligate aerobes. Obligate aerobes can grow only in the presence of oxygen. Glucose is oxidized to pyruvic acid, but the latter does not remain as the final electron acceptor. Instead, pyruvic acid is completely oxidized to carbon dioxide and water in a process called **aerobic respiration** (to be discussed later). Some microorganisms can use inorganic molecules other than oxygen, such as nitrate, as final electron acceptors.

2. Facultative anaerobes. Facultative anaerobes can grow either in the presence or in the absence of oxygen. The facultative anaerobe in the presence of oxygen completely oxidizes the organic molecule to car-

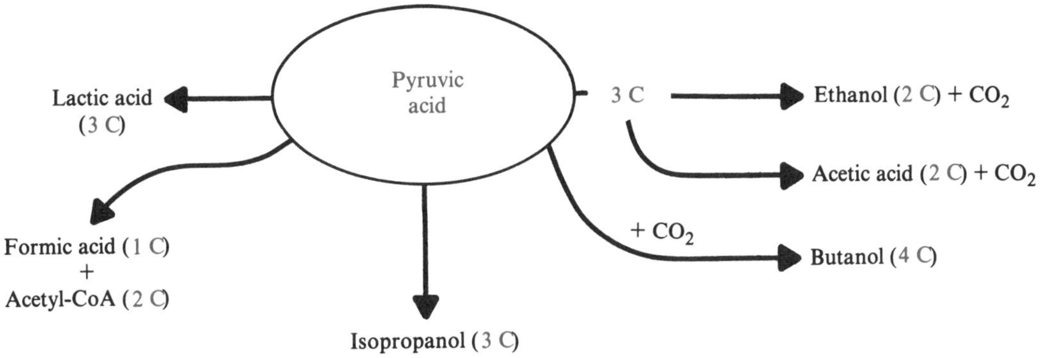

FIGURE 3-8
Some products of pyruvate metabolism. The number of carbon atoms in each molecule is indicated in parentheses.

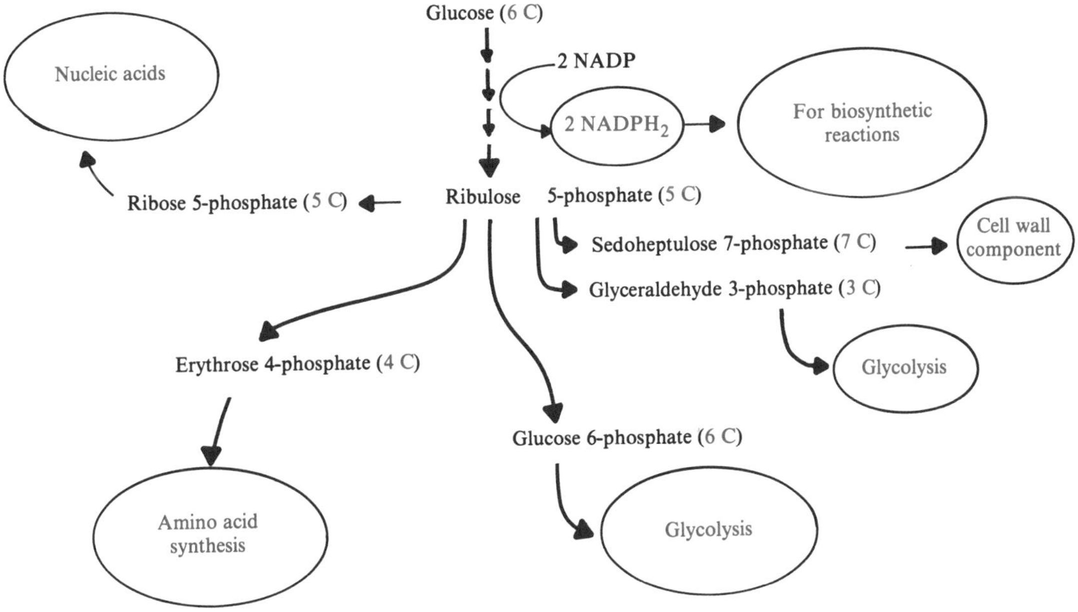

FIGURE 3-9
Simplified scheme of pentose phosphate pathway.

bon dioxide and water. When oxygen is absent, the organic electron donor is incompletely oxidized in the fermentation process to molecules such as lactic acid.

3. Obligate anaerobes. Obligate anaerobes can grow only in the absence of oxygen. In fact, oxygen often kills these microorganisms. Fermentation is one major mechanism used by obligate anaerobes to obtain energy; the other is anaerobic respiration. Obligate anaerobes can produce a variety of end products, such as organic acids from pyruvic acid metabolism (see Fig. 3-8). These organic acids form a species-specific profile that can be identified in the clinical laboratory by gas chromatography.

Other Pathways of Glucose Oxidation

In addition to the EMP pathway, other pathways of glucose catabolism are available to most microorganisms. They include the pentose phosphate pathway and the Entner-Doudoroff pathway.

The **pentose phosphate pathway** consists of a large number of reactions in which glucose is converted to a 5-carbon sugar, ribulose 5-phosphate. This pathway is significant for the following reasons (Fig. 3-9):

1. A number of 3-, 4-, 5-, 6-, and 7-carbon sugars are produced. These sugars are phosphorylated and can be oxidized to pyruvic acid with the production of energy via substrate phosphorylation.
2. The sugars discussed in item 1 can also be used as the framework for certain cellular components of the cell. For example, the genetic material of the cell, DNA and RNA, is made up of 5-carbon sugars, called deoxyribose and ribose, respectively.
3. Nicotinamide adenine dinucleotide phosphate (NADP) acts as a carrier of electrons and protons in the form of $NADPH_2$. Unlike $NADH_2$, $NADPH_2$ is

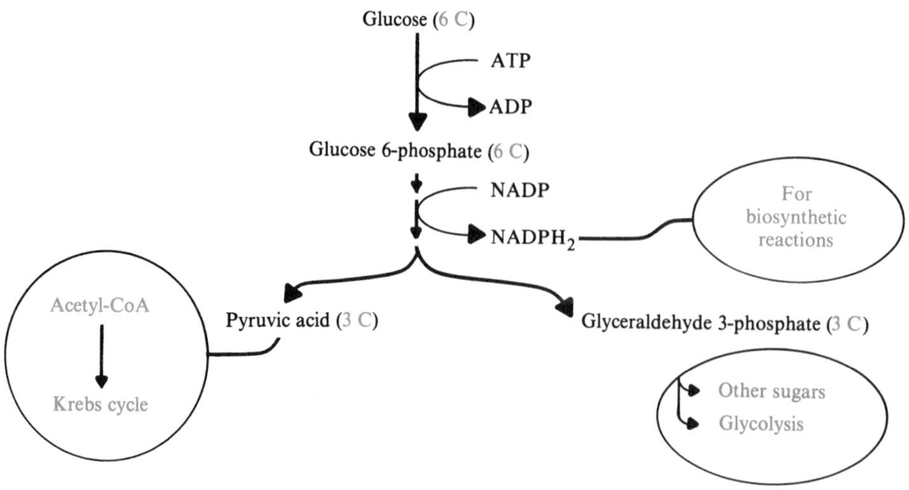

FIGURE 3-10
Entner-Doudoroff pathway. The number of carbon atoms is indicated in parentheses. How products are used in metabolism is indicated in color.

used in biosynthetic processes. The hydrogens are fixed to carbon skeletons to produce organic molecules.

Another pathway of glucose oxidation is called the **Entner-Doudoroff** pathway (Fig. 3-10). In this pathway glucose is rearranged and cleaved to form the product glyceraldehyde 3-phosphate and pyruvic acid. Glyceraldehyde 3-phosphate can, as in glycolysis, be oxidized to release energy in the form of ATP but it can also be used to produce larger sugars.

Molecules Other Than Sugars Can Be Fermented

Amino acids, purines and pyrimidines, and organic acids can be fermented by some microorganisms. Of particular significance are the strictly anaerobic bacteria such as *Clostridium* whose species cause wound infections such as tetanus and gas gangrene.

RESPIRATION

Respiration is a cellular-energy-generating system in which the electrons released by oxidation are transferred to an **electron transport chain.** The electron transport chain is located in the cytoplasmic membrane of bacteria and mitochondrial membrane of eukaryotes. The final electron acceptor may be oxygen (aerobic respiration) or an inorganic molecule other than oxygen (anaerobic respiration).

Aerobic Respiration

Microorganisms that use aerobic respiration (or even anaerobic respiration) as a means of obtaining energy also utilize most of the reactions in glycolysis. The major difference is that in aerobic respiration pyruvate can be completely oxidized to carbon dioxide and water and the electrons and protons released are transported to an elec-

tron transport chain. Respiration occurs in the following way:

Electrons and protons captured by NAD during glycolysis are transported to the electron transport chain. Pyruvic acid loses a carbon, as carbon dioxide, and is converted to a 2-carbon fragment (called an **acetyl group**) in the presence of two coenzymes: **coenzyme A (CoA)** and NAD. In the reaction the acetyl group binds to CoA to form acetyl-CoA and NAD is reduced to $NADH_2$:

$$H-\underset{\underset{H}{|}}{\overset{\overset{H}{|}}{C}}-\overset{\overset{O}{\|}}{C}-COOH + CoA + NAD \rightarrow$$

Pyruvic acid

$$H-\underset{\underset{H}{|}}{\overset{\overset{H}{|}}{C}}-\overset{\overset{O}{\|}}{C}{\sim}CoA + NADH_2$$

Acetyl-CoA

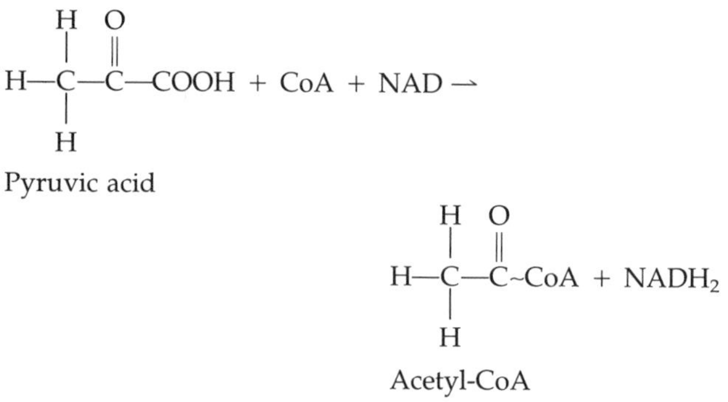

The $NADH_2$ generated in this reaction can transfer its electrons and protons to the electron transport chain while the acetyl-CoA is ready to be oxidized in a series of reactions called the **Krebs** or **citric acid cycle.** The Krebs cycle is a pathway in which the remaining carbons of the acetyl group are converted to carbon dioxide and in the process electrons and protons are released. If we look at the Krebs cycle more closely (Fig. 3-11), the following intermediates and products are formed:

1. Acetyl-CoA condenses with a 4-carbon unit, **oxalo-acetate,** to form the 6-carbon **citric acid.**
2. Citric acid undergoes a series of reactions to form **isocitric acid.** Isocitric acid is oxidized to a 5-carbon molecule, **alpha-ketoglutaric acid,** with the release of a molecule of CO_2 and the reduction of NAD to $NADH_2$.

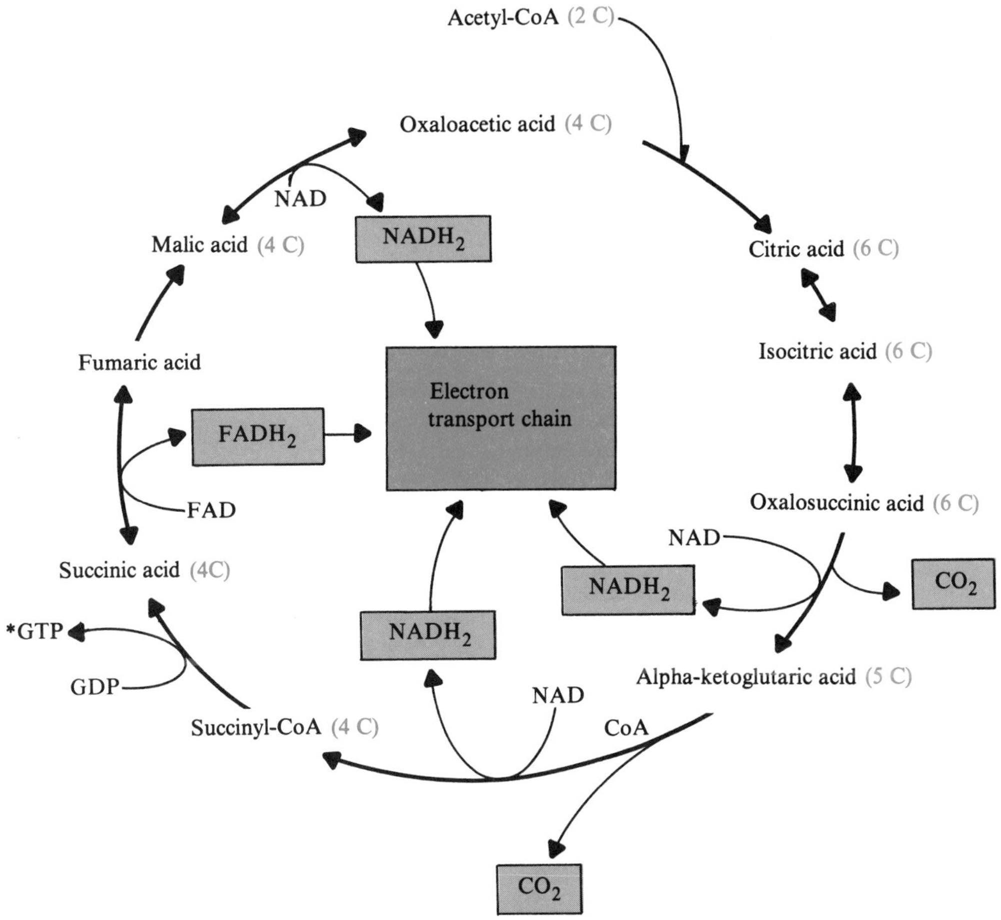

FIGURE 3-11
The Krebs or citric acid cycle. This cycle oxidizes acetyl-CoA with the release of carbon dioxide and four pairs of electrons. Electrons picked up by NAD and flavin adenine dinucleotide (FAD) are carried to the electron transport chain. *GDP (guanosine diphosphate) is converted to guanosine triphosphate (GTP). GTP is converted to ATP in the following reaction: GTP + ADP $\leftrightharpoons$ GDP + ATP.

3. Alpha-ketoglutaric acid is further oxidized in the presence of CoA to a 4-carbon unit, **succinyl-CoA,** with the liberation of one molecule of CO_2 and the reduction of NAD to $NADH_2$.
4. Succinyl-CoA loses the CoA unit, and energy is trapped by guanosine diphosphate (GDP) to form guanosine triphosphate (GTP). ATP is later produced from the reaction:

$$GTP + ADP \rightleftharpoons GDP + ATP$$

5. Succinic acid is oxidized to **fumaric acid** and another coenzyme, flavin adenine dinucleotide (FAD) is reduced to $FADH_2$.
6. **Malic acid** is oxidized to oxaloacetic acid, and NAD is reduced to $NADH_2$.

What the Krebs cycle has accomplished is that it has (1) oxidized a molecule of acetyl-CoA, producing two molecules of CO_2; (2) released four pairs of protons and electrons, which are captured by NAD or FAD for transfer to the electron transport chain; (3) generated one molecule of ATP via GTP formation; and (4) produced a series of intermediates that, as we will see later, are used in biosynthesis.

The potential energy of the electrons in reduced NAD and FAD, formed in the Krebs cycle, is transferred to the electron transport chain. The chain is made of up coenzymes, proteins, and nonproteins that act as carriers (Fig. 3-12). The first components of the chain are **flavoproteins** called **NAD dehydrogenase** and **FAD dehydrogenase,** both of which carry protons and electrons. A nonprotein carrier called **quinone** also carries protons and electrons and is situated in the middle of the chain, while the remaining carriers are proteins called **cytochromes.** Cytochromes (abbreviated **cyt**) carry only electrons and are designated by letters (cyt b, cyt c, etc.). The electron transport chain is comparable to the water wheels described previously in the section Electrons, Oxidation, and Energy. The dehydrogenase is the first wheel at the top of the chain, while at the bottom oxygen, the last wheel, is the final electron acceptor. Let us examine how electron and proton transfer occurs and where ATP is produced.

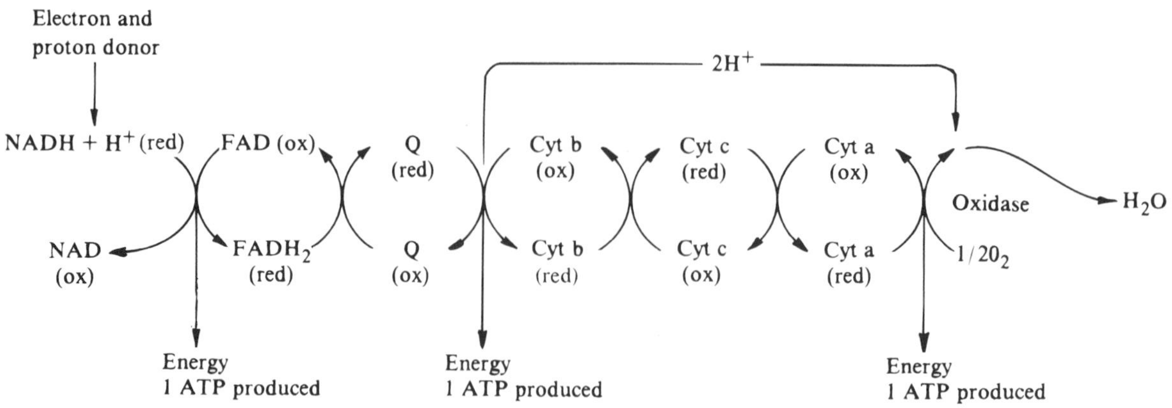

FIGURE 3-12
Electron transport chain. NAD accepts electrons and protons from oxidized substrates and transfers them to the electron transport chain found in the cytoplasmic membrane of the prokaryotic cells. These components include flavoproteins and their prosthetic group flavin adenine dinucleotide (FAD), quinones (Q), and cytochromes (Cyt) b, c, and a. Hydrogens are transferred only as far as FAD, while electrons are used in the alternate reduction (red) and oxidation (ox) of all the respiratory transport components. The final product of oxidation is water. Energy is released in sufficient concentration at three sites in the transport chain to produce a molecule of adenosine triphosphate (ATP). Three ATPs are produced for each pair of electrons transported the entire length of the chain. If reduced FAD is the original carrier (for example, FAD is used in the Krebs cycle), only two molecules of ATP are produced. The electron transport chain is believed to be a proton pump in which ATP synthesis is coupled to proton transfer.

1. The electrons and protons generated during respiration are transferred by NAD and FAD from the cytoplasm to other electron transport components.
2. Each of the components in the chain becomes alternately reduced (if it picks up electrons from the previous carrier) and oxidized (if it releases electrons to the next carrier). The electrons picked up by NAD are at a very high energy level, and if they were transferred in a single step to oxygen (bypassing the intermediate carriers) a tremendous amount of energy would be released. The ATP molecule has a limited amount of energy it can trap and much of the energy released in a single oxidation would be lost as heat. Intermediate carriers provide a means of releasing small increments of energy.*
3. Each oxidation step in the electron transport chain releases energy, and there are three sites where there is sufficient energy release for capture by ATP via electron transport phosphorylation. Thus, the transport of a pair of electrons from NAD to oxygen results in the release of three ATP molecules. If the original electron carrier is FAD (as in the Krebs cycle), only two ATP molecules are produced:

$$NADH_2 + 3\ ADP + \tfrac{1}{2}\ O_2 + 3\ PO_4 \rightarrow NAD + 3\ ATP + H_2O$$

$$FADH_2 + 2\ ADP + \tfrac{1}{2}\ O_2 + 2\ PO_4 \rightarrow FAD + 2\ ATP + H_2O$$

* This simplistic discussion of energy release and ATP synthesis is far from complete. We now know that electron flow is coupled to ATP synthesis by means of differences of electrical potential and differences of pH across the cytoplasmic membrane. This chemical and electrical difference is due to the movement of protons **(proton motive force)** across the cytoplasmic membrane. (See Additional Readings at the end of this chapter for a discussion of the proton motive force.)

4. The last carrier in the chain is called **cytochrome oxidase,** which transfers its electrons to oxygen. The hydrogen atoms that combine with oxygen to form water are those that were released by quinones during electron transport.

Energy Profile for Aerobic Respiration. The total amount of energy, in the form of ATP, that can be produced from the complete oxidation of one molecule of glucose is now examined:

1. 2 $NADH_2$ produced during glycolysis	6 ATP
2. Substrate phosphorylation in glycolysis	4 ATP
3. $NADH_2$ produced during conversion of pyruvic acid to acetyl-CoA	6 ATP
4. 6 $NADH_2$ produced in Krebs cycle	18 ATP
5. 2 $FADH_2$ produced in Krebs cycle	4 ATP
6. Conversion of GTP to ATP in Krebs cycle	2 ATP
Total ATP gained	40
Subtract 2 ATP consumed in glycolysis	−2
Net gain of ATP	38 per molecule of glucose oxidized

As you can see, aerobic respiration results in the gain of substantial amounts of ATP (38 molecules) as compared to fermentation (2 molecules) when the latter is the only source of energy.

Anaerobic Respiration

Respiration does not always involve oxygen as the final electron acceptor. Alternative electron acceptors, such as nitrate (NO_3), sulfate (SO_4), and carbonate (CO_3) or organic molecules such as fumaric acid can be used by some bacterial species, especially the soil species. When the

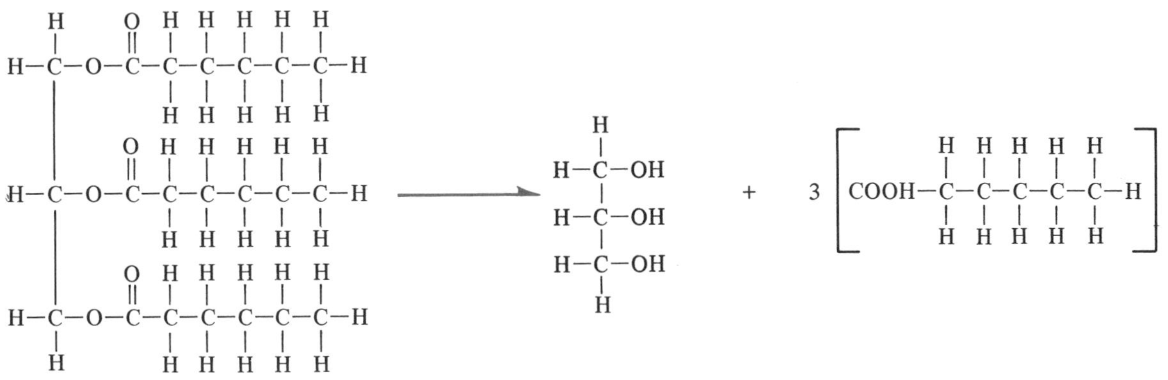

Lipid Glycerol 3 (Fatty acid)

FIGURE 3-13
Lipid degradation by lipases produces glycerol and fatty acids.

electron acceptor in respiration is a molecule other than oxygen, the process is called anaerobic respiration.

Sources of Electrons Other Than Carbohydrates

Carbohydrates are not the only source of electrons for energy formation. Organic molecules, such as lipids and proteins, can be metabolized to release electrons and produce intermediates that find their way into the Krebs cycle or glycolytic cycle. **Lipases** can cleave lipids into their component parts, glycerol and fatty acids (Fig. 3-13). Glycerol can enter the glycolytic cycle while fatty acids are oxidized in a process called **beta oxidation.** Beta oxidation brings about the release of two carbon fragments and their conversion of acetyl-CoA. Acetyl-CoA can directly enter the Krebs cycle.

Proteins are catabolized by **proteases** into their component amino acids. Amino acids lose their amino groups in a process called **deamination,*** and this can result in the formation of organic acids such as pyruvic acid, alpha-ketoglutaric acid, or others that make up the Krebs cycle.

Biosynthesis: A Process That Utilizes Energy

Many cellular components and enzymes are degraded during the life cycle of a cell and biosynthesis is needed to replenish them at normal levels. In order for biosynthetic pathways to become engaged, three processes or conditions must be operating. First, there must be a **source of carbon skeletons;** second, there must be a **source of reducing power** in the form of hydrogens; and, third, there must be a **source of energy.** Energy sources have already been discussed. We now look at the other factors. In addition we also discuss how these biosynthetic processes can be regulated.

* See page 30 for an example of a deamination reaction.

THE NEED FOR CARBON SKELETONS

Very few molecules enter the cell and become directly incorporated into macromolecules, the components of cellular structures. Macromolecules are made up of basic building blocks: amino acids for proteins, purines and pyrimidines for nucleic acids, and simple sugars for polysaccharides. In addition, large molecules such as lipids are also made up of the building blocks glycerol and fatty acids. The building blocks are derived from carbon skeletons produced in pathways that are also involved in energy production. Let us look at the various metabolic pathways and see what they provide in the way of carbon skeletons.

Glycolysis

1. Glucose can be rearranged and converted to glucose 1-phosphate, which can be energized by ATP to form ADP-glucose:

   Glucose 1-phosphate + ATP ⇀

   ADP-glucose + P-P (pyrophosphate)

   The glucose on ADP-glucose can be transferred to a growing polysaccharide chain to produce glycogen, a storage form of glucose in the bacterial cell.
2. Glucose-phosphate also serves as a precursor for the synthesis of other 6-carbon sugars.
3. Glyceraldehyde 3-phosphate is used in the synthesis of the amino acids serine, glycine, and cysteine.
4. Phosphoenolpyruvate is used in the synthesis of the amino acids tyrosine, phenylalanine, and tryptophan.
5. The carbons of pyruvic acid are used in the synthesis of the amino acids alanine, valine, and leucine.
6. Dihydroxyacetone phosphate is a precursor in lipid synthesis because it can be converted to glycerol.

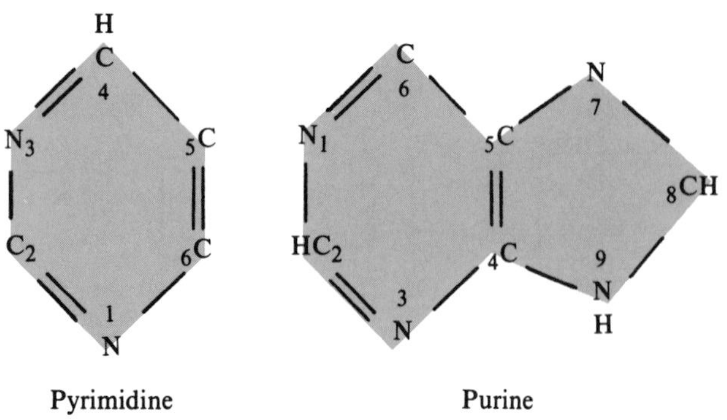

FIGURE 3-14
Pyrimidine and purine, showing atom number and position.

Pentose Phosphate Pathway

1. A 4-carbon sugar, erythrose 4-phosphate, is utilized in the synthesis of the amino acids tyrosine, phenylalanine, and tryptophan.
2. Five-carbon sugars, such as ribose phosphate, are used as the sugar component of the nucleic acids deoxyribonucleic acid (DNA) and ribonucleic acid (RNA).

Krebs Cycle

1. Alpha-ketoglutaric acid is a precursor to the amino acids lysine, glutamic acid, proline, and arginine.
2. Oxaloacetic acid is a precursor to the amino acids aspartic acid, threonine, isoleucine, lysine, and methionine.
3. Acetyl-CoA provides its carbons for the fatty acid components of lipids. Acetyl-CoA becomes bonded to a special carrier called **acyl carrier protein (ACP).** ACP acts as a primer by adding 2 carbon units to the growing fatty acid chain. Fatty acids may be up to 18 or more carbons in length.

So far we have not discussed the biosynthesis of the purines and pyrimidines (Fig. 3-14), which are the building blocks of nucleic acids. The principal precursor for them is the amino acids (Table 3-2). The replication of nucleic acids is discussed in Chapter 5.

TABLE 3-2
Origin of the Atoms of Purine and Pyrimidine Bases

Atom and position*	Molecule the atom is derived from	
	Purine	Pyrimidine
N-1	Aspartic acid (amino acid)	Aspartic acid (amino acid)
C-2	Formic acid	CO_2
N-3	Glutamine (amino acid)	NH_3
C-4	Glycine (amino acid)	Aspartic acid
C-5	Glycine	Aspartic acid
C-6	CO_2	Aspartic acid
N-7	Glycine	—
C-8	Formic acid	—
N-9	Glutamine	—

* The atom number and position are illustrated in Figure 3-15.

THE NEED FOR REDUCING POWER

Once carbon skeletons have been supplied for biosynthesis, they must be reduced by adding hydrogen atoms. The source of these hydrogens is $NADPH_2$, which is generated in the pentose phosphate pathway discussed earlier (see Other Pathways of Glucose Oxidation). One very important biosynthesis that requires considerable reduced NADP is the formation of fatty acids. Fatty acids consist of long chains of hydrocarbons and many of the hydrogens are supplied by $NADPH_2$.

Control of Metabolic Activity

Since enzymes are the cells' mechanism for speeding up chemical reactions, it stands to reason that enzymes are involved in controlling the reactions in a positive or negative way. Controlling what reactions are to be used by the cell at any one time is a useful technique for conserving energy and producing only what the cell needs. There are two basic types of metabolic control:

1. Control of enzyme synthesis. This type of control involves mechanisms operating at the level of the gene. This aspect of control is discussed later in Chapter 5.
2. Control of enzyme activity. This technique involves the turning on or turning off of enzyme activity and is associated with a special class of enzymes called **allosteric enzymes.**

ALLOSTERIC ENZYMES AND METABOLIC CONTROL

One of the distinguishing physical characteristics of allosteric enzymes is that they consist of subunits, often 4 or multiples of 4. The subunits can assume different conformations in response to the binding of molecules, such as substrates, to active sites. Each subunit may contain an active site and the binding of a substrate molecule to one subunit increases the binding of the second substrate molecule, and so on (Fig. 3-15). The subunits of allosteric enzymes also possess **regulatory sites** that are distinct from the active site. Regulatory sites bind molecules, other than substrates, that change the conformation of the subunits and may cause an increase or decrease in the activity of the enzyme. Thus, the allosteric enzyme possesses sites that determine what products will be produced in the cell. The primary type of cellular control mechanism associated with allosteric enzymes is called **feedback inhibition.**

Feedback Inhibition

Feedback inhibition is the type of control most frequently associated with biosynthetic reactions, but catabolic reactions are also involved. This type of control assumes that when a product (or products) in a metabolic pathway begins to accumulate it can feed back on the first enzyme in the pathway and shut off not only the synthesis of the final product or products but also any intermediates in

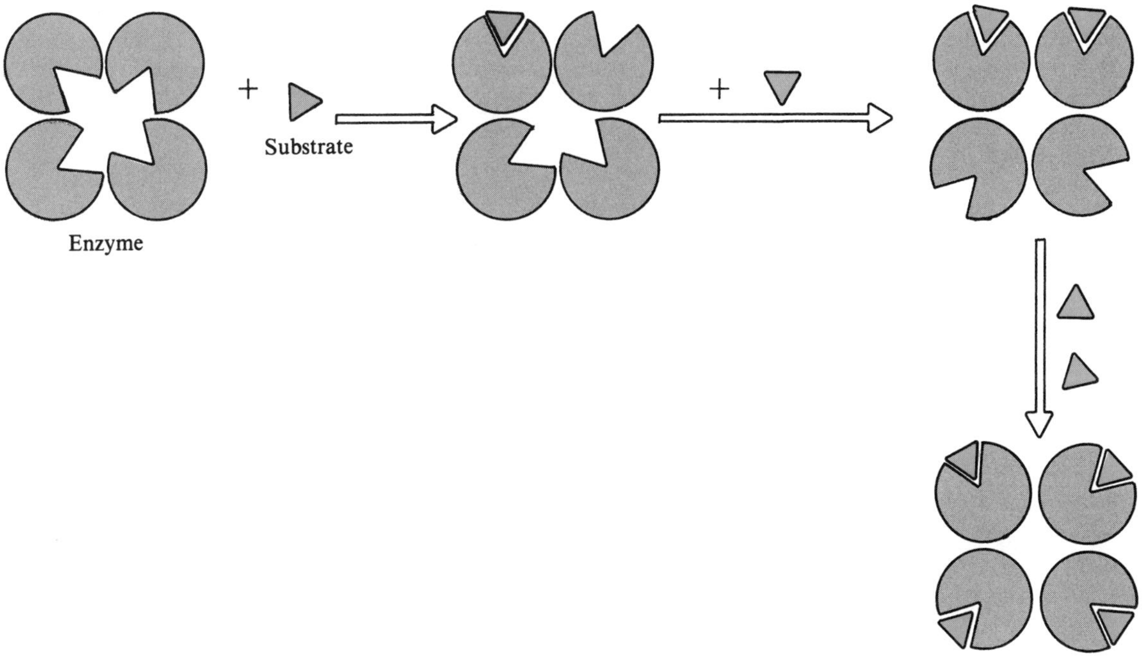

FIGURE 3-15
How binding of substrate molecules to the active sites on the subunits of allosteric enzymes increases activity. Binding of one substrate molecule causes a change in the conformation of the enzyme and results in an increase in the rate of binding of a second substrate molecule. The binding of two substrate molecules in turn increases the rate of binding of substrate molecules to the remaining active sites.

the pathway. In the following example, the final product D of the metabolic sequence feeds back and shuts off enzyme E_1. In the absence of product B, neither C nor D is produced. Enzyme E_1 in the sequence acts as the allosteric enzyme.

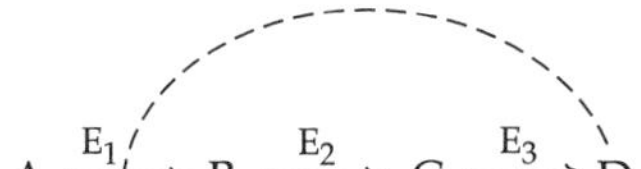

Some metabolic pathways are branched, and more than one product is involved in the control mechanism. The cell must control the amounts of all the different products. Under some environmental conditions, only one of the products may accumulate in the cell. Shutting down the first enzyme will prevent the formation of both products. In the following example, the primary products are D, F, and H, and the allosteric enzymes are E_1, E_4, and E_6.

$$A \xrightarrow{E_1} B \xrightarrow{E_2} C \xrightarrow{E_3} D \begin{array}{c} \nearrow^{E_4} E \xrightarrow{E_5} F \\ \searrow_{E_6} G \xrightarrow{E_7} H \end{array}$$

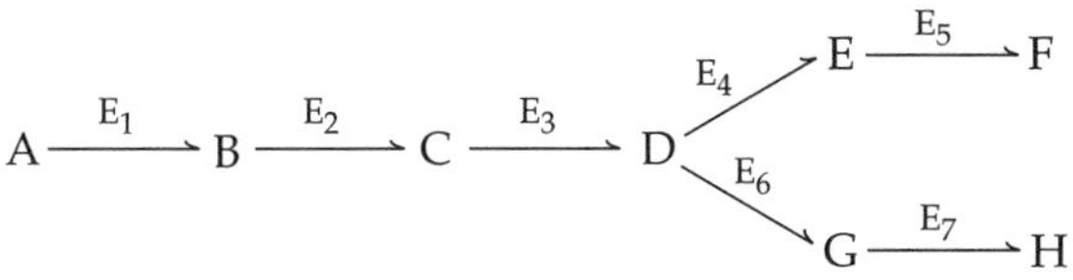

Control of branched pathways can take place in the following ways:
1. Cumulative feedback inhibition. In the preceding diagram, neither product F nor product H alone

could completely reduce the activity of the enzyme E_1; for example, each might reduce activity by 50 percent. Together, however, they totally shut off the activity of enzyme E_1.
2. Sequential feedback inhibition. Products F and H feed back on enzymes E_4 and E_6, causing accumulation of product D. Product D in turn feeds back on enzyme E_1, inhibiting its activity.
3. Multivalent feedback inhibition. Neither product F nor product H has any effect individually on the activity of enzyme E_1, but together they inhibit activity.

Summary

1. Metabolism can be divided into two basic processes: catabolism, or energy production from the degradation of molecules, and anabolism, or the biosynthesis of molecules. Both processes require catalysts in the form of special proteins called enzymes.
2. Enzymes lower the energy of activation of a reaction. They exist in a special conformation that produces an active site for binding substrate. It is at the active site that bond breaking and bond making occur. Some enzymes require cofactors to be active and these may be in the form of vitamins or inorganic ions.
3. Enzymes are affected by pH, temperature, concentration of substrate, and inhibitors. Most enzymes exhibit maximum activity at pHs between 5 and 8 and at temper-

atures between 30 and 37 C. Very high temperatures can cause the protein to unfold or denature, with loss of activity. Inhibitors of enzymes are of two types: competitive, in which the inhibitor competes with the normal substrate for the active site, and noncompetitive, in which the inhibitor does not bind at the active site but at another site that induces a conformational change affecting the active site.

4. The names of enzymes are written with the suffix "-ase." Enzymes can be classified into various groups depending on the type of reaction they catalyze. The major groups of enzymes are oxidoreductases, transferases, hydrolases, lyases, isomerases, and ligases. Enzymes are also classified according to their biological activity, that is, endoenzymes and exoenzymes. Microbial enzymes are used in medical endeavors.

5. Infectious microorganisms obtain their energy from the oxidation of organic molecules. Energy is locked up in the electrons released during the oxidation process. Electrons can be transferred by carriers to the electron transport chain, which is located in the cytoplasmic membrane of prokaryotes and mitochondria of eukaryotes. During the movement of electrons in the electron transport chain, energy is released and is then captured during the phosphorylation of ADP to ATP.

6. In addition to electron transport phosphorylation, there is substrate phosphorylation. In this process energy is associated with a high-energy phosphate trapped in a substrate molecule. The high-energy phosphate is used to phosphorylate ADP to ATP.

7. Two metabolic processes that generate energy in the cell are fermentation and respiration. Fermentation is an anaerobic process that usually involves the oxidation of a sugar. The fermentation of glucose is referred to as glycolysis. During glycolysis, energy is released in the form of ATP via substrate phosphorylation. The final electron acceptor in glycolysis is pyruvic acid, which can be converted to a multitude of products, depending on the species of microorganism.

8. Glucose can be oxidized to produce energy in two other pathways: the pentose phosphate pathway and the Entner-Duodoroff pathway. The pentose phosphate pathway also serves to produce a variety of 3-, 4-, 5-, 6-, and 7-carbon sugars that can be utilized by the cell in various processes. In addition, $NADPH_2$ which is required in biosynthetic reactions is produced. The Entner-Doudoroff pathway produces glyceraldehyde 3-phosphate and pyruvic acid, as in glycolysis, but uses a different route.

9. Respiration is an oxidation process in which the energy of the electron is released during its transport in the electron transport chain. The final electron acceptor may be oxygen (aerobic respiration) or other molecules (anaerobic respiration). The electrons produced during respiration are derived from the oxidation of sugars, as in glycolysis, and in the Krebs cycle, but other organic molecules, such as lipids, can also be a source of electrons. Electrons are transported to the electron transport chain by carriers such as NAD and FAD.

10. The Krebs cycle represents a process in which the pyruvate molecule, generated during glycolysis, is completely oxidized to carbon dioxide. Many intermediates produced in the Krebs cycle, such as alpha-ketoglutarate, are also used in biosynthetic reactions especially in the synthesis of amino acids.

11. The electron transport chain consists of coenzymes, proteins, and nonproteins extended across the cytoplasmic membrane. NAD dehydrogenase and FAD dehydrogenase and quinone of the electron transport chain transport both protons and electrons, while the cytochromes, the last members of the chain, transport only electrons. The final electron acceptor in aerobic respiration, oxygen, is converted to water. Final electron acceptors in anaerobic respiration include such molecules as nitrate and sulfate. The net gain of ATP from aerobic respiration, using glucose, is 38, as compared to 2 for fermentation.

12. Biosynthesis in the cell requires energy, reducing power and carbon skeletons. The carbon skeletons give rise to various building blocks, such as amino acids, sugars, and purines and pyrimidines, which will be the foundation of macromolecules. The carbon skeletons are produced by the same pathways that were used to generate energy in the cell. Reducing power is provided mainly by $NADH_2$ produced in the pentose phosphate pathway.

13. Metabolic processes can be controlled by regulating enzyme synthesis (see Chapter 5) or by controlling enzyme activity. Control of enzyme activity in the cell is brought about by allosteric enzymes, which consist of protein subunits that have regulatory sites in addition to active sites. Regulatory sites can bind molecules other than the substrate and they can increase or decrease enzyme activity.

14. Allosteric enzymes are especially evident in biosynthetic reactions, where they are usually found in the first reaction of a pathway that utilizes several enzymes to generate a product. One type of allosteric enzyme control is called feedback inhibition. In feedback inhibition the end product of the pathway inhibits the first enzyme of the pathway.

Questions for Study

1. What are allosteric enzymes? Look at some of the steps in the various metabolic pathways and indicate where you think an allosteric enzyme would be needed.
2. What is the importance of sulfur in metabolism?
3. Discuss the relationship of catabolism to anabolism. Which one depends on the other or do they both depend on each other?
4. What is the distinction between biological oxidation and reduction? Make a list of some important oxidations and reductions that occur in the various metabolic pathways.

5. What important characteristic distinguishes NAD from NADH in metabolic processes? Give examples.
6. Make a list of the products generated from the metabolism of pyruvate. Find out what microbial species are known to produce these individual products in significant quantities.
7. What is the primary function of the following pathways: (1) glycolysis, (2) Krebs cycle, and (3) pentose phosphate pathway? Are these pathways catabolic or anabolic or both? Explain.
8. What are the primary differences between aerobic and anaerobic respiration?

CHAPTER 4

Microbial Growth

OBJECTIVES

To describe briefly the stages of bacterial growth and the biochemical changes occurring in each stage

To list the chemical factors affecting growth and the function of each

To describe how oxygen is handled by the four groups of bacteria based on their oxygen requirements

To describe the physical factors affecting growth

To differentiate between synthetic and nonsynthetic media, enriched and enrichment media, and selective and differential media and to give examples of each type

To outline the various ways in which anaerobes can be cultivated

To discuss how pure cultures can be obtained in the laboratory

To discuss the various types of primary isolation media and their function

To outline the various ways in which microbial growth can be measured

To define the terms culture, logarithmic, nutrient, aerotolerant, plasmolysis, pure culture, and lyophilization

OUTLINE

- GROWTH OF BACTERIAL CELLS
  - The Growth Curve
    - Lag Phase
    - Log Phase
    - Stationary Phase
    - Death and Decline Phase
- CHEMICAL REQUIREMENTS FOR GROWTH
  - Water
  - Carbon
  - Nitrogen
  - Sulfur and Phosphorus
  - Oxygen
    - Products of Oxygen Metabolism
  - Minerals
- PHYSICAL REQUIREMENTS FOR GROWTH
  - Hydrogen Ion
  - Temperature
    - Psychrophiles
    - Mesophiles
    - Thermophiles
  - Practical Aspects of Temperature Control
  - Osmotic Pressure
- CULTIVATION OF MICROBIAL SPECIES
  - Types of Culture Media
    - Media Based on Chemical Content
    - Media Based on Laboratory Use
  - Cultivation of Anaerobes
- TECHNIQUES FOR ISOLATING BACTERIA
  - Pure Cultures
    - Streak Plate
    - Pour Plate
    - Membrane Filter
  - Media Used for Primary Isolation of Bacteria
- PRESERVATION OF ISOLATED MICROORGANISMS
  - Freezing
  - Freeze-drying (Lyophilization)
- LABORATORY MEASUREMENT OF MICROBIAL GROWTH
  - Cell Count
    - Microscopic
    - Standard Plate Count
  - Cell Density

Growth is the coordination of chemical and physical processes in the cell that ideally result in cell division. The cellular chemical and physical processes are also influenced by external chemical and physical forces. For laboratory technicians a knowledge of growth is important because they are concerned with cultivating microorganisms for clinical and investigative purposes. Nurses, hygienists, and physicians may be concerned with microbial growth because under certain circumstances they utilize procedures that prevent microbial growth. The average citizen each day tries to prevent spoilage of foods or destruction of various articles susceptible to microbial attack. Industrial microbiologists are often concerned with enhancing microbial growth in order to provide increased synthesis of a commercially marketable microbial product such as vitamins or organic acids.

In this chapter we examine the chemical and physical factors affecting growth and how a knowledge of microbial growth is utilized in the microbiological laboratory. Later in Chapter 15 we discuss more specific aspects of microbial growth in relationship to infectious disease.

FIGURE 4-1
Asexual reproduction in bacteria. A. Diagrammatic representation. The cell wall begins to invaginate while DNA duplicates. As cell wall invagination continues, each side will possess a molecule of DNA. Cell wall invagination continues until the cell splits into two units or progeny of equal size.

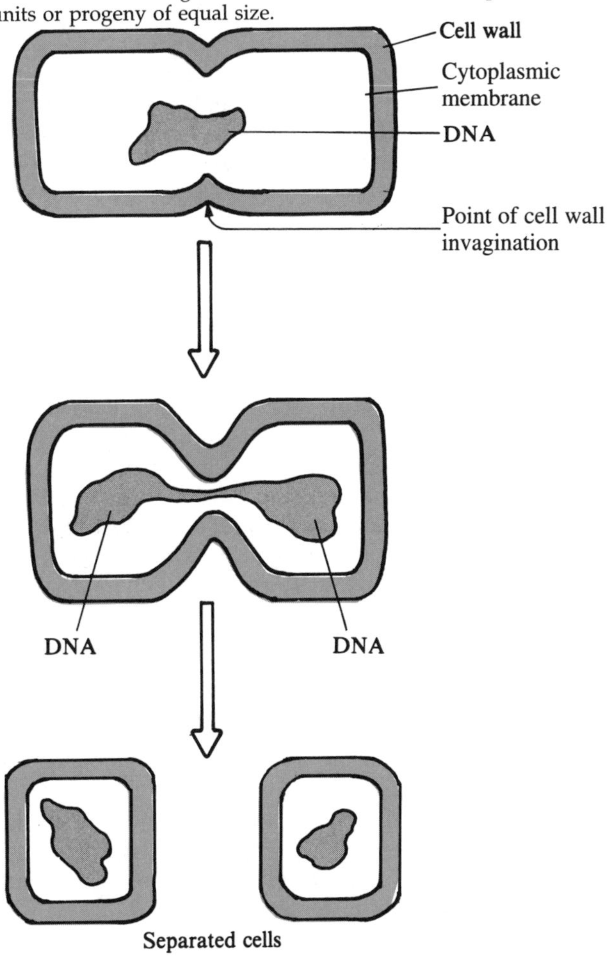

Growth of Bacterial Cells

Bacterial cells can be grown in various nutrient-containing preparations called **culture media.** The population of cells in the medium is called a **culture.** A microbial cell grows by increasing its cellular constituents and then dividing into two cells. Bacterial cells divide by an asexual process called **binary fission** (Fig. 4-1). When the cell divides, each of the progeny possesses a copy of the DNA, as well as other cellular components, that will enable them also to grow and divide. The division process continues in a geometric way; that is, after the first cell divides into two cells, the population doubles: 4, 8, 16, 32, 64, and so on. The time required for a single cell or population of cells to double is called the **generation time** or **doubling time.** The generation time can be calculated mathematically by determining the number of cells in samples taken from broth cultures at various time intervals during geometric growth. For example, suppose we remove one sample at time 0 and three samples each at 30-minute intervals. The number of bacteria found at each interval is found to be 100, 200, 400, and 800, respectively. We can see from these experimental results that the doubling time is 30 minutes. This type of data could be graphed by using an arithmetic scale but in the laboratory a culture containing 800 bacteria would not be visible to the naked eye and would be difficult to measure. Bacterial growth becomes visible as a turbid solution only when there are at least 1×10^7 (10 million) bacteria per milliliter. In the laboratory, cultures often contain up to 5×10^9 (5 billion) bacteria per milliliter. To graph this kind of data requires a logarithmic scale (Fig. 4-2).

FIGURE 4-2
Bacterial growth plotted logarithmically and arithmetically. One can see from the graph that measurements of growth at time intervals on the arithmetic scale are difficult to evaluate at early times and later when the cell number goes beyond 1000.

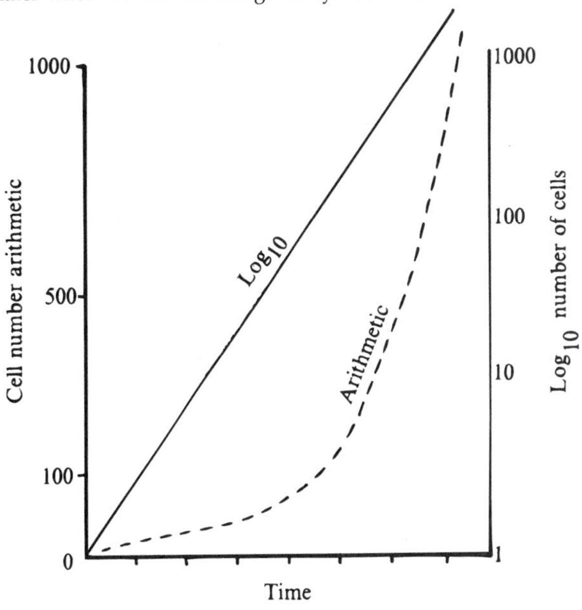

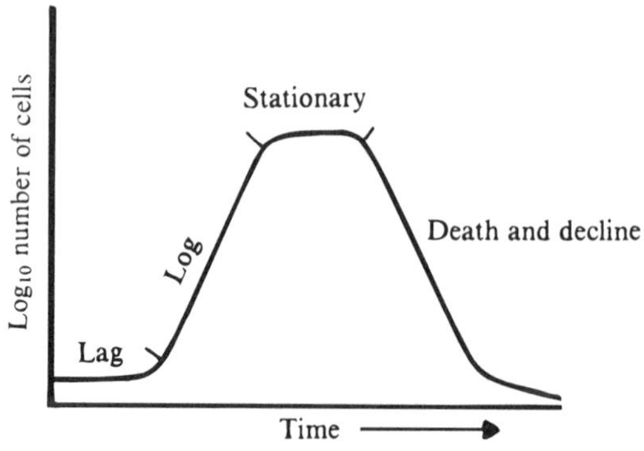

FIGURE 4-3
Growth curve of bacterial culture.

THE GROWTH CURVE

A population of bacterial cells goes through a number of phases from the time it is introduced into a medium until it ceases growth. When these phases are graphed, they produce a typical growth curve (Fig. 4-3). The growth curve includes the **lag, log, stationary,** and **death and decline phases.**

Lag Phase

When microorganisms are introduced into a growth medium, there is usually a period of adjustment to the new chemical and physical environment. There is a lag in cell division and the population does not divide at all or divides in a nongeometric fashion. This phase produces an almost horizontal line on the growth curve. Near the end of the lag phase the rate of cell division begins to accelerate.

Log Phase

The term **log** is an abbreviation for logarithmic, which means that the population of cells is dividing in a geometric or logarithmic fashion. During the log phase, cell division is occurring at a constant rate, for example, every 30 minutes. The reason for this constancy in the log phase is that all components in the cell, such as DNA, RNA, protein, and cell wall, are doubling their mass at a specific rate just like cell division. The growth rate of bacterial species varies and depends on

1. The microbial species. Every species because of its genetic potential has a minimum and maximum rate of growth. In the log phase microorganisms are growing more efficiently than in any other phase of growth.
2. Temperature. An increase in temperature up to a certain limit increases the rate of growth. For example, a culture of *Escherichia coli* grown at 30 C may have a generation time of 1 hour but at a temperature of 37 C may have a generation time of 30 minutes or less.
3. Growth-supporting ability of the culture medium. A medium containing a high concentration of preformed organic nutrients will support a faster growth rate than a nutritionally poor medium. Of course the nutrients must be ones that can be metabolized by the microbial species in question.

Stationary Phase

When bacteria are cultivated in a medium in which nutrients are not replenished, a point is reached during which the growth rate declines. Many bacteria in a nutrient-depleted medium will be dying while others will be dividing—the living ones using nutrients from dying cells. In the stationary phase there is a balance between the number of cells dying and the number dividing. This equilibrium is represented as a horizontal line in the growth curve when plotted on semi-log paper (see Fig. 4-3). In addition to nutrient depletion, other factors are also responsible for the decline in growth and include

1. pH changes. Acids are the common metabolic excretion product and cause a reduction in pH of the medium.
2. Accumulation of toxic waste products. Some of these toxic wastes may also be the acids described in 1.
3. Reduced concentration of oxygen (if the organism is aerobic) in the medium is usually due to overcrowding and rapid depletion of oxygen.

The chemical and physical changes occurring during the stationary phase can induce the formation of endospores by bacteria such as *Bacillus* and *Clostridium* and loss of vegetative cells.

Death and Decline Phase

The death and decline phase of growth is essentially the reverse of the logarithmic phase; that is, the cells in the population are dying in a geometric fashion. Factors responsible for the death phase include those given for the stationary phase as well as the release of lytic enzymes by some groups of bacteria when they lyse or burst.

Chemical Requirements for Growth

Chemicals required for growth are called **nutrients.** Nutrients may be in the form of inorganic or organic compounds or a combination of both. Let us suppose that we wish to cultivate two species of bacteria, *E. coli,* an inhabitant of the intestinal tract, and a species of *Streptococcus* from the oral cavity. Following cultivation we may wish to determine some of their growth characteristics. Our first task is to prepare a medium and determine what is needed. Most media used today are commercially prepared, but it is still important to understand why the constituents were chosen and their function in the cell.

WATER

We need water to dissolve the required nutrients. This will allow the nutrients to be transported across the cytoplasmic membrane into the cell. In addition, many biochemical reactions require water to break down (hydrolyze) certain compounds.

CARBON

Most microorganisms, including those infectious for humans, must be supplied carbon in an organic form (only a few bacteria can use inorganic carbon, such as carbon dioxide, as their carbon source). Organisms using organic molecules as a source of carbon are called **heterotrophs.** The organic carbon source one should use depends on the genetic potential of the bacterial cell—that is, can the bacterial cell produce enzymes that will metabolize the carbon source? The most common sources of carbon for bacterial cells are sugars, such as glucose, because they are easily degraded in glycolysis and because they can also serve as energy sources. When glucose is catabolized, it provides the carbon skeletons for the various precursor materials (such as amino acids). *E. coli* can use glucose for all of its biosynthetic needs but this is not true for the *Streptococcus* species. Some biosynthetic reactions are absent in *Streptococcus* and the precursor material must be present in the medium. The organic precursor materials that must be supplied in the medium are called **growth factors** and may include amino acids, purines and pyrimidines, and vitamins. Vitamins are used as coenzymes (see Table 3-1).

The carbon source for some microorganisms could be a macromolecule such as the polysaccharide cellulose. However, the microorganism must be able to produce the enzyme cellulase that can be excreted from the cell (exoenzyme) to degrade the macromolecule into its constituent subunits, that is, glucose. Macromolecules are not transportable through the cytoplasmic membrane, but their smaller subunits, such as glucose, are transportable.

NITROGEN

Nitrogen is a major element of proteins and is also found in the purines and pyrimidines. The microbial cells' nitrogen requirements are usually supplied via an inorganic molecule, such as ammonia (NH_3) or nitrate (NO_3), but nitrite (NO_2) and nitrogen gas (N_2) can also be used by some microorganisms. Inorganic forms of nitrogen are first converted by the cell into ammonia (Fig. 4-4), which then becomes the amino group in an amino acid. For an organism such as *Streptococcus,* with limited biosynthetic potential, inorganic nitrogen may be used to synthesize most of the amino acids, but the various vitamins must be supplied in the medium (see Table 4-2 and Cultivation of Microbial Species).

Proteins can be a source of nitrogen, as well as carbon and energy, provided the microbial cell produces exoenzymes, such as proteases, that degrade them. A partially digested protein called **peptone** is a component of several commercially available media and it serves these purposes.

Nitrogen gas (N_2) as a source of nitrogen is used primarily by organisms found in soil and water. They take up the gas and add hydrogens to it to make ammonia, a process called **nitrogen fixation.** This process can be utilized by only a few infectious microorganisms, such as *Klebsiella,* and then only when more normal nitrogen sources, such as nitrate, are absent. Neither *E. coli* nor *Streptococcus* can use nitrogen gas.

SULFUR AND PHOSPHORUS

Sulfur, which is an element found in some amino acids, is usually supplied to the microbial cell in the form of inorganic sulfate. The sulfate is converted to hydrogen sulfide (H_2S), which is used in the synthesis of the amino acid cysteine. Inorganic phosphate is the most widely used source of phosphorus for microorganisms. Phosphorus is important in the synthesis of the nucleic acids DNA and RNA. One of the components of these nucleic acids is adenosine triphosphate (ATP), which is the energy molecule of the cell (see Chapter 3). Phosphate in the medium is also important as a buffer when it is in the form of mono- or dipotassium phosphate (KH_2PO_4 and K_2HPO_4, respectively). Buffers absorb hydrogen ions generated during microbial metabolism when acids are produced. This buffering capacity enables the medium to support more growth since most bacteria are unable to grow at low or acid pHs.

OXYGEN

We have already observed in Chapter 3 that oxygen plays an important role in the growth of microorganisms because it is a terminal electron acceptor in respiration. Although some organisms may not require oxygen for

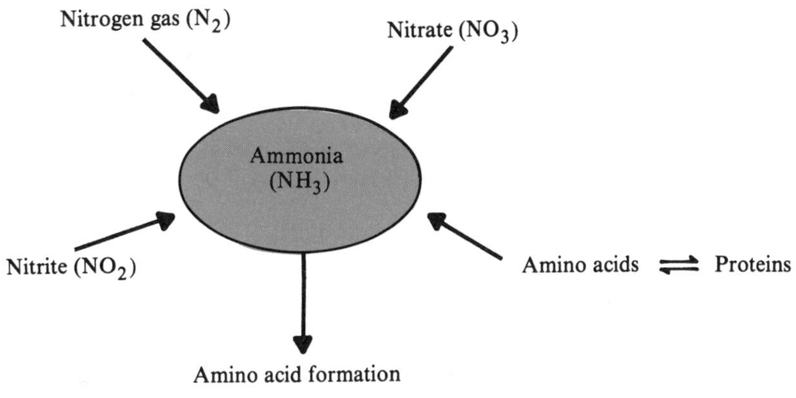

FIGURE 4-4
The flow of nitrogen from inorganic to organic forms and vice versa within the cell. Ammonia (NH_3) is the central nitrogen compound because it is used in the synthesis of amino acids.

growth, they do respond to its presence in different ways. Let us see how and why microorganisms respond so differently to this element.

Products of Oxygen Metabolism

Many microorganisms possess enzymes that reduce oxygen not only to water, as in aerobic respiration, but also to toxic products. Two of the most important of these toxic intermediates are **hydrogen peroxide** and **superoxide.** The oxygen atom in each of these molecules, in terms of electronic configurations, is different from molecular or atmospheric oxygen. These toxic molecules are also produced by mammalian white blood cells and are the basis of mammalian resistance to microbial invasion (see Chapter 9). Microorganisms have evolved enzymatic mechanisms for removing the toxic intermediates of oxygen metabolism and converting them to molecular oxygen. The enzymes involved are **catalase,*** which converts hydrogen peroxide to water and oxygen:

$$H_2O_2 \xrightarrow{\text{catalase}} H_2O + O_2$$

and **superoxide dismutase,** which converts superoxide to hydrogen peroxide and molecular oxygen (the peroxide can be metabolized by catalase). Based on oxygen requirements, microorganisms are divided into four groups. We will see how each tolerates oxygen and its toxic intermediates.

1. **Obligate aerobes.** Obligate aerobes are totally dependent on oxygen for growth. The oxygen requirement is usually expressed as 1 atmosphere, or 20%, the concentration of oxygen in air at 1 atmosphere. Obligate aerobes produce hydrogen peroxide and superoxide but they also possess the enzymes catalase and superoxide dismutase, which enable them to tolerate high concentrations of oxygen.
2. **Microaerophiles.** Microaerophiles grow in the presence of oxygen but can tolerate only so much oxygen (about 0.2 atmosphere, or 4%). Microaerophiles produce the necessary enzymes to break down hydrogen peroxide and superoxide, but if too many toxic products are formed, the enzymatic system of the bacterium becomes overloaded and growth is inhibited.
3. **Facultative anaerobes.** Facultative anaerobes can grow in the presence of oxygen or in its absence. In the presence of oxygen they use aerobic respiration for energy production but in its absence fermentation or anaerobic respiration is the major source of energy. Facultative anaerobes grow best under aerobic conditions and produce catalase and superoxide dismutase to break down hydrogen peroxide and superoxide that accumulate.
4. **Obligate anaerobes.** Obligate anaerobes can grow only in the absence of oxygen. Obligate anaerobes such as *Clostridium* are found in the soil, but anaerobes can also be found in certain environments in the human host. These anaerobic environments include the intestinal tract and areas such as the pockets lying between the teeth and gums (gingival crevice). The effect of oxygen on obligate anaerobes is variable. Oxygen can be lethal to some obligate anaerobes simply because the microorganisms possess enzymes that reduce oxygen to hydrogen peroxide and superoxide but lack enzymes that degrade them to nontoxic compounds. Other obligate anaerobes (called **aerotolerant** species) are tolerant of oxygen simply because they lack enzymes that reduce oxygen to water or any toxic intermediates.

* Peroxidase can also break down hydrogen peroxide but oxygen is not produced.

MINERALS

Mineral requirements of microorganisms vary considerably. Some minerals such as calcium, magnesium, potassium, and iron are needed by practically all bacteria. Other minerals such as sodium, zinc, molybdenum, cobalt, copper, and manganese are usually required in small or trace amounts. In most instances it is not necessary to add trace elements to laboratory media since many are normal contaminants of tap or even "distilled" water. The more important minerals and their function in microbial metabolism are summarized in Table 4-1. Iron plays a very important role in the infectious disease process; this is discussed in detail in Chapter 15.

TABLE 4-1
Important Minerals and Their Function in Microbial Metabolism

Element	Function
Magnesium	Stabilization of nucleic acids and ribosomes; required in some enzymatic reactions
Potassium	Required in some enzymatic reactions; important in protein synthesis
Iron	Important component of the cytochromes; important in diphtheria toxin production by *Corynebacterium diphtheriae;* important factor in bacterial disease (see Chapter 14).
Calcium	Cofactor for some enzymes; required for attachment of some bacterial viruses to the bacterial cell; important in spore formation by bacteria
Zinc	Cofactor for some enzymes
Molybdenum	An important component of the enzyme involved in nitrogen fixation
Cobalt	Component of vitamin B_{12}
Manganese	Cofactor for some enzymes and can substitute for magnesium
Sodium	Required primarily by marine microorganisms

Physical Requirements for Growth

Many physical factors affect microbial growth, and manipulation of these factors can allow one to select specific microbial species. For the clinical microbiologist some of these physical factors are provided for in commercial media. Let us briefly examine how variations in some of these physical factors affect growth.

HYDROGEN ION

Most bacteria grow best at pHs between 6 and 8 while fungi show optimum growth at pHs between 5 and 6. This is the principal reason why most microorganisms are unable to cause infections in the stomach, where the pH is approximately 2.0. Commercial media contain buffers to prevent a rapid drop in pH during bacterial growth on carbohydrates, such as glucose and other sugars. These buffers may be in the form of phosphates or organic molecules such as peptones or amino acids. The latter are often metabolized to alkaline products rather than acid products.

TEMPERATURE

Based on temperature requirements for optimal growth, microorganisms have been divided into three types: **psychrophiles, mesophiles,** and **thermophiles.** When the growth rate of psychrophiles, mesophiles, and thermophiles is plotted, each group exhibits a characteristic minimum, optimum, and maximum temperature of growth (Fig. 4-5). The minimum temperature is the lowest temperature at which the organisms grow. The optimum temperature is the temperature at which growth is best. The maximum temperature is the highest temperature at which growth is possible and beyond which growth is not possible. At maximum temperatures of growth the enzymatic machinery of the cell is still operating but the enzymes are more rapidly inactivated than would occur at lower temperatures.

Psychrophiles

Psychrophiles have a temperature range for growth between −10 and 20 C. They are found in many aquatic and soil environments of temperate regions as well as extremely cold regions of the earth. Food and dairy products are sometimes contaminated by psychrophiles, whose growth is stimulated when foods are refrigerated. Psychrophilic temperatures are usually not lethal to organisms that grow best above 25 C but they do inhibit growth.

Mesophiles

The microorganisms that cause disease in humans are characteristically mesophiles. They prefer growth at temperatures between 30 and 37 C, the latter being the normal body temperature.

Thermophiles

Thermophiles show a temperature range for growth between 45 and 70 C. They are found in hot sulfur springs and other areas where high temperatures are maintained. Thermophiles for the most part are incapable of growth at the usual temperatures of the body and are not involved in infectious diseases of humans.

FIGURE 4-5
Comparison of growth rates of psychrophiles, mesophiles, and thermophiles at minimum, optimum, and maximum temperatures.

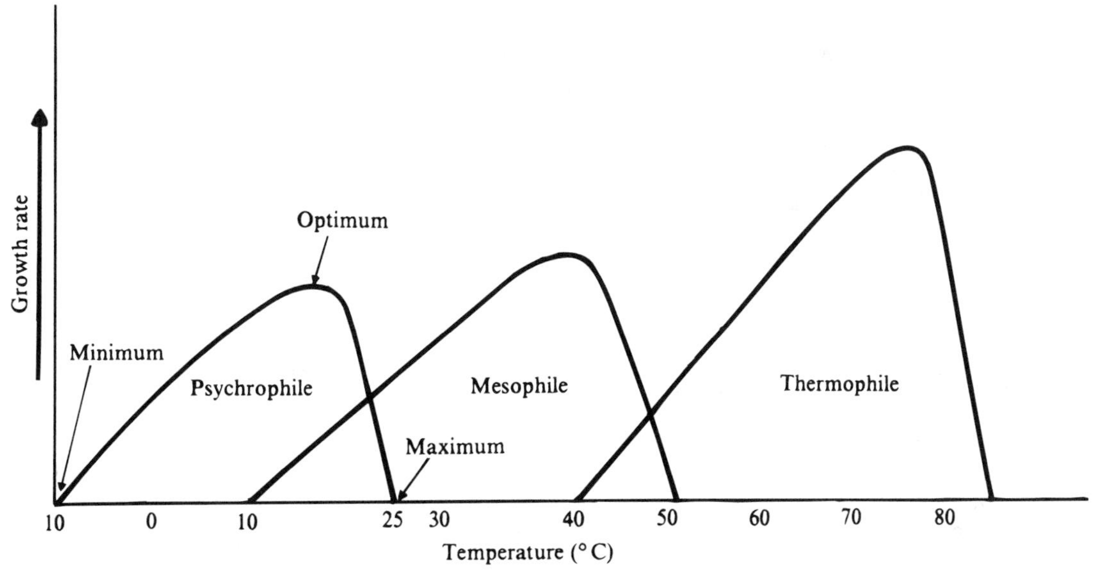

PRACTICAL ASPECTS OF TEMPERATURE CONTROL

Low temperatures are used as a technique for the preservation of foods by inhibiting microbial growth. Refrigeration temperatures (2–7 C) are suitable for the storage of a large number of perishable foods. Food-poisoning microorganisms, except for *Clostridium botulinum* type E, are prevented from growth at temperatures below 6 C. Still, many microorganisms can grow, albeit slowly, at temperatures from 0 to −34 C. Several yeasts, for example, are capable of growth at temperatures between −18 and −34 C. Generally speaking, gram-positive cocci such as *Staphylococcus* are more resistant to low temperatures than are gram-negative rod-shaped bacteria such as *Salmonella*.

The freezing of microorganisms that cannot grow at freezing temperatures is a method of preserving microorganisms in the laboratory. Once deepfreezing temperatures (−50 to −95 C) have been reached, a great percentage of the microorganisms die. The cells surviving the initial freezing die gradually in the frozen state. The rate at which they die depends on (1) whether the freezing is slow or fast, (2) the composition of the medium in which the microorganisms were frozen, (3) the length of storage in the frozen state, and (4) the temperature at which the microorganisms were frozen. Several changes that contribute to the loss of viability occur in the cell during freezing:

1. Free water in the cell forms ice crystals, which lead to dehydration of the cell and an increase in the concentration of electrolytes.
2. The dehydration from ice crystal formation also changes the colloidal state of cytoplasmic proteins.
3. Some cellular proteins are denatured by freezing, apparently because of the removal of sulfhydryl groups.
4. There is a decrease in pH, as well as loss of gases such as carbon dioxide and oxygen, following freezing. Thus, metabolism and respiratory activity are suppressed. Once the frozen culture has thawed, many cells have increased nutritional requirements that remain for several generations. Apparently the freezing process has injured the cytoplasmic membrane and a restoration of normal activity does not occur until several generations have elapsed.

High temperatures, such as those between 62 and 71 C, are used in pasteurization processes while temperatures above 100 C are used in sterilization procedures, which are discussed in Chapter 7.

OSMOTIC PRESSURE

The concentration of solutes in a medium is an important factor controlling the growth of microorganisms. Maintaining a relatively constant ionic strength in the cell is important because the stability and activity of enzymes and other macromolecules are dependent on it. Several types of commercially available media contain sodium chloride (NaCl) to maintain the ionic strength of the medium. If the solute concentration outside the cell is higher than inside the cell, water will flow from the cytoplasm of the cell to the outside. This loss of water from the cell causes the cell protoplast to shrink, a condition called **plasmolysis.** Plasmolysis prevents growth. This technique is used in industry for curing hams and other meats by adding high concentrations of salt or sugar (sucrose).

Cultivation of Microbial Species

In previous paragraphs we discussed what chemical and physical factors are required for the growth of microorganisms. Now we examine the actual types of culture media used to cultivate a population of bacteria.

TYPES OF CULTURE MEDIA

The laboratory medium can be in the form of a liquid, in which instance it is called a **broth,** or in the form of a semisolid, in which case **agar** is added to the broth. Agar, a carbohydrate isolated from seaweed, is not digested by bacteria and does not serve as a nutrient in the medium. Agar is added to the broth and the mixture is sterilized and then cooled. Cooling results in the formation of a semisolid medium permitting the isolation and possible differentiation of bacteria on its surface. Laboratory media are classified according to their chemical content and laboratory use.

Media Based on Chemical Content

A medium in which the exact chemical composition is known is called a **synthetic** or **defined medium.** It may be a simple salts solution with a carbon source, or it may include many organic components (Table 4-2). A medium in which the exact chemical composition is not known

TABLE 4-2
Chemical Composition of a Defined and Complex Medium*

Defined medium (mg/liter)	Complex medium (mg/liter)
$CaCl_2$ (15)	Cysteine (15)
$MgSO_4$ (120)	Sodium glutamate (500)
$(NH_4)_2SO_4$ (1200)	$(NH_4)_2SO_4$ (1200)
Na_2HPO_4 (7000)	Sodium acetate (10,000)
NaH_2PO_4 (200)	Na_2HPO_4 (7000)
Glucose (10,000)	NaH_2PO_4 (1200)
	Folic acid (0.005)
	Biotin (0.0025)
	Para-aminobenzoic acid (0.1)
	Thiamine (0.5)
	Riboflavin (0.5)
	Pyridoxal (1.0)
	Pantothenate (0.5)
	Nicotinic acid (1.0)
	Glucose (10,000)

* The defined medium is a basal salts medium used to cultivate organisms such as *Escherichia coli.* The complex medium is used to cultivate bacteria such as some oral streptococci.

TABLE 4-3
Composition of a Complex Medium, Nutrient Broth

Component	Concentration (gm/liter)
Peptone	5.0
Beef extract	3.0
Sodium chloride	8.0
Water	1000 ml

is called **nonsynthetic** or complex. **Nutrient broth** is an example of a complex medium (Table 4-3).

Most microbiological media are commercially available in the form of powder or crystals. The media are dissolved in water and sterilized to destroy any living organisms and then are cooled before laboratory use. A temperature is selected, usually 30 or 37 C, for cultivation of the bacteria. Because of the diverse requirements of some bacteria, it is sometimes necessary to add specific components to the commercial medium or adjust other factors. For this reason there now exists a classification of media based on specific laboratory use.

Media Based on Laboratory Use

An **all-purpose medium** is designed to support the growth of most microorganisms. Examples of all-purpose media are nutrient broth, nutrient yeast, and trypticase soy broth.

Enriched media contain a basal growth-supporting medium to which nutritive supplements are added. **Blood agar** is an enriched medium. Blood agar base contains an infusion of beef heart muscle, tryptose, salt, and agar. After sterilization this medium is allowed to cool to 50 C and to it is added 5% sterile defibrinated sheep or horse blood.

Some media can be **selective;** that is, they are used to select for wanted species of bacteria and select against unwanted species of bacteria. This selection is generally achieved in either a synthetic or nonsynthetic medium by the addition of specific chemical components. Many selective media incorporate dyes such as crystal violet or antibiotics to inhibit the growth of undesirable species. Other selective procedures include (1) addition of specific energy or carbon sources, (2) adjusting the pH, (3) increasing the osmotic properties, and (4) adjusting the oxygen tension. Some bacteria, such as the *Neisseria,* require low levels of oxygen but increased concentrations of carbon dioxide. Carbon dioxide incubators that electronically control the level of carbon dioxide for growth are available.

Some media are **differential;** that is, they enable one to distinguish between various genera and species of bacteria. Although two or more types of bacteria can grow on this medium, some agent in the medium allows them to be differentiated. Often the separation is based on color differences in the isolated colonies. An example of this kind of medium is eosin-methylene blue (EMB) agar, which differentiates *E. coli* from *Enterobacter aerogenes.* The *E. coli* colonies on EMB agar are dark with a metallic sheen, while most *E. aerogenes* colonies are pink with a blue center and rarely have a metallic sheen. Most of the differential media are also selective and contain many kinds of growth-inhibiting agents.

An **enrichment medium** is used to inhibit the growth of an unwanted bacterial species that greatly outnumbers the wanted species in a specimen. For example, some fecal specimens containing the infectious agent *Salmonella* are outnumbered by the bacteria that are indigenous to the intestinal tract. An enrichment medium contains an agent such as selenite or tetrathionate that inhibits the growth of the unwanted species and favors the growth of the wanted species.

Transport media are especially designed to preserve microorganisms during their transit following isolation from the patient until they are cultivated in the laboratory. The medium is usually a buffered salts medium that prevents microbial growth. Some transport media contain agents that absorb oxygen, and these are used in transporting anaerobes to the laboratory.

CULTIVATION OF ANAEROBES

Obligate anaerobes grow only in the absence of air and some are sensitive to any level of oxygen. The cultivation of anaerobes, therefore, requires special precautions and the use of techniques that are not used in the cultivation of aerobic microorganisms. The most widely used and least expensive way to isolate anaerobes is by the **anaerobic jar method.** The jar, made of polycarbonate, is called the **GasPak** and is equipped with a removable lid that can form an airtight seal. The GasPak system (Fig. 4-6) is ordinarily used in clinical laboratories. A specified amount of water is added to the contents of a disposable aluminum foil envelope. The envelope is placed in the GasPak jar along with the inoculated cultures. The jar is sealed, and the water added to the envelope generates the production of hydrogen and carbon dioxide gases. With the aid of a catalyst (platinum) that is in the lid of the jar, any oxygen in the GasPak combines with hydrogen gas to form water, thus producing an anaerobic environment.

Another simple technique for cultivating anaerobes is the **Bio-Bag** (Fig. 4-7). The Bio-Bag consists of a clear, gas-impermeable bag, an ampule containing an indicator, and a gas generator ampule. One or two plates are placed inside the bag and then the bag is sealed. The indicator ampule is crushed and the gas generator is activated. In about half an hour any oxygen in the bag is removed. The plates are easily observed and the organisms grow and remain viable for up to 1 week.

A technique for isolating anaerobes in laboratories specializing in such procedures is the **anaerobic glove box.** The anaerobic glove box is made of a flexible vinyl plastic with openings for neoprene gloves (Fig. 4-8). The box may enclose up to 30 cubic feet. A mixture of nitrogen, hydrogen, and carbon dioxide gases fills the box and maintains its shape. Agar media are prepared outside the box and are placed in the box until the oxygen has been removed. Specimens are then inoculated onto the prepared agar

FIGURE 4-6
The GasPak for isolation of anaerobes. The GasPak is an anaerobic system consisting of a polycarbonate jar, lid holding a charged catalyst reaction chamber, GasPak disposable hydrogen-plus–carbon dioxide generator envelope, and disposable anaerobic indicator. (Courtesy of BBL Microbiology Systems, Division of Becton, Dickinson and Company, Cockeysville, MD.)

FIGURE 4-7
Bio-Bag environmental chamber (type A), a disposable environmental system for the isolation of anaerobic bacteria. The chamber is sized to hold either a plate or the miniature identification systems currently used in clinical laboratories. (Courtesy of Marion Laboratories, Inc., Kansas City, MO.)

plates within the box. An incubator may be placed in the box for incubation of the culture.

Isolation of anaerobes can be an important part of clinical microbiology because some anaerobes, such as species of *Clostridium*, are causes of fatal diseases. Non-sporeforming anaerobes, such as *Bacteroides, Fusobacterium,* and others, are more difficult to isolate than *Clostridium* species and special procedures are required for their isolation. These procedures may include special containers for transport of the clinical specimen and complex media containing blood and various supplements for cultivation, as well as special environments for cultivation such as those discussed.

Techniques for Isolating Bacteria

PURE CULTURES

In medical microbiology the cultivation and isolation of a single species is a necessary prerequisite for identifying bacteria. The isolation of a single species from a mixed culture is called the **pure culture technique.** Several

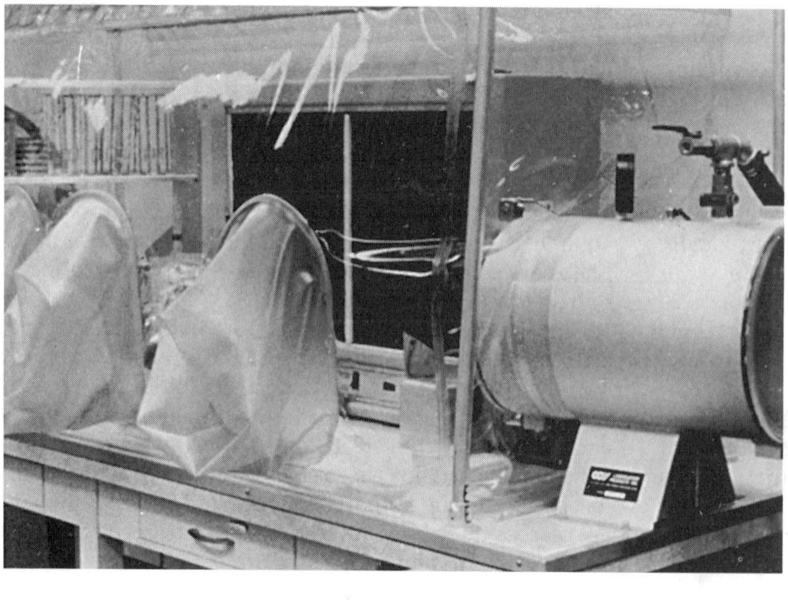

FIGURE 4-8
The anaerobic glove box. (Courtesy of Coy Laboratory Products, Inc., Ann Arbor, MI.)

methods are available for obtaining pure cultures. In each case a culture or specimen containing microorganisms (called the **inoculum**) is introduced **(inoculated)** onto appropriate media for incubation at a specific temperature and time. We first examine the basic mechanisms for isolating a pure culture and then look at types of isolation media.

Streak Plate

In the streak plate technique a small inoculum of the mixed population is streaked directly onto the surface of an agar medium. The streaking is performed with an inoculating loop. This procedure thins out the microbial population on the surface of the agar and where a single organism has been deposited, a colony, which contains only one kind of bacterium, will develop after suitable incubation (Fig. 4-9). From one such colony an inoculum is streaked onto the surface of a second agar plate and the colonies that develop there are also examined. This subculture procedure ensures that only one kind of microorganism is present in the initially isolated colony. The pure culture can be used to conduct further laboratory investigations.

Pour Plate

In the pour plate procedure the mixed population is first diluted and a small quantity is transferred to the bottom of a sterile Petri dish. Melted agar (50 C) is then poured into the Petri dish to cover the bacteria. The dish is gently tilted to obtain uniform distribution of organisms. Colonies will develop on the surface of the agar as well as in the agar. This technique may be used for the isolation of anaerobes or microaerophiles tolerant of low levels of oxygen.

FIGURE 4-9
The streak plate technique for isolation of colonies of bacteria. The area of heavy growth indicates the initial site of inoculation. A second streak was made at right angle to the first, and a third at right angle to the second. As the growth is thinned out, individual cells are deposited on the agar, giving rise to discrete colonies.

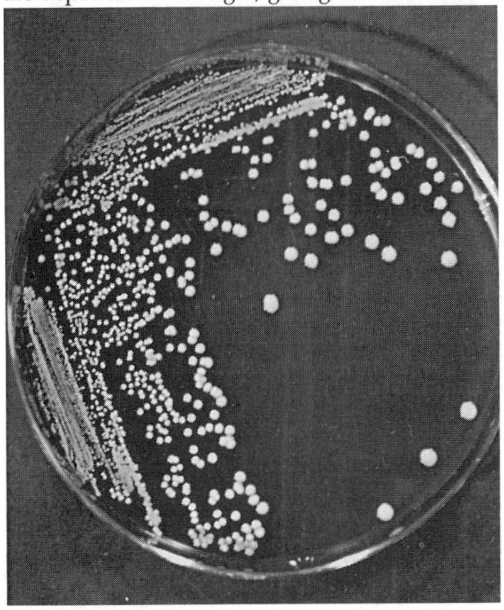

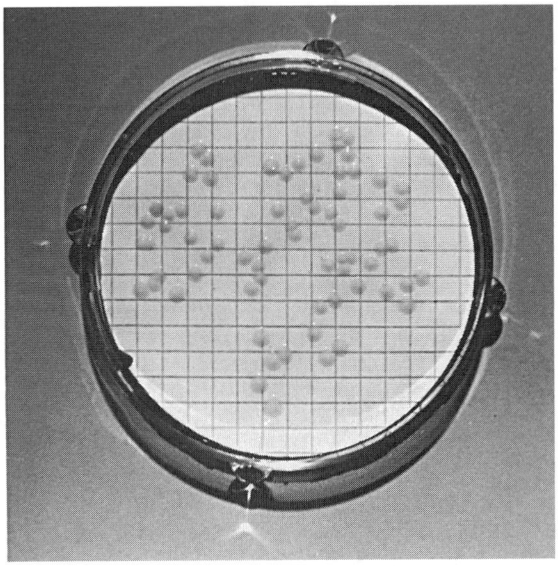

FIGURE 4-10
Colonies as they would appear on a membrane filter placed on an agar surface. (Courtesy of Stanley Livingston.)

Membrane Filter

Membrane filters are thin porous sheets composed of cellulose esters or related materials. Once the sample is filtered, the filter can be placed on top of an agar medium, and after suitable incubation colonies will develop (Fig. 4-10). In clinical microbiology the membrane filter technique has some applications when (1) the organism may be in small numbers in a large volume of fluid, (2) the fluid from which the organism is being isolated inhibits microbial growth (for example, spinal fluid or urine), and (3) total viable counts can be determined from urine samples and tedious dilution techniques are thereby avoided.

MEDIA USED FOR PRIMARY ISOLATION OF BACTERIA

Speed, specificity of the testing procedure, and economy of the test are three factors to be considered in diagnostic procedures in the clinical microbiology laboratory. When an organism can be identified quickly and with certainty, the patient can be treated more rapidly and the probability of cure is enhanced. The choice of the medium for isolation of the microbial species is, therefore, extremely important. It is usually dictated by the source of the specimen—feces, urine, and so on—and by the type of infectious agent suspected of causing the infection. A number of physiologically different microorganisms could conceivably be the cause of the infection. The clinical microbiologist generally uses more than one type of medium, as well as different environmental conditions for primary isolation; that is, the culture will be incubated both anaerobically and aerobically. The most commonly recommended primary isolation media are

1. **Thioglycolate.** Thioglycolate contains, in addition to nutrients for growth, thioglycolic acid and a small amount of agar. These components provide a reduc-

ing environment; that is, oxygen is depleted from the medium. Thus, some anaerobes can be cultivated without resorting to special anaerobic techniques.

2. **Blood agar.** Blood agar is an all-purpose medium that supports the growth of a wide range of pathogens, even those with very fastidious requirements. It also permits the evaluation of the hemolytic activity of microorganisms. Some microorganisms will completely lyse the red blood cells, and on blood agar the result is a clearing around the colony. This type of hemolysis is called **beta hemolysis.** Incomplete hemolysis or **alpha hemolysis** causes a greening around the colony. Absence of hemolysis is called **gamma hemolysis** (Fig. 4-11).

FIGURE 4-11
Hemolytic activity. A. Colonies show no hemolytic activity (gamma hemolysis). B. Colonies show beta-hemolytic activity, complete lysis of red blood cells in the area around the colonies. (From J. LeBlanc and L. N. Lee, *J. Bacteriol.* 150:835, 1982.)

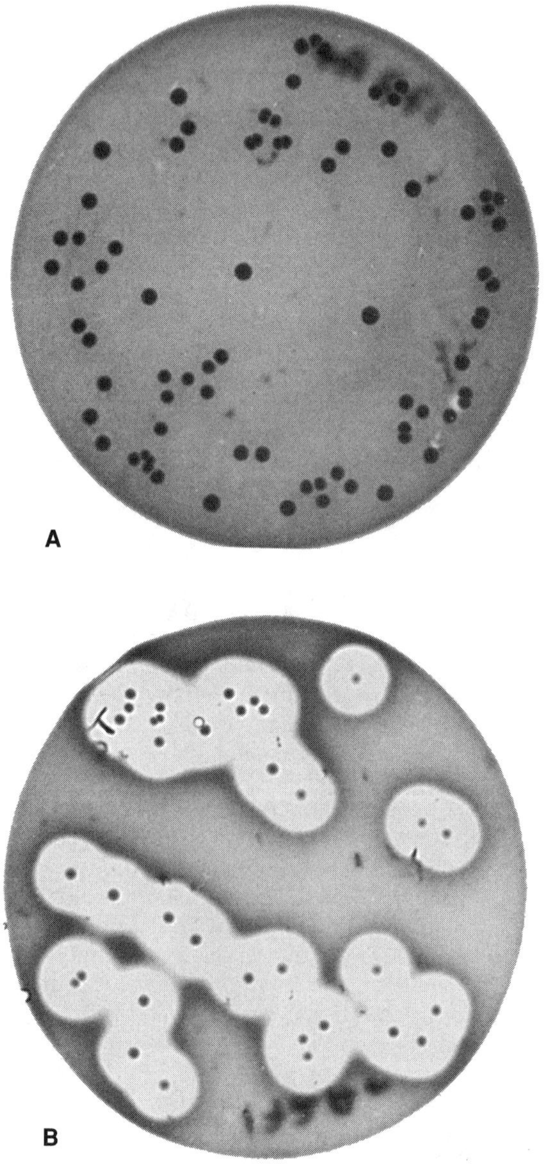

3. **Phenylethyl alcohol agar.** This agar medium is selective for the isolation of gram-positive cocci. The agents in this medium inhibit gram-negative species. Red blood cells may also be used in the medium for determining hemolytic activity of the coccal species.
4. **Eosin-methylene blue (EMB) agar.** EMB agar and MacConkey agar are selective media used in the isolation of gram-negative species, particularly those that infect the intestinal tract. Agents in these media inhibit gram-positive species; the inhibitors are often dyes that are toxic and interfere with electron transport.
5. **Chocolate blood agar.** This agar medium contains blood that has been heated until the medium turns brown. It has been used for the isolation of *Hemophilus* and *Neisseria.* When antibiotics (vancomycin, colistin, and nystatin) are added to it, it is called Thayer-Martin medium and it becomes selective for the isolation of *Neisseria gonorrhoeae* and *Neisseria meningitidis,* the agents of gonorrhea and bacterial meningitis, respectively.

Preservation of Isolated Microorganisms

Sometimes it is not possible to perform tests immediately on isolated bacteria and many bacteria do not survive for any length of time outside the host. Microorganisms can be preserved by a number of techniques, but the most widely used are freezing and freeze-drying.

FREEZING

Most bacteria can be frozen in various types of media. The specimens are frozen rapidly to a temperature of -20 to -30 C to maintain the majority of cells in a viable state. Ultra-low temperatures obtained by using liquid nitrogen have been successfully employed for storage and preservation of all biological cell types, including fungi, viruses, and red blood cells.

Freeze-drying (Lyophilization)

Ice crystal formation produced during the freezing process can damage cells. If the specimen is first frozen in a bath containing dry ice and acetone or some other mixture, the water in the cell can be removed by sublimation (as a gas) and damage to many of the cells can be prevented. This technique is commonly used for preservation of cultures and for shipment of cultures in the mail.

Laboratory Measurement of Microbial Growth

There are a number of ways to calculate microbial growth. In the research laboratory, for example, investigators can determine the concentration of macromolecules such as

DNA, RNA, protein, and so on, in a population of cells and these become parameters of growth. In the clinical laboratory, however, investigators are often more concerned with the actual number of bacteria in a specimen because this often relates to the intensity of infection in a patient. Two of the most commonly used techniques for determining bacterial numbers are cell count and cell density measurements.

CELL COUNT

Microscopic

Using the microscope, one can count bacterial cells directly when a small portion of the culture is spread on a calibrated slide called the **Petroff-Hauser counter.** This device is similar to the hemocytometer used to count red blood cells. Calibrated ruled areas are etched into a special glass slide (Fig. 4-12). An aliquot of bacteria is introduced under the coverslip that covers the ruled area. The ruled area is observed microscopically, and the microorganisms are counted. Since the depth of fluid above the calibrated area is known, the number of organisms per unit volume can be calculated. This method cannot, however, distinguish live from dead cells.

Standard Plate Count

Cells can be counted indirectly by determining the number of cells that, when spread on the surface of an agar medium, give rise to distinct colonies. The standard plate count technique usually involves some type of dilution that reduces the number of cells to a countable number (30–300 cells) before plating on suitable media. The colonies are counted, and that figure times the dilution factor will give the total number of viable bacteria per milliliter in the original culture before dilution (Fig. 4-13). This technique is one of the most widely used in microbiology laboratories. In addition to spreading directly onto the agar surface, the sample may also be filtered through a membrane filter that will retain the bacteria. The filter may then be placed over an agar surface and, after suitable incubation, the colonies may be counted (see Fig. 4-10).

CELL DENSITY

As the population in a culture increases, the turbidity or density of the broth culture also increases. Changes in turbidity can be detected by a device called a **spectrophotometer,** which records them in units called optical density (OD) units or absorbance (A) units (Fig. 4-14). When the measurements are correlated and graphed, they can save the researcher a considerable amount of time. In subsequent experiments, for example, an optical density reading alone is all that is required if the researcher wishes to know the population of cells. This technique can be applied only when one uses the same organism under the same environmental conditions and during logarithmic growth.

Summary

1. Bacteria reproduce asexually in a process called binary fission. They reproduce geometrically, with doubling times varying from a few minutes to several hours depending on the species.

2. Bacteria in culture exhibit a growth cycle that includes phases such as lag, log, stationary, and death and decline. The lag phase is a period of adjustment to the growth medium. The log phase is a period of constancy in which the rate of growth of a microbial species can be determined. The growth rate depends on the type of microbial species, temperature, and growth-supporting ability of the medium. The stationary phase is characterized by an equilibrium between the number of cells dying and the number dividing. The death and decline phase is a period of geometric decline brought about by toxic products and nutrient loss.

3. The major nutrients required for growth include water, carbon, nitrogen, sulfur, phosphorus, oxygen, and

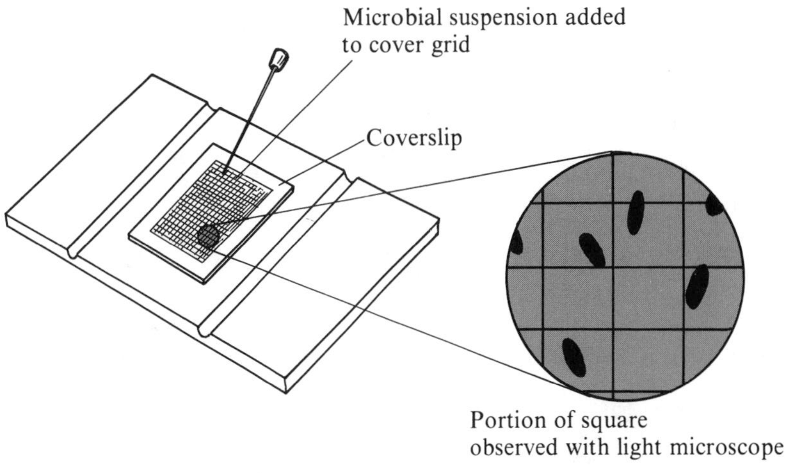

FIGURE 4-12
Petroff-Hauser counter. The large square is observed microscopically after the addition of an aliquot of a culture. The volume of fluid on the large square is known, and this number is multiplied by the number of bacteria observed times the original dilution factor. The product is the concentration of bacteria per milliliter present in the culture sample.

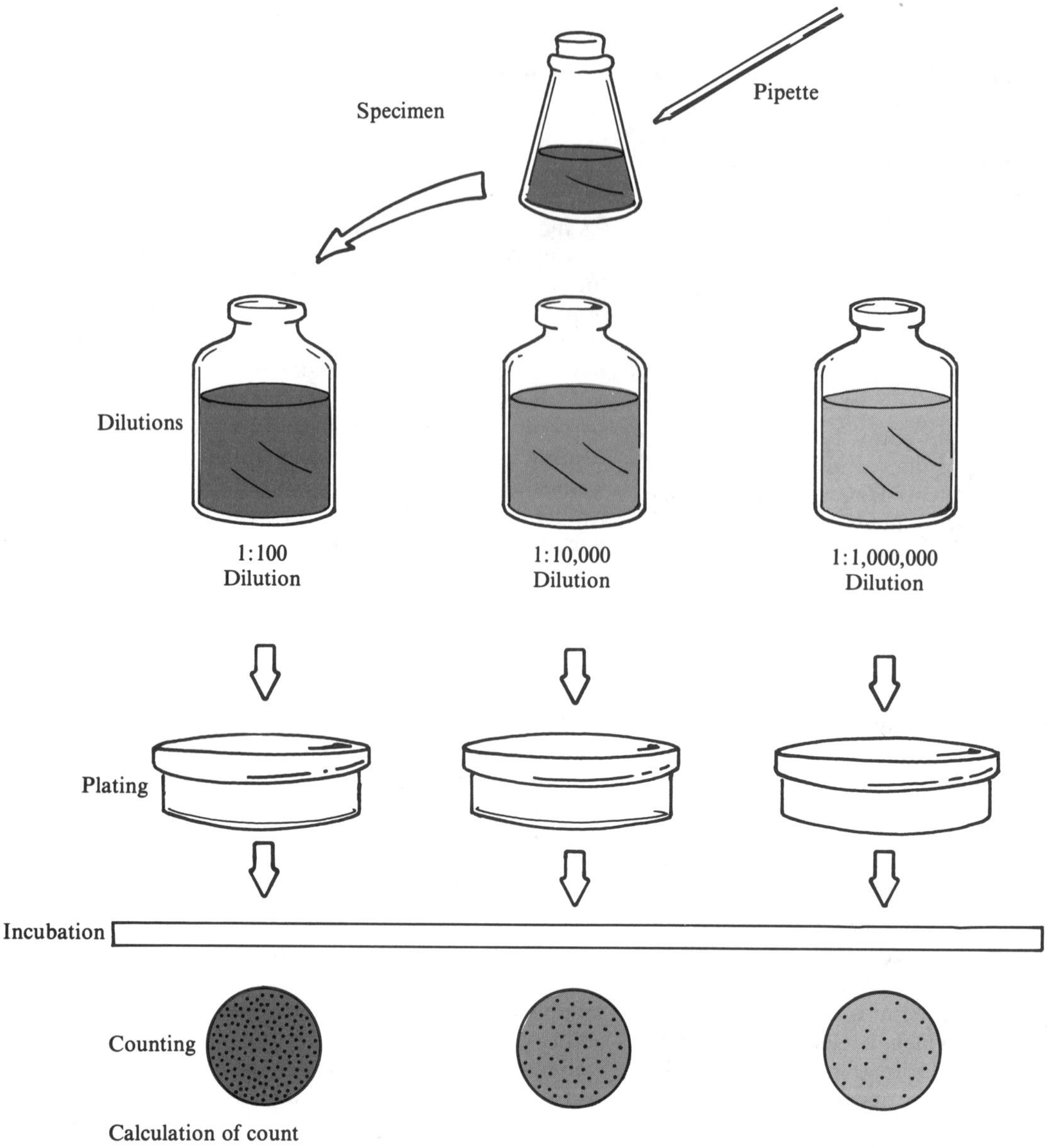

FIGURE 4-13
Dilution technique for determining the viable cell number in a bacterial culture. (Adapted from M. J. Pelczar and R. D. Reid, *Microbiology*. New York: McGraw-Hill, 1972.)

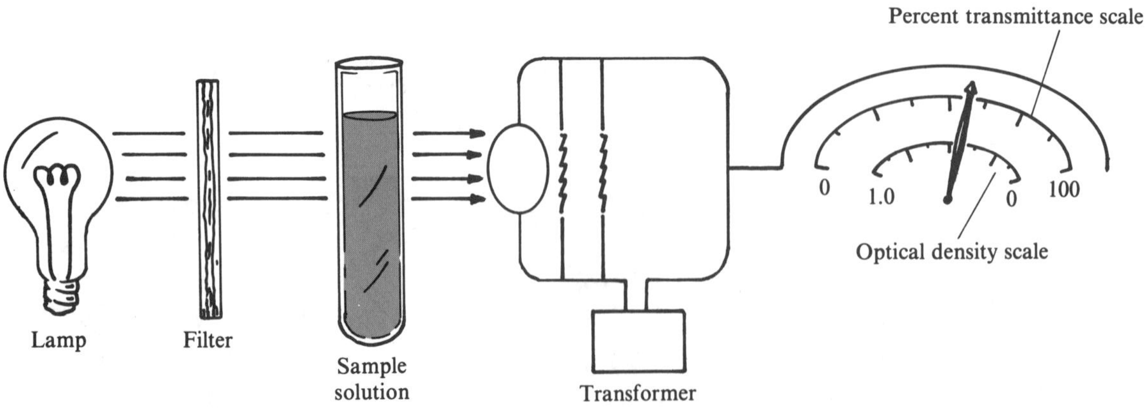

FIGURE 4-14
Spectrophotometer. A sample of bacteria in solution acts as colloidal suspension that intercepts light passing through it. Some light is absorbed; the remainder, passing through, activates a photocell, which in turn registers the percentage of transmittance on a galvanometer. The higher the percentage of transmittance, the fewer the cells in suspension. The amount of light absorbed by the suspension is reflected in the optical density (OD). The greater the number of cells in suspension, the greater the optical density.

minerals. Water is needed for the transport of nutrients and in the hydrolysis of molecules in the cell. Organic carbon serves both as a carbon and as an energy source in organisms referred to as heterotrophs. Organic molecules that cannot be synthesized from a carbon source and are required in the culture medium are called growth factors. Minerals are required only in trace amounts, and these are usually supplied in the water supply.

4. Nitrogen is most frequently utilized by bacteria in the form of inorganic molecules such as nitrate, nitrite, ammonia, and nitrogen gas. These forms are converted to ammonia, which is then incorporated into the organic phase as an amino acid. Sulfur and phosphorus are usually supplied to the cell in inorganic forms such as sulfate and phosphate, respectively. Phosphate also acts as a buffer against acids produced during growth.

5. Oxygen is required by aerobic, microaerophilic, and facultatively anaerobic bacteria but not by obligate anaerobes. Oxygen is a final electron acceptor that is usually converted to toxic products such as hydrogen peroxide and superoxide. Organisms that utilize oxygen, however, also produce enzymes, such as catalase and superoxide dismutase, that inactivate the toxic products. For some obligate anaerobes oxygen is toxic but in other anaerobes oxygen can be tolerated because it is not reduced to toxic intermediates.

6. The major physical factors affecting growth are pH, temperature, and osmotic pressure. The pH of bacterial culture media is between 6 and 8, while fungi grow best at pHs below 6.0. Buffers, such as phosphate and proteins, are used in culture media to prevent rapid drops in pH due to accumulation of acids.

7. Bacteria can be classified as psychrophilic, mesophilic, and thermophilic based on their optimum temperatures for growth. Psychrophiles have an optimum temperature range between 0 and 20 C; mesophiles, between 30 and 37 C; and thermophiles, between 45 and 70 C. Temperatures between 62 and 71 C are used in pasteurization processes while temperatures at 100 C and above are used to sterilize. Low temperatures including freezing can injure and kill bacteria but some microorganisms can survive low temperatures for various lengths of time.

8. Osmotic pressure in culture media is usually supplied in the form of salt (NaCl). Some foods are prepared in high concentrations of salt or sugars to induce plasmolysis of bacteria and thus preserve food.

9. Culture media can be in the form of a liquid, called broth, or a semisolid produced by using the carbohydrate called agar. Media can be classified based on chemical content and laboratory use. On the basis of chemical content media may be synthetic, that is, the exact composition is known, or nonsynthetic, that is, the exact chemical composition is not known.

10. Media based on laboratory use are divided into all-purpose, enriched, selective, differential, enrichment, and transport. All-purpose media provide nutrients for growth of most microorganisms. Enriched media contain a basal growth medium plus additional nutrients, such as blood, for growth of more fastidious microorganisms. Selective media contain additives that select against some bacteria and for other bacteria. A differential medium contains additives that allow one to distinguish different species on an agar surface. An enrichment medium inhibits the growth of unwanted species that are in excess in a specimen and induces the growth of wanted species. A transport medium is used for specimens removed from patients that must be carried back to the laboratory without harming the microorganisms that are present.

11. Cultivation of anaerobes requires techniques that remove or replace oxygen. The anaerobic jar is a widely used device in which gases, such as hydrogen, are generated and combine with oxygen to form water. A smaller version of an anaerobic container is the Bio-Bag. For larger operations there is the flexible vinyl plastic glove box, which contains gases that maintain the shape of the box and remove oxygen.

12. Pure culture techniques are used to isolate a single species from a mixed culture. There are three basic methods for obtaining a pure culture. The streak plate physically separates individual cells on an agar surface using an inoculating loop. In the pour plate technique bacteria are diluted and distributed in molten agar to effect their separation. Small numbers of bacteria in a fluid can be separated out of the fluid by use of the membrane filter technique. Bacteria retained on the filter can be cultivated on an agar surface.

13. The media for isolation of bacteria from laboratory specimens include thioglycolate for some anaerobes, blood agar for detecting the hemolytic activity of bacteria, phenylethyl alcohol agar for isolating gram-positive cocci, eosin-methylene blue agar for isolating gram-negative species, and chocolate blood agar for isolation of *Hemophilus* and *Neisseria* species.

14. Microorganisms can be preserved by freezing or freeze-drying, but freeze-drying is the more efficient technique.

15. Microbial growth can be detected in various ways. Microscopic cell counts using the Petroff-Hauser counter measure both live and dead cells. Standard plate counts measure only viable cells. Cell density is an indirect means of measuring growth by using a spectrophotometer.

Questions for Study

1. A sterile glucose solution (only glucose plus water) is observed to contain a number of cells of a *Klebsiella* species. Explain how this organism obtains its necessary nutrients under these conditions.
2. Suppose you suspect an individual to have an intestinal infection caused by a nonindigenous species of bacteria. What kind of media would you use to isolate the suspected pathogen? Explain your answer.
3. An individual receives antibiotic chemotherapy to destroy the organism causing abscesses. You exam-

ine the periphery of one of the abscesses and discover killed microorganisms. Your first inclination is to discontinue therapy but your supervisor says this might not be appropriate. Why would the supervisor suggest this and what is the reasoning behind his or her answer?

4. Suppose you were asked to kill a population of bacteria with a disinfectant. The disinfectant kills microorganisms at the rate of 10 per minute (one log factor). What is the least amount of time it will take to kill all the microorganisms, assuming the original population of bacteria was 10^9?
5. A basal salts medium can be used to cultivate *E. coli.* List the individual minerals and nutrients and explain their function in metabolism.
6. What are the conditions under which superoxide is produced by bacteria? Is superoxide produced by all bacteria? If not, why not?
7. If anaerobes can grow only in the absence of oxygen, what happens to oxygen if it is present?
8. You are given a liter of urine that supposedly contains 10^3 gram-negative microorganisms. How would you go about determining the exact number of viable bacteria and that they were gram-negative?

CHAPTER 5

Microbial Genetics

OBJECTIVES

To discuss the basic chemical structure of DNA and how it is physically arranged in the cell

To explain the relationship between DNA structure and replication

To list the enzymes associated with DNA replication and transcription and their specific functions

To outline the basic steps in protein synthesis

To describe the differences and similarities between a repressible and inducible operon

To explain what is meant by the genetic code and how mutations affect it

To explain how mutations may arise in the cell and how some of them can be repaired

To describe how mutants can be detected and isolated

To distinguish the three methods of DNA transfer: transformation, transduction, and conjugation

To describe the importance of plasmids to bacteria and how they are transferred

To define the terms transcription, genotype, phenotype, plasmid, codon, anticodon, inducible, constitutive, insertion sequence, transposon, auxotroph, prototroph, and sex factor

OUTLINE

NUCLEIC ACIDS: THE BASIS OF HEREDITY

DNA STRUCTURE AND REPLICATION
- Mechanism of DNA Replication

DNA TRANSCRIPTION
- DNA and the Genetic Code

TRANSLATION OF THE GENETIC CODE: PROTEIN SYNTHESIS

CONTROL OF PROTEIN SYNTHESIS
- Induction and Repression
- The Operon
  - Inducible Operons
  - Repressible Operons

MUTATION
- Spontaneous Mutations
- Induced Mutations
  - Physical Agents
  - Chemical Agents
- How Mutations Affect the Genetic Code
- Repair of Mutations
- Mutant Isolation and Detection
- Detection of Chemical Carcinogens

DNA TRANSFER OTHER THAN IN CELL DIVISION
- Transformation
- Conjugation
  - Hfr Cell Formation
- Transduction

PLASMIDS
- Characteristics Associated with Plasmids
  - R Plasmids
  - Resistance to Heavy Metals
  - Virulence Determinants

DNA TRANSFER AND INFECTIOUS DISEASE

A student might think that a discussion of microbial genetics and how microorganisms store and transfer genetic information would be boring and hardly worth the effort. Quite the contrary. The rapid development of molecular genetics, in conjunction with the ability of scientists to manipulate and transfer genes, has elicited considerable interest among physicians, scientists, and the public in general. Our ability to manipulate the hereditary material of microorganisms and even of our own species has far-reaching consequences.

The primary purpose of this chapter is to discuss the functions of the hereditary material in microorganisms and to examine how manipulation of the genetic material is being used to advance industrial and medical microbiology.

Nucleic Acids: The Basis of Heredity

The characteristic traits that are expressed in one generation and transferred to another generation have their origin in the nucleic acids of the cell, that is, deoxyribonucleic acid (DNA) and ribonucleic acid (RNA). All cellular organisms have DNA as the carrier of their heredity; however, acellular microorganisms, such as some viruses, substitute RNA for DNA.

The hereditary material consists of specific sequences of purine and pyrimidine bases (see Fig. 3-14) that are divided into units of information called **genes.** All the genes of the organism make up what is referred to as the **genotype** of the cell. The translation of the information in the genes leads to the expression of specific traits by the organism called the **phenotype.**

The genetic information of the bacterial cell can be carried on a single molecule of DNA, which is called a **chromosome.** Eukaryotes, however, require more than one chromosome or DNA molecule to carry all their hereditary information. Many bacteria also have smaller pieces of DNA, called **plasmids,** that are not part of the chromosome (extrachromosomal). Plasmid DNA confers traits that enable the bacteria to survive more efficiently in their environment.

The DNA molecule performs specific functions in the bacterial cell and includes the ability to

1. Duplicate (replicate) itself for transfer to progeny (daughter cells) during cell division.
2. Transcribe itself into a nucleic acid molecule that can be translated into protein.
3. Control the synthesis of proteins.
4. Mutate and change specific characteristics.
5. Duplicate and transfer itself to other species in processes other than cell division.

We now examine each of these functions in more detail.

FIGURE 5-1
Nucleotide arrangement as demonstrated in a portion of the DNA molecule. Each strand consists of a sugar phosphate backbone with purine (adenine and guanine) and pyrimidine (thymine and cytosine) bases attached to a sugar group. Bases between strands are paired by hydrogen bonds (. . . .). The strands are antiparallel. The strand on the left is called the 5′ end; that is, it is arranged in the 5′ to 3′ direction. The strand on the right is arranged in the 3′ to 5′ direction.

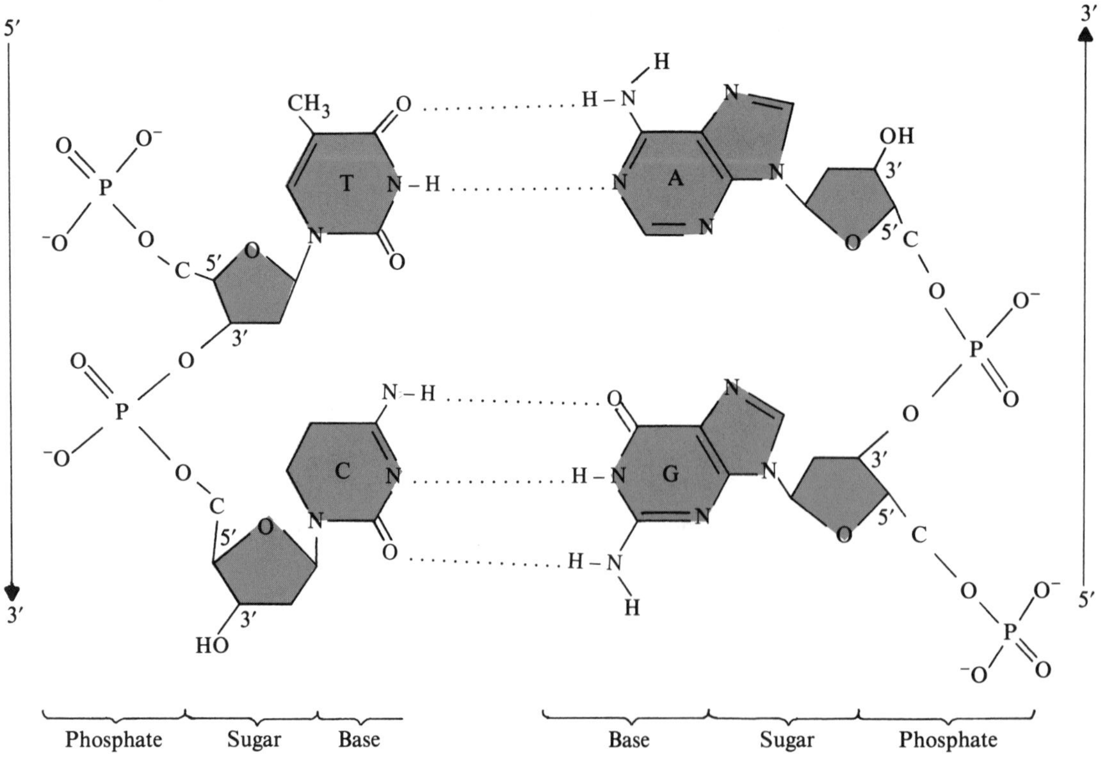

DNA Structure and Replication

The DNA molecule of bacteria consists of two chains of chemical units called **nucleotides.** A single molecule of bacterial DNA may contain from 10 to 40 million nucleotides. A nucleotide consists of a base, either a purine or pyrimidine, to which is attached a sugar phosphate group. Each chain consists of alternating sugar phosphates with a purine or pyrimidine base attached to each sugar group (Fig. 5-1). The bases in DNA are of four different types: adenine and guanine, which are purines, and thymine and cytosine, which are pyrimidines. The two nucleotide chains are attached to each other by virtue of the bonding of hydrogen atoms between a specific purine base on one strand and a specific pyrimidine base on the other strand. In DNA, adenine binds to thymine and guanine binds to cytosine. This is called a **base pair** arrangement; that is, adenine on one strand is **complementary** to thymine on the other strand and guanine on one strand is complementary to cytosine on the other strand. If you look at Figure 5-1 you will notice that one strand appears to be upside down; that is, the strands are antiparallel. One strand has a free hydroxyl (OH) group attached to carbon 3 of the sugar, while on the opposite strand the free hydroxyl is on carbon 5 of the sugar. Each strand has a 3′ and a 5′ end.

Double-stranded DNA exists in the cell in the form of a helix, with the two ends of the molecule joined to form a circle (Fig. 5-2). In its circular form the DNA molecule is much longer than the cell; therefore, the circle is folded on itself in order to fit into the bacterium.

MECHANISM OF DNA REPLICATION

The transmission of genetic material from parent to progeny requires an exact duplication of the original or parental DNA strands. Major errors in the duplication process could be disastrous, leading to conditions that prevent normal cell growth and development.

Because the bacterial chromosome is in a coiled state in the cell, it must be unwound to be duplicated. The DNA molecule replicates in a **semiconservative manner.**

FIGURE 5-2
Configuration of DNA molecule. A. Helical nature of the DNA molecule. B. Circular nature of DNA. The figure on the left is a closed circle while that on the right shows how twisting of the circle reduced the circle size.

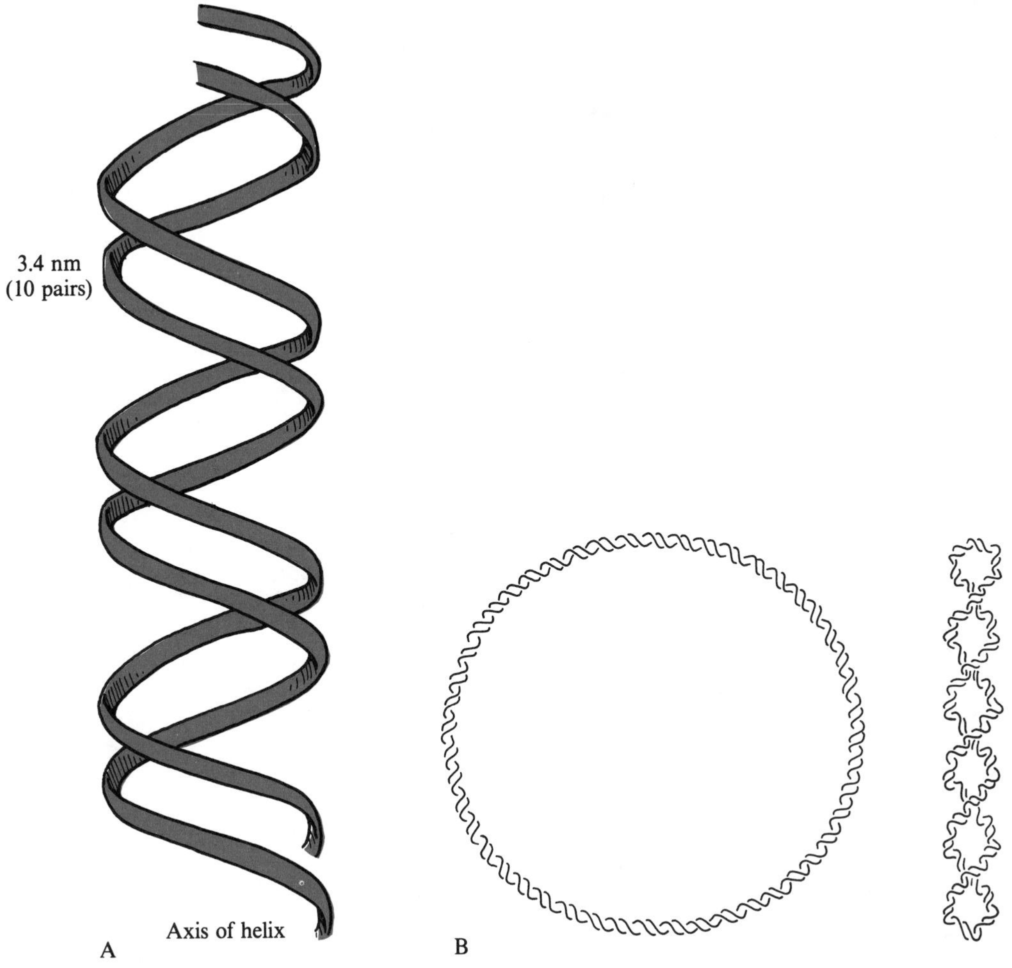

Each strand of the parent DNA serves as a template for the formation of a complementary strand (Fig. 5-3). The mechanism by which the DNA molecule undergoes this duplication process in the cell is believed to occur in the following way (Fig. 5-4):

The bacterial chromosome possesses a site for unwinding DNA and for initiation of DNA replication, referred to as the **origin.** The origin is recognized and activated by specific proteins such as

1. **Unwinding proteins.** One strand of the DNA mole-

FIGURE 5-3
Semiconservative replication of DNA. Microbial cells are grown in a medium containing heavy nitrogen (N^{15}). A. Both strands of DNA are labeled with heavy isotope. B. After transfer to a medium containing light nitrogen (N^{14}), this generation of cells contains DNA that has one light and one heavy strand. C. One-half of progeny in this generation of cells contain hybrid DNA ($N^{15}N^{14}$). D. One-fourth of the progeny contain hybrid DNA while three-fourths contain light DNA.

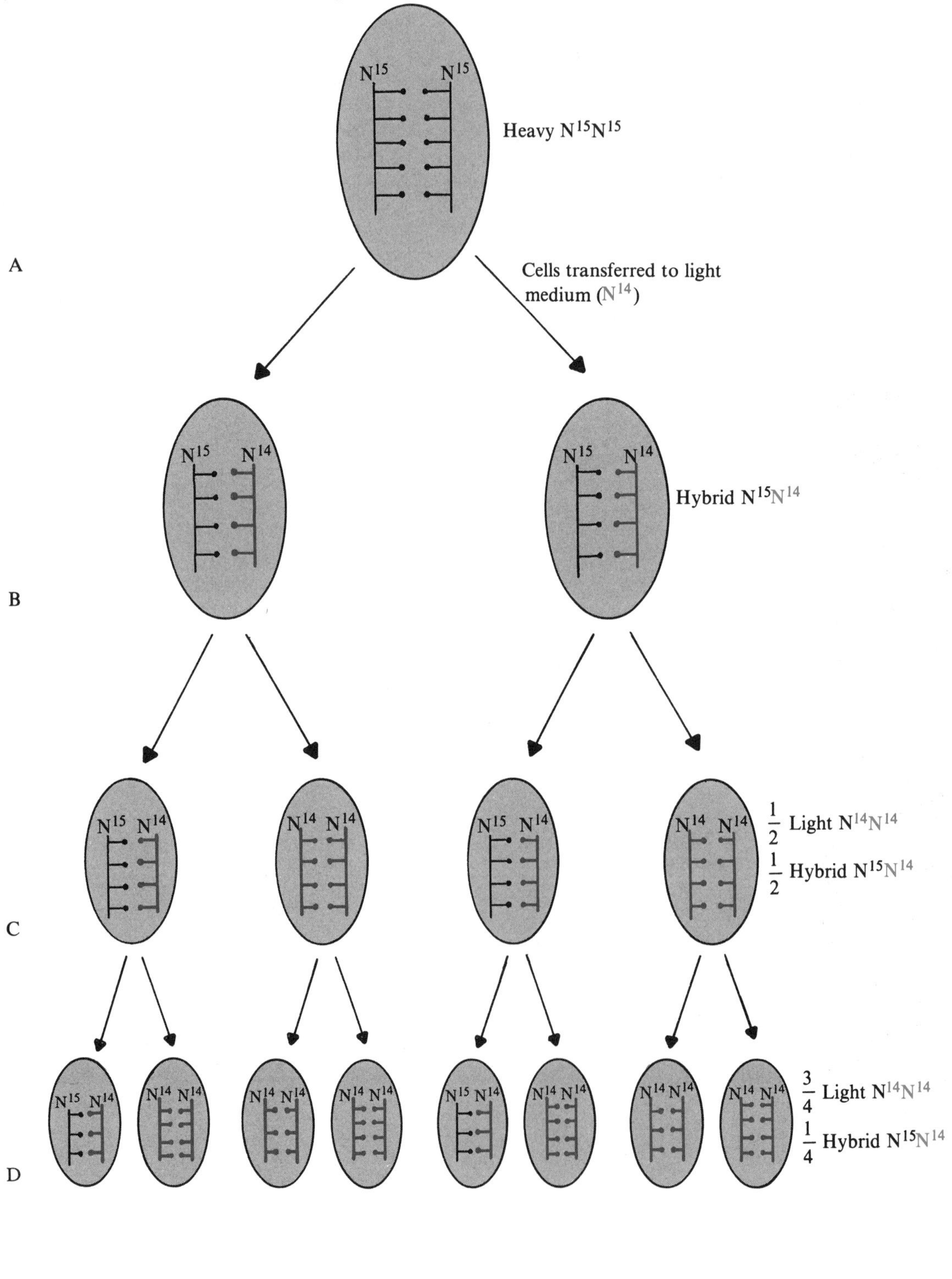

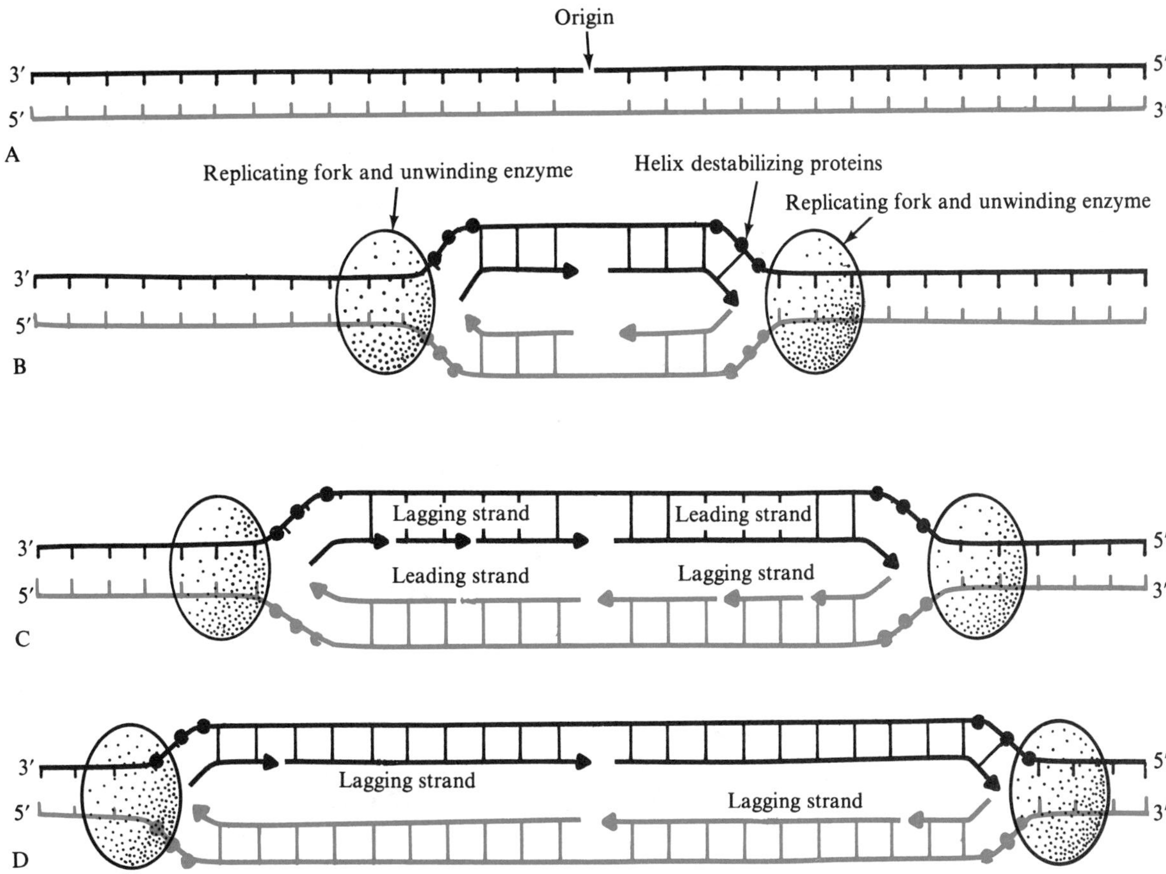

FIGURE 5-4
Replication of DNA in bacteria. A. A double-stranded DNA molecule is nicked by an enzyme at the origin. B. An unwinding enzyme produces two replicating forks. Single strands are prevented from unwinding by helix-destabilizing proteins. C. Behind each replicating fork, one new DNA strand grows continuously **(leading strand)** and the other grows in a series of fragments **(lagging strand).** D. As DNA synthesis continues, the fragmented pieces of DNA nearest the origin become linked by DNA ligase. Please note that the RNA primers have been omitted for clarity.

cule is nicked by an enzyme; thus, the tension in the circular helix is released. The unwinding of DNA is caused by unwinding proteins that promote separation of the two parental strands. Unwinding produces two **replicating forks,** one on either side of the origin (see Fig. 5-4), which will move away from the origin during the replication process.

2. **Helix-destabilizing proteins.** Any unwound single-stranded DNA will be prevented from rewinding by the attachment of helix-destabilizing proteins.
3. **DNA polymerase.** The actual synthesis of new (daughter) DNA is catalyzed by the enzyme DNA polymerase. The substrates for the enzyme are the four deoxyribonucleotide triphosphates, that is, dATP (deoxyadenosine triphosphate), dGTP (deoxyguanosine triphosphate), dCTP (deoxycytosine triphosphate), and dTTP (deoxythymidine triphosphate). Just before DNA synthesis, short RNA strands called **primer RNA** are laid down in the 5′ to 3′ direction.

DNA polymerase synthesizes DNA only in the 5′ to 3′ direction because the enzyme requires a free 3′ hydroxyl group; that is, nucleotides are added to the free 3′ end. Since the two strands are antiparallel, the continuous addition of deoxyribonucleotides to the RNA primer can occur only on one strand (see Fig. 5-4). The DNA strand replicating continuously is called the **leading strand.** The 5′ end of the leading strand is located at the origin and its 3′ end at the moving replicating fork. The opposite or **lagging strand** is elongated by a different mechanism, because the 3′ position is at the origin while the 5′ end is at the replication fork. If nucleotides were sequentially added to the end of the lagging strand at the replication fork, then this strand's growth would proceed in a 3′ to 5′ direction. This does not take place. Instead, growth takes place by the synthesis of a number of short polynucleotide chains between the replication fork and the origin. Each short chain is laid down in the direction 5′ to 3′ and these are later linked together and to the 5′ end of the lagging strand. Each short DNA chain is actually attached to the 3′ ends of the individual primer RNA strands, which were laid down before DNA synthesis. Later the RNA primers are removed and the regions that are left vacant are filled in with deoxyribonucleotides. The smaller units of DNA synthesized on the lagging strand are united by the enzyme called **DNA ligase.** As a result, the overall direction of growth of the lagging strand is the same as that of the leading strand.

DNA Transcription

The information contained in the DNA molecule cannot be used by the cell until it is transcribed into a form that is translatable. **Transcription** is merely the process in which one strand of DNA serves as a template for the synthesis of a single-stranded RNA molecule, called **messenger RNA (mRNA).** RNA differs from DNA in that RNA possesses the sugar ribose instead of deoxyribose, and uracil takes the place of thymine. The base pairing between a DNA strand and an RNA strand is

DNA	**RNA**
A	Ü
T	A
C	G
G	C

It is the information on the mRNA molecule that can be translated into usable information by the cell. This usable information is in the form of amino acids that are assembled into specific proteins. Thus the flow of information in the cell is as follows: DNA → RNA → Protein.

The transcription of DNA into mRNA requires the enzyme **RNA polymerase,** which assembles the nucleotides adenosine triphosphate (ATP), uridine triphosphate (UTP), guanosine triphosphate (GTP), and cytosine triphosphate (CTP) into an RNA chain (Fig. 5-5). Bacteria may have a thousand or more genes and the transcription of each one is under the control of specific sites on the DNA, which is discussed later under Control of Protein Synthesis. Keep in mind that a DNA strand can also be transcribed into RNA molecules other than mRNA, for example, ribosomal RNA (rRNA) and transfer RNA (tRNA), whose functions are described shortly.

DNA AND THE GENETIC CODE

It is the particular sequence of nucleotides in a gene that determines the specific amino acid composition of the polypeptide* for which it codes. The nucleotides on the mRNA are arranged as a linear sequence of coding units or **codons** (also called **triplets**). Each codon consists of three successive purine or pyrimidine bases. The sequence of codons on the mRNA contains the necessary information to (1) initiate polypeptide synthesis, (2) designate the sequence of amino acids in the polypeptide, (3) terminate the synthesis of the polypeptide, and (4) release the completed polypeptide.

Since there are four different purine or pyrimidine bases and the code is a triplet code, the total number of possible code words is 64 ($4 \times 4 \times 4$). The maximum number of different amino acids in the polypeptide is 20; thus, each amino acid can have at least 3 code words. Codons that specify amino acids are referred to as **sense codons.** Three of the codons do not code for an amino acid and are referred to as **nonsense codons** (Table 5-1).

Translation of the Genetic Code: Protein Synthesis

mRNA is translated into polypeptides in a process that takes place on the ribosome. **Ribosomes** are small structural components in the cell that are composed of RNA molecules, called **ribosomal RNA,** and a variety of proteins. Bacterial ribosomes are composed of two subunits, 50S and 30S (S refers to **Svedberg,** which is a relative size unit derived from sedimentation studies). Before polypeptide synthesis begins, each amino acid is **activated** and brought to the ribosome by means of another RNA called **transfer RNA** (tRNA). There are 20 different tRNA molecules, one for each amino acid. The amino acid is attached

* Proteins are made up of amino acids linked together by bonds called **peptide bonds;** hence the name **polypeptide.** Most proteins are made up of more than one polypeptide molecule.

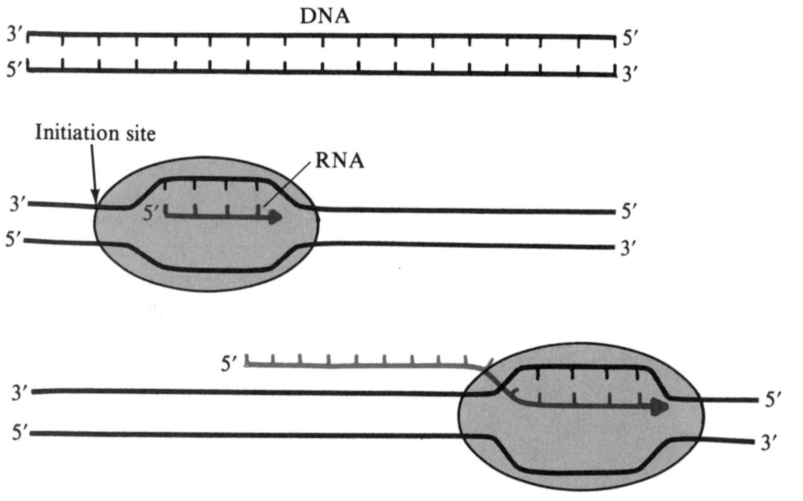

FIGURE 5-5
Transcription of DNA into RNA. Transcription begins at an initiation site where the DNA unwinds and RNA polymerase binds. Only one strand is transcribed and this is in a 5′ to 3′ direction. RNA polymerase moves along the DNA with ribonucleotides being added to the 3′ end of the growing chain.

TABLE 5-1
The Genetic Code

First letter	Second letter U	C	A	G	Third letter
U	Phe	Ser	Tyr	Cys	U
	Phe	Ser	Tyr	Cys	C
	Leu	Ser	Nonsense	Nonsense	A
	Leu	Ser	Nonsense	Trp	G
C	Leu	Pro	His	Arg	U
	Leu	Pro	His	Arg	C
	Leu	Pro	Gln	Arg	A
	Leu	Pro	Gln	Arg	G
A	Ileu	Thr	Asn	Ser	U
	Ileu	Thr	Asn	Ser	C
	Ileu	Thr	Lys	Arg	A
	Met	Thr	Lys	Arg	G
G	Val	Ala	Asp	Gly	U
	Val	Ala	Asp	Gly	C
	Val	Ala	Glu	Gly	A
	Val	Ala	Glu	Gly	G

U = uracil; C = cytosine; A = adenine; G = guanine; Phe = phenylalanine; Ser = serine; Tyr = tyrosine; Cys = cysteine; Leu = leucine; Trp = tryptophan; Pro = proline; His = histidine; Arg = arginine; Gln = glutamine; Ileu = isoleucine; Thr = threonine; Asn = asparagine; Lys = lysine; Met = methionine; Val = valine; Ala = alanine; Asp = aspartic acid; Gly = glycine; Glu = glutamic acid.

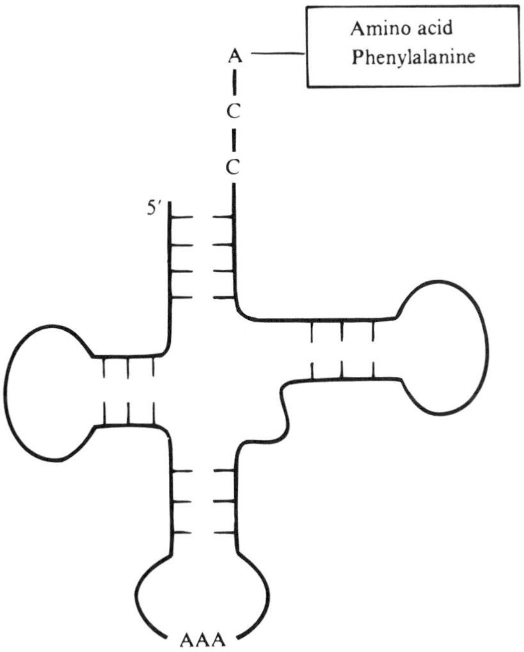

FIGURE 5-6
Basic structure of transfer RNA (tRNA). tRNA is single-stranded but the molecule folds and some hydrogen bonding (———) occurs between bases, which gives the molecule the appearance of a clover leaf. One end of the tRNA chain ends in CCA and this is the site for attachment of an amino acid (in this example, it is phenylalanine). One of the loops on the RNA molecule contains a triplet base called the anticodon (in this example, it is AAA that is complementary to one of the codons for phenylalanine, which is UUU; see Table 5-1).

to one end of the tRNA and in this form is called **aminoacyl tRNA,** while the other end of the tRNA possesses a sequence of bases called the **anticodon** (Fig. 5-6). If, for example, the tRNA carried the amino acid phenylalanine and the code word on the mRNA for phenylalanine was UUU, then the anticodon on the tRNA carrying the amino acid would be AAA. Thus, the anticodon sequence is complementary to the codon sequence and this provides a potentially errorless translation. The process of protein synthesis occurs in a series of steps referred to as **initiation, elongation,** and **termination.**

The synthesis of the polypeptide takes place by the linear movement of ribosomes along the mRNA so that each codon is translated in sequence. The first aminoacyl tRNA attaches to an **initiation site** on the mRNA and with a ribosome forms an initiation complex. The ribosome moves to the next codon and a second aminoacyl tRNA, with the proper anticodon, attaches to the ribosome. The two amino acids are joined by a bond called a **peptide bond** (Fig. 5-7). The peptide becomes attached to the second aminoacyl tRNA while the first tRNA is released and is free to go back into the cytoplasm and pick up another amino acid. This process continues in a sequential manner until the last codon on the mRNA is reached and the complete polypeptide has been synthesized. After the first ribosome has moved away from the initiation site, another ribosome can attach to the initiation site and the synthesis of a second molecule of the polypeptide is begun. Thus, each ribosome on the mRNA is carrying a polypeptide of varying length. Termination and release of the polypeptide are due to the presence of nonsense codons (see Table 5-1). When the polypeptide is released into the cytoplasm, the ribosome separates from the mRNA and it (ribosome) can be used again to initiate polypeptide synthesis.

Control of Protein Synthesis

The metabolic potential of most microbial cells is vast, and synthesis of all of the enzymes used in metabolism is not necessary. The cell will coordinate its genetic potential with the availability of nutrients to determine which enzymes are needed for growth. Protein synthesis is therefore not an unrestricted metabolic process but is under the control of a genetic mechanism subject to induction and repression.

INDUCTION AND REPRESSION

The concentration of many enzymes in the cell is directly associated with specific nutrients in the cell's environment. Enzymes that show an increase in concentration in the presence of specific nutrients are called **inducible enzymes.** The enzyme beta-galactosidase, for example, is an inducible enzyme that is produced when its substrate, lactose, a disaccharide (carbohydrate composed of two sugars), is present in the cell's environment. If lactose is

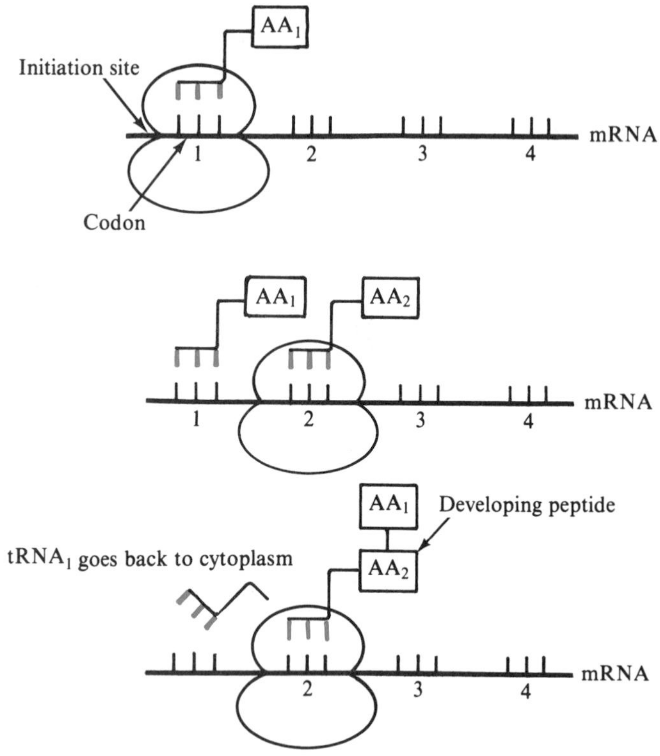

FIGURE 5-7
Mechanism of protein synthesis. Ribosome binds to a messenger RNA (mRNA) initiation site along with aminoacyl tRNA(AA_1) possessing an anticodon that is complementary to codon 1. The ribosome moves to a second codon, and anticodon of aminoacyl tRNA(AA_2) binds to it. A peptide bond is formed between amino acids 1 and 2 and peptide becomes attached to the second tRNA. The first tRNA is free to return to the cytoplasm. The process continues until the termination triplet is reached and polypeptide is released.

not present, the cell produces a protein that represses the synthesis of beta-galactosidase. Not all enzymes are subject to this dual induction-repression response. Some enzymes in the cell, called **constitutive enzymes,** are produced whether the natural substrate is present or not. Constitutive enzymes can be controlled by mechanisms that affect enzyme activity; this type of control is discussed in Chapter 3. Much of our knowledge concerning induction and repression is the result of work by two French microbiologists, Jacob and Monod. They were instrumental in developing the operon theory of control.

THE OPERON

The operon consists of a cluster of genes and nucleotide sequences (they do not code for any polypeptide) that control the synthesis of proteins in the cell. For example, the formation of some molecules in the cell may require from 2 to 10 different enzymes. The genes that code for these enzymes are clustered together in the operon. The synthesis of these enzymes can be genetically turned on or turned off to suit the particular needs of the cell. The operon and associated areas consist of the following components (Fig. 5-8):

1. **Structural genes.** Genes coding for enzymes involved in the formation of a specific molecule in the cell are called structural genes.
2. **Operator.** The operator is not a gene but a sequence of nucleotides that are adjacent to the structural genes. The operator is able to bind a protein called the **repressor protein** and this prevents transcription of the structural genes.
3. **Promoter.** The promoter is not a gene but a special sequence of nucleotides lying outside the operator. The promoter is the site for binding RNA polymerase, which is required for transcription of the structural genes.
4. **Regulator gene.** The regulator gene lies outside the operon. It codes for the synthesis of the **repressor** protein molecule, whose site of action is the operator.

Let us examine each type.

Inducible Operons

Inducible operons are primarily involved in controlling enzymes that are associated with degradative systems in the cell, that is, processes that release energy. The lactose **(lac)** operon is an example of an inducible operon. The lac operon possesses three structural genes: the **beta-galactosidase gene (Z),** which codes for the enzyme that cleaves lactose into glucose and galactose sugars; the **permease gene (Y),** which codes for a protein that transports lactose into the cell; and the **transacetylase gene (A),** which is involved in utilization of galactosides other than lactose.

In the absence of lactose (a condition in which the bacterial cell does not need beta-galactosidase), the regulator gene produces a repressor protein that binds to the operator and transcription of structural genes by RNA polymerase is prohibited (Fig. 5-8A). When lactose is present, the repressor protein attaches to this sugar and the complex is unable to bind to the operator. Under these circumstances RNA polymerase is free to transcribe the structural genes (Fig. 5-8B).

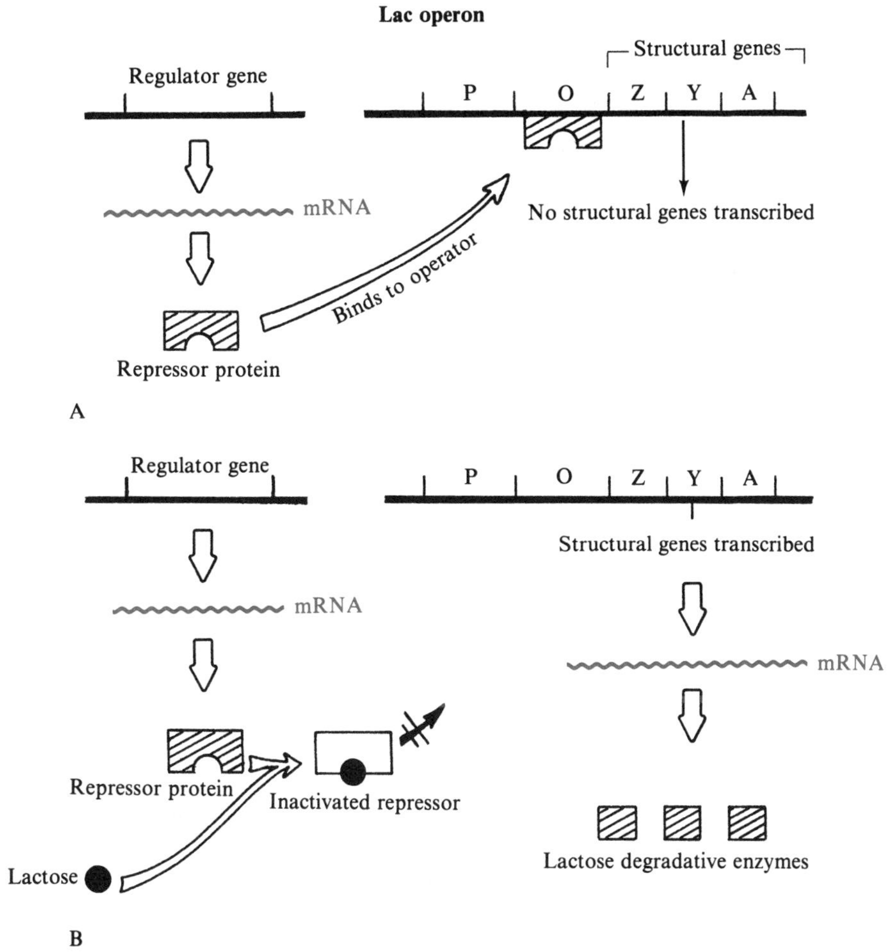

FIGURE 5-8
Inducible operon. A. Lactose (lac) operon in the absence of the inducer lactose. Repressor protein is synthesized and binds to the operator (O). Structural genes are not transcribed. B. Lactose operon in the presence of the inducer. Lactose binds to the repressor and inactivates it. Inactivated repressor is unable to bind to the operator and structural genes are free to be transcribed.

Repressible Operons

Repressible operons are involved primarily in biosynthetic systems, for example, pathways associated with amino acid synthesis. In this system the repressor protein does not bind to the operator until it first complexes with a **co-repressor** molecule. The co-repressor molecule is the end product of biosynthesis. For example, the tryptophan operon controls the synthesis of enzymes involved in tryptophan formation in the cell. If tryptophan is already present in the culture medium, the bacterial cell does not need to synthesize its own tryptophan. Tryptophan acts as a co-repressor and binds to the repressor protein, forming a complex that binds to the operator and prevents transcription of the tryptophan structural genes (Fig. 5-9).

Inducible and repressible operons help the cell conserve energy by preventing the unnecessary synthesis of enzymes at a particular time in the bacterial cell cycle. Recall that another form of control, called feedback inhibition, also helped conserve energy by reducing the activity of enzymes that were already present in the cell (see Chapter 3).

Mutation

The term **mutation** refers to change or modification in a specific characteristic of the organism. These changes or modifications are the result of alterations in the base sequence of the hereditary material. Mutation may bring about advantages or disadvantages to the cell. Some mutations may be lethal, while others may help the organism to survive in its environment. The induction of mutations is called **mutagenesis** and the agents involved are called **mutagens.** Mutations play an important role in many fields of microbiology. They are used by research scientists to delve into the various aspects of structure and function, metabolism, and reproduction of microorganisms. The results from such studies have been helpful in

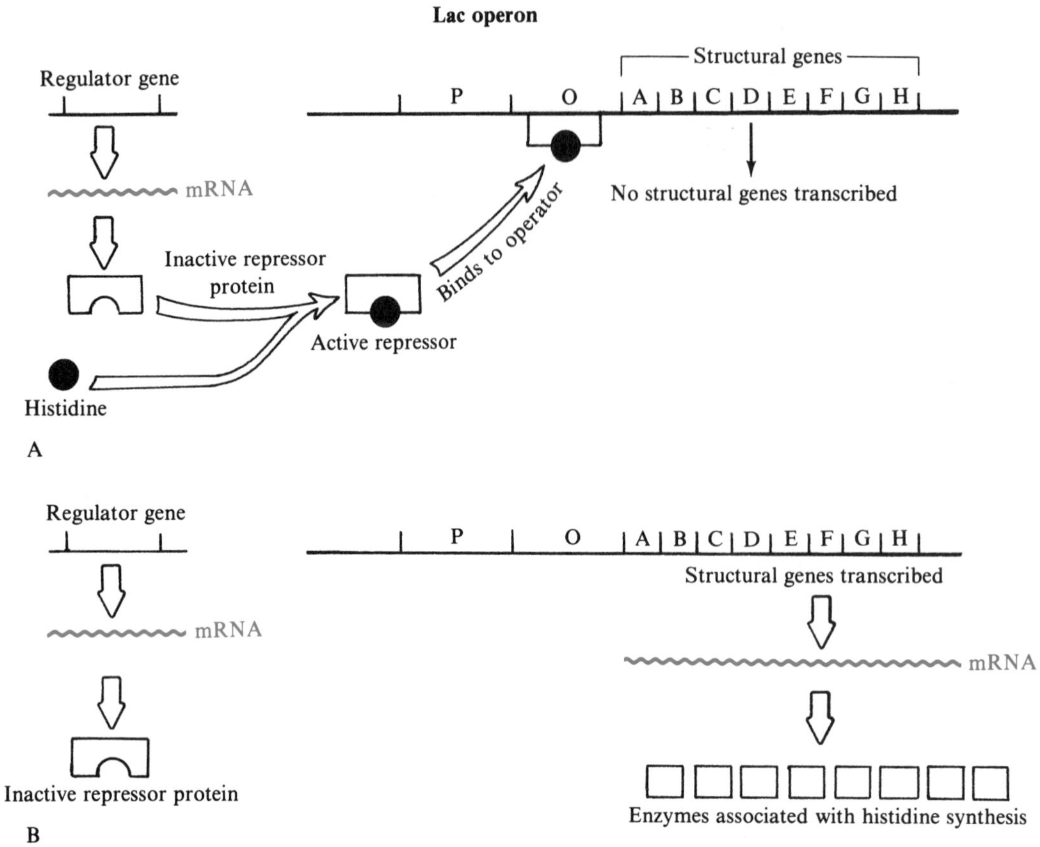

FIGURE 5-9
Repressible operon. A. Operon involved in controlling enzymes associated with synthesis of the amino acid histidine. In this example, histidine is in excess. Histidine acts as a co-repressor and activates the repressor, which prevents transcription of structural genes. B. Histidine operon in the absence of histidine in the cell. The inactive repressor has no effect on the operator, and structural genes are transcribed.

understanding the genetic systems of higher organisms, including humans. Mutation is also important in areas of applied microbiology. Increased synthesis of industrially useful products resulting from microbial metabolism is due to the ability of microbiologists to select naturally occurring mutants or to induce mutations.

Mutations may arise in two general ways: They may arise spontaneously or they may be induced. The probability of a mutation arising spontaneously may be only one in a million; that is, the mutation rate is 1×10^{-6}. For example, if the mutation rate for "inability to metabolize lactose" is 1×10^{-6}, then in a population of 1 million bacteria that are able to metabolize lactose, there is the probability that one of them will be a mutant and unable to metabolize lactose. Some areas of the DNA are more susceptible to mutation than others and are called **hot spots.** Thus, the mutation rate for a hot spot may be 1 in 10,000 (1×10^{-4}) while in another gene the mutation rate may be 1 in every 10 million (1×10^{-7}). The frequency at which mutations may arise can be increased substantially by inducing them with a mutagenic agent. Mutagens include both physical and chemical agents.

SPONTANEOUS MUTATIONS

Spontaneous mutations occur in the absence of human intervention. For example, purine and pyrimidine bases can temporarily exist in different electrochemical forms, which results in mispairing. Adenine instead of pairing with thymine can pair with cytosine. Guanine, which normally pairs with cytosine, can pair with thymine. When DNA duplicates, the mispairing leads to a permanently altered base pair in the bacterial cell (Fig. 5-10). When this altered base pair is transcribed as part of a gene, the mRNA may be transcribed incorrectly, thus producing an altered polypeptide.

Spontaneous mutations may also occur by a biological mechanism. It has been observed that specific nucleotide sequences or elements, called **insertion sequences** (IS), are present in the DNA molecule. IS are usually less than 2000 nucleotide sequences in length and are capable of moving from one location to another. IS elements do not confer any known phenotype on the cell, but they can insert themselves within or between genes and thus affect the activity of genes at the site of insertion or distal to it (Fig. 5-11). IS elements are known to prevent transcription

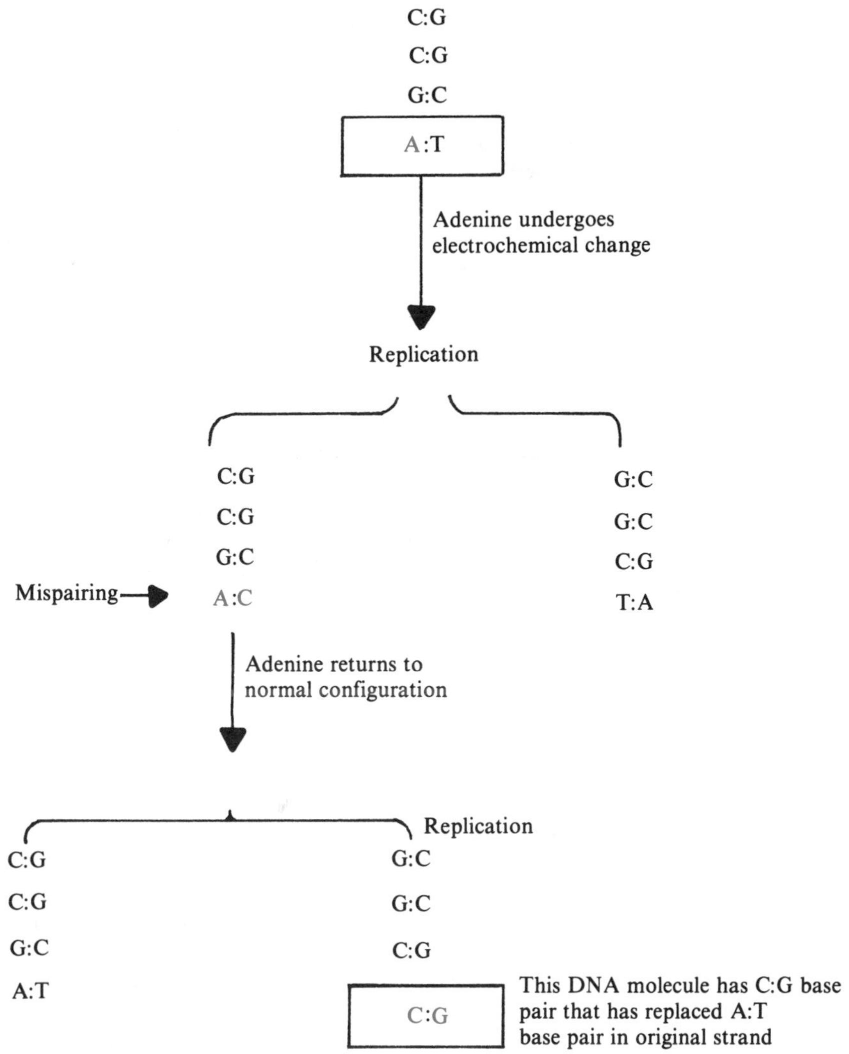

FIGURE 5-10
Spontaneous mutation involving the base adenine.

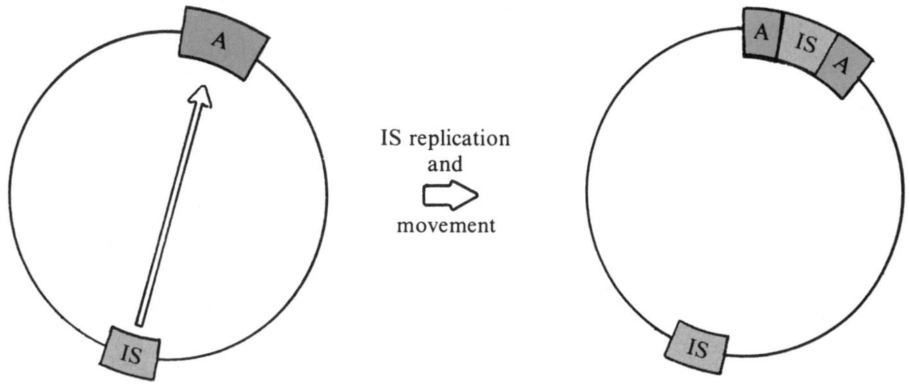

FIGURE 5-11
Movement of insertion sequence (IS). IS element replicates and inserts a copy within the A gene.

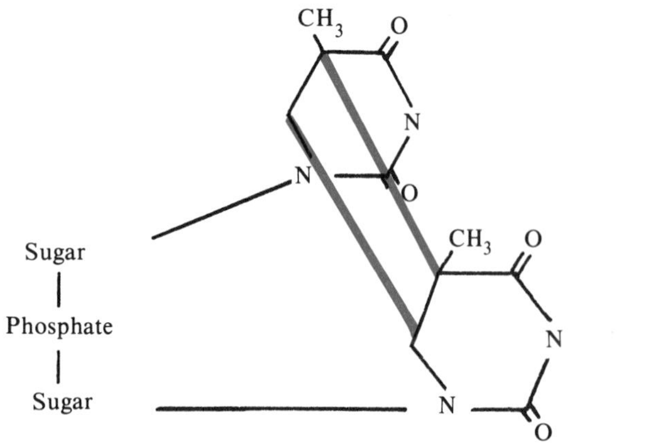

FIGURE 5-12
Thymine dimer formation. Ultraviolet light causes covalent bonding between adjacent thymines on the same DNA strand.

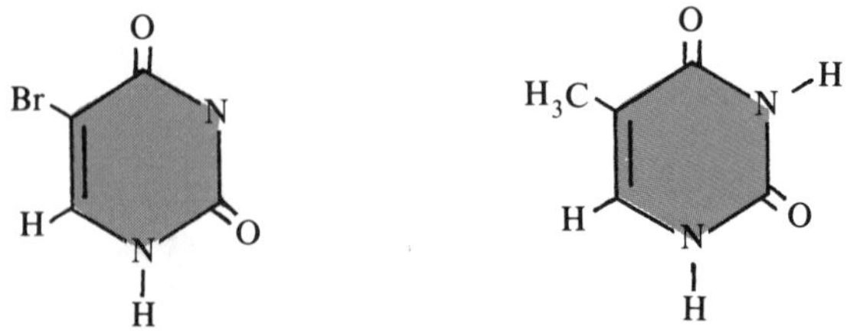

5-Bromouracil Thymine

FIGURE 5-13
Structural similarity between 5-bromouracil and thymine.

of structural genes or to reduce the rate of their transcription.

INDUCED MUTATIONS

Physical Agents

Physical agents that induce mutations include x-rays, gamma rays, and ultraviolet (UV) light. X-rays and gamma rays are extremely energetic and when they bombard cells, impart this energy to various molecules. The impact of these rays causes the discharge of electrons from molecules (called ionization) and the latter become very reactive (ions) and damage the DNA. For example, water struck by x-rays changes to a reactive form (the hydroxyl radical) that breaks the sugar phosphate backbone of DNA.

Ultraviolet light is not so energetic as x-rays or gamma rays but it is readily absorbed by molecules such as proteins and nucleic acids. Pyrimidines in particular absorb ultraviolet light and form abnormal bonds with adjacent pyrimidines on the DNA strands. This abnormal bonding produces what are referred to as **dimers** (Fig. 5-12) of thymine (thymine-thymine) and cytosine (cytosine-cytosine). Dimers are very inflexible and have a tendency to become obstacles to normal DNA replication.

Chemical Agents

A variety of chemicals, from simple molecules such as nitrous acid (HNO_3) to more complex molecules such as acridines, can react with DNA to cause changes in the sequence of bases. The altered purine or pyrimidine bases have a tendency to mispair with other bases. For example, nitrous acid removes the amino group (deamination) from purine and pyrimidine bases. Deamination of cytosine leads to cytosine pairing with adenine instead of guanine.

Some chemical agents, such as 5-bromouracil, are structurally similar to the normal DNA bases (Fig. 5-13) and are incorporated into the DNA in place of the normal base during replication. These structurally similar compounds are referred to as **analogues;** they can mispair with other bases and this leads to mutations.

Another group of chemical agents are those like the **acridines** (proflavin, for example) that because of their chemical and physical properties can slip in between bases on the DNA strand. This activity distorts the DNA molecule and produces large gaps between normal bases. The outcome is that following replication deletions or insertions of bases can occur in the DNA.

HOW MUTATIONS AFFECT THE GENETIC CODE

When mutations are produced, they affect the coded information on the DNA. Transcription of altered DNA leads to the formation of an altered mRNA. Finally, translation of the affected mRNA affects the polypeptide product in a variety of different ways, depending on the mutation (Fig. 5-14):

1. No effect. Mutation may result in a change to an alternate code word. Recall that there are at least three different code words for a single amino acid.
2. Missense mutation. A single base pair change leads to a change in the codon and its translation into a different amino acid. The activity of the polypeptide may or may not be affected, depending on the type of amino acid and its location in the peptide chain.
3. Nonsense mutation. A single base change in the DNA can occasionally lead to premature chain termination on the mRNA if nonsense codons are formed.
4. Frameshift mutation. The deletion or addition of a single base can cause the reading frame of the message to be shifted one base. The message distal to the site of insertion or deletion will code for a new set of amino acids. This usually leads to the formation of a nonfunctional polypeptide, but, again, this depends on the site of mRNA alteration.

REPAIR OF MUTATIONS

Even in the absence of mutagens, mutations can occur in the DNA during the replication process. Damage to DNA is repaired by a variety of different enzymatic mechanisms. When DNA damage does occur, a series of cellular changes called the **SOS** (international distress signal) re-

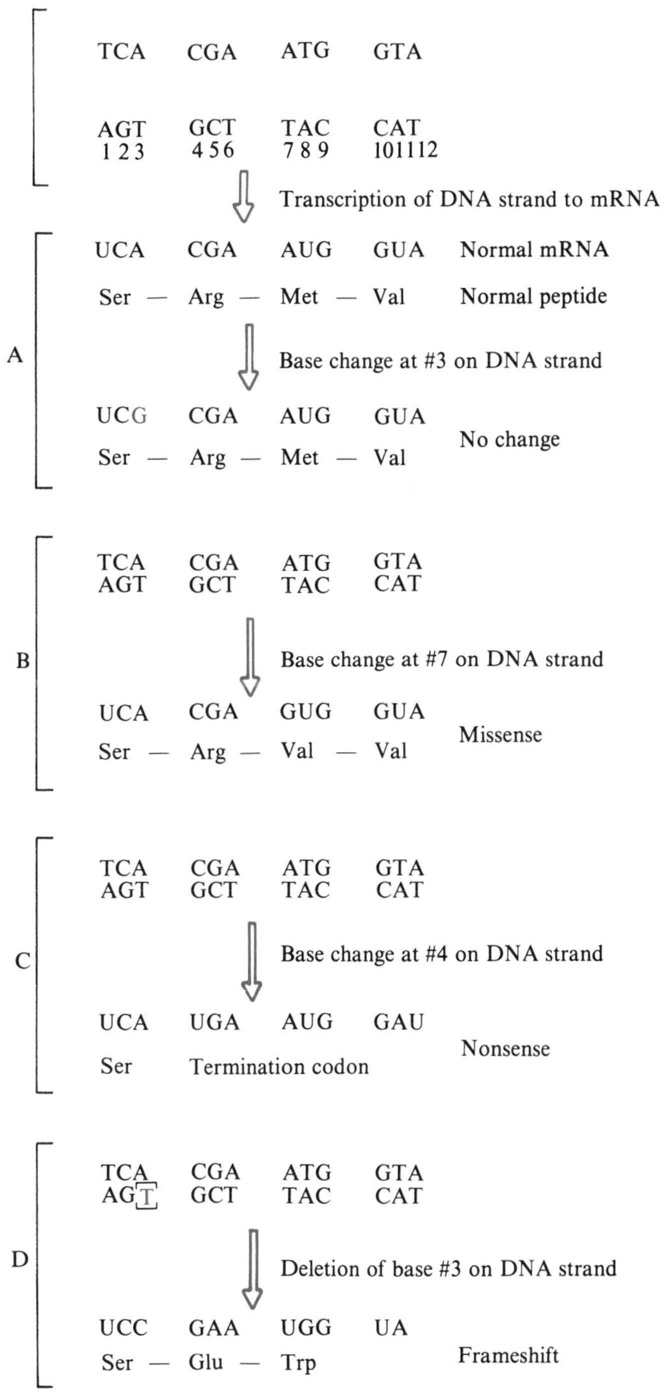

FIGURE 5-14
Effects of mutation on the genetic code. A. Genetic change that produces no change in the peptide. B. Mutation that causes missense or change in the amino acid. C. Mutation results in the formation of a nonsense or terminating codon. D. Mutation in which a base is deleted, resulting in a frameshift or change in all the amino acids distal to the initiation mutation. Ser = serine; Arg = arginine; Met = methionine; Val = valine; Glu = glutamic acid; Trp = tryptophan.

sponse takes place. One of the changes is that cell division is inhibited. The other is that the activities of the bacterial cell are focused on repairing the DNA damage. Some enzymes are induced by the cell to remove specific altered purine or pyrimidine bases. This excision event is followed by the use of enzymes such as DNA polymerase and DNA ligase to insert the correct bases and zip up the sugar phosphate backbone, respectively. A common repair mechanism induced by ultraviolet damage is called **excision repair** (Fig. 5-15). In this process an eyzymatic incision is made on one side of the thymine-thymine or cytosine-cytosine dimers. A second enzyme removes the dimer as well as several adjacent bases. All the bases are replaced with the help of DNA polymerase and the sugar phosphate backbone is zipped up by DNA ligase.

Despite the various mechanisms for DNA repair, mutations do occur and sometimes it is the repair process that is faulty.

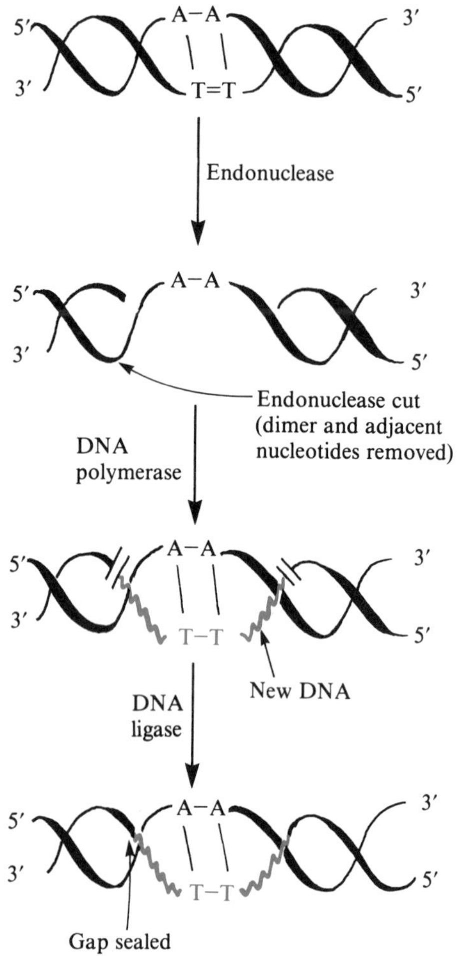

FIGURE 5-15
Excision repair of DNA damaged by ultraviolet light. (Adapted from E. M. Witkin, *Bacteriol. Rev.* 40:869, 1976.)

MUTANT ISOLATION AND DETECTION

Some mutations result in visible changes that are easily detected. In bacteria these changes may involve colony pigmentation, colony size, and colony texture. Other mutations affect the growth of microorganisms. Many microorganisms are capable of synthesizing all their organic material using a simple carbon source and basic salts (see Chapter 4). Mutants in which the phenotypic change involves the requirement of a growth factor are called **auxotrophs,** while the parent organisms that have no such requirements are called **prototrophs.** Auxotrophic mutants can be isolated by using a technique called **replica plating** (Fig. 5-16). In this technique a sample of cell culture is spread on an agar plate (master plate) that is supplemented with nutrients that will permit the growth of auxotrophs and prototrophs. Colonies will appear on the plate after suitable incubation, and the pattern of these colonies on the plate can be transferred to a velveteen cloth. Each tuft of the velveteen cloth acts like an inoculating needle. The velveteen cloth is pressed onto an agar surface that has a minimal medium; that is, it will support the growth of prototrophs but not auxotrophs. By comparing the colony distribution on the master plate with those on the plate containing minimal medium, the auxotroph can be isolated. If one wishes to determine the specific requirement of the auxotroph, one can replica plate from the master plate to minimal media plates containing specific amino acids, vitamins, and so on.

DETECTION OF CHEMICAL CARCINOGENS

Scientists as well as the general public are very aware of the need to detect chemicals that can cause cancer **(carcinogens).** It is believed that mutations induced by chemical agents can lead to cancer. Bruce **Ames** devised a **test** (that bears his name) that is used to screen compounds that may be potential carcinogens. The basis of the test is whether or not a chemical compound can cause the reversion of a well characterized mutation in one of the histidine genes in the bacterial species *Salmonella typhimurium.* The tester bacterial strain is added to a mixture containing rat liver extract plus the suspected chemical carcinogen (Fig. 5-17). Rat liver extract is used because many potentially carcinogenic chemical compounds that enter the body must be activated by mammalian enzymes to exhibit mutagenic or carcinogenic effects. The mixture is allowed to incubate and is then inoculated onto a medium devoid of histidine. The auxotrophic *Salmonella* will grow on the medium only if the suspected carcinogen has caused a reversion of the original mutation in the tester strain.

DNA Transfer Other Than in Cell Division

In the previous paragraphs we discussed how mutations cause a change in the phenotype of the cell. In the following paragraphs we show how microorganisms can change their genetic constitution when genes are transferred in processes other than cell division. There are three general mechanisms for gene transfer: transformation, conjugation, and transduction. In each of these processes there is a transfer of genes from the donor to recipient DNA. This genetic exchange is called **recombination.** Most recombination occurs between two DNA segments that are homologous; that is, they have similar nucleotide sequences (the sequence of events that leads to formation of recombinant DNA is diagrammed in Fig. 5-18). The central feature of this model is that recombinant DNA molecules are formed by breaking and rejoining of intact DNA molecules of similar genotype. Let us now examine the three mechanisms in which genes can be transferred.

TRANSFORMATION

Transformation is the most primitive of the mechanisms for gene transfer among bacteria and is known to occur in only a few genera. The probability that transformation has contributed much to genetic variety is very small for most microorganisms. Transformation involves the tak-

FIGURE 5-16
Replica plating technique. A culture may be treated with a mutagen to produce mutants, or an untreated culture may be used for recovery of spontaneous mutants. An aliquot of the culture is spread on an agar medium that supports the growth of mutants as well as nonmutants. Only enough culture medium is added so that fewer than 100 colonies are distributed over the surface of the agar. A velveteen pad is used to press over the colonies (master plate) and they are transferred to an agar surface containing minimal medium (which will not support the growth of mutants). Colony X does not grow on this plate. Cells from the mutant colony can be tested by setting up a new master plate and replica plating to medium that is deficient in specific nutrients such as amino acids. Thus, specific amino acid mutants can be recovered.

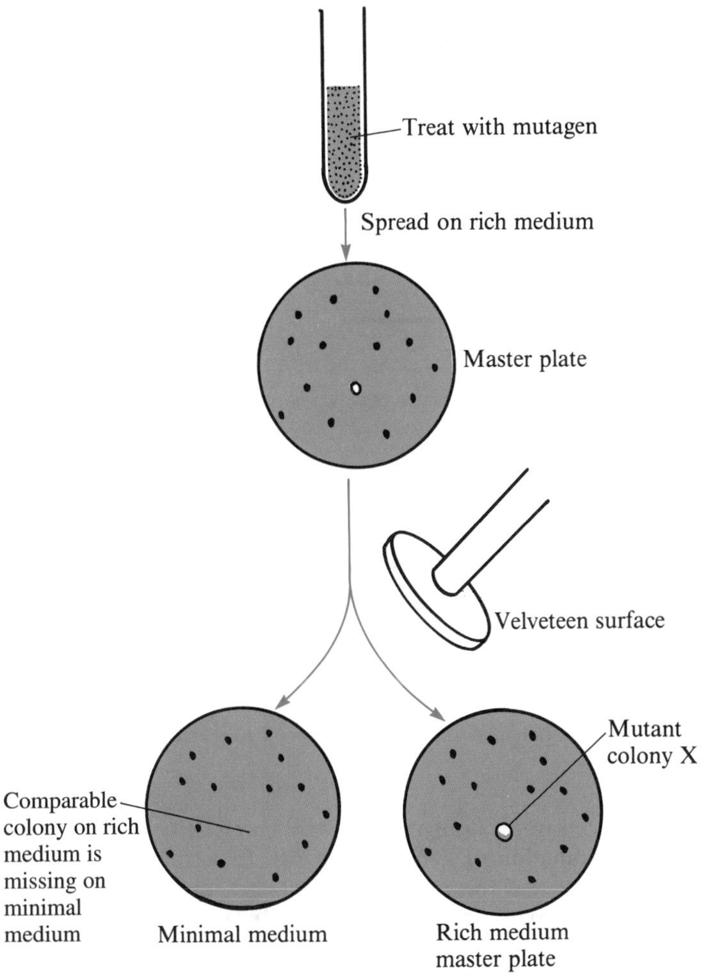

FIGURE 5-17
Ames test for carcinogenicity. A mixture containing liver extract, potential carcinogen, and *Salmonella* species with a specific mutation in the histidine operon (his$^-$) is incubated. An aliquot is transferred to an agar medium that does not contain histidine. The plate is incubated, and any bacteria that have reverted to his$^+$, because of the mutagenic effect of the carcinogen, will grow on the plate and produce colonies. Liver extract contains enzymes that are normally involved in the biochemical transformation of a chemical to an active mutagen.

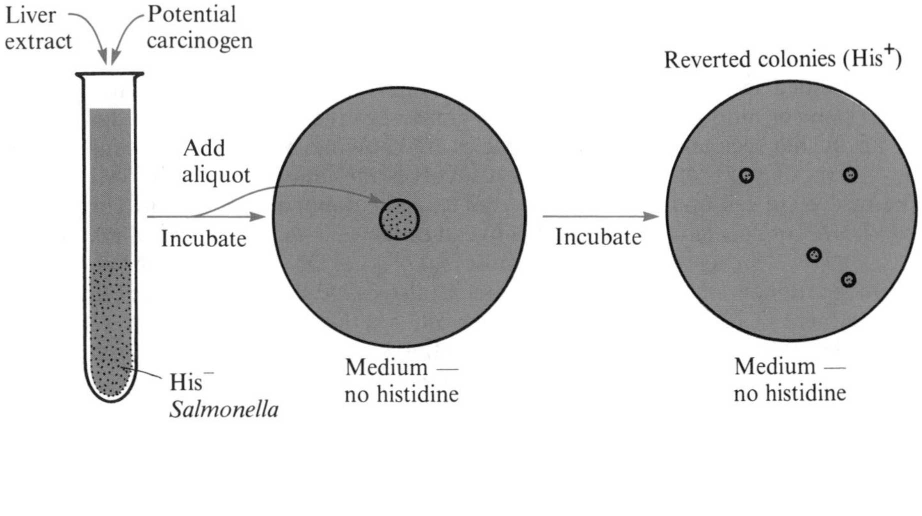

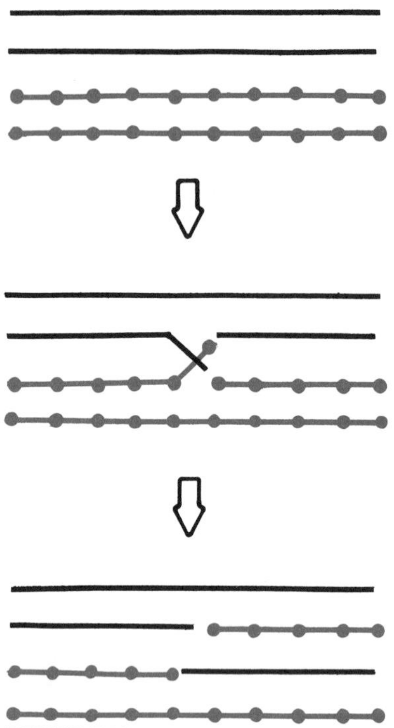

FIGURE 5-18
How recombination takes place between homologous DNA strands.

ing up of cell-free fragmented DNA by a recipient cell and the recombination of genetic elements. Experimentally, DNA is extracted from the donor cell and fragments of DNA are mixed with a population of viable recipient cells of a related species. The recipient cell will take up pieces of the DNA. Transformation has been studied primarily in gram-positive organisms such as *Bacillus subtilis* and species of *Streptococcus*. The overall process of transformation can be divided into the following steps (Fig. 5-19) (these apply only to gram-positive bacteria; there are some variations in gram-negative species):

1. Development of competence. **Competence** refers to the ability of a cell to take up DNA. Transformable bacteria become competent only under certain growth conditions. Log phase cultures of streptococci, for example, release a protein competence factor that induces competence for the entire cell population.
2. Binding of DNA. Competent cells are believed to carry receptor sites for binding DNA. Only double-stranded DNA is bound; single-stranded DNA or RNA is not bound. DNA from the same or different bacterial species can be taken up by the recipient cell.
3. Uptake of DNA. DNA is taken up by the cell and converted to single-stranded DNA of specific lengths.
4. Integration of DNA. Single-stranded donor DNA with sequences homologous to recipient DNA can enter into a recombination event. The donor single strand physically displaces a homologous strand of the recipient chromosome. Donor DNA that is not homologous does not engage in recombination and is eventually degraded by enzymes (nucleases).

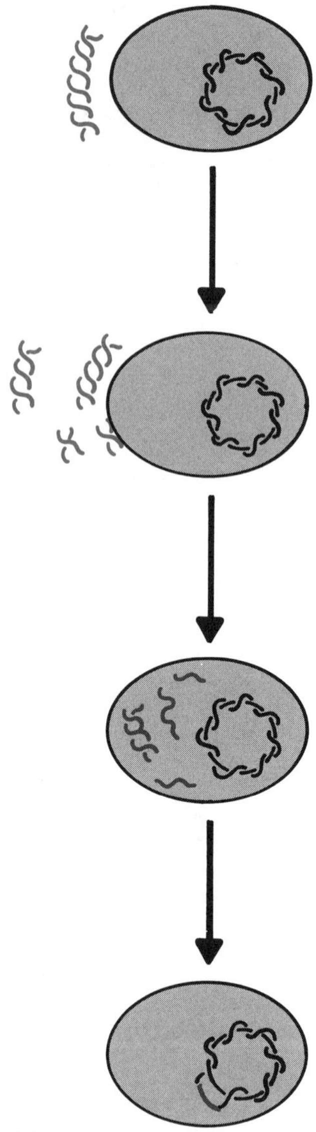

FIGURE 5-19
Transformation process. See text for details of this process.

CONJUGATION

Conjugation is an important means of gene transfer, especially among gram-negative bacteria. Only a few gram-positive species are known to be involved in conjugation. Conjugation involves the interaction of two cell mating types, referred to as the **donor** and **recipient.** The genetic transfer between donor and recipient is mediated by an extrachromosomal piece of DNA known as the **sex factor,** or fertility factor (also called **F factor**) found in the donor cell. The donor cell is called $\mathbf{F^+}$; the recipient cell, which does not contain the sex factor, is called $\mathbf{F^-}$. The sex factor is double-stranded DNA that is about one-fortieth the size of chromosomal DNA. The sex factor is not under control

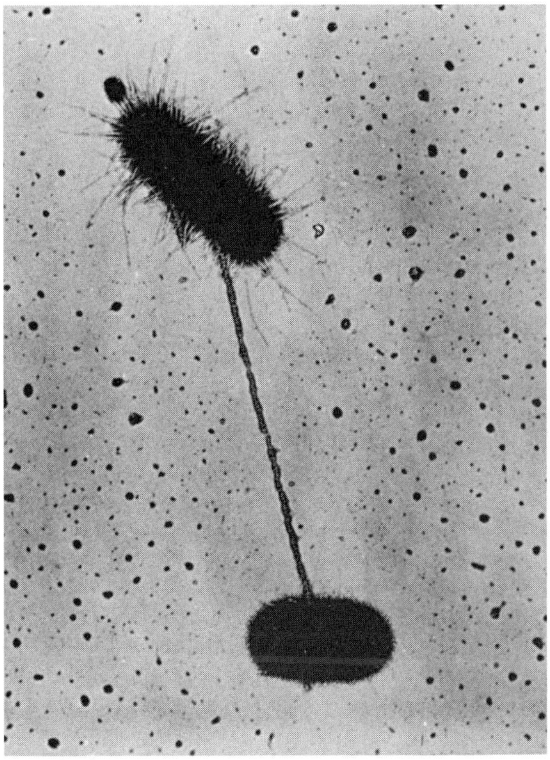

FIGURE 5-20
Electron micrograph showing conjugation between the donor cell containing the sex factor (F^+) and the recipient cell (F^-). The highly piliated cell *(top)* is the donor. (Courtesy of C. C. Brinton.)

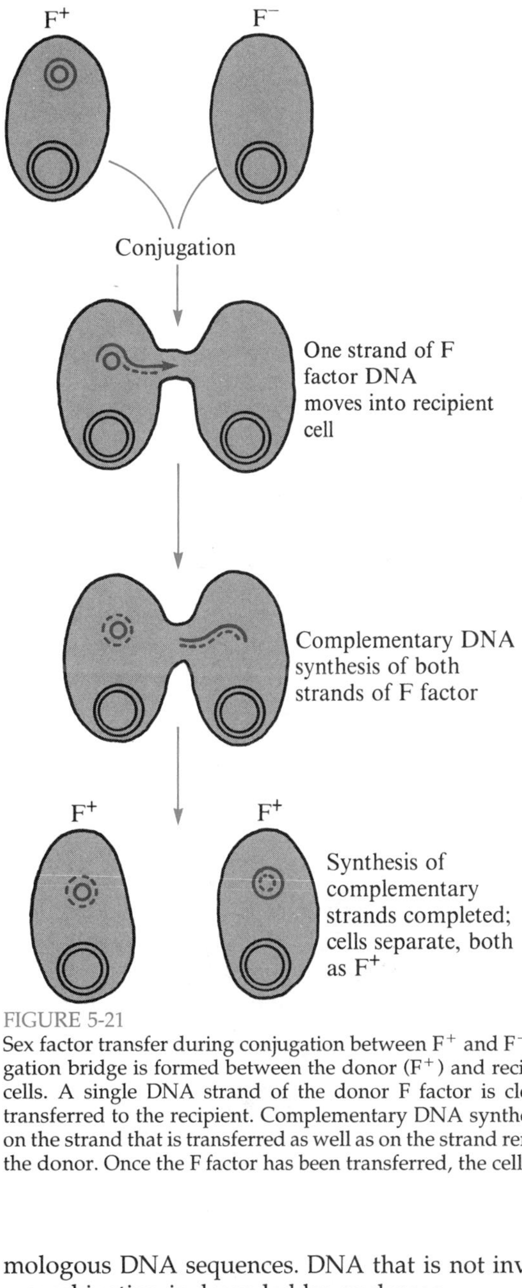
F+
F−
Conjugation
One strand of F factor DNA moves into recipient cell
Complementary DNA synthesis of both strands of F factor
F+
F+
Synthesis of complementary strands completed; cells separate, both as F+

FIGURE 5-21
Sex factor transfer during conjugation between F^+ and F^-. A conjugation bridge is formed between the donor (F^+) and recipient (F^-) cells. A single DNA strand of the donor F factor is cleaved and transferred to the recipient. Complementary DNA synthesis occurs on the strand that is transferred as well as on the strand remaining in the donor. Once the F factor has been transferred, the cells separate.

by the bacterial chromosome and it can replicate autonomously. The F factor possesses several genes that code for the formation of sex pili that aid the donor in attaching to a recipient cell (Fig. 5-20). The sex pili are believed to retract into the donor cell, thereby bringing the donor and recipient closer together. How the channel for transfer of donor DNA is produced is not known. During the conjugation process (Fig. 5-21) a copy of the sex factor is made and one of its single strands is transferred to the recipient. The complementary strand of the donor single strand is synthesized in the recipient, which is now converted to an F^+.

Hfr Cell Formation

The fertility factor does not always exist outside the chromosome but occasionally is integrated into the bacterial chromosome (Fig. 5-22). In an integrated state the sex factor is under control of chromosomal replication. The cells possessing the integrated form of the sex factor are called **Hfr (high frequency of recombination).** During conjugation and chromosome transfer most of the sex factor genes are not transferred. The reason for this is that they represent some of the last genes to be transferred, and because the conjugation bridge is very fragile and is broken before they can be transferred.

Once the donor DNA is transferred, recombination can take place and again involves an exchange between homologous DNA sequences. DNA that is not involved in recombination is degraded by nucleases.

TRANSDUCTION

Transduction involves the transmission of DNA from donor bacterium to recipient bacterium but, unlike conjugation and transformation, the DNA is transferred by a bacterial virus called a **bacteriophage**. To understand transduction we must first discuss how bacterial viruses operate (Fig. 5-23). Viruses infect bacterial cells by injecting viral DNA into the bacterial cytoplasm. The virus takes over the machinery of the cell and produces more virus. After so many virus particles have been produced, the bacterial cell lyses and the progeny viruses are released and are capable of infecting other bacteria. During the formation of virus the bacterial DNA is eventually

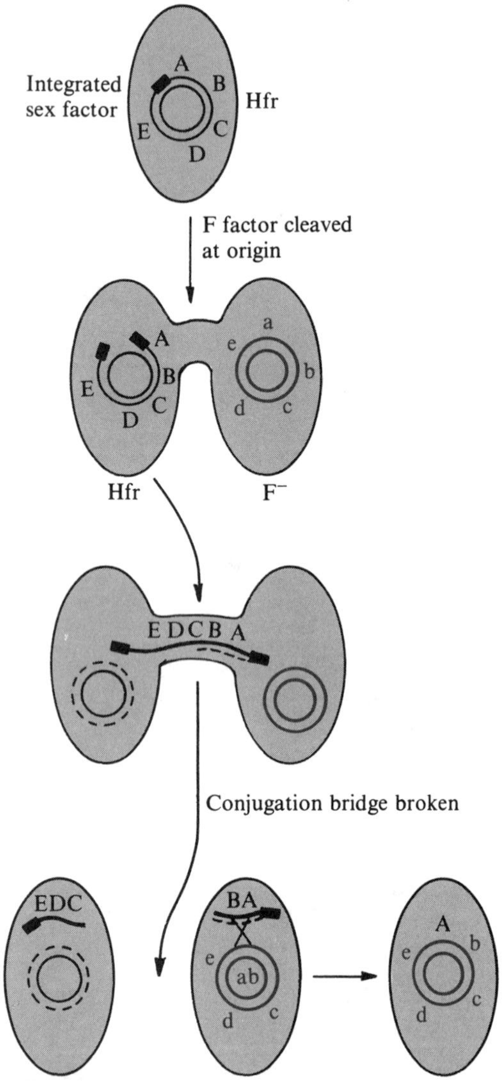

FIGURE 5-22
Conjugation process involving Hfr and F^-. A conjugation bridge is formed between donor (Hfr) and recipient (F^-) cells. The sex factor on the Hfr chromosome is cleaved, and a single-strand transfer is initiated. There is complementary synthesis of the transferred DNA strand as well as the remaining single strand in the Hfr cell. The conjugation bridge is broken, and only genes A and B are transferred to the recipient. Recombination between homologous genes results in the incorporation of Hfr gene A into the recipient chromosome.

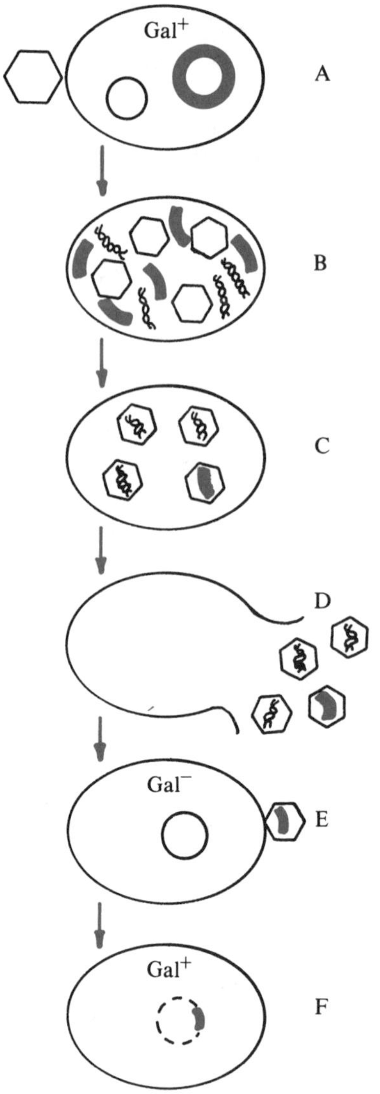

FIGURE 5-23
Generalized transduction. A. Bacterial cell with a functional galactose gene (gal^+) is infected by a virus (bacterial DNA is red; viral DNA is black). B. Bacterial DNA is degraded. C. Bacterial cell lyses, releasing virus, one of which carries the bacterial (gal^+) gene. E. Another bacterial cell that carries a nonfunctional galactose gene (gal^-) is infected by the transducing virus. F. The transduced gal^+ gene engages in recombination with a gal^- gene of bacterial chromosome, converting the cell to gal^+. The bacterial cell does not lyse because there was no viral information in the infecting viral particles.

broken up into smaller pieces, and some of them become accidentally packaged into the virus particle in place of viral DNA. The virus carrying the bacterial DNA is called a **transducing virus.** When the transducing virus infects a bacterial cell, the bacterial DNA it carries can exchange with the DNA of the infected bacterial cell, provided the sequences are homologous. Since any bacterial gene can be carried by the transducing virus, the transduction process is called **generalized transduction.** Another type of transduction called **specialized transduction** can also take place and this is discussed in Chapter 31.

Plasmids

Plasmids are circular double-stranded molecules of DNA that are found outside the bacterial chromosome. They are from one-tenth to one-ten-thousandth the size of the bacterial chromosome. Plasmids are autonomous and are not controlled by the bacterial chromosome. As few as 1 or as many as 100 plasmid molecules may be present in the cell. Plasmids can be divided into two classes: **conjugative** and **nonconjugative.** A conjugative plasmid possesses the genes for pilus formation and this permits transmission of copies of itself to a recipient during conjugation. Nonconjugative plasmids do not possess the information that can affect their own transfer. Nonconjugative plasmids can be transferred by such processes as transduction or transformation or by conjugation, but in the latter instance only if the bacterial cell also contains conjugative plasmids.

CHARACTERISTICS ASSOCIATED WITH PLASMIDS

Both conjugative and nonconjugative plasmids contain information that confers important characteristics to the bacterial cell. Plasmid-associated characteristics, although not indispensable, are important for helping the bacterium to cope in its particular environment. We discuss only the characteristics that have medical significance.

R Plasmids

R plasmids possess information for resistance to antimicrobial compounds such as antibiotics. R plasmids are readily dispersed because of two important features: They are conjugative and they carry genetic elements called **transposons.** There is little difference between a transposon and an IS element except that transposons possess information for antibiotic resistance while IS elements do not. A transposon can replicate and transfer a copy of itself to other genetic elements (other plasmids, chromosomal DNA). This promiscuity is one of the reasons why bacteria quickly become resistant to antimicrobials. The conjugative ability of R plasmids resides on a segment called the **resistance transfer factor** or **RTF.** RTF carries information for pilus formation and is similar to the F factor. The antimicrobial resistance genes (designated *r*), of which there may be one or several on the R plasmid, are usually clustered together.

R plasmids can be transferred from nonpathogenic bacteria to pathogenic bacteria and vice versa because conjugation can be between the same or different species of bacteria. When antimicrobials, such as penicillin or tetracycline, are administered to patients over a long period of time, there is a selection process that favors the emergence and growth of drug-resistant strains. These drug-resistant strains can be transferred to individuals who do not harbor drug-resistant strains—a situation that occurs repeatedly in the hospital.

Resistance to Heavy Metals

Heavy-metal ions such as cobalt and mercury are inhibitory to the growth of bacteria. There are plasmids, found primarily in the gram-positive staphylococci, that code for resistance to heavy metals. Heavy-metal ions are in such antimicrobial preparations as silver nitrate. Metal ion plasmid resistance is often associated with antibiotic resistance factors. Thus, the transfer of metal ion resistance via plasmids from one cell to another is often accompanied by antibiotic resistance as well.

Virulence Determinants

The ability of some microorganisms to cause disease (referred to as virulence) is associated with special determinants carried on plasmids. These determinants often code for toxins that are detrimental to the host, but not always. Some of the principal virulence determinants coded by plasmids are found in the following bacteria:

1. *Escherichia coli.* Some *E. coli* strains produce two types of toxins that affect the intestinal tract: heat-labile (LT) and heat-stable (ST). Both toxins are plasmid-associated.
2. *Staphylococcus aureus.* An affliction of the skin of newborns called scalded skin syndrome is caused by certain strains of *S. aureus.* The toxin is plasmid-associated.
3. *Clostridium perfringens.* One type of diarrheal disease in domestic animals is caused by *C. perfringens* type C. The disease is associated with a toxin that is encoded on a plasmid.
4. *Streptococcus* species. Several species of *Streptococcus* produce **hemolysins** (lyse red blood cells) that are encoded on plasmid DNA.

DNA Transfer and Infectious Disease

The question we should now ask is "What is the significance of bacterial DNA transfer with respect to infectious disease?" Bacteria are not totally autonomous and their survival depends on associations with other microorganisms, especially other bacteria. All bacterial species possess accessory elements such as plasmids. Therefore, gene exchange among bacterial species involves both chromosomal and accessory DNA. Which genes will be retained for any length of time depends on several factors, including (1) whether a chromosomal gene or small replicon gene is being exchanged—chromosomal genes are more likely to be retained than are genes from accessory elements, (2) restriction enzymes that may degrade donor DNA (see Chapter 6 for further details), (3) host-recipient incompatibility (for example, gene transfer between gram-positive and gram-negative bacteria has not been observed), and (4) whether the gene offers some immediate advantage to the host. Let us look at the mammalian intestinal tract as an example of how DNA transfer is associated with infectious disease.

A large population of different bacterial species is maintained in the intestinal tract. Each species possesses mobile accessory DNA elements such as plasmids, transposons, and viruses. Thus, each bacterium lives in an environment containing a large gene pool that is potentially exchangeable. Most of the genes located on mobile genetic elements code for metal resistance, antibiotic resistance, bacteriocin production, or toxin production. Let us assume that an individual is infected with an organism that possesses a plasmid gene coding for resistance to the antibiotic tetracycline. The resistance plasmid could be transferred to other bacterial species in the intestinal tract. The gene would most likely be retained only if tetracycline were administered to the infected individual. Once the administration of tetracycline is discontinued, the plasmid becomes eliminated because it is no longer useful to the bacterium. Sometimes antibiotic resistance and toxin genes are flanked by transposons. This permits the DNA encoding the virulence factor(s) to be integrated into the recipient's genome. Under these circumstances a normally nonpathogenic recipient bacterium could become transformed into a pathogen. In some Third World countries, antibiotics are considered over-the-counter drugs. Continual use of antibiotics obtained in this way often results in the individual possessing intestinal microorganisms that display resistance to as many as six or more antibiotics. Antibiotic resistance transfer is discussed at more length in Chapter 6.

Summary

1. DNA, the basis of heredity, performs specific functions in the bacterial cell: (a) duplication for transfer during cell division; (b) transcription into messenger RNA (mRNA), which can be translated into protein; (c) control of protein synthesis; (d) ability to mutate; and (e) transfer of genes in processes other than cell division.

2. Bacterial DNA is a double-stranded molecule in which a sequence of nucleotide bases on one strand is complementary to the sequence of nucleotide bases on the opposite strand. In the cell the DNA exists in the form of a circle that is folded on itself.

3. The DNA molecule is replicated in a semiconservative manner in which each strand acts as a template for synthesis of a complementary strand. Replication of DNA begins at the origin and involves both strands. DNA synthesis proceeds in opposite directions from the origin. Replication is initiated by an enzyme that nicks one strand at the origin while other proteins, such as unwinding proteins and helix-destabilizing proteins, unwind the DNA and prevent it from rewinding, respectively.

4. Synthesis of DNA is catalyzed by the enzyme DNA polymerase, which adds nucleotides in the 5′ to 3′ direction. Since the two strands are antiparallel, one strand adds nucleotides continuously. The other strand lags behind because short RNA primers must first be produced along the lagging strand.

5. One of the DNA strands is transcribed into mRNA by the enzyme RNA polymerase. The nucleotides in the mRNA are arranged as a linear sequence of coding units or triplets called codons. There are 64 possible codons, a minimum of 3 for each of the 20 different amino acids. Three triplets do not code for amino acids and are called nonsense.

6. Information on the mRNA is translated into a polypeptide when it engages a ribosome and the first aminoacyl transfer RNA (tRNA) is brought to it to form an initiation complex. As the ribosome moves down the mRNA, amino acids are brought by tRNA molecules whose anticodons are complementary to the codons. When each amino acid arrives, a new peptide bond is formed. The message is terminated when a nonsense triplet has been reached. The completed polypeptide is released into the cytoplasm.

7. Some enzymes in the cell are inducible and are under the control of genetic mechanisms. The genetic unit controlling inducible enzymes is called an operon. The operon, which consists of structural genes, an operator, and promoter, is itself under the control of a repressor protein encoded by the regulator gene.

8. Operons are of two basis types: inducible and repressible. Inducible operons are turned off by an active repressor protein but in the presence of inducer the repressor becomes inactive and the structural genes of the operon are turned on. In a repressible operon the repressor molecule becomes active only in the presence of a corepressor molecule, which is usually the end product of a biosynthetic pathway.

9. Mutations may arise spontaneously without human intervention or they may be induced. Spontaneous mutation may involve electrochemical changes in a base that permit it to mispair during replication. Many spontaneous mutations are caused by short units of DNA called insertion sequences (IS). IS elements can replicate and insert themselves into other DNA molecules and interfere with normal gene transcription.

10. Induced mutations may be caused by physical or chemical agents. Physical agents such as x-rays or gamma rays can energize molecules in the cell that damage DNA. Ultraviolet light is absorbed by pyrimidines to form dimers that interfere with replication.

11. Chemical mutagens cause changes in the DNA that usually involve mispairing events. Some chemicals alter the purine or pyrimidine base while others are analogues and are incorporated into the DNA in place of the normal base. Some chemicals can insert themselves between bases, and this ultimately results in the addition or deletion of bases following DNA replication.

12. The effect of mutation on the genetic code may be (a) no effect, (b) to change a codon that causes missense, (c) to produce a nonsense triplet that terminates the message, and (d) to insert or delete a base that causes a shift in the reading frame of the message. These effects may or may not affect the polypeptide, depending on their location in the message.

13. Mutations can be repaired by enzymes that are induced following an SOS response. There are repair enzymes that can remove specifically damaged bases and replace them with the correct base. Ultraviolet light damage can be repaired by enzymes that remove the dimer and additional bases in a process called excision repair.

14. Some bacterial mutants can be detected visually but mutants with growth requirements are detected by replica plating techniques. Mutants of *Salmonella typhimurium* are used commercially to determine the potential of chemicals to be carcinogenic. The test (Ames test) is based on the ability of the potential carcinogen to produce mutations in *S. typhimurium* that reverse the effects of the original mutations.

15. Bacteria can transfer copies of their genes to other bacteria in processes other than cell division. After the gene is transferred, it enters into a recombination event with the host gene and homologous sequences are exchanged. Transformation is a process in which cell-free DNA is taken up by the cell. Conjugation is a process in which there is DNA transfer from a donor that contains a fertility factor (F^+) to a recipient that does not contain the sex factor (F^-). If the sex factor is outside the chromosome (F^+), only the sex factor is transmitted, but if the sex factor is integrated into the chromosome (Hfr), all or part of the chromosome is transferred. Transduction is a process in which a bacterial virus picks up bacterial DNA from an infected host and transfers it to a new bacterial host.

16. Plasmids are small extrachromosomal pieces of DNA carrying traits that are not indispensable to the bacterium. Some plasmids can affect their own transfer (conjugative) while others cannot (nonconjugative). Some of the characteristics encoded in plasmids are antibiotic resistance, heavy-metal resistance, and virulence determinants.

Questions for Study

1. Describe the function of the types of RNA molecules that can be transcribed from genomic DNA.
2. Describe what is meant by conservative replication. What would be the consequences of such replication by cells?
3. What are the major proteins associated with the replication process?
4. What area of the operon is not a gene? What would be the significance of mutations affecting genes and nongenes in the operon?
5. What is the distinction between a repressible and inducible operon?
6. If spontaneous mutations are not caused by environmental factors, what does cause them?
7. Characterize the following: missense mutations, nonsense mutations, and frameshift mutations.
8. Describe the three basic ways that bacteria are involved in DNA transfer other than cell division. Which one(s) is (are) predominant in drug resistance transfer?

CHAPTER 6

Biotechnology and Medicine

OBJECTIVES

To understand the term biotechnology and its relationship to genetics

To outline briefly the technique for producing recombinant DNA

To describe the technique for selecting clones that possess recombinant DNA

To describe the technique for selecting recombinant clones that possess the desired gene

To discuss how a eukaryotic gene can be expressed in a prokaryotic host

To describe the technique of the polymerase chain reaction and why it is important in clinical medicine

To outline briefly some applications of genetic engineering to medicine

To define the terms genetic engineering, restriction endonuclease, cloning, annealing, gene probe, denaturation, and complementary DNA

OUTLINE

GENETIC ENGINEERING AND RECOMBINANT DNA

OVERVIEW OF EVENTS IN PRODUCING RECOMBINANT DNA
- Donor DNA
- Vectors
- Cloning
- Selection of Recombinant Clones
- Purifying Cloned DNA
- Expression of Foreign Genes

POLYMERASE CHAIN REACTION

MEDICAL APPLICATIONS OF GENETIC ENGINEERING
- Drug Production
- Vaccine Development
- Gene Therapy

In the previous chapter we focused primarily on the underlying principles of genetics and the mechanisms of gene transfer. In this chapter we concentrate on some of the practical aspects of genetics, particularly in the domain of infectious disease. This practical application of genetics has become part of a rapidly expanding field of science called **biotechnology.**

Genetic Engineering and Recombinant DNA

The phrase **recombinant DNA** refers to the creation of DNA molecules from different biological sources. Recombinant DNA technology is commonly termed **gene splicing** or **genetic engineering.** The single most important event that advanced the development of genetic engineering was the discovery of **restriction enzymes** or **restriction endonucleases.** The term restriction refers to the ability of the enzyme to recognize and cleave specific sequences in a foreign DNA molecule. There are literally hundreds of restriction enzymes from a variety of sources that recognize different DNA sequences (Fig. 6-1). Some restriction endonuclease enzymes create double-stranded breaks, and thus produce staggered ends (Fig. 6-1). The staggered ends with complementary bases are called "sticky" because they combine with similar sequences produced by the same enzyme on other DNA molecules. The joining of complementary sticky ends from different sources is called **annealing.**

Overview of Events in Producing Recombinant DNA

One of the attributes of recombinant DNA technology is that it allows one to take genes from a variety of sources and use them to make products of commercial interest. The basic approach in genetic engineering is twofold: (1) to take a gene of specific interest and join it to a DNA molecule capable of replication, and (2) to provide an environment in which the gene of interest can be reproduced in large numbers, a procedure called **cloning.** The basis of this approach is illustrated in Figure 6-2 and is discussed in the following sections.

DONOR DNA

The gene or DNA sequence to be isolated from an organism for producing a specific protein product or performing a specific function is referred to as **donor** or **passenger DNA.** The term donor implies that its DNA will be annealed to a larger piece of DNA called a **vector** or **vehicle.**

VECTORS

The vector used to carry the gene of interest should have the following attributes: (1) be able to replicate, (2) be capable of introduction into a cell, and (3) possess some attribute making its presence recognizable. The three most common vectors are plasmids, bacteriophage, and cosmids (cosmids possess the virtues of plasmids and bacteriophage). Let us assume that we will use a plasmid as a vector. A frequently used plasmid is pBR322. pBR322 contains genes for ampicillin and tetracycline resistance. In addition, it also possesses several restriction sites that occur only once on the plasmid. If foreign DNA is inserted into the ampicillin resistance gene, the resistance gene becomes inactivated. This property enables the investigator to identify bacteria that possess the plasmid, because the bacterium cannot grow in the presence of the antibiotic. Plasmid DNA is treated with the same restriction endonuclease as donor DNA. The fragments generated can hybridize with donor DNA, producing a hybrid plasmid. Once the donor DNA is inserted into the vector DNA, DNA ligase is used to form phosphodiester bonds and seal the open ends. This results in the formation of a circular hybrid plasmid.

FIGURE 6-1
Recognition site for two restriction endonucleases. A. Enzyme from *Escherichia coli*, called EcoRI, cuts DNA to produce a molecule with 5′ tails. B. Enzyme from *Providencia stuartii*, called PstI, cuts DNA to produce 3′ tails.

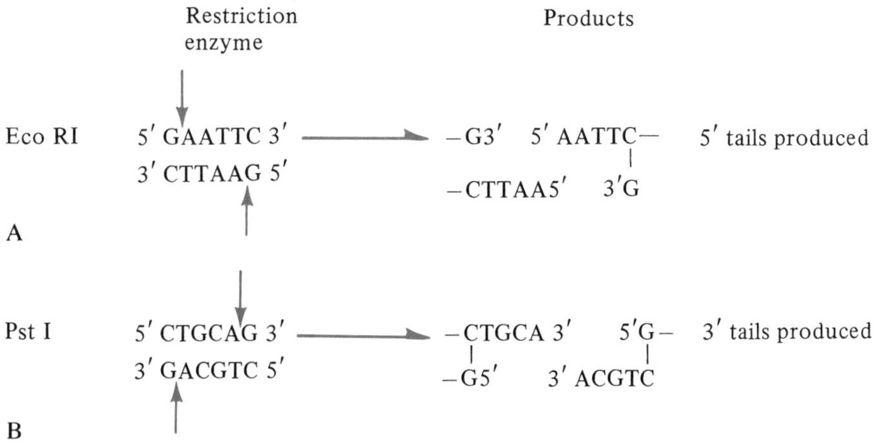

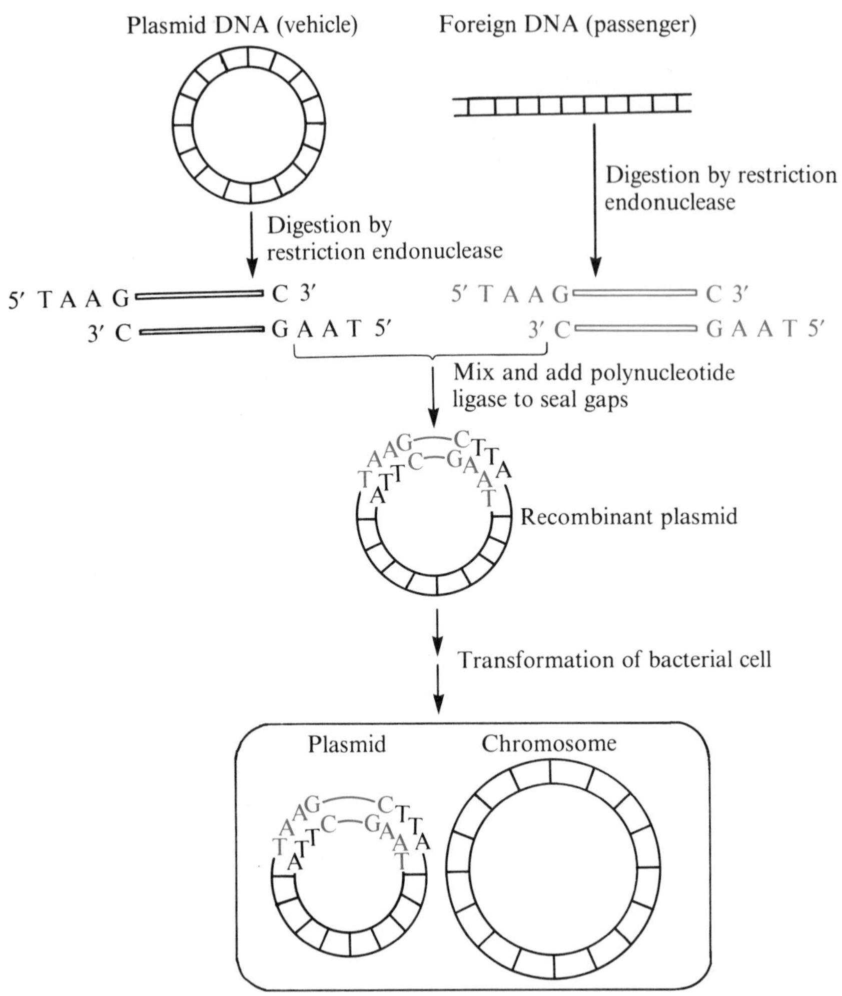

FIGURE 6-2
Recombinant DNA experiment. Plasmid DNA (bacterial source) plus foreign DNA (eukaryotic source) are digested by endonuclease. DNA fragments are produced with complementary "sticky" ends. Some foreign DNA will bond with plasmid DNA. The plasmid circularizes and can be used to transform a bacterial cell. The foreign DNA (gene) can be expressed in the bacterium. (From R. F. Boyd, *General Microbiology*, 2nd ed. St. Louis: Mosby, 1988.)

CLONING

The next step after producing recombinant plasmids is to insert them into a suitable host organism. The principal host organism has been the bacterium *Escherichia coli* but other hosts might include the bacterium *Bacillus subtilis*, as well as eukaryotic yeasts. The recombinant plasmid can be introduced into a bacterial cell by treating the latter with calcium chloride (calcium chloride increases the permeability of the bacterial cell wall to the plasmid), a process called **transformation.** Each transformed bacterium is allowed to reproduce on a suitable agar surface to produce colonies.

Each bacterial cell in a colony has the same genetic constitution and therefore each colony can be called a **clone** of cells. If a single colony or a portion of the colony is transferred to another agar surface, all the progeny will contain copies of the same genetic sequence. This natural amplification process results in the generation of millions of copies of a particular DNA sequence.

SELECTION OF RECOMBINANT CLONES

Not all bacterial cells in the transformation process will be transformed. In addition, some transformed cells will not contain the desired DNA sequence. The first procedure is to determine which clones have incorporated the plasmid vector. This is a relatively simple task that is based on antibiotic resistance and the use of host *E. coli* cells that are sensitive to ampicillin and tetracycline. Plasmid pBR322, discussed previously, can have foreign DNA incorporated into the ampicillin resistance gene if a particular restriction enzyme is used. This results in inactivation of the ampicillin resistance gene (Fig. 6-3). Three types of cells are the consequence of this transformation process:

1. Cells that have not been transformed and are sensitive to both tetracycline and ampicillin.
2. Transformed cells in which the vector does not contain foreign DNA. These cells are resistant to both antibiotics.

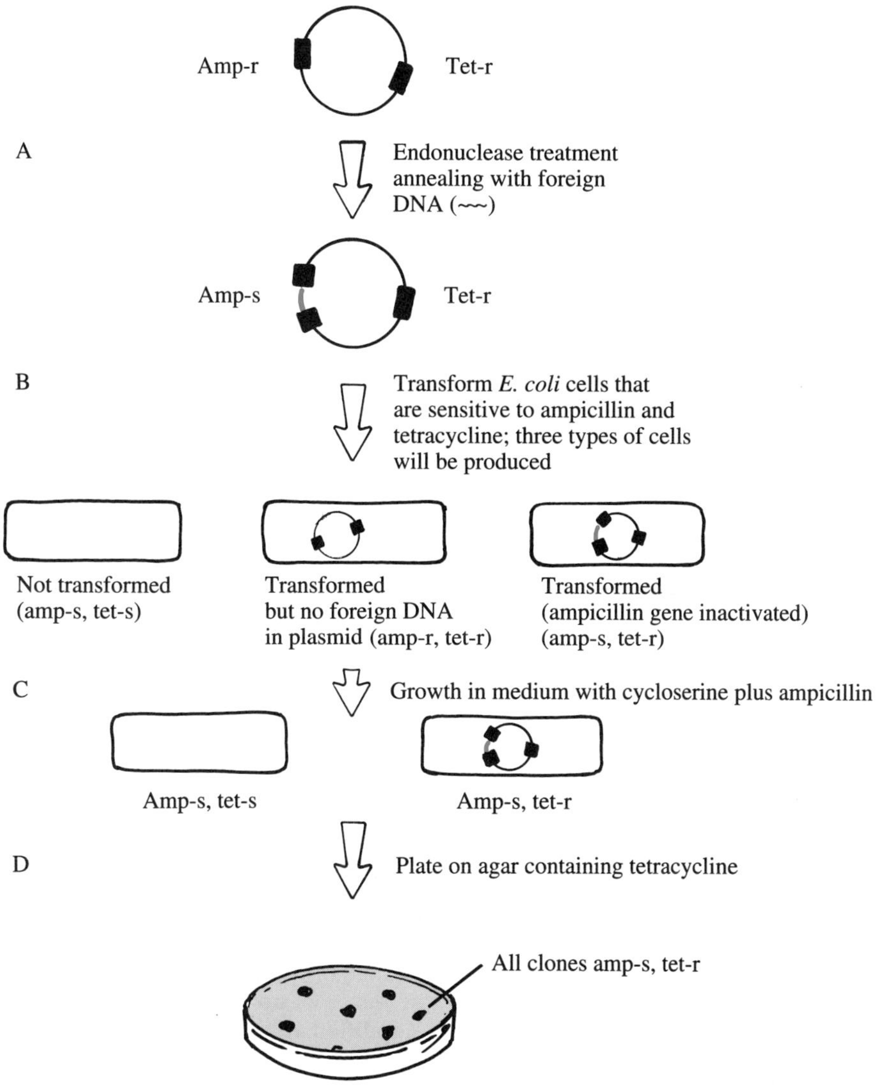

FIGURE 6-3
Technique for isolating pBR322 plasmid that contains foreign DNA. A. Endonuclease treatment of plasmid is followed by annealing of foreign DNA into plasmid. If foreign DNA is inserted, the ampicillin gene becomes inactivated (amp-s). B. *E. coli* cells sensitive to ampicillin and tetracycline are subjected to transformation, resulting in three types of cells being produced. Some cells will not be transformed, some will be transformed but the plasmid does not contain foreign DNA, and others will be transformed with recombinant plasmid. C. Cells grown in medium containing cycloserine and ampicillin. Cycloserine kills growing cells (amp-r,tet-r) but only inhibits amp-s cells. D. Cells plated on agar containing tetracycline. Only cells with recombinant plasmid (amp-s,tet-r) will grow. Amp-s = ampicillin-sensitive; amp-r = ampicillin-resistant; tet-s = tetracycline-sensitive; tet-r = tetracycline-resistant.

3. Transformed cells containing a recombinant vector that has an inactivated ampicillin gene. These cells are ampicillin-sensitive and tetracycline-resistant.

The cell mixture is first grown in a medium containing cycloserine plus ampicillin. Cycloserine kills growing cells (amp-r,tet-r) but only inhibits growth of ampicillin-sensitive cells. The next stage in the procedure is to plate the cells on agar containing tetracycline. Only recombinant clones (amp-s,tet-r) will grow on the agar.

The second procedure is to identify the clones that have the *desired* DNA sequence. Several techniques can be used and include the following:

1. Product detection. If the desired gene codes for a protein that is not present or is defective in the host cell, the protein can be detected. For example, the protein to be assayed may exhibit a color.
2. An immunological technique can be used if specific antibodies are available to the gene product.
3. The simplest procedure involves hybridization with a nucleic acid probe (Fig. 6-4). A portion of each colony is transferred from the agar surface to a filter paper. The filter paper is treated with sodium hydroxide to lyse the cells and release denatured DNA. The paper is then dried to fix the denatured DNA

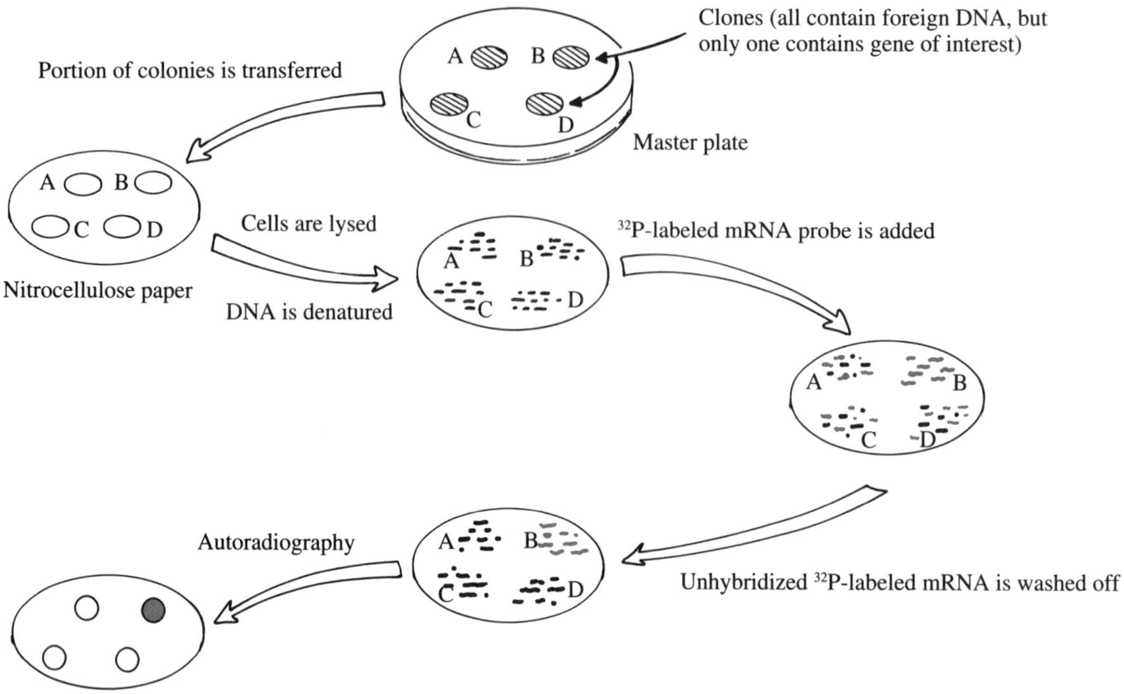
Clones (all contain foreign DNA, but only one contains gene of interest)
Portion of colonies is transferred
A B C D
Master plate
Nitrocellulose paper
Cells are lysed
DNA is denatured
³²P-labeled mRNA probe is added
Autoradiography
Unhybridized ³²P-labeled mRNA is washed off
Dark spot on film indicates that clone B contained foreign DNA

FIGURE 6-4
Hybridization assay for the detection of plasmid containing desired gene in cloned cells. See text for details.

to the surface. The paper is treated with a phosphorus 32 (^{32}P)–labeled probe (messenger RNA or complementary DNA) that is complementary to the DNA of the gene being sought. The paper is subjected to conditions that favor renaturation. The paper is washed and any unbound ^{32}P-labeled probe is removed while hybridized ^{32}P-labeled probe remains on the paper. The paper is dried and subjected to autoradiography. A dark spot on the paper indicates colonies that contain the desired gene. The ^{32}P-labeled nucleic acid used in this experiment is one example of what is referred to as a **gene probe.** How gene probes are generated and how they can be used clinically are discussed in Under the Microscope 3.

PURIFYING CLONED DNA

Once the desired clone has been identified on the master plate and propagated, the specific DNA sequence can be purified. The desired DNA fragment is cut out of the plasmid by restriction enzymes and separated from the vector DNA fragments by electrophoresis.

EXPRESSION OF FOREIGN GENES

Cloned genes are not always expressed in host cells unless some modification has been made in the cloning vector. Vectors require the necessary transcription and translation signals that permit expression of the desired gene. This is especially true if the foreign gene is eukaryotic while the host cell is prokaryotic. Somatostatin, a mammalian hormone that regulates growth, was one of the first medically important peptides to be synthesized successfully using recombinant DNA technology. The synthetic somatostatin gene was spliced into the vector pBR322 and then modified by attaching part of the *E. coli* lac operon to it (Fig. 6-5). This procedure permits a eukaryotic gene (somatostatin) to be controlled by a prokaryotic operon (lac operon).

The recombinant plasmid was then introduced into *E. coli* and allowed to replicate. The somatostatin gene was transcribed along with the beta-galactosidase gene fragment. The fusion protein that was produced contained somatostatin plus beta-galactosidase. The fused proteins were separated by cyanogen bromide. The somatostatin polypeptide folded into an active molecule and was later purified.

Polymerase Chain Reaction

One of the outgrowths of in vitro gene amplification has been the development of the polymerase chain reaction (PCR). PCR can be used to amplify genes without the need for culture. PCR, which allows the amplification of a single copy of a DNA sequence by more than a millionfold, is based on the repetition of three steps: (1) denaturation, (2) reannealing (hybridizing), and (3) enzymatic

UNDER THE MICROSCOPE 3

Gene Probes

Gene probes can be obtained in different ways but many are constructed by isolating complementary DNA. For example, if the desired gene is expressed in a specific tissue or cell, its messenger RNA (mRNA) is often expressed more abundantly than any other. The gene for insulin production, for example, is associated with specific pancreatic cells. The desired mRNA can be used as a template for producing DNA. Such a process is possible because of the discovery of the animal virus enzyme called **reverse transcriptase.** With this enzyme, double-stranded DNA can be synthesized. DNA prepared in this way is referred to as **complementary DNA** or **cDNA** (see figure below). Complementary DNA copies are purified, then spliced into the appropriate vector, and finally cloned to yield the gene probe. The probe can be labeled radioactively (^{32}P) or biochemically (biotin) and then denatured into single strands. Most gene probes are DNA, but RNA also can be used. Probes also can be propagated if the gene codes for a protein of known amino acid sequence. In the laboratory, oligonucleotides can be constructed to code for a specific amino acid sequence in the desired protein.

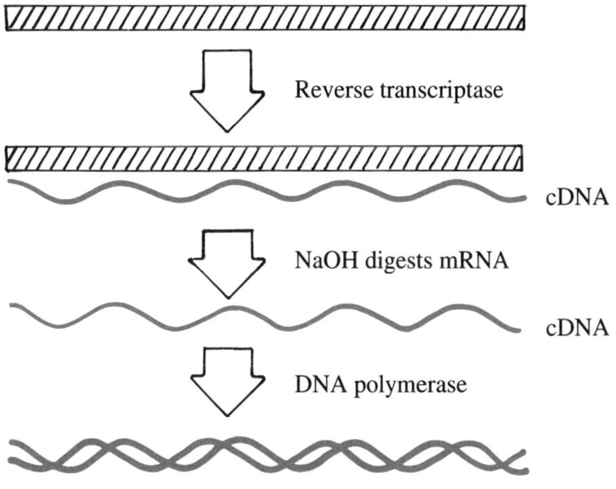

A simplified description of the technique for synthesis of double-stranded complementary DNA (cDNA) from messenger RNA (mRNA).

The labeled probe is now capable of hybridizing with either a DNA or an RNA strand of complementary sequences. In the clinical setting, for example, we may wish to identify a microorganism based on a particular phenotypic characteristic (a toxin). The DNA from the clinical sample is denatured to isolate single-stranded DNA and is attached to a filter. The DNA probe (contains the DNA sequence for the toxin coding gene) is passed over the filter. This allows hybridization between DNA single strands to occur with the formation of double-stranded duplexes. Unreacted single-stranded DNA is washed off the filter. One of the problems with the use of probes is that the unknown clinical source may be in short supply. One technique is to amplify the probe nucleic acid; another is to amplify the target sequence. One of the most widely used target sequence amplification techniques is called polymerase chain reaction (PCR) (see Polymerase Chain Reaction in this chapter). These reactions are used to increase the signal from bound probes. A wide variety of gene probes are now available for the identification of several species of bacteria. Many of these probes are ribosomal RNA (rRNA) probes. rRNA is a useful probe for two reasons:

1. rRNA sequences occur in each ribosome of an organism and provide a natural amplification system, and
2. rRNA sequences are highly conserved (not subject to random mutations) among all microorganisms and can be used for nucleic acid sequencing or PCR amplification.

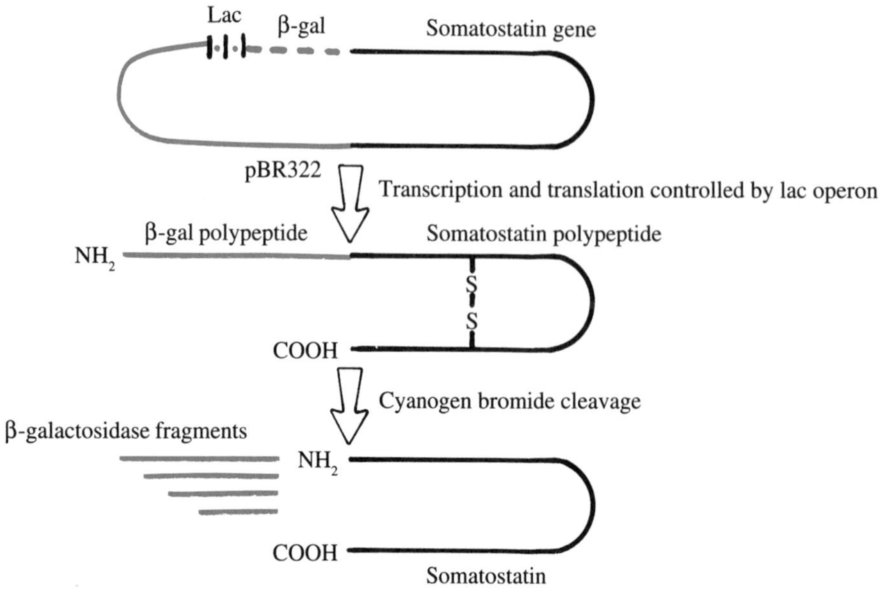

FIGURE 6-5
Synthesis of somatostatin by recombinant DNA. Plasmid pBR322(−) containing the lactate (lac) operon (———) is joined to the gene coding for somatostatin synthesis.

nucleotide addition. The steps are outlined below (Fig. 6-6).

Step 1. **Denaturation** of the target double-stranded DNA is accomplished by high temperatures that dissociate complementary strands.

FIGURE 6-6
Polymerase chain reaction.

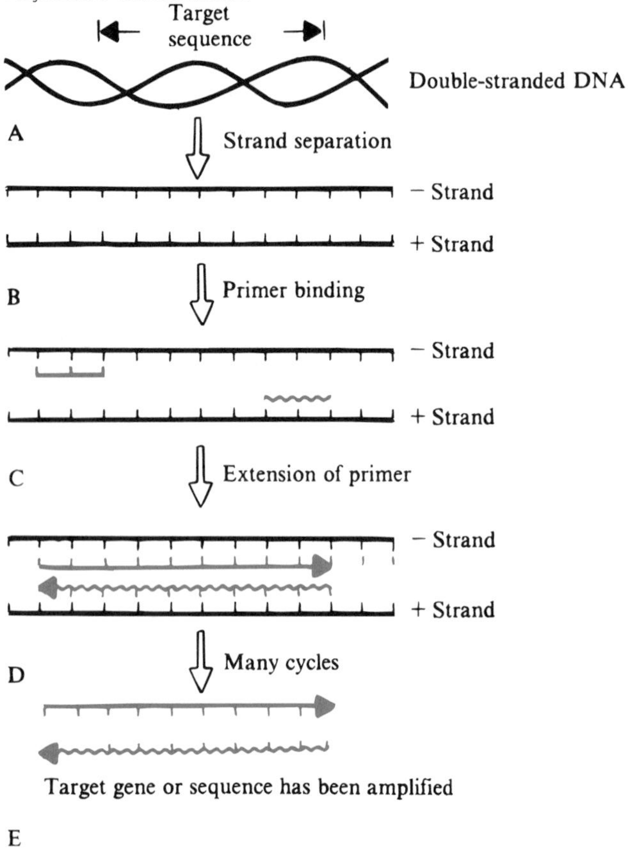

Known primers that flank the target sequence are then produced and will be added later. The primers constitute a pair of synthetic oligonucleotides that flank the DNA segment to be amplified. The primers are complementary to opposite strands of the target sequence. The sequence of the primers is determined by the sequence of the DNA to be amplified. The primers are usually 20 to 30 bases in length and not complementary to each other.

Step 2. The primers are **annealed** to the target when the temperature is lowered to 40 to 50 C. Because the primers are in excess, the formation of primer-target duplexes occurs in preference to the reassociation of two complementary template strands.

Step 3. **Nucleotide addition** is accomplished by adding thermostable DNA polymerase to the reaction. The primers serve as the starting points for enzymatic addition of nucleotides. The original DNA strands serve as templates for the new DNA being made. Primer extension doubles the number of DNA molecules that were initially present. During the second and subsequent cycles the original DNA segment and the newly generated complementary DNA become templates.

Usually the PCR cycle is repeated 20 to 40 times before the amplified product can be detected by gel electrophoresis or DNA hybridization with a ^{32}P-labeled probe.

PCR has provided a revolution in genetic sequencing. It will have profound effects on the work of genome mappers (for example, the human genome mapping and sequencing project), forensic scientists, acquired immunodeficiency syndrome (AIDS) researchers (detecting DNA of the human immunodeficiency virus [HIV] in infants), and investigators seeking to improve genetic disease (sickle cell anemia, phenylketonuria) detection. PCR is also being used to detect human papillomavirus to determine the relationship between the virus and cervical cancer (see Chapter 32).

Medical Applications of Genetic Engineering

Genetic engineering has had profound effects in agriculture and industry. Some products of this application are bacteria that can metabolize toxic wastes, plants with resistance to frost and specific pests, and crop plants with resistance to herbicides. We reserve this discussion for the medical applications of genetic engineering.

DRUG PRODUCTION

Some drugs that under ordinary conditions can be obtained only in minuscule amounts or are difficult to process are potential subjects for genetic engineering. Some of the medically important peptides or proteins synthesized by genetic engineering are outlined in Table 6-1. One of the more recent important drugs is DNase. In late 1993 the Food and Drug Administration approved the use of recombinant human-type DNase for the treatment of cystic fibrosis. DNase reduces the frequency of respiratory tract infections and improves lung function in patients with cystic fibrosis. Cystic fibrosis typically induces thick mucous secretions in the lungs, which lead to recurrent infections with *Pseudomonas aeruginosa*. When leukocytes combat these infections, bacterial DNA is released and causes further obstruction of the airways. DNase administered as a mist digests the extraneous DNA and thereby reopens airways.

VACCINE DEVELOPMENT

Traditional vaccines are prepared by processing the whole organism (whooping cough vaccine, viral vaccines) or specific microbial components (for example, the protein toxins of some bacterial species). **Recombinant vaccines** represent a breakthrough in disease prevention. One significant recombinant vaccine is the vaccine against hepatitis B virus (HBV). The gene coding for one of the surface proteins (hepatitis B surface antigen) of this virus has been cloned in yeast (see Chapter 32).

TABLE 6-1
Medically Important Peptides or Proteins Produced by Genetic Engineering

Peptide or protein	Use
Interferons	Antiviral and antitumor agents
Blood clotting factor VIII	Treatment of hemophilia
Growth hormone	Promotion of growth
Insulin	Treatment of diabetes
Interleukins	Treatment of tumors and immune disorders
Somatostatin	Treatment of acromegaly
Streptokinase	Anticoagulant
Tumor necrosis factor	Cancer treatment
DNase	Cystic fibrosis treatment

GENE THERAPY

One of the dreams of medical geneticists—to cure genetic defects—may soon become a reality. The basis of this technique is that one can insert into the host chromosome a functional gene that corrects a genetic defect. At present the only human tissues that can be used for gene transfer are bone marrow cells and skin cells (somatic cells). These cell types can be extracted from the body, grown in culture, and reimplanted into the patient. Functional genes can be transferred efficiently to cells if they are part of a virus. Recently, an individual lacking adenosine deaminase, the enzyme that destroys toxic metabolic by-products, was treated with gene therapy. The procedure is carried out as follows:

1. The functional gene is inserted into the genome of a **retrovirus.** The virus is allowed to replicate.
2. Defective bone marrow cells are removed from the patient and infected with virus containing the functional gene. The functional gene recombines with the chromosome of the defective cell.
3. The repaired bone marrow cells are reinfused into the patient. Since most of the bone marrow cells will differentiate into red blood cells, lymphocytes, and so on, these descendants also will possess the functional gene.

To date this technique is suitable for diseases in which the defect is in the patient's bone marrow, for example, a disorder in which there is a missing enzyme or protein. However, use of gene therapy presents new ethical issues. If gene therapy can be applied to somatic cells, can and should it be applied to germ (sex) cells? Will society allow manipulation of sex cells, permitting the "new" gene to be passed on to the patient's children? The technology that will bring this issue to the forefront is not far off.

Summary

1. The discovery of restriction endonucleases led to the development of genetic engineering. Genetic engineering is a technology that removes genes from a variety of sources and clones them in a microbial host.
2. The basic approach in genetic engineering is to remove DNA from any source and join it to a vector DNA molecule capable of (a) replication, (b) introduction into a host cell, and (3) possession of a recognizable trait. The resulting hybrid is called a recombinant DNA molecule.
3. Once recombinant DNA has been produced, it is used to transform host cells, usually *E. coli*. As the host cell divides, it acts as a natural amplification machine; that is, recombinant DNA becomes cloned.
4. Selection of the recombinant DNA clone is accomplished by using a vector that possesses a recognizable trait such as antibiotic resistance or sensitivity. Identifying

the clone containing the desired gene is achieved by nucleic acid hybridization.

5. Expression of eukaryotic genes in a prokaryotic host requires some modifications. Specific transcription and translation signals can be fused to the vector before the transformation process occurs.

6. An important development in biotechnology has been the technique called the polymerase chain reaction. The value of this technique is that it permits rapid amplification of DNA sequences without the use of culture.

7. Genetic engineering has been applied to the medical field in areas such as vaccine development, drug production, and gene therapy. The advantage of this technique is that large amounts of a product, whose gene may be in a plant or animal, can be manufactured in a microbial cell.

Questions for Study

1. What is the most important characteristic of plasmid pBR322 as a vector in recombinant DNA technology?
2. What is the purpose of calcium chloride in the cloning transformation process?
3. What is the role of DNA ligase in producing recombinant DNA?
4. Assume you are using pBR322 as a vector, and a restriction enzyme that inserts into the gene coding for tetracycline resistance. Outline the technique for isolating the recombinant clone.
5. Utilizing some of the references listed under Additional Readings, describe the procedure for isolating recombinant clones using bacteriophage as a vector.
6. Describe how the Southern blotting technique is used to isolate a particular gene from a complex mixture of DNA (see Additional Readings).
7. Outline the necessary steps in cloning a prokaryotic gene in a yeast cell. What are some of the problems? (See Additional Readings.)

PART

II Control of Microorganisms

CHAPTER

7 Sterilization and Disinfection

OBJECTIVES

To define the commonly used sterilization and disinfection terms and use them in specific contexts, and especially to differentiate between antisepsis and disinfection

To appraise conditions or factors that affect sterilization and disinfection procedures and agents

To name the commonly used modes of attaining sterility; to point out the advantages and the limitations of each; and for each mode, to state the minimum conditions that must be applied to ensure sterility

To give the mechanisms of action, the good and bad features, and the typical applications for moist and dry heat, filtration, ultrasound, and radiation as they pertain to the control of microorganisms

To comment on sterilization indicators, specifically their composition, rationale for use, interpretation of readouts, and reliability

To give the good and bad features and the typical applications of representative disinfectants from each of the major chemical disinfectant groups, specifically hexachlorophene, 70% alcohol, bleach, tincture of iodine, iodophors, glutaraldehyde, and chlorhexidine

OUTLINE

TERMINOLOGY
GENERAL CONSIDERATIONS
- Problem Microorganisms
  - Bacterial Endospores
  - Mycobacteria
  - Hepatitis Viruses and Human Immunodeficiency Virus
  - *Pseudomonas* Species
- Interfering Matter
- No Universal Method
- Principal Modes of Achieving Sterility

PHYSICAL METHODS
- Heat
  - Rate of Thermal Death Determination
  - Moist Heat
    - Boiling
    - Steam at Atmospheric Pressure
    - Steam Under Pressure—Autoclaving
    - Sterilization Indicators
    - Pasteurization
  - Dry Heat
    - Dry Heat Sterilization
    - Incineration
- Filtration
- Ultrasonic Cleaners
- Radiation
  - Ultraviolet Radiation
  - Ionizing Radiation

CHEMICAL METHODS
- Qualities of a Universal Disinfectant
- Classes of Disinfectants
  - Phenol and Phenolics
  - Alcohols
  - Halogens
    - Chlorine
    - Iodine
  - Surfactants
    - Soaps
    - Detergents
  - Alkylating Agents
    - Formaldehyde
    - Glutaraldehyde
    - Ethylene Oxide

OUTLINE *(continued)*

Heavy Metals
Chlorhexidine
DISINFECTION OF CRITICAL INSTRUMENTS
Arthroscopes and Laparoscopes
Cardiac Catheters
Hemodialyzers
DISINFECTION OF SEMICRITICAL INSTRUMENTS
DISINFECTION OF NONCRITICAL ITEMS
PRACTICAL RECOMMENDATIONS

Infectious disease agents are controlled in four ways: by public sanitation measures, by sterilization and disinfection procedures, by chemotherapeutic agents, and by the body's defensive mechanisms. This chapter is concerned with sterilization and disinfection procedures that are used to destroy microorganisms before they enter the body.

Terminology

Sterilization and disinfection terms are given in Table 7-1. Additional explanatory comments follow.

Sterility indicates freedom from viable forms of microorganisms. It is an absolute state—there are no degrees of sterility. Either an object is sterile or it is not. There may be billions of killed bacteria present, as in some vaccines, but if not a single viable bacterium is present, the preparation is sterile. A preparation may be sterile and yet be harmful because of the presence of microbial products. Injection fluids, for example, may be sterile but contain fever- or shock-inducing molecules (endotoxins) that are derived from microorganisms.

The breakdown of living tissue by the action of microorganisms is known as **sepsis.** It is accompanied by an acute inflammatory reaction. Pus formation is a prominent feature of bacterial sepsis. Toxic microbial products may contribute to the septic process. The host has an intense, overwhelming infection, toxemia, or both when sepsis exists.

TABLE 7-1
Sterilization and Disinfection Terminology

	Noun				
Process	**Agent**	**State or condition**	**Verb**	**Adjective**	**Action, agent, or state**
Sterilization	Sterilant (if a chemical)	Sterility	Sterilize	Sterile, sterilized	Completely destroys or removes all microorganisms; renders treated microorganisms permanently incapable of reproducing
	-cide			-cidal	Kills the form of microorganism named in the prefix: bactericide, sporicide, tuberculocide, fungicide, etc.
	-stat	-stasis		-static	Prevents multiplication of the type of microorganism named in the prefix without necessarily killing it: bacteriostat, fungistat, etc.
		Asepsis		Aseptic	"Without sepsis": the absence or the exclusion of sepsis
	Antiseptic	Antisepsis	Antisepticize		"Against sepsis": the application of nonchemotherapeutic agents to living tissue with the objective of at least preventing the multiplication of pathogenic microorganisms (does not ordinarily include spores)
Disinfection	Disinfectant		Disinfect	Disinfected	Prevents infection: carried out with chemical agents (disinfectants) or by physical means (e.g., boiling, pasteurization) on inanimate objects with the objective of at least killing (with the exception of spores) all harmful forms (e.g., pathogens)
	Germicide			Germicidal	Kills all types of microorganisms but not spores necessarily; used on body surfaces and on inanimate objects
Degermination			Degerm		Removes microorganisms, especially transients on the skin, by chemical (antiseptics/soaps) and mechanical (scrubbing) means
Sanitization			Sanitize		Reduces the number of microorganisms on inanimate objects (tableware, garments) to a safe level as judged by public health standards

Disinfection at the very least destroys harmful (pathogenic) microorganisms that are in the vegetative state. The target microorganisms in the health fields, for example, are the microorganisms that can cause infection. A disinfected object should not be expected to be sterile; it may harbor viable nonpathogens and spores of pathogens. According to the strict interpretation of the term, **disinfection is carried out on inanimate objects,** not on living tissue.

General Considerations

PROBLEM MICROORGANISMS

The specific population of microorganisms on or within a component to be sterilized or disinfected is not usually known. Therefore, the assumption is made that the most resistant microbial forms—bacterial endospores—are present.

Bacterial Endospores

Bacterial endospores are the most resistant form of microbial life. Some spores withstand as much as 16 hours of boiling. A procedure must be sporicidal if sterility is to be established.

Mycobacteria

The mycobacteria, of which the bacterium causing tuberculosis is the most important, are noted for their resistance to disinfectants. The mycobacterial cell surface is rich in wax-like lipids. Mycobacteria, however, are as sensitive to heat as most other bacteria.

Hepatitis Viruses and Human Immunodeficiency Virus

The hepatitis B virus (HBV) and hepatitis C virus (HCV) are problem agents. They are difficult to control because of the situations in which transmission most frequently occurs (sexual transmission and contact with blood or blood products). The viruses are not cultivatable and there is no easy way to check the effects of disinfectants. Blood is also the single most important source of the human immunodeficiency virus (HIV). Precautions against HIV infection are the same as those for the hepatitis viruses (see Chapter 32 for a discussion of precautions by health care workers).

Pseudomonas Species

Species of *Pseudomonas* are problems for hospitalized patients who are compromised by underlying conditions or diseases. These organisms are able to proliferate in distilled and deionized water. In addition, they produce a slime that is a barrier to disinfectants. See Chapter 22 for a more detailed discussion of *Pseudomonas.*

INTERFERING MATTER

Organic material such as pus, blood, saliva, urine, and feces can harbor microorganisms and protect them from disinfection. The hepatitis viruses are particularly resistant to disinfectants when they are present in organic matter such as dried blood. Before disinfecting reusable instruments, for example, it is necessary to remove the interfering material.

NO UNIVERSAL METHOD

No given sterilization or disinfection procedure is applicable to every situation. The biological or physical nature of the object being treated differs from one situation to another. These differences dictate the mode of treatment to be employed. **Heat** is the surest, most practical, and most widely used means to control microorganisms. In some situations, however, heat is not appropriate because of the thermolability or thermosensitivity of the object being treated. Treatment of an instrument will surely differ from treatment of the oral mucosa.

PRINCIPAL MODES OF ACHIEVING STERILITY

The routinely used methods for obtaining sterility are **autoclaving** with saturated steam under pressure, **elevated dry heat** (hot air), and gassing with **ethylene oxide** (ETO). This is not to say that other devices or chemical agents do not produce sterility.

Physical Methods

HEAT

Rate of Thermal Death Determination

It is useful to determine the heat susceptibility of a given microorganism so the extent of treatment to be applied in a given situation is understood. Establishing the rate of kill lends the element of predictability to the heating process. The rate can be determined from the **decimal reduction time (D value).** The D time is the time in minutes required to kill 90 percent (1 log unit) of the population at a given temperature. When plotted, the D time values usually exhibit a straight line (Fig. 7-1). Thus, if 90 percent of the population dies in 1 minute, then 90 percent of the remaining 10 percent dies in the next minute, 90 percent of the remaining 1 percent dies in the next minute, and so on.

Moist Heat

Most mesophilic bacteria in the vegetative form are killed by moist heat at a temperature of 60 C applied for 30 minutes. Vegetative forms of bacteria, yeasts, and molds are killed in 5 to 10 minutes at 80 C. Mold spores require 30 minutes at 80 C. The heat resistance of most viruses is similar to that of the vegetative forms of other microorganisms. Bacterial spores have a much greater thermoresistance than do vegetative forms. Therefore, a moist heat temperature of at least 121 C is applied for at least 15 minutes to destroy the most resistant of spores.

The mode of action of moist heat is generally stated to be via the coagulation of proteins. Thermal death, however, probably results from more subtle changes such as

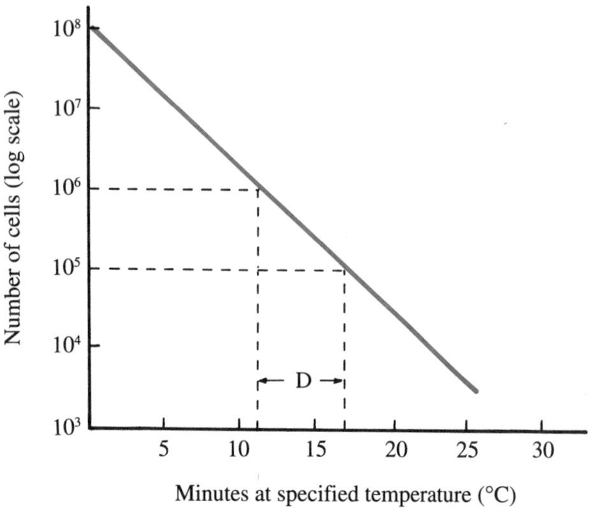

FIGURE 7-1
Determination of decimal reduction time (D). A sample of cells, for example, 1×10^7 cells per milliliter, is exposed to a given temperature over a specified period of time. At various times (minutes) the culture is measured for the number of microorganisms that have been killed. The data are plotted and a straight line is obtained. By drawing lines from the ordinate corresponding to 1 log unit (between 10^5 and 10^6 in the example) to the curve and then extrapolating to the abscissa, the decimal reduction time can be determined. In the above example, D is approximately 5 minutes; that is, it takes 5 minutes to reduce the population by a factor of 10. Theoretically, the population is reduced by a factor of 10 every 5 minutes.

inactivation of enzymes, changes in nucleic acid(s), and cytoplasmic membrane changes.

Boiling. Boiling is not reliably sporicidal and so it cannot be relied on to achieve sterility within a practical period. It is, however, an efficient means of physical disinfection. Vegetative forms of infectious agents are readily killed by boiling in a matter of minutes.

Steam at Atmospheric Pressure. Steam contains latent heat that is generated during vaporization. The latent heat is released when steam condenses on a colder surface. The condensation releases not only heat but also moisture, which is necessary for protein coagulation to occur. The shrinking in volume of the steam during condensation creates a negative pressure, thereby drawing in more steam. As the heated object reaches the temperature of the steam, condensed water returns to the vapor phase. Steam under pressure is used in the process of autoclaving.

Steam Under Pressure—Autoclaving. Moist heat at a temperature of 121 C applied for 15 minutes is known to kill the spores of virtually every species. To obtain a moist heat temperature of 121 C, saturated steam is placed under pressure of 15 pounds per square inch (psi). The pressure as such has no deleterious effect on microorganisms, but is needed to raise the moist heat temperature to 121 C. The value generally quoted for achieving sterility by using steam under pressure is 15 psi (121 C) applied for 15 minutes. The values change according to time-temperature relationships (Table 7-2). As the temperature is raised (via a rise in pressure), the required time of exposure diminishes. Thus, at 20 psi, the temperature becomes 126 C and the sterilization time is 10 minutes.

Moist heat sterilization ordinarily is performed in a sealed chamber called an **autoclave.** It is the preferred method of sterilization when it is applicable. To request that something be autoclaved is tantamount to requesting it be sterilized. The home pressure cooker in essence is an autoclave but it lacks the double-walled construction and the control devices of commercial autoclaves.

Sterilization Indicators. Since saturated steam autoclaving is the principal mode of achieving sterility, at this junction it is fitting to describe sterilization indicators. The two likely causes of sterilization failures are malfunctioning equipment and inadequate treatment. Loads differ in size and nature (e.g., hard-surfaced objects vs. absorbent items), and these in turn affect the length of time that is required to attain sterilizing conditions.

The commonly used indicators and checks are chemicals that undergo a color change and cultures testing for spores of selected bacterial species. The chemical indicators that exhibit a color change have the chemical imprinted on tapes and wrappers for surface exposure indication and on tabs that are used for insertion into the interior of items. The chemical color change indicators offer the advantage of immediate readout, and they bear the evidence of exposure directly on the exposed article. They are not accurate indicators of sterilization but they are useful for evaluating that the proper temperature has been attained.

The culture test (biological monitor) is regarded as the

TABLE 7-2
Minimum Sterilization Exposure Period—Wrapped and Unwrapped Goods, Gravity Cycle Only

	Autoclave setting	
Items	**(121°C) (250°F) (minutes)**	**(132°C) (270°F) (minutes)**
Dressings, wrapped in muslin or equivalent	30	15
Glassware, empty, inverted	15	3
Instruments, metal only, any number (unwrapped)	15	3
Instruments, metal, combined with suture, tubing, or other porous materials (unwrapped)	20	10
Instruments, wrapped in double-thickness muslin or equivalent	30	15
Linen packs (maximal size 12″ × 12″, maximal weight 12 pounds)	30	—
Treatment trays, wrapped in muslin or equivalent	30	15
Utensils, unwrapped	15	3
Utensils, wrapped in muslin or equivalent	30	15

SOURCE: Courtesy of American Sterilizer Co., Erie, PA.

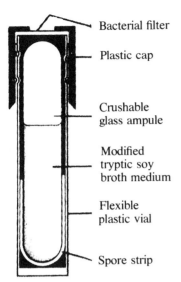

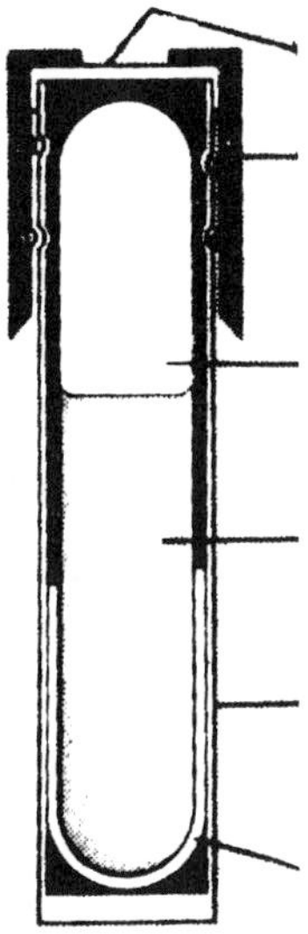

FIGURE 7-2
Biological sterilization indicator. The capsule contains a strip impregnated with bacterial spores, a pH indicator, and culture medium in a crushable ampule. After removal from the sterilizer, the ampule is crushed, releasing the culture medium onto the spore strip. A yellow color after incubation indicates incomplete sterilization. (The capsule is part of the ATTEST system manufactured by the 3M Co., St. Paul, MN.)

most reliable of the sterilization indicators. The major disadvantage is the requirement for an incubation period. The spores of several species of bacteria with known thermoresistance or a known resistance to ETO are commercially available in ampules or impregnated in filter paper strips (Fig. 7-2). The species whose spores are commonly used are *Bacillus stearothermophilus* for moist heat, *Bacillus subtilis* var *globigii* for ETO, and *B. subtilis* var *niger* for dry heat. The Joint Commission on Accreditation of Hospitals and the Communicable Disease Center recommend that steam autoclave and ETO sterilizers be tested at least once a week with appropriate spore indicators.

Pasteurization. Pasteurization utilizes mild heat to destroy pathogenic vegetative forms in liquids without altering the liquid's palatability. The pasteurization of milk, for example, is expected to kill vegetative pathogens that are derived from infected cattle and from human environmental contamination. Infectious diseases associated with the transmission of raw milk include tuberculosis, brucellosis, streptococcal and *Campylobacter* infections, typhoid fever, dysentery, diphtheria, and Q fever.

There are two pasteurization techniques. In the **holding** or **batch method,** milk in vessels is pasteurized at a temperature of 62.0 C for 30 minutes. In the **flash method** or **continuous flow method,** thin films of milk stream over pipes or plates that are held at 71.7 C. An exposure time of only 15 seconds is required to pasteurize with the flash method.

Dry Heat

Biomolecules exhibit less thermosensitivity to dry heat than to moist heat. Damaging alterations of proteins by dry heat are the result of oxidation, desiccation, and changes in osmotic pressure. Dry heat is slower and requires temperatures higher than those used in moist heat sterilization.

Dry Heat Sterilization. Dry heat is customarily used at 160 C for at least 2 hours or 170 C for at least 1 hour. Dry heat temperatures below 140 C do not destroy spores within a reasonable time period. Mechanically convected ovens are used to provide evenly distributed heat. Dry heat is the method of choice for sterilizing powders, oils, and thermostable materials that are adversely affected by moisture.

Incineration. Discardable, combustible items such as masks, gloves, and wipes that are soiled with blood or body fluids should be disposed of in sturdy, impervious bags. Flaming is a convenient way to kill microorganisms or to sterilize inexpensive heat-tolerant implements.

FILTRATION

Several porous materials are used to remove microorganisms from liquids and from the air. There are many applications of filters in microbiology: sterilization of liquids and air; separation of microorganisms of different sizes; preparation of cell-free solutions of toxins, antigens, and so on; and determination of virus size.

Membrane filters are the principal filters used in laboratories today. Membrane filters are paper-thin, sieve-like elements composed of inert cellulose esters and other polymeric materials. The size of the pores is comparatively uniform in any one filter, and the flow rate is much superior to that of depth filters because of the numerous pore openings. The pores range in size from those that retain the smallest viruses to those that retain only some of the larger protein molecules (Fig. 7-3). Some filters can be made transparent so the materials collected on the surface can be stained and examined under the microscope. Body fluids such as urine can be run through a filter and then aseptically placed on an agar medium. Organisms present in the fluid grow on the filter surface and can be counted.

A popular application of filters is in air control systems for removing particles, including microorganisms. **High-efficiency particulate air filters (HEPA filters)** remove particles as small as 0.3 μm with 99.97 percent efficiency. They are used in "clean room" installations and in biohazard hoods.

ULTRASONIC CLEANERS

High-frequency sound waves, above the human auditory level, have applications in the health-related fields. They are used primarily as a **presterilization mode** to remove interfering matter. They can remove blood, pus, and other organic soil from instruments and glassware before the sterilization procedure commences.

$1\ \mu m = 1\ \text{micrometer} = \frac{1}{1,000,000}\ \text{meter}$

$1\ \mu m = 3.937 \times 10^{-5}\ \text{inch}$

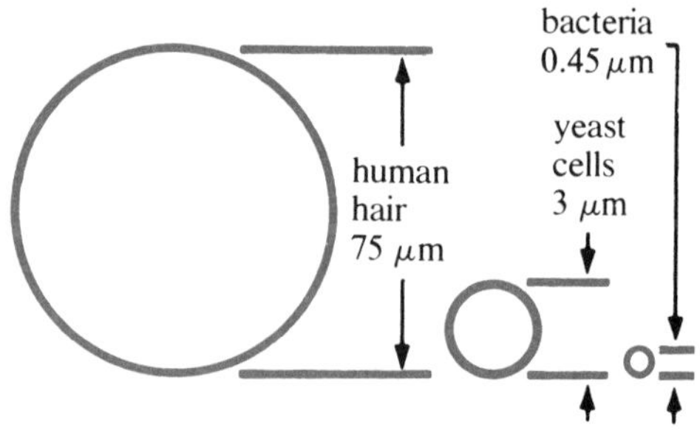

Pore Size Reference Guide

0.2 µm	will retain all bacteria
0.45 µm	will retain all coliform groups
0.8 µm	will retain airborne particles for analysis
1.2 µm	will retain all nonliving particles considered dangerous in fluids intravenously administered
5 µm	will retain all significant cells from body fluids for analysis

FIGURE 7-3
Reference guide to pore size of membrane filters. (Courtesy of Gelman Sciences, Inc., Ann Arbor, MI.)

RADIATION

Ultraviolet Radiation

The practical application of ultraviolet (UV) radiation in the control of microorganisms is primarily to reduce the population of microorganisms in the air. UV lamps are referred to as **germicidal lamps.** Most germicidal lamps are low-pressure mercury-vapor lamps that generate UV rays with a predominant wavelength of 2537 Å.

There are UV barrier installations by which incoming ducted air of buildings is irradiated with germicidal lamps. The air and surfaces of hospital rooms, operating rooms, entryways, nurseries, gymnasiums, and cafeterias can be irradiated by louvered or shielded ceiling fixtures. The fixtures are designed so the UV energy is reflected through a maximum distance without striking the occupants of the room. Warmed air normally rises to the ceiling, carrying with it the microorganism-bearing droplet nuclei (minute particles of mucus that are aerosolized during talking, sneezing, and coughing; see also Chapter 15).

There are two major drawbacks associated with UV irradiation when it is used in the control of microorganisms. UV rays have low penetrability. Organisms must be directly exposed to the incident rays. Organisms within solids or those shielded by any covering remain unaffected by UV. Precautions must be taken to avoid prolonged exposure of humans to intense UV radiation. Overexposure to UV lamp irradiation causes skin erythema and conjunctivitis.

Ionizing Radiation

Electromagnetic rays have profound effects when they are directed at microorganisms. Short-wavelength electromagnetic rays include x-rays, which are produced by electron accelerators, and gamma rays, which are produced by decay of radioactive substances.

Ionizing radiation, when used for sterilizing, offers the advantage of avoiding both heat and moisture (gamma rays can penetrate 2 feet of water), and allows prepackaging and sealing of items to be sterilized. Ionizing radiation is especially useful for sterilizing pharmaceuticals and disposable medical supplies such as syringes and catheters. The disadvantages are the expensive equipment and the safety measures required, and the effects on materials. For example, fabrics can lose their tensile strength after radiation.

Chemical Methods

Chemical agents used for the control of microorganisms on body surfaces and on inanimate objects are grouped under the general heading of disinfectants or germicides. In certain contexts, the word **disinfectant** or **germicide** represents all the chemical agents that are used in sterilization and disinfection.

There are several situations in which it is not possible to achieve sterility or in which sterility is not necessary. In many instances all that is needed is to reduce the population of microorganisms to a safe level or to rid an object of habitually pathogenic vegetative forms.

Sterility can be attained with chemicals when they are used under prescribed conditions. Such chemicals are referred to as **chemosterilizers** or **sterilants.** They include **ethylene oxide (ETO), betapropiolactone,** some **phenolics** and **halogens, strong acids** and **alkalis, formaldehyde** and **glutaraldehyde,** and **peracids.** Situations in which chemosterilizers apply (with the exception of ETO) are limited.

QUALITIES OF A UNIVERSAL DISINFECTANT

Just as no single physical method is applicable to every sterilization or disinfection problem, no one chemical agent can contend with the many variables that are part of differing control problems. An ideal disinfectant would have the following qualities:

1. It would be able to destroy all forms of microorganisms, including bacterial spores, within a practical period.
2. Soil would not interfere with its actions.

TABLE 7-3
Disinfectants and Antiseptics[a]

Class	Disinfectant[b]	Antiseptic	Other properties
Gas			
Ethylene oxide	+2 to +4	0	Toxic; good penetration; requires relative humidity of 30% or more; bactericidal activity varies with apparatus used; absorbed by porous materials. Dry spores highly resistant; moisture must be present, and presoaking is desirable.
Liquid			
Glutaraldehyde, aqueous	+3	0	Sporicidal; active solution unstable; toxic.
Formaldehyde + alcohol	+2	0	Sporicidal; noxious fumes; toxic; volatile.
Formaldehyde, aqueous	+1 to +2	0	Sporicidal; noxious fumes; toxic.
Phenolic compounds	+3	±	Stable; corrosive; little inactivation by organic matter; irritate skin.
Chlorine	+1	±	Flash action; much inactivation by organic matter; corrosive; irritate skin.
Alcohol	+2	+3	Rapidly -cidal; volatile; flammable; dries and irritates skin.
Iodine + alcohol	0	+4	Corrosive; very rapidly -cidal; causes staining; irritates skin; flammable.
Iodophors	+1	+3	Somewhat unstable; relatively bland; staining temporary; corrosive.
Iodine, aqueous	0	+2	Rapidly -cidal; corrosive; stains fabrics; stains and irritates skin.
Quaternary ammonium compounds	+1	+2	Bland; inactivated by soap and anionics; absorbed by fabrics.
Hexachlorophene	0	+2	Bland; insoluble in water, soluble in alcohol; not inactivated by soap; weakly -cidal.
Mercurial compounds	0	+1	Bland; much inactivated by organic matter; weakly -cidal.

± = some compounds may or may not be effective antiseptics.
[a] More detailed information must be obtained from descriptive brochures, journal articles, and books. Selection of the most appropriate germicide should be based on whether it is to be used as a disinfectant or as an antiseptic and on the estimated level of antimicrobial action needed.
[b] Maximal usefulness is denoted by +4.
SOURCE: From E. H. Spaulding, *Manual of Clinical Microbiology*, 2nd ed. Washington, D.C.: American Society for Microbiology, 1974.

3. It would be nonirritating, nonallergenic, and nontoxic.
4. It would be noncorrosive and nondiscoloring, and would not leave unsightly residues on objects.
5. It would demonstrate wettability and penetrability.
6. It would be soluble in water.
7. It would be chemically stable.
8. Dilution would not adversely affect its activity.
9. It would not have a disagreeable odor or be expensive.

No disinfectant meets all these qualifications. Disinfectants must be chosen on the basis of their intrinsic properties and on the basis of the job at hand (Table 7-3).

CLASSES OF DISINFECTANTS

Phenol and Phenolics

Phenol, formerly called carbolic acid, figured in a medical classic. Lister used sprays of phenol to lessen infection rates in patients undergoing surgery. Today dilutions of pure phenol are not used as antiseptics because of phenol's irritant and anesthetizing qualities.

Phenol is the parent compound of many disinfectants referred to as phenolics (Fig. 7-4). Since phenol and phenolics are among the more active compounds in the presence of organic matter, they are suitable agents for disinfecting saliva, feces, and similar matter. They are stable

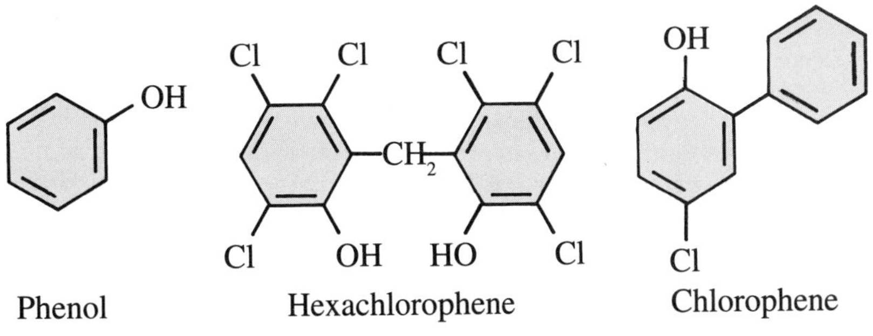

FIGURE 7-4
Phenol and two phenol-related compounds.

and persist on surfaces for long periods of time after application. Dried residues become active when rehydrated. Thus, they have a combination of desirable features that many other disinfectants lack and they are tuberculocidal.

Hexachlorophene is a bisphenol, that is, two molecules of phenol joined (see Fig. 7-4), that is absorbed through the intact skin. At one time hexachlorophene was especially valuable in controlling hospital nursery staphylococcal infections. However, since 1972 its usage has changed. Studies of newborn infants who received three or more daily baths in 3% hexachlorophene for more than 3 days revealed that brain damage developed in some premature infants. Hexachlorophene is now restricted to prescription use. It is not to be used in hospital nurseries unless a staphylococcal epidemic is flourishing.

Other effective phenol-related compounds are chlorophene (see Fig. 7-4) and orthophenylphenols. Cresols and xylenols are phenolic-related compounds that are coal tar derivatives. They are used for sanitation.

Alcohols

Alcohols are bactericidal, tuberculocidal, and fungicidal but not sporicidal. Enveloped viruses are susceptible to the alcohols because the latter strip away the lipid components. The mode of action of alcohols is primarily that of denaturation of proteins. Ethyl and isopropyl alcohols are the only alcohols that are extensively used. The recommended concentration is 70% even though concentrations from 60 to 95% seem to kill as fast. In recent studies ethyl alcohol was shown to have consistently high antimicrobial activity on environmental surfaces regardless of the test method, test organism, or contact time. The major disadvantage is that if the effective concentration is bypassed by dilution, the antimicrobial activity is slow and uncertain.

Halogens

Most disinfectants categorized as halogens are inorganic halogen compounds. The mode of action is oxidation and halogenation of proteins. The commonly used halogens are **chlorine** and **iodine.** All halogens, especially chlorine, are important as components in other disinfectants.

Chlorine. Elemental chlorine and inorganic chlorine compounds are employed principally for sanitation, purification, and disinfection. Elemental chlorine is used for water purification. **Hypochlorites** and other chlorine-releasing compounds serve as bleaching agents and as sanitizing agents in dairies, abattoirs, and swimming pools, and for housekeeping. Organic matter interferes with the antimicrobial activity of the chlorine compounds to a considerable extent. Household bleach is an effective germicide. The active ingredient is **sodium hypochlorite ($NaOCl$)** at 5.25% concentration. It is diluted 1 : 10 to 1 : 100, depending on the amount of organic matter present on the surface to be disinfected. It is corrosive to some metals, especially aluminum. Dilutions should be prepared fresh daily.

Iodine. Iodine compounds currently are the most popular for wound and skin antisepsis and for preoperative skin antisepsis. They also are used as general disinfectants for thermometers and surgical appliances and for purification of water. They are bactericidal and sporicidal.

Molecular iodine is not readily soluble in aqueous solution. Therefore it usually is dissolved in alcohol to provide **tinctures.** The ready evaporation of alcohol creates problems because strong iodine concentrations can cause tissue necrosis. Tinctures of iodine formulations contain differing percentages of iodine and of alcohol; 1, 5, and 7% tincture formulations destroy 90 percent of skin bacteria in 90, 60, and 15 seconds, respectively.

The disadvantages of the tinctures were overcome by the development of a group of compounds called **iodophors.** Iodophors consist of elemental iodine solubilized by carriers such as nonionic surfactants and povidone and polyethylene glycols. The carriers increase solubility and provide a sustained-release reservoir of iodine. Iodophor activities are not as great as the tinctures but they do not stain and are nontoxic. Some proprietary iodophors include Wescodyne, Betadine, Prepodyne, and Surgidine.

Surfactants

Surfactants are surface-active agents that have the property of concentrating at interfaces. They lower surface tension. They are good solubilizing and wetting agents. Surfactants include the soaps and detergents.

Soaps. Cosmetic soaps are usually sodium and potassium salts of long-chain fatty acids. They are invaluable in controlling microorganisms, even though many of them have no direct antimicrobial activity. Their usefulness resides in their ability to degerm the skin by mechanically removing microorganisms. They emulsify the oily layer of the skin, where most of the transient and cross-infecting microorganisms are enmeshed. The lipid layer with its contents of microorganisms is broken up and vanishes down the drain in the rinse water. In addition to the emulsifying and degerming action, about 50 percent of the cosmetic soaps are designed to have some direct antimicrobial activity. They contain a bacteriostatic or bactericidal compound that potentially reduces cross contamination, body odor, and superficial cutaneous infections.

Detergents. Detergents are synthetic surfactant cleansing agents. They are regarded as superior to the soaps as cleansing agents because they do not form precipitates and deposits with water minerals as soaps do. They are divided into the **anionic, cationic,** and **nonionic** detergents on the basis of the polarity and activity of their polar groups.

Anionic detergents are used in laundry powders and liquids. They are not disinfectants. Like soaps they remove microbial contaminants with the grime and dirt of soiled articles.

Members of the **cationic detergent** group have been among the most popular disinfectants, antiseptics, and sanitizers. The lipid-containing negatively charged membrane of the bacterial cell attracts the positively charged components of the lipophilic alkyl chain portion of the cationic detergent molecule. The lethal action of cationic

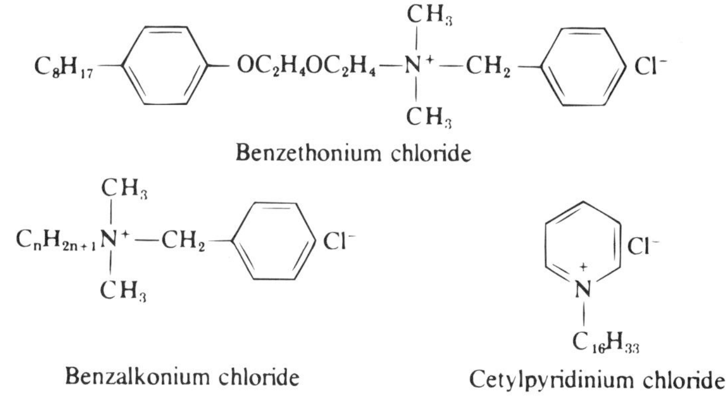

FIGURE 7-5
Three popular cationic detergents.

detergents is primarily ascribed to cell membrane disruption. Enveloped viruses are also inactivated by cationic detergents.

Only three main types of cationic detergents are popularly used as antimicrobial agents: **benzalkonium chloride (Zephiran), benzethonium chloride (Phemerol),** and **cetylpyridinium chloride (Ceepryn)** (Fig. 7-5).

Cationic detergents are bland (colorless, tasteless, odorless), very stable, nontoxic, and inexpensive, and remain active at high dilutions. These good qualities have to be weighed against several shortcomings. They are not sporicidal or tuberculocidal. *Pseudomonas* organisms appear to be refractory to them at low concentrations. Cationic detergents are readily absorbed by surfaces such as gauze and cotton, which are sometimes used to cushion instruments being decontaminated or being kept sterile in disinfectant solutions. Organic matter interferes with their action. They are readily neutralized by soaps and anionic detergents. If soap is used to remove gross contamination or soil from the skin or from an object, follow-up use with a cationic detergent may be self-defeating and deceiving if a soap residue remains. The cationic detergent loses its antimicrobial activity because it chemically interacts with the soap.

Nonionic detergents have no antimicrobial properties.

Alkylating Agents

Alkylating agents exert their antimicrobial effects by substituting alkyl groups for the hydrogen of reactive groups of enzymes, nucleic acids, and proteins. Labile reactive hydrogens are available on carboxyl (—COOH) groups, sulfhydryl (—SH) groups, amino (—NH_2) groups, and hydroxyl (—OH) groups. Some of the alkylating agents are used in the gaseous phase or vapor phase, some as liquids, and some in either the gaseous or the liquid state.

Formaldehyde. Formaldehyde is sometimes employed in the gaseous state as a fumigant. In solution as **formalin,** it is known for its uses as a fixative for anatomical and pathological tissue specimens, as an inactivator in vaccines, and as a component of embalming fluids. Sterilization and disinfection applications are limited because it is a tissue irritant.

Glutaraldehyde. A chemical relative of formaldehyde, glutaraldehyde has two reactive aldehyde groups (Fig. 7-6). It is highly rated as a disinfectant and has a wide spectrum of activity. When used in a 2% solution, it is bactericidal, tuberculocidal, and virucidal in 10 to 90 minutes and sporicidal in 10 hours. Glutaraldehyde disinfectants along with iodine compounds and bleach are recommended for use against hepatitis viruses when sterilization is not feasible. Since glutaraldehyde is irritating to the skin and mucous membranes and very irritating to the eyes, it is not used as an antiseptic. Commercially available glutaraldehyde preparations include Cidex, Sporicidin, Glutarex, and Banacide.

Ethylene Oxide. The gas ETO is a cyclic ether (see Fig. 7-6). The major advantage of this penetrative gas is that it can sterilize without high levels of heat or moisture. A wide range of articles that are affected by elevated heat are sterilized with ETO: catheters, disposable medical items, dental handpieces, sutures, and heart-lung machines.

ETO forms explosive mixtures with air. Therefore, it is diluted with inert gases such as carbon dioxide, nitrogen, and halogenated hydrocarbons. ETO is toxic if inhaled, and it is a vesicant (it can cause blisters) on contact. It is slow-acting, requiring 4 hours at 50 to 56 C or 6 to 12 hours at room temperature to produce sterility. Special equipment is necessary. Many hospitals now have ETO

FIGURE 7-6
Alkylating agents.

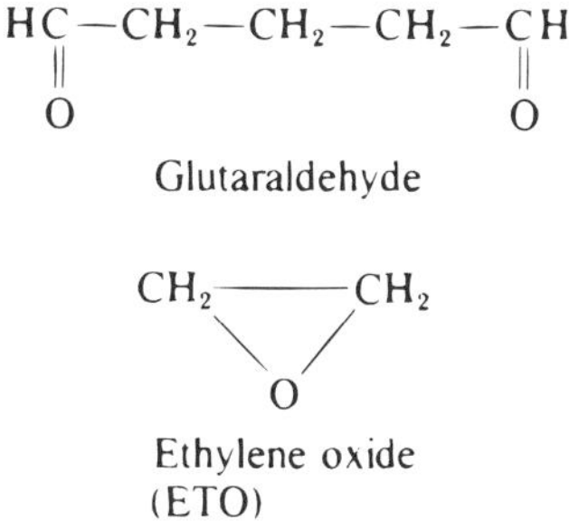

autoclaves as part of their standard sterilizing equipment. Items treated with ETO that are to be used in patient contact must first be aerated to remove residual ETO.

Heavy Metals

Most of the heavy-metal disinfectants contain **mercury** or **silver.** Metal-containing disinfectants have been largely replaced by more effective compounds. Organomercurial antiseptics have been superseded by iodine compounds, cationic detergent formulations, and alcohol. The one silver compound to be noted is **silver nitrate.** It is the law in most states that a 1% prophylactic silver nitrate solution or certain antibiotics be instilled into the eyes of all newborns to prevent the development of gonococcal conjunctivitis. A recent burn treatment technique also incorporates silver nitrate.

Chlorhexidine

Special mention is due an antiseptic with the generic name chlorhexidine. A 4% chlorhexidine preparation (the commercial product is called Hibiclens or Hibitane) is used for surgical scrubs, for handwashing by health care personnel, and as a skin wound cleanser. Chlorhexidine persists on the skin whereas iodophors do not; it is not appreciably absorbed into the blood from the skin as hexachlorophene is; it is generally nonirritating; and it is active against gram-positive and gram-negative bacteria.

Disinfection of Critical Instruments

Critical instruments are those that enter sterile tissue or the vascular system. These instruments include arthroscopes, laparoscopes, cardiac catheters, and hemodialyzers. Improper sterilization of these instruments has led to clusters of hospital-associated infections.

ARTHROSCOPES AND LAPAROSCOPES

Because of the heat sensitivity of these instruments, disinfection has replaced sterilization as a common reprocessing method. Recently, heat-tolerant instruments have become available and autoclaving is now possible. High-level disinfection using formaldehyde plus dimethoxytetrahydrofuran has been used with success. Many individuals, however, are sensitive to residual formaldehyde and use of this technique must be evaluated.

CARDIAC CATHETERS

Many hospitals reprocess and reuse disposable cardiac catheters. Several studies indicate that this process does not result in any unfavorable consequences. The sterilizing agent used is ETO.

HEMODIALYZERS

Disposable hemodialyzers can be reprocessed using high-level disinfection without the worry of complications. The most commonly used chemical germicides include formaldehyde, peroxyacetic acid, and glutaraldehyde. Formaldehyde in a 4% solution instead of the normal 2% solution is recommended to destroy nontuberculous mycobacteria.

Disinfection of Semicritical Instruments

Semicritical instruments are those that come in contact with mucous membranes but do not penetrate the bloodstream or invade sterile tissue. Fiberoptic endoscopes, bronchoscopes, anesthesia, and respiratory equipment are semicritical devices. Flexible endoscopes have been implicated in the transmission of a variety of microbial species including *Salmonella, Helicobacter pylori,* and *Pseudomonas aeruginosa*. Under ideal conditions the endoscope should be sterilized after use in a patient but most of the time these instruments are only disinfected. Fiberoptic endoscopes are heat-labile and cannot be autoclaved. Repeated use of ETO for sterilization results in deterioration of the endoscope. The most practical and efficient technique is to clean the instrument followed by treatment with a chemical germicide. Germicides include 2% glutaraldehyde, which can be applied to the instruments for 20 to 30 minutes.

Automated endoscope washers are extensively used; however, they have been documented in some cases to be the source of contamination. Experimental studies indicate that manual cleaning of the endoscope with a neutral detergent can reduce contamination by more than 99.97 percent. If this procedure is followed by disinfection with 2% glutaraldehyde, contamination is virtually eliminated.

Anesthesia and respiratory equipment can become vectors of infectious agents. Mechanically ventilated patients should be supplied with a decontaminated set of connecting tubes every 24 to 48 hours. A heat- and moisture-exchange filter placed near the patient's mouth can protect the ventilator circuit and keep it dry. For a discussion of the disinfection of ventilation circuits, see *AORN J.* 53: 775, 1991; *Am. J. Med.* 91:264S, 1991.

Disinfection of Noncritical Items

Noncritical items for disinfection come in contact only with the intact skin of the patient. Noncritical items include bedpans, urinals, washbowls, crutches, and so on. There are no specific guidelines for disinfection of such equipment. Bedpans, for example, may require high-level disinfection but there are no sufficient data to implicate them in microbial transmission. Nondisposable bedpans, urinals, and washbowls can be cleaned and disinfected in flushing disinfectors (see *Am. J. Med.* 91:264S, 1991; *J. Hosp. Infect.* 18:264, 1991).

Practical Recommendations

To prevent self-infection, the cross infection of patients, and contamination of the environment, it is important to keep these suggestions in mind.

1. Make liberal use of soap and water.
2. Keep immunizations current.
3. Keep contaminated fingers from the mouth.
4. Use germicides according to the manufacturer's instructions. Allow the prescribed time for them to act.
5. Be especially wary of needlestick injuries. Wear heavy-duty gloves when processing needles and sharp instruments.
6. Use the recommended barrier techniques when they are called for: face masks, disposable gloves, protective eyewear, and gowns.
7. Most important, "think through" or "see in the mind's eye," as Lister phrased it, how transmission of microorganisms might occur. Imagine the contaminating material is stained with a fluorescent, eye-catching dye. The contamination from a wound dressing might show up on the hands of the nurse, the instruments that were used to remove the dressing, the hospital bedstand, the bedclothes, the floor, the patient's gown, the nurse's clothing—anywhere in the room. With this mental picture should come the realization that every move must be made in such a manner as to provide the fewest opportunities for disseminating microorganisms. Asepsis procedures should not be performed in a haphazard manner. All efforts should be made to utilize available methods to prevent or minimize infection.

Summary

1. The terms requiring an understanding are sterile, asepsis, antisepsis, disinfection, sanitation, and germicide, and the suffixes -cide and -stasis.

2. One should always assume that highly resistant microbial forms are present when treating various objects. The level of kill in a microbial population is rarely tested. Sterilization and disinfection procedures should be carried out as prescribed.

3. The microorganisms posing special problems are bacterial endospores, mycobacteria, hepatitis viruses and human immunodeficiency virus (HIV), and *Pseudomonas* species.

4. Interfering matter, such as blood and feces, affects the activity of antimicrobial agents.

5. The principal modes of attaining sterility are autoclaving in saturated steam, use of elevated dry heat, and exposure to ethylene oxide.

6. Because sterilizing devices are subject to physical stresses and because sterilizing conditions vary, use of sterilization indicators is advised.

7. The physical methods of controlling microorganisms include boiling, saturated steam autoclaving, and pasteurization; dry heat methods such as elevated hot air and incineration; filtration; ultrasonic devices; and irradiation using ultraviolet light or ionizing radiation.

8. The major classes of disinfectants are phenol and phenolics, alcohols, halogen compounds, surfactants (soaps and detergents), alkylating agents, and heavy-metal compounds.

Questions for Study

1. Observe the medical devices, instruments, patient's clothing, and other objects in a patient's hospital room and determine which can be sterilized or disinfected and the method used.
2. What personal hygiene procedures on the part of a nurse or nursing assistant would ensure a reduction in hospital-associated infections? Explain the reasons for your suggestions.
3. Make a list of the disinfectants and antiseptics that are used in your hospital or physician's office. What is the active ingredient in each of them? Does this compare with the ingredients discussed in this chapter?
4. Are there any disinfectants that can be used as antiseptics? If so, how is this accomplished? If not, why not?
5. What is the basis for saying that soaps without an added antimicrobial agent may be as effective in preventing hospital-associated infections as those with the antimicrobial agent?
6. Examine some of the household items that are used for sanitization. What is the active ingredient in them that would be considered antimicrobial?

CHAPTER

8 Chemotherapy

OBJECTIVES

To describe the characteristics of certain drugs that make them suitable as chemotherapeutic agents

To list the major chemotherapeutic drugs that are inhibitors of cell wall synthesis, cytoplasmic membrane function, protein synthesis, nucleic acid synthesis, and cell metabolites

To describe briefly the mechanisms of action of penicillin on the cell wall

To describe the various ways in which protein synthesis can be inhibited by chemotherapeutic agents

To outline the factors that a physician must consider when deciding on a drug for chemotherapy

To describe how microorganisms are able to develop resistance to an antimicrobial

To describe what types of tests are used to measure a microorganism's susceptibility to antimicrobials

To define the terms antibiotic, chemotherapeutic agent, beta-lactamase, penicillin-binding protein, prophylaxis, antimetabolites, minimal inhibitory concentration (MIC), transposon-associated resistance, and Kirby-Bauer method

OUTLINE

GENERAL CHARACTERISTICS OF CHEMOTHERAPEUTIC AGENTS
- Antimicrobial Activity Measurement and Other Factors
- Selective Toxicity and Therapeutic Index

CHEMOTHERAPEUTIC AGENTS
- Inhibitors of Cell Wall Synthesis
  - Penicillins
    - Mechanism of Action
    - Beta-lactamases and Resistance to Penicillin
  - Cephalosporins
  - Carbapenems
  - Bacitracin
  - Vancomycin
- Inhibitors of Cytoplasmic Membrane Function
  - Polyenes
  - Azoles
  - Polymyxins
- Inhibitors of Protein Synthesis
  - Aminoglycosides
  - Tetracyclines
  - Chloramphenicol
  - Erythromycin
  - Lincomycin and Clindamycin
  - Spectinomycin
- Inhibitors of Nucleic Acid Synthesis
  - Rifampin
  - Nalidixic Acid and the Quinolones
  - Flucytosine
  - Amantadine
  - Ribavirin
  - Idoxuridine
  - Vidarabine
  - Acyclovir
  - Zidovudine
- Antimetabolites
  - Sulfonamides
  - Para-aminosalicylic Acid and the Sulfones
  - Trimethoprim
  - Ethambutol

OUTLINE *(continued)*

Isoniazid
Nitrofurans
Factors in Selecting a Drug for Chemotherapy
Dosage
Route of Administration
Drug Combinations
Prophylaxis
Toxicity
Drug Resistance
The Genetics of Drug Resistance
Mechanisms of Drug Resistance
Interference with Transport
Enzymatic Inactivation
Alteration of the Microbial Target
Synthesis of Resistant Metabolic Pathways
Quantitative and Qualitative Determination of Antibiotic Activity
Quantitative Tests
Broth Dilution Test
Agar Dilution Method
Qualitative Tests
Disk Diffusion Test
The E Test
Antibiotic Concentration in the Patient's Serum

Chemotherapeutic agents are a class of compounds used in the treatment of disease. They fall into two general categories: those produced **synthetically** by chemists and those produced biologically by microorganisms, that is, **antibiotics.** This separation is rather imprecise because scientists can also produce semisynthetic drugs. This feat is accomplished by first recovering from the microbe the chemical nucleus of the biologically active compound. Then the chemist can synthetically add various chemical groups to the nucleus to improve the drug's characteristics.

Chemists began synthesizing antimicrobial agents in the late 1800s and early 1900s. Antibiotics were not discovered until the 1930s. Antibiotics were shown to be produced in small amounts by soil bacteria and fungi. Microbiologists seized on this natural metabolic process and began manipulating the growth characteristics of microorganisms in order to increase the amount of antibiotic produced. Today the commercial production of antibiotics and other antimicrobials is on a large scale. In the United States alone, antibiotic production accounts for over 1½ billion dollars per year.

In this chapter we describe the various characteristics of antimicrobial agents and the factors that influence the choice of antimicrobials for therapy. We also discuss the mechanisms of antimicrobial resistance among microorganisms and how the clinician uses various tests to determine what antimicrobial can be used by the physician.

General Characteristics of Chemotherapeutic Agents

ANTIMICROBIAL ACTIVITY MEASUREMENT AND OTHER FACTORS

The antibiotic activity of a microbe isolated from the soil can be measured in several ways. One method is to produce a culture filtrate from the antibiotic-producing microorganism (or a synthetic agent produced in the laboratory). The test material can be put into regularly spaced holes punched into the agar, or it may be introduced into cylinders placed on the surface of an agar plate seeded with a test microorganism. Antibacterial activity is noted as a clear zone around the agar well or the cylinder (Fig. 8-1).

The potential antimicrobial is usually tested against several groups of microorganisms to determine its **spectrum of activity.** A **broad-spectrum drug** is one that has activity against gram-positive as well as gram-negative species. A **narrow-spectrum drug** affects only one group of microorganisms or perhaps only one species.

Antimicrobial activity is not the only factor that must be considered in selecting a drug for commercial use. A variety of tests must be performed to measure the following:

1. Stability to heat
2. Solubility in water
3. Toxicity (see below)
4. Rate of excretion of drug from the host

The two most important criteria for the use of a drug as a chemotherapeutic agent are that (1) **it must exert antimicrobial activity at very low concentrations** and (2) **it should be relatively nontoxic.**

FIGURE 8-1
Cylinder method for determining bacterial sensitivity to drugs. Cylinders are placed on agar plates and filled with a specified quantity of antibiotic. Antibiotic is considered effective if a zone of no growth develops. Note the variation in the width of zones of inhibition. The width may be due to the type of antibiotic placed in the cylinder or to a variation in the concentration of one antibiotic. (From L. P. Garrod and F. O'Grady, *Antibiotics and Chemotherapy*, 5th ed. London: Churchill Livingstone, 1973.)

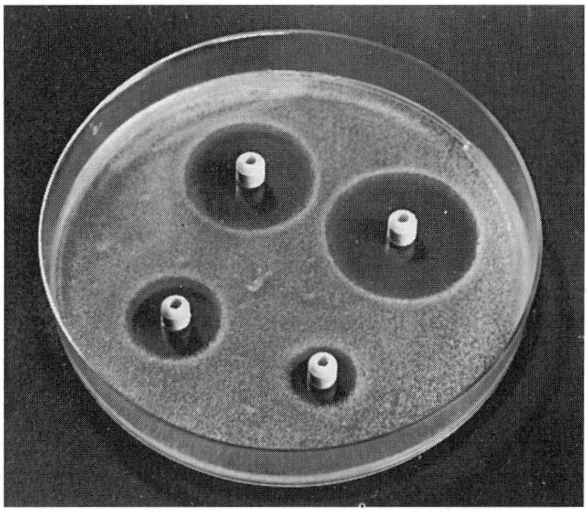

SELECTIVE TOXICITY AND THERAPEUTIC INDEX

A chemotherapeutic agent is one that is **selectively toxic;** that is, it is toxic to the microbial cell but relatively nontoxic to the host cell. Selective toxicity is possible because of occasional differences in the biochemistry of the host and microbial cell. For example, penicillin inhibits the synthesis of bacterial cell wall, a component that is not present in mammalian cells. Sometimes the drug may be specific for a microbial enzyme that is not present in mammalian cells, but this is rare. The biochemical activities of microorganisms are so similar to those in mammalian cells that the drug will affect both cell types. However, the drug to be used often shows greater affinity for the microbial component than the mammalian one. For example, protein synthesis occurs in all cell types but the ribosomes of mammalian cells differ from those of bacterial cells. Several drugs that possess greater affinity for the bacterial ribosome than the mammalian ribosome are available. This represents **selective toxicity.**

Antimicrobials may have a low or high selective toxicity. Some drugs have a **low selective toxicity;** that is, they are nearly as toxic to the mammalian cell as they are to the infectious microbe. A measure of a drug's selective toxicity is called the **therapeutic index.** The therapeutic index represents the ratio between the minimum toxic and maximum therapeutic concentrations of a drug. A high therapeutic index indicates that the concentration of drug that is therapeutic is virtually nontoxic to host tissue. A low therapeutic index indicates that the concentration of drug that is therapeutic is also harmful to host tissue.

Chemotherapeutic Agents

Chemotherapeutic agents either kill (**-cidal,** for example, **bactericidal**) the infectious agent or arrest (**-static,** for example, **bacteriostatic**) its growth. In very life-threatening situations a chemotherapeutic agent that quickly kills the infectious agent may be required. Chemotherapeutic agents that arrest growth enable the host, over time, to mount an immunological defense in the form of antibody

FIGURE 8-2
Structure of penicillin nucleus (6-aminopenicillinic acid) and some of its more clinically useful derivatives.

Penicillin nucleus

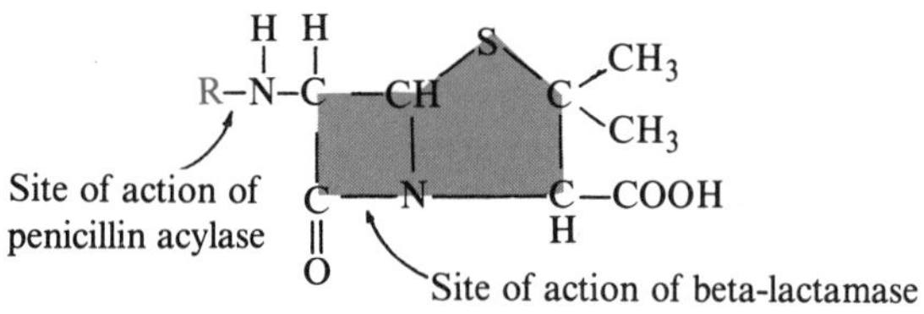

NAME OF DERIVATIVE	SIDE CHAIN	CHARACTERISTICS
Penicillin G (benzyl penicillin)	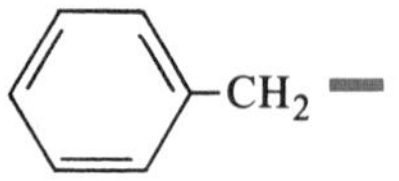	Inexpensive, acid labile, susceptible to beta-lactamases of gram-negative and gram-positive bacteria; ineffective orally
Penicillin V (phenoxymethyl penicillin)	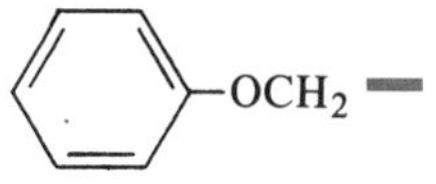	Acid resistant; can be taken orally; narrow spectrum
Oxacillin	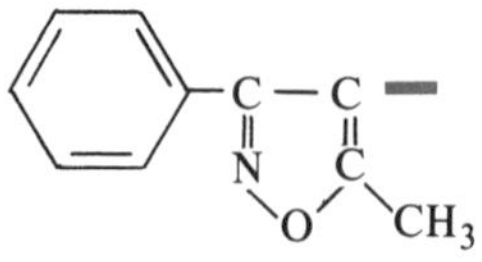	Can be taken orally; not susceptible to beta-lactamases; narrow spectrum
Ampicillin	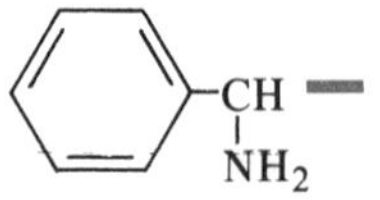	Sensitive to beta-lactamases; broad spectrum; acid resistant
Carbenicillin	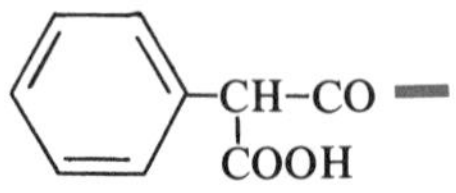	Cannot be administered orally; resistant to gram-negative beta-lactamases; active against *Pseudomonas*
Methicillin	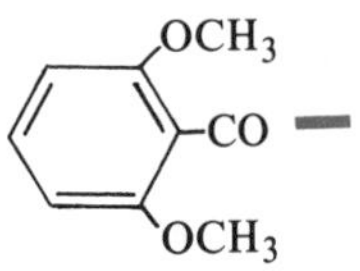	Relatively resistant to beta-lactamases; most effective against *S. aureus* resistant to penicillin G

production. These antibodies can protect the individual from future infections from the same infectious agent. In general, the antimicrobial activity of chemotherapeutic agents relates to their ability to affect metabolism in several ways.

INHIBITORS OF CELL WALL SYNTHESIS

The most important drugs that inhibit cell wall synthesis are the penicillins, the cephalosporins, bacitracin, and vancomycin. These drugs are effective only in bacterial cells that are actively synthesizing cell wall peptidoglycan precursors. All these drugs are bactericidal.

Penicillins

Penicillin comes as close as any drug to being the model antibiotic because of its low toxicity and the minimal concentration required for antibacterial activity. Penicillins and cephalosporins belong to a class of compounds called **beta-lactams.** This designation is based on the common nucleus of these antibiotics, which contains a beta-lactam ring (Fig. 8-2). Except for penicillin G (benzyl penicillin) all penicillins are semisynthetic (Fig. 8-2). Addition of side chains to the penicillin nucleus has resulted in agents with features that include a different spectrum of activity, resistance to microbial enzymes, and resistance to stomach acids.

Special dosage forms of penicillin are often used in treatment. The potassium salt of penicillin G dissolves readily in body fluids. Even with intramuscular injections penicillin is quickly absorbed from the site of injection into the bloodstream. The rate of dissolution of penicillin can be reduced if penicillin is combined with **procaine.** A single intramuscular injection of penicillin procaine can produce a therapeutic level of drug for 24 hours in the bloodstream. The same dose of penicillin in water is effective for only 4 to 5 hours.

In its aqueous form penicillin is rapidly excreted from the kidneys. A preparation called **penicillin benzathine** is used to circumvent this problem. Penicillin benzathine consists of two molecules of benzyl penicillin bound to dibenzylmethylenediamine. Given intramuscularly, this preparation produces high levels of the drug in the serum for several days.

Penicillin and its derivatives are the least toxic of all the drugs used in chemotherapy. When doses approach 40 to 50 million units, however, neurotoxicity can result. The most adverse effect caused by administration of penicillin is an allergic response, observed in up to 8 percent of the population who receive the drug (Fig. 8-3). All persons are at potential risk of such allergic reactions because penicillins are found everywhere in the environment as a result of agricultural, industrial, and medical uses. It should be noted that only about 10 percent of persons who report a history of severe allergic reactions to penicillin are still allergic. With the passage of time after a severe allergic reaction to penicillin, most persons stop expressing penicillin-specific IgE.

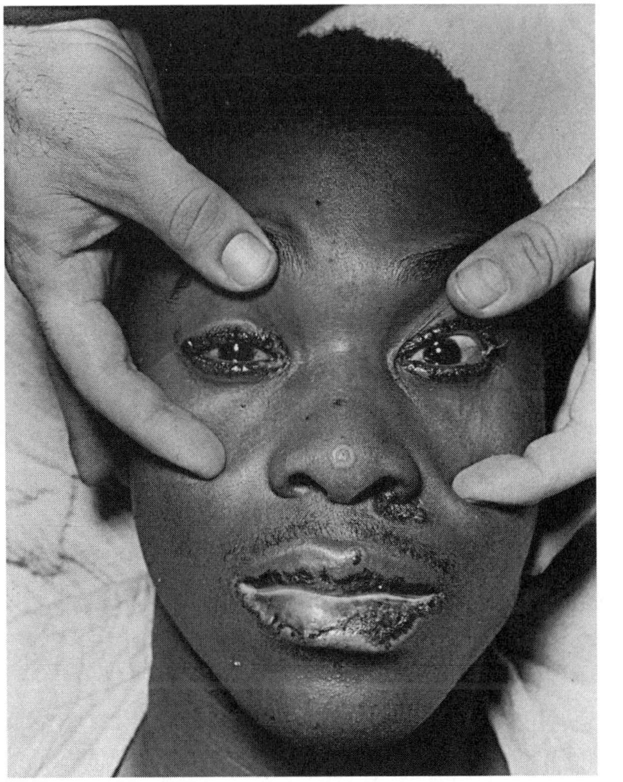

FIGURE 8-3
Penicillin allergy. (Courtesy of the Centers for Disease Control, Atlanta, GA.)

Mechanism of Action. The exact mechanism by which penicillin is lethal to bacteria is still not known and more than one mechanism may be involved. The discovery of **penicillin-binding proteins (PBP)** and the identification of a transpeptidase as the lethal target of beta-lactam antibiotics have shed some light on the controversy.

PBP are located in the cytoplasmic membrane and there are three to eight distinct types in a given microorganism. PBP are involved in the synthesis of bacterial cell wall. When beta-lactams enter the cytoplasmic membrane, they bind to PBP and form a complex. The affinity of PBP for beta-lactams is variable. Affinity is related to the type and concentration of the beta-lactam as well as the type of PBP affected. The binding of beta-lactams to different PBP affects certain morphological responses associated with cell wall synthesis (Fig. 8-4).

PBP 1 is associated with the enzymes involved in cell elongation. PBP 2 is affiliated with cell shape while PBP 3 is related to septum formation. The addition of a penicillin to a culture of rod-shaped bacteria will sometimes cause immediate lysis, while with other penicillins the cells may round up, forming ovoid cells. With other penicillins there may be the formation of filaments. It now appears that the initial action of beta-lactams is to inhibit bacterial growth by affecting the activity of an enzyme involved in peptidoglycan metabolism. The most likely candidate for this is a **transpeptidase,** that is, the enzyme that connects peptides in the peptidoglycan strands. Breakage of strand linkages is believed to be followed by an irreversible response in which a hydrolytic enzyme

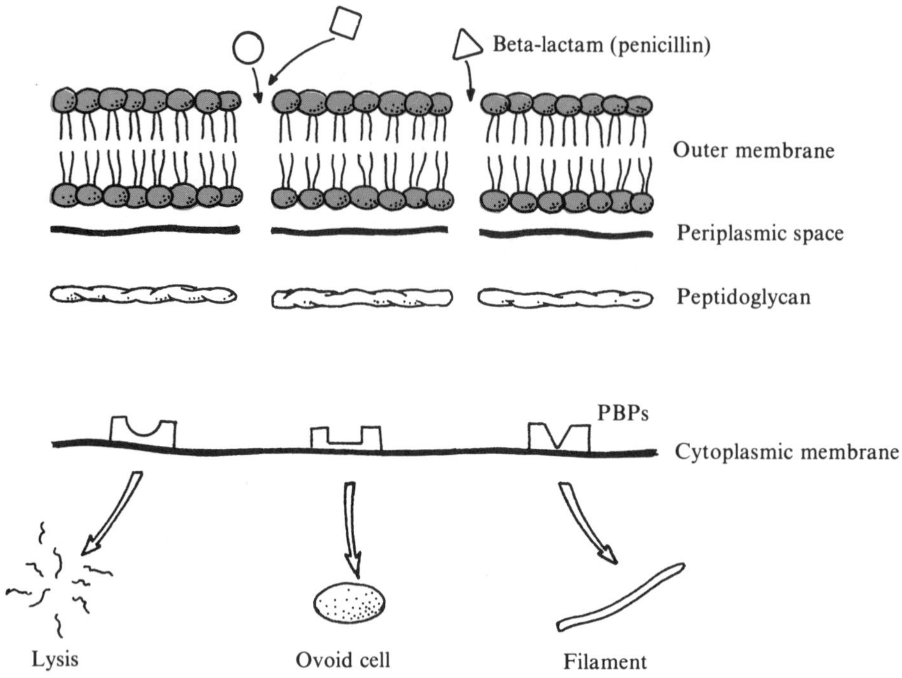

FIGURE 8-4
Movement of beta-lactams through the cell envelope and their effect on the bacterial cell. The affinity of a beta-lactam for penicillin-binding proteins (PBP) varies depending on the structure of the beta-lactam antibiotic. The effect on the bacterial cell is associated with the type of PBP.

acts autocatalytically. The enzyme breaks covalent bonds in the peptidoglycan strands, thus exposing the cytoplasmic membrane to the environment. This ultimately leads to lysis of the cell (see Fig. 8-4).

Beta-lactamases and Resistance to Penicillin. Resistance to antibiotics is discussed in more detail later under Drug Resistance; however, penicillin resistance is discussed here because penicillin and its derivatives are the most widely used antimicrobial agents and the least toxic. Microorganisms have three mechanisms for resistance to beta-lactams: alteration of the drug's target, diminished permeation, and production of inactivating enzymes. The major reason why many microorganisms are resistant to penicillin and other beta-lactams is a microbial enzyme called **beta-lactamase.** There are several classes of beta-lactamases and each splits the beta-lactam ring, thereby inactivating the antibiotic (see Fig. 8-2). Beta-lactamases are found primarily in the periplasmic space, where they are believed to be responsible for the assembly of peptidoglycan. They have been found in most gram-positive and gram-negative bacteria and their ability to inactivate penicillin can vary from one penicillin to another. The genetic determinants for beta-lactamase may be chromosome- or plasmid-associated.

Sensitivity to beta-lactamases is now the single most important consideration in the development of new beta-lactams. One solution to the problem has been to use combinations of beta-lactams to broaden the scope of antibacterial activity. Another solution is to couple beta-lactamase inhibitors to the beta-lactams. Inhibitors such as **clavulanic acid, sulbactam,** and **tazobactam** have proved to be invaluable in certain treatment regimens. They do not, however, inhibit all beta-lactamases. *Enterobacter, Citrobacter,* and *Serratia* species and *Pseudomonas aeruginosa* are not affected by the inhibitors.

Methicillin resistance by *Staphylococcus aureus* has become a major concern in the medical community. Resistance to methicillin also confers resistance to other beta-lactams. This characteristic is discussed in Chapter 17.

Cephalosporins

Cephalosporins are beta-lactam antibiotics similar in structure and activity to penicillins (Fig. 8-5). Semisynthetic derivatives have been prepared, with **cephalothin** being the first marketed derivative of cephalosporin C.

Many cephalosporins show resistance to the beta-lactamases of several species of bacteria. Cephalosporins are useful alternatives to penicillins, particularly when the patient is allergic to penicillin or is infected by a penicillin-resistant species. There are now second- and third-generation cephalosporins that are currently used in treatment: **Cefamandole, cefotaxime, cefoxitin, cefazolin,** and **cefoperazone** are but a few of them. Many of the new cephalosporins are active against gram-negative species as well as gram-positive ones. Cefoxitin and cefuroxime, for example, are routinely used prophylactically in surgical procedures. Cefotaxime is now the drug of choice in the treatment of bacterial meningitis due to ampicillin-resistant strains of *Hemophilus influenzae* type b, *Streptococcus pneumoniae,* and *Neisseria meningitidis.* Other recently in-

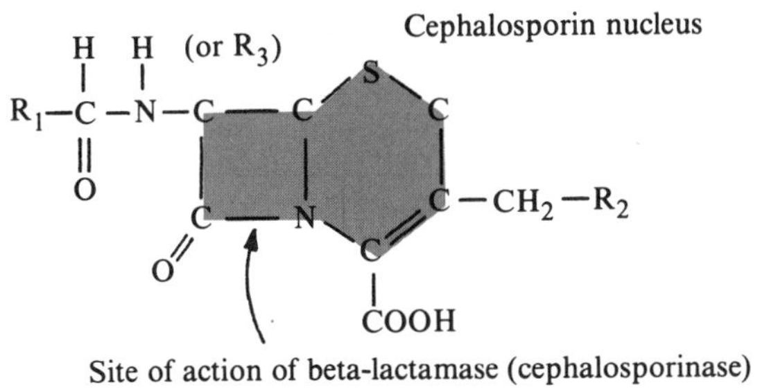

NAME OF DERIVATIVE	SIDE CHAIN R_1	SIDE CHAIN R_2	CHARACTERISTICS
Cephalothin	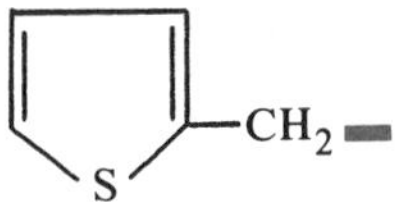	$-OCOCH_3$	Can be given only IM or IV; used for severe staphylococcal infections
Cefazolin	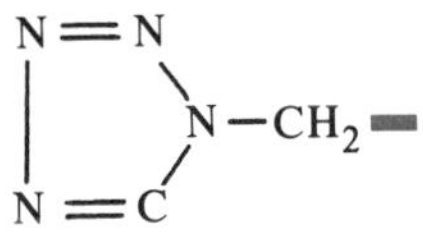	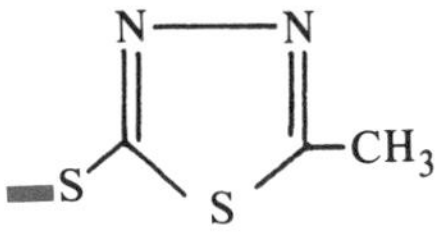	Can be given only IM or IV; more active than cephalothin against *E. coli* and *Klebsiella;* more susceptible to beta-lactamase than cephalothin
Cefamandole	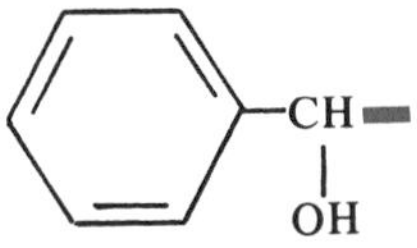	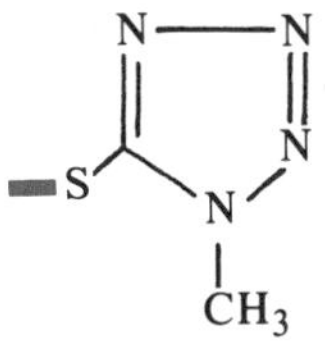	Inhibits enterobacteriaceae to greater degree than cephalothin; active against *Hemophilus influenzae;* administered parenterally
Cefoxitin*	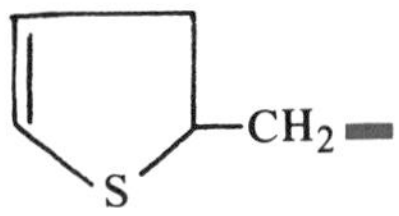	$-OCONH_2$	Diminished activity against gram-positives but greater activity against gram-negative organisms than cefamandole; administered primarily IV
Cefotaxime	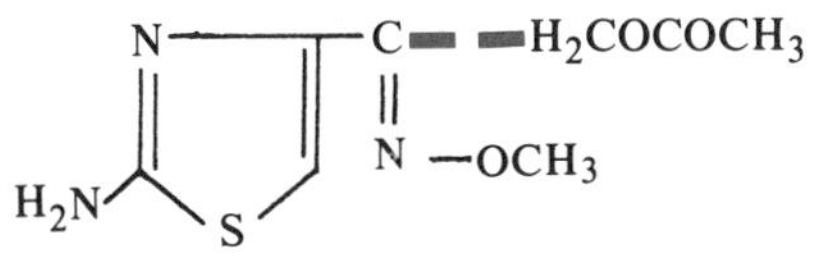		Marked resistance to beta-lactamases of certain gram-negative bacteria such as *Hemophilus influenzae;* active against *Pseudomonas*

*Cefoxitin has an R_3 side chain of $-OCH_3$

FIGURE 8-5
Structure of the cephalosporin nucleus (7-aminocephalosporanic acid) and some of its more important derivatives. IM = intramuscularly; IV = intravenously.

troduced cephalosporins include **cefixime, cefprozil, cefpodoxime,** and **cefibuten.** Cefprozil is used in the treatment of acute bacterial respiratory infections.

Carbapenems

Carbapenems differ from the penicillins in that they have a carbon atom replacing the sulfur atom on the thiazolidine ring. **Imipenem** is the first of this class of drugs to be marketed in the United States. Imipenem has the widest spectrum of activity of any drug currently available. It is effective against gram-positive bacteria (except methicillin-resistant staphylococci), many gram-negative cocci and Enterobacteriaceae, and many anaerobes. The drug has potential for use as a monotherapeutic agent, for example, in intraabdominal infections where there is a mixed flora. Imipenem is toxic to the kidneys and has been known to cause seizures in those with renal failure or underlying central nervous system pathology. The drug should not be used if *Pseudomonas* species are believed to be associated with infection.

Bacitracin

Bacitracin is a peptide antibiotic originally isolated from the bacterium *Bacillus subtilis*. It is active against gram-positive bacteria but not gram-negative species. The drug is not absorbed from the intestinal tract and is very toxic to the kidneys (nephrotoxicity). Its primary use has been as a topical agent in combination with other topical agents such as polymyxin and neomycin.

Bacitracin inhibits cell wall synthesis by preventing the transfer of peptidoglycan precursors to the growing cell wall.

Vancomycin

Vancomycin is a drug with limited usefulness in the clinical situation. Its use has been restricted to the treatment of staphylococcal infections in which the infectious agent is resistant to methicillin or oxacillin. Vancomycin is also used in the treatment of antibiotic-associated pseudomembranous colitis (see Chapter 19). Vancomycin blocks the late stages of peptidoglycan synthesis.

Vancomycin resistance among certain clinical isolates is becoming an increasing problem for the physician. This resistance is now being seen in isolates of *Enterococcus* and certain staphylococcal isolates (but not *S. aureus* or streptococcal isolates). Enterococcal and coagulase-negative staphylococcal species are major causes of hospital-associated bacteremia. This vancomycin resistance is often accompanied by multiple resistance to antimicrobial agents.

The most common adverse effects of vancomycin include a group of signs or symptoms known as **red man syndrome** or **RMS.** RMS is characterized by pruritis, erythema, and in severe cases, angioedema, hypotension, and cardiovascular collapse. The severity of the reaction correlates with the amount of histamine released into the plasma following drug administration.

INHIBITORS OF CYTOPLASMIC MEMBRANE FUNCTION

Polyenes

Polyenes are primarily antifungal agents produced mainly by Streptomycetaceae. The principal polyenes are **amphotericin B** and **nystatin,** but minor ones include candicidin, pimaricin, trichomycin, and hamycin. Polyenes have an affinity for lipids and bind irreversibly to cytoplasmic membrane sterols such as ergosterol. Polyene binding creates large pores in the eukaryotic membranes. This action leads to alterations in permeability resulting in loss of nutrients and other compounds.

Polyenes such as amphotericin B have low solubility in water and most preparations are made up in sodium deoxycholate. Polyenes are relatively toxic and most adverse effects involve the kidneys. Amphotericin B is used intravenously in the treatment of systemic fungal infections. Many years of research have gone into the development of techniques for reducing polyene toxicity. For example, amphotericin B is often administered with **flucytosine.** This combination permits the use of smaller doses of amphotericin B. Recent work has concentrated on the development of lipid vehicles for administration of the drug (see Under the Microscope 4).

UNDER THE MICROSCOPE 4

Amphotericin B and Liposomes

The treatment of disseminated fungal infections in immunocompromised patients is difficult because the most efficacious drug, amphotericin B, has a narrow therapeutic index. Toxicity from the short-term effects of amphotericin B therapy includes fever, chills, vomiting, and cardiotoxicity, while long-term therapy is associated with hypomagnesemia,* renal toxicity, and anemia.

A promising new drug delivery system that results in more effective antifungal activity is now under investigation. The new technique involves the encapsulation of drugs such as amphotericin B in liposomes (L-AmB). Liposomes are synthetic vesicles; that is, they are bubbles composed of a phospholipid bilayer. Liposome preparations of amphotericin B are easily reproduced by dissolving the drug in methanol and adding this preparation to a phospholipid-chloroform solution.

Liposomes have an affinity for organs rich in endothelial cells such as liver, lung, spleen, kidney, and bone marrow. This attraction is particularly advantageous because disseminated fungal infections localize in these areas. Liposomes have an affinity for ergosterol, the steroid present in the fungal cell membrane.

Current studies in animal systems and in humans indicate that amphotericin encapsulated in liposomes is less toxic than free amphotericin B during the course of therapy. Thus, patients were shown to be capable of tolerating higher concentrations of the drug and to respond more favorably to therapy.

* Hypomagnesemia is a condition in which there is a deficiency of magnesium in the body that results in twitching and convulsions.

Nystatin, a widely used polyene, is used primarily as a topical agent in the treatment of disease caused by the yeast *Candida.*

Azoles

Azoles are primarily broad-spectrum antifungal agents. Azoles interfere with eukaryotic lipid biosynthesis and thus affect membrane permeability. Three major antifungal azole drugs are presently in clinical use: **ketoconazole, fluconazole,** and **itraconazole.** Other azoles are listed in Table 33-1. One of the documented concerns about the use of some azoles is their rapid degradation in the liver during concurrent therapy with drugs such as rifampin. The clinical effectiveness of some azoles is decreased substantially under these conditions.

Ketoconazole has a broad spectrum of activity and can be taken orally. It is used as an alternative to amphotericin B in systemic disease. Adverse reactions to the drug include nausea, vomiting, and some liver dysfunction.

Fluconazole can be administered orally and intravenously and is capable of penetrating the blood-brain barrier. This drug was approved in 1990 for treatment of cryptococcal meningitis and candidiasis (thrush). These diseases have had devastating effects on patients with acquired immunodeficiency syndrome.

Itraconazole is used in the treatment of superficial fungal infections. Itraconazole cannot as yet be administered intravenously. The drug is administered with cyclodextrin for solubilization and rapid absorption in the intestine.

Polymyxins

The polymyxins are polypeptide antibiotics produced by *Bacillus polymyxa*. Only polymyxin B and polymyxin E are used clinically. Polymyxins are antibacterial agents active against gram-negative species. They interact with bacterial membrane lipids and cause leakage of cellular contents. Polymyxins are nephrotoxic and are therefore used primarily as topical agents. Polymyxin B is not absorbed from the intestinal tract and for that reason the drug is occasionally administered for intestinal infections.

INHIBITORS OF PROTEIN SYNTHESIS

Aminoglycosides

Aminoglycosides are the major inhibitors of protein synthesis. They are antibacterial compounds that can act as -static or -cidal agents. Despite their toxicity, aminoglycosides remain bactericidal against many organisms that are difficult to treat such as *P. aeruginosa* and *Enterobacter.* They act synergistically (see Drug Combinations) with many beta-lactams and in drug combinations are frequently used to treat serious gram-negative infections. Recent increases in bacterial resistance to these drugs have reduced their frequent use. The characteristics of aminoglycosides are described in Table 8-1.

TABLE 8-1
Characteristics of the Aminoglycosides

Aminoglycoside	Principal clinical use	Comments
Streptomycin	Treatment of tuberculosis but always with other drugs; treatment of tularemia and plague; combined with penicillin in treatment of endocarditis caused by enterococci and viridans streptococci	Most microorganisms develop resistance to drug when used alone; therefore it is used only under special circumstances
Kanamycin	Used primarily as a topical drug or for oral therapy	Lacks activity against pseudomonads; susceptible to inactivation by a number of aminoglycoside-modifying enzymes
Gentamicin	Widely used in treatment of infections caused by facultative and aerobic bacilli, for example, the Enterobacteriaceae	Effective against pseudomonads and most Enterobacteriaceae; resistant strains found primarily in hospitals
Tobramycin	Spectrum of activity similar to gentamicin's	More active against *Pseudomonas aeruginosa* than is gentamicin; resistant strains primarily in hospitals
Sisomicin	Spectrum of activity similar to gentamicin's	Similar to tobramycin in its activity against *P. aeruginosa*
Amikacin	Has broadest spectrum of activity of aminoglycosides; particularly effective against *Pseudomonas* species	Produced from the acylation of kanamycin; resistant to aminoglycoside-modifying enzymes; no major resistant strains detected
Neomycin	Used primarily as a topical agent because of toxicity; activity spectrum similar to kanamycin	Occasionally administered orally as an antiseptic before bowel surgery
Fortimicin A	Activity parallels that of amikacin but has greater activity against *Serratia marcescens*	Resembles kanamycin in its poor activity against *P. aeruginosa*
Netilmicin	Resistant to enzymes that modify gentamicin and sisomicin; effective against more strains of enteric bacilli than is gentamicin	A semisynthetic derivative of sisomicin
5-Episisomicin	More active against *P. aeruginosa, S. marcescens, Providencia* species than is gentamicin	A semisynthetic derivative of sisomicin

Aminoglycosides show toxicity for the hearing mechanism (ototoxicity) and for the kidney (nephrotoxicity). Toxicity depends on dosage, immune status of the host, host renal function, and the drug being used.

The mechanism of action of aminoglycosides is believed to be as follows:

1. A small amount of antibiotic penetrates the bacterial cell and binds to ribosomes. Ribosome binding causes a misreading of messenger RNA (mRNA) and results in the formation of abnormal protein.
2. Some of the abnormal protein is incorporated into the cytoplasmic membrane, producing pores that enable more antibiotic to enter the bacterial cell. This results in an increase in the rate of abnormal protein formation.
3. The concentration of antibiotic reaching the cytoplasm is so high that it totally blocks the binding of ribosomes to mRNA and protein synthesis is shut down.
4. The binding of antibiotic to all of the ribosomes is irreversible and the bacterial cell dies.

See Table 8-1 for the descriptions of naturally occurring and semisynthetic aminoglycosides.

Tetracyclines

Tetracyclines (Fig. 8-6) are bacteriostatic agents that bind to the 30S ribosome and block the binding of aminoacyl transfer RNA (tRNA) to the A site. Tetracyclines have the broadest spectrum of activity of all antibiotics. They inhibit gram-positive and gram-negative bacteria, rickettsiae, mycoplasmas, spirochetes, chlamydiae, and some protozoa.

Although relatively nontoxic, tetracycline is not always appropriate for therapy. Continued use of tetracyclines can eliminate the bacterial flora predisposing the patient to disease by indigenous fungi such as *Candida*. Infections caused in this way are called **superinfections.** Tetracyclines can stain developing teeth; therefore, the drug should not be administered to children under 5 years old. They also cause fatty degeneration of the liver in pregnant women.

Tetracyclines are the drug of choice in the treatment of rickettsial and chlamydial infections and are frequently used to treat upper respiratory tract disease. Tetracyclines are also used in the treatment of acne (see Under the Microscope 17, Chapter 20).

FIGURE 8-6
Structure of the tetracycline nucleus and some of its derivatives.

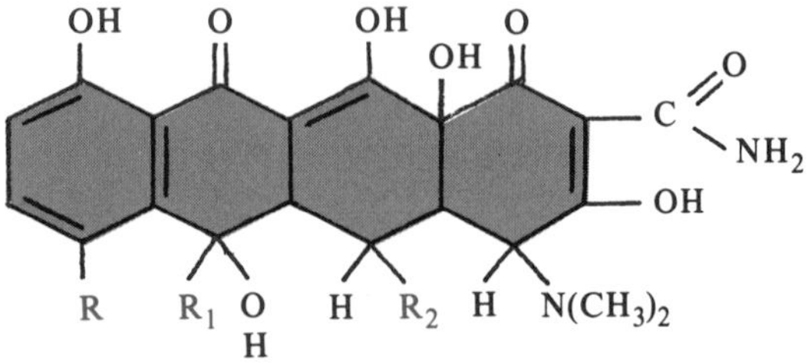

Chloramphenicol

Chloramphenicol is a bacteriostatic agent that inhibits protein synthesis by binding to the 50S ribosome and blocking peptidyl transfer. It has broad-spectrum activity but is very toxic. Toxicity is associated with inhibition of protein synthesis in bone marrow cells. Toxicity can give rise to anemia and leukopenia, and repeated administration may result in fatal aplastic anemia. It is still the drug of choice for typhoid fever, and for meningitis in patients who are allergic to penicillin.

Erythromycin

Erythromycin belongs to a group of drugs called **macrolides.** Macrolides are considered among the best-tolerated antimicrobial agents. For this reason they have been used as alternative drugs when other drugs are too toxic or when an individual is allergic to penicillins. One of the main drawbacks of erythromycin is acid stability. Newer derivatives of erythromycin that have shown acid stability include azithromycin, spiramycin, josamycin, roxithromycin, and calithromycin.

Macrolides are taken orally and their use is primarily for intracellular pathogens such as *Chlamydia, Campylobacter,* and *Mycobacterium avium-intracellulare* complex. Erythromycin is the drug of choice in legionnaires' disease and pneumonia caused by *Mycoplasma pneumoniae.*

Erythromycin affects protein synthesis by binding to free ribosomes but not polysomes. The ribosome-bound drug allows the formation of a small peptide but then prevents further elongation of the peptide.

Lincomycin and Clindamycin

Lincomycin and clindamycin resemble erythromycin in their spectrum of activity and pharmacological characteristics. **Clindamycin** is a derivative of lincomycin and is the drug of choice in the treatment of serious anaerobic pulmonary infections. In addition, clindamycin is the main alternative therapy for patients with the protozoal disease toxoplasmic encephalitis who are intolerant of sulfonamides. **Lincomycin** is used in treating staphylococcal and streptococcal infections that do not respond to penicillin therapy or when the patient is allergic to penicillin.

Two of the major side effects of clindamycin and lincomycin therapy are diarrhea and **pseudomembranous colitis.** These toxic effects are controllable and are described in Chapter 19.

Both lincomycin and clindamycin inhibit protein synthesis by preventing peptidyl transfer.

Spectinomycin

Spectinomycin is not a true aminoglycoside but is very similar structurally. It inhibits protein synthesis much as chloramphenicol does. Its principal use is as an alternative to ceftriaxone in the treatment of pediatric gonococcal infections.

INHIBITORS OF NUCLEIC ACID SYNTHESIS

Inhibitors of nucleic acid synthesis include antibacterial drugs such as nalidixic acid and rifampin, the antifungal drug flucytosine, and several antiviral agents. A more complete list of antiviral drugs is provided in Table 31-6.

Rifampin

Rifampin is a semisynthetic derivative of the antibiotic rifamycin B. Rifampin inhibits RNA synthesis by binding to a subunit of the DNA-dependent RNA polymerase of the bacterial cell. This binding ultimately interferes with the initiation of transcription by the enzyme. Mammalian RNA polymerases are not affected by the drug. Rifampin has activity against mycobacteria and gram-positive species but is less effective against gram-negative species. It is used with drugs such as streptomycin and ethambutol in the treatment and prophylaxis of tuberculosis.

Nalidixic Acid and the Quinolones

Nalidixic acid is a synthetic **quinolone** and is unlike all other antimicrobial agents (Fig. 8-7). It is most effective against gram-negative species but not anaerobes. Its use is restricted to specific situations. It has been used with other drugs to prevent infections in cancer patients undergoing therapy. The drug selectively suppresses the bacteria in the intestinal tract that are the major causes of urinary tract infection in compromised patients.

The bacteriostatic activity of nalidixic acid like other quinolones is due to its effect on the enzyme DNA gyrase. DNA gyrase is one of the enzymes associated with DNA replication.

The newer quinolones such as the **fluoroquinolones** show greater activity and decreased tendency to form resistant mutants than does nalidixic acid. Determinants of fluoroquinolone resistance are chromosomally associated and not plasmid-associated as are determinants of nalidixic acid resistance. Some of the newer fluoroquinolones include **norfloxacin** used in the treatment of urinary tract infections and infectious diarrhea. **Ciprofloxacin** is approved for use in the oral treatment of urinary tract infections, respiratory tract infections, diarrheal disease due to *Salmonella* and *Shigella* species, and bone infections due to *P. aeruginosa.* **Ofloxacin** has been approved for the treatment of urinary tract and respiratory tract infections and for eradicating *Chlamydia trachomatis,* an agent of a sexually transmitted disease.

There has been a continued increase in methicillin-resistant *S. aureus* to the fluoroquinolones. Consequently, these drugs cannot be considered appropriate therapy for suspected methicillin-resistant *S. aureus* infections.

FIGURE 8-7
Structure of nalidixic acid.

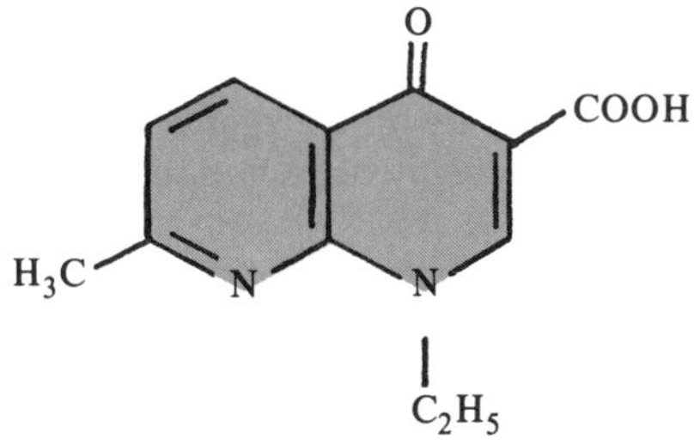

Flucytosine

Flucytosine is a fluorinated pyrimidine originally developed as an antimetabolite for use in cancer chemotherapy. It has a narrow spectrum of activity that is limited to systemic yeast infections when it is administered with amphotericin B.

Fluorocytosine is deaminated in the cytoplasm of the fungal cell to 5-fluorouracil. The latter is subsequently phosphorylated and incorporated into RNA. This fluorinated RNA derivative interferes with normal protein synthesis. Flucytosine can also interfere with DNA synthesis (Fig. 8-8).

Toxic effects from flucytosine therapy are minimal and include nausea, vomiting, and diarrhea.

Amantadine

Amantadine inhibits the primary transcription process in the influenza A virus and thus prevents uncoating of the virus capsid. Amantadine is used for the prevention of influenza A, but it is not a substitute for the influenza vaccine. Maximum effectiveness of the drug is obtained only when it is administered at the start of the influenza season. The drug must be maintained daily as long as virus exposure is certain (usually 6–8 weeks). Side effects from the drug include dizziness, depression, and drowsiness, particularly in the elderly.

Rimantadine is an analogue of amantadine that also is used in the prophylaxis of influenza A virus infection. The drug has fewer side effects than amantadine.

Ribavirin

Ribavirin (Virazole) is a synthetic nucleoside resembling guanosine. It is active against both DNA and RNA viruses. The drug appears to inhibit an early viral replication step that leads to synthesis of viral nucleic acids. Ribavirin has been approved by the Food and Drug Administration (FDA) for use in the treatment of respiratory syncytial virus and Lassa fever virus infections. Aerosolization of the drug is effective in the treatment of both viral infections.

Idoxuridine

Idoxuridine (5-iodo-2′-deoxyuridine or IDU) is a halogenated analogue of thymidine and is incorporated in place of thymidine into cellular as well as viral DNA. IDU is used as an ophthalmic solution in the treatment of herpes keratitis. Since the infected cells of the eye do not divide, only viral DNA incorporates IDU and host toxicity is avoided.

Vidarabine

Vidarabine (adenine arabinoside or ara-A) has a spectrum of activity similar to that of IDU. The drug is particularly effective against herpesvirus infections. It is used as an ophthalmic solution in the treatment of herpes keratitis. Although vidarabine has been used to treat herpes encephalitis, herpes simplex and varicella-zoster infections

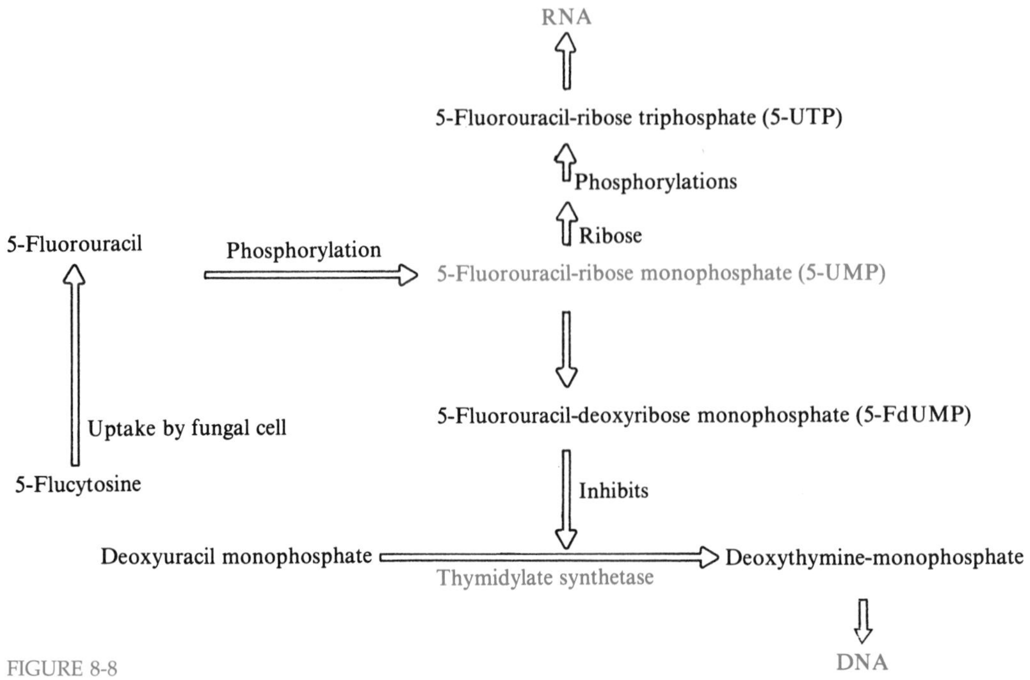

FIGURE 8-8
Action of flucytosine in fungi. Flucytosine is taken into the cytoplasm of the fungal cell, where it is converted to 5-fluorouracil-ribose monophosphate (5-UMP). The latter can be phosphorylated and incorporated into RNA and interfere with normal protein synthesis, or it can be converted to a deoxy form (5-FdUMP), which is an inhibitor of thymidylate synthetase.

in the immunocompromised host, and neonatal herpes, these diseases are almost entirely treated with acyclovir now (see Acyclovir).

Acyclovir

Acyclovir is an antiviral agent that is particularly effective in the treatment of herpes simplex virus infections. The drug is available as an ointment, as pills or capsules, or in an intravenous suspension. In addition to its use for severe infections that were originally treated with vidarabine, the drug is effective in shortening the course of initial genital herpesvirus infection when it is administered orally or intravenously. Acyclovir also shortens the course of common cold sores when it is administered in ointment form.

Acyclovir is a unique antiviral agent in that it is selectively metabolized by virus-infected cells. To be effective, the drug must be phosphorylated, which occurs efficiently only in virus-infected cells (Fig. 8-9). The phosphorylation is carried out only by a virus-coded thymidine kinase. The phosphorylated acyclovir is further phosphorylated to acyclovir triphosphate. The latter is a potent inhibitor of herpes simplex–induced DNA polymerase. Acyclovir triphosphate has little or no effect on host cell DNA polymerase.

Zidovudine

Zidovudine (azidothymidine or AZT) was initially synthesized in 1964 for use as an anticancer drug. Like acyclovir, AZT is converted into an active triphosphate by cellular kinases. AZT triphosphate inhibits the human immunodeficiency virus (HIV), which causes AIDS. The site of inhibition by AZT is the enzyme that converts viral RNA into viral DNA. AZT is toxic but it nevertheless prolongs the survival of patients with advanced HIV infection. The major adverse effects are anemia and granulocytopenia. (See Chapter 32 for further discussion of AZT in AIDS patients.)

ANTIMETABOLITES

Antimetabolites are defined as compounds that are structurally similar to normal cellular metabolites and may compete with them for attachment to an enzyme surface.

Sulfonamides

The sulfonamides were among the first synthetic agents used successfully in the treatment of disease. Important derivatives of the sulfonamides are **sulfanilamide, sulfadiazine, sulfamethoxazole, sulfathiazole, sulfasoxazole,** and **sulfapyridine.** Overuse of many of the sulfonamides resulted in large-scale resistance by microorganisms. Still, some of these drugs are the mainstay of certain therapeutic regimens.

Sulfonamides are still used in the treatment of urinary tract infections, particularly in children and infants. Sulfonamides are very soluble in urine. Oral sulfonamides are sometimes recommended as a prophylaxis for travel-

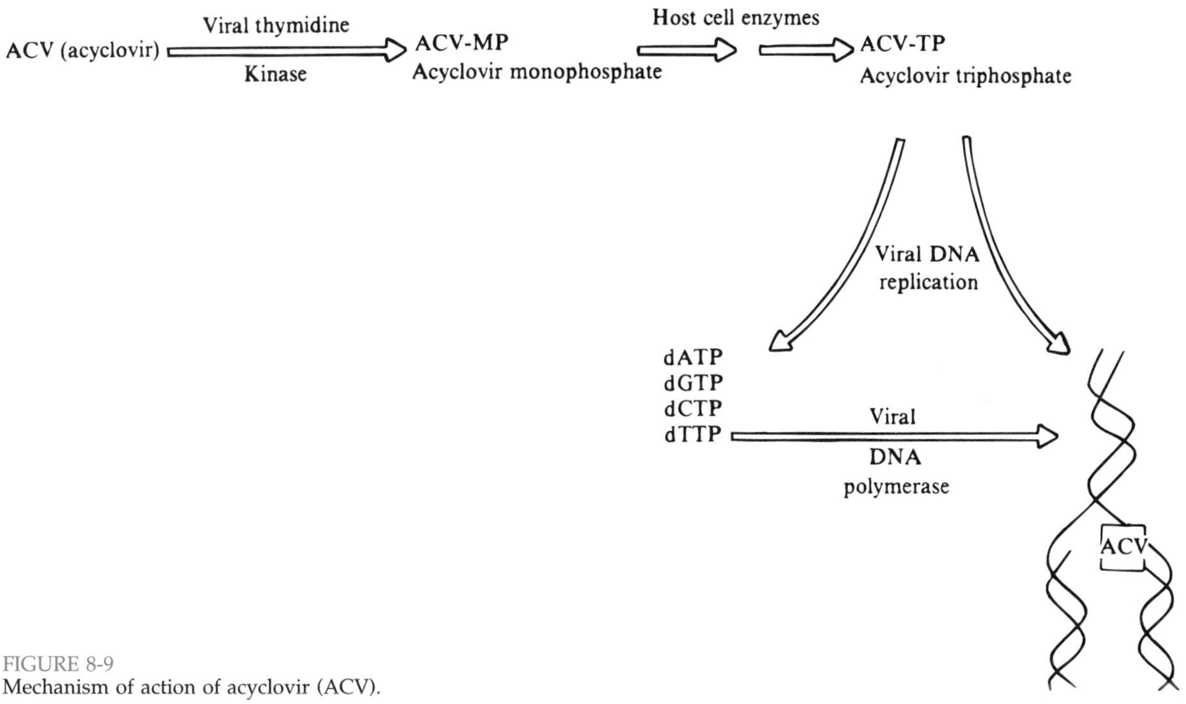

FIGURE 8-9
Mechanism of action of acyclovir (ACV).

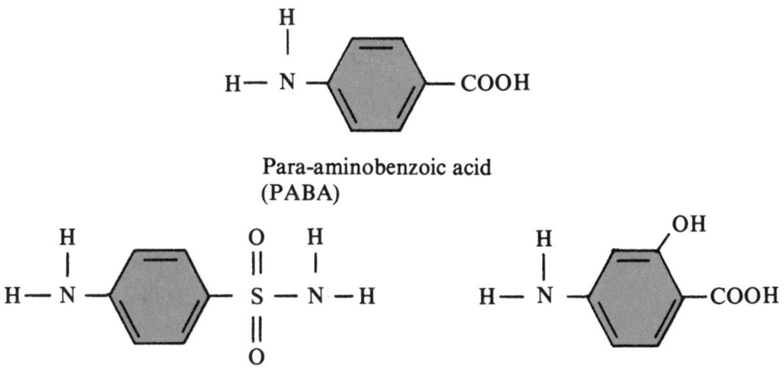

FIGURE 8-10
Structural relationship between the antimetabolites sulfanilamide and para-aminosalicylic acid and the metabolite para-aminobenzoic acid.

er's diarrhea caused by *Escherichia coli.* Sulfadiazine silver is used topically for burn patients. Sulfadiazine with pyrimethamine is used in the treatment of toxoplasmosis. The combination of sulfamethoxazole and trimethoprim has proved especially effective against several intestinal and urinary tract pathogens.

Sulfonamides are bacteriostatic and owe their effectiveness to their similarity to para-aminobenzoic acid (PABA) (Fig. 8-10). PABA is a component of the vitamin **folic acid,** one of the B vitamins. Sulfonamides prevent the synthesis of bacterial folic acid. Folic acid is a coenzyme important in amino acid metabolism and purine nucleotide synthesis (Fig. 8-11).

The sulfonamides are for the most part readily tolerated; however, they do have some undesirable side effects. They can bind to plasma proteins that are normally occupied by bilirubin. In the newborn, bilirubin can penetrate the blood-brain barrier, causing encephalopathy (kernicterus). Therefore, sulfonamides should not be administered to pregnant women. Approximately 1 to 3 percent of patients receiving sulfonamide exhibit hypersensitivity to the drug. Persons with glucose 6-phosphate dehydrogenase deficiency experience a minor anemia caused by the instability of red blood cells. The anemia is severely exaggerated if these patients are treated with sulfonamides or nitrofurans.

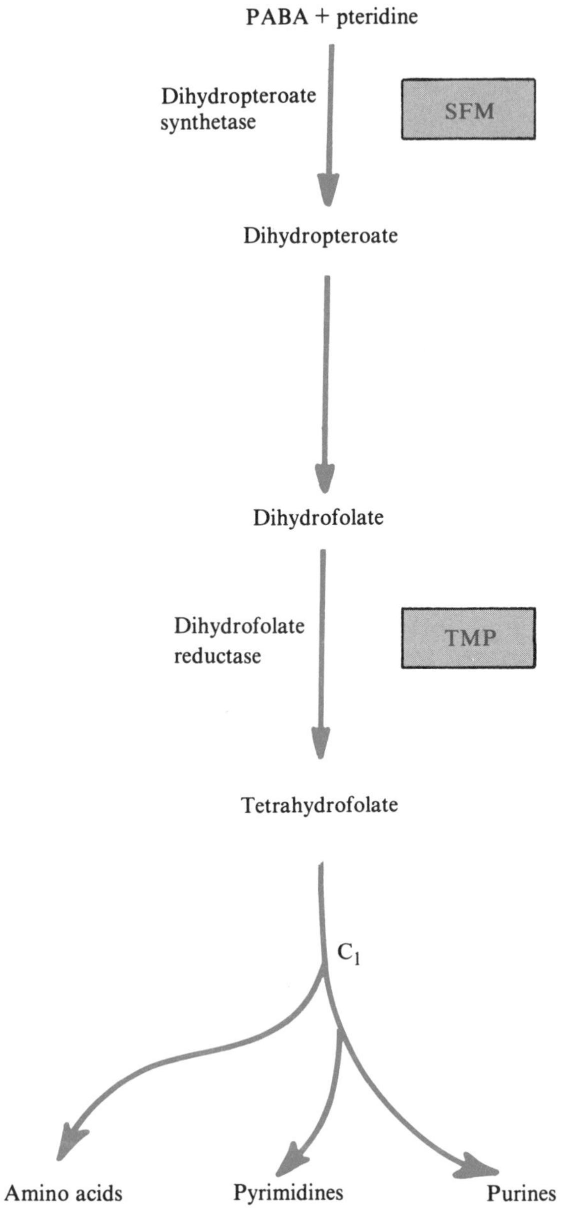

FIGURE 8-11
Reaction pathway in which para-aminobenzoic acid (PABA) is involved in the synthesis of amino acids, purines, and pyrimidines. The drugs that act as antimetabolites in the pathway are enclosed in boxes. C_1 = one carbon unit; SFM = sulfonamide; TMP = trimethoprim.

Para-aminosalicylic Acid and the Sulfones

Para-aminosalicylic acid (PAS) and the sulfones are analogues of PABA. PAS shows little activity against most organisms except *Mycobacterium tuberculosis.* The drug was once used in combination with other drugs in the treatment of tuberculosis but other drugs have replaced it.

The sulfones are used almost exclusively in the treatment of leprosy. **Dapsone** is the more frequently prescribed sulfone. Sulfones are known to cause hemolytic and nonhemolytic anemia.

Trimethoprim

Trimethoprim is a structural analogue of pteridine, a component of the folic acid molecule. It is a potent inhibitor of the enzyme dihydrofolate reductase in bacteria and interferes competitively with the conversion of dihydrofolic acid to tetrahydrofolic acid (see Fig. 8-11). Trimethoprim interferes with normal amino acid and purine and pyrimidine synthesis.

Trimethoprim is used in combination with sulfamethoxazole, the combination abbreviated TMP-SMZ. TMP-SMZ is bactericidal and is used most frequently in the treatment and prophylaxis of several hospital-associated diseases, particularly those caused by gram-negative bacteria. It is one of the best therapeutic agents in the treatment of *Pneumocystis* pneumonia associated with AIDS.

Serious toxicity from TMP-SMZ therapy is rare but when it occurs, the most likely complications are severe skin lesions and the combination of thrombocytopenia and leukopenia.* TMP-SMZ should not be administered to pregnant women or those known to be sensitive to sulfonamides.

Ethambutol

Ethambutol is used exclusively in the treatment of tuberculosis. It affects only growing microorganisms and is believed to interfere with RNA synthesis. Ethambutol is beneficial in combination with other drugs for the treatment of tuberculosis because it helps delay the emergence of drug-resistant strains. At high dosage, ethambutol can affect visual acuity.

Isoniazid

Isoniazid (INH) is important in the treatment of tuberculosis. It is employed in combination with other drugs such as streptomycin or rifampin. Isoniazid is particularly effective in the treatment of tuberculosis because it is readily absorbed from the intestinal tract and is only mildly toxic to the host in low dosages. Isoniazid resembles nicotinamide in structure and competes with it for incorporation into nicotinamide adenine dinucleotide (NAD), an important coenzyme in metabolism.

Isoniazid is relatively nontoxic when administered in small doses. In 50 percent of the population (only 15 percent in Orientals), it is inactivated very slowly in the body. This can result in a cumulative toxicity demonstrated by neuritis. The latter can be prevented by simultaneous administration of pyridoxine.

Nitrofurans

Nitrofurans have various antibacterial, antiprotozoal, and antifungal activities. As bacteriostatic and bactericidal agents, they are used in the treatment of urinary tract infections. **Nitrofurantoin** is the most widely prescribed of the nitrofurans. It is frequently used for hospitalized patients to prevent urinary tract infections following cath-

* Thrombocytopenia is a condition in which there is a decrease in the number of blood platelets. Leukopenia is a condition in which there is a decrease in the number of leukocytes below normal blood levels.

eterization. Although its exact mechanism of action is unknown, nitrofurantoin is believed to affect carbohydrate metabolism in the bacterial cell by interfering with acetyl-coenzyme A activity.

FACTORS IN SELECTING A DRUG FOR CHEMOTHERAPY

The choice of drug for therapy is dictated primarily by the type of microorganism causing the disease. In some instances, a direct relationship exists between the disease and the microorganism involved. Diphtheria, for example, is always caused by *Corynebacterium diphtheriae.* In other diseases, such as pneumonia, a variety of microorganisms could be the cause of infection. We now discuss some of the principal factors to consider in selecting an agent for therapy.

Dosage

The dosage of drug to be given to the patient may be affected by many factors, including the rate of excretion or inactivation of the drug, its toxic potential, the age of the patient, and the presence of underlying organic illness. Dosage selection is correlated with the **minimal inhibitory concentration (MIC)** of the drug (the smallest amount of drug that inhibits growth; see under Broth Dilution Test, later in this chapter) and the amount that will produce the MIC in the serum of the patient. The general recommendation is that the concentration of the drug in the serum be three to five times the MIC to ensure effective therapy. In very serious infections the ratio of serum level to MIC may be as much as 100:1, for example, in penicillin therapy for meningitis infections caused by species of *Neisseria.*

Route of Administration

Many drugs are not absorbed from the intestinal tract, and others are destroyed by acids in the gut. This kind of information is important in deciding whether a drug is to be given orally, parenterally, or topically. In severely ill patients the parenteral route is preferred because the drug will appear more rapidly at the site of infection and at higher concentrations than with the oral route. A sizable percentage of drug is excreted in the feces if it is administered orally. Drugs not absorbed from the intestinal tract are effective in the treatment of gastrointestinal disorders when high concentrations of the drug are required.

Drug Combinations

There are four primary reasons for using a combination of drugs in therapy:

1. To provide a broader spectrum of activity. For example, in life-threatening sepsis in which the offending bacterial agent is not known, drug combinations can reasonably ensure destruction of any gram-negative or gram-positive species.
2. To minimize toxicity. Therapeutic regimens that use two or more drugs in combination are at lower dosages than would be required in monotherapy. For example, flucytosine is used in combination with amphotericin B. Under these circumstances amphotericin B can be used at a much lower dosage than would be required when amphotericin is used alone.
3. To minimize resistance. Drugs in combination prevent or minimize the likelihood of emergence of drug-resistant strains. This strategy has been used for many years in the treatment of tuberculosis. The probability of emergence of strains resistant to both drugs of a combination is approximately equal to the product of the probabilities of resistance to individual agents.
4. To provide a **synergistic effect.** Drug combinations provide either an inhibitory or a lethal effect that is greater than would be expected from the sum of the activities of the individual agents (Fig. 8-12).

Not all drug combinations produce a synergistic effect. Some combinations produce an **indifference** in which the combined effect of the two drugs is no greater than the effect of either one administered separately (Fig. 8-12). Some combinations produce an **additive** effect in which the effect of the combination is equal to the sum of each drug administered separately (Fig. 8-12). Lastly, some combinations are **antagonistic** and the combined effect is less than that of either drug administered separately (Fig. 8-12).

Some synergisms are bactericidal and there are four mechanisms for achieving this type of result. First, a cell wall–active agent can be combined with an aminoglycoside (penicillin plus streptomycin in the treatment of enterococcal endocarditis). Second, a beta-lactam can be combined with inhibitors of beta-lactamase (the beta-lactamase inhibitor is a beta-lactam that has a higher affinity for the enzyme; ampicillin plus cloxacillin). The third mechanism is blockade of sequential steps of a critical metabolic pathway (trimethoprim and sulfamethoxazole inhibit sequential steps in folic acid synthesis). Fourth, for certain double beta-lactam interactions each drug exhibits a preferential affinity for the targets or PBP, for example, amdinocillin plus aztreonam.

Prophylaxis

Prophylactic administration of antimicrobials has become an important component of the physician's arsenal in the prevention of infections. Prophylaxis is especially useful for various surgical procedures that are subject to contamination by indigenous or endogenous microorganisms. The most effective period of prophylaxis is the 2 hours before the initial surgical incision. The duration of the prophylaxis is still controversial. Many studies indicate no benefit after the first postoperative day. However, many surgeons maintain that individuals in whom there are invasive life-supporting cannulas and tubes require long-term antibiotic prophylaxis. Some of the surgical procedures requiring antibiotic prophylaxis include cesarean section, vaginal or abdominal hysterectomy, orthopedic procedures with hardware insertion, major head and neck surgery, and various gastrointestinal procedures. **Cefazolin** and **cefoxitin** are the primary antimicrobial agents used in these surgical procedures. Other circumstances in which antimicrobial prophylaxis is recommended include

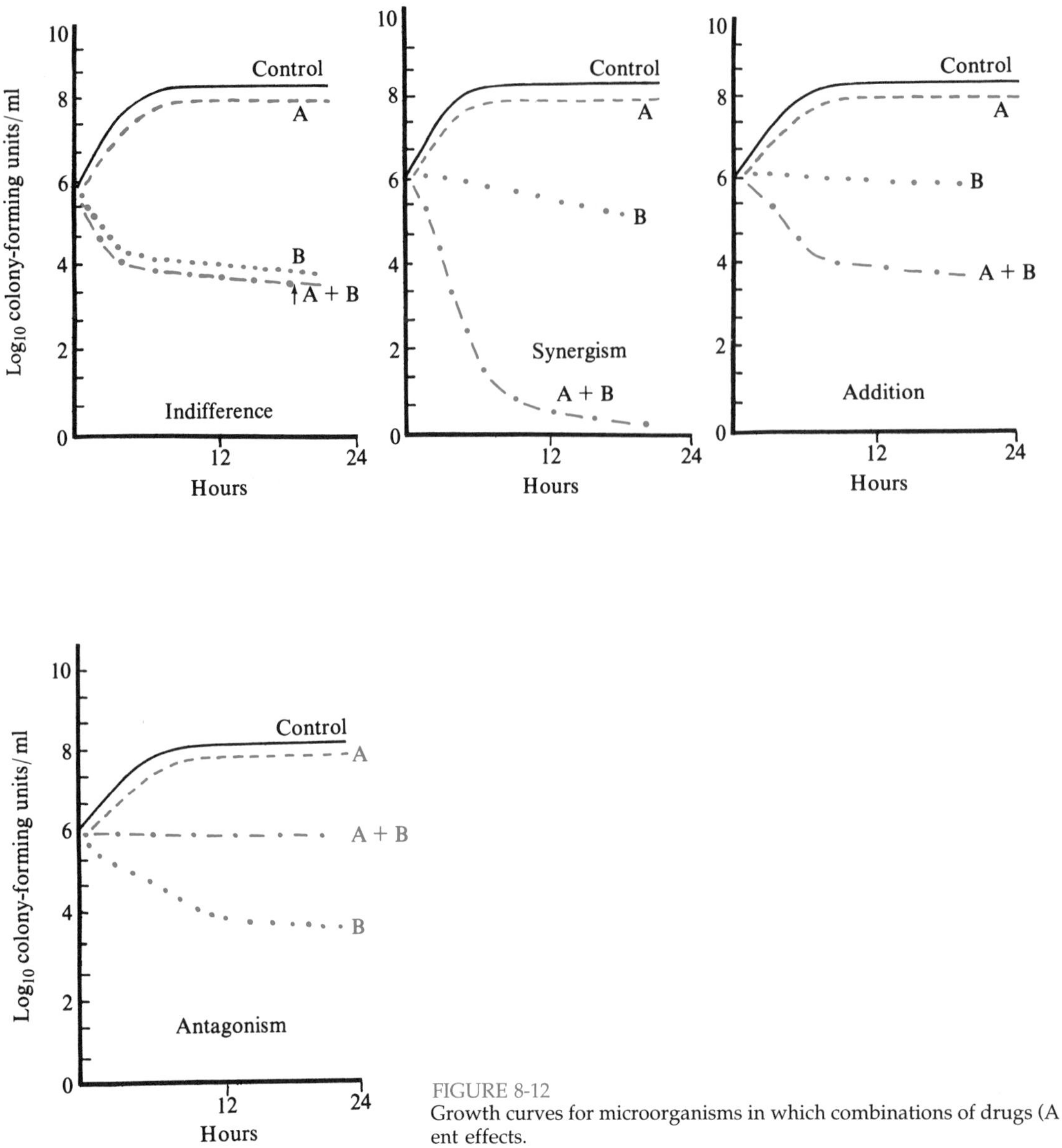

FIGURE 8-12
Growth curves for microorganisms in which combinations of drugs (A and B) produce different effects.

1. Dental extraction. Chemotherapy is considered before dental extraction only if the patient has a history of rheumatic fever, subacute bacterial endocarditis, or congenital heart defects. Extraction leads to displacement of oral microorganisms, particularly species of *Streptococcus,* into the circulation. These microorganisms can be implanted on heart tissue and can lead to serious disease.
2. Rheumatic fever. Penicillin is given prophylactically to rheumatic fever patients to prevent recurrence of streptococcal infection in heart tissue.
3. Tuberculosis. Isoniazid is administered prophylactically to those who are closely associated with tuberculosis patients. It is also used to prevent development of progressive tuberculosis.

Toxicity

The toxic potential of a drug is a major factor in the selection of a chemotherapeutic agent. This is especially true if the drug is to be administered to children, pregnant women, the elderly, and persons with organic diseases. In patients with underlying renal disease, antibiotics may persist in the body for extensive lengths of time because of the inability of the kidneys to excrete them. Drugs such as polymyxin, amphotericin B, and bacitracin should be used with extreme caution since they are directly toxic to kidney tissue. The physician must also be aware of drug interactions between the antimicrobial agent and drugs used by the patient for the treatment of noninfectious diseases.

DRUG RESISTANCE

After the introduction of penicillin and other antibiotics, antibiotic-resistant bacteria emerged. The discovery and development of newer agents with broader spectra of activity helped control infections caused by antibiotic-resistant bacteria. With each new class of antibiotic, newly resistant bacteria emerged. Antibiotic resistance is now a disturbing problem in the medical community. For example, strains of the organism causing tuberculosis are now resistant to several of the drugs that are used to control it; the organism causing gonorrhea has demonstrated multiple antimicrobial resistance; and *S. aureus,* which at one time was relatively easy to control, is exhibiting multiple resistance. Essentially, the basis of antibiotic resistance is **intrinsic** (a natural property of an organism) or **acquired** (mutational or plasmid/transposon-encoded). Increases in the number of drug-resistant strains may be due to the following:

1. Indiscriminate antibiotic use by the physician, for example, prolonged antimicrobial prophylaxis after surgery.
2. Feeding of subtherapeutic levels of antimicrobials to farm animals, a practice that increases the pool of drug-resistant species (*Salmonella* species, for example).
3. Inappropriate use of antibiotics by nonphysicians in developing countries. In some countries antibiotics can be purchased without a prescription. Antibiotics used improperly (for example, over a period of weeks) can lead to the selection of drug-resistant strains. If the dosage is too low, the infectious agent may not be inhibited, and this can lead to overgrowth as well as selection of drug-resistant strains.
4. Patient apathy toward the antimicrobial regimen prescribed by the physician. This is one of the causes of multiresistance by the organism causing tuberculosis.

The Genetics of Drug Resistance

There are several ways in which drug resistance can emerge in a microbial species.

1. **Transformation.** Cell-free DNA carrying a resistance gene can be released by a dying bacterial cell and taken up by a viable bacterial cell. The resistance gene is incorporated into the genome of the recipient cell.
2. **Transduction.** A bacteriophage acts as a vector and transfers DNA containing a resistance gene from one bacterial cell to another.
3. **Conjugation.** DNA containing a resistance gene is transferred from one bacterial cell to another in the conjugation or sexual process. The DNA transferred may be chromosomal or plasmid in origin.
4. **Mutation.** Mutations in regulatory genes can lead to increased expression of enzymes such as cephalosporinases that are encoded on the chromosome. Mutations can also lead to alterations in permeability (an intrinsic property) that prevent entrance of the drug into the cytoplasm.

Most antibiotic resistance genes are located on small pieces of DNA called **transposons** (also called **jumping genes**). Transposons are equipped with the information that allows them to move independently as a copy of themselves to other DNA sites. These DNA sites may be on the same chromosome, on a plasmid such as transmissible R factors, or on a bacteriophage. The transposon is, therefore, the major fundamental unit of drug resistance because it permits drug resistance genes to be spread from one generation to another within a strain and to other bacterial species. This promiscuous transfer and genetic exchange between different bacterial species allow the development of **multiple drug-resistant strains.**

Mechanisms of Drug Resistance

Four major mechanisms are responsible for the ability of microorganisms to resist the action of antimicrobials: interference with transport across the cell wall or cytoplasmic membrane (an intrinsic property), enzyme modification of the drug, alteration of the antimicrobial target in the microbe, and synthesis of resistant metabolic pathways. More than one mechanism may be available to a single microbial species and this is one reason why treatment of some infections is so difficult.

Interference with Transport. Interference with antimicrobial transport is frequently associated with chromosomal mutations. Such mutations result in alterations of the structure of cell wall or cytoplasmic membrane components or changes in sugar transport systems. Antimicrobial resistance in some species of *Salmonella,* for example, is related to the reduction in size or change in chemistry of **porin** channels in the cell wall.

Some drugs reach the periplasmic space but cannot be transported across the cytoplasmic membrane because they are modified by enzymes. These modifying enzymes also inactivate the drug—a characteristic discussed in the next section.

Enzymatic Inactivation. The most frequent antimicrobial resistance mechanism in bacteria is plasmid-mediated enzymatic inactivation (Table 8-2). Most of the enzyme inactivators are located in the periplasmic space. They include the beta-lactamases (beta-lactamases of *S. aureus* are excreted extracellularly; the same enzymes of gram-nega-

TABLE 8-2
Modifying Enzymes of the Aminoglycosides

Enzyme	Antibiotic substate
Acetyltransferase	Kanamycin, tobramycin, amikacin, sisomycin, neomycin, gentamicin
Adenyltransferase	Tobramycin, amikacin, kanamycin, neomycin, gentamicin, streptomycin, spectinomycin
Phosphotransferase	Neomycin, kanamycin, streptomycin, gentamicin

tive organisms are found in the periplasmic space) and enzymes that acetylate, adenylate, or phosphorylate various aminoglycosides. The major drug-inactivating enzyme located in the cytoplasm is chloramphenicol transacetylase. Drug modification occurs at a specific amino or hydroxyl group. Some drug modification sites are common to many of the aminoglycosides, and thus cross resistance is common.

How modification of aminoglycosides renders them inactive is not known but may be the result of (1) competition with unmodified aminoglycosides for the drug's target site, (2) ineffective binding to ribosomes, or (3) inability to interfere with ribosome function. Several determinants of aminoglycoside resistance are found on transposable elements. In some instances the transposon resistance factor is associated with as many as four or five resistance determinants. Thus a wide spectrum of cross resistance can be found in microorganisms when these transposons have been disseminated.

Alteration of the Microbial Target. Alteration of the microbial target is usually associated with a chromosomal mutation, but plasmids may also be involved. Two of the most widely examined instances involving alteration of a microbial target are PBP and the 30S ribosome.

The catalytic actions associated with the various PBP have already been discussed. If PBP are absent or are altered in such a way that their affinity for beta-lactams is decreased, then penicillin resistance may ensue.

Streptomycin resistance is associated with the loss or alteration of a single protein in the 30S ribosomal subunit. These mutations result in decreased ribosomal binding of streptomycin.

Synthesis of Resistant Metabolic Pathways. Synthesis of resistant metabolic pathways is associated with resistance to sulfonamides and related antimetabolites. An altered enzyme allows the organism to bypass the competitive inhibition of these drugs (see Fig. 8-11). This type of resistance has been observed in the Enterobacteriaceae during treatment with trimethoprim. These organisms are known to contain plasmid-coded dihydrofolate reductases or dihydropteroate synthetases that are resistant to the drug.

QUANTITATIVE AND QUALITATIVE DETERMINATION OF ANTIBIOTIC ACTIVITY

Both qualitative and quantitative measurements of potential antibiotics must be made to determine their usefulness as chemotherapeutic agents. In these procedures the unknown antibiotic is tested against microbial species such as *E. coli*, *S. aureus*, and *P. aeruginosa*. These organisms are fast growers and are known to be sensitive to antibiotics. The same tests are applied in the clinical setting to determine the susceptibility of an unknown pathogen, recently isolated from an infected patient, to known antibiotics. Susceptibility tests are important for evaluating which antibiotic can be used by the physician in disease treatment.

Quantitative Tests

Broth Dilution Test. In the broth dilution test the MIC and **minimal bactericidal concentration (MBC)** of the drug can be determined. A standard inoculum of the test organism is seeded into tubes of sterile broth containing decreasing concentrations of the antibiotic (Fig. 8-13). After 24 hours of incubation at 35 C the MIC is determined by finding the lowest concentration of drug inhibiting bacterial growth.

The MBC can be found by subculturing material from the tubes showing no visible growth into broth tubes that contain no antibiotic. Subculturing dilutes out the antibiotic. The lowest concentration of drug in the original culture that leads to no growth is the MBC. Major disadvantages of the broth dilution technique are that (1) only one organism can be run in a single series of tubes, (2) contamination is difficult to detect in broth, and (3) the test is expensive if large numbers of bacterial strains are being surveyed. The development of **microdilution trays** in frozen or dried form and **automated dispensing devices** has reduced the cost and time required to carry out these procedures. In some commercially available systems an automated photometric device is available to read the results of microdilution tests. The broth microdilution test has become the most popular of the current methods available to clinical laboratories in the United States. The reader device for these tests can be connected to a personal computer, which generates printed reports and facilitates data storage.

Most clinical laboratories do not use the broth dilution test as a routine method for determining antimicrobial susceptibility. Instead, they use it as a supplemental procedure to the disk diffusion method. Broth dilution is used primarily for determining the MIC of test organisms at several concentrations of drug. These data then are used in determining the dosage that will be effective in treating human infections. The data will be correlated with results obtained with the disk diffusion technique (discussed later).

Broth microdilution is useful in determining anaerobe susceptibility. Commercial broth microdilution panels are available. Anaerobe susceptibility testing is not appropriate under all conditions. Anaerobe susceptibility testing should be utilized for isolates from central nervous system (CNS) infections, endocarditis, osteomyelitis, joint infections, prosthetic device infections, and recurrent or refractory bacteremia. Organisms considered appropriate for testing are species of *Bacteroides*, *Clostridium*, and *Fusobacterium*.

Agar Dilution Method. The agar dilution method is a simplified procedure for testing the effect of an antibiotic against many bacterial strains. In the test the antibiotic at various concentrations is mixed with molten agar, poured into Petri dishes, and allowed to harden. Standard aliquots of the test microorganisms are transferred to each of the agar plates by an inoculum-replicating apparatus. As many as 36 different bacterial isolates can be seeded on one plate (Fig. 8-14). Three areas on the plate are reserved for the control cultures, *S. aureus*, *E. coli*, and *P. aeruginosa*. All the plates containing the various concentrations of antibiotic are read after 18 to 24 hours of incubation. The MIC is read as the lowest concentration of antibiotic that inhibits growth. Both the broth and agar dilution techniques yield more precise results, but because of heavy work loads most laboratories use the disk diffusion test.

Qualitative Tests

Disk Diffusion Test. The disk diffusion test is an agar diffusion technique and is one of the most widely used procedures for determining bacterial susceptibility to antimicrobials. In the test, paper disks impregnated with known amounts of antibiotic are placed on an agar medium seeded with a known species of bacteria. As the antibiotic diffuses into the medium, it produces a gradient of antibiotic concentration. After suitable incubation, antibiotic activity is determined by the width of the zone of no growth around the antibiotic disk (Fig. 8-15).

The size of the zone of inhibition can be correlated with the clinical susceptibility of the microorganism to the antibiotic, provided standard conditions are maintained. One standardized test is called the **Kirby-Bauer** method. In this technique, Mueller-Hinton agar, a standard inoculum, and a single antibiotic disk of standardized potency (usually 30 μg for many antibiotics) are used. Zones of inhibition are described as susceptible, intermediate, and resistant. The breakpoint between the zones for each antibiotic is obtained from published tables. The Kirby-Bauer tables have taken into account the MIC of the organism obtained from broth or agar dilution techniques, the blood

FIGURE 8-13
Broth dilution test used to determine minimal inhibitory concentration (MIC) and minimal bactericidal concentration (MBC) of antimicrobial compounds. A. Each broth tube contains 9.0 ml of sterile broth with a different concentration of antimicrobial. To each tube is added 0.5 ml of broth and 0.5 ml of a known concentration of microorganisms. The concentration of microorganisms in each broth tube is so small that there is no visible turbidity. Tubes are incubated at 35 C for 12 to 18 hours. B. Tubes are examined for macroscopic growth. The lowest concentration of drug showing no growth is the MIC. In this case it is 2.5 μg/ml. C. To determine MBC, loopfuls are removed from tubes showing no visible growth and are streaked on agar plates. The plates showing no growth indicate drug concentrations that destroy the microorganisms (10 μg/ml).

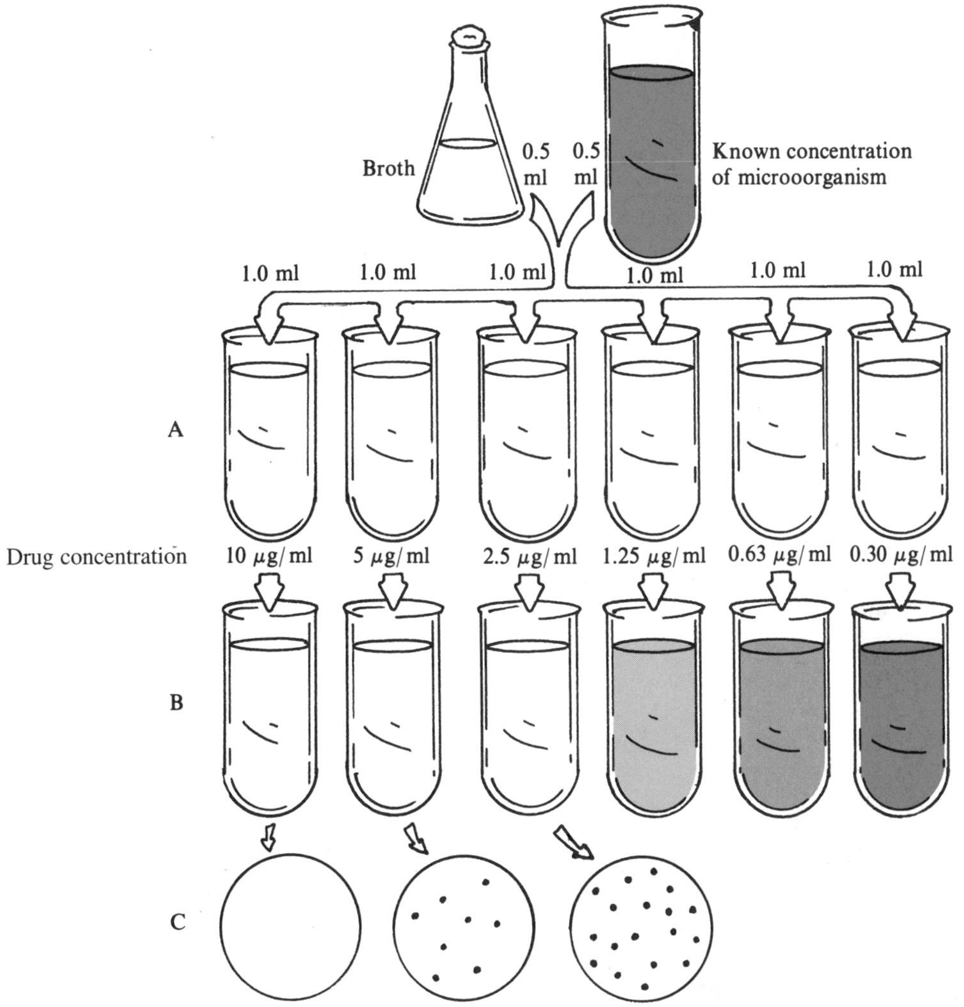

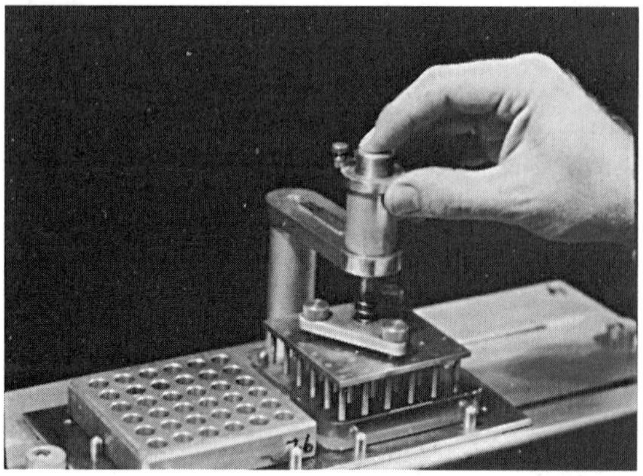

FIGURE 8-14
Steers inoculum-replicating device. The plate on the left contains 36 reservoirs for bacterial inocula. The bottom plate on the right contains antibiotic-containing medium on which bacteria will be seeded. (From J. A. Washington II, *Mayo Clin. Proc.* 44:811, 1969.)

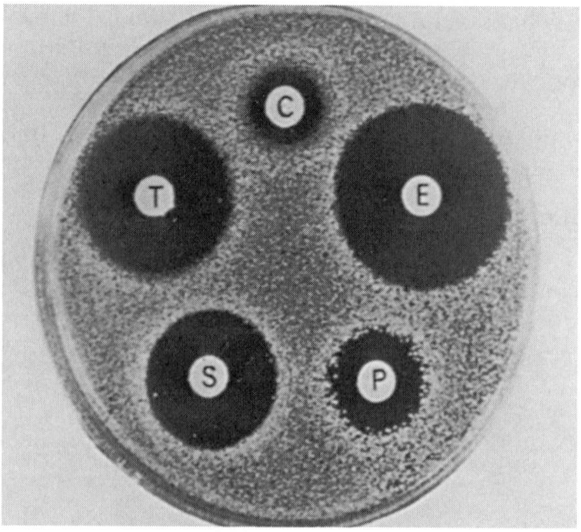

FIGURE 8-15
Disk diffusion test. An agar medium is inoculated with a strain of *Staphylococcus aureus*. Disks containing specified amounts of antibiotic are placed on the agar. The type of antibiotic in each disk is indicated by the letter: *T*, tetracycline; *C*, chloramphenicol; *E*, erythromycin; *P*, penicillin; *S*, streptomycin. Inhibition of growth of *S. aureus* is evidenced by a clear zone around the antibiotic disk. (From L. P. Garrod and F. O'Grady, *Antibiotics and Chemotherapy*, 5th ed. London: Churchill Livingstone, 1973.)

levels obtained with normal dosage of the antibiotic, and the distribution of zone sites among species with known responsiveness to the antibiotic (Table 8-3).

The disk diffusion test provides information that is adequate for guiding the therapy of most infections. Disk diffusion is not applicable for slowly growing organisms, obligate anaerobes, or microorganisms requiring higher than usual levels of carbon dioxide. The reason is the test has been standardized for fast-growing aerobic and facul-

TABLE 8-3
Examples of Zone Size Interpretative Standards for Some Antimicrobial Agents Used in the Treatment of Infectious Disease

Antimicrobial agent	Disk content	Inhibition zone diameter (to nearest mm)		
		Resistant	**Intermediate***	**Susceptible**
Amikacin	30 μg	≤14	15–16	≥17
Ampicillin				
Gram-negative enterics	10 μg	≤13	—	≥17
Staphylococci	10 μg	≤28	—	≥29
Carbenicillin				
Enterobacteriaceae	100 μg	≤19	—	≥23
Pseudomonas	100 μg	≤13	—	≥17
Cefoxitin	30 μg	≤14	—	≥18
Chloramphenicol	30 μg	≤12	13–17	≥18
Clindamycin	2 μg	≤14	15–20	≥21
Erythromycin	15 μg	≤13	14–22	≥23
Gentamicin	10 μg	≤12	13–14	≥15
Moxalactam	30 μg	≤14	—	≥23
Nalidixic acid	30 μg	≤13	14–18	≥19
Penicillin G				
Staphylococci	10 units	≤28	—	≥29
Sulfonamides	250 or 300 μg	≤12	—	≥17
Tetracycline	30 μg	≤14	15–18	≥19
Trimethoprim	5 μg	≤10	—	≥16
Vancomycin	30 μg	≤9	10–11	≥12

* *Intermediate* indicates that the test result be considered equivocal or indeterminate.
SOURCE: Adapted from Table 2, in *Performance Standards for Antimicrobial Disk Susceptibility Tests*, 4th ed., M2-A4, by the National Committee for Clinical Laboratory Standards. The interpretative data are valid only if M2-A4 methodology is followed. Used with permission.

TABLE 8-4
Characteristics of Some Important Chemotherapeutic Agents

Drug and site of inhibition	Microbial group involved and specific clinical use
Cell wall inhibitors	
Penicillins (see also Fig. 8-2)	Bacteria; effective against gram-positive and gram-negative, depending on preparation used
Cephalosporins (see Fig. 8-5)	Bacteria; effective against gram-positive and gram-negative, depending on preparation used
Bacitracin	Bacteria; used primarily in topical preparations because of tissue toxicity
Vancomycin	Bacteria; for staphylococcal infections that do not respond to penicillins, treatment of antibiotic-associated pseudomembranous colitis
Cytoplasmic membrane inhibitors	
Amphotericin B	Fungi; treatment of systemic fungal infections by *Candida, Histoplasma,* and *Blastomyces*; combined with flucytosine to reduce potential toxicity to kidney
Nystatin	Fungi; topical agent in treatment of *Candida* infections
Imidazoles (ketoconazole, miconazole, etc.)	Fungi; ketoconazole for systemic fungal infections but others used primarily as topical agents
Polymyxins	Bacteria; because of toxicity to kidneys, used primarily in topical preparations
Protein synthesis inhibitors	
Aminoglycosides (streptomycin, amikacin, etc.; see Table 8-1)	Bacteria; see Table 8-1
Chloramphenicol	Bacteria; toxicity reduces its use to treatment of typhoid and meningitis in which the patient is allergic to penicillins
Erythromycin	Bacteria; absence of toxicity makes it suitable alternative to other drugs that are toxic or cause allergic reactions; drug of choice in legionnaires' disease and pneumonia caused by *Mycoplasma pneumoniae*
Lincomycin	Bacteria; used to treat staphylococcal infections that do not respond to penicillins
Clindamycin	Bacteria and some protozoa; anaerobic pulmonary infections
Tetracyclines	Bacteria; rickettsial and chlamydial infections
Nucleic acid synthesis inhibitors	
Rifampin	Bacteria; treatment of tuberculosis, combined with other drugs
Nalidixic acid and fluoroquinolones	Bacteria; primarily in preventing gram-negative urinary tract infections in compromised patients
Flucytosine	Fungi; yeast infections (*Candida*) but also combined with amphotericin B to reduce toxicity in treatment of systemic infections
Ribavirin	Virus; respiratory syncytial virus and Lassa fever virus
Amantadine	Virus; influenza A virus infections
Idoxuridine	Virus; herpes simplex virus type 1 infections of the eye
Vidarabine	Virus; herpes zoster (shingles), herpes simplex encephalitis, and chickenpox in immunocompromised patients
Acyclovir	Virus; genital herpes infections
Zidovudine (AZT)	Virus; human immunodeficiency virus (HIV)
Antimetabolites	
Sulfonamides	Bacteria, some urinary tract infections; topical forms for burn patients; oral preparations to prevent traveler's diarrhea
Para-aminosalicyclic acid	Bacteria; only in tuberculosis
Ethambutol	Bacteria; used exclusively in treatment of tuberculosis
Trimethoprim	Bacteria; used primarily in combination with a sulfonamide, sulfamethoxazole, for treatment of hospital-associated diseases of respiratory, urinary, and gastrointestinal tracts; also used in treatment of *Pneumocystis carinii* pneumonia in AIDS patients
Isoniazid	Bacteria; tuberculosis
Nitrofurans	Bacteria, fungi, protozoa; nitrofurantoin used to prevent urinary tract infections following catheterization

tatively anaerobic organisms. Disk diffusion tests are still the most economical of the susceptibility tests to perform. They are also easy to perform and reproducible, and provide category (inhibition zones) results that are easily interpreted by the physician.

The E Test

The E test is a recently developed technique that is a modification of the disk diffusion and the agar dilution methods. This test provides a simple, cost-effective, and rapid method for measuring the **MIC of single antimicrobial agents.** The test is based on diffusion of an antibiotic gradient from a plastic strip (Plate 2) on inoculated agar media. The resulting elliptical zone of bacterial inhibition is read at the point of intersection of the ellipse with an MIC scale on the strip. The test allows one to determine the MIC of an organism to one or more selected antibiotics rather than to a predetermined panel of antimicrobial agents. The E test is particularly useful in cases in which the MIC of penicillin is required for suspected penicillin-resistant pneumococci, or for measuring the MIC of ampicillin and vancomycin for *Enterococcus faecium* isolates from serious infections.

Antibiotic Concentration in the Patient's Serum

The determination of antibiotic concentration in the serum is justified when an antibiotic exhibits a narrow range between therapeutic and toxic concentrations. Therefore, serum assays may be necessary to treat life-threatening infections. Some of the toxic drugs that need to be measured include the aminoglycosides, vancomycin, and chloramphenicol. The enzymatic assay is one commonly employed technique. For example, in one type of assay enzymes that acetylate or adenylate the antimicrobial agent are used. The modified antimicrobial agent is separated from the mixture and quantified. Other methods for assay include immunoassays, chromatography, and chemical assays.

Summary

1. Chemotherapeutic agents are drugs that are selectively toxic. This selectivity may be due to absence of the target in mammalian cells or to microbial targets that are biochemically different from their mammalian counterparts. Selective toxicity can be expressed as a ratio between the maximum toxic level and the maximum therapeutic level.

2. Chemotherapeutic agents can be synthesized totally or partially in the laboratory or they may be produced biologically by microorganisms, that is, antibiotics. Chemotherapeutic agents may have a broad or narrow spectrum of activity. They may inhibit (-static) or kill (-cidal) microbes.

3. Antimicrobial activity of newly isolated chemotherapeutic agents can be determined by using a plate diffusion technique with test microorganisms. Several factors must be considered in evaluating the potential of a chemotherapeutic agent but the two most important are that (1) the drug is active at very low concentrations and (2) the drug is relatively nontoxic to mammalian tissue.

4. The characteristics of the various chemotherapeutic agents are outlined in Table 8-4.

5. Several factors must be taken into account before the physician prescribes a drug regimen: (1) the correct dosage based on the minimal inhibitory concentration (MIC) of the drug, (2) route of administration of the drug, (3) toxicity of the drug, (4) whether a drug combination should be used, and (5) whether the drug can be used prophylactically.

6. Drug resistance in bacteria is related primarily to transfer of resistance determinants via conjugation, transformation, and transduction. Most antibiotic resistance genes are located on transposons, which can be transferred to future generations of the same or different species.

7. The mechanisms that permit bacteria to resist antimicrobials are (1) interference with transport of the drug, (2) enzymatic inactivation of the drug, (3) alteration of the drug's target site, and (4) synthesis of resistant metabolic pathways.

8. Drug combinations are being used increasingly in the treatment of infectious disease. The major reasons for using them are to (1) provide a broader spectrum of activity, (2) minimize toxicity, (3) minimize resistance, and (4) provide a synergistic effect.

9. Quantitative and qualitative tests are used in the clinical laboratory to determine what antimicrobial will be effective in treatment. The most widely used test is a qualitative one called the disk diffusion test. This test provides zones of microbial inhibition described as susceptible, intermediate, and resistant.

10. Quantitative determinations of antibiotic activity are provided by two methods called broth and agar dilution tests. They are used primarily to determine the MIC of various drugs.

11. Quantitative determinations of antibiotic levels in the serum are important when the drug has a narrow range between therapeutic and toxic concentrations.

Questions for Study

1. If drug-resistant mutants for one drug arise at the rate of one per 10^5 colonies, what would be the rate if two drugs in combination were used and resistant mutants arose at the rate of one per 10^3 colonies? What would be the effect if three or more drugs were used in treatment? Explain the implications of this type of therapy.
2. If antibiotics are capable of inhibiting or killing bacteria, explain how the bacteria responsible for producing some of these antibiotics can survive. For

example, the antibiotic chlortetracycline is produced by the bacterium *Streptomyces aureofaciens.* Give several examples of how this immunity to the antibiotic might be accomplished.

3. There are certain clinical settings in which the rapid killing of gram-negative bacteria has aggravated the condition, for example, typhoid fever, gram-negative bacterial sepsis, and neonatal meningitis due to gram-negative enteric bacilli. The aggravation was observed when cell wall inhibitors were used in treatment. Can you offer some explanation for this?
4. Explain the attributes of using drugs in combination for infectious disease. On your own, find out from physicians, textbooks, or journal articles what diseases or conditions require the use of drugs in combination.
5. What is the explanation as to why there seem to be fewer drugs for treatment of fungal infections? Viral infections?
6. In addition to knowing the minimal inhibitory concentration for a specific drug, what other considerations must be addressed before a drug is prescribed for therapy? Does body site of the infection influence the choice or dosage of a drug? Explain.
7. Describe the mechanisms by which antibiotic resistance genes on chromosomes as well as plasmids can be transferred to other chromosomes or genetic units.
8. Without the use of drug-inactivating enzymes, how can bacteria develop resistance to antimicrobials?
9. What are penicillin-binding proteins and how are they involved in microbial sensitivity to penicillin?
10. Make a list of antibiotics or other antimicrobials that have been prescribed for you or members of your family in the past 5 years. For what condition or infection were they prescribed? Do you think they were appropriate? If not, why not?

PART III

Immunology

CHAPTER 9

Nonspecific Host Resistance

OBJECTIVES

To differentiate in simple terms between specific and nonspecific immunity

To discuss the characteristics of the cell types involved in antimicrobial defense

To discuss the noncellular mechanisms of antimicrobial defense

To describe phagocytosis with respect to antigen, particularly as it relates to recognition, internalization, digestion, and presentation

To describe the mechanisms by which intracellular parasites evade phagocytosis

To discuss inflammation with respect to inducers of the process and molecules released during the process

To describe how interferons are able to protect cells against viral infection

OUTLINE

NONSPECIFIC VS. SPECIFIC IMMUNITY

CELLULAR MECHANISM OF ANTIMICROBIAL DEFENSE
- Phagocytic and Nonphagocytic Cells
  - Polymorphonuclear Granulocytes
    - Neutrophils
    - Basophils and Mast Cells
    - Eosinophils
  - Mononuclear Phagocytes
    - Phagocytosis
    - Antigen Presenting
- Dynamics of Phagocytosis
  - Inflammation
    - Acute Inflammation
    - Chronic Inflammation
  - Phagocytic Process
    - Recognition
    - Vacuole Formation
    - Phagolysosome Formation
    - Oxidative Killing
    - Nonoxidative Killing
  - Macrophage Activation
- Deleterious Effects of Phagocytosis
  - Tissue Destruction
  - Intracellular Survival of Some Microorganisms
- Defects in Phagocytic and Inflammatory Processes
  - Motility and Chemotaxis Disorders
  - Phagocytosis Disorders
  - Microbicidal Disorders
  - Neutropenia

NONCELLULAR MECHANISMS OF DEFENSE
- Plasma
- Tissue Factors
  - Interferons
  - Complement System
- Platelets

At one time or another, all of us have recovered from infectious diseases such as colds, the flu, measles, and mumps. Recovery from such diseases indicates that our bodies are, to varying degrees, capable of protecting us from the harmful effects of infectious agents. The system that affords us this protection is called the **immune system.** The immune system is capable of recognizing foreign substances that are not part of our natural makeup or **self.** For example, infectious agents that invade the body are considered an example of nonself. Your cells or tissues are not considered foreign to you but are foreign **(nonself)** if they are introduced into another individual. The purpose of this and following chapters is to (1) show how foreign substances are recognized and (2) demonstrate the consequences of this recognition for the foreign substance as well as the host.

Nonspecific vs. Specific Immunity

The immune system can handle infectious agents in either a nonspecific **(innate)** or a specific **(adaptive** or **acquired)** way. When any infectious agent enters the host, the innate immune system of chemical (e.g., lysozyme, sebaceous gland secretions) and physical (e.g., integument) factors and immune cells (e.g., macrophages, neutrophils) is engaged. Sometimes the nonspecific immune process requires additional help in the form of a specific response. The specific immune response utilizes the machinery of the nonspecific response plus additional factors.

The specific immune system is often viewed as being composed of two branches whose roles are different depending on whether the infectious agent is extracellular or intracellular. One branch referred to as the **humoral** (*humoral* meaning "fluid") **immune response** is associated primarily with **extracellular pathogens.** Humoral immunity is associated with the formation of protein molecules called **antibodies.** Antibodies can be defined as a group of proteins that are formed in response to the presence of a foreign agent. In turn, antibodies react with the foreign agent and help destroy it. The class of proteins that all antibodies belong to is called **immunoglobulins,** which are discussed in Chapter 10. Antibodies are produced by a class of lymphocytes called **B cells.** The foreign agent capable of stimulating the formation of antibodies is referred to as the **antigen.**

The other branch of the specific immune system, referred to as **cell-mediated immunity,** deals primarily with **intracellular pathogens.** Cell-mediated immunity is associated primarily with lymphocytes called **T cells.** There is a reason why we need a system to deal with intracellular parasites. By themselves antibodies are unable to penetrate host-infected cells. Consequently an additional immune response is needed. Cell-mediated immunity, as the name implies, is based on the immune system utilizing specific cells to deal with the invader. Later in Chapter 12, we discuss the specifics of humoral and cell-mediated immunity.

In Chapter 14 we discuss how the integument and mucosal surfaces of the body help prevent invasion by microbial agents. In this chapter, we describe some of the noncellular and cellular components of the circulatory system that are engaged in nonspecific host defense. Most of the discussion centers on the cellular mechanism of antimicrobial defense, that is, the role of phagocytic and nonphagocytic cells.

Cellular Mechanism of Antimicrobial Defense

A variety of cell types are involved in resistance and immunity to infection. Some cell types are discussed in this chapter while others, which are associated with specific or adaptive immunity, are characterized in following chapters. Figure 9-1 provides an overview of the cell types and their origin.

PHAGOCYTIC AND NONPHAGOCYTIC CELLS

The basis of a nonspecific cellular mechanism of defense is centered on the ability of certain white blood cells to ingest and digest microorganisms. There are two types of white blood cells associated with nonspecific host resistance: **polymorphonuclear granulocytes** and **mononuclear phagocytes (macrophages).**

Polymorphonuclear Granulocytes

Polymorphonuclear granulocytes are short-lived (12–24 hours) and, as their name implies, possess a multilobed nucleus and granules. The granules contain hydrolytic enzymes capable of digesting most organic material. Polymorphonuclear granulocytes make up approximately 70 percent of the normal white blood cell (leukocyte) count. They are divided into three types based on staining, morphological, and developmental properties: **neutrophils, basophils** and **mast cells,** and **eosinophils.**

Neutrophils. Neutrophils, which are sometimes referred to as polymorphonuclear neutrophils (PMN), make up 90 percent of the blood granulocytes. They possess receptors for immunoglobulins and are active in the digestion of ingested microorganisms. Neutrophils possess two types of granules: a primary granule, which contains acid hydrolases, myeloperoxidase, and lysozyme, and a secondary granule that contains lactoferrin and lysozyme (see Phagocytosis). Neutrophils are the first to reach the site of infection but they succumb quickly in battle. Neutrophils have also been described as a source of endogenous peptide antibiotics (see Under the Microscope 5).

Basophils and Mast Cells. Basophils and mast cells make up less than 1 percent of the total white blood cell count. Mast cells, which are similar in many ways to basophils, are not found in blood but appear in peripheral tissue. Both cell types possess receptors for the immunoglobulin class called IgE. Basophil and mast cell granules, when

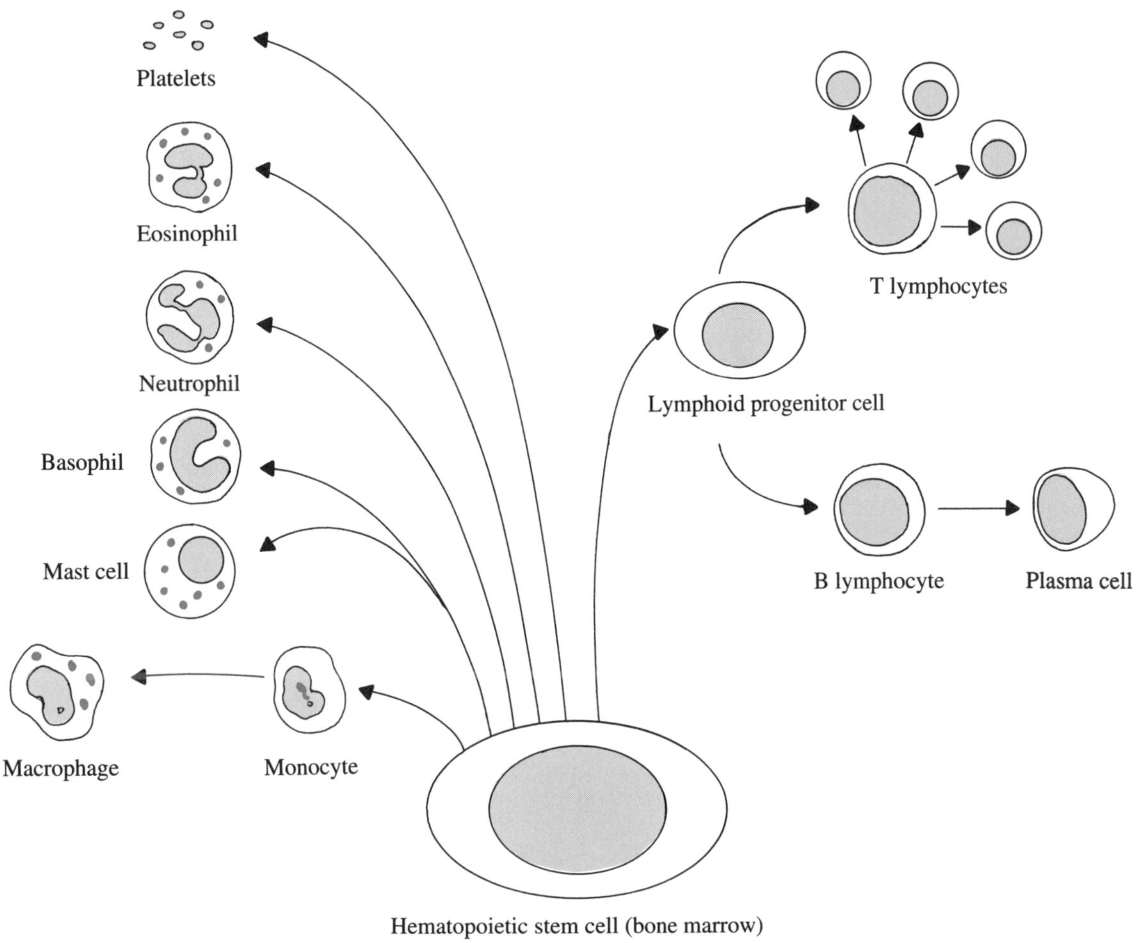

FIGURE 9-1
Cell types involved in immune response. Cell types are derived from bone marrow stem cells. Cell types on the right are associated only with a specific immune response. Cell types on the left are associated with a nonspecific immune response but can be part of a specific immune response if the latter becomes activated.

released following stimulation,* contain pharmacologically active substances such as histamine. Histamine affects blood vessels and smooth-muscle function. The granules stain (Wright's stain) an intense deep violet blue on blood smears. Mast cells are found primarily in the mucosa of the lungs and intestine as well as in the connective tissue surrounding the blood vessels. Mast cells are regarded as "sentinel" cells because of their location and ability to react with foreign substances. For example, they interact with substances that are associated with hypersensitivities (i.e., allergies—see Chapter 13). Substances that cause allergies usually make contact with the host via the respiratory or intestinal tract, the two sites where mast cells are located. However, mast cells may play a positive role by helping to destroy animal parasites such as worms (helminths—see Chapter 34). For the most part, however, mast cells do not play a major role in nonspecific immunity.

* Release of enzymes and other chemicals from granules is called **degranulation.** Degranulation occurs following antigen binding to membrane-bound IgE.

Eosinophils. Eosinophils account for approximately 3 to 5 percent of the leukocyte count in normal blood. Like basophils, they possess immunoglobulin receptors but unlike neutrophils their primary function is not digestion of ingested microorganisms. The granules of eosinophils are acidophilic (affinity for the acid dye eosin) and are released outside the cell. Eosinophilic granules destroy primarily animal parasites such as protozoa and worms. Two of the proteins in the granules are **major basic protein (MBP)** and **eosinophil cationic protein (ECP).**

Mononuclear Phagocytes

The bone marrow is the origin of stem cells that give rise to **monocytes.** Monocytes eventually reach the bloodstream. Monocytes migrate from the blood into various tissues and organs where they enlarge and form **macrophages.** Macrophages are widely deployed throughout the body. Some are **fixed,** primarily along blood vessels of the spleen, lymph nodes, liver, and bone marrow. Others are motile and are called **wandering** or **free macrophages.** Depending on their location and their histological appearance, macrophages are given more specific names,

UNDER THE MICROSCOPE 5

Defensins: Natural Peptide Antibiotics Produced by Humans and Animals

Antibiotics generally are thought of as being produced by fungi and bacteria. Defensins are a newly defined family of broad-spectrum antibiotic peptides found in the leukocytes of humans and other mammals. Defensins comprise a group of similar carbohydrate-free peptides, containing 29 to 34 amino acids. Each defensin includes six cysteine residues that form three characteristic intramolecular disulfide bonds. Human neutrophils contain four defensins: human neutrophil protein (HNP)-1, -2, -3, and -4. Together, these four defensins constitute 30 to 50 percent of the total protein in the human neutrophil's azurophilic granules, where they are strategically located for extracellular secretion or for delivery to phagocytic vacuoles. Defensin-positive neutrophil cells, for example, are found within blood capillaries adjacent to the air spaces in human lung tissue. Macrophages constitute the lung's first line of cellular defense against inhaled microorganisms, but neutrophils readily enter air spaces to protect the lung when infection occurs.

Although defensins are most prominent in neutrophils, at least two rabbit defensins are synthesized in alveolar macrophages. Defensin-like molecules are abundant in preparations of murine small intestine and are not limited to mammals. Certain insect larvae contain defensin-like molecules in their hemolymph (body fluid).

The microbial targets susceptible to mammalian defensins include a variety of gram-positive and -negative bacteria, fungi, and certain viruses. Experimentally human defensin HNP-1 kills a smooth strain of *Escherichia coli* by sequentially affecting the permeability of the outer and inner membranes. The bacteria have to be under conditions that support growth or active metabolism to be susceptible to HNP-1.

Defensins express biological properties other than antimicrobial activity. They exert potent but nonselective cytotoxic activity in vitro against various actively metabolizing human and mouse tumor cells. They may play an important role in cell differentiation and function. They exert selective in vitro chemotactic activity for blood monocytes.

Perhaps future therapeutic agents will be patterned for endogenous antibiotics such as defensins.

Excerpted from R. I. Lehrer, T. Ganz, and M. E. Selsted, *ASM News* 56:315, 1990.

such as **Kupffer cells** in the liver, **microglia** in the brain, **alveolar** or **"dust cells"** in the lung, and **peritoneal macrophages** in the gut. Irrespective of location, they are all macrophages.

Morphologically, macrophages assume a wide variety of shapes determined by their habitats. In suspension, they are round and about 14 to 20 μm in diameter. The nucleus may be round, elongated, or bean-shaped. The peripheral cytoplasm is usually clear and constantly forming and reforming veil-like ruffles.

Two of the most important functions of mononuclear phagocytes in the host are **phagocytosis** and **antigen presenting.**

Phagocytosis. Macrophages and neutrophils are referred to as **professional phagocytes;** that is, their predominant role is to remove foreign substances. In this capacity they engulf foreign substances, kill microorganisms if those are the entrapped material, and then break down the trapped material for excretion and reutilization. Macrophages are long-lived, being replaced at a rate of about 1 percent per day; hence they are capable of sustained activity.

Antigen Presenting. Antigen presenting cells (APC) are found primarily in the skin, lymph nodes, spleen, and thymus. These body sites (except the thymus*) represent areas where macrophages are most likely to encounter foreign substances (nonself antigens). Macrophages ingest the foreign material and degrade it into small fragments, some of which are antigenic. The antigenic fragments are bound to major histocompatibility complex (MHC) proteins (see Chapter 11) and transported to the surface of the APC (Fig. 9-2). The surface antigen acts like a beacon and attracts antigen-reactive lymphocytes that induce a specific immune response, that is, humoral and cell-mediated immunity. The role of the macrophage in specific immune responses is discussed at length in Chapter 12. Macrophages possess many receptors for contact with a variety of immune system molecules. Consequently, macrophages are associated with many immune functions of both a specific and a nonspecific nature (Table 9-1).

DYNAMICS OF PHAGOCYTOSIS

When some foreign substances, for example, microorganisms, enter the body, a variety of immune cells migrate

* Thymus presents self antigens.

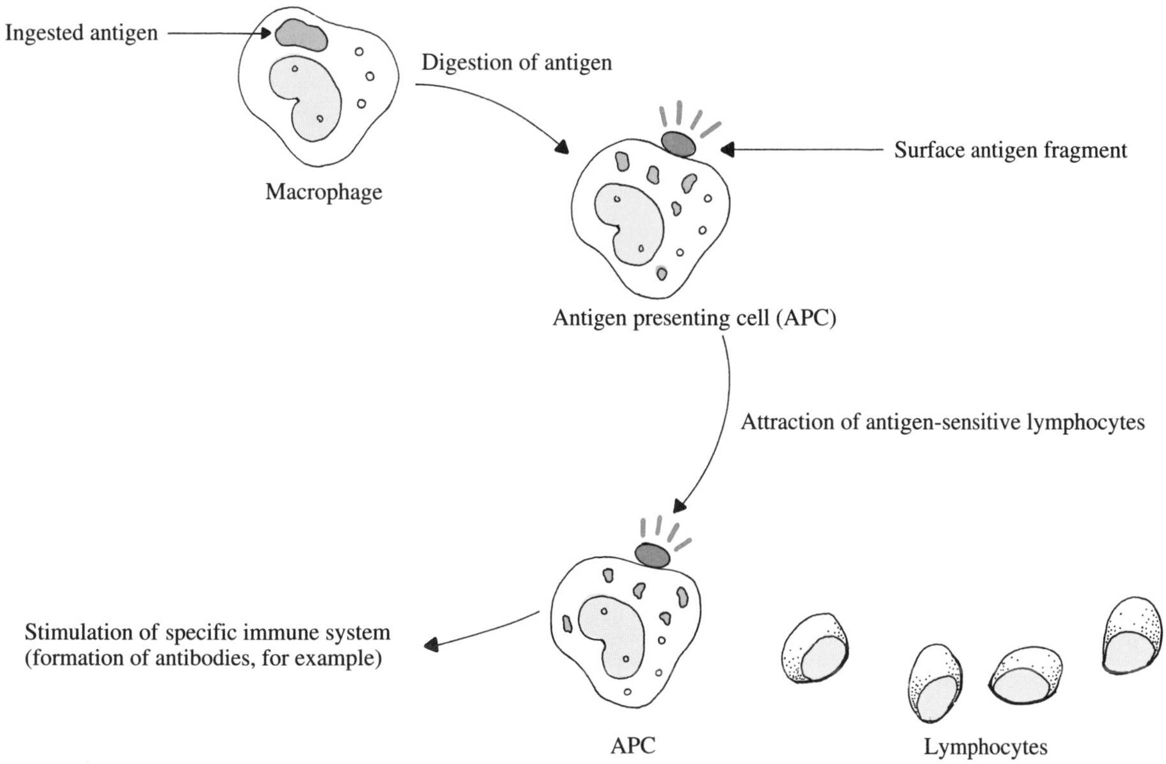

FIGURE 9-2
Antigen presenting cell (APC) formation. Macrophages ingest foreign material (*colored*) and digest it into fragments. Some of the fragments are transported to the macrophage surface, creating an APC. Surface antigen attracts lymphocytes that recognize antigen and engage in a specific immune response, for example, formation of antibodies.

TABLE 9-1
Specific and Nonspecific Immune Functions of Macrophages

Microbicidal activities

Macrophages destroy ingested microorganisms via release of hydrolytic enzymes and other proteins; this may take place in the presence or absence of antibodies and lymphocytes.

Inflammation and fever

Macrophages release proteins and other factors (interleukin-1 [IL-1], prostaglandins, complement, and clotting factor) that can stimulate and maintain the inflammatory process.

Activation of lymphocytes

Macrophages process foreign antigens and present them to lymphocytes. Lymphocytes in turn induce antibody formation as well as the cell-mediated immune response.

Tumor destruction

Macrophages are stimulated and activated by various immune cell products that enable them to phagocytize and destroy tumor cells.

to the site of infection or injury. During microbial infection the function of the immune cells is to localize and destroy the intruders before they can spread to other parts of the body. The signal that often attracts phagocytic cells to the site of infection is a process called **inflammation.**

Inflammation

A variety of agents or substances, in addition to microbial agents, can elicit an inflammatory response. These agents include drugs, pollen, inert physical materials such as wood, and pieces of metal. Inflammatory reactions can be classified according to their duration: **acute** or short duration, and **chronic** or long duration.

Acute Inflammation. Acute inflammation starts immediately after the tissue has been insulted. The classic symptoms of inflammation are pain, redness, heat, and swelling. The initial events of inflammation include smooth-muscle cell constriction, which causes dilation of blood vessels; increased capillary permeability; and leukocyte migration to the site of injury (Fig. 9-3). These events are mediated by vasoactive (affecting blood vessels) agents such as **histamine** and **prostaglandins.** Both of these molecules are derived from injured cells and later from cells that infiltrate the area. Histamine, for example, is released from the mast or "sentinel" cells located near the site of injury.

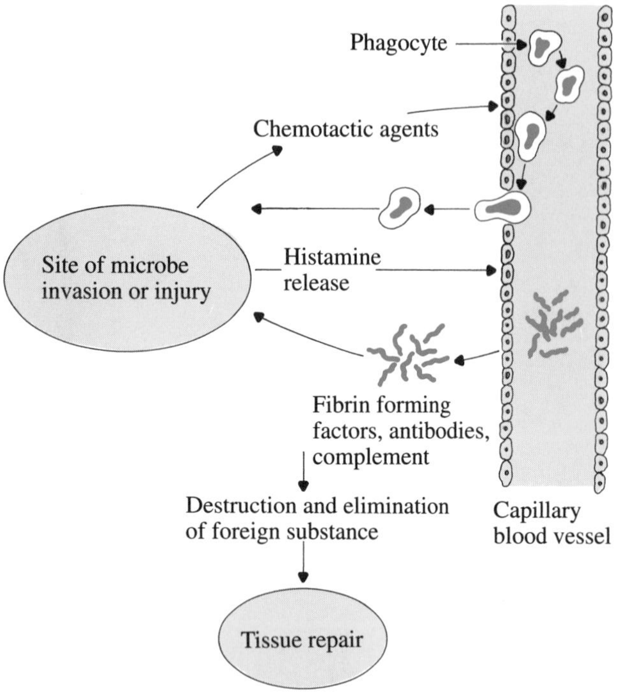

FIGURE 9-3
Inflammation process. At the site of inflammation due to microbe invasion or to the presence of other foreign substances, a number of chemotactic agents (e.g., histamine) are released. These substances diffuse into capillaries. Phagocytes in the circulation, attracted to the site of inflammation, pass through capillary walls (a process called **diapedesis**). Vasoactive substances from the site of inflammation also diffuse into capillaries and promote the passage of plasma elements such as fibrin forming factors, antibodies, and complement to the site of inflammation. After the foreign substance has been destroyed, tissue repair follows.

Migration of leukocytes, particularly neutrophils and macrophages, from the capillaries to the site of injury is due to a process called **chemotaxis** (attraction to a site induced by a chemical agent). The chemotactic agents released at the site of injury include bacterial or viral products, products released from damaged cells or tissues, enzymes from degraded neutrophils, complement fragments, blood clotting factors, and others. Activated clotting factors provide **fibrin**, which helps to localize the infectious agent or irritant.

Phagocytes, particularly neutrophils, carry out their functions of ingestion and digestion (see Phagocytic Process). The site of infection or injury is literally a battlefield where dead and digested microorganisms as well as dead and disintegrating neutrophils are found. This accumulation of dead and dying cells and other debris is called **pus.** Some of the chemotactic factors, which are degranulation products from neutrophils, attract macrophages to the battlefield. Macrophages help phagocytose whole microorganisms, damaged cells and tissues, dead neutrophils, and fibrin deposits.

Once the phagocytic process is completed, the next step in acute inflammation is tissue repair. Tissue repair is affected by compounds such as **fibroblast activating factor (FAF).** FAF stimulates fibroblast proliferation and stimulates collagen formation by fibroblasts.

Chronic Inflammation. If the offending microorganisms or materials persist, the inflammatory process progresses into the chronic state. The cell types characteristic of **chronic inflammation** are macrophages, lymphocytes, and plasma cells (antibody-producing cells). The continuous arrival of macrophages and the presence of local fibroblasts can lead to the formation of two cell types: epithelioid cells (macrophages that form groups of epithelial-appearing cells) and **multinucleated giant cells** (macrophages that coalesce to form a large cell with many nuclei). Fibroblasts in the area may deposit excessive collagen and form dense fibrous scar tissue. The formation of **granulomas** (chronic inflammatory lesions characterized by epithelioid and giant cells, and extensive fibrosis) often is an undesirable outcome. In syphilis, tuberculosis, and some worm and fungus infections, there may be extensive tissue destruction due to granuloma formation. On the positive side, granulomas do isolate the focus of infection. Chronic inflammation usually is accompanied by immune responses if the irritant is immunogenic (can stimulate antibody formation).

Excessive inflammation, both acute and chronic, and serious tissue injuries characterize a wide variety of human diseases, as will be seen in the description of hypersensitivities in Chapter 13.

One of the systemic effects of inflammation is **fever,** which is discussed in Chapter 14.

Phagocytic Process

Recognition. Once phagocytic cells are attracted to the site of inflammation, they must have a mechanism for recognizing the infectious agent. As we previously stated, phagocytes have a variety of receptors on their surface and some of these will recognize the infectious agent. Phagocytic cells are better equipped to recognize the infectious agent, however, if the latter is properly marked. The marking process, referred to as **opsonization** (to prepare for a meal), may involve the following: The microorganism may be coated with one or more of a group of serum proteins such as **complement** or immunoglobulins IgM or **IgG.*** The phagocyte is then able to bind the infectious agent via the receptor-antibody or receptor-complement bridge (Fig. 9-4). In the presence of antibody plus complement, the infectious agent is lysed. Consequently, phagocytosis is enhanced in the presence of the two opsonins.

Vacuole Formation. The infectious agent, after being bound to the phagocyte, is engulfed in a process called **endocytosis.** In this process the contacted portion of the cytoplasmic membrane of the phagocyte engulfs the particle, and the involved segment of the membrane is pinched off (Fig. 9-5). This action creates an internalized vacuole, called a **phagosome,** that encloses the infectious microorganism.

* Additional opsonins have been identified recently and include **fibronectin** and mannose-binding protein from serum.

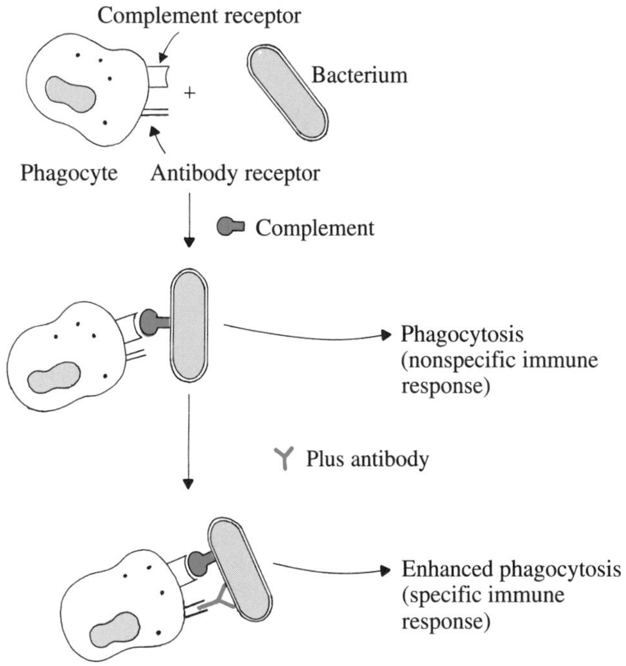

FIGURE 9-4
Marking the bacterial cell by opsonization. The phagocytic cell possesses receptors for complement (the opsonin) and for antibody. Complement alone can mark bacterium and attract the marked cell to a phagocyte via a complement-receptor bridge—a nonspecific immune response. In the presence of antibody, the bacterium is marked with antibody as well as complement and a specific immune response is initiated.

FIGURE 9-5
Vacuole and phagolysosome formation in the phagocytic process.

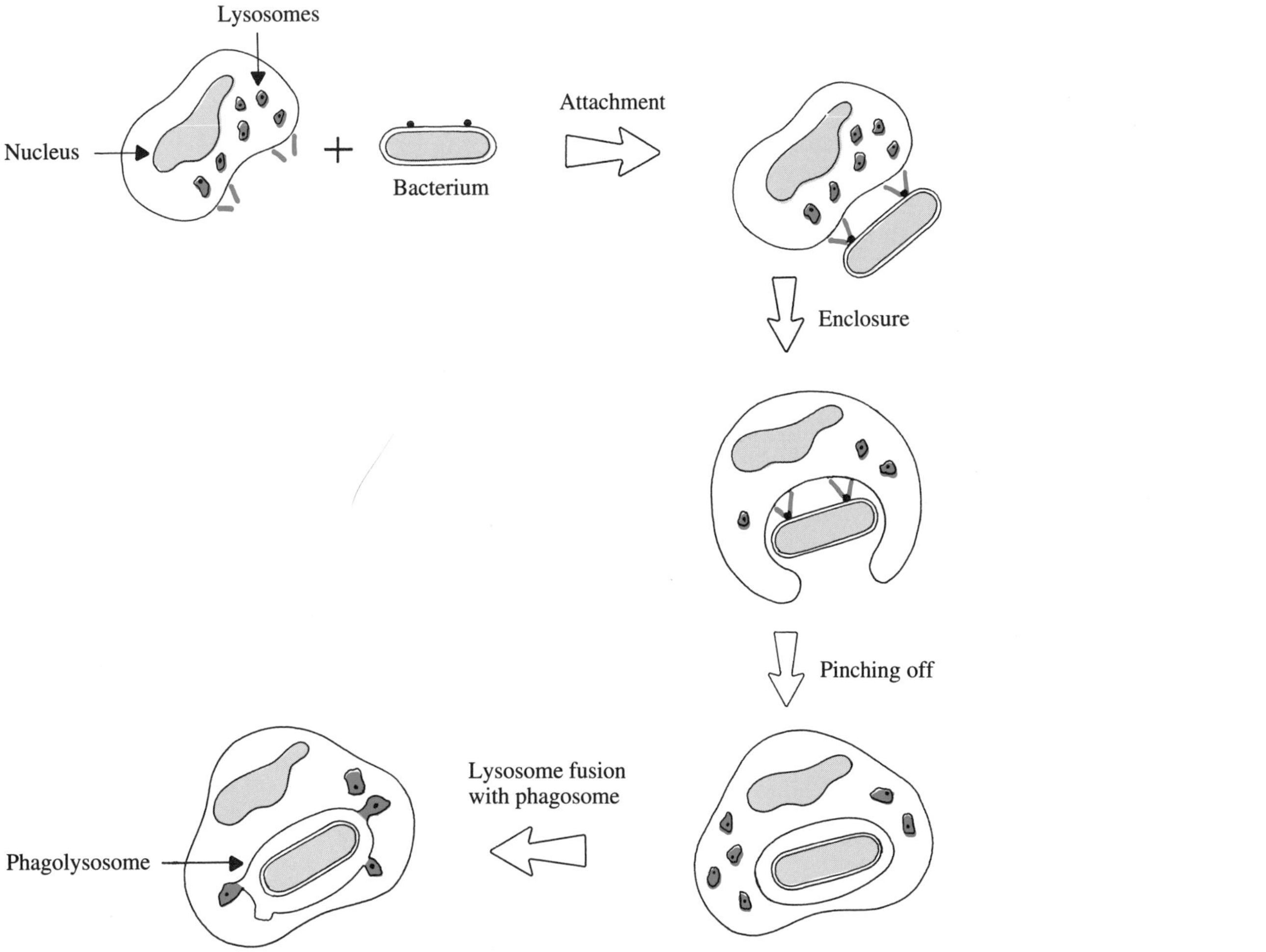

Phagolysosome Formation. The phagocytic cell, like most mammalian cells, contains an organelle called the **lysosome.** The lysosome membrane encloses a collection of over 60 enzymes. Some of these enzymes (proteases, lipases, nucleases, etc.) are hydrolytic and active at acid pH. They are referred to as **acid hydrolases.** Other lysosomal enzymes include **myeloperoxidase** (this enzyme gives a greenish tinge to abscess fluid) and neutral proteases. All of these enzymes contribute to microbial killing and lysis. They are in the form of aggregates called **primary (azurophilic) granules.**

Within the activated phagocytic cell there is a fusion of the lysosome with the phagosome to form a **phagolysosome** (Figs. 9-5 and 9-6). During fusion there is **degranulation** or the release of lysosomal enzymes. The degradative enzymes, now enclosed within the phagolysosome membrane, begin the killing and digestion of microorganisms. Microbicidal activity in the phagolysosome can be gener-

FIGURE 9-6
Oxygen-dependent phagocytosis. Oxygen enters the phagocyte and induces glucose 6-phosphate to enter the hexose monophosphate pathway (HMP). NADPH oxidase is activated by this shift and converts oxygen to superoxide (O_2^-). Superoxide enters the phagosome and is converted to intermediates such as hydrogen peroxide (H_2O_2'), hydroxyl radical (OH^-), and singlet oxygen (O_2'). These intermediates are microbicidal. Fusion of lysosome with phagosome releases myeloperoxidase, which reacts with hydrogen peroxide and chlorine to form hypochlorous acid. These compounds are also microbicidal. Other lysosome enzymes are degradative. Secondary granules fuse with phagolysosome and release enzymes and products that are also microbicidal. Following the digestion process, some bacterial remains are undigested in the phagolysosome. The phagolysosome shrinks and moves to the cell surface as a residual body. The undigested remains are expelled from the cell via exocytosis when the residual body fuses with the cell membrane (exocytosis).

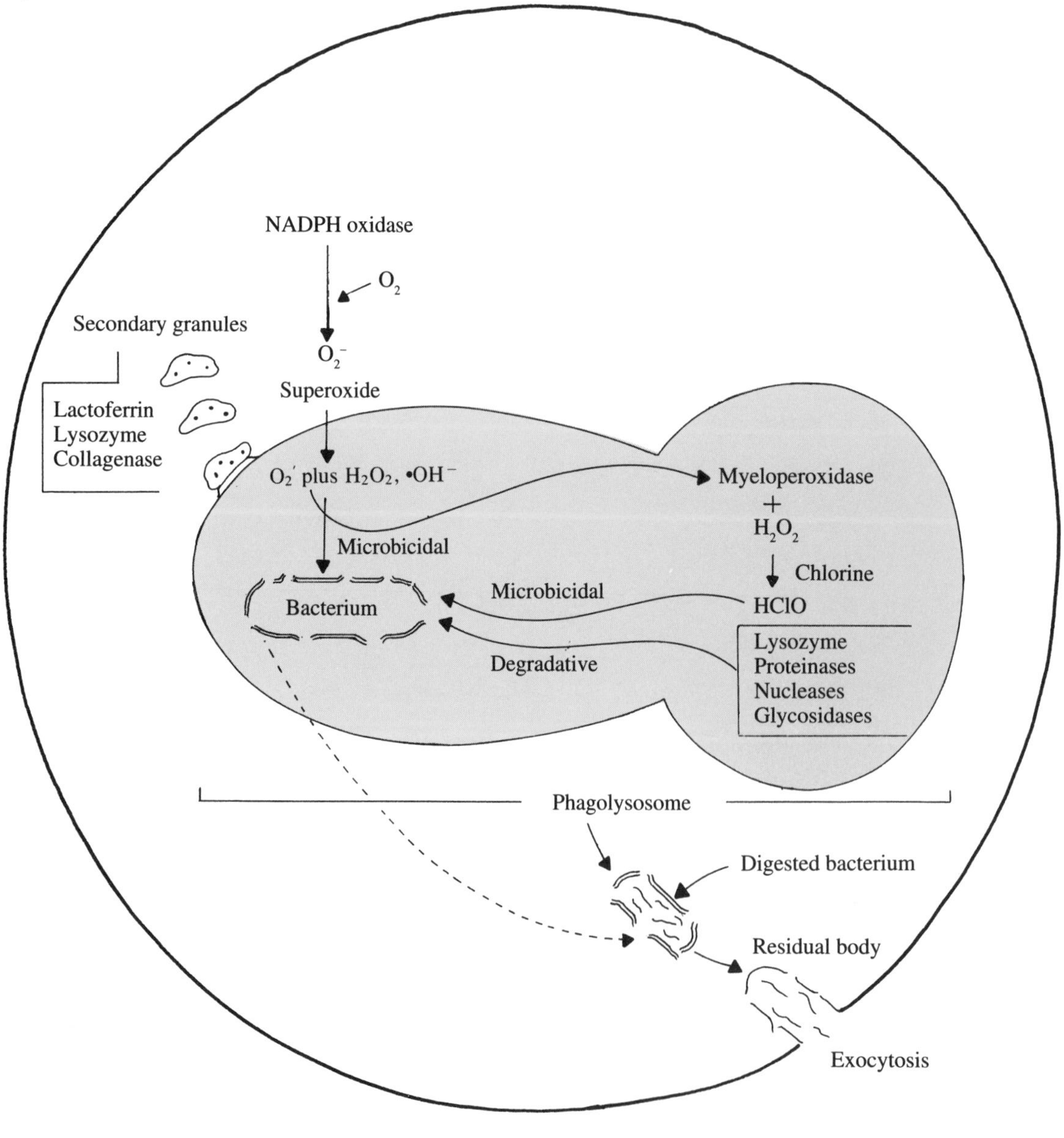

ated in two different pathways, discussed below: nonoxidative and oxidative.

Granules not associated with the lysosome are also present in the phagocytic cell and are referred to as **secondary granules.** Some of the important substances in secondary granules are **lysozyme** and **lactoferrin.** Lactoferrin (see Nonoxidative Killing and Chapter 14) is a binder (chelator) of iron and in this capacity limits the amount of iron available for bacterial growth. Secondary granules also contain a substance that acts as a chemoattractant. The principal function of secondary granules, therefore, is to enhance the recruitment of neutrophils and macrophages to the site of inflammation. After phagocytosis, as much as 80 percent of the contents of secondary granules are found outside the cell.

Oxidative Killing. Neutrophils and tissue macrophages utilize the energy of glycolysis to engulf microorganisms. When neutrophils (but not macrophages) are activated, there is a 100-fold increase in oxygen consumption. This activity is called the **respiratory burst** (see Fig. 9-6). During the respiratory burst a membrane-bound enzyme, **NADPH oxidase,** is activated in the neutrophil. NADPH oxidase reduces oxygen (O_2) to a highly activated superoxide (O_2^-) molecule. Superoxide is an unstable molecule that can be reduced to other highly reactive intermediates such as hydroxyl radical (OH^-), hydrogen peroxide (H_2O_2), and singlet oxygen (O_2'). All of these highly reactive species can directly damage bacteria and they can take place in the phagosome without fusion with the lysosome. When lysosome fusion occurs, **myeloperoxidase** is released, and in the presence of hydrogen peroxide and chloride ion produces **hypochlorous acid,** a potent microbicidal agent. Other halides such as iodine can also be used in the myeloperoxidase–hydrogen peroxide reaction to create a molecule that can iodinate bacteria.

Nonoxidative Killing. Nonoxidative killing is a process that occurs in macrophages (but not neutrophils) and is not mediated by myeloperoxidase (hydrogen peroxide is not formed). The lysosomal cationic proteins are the principal microbicidal agents. Lysozyme and lactoferrin are also involved in phagocytic function. Lactoferrin, mentioned earlier as a component of secondary granules, limits bacterial growth by making iron unavailable as a nutrient. Lysozyme plus cationic proteins can digest the bacterial cell wall. Once hydrolytic enzymes digest macromolecules into monomeric units, the latter are transported from the phagolysosome into the cytoplasm of the macrophage.

After digestion has been completed, a shriveled phagolysosome, called a **residual body,** attaches to the cytoplasmic membrane of the macrophage. Any undigested material is discharged to the exterior in a process called **exocytosis** (see Fig. 9-6).

Macrophage Activation

The activity of macrophages can be increased by a process called activation. Macrophage activation may be induced by microbial components such as lipid A or lipopolysaccharide. Some of the most important activators are the mediators called **cytokines.** Cytokines are molecules released by antigen-stimulated immune cells. One cytokine that stimulates macrophages is called **interferon gamma (IFN-γ).** IFY-γ induces a resting macrophage to escalate activities by enlarging its content of lysosomes and lysosomal enzymes (Fig. 9-7). Consequently the macrophage is more effective in destroying microbial agents; that

FIGURE 9-7
Macrophage activation. An antigen presenting cell attracts a T cell that recognizes the antigen. The T cell is induced to produce lymphokines which can stimulate resting macrophages to become activated. Activated macrophages possess increased numbers of lysosomes and hence have increased phagocytic potential.

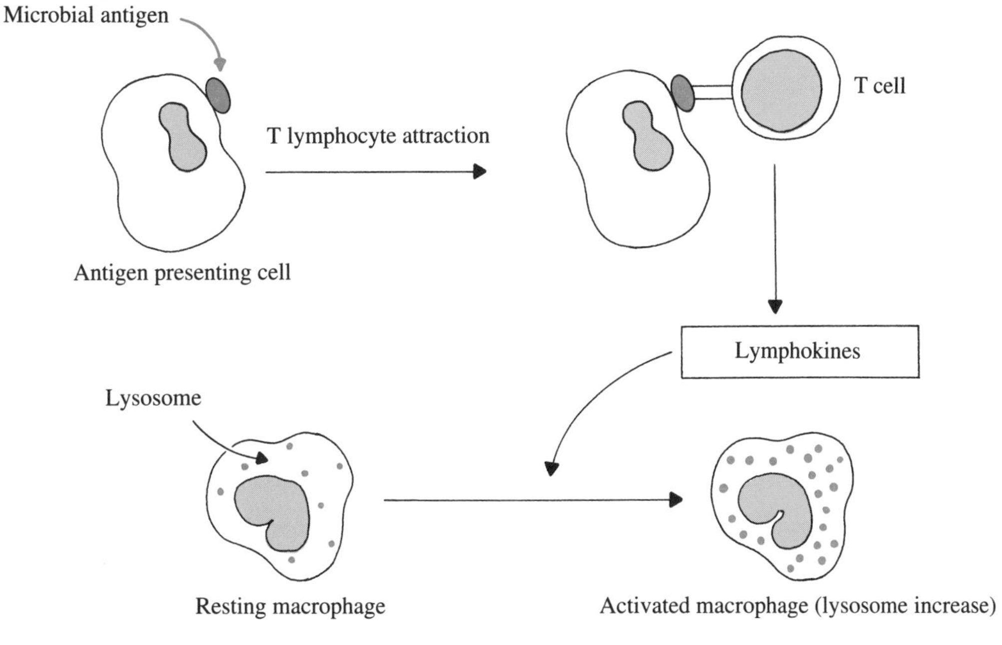

is, more superoxide and other microbicidal agents are produced. For example, in the disease tuberculosis the infectious agent exists as an intracellular pathogen. Only activated macrophages are capable of destroying the microbial agent. Macrophage activation is also required for the destruction of tumor or cancer cells (see Chapter 13).

Since macrophage activation requires the help of cytokines whose activities are immune-specific, cytokines are discussed again in Chapter 11.

DELETERIOUS EFFECTS OF PHAGOCYTOSIS

Tissue Destruction

Destruction by phagocytes is not confined solely to the interior of the phagocytic cell. The contents of lysosome granules and of specific granules, and toxic oxygen products, can be released into the tissues. This can occur if the materials are too large, too numerous, or too inaccessible to be endocytosed. The released cell products can affect normal body components, resulting in serious tissue damage. This is a major factor in immune-complex diseases such as streptococcal glomerulonephritis and rheumatoid arthritis (see Chapter 13).

Intracellular Survival of Some Microorganisms

Some microorganisms can evade ingestion by phagocytes because of various microbial surface components such as capsules. Even though most microorganisms can be ingested by phagocytic cells, some are able to evade the digestion process. These microorganisms not only survive the ingestion process but also are capable of thriving and even multiplying within the macrophage. Evasion of the phagocytic process is prominently illustrated by two bacterial genera—*Coxiella* and *Rickettsia*—and mycobacteria (*Mycobacterium tuberculosis*). *Coxiella* organisms are resistant to acid hydrolases in the phagolysosome while *Rickettsia* species release an enzyme (phospholipase) that lyses the phagosome membrane, thereby preventing fusion with the lysosome (Fig. 9-8).

DEFECTS IN PHAGOCYTIC AND INFLAMMATORY PROCESSES

Defects in lymphocytes can result in a variety of disorders affecting phagocytosis and inflammation. Although these disorders are usually rare, they are potentially life-threatening.

FIGURE 9-8
Host-parasite response to phagocytosis by most bacteria (A), by *Coxiella* (B), and by *Rickettsia* (C).

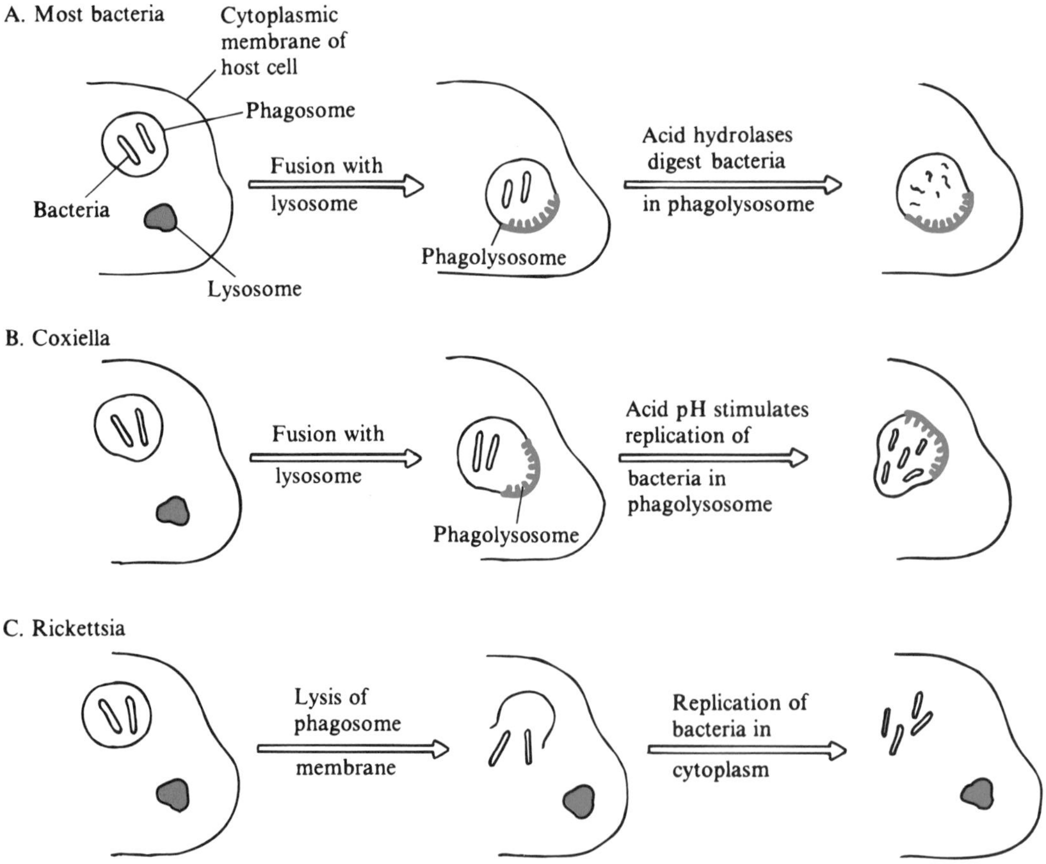

Motility and Chemotaxis Disorders

Motility and chemotaxis disorders result in the inability of neutrophils to migrate to the site of infection following interaction with chemoattractants. This response may be due to a defect in the production of **actin,** a structural protein associated with motility. The administration of some drugs, for example, corticosteroids, can also inhibit the chemotactic activity of neutrophils. Finally, some individuals may have a genetic defect that impairs the formation of chemotactic factors. Decreased neutrophil chemotaxis can be seen in the childhood disease **Chédiak-Higashi syndrome.** This syndrome is an inherited disorder affecting phagocytic function. It is characterized by symptoms which include albinism, central nervous system abnormalities, and recurrent bacterial infections.

Phagocytosis Disorders

Phagocytosis disorders are associated with the inability of neutrophils to engulf bacteria or the inability to degranulate or both. Primary granules contain substances that participate in microbicidal events. Secondary granules function primarily as inflammatory mediators (PMN recruitment at the site of infection). Defects in granule content, for example, myeloperoxidase deficiency, can result in the inability of neutrophils to kill the fungus *Candida albicans.* Deficiency in secondary granules can lead to recurrent skin infections (PMN cannot be mobilized to the site of injury). In Chédiak-Higashi syndrome there is impairment in the formation of phagolysosomes and this results in decreased bactericidal activity.

Microbicidal Disorders

Microbicidal disorders are usually the result of deficiencies in myeloperoxidase or an inability to generate superoxide, hydrogen peroxide, and hypochlorite. Lack of microbicidal activity is observed in **chronic granulomatous disease (CGD).** CGD, in most patients, is inherited as an X-linked trait. Boys, starting at about the age of 1 year, show an increased susceptibility to recurrent infections with pyogenic cocci such as staphylococci and other organisms that are normally low in virulence. Recurrent disseminated abscesses and pneumonia, often accompanied by enlargement of lymph nodes, spleen, and liver, and chronic dermatitis are common findings. Tissue biopsy specimens reveal granuloma formation in virtually every organ. Although at one time the prognosis was poor, early diagnosis, aggressive chemotherapy, and surgery have improved the long-term prognosis. IFN-γ and various antibiotics administered prophylactically have significant effects on the management of this disease.

Neutropenia

A quantitative abnormality can also affect phagocyte function. For example, an adequate number of leukocytes is needed to affect the inflammatory response. Sometimes there is a substantial decrease in the number of leukocytes in the circulation, a condition called **neutropenia.** Neutropenia can be the result of bone marrow injury due to ionizing radiation or drugs, marrow replacement, nutritional deficiencies, or congenital stem cell defects.

Noncellular Mechanisms of Defense

A host of substances found in the circulatory system and tissues are capable of providing the host with some means of protection from infection.

PLASMA

The fluid portion of uncoagulated blood is called **plasma.** Plasma contains many substances: proteins, carbohydrates, lipids, water, hormones, salts, and gases. The principal proteins are albumin, fibrinogen, and globulins. Fibrinogen is converted into fibrin in blood coagulation and in inflammation. One type of globulin is the gamma globulin, which is particularly important as **immunoglobulins** in acquired immunity. Immunoglobulins function as the antibodies of the humoral immune response (see Chapter 12). Various complement components (see below) also are globulins. When plasma exits from the bloodstream into the tissues in an inflammatory response, it leads to **edema** (swelling). Edema fluid facilitates the emigration and mobility of phagocytes, conveys antibodies into the tissues, and dilutes toxic elements. Edema fluid in the tissues may lead to blockage and blanching.

TISSUE FACTORS

There are certain, less well defined antimicrobial chemical substances that contribute to nonspecific host resistance and these are described in Table 9-2. We discuss two of them—interferon and complement—in more detail.

TABLE 9-2
Some Chemical Factors Associated with Nonspecific Host Resistance

Chemical	Source	Microorganisms affected
Fatty acids	Intestinal tract, skin glands	Gram-negative bacteria
Transferrin, lactoferrin	Leukocytes, milk, serum	Gram-positive and gram-negative bacteria
Spermine, spermidine	Pancreas, prostate	Gram-positive bacteria
Lysozyme	Serum, leukocytes, tears, saliva	Gram-positive and gram-negative bacteria
Complement	Serum	Bacteria, viruses, and protozoa
Interferon	Most cells except neutrophils	Viruses, some intracellular protozoa
Myeloperoxidase, xanthine oxidase	Neutrophils, milk	Bacteria, viruses, protozoa

Interferons

Interferons are a family of low molecular weight proteins that are synthesized by cells in response to virus infection. They also are synthesized in response to immune stimulation, molecules such as endotoxins and polysaccharides, and certain bacterial species. Interferons are classified as interferon alfa (IFN-α), beta (IFN-β), and gamma (IFN-γ). The primary natural sources are leukocytes for IFN-α, fibroblasts for IFN-β, and T lymphocytes for IFN-γ.

Interferons were first discovered when it was determined that infection with one virus interferes with infection by another virus. Virus interference is probably the most important of the nonimmunological antiviral defense mechanisms. It serves as an early protective device while the immune response is still relatively ineffective. Infected cells release interferons a few hours after viral infection, and higher levels are attained within a few days. The released interferons bind to receptors on nearby healthy cells. Interferons are not virus-specific but they are relatively species-specific. Interferons induced in response to one virus may be equally effective against an unrelated virus. Human interferon is most effective in humans while bovine interferon is most effective acting on bovine cells, and so on.

Interferons cause antiviral resistance in an indirect way (Fig. 9-9). They bind to the cell surface and activate cellu-

FIGURE 9-9
Proposed mechanism of interferon action. The infecting virus (1) produces new viral particles and also (2) induces the cell to produce interferon mRNA (IF-mRNA), which (3) is translated into interferon molecules. (4) Interferon released by the cell may inhibit development of the virus in the same cell, or it may bind to adjacent cells and (5) induce them to produce antiviral proteins (6), such as a nuclease (7) that cleaves any potential viral mRNA, and a protein kinase (8) that inhibits viral protein synthesis. (Adapted from R. F. Boyd, *General Microbiology*, 2nd ed. St. Louis: Mosby, 1988.)

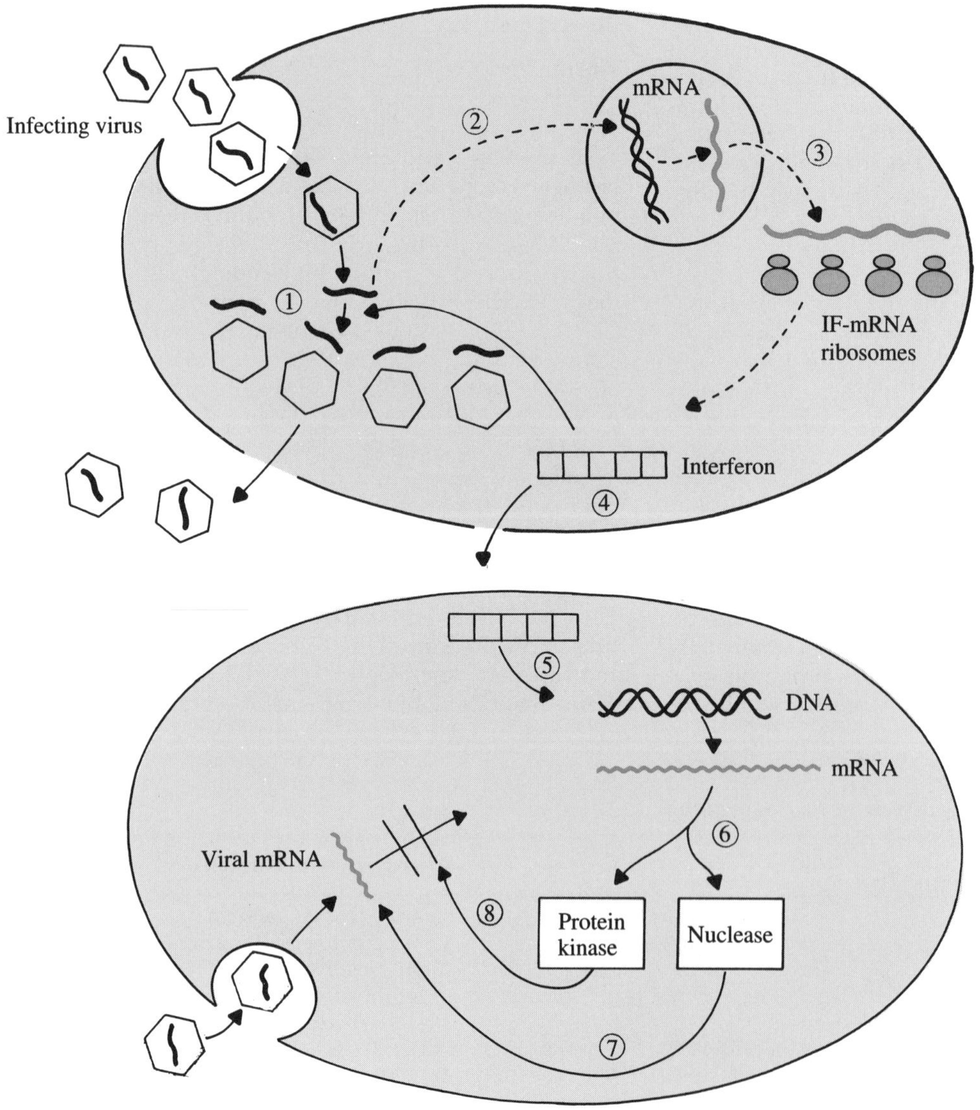

lar genes that code for antiviral proteins. The principal target of antiviral proteins is the translation mechanism. Antiviral proteins include a **protein kinase** and a **nuclease.** Protein kinase inhibits viral protein synthesis by inactivating an initiation factor, while nuclease preferentially cleaves viral messenger RNA (mRNA). Both blocking actions require the presence of double-stranded RNA. The presence of double-stranded RNA alerts the cell to the presence of an infecting virus.

Interferons also inhibit multiplication of cells. The molecular basis of this activity is unknown. The inhibitory activity often is greater against cancer cells than against normal cells. Interferons are produced in small amounts in hosts. Now they can be produced in quantity by tissue-culture cell lines utilizing recombinant DNA technology. A new human interferon-based topical gel appears to diminish significantly the symptoms of recurrent genital warts. IFN-α recently was shown to have significant activity against hepatitis B and C viruses. The Food and Drug Administration (FDA) also has approved the use of interferon for hairy cell leukemia, chronic myelogenous leukemia, and Sézary syndrome.

An equally important role for the interferons, especially IFN-γ, is as a modulator of immune reactivity. This is described in the text with the cytokines (see Chapter 11).

Complement System

The complement system is made up of more than 25 plasma proteins that play a major role in host defense. The complement proteins do not act alone in destroying microorganisms. They must first be activated, after which they interact synergistically with other host factors to bring about their effects on the parasite. For example, the complement system can be activated by the endotoxin of gram-negative bacteria. As we previously indicated (see Fig. 9-4), a bacterial cell is "marked" for phagocytosis when a complement protein binds to the microbial surface (opsonization). This marking by **complement without antibody** is characteristic of a nonspecific immune response. Complement is also involved in a very specific way when the infectious agent is marked with antibody as well as complement. This antibody-dependent complement activation induces the specific or acquired immune system, that is, the humoral and cell-mediated immune systems (see Chapter 12 for details).

In addition to pathogen destruction, activation of complement can promote inflammation, foreign cell lysis, tissue damage, pathogen localization, and chemotaxis. Complement deficiencies lead to serious consequences with respect to resistance to infection. These aspects of complement are discussed in Chapter 13.

PLATELETS

Platelets are cytoplasmic fragments from megakaryocytes. They are cell-like structures that do not possess a nucleus. Platelets are mostly recognized for their role in blood clotting; however, they also play a role in inflammation and other immune functions. Platelets release vasoactive substances, such as histamine, that increase vascular permeability. They also release **platelet activating factor (PAF),** which is associated with an allergic response called anaphylaxis (see Chapter 13 for details).

Summary

1. First-line nonspecific host resistance is provided by the intact integument and by substances, cells, and structures on its surface (see Chapter 14). The circulatory system also provides cellular and noncellular factors that aid in preventing infection or purging the host of foreign substances.
2. Ingestion and digestion of foreign substances are associated with a process called phagocytosis. Cells associated with antimicrobial defense include both phagocytic and nonphagocytic types—polymorphonuclear granulocytes and mononuclear phagocytes. Table 9-3 outlines the functions of these cell types.
3. The phagocytic process usually is initiated when phagocytes are attracted to the site of inflammation. Phagocytosis requires a recognition stage, which may or may not involve special markers. Special markers, such as complement and IgG, elevate the efficiency of phagocytosis. The foreign substance is engulfed in a vacuole, which later fuses with lysosomes. Lysosomes contain microbicidal and degradative enzymes.
4. The killing of a microbial agent can take place in the absence or presence of oxygen; that is, the process may be NADPH oxidase–dependent or –independent. Once phagocytosis is completed, the debris is removed from the site of inflammation and the tissue is repaired.
5. Phagocytosis is not always beneficial. The products of inflammation and phagocytosis can cause tissue destruction. In addition, the phagocyte may serve as a refuge for some bacteria, viruses, and other infectious agents.
6. Defects can exist in the phagocytic and inflammatory processes. These defects can be due to (1) conditions that decrease leukocyte count, (2) deficiencies in degranulation, (3) inability to produce superoxide, and (4) defects involving chemotaxis and motility of neutrophils.
7. Noncellular mechanisms of defense include plasma factors, tissue factors, and platelets. Plasma contains a variety of proteins, the most important of which are immunoglobulins and complement. They may be involved in specific as well as nonspecific immune resistance.
8. The most important tissue factors are the proteins interferon and complement. Interferon is particularly important in resistance to viruses. Commercially produced interferons are being used to treat some diseases. Complement is a composite of several proteins, some of which help mark a foreign substance for nonspecific phagocytosis. Complement is also associated with the promotion of inflammation and engagement in specific immune phagocytosis.
9. Blood platelets are associated with inflammation by virtue of their ability to release vasoactive substances such as histamine. In addition, they can release factors that activate complement.

TABLE 9-3
Characteristics of Leukocytes Involved in Nonspecific Immunity

Cell type	Percent of total white blood cell count	Function
Polymorphonuclear granulocytes		
Neutrophils	60	Most active in phagocytosis; first to reach site of infection
Basophils	<1	Process antigens associated with allergies; release vasoactive substances associated with inflammation
Mast cells	<1	Found primarily in lung and intestinal mucosa and lining of blood vessels; release vasoactive substances associated with inflammation; like basophils, are associated with allergies; can destroy animal parasites
Eosinophils	3–5	Engage in animal parasite destruction by extracellular release of granules
Mononuclear phagocytes		
Monocyte/macrophage	30–35	As macrophages widely distributed in tissues; primary functions are phagocytosis and presenting antigen to lymphocytes (see Table 9-1)

Questions for Study

1. In very general terms, what are the similarities between nonspecific and specific immunity? The differences?
2. List the polymorphonuclear granulocytes. What is their specific role in the immune response?
3. Do professional phagocytes have any role other than destroying infectious or foreign agents? Explain.
4. Describe what positive and negative roles inflammation has in the immune response.
5. List some circumstances in which phagocytic activity or the inflammatory process may be hindered (you may wish to consult other texts for this information).
6. Without consulting the tables in this chapter, list some chemical factors associated with nonspecific host resistance.
7. From the Henderson article on platelets, describe the probable roles of platelets in bacterial infections and animal parasite infections.

CHAPTER

10 Antigens and Antibodies

OBJECTIVES

To describe the physical, biochemical, and biological properties of antigens

To describe the structure of immunoglobulins and how this structure relates to function

To outline the biological properties of the five immunoglobulin classes

To describe the forces that are involved in antigen-antibody binding

To discuss the mechanism of antibody diversity

To discuss briefly immunoglobulins as antigens

OUTLINE

ANTIGENS
- Immunogenicity
- Specificity

IMMUNOGLOBULINS (ANTIBODIES)
- Structure of the Basic Immunoglobulin Molecule
  - Heavy Chains and Light Chains
- Immunoglobulin Structure in Detail
  - Fragments, Chains, and Domains
- Immunoglobulin Polymers
- Antigen-Antibody Binding
- Biological Properties of the Five Immunoglobulin Classes

ANTIBODY DIVERSITY
- Immunoglobulin Genes
  - Light Chain Reorganization
  - Heavy Chain Variable Chain Reorganization
  - Heavy Chain Switch and Immunoglobulin Function

IMMUNOGLOBULINS AS ANTIGENS
- Isotypic Determinants
- Allotypic Determinants
- Idiotypic Determinants

ANTIGENS AND ANTIBODIES IN IMMUNODIAGNOSIS

In previous chapters we discussed how the nonspecific immune system responds to infectious agents or other foreign substances. Now we would like to introduce some aspects of the **specific immune response.** The preciseness of the specific immune response is related directly to characteristics of the antigen (foreign agent) stimulating it as well as the immunoglobulin induced by the antigen. In this chapter we discuss the molecular aspects of these two types of molecules and the functions they perform in the immune response.

Antigens

An antigen (commonly abbreviated Ag) is usually a foreign molecule that induces the host's immune system to generate antibodies. Different antibodies bind to different antigens since each antibody is specific for a particular antigen. Therefore, antigens possess two unique properties: the ability to induce antibody production and specificity. The ability of antigens to stimulate antibody production is also referred to as **immunogenicity.** Antigens, because of their immunogenic potential, are also referred to as **immunogens. Specificity** refers to the capacity of the antigen to combine with antibodies or immune cells.

IMMUNOGENICITY

The immunogenicity of antigens is dependent on their foreignness, high molecular weight, and chemical complexity.

1. Foreignness. Typical foreign antigens that the immune system responds to include the various types of infectious agents and their products (for example, toxins), proteins or foreign serum, mismatched transfused red blood cells, transplanted tissues, capsular and other polysaccharides, and vaccines. Out of necessity, the immune system ordinarily does not react with its own molecules. Generally, the greater the chemical and structural disparities between the antigen and similar molecules in one's own body, the more immunogenic the foreign material.

   What are frequently called antigens, for example, bacterial cells, in actuality are a composite of many diverse antigenic molecules. The various structural and molecular components of a bacterial cell—capsules, flagella, pili, cell wall components such as lipopolysaccharides, and subfractions—are all antigens. Disassembly of the bacterial cell into various antigenic components occurs during the phagocytic process.
2. Molecular weight. The immunogenicity of a molecule is usually dependent on its molecular weight. The most potent antigens are proteins with molecular weights of 10,000 or more. Small molecules such as amino acids or simple sugars are not immunogenic. For the most part, larger molecules are better antigens than smaller ones. Some small chemical groups can stimulate antibody formation if they are complexed or associated with proteins. These small chemical groups are called **haptens.** As we describe in Chapter 13, some naturally occurring allergenic (capable of causing allergies) substances, such as metals, are haptens.
3. Chemical complexity. Polysaccharides, such as starch or glycogen, possess repetitive sugar units (homopolymers) and are poorly immunogenic despite their high molecular weight. Mixed polymers (heteropolymers), for example, polysaccharides possessing more than one type of sugar, are good immunogens. Lipids and nucleic acids by themselves are poorly immunogenic or nonimmunogenic unless they are complexed with another molecule such as a protein. Again proteins are better immunogens than are other macromolecules.

The immunogenicity of antigens can be enhanced by mixing them with certain compounds or molecules called **adjuvants.** Adjuvant properties can be further enhanced by the addition of a microbial antigen. For example, Freund's complete adjuvant is a water-in-oil emulsion containing the heat-killed bacterium *Mycobacterium tuberculosis.* Some vaccines contain adjuvants.

SPECIFICITY

Antigen specificity refers to the ability of a single antigen to interact selectively with a corresponding antibody and not with other antibodies that were induced by other antigens.

On the antigen molecule are small, discrete sites of specific chemical composition and molecular configuration or shape. These sites are called **antigenic determinants**

FIGURE 10-1
Formation of antigenic determinant (epitope) of antigen. A polypeptide containing 90 amino acids folds into a shape that provides a site for the binding of antigen (*colored*). Amino acid residues are numbered. S—S = sulfur-sulfur binding; SH = sulfhydryl group.

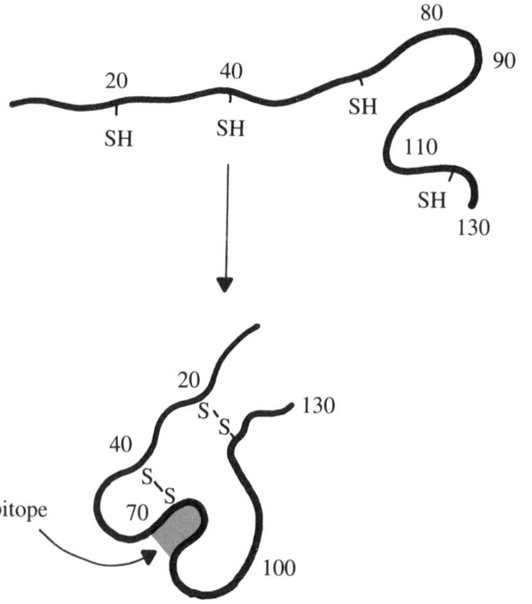

or **epitopes.** Most naturally occurring epitopes are made up of five to six amino acid or sugar residues. The spatial relationship of these residues results in the epitope having a specific shape (Fig. 10-1). Large proteins or polysaccharides may contain several identical or different epitopes. We may succinctly define epitopes as molecular shapes recognized by antibodies or immune cells.

The sites on the antibody to which the epitope binds are called **paratopes.** The specificity between epitope and paratope may be based on the sequence of residues (amino acids, sugars) in the epitope or on the conformation or folding of the epitope.

Immunoglobulins (Antibodies)

Immunoglobulins (commonly abbreviated Ig) are glycoproteins that are important in humoral immunity. They are produced by a group of white blood cells or lymphocytes called **B cells.** In the context of antigen-antibody response, immunoglobulins perform two important functions:

1. Some immunoglobulins, as we already indicated, are produced in response to the presence of antigens. They bind to the antigens that induced them and are responsible for increasing the efficiency of antigen degradation.
2. Some immunoglobulins are bound to the surface of B cells where they act as receptors for any foreign antigen entering the host.

Both of these functions are intimately tied together and are discussed at length later in Chapter 12. There are five immunoglobulin classes—IgG, IgM, IgA, IgD, and IgE. The basis of this classification is related to differences in their high molecular weight polypeptide chains called **heavy** or **H chains.**

STRUCTURE OF THE BASIC IMMUNOGLOBULIN MOLECULE

Heavy Chains and Light Chains

Immunoglobulins have a basic pattern of four polypeptide chains (Fig. 10-2). Two of the chains, which are identical, are of a higher molecular weight and are called heavy or H chains. The two **light** or **L chains,** which are also identical, have a lower molecular weight. The light chains are approximately one-half the length of the H chains. Each immunoglobulin class has a distinctive H chain type. L chains are of two types, kappa (κ-type) or lambda (λ-type). Each immunoglobulin molecule, regardless of its H chain, has one type of L chain but never both types.

Each L chain is linked to an H chain by disulfide bonds, thereby producing two identical subunits. Each H chain–L chain subunit is in turn held together by disulfide bonds, producing the typical four-chain polypeptide immunoglobulin unit.

The immunoglobulin is diagrammatically represented in the shape of Y. The arms of the Y represent the N or amino (NH_2) terminal while the tail of the Y represents the C or carboxy (COOH) terminal.

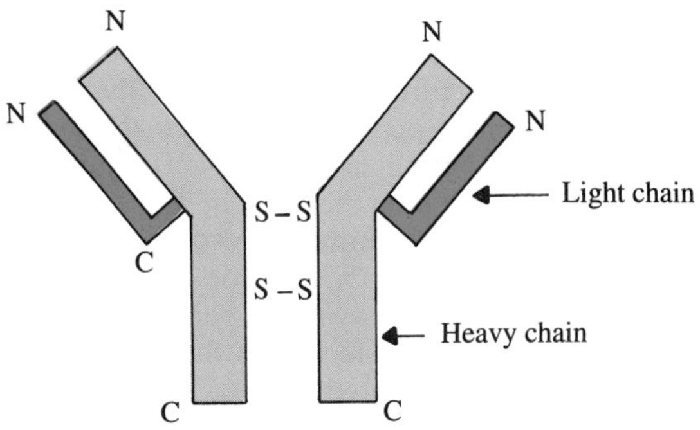

FIGURE 10-2
Basic structure of immunoglobulin molecule. The basic immunoglobulin unit, which is common to all immunoglobulin classes, consists of two identical heavy chains and two identical light chains. Heavy chains are held together by sulfur-sulfur bonds.

IMMUNOGLOBULIN STRUCTURE IN DETAIL

IgG is the most abundant of the immunoglobulins in the serum and its structure can be considered to be typical. The following discussion centers on this immunoglobulin.

Fragments, Chains, and Domains

Enzymatic digestion of IgG into chain fragments was used to elucidate immunoglobulin structure as well as func-

FIGURE 10-3
Enzymatic digestion of IgG. Digestion of IgG with pepsin and papain. Pepsin cleaves the heavy chain while papain affects the hinge region. Two Fab fragments plus an Fc fragment are released.

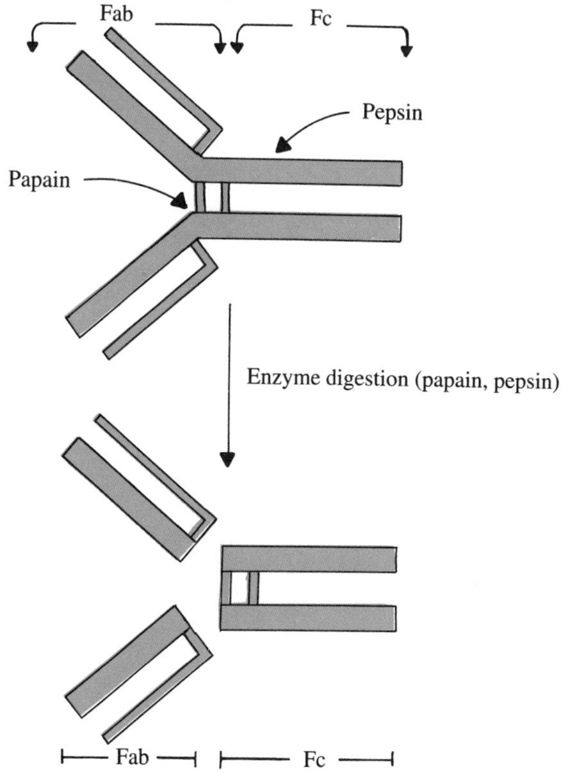

tion. One of the fragments that had antigen binding capabilities was called **Fab** (antigen binding fragment). Each arm of the basic Y structure is an antigen binding fragment. The other fragment produced by enzymatic digestion was termed **Fc** (crystallizable fragment). Fc represents the tail of the basic Y structure (Fig. 10-3). The contribution of the Fc region to the immune response includes

1. The ability to bind to specific receptors (Fc receptors) on phagocytic cells such as macrophages and neutrophils. This interaction facilitates the capture and ingestion of antibody-coated antigens such as bacteria (see Chapter 9 for discussion of this process).
2. The ability to bind complement, a serum component that is important in the immune response (see Chapter 12 for a detailed discussion of complement).
3. Mediation of the passage of maternal IgG antibodies across the placenta.

The fragments produced from enzymatic digestion of the immunoglobulin molecule have enabled scientists to differentiate specific areas or **domains** (Fig. 10-4). These domains have evolved to perform specific functions. Some domains are characterized by their variability in amino acid sequences and are referred to as **variable (V) regions.** Other regions are characterized by their constancy in amino acid sequences and are referred to as **constant (C) regions.** Variability is observed in the Fab region where antigen binds to the immunoglobulin. The paratope of the immunoglobulin molecule must discriminate between different antigenic determinants. The area of constancy, for example, Fc, represents the domains that bind specific immune components or cells (complement, macrophages, K cells, etc.).

In summary the antibody molecule, based on its structure, can be seen to perform two basic functions: (1) bind to different antigens because of its variable region and (2) use its Fc region to bind to the Fc receptors on immune cells and components of the host.

IMMUNOGLOBULIN POLYMERS

The basic immunoglobulin molecule exists as a monomer, that is, a single structural unit composed of two H and L chains. However, IgM and IgA can exist as polymers in which two (dimer), three (trimer), or five (pentamer) immunoglobulin units are joined. Polymers have a **J chain** (joining chain) that is believed to initiate assembly of the polymer (Fig. 10-5).

FIGURE 10-4
Variable and constant domains of the immunoglobulin molecule. IgG possesses six domains produced from disulfide bonding; two in the light chain, V_L and C_L, and four in the heavy chain, C_H1, C_H2, C_H3, and V_H. These domains possess specific functions. The site of carbohydrate (CHO) attachment is also indicated.

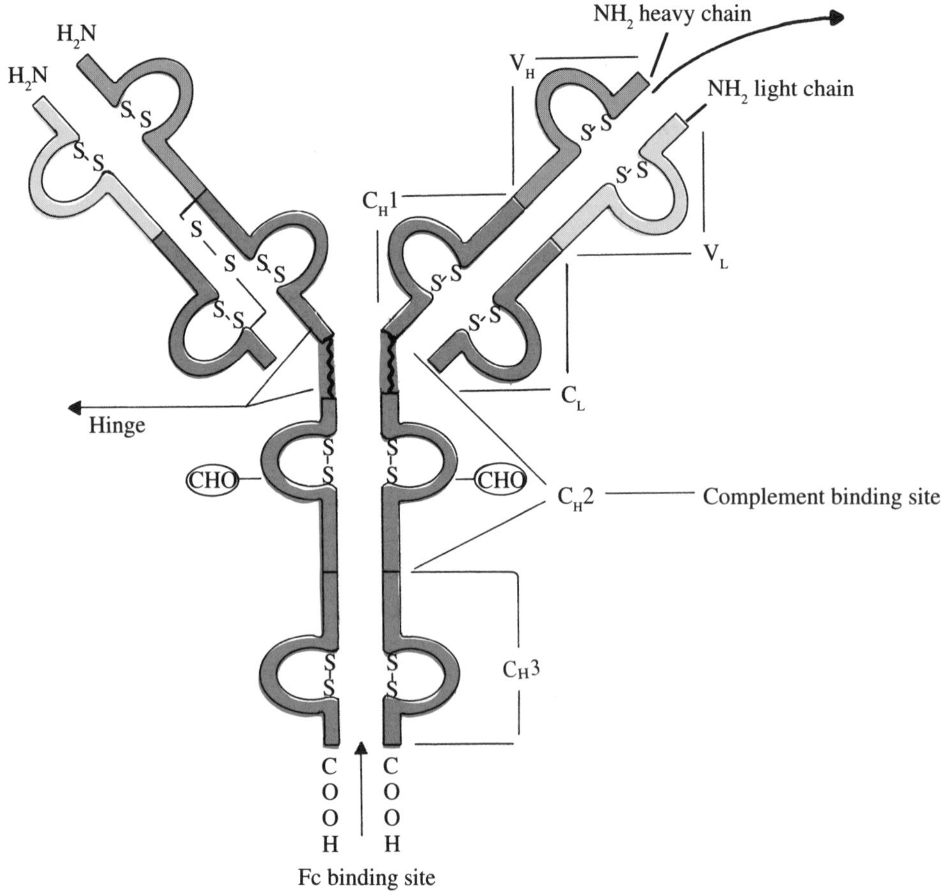

FIGURE 10-5
Structures of the immunoglobulin classes.

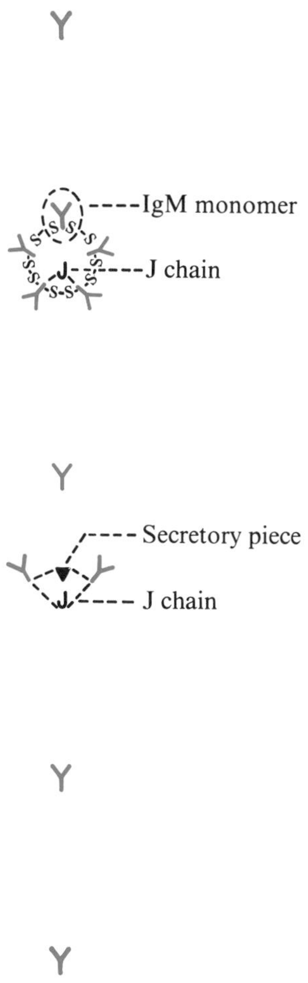

IgG — A monomer (single unrepeating unit). Most common antibody in serum.

IgM — Appears as a monomer on surface of immature B cells where it serves as antigen receptor.

— Appears as a pentamer in serum. Earliest Ig formed in response to antigen.

IgA — Appears as a monomer in serum. Formed in spleen and lymph nodes.

— Appears as a dimer and trimer on mucosal surfaces. Produced as a dimer with J chain in lamina propria of gut, lung, and glands. Secretory piece added upon transport across epithelial cells.

IgD — A monomer. Appears on surface of immature B cells where it expresses the same antigen receptor as IgM.

IgE — A monomer. Attaches to mast cells. Serves as the reaginic antibody of human anaphylaxis.

ANTIGEN-ANTIBODY BINDING

The variable regions of the H and L chains are folded in such a way as to create a specific shape for antigen binding. Once the antigen nestles into its binding site, there is an interaction between the chemical groups on the antigen and the amino acids of the binding site (Fig. 10-6). This interaction may be tight or loose, depending on the distance between the chemical groups. For example, if a chemical group on the antigen is negatively charged and is close to a positively charged amino acid residue of the binding site, there will be a strong attractive or electrostatic force (Fig. 10-7). If the chemical groups on the antigen and binding site are of the same charge, a repulsive force is generated. In addition to electrostatic forces there are other attractive interactions, including hydrogen and hydrophobic bonding.

The intermolecular forces between antigen and antibody will not be adequately established unless there is a good fit between antigen and antibody (see Fig. 10-7). Antibodies are capable of distinguishing between small differences in antigen configuration or shape. An antigen that fits poorly into the antigen binding site will not pro-

FIGURE 10-6
Binding of antibody to antigen via chemical groups on the antigenic determinant and Fab portion of the antibody molecule.

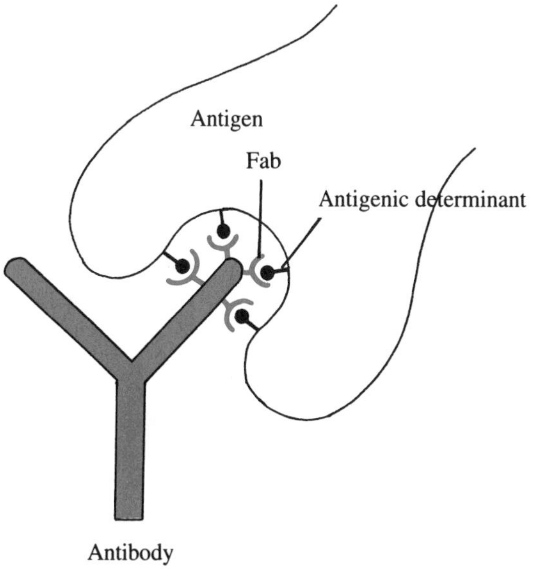

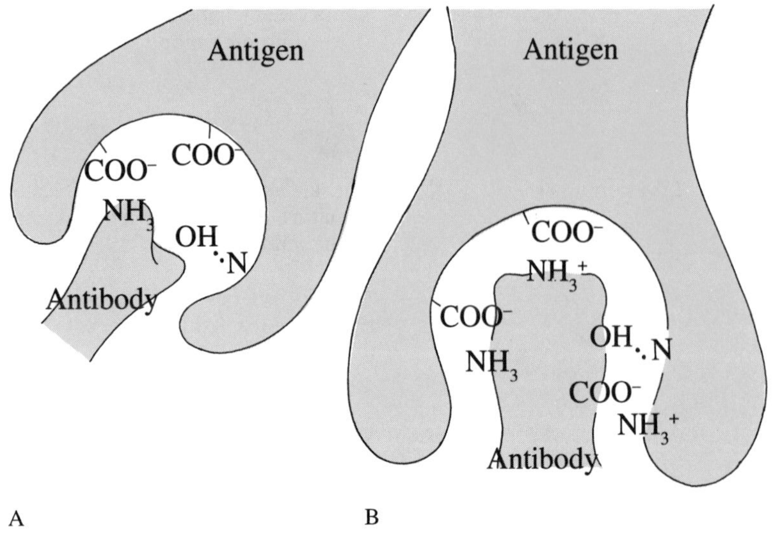

FIGURE 10-7
Degree of fit between antibody chemical group and antigen. A. Ionic attraction between COO^- and NH_3^+, and hydrogen bonding between OH and N groups. Repulsion between COO^- groups produces a poor fit between antigen and antibody. B. All ionic and hydrogen bond interactions are attractive and antibody produces a good fit with antigen.

vide the opportunity for attraction forces to operate. Consequently the specificity between antigen and antibody is sharply reduced. Undoubtedly, specificity is controlled by antigen shape as well as by the chemical nature of the determinants.

BIOLOGICAL PROPERTIES OF THE FIVE IMMUNOGLOBULIN CLASSES

The physicochemical and biological properties of the five immunoglobulin classes are summarized in Table 10-1.

1. **IgG.** Beginning about the age of 2 years and into the fourth decade of life, IgG makes up about 75 to 80 percent of the immunoglobulin in normal serum. It is also found in tissue spaces. It is the only immunoglobulin that crosses the placental barrier. IgG transfer across the placenta temporarily protects the newborn child against certain infectious diseases to which the mother has antibodies (Fig. 10-8). Functionally, IgG is a major inactivator of extracellular viruses and bacteria. In addition, IgG coats antigens in preparation for phagocytosis in the process known as **opsonization.** One of IgG's exclusive functions is the inactivation of toxins. IgG is also involved in hypersensitivity reactions, which are discussed in Chapter 13.
2. **IgM.** Functionally, IgM is similar to IgG but differs from it in very significant ways. IgM is found primarily in the serum where it constitutes only about 7 to 10 percent of all serum immunoglobulins. IgM is not ordinarily found in the extravascular spaces. IgM is the largest of the immunoglobulins and exists primarily as a pentamer and secondarily as a monomer (see Fig. 10-5). There are specific properties re-

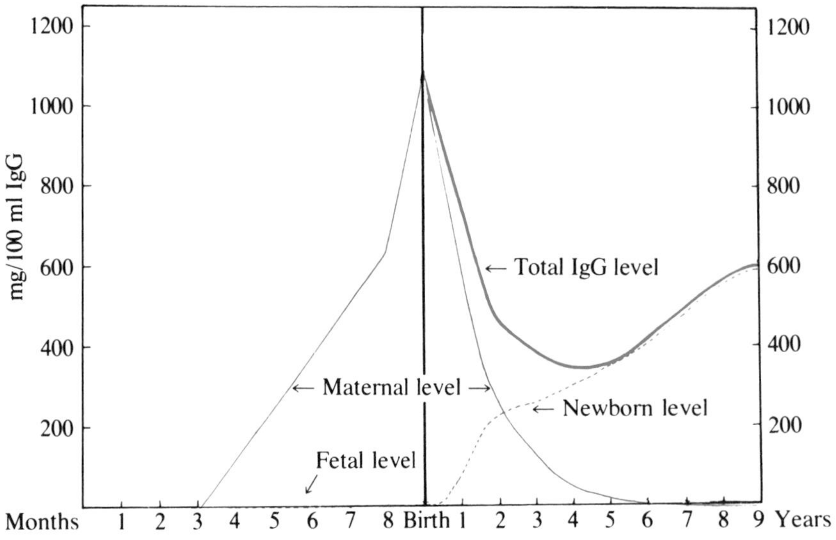

FIGURE 10-8
Probable IgG levels in the fetus and newborn. (From M. R. Allansmith. In F. Falkner, ed., *Human Development*. Philadelphia: Saunders, 1966.)

TABLE 10-1
Selected Physicochemical and Biological Properties of Immunoglobulins

	IgG	IgM	IgA	IgE	IgD
H chain class	Gamma (γ)	Mu (μ)	Alpha (α)	Epsilon (ϵ)	Delta (δ)
Physicochemical properties					
Sedimentation (rate)	7	19	7–11	8	7
Molecular weight (daltons)	146,000	900,000	160,000	200,000	180,000
Serum concentration (mg/ml)	6–8	0.4–2.0	1.4–4.0	Trace	0.03
Half-life in serum (in days)	21–23	5	6	2.5	3
Number of four-chain units	1	5	1–3	1	1
Antigen binding sites	2	10	2–6	2	2
Biological properties					
Types of antibody	Agglutinin Precipitin Opsonin Neutralizing	Agglutinin Precipitin Opsonin Neutralizing	Secretory antibody on mucous surfaces Aggregates activate complement through the alternative pathway	Reagin; skin-sensitizing Aggregates activate complement through the alternative pathway	?
Fixes complement	+	+	–	–	–
Crosses placenta	+	–	–	–	–
Binds to Fc receptors on neutrophils and macrophages	+	–	–	–	–
Other distinct properties	Blocking antibody of atopic allergy hyposensitization; Rh isoagglutinin; prominent in secondary response	First Ig formed; ABO antibodies; receptor on B cell membrane	Found in serum and external secretions; provides local/topical immunity	Reaginic antibody of anaphylaxis and atopic allergies; attaches to mast cells	Receptor on B cell membrane

+ = positive; – = negative.

lated to the pentamer. For example, IgM cannot cross the placenta. The immunity of newborns to certain infectious diseases is due to the transfer of IgG antibodies, and not the larger IgM antibodies.

The five immunoglobulin units of the IgM pentamer also provide 10 identical antigen binding sites (only two for IgG). The IgM molecule provides more sites for binding infectious agents or other antigens than does IgG. IgM also possesses five Fc sites, which makes it more efficient than IgG in initiating a response when it binds to complement (see Chapter 9). The early production of IgM accounts for its initial presence at the site of infection.

As a monomer IgM is found on the surface of mature B lymphocytes, where they act as sites for binding of antigen. In addition, IgM monomers are found in high concentrations in patients with certain diseases such as lupus erythematosus and rheumatoid arthritis.

3. **IgA.** IgA represents about 10 percent of the total immunoglobulins in the serum. IgA, however, is the principal immunoglobulin found in external secretions. These secretions include saliva, tears, colostrum (milky fluid secreted by mammary glands near time of birth), and secretions on the surface of the intestinal, respiratory, and genital tracts. IgA occurs in various polymeric forms but primarily as a monomer and dimer. The IgA dimer possesses a J chain plus another chain called the **secretory piece,** and hence is termed secretory IgA or sIgA. The secretory

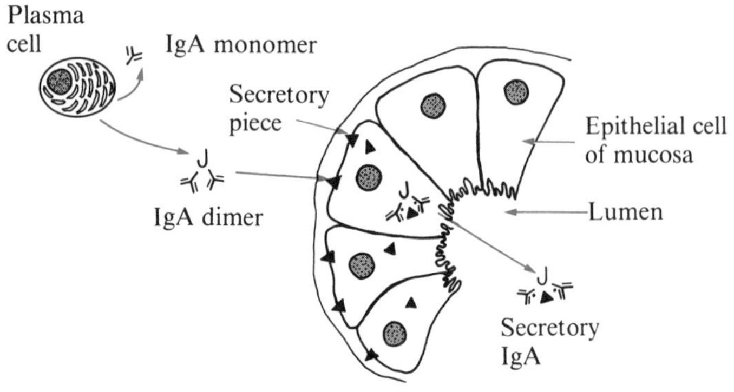

FIGURE 10-9
Secretory IgA formation. IgA dimers (two units of IgA and a J chain) are formed in submucosal plasma cells. The secretory piece initially is located across the cell membrane of mucosal epithelial cells, where it serves as a receptor of the IgA dimer. The IgA dimer–secretory piece complex is transported through the cytoplasm of the epithelial cell and secreted through the opposite side of the cell. The secreted IgA provides local, topical immunity on the mucosal surface.

piece is believed to aid in the transport of IgA across mucosal surfaces (Fig. 10-9).

It is at the mucosal surface where IgA protects the host from infectious agents. Secretory IgA functions as a topical, local immune system. Most of the microorganisms and foreign antigens that enter the body must first attach to the mucosa. sIgA prevents that attachment and subsequent penetration. Microbial species such as *Vibrio cholerae, Streptococcus mutans,* and *Neisseria gonorrhoeae* will not bind to epithelial surfaces in the presence of sIgA. Local sIgA also neutralizes virus and thus plays a role in protecting the host from reinfection by respiratory viruses.

sIgA is relatively resistant to proteolytic enzymes, due to the presence of the secretory component. In some infections, however, the microbial agent is able to produce proteolytic enzymes that digest sIgA. This virulence factor makes the host more susceptible to infection.

4. **IgD.** IgD makes up less than 1 percent of the serum immunoglobulins. Its primary function, like that of monomeric IgM, is as a receptor on the surface of B lymphocytes where it binds antigen.
5. **IgE.** IgE is found in trace amounts in the serum. IgE can be found in higher levels in individuals with certain allergic conditions such as hay fever as well as in those with certain animal parasite infections such as hookworm. During severe allergic reactions, such as anaphylactic shock, IgE antibodies, via their Fc regions, bind to tissue mast cells and basophils. These latter cells release histamines and other products associated with the symptoms of allergy (see Chapter 13 for further discussion of hypersensitivities or allergies).

Antibody Diversity

In response to various antigens in the environment, a human produces virtually millions of antibodies, each with a different specificity. In addition, the amino acid sequences in the constant region of each immunoglobulin class are identical while the variable part of the molecule has differing amino acid sequences. How could each of us produce all of these antibodies if there are at the most 1 million genes in the human genome?

IMMUNOGLOBULIN GENES

In the 1960s Dreyer and Bennett reasoned that mutation alone could not account for antibody diversity. They proposed that separate gene sequences in a germ cell encoded for multiple variable (V) regions and for the constant (C) region. This result led to the concept that there are two genes for a single protein chain (i.e., for an immunoglobulin chain). In addition, there must be a mechanism for joining the two genetic components in the somatic cell to form a single transcriptional unit. Evidence obtained in animal studies using modern DNA manipulation techniques proved the proposal to be correct.

The studies originally conducted in mice showed that the V and C genes are far apart in the germ line (embryonic DNA) and move closer together by recombination in the DNA of lymphocyte precursor cells (somatic cells, Fig. 10-10). There are also genes that code for J (joining) sequences of portions of the V_L and V_H domains. The V, J, and C region gene sequences are separated by noncoding sequences, called **introns*** that serve as "spacers."

Light Chain Reorganization

During the development of the B cell, a V gene segment is translocated via recombination to a site next to a J segment. This results in the formation of a contiguous VJ sequence without intervening introns. The VJ segment remains separated from the C segment. Any of the multiple V gene segments can be joined to any of the J gene sequences. Once VJ recombination has taken place, the cell is committed to synthesizing an antibody whose antigen binding specificity is encoded by that VJ sequence. The DNA that originally was located between the chosen V segment and the chosen J segment is deleted. Thus, if there were 200 V gene segments and the sixth was the chosen segment, V segments 7 to 200 will be deleted (the V segments are on the 5′ upstream end of the gene) and segments 1 to 6 will remain. Likewise with the J segment,

* Introns are untranslated intervening sequences in the DNA; exons are informational areas in the DNA that can be translated into products.

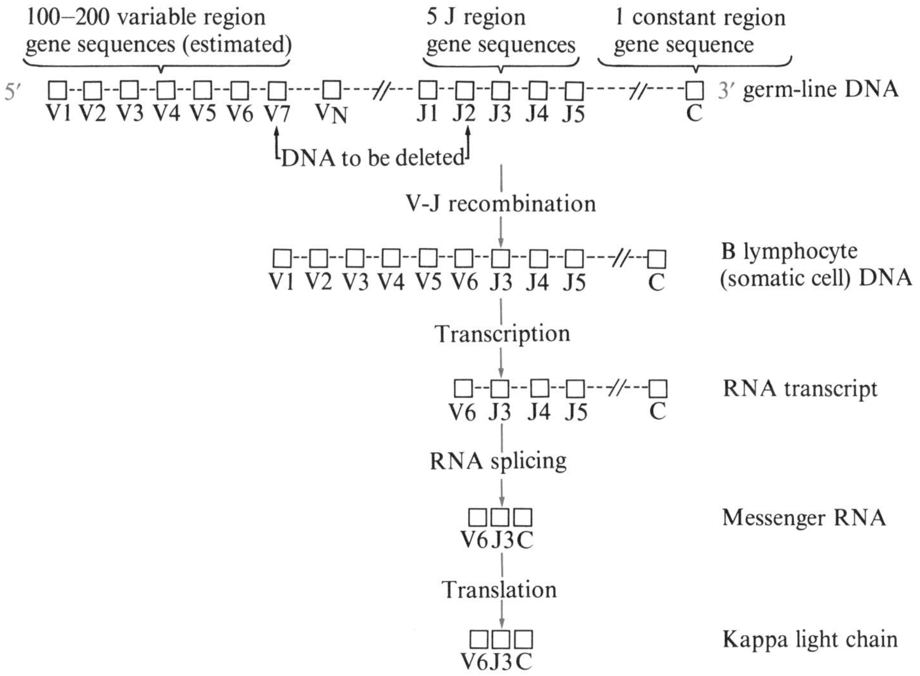

FIGURE 10-10
Antibody diversity generation in kappa light chain (human). Germ-line DNA for the light chain contains multiple variable (V) and joining (J) gene sequences and a single constant (C) region gene sequence. There is a long intervening DNA sequence (intron) between the V and J segments and a shorter sequence between the J and C segments. During recombination in the somatic cell (the B cell), segments of DNA are deleted as the chosen V gene sequence comes to be translocated next to one of the J segments. The entire gene is transcribed. The intervening sequences and the extra J's are spliced out to yield the messenger RNA that is to be translated into the kappa chain. (Not illustrated: A leader segment accompanies these steps; the leader is cleaved away as the chain exits through the B cell membrane.)

if J3 were chosen, then J1 and J2 will be deleted and J3, J4, and J5 will remain. The resulting gene, which contains V segments 1 to 6, J segments 3 to 5, introns, and the constant segment, will be transcribed into high molecular weight RNA. This RNA will later be processed to form a functional message that will be translated into an immunoglobulin light chain.

Heavy Chain Variable Chain Reorganization

Heavy chain recombination, which contributes to the formation of the Fab portion of the immunoglobulin molecule, is like that described for light chain events. There is one major difference between the two of them. The variable region of the heavy chain has an additional gene segment, called the **D (diversity)** gene segment. V and J recombinations with alternative sequences in the D segment afford additional chances for variability.

This capability of recombining selected sequences of germ-line DNA into a single active sequence in somatic cells explains how a large repertoire of antibodies can be generated without having to have a germ-line gene for each antibody specificity. In humans, for example, each light chain is thought to have between 50 and 200 separate V genes and 5 J genes, and each heavy chain between 100 and 200 V genes, 4 J genes, and 12 D genes. If we assume that 200 V_L plus 5 J_L, plus 200 V_H plus 4 J_H plus 12 D_H genes randomly associate, the total number of different antibody molecules that could be synthesized from this gene pool would be 9.6×10^6. This illustrates how a limited amount of DNA (421 genes) can generate a potential 10 million antibody specificities.

The rearrangement of antibody gene segments is but one way of generating antibody diversity. There are two other ways. First, gene mutations in the variable region occur during B cell development in the bone marrow. Different polypeptide sequences can be produced by the B cell clones. Second, generation of different codons during splicing of VDJ junctions can also lead to generation of different polypeptides. For example, the precise site at which the V and J segments join may vary, resulting in nucleotide codon differences (Fig. 10-11).

Heavy Chain Switch and Immunoglobulin Function

A type of diversity that involves the biological functions of the antibody molecule occurs at the heavy chain end of the immunoglobulin molecule and is called **heavy chain switch** (Fig. 10-12). Antibody diversity takes place in the variable region by the time the B cell membrane has receptor immunoglobulin molecules and before contact with foreign antigen occurs. Only B cells whose surface immunoglobulin interacts with antigen go on to secret antibod-

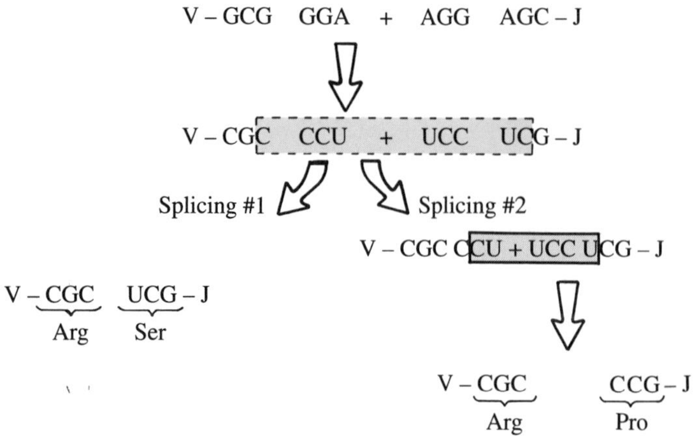

FIGURE 10-11
Antibody diversity generated by splicing between V and J regions. Original DNA sequences in V and J junctions are illustrated along with the primary RNA transcript. Depending on the site of splice (———), the same VJ joining could produce polypeptides differing in one amino acid. V = variable sequence; J = J chain sequence; Arg = arginine; Ser = serine; Pro = proline.

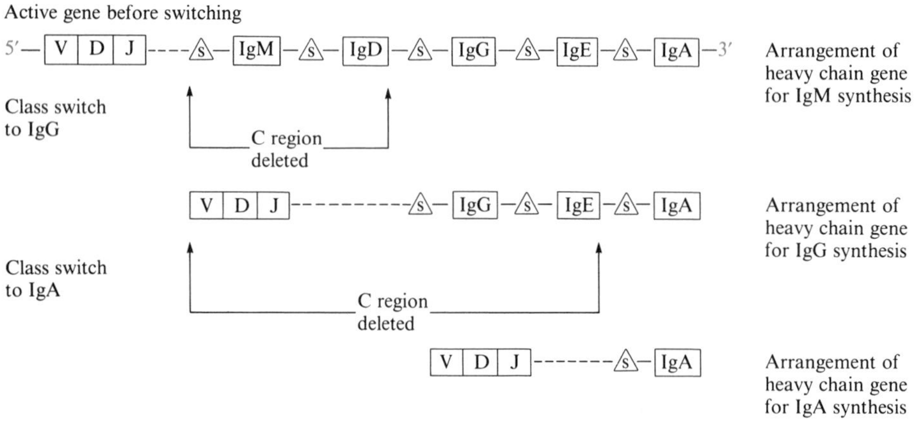

FIGURE 10-12
Heavy chain switch (S/S recombination). The recombinational steps on the 5′ (left) side of the active gene that produced the V, D, and J sequence (the variable region) are shown in Figure 10-11. The D (diversity) gene segment is found only in heavy chains. The constant (C) region gene sequences are lined up in the order of IgM, IgD, IgG, IgE, and IgA. Each constant region gene is preceded by a switching signal (S). This arrangement leads to IgM synthesis if there is no gene switching. The switch to IgG secretion involves deletion of the S, IgM, S, IgD sequence and the translocation of the VDJ transcription unit to a position next to the IgG gene sequence. The switch to IgA secretion involves deletion of the S, IgM, S, IgD, IgG, S, IgE sequence and the translocation of VDJ to a position next to the IgA sequence.

ies. Upon antigen recognition, the cell is driven **(antigen-driven)** along its developmental pathway to form a clone of lymphocytes that produce an antibody of a single specificity (a **monoclonal antibody**). End line B cells, now called plasma cells, begin their antibody secreting functions by first making IgM.

Other immunoglobulin classes can be made by B cells while retaining the same antigen binding sites on the Fab region. The switch involves a second recombinational event, called **S/S recombination.** The switch from one class to another is accomplished through recombination of switching sequences (S) that exist in the introns between the exons of each H chain class. Starting from the VJ region, the DNA sequences for the constant region of the heavy chains of the immunoglobulin classes are lined up in the order of IgM, IgD, IgG3, IgG1, IgA1, IgG2, IgG4, IgE, and IgA2 (there are four subclasses of IgG and two subclasses of IgA). If the heavy chain switch is to IgG (the most frequent switch), IgM and IgD sequences encoding the constant regions are deleted. If the switch is to IgA2, then the sequences encoding the constant regions of IgM, IgD, IgG, and IgE are deleted. The functional implication of the switches is that antigen binding sites of a particular immunoglobulin molecule can associate with any of the five immunoglobulin classes. The immunoglobulin acquires the biological functions characteristic of each immunoglobulin class.

Immunoglobulins as Antigens

An immunoglobulin is a polypeptide whose messenger RNA (mRNA) has been spliced together from mRNAs coding for different parts of the immunoglobulin mole-

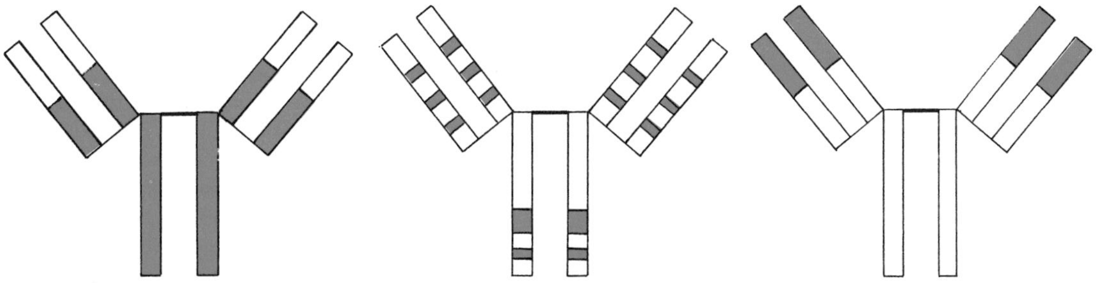

FIGURE 10-13
Antibody variation. Isotypic, allotypic, and idiotypic determinants involve certain amino acid residues in the colored areas.

cule. This creates variability in the immunoglobulin molecule; that is, there are differences in the amino acid sequences of various parts of the molecule. Since immunoglobulins are proteins, they can also be antigens and their variability creates different antigenic determinants on the molecule. As antigens, immunoglobulins carry three types of antigenic determinants referred to as **isotypic, allotypic,** and **idiotypic** (Fig. 10-13).

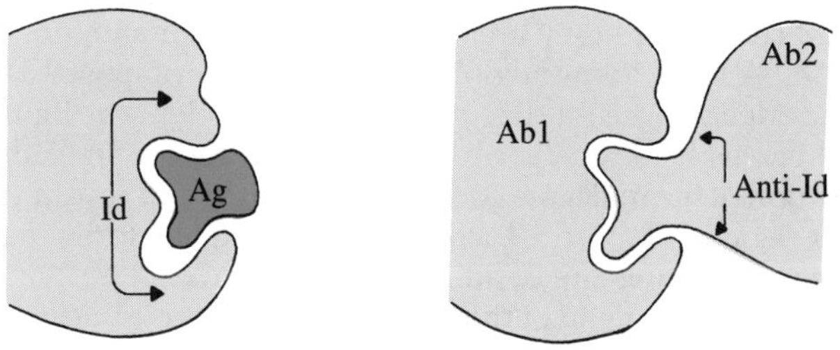

FIGURE 10-14
Anti-idiotypic antibody (Ab2) competes with antigen (Ag) for a binding site on antibody 1 (Ab1). Idiotopes (Id) (antigenic determinants) of antibody 1 bind antigen. Antibody is produced in response to isotopes of antibody 1. Antibody 2 mimics antigen and therefore competes with it for antigenic determinants on antibody 1.

ISOTYPIC DETERMINANTS

The term isotype refers to the genetic variation within a family of polypeptides. Each isotype is represented as a distinct gene and is present in all members of a species. Isotypic determinants distinguish H chain classes (IgG, IgA, IgM, IgE, and IgD), subclasses (e.g., IgG1, IgG2), and the lambda L chain (there is only a single class of kappa). All of these variations occur in the constant domain of all immunoglobulins (see Fig. 10-13).

ALLOTYPIC DETERMINANTS

Allotypic variation refers to genetic variation involving different alleles at a specific gene locus (alleles are alternate forms of the gene). For example, not all individuals possess the same blood groups. Allotypic variation involves primarily the heavy chain constant regions (see Fig. 10-13). H chains are the same in an immunoglobulin and only one allotype is expressed (called the allelic exclusion principle) in an individual. Allotypes have been used to identify peoples and demonstrate familial relationships. They are also important in tissue typing.

IDIOTYPIC DETERMINANTS

The antigenic determinants that distinguish one monoclonal immunoglobulin from others having the same isotypes and allotypes are called **idiotopes.** A set of idiotopes is called an **idiotype (Id)** and is located in the Fab or antigen binding region (see Fig. 10-13).

An antibody with its idiotypes can induce the formation of a second antibody. The second antibody binds only to the first antibody that induced it. The second antibody is called an anti-idiotype (Fig. 10-14). Therefore, the anti-idiotype competes with antigen for the binding site on the first antibody. Anti-idiotypic antibodies may be formed naturally or induced artificially. By such antibody-antibody reactions the immune system interacts with itself and thus is involved in immune regulation. In addition, anti-idiotypes have potential for therapeutic use (see Chapter 12).

Antigens and Antibodies in Immunodiagnosis

The antigen-antibody reactions discussed here take place within the mammalian host (in vivo). Several of these reactions also take place outside the animal host (in vitro) under controlled laboratory conditions. These reactions are not only specific but also readily detectable. The subdiscipline of immunology that exploits these interactions is designated **serology.** The more common serological tests used in the diagnosis of infectious disease are discussed in Appendix B.

Summary

1. Antigens possess two distinct properties: immunogenicity and specificity. Immunogenicity refers to their ability to induce the formation of antibodies, while specificity refers to their capacity to bind to antibodies in a specific way.

2. Immunogenicity of antigens is related to their foreignness, molecular weight, and chemical composition (i.e., the antigen is nonself, has a molecular weight of 10,000 or more, and consists of different chemical groups). The specificity of antigens is based on the chemical groups involved and their configuration.

3. Immunoglobulins, produced by B cells and their derivatives, can react with the antigens that induced them. Some immunoglobulins become part of the surface of B cells where they are receptors for foreign antigen.

4. A basic immunoglobulin molecule is composed of two identical heavy (H) chains and two identical light (L) chains held together by sulfur-sulfur bonds. The Fab portion of the molecule contains variable (V) and constant (C) regions of H and L chains. The V regions form the antigen binding site of an antibody molecule.

5. The other end of the immunoglobulin molecule, the Fc region, is composed of constant (C) regions of H chains. The biological functions of the Fc region include binding of immunoglobulins to host immune cells, binding of complement, and facilitation of the transplacental passage of IgG.

6. The magnitude of binding of antigen to antibody depends on the interaction of their chemical groups and configuration of the antigen.

7. There are five immunoglobulin classes—IgG, IgM, IgA, IgD, and IgE. They are composed of a basic unit, which depending on the immunoglobulin, can exist in a monomeric, dimeric, trimeric, or pentameric form. Immunoglobulin classes have specific functions (see Table 10-1).

8. Antibody diversity is due to intrachromosomal recombination in somatic cells of selected V, J, D, and C gene sequences to form a single transcription unit. This mechanism allows the generation of a large repertoire of immunoglobulin receptors of differing specificities without requiring an individual germ-line gene for each antibody specificity.

9. Another recombinational event, the heavy chain switch, occurs at the other end of the immunoglobulin molecule after antigen recognition. Through S/S recombination, an antigen binding site can associate with any of the five immunoglobulin classes and thereby acquire the biological functions characteristic of that class.

10. Immunoglobulins, which can act as antigens, carry three types of antigenic determinants: isotypic, allotypic, and idiotypic. The immune system, therefore, can interact with itself.

Questions for Study

1. Are all antigens immunogens? Are all immunogens antigens? Explain.
2. Draw a simplified diagram of an immunoglobulin. Label the important binding sites and what binds to them.
3. What is the influence of the Fc region of an immunoglobulin in the immune response?
4. Briefly describe the three ways in which antibody diversity can be generated.
5. List at least two functions for each of the immunoglobulin classes.
6. What is an anti-idiotype?

CHAPTER

11

Cells and Tissues of the Immune System

OBJECTIVES

To outline the various tissues and organs that make up the immune system

To describe how an infectious agent is processed once it enters the host

To discuss the biological importance of the major histocompatibility complex (MHC) and what is meant by MHC restriction

To discuss the various activities of cytokines and how they are involved in the immune response

To describe the functions of surface markers and receptors on T cells

To discuss the biological activities of the various T cell subpopulations

To describe the process of B cell activation

To explain the concept of clonal selection as it applies to the humoral response to antigenic determinants

To describe the mechanism of NK cell activity

OUTLINE

PRIMARY LYMPHOID ORGANS AND TISSUES

SECONDARY LYMPHOID ORGANS AND TISSUES

MAJOR HISTOCOMPATIBILITY COMPLEX
- Class I Antigens
- Class II Antigens
- Class III Antigens

CYTOKINES
- Interleukin-1
- Interleukin-2
- Interleukin-6
- Interferons

LYMPHOID CELLS
- T cells
  - Surface Markers (Differentiation Antigens)
  - Surface Receptors
  - T Lymphocyte Subsets
- B Cells
  - Plasma Cells
  - Memory Cells
  - Clonal Selection

NON-T, NON-B LYMPHOCYTES
- Natural Killer Cells

MONONUCLEAR AND POLYMORPHONUCLEAR PHAGOCYTES

During mammalian evolution, several cells, tissues, and organs were formed to defend the body against attack by infectious agents and other nonself antigens. In Chapter 9 we saw how the body in a nonspecific way offered a first line of defense against infectious agents. In this chapter we examine primarily the types of cells that are involved in the immune response in a very specific way.

Specific immune cells arise from **stem cells,** which are found primarily in the bone marrow, thymus, and liver of all adults. Stem cells give rise to **progenitor cells,** which can differentiate into a variety of cells such as red blood cells, neutrophils, eosinophils, basophils, macrophages, platelets, and lymphocytes. Macrophages and lymphocytes are organized into tissues and organs collectively referred to as the **lymphoid system.** The lymphoid system is actively engaged in the entrapment and processing of infectious agents and other foreign substances that enter the body.

Primary Lymphoid Organs and Tissues

The primary lymphoid organs are the **thymus** and **bone marrow** (Fig. 11-1). The thymus, which overlies the heart, is the site for differentiation of stem cells into lymphocytes called **T cells.** Functional T cells (cells that have not responded to antigen) migrate to secondary lymphoid organs (see Fig. 11-1). In the secondary lymphoid organs they respond to foreign antigens that enter the host. The thymus is most active early in childhood. If the thymus is surgically removed shortly after birth, normal cell-mediated immune responses are curtailed. For example, the child becomes susceptible to viral infections and other intracellular parasites (see Chapter 12 for discussion of function of cell-mediated immunity).

Bone marrow can be found in the cavities of most bones of the body. It is the source of all classes of blood cells. Bone marrow is also the primary source of lymphocytes called **B cells.** B cells (specifically plasma cells) are the factories where antibody is produced in the host. Bone marrow can serve as a secondary lymphoid organ where T and B cells can migrate and engage foreign antigens.

Secondary Lymphoid Organs and Tissues

Secondary lymphoid organs include the spleen, lymph nodes, and scattered lymphoid tissue (see Fig. 11-1). It

FIGURE 11-1
Primary and secondary lymphoid organs.

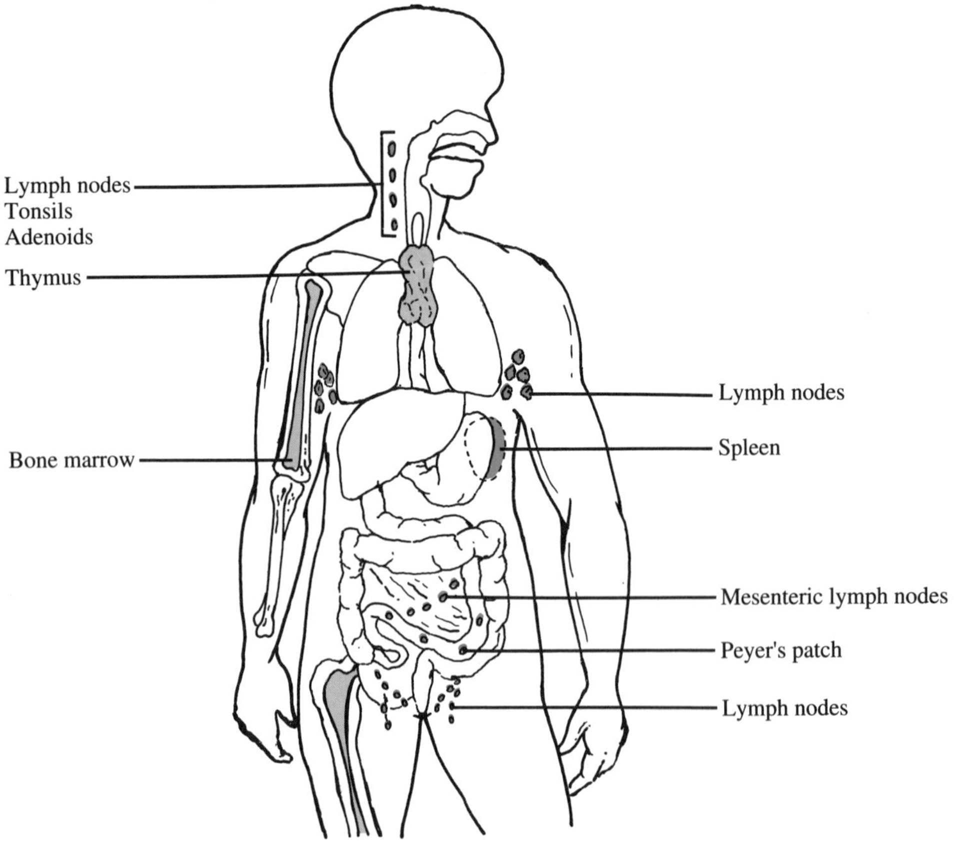

is in the secondary organs that the immune response is properly initiated. Foreign antigens or infectious agents that enter the host are trapped by macrophages and concentrated in the various secondary lymphoid tissue. Since there is a direct connection between lymph tissue and the venous system (i.e., the thoracic duct that enters the subclavian vein), foreign antigen is circulated throughout the lymph system and processed.

The spleen contains two major types of tissue: red pulp and white pulp. The white pulp, which contains the lymphoid tissue, is made up of B cells and T cells plus macrophages and specialized antigen presenting cells (see Chapter 9 for discussion of these cells).

Lymph nodes are small, bean-shaped organs distributed throughout the body (Fig. 11-2). They serve as a junction between the tissue periphery and the thoracic duct by draining tissue fluid or lymph. When antigen enters the node, for example, in the form of a bacterial cell, it may be engulfed by phagocytic macrophages. The antigens released by digestion of the bacterial cell can then be presented to migrating or localized T or B cells. Sometimes the proliferation of immune cells as well as the processing of antigen is so intense that the nodes become enlarged and inflamed. Enlarged nodes are referred to as **buboes,** for example, the enlarged nodes observed in bubonic plague. Processed antigen and lymph cells may be removed via an efferent lymphatic duct and thence into the thoracic duct.

FIGURE 11-2
Lymph node network.

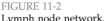

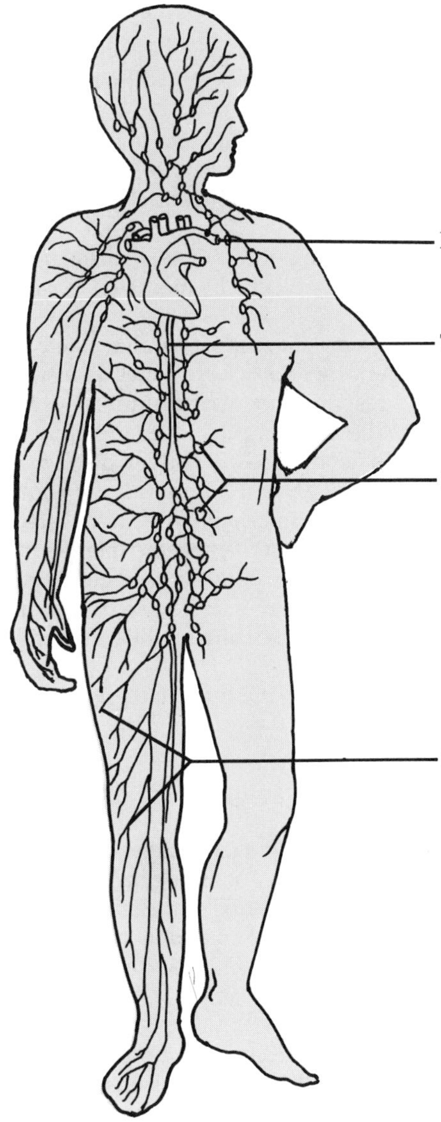

Diffuse lymphoid tissue can be found scattered in several organs such as the submucosal areas of the gastrointestinal, respiratory, and genitourinary tracts. These are the lymph areas that an antigen initially encounters after it has entered the host. The tonsils, adenoids, Peyer's patches in the intestine, and appendix constitute what is referred to as mucosal-associated lymphoid tissue or **MALT.**

The ability of lymphocytes to recognize various substances is often dependent on the presence of cell membrane proteins called **major histocompatibility complex (MHC) proteins.** In addition, the processing of foreign antigen and the production of antibodies by lymphocytes cannot take place without the help of mediators called **cytokines.** Therefore we discuss MHC proteins and cytokines before discussing the characteristics of T cells and B cells.

Major Histocompatibility Complex

During the early part of the twentieth century, scientists recognized that experiments involving grafts or transplanted tissues from one individual to another were invariably unsuccessful. These failures led to the realization that cell membrane antigens are involved in immune reactions. These antigens are coded by genes called **major histocompatibility genes.** Tissue compatibility or histocompatibility is a very important aspect of immunology. Every individual has a specific set of histocompatibility genes. In humans the histocompatibility system is referred to as the **HLA (human leukocyte-associated antigens) gene cluster.**

The HLA complex consists of four main regions termed A, B, C, and D and these in turn are divided into subregions. There are many distinct genes in the MHC. Their products (MHC antigens or proteins) are designated **Class I, Class II, and Class III** molecules. Homology exists between Class I and Class II molecules and between these molecules and homologous regions on immunoglobulin molecules. Thus, the MHC proteins are an important part of the family of molecules involved in the immune response. At each HLA subregion there are several distinct antigenic specificities and like immunoglobulins, they provide diversity. In summary, MHC gene products are essentially markers that distinguish "self" from "nonself." They are involved not only in graft rejection but also in the regulation of immune responsiveness. Let us examine in more detail MHC proteins or class antigens.

CLASS I ANTIGENS

The antigens of Class I are considered the classic transplantation antigens and are found in most nucleated mammalian cells. Class I genes are encoded in the A, B, and C regions. Their products are involved in signaling effector T cells during cell-mediated immunity. Each Class I antigen bears many antigenic determinants. Cytotoxic T cells (T_C) cells respond to Class I antigens on foreign cells and destroy them. Class I antigens are also involved with immune surveillance. During viral infection T_C cells recognize not only the viral antigen on the cell surface of the infected cell but also Class I antigens. The requirement that foreign antigen and host MHC be present is called **MHC restriction. MHC-restricted cell-mediated immunity** is associated with Class I molecules and Class II molecules.

CLASS II ANTIGENS

Class II antigens are displayed on B cells and macrophages (antigen presenting cells). They are primarily involved in the recruitment of helper (T_H), delayed-type hypersensitivity (T_D), and suppressor (T_S) cells. Class II genes are encoded in the D region. Class II molecules are presented to T_H cells in association with foreign antigen. For example, recognition of antigen by a T_H cell requires the binding of the T cell receptor with the foreign antigen and Class II antigen of the antigen presenting cell (Fig. 11-3). Class II antigens restrict responses to a self-MHC molecule alone.

CLASS III ANTIGENS

Class III antigens include complement components C2 and C4, which are discussed in Chapter 12.

FIGURE 11-3
Major histocompatibility complex (MHC) restriction involving T_H cells and antigen presenting cells (APC). The antigen presenting cell shows MHC Class II proteins plus foreign antigen displayed on its surface. Recognition between the APC and T_H cell involves interaction of foreign antigen and T cell receptor (TCR) as well as interaction between Class II proteins and CD4 protein.

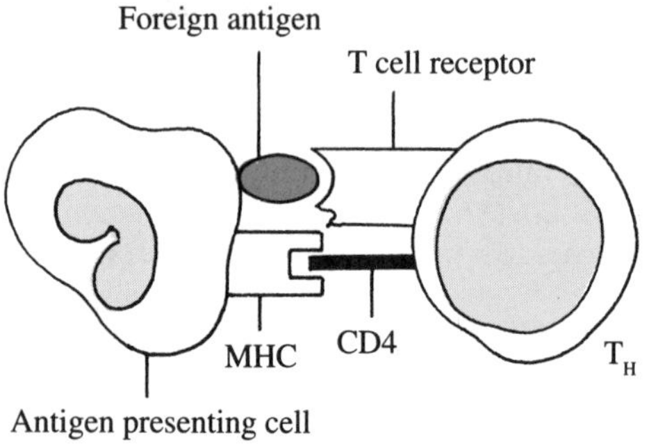

Cytokines

Cytokines are polypeptide hormones produced primarily by leukocytes in response to exogenous molecules (e.g., bacterial products) as well as endogenously produced molecules. Cytokines produced specifically by lymphocytes are called **lymphokines,** while those produced by monocytes are called **monokines.** Cytokines can affect the cells that produced them, or adjacent cells or tissues, or they may act systemically. Some of the ways cytokines can affect the immune response are

1. As **mitogen-like molecules.** Cytokines are not mitogens but they exhibit some of the characteristics of mitogens. Mitogens are substances that promote cell division or mitosis. For example, the lipopolysaccharide (LPS) of gram-negative bacteria can stimulate the proliferation of B cells. Another class of mitogens is **lectins.** Lectins are glycoproteins produced by plants that can activate T cells to proliferate. Mitogens are frequently used to study lymphocyte function.
2. As **chemotaxins.** Some cytokines attract phagocytes and eosinophils to the site of infection, thereby intensifying the immune response.
3. As **mediators of differentiation.** Some cytokines are able to induce lymphocytes, for example, B cells, to differentiate into antibody-producing cells on antigen stimulation.
4. As **cytotoxins.** The killing of tumor cells or the inhibition of tumor cell growth can be mediated by specific cytokines.
5. By **activation** of macrophages. Macrophage activation is an important function of cytokines. It results in an intensified response (increased numbers of lysosomes, etc.) to the invading microorganism.

The term **interleukin** is now used to convey the meaning of a mediator that serves as a communication link between leukocytes. Specific interleukins usually affect more than one target cell type, and a specific interleukin may have several effects on the cells of a single target cell population. Interleukins may still be referred to as lymphokines or monokines, depending on the source cell type.

Table 11-1 illustrates some of the important cytokines. We elaborate on only a few of them.

INTERLEUKIN-1

Interleukin (IL)-1 is produced by macrophages and other cell types in response to antigens or mitogens (LPS, for example). IL-1 is primarily a mediator of the acute-phase response. For example, IL-1 acts as an endogenous pyrogen to induce fever (see Chapter 14). IL-1 induces release of hematopoietic growth factors (Table 11-1) and hence is a regulator of hematopoiesis.

IL-1 has direct or indirect effects on immune cells. It increases the secretion of IL-2 by T cells in response to antigens. IL-1 also increases specific resistance to infection by amplifying polymorphonuclear leukocyte (PMN) mi-

TABLE 11-1
Cytokines and Their Functions*

Factor	Source	Principal functions
Interleukins		
IL-1	Macrophage, nucleated cells in response to injury	Proliferation and differentiation of B and T cells; induces fever; activates PMN and monocytes
IL-2	Activated T cells	Promotes secretion of other lymphokines; promotes differentiation of B and T cells; amplifies cytotoxic activity of T and NK cells
IL-3	Activated T cells	Fosters growth and differentiation of bone marrow stem cells
IL-4	T_H cells	Enhances multiplication of B cells and T_C cells; elevates production of IgG and IgE; increases MHC Class II expression by resting cells
IL-5	T_H cells	Induces differentiation of eosinophils; stimulates production of IgA and IgM
IL-6	Macrophage, T_H cells, fibroblasts	Promotes B cell differentiation into plasma cells; induces Ig production; stimulates T cell IL-2 or IL-4 production
IL-7	Spleen, thymus	Growth factor for B and T cells
IL-8	Macrophage, T cells, fibroblasts, endothelial cells	Neutrophil chemotactic factor
Interferons		
IFN-α	Monocytes, lymphocytes	Antiviral activities
IFN-β	Fibroblasts, epithelial cells	Antiviral activities; increases NK cell functions
IFN-γ	T_H cells, NK cells, T_C cells	Similar to IFN-α and IFN-β; augments PMN and macrophage function; enhances production of IgG subclasses
Tumor necrosis factor (TNF)	LPS-stimulated macrophages, T_H cells	Induces fever; mediates endotoxic shock; antitumor activity; enhances B cell proliferation; enhances PMN and monocyte function; enhances production of other cytokines
Hematopoietic growth factors		
GM-CSF	T cells, monocytes, fibroblasts	Stimulates proliferation of neutrophil, monocyte, and eosinophil progenitors; enhances function of mature corresponding cells
G-CSF	Monocytes, fibroblasts, endothelial cells	Stimulates proliferation of neutrophil progenitors; enhances function of mature neutrophils
M-CSF	Monocytes, fibroblasts, endothelial cells	Stimulates proliferation of monocyte progenitors; enhances function of monocytes

PMN = polymorphonuclear leukocyte; LPS = lipopolysaccharide; Ig = immunoglobulin; T_H = helper T cells; T_C = cytotoxic T cells; NK = natural killer; GM-CSF = granulocyte-macrophage colony-stimulating factor; G-CSF = granulocyte colony-stimulating factor; M-CSF = macrophage colony-stimulating factor.
* This table contains only some of the sources and activities of cytokines.

gration to the site of injury and increasing PMN production of microbicidal molecules such as superoxide and hydrogen peroxide.

IL-1 also induces synthesis of other cytokines such as IL-6, IL-8, and tumor necrosis factor (TNF). IL-1 and TNF play an important role in the pathophysiology of bacterial meningitis. These mediators are released in excess during infection by agents such as *Neisseria meningitidis*. They cause a worsening of the inflammation and increase the severity of complications of infection (see Under the Microscope 6).

INTERLEUKIN-2

The most important function of IL-2 is to initiate proliferation of T cells activated by specific antigen. IL-2 is produced by antigen-activated helper T cells on receiving the IL-1 signal from macrophages. IL-2 production is defective in some diseases such as infection with human immunodeficiency virus (HIV) and some autoimmune diseases. IL-2 effects on other cells are outlined in Table 11-1. The role of IL-2 as a chemotherapeutic agent is discussed later.

INTERLEUKIN-6

IL-6 like IL-1 can act as a stem cell activator. IL-6 along with IL-1 and TNF is one of the major mediators in the host's response to infection or inflammatory processes. IL-6 is produced by a variety of cells including T cells, natural killer (NK) cells, PMN, and monocytes/macrophages. The physiological effects of IL-6 include induction of fever, activation of T cells and NK cells, and induction of immunoglobulin synthesis by preactivated B cells.

Under the Microscope 6

Tumor Necrosis Factor, Endotoxin, and Gram-Negative Septicemia

It is currently believed that interaction of endotoxin with the macrophage may be the primary event in initiating all of the biological effects of endotoxin. This interaction results in the release of several mediators: tumor necrosis factor (TNF), interleukins (IL)-1, -6, and -8, and platelet activating factor (PAF). Of particular importance is TNF. Excess amounts of TNF are released during the acute phase of bacterial infection and cause worsening of inflammation. TNF in the plasma is correlated with the shock syndrome and fatal outcome in patients with gram-negative septicemia. TNF causes vascular endothelial damage, and an increase in vascular permeability which leads to vascular leakage.

Many years of research have gone into the development of techniques for treating the effects of gram-negative septicemia. Antibiotic administration and infection control have not significantly reduced the incidence over the years. Type-specific immunization does not appear to be a practical alternative since there are too many serotypes of *Escherichia coli* and *Klebsiella pneumoniae,* the most habitual offenders. Immunotherapy, however, does appear to be a viable alternative. Two avenues of approach involve therapies directed at endotoxin or the mediators, such as TNF. In recent studies, monoclonal antibodies directed to the lipid A fraction reduced the morbidity and mortality of gram-negative septicemia. The reduction in mortality rates was most significant in patients in whom septic shock developed. This type of therapy is available in Europe but has not yet been approved by the Food and Drug Administration. Several trials using anti-TNF antibodies in patients with septic shock are underway (1992–1993). IL-1 appears to have a synergistic effect in the presence of TNF. The discovery of a natural IL-1 receptor antagonist has led to the development of a natural form of immunotherapy. IL-1 receptor antagonist counteracts the effects of endotoxin and increases the rate of survival from endotoxic shock.

INTERFERONS

Interferon (IFN) was originally described as a protein mediator that prevented viral replication in host cells (see Chapter 9). This antiviral activity is actually due to a group of proteins (IFN-α, IFN-β, and IFN-γ). We have since learned that interferons also play a role in the regulation of the immune system. Interferons, depending on their type, reduce the growth of certain tumors and normal bone marrow cells. They also defend against protozoal or bacterial infections by enhancing phagocytic activities and macrophage activation.

IFN-γ has multiple effects on the immune response (Table 11-2). What sets IFN-γ apart from other interferons is its ability to activate macrophages. This is of critical importance in the resolution of infections caused by intracellular pathogens such as protozoa. IFN-γ is produced by antigen-stimulated T_H and by activated NK cells. It helps activate T_C cells, enabling them to destroy infected host cells, and it increases the ability of B cells to produce antibodies. IFN-γ can also induce Class II MHC antigens, which are needed for recognition of foreign antigen by T_H cells (see Table 11-2).

Interleukins hold great promise as therapeutic agents. Studies are under way using interleukin to enhance an immune response to cancers and intractable infections. For example, T cells or NK cells obtained from patients are stimulated by IL-2 to proliferate in large numbers in vitro. The treated cells are infused back into the patient. IFN-γ has been approved for the treatment of chronic granulomatous disease (CGD), an inherited condition (see Chapter 13 for discussion). The use of cytokines as biological agents is discussed in detail in Chapter 12.

TABLE 11-2
Some Effects of Interferon Gamma (IFN-γ)

Enhances cell killing by killer cells such as cytotoxic T lymphocytes (CTL), NK cells, and K cells
Enhances suppressive activity of supressor T cells (T_S cells)
Inhibits migration of macrophages
Activates macrophages and promotes phagocytosis and intracellular destruction by macrophages
Enhances expression of Fc receptors on macrophages
Increases expression of histocompatibility antigens (Class I and Class II MHC antigen) on various cells, including macrophages, tumor cells, and endothelial cells
With B cell differentiation factor (BCDF), stimulates B cell proliferation and increases antibody production by B cells

Lymphoid Cells

Mature lymphoid cells are produced in the thymus and bone marrow. They make up approximately 20 percent of the total leukocyte (white blood cell) population. Lymphoid cells enter the circulation and can be distributed to various secondary lymphoid organs. They can be divided into two classes: **T cells** and **B cells.** Both cell types are approximately 8 to 12 μm in diameter and are almost entirely filled by the nucleus. An infectious agent entering the host will eventually encounter T cells and B cells. Encounters with B cells result in antibody formation with indirect help from T cells. Both classes of lymphoid cells possess surface markers and receptors that help differentiate between them. Surface markers and receptors also differentiate subpopulations within a class.

T CELLS

Surface Markers (Differentiation Antigens)

As the T cell matures in the thymus, it differentiates into subpopulations of cells, each with specific functions. All of these T cell subpopulations possess surface markers that distinguish them from B cells. These markers or antigens are symbolized by the letters **CD** (cluster designation) and include a very large number of glycoproteins (CD1, CD2, etc.). Different combinations of CD glycoproteins also can be related to different subpopulations of T cells. For example, $CD4^+$ T cells (they possess markers CD2, CD3, CD4, and CD7) exhibit delayed hypersensitivity functions while $CD8^+$ T cells (they possess markers CD2, CD3, CD7, and CD8) show cytotoxic activity. $CD4^+$ cells possess the CD4 proteins that happen to be the receptor for HIV, the causative agent of acquired immunodeficiency syndrome (AIDS). CD4 also appears on the surface of macrophages.

Surface Receptors

In addition to surface markers there are also **surface receptors** on lymphocytes. Surface receptors are capable of binding to foreign antigen, complement, lymphokines, viruses, and erythrocytes. Binding of any one of these substances stimulates the lymphocyte into an active state. We are primarily interested in the antigen receptor or **T cell receptor (TCR).**

The **T cell receptor** is acquired as T cells differentiate into different subpopulations. The T cell receptor is a protein composed of two polypeptide units encoded by genes that resemble those that encode antibody molecules. In other words, they are assembled from separate DNA segments and have variable and constant regions (see Antibody Diversity in Chapter 10). Thus, there is a large enough repertoire of T cell receptors to recognize an essentially unlimited number of target antigens. The T cell receptor does not react with free antigen; instead the antigen must be part of the surface of another cell (bound to MHC protein, see paragraph below), for example, an antigen presenting cell (see Fig. 11-3).

Antigen recognition is also dependent on the presence of specific cell MHC proteins. The cell is activated only by an antigen presenting cell of the same histocompatibility type. It is not activated by the histocompatibility marker alone because this would cause the body to attack itself. The T cell will, however, respond to an MHC-encoded protein from another individual without antigen. It is this latter response that accounts for the rejection of grafted or transplanted tissue (Fig. 11-4). A T lymphocyte with the correct antigen recognition will bind to the antigen-MHC complex on the antigen presenting cell and this results in activation of the lymphocyte. T lymphocyte activation results in the release of immune regulators or lymphokines (Chapter 13 discusses in detail T cell activation).

T Lymphocyte Subsets

Maturation of T cells in the thymus involves (1) acquisition of MHC restriction properties, (2) acquisition of anti-

FIGURE 11-4
T cell receptor (TCR) recognition of antigen. A. The T cell will not bind free antigen. B. The T cell recognizes nonself (foreign cell) and will destroy it (e.g., graft rejection). C. The T cell will not recognize self antigen presenting cell (APC) in the absence of antigen; otherwise it would be self destruction. D. The T cell recognizes the APC only with foreign antigen.

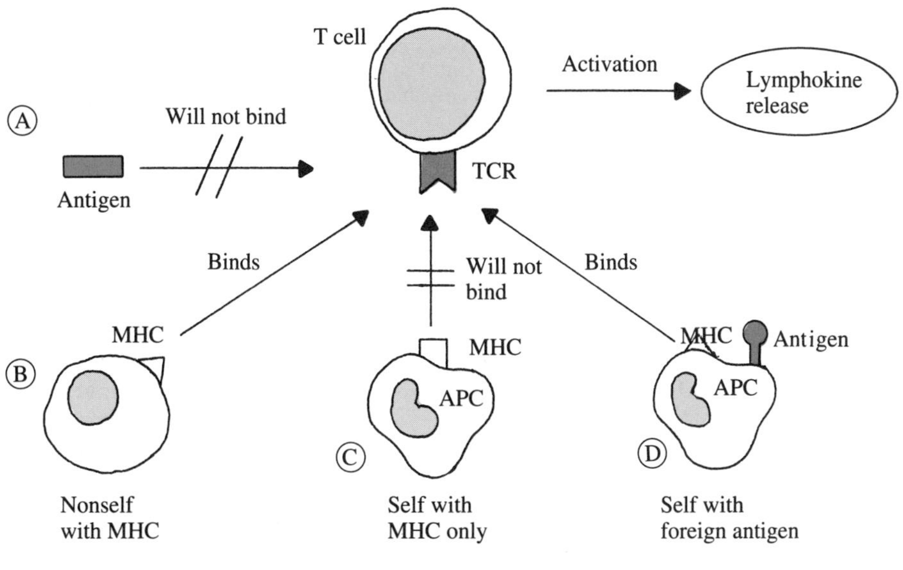

gen receptors, and (3) differentiation into four functionally distinct subsets. The subsets include helper T cells (T_H), suppressor T cells (T_S), cytotoxic T cells (T_C), and delayed-type hypersensitivity cells (T_D or T_{DTH}).

Helper T cells (T_H cells) are regulators that enhance the expression of other lymphocytes and macrophages. T_H cells do not interact directly with free antigen. They recognize antigen on antigen presenting cells only in association with Class II MHC proteins recognized as self. The recognition activates T_H cells to cause the growth of antigen-specific clones of lymphocytes and their differentiation into an effector function. Effector function is usually manifested by the secretion of **lymphokines** (for example, interleukins and IFN-γ), the hormone regulators of the immune response. Another effector function includes cytotoxicity (see discussion on cytotoxic T cells below). The relationship between T_H cells and B cells is discussed under B Cells.

Suppressor T cells (T_S cells) suppress the expression of immune functions by other lymphocytes. Suppressor cells are believed to secrete soluble factors that affect the functional roles of T or B cells. For example, binding to a plasma cell can suppress antibody formation. Suppressor cells can bind to an effector cell (T_H, for example) directly or by an antigen that acts as a bridge between both cell types.

Cytotoxic T cells (T_C cells) are able to bind to certain target cells and lyse or kill them. The binding is based on the presence of specific receptors. The target cell, before it can be bound to a T_C cell, must possess the Class I MHC proteins as well as foreign antigen (most somatic cells exhibit Class I MHC proteins). Once T cells bind to target cells, there is a change in the permeability of the cell membrane of the target cell and this results in cell death. Let us explore this process in more detail.

One of the major targets of T_C cells are mammalian cells that have been infected with virus (Fig. 11-5). Once a virus penetrates the cell, the former is protected from any antibody that might be circulating in the bloodstream of the host. Consequently, humoral immunity is of little value. However, virus is susceptible to the cell-mediated immune response of the host. When a virus infects a cell, some viral antigens become entrapped in the cytoplasmic membrane of the infected cell (actually viral antigen binds to MHC proteins in endoplasmic reticulum and is then transported to cell membrane). Viral antigens along with MHC proteins are recognized by T_C cells. Once the recognition has taken place, there is a fusion of the membranes of the cytotoxic T_C cell and the host cell. Special protein molecules, called **perforins,** are released by the T_C cell and inserted into the cytoplasmic membrane of the host cell. This results in the formation of large pores and the flow of water and salts into the target cell. The target cell swells and lyses, releasing a virus that is unable to replicate. The T_C cell is not adversely affected by this process and is capable of binding to and killing other virally infected cells.

Delayed-type hypersensitivity cells (T_D or T_{DTH} cells) are involved in the following reactions: (1) protection against intracellular parasites such as some bacteria, viruses, fungi, and protozoa; (2) protection against tumor cells; (3) inflammation resulting from infection by parasites such as *Mycobacterium tuberculosis;* and (4) rejection of grafts (see Chapter 13). Delayed-type hypersensitivity (DTH) refers to a slowly developing inflammatory response to an antigen. Tuberculosis is the most frequently described type of delayed-type hypersensitivity; that is, an inflammatory response (tubercles in the lungs, for example) develops slowly due to a hypersensitivity to the

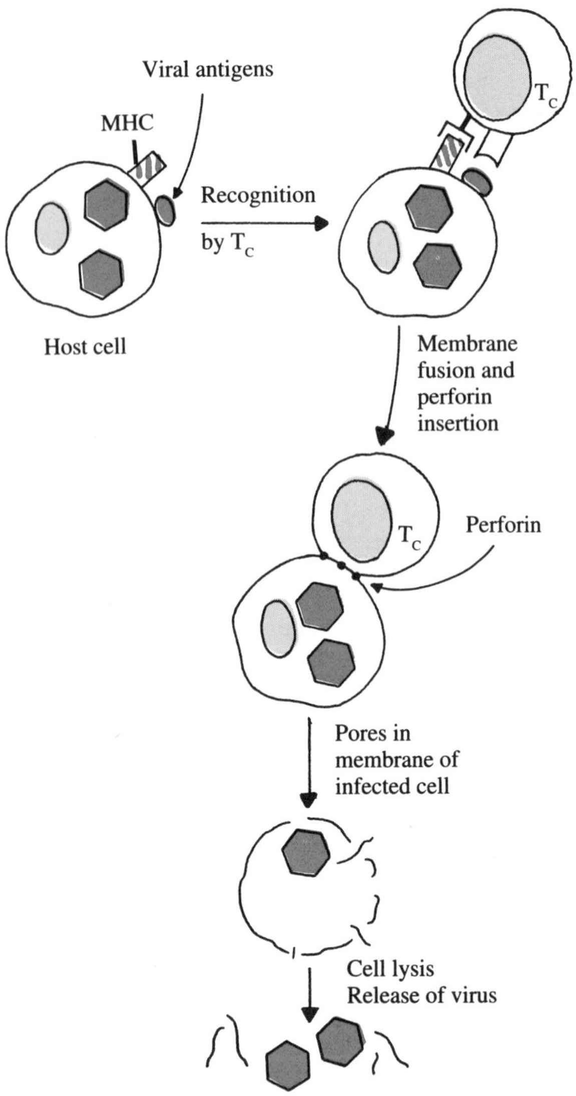

FIGURE 11-5
Action of cytotoxic T cells (T_C) on virus-infected cell. During virus infection, viral proteins are left on the cytoplasmic membrane of the host cell. The infected cell with antigen and MHC proteins is recognized by the T_C cell. Membranes of the host cell and T_C cell fuse with release of lysosomal-like enzymes (perforins) into the host cell membrane. Pores created by perforins result in osmotic shock and lysis of the cell. The virus released following cell lysis is subject to immune response and destruction.

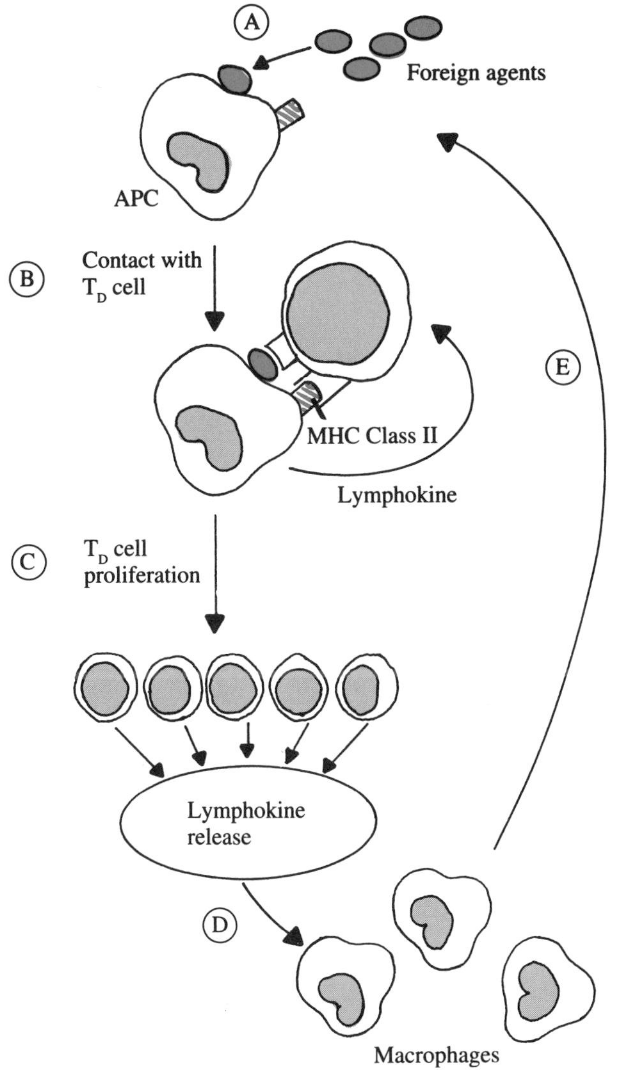

FIGURE 11-6
Generation of T_D cells and their role in parasite removal. A. One of the infectious agents at the site of infection is ingested by a macrophage and presented to the T_D cell. B. Once contact is made with the T_D cell, the macrophage releases lymphokine (interleukin-1), which causes the T_D cell to proliferate. C. Clones of T_D cells release lymphokines (e.g., macrophage chemotactic factor) that recruit macrophages. D. Macrophages migrate (E) to the area where the infectious agents are concentrated. APC = antigen presenting cell.

antigens of the bacterium causing tuberculosis *(M. tuberculosis).*

Macrophages process foreign antigen and present it to the T_D cell in association with Class II MHC proteins (Fig. 11-6). Activated macrophage releases lymphokines (for example, IL-1), which causes T_D cells to proliferate. Proliferating T_D cells in turn release a lymphokine that attracts macrophages to the site where the foreign antigen was encountered. Activated macrophages release many toxic molecules in addition to lymphokines. The toxic components include hydrogen peroxide, superoxide, and hydroxyl radical. They cause inflammation and destroy bacterial cells as well as healthy cells in the area.

B CELLS

B cell development was first discovered in birds in a cloaca-associated organ called the **bursa of Fabricus,** hence, the term B cell. B cell development in humans, however, is associated with the bone marrow (see Fig. 11-1).

The characteristic marker of the B cell is its surface immunoglobulin (produced within the B cell), which acts as a receptor for antigen. The surface immunoglobulin of circulating B cells belongs to the IgM and IgD classes (see Fig. 10-5). During B cell development some immature B cells frequently come into contact with self antigens. These immature B cells are eliminated so the host becomes tolerant of its own antigens. Once the B cell matures, it can be activated. Activation induces the B cell to differentiate into two populations of cells: **plasma cells** and **memory cells.**

Antibody production by B cells requires the involvement of T_H cells **(T-dependent activation).** Some antigens, however, are able to activate B cells to produce antibody without T cell help **(T-independent activation).** T-dependent activation occurs in the following way (Fig. 11-7):

1. Protein antigens are taken up by macrophages, fragmented, and then bound to MHC Class II proteins on the cell surface. At the same time protein antigens (not on the activated macrophage) bind to the immunoglobulin receptor on B cells. Antigen on the B cell is also engulfed, fragmented, and bound to the cell surface.
2. Binding of antigen on the B cell surface is not enough to activate it. The B cell requires the assistance of T_H cells. T_H cells recognize the antigen–MHC Class II protein complex on the activated macrophage. This recognition process also involves the release of IL-1 from the macrophage and its transmission to the T_H cells. T_H cells are now activated.
3. Activated T_H cells enlarge, proliferate, and interact with the B cells presenting antigen. During this stage T_H cells also send a signal to the B cells in the form of IL-2 but other interleukins (IL-4, IL-5, and IL-6) and IFN-γ are probably involved. The B cells are now activated.
4. Activated B cells multiply and differentiate. B cells differentiate into plasma cells that secrete specific antibody.

A few antigen molecules can activate B cells without T cells. These antigens are large polymers that have repeating antigenic determinants, for example, LPS, dextran, levan, and flagellin of bacterial flagella. B cells react with antigen in its native state by their surface immunoglobulin. The antigen is internalized and processed in a manner similar to that occurring in macrophages. Plasma cells and memory cells are produced during B cell activation. T cells participate indirectly by releasing lymphokines that stimulate B cell proliferation. The antibody responses to

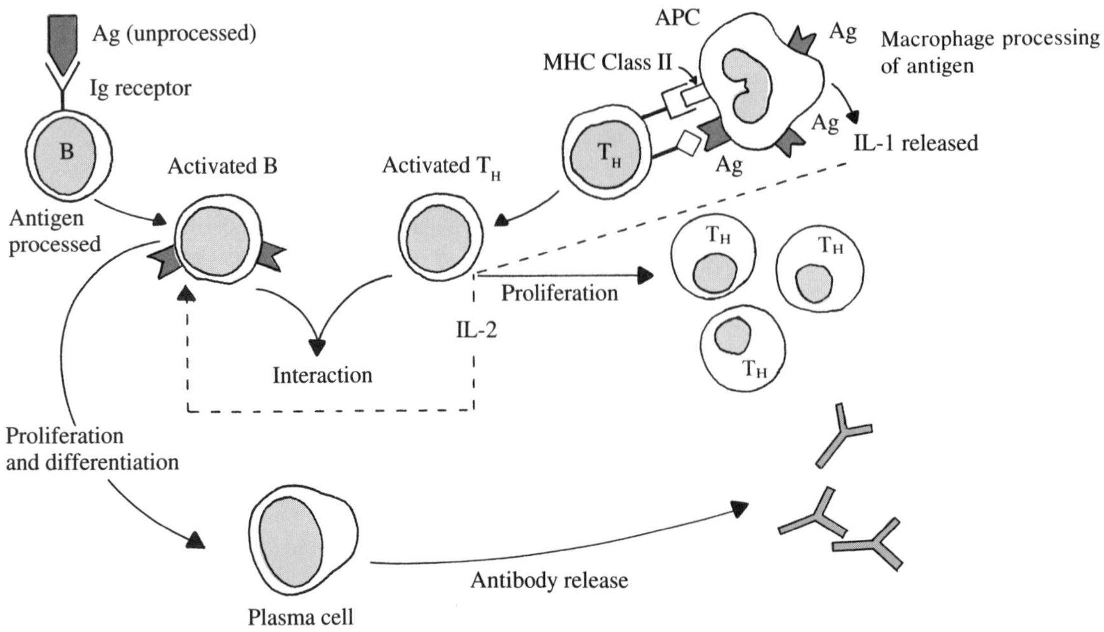

FIGURE 11-7
B cell activation. Antigen (Ag) is processed by a macrophage and bound to the cell surface with MHC Class II proteins. The macrophage is now an antigen presenting cell (APC). Antigen is presented by the APC to the T_H cell, which becomes activated. Interleukin (IL)-1 released by the APC causes a proliferation of T_H cells. Antigen also is processed by the B cell and the latter becomes activated. The B cell and T_H cell interact with the release of IL-2. IL-2 stimulates B cells to divide and differentiate into plasma cells. Plasma cells produce and release specific antibody.

T-independent antigens are weak, generally weaker than those that are T-dependent.

Plasma Cells

Plasma cells are short-lived (3–5 days) compared to circulating memory B cells, which may live for years. Plasma cells do not possess a surface immunoglobulin receptor. They are normally found in the secondary lymphoid organs (i.e., spleen, lymph nodes, and Peyer's patches). The plasma cell produces antigen-specific antibodies (i.e., the same specificity as the parent B cell). The antibody produced by plasma cells may be of any class (IgG, IgE, IgA, etc.) but a single plasma cell produces only one class of immunoglobulin.

Memory Cells

The memory B cell is distinguished from the plasma cell by the presence of an immunoglobulin surface marker. Memory cells display the same antigen recognition as their parent B cell precursors. Thus, the memory cell is waiting for a second dose of the antigen that originally activated the parent B cell. If there is a later encounter with the antigen, the memory cell can differentiate into a second wave of plasma cells and memory cells (see Clonal Selection).

Clonal Selection

Both B and T cells possess receptors for antigen. As discussed earlier, B cells have a surface immunoglobulin that can recognize virtually any antigen. T cells possess the T cell receptor that performs the same task. Prior to antigen contact, B and T cells are committed to a single specificity. Antigen-activated B and T cells engage in a **primary response** and differentiate into two clones of cells: **effector cells** and **memory cells** (Fig. 11-8). For example, an effector B cell clone could be plasma cells that produce antibodies, while an effector T cell clone might be T_C cells that possess cytotoxic activities. Memory cells (B or T cells) act as sentinels surveying all the foreign antigens or invading microorganisms that pass their way. In the presence of the same antigen the memory cells are stimulated to engage in a **secondary response.** The already primed memory cells differentiate into a new wave of effector cells and memory cells. The secondary response is quicker and more intense than the primary response.

Vaccines represent an example of how the memory system works. A vaccine contains commercially prepared antigens of an infectious microorganism (but it does not cause disease). When the vaccine is injected into the individual, it induces a primary response: production of specific antibodies and memory cell formation. If the vaccinated individual at some later time becomes infected with the same organism, the primed memory cells respond to the same antigen quickly and with intensity. The infectious microorganism is rapidly dispatched and the individual shows no disease symptoms or, at the very most, mild symptoms.

In 1959, F. M. Burnet developed clonal selection as a

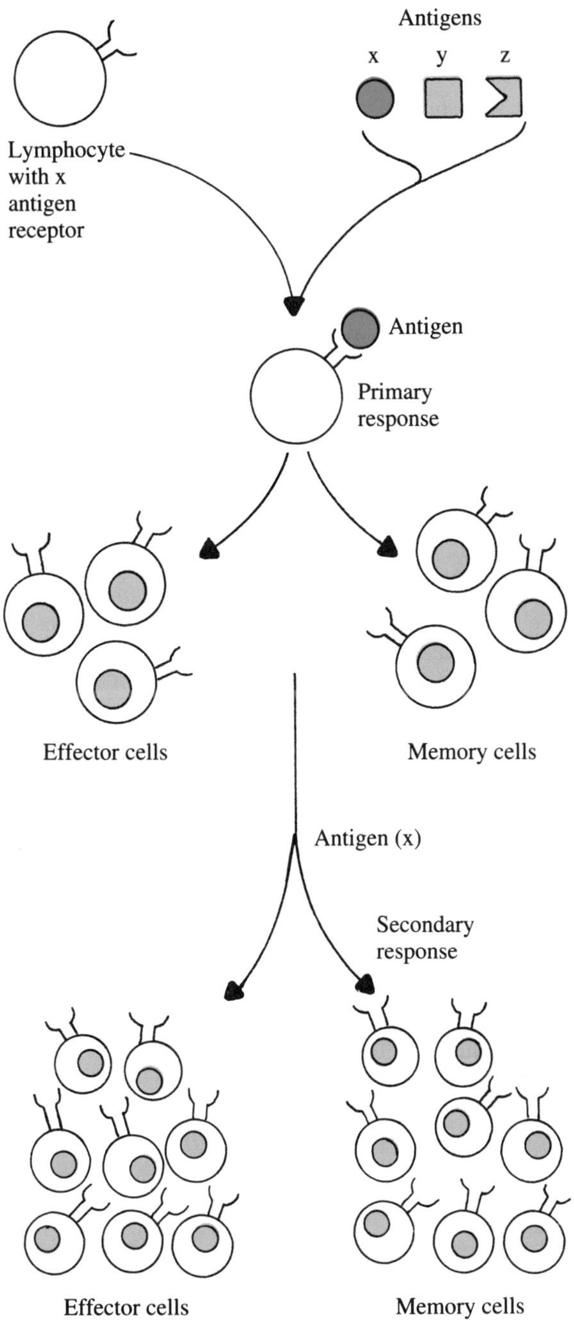

FIGURE 11-8
Clonal selection (see text for details).

model to explain antibody formation. This model, which can also apply in most respects to T cells, can be summarized as follows:

1. In every person there is a large array of previously genetically programmed clones of lymphocytes. Each clone bears specific surface receptors capable of reacting only with a single specific antigenic determinant.
2. Theoretically, a person possesses a fixed repertoire of receptors that can recognize all the antigens that the individual will ever encounter.
3. Incoming antigen selectively stimulates the proliferation of only that clone of lymphocytes that exhibit preordained complementary antigen-specific receptors.
4. The specificity of the antibodies produced by the proliferated B lymphocytes is identical to that of the antigen receptor immunoglobulins.

Non-T, Non-B Lymphocytes

There are some cells called **null cells** that do not express either T or B lymphocyte characteristics. These cells are cytotoxic cells and are referred to as **natural killer cells (NK cells).**

NATURAL KILLER CELLS

NK cells are large granular lymphocytes that make up approximately 5 percent of the lymphocytes in the blood. They are distributed in a variety of organs as well as lymphoid tissues, especially the spleen and lymph nodes. Unlike cytotoxic T cells, NK cells do not exhibit a finely tuned immunological specificity and memory. They can kill tumor cells without prior immunization and without restriction by MHC proteins. NK cells along with macrophages provide a first line of defense against malignancies such as cancer.

The cytotoxic effect of NK cells is apparently enhanced by lymphokines (see Cytokines) and this response has been used in treatment. In one experiment peripheral leukocytes were removed from a cancer patient and exposed to IL-2. These **lymphokine-activated cells (LAK cells)** were reinjected into the patient to reduce the size of the tumors. However, high doses of IL-2, to maintain activation of lymphocytes, also cause serious life-threatening side effects and their use is restricted.

NK cells also appear to protect against viral infections. This activity is enhanced by cytokines produced in response to viral infection.

NK cells possess a surface receptor for the Fc domain of IgG (Fig. 11-9). The receptor is identified with another activity of NK cells, called **antibody-dependent cell-mediated cytotoxicity (ADCC).** ADCC activities take place without complement.

Mononuclear and Polymorphonuclear Phagocytes

Both mononuclear and polymorphonuclear phagocytes are important in the immune response and both were discussed earlier in Chapter 9. These leukocytes can engage in activities that are shared by both specific and nonspecific immune responses: (1) Macrophages become activated only with the help of T lymphocytes, (2) antigen presenting cells interact with T lymphocytes to affect an immune response, and (3) the phagocytic activity of macrophages can be enhanced in the presence of specific

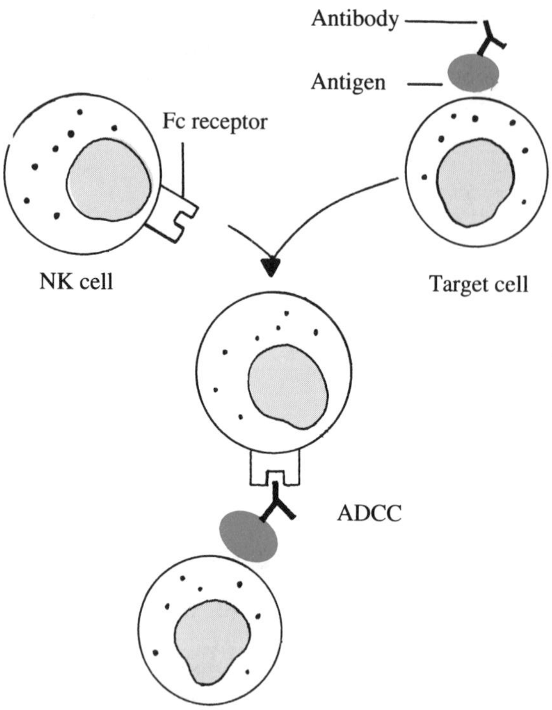

FIGURE 11-9
Natural killer (NK) cell and cell-mediated cytotoxicity. The NK cell with an Fc receptor recognizes the antibody-antigen complex on the target cell. Binding of the two cells brings about antibody-dependent cell-mediated cytotoxicity (ADCC).

antibody. All of these examples illustrate how specific and nonspecific immunity can be intertwined. How the two systems are integrated is the topic of Chapter 13.

Summary

1. The immune system is made up of a variety of tissues, organs, and cells collectively referred to as the lymphoid system. The lymphoid system deals with foreign tissues, cells, or antigens in either a nonspecific or a specific way.

2. The lymphoid tissue and organs are integrated into a network that involves primary and secondary components. Primary organs are the thymus and bone marrow. The thymus is the site of T lymphocyte formation while the bone marrow is the primary source of red blood cells and B lymphocytes.

3. Secondary organs and tissues include the spleen, lymph nodes, and scattered lymphoid tissue. Foreign antigens that enter the host will be trapped and carried to secondary sites and processed.

4. Lymphoid cells include T cells and B cells. T cells possess surface markers and receptors such as the T cell receptor that distinguish them from B cells. Antigen recognition and processing by lymphocytes is dependent on major histocompatibility complex (MHC) proteins and cytokines.

5. The MHC is a cluster of genes that encode products that mark cells and enable the immune system to distinguish self from nonself. There are two major classes of MHC: Class I molecules, which are found on all nucleated cells, and Class II molecules, which are displayed on antigen presenting cells and B cells.

6. Cytokines are hormones produced primarily by leukocytes that serve as a communication link between them. They can act as activators or inhibitors depending on the cell type producing them and the target cell.

7. T lymphocytes differentiate into four functional groups (Table 11-3).

8. B cells possess a characteristic surface immunoglobulin as well as Class II MHC antigens. B cell activation can take place in the presence or absence of T cells. T-independent activation occurs when certain polymers with repeating units directly bind to B cells. T-dependent activation requires antigen presenting cells, T_H cells, and B cells. Activated B cells differentiate into plasma and memory cells.

9. The clonal selection theory basically states that each person has genetically programmed clones of lymphocytes with the ability to recognize an array of antigenic

TABLE 11-3
Characteristics of T Lymphocyte Subsets

Subset	Differentiation antigen	Function
T_H	CD4	Helps other lymphocytes to enhance their expression, e.g., B cells to produce antibody; does not bind free antigen and recognizes antigen only in association with Class II MHC proteins
T_S	CD5, CD8	Causes antigen-specific suppression of cellular and humoral immune responses; blocks activation of T_H or B cells; causes antigen-specific suppression of delayed-type hypersensitivity; no clear-cut MHC restriction
T_C	CD5, CD8	Does not bind free antigen; recognizes antigen in association with MHC Class I molecules; lyses target cells and kills virus-infected cells
T_D	CD4	Recruits macrophages, neutrophils, etc. to dispense of antigen they cannot dispose of directly: antigen stimulation mediates a delayed-type hypersensitivity which involves Class II MHC proteins

determinants on foreign antigens. Each clone is specific for a given epitope.

10. Some immune cells do not express either T or B lymphocyte characteristics. These cells are referred to as natural killer (NK) cells. NK cells can kill tumor cells without prior immunization or without MHC restriction proteins. NK cells may also be involved in an antibody-dependent cytotoxic activity.

11. Mononuclear and polymorphonuclear phagocytes, which represent the host's nonspecific defense against foreign antigens, share their activities with the contributors of the specific immune response.

Questions for Study

1. Assuming that an infectious agent has entered the respiratory tract, briefly describe the series of events that occur in the capture and processing of, and the antibody response to the infectious agent.
2. Prepare a table listing the similarities and differences between B cells and T cells (don't forget surface markers and receptors).
3. In what ways, if any, is T cell activation similar to or different from B cell activation?
4. Is the destructive activity of T_D cell responses direct or indirect? Explain.
5. Summarize in your own words how clonal selection works.
6. On what type of cells are Class I MHC antigens found? Class II MHC antigens? What cell types are Class II MHC antigens attracted to?
7. In what ways is the process of cytotoxicity of T_C cells different from that of NK cells?

CHAPTER

12 The Immune Response (Humoral vs. Cell-Mediated Immunity)

OBJECTIVES

To discuss the functions of complement in specific and nonspecific immunity

To compare briefly the similarities and differences in the classic and alternative complement pathways

To discuss how microorganisms evade the actions of complement

To outline the nonspecific and specific immune responses of the host to bacteria, viruses, fungi, and animal parasites

To differentiate between active and passive immunity and between naturally acquired and artificially acquired immunity

To discuss how the following immunogenic materials are prepared and used in immunization: toxoids, attenuated vaccines, subunit vaccines, recombinant vaccines, anti-idiotypic antibodies, and synthesized immunogens

To describe what is meant by passive immunization and immunotherapy and outline current options for immunotherapy

To define the terms opsonins, anaphylatoxin, membrane attack complex, properdin, sialic acid, toxoid, immunotoxin, and anamnestic response

OUTLINE

CHEMICAL REGULATORS OF THE IMMUNE RESPONSE
- Complement
  - Classic Pathway
  - Alternative Pathway
  - Aspects of Complement Regulation
  - Complement Functions
  - Complement Deficiencies and Disease
  - Complement Evasion by Parasites

NONSPECIFIC DEFENSES AGAINST MICROORGANISMS
- Bacteria
- Viruses

SPECIFIC DEFENSES AGAINST MICROORGANISMS
- Bacteria
- Viruses
- Fungi and Animal Parasites

IMMUNITY THROUGH VACCINATION
- Immunization Practices
  - Active Immunization
  - Passive Immunization and Immunotherapy

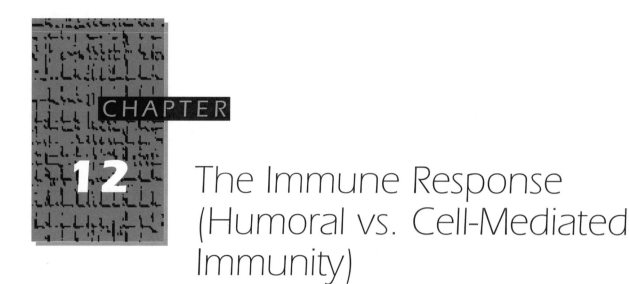

Up to this point we have identified most of the players associated with the specific and nonspecific immune response. In this chapter we discuss how these players defend the host against specific infectious agents such as bacteria, viruses, and animal parasites. As you follow the descriptions, you will notice that most of the immune cells and products discussed were detailed in previous chapters. We therefore encourage you to review these previously discussed topics in case you have forgotten them. Before reading this chapter, it also would behoove you to reexamine the discussion on cytokines in Chapter 11. First, however, we discuss in more detail complement and its role as a factor in pathogen destruction and as a regulator of the immune response. The last part of this chapter is devoted to how immunity may be acquired through various immunization practices.

Chemical Regulators of the Immune Response

COMPLEMENT

The complement system is an array of approximately 19 plasma proteins and at least 9 membrane proteins that can act in a nonspecific as well as a specific way in host defense. One of the primary functions of the complement system is to assist or complement the effects of antibody in the activation or destruction of pathogens (other functions are discussed later in the chapter).

Complement proteins in the plasma or other body fluids are normally in an inactive state. The proteins are activated by the presence of

1. Antibody on a cell surface;
2. Immune complexes, that is, antigen-antibody complex; or
3. A surface component of a microbial cell, for example, the lipopolysaccharide of gram-negative bacteria.

The complement system has two pathways that can be activated: the **classic pathway** and the **alternative pathway.** There is a basic series of complement factors that are numbered C1 through C9. Factors C1, C4, and C2 are involved only in the classic pathway. The factors denoted in the alternative pathway are designated by capital letters B, H, D, I, and P. Peptide fragments derived from proteolysis of complement are described by the suffixes a, b, and so on, for example, C3a. Once activation takes place, there is a cascade of reactions in which one protein activates another protein in the sequence. The activation is actually a cleaving of a protein in the series. The cleaved protein fragments then exhibit new enzymatic or physiological activity.

Let us now explore the two complement pathways in more detail (Fig. 12-1).

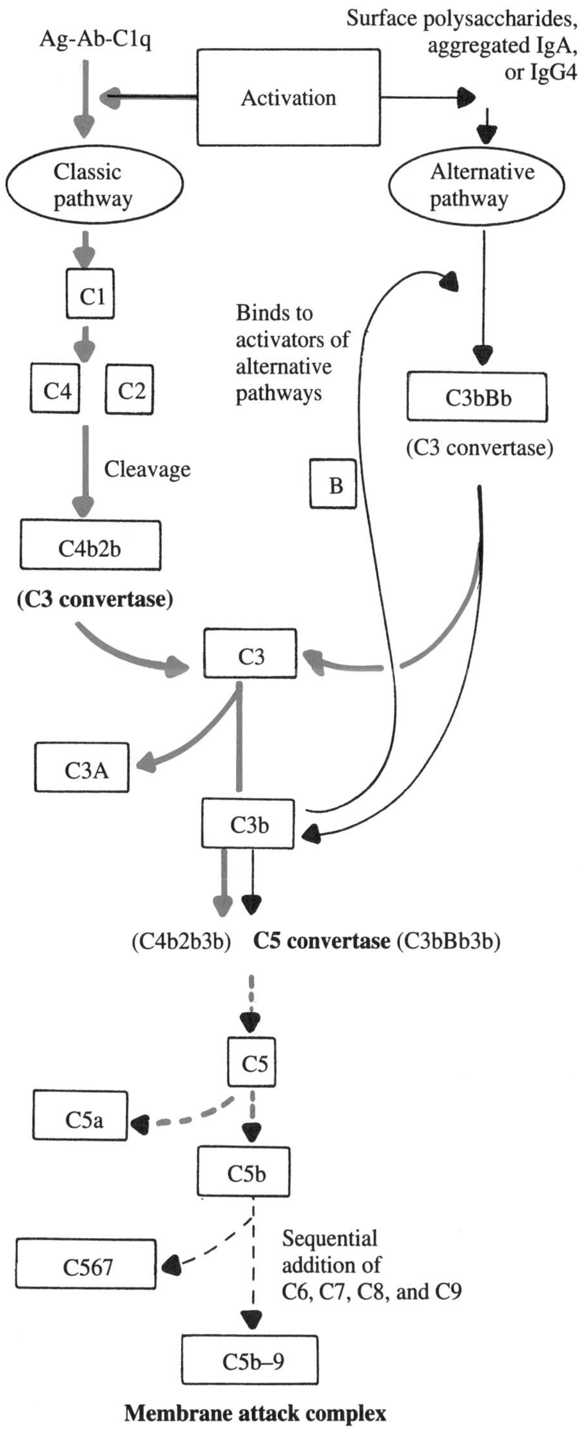

FIGURE 12-1
Classic and alternative complement pathways. The red arrows indicate the reactions associated with the classic pathway and the black arrows indicate alternative pathway reactions. An interrupted arrow indicates that the reactions and products are part of both systems. See Table 12-2 for a description of the biological effects of the various complement fragments generated in the pathways. Complement components are enclosed in boxes. Ab = antibody; Ag = antigen; B = factor B.

Classic Pathway

The classic pathway is associated with specific immune responses. The pathway is activated when there is an immunological recognition of antigen with antibody. Inactive complement component C1 in the serum interacts

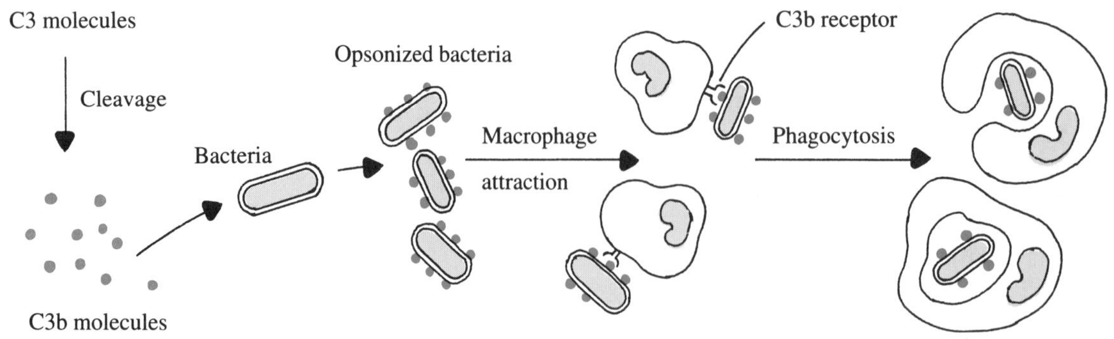

FIGURE 12-2
C3b coating of bacteria. C3 complement molecules are cleaved into C3b molecules, which act as opsonins and bind to bacteria. Macrophages with receptors for C3b bind to opsonized bacteria and phagocytose them.

with the Fc portion of the antibody molecule. Binding of at least two distinct immunoglobulin fragments is required for complement activation. Only IgM and certain subclasses of IgG (IgG1, IgG2, and IgG3) comply with this requirement. A single IgM molecule on the cell membrane can activate but more than one IgG molecule is required for complement activation (Fig. 12-1). IgE and IgA are not activators.

The C1 protein is actually composed of three different proteins: C1q, C1r, and C1s. Only C1q acts as the antibody recognition factor; that is, it recognizes its binding sites on antibody. After binding to antibody, C1q undergoes a conformational change and becomes a proteolytic enzyme whose substrate is C1r (C1r in enzyme form acts on C1s).

The substrates of activated C1s (it is still part of the three-protein complex) are **C4** and **C2** (these proteins were numbered before discovery of the initiation sequence; thus, C4 precedes C2). Cleavage of C4 and C2 results in the release of peptide fragments **C4a, C2a, C2b,** and **C4b.** C2b associates with C4b to produce **C4b2b,** which is enzymatically active and is referred to as **C3 convertase.** The substrate for C3 convertase is **C3,** which is cleaved into **C3a** and **C3b.** C3a acts as an **anaphylatoxin;** that is, it promotes the mast cell release of histamine which affects vascular permeability and smooth-muscle contraction. Anaphylatoxins produce an inflammatory response that can aid in the localization and destruction of an infectious agent.

Thousands of C3 molecules are cleaved into C3a and C3b molecules. Each of the C3b fragments can bind to cell membrane and interact with components of the alternative pathway to produce a C3 cleaving enzyme. Thousands of C3b molecules act as *opsonins* and coat microorganisms or immune complexes. Phagocytes with receptors for C3b molecules will bind to the antibody-coated foreign material (Fig. 12-2). **C3b formation is one of the major biological functions of both complement systems.**

Some C3b molecules join membrane-bound C4b2b to form the next enzymatically active unit, **C4b2b3b,** also called **C5 convertase.** C5 convertase cleaves **C5** into two products, **C5a** and **C5b,** and this concludes the enzymatic phase of the pathway. C5a has chemotactic activity as well as anaphylatoxin activities. C5b becomes attached to the membrane.

The final phase of the classic pathway involves the formation of a multicomponent complex. The binding of C5b to cell membrane begins the binding in succession of complement components **C6, C7, C8,** and **C9.** The **C5b–9** complex affects the permeability of the cell membrane. This alteration results in the flow of water into the cell, thereby causing lysis. The C5b–9 complex is called the **membrane attack complex** or **MAC.** Apparently, polymerized C9 of the complex inserts into the membrane of the cell, producing large pores or channels. The channels allow for the flow of water into the cell and subsequent cell lysis (Fig. 12-3).

Alternative Pathway

The alternative pathway provides a different method for the conversion of C3 to C3b. Proteins in the alternative pathway are essentially similar to those of the classic pathway. However, there are major differences: First, the alternative pathway can be activated without antibody. **Thus, the pathway represents a nonspecific and immediate immune defense mechanism.** Second, C1, C4, and C2 proteins are not required in the alternative pathway. Third, activation occurs in the fluid phase as well as on target cell surfaces. Thus, fluid-phase components can be deposited indiscriminately on both the microbial and the host cell, leading to inflammatory responses. Fourth, cleavage of C3 depends on three serum proteins—**properdin (P), factor B (B),** and **factor D (D)**—that do not participate in the classic pathway.

The alternative pathway is activated by molecules with repeating chemical structures such as some polysaccharides, lipopolysaccharides of gram-negative bacteria, and teichoic acid of gram-positive bacteria. Aggregated immunoglobulins of classes that do not bind C1q (for example, IgA and IgG4) can also act as activators. On the target membrane a C3b fragment is cleaved from C3. Factor B binds to C3b and this C3bB complex is susceptible to cleavage by factor D. The cleavage results in the formation of C3bBb, a **C3 convertase.** C3bBb is relatively unstable but properdin can increase this enzyme's stability. C3bBb

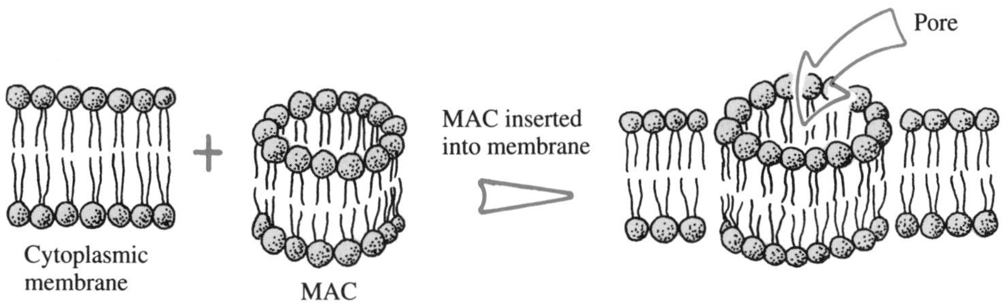

FIGURE 12-3
Diagrammatic illustration of how the membrane attack complex (MAC) alters the permeability of the host cell.

cleaves C3 and liberates C3a and C3b fragments. Many C3b molecules bind to the same membrane site as the first C3b molecule. The C3b molecules in turn capture more B molecules, and more C3 convertase is produced. Thus, there is a massive deposition of C3b molecules on the target membrane. C3bBb can combine with one or more molecules of C3b to produce **C5 convertase.** This reaction leads to formation of the membrane attack complex.

The utilization of complement components in the formation of the membrane attack complex is called **complement fixation.** Complement fixation is an important clinical laboratory test (see Appendix B).

Aspects of Complement Regulation

The complement systems can be regulated by several proteins that act on the level of activation, amplification, and effector function. Some of the important regulatory devices are those that help protect healthy host cells from the detrimental effects of complement. There are membrane-bound proteins that can inactivate complement proteins or cause their rapid decay. For example, when C3 convertase is bound to targeted microbial cells, it initiates rapid activation and amplification, but on healthy cells the convertase is subject to rapid decay. One of the chemical constituents on host cells that is involved in this control is **sialic acid.** Sialic acid is a component of the capsules of several bacteria; thus, there is a molecular mimicry between some infectious agents and the host. Group B streptococcus, for example, possesses capsules containing sialic acid. When this organism invades a host (a newborn) that lacks antibodies against its capsule, there is a limited immune response. Basically the infectious agent goes unrecognized.

Host bystander cells also are resistant to the potentially devastating effects of the membrane attack complex. There is a plasma protein that binds to host cells and helps prevent binding of the attack complex. Healthy cells also are able to shed the attack complex from their surface and replace any cell membrane lipids that have been destroyed.

Complement Functions

Complement plays several major roles in specific as well as nonspecific responses. Although some of these have been alluded to previously, here we categorize them for quick reference by the student.

1. **Anaphylatoxins.** C5a, C3a, and C4a are stimulators of the inflammatory response. They promote mast cell degranulation and release of histamine, which can cause smooth-muscle contraction and increased vascular permeability.
2. **Chemotaxins.** C5a and C567 act as chemotactic factors. They stimulate the migration of phagocytes to the site of infection. In addition, they also stimulate neutrophils to increase their adherence to the inflammatory site, to degranulate, and to increase their oxidative burst.
3. **Immune complex** clearance. Immune complexes are composed of soluble antigen and antibodies that can deposit on healthy host cells and cause inflammatory diseases. Complement components can keep the immune complexes solubilized and foster their binding to the C3b receptor on red blood cells. Red blood cells carry the immune complexes to the liver, where they can be destroyed. Immune-complex diseases are discussed in Chapter 13.
4. **Lymphocyte modulator.** C3 or its fragments appear to enhance or inhibit the activities of T cells and B cells.
5. **Opsonization.** C3b fragments bind to microbial surfaces and act as a bridge between the microbe and the effector cells possessing receptors. In the presence or absence of antibody, opsonization with C3b promotes phagocytosis and digestion of bacteria. Binding of C3b to virus also can result in the latter's neutralization.
6. **Cytolysis.** When inserted into the cell membrane of targeted cells, the membrane attack complex causes cell death and lysis. Among bacterial species, only gram-negative ones are affected in this way. Complement in association with antibody can lyse host cells carrying viral antigen, or directly damage enveloped viruses.

Complement Deficiencies and Disease

Complement deficiency states may be acquired or inherited. Acquired defects are common and can be due to various disease states or conditions. Burn patients, patients with liver disease, and patients with chronic immune-complex diseases are examples of individuals in whom an acquired complement deficiency may exist. Successful treatment of the underlying condition can usually resolve such deficiencies.

Inherited complement deficiencies are quite uncommon and are usually due to some inborn error of metabolism. The most frequent complement deficiencies involve C2, C4, C7, and C8 factors. Complement deficiencies also may involve regulatory components such as properdin in the alternative pathway. Some generalizations can be made about complement deficiencies:

1. C1, C2, C3, and C4 deficiencies. Immune disorders, such as lupus erythematosus, are observed in individuals lacking these early complement components. In addition, this population is susceptible to systemic and recurrent respiratory infections caused by encapsulated bacteria such as *Neisseria meningitidis, Streptococcus pneumoniae,* and *Hempohilus influenzae.* In individuals with rare C3 deficiency, collagen vascular disorders and recurrent infections by encapsulated bacteria such as those discussed above often develop.
2. C5 through C9 deficiencies. Diminished chemotactic activity results from C5 deficiency alone. C5 through C9 deficiencies may result in the inability to generate microbicidal activity (membrane attack complex). These deficiencies lead to infection, primarily by *Neisseria* species, especially *N. meningitidis.*

Prevention of infection in complement-deficient individuals can be accomplished by immunization with appropriate vaccines, that is, vaccines for *H. influenzae* type b, *S. pneumoniae,* and *N. meningitidis.* Those already infected should be treated with the appropriate antibiotics.

Complement Evasion by Parasites

Microorganisms have evolved strategies for evading the actions of complement. These strategies include (1) preventing activation of complement cascade, (2) blocking the formation of C5b–9, and (3) preventing lysis by the C5b–9 complex.

Lipopolysaccharide components of some gram-negative bacteria can inhibit C1 activation in the classic pathway. The mere change of a single sugar molecule in the lipopolysaccharide of *Salmonella* species, for example, can affect complement activation. In the alternative pathway, inhibition of C3 activation is caused by the capsular material of gram-positive and gram-negative bacteria. Sialic acid, mentioned previously, is one such capsular component that prevents activation.

Some microorganisms are capable of releasing molecules that inactivate complement molecules. *Staphylococcus aureus,* for example, sheds a soluble sialic acid which binds the early complement components. This depletes the complement components from the classic pathway. Microbial proteases, released by bacteria such as *Pseudomonas aeruginosa,* can attack and destroy complement components.

The increased virulence of group A streptococci with surface M protein, as opposed to those without M protein, is believed to be due to the inability of C3 to bind M protein–bearing strains.

Prevention of C5b–9 formation is due to microorganisms releasing molecules that either bind or degrade complement. Microorganisms, such as species of *Salmonella,* allow the binding of C5b–9 complex on the membrane but the binding is so weak that lysis is prevented. Apparently, the determining factor is lipopolysaccharide chain length. Long-chain lipopolysaccharides prevent access of the C5b–9 complex to the areas of the outer membrane that are susceptible to lysis.

Nonspecific Defenses Against Microorganisms

Although nonspecific immune defenses were discussed previously, we briefly reiterate them because they are intimately tied to specific immune responses. We concentrate on describing immune responses to bacteria and viruses because we know more about them than other infectious agents.

BACTERIA

When a bacterial cell reaches an epithelial surface, it encounters chemical and physical barriers that may prevent infection. The ability of the host to mount effectively an immune response often depends on the relationship between immune components and the bacterial cell wall or structures located outside of it (pili, flagella, capsules, etc.). Many bacteria that we consider nonpathogenic in the healthy host can be destroyed without the aid of a specific immune response. If the infectious agent survives the first line of host defenses, it will engage local macrophages. The scenario for the host's nonspecific response is illustrated in Figure 12-4:

1. Bacterial surface components activate the alternative complement pathway and C3b is deposited on the bacterium.
2. C3b deposition on the bacterium promotes opsonization and digestion by polymorphonuclear leukocytes.
3. Polymorphonuclear leukocytes release lactoferrin, which limits the availability of free iron and inhibits bacterial growth.
4. Complement factors such as C5a act as chemotaxins and promote the migration of polymorphonuclear leukocytes and macrophages to the site of infection.
5. C3a and C5a as anaphylatoxins also promote mast cell degranulation.
6. Tissue injury and inflammation trigger the blood clotting system and the deposition of fibrin. Fibrin prevents the spread of the bacteria.

VIRUSES

The nonspecific mechanisms of resisting viruses are based primarily on, first, the presence of secretory IgA (sIgA) on mucosal surfaces. Binding of sIgA to virus can prevent its attachment to the epithelial surface and thus block virus penetration of the host. sIgA seems to be effective

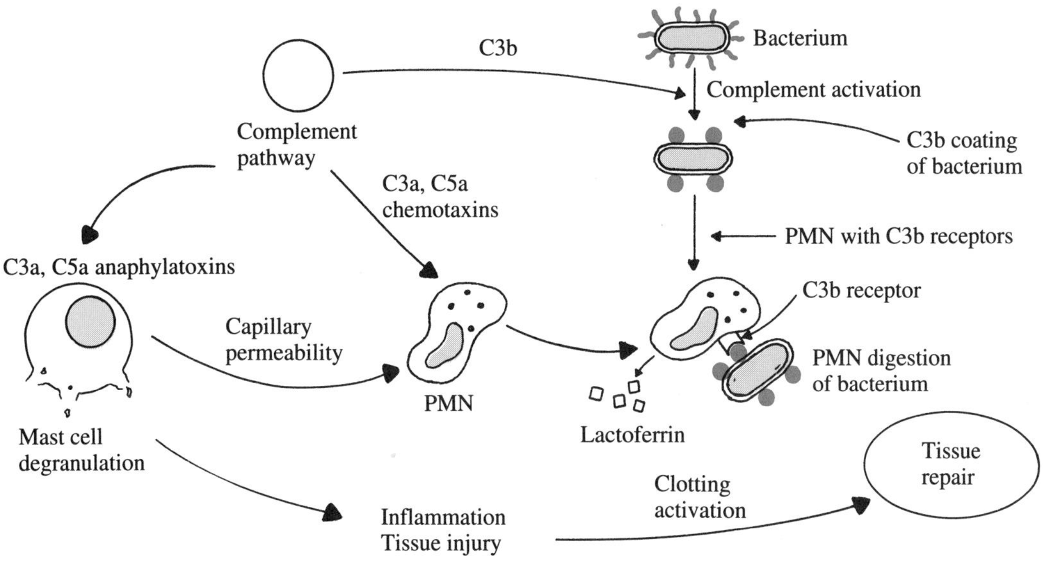

FIGURE 12-4
Nonspecific immune response following bacterial invasion. Surface components of bacterium activate the complement system, and C3b is deposited on the bacterial surface. Polymorphonuclear leukocytes (PMN) with C3b receptor phagocytose bacterium. Polymorphonuclear leukocytes also release lactoferrin, which limits the availability of iron and prevents bacterial growth. Complements C3a and C5a as chemotaxins promote the migration of other polymorphonuclear leukocytes to the site of infection. C3a and C5a as anaphylatoxins cause mast cell degranulation, which increases capillary permeability and flow of more polymorphonuclear leukocytes to the site of infection. Inflammation and tissue injury from bacterial destruction activate the clotting mechanism and tissue repair ensues.

in neutralizing some viruses. This effectiveness is probably due to the four Fab portions of the immunoglobulin for epitope binding. Second, interferon is produced by infected cells and can prevent the viral infection of adjacent healthy cells. Natural killer (NK) cells also play a major role in limiting viral infection by attacking virally infected cells.

Specific Defenses Against Microorganisms

BACTERIA

Antigen from the invading organism can induce immune responses involving both B and T cells. Antigen will move via lymph tissue to lymph nodes where it will encounter lymphocytes. The antigen may be free or it may be on the surface of an antigen presenting cell. Within the lymph node different populations of lymphocytes are stimulated, depending on the particular antigen (remember that both B and T cells have a diverse repertoire of antigen binding specificities).

Most often antigen presenting cells (macrophages, for example) make contact with T_H cells by the cross-linking of several receptors (Fig. 12-5). This interaction triggers the antigen presenting cell to release the lymphokine interleukin (IL)-1. IL-1 activates T_H cells to produce IL-2, interferon gamma (IFN-γ), and other lymphokines. IL-2 can perform several functions, including (1) stimulating the T_H cell that produced it to grow and divide, (2) inducing cytotoxicity of T_C cells, (3) stimulating NK cell activity, and (4) activating B cells. IFN-γ increases the phagocytic activity of macrophages but this can also lead to tissue damage and inflammation.

Bacterial antigen also can evoke a response from B cells, with or without the help of T cells. Activated T_H cells release IL-4, the interleukin that promotes B cell growth and differentiation. IL-6 released from T_H cells induces B cells to differentiate into plasma cells and memory cells. This primary immune response results in the formation of antibodies but there is a lag in their formation (Fig. 12-6). IgM antibodies are the first to be produced, usually from the fifth to seventh day after exposure to antigen and peaking about the fourteenth day. IgG appears about the tenth day after antigen exposure and peaks several weeks later. Antibody affects bacterial infection in the following ways:

1. Some antibodies are capable of neutralizing toxins and various spreading factors (hyaluronidase, for example) produced by the infectious agent.
2. Antibody can bind to antigens on the surface of the bacterial cell and with the assistance of complement, can act as opsonins. Hence, phagocytosis of bacteria is enhanced.
3. Antibody to pili, capsules, flagella, and so on can prevent the attachment of microbes to epithelial surfaces.

Memory cells, produced by the host during the primary response to antigen, are poised to respond to the antigen

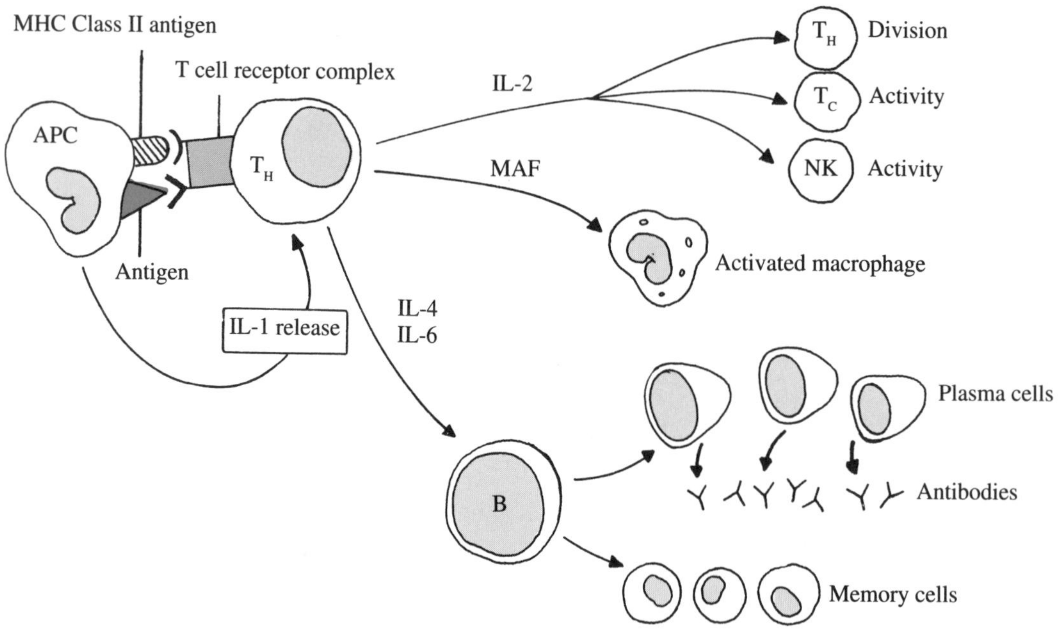

FIGURE 12-5
Specific immune response in bacteria. Antigen on the antigen presenting cell (APC) makes contact with the T_H cell via T cell receptor complex. The activated antigen presenting cell releases interleukin (IL)-1, which activates the T_H cell to release IL-2. IL-2 is autocatalytic and increases T_H cell division. IL-2 increases T_C and NK cell activity. The activated T_H cell releases macrophage activating factor (MAF), which increases the phagocytic activity of macrophages. The T_H cell also releases IL-4 and IL-6, which stimulate the B cell to differentiate into antibody-producing plasma cells and memory cells (relationship of B cell activation and antigen presentation is discussed on page 173).

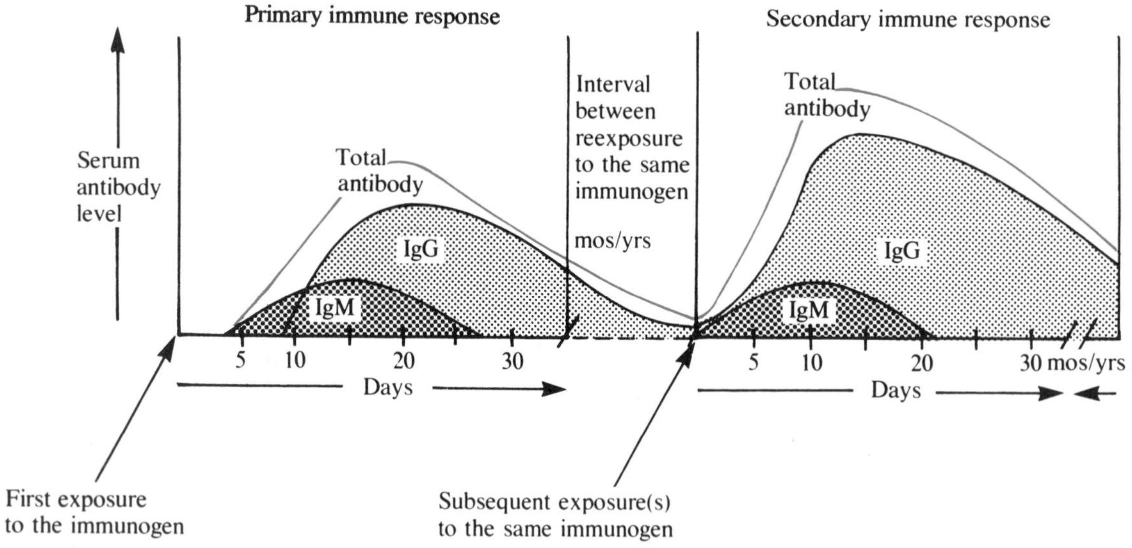

FIGURE 12-6
Primary and secondary immune responses. In the primary response, IgM is the first to appear in the serum. It appears on the fifth to seventh day and peaks at about 14 days. IgG appears at about the tenth day and peaks several weeks later. In the secondary immune response, both IgM and IgG appear to increase within 2 to 3 days. In the secondary immune response, the lag period is shorter, the total antibody level far surpasses that of the primary immune response, antibody is formed over a longer period of time, and much more IgG is formed than IgM.

a second time. This secondary response (for example, vaccine booster doses) results in a prompt and elevated production of IgG antibodies (Fig. 12-6). This prompt elevated response is called an **anamnestic response.**

VIRUSES

Viruses are intracellular parasites that usually invade epithelial surfaces and then enter the blood (viremic phase) before reaching their target organ. Specific immune responses are activated only by the surface antigen of free virus or by viral proteins exposed on the surface of virally infected cells (Fig. 12-7). Response to viral antigens is almost exclusively T cell–dependent; that is, even B cell activation requires T cell help. Individuals with T cell dysfunction are especially susceptible to viral infections. Viruses released into the bloodstream can be attacked directly by antibodies, such as IgG and IgM, and neutralized. Once the virus reaches the target organ, it is subject to specific effects of antibody, complement, and cell-mediated responses as well as nonspecific responses such as interferon. The effects of antibody and complement include the following:

1. Antibody-coated virus is prevented from entry into the cell and assembly into mature virus.
2. Antibody plus complement can bind to the viruses with lipid envelopes on their surface. The consequence of this is that the lipid membrane of the virus is disrupted and the virus becomes inactivated.
3. Antibody plus the C3 factor of complement can coat virus. Phagocytes via their C3 receptors bind the opsonized virus, which can lead to phagocytic destruction (but also may lead to intracellular survival of virus).
4. Antibody plus complement can recognize viral antigen on virally infected cells, leading to lysis of the cell. Free virus released from the lysed cell is subject to other host defensive measures.

Antibody also is involved in cell-mediated responses. NK cells, for example, are cytotoxic because they possess Fc receptors that recognize specific antibody-coated virus. Cytotoxic T cells, stimulated by IL-2 from antigen-activated T_H cells, recognize viral antigen and self Class I MHC proteins. This results in lysis of virally infected cells. T_D cell populations also can be stimulated by viral antigen. Whether T_D cells assist the host in recovery from viral disease has not been determined.

FUNGI AND ANIMAL PARASITES

Immunity to fungal infections is believed to be similar to that for bacterial infections, but in reality we still know little about them. Humoral immunity appears to play a minor role in protecting the host from fungal disease. Fun-

FIGURE 12-7
Immune responses following interaction of a virus with the host cell.

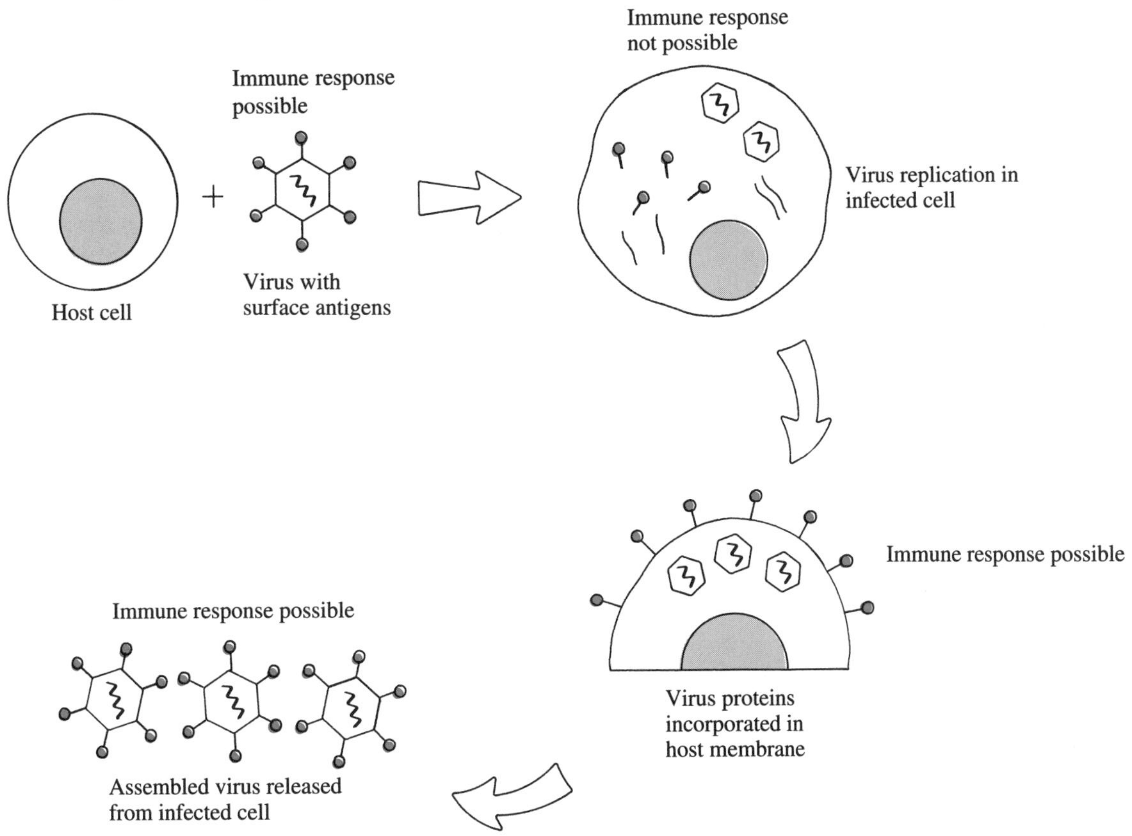

gal antigens, like those of the mycobacteria, induce a delayed-type hypersensitivity. Delayed-type hypersensitivity can result in granuloma formation, that is, the presence of epithelioid cells and giant cells (see Fig. 31-10). This type of reaction is a consequence of the persistence of fungal antigen, for example, a macrophage that cannot digest the fungal pathogen. Delayed-type hypersensitivities are discussed in more detail in Chapter 13. Absence of delayed-type hypersensitivity can result in chronic infections. For example, patients with acquired immunodeficiency syndrome (AIDS) who lack helper T cell activity are susceptible to indigenous fungal infection by *Candida albicans* and many other fungi, viruses, and animal parasites.

Animal parasites include protozoa as well as worms (helminths). These infectious agents are much larger than bacteria and viruses and many possess complex life cycles. Smaller animal parasites, such as the protozoa, are intracellular infectious agents, while the larger worms are extracellular. In general, protozoa stimulate formation of IgG and IgM antibodies, while worms stimulate IgG, IgM, and IgE. IgE sensitizes local mast cells, which causes the latter to degranulate and to release a factor that attracts eosinophils to the site of pathogen invasion (Fig. 12-8). In addition, T cells activated by antigen release a factor that stimulates proliferation of eosinophils. Eosinophils can combine with antibody to kill worms by antibody-dependent cytotoxicity (ADCC). Antibody can affect animal parasite infections in the following ways:

1. Preventing spread. Some protozoa have specific receptors for binding to host cells. Antibody binding to these receptors prevents attachment of the parasite to epithelial surfaces.
2. Enhancing phagocytosis. Complement plus antibody bind to protozoan parasites and then interact with the macrophage. The macrophage has Fc receptors as well as complement (C3b) receptors.
3. Cytotoxicity. Antibody bound to parasite may be recognized by cytotoxic cells such as eosinophils, neutrophils, and macrophages. Complement can enhance this reaction.
4. Complement-mediated lysis. Antibody bound to parasitic worms stimulates the classic complement pathway. Antibody plus complement bound to parasite causes direct damage to the cytoplasmic membrane.

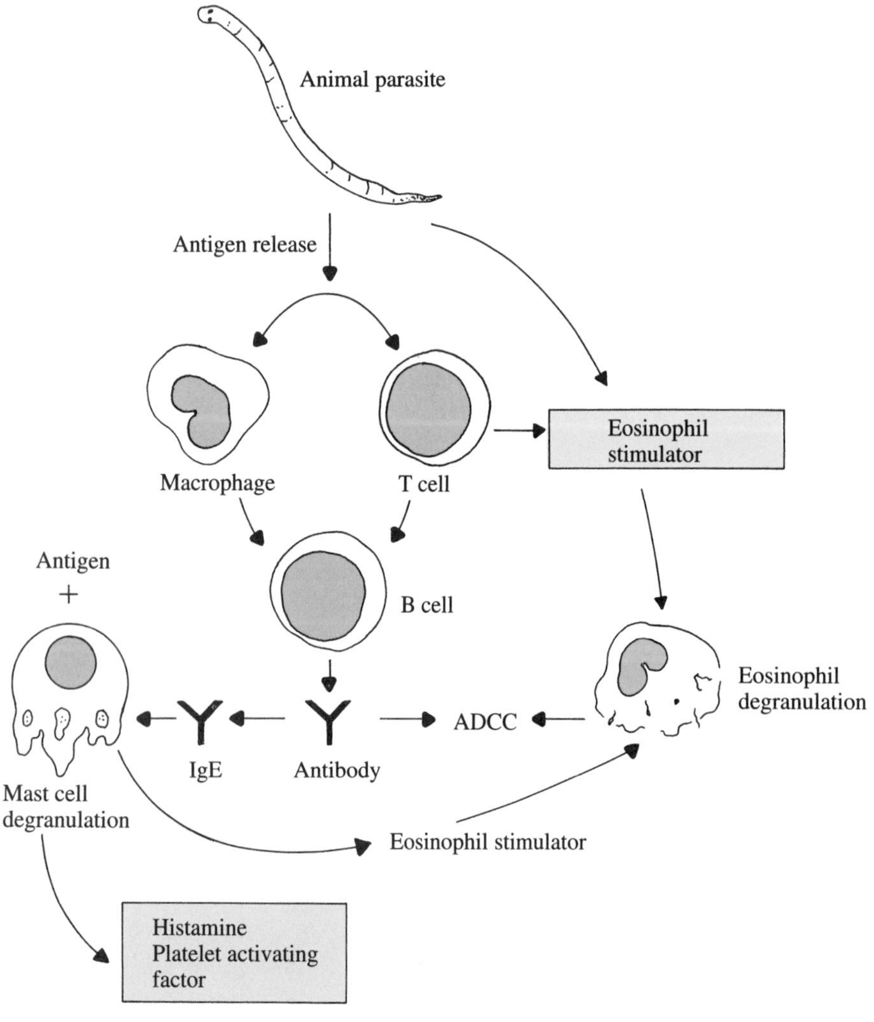

FIGURE 12-8
Immune response to animal parasite infection. Antigens of a parasite stimulate macrophages and T cells to interact with B cells. B cells produce IgE-specific antibody. IgE sensitizes mast cells, which in the presence of antigen degranulate and release factors such as histamine and platelet activating factor. Mast cells, as well as the parasite, release eosinophil stimulator that promotes the latter's proliferation and chemotactic activity. Eosinophils in association with antibody kill the parasite by antibody-dependent cytotoxicity (ADCC). Eosinophils (not shown) also release enzymes that control substances released from mast cells. Mast cell factors such as histamine control vascular permeability and inflammation at the site of infection.

Immunity Through Vaccination

You have seen that innate and acquired immunity are the host's major mechanisms for responding to infectious agents. However, in addition to being a natural response, acquired immunity can also be artificial, active or passive. The types of acquired immunity are described below.

1. Naturally acquired. The antigen, usually an infectious agent, or antibodies are transmitted to the individual under natural circumstances. Exposure to antigen or contact with antigen is unintentional.
2. Artificially acquired. The antigens or antibodies are introduced by artificial means, ordinarily by using a vaccine or an antiserum, respectively.
3. Active. Antibodies are produced by the individual either as the result of an infection (natural) or by injected vaccines.
4. Passive. Antibodies are not produced by the individual. Instead, antibodies may have been injected in the form of an antiserum or immune globulins that were obtained from animals or from other humans (artificially acquired passive immunity). The antibodies may have been transmitted under natural circumstances, as in the transfer of maternal antibodies across the placenta to the fetus or the transmission of antibodies via colostrum (naturally acquired passive immunity). The passive immune state is of short duration—weeks to months. The proteins of administered serum are foreign, and the body may react to them as it does to foreign antigens.

IMMUNIZATION PRACTICES

Active Immunization

The material that is deliberately introduced to evoke the active immune state is referred to as a **vaccine, immunogen, immunizing material,** or **antigen.** For instance it may be designated **toxoid** when it is a modified toxin, or **bacterin** when it is a suspension of modified bacteria. The purpose of a vaccine is to put the immune system on the alert against a particular infectious agent. The type or composition of the vaccine may vary considerably and can be divided into the following:

1. Toxoids. The exotoxins of some bacteria, notably of the tetanus and diphtheria bacteria, are converted in the laboratory to a nontoxigenic form by treatment with formalin or other modalities (see Appendix E for licensed vaccines and toxoids).

2. Whole-cell killed vaccines. Some vaccines consist of suspensions of inactivated intact microorganisms. The whooping cough, typhoid fever, and plague vaccines are whole-cell vaccines. Whole-cell vaccines sometimes produce serious side effects. There are efforts to define a subunit of the whole cell that confers immunity and avoids unwanted side effects.

3. Attenuated vaccines. Several effective vaccines consist of living microorganisms that, through laboratory processing, have lost their virulence or their virulence has been reduced. This process is called **attenuation.** Attenuated microorganisms can still multiply in the host but lack the ability to cause disease. It is a general tenet of immunization practices that living microorganisms induce a higher and longer-lasting level of immunity than do nonliving microorganisms. Another advantage of attenuated vaccines relative to killed vaccines is that the aborted infection is assumed to invoke an effective cell-mediated immunity that includes cytotoxic T cell responses. Furthermore, the need for booster doses may be lessened.

The attenuation process commonly involves adapting microorganisms to conditions they do not face in the host. Consequently, the microorganism's ability to multiply unrestrictedly in the host is lost. The method of virus attenuation often involves prolonged growth of the virus in cells of a species that the virus normally does not infect. Thus, poliovirus is grown in monkey tissue culture, yellow fever and influenza viruses in embryonated hen's eggs, German measles virus in duck embryo, and so on.

4. Purified antigens, subunit vaccines. Intact microorganisms are a composite of various antigens. The bacterial envelope, for example, has structures or molecular components such as capsule, slime layer, pili, lipopolysaccharide, flagella, and teichoic acid. These components are antigenic and sometimes harmful. The immunity an individual develops against a given microorganism very often is directed against a predominant antigen ("protective antigen"). More specifically, immunity is directed against only one of a few antigenic determinants of that antigen. Once the specific antigen is identified, the vaccine, whenever feasible, is made of the isolated purified antigen.

A **subunit vaccine** is composed of that fraction or a part of the whole microorganism that is known to contain the antigenic molecules that stimulate immunity. Antibodies against the capsular antigens of several pathogenic bacteria protect against disease caused by the pathogens. Vaccines containing purified capsular polysaccharides are available against strains of *S. pneumoniae, N. meningitidis,* and *H. influenzae.*

Some vaccines are polyvalent, meaning that the vaccine is composed of several to many variants of the antigen. The current vaccine against *S. pneumoniae,* for example, contains polysaccharides from 23 of the more than 80 capsular strains of this organism. The 23 strains represented in the vaccine account for the majority of cases of pneumococcal lobar pneumonia.

5. Recombinant vaccines. If the protective antigen of a microorganism is known, it can be purified beyond the subunit stage by isolating the genetic material of the microorganism. Segments of nucleic acid, including those that code for the antigen, are inserted into bacteria, yeasts, or animal cells. Large quantities of purified antigen can be produced in this way. The gene that codes for the surface antigen of the hepatitis B virus, for example, has been cloned in yeast cells. This vaccine is as immunogenic as the vaccine that is prepared from hepatitis B surface antigen obtained from human plasma.

Pure preparations of antigen as obtained by recombinant DNA technology may have limited immunogenicity. This is because the antigens are not effectively processed in the host and delivered to antigen-responsive cells. A way around this difficulty is to insert the genes into a nonvirulent carrier organism such as a modified vaccinia virus. The gene for the glycoprotein antigen of the rabies virus, for example, has recently been inserted into the vaccinia virus. Edible bait containing the virus has been tested for its ability to confer protection against rabies in wild and domestic animals and has proved successful.

6. Anti-idiotypic antibodies. Anti-idiotypic antibodies are being evaluated as vaccines in animals. An anti-idiotypic antibody is a second-generation image of an immunogen. For example, if an antigen is a key, then the antigen combining site of the antibody is the wax impression of that key. Thus, the idiotype is the impression of the original key. The anti-idiotype is the second key made from the wax impression of the first. Hence, the anti-idiotype carries the image of the foreign antigen as part of its structure (Fig. 12-9). Theoretically, injecting anti-idiotype antibodies into the host will evoke the correct type of protective antibodies. The advantage of this approach is that the individual is not exposed to the potentially damaging side effects from whole or parts of infectious microorganisms. If the availability of the antigen to be used for a vaccine is limited, then anti-idiotype antibodies would be a solution. Anti-idiotype serum is made in another animal (rabbit, for example) and it is possible that it could

FIGURE 12-9
Vaccines from anti-idiotypic antibodies. A. Virus with surface antigen is injected into a mouse, resulting in a group of monoclonal antibodies being produced. The antibodies (Ab_1) showing the most antiviral activity are chosen (B) for injection into a syngeneic mouse (reacts only to Ab_1 idiotype). The monoclonal antibodies collected are anti-idiotypic (Ab_2) and contain exact images of part of the viral antigen. Ab_2 is used as a vaccine and is injected into a mouse. Ab_2 stimulates the formation of Ab_3 antibodies, which are the same as Ab_1, and they neutralize virus.

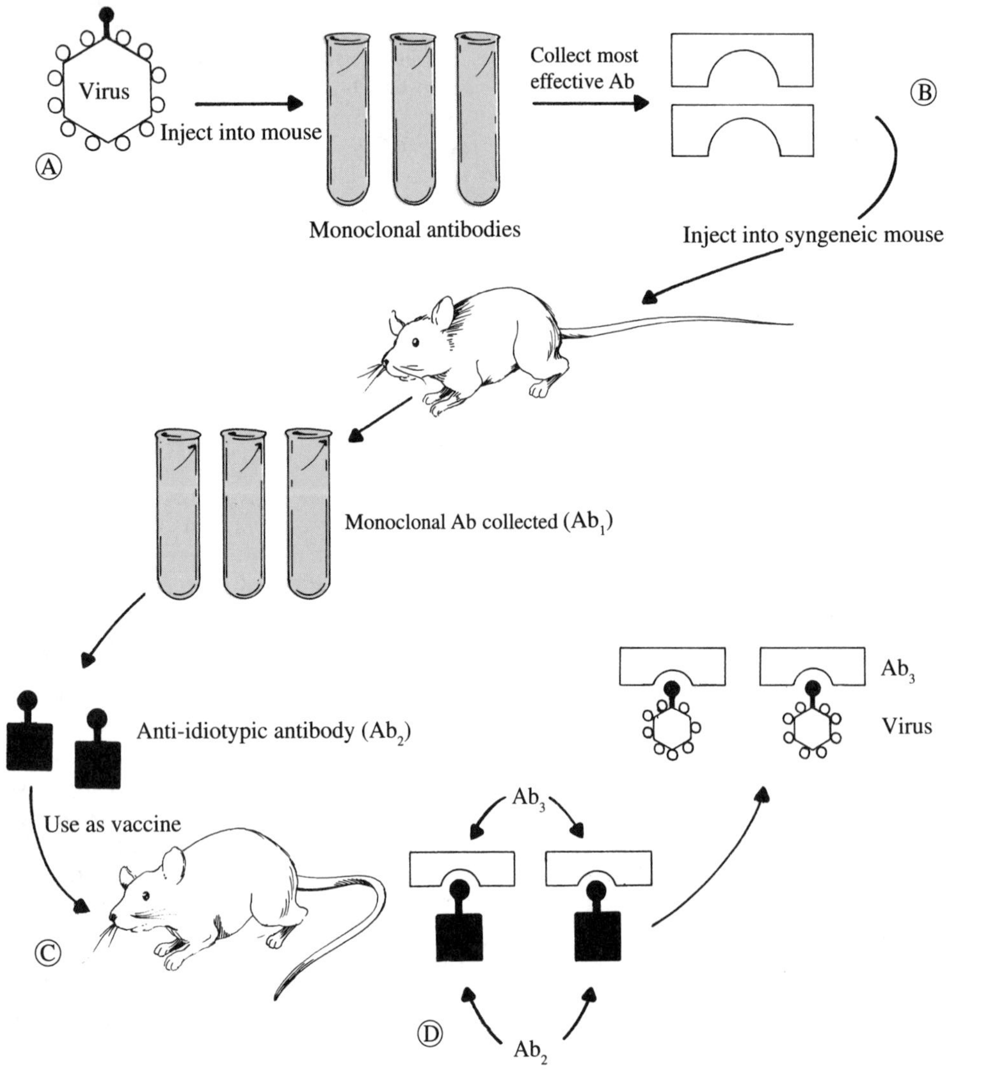

cause fever and allergic reactions in some people. No anti-idiotype vaccine has yet been approved for use in humans.

7. Synthesized immunogens. Future vaccines may consist of synthesized immunogens. Monoclonal antibodies are precisely specific for epitopes. They can be used to identify the epitopes responsible for protection among the sites of the entire antigen molecule. Once the isolated epitope is analyzed for amino acid composition and sequence, it can be synthesized. A pure preparation of the synthesized sequence alone usually is nonimmunogenic. It would be necessary to couple the sequence to a carrier molecule or insert it into a nonvirulent carrier microorganism.

In 1990, the Immunization Committee of the American College Health Organization provided recommendations (Table 12-1) to colleges and universities to use as guidelines for establishing and implementing a comprehensive Prematriculation Immunization Requirement (PIR). Universities have protected their students from vaccine-pre-

TABLE 12-1
Prematriculation Immunizations Recommended by the American College Health Association, 1990

Vaccine	Age indicated	Major indications[a]	Major precautions[a]
MMR (if given instead of individual vaccines)	First dose at 12 months;[b] second dose at school entry or later	All entering college students born after 1956 should have two doses of live measles vaccine; susceptible travelers	Pregnancy; history of anaphylactic reaction following egg ingestion or receipt of neomycin; immunosuppression; appropriate for HIV antibody–positive persons
Measles vaccine	First dose at 12 months;[b] second dose at school entry or later	All entering college students born after 1956 should have two doses of live measles vaccine; susceptible travelers	Pregnancy; history of anaphylactic reaction following egg ingestion or receipt of neomycin; immunosuppression; appropriate for HIV antibody–positive persons
Rubella vaccine	12 months[b]	Both males and females without verification of live vaccine on or after first birthday or laboratory evidence of immunity; susceptible travelers	Pregnancy; history of anaphylactic reaction following receipt of neomycin; immunosuppression; appropriate for HIV antibody–positive persons
Mumps vaccine	12 months[b]	All entering college students born after 1956 should have had one dose of live mumps vaccine or a history of mumps	Pregnancy; history of anaphylactic reaction following egg ingestion or receipt of neomycin; immunosuppression; appropriate for HIV antibody–positive persons
Tetanus-diphtheria toxoid	Primary series in childhood, booster 14–16, booster every 10 years	All persons	History of a neurological hypersensitivity reaction following a previous dose
Polio vaccine: killed vaccine (E-IPV), live vaccine (OPV)	Primary series in childhood, booster only if needed for travel after age 18	Persons traveling to areas where wild poliovirus is endemic or epidemic; OPV not indicated for persons over 18 years unless previously immunized with OPV	OPV should not be given to immuno-compromised persons or to HIV antibody–positive persons

[a] Refer to appropriate Immunization Practices Advisory Committee (ACIP) recommendations for more details.
[b] Public health authorities recommend that a first dose of MMR be given at 15 months of age; however, vaccine administered at 12 months of age is still accepted as a first dose.

ventable disease outbreaks by requiring them to have proof of vaccination before admission. This procedure is a safeguard against costly tracking procedures and emergency immunization.

Passive Immunization and Immunotherapy

It is sometimes necessary to immunize an individual with antibodies that have been produced in an animal or that are obtained from another human. The patient may have been exposed to an infectious agent to which he or she has not been actively immunized or for which active immunization is not routine practice (infectious hepatitis). In the first instance, even if active immunizing material were available, it is not possible for the patient to produce a sufficient level of antibodies to fight off the current infection. Antisera developed in animals or gamma globulins obtained from humans are used to provide temporary, immediate protection. These procedures are referred to as **passive immunotherapy.**

The use of animal (foreign or heterologous) antisera for humans has declined. Foreign antisera in vivo has a short half-life of between 7 and 23 days. The antisera level diminishes in the patient because of dilution, catabolism, immune complex formation, and elimination. Foreign antisera can cause anaphylactic reactions on second exposure, and serum sickness (painful joints, fever, and rash). Animal antisera still used in humans are equine diphtheria antitoxin, polyvalent botulinum antitoxin, and equine antilymphocyte serum.

Human gamma globulin has few side effects and is not eliminated as rapidly as animal antisera. Gamma globulin preparations are of two types. **Immune serum globulin (ISG)** is prepared from pooled plasma or serum obtained from a group of donors. This preparation is acquired irrespective of infection or immunization history of the donor (with certain precautions).

When gamma globulin from several individuals is pooled, it is likely to contain antibodies to the common infectious diseases. ISG is used before and after exposure to hepatitis A and for **hypogammaglobulinemia,** that is, individuals at risk who have low levels of gamma globulin. ISG also can be used for measles in nonimmunized children who have been exposed to measles or who are immunosuppressed. The second type of gamma globulin is obtained from individual donors who have been deliberately and actively immunized against a given disease. These preparations are specifically named—tetanus (TIG), hepatitis B (HBIG), rabies (RIG), and varicella-zoster (chickenpox-shingles or VZIG) immune globulin are some of the better-known preparations. Immune globulins and antitoxins used in the United States are outlined in Appendix E.

Immunotherapy is receiving considerable attention because of its potential in treating and preventing infections in the immunocompromised. A wide range of molecules including interferons, interleukins, hematopoietic cytokines, and monoclonal antibodies are now available for the prevention and treatment of infections in the immunocompromised host. Some of the biological agents currently under investigation include

1. **Interferon gamma.** Chronic granulomatous disease is an inherited immune disorder in which most patients suffer from recurrent infections by *S. aureus, Pseudomonas cepacia,* and *Chromobacterium violaceum.* When administered with antibiotics, IFN-γ reduces the duration of hospitalization from these infections. IFN-γ induces macrophages and neutrophils to synthesize products of oxidation.
2. **Interferon alfa.** IFN-α has antitumor and antiretroviral* activities. IFN-α regulates lymphocyte and NK cell activities. AIDS patients, who frequently have a cancer called Kaposi's sarcoma, respond to IFN-α by showing increased immune cell activity. IFN-α also inhibits the replication of the virus causing AIDS.
3. Hematopoietic growth factors. Chemotherapies for AIDS patients result in neutropenia and anemia. Hematopoietic growth factors such as **granulocyte-macrophage colony-stimulating factor (GM-CSF)** and **granulocyte colony-stimulating factor (G-CSF)** can reverse the neutropenia induced by chemotherapy. **Erythropoietin,** another growth factor, can correct the anemic condition in AIDS patients.

   Neutropenia is also associated with autologous bone marrow transplantation in cancer patients. Many of the deaths in these patients are due to bacterial and fungal infections. Use of G-CSF and GM-CSF has resulted in the reduction of myelosuppression and the acceleration of hematopoietic recovery.
4. Immunoglobulins. Immunoglobulins are being evaluated for preventing and treating infections in critically ill patients. Trauma or surgery patients have decreased levels of IgG and their neutrophils show reduced antimicrobial activity. Intravenous immunoglobulin preparations given prophylactically appear to reduce infection rates, particularly pneumonia. Intravenous immunoglobulins are now being used routinely in bone marrow transplant recipients to prevent infection by cytomegalovirus.

   A pressing problem in the immunocompromised is infection by gram-negative bacteria. The endotoxin of these bacteria is responsible for shock and considerable mortality. Monoclonal antibodies to the endotoxin are being investigated in the hopes of preventing gram-negative sepsis.
5. Immunotoxins. The selective destruction of tumor cells without harming healthy cells has been the goal of the medical community for several generations. A technique that may accomplish this goal is being evaluated. The strategy involves coupling a plant toxin called **ricin** to monoclonal antibodies. Ricin was selected because of its potency, humans rarely

* Retroviruses are RNA viruses, one of which is the human immunodeficiency virus (HIV).

demonstrate prior immunity to it, and it is biochemically characterized. Ricin can nonselectively bind to any cell and kill it. The binding fraction of the molecule is removed and replaced with an antibody that selectively binds to a target cell. For example, in autoimmune diseases antibodies are induced by and react with an individual's own tissue. It may be possible, using immunotoxins, to eliminate the set of lymphocytes that make such antibodies. Someday immunotoxins may play a role in destroying cancer cells and in solving the transplantation problem.

Summary

1. The specific immune response consists of cells (cell-mediated immunity) and antibodies (humoral immunity) that recognize foreign antigens and seek to destroy them. The interaction of the two systems is dependent on mediators and regulators such as cytokines and complement, respectively.

2. Complement is an array of plasma and membrane proteins that play a role in nonspecific as well as specific resistance. There are two pathways, classic and alternative, whose primary function is to produce C3b. C3b deposition on microorganisms marks them for destruction. Other complement functions include cytolysis, immune complex clearance, and chemotaxin and anaphylatoxin activities. See Table 12-2.

3. Complement deficiencies lead to serious conditions including lupus erythematosus as well as susceptibility to recurrent infections by bacterial species.

4. Many microorganisms are endowed with the ability to evade the effects of complement by (a) preventing activation of complement, (b) blocking the formation of C5b–9 complex molecules, or (c) preventing lysis by the C5b–9 complex.

5. Cell-mediated immune responses to bacteria involve presentation of antigen to T_H cells. T_H cells release a lymphokine that stimulates T_H cell growth as well as increasing T_C, B cell, and NK cell activity. T_H cells also release interferon gamma (IFN-γ), which activates macrophages and increases their phagocytic activities.

6. The humoral response to bacteria also involves T_H cells that release lymphokines to stimulate B cell growth and differentiation. Activated B cells differentiate into antibody-producing plasma cells and memory cells. Antibody can neutralize bacterial toxins, bind to complement-coated bacteria, and phagocytose them. It can also bind to bacterial surface components and prevent their attachment to epithelial surfaces.

7. The immune response to virus is T cell–dependent. IgG and IgM antibody bind to free virus in blood and neutralize it. At a target organ, virus is subject to cell-mediated and humoral immunity. Antibody and complement can bind to envelope-free virus, to viral antigens on infected cells, and to enveloped virus to effect their destruction. Antibody alone can coat virus and prevent its replication. Antibody is also involved in cell-mediated responses involving NK cells, T_C cells, and T_D cells.

8. Immunity to fungal infections is primarily cell-mediated and often involves delayed-type hypersensitivities.

9. Animal parasites are affected by humoral and cell-mediated responses. In particular, worm infections result in the enlistment of eosinophils. Eosinophils in the presence of antibody kill the worm by antibody-dependent cytotoxicity. Antibody can also enhance phagocytosis of protozoa, or cause complement-mediated lysis of worms and protozoa.

10. Immunity can be acquired by immunization. Immunization practices may be active or passive. Active immunization involves the use of vaccines, which include toxoids, whole-cell killed vaccines, attenuated vaccines, subunit vaccines, recombinant vaccines, anti-idiotypic antibodies, and synthesized immunogens.

TABLE 12-2
Biological Effects of the Major Complement Factors

Complement component	Receptors for	Biological response
C3a	Phagocytes, mast cells, basophils, some leukocytes	Anaphylatoxin that induces histamine release, which can cause smooth-muscle contraction; causes macrophages to release IL-2, which enhances immune response
C4a	Mast cells, polymorphonuclear leukocytes	Anaphylatoxin
C5a	Phagocytes, mast cells	Chemotactic factor for neurophils; triggers oxidative burst in neutrophils; histamine release by mast cells, thus same as C3a; can bind to suppressor T cells and suppress immune response; anaphylatoxin
C3b	Phagocytes, some lymphocytes	Opsonin that enhances phagocytosis; activates alternative pathway
C567	Phagocytes	Chemotaxin and promotes migration of phagocytes
C5b–9	Phagocytes	Membrane attack complex; cell membrane integrity is disrupted, leading to influx of water and cell lysis

11. Passive immunization involves the use of antibodies produced in an animal or another human. Human gamma globulin may be obtained from pooled plasma or from individual donors who have been deliberately immunized against a specific disease.

12. A variety of biological agents are available for use in the treatment and prevention of infections in the immunocompromised. These biological agents include IFN-α, IFN-γ, hematopoietic growth factors, immunoglobulins, and immunotoxins.

Questions for Study

1. What is the difference in the kinetics of the first and second exposures to the same antigen?
2. Demonstrate by means of an illustration that you know the differences between the specific immune response to viruses and that to bacteria.
3. Explain the conditions under which mast cell degranulation occurs.
4. Make a list of all the vaccinations you have had and describe how the immunogenic material was prepared.
5. What determines whether the classic or alternative complement pathway is activated in response to an infectious agent?
6. Demonstrate by means of an illustration the sequence of events that occurs when a bacterial cell invades the host and activates the classic complement pathway.
7. How is sialic acid involved in complement regulation?
8. Why is the host able to respond immunologically to virus if the virus multiples in the cytoplasm of the cell?
9. Make a table of some of the important cytokines, indicating their function in the immune response and how they might be used in immunotherapy.

CHAPTER 13

Immunological Disorders

OBJECTIVES

To describe in very brief terms what immunological disturbances are responsible for immunodeficiency diseases, hypersensitivities, autoimmune diseases, and graft rejection

To discuss the basic differences between anaphylactic, immune complex, and cytotoxic hypersensitivity reactions and to identify the antibodies, cells, mediators, and mechanisms involved in each reaction

To describe the cell types and mediators associated with delayed-type hypersensitivities

To outline the theories that explain autoimmunity and to list the factors that can induce an autoimmune response

To describe the role of the immune system in graft rejection and to discuss the approaches used to prolong graft survival

To describe the T cell response to tumors and mediators involved

To describe the active and passive techniques in tumor immunotherapy

OUTLINE

IMMUNODEFICIENCY DISEASES
- Stem Cell Disorders
- B Cell and T Cell Disorders
- Phagocytic Disorders
- Acquired Immunodeficiencies

HYPERSENSITIVITIES, OR ALLERGIES
- Type I Hypersensitivities
  - Mechanism
  - Systemic Anaphylaxis
  - Atopy (Localized Allergies)
- Type II Hypersensitivities (Cytotoxic Diseases)
- Type III Hypersensitivities (Immune-Complex Diseases)
  - Mechanism
  - Arthus Reaction and Serum Sickness
- Type IV Hypersensitivities (Delayed or Cell-Mediated)
  - Mechanism
  - Hypersensitivity of Infection (Tuberculin Hypersensitivity)
  - Allergic Contact Dermatitis

AUTOIMMUNE DISEASES
- Possible Mechanisms for and Induction of Autoimmunity
- Types of Autoimmune Diseases
  - Organ-Specific
  - Systemic

GRAFT REJECTION AND TRANSPLANTATION IMMUNOLOGY
- Transplant Terminology
- Rejection Mechanisms
- Preventing Graft Rejection
  - Tissue Typing
  - Immunosuppression
- Immunologically Privileged Sites and Tissues

TUMOR IMMUNOLOGY (CANCER AND THE IMMUNE SYSTEM)
- T Cell Response to Tumors
- Immunological Escape
- Tumor Immunotherapy
  - Active Immunotherapy
  - Passive Immunotherapy

The human immune system has evolved into an efficient defense mechanism. Occasionally, the immune system is altered or affected in such a way as to result in damage. Host tissue may be directly damaged or the host becomes subject to recurrent or severe infection by microbial agents. These effects may be due to (1) **immunodeficiency diseases,** which are deficiencies in immune components; (2) **hypersensitivities (allergies),** which result from overaggressive behavior of a normal immune response; (3) **autoimmune diseases,** due to a breakdown in discrimination of self antigens; (4) **graft rejection,** which is the rejection of transplantation antigens; and (5) **tumor formation,** which results from defective immune responses. We examine these immune responses and provide examples.

Immunodeficiency Diseases

Immunodeficiency diseases may be the result of genetic, developmental, or acquired defects in immune components. The defect may be in the stem cells, in the T or B cell immune system, or in the nonspecific phagocytic process.

STEM CELL DISORDERS

Most stem cell disorders involve the cells that are precursors to mature functional T and B lymphocytes, although other immune cells may be involved. These disorders are characterized in Table 13-1.

B CELL AND T CELL DISORDERS

B and T cell disorders may be due to a genetic or developmental defect. B cell disorders involve a deficiency in gamma globulins and are referred to as **hypogammaglobulinemias.** The primary consequence of B cell disorders is a susceptibility to bacterial infections.

Individuals with T cell disorders are susceptible to severe infections by viruses, fungi, and any other intracellular parasite (pathogens that ordinarily are destroyed by cell-mediated immune responses). Persons affected with these disorders seldom live beyond puberty. Even though T_H cells are important in B cell activation, persons with T cell disorders still produce enough antibody to mount some resistance to extracellular bacterial pathogens. Table 13-2 characterizes some of the major conditions caused

TABLE 13-1
Immunodeficiency Diseases Caused by Stem Cell Defects

Disorder	Cell type deficiency	Effect on host	Other characteristics and treatment
Severe combined immunodeficiency disease (SCID)	B and T cells	Severe recurrent infections	Phagocytosis is normal; antibiotics, bone marrow transplantation
ADA enzyme deficiency	T cell	Severe bacterial and viral infections	Genetically inherited SCID; antibiotics, bone marrow transplantation
Ataxia* telangiectasia	T and B cells	Bacterial and viral infections	Developmental defect occurring prior to stem cell maturation; antibiotics
Wiskott-Aldrich syndrome	T and B cells, monocytes, platelets	Bleeding, recurrent infections, eczema	X-linked recessive syndrome; IgM levels low but IgA and IgE elevated; antibiotics, bone marrow transplantation

ADA = adenosine deaminase.
* Ataxia (uncoordinated muscle movement), telangiectasia (vascular dilation).

TABLE 13-2
Infections Caused by T and B Cell Dysfunction

Type of infection	Site of dysfunction
Severe and/or recurrent infection with pyogenic bacteria	B cells
Severe viral infections caused by	T cells (SCID). See Under the Microscope 7.
Herpesviruses (cytomegalovirus, varicella virus)	
Hepatitis virus, echovirus, vaccine-strain poliomyelitis	B cells (deficiency of IgG, IgM, IgA)
Resistant superficial candidiasis	T cells (SCID, CMC, steroid therapy)
Systemic infection with opportunistic fungi (*Nocardia, Aspergillus, Candida*)	T cells (Hodgkin's disease)
Pneumonia caused by *Pneumocystis carinii*	T cells (SCID, treated leukemia)
Infection by *Giardia lamblia*	B cells (deficiency of IgG, IgM, or IgA)
Sudden severe sepsis	B cells (deficiency of IgM)

SCID = severe combined immunodeficiency disease; CMC = chronic mucocutaneous candidiasis.

UNDER THE MICROSCOPE 7

Treatment for SCID Patients Who Are ADA-Deficient

Severe combined immunodeficiency disease (SCID) affects about 1 out of 100,000 babies. SCID is also known as the boy-in-the-bubble disease, after David, a patient who survived with SCID until the age of 12 by living in a sterile plastic bubble. David died in 1984 of blood cancer after he underwent bone marrow treatment that was designed to free him from life in the bubble. Most SCID patients do not live in circumstances so extreme as those of the boy in the bubble.

One form of SCID is due to an inherited lack of the enzyme adenosine deaminase (ADA). All mammalian cells contain ADA but its deficiency appears to be deleterious only for lymphocytes. Children with the ADA deficiency constantly have infections and fevers, spend much time in isolation at a hospital, and require frequent blood transfusions. In 1990 the Food and Drug Administration gave the first-ever approval of the treatment for human disease using gene therapy. Approval was given for experimental gene therapy for two diseases, SCID due to ADA deficiency and the cancer malignant melanoma. The process involves inserting curative genes into human T lymphocytes. T lymphocytes are removed from patients and cultured. In ADA deficiency normal genes that code for ADA will be inserted into the lymphocytes of SCID patients. After the treated lymphocytes have multiplied in culture, they will be returned to the patient. The ADA-engineered lymphocytes will have to be replenished periodically. Patients will also be treated with a purified preparation of ADA that is bound to polyethylene glycol. The preparation prolongs the lifetime of ADA in the body.

If experimental gene therapy is successful, it will initiate a revolution in medical treatment for a number of serious human diseases.

by B and T cell dysfunction (see also Under the Microscope 7).

PHAGOCYTIC DISORDERS

Defects in the nonspecific phagocytic processes of neutrophils and macrophages are discussed in Chapter 9.

ACQUIRED IMMUNODEFICIENCIES

Acquired immunodeficiencies arise as a result of malignancies, age, infection, ionizing radiation, and drugs that affect the lymphoid system.

Malignancies that affect the immune system are **monoclonal gammopathies, leukemias,** and **lymphomas.** Monoclonal gammopathies develop when plasma cell cancers, called **myelomas** or **plasmacytomas,** produce excesses of whole immunoglobulin molecules or immunoglobulin chains. The immunoglobulins have no defined antibody function. There are numerous monoclonal gammopathies, some of which are Waldenström's macroglobulinemia, multiple myeloma, and heavy or light chain disease. **Malignant myeloma** is the most common. When fully developed, the disease affects the bone marrow, the skeletal and nervous systems, and the kidneys. **Leukemias** are usually blood-borne malignancies of various types of white blood cells, all of which in some way affect immunity. **Lymphomas** grow as isolated tumors, often in lymph nodes and other lymphatic tissue.

The most common acquired immunodeficiency is acquired immunodeficiency syndrome (AIDS). AIDS is a complication resulting from infection of helper T cells by the human immunodeficiency virus (HIV). This devastating infection is discussed in detail in Chapter 32.

Hypersensitivities, or Allergies

An acquired immune response to an antigen for the second time can sometimes go awry, causing tissue damage. This type of response is referred to as a **hypersensitivity** or **allergy.** Hypersensitivities are categorized on the basis of the schema proposed by Gell and Coombs. According to this schema, allergic reactions are divided into four types:

- Type I—immediate type, anaphylactic
- Type II—cytotoxic
- Type III—immune complex
- Type IV—delayed-type, cell-mediated

Types I, II, and III are antibody-mediated while type IV is cell-mediated.

TYPE I HYPERSENSITIVITIES

Type I hypersensitivities are immediate in that they develop usually in 5 to 30 minutes after reexposure to an antigen. The reaction of the host to the antigen is termed **anaphylaxis** (unprotected). Anaphylaxis may be characterized by a localized response (e.g., asthma) or by a systemic one. Systemic anaphylaxis, for example, from a bee sting, is life-threatening. The term **allergy** is usually reserved for type I hypersensitivities.

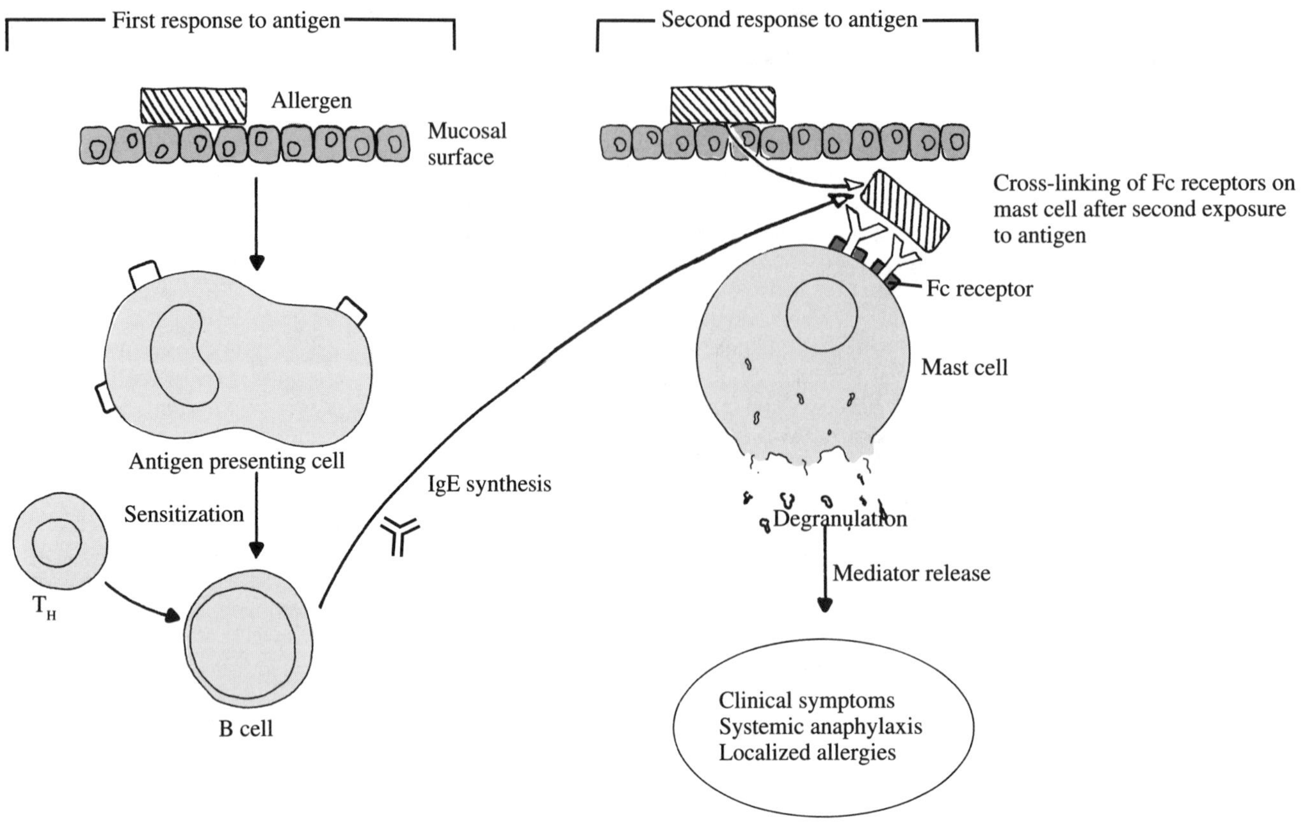

FIGURE 13-1
Scheme for type I hypersensitivity. During the first response to antigen, B cells with help from T_H cells produce specific IgE. IgE sensitizes mast cells. On second exposure to antigen, there is cross-linking of mast cell Fc receptors by surface-bound antigen. The cross-linking triggers degranulation and release of pharmacologically active mediators.

Mechanism

Before the symptoms of a hypersensitivity can be expressed, the individual must first be sensitized to the antigen. The antigen is referred to as an **allergen,** and at first contact with the host induces the synthesis of IgE (Fig. 13-1). IgE binds to mast cells and basophils. The mast cells, which are fixed around blood vessels or in connective tissue, become sensitized.

A second exposure of the mast cells to the allergen results in a cross-linking of the IgE receptors followed by degranulation. Degranulation causes the release, from the cytoplasm, of pharmacologically active mediators such as histamine. Binding of allergen also induces lipid metabolism in the cytoplasmic membrane of the mast cells. Lipid metabolism results in the synthesis of prostaglandins, thromboxanes, and leukotrienes. Collectively these mediators may act as chemoattractants, activators or effectors of smooth muscle and mucosal surfaces. Table 13-3 describes the effects of mast cell mediators.

Systemic Anaphylaxis

The allergens associated with systemic anaphylaxis include therapeutic agents including antibiotics and venom of bees, wasps, hornets, and other *Hymenoptera* (see Under the Microscope 8). The allergens evoking a response are therefore usually injected. Essentially there are three syndromes of systemic anaphylaxis:

1. Extensive swelling of the upper respiratory tract, which leads to airway obstruction and asphyxiation. Hypersecretion of mucus also occurs.
2. Spasms of the bronchioles in the lower respiratory tract, which lead to asphyxiation.
3. Vascular collapse (shock) without respiratory distress.

The **signs** and **symptoms** associated with a systemic anaphylactic reaction include the following:

1. **Erythema,** a reaction of the skin in which there is a reddening
2. **Urticaria (hives),** a raised, blanched area on the skin
3. **Pruritus,** intense itching
4. **Hypotension,** shock resulting from increased vascular permeability and collapse
5. Upper respiratory tract obstruction primarily as a result of laryngeal edema
6. Asthma-like syndrome involving the lungs
7. Smooth-muscle spasms evidenced particularly in the genitourinary and gastrointestinal tracts as abdominal pain, diarrhea, vomiting, or incontinence

TABLE 13-3
Mediators Released by Mast Cells and Their Effect on Host

Mediator	Cytoplasm (C) or membrane (M) derived	Function
Histamine	C	Inflammatory activator; vasodilation, vascular permeability, smooth-muscle contraction (bronchioles), mucus secretion, mucosal edema
PAF	M	Inflammatory activator; induces platelet lysis, formation of microthrombi
Heparin	C	Anticoagulant
NCF	C	Inflammatory activator; chemoattractant for neutrophils which clean up cell debris
ECF-A	C	Chemoattractant for eosinophils which release antihistamine-like substances
Leukotrienes (LTA_4–LTE_4)	M	Muscle spasmogens; smooth-muscle contraction and vascular permeability; chemoattractant for macrophages and basophils
Prostaglandins	M	Contraction of bronchial muscle, platelet aggregation, vasodilation
Thromboxanes	M	Same as prostaglandins
Kininogenase	C	Inflammatory activator; generate kinins from tissue kininogens and leads to vasodilation and edema
Tryptase	C	Unknown, may be involved in cutaneous responses

PAF = platelet activating factor; NCF = neutrophil activating factor; ECF-A = eosinophil chemotactic factor of anaphylaxis.

UNDER THE MICROSCOPE 8

The Imported Fire Ant and Anaphylactic Reactions

Local and systemic anaphylactic reactions to *Hymenoptera* venoms usually are associated by the public with the stings of bees, wasps, hornets, and yellow-jackets. Imported fire ants, however, are a major cause of such reactions in all or parts of the states of Texas, Louisiana, Mississippi, Alabama, Georgia, Florida, South Carolina, and North Carolina. Surveys indicate that as high as 58 percent of the population in some areas are stung by imported fire ants and that up to 1 percent of those suffer hypersensitivity reactions. The ants will attack humans or animals that disturb their nests. Each ant will attack repeatedly if left undisturbed.

The fire ant is so named because its venom elicits a sharp, burning sensation. The venom contains chemically unique alkaloids that cause allergic and toxic reactions. The toxic reaction is an intense, necrotizing inflammatory reaction that produces a characteristic sterile pustule within 24 hours at the sting site. The hypersensitivity reactions include diffuse erythema, pruritus, and hives manifested in the skin, respiratory distress due to laryngeal edema and bronchospasms, nausea, shock, coma, and death. Treatment of an ongoing reaction is the same as for any anaphylactic reaction. Skin testing with whole body extract (WBE) of fire ants or venom and the RAST test are used for diagnosis. Immunotherapy (desensitization) with WBE is recommended for selected patients who have had a systemic reaction.

From R. F. Lockey, *Hosp. Pract.* 25(3):109, 1990.

Prevention and management of systemic anaphylactic reactions are especially important since the condition may be life-threatening. It is necessary to take histories, to conduct appropriate tests, and to heed warnings from previous reactions. It is also important to know the conditions that are likely to produce such reactions before injections are considered.

Treatment of systemic anaphylaxis is based on using drugs that antagonize the effects of mast cell mediators. **Epinephrine** is the drug of choice. Epinephrine is a physiological antagonist of histamine. It dilates bronchioles, has a vasoconstricting influence, and aids in the resorption of edema fluid. Epinephrine also blocks the release of mast cell mediators and is a direct stimulator of the heart. If shock is severe, drugs must be administered to maintain blood pressure. Upper airway obstruction owing to laryngeal edema may necessitate some form of airway maintenance.

Atopy (Localized Allergies)

The term **atopy** was originally coined to describe the clinical features of type I hypersensitivities such as hay fever and eczema. Today, atopy is used to encompass a variety of chronic or common allergic states. These allergic states include hay fever, asthma, hives, and food allergies.

The **mechanism** by which localized allergies are expressed is basically the same as for systemic anaphylaxis. Mast cell activation is what makes the allergy localized. The most obvious differences between systemic and localized anaphylaxis is in degree; localized allergies are not usually life-threatening. In addition, the allergens in localized allergies usually evoke a response by contact with mucosal surfaces rather than skin injection as in systemic anaphylaxis.

Localized allergies are of such a type that they require a physician for diagnosis, treatment, and control. Table 13-4 characterizes some of the common clinical allergies. It is estimated that 10 percent of the population has minor allergies that are detected when the individuals are appropriately tested.

A history of allergy among close relatives can be obtained among a majority of allergic patients. The allergic syndrome in the offspring is not necessarily the same as that of the parents. The allergic substance may well be different. Indeed, the target organ within the same individual may change. The first allergic disease experienced in infancy may be a food allergy with gastrointestinal involvement. This response is followed by allergic dermatitis in childhood, eventually developing into asthma in young adulthood.

Allergy testing, which can detect minor allergies in the population, is usually in the form of skin testing or a laboratory test known as the **radioallergosorbent test (RAST test,** see Appendix B). Many of the antigen preparations for allergy testing are commercially available, but some may have to be tailored by the allergist to the patient's history or idiosyncrasies.

In **skin tests** the introduction of the allergen to which the patient is allergic leads within minutes to the **wheal-and-erythema reaction** (Fig. 13-2). The site first reddens. As edema fluid collects in the area, the central portion becomes raised and blanched while the periphery becomes erythematous. In the **scratch test** the surface of the skin is abraded with a dull needle or implement. A droplet of allergen is instilled in the abraded area. Skin testing may be intradermal; that is, measured amounts of allergen are injected between the layers of the skin. The **intradermal test** is the more sensitive of the two tests. In the **patch test** the suspected allergen is either directly taped to the skin or applied to gauze or cotton that is taped to the skin.

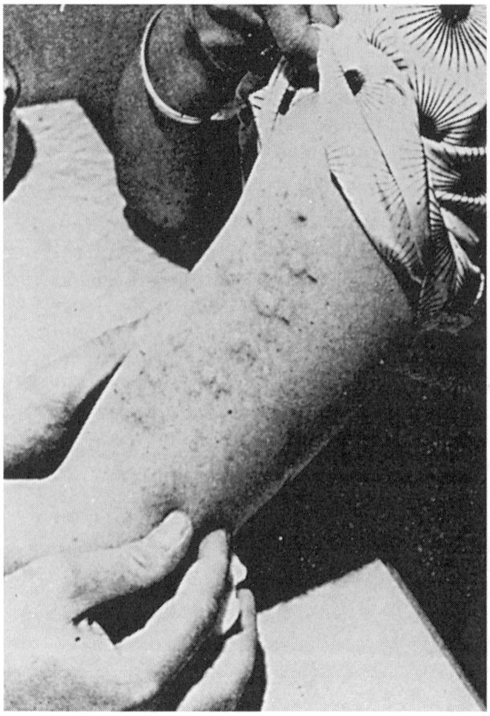

FIGURE 13-2
Whealing reactions following intradermal testing. (From B. F. Feingold, *Introduction to Clinical Allergy,* 1973. Courtesy of Charles C. Thomas, Publisher, Springfield, Illinois.)

Prevention of clinical allergies can be accomplished many times by avoiding the allergen. When this is not

TABLE 13-4
Common Clinical Allergies

Allergic respiratory disease (ARD)
- Pollinosis—seasonal allergic rhinitis. Pollens are from trees and grasses in spring and early summer, weeds in late summer. Pollens are mostly wind-borne but also insect-borne.
- Perennial allergic rhinitis (PAR)—year round. Common allergens are house dust and animal epidermals (hair, feathers, dander). Among the many allergens of house dust are mold spores, animal epidermals, and mites.
- Bronchial asthma. Common allergens are those cited under ARD and PAR. The air sacs are overdistended, plugs of mucus fill bronchial passages, smooth muscles enlarge (hypertrophy) to thicken and narrow the walls of the bronchi. Symptomatic relief is obtained by bronchodilators that relax the muscles of the bronchi, and by expectorants and liquefacients that dissolve and expel the mucous plugs and the other accumulations.

Gastrointestinal allergies—colic and possibly ulcerative colitis

Allergic skin disorders
- Atopic dermatitis. This can be divided into stages: infant, childhood, and adolescent-adult.
- Allergic contact dermatitis (ACD). A variety of allergens (contactants), many serving as haptens, elicit nonatopic skin allergies via the delayed hypersensitivity mechanism.

possible, the patient's sensitivity can be reduced by a process called **hyposensitization.** Hyposensitization is performed by parenteral injections of the corresponding allergen. Good success has been attained, for example, for hay fever and insect sting allergies. The parenterally introduced allergen ("allergy shots" to the patient) elicits the formation of allergen-specific IgG antibodies. In addition, suppressor T cell activity is enhanced while IgE levels fall. The correlation between these responses and clinical improvement is believed to be associated with the action of IgG, which functions as a blocking antibody.

Treatment of clinical allergies relies on the use of antihistamines, decongestants, bronchodilators, vasoconstrictors, expectorants, and corticosteroids. Antihistamines, of little value in systemic anaphylaxis because of the extent of the reactions, are mainstays in allergic rhinitis and urticaria.

TYPE II HYPERSENSITIVITIES (CYTOTOXIC DISEASES)

Type II hypersensitivities are mediated by IgG/IgM antibody and complement. They cause damage to cells such

FIGURE 13-3
Type II hypersensitivity reaction. A. Antigen (Ag)-antibody (Ab) complexed on a target cell activates complement. B. Formation of the C5–9 membrane attack complex causes lysis. C. C3b deposited on the target cell attracts neutrophils to the scene. D. Neutrophils cannot phagocytose the target cell because it is too large. E. Neutrophils release lysosomes to the outside and the target cell is lysed.

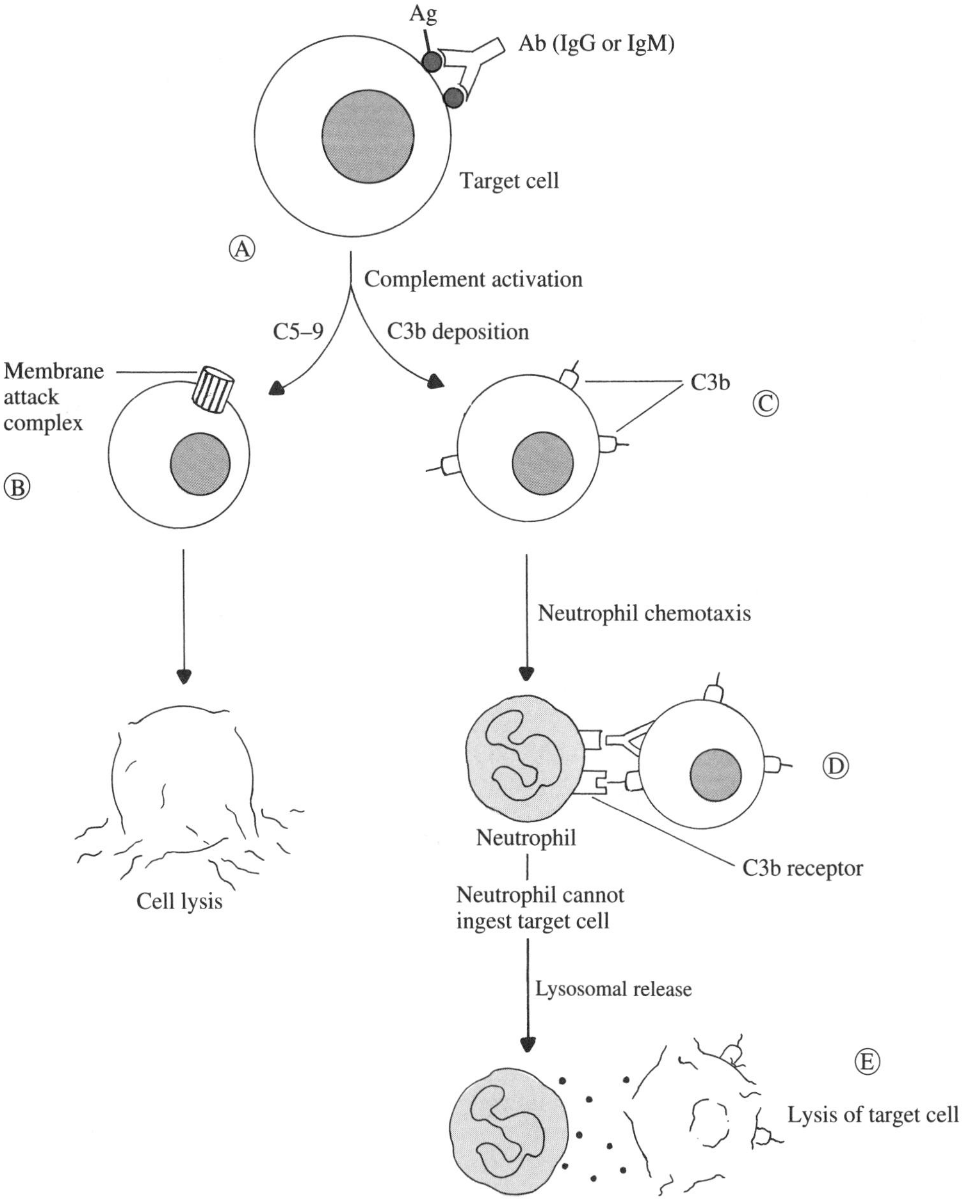

as blood cells, platelets, and tissue cells. In these reactions antigens may be (1) part of the patient's own cells, (2) soluble foreign antigen, or (3) antigen-antibody complexes that attach to the cells. The binding of antigen-antibody to the cell triggers the activation of complement and the subsequent lysis of the cell. Lysis can occur in two ways: First, the C5–9 membrane attack complex (MAC) can be formed, and second, a complement factor (C3b) can be deposited on the surface of the target cell, making it susceptible to destruction by neutrophils and macrophages. This opsonization process does not result in ingestion of the target cell because the latter is too large. Instead, the neutrophil releases its lysosomes to the outside and this causes damage to the target cell (Fig. 13-3).

Clinical type II hypersensitivities include blood transfusion reactions and Rh incompatibility reactions (see Appendix B), autoimmune hemolytic anemia, and drug-induced reactions. Drugs sometimes act as haptens and attach to blood cells. Agranulocytosis (decrease in granulocytes) may develop when an antibiotic such as chloramphenicol attaches to granulocytic leukocytes. Hemolytic anemia may develop when phenacetin (an analgesic) binds to erythrocytes.

TYPE III HYPERSENSITIVITIES (IMMUNE-COMPLEX DISEASES)

An immune complex is any antigen-antibody complex found in the body. Normally these complexes are removed or cleared by the immune system, with no damage to the host. There are conditions, however, in which the immune complex leads to hypersensitivity and damage to host tissue. The immune system in immune-complex disease becomes overloaded and is unable to phagocytose and destroy the antigen-antibody complex. Overloading is observed in some persistent or chronic microbial infections such as leprosy and hepatitis and in some autoimmune diseases such as rheumatoid arthritis and systemic lupus erythematosus.

Mechanism

Most immune complexes are removed by polymorphonuclear leukocytes and macrophages in the liver, spleen, and lung. Clearance of the immune complexes appears to depend on their size, immunoglobulin class, and relative concentration of antigen and antibody. Size appears to play the most important role in this process. The inability to remove immune complexes results in their persistence and this can lead to deposition of the immune complex in certain tissues. The tissues most often affected are the walls of blood vessels (endothelium), basement membrane of kidney tubules (glomeruli), and synovial tissue (membranes that secrete viscous fluid into joints). Once deposition of the immune complex occurs, a series of immunological events is set into motion (Fig. 13-4):

1. Complement is activated and anaphylatoxic factors C3a, C4a, and C5a are released. These factors act on basophils and mast cells to release vasoactive amines (histamine, for example), causing an inflammatory response.
2. C5a as a chemotactic factor attracts polymorphonuclear leukocytes. These cells, unable to ingest and eliminate the immune complex, release lysosomes into the extracellular fluid. This leads to damage of host cells to which the immune complex is bound as well as damage to healthy cells in the vicinity. Polymorphonuclear leukocytes retain their viability and can release additional lysosomes.
3. Platelet activation by immune complexes causes the release of vasoactive amines, which lead to increased vascular permeability. In addition, platelet binding of the immune complex causes aggregation of platelets and formation of thrombi. Thrombi bind to the basement membrane of the blood vessel wall. The net result is hemorrhagic necrosis and other forms of tissue destruction.

Arthus Reaction and Serum Sickness

These conditions are prototypes of immune-complex disease. In the Arthus reaction a soluble antigen is injected into the skin of an experimental animal, such as a rabbit, at intervals of about one week. This progressively leads to formation of an ever-increasing inflammatory focus that becomes necrotic. In serum sickness the administration of a single large dose of a soluble antigen brings about a systemic condition in 6 to 12 days. The antigens inducing this response include antiserum or chemotherapeutic agents designed to persist in the body. The patient experiences arthralgia (painful swollen joints), fever, rash, and enlargement of the lymph nodes. The large or persisting dose of antigen allows enough antigen to remain and form complexes when sufficient antibody has been formed.

The tissue pathology and clinical manifestations of the Arthus reaction and of serum sickness were known for many years before the underlying immune events were understood. Recently, several of these poorly understood diseases were found to be attributable, at least partially, to reactions of immune complexes. These immune-complex diseases include rheumatoid arthritis, systemic lupus erythematosus, acute viral hepatitis, Hashimoto's thyroiditis, scleroderma, poststreptococcal glomerulonephritis, and other diseases. Some immune-complex diseases are attributable to dirty environments that exist at the workplace or that are associated with hobbies. These diseases include farmer's lung, maple bark disease, bagassosis (caused by contact with sugar cane fiber), and pigeon breeder's lung.

TYPE IV HYPERSENSITIVITIES (DELAYED OR CELL-MEDIATED)

Delayed-type hypersensitivities (DTH) are those that take more than 12 hours to appear. DTH are initiated by the recognition of a cell-bound antigen by a T cell. The effector cells in this process are activated T cells and macrophages. Unlike other hypersensitivities, DTH cannot be transferred from one animal to another in the serum.

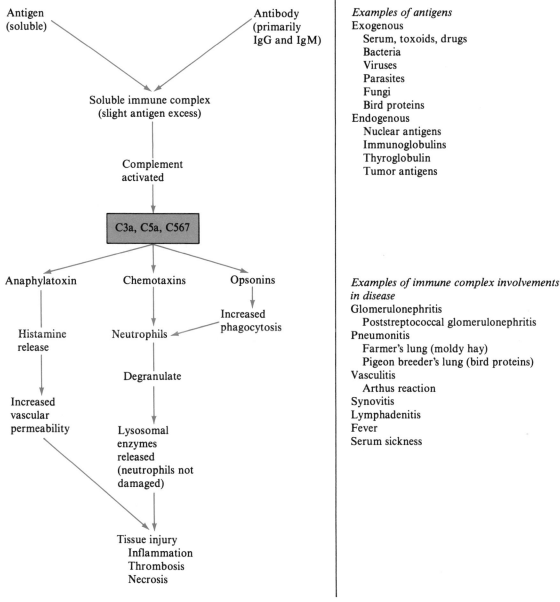

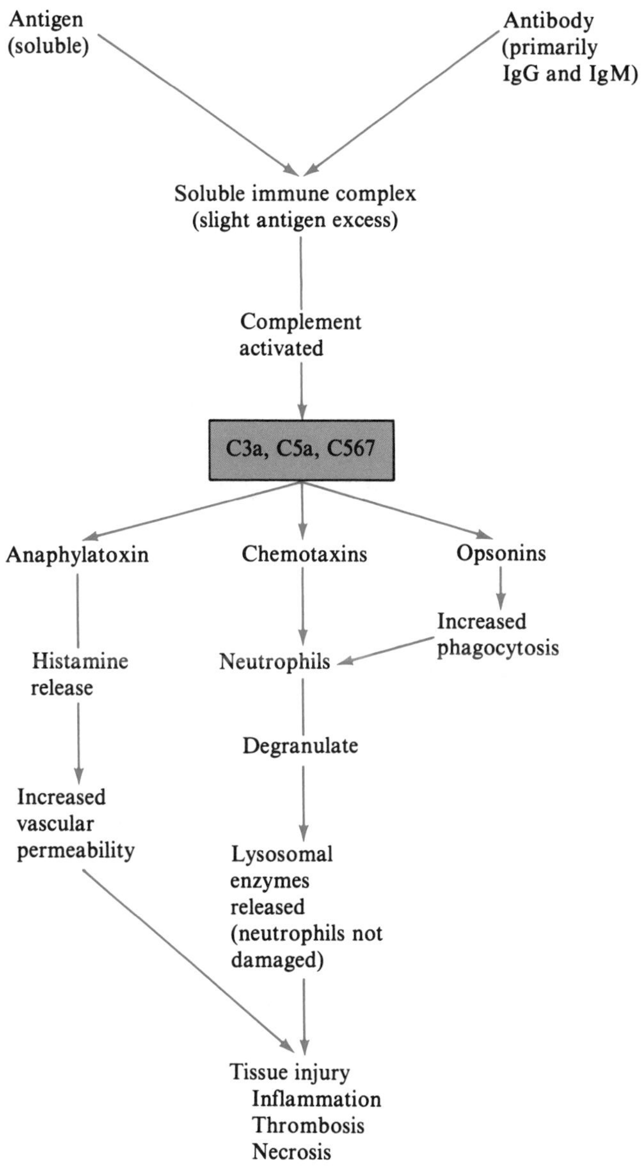

Examples of antigens

Exogenous
- Serum, toxoids, drugs
- Bacteria
- Viruses
- Parasites
- Fungi
- Bird proteins

Endogenous
- Nuclear antigens
- Immunoglobulins
- Thyroglobulin
- Tumor antigens

Examples of immune complex involvements in disease

Glomerulonephritis
- Poststreptococcal glomerulonephritis

Pneumonitis
- Farmer's lung (moldy hay)
- Pigeon breeder's lung (bird proteins)

Vasculitis
- Arthus reaction

Synovitis

Lymphadenitis

Fever

Serum sickness

FIGURE 13-4
Immune-complex disease. The antigen-antibody complexes are formed in the blood and tissue spaces. They are deposited in the walls of blood vessels, in basement membranes, and in joint synovia.

Mechanism

The cellular reactions associated with DTH are outlined below and in Figure 13-5.

1. Foreign antigen is taken up by macrophages or dendritic cells and cleaved into peptide fragments. The peptides complex with major histocompatibility complex (MHC) (Class I or II proteins) at the membrane surface. The cells thus become antigen presenting cells (APC).
2. T cells that recognize the APC peptide fragment plus the MHC Class II protein become activated and differentiate into two clones: T_D and T_C cells.
3. T_D cells, on recognition of antigen, release lymphokines that activate macrophages. Macrophages are attracted to the site where antigen is located. Activated macrophages secrete substances such as interleukin (IL)-1 and tumor necrosis factor (TNF). IL-1 is a stimulator of T cells and is associated with fever and other inflammatory responses. TNF displays cytotoxic activities for tumor cells and is also an inducer of fever. The presence of activated macrophages results in destruction of parasites and tumor cells and also causes damage to surrounding healthy tissues.

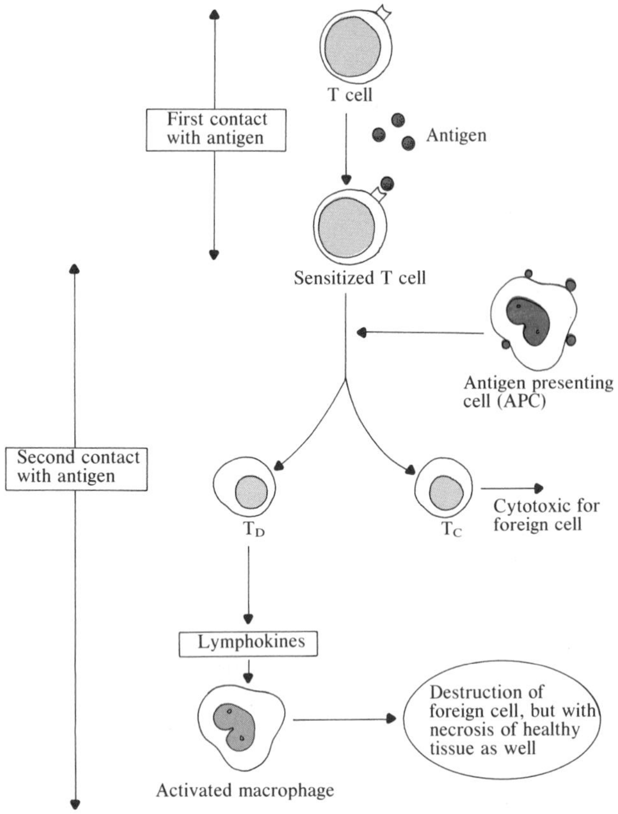

FIGURE 13-5
Type IV hypersensitivity reaction. Initially foreign antigen sensitizes the T cell. On second contact with antigen, a sensitized T cell is presented antigen by the antigen presenting cell (APC). The T cell differentiates into T_D and T_C cells. T_C cells are cytotoxic for the foreign cell. T_D cells, in the presence of foreign antigen, release lymphokines and attract and activate macrophages. Macrophages destroy the foreign cell plus some healthy tissue.

Hypersensitivity of Infection (Tuberculin Hypersensitivity)

The immune response of individuals to the bacillus causing tuberculosis *(Mycobacterium tuberculosis)* has been the model for DTH. However, other infectious agents such as some animal parasites, fungi, and viruses also can cause DTH. In tuberculosis the bacterium assumes an intracellular habitat within the macrophage and thus requires cell-mediated responses to eliminate it. The bacillus can multiply in the macrophage and infect other macrophages at the site of infection. The initial infection sensitizes the host and later, as other bacilli or their products are released, a DTH is initiated. Under these circumstances many macrophages and other cell types accumulate at the site of infection and die. Necrotic material forms, probably including healthy tissue that was sacrificed to contain the infection. The reaction basically is that of a chronic inflammation.

Diagnostic skin tests are available for certain infectious diseases. Circulating sensitized T cells respond to skin test antigens in a positive test reaction. There are no live multiplying organisms in the test antigen, so the lesion at the challenge site resolves in time. Commercially prepared extracts of the various infectious agents are used for skin testing.

The most widely applied of the delayed hypersensitivity tests is the **tuberculin test.** A purified preparation of tuberculoprotein, referred to as **purified protein derivative (PPD),** is used in tuberculosis skin testing. In a positive reaction an indurated inflammatory reaction begins to appear after 6 to 12 hours. The reaction reaches its greatest intensity in 24 to 72 hours, and gradually subsides. The degree of sensitivity of the patient and the amount of tuberculin applied in the skin test are related to the size of the reaction and the amount of tissue damage in the skin test site.

Allergic Contact Dermatitis. Allergic contact dermatitis is an allergic response that occurs when certain chemicals come in contact with the skin. The most common causes are simple chemical ingredients of soaps and cosmetics, industrial chemicals, ointments, chemotherapeutic agents (especially those that are topically applied), and plant substances, to mention a few. The classic example of ACD involves plants in the genus *Rhus*—poison ivy, poison oak, and poison sumac—in which the active allergenic factor is an **oleoresin.**

ACD allergens are substances of relatively simple chemical composition. In an earlier chapter we emphasized that antigens are usually large molecules. Then how can simple chemicals such as mercury and nickel and certain molecules of the *Rhus* plant be allergenic? The commonly accepted theory is that they act as partial antigens or haptens. The chemicals conjugate with proteins of the skin. The complete antigen consists of the haptens of the allergic substance as well as the proteins of the skin. The haptens are the determinant groups, while the proteins of the skin act as carrier molecules.

Acute ACD occurs, on average, 18 to 24 hours after a sensitized individual encounters the allergen. The reaction may range from a well defined erythematous area to extensive areas of vesiculation (bullae). The vesiculated (blistered) lesions may ooze, crust, and become infected (Fig. 13-6). Oleoresin of *Rhus* plants may be spread by rubbing or contact before the vesicular reaction occurs.

A sensitized person experiencing a reaction may not always have a history of direct contact with the allergen. With poison ivy, for example, pets and clothing may be the indirect bearers of the stimulus. Burning of the plants may vaporize the allergenic components and the smoke, coming in contact with exposed parts of the body, may elicit a violent response.

The customary mode of testing for hypersensitivity is the **patch test,** described previously under Atopy (Localized Allergies). Treatment is usually conservative, in the form of compresses and soaks. Steroids are used for severe ACD.

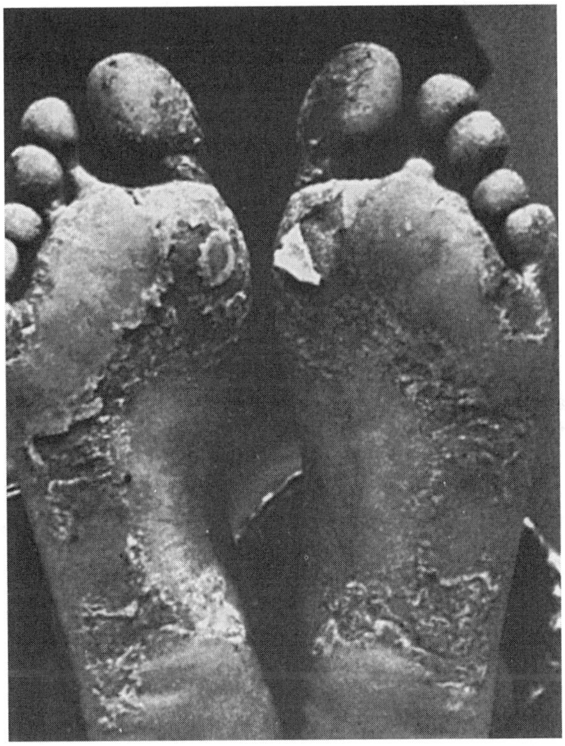

FIGURE 13-6
Pruritic scaly eruptions caused by delayed hypersensitivity reaction to adhesive in the lining of tennis shoes. (From S. M. Connolly, *Postgrad. Med.* 74:227, 1983. By permission of Mayo Foundation.)

Autoimmune Diseases

Occasionally, the body responds to its own cells in a negative fashion, producing autoantibodies. The diseases associated with autoantibodies are called **autoimmune diseases.** Autoimmune diseases occur in patients with type II, III, and IV hypersensitivities. In the following paragraphs we briefly examine self-tolerance and the factors that result in its breakdown. In addition we discuss the factors that trigger autoimmunity.

POSSIBLE MECHANISMS FOR AND INDUCTION OF AUTOIMMUNITY

The pathology observed in autoimmune diseases is the result of the interaction of many factors in the immune system network. How the system of self-tolerance is broken down is not completely understood but there are some theories, including the following:

1. Defects in thymus and bone marrow, which could influence the interaction between B and T lymphocytes and self antigens.
2. Malfunction of suppressor lymphocytes. It is believed that T_S cells control the normal response to self antigens. Interference with T_S activity could lead to a positive response between lymphocytes and self antigens.
3. Enhanced T_H cell activity. T_H cells normally do not induce an autoimmune response when self-reactive B or T cells are present. If T_H cells are activated, they could induce B cells to produce antiantibodies.

A breakdown in the system of immune tolerance makes the host potentially susceptible to a variety of autoimmune diseases. The triggers for development of autoimmune disease include the following:

1. Drugs. Drugs bind to cells and may cause alteration of the surface antigens. The host responds to the cells as if they were foreign.
2. Self antigens that share identical or similar antigens to foreign antigens. For example, *Streptococcus pyogenes* is the causative agent of "strep throat." This infection can lead to a complication called rheumatic fever, which affects heart muscle. Antibodies produced against *S. pyogenes* can react with heart muscle. Thus, the antigens on *S. pyogenes* are similar or identical to those on heart muscle **(cross-reacting antigens).**
3. Expression of hidden antigens. Self antigens that are not normally exposed to the immune system, such as the lens of the eye or spermatozoa, can be exposed by injury, surgery, or infection. Autoantibodies can lead to conditions such as **uveitis** (inflammation of the middle coat of the eye) and aspermatogenesis, respectively.
4. Viral infection. Viruses are able to display their own antigens on the surface of the infected cell. In addition, the genome of many viruses can integrate into the host's genome and can influence surface antigens on the cell. Scientists have suggested that some diseases such as systemic lupus erythematosus, diabetes, and multiple sclerosis are preceded by viral infection and an autoimmune response.

TYPES OF AUTOIMMUNE DISEASES

Autoimmune diseases may be broken down into two types: those that are **organ-specific** and those that are **systemic** in nature. We discuss two examples of each type.

Organ-Specific

Autoimmune thyroid diseases can fall into different clinical categories but one of the more common forms is called **Hashimoto's thyroiditis.** This disease is more common in middle-aged women. The gland becomes infiltrated with lymphocytes and phagocytes and enlarges (goiter). Patients with the disease possess antibodies to the thyroid hormone thyroglobulin. Treatment relies on hormone replacement therapy.

Myasthenia gravis is a disease in which myasthenia gravis autoantibodies develop against acetylcholine receptors at neuromuscular junctions. This action blocks muscle contraction that normally occurs when acetylcholine released from neurons binds to the acetylcholine receptor. Victims experience extreme muscle weakness. There may be difficulties in chewing, swallowing, and breathing that eventually lead to respiratory failure.

Systemic

In **rheumatoid arthritis,** antibodies primarily of class IgM (these antibodies are referred to as **rheumatoid factor**) are formed against the Fc portion of the patient's own IgG molecules. IgG, thus, serves as an antigen. The IgM-IgG immune complexes are deposited in the synovia of joint spaces. Complement is activated by the complexes and intense inflammation ensues, progressively breaking down collagen and cartilage in the joints.

Systemic lupus erythematosus is a chronic inflammatory disease affecting primarily middle-aged women. Immunological reactions involve numerous self antigens with a variety of host tissues and organs. The disease is characterized by a butterfly rash resembling the color of a wolf (*lupus* in Latin means "wolf").

Systemic lupus erythematosus reflects a loss of tolerance to several self antigens such as DNA, RNA, and other cytoplasmic elements. The major autoantibody is anti-DNA (of the IgG and IgM classes) that can complex with free DNA to form an immune complex. Immune complexes become deposited on tissues and activate complement. The ensuing inflammatory process damages tissues. Immune complexes can be deposited on the glomeruli of the kidneys, on arterioles, in joints, and on heart tissue. Thus, several vital organs can be compromised by the disease. Clearance of immune complexes puts the disease in remission.

Graft Rejection and Transplantation Immunology

Transplantation has become an important area in medicine in recent years. For the most part, it is relatively easy to transplant tissue from one body site to another. For example, in burn patients, skin can be transplanted from one region of the body to another. Transplantation from one individual to another (unless they are identical twins) is difficult. Such procedures are intricate because the body's immune system recognizes the transplanted tissue or organ as nonself and rejects it.

TRANSPLANT TERMINOLOGY

The most important determinants responsible for graft rejection are the cell membrane antigens coded for by a cluster of genes called the major histocompatibility complex or MHC. In humans the MHC is designated **HLA,** for human leukocyte antigens. MHC was discussed earlier in Chapter 11. The antigens of the graft involved in immunorejection are called **transplantation antigens.** The speed at which a graft rejection occurs is directly related to the degree of antigenic difference between donor and recipient. There is a transplantation terminology used to describe grafting between donor and recipient (Table 13-5). For example, **autografts** and **isografts** are not immunorejected because their antigens are identical with the recipient's antigens. Most grafts between humans are **allografts;** that is, they are members of the same species but they are not genetically identical. The tissues of the donor are foreign to the recipient and are therefore antigenic. **Xenografts** are cell, tissue, or organ grafts between members of two different species.

REJECTION MECHANISMS

T cells are mainly responsible for graft rejection. Except for hyperacute rejection, antibodies play only a minor role. Once the graft is in place, blood vessels communicate with it and thus expose it to blood cells. The recipient's T_H cells become sensitized when they recognize the foreign membrane antigens and MHC Class II proteins of the

TABLE 13-5
Transplantation Terminology

Prefix	Meaning	Combining suffixes	Transplantation parlance
Auto-	Self	-graft -geneic -antigen -antibody	An autograft is a self graft, e.g., skin from one site of the patient's body moved to another site on the patient's body
Iso-	Equal; identical with another	-graft -geneic -antigen -antibody	An isograft is a graft between isogeneic individuals, i.e., between genetically identical individuals such as identical (uniovular) twins
Allo- (homo-)	Similar; like another	-graft -geneic -antigen -antibody	An allograft is a graft between allogeneic individuals, i.e., between nonidentical members of the same species
Xeno- (hetero-)	Dissimilar; unlike another; foreign	-graft -geneic -antigen -antibody	A xenograft is a graft between xenogeneics, i.e., between members of different species, as a graft from ape to human

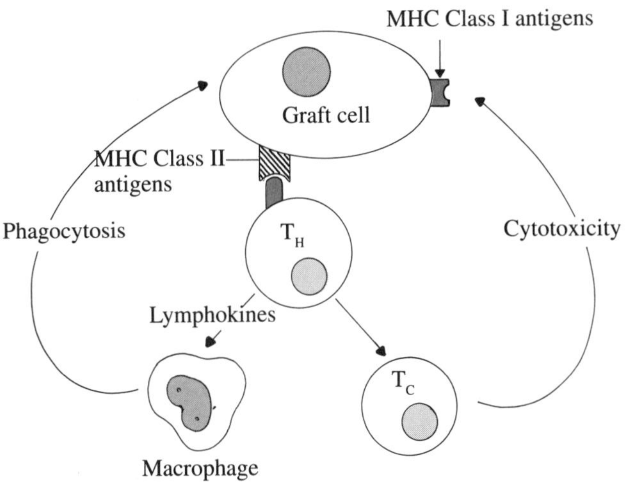

FIGURE 13-7
Mechanism of graft-cell destruction. T_H cells recognize MHC Class II antigens on the graft cell. T_H cells are activated to release lymphokines, which stimulate and attract macrophages to the graft site. T_H cells also activate T_C cells, causing them to divide and migrate to the site of the graft where they recognize MHC Class I antigens.

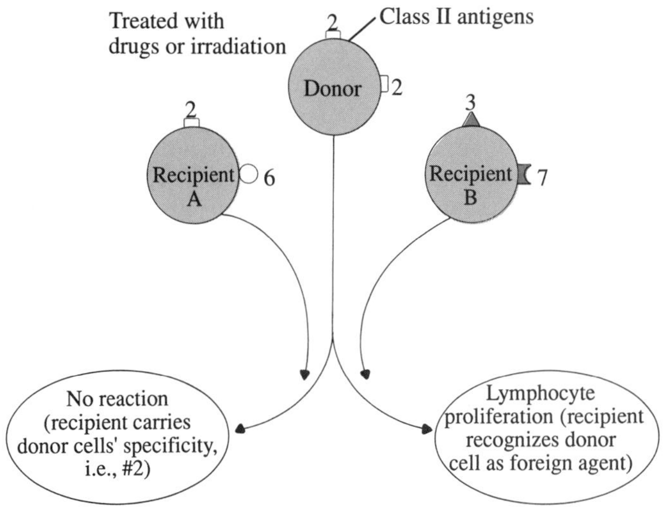

FIGURE 13-8
Histocompatibility testing using mixed lymphocyte culture (MLC) assay. Donor lymphocytes are treated with drugs or irradiation to prevent proliferation. Antigen specificities are represented by differently numbered shapes. Two different recipient populations (A and B) are shown. Recipient A with number 2 class antigen does not recognize as foreign the donor with number 2 antigens and thus no reaction occurs. Recipient B with number 3 and 7 antigens recognizes the donor as foreign and proliferates.

donor. This results in the release of lymphokines, which stimulate macrophages to infiltrate the blood vessels of the graft. Macrophages help phagocytize the foreign tissue cells. Activated T_H cells may also promote activation and expansion of T_C cells. T_C cells can recognize a specific MHC Class I antigen on the donor. T_C cells reach the graft and destroy it by cytotoxic processes (Fig. 13-7).

PREVENTING GRAFT REJECTION

Immunorejection under normal circumstances is a beneficial reaction: Without it the body would serve as a culture medium for any cell or tissue it contacts. What scientists have been seeking for many years is a technique for preventing immunorejection in transplantation procedures. There are two general approaches used to increase the survival of grafts: (1) **tissue typing,** to select donors with as few HLA mismatches with the recipient as possible, and (2) reducing the immune responses **(immunosuppression)** of the recipient.

Tissue Typing

The purpose of tissue typing is to match the tissue antigens of the donor and recipient as closely as conditions allow. The genes for HLA are located on a small segment of human chromosome 6. The products of some of the gene loci on this segment can be serologically identified.

In kidney grafting, long-term survival of the graft occurs in a high percentage of patients when there is a sibling donor who is serologically matched with the recipient at both the HLA-A and HLA-B (Class II) loci and the HLA-DR (Class I) loci and when appropriate immunosuppression accompanies the grafting. Once the donor has been selected on the basis of HLA matching, the donor's lymphocytes and recipient's lymphocytes are cultured for several days. The test is called the **mixed leukocyte reaction (MLR).** The object is to detect lymphocyte proliferation. For example, when lymphocytes from genetically dissimilar individuals are cultured together, transformation and mitosis occur. Each population of lymphocytes reacts against "foreign" determinants on the surface of the other lymphocyte population. The greater the proliferation, the greater the disparity between donor and recipient. The important proliferation is that of the recipient's lymphocytes because it reflects the degree of immunorejection. Therefore, the MLR test usually is modified by first treating the donor's lymphocytes with drugs or irradiation to inhibit donor cell multiplication. Donor lymphocytes act only as stimulators (Fig. 13-8).

Immunosuppression

The purposes of immunosuppressive procedures are to destroy lymphocytes before they recognize antigen, to prevent antigen-stimulated lymphocytes from proliferating, and to reduce inflammation. Immunosuppressive modalities include the following:

1. Immunosuppressive drugs. Azathioprine, mercaptopurine, and cyclophosphamide functioning as antimetabolites interfere with RNA or DNA synthesis. Proliferating lymphocytes and regrettably, other proliferating cells of the body, such as bone marrow cells and intestinal epithelial cells, are nonspecifically affected by these drugs. Cyclosporine, a more recent addition to the immunosuppressive drug armamentarium, appears to have a greater specificity for lymphocytes than for other cell types. Its primary

action is to inhibit the production of IL-2 and the IL-2 receptor, thereby preventing T cells from receiving the signal to divide. Corticosteroids have a similar action, and so they are frequently used, very effectively, in combination with cyclosporine.
2. Anti-inflammatory agents. Adrenocortical hormones depress phagocyte chemotaxis. They stabilize lysosome membranes, thereby affecting the ability of lysosomes to release graft-destroying hydrolytic enzymes.
3. Immunological measures. Equine antilymphocytic serum (ALS) is administered specifically to destroy T cells. The procedure is of variable effectiveness. Already proved effective in experimental animals is an anti–IL-2 monoclonal antibody that is covalently linked to the cytotoxic part of the diphtheria toxin molecule. The anti–IL-2 antibodies bind to T cells that were activated by recognition of donor MHC antigens. The attached toxin enters and selectively kills the T cells.
4. X-radiation. X-radiation destroys lymphoid tissue. Irradiation has largely been replaced by other immunosuppressive modalities. Furthermore, to be effective it must be done several days before transplantation. However, when cadaver organs are required, it usually is not possible to know beforehand when a suitable organ will be available.

Since most of these suppressive procedures affect the whole immune system, the immunocompromised patient has lowered resistance to infectious agents, including many opportunistically pathogenic microorganisms. However, the rate of infections has declined in recent years because transplant specialists have learned that patients do not require intensive antirejection therapy, as was once thought necessary.

IMMUNOLOGICALLY PRIVILEGED SITES AND TISSUES

Allografts to certain sites ordinarily are not immunorejected. For example, the avascularity of corneas apparently makes the foreign antigens of the graft inaccessible to the immune response. Tissue typing is not advantageous unless a second graft is required because of vascularization of the first graft. Grafts that become vascularized often are treatable with topical steroids to provide localized immunosuppression. Brain, because it lacks lymphatic drainage, and testicular antigens, because they are sequestered, are referred to as privileged sites or tissues.

Tumor Immunology (Cancer and the Immune System)

Tumors or neoplasms are abnormal growths of tissue to which the host's immune system may or may not respond. Many tumors are characterized by a transformation process in which there is an alteration of the surface antigens. Transformation may be due to chemical or physical agents or it may result from viral infection (see Chapter 31 for a discussion on viruses and cancer). How the immune system responds to the tumor depends on whether the new surface antigens are weakly or strongly immunogenic. In some instances the tumor cell can evade the immune response, a condition referred to as "immunological escape." In the following paragraphs we examine the host's response to tumors.

T CELL RESPONSE TO TUMORS

T lymphocytes play the most important role in tumor destruction. Tumor-associated antigens are shed and bind to APC. APC stimulate the activity of T and B cells, which in turn increase the activity of other cell types (Fig. 13-9). The cell types that may be involved in tumor destruction include

1. NK cells. T_H cells stimulated by tumor antigen release interferon gamma (IFN-γ) and IL-2, which recruit NK cells.
2. Macrophages. Macrophages are recruited and activated by IFN-γ. Activated macrophages exhibit cytolytic activity for tumor cells.
3. T_C cells. Cytotoxic lymphocytes, also recruited and activated by IFN-γ and IL-2, recognize tumor cells in association with MHC proteins.
4. Antibody-dependent cellular cytotoxicity (ADCC). Antibody released by plasma cells can bind to tumor cells. The Fc region of the bound antibodies attracts immunologically nonspecific cells such as macrophages, neutrophils, and NK cells. Complement may or may not be involved.

IMMUNOLOGICAL ESCAPE

One of the paradoxes of tumor immunology is how some immunogenic tumor-associated antigens escape the immune system. Immunological escape occurs when the factors favoring tumor growth outweigh the factors favoring tumor destruction. Factors contributing to immunological escape are

1. Antigen masking. Some tumor cell antigens are covered with molecules such as polysaccharides that prevent them from being recognized by lymphocytes or are poorly recognized.
2. Genetic factors. Some individuals with certain MHC determinants are poor inducers of a cytotoxic T cell response.
3. Blocking factors. Tumor-specific antigens when shed could bind to tumor-specific antibody. This antigen-antibody complex could bind directly to T_C cells and prevent their attachment to tumor cells. The antigen-antibody complex could also bind to T_H cells and prevent them from recognizing the tumor.
4. Dose response. Low doses of tumor cells may sneak through and not be recognized by the immune system. By the time the tumor cells grow and become

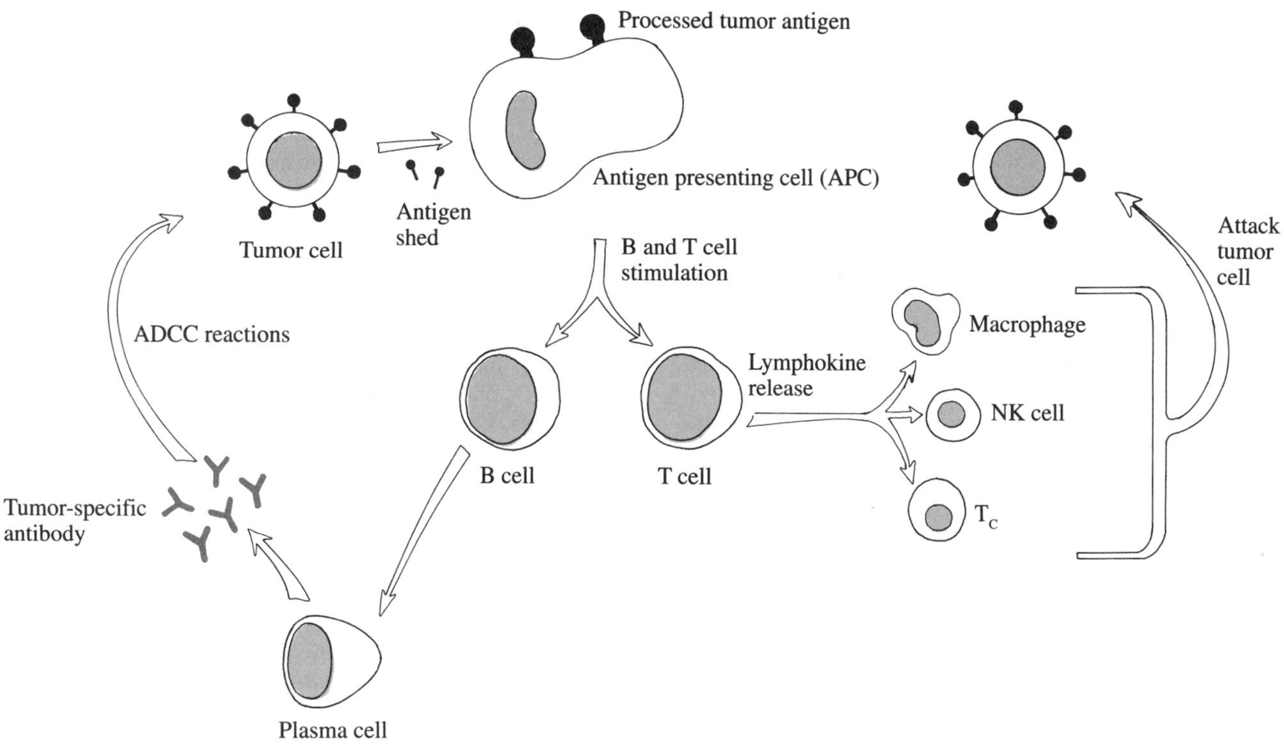

FIGURE 13-9
T cell response to tumors. The tumor cell sheds antigen, which is taken up by the antigen presenting cell (APC) and processed. APC stimulates B and T cells. B cell stimulation leads to the formation of tumor-specific antibody and involvement of antibody-dependent cytotoxicity (ADCC) reactions. Activated T cells (T_H) release lymphokines (interferon gamma), which activate and attract NK cells, macrophages, and T_C cells. The latter cells attack the tumor cell.

established, the immune system is too late in its response. In experimental animals low doses of tumor cells do sneak through and develop into tumors. Higher doses are recognized and eventually rejected.

TUMOR IMMUNOTHERAPY

Tumor immunotherapy can be divided into two broad categories: active and passive.

Active Immunotherapy

A variety of techniques are used to induce the patient's immune system to increase its production of immune products against tumor antigens, and include the following:

1. Stimulating the immune system to expand its responses. A variety of synthetic chemicals and certain microorganisms or their derivatives are used as immunostimulants. Two of the microorganisms used for this purpose are *Corynebacterium parvum* and mycobacteria. Mycobacteria are in the BCG vaccine used for immunization against tuberculosis.
2. Modifying the tumor cell surface to increase antigenicity. The tumor cell surface is altered by treatment with synthetic chemicals. Many tumor cells produce the polysaccharide called **sialomucin,** which serves as a protective coating for the cell surface, masking tumor antigens. The enzyme neuraminidase attacks sialomucin and thus exposes surface antigens.
3. Formation of tumor hybrids. Tumor cells from one species are fused with normal cells from another species, thereby making the hybrid cell more immunogenic because of the foreign antigens.
4. Use of cytokines. Interferons and IL-2 have antitumor effects in human models. Both are now available in quantity through recombinant DNA techniques. The postulated antitumor activities of interferons are that they directly prevent tumor cells from proliferating; they induce an increase of activated effector lymphocytes; and they induce tumor cell membrane antigens, thus allowing for better recognition by the immune system. IL-2 fosters lymphocyte activation and proliferation, NK cell activation, and the release of other lymphokines and hormones.

Passive Immunotherapy

Passive immunotherapy involves the transfer of antitumor antibody to cancer patients to cause tumor regression or prevent recurrence of the tumor. Some of the procedures involve the use of monoclonal antibodies and gene therapy.

Monoclonal antibodies, antibodies of a single kind (see preparation of monoclonal antibodies in Appendix B), can be produced in quantity using recombinant DNA technology. Monoclonal antibodies offer the advantages that they can be produced in quantity and they are specific. The specificity is related to the overexpression of tumor-associated antigen (TAA), compared to normal tissues. Production of human source monoclonal antibodies has not been very successful, in contrast to the readily available mouse antibodies. Recently, recombinant DNA technology has been used to couple mouse genes that code for the Fab portion of a monoclonal antitumor antibody with human genes that code for the Fc portion of the immunoglobulin molecule. The objective of the hybridization is to prevent an immune response to the mouse antigens and the later elimination of the tumor-specific monoclonal antibodies.

Another promising and highly important application of monoclonal antibodies is as a tumor seeking device. Radioactive labels are conjugated to tumor-specific monoclonal antibodies and tumor deposits or metastases are localized through use of appropriate radioactivity sensing devices. Other tumor destroying techniques can then be directed at the metastases. Monoclonal antibodies can also be used to deliver cytotoxic agents such as ricin (see Chapter 12 for discussion of this technique).

Experimental gene therapy was approved late in 1990 (see Under the Microscope 7) for the treatment of patients with advanced malignant melanomas. Genetic manipulation is used to amplify the natural cancer killing potential of tumor infiltrating lymphocytes (TIL). TIL obtained from cancer patients are cultured to yield billions of cells. Genes are inserted into the TIL that commands the cells to produce **TNF** and **IL-2.** The genetically engineered TIL, when reintroduced into the patient, are expected to localize in the tumor itself and produce the tumor killing factors. Experiments in mice have shown that cells genetically altered by TIL are very vigorous against cancer cells.

Summary

1. Immune responses are not always beneficial and can result in a variety of immunological disorders such as allergies, autoimmune diseases, and graft rejection.

2. Immunodeficiency diseases may be due to genetic, developmental, or acquired defects in immune components. These defects may affect stem cells, B and T cells, or phagocytes. Acquired immunodeficiencies may be the result of infections, age, ionizing radiation, or drugs that alter the immune system.

3. Allergies or hypersensitivities are divided into four types based on the mechanism of allergic injury. Types I, II, and III are of the immediate type (12 hours or less) and antibody-mediated. Type IV hypersensitivities are delayed (more than 12 hours) and are cell-mediated.

4. Type I hypersensitivities are of two types, depending on the allergen: systemic anaphylaxis, which can be fatal, and localized allergies, which are seldom fatal. On exposure to allergen, the host synthesizes IgE, which binds mast cells and sensitizes them. A second exposure to allergen activates mast cells to release pharmacologically active substances that bring about inflammation and a host of other responses.

5. Type II hypersensitivities are mediated by antibody and complement and cause damage to blood cells, platelets, and tissue cells. These hypersensitivities are seen most often in drug reactions.

6. Type III hypersensitivities are associated with immune complexes, which are initially small and some are cleared. A pathological response occurs when some immune complexes escape clearance and are deposited on blood vessel walls, kidney basement membrane, and synovial tissue. Immune complexes activate complement, causing inflammation and eventual destruction of healthy tissue.

7. Type IV hypersensitivities are associated with T cell activities. The allergen may be a microbial product of infection, such as tuberculin in *M. tuberculosis* infection. The allergen may also be a simple industrial or plant chemical that gives rise to allergic contact dermatitis. Activated T cells attract macrophages which are responsible for tissue damage.

8. Tolerance to self antigens is primarily due to clonal deletion and clonal anergy. Defects in the immune system can lead to autoimmune diseases which may be triggered by drugs, cross-reacting antigens of infectious agents, viral infection, or expression of secluded antigens. Autoimmune diseases are divided into two types: those that are organ-specific (e.g., myasthenia gravis) and those that are systemic (e.g., rheumatoid arthritis).

9. Grafts are usually rejected because the donor's immune system considers them nonself. Activated T cells are primarily responsible for graft rejection. Tissue cell destruction may be caused by macrophages, or cytotoxic T cells. Graft survival can be enhanced by using tissue typing to determine the degree of relatedness between donor and recipient and by employing immunosuppressive techniques.

10. Allografts to certain sites such as the brain and cornea are not rejected because they lack lymphatic drainage.

11. Tumors can escape immune surveillance even though some possess altered antigens. The altered antigens are not recognized or are poorly recognized. T cells play the most important role in destruction of tumor. Once tumor antigen is recognized, a variety of cells including NK cells, macrophages, and cytotoxic T cells can destroy the tumor.

12. Immunotherapy for tumors is divided into active and passive approaches. Active approaches rely on using synthetic chemicals, microbial products, and cytokines, for example, to stimulate the immune system of the cancer patient. Passive approaches involve the transfer of antitumor antibody to cause tumor regression or prevent tumor recurrence. Monoclonal antibodies and gene therapy are the most important passive approaches.

Questions for Study

1. Describe how IgE can have beneficial as well as detrimental effects in the immune response.
2. Survey your class for various types of allergies. Classify the allergies and describe the immunological response to each of them.
3. Describe the role, if any, of complement in hypersensitivities.
4. Using other references, determine what infectious agents give rise to hypersensitivity responses. What is the immunological basis for these sensitivities? What skin tests, if any, are used to determine this sensitivity?
5. What are the roles of mast cells in hypersensitivities?
6. Using other references, determine the immunological basis of blood transfusions.
7. Diagrammatically illustrate the cell types and mediators involved in the various types of hypersensitivities.

PART

IV Host-Parasite Interaction

CHAPTER

14 Microorganisms as Commensals and Parasites

OBJECTIVES

To differentiate between a commensal and a parasite, an intracellular and extracellular parasite, an infection and disease, pathogenicity and virulence, and exotoxin and endotoxin

To describe the various chemical and physical characteristics of the skin, mucosal surfaces, respiratory tract, genitourinary tract, and epithelial and subepithelial surfaces that resist invasion by microorganisms

To explain how the immunological state of the host, genetic constitution, nutrition, occupation, and underlying conditions affect the host's resistance to disease

To outline briefly what microbial factors contribute to the initiation of the infectious disease process

To explain how some microorganisms avoid host defense mechanisms

OUTLINE

MICROORGANISMS AS COMMENSALS AND PARASITES
- Commensalism
- Parasitism
  - Extracellular Parasites
  - Intracellular Parasites

TERMINOLOGY ASSOCIATED WITH THE INFECTIOUS DISEASE PROCESS

HOST FACTORS AFFECTING THE DISEASE PROCESS
- Portal of Entry
  - Skin
  - Mucosal Surfaces
  - Respiratory Tract
  - Oropharynx
  - Intestinal Tract
  - Genitourinary Tract
- Subepithelial Factors
- Factors Influencing Host Resistance to Infection
  - Immunological State of the Host
  - Genetic Constitution of the Host
  - Race
  - Nutrition
  - Occupation
  - Underlying Conditions

MICROBIAL FACTORS AND THE DISEASE PROCESS
- Adherence to Host Tissue
  - Adhesins
- Invasion of the Host
  - Invasion of Host Cells
- Toxins
  - Exotoxins
  - Endotoxins
- Endotoxin and Gram-Negative Septicemia
- Avoiding Host Defense Mechanisms
  - Antiphagocytic Factors
  - Antigenic Variation (Changing Surface Chemistry)
  - Serum Resistance

One important area of microbiological research involves the host-parasite relationship. A knowledge of the chemistry and molecular biology of this process will eventually lead to the development of vaccines to prevent disease. The purpose of this chapter is to describe the factors, both microbial and host-related, that are associated with the disease process.

Microorganisms as Commensals and Parasites

The human body is a shelter and source of nutrients for many microorganisms, primarily bacteria and secondarily fungi. Microorganisms that benefit from this association without harming the host are referred to as **commensals.** A **parasitic** relationship is one in which the microorganism benefits at the expense of its host. Let us look more closely at these two associations.

COMMENSALISM

Before birth the fetus is essentially in a sterile environment, but at delivery microorganisms come into contact with the infant. Some of these microorganisms are derived from the mother or others who come into contact with the infant. Most microorganisms are transient passersby that are destroyed by conditions in the host, but others establish themselves and produce microcolonies. This latter group has therefore **colonized** the host. As several types of microorganisms colonize a particular body site, the **microflora** are established. The factors that influence the kind and number of microorganisms at any body site are (1) the availability or unavailability of oxygen, (2) the availability of appropriate receptor sites for attachment, (3) the pH of the host site, (4) the availability of nutrients, (5) the influence exerted by other microorganisms at the site, and (6) the immunological response of the host to the presence of the microorganism.

Not all areas of the body are occupied by commensal species. There are appreciable numbers of microorganisms in the upper respiratory tract, lower intestinal tract, and skin (see Appendix D). Areas such as the esophagus, urinary tract, and stomach contain few microorganisms. The blood, spinal fluid, urine, and endothelial tissues are normally sterile.

The indigenous microflora remain with the host for life, with only minor changes resulting from disease, dietary alterations, or hormonal changes. Many of the indigenous microorganisms may be important in maintaining the health of the host. For example, in some animals microorganisms of the intestinal tract are capable of synthesizing vitamins such as pantothenic acid, riboflavin, and vitamin B_{12}. It has been suggested that certain vitamin deficiencies in the human diet can be remedied by bacterial vitamin synthesis in the intestinal tract. Experiments on germ-free animals have also demonstrated that without intestinal microflora there is a reduction in the size and plasticity of the digestive tract, compared with that in conventional animals. In addition, some commensals produce metabolic products that are effective in preventing invasion by parasites. For example, commensals in the intestinal tract produce fatty acids that inhibit ingested bacteria that attempt to colonize the host.

There is a dynamic relationship among commensals that make up the microflora of any particular body site. In general terms, the gram-positive bacteria control the number of gram-negative bacteria and vice versa, while both groups of bacteria control the concentration of yeasts. Any established member of the normal microflora is recognized as such and the host's immune system does not respond to it as a foreign body.

PARASITISM

Any microorganism that can inhabit the human body is a potential parasite and this includes commensals. Commensals cause disease only when the host's defenses have been compromised by such things as age, underlying disease, poor nutrition, burns, and so on. Parasitism may or may not result in damage to the host. Many parasites, such as the human immunodeficiency virus (HIV) which causes the acquired immunodeficiency syndrome (AIDS), bring about devastating changes in the host. If the host dies, one chain of transmission of the parasite to other hosts is lost. The most successful parasite is one that obtains enough nutrients to multiply in the host without causing major damage. In this way the way the parasite can be maintained indefinitely within its population of hosts.

Most successful parasites are able to colonize the host because the host has been compromised by some condition or disease. In addition, the parasite may possess such potent weapons that it can overcome the host's normal defense mechanisms. Once the parasite enters its host, it may take up residence in one of two ways. First, the parasite may be capable of entering various cells of the body, that is, exist as an **intracellular parasite.** Second, it may remain attached to the surface of host tissue, that is, become an **extracellular parasite.** Let us examine both options.

Extracellular Parasites

Extracellular parasites are exposed to many of the host's defensive forces that are exerted at cell or tissue surfaces (see Toxins). An important characteristic of many extracellular parasites is the ability to produce potent **toxins** or other proteins that enable them to colonize and damage tissue. Many of these microbial products quickly induce an inflammatory response (see Chapter 9), which helps the host recover from the disease. Extracellular parasites usually cause diseases referred to as **acute;** that is, the symptoms of disease appear for only a short period and then quickly subside. Recovery from diseases caused by extracellular parasites often occurs within a few days.

Intracellular Parasites

Only a few microorganisms, except viruses, are able to carry out their life cycle within the environment of a host cell. When invaded by a microorganism, the host cell is not an entirely peaceful environment. Many host cells,

TABLE 14-1
Some of the Major Intracellular Parasites

Parasite	Obligate (O) or facultative (F)
Virus	
All viruses	O
Bacteria	
Mycobacterium tuberculosis	F
Neisseria gonorrhoeae	F
Salmonella typhi	F
Legionella pneumophila	F
Brucella species	F
Listeria monocytogenes	F
Francisella tularensis	F
Rickettsia species	O
Chlamydia species	O
Protozoa	
Plasmodium vivax	O

such as macrophages, possess molecules that can degrade and kill invading microorganisms. The intracellular parasite must be equipped with special attributes that enable it to defend itself against cellular obstacles. Even as important, the parasite must not impair any host functions that are essential to the parasite's own survival and multiplication. For example, the protozoan *Plasmodium vivax*, which causes malaria, must remain in the red blood cell of its host to use certain coenzymes that the parasite cannot produce. A quickly killed red blood cell is of no use to the parasite.

Despite the potential pitfalls for microorganisms living within host cells, there are advantages to intracellular living. As we have already mentioned, some microorganisms are totally dependent on certain metabolic products found only in the intracellular environment. In addition, the intracellular parasite is not directly exposed to various immune forces such as antibodies, immune cells, complement, and other immune factors found in the bloodstream.

Intracellular parasites are of two types (Table 14-1): those that can live inside or outside host cells **(facultative intracellular parasites)** and those that can replicate only inside host cells **(obligate intracellular parasites).** Diseases caused by intracellular parasites (except viruses) are usually **chronic** in nature. Thus, disease symptoms appear over an extended period (weeks to months) because immune factors are not in direct contact with the parasite.

Terminology Associated with the Infectious Disease Process

The terms **infection** and **disease** are often used synonymously in discussions of the host-parasite relationship. When microorganisms make contact with a host, three things can happen: (1) The host does not respond to the presence of the microorganism and the latter acts as a **colonizer;** (2) the host responds to the microorganism by producing antibodies—thus, an infection takes place; and (3) the host produces antibodies in response to the microorganism and the latter causes tissue damage—that is, a **disease** occurs.

Terms that also deserve explanation are **pathogenic** and **virulence.** Microorganisms that are able to cause disease are said to be pathogenic (noun, pathogen). As you have probably surmised, some microorganisms are more pathogenic than others. For example, a strain of *Streptococcus pneumoniae* (strain A) that does not produce a capsule is unable to cause the type of disease that is associated with a capsule-producing strain (strain B). Thus, strain B is more pathogenic than strain A. Pathogenicity is a very qualitative term that describes a microorganism's disease-producing potential. A more quantitative measurement of a microorganism's disease-producing abilities is termed virulence. The virulence of microorganisms is related to their capacity either to invade tissue **(invasiveness)** or to produce **toxins** that affect host tissue. Among the literally thousands of microbial species, probably no more than 300 can be described as virulent. Virulence determinations often measure the number of microorganisms or amount of microbial product, such as toxins, that can cause death or disease in 50 percent of the test animals (Fig. 14-1). These measurements are referred to as LD_{50} (median lethal dose) or ID_{50} (median infectious dose), respectively.

Virulence is a property that can be modified in the laboratory. A highly virulent microorganism may lose its virulence on serial passage of the microbe in unnatural hosts. Some microorganisms demonstrate variations in their virulence, depending on their location in the host. For example, there may be variations in the type of microbial surface proteins required for adherence or there may be loss of a toxin. Environmental factors such as nutrient supply and temperature also have been observed to control virulence. Iron, for example, has been recognized as a factor in the formation of diphtheria toxin (see Chapter 20, Pathogenesis). The loss or substantial reduction of virulence is referred to as **attenuation.** Our ability to attenuate microorganisms enables us to produce vaccines. Many vaccines (polio, measles, and mumps vaccines) are merely attenuated microbial agents. When attenuated vaccines are injected into the body, they do not cause disease but they can stimulate the formation of antibodies that can ward off future infections.

There are situations in which highly pathogenic microorganisms may not be pathogenic. For example, some individuals, because of certain inherited genetic traits, can be infected by a pathogen but not show symptoms of disease. Individuals who harbor these pathogens and show no disease symptoms are called **carriers** (see Chapter 15, Animate Reservoirs).

The diseases caused by microbial agents are not always

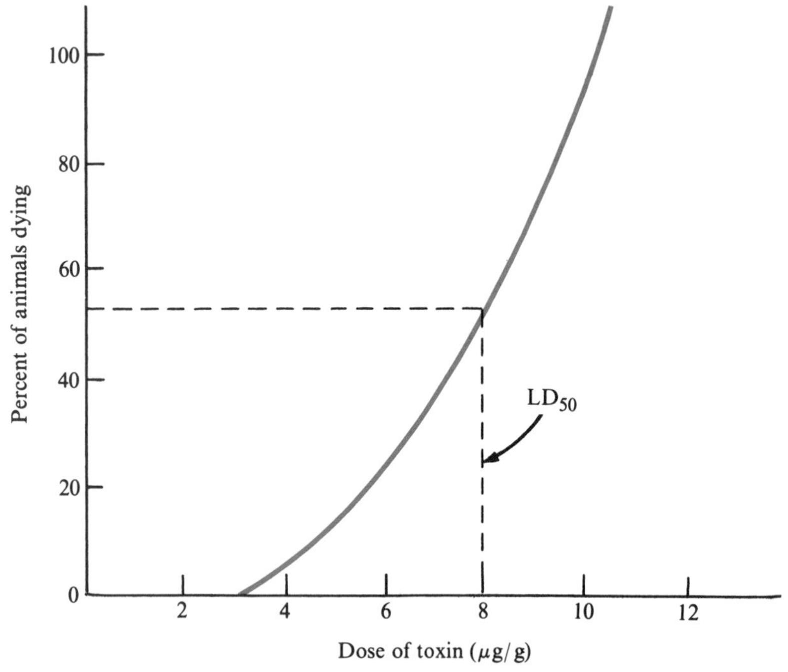

FIGURE 14-1
Determination of the 50 percent lethal dose (LD_{50}) for a toxin. Various doses of toxin are injected into animals. The percentage of animals that die is plotted and the LD_{50} is extrapolated. In this figure 8 μg of toxin per gram of animal is the LD_{50}.

the same in terms of location or host response. The following terms explain the various types of disease:

Local. A disease that is restricted to a confined area.
Focal. A localized site of disease from which bacteria and their products are spread to other parts of the body.
Systemic. A disease in which the microorganism or its products can spread throughout the body, not necessarily from a localized site.
Primary. A disease caused by one microbial species.
Secondary. A primary disease complicated with a second pathogen (for example, pneumonia following primary influenza).
Mixed. A disease caused by two or more microorganisms.
Inapparent or Subclinical. A disease that does not give rise to any detectable overt symptoms.
Latent. A disease in which the microbial agent persists in the tissues in a dormant state and later becomes activated to induce symptoms.
Bacteremia. A transitory disease in which bacteria present in the blood are usually cleared from the vascular system with no harmful effects. Other microbial agents, such as fungi **(fungemia)** and viruses **(viremia),** may also be present in the blood.
Septicemia. A condition in which the blood serves as a site of bacterial multiplication as well as a means of transfer of the infectious agent from one site to another.
Pyemia. The presence of pyogenic (pus forming, such as staphylococci and streptococci) bacteria in the blood as they are being spread from one site to another in the body.
Toxemia. The presence of microbial toxins in the bloodstream.

The properties of pathogenicity and virulence are not stable and are influenced by host as well as microbial factors. In the following paragraphs we discuss how these factors affect the outcome of host-parasite interactions.

Host Factors Affecting the Disease Process

PORTAL OF ENTRY

The body surface presents various sites for the entry of microorganisms. Each site offers resistance to the establishment of microorganisms not indigenous to the host. Moreover, microorganisms that make up the normal microbial flora release metabolic products that prevent colonization by potential pathogens acquired from the environment.

Skin

The tough, thick outer layer of the skin (Fig. 14-2) is a natural barrier to invading microorganisms. The cells of the outer layer of skin have a rapid turnover (14 days). Most are released into the environment (a process called **desquamation**). Pathogenic microorganisms, therefore, have only a limited time in which to invade the host. Secretions from sebaceous glands (sebum) are broken down into fatty acids by resident microorganisms (for example, *Corynebacterium, Staphylococcus epidermidis*). The fatty acids cover the skin's surface and have an antimicrobial effect on *Staphylococcus aureus* and streptococci. Fatty acids have a stimulatory effect on commensal *Propionibacterium* species. *Propionibacterium* organisms produce propionic acid, which has an antimicrobial effect on many

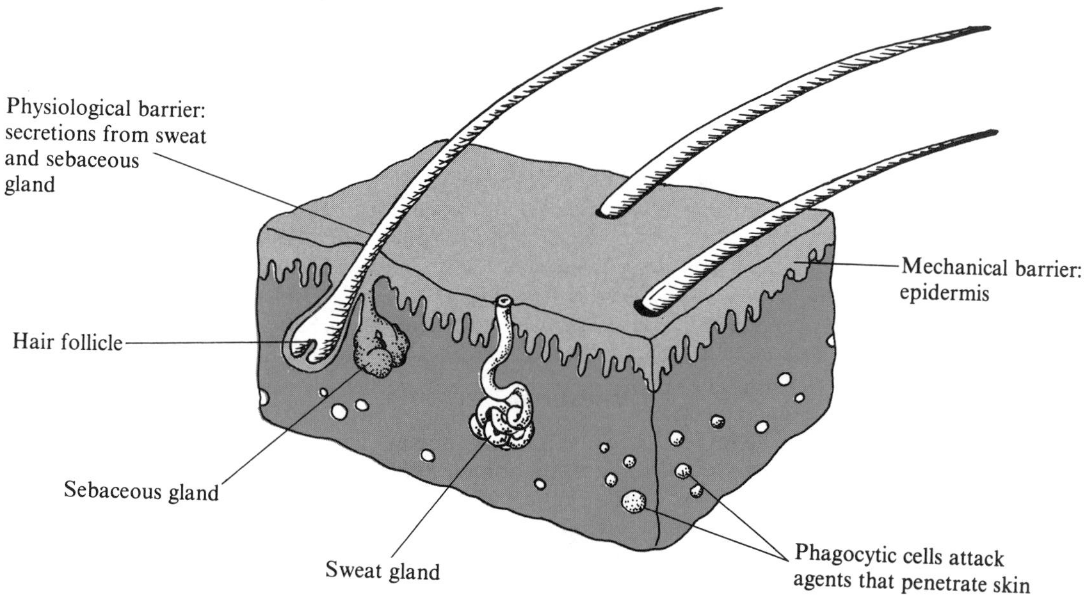

FIGURE 14-2
Cross section of the skin demonstrating the barriers to infectious agents.

species of bacteria. Sweat contains secretory IgA, which probably explains why sweat glands are not colonized by bacteria.

Resident microorganisms are not pathogenic unless the skin becomes abraded and the individual's natural immune mechanisms become depressed. Microorganisms may enter the host through skin abrasions, or they may be transferred by the bite of animals or insects. The rabies virus, for example, can be transmitted to humans by the bite of dogs, carnivorous wild animals (especially skunks, raccoons, foxes, and coyotes), and bats. Other infectious agents, including the causal agents of plague, malaria, and Rocky Mountain spotted fever, are transmitted by insect bites. Another means of entry into the host is via needles or by implantation of prosthetic devices. Skin commensals such as *S. epidermidis* are all too often causes of severe infections following placement of prosthetic heart implants (see Chapter 17, Coagulase-Negative Staphylococci).

Mucosal Surfaces

The mucosal surface is one of the first surfaces on which microorganisms make contact with the host. The gastrointestinal tract, respiratory tract, salivary and lacrimal glands, biliary system, and portions of the genitourinary tract all have mucosal surfaces. Many of these surfaces are in contact with the external environment. A variety of host defense mechanisms are available at the mucosal surface to prevent parasite colonization.

1. Immunological defenses. The most important component of the immunological defense at the mucosal surface is secretory IgA. Secretory IgA prevents microbial attachment at the mucosal surface (see Chapter 10 for details). It should be pointed out that some pathogenic bacteria, such as species of *Neisseria, Hemophilus,* and *Streptococcus,* produce a protease that cleaves secretory IgA. Protease production may therefore be considered a virulence factor.
2. Microflora. The sites at which an invading microorganism may enter the host (skin, respiratory tract, digestive tract) are usually colonized by an indigenous population of microorganisms (see Appendix D). Indigenous microorganisms can act antagonistically toward potential invaders by (1) producing substances such as bacteriocins (see Chapter 15, Bacteriocin Typing) that are lethal for closely related species or inhibitory to unrelated species; (2) competitive inhibition—that is, the indigenous species occupies body sites, making them unavailable to the invader; and (3) fatty acid production by anaerobes in the intestinal tract. *Shigella* and *Salmonella* species are inhibited by fatty acids.
3. Mucins. Mucins are hydrophilic glycoproteins that form a film in the intestinal tract and a partial coat in the respiratory tract. Mucins lubricate and waterproof the mucosal surface, but they also prevent adherence of some microorganisms or their toxic products. Microorganisms bound by mucins may be removed via ciliary action in the respiratory tract or by peristalsis in the intestinal tract.
4. Lysozyme, lactoferrin, and peroxidase. These substances on the mucosal surface aid in the defense against microbial invasion. Lysozyme, which is found in tears, nasal secretions, breast milk, and genital fluids, acts directly on the bacterial cell wall (see Chapter 2, Osmosis and Cells Without Cell Walls, for details). Lactoferrin is an iron binding protein whose importance is discussed later in the chapter.

Peroxidase is found in saliva and, in combination with thiocyanate and hydrogen peroxide, is active against several bacteria, fungi, and viruses (see Chapter 9, Fig. 9-6 for details).

Respiratory Tract

Inhaled air contains suspended particles of various sizes. The inhaled particles may include dust; epithelial cells shed from skin, which may contain microorganisms; freely suspended molds or bacterial spores; and suspended aerosols from sneezing and coughing, which may also contain microorganisms. Particles that are 10 μm in diameter or larger seldom reach the lungs because of the mucociliary blanket that covers the respiratory tract (Fig. 14-3). Cilia lining the nasal cavity trap particles and sweep them to the throat, where they are swallowed. The lower part of the respiratory tract contains macrophages that aid in resistance (see Chapter 9). When host defense mechanisms for the respiratory tract become defective, some microorganisms are equipped to adhere strongly to the respiratory epithelium (Fig. 14-4) and may be the cause of serious infections such as whooping cough and bacterial and viral pneumonias. Other agents, such as the causative agent of tuberculosis, can be ingested by macrophages but remain infective because immune responses are impaired.

Pulmonary secretions contain antibodies such as IgG and IgM, as well as complement, lysozyme, and **fibronectin.** Fibronectin is a glycoprotein found in plasma as well as extracellular matrices. Fibronectin can bind gram-positive bacteria, such as staphylococci and streptococci, and promote phagocytosis.

FIGURE 14-3
Diagram of the respiratory tract showing the barriers to infectious agents. Alveoli contain phagocytic cells that engulf parasites.

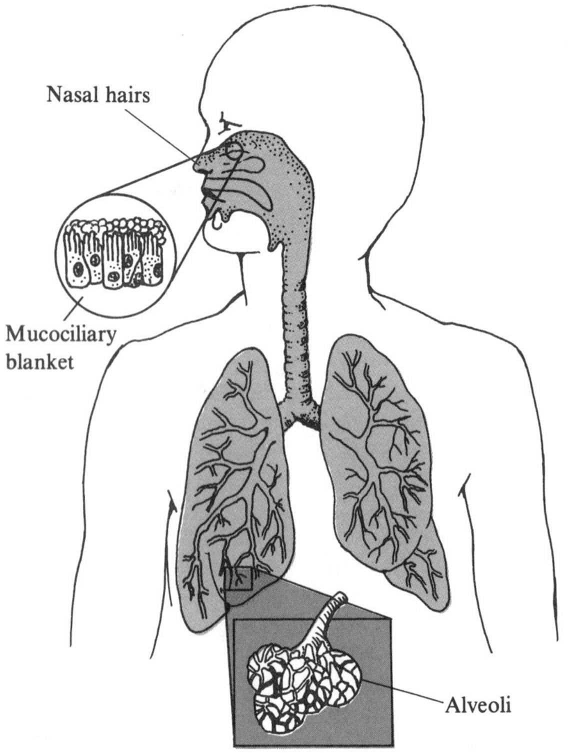

Oropharynx

Microorganisms in the oral cavity are numerous (see Appendix D). Gingival fluid has as many as 1×10^{10} microorganisms per milliliter. Saliva is responsible for flushing out microorganisms from the oral cavity. When salivary flow is impeded, for example, by anesthesia, the numbers of microorganisms increase. Saliva also contains such microbial inhibitors as lysozyme and secretory antibodies.

Intestinal Tract

Many microorganisms can enter the intestinal tract by ingestion of food and drink. Those that are indigenous to the oral cavity are also swallowed. Organisms that survive the acid conditions of the stomach, for example, by being wrapped in a bolus of food, enter the intestinal tract and encounter antimicrobial forces such as acids, bile salts, and enzymes. Commensal bacteria are associated primarily with the intestinal epithelium. Commensals prevent pathogen colonization by techniques described under Host Factors Affecting the Disease Process. The mucus lining the epithelial surface is a mechanical barrier to pathogen colonization. This mucus layer also contains secretory IgA which protects against infection. Still, these barriers to infection can be breached by certain microorganisms such as *Salmonella typhi* and *Vibrio cholerae.* The latter can attach to microvilli on the epithelial surface and enter the epithelial cell by a process similar to phagocytosis (see below). Commensal bacteria, however, do not penetrate epithelial cells.

Genitourinary Tract

Under normal conditions, urine in the bladder is a sterile fluid. When it contains large numbers of microorganisms, serious infection is often indicated. Infections of the urogenital tract occur more frequently when structural abnormalities prevent normal flow or flushing action of urine. Women are more prone to such infections because of the shortness of the urethra and its proximity to the anus with its indigenous microflora. A group of bacteria called the lactobacilli dominate the vaginal flora of normal healthy women. *Lactobacillus* species break down glycogen, a component of the vaginal epithelium, into lactic acid. Lactic acid maintains the acidity of the vagina and prevents infection by pathogenic species. Pathogens able to colonize the vagina can dominate the microflora and ascend to infect the bladder.

SUBEPITHELIAL FACTORS

Many parasites are not endowed with invasive factors that enable them to penetrate the epithelial surface. Some infectious agents summon a disease response by remaining on the epithelial surface. For example, *Corynebacterium diphtheriae,* the agent of diphtheria, multiplies on the epithelial surface of the respiratory tract. There it produces

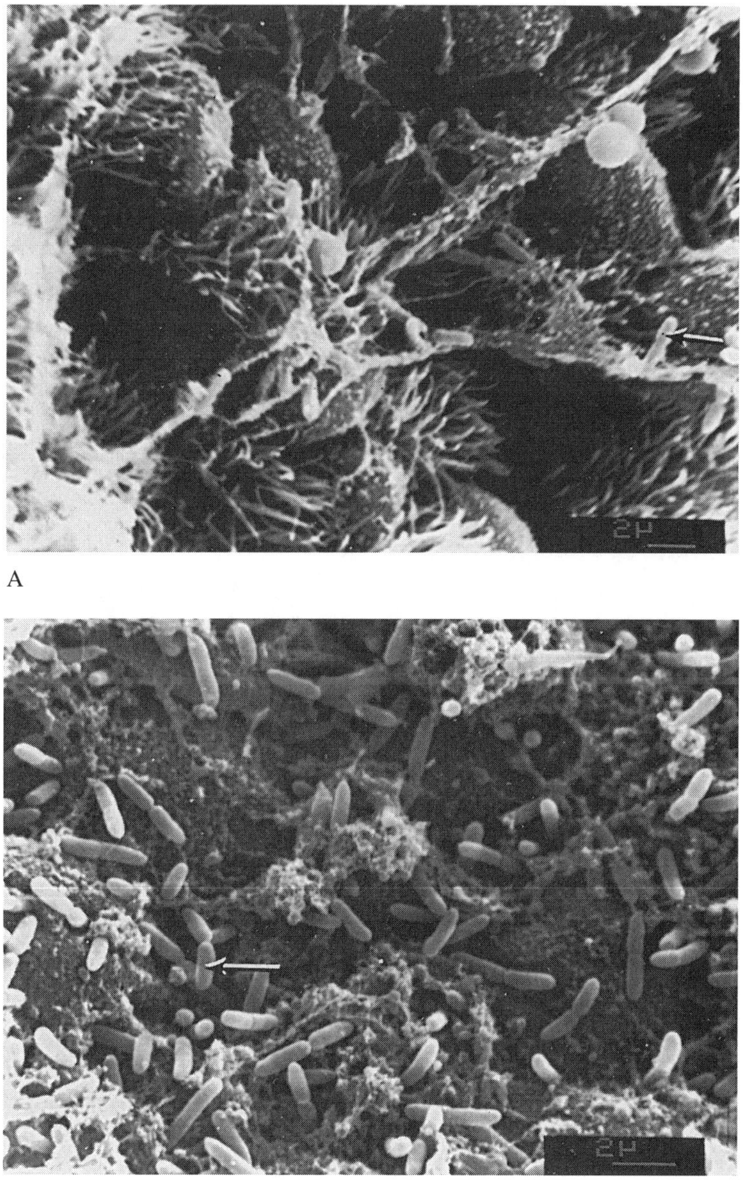

A

B

FIGURE 14-4
Effect of an environmental factor on the adherence of microorganisms to respiratory epithelium. A. Normal tracheal cells, in which a few rare bacteria *(arrow)* can be found adhering to cilia. B. Tracheal cells that have been injured with acid. Many bacilli *(arrow)* can be seen to adhere. (From R. Ramphal and M. Pyle, *Infect. Immun.* 41:345, 1983.)

a toxin that penetrates the bloodstream and is carried to other parts of the body. Respiratory viruses as well as viruses causing warts are also examples of infectious agents remaining on epithelial surfaces.

Microorganisms that penetrate the epithelial surface encounter three antimicrobial defense mechanisms: (1) tissue fluids, (2) the lymph system, and (3) phagocytic cells (see Chapter 9 for details of these mechanisms). Sometimes the microorganism can evade these antimicrobial forces. The agent of tuberculosis, *Mycobacterium tuberculosis,* is engulfed by phagocytes but is resistant to phagocytic digestion. The phagocyte provides the organism a habitat for avoiding the host's other defense mechanisms such as tissue factors and antibodies. This is one reason why diseases such as tuberculosis are **chronic** and difficult to cure.

FACTORS INFLUENCING HOST RESISTANCE TO INFECTION

Immunological State of the Host

As stated previously, the major factor that determines the outcome of microbial infection is the immunological state of the host. Today diseases such as measles are not nearly as devastating as they were several hundred years ago. Present populations have developed a more benign relationship with the microorganisms causing disease. Repeated infections in a community have resulted in the selection of resistant individuals. That this process has taken place is evident from studies of infectious diseases that have occurred in isolated communities throughout the world.

Immunosuppressed or immunocompromised individuals are more susceptible to disease than are normal healthy individuals. Compromised individuals are also more likely to be infected by what we would normally consider "nonpathogenic" or opportunistic microorganisms. The AIDS patient, in whom the immune system is depressed, is a classic example of how opportunistic microorganisms gain a foothold. In normal individuals *Pneumocystis carinii* is of little or no consequence, but in AIDS patients it is one of the leading causes of death. The use of immunosuppressive drugs such as corticosteroids or radiation treatment interferes with normal immune responses. These treatments make the host susceptible to a host of microbial agents. Individuals may also be immunocompromised because they have defects in which no immunoglobulins or abnormal ones are produced.

In children and older adults the immune system is also depressed. These two groups are frequently more susceptible to respiratory diseases such as pneumonia.

Genetic Constitution of the Host

The genetic constitution of the host contributes to the susceptibility to infectious disease since nonspecific and specific immune defense mechanisms are also genetically controlled. Our genes determine the type and chemistry of anatomical or physiological barriers as well as the type and chemistry of cellular and biochemical defense mechanisms. For example, host cells and tissues may not possess the appropriate receptors for microbial adhesion. Additionally, the temperature of a particular site may not be conducive to microbial multiplication. Host genetic composition also functions at the level of the immune response.

Products of human leukocyte antigen (HLA) genes are involved in antigen presentation to the immune system. There is considerable evidence that susceptibility to rheumatic fever, for example, operates via immune response genes. In rheumatic fever there is cross reactivity between microbial antigens and self antigens of the heart (see Chapter 17).

Race

A biochemical basis for racial immunity is known and involves the disease malaria. Individuals with the sickle cell trait have a genetic defect in which the red blood cell shows a resistance to the parasite causing malaria. In contrast, humans with the sickle cell trait are also more susceptible to extraintestinal *Salmonella* infection than are healthy individuals.

Nutrition

The nutrition of the individual may also contribute to the disease process. In general, one can say that if the health of the host is seriously impaired by inadequate nutrition, infections are more likely to occur. Considerable evidence has shown that **iron** plays a role in the host's susceptibility to disease. Iron is required by most living organisms. It is a component of cytochromes and is involved in electron transport (see Chapter 3). Iron is found in high concentrations in the host (approximately 4.5 gm in an adult human), but most of this is unavailable to an infecting microorganism. Any free iron in the host is in an insoluble ferric form (Fe^{3+}). This creates a condition in which the pathogen must compete with the host.

Iron in host tissue is normally complexed with iron binding proteins that are found in most body fluids such as **transferrin, lactoferrin,** and **ferritin.** Some bacteria have evolved special mechanisms for accumulating iron and transporting it into their cytoplasm. These bacterial iron transport systems are associated with the iron binding compounds called **siderophores** (Fig. 14-5). Bacterial siderophores are able to remove iron from transferrin and other iron binding molecules. The mechanism by which the bacterial cell removes iron from the siderophore is not known.

Transferrin and lactoferrin exhibit bacteriostatic effects in the host, but this activity is lost when these molecules become saturated with iron. Lactoferrin is present in high concentrations in human milk and is probably responsible for inhibiting microorganisms, such as *Escherichia coli*, that cause gastroenteritis. Breast milk has occasionally been used to stop outbreaks of enteritis when all other methods of treatment have failed. The bottom line is that **iron overload** increases the risk of infection while host iron-withholding systems decrease the risk of infection (see Under the Microscope 9).

Occupation

Occupation is an important factor in susceptibility to infection. One would expect more infections of tularemia (rabbit fever) and brucellosis in persons who are exposed to animals and animal hides—hunters, stockyard workers, and veterinarians. Hepatitis, which can be acquired through infected blood or blood products, is more prevalent among surgeons, nurses, and others who work in hospitals than in the general population.

Underlying Conditions

Underlying conditions or diseases are major predisposing factors to infection. Diabetics, for example, whose disease is not under control by insulin or diet are particularly prone to tuberculosis and staphylococcal infections. The patient with heart disease is also susceptible to infections of heart tissue. Some streptococci in the oral cavity, for

FIGURE 14-5
Structure of one type of siderophore. Sites of iron binding are in color.

$$NH_2(CH_2)_5 N - C(CH_2)_2 CONH(CH_2)_5 N - C(CH_2)_2 CONH(CH_2)_5 N - C - CH_3$$

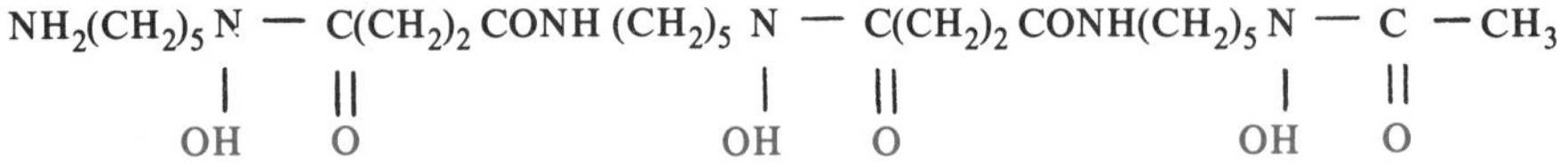

UNDER THE MICROSCOPE 9

Avoiding Iron Overload

Infection at body sites is often associated with the presence of excess iron. Iron not only is required for microbial growth but also suppresses chemotaxis, phagocytosis, and the microbicidal activity of mononuclear and polynuclear leukocytes. As we discussed previously, lactoferrin and transferrin are effective in reducing the amount of iron that is available for utilization by microbial cells. When molecules of lactoferrin become about 40 percent saturated, they are ingested by macrophages and the metal is assimilated into the iron seclusion protein **ferritin.**

Recently researchers discovered how the withholding of iron might defend the host against intracellular pathogens. Interferon gamma induces a flavoprotein that converts ·-arginine to ·-citrulline plus nitric oxide. Nitric oxide causes the efflux of nonheme iron from infected host cells. In addition, macrophages, in the absence of ·-arginine, induced by interferon gamma can lower their net uptake of iron, thereby suppressing intracellular growth of intracellular pathogens such as *Legionella pneumophila* and *Listeria monocytogenes.*

Despite the host's ability to withhold iron from potential pathogens, infections still occur. Cultural and clinical conditions can compromise the iron-withholding defense system. These include the following:

1. Transferrin or ferritin deficit
2. Hemoglobin disorders such as thalassemia or sickle cell anemia
3. Multiple transfusions of whole blood or erythrocytes
4. Reduction in normal menstrual flow
5. Ingestion of iron tablets
6. Excessive consumption of red meats

Further details of this system can be found in the article by Weinberg, listed under Additional Readings.

example, may be displaced into the bloodstream during oral surgery. In healthy persons these microorganisms are rapidly cleared from the circulation. In the patient with heart disease the streptococci adhere to the damaged heart tissue and set up foci of infection.

Microbial Factors and the Disease Process

ADHERENCE TO HOST TISSUE

The human species possess several physical and chemical barriers to infectious agents. These barriers are, except for minor differences, the same in all individuals. The similarity of these barriers has resulted in the evolution of microorganisms that utilize mechanisms based on a common or similar theme.

Unless the microorganism enters the host via an insect bite or inoculation by needle or implant device, it will adhere to some body surface. Adherence represents the first and most important microbial mechanism for initiating the infectious disease process.

Adherence to tissue at some body sites can be a formidable event. For example, in the respiratory tract a microorganism must deal with the mucociliary blanket before attachment can be made. Attachment requires the participation of a **receptor** on the host and a molecule on the surface of the microbe called an **adhesin.** In chemical terms host receptors are invariably carbohydrates while adhesins are usually proteins.

Adhesins

Pili are prominent adhesins found in many gram-negative species such as members of the Enterobacteriaceae. Strains of *E. coli* possess one type of pilus, referred to as **type 1 pili** (Fig. 14-6). Type 1 pili bind to receptors containing the sugar mannose. *E. coli* can produce other types of pili depending on the type of tissue or condition encountered. Two or more pili are not usually expressed simultaneously.

Gram-positive organisms, such as *Streptococcus pyogenes,* adhere to epithelial cells of the skin and nasopharynx. Epithelial cell surfaces are covered with the plasma glycoprotein **fibronectin.** Fibronectin acts as a receptor for the **lipoteichoic acid** adhesin of *S. pyogenes* (Fig. 14-7). Fibronectin represents a classic example of the delicate balance between health and disease. Fibronectin binds to bacteria to promote phagocytosis but it also may bind to epithelial surfaces to promote microbial adhesion.

The gram-negative bacterium *V. cholerae* attaches to receptors on the intestinal wall by adhesins located on the surface of the flagellum. *V. cholerae* would normally be discharged out of the intestinal tract by peristalsis but the flagellum propels it to a suitable surface for attachment. This propulsion, which represents a chemotactic process, was discussed in Chapter 2.

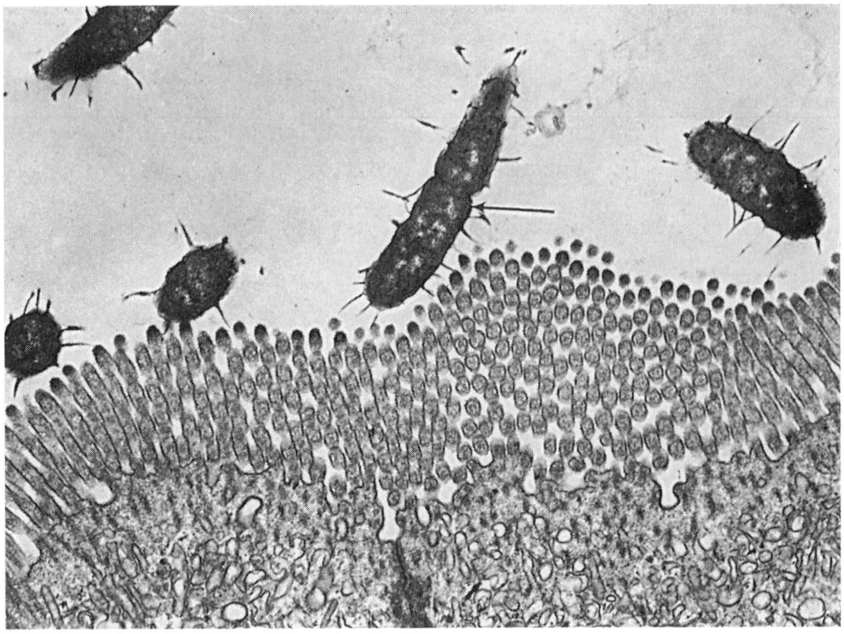

FIGURE 14-6
Electron micrograph demonstrating attachment of *Escherichia coli (arrow)* to the intestinal epithelium. The pili can be seen to project from the surface of the bacterial cells and are in contact with the host cell surface. (From H. W. Moon, B. Nagy, and R. E. Isaacson, *J. Infect. Dis.* 136[Suppl.]:124, 1977.)

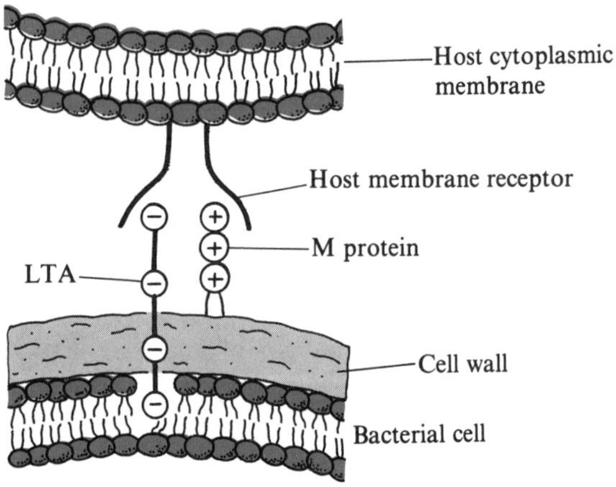

FIGURE 14-7
Lipoteichoic acid (LTA) attachment process. LTA associated with the cytoplasmic membrane of the bacterial cell is negatively charged. Positively charged M protein of *Streptococcus pyogenes* binds to LTA at the surface, leaving exposed lipid ends that bind to receptors on the host cell.

Once a microorganism becomes attached to a tissue or cell surface, it may remain there as an **extracellular parasite** or it may invade cells to become an **intracellular parasite** (see Parasitism). Some extracellular parasites cannot penetrate host cells because of temperature restrictions. For example, many fungi that cause superficial infections cannot multiply at the general temperature of the body (37 C). They can, however, multiply at lower temperatures on the surface of the body. Extracellular parasites, such as the agent of diphtheria *(C. diphtheriae)*, are unable to withstand host defense mechanisms and are restricted to the epithelial surface of the respiratory tract (see Under the Microscope 10).

INVASION OF THE HOST

Some microorganisms do not remain on the epithelial surface but instead penetrate to subepithelial layers where antimicrobial defense mechanisms await them (see Subepithelial Factors). Microbes surviving this encounter can enter lymphatics and be delivered to lymph nodes for destruction. The microorganisms able to withstand the battle in the lymph nodes can be spread throughout the body. Occasionally microorganisms may damage small blood vessels in the subepithelium and directly enter the bloodstream. The ability to penetrate below the epithelium is a trait referred to as **invasiveness.** Several microbial products associated with invasiveness and spread of microorganisms throughout the body are listed in Table 14-2. Most invasive factors are enzymes. Their activities are believed to play some role, but not the only one, in the pathogenesis of infectious agents.

Spread via lymphatics and direct invasion of the bloodstream are not the only avenues of microbial dissemination. Occasionally microorganisms invade the cerebrospinal fluid by spanning the blood-cerebrospinal junction in the meninges. Organisms such as the bacteria *Neisseria meningitidis* and *Hemophilus influenzae* and the fungus *Cryptococcus neoformans* can perform this feat. Each of these microorganisms is an agent of meningitis. An additional avenue of microbial spread is via peripheral nerves

UNDER THE MICROSCOPE 10

Biofilms and Adhesion

Biofilms are a complex of organic material of bacterial origin covering the surface of some inert or biological material. The inert or biological material is invariably immersed in a natural aquatic environment. Microorganisms adhere to and are immobilized within the biofilm, which acts as a habitat for growth and degradation of chemical substances. Biofilms play a vital role in minimizing the buildup of pollutants in waste management systems (for example, the trickling filters used in sewage treatment) by degrading organic compounds and transforming inorganic compounds.

Biofilms also play a role in medicine in both a positive and a negative way. For example, the lumen of the intestinal tract is covered by a biofilm of bacteria. The intestinal biofilm prevents adhesion of potentially pathogenic bacteria that may enter the intestinal tract. In the vagina there is a biofilm of **lactobacilli** that protects females from urinary tract infections. In contrast, insertion of prosthetic devices, such as heart valves, into the human body also gives rise to biofilms. In this instance, bacteria such as *Staphylococcus epidermidis* release a slime layer that attaches to the heart valve. The valve biofilm acts as a focus of infection and releases microorganisms into the bloodstream (see Chapter 17). In cystic fibrosis patients the organism *Pseudomonas aeruginosa* releases large amounts of a slimy carbohydrate (alginate) that attaches to the air passages, preventing normal breathing. Bacteria in this biofilm are protected from the action of antibiotics because the organic matrix of the biofilm limits diffusion of such molecules. Treatment of such disorders is very difficult.

Studies are now under way to determine if the coating of prosthetic devices such as catheters with lactobacilli can prevent biofilm formation by pathogens such as *Escherichia coli*. Catheter-associated infections are discussed in Chapter 35.

TABLE 14-2
Microbial Products Associated with Invasiveness and Spread of Microorganism in the Host

Invasive fiber	Organism	Function
Coagulase	Staphylococci	Causes formation of fibrin, which may deposit on surface of microorganism and inhibit phagocytosis
Streptokinase (fibrinolysin)	Streptococci	Transforms plasminogen to plasmin, an active proteolytic enzyme that digests fibrin; importance in disease not totally understood
Hyaluronidase	Streptococci, staphylococci, and clostridia	Splits hyaluronic acid, a component of connective tissue
Hemolysins	Many bacteria, especially streptococci, staphylococci, and clostridia	Lyse red blood cells
Lecithinase	Clostridia	Splits lecithin, a component of cytoplasmic membranes
Collagenase	Clostridia	Digests collagen, a component of connective tissue
Extracellular polymeric substances (capsules and slime layers)	Several bacteria, including pseudomonads, staphylococci, streptococci, and others	Inhibits phagocytosis and in some instances may be important in adhering to host tissue

to the central nervous system. For example, cold sores are caused by a herpesvirus that can travel along a peripheral nerve to produce a localized infection involving the lips or contiguous areas (see Chapter 32).

Invasion of Host Cells

We know that several antimicrobial factors are present in the bloodstream and lymph—antibodies, complement, macrophages, and so on. It would seem that the cytoplasm of the cell, which is rich in nutrients and free of competing organisms, would be a safe haven for the microbe. The intracellular parasite, however, is faced with new challenges (degradative enzymes, changes in pH, and other antimicrobial forces). Invasion of host cells is a prerequisite for viral infection but only a few bacteria are capable of penetrating the cell and surviving in this new environment. In the following paragraphs we examine the technique for invasion of host cells.

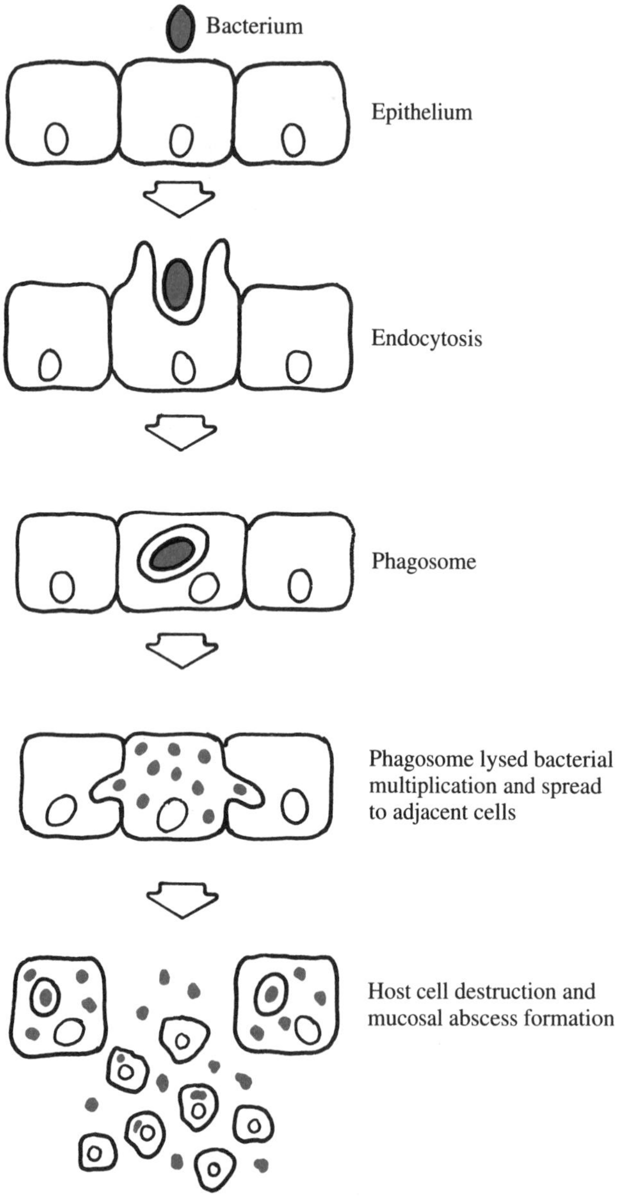

FIGURE 14-8
Shigella invasion in intestinal epithelium.

Epithelial cells are considered nonphagocytic cells; that is, they do not routinely endocytose microbial cells. Yet some bacteria, such as *Salmonella, Shigella,* and *Yersinia* species are able to enter epithelial cells and act as intracellular parasites. These bacteria possess several genes that code for proteins controlling the invasion process. If these proteins are not induced, the invasion process does not take place. Microbial adherence to the epithelial surface is followed by rearrangement of actin filaments and other cytoskeletal proteins that are distributed throughout the host cell membrane. These proteins surround the invading microorganism and help to internalize it (Fig. 14-8). Once the bacterial cell is internalized, host proteins return to their normal membrane distribution. Salmonellae, once inside the cell, are enclosed within a vacuole. Salmonellae grow readily in the vacuole and quickly cause its expansion. Endocytosis of shigellae eventually results in lysis of the phagocytic membrane. Shigellae multiply freely in the cytoplasm.

TOXINS

The virulence of most bacteria that are not intracellular parasites is a consequence of toxin production. Toxins are one of the major causes of tissue damage and are of two types: **exotoxins** and **endotoxins.** Characteristics differentiating the two groups are outlined in Table 14-3. Toxins are not characteristically found in microorganisms other than bacteria.

Exotoxins

Exotoxins are heat-labile proteins released outside the bacterial cell. Exotoxins are produced by both gram-positive and gram-negative bacteria. Some of the most potent poisons known are exotoxins such as diphtheria, tetanus, and botulism toxins. Exotoxins whose site of action is the intestinal tract are called **enterotoxins.**

Most exotoxins are highly antigenic and the antibodies produced from their stimulation are called **antitoxins.** Chemically modified exotoxins are used as vaccines (see Chapter 12 and Appendix E) and are referred to as **toxoids.** For example, the diphtheria and tetanus toxoids make up part of the trivalent vaccine DPT (diphtheria, pertussis, tetanus). The major exotoxins produced by pathogenic bacteria and their activities are listed in Table 14-4. Most exotoxins are composed of two subunits; one is nontoxic but binds to specific cell surface receptors. The nontoxic subunit facilitates the entry of the second, or toxic, subunit into the host cell (Fig. 14-9). The exotoxins of *E. coli* and *V. cholerae* exert their activity in the intestinal lumen. Both of these species cause diarrhea via the action of toxin on the enzyme adenyl cyclase located in the mammalian cytoplasmic membrane. The enzyme catalyzes the following reaction.

$$\text{Adenosine triphosphate (ATP)} \xrightarrow{\text{adenyl cyclase}} \text{adenosine } 3',5'\text{-cyclic monophosphate (cAMP)}$$

The increase in cAMP causes a change in the electrical potential of the mammalian cytoplasmic membrane. This results in a leakage of fluids and electrolytes (see Under the Microscope 11).

Endotoxins

As discussed in Chapter 2, an endotoxin is a molecular complex found in the gram-negative cell wall. The complex is made up of a core of oligosaccharides to which a lipid, called **lipid A,** is bound. Also bound to the core are the O-specific side chains that are polymers of oligosaccharide units. The latter carry the antigenic determinants responsible for the serological specificity of the bacterium

TABLE 14-3
Characteristics Differentiating Exotoxins from Endotoxins

Exotoxins	Endotoxins
Most are polypeptides with molecular weights between 1×10^4 and 9×10^5	Low molecular weight component of lipopolysaccharide complex; lipid A is toxic component
Excreted by living cells	Part of the cell wall of gram-negative bacteria and can be released when the cell lyses or during vegetative growth
Relatively unstable to temperatures above 60 C	Relatively stable to temperatures above 60 C for several hours with no loss of activity
Antigenic (stimulates formation of antibodies)	Lipid A is not antigenic
Can be converted to a toxoid	Cannot be converted to a toxoid
Does not produce fever in the host	Produces fever in the host
Very toxic in microgram quantities to laboratory animals	Weakly toxic; hundreds of microgram quantities required to be lethal for animals

(Fig. 14-10). Endotoxin is released usually when the cell is lysed, but can also be released during vegetative growth.

Endotoxin has been isolated from gram-negative bacteria, and its biological properties have been determined through studies of several susceptible animals. The effects of endotoxin on the cardiovascular, respiratory, and blood clotting mechanisms have been known to lead to intravascular coagulation, septic shock, and death.

Endotoxin and Gram-Negative Septicemia. Bloodstream infection with gram-negative bacteria remains one of the major clinical problems facing the physician. Fatality rates from gram-negative septicemia (25–50 percent) remain as high today as they did 25 years ago. Estimates of the number of episodes of bacteremia involving gram-negative bacilli annually in the United States range from 71,000 to more than 300,000. One of the critical virulence factors in gram-negative infection is endotoxin. Some of the clinical features of gram-negative septicemia found in animals are also found in humans. The clinical features are as follows:

1. **Fever.** Endotoxin can induce fever in susceptible animals. Fever is mediated by endogenous pyrogens (*pyro* means "heat") produced by leukocytes (interleukin [IL]-1, for example). Endogenous pyrogens are released into the arterial blood. They act on the body's thermostat, the anterior hypothalamus of the brain, which contains thermosensitive nerve cells. The hypothalamus in turn releases molecules, called **prostaglandins (arachidonic acid,** for example), which become metabolized. Metabolized prostaglandins cause the hypothalamic thermostat to be raised to a higher level. The new thermostatic reading signals various efferent nerves. For example, the nerves innervating peripheral blood vessels cause them to constrict and this conserves heat. The increased heat of the body from vasoconstriction continues until the temperature of the blood supplying the hypothalamus matches the elevated thermostat reading. The thermostat can be reset to normal when the concentration of endogenous pyrogen falls.

Endogenous pyrogens are produced primarily by

TABLE 14-4
Important Exotoxins Associated with Disease in Humans

Toxin or disease	Microorganism	Mechanism of action
Exotoxin A	*Pseudomonas aeruginosa*	Inhibits peptide chain elongation
Enterotoxin	*Bacillus cereus*	Similar to cholera toxin
Enterotoxin (traveler's diarrhea, infant diarrhea)	*Escherichia coli*	Same as cholera toxin
Scalded skin syndrome	*Staphylococcus aureus*	Separation of the epidermis
Erythrogenic toxin (scarlet fever)	*Streptococcus pyogenes*	Produced only by strains of streptococci carrying a bacteriophage that is nonvirulent; toxin causes a rash
Enterotoxin (food poisoning)	*Staphylococcus aureus*	Neurotoxin that affects motility of the gut
Diphtheria toxin	*Corynebacterium diphtheriae*	Inhibits peptide chain elongation during protein synthesis
Cholera enterotoxin	*Vibrio cholerae*	Stimulation of adenyl cyclase and increase in cAMP, leading to fluid and electrolyte loss from the gut
Tetanus or lockjaw	*Clostridium tetani*	Neurotoxin blocks function of inhibitory synapses in the spinal cord, thus causing muscular spasms
Botulism (types A, B, and E toxins)	*Clostridium botulinum*	Neurotoxin that blocks release of acetylcholine or blocks its production at synapses or neuromuscular junctions
Enterotoxin	*Clostridium perfringens*	Causes hypersecretion of electrolytes and water in the intestine
Alpha toxin (gas gangrene)	*Clostridium perfringens*	Splits lecithin, a component of cytoplasmic membranes

cAMP = adenosine 3′,5′-cyclic monophosphate.

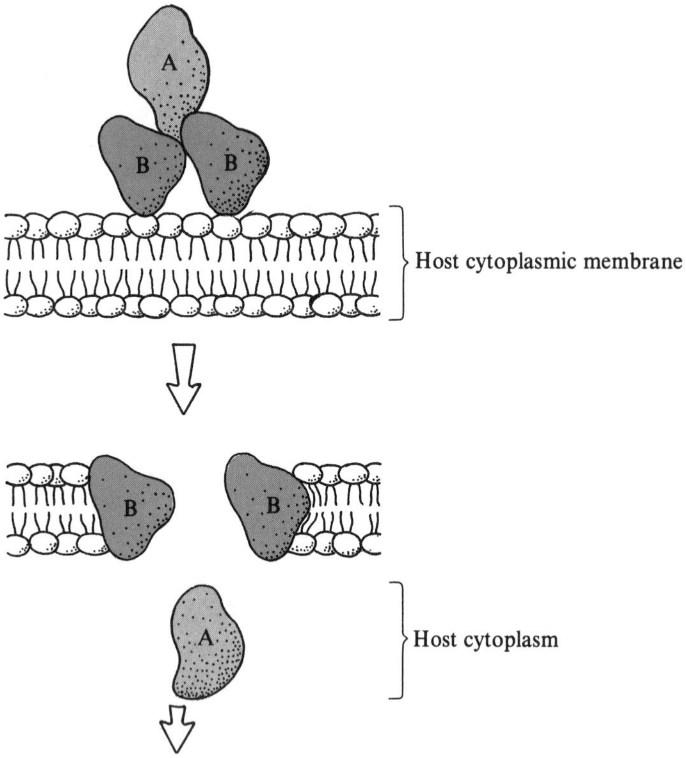

FIGURE 14-9
Possible mechanism for entry of exotoxins, such as cholera toxin, possessing different subunits A and B. B subunits of toxin bind to the cytoplasmic membrane of the host cell and insert themselves across it. This provides an avenue for diffusion of A, or toxic subunit, into the cell cytoplasm.

UNDER THE MICROSCOPE 11

Adenyl Cyclase and Bacterial Virulence

Mammalian adenyl cyclases are the targets of various hormones and neurotransmitters that control the levels of adenosine 3′,5′-cyclic monophosphate (cAMP) in the cell. cAMP activates specific protein kinases in the cell and the kinases in turn phosphorylate different proteins. Phosphorylated proteins are involved in a variety of cellular responses involving growth and metabolism. We now know that the activity of a number of microbial toxins is associated with the regulation of cAMP of host cells. This group includes toxins from *Vibrio cholerae, Escherichia coli, Bacillus subtilis, Bordetella pertussis,* and *Bacillus anthracis.*

In the above examples, except for *B. pertussis* and *B. anthracis,* the toxins interact with host adenyl cyclases. With *B. pertussis* and *B. anthracis,* however, the adenyl cyclase is provided by the microorganism and is found on the microbial surface. When the bacterium makes contact with host cells, the bacterial enzyme penetrates the host cell membrane. Inside the host cell the bacterial adenyl cyclase is activated by a host protein called **calmodulin.** The subsequent increase in cAMP can result in different effects on the host cell including increased secretory activity. In skin cells, for example, *B. anthracis* toxin (the cause of anthrax) causes edema but in phagocytic cells, such as alveolar macrophages, the toxin impairs phagocytic activities. More will be said about the specific activities of microbial toxins in later chapters.

macrophages. The principal endogenous pyrogen is a protein called **interleukin-1** (IL-1). Interferon and tumor necrosis factor (cachectin) can also induce fever. Exogenous pyrogens are induced primarily by molecules such as microbial components, toxins, or other products that are not indigenous to the body (Fig. 14-11).

Fever enhances the inflammatory response and at the same time interferes with microbial growth as well as replication of tumor cells. This positive response must be weighed against the detrimental aspects of fever. Fever may result in increased heart rate, which would be deleterious to those with compromised cardiovascular function. Fever also increases the basic metabolic rate by 7 to 8 percent for each degree (Fahrenheit) of temperature

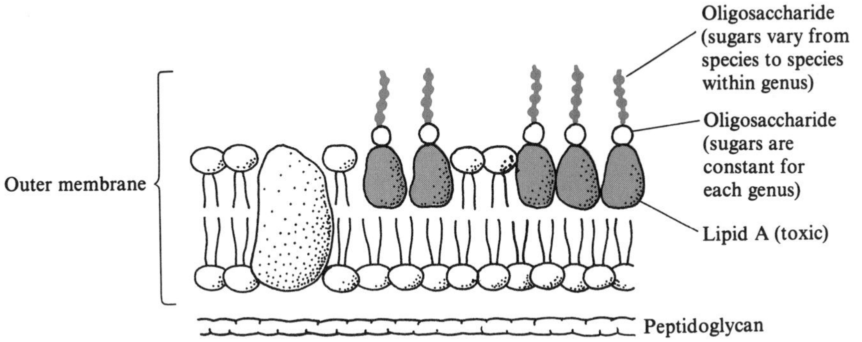

FIGURE 14-10
Relationship of endotoxin to gram-negative cell wall. The endotoxin represented in color is a lipopolysaccharide. Lipid A, the toxic component of endotoxin, is inserted into the membrane and is complexed with two types of oligosaccharides. The outermost oligosaccharide is sometimes called the O or somatic region. Variations in the sugars of this region enable the microorganism to differentiate into specific serological groups.

FIGURE 14-11
Mechanism of fever induction following infection.

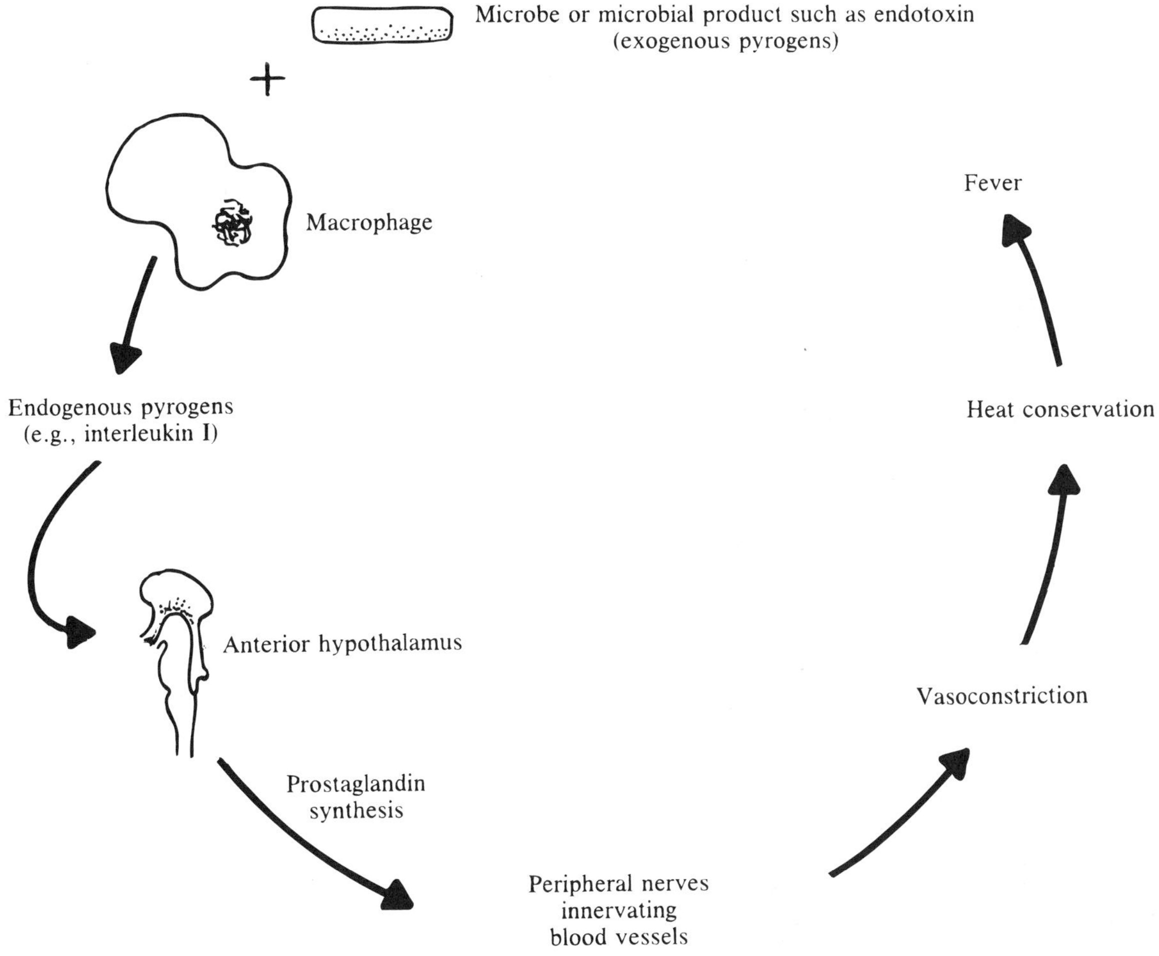

elevated. This usually results in increased caloric demand and mild to severe dehydration.

2. **Activation of the coagulation mechanism.** Intravascular coagulation is one of the manifestations of gram-negative septicemia, although it also occurs in other types of infections. Endotoxin activates components of the clotting mechanism and thus leads to the formation of fibrin. If fibrin becomes trapped in the small blood vessels, intravascular coagulation and shock can follow.

3. **Depression of the reticuloendothelial system.** Macrophages make up the reticuloendothelial system. Endotoxin prevents macrophages from clearing the fibrin polymers that become trapped in the small blood vessels.

4. **Vascular collapse.** In animals endotoxin is known to cause the release of cytokines from cells of the immune system. Some of these cytokines affect the circulatory system and they can cause increased vascular permeability and dilatation (see Under the Microscope 6). The circulatory changes lead to impaired blood flow to vital organs—kidneys, liver, brain, and lung—and ultimately to shock and possibly death.

AVOIDING HOST DEFENSE MECHANISMS

Antiphagocytic Factors

Once microorganisms have penetrated beneath the surface of the skin, they are exposed to cellular elements such as phagocytic macrophages (see Chapter 9 for a discussion of phagocytosis). Several microorganisms are virulent because they can avoid the phagocytic process. An important microbial antiphagocytic device is the capsule that prevents complement deposition on the bacterial surface. The capsules of *S. pneumoniae, Klebsiella pneumoniae, Bacillus anthracis, H. influenzae, N. meningitidis,* and *Yersinia pestis* resist the process of phagocytic ingestion.

Group A streptococci utilize a surface protein, called **M protein,** to evade phagocytic ingestion. M protein prevents opsonization by complement by binding fibrinogen. Another cell wall protein called **protein A** is a component of *S. aureus.* Protein A also inhibits ingestion by phagocytes.

Some microorganisms become ingested during the phagocytic process but are able to resist the digestion process in the immune cell. Bacteria capable of resisting digestion include species of *Mycobacterium, Salmonella, Coxiella,* and *Rickettsia.* The mechanism of this resistance is explained in more detail in later chapters.

Antigenic Variation (Changing Surface Chemistry)

Microbes can avoid host immune responses by altering the chemistry of surface antigens. *Neisseria gonorrhoeae* possesses two mechanisms for altering surface antigens. A single strain, for example, can express several different surface **PII proteins.** In addition, *N. gonorrhoeae* can modify the antigenicity of its pili. Whatever the mechanism, this periodic switching helps avoid the immune response.

Borrelia species, the cause of relapsing fever, also use a mechanism similar to *N. gonorrhoeae* pilin variation. *Borrelia* organisms induce antibodies that respond to a specific surface protein. As *Borrelia* organisms are being destroyed, some strains change the chemistry of their surface proteins. Once the change has been made, the host's circulating antibodies do not recognize the new protein and require time to respond to it. Eventually, after several changes in surface proteins, the host's immune system becomes overtaxed.

Other microorganisms, such as the helminth *Schistosoma,* can also change their surfaces but in a way different from *N. gonorrhoeae* and *Borrelia* species. *Schistosoma* organisms, after invading the host, assume residence in the veins of the bladder and intestine. They avoid detection by the host's immune system by coating themselves with the proteins that normally coat red blood cells and other host cells. Thus, the parasite goes unrecognized because its surface does not contain foreign molecules.

Serum Resistance

Some microorganisms are able to avoid complement lysis, a technique referred to as **serum resistance. S protein** is a component of human serum that functions as an inhibitor of the terminal membrane attack complex. Bacteria that bind S protein through various cell surface receptors can escape complement lysis. Binding has been observed with streptococci and *S. aureus.*

The **O antigens** of *Salmonella* species are also resistant to complement. This resistance is due to steric hindrance of the C5b–9 complement complex, inhibiting its access to specific areas in the outer membrane of *Salmonella.* The sialic acid capsules of *E. coli* strains and *N. meningitidis* group B also bestow serum resistance by preventing productive complement activation.

Summary

1. Microorganisms can inhibit many sites in the human body. Some of the microorganisms become permanent residents (commensals) but others can be parasitic. Factors determining the fate of microbial species include the presence or absence of oxygen, presence of receptors for attachment, availability of nutrients, and immunological response of the host.

2. Most successful parasites merely live off their hosts without causing major damage to tissue. Parasites colonize the host either because the host has been compromised by some underlying condition or because the parasite possesses mechanisms for overcoming host defenses.

3. Parasites can live outside or inside host cells. Extracellular parasites usually produce toxins or release products that enable the host to respond quickly to infection. Extracellular parasites usually produce acute infections.

4. Intracellular parasites may be of two types: those that can survive only intracellularly and those that can live intracellularly as well as extracellularly. Intracellular parasites use the host cell for important metabolites or as a mechanism for evading immune products in the bloodstream. Many intracellular parasites produce chronic disease.

5. Microorganisms that inhabit the host but do not induce an immune response are merely colonizers, but if antibodies are produced, the microorganism causes infection. If tissue is destroyed during infection, the microorganism causes disease.

6. The disease-producing potential of microorganisms is referred to as pathogenicity. A more quantitative term is virulence, which refers to the number of microorganisms or amount of microbial product that can cause disease in 50 percent of the subjects tested. Microbial virulence can be attenuated in the laboratory and this is the mechanism for producing vaccines.

7. Host defense mechanisms are initiated at the site of entry, the epithelium, as well as in subepithelial tissue, including the bloodstream. The skin is a thick epithelial covering that offers physical resistance to microbial penetration. The skin also contains chemical antimicrobial factors such as fatty acids.

8. The mucosal surface is an important defense against infection. It contains secretory IgA, has a resident microflora, has a film of mucin, and contains substances such as lysozyme, lactoferrin, and peroxidase. All of them help to prevent attachment of microorganisms or to destroy microorganisms that come in contact with the mucosal surface.

9. The respiratory tract is a barrier to infection primarily because of its mucociliary blanket. The flushing action of saliva helps to reduce microbial numbers in the oropharynx. The acidity of the stomach and the acids, bile salts, and enzymes present in the intestinal tract help prevent microbial colonization. In the genitourinary tract the acidity of the vagina inhibits microbial activity while the flushing action of urine deters microbial colonization.

10. Three host defense mechanisms exist below the epithelial surface: tissue fluids, which contain antimicrobial factors such as antibodies; the lymph system, which carries microorganisms to lymph nodes for destruction; and phagocytic cells in the bloodstream and at tissue surfaces.

11. The host's resistance to infection can also be influenced by factors such as the immunological state, race, nutrition, occupation, and underlying conditions of the host.

12. Microorganisms are equipped to invade host tissue through the release of various enzymes and other proteins. Much of the damage to host tissue is due to two types of toxins, exotoxins and endotoxins.

13. Exotoxins are proteins released by the bacterium into the environment. Most exotoxins are made up of two subunits, one used to bind to the host cell and to facilitate the entry of the second subunit. The second subunit is the toxic component. Exotoxin activities are described in Table 14-4.

14. Endotoxins are part of the lipopolysaccharide of the outer membrane of the gram-negative bacterial cell wall. Lipid A is the toxic component. Endotoxin released during bacteremia can affect the host by (1) inducing fever, (2) activating the coagulation mechanism and causing intravascular coagulation, (3) depressing the reticuloendothelial system, and (4) causing vascular collapse.

15. Some microorganisms can avoid host defense mechanisms by preventing phagocytosis. The bacterial capsule and some surface proteins are the major antiphagocytic factors. Other microorganisms can also alter their surface chemistry so the host's immune system has problems in recognition. Finally, complement lysis can be prevented by microbial surface components as well as some natural serum proteins.

Questions for Study

1. Now that you have finished the chapters on immunology and host-parasite relationships, in a lengthy paper, describe all the events that occur when a bacterial cell infects a body site (respiratory tract, intestinal tract, etc.). In your description, list all the barriers to infection including physical, chemical, and cellular. Also describe the potential bacterial factors that might favor infection. Do the same for viral infection of the host.
2. Explain the relationship that exists between gram-negative septicemia and tumor necrosis factor.
3. Describe some well known bacterial toxins. What, if anything, do some of them have in common?
4. What determinants, both parasite and host, provide the mechanism for colonization and invasion?
5. Outline the chemical and physical factors of the following body sites that provide a barrier to infection: respiratory tract, intestinal tract, and vagina.
6. Without referring to the glossary or the chapter, define the following terms: commensal, microflora, acute disease, infection, disease, virulence, attenuation, latent disease, mucin, fibronectin, siderophore, lactoferrin, adhesin, and toxoid.

CHAPTER 15

Epidemiology

OBJECTIVES

To describe the various stages and symptoms associated with acute disease

To understand the mechanisms that enable microorganisms to persist in the host

To differentiate between reservoirs and sources of disease

To list the diseases that are transmitted from animals to humans

To list the diseases that are transmitted to humans from contaminated water or food

To describe how microorganisms can be transmitted by air

To explain briefly the laboratory techniques used to identify the source of a disease

To define the terms chronic disease, subclinical infections, pyrogen, carrier, zoonoses, vector, droplet nuclei, fomite, epidemic, endemic, herd immunity, morbidity, index case, biotype, serotype, and DNA probe

OUTLINE

CLINICAL STAGES OF DISEASE IN THE HOST
- Acute vs. Chronic Disease
  - Acute Disease
    - Incubation Period
    - Prodromal Period
    - Acute Period
    - Convalescent Period
  - Chronic Disease

RESERVOIRS AND SOURCES OF DISEASE
- Animate Reservoirs
  - Human
  - Animal
  - Insect
- Inanimate Reservoirs

TRANSMISSION OF INFECTIOUS MICROORGANISMS
- Contact
  - Direct
  - Indirect
    - Water
    - Food
    - Fomites
- Air
- Horizontal vs. Vertical Transmission
  - Vertical Transmission

PATTERNS OF DISEASE IN THE COMMUNITY
- Endemic, Epidemic, and Sporadic Disease
- Incidence and Prevalence
- Herd Immunity
- Descriptive Epidemiology
  - Host Factors
  - Place
  - Time

LABORATORY TECHNIQUES IN EPIDEMIOLOGY
- Conventional Methods
  - Biotyping
  - Serotyping
  - Antibiograms
  - Phage Typing
  - Bacteriocin Typing

OUTLINE (*continued*)

Molecular Methods
Plasmid Profiles
DNA Probes
Polymerase Chain Reaction

In the previous chapter we discussed the one-on-one relationship between host and parasite. Epidemiology (from the Greek *epidemios,* which means "among the people") is concerned with disease as it applies to populations of individuals. The science of epidemiology may be involved with infectious as well as noninfectious disease. The role of the epidemiologist is to gather statistics that will indicate the prevalence or frequency of disease. Our discussion of epidemiology is directed at how infectious diseases are spread, how they are controlled, and how they may be identified, as well as their frequency and prevalence in a population.

Clinical Stages of Disease in the Host

To understand the various aspects of disease in a population we should first have some knowledge of the clinical stages of infectious disease in the individual.

ACUTE VS. CHRONIC DISEASE

Individuals infected by a pathogenic microorganism will respond to it in various ways. Sometimes the host's immune system will inhibit the pathogen before it can elicit symptoms or the symptoms will be so slight as to be almost imperceptible. Such infections are called **subclinical** or inapparent. When the pathogen overcomes the host's defense mechanisms, the manifestations of disease may ensue and proceed in an acute or chronic manner.

Acute Disease

Acute disease is characterized by symptoms that usually appear quickly, become very intense, and then subside when the host's immune system has overwhelmed the pathogen or its toxic products. Acute disease is the type of disease with which most of us are acquainted, for example, the childhood diseases such as measles and chickenpox and the various types of influenza. One can always determine the approximate length of time it will take to recover from such diseases. Both acute and chronic diseases proceed in such a way that they can be divided into various stages: **incubation, prodromal, acute,** and **convalescent.** These stages in chronic disease, however, cannot be as precisely identified as in acute disease.

Incubation Period. The incubation period is that period of time from the moment the infectious agent enters the host until the first symptoms of disease appear. This period may be as short as a few hours or as long as several years. The time interval is influenced by how fast the infectious agent can multiply and how quickly the microorganisms or the microbial products affect host tissue. Food poisoning caused by the ingestion of preformed toxin in contaminated food often produces symptoms within 8 to 24 hours. Other diseases, in which the infectious agent is taken into the body, may have incubation periods of one to several weeks. Many of the fungal pathogens, for example, have long incubation periods in the host. One must remember that the incubation period is greatly influenced by the virulence of the microorganism, the antigenic potential of the microorganism or its products, and the immunological state of the host. Measles affecting a normal healthy child in the community may have an incubation period of 7 to 10 days, but the same virus infecting a hospitalized patient could have an incubation period of 1 to 2 days. The average incubation period for most diseases is between 10 and 21 days.

Prodromal Period. The term **prodromal** is derived from the Greek word that means "running before." In terms of the infectious disease cycle **prodromal** refers to the warning symptoms that indicate the onset of disease. This is the period in which the individual characterizes his or her general state of health as "not feeling well." The technical term for this symptom is **malaise.** It may include such symptoms as headache, upset stomach, or slight fever. The infectious agent during the prodromal period has multiplied only to the extent that its products have induced a slight response by the host.

Acute Period. The acute period is the stage in which the symptoms of disease are at their peak. During this period the infectious microorganisms have reached a population level that induces the host to respond with immunological intensity. The intensity of this immunological response as well as the intensity of the symptoms are related to the number of host-parasite encounters. If the encounter is the first of its kind, then the symptoms of disease are usually very intense and the maximum immunological response takes longer to develop. A rapid immunological response and less intense symptoms will develop if the disease represents a repeat encounter between host and parasite.

The types of symptoms associated with the acute disease period vary from disease to disease, but some symptoms are more prevalent in most diseases than others. **Fever** is one of the most common symptoms of disease and was discussed in Chapter 14.

Skin or epithelial lesions are a frequent response to infection by many microorganisms and result from (1) localization of the microorganisms near the body surface, (2) the effects of a microbial toxin near the body surface, or (3) an inflammatory response (hypersensitivity) to a microbial antigen. Multiple lesions that appear on the body surface are called **rashes.** The rashes produced by viruses often go through a succession of forms such as the following:

Macule. A macular lesion is flat and usually red.

Papule. A papular lesion is firm and elevated.

Vesicle. A vesicular lesion contains fluid.

Pustule. A pustular lesion contains pus, often a result of secondary bacterial infection.

Rashes that are localized on the body surface can be of diagnostic importance.

Other symptoms of disease may include cough, which is associated with respiratory disease. Intestinal diseases are usually characterized by the symptoms of vomiting, diarrhea, or dysentery (bloody diarrhea).

Convalescent Period. Convalescence refers to the recovery period from a disease. Convalescence is associated with a sharp decline in symptoms such as fever or headache associated with the disease in question. The subsiding of symptoms is correlated with maximum antibody levels in the host and usually means the pathogen is being eradicated.

Chronic Disease

Some microorganisms are capable of persisting in the host for long intervals because they can avoid the normal immunological responses of the host. Persistent infections can be divided into chronic, latent, and slow. We concern ourselves with chronic infections since latent and slow infections are more characteristic of viruses, discussed in Chapter 31. Chronic infections are those in which the symptoms of disease are expressed over a long period of time. Many times in chronic disease the infectious agent is an intracellular parasite that localizes in phagocytes. The organism can, therefore, be transported to various organs and body sites where microbial multiplication or even lysis of microorganisms releases products that give rise to the original symptoms of disease or new symptoms. The symptoms arising during relapses are often due to hypersensitivity reactions by the host. Chronic diseases such as brucellosis and tuberculosis are believed to be due to the inability of the host to respond with any immunological efficiency. Apparently the microbial antigens are not sufficiently immunogenic to make the host produce antibodies that can eliminate the pathogen.

Reservoirs and Sources of Disease

Pathogenic microorganisms, if they are going to retain their potential to cause disease, must have a place where they can maintain themselves and replicate. This place of survival and replication is called the **reservoir,** and it may be animate or inanimate. Viruses, which are obligate intracellular parasites, replicate only in living cells and are harbored in a variety of living hosts. Animate reservoirs are also required for bacterial species such as the streptococci and staphylococci, even though they are not obligate parasites. Reservoirs may also be inanimate. Many microorganisms replicate in soil, water, and food, provided nutrients are available. Many bacterial species that cause disease in the hospital, such as *Pseudomonas* and *Klebsiella* species, may be found in both inanimate and animate reservoirs.

Sources of disease are objects or places, either animate or inanimate, from which the infective agent passes to the host. Sometimes the reservoir and source are one and the same. The organism that causes pneumonia *(Streptococcus pneumoniae)*, for example, is harbored by humans in the oral cavity. If the infected individual comes into direct contact with another individual (by kissing, for example) and causes disease, the reservoir and source are the same. There are also many examples in which the reservoir and source are not the same. If the reservoir of disease is the kidney of an animal, the infectious microorganism may infect a human in two ways. Humans may eat the kidneys of the diseased animal, in which case the reservoir and source are the same. The live animal may also contaminate a water supply through urination. Ingestion of the contaminated water by humans could also lead to disease, and in this instance the source of the disease would be water. The length of time that the microorganism remains viable in the source depends on environmental as well as microbial factors.

ANIMATE RESERVOIRS

Human

Humans not only represent the most important reservoir of microbial agents but also in many instances they are the only reservoir. Many viral agents, such as the measles, rubella, mumps, influenza, and poliomyelitis virus, and bacterial agents, such as those causing sexually transmitted disease, whooping cough, and diphtheria, are maintained only in human reservoirs.

As stated previously, humans also harbor microorganisms that cause **persistent** infections. The two most important consequences of persistence is that (1) the microorganisms remain in the community for extended periods of time and (2) there can be reactivation of disease when the immunological state of the host becomes temporarily or permanently impaired. Two diseases that illustrate persistence are typhoid fever and tuberculosis, caused by the bacteria *Salmonella typhi* and *Mycobacterium tuberculosis,* respectively. During recovery from typhoid fever the host may harbor bacteria in the gallbladder and disease symptoms are not apparent. Periodically (over months to years), bacteria multiply and are shed from the gallbladder into the intestinal tract and hence into the environment via feces. The individual shedding the microorganisms is a **carrier.** The carrier can shed microorganisms that may contaminate food or water. Thus, the carrier becomes a permanent source of infections for others. In tuberculosis the infecting bacteria can be walled off in calcified lesions (such as in the lung) that are not affected by the host's immune system. The bacteria remain viable in the lesions for many years. The lesions can rupture at any time, releasing viable bacteria that multiply in tissue and thus cause a reactivation of disease. Reactivation also makes the host a new source of infection.

Even though the carrier state may be a result of microbial persistence, not all carriers are alike. **Convalescent carriers,** for example, are those who are recovering from the disease and in whom the infectious agent remains and multiplies without causing overt symptoms (as in typhoid fever, for example). **Healthy carriers** are those who do not have the disease but still carry infectious microorganisms. Those who carry strains of *Staphylococcus aureus,* which are causes of food poisoning, are examples of healthy carriers. The carrier harbors the staphylococci in the nares (nostrils) and, when he or she handles food, contaminates it with staphylococci. Detection of the carrier state is very important in severing the chain of transmission that may involve hundreds or even thousands of individuals.

Animal

Animals, particularly domestic animals, are important reservoirs and sources of disease to humans. A disease that occurs primarily in animals and is secondarily transmitted to humans is called a **zoonosis.** *Salmonella* species are normally found in the intestinal tract of animals such as poultry or cattle. When they contaminate food ingested by humans, the salmonellae can cause disease (salmonellosis). Table 15-1 describes the zoonoses. Many times when animals are reservoirs, the human represents a dead end in terms of disease transmission because the disease cannot be transferred from human to human. For example, Q fever and brucellosis are diseases of animals that can be acquired through contact with the animals or animal products. There are exceptions, of course, such as in the case of the disease salmonellosis. Salmonellosis may be acquired from animals but the infected human can also serve as a source of disease to other humans.

Insect

Two classes of arthropods, Insecta and Arachnida, are important in the transfer of infectious agents from one host to another. Arthropods are therefore called **vectors** in the disease process. The class Insecta includes flies, mosquitoes, fleas, lice, and true bugs; Arachnida includes ticks and mites. Insect vectors may be divided into two types: mechanical and biological. **Mechanical vectors** are

TABLE 15-1
Diseases of Animals (Zoonoses) That Are Transmissible to Humans

Disease	Transmission to humans	Animal reservoir
Bacterial		
Salmonellosis	Ingestion of contaminated food or water	Dogs, cats, farm animals, poultry, reptiles, rodents
Brucellosis	Drinking raw milk or direct contact with animal	Dogs, farm animals, rodents
Tularemia	Ingestion of or contact with contaminated meat and arthropod vectors	Rodents and rabbits
Anthrax	Contact with contaminated animal hides or products	Farm animals
Leptospirosis	Contact with contaminated water	Dogs, cats, wild rodents, farm animals
Bubonic plague	Rat flea but human-to-human transmission in pneumonic plague	Rodents such as ground squirrels, rats, chipmunks
Rickettsial disease (scrub typhus and murine typhus)	Ticks, fleas, mites	Primarily wild rodents
Q fever	Ingestion of raw milk, inhalation of contaminated dust, or contact with contaminated animal	Farm animals (cattle, sheep, goats)
Cat-scratch fever	Scratch or bite of cat	Cats
Viral		
Rabies	Bite of animal or contact with infectious saliva or tissue, inhalation of aerosols	Dogs, cats, farm animals, and wild animals, particularly skunks and raccoons
Equine encephalitis	Horses to mosquitoes to humans	Horses, pheasants, domestic pigeons
Parasitic (Helminths)		
Echinococcosis	Ingestion of eggs deposited on raw fruit	Foxes, dogs, and cats are principal hosts, but life cycles in nature completed in voles and mice
Trichinosis	Ingestion of contaminated meat, usually pork	Pigs and bears are most important reservoirs

TABLE 15-2
Major Vector-Borne Diseases of Humans

Vector	Disease	Microbe classification
Mosquito	Animal parasite diseases	
Culex, Anopheles, and *Aedes* species	Filariasis	*Wuchereria* and *Brugia* species
Anopheles species	Malaria	*Plasmodium* species
	Viral diseases	
Aedes species	Dengue fever	Flavivirus
	Yellow fever	Flavivirus
	St. Louis encephalitis	Flavivirus
Culex species	Eastern equine encephalitis	Alphavirus
	Western equine encephalitis	Alphavirus
	St. Louis encephalitis	Flavivirus
Tick	Bacterial diseases	
	Relapsing fever	*Borrelia recurrentis*
	Rocky Mountain spotted fever	*Rickettsia rickettsii*
	Q fever	*Coxiella burnetii*
	Tularemia	*Francisella tularensis*
	Lyme disease	*Borrelia burgdorferi*
	Viral diseases	
	Colorado tick fever	Orbivirus
	Crimean hemorrhagic fever	Nairovirus
Mite	Bacterial diseases	
	Q fever	*Coxiella burnetii*
	Rickettsialpox	*Ricksettsia akari*
Flies	Animal parasite diseases	
Deerfly	Eye worm	*Loa loa*
Tsetse flies	Sleeping sickness (African)	*Trypanosoma* species
Blackflies	Leishmaniasis	*Leishmania* species
	Onchocerciasis	*Onchocerca volvulus*
	Bacterial diseases	
Deerfly	Tularemia	*Francisella tularensis*
Muscoid flies	Yaws	*Treponema pertenue*
	Viral diseases	
Sandfly	Sandfly fever	Phlebovirus
	Vesicular stomatitis	Vesiculovirus
Lice	Bacterial diseases	
	Epidemic typhus	*Rickettsia prowazekii*
	Trench fever	*Rochalimaea quintana*
Fleas	Bacterial diseases	
	Endemic typhus	*Rickettsia typhi*
	Bubonic plague	*Yersinia pestis*
True bugs (reduviids)	Animal parasite diseases	
	Chagas' disease (American trypanosomiasis)	*Trypanosoma cruzi*

SOURCE: R. F. Boyd, *General Microbiology*, 2nd ed. St. Louis: Mosby, 1988.

invertebrate animals that carry the infectious agent on their appendages and are not involved in the life cycle of the infectious agent. Flies, for example, may pick up *Salmonella* organisms from animal feces and transmit them to humans via contaminated food. Thus the fly is not a true reservoir of the infectious agent. **Biological vectors** are invertebrate animals that serve as host and reservoir of the microbial agent. Many arthropods feed on animals and humans and during the blood feast acquire the infectious microorganism. The infected arthropod can feed on other hosts, which may include humans, and thus transmit the infectious microorganisms from one host to another. Occasionally the arthropod is required in the developmental cycle of the microbial agent. The protozoal agent that is the cause of malaria requires the mosquito to undergo its sexual cycle. In the epithelial cells of the mosquito stomach the protozoan matures and then migrates to the salivary glands. When the mosquito bites a human, the pathogen is injected into the human host. The insect vectors and the diseases with which they are associated are outlined in Table 15-2.

INANIMATE RESERVOIRS

Inanimate reservoirs or sources of disease are soil, water, and food. Many microorganisms can carry out their life cycle in **soil** and water, and, fortunately for us, most are not pathogenic for humans. Most fungal species, for example, exist in the soil as spores. When some of these spores are inhaled by a susceptible host, they germinate and engage in vegetative growth and produce disease. Bacteria that produce the deadliest toxins known to humans are indigenous to the soil. Species of *Clostridium* such as *C. botulinum* and *C. tetani* exist in the soil as spores. *C. botulinum* may contaminate food and under anaerobic conditions produces the toxin associated with food poisoning (botulism). If *C. tetani* spores contaminate a wound, they germinate and produce a toxin responsible for the symptoms of the highly fatal disease called **tetanus.** Animal parasites such as the parasitic worms (helminths) are usually passed as eggs from the intestinal tract of the animals they parasitize. These eggs may remain in an infective state until they are picked up by another host. Very few microorganisms pathogenic for humans are capable of vegetative growth or a free-living existence in the soil.

Pure **water** is unable to support the growth of microorganisms, but most water contains minerals and organic nutrients that have been derived from the surrounding soil or air. Humans also contaminate waters either directly or indirectly via raw or processed sewage. Pathogenic as well as nonpathogenic microorganisms may find their way from humans or animals into water supplies. Some potential pathogens for humans live in the fish and shellfish that inhabit inland and coastal waters. Thus, water supports their existence and also contributes to their potential for infecting humans.

Food is an important reservoir for microorganisms infectious for humans. Human disease may result from ingestion of the meat of the infected animal or ingestion of originally uninfected meat that has been contaminated. Several bacterial and animal parasite diseases can be acquired by humans from the ingestion of meat from diseased animals. Eggs may be infected with *Salmonella* and when eaten raw can cause human disease. Cows carry several microorganisms infectious for humans. Ingestion of infected meat or milk may cause disease in humans. Tuberculosis, brucellosis, and Q fever are the most frequently encountered diseases resulting from the ingestion of infected meat or milk; however, diseases caused by species of *Campylobacter* and *Streptococcus* can also occur. These diseases are associated with drinking raw milk. Pasteurization ordinarily destroys these organisms. Some worms infect animals and are encysted in muscle. Ingestion of uncooked pork, for example, can lead to the disease called **trichinosis.**

Foods may be accidentally contaminated with potentially infectious microorganisms. Shellfish such as oysters, for example, may be harvested from waters that are polluted with human sewage. Ingestion of such foods uncooked can lead to such diseases as viral hepatitis. Carriers may contaminate food and be a source of disease to humans. Diseases such as salmonellosis, shigellosis, amebiasis, and cholera can be acquired in this way. Some microorganisms that contaminate foods produce toxins that when ingested cause gastrointestinal symptoms (see Transmission of Infectious Microorganisms). When properly refrigerated, smoked, canned, or pasteurized, however, foods are safe to eat and will not cause disease.

Transmission of Infectious Microorganisms

Disease transmission refers to the method of transfer of infectious microorganisms from the source (which may or may not be the same as the reservoir) to the host. Transmission may occur by contact, through the air, or by means of a vector. (Transmission by vectors was discussed under Reservoirs and Sources of Disease.) Sometimes an organism may have more than one route of transmission.

CONTACT

Spread of microorganisms by contact occurs when the potential victim has contact with the source of the microorganisms. This contact may be either direct or indirect.

Direct

Direct contact refers to transmission of microorganisms from person to person by close personal association. Handshaking, kissing, sneezing, coughing, and sexual contact represent the most usual ways that microorganisms are transferred by direct means (Fig. 15-1).

Sexually transmitted diseases have become rampant in many parts of the world, especially in developed countries like the United States. To most people, sexually transmitted diseases are represented by the traditional diseases syphilis and gonorrhea. Greater sexual freedom, as well as changes in sexual practices, has resulted in recent years in an increasing number of sexually transmitted diseases of unusual types. For example, chlamydial infection is now more common than gonorrhea, and the incidence of genital herpes is believed to be as high as 1 million or more cases per year. Homosexual activity can also lead to diseases usually considered to be primarily enteric. Enteric diseases such as giardiasis, salmonellosis, and shigellosis are now frequently encountered in the gay community. A list of the sexually transmitted diseases is presented in Table 15-3. The complications of sexually transmitted disease, especially in women, have created great concern. Increased health expenditures, loss of productivity, and human suffering have resulted from sexually transmitted disease complications such as pelvic inflammatory disease. These complications have led to loss of fertility as well as detrimental effects in the newborn.

Sneezing and coughing may also be considered a method of direct spread, provided the individuals are within a few feet of each other. The microorganisms are expelled in droplets that are carried only a few feet and then drop to horizontal surfaces. Direct spread of this kind is characteristic of measles, a viral disease.

Direct contact may also be responsible for the transmission of diseases that are caused by the patient's own mi-

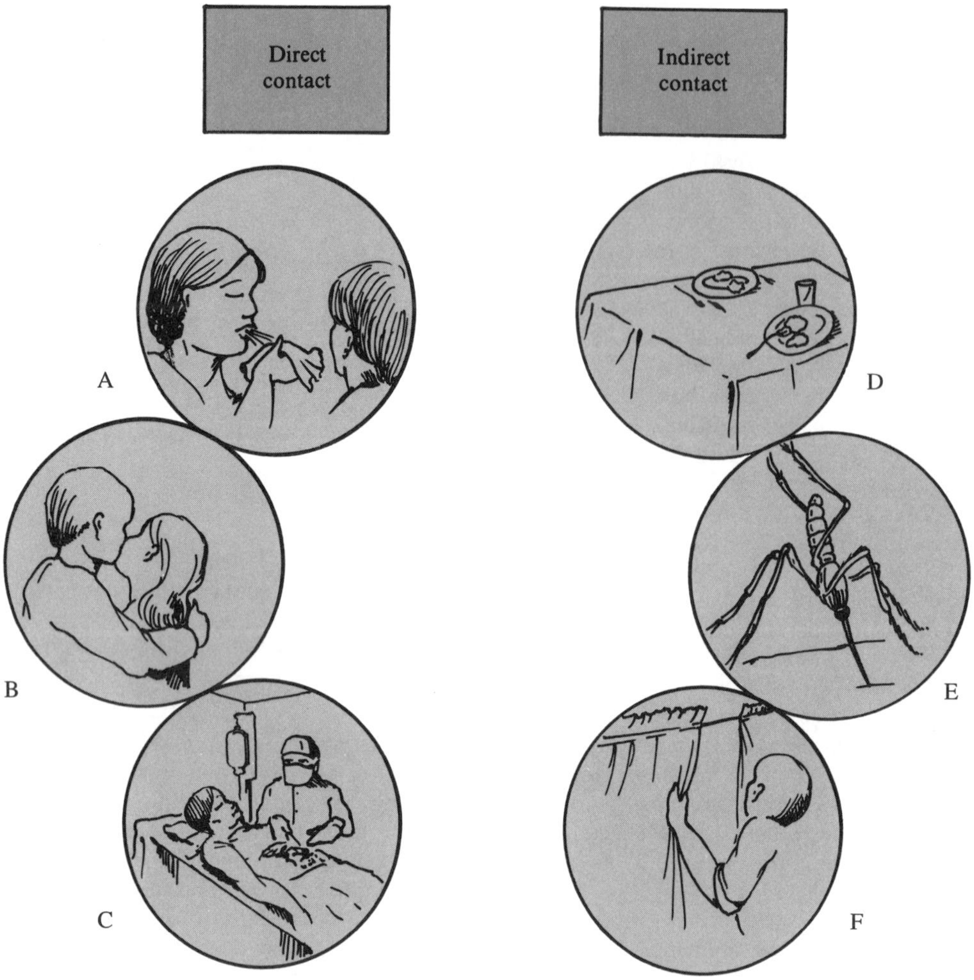

FIGURE 15-1
Routes of transmission for infectious agents. On the left are direct routes of transmission. A. Sneezing disperses microorganisms that will directly infect an individual within 3 feet of its origin. B. Kissing or direct contact between individuals, as in sexual intercourse, transmits microorganisms. C. During surgery an individual's indigenous microflora can be transferred by the surgeon to another body site, and this may result in infection. On the right are indirect routes of transmission. D. Food, water, or eating utensils may be contaminated with microorganisms that can be acquired by a person coming in contact with them. E. A mosquito can transfer infectious microorganisms from a source such as an animal to a new host. F. Microorganisms may be in particles that contaminate articles such as curtains. Handling the curtain can disperse the microorganisms, which can be inhaled or come in contact with other exposed tissue.

crobial flora. These infections, sometimes referred to as **endogenous,** are frequently encountered in the hospital environment. Patients, because of either examination or treatment procedures, can have indigenous microbial species transferred from one body site to another. During surgery, for example, intestinal microorganisms may be accidentally displaced from the intestinal tract into the bloodstream, where they replicate rapidly and cause disease (see Chapter 35).

Indirect

Indirect transmission occurs when the infectious microorganism is carried from one person to another on various intermediate objects such as food, dust, water, or **fomites** (inanimate objects other than food or water). The intermediate objects may be contaminated from an animate or inanimate source (see Fig. 15-1).

Water. Water is a common vehicle for the transmission of infectious microorganisms. An outbreak of waterborne disease is defined as an incident in which two or more persons experience similar illness after consumption or use of water intended for drinking and epidemiological evidence implicates water as the source of the illness. Community as well as noncommunity water systems may be involved. Many outbreaks occur in recreational areas where wells or other water sources become fecally con-

TABLE 15-3
Characteristics of the Sexually Transmitted Diseases[a]

Disease	Causal agent	Type of parasite	Cause of infertility, abortion, or infection to fetus	No. of cases reported to CDC, 1992	Estimated no. of infections per year
Gonorrhea	*Neisseria gonorrhoeae*	Bacterium	Yes	501,409	2.5 million
Syphilis	*Treponema pallidum*	Bacterium	Yes	33,973[b,c]	340,000
Nongonococcal urethritis	*Chlamydia trachomatis, Ureaplasma urealyticum*	Bacteria	No	NR	4–5 million
Trichomoniasis	*Trichomonas vaginalis*	Protozoan	No	NR	1.0 million
Venereal warts	Human papillomavirus	Virus	No	NR	12–24 million
Genital herpes	Herpes simplex virus	Virus	Yes	NR	30 million
Lymphogranuloma venereum	*Chlamydia trachomatis*	Bacterium	No	302	?
Soft chancre (chancroid)	*Hemophilus ducreyi*	Bacterium	No	1,886	?
Granuloma inguinale	*Calymmatobacterium granulomatis*	Bacterium	No	6	?
Candidiasis	*Candida albicans*	Fungus	Yes	NR	?
Scabies	*Sarcoptes scabiei*	Arachnid (mite)	No	NR	?
Pediculosis pubis	*Phthirus pubis*	Insect (louse)	No	NR	?
Enteric disease	*Salmonella* species	Bacterium	No	NR	?
	Shigella species	Bacterium	No	NR	?
	Campylobacter fetus subspecies *jejuni*	Bacterium	Yes	NR	?
	Entamoeba histolytica	Protozoan	No	NR	?
	Giardia lamblia	Protozoan	No	NR	?
AIDS (acquired immunodeficiency syndrome)	Human immunodeficiency virus (HIV)	Virus	No	45,472	?

CDC = Centers for Disease Control; NR = not reportable.
[a] See also Appendix F for more recent data.
[b] Primary and secondary cases only.
[c] Civilian cases only.

taminated. From 40 to 50 outbreaks, involving about 4000 to 5000 cases, occur each year in the United States. The most frequently recovered pathogen is *Giardia lamblia,* a protozoan that causes gastrointestinal disease. The infectious agents associated with waterborne disease are outlined in Table 15-4.

Water is also an important vehicle for extraintestinal infection. A number of pathogens can be acquired through occupational, recreational, and even therapeutic contact with water. Waterborne pathogens can enter the human through intact or abraded skin, for example, hot tub–associated dermatitis; inhalation and aspiration, for example, contaminated aerosolized medications or humidifiers; or simply application of water to eyes, ears, nose, oral cavity, and mucosa of the genitourinary tracts. Extraintestinal infections are primarily superficial infections involving the skin but severe systemic disease may occur in those who are immunologically deficient. The spectrum of microbial agents that can cause such water-related diseases includes bacteria, fungi, viruses, and protozoa. Two of the most important recognized agents of water-related extraintestinal infections are bacteria, that is, *Legionella pneumophila,* the cause of legionnaires' disease, and marine *Vibrio* species that cause wound infections.

Food. A foodborne disease outbreak is defined as an incident in which two or more persons experience a similar illness, usually gastrointestinal, after ingestion of a common food and epidemiological analysis implicates the food as the source of the illness. Over 60 percent of foodborne disease outbreaks are associated with restaurants; the remainder are associated with foods eaten at home (Table 15-5). Factors that contribute to foodborne illness are (1) improper holding temperatures for food, (2) poor personal hygiene, (3) contaminated equipment used in the processing of food, (4) inadequate cooking, and (5) food obtained from an unsafe source. The microbial agents most frequently implicated in foodborne illness are *Salmonella* species, *Campylobacter* species, *S. aureus,* and *Clostridium perfringens.* They are responsible for nearly 80 percent of the outbreaks in the United States. *Campylo-*

TABLE 15-4
Infectious Agents Associated with Waterborne Disease*

Causal agent	Incubation period	Clinical syndrome
Bacterial		
Escherichia coli	6–36 hr	Gastrointestinal syndrome, usually diarrhea
Salmonella species	6–48 hr	Gastrointestinal syndrome, usually diarrhea
Shigella species	12–48 hr	Gastrointestinal syndrome, usually diarrhea
Campylobacter jejuni	2–5 days	Gastrointestinal syndrome, usually diarrhea
Yersinia enterocolitica	3–7 days	Gastrointestinal syndrome, usually diarrhea
Parasitic		
Giardia lamblia	1–4 wk	Gastrointestinal syndrome, usually chronic diarrhea, cramps, fatigue, and weight loss
Entamoeba histolytica	2–4 wk	Gastrointestinal syndrome, variable from acute fulminating dysentery with fever, chills, and bloody stools to mild diarrhea and abdominal cramps
Cryptosporidium	5–21 days	Cholera-like diarrhea, abdominal cramps
Viral		
Hepatitis A	2–4 wk	Fever, nausea, vomiting, dark urine
Norwalk and Norwalk-like agents	24–48 hr	Gastrointestinal syndrome, vomiting, watery diarrhea, abdominal cramps, often headache
Rotavirus	24–72 hr	Gastrointestinal syndrome, vomiting, watery diarrhea, abdominal cramps, often with dehydration
Enterovirus	5–10 days	Other syndromes than gastrointestinal: poliomyelitis, aseptic meningitis, and herpangina

* Heavy metals may also be associated with waterborne disease, but they are not included here.

TABLE 15-5
Microorganisms Associated with Reportable Foodborne Disease Outbreaks in the United States*

Etiological agent	Relative frequency	Common vehicle
Bacterial		
Bacillus cereus	Infrequent	Contaminated rice
Campylobacter species	Frequent	Undercooked chicken, unpasteurized milk
Clostridium perfringens	Frequent	Improper storage or cooking of meats or meat products
Clostridium botulinum	Infrequent	Home-canned vegetables or fermented foods
Escherichia coli	Infrequent	Contaminated and undercooked hamburger
Salmonella species	Frequent	Undercooked chicken, eggs, unpasteurized milk
Shigella species	Infrequent	Food contaminated by food handlers in crowded conditions
Staphylococcus aureus	Frequent	Pastries, custard, salad dressing, sliced meats
Streptococcus group A	Infrequent	Any foods contaminated by carrier
Vibrio cholerae	Infrequent	Fish, raw oysters
Vibrio parahaemolyticus	Infrequent	Raw seafood
Animal parasite		
Trichinella spiralis	Infrequent	Pork, wild animal meat
Viral		
Hepatitis A	Frequent	Potato salad, frozen custard
Norwalk virus	Infrequent	Shellfish

*Foodborne disease may also be caused by chemicals, for example, heavy metals, mushrooms, and contaminated fish, which are not included in this table.

bacter species are now considered the most frequent cause of bacterial diarrhea in the United States. A major factor responsible for some outbreaks is improper holding temperature. Foodborne disease may be divided into two types: **food infections** and **food poisonings.** Food infections result from the ingestion of microorganisms, such as *Salmonella,* found in the food. Salmonellae produce a toxin in the victim's intestine that causes gastrointestinal symptoms. Food poisonings are the result of ingestion of toxins that were liberated during growth of microorganisms in the food. Microbial growth occurs because the contaminated food was left at an improper holding temperature. *S. aureus,* for example, may be transmitted by food handlers, and if the food is left at a temperature that supports microbial growth the microorganisms multiply and produce a toxin that, if ingested, causes gastrointestinal disease.

In recent years *Listeria monocytogenes* has become established as a foodborne pathogen. This organism is psychrophilic and capable of growth at refrigeration temperatures. *L. monocytogenes* is especially virulent in compromised patients, for example, in those with underlying malignancy or in pregnant women. Neonatal or adult disease can result in meningitis. Stillbirths may also occur in the neonate. Major outbreaks of listeriosis have occurred since 1981 and case-fatality ratios have been high in each outbreak.

Fomites. Inanimate objects (fomites) are also involved in disease transmission. Contamination of inanimate objects is a frequently encountered means of disease transmission in the hospital. Catheters, needles, and other objects may be contaminated by hospital personnel. When these devices come into contact with the patient, the contaminating microorganisms may initiate disease (see Chapter 35).

AIR

Microorganisms cannot use air as a reservoir, but they can use it as means of dissemination. Airborne transmission implies that the organisms travel longer distances than in the direct type of transmission between individuals, which usually involves distances of only a few feet. Wind currents, humidity, and other environmental factors influence the distance microorganisms can travel in the wind currents or as vegetative forms that have been aerosolized and carried by currents of air. Many of the fungal diseases, for example, result from the inhalation of spores that contaminate the environment and are carried in the air.

Indoors, microorganisms are also disseminated either in dust or as droplet nuclei. **Dust** is material that has settled to surfaces and is subject to dissemination by air currents or various physical actions (shaking a dust mop, for example). The dust particles may remain suspended in the air for various lengths of time. Some microorganisms such as staphylococci and streptococci can remain viable in dust for up to three months. This is a characteristic that is more common among the gram-positive bacteria than gram-negative bacteria. The cell envelope of gram-positive bacteria is considerably thicker and more resistant to drying and ultraviolet radiation than that of gram-negative bacteria. **Droplet nuclei** are particles of mucus that have been expelled from humans by sneezing or coughing. These mucus particles contain microorganisms and because of their small size (5 μm or smaller) remain suspended in air for long periods of time. Tuberculosis is a disease that is transmitted by droplet nuclei.

Aerosols generated by spraying water into the air (e.g., at water treatment facilities or in humidifiers or water coolers) may also contain microorganisms that are infectious for humans. Legionnaires' disease, for example, is caused by a microorganism whose primary habitat is water and is transmitted to humans by aerosols.

HORIZONTAL VS. VERTICAL TRANSMISSION

Microorganisms must spread from one individual to another if they are to persist and cause disease. If an individual infected with the measles virus, for example, does not make contact with other individuals, the virus will die in the host. Microorganisms can be spread horizontally or vertically. **Horizontal spread** is the transfer of disease by everyday contact, that is, by air, water, food, contact, or vectors. **Vertical spread** involves transfer of infectious agents from parent to offspring via sperm, ovum, placenta, milk, or direct contact.

Vertical Transmission

The vertical transmission of infectious agents may occur after birth (postnatal), before birth (congenital), or during birth (perinatal). Congenital transmission involves transfer of the microbial agent across the placenta; perinatal infection occurs during passage through the birth canal. The microbial agents associated with congenital and perinatal infections are outlined in Table 15-6. Transmission across the placental membrane results in deposition of the microbial agent into the fetal blood. The infectious agent can then be disseminated to any organ or tissue of the fetus. Transmission during passage through the birth canal results initially in infection of the skin, eyes, or respiratory tract of the infant. Depending on its virulence, the microbial agent may later invade the bloodstream. The infant, after infection, often sheds the microbial agent because of immune tolerance. The infected host may produce antibodies to the infectious agent, but they are not sufficient to neutralize the microorganism. Infections can be devastating to the newborn, resulting in malformations, damage to various organs or tissues, and even death.

Transmission after birth (postnatal) occurs when the parent (1) experiences a primary infection at or just after the birth, (2) experiences a reactivation of a latent infection (some persistent viruses, for example, are activated during pregnancy), or (3) has been shedding virus continuously during pregnancy. Hepatitis virus, for example, is carried in the blood of the mother and is transmitted during or shortly after birth. A mother who sheds microorganisms in the milk during lactation represents one of the most common means of postnatal transmission. Other vehicles of transmission include feces, urine, saliva, blood, and contact with skin mucosa.

TABLE 15-6
Microbial Agents Associated with Congenital or Perinatal Disease in Infants

Agent	Consequences of infection
Congenital infection	
Cytomegalovirus	Hepatitis, jaundice, congenital heart disease, mental retardation
Rubella virus	Abortion, congenital malformation, deafness, cataracts, heart defects, encephalitis
Poxvirus (smallpox)	Abortion, stillbirth, congenital smallpox
Varicella-zoster virus	Low birth weight, bilateral cataracts, atrophic limbs, mental retardation, congenital varicella
Vaccinia virus	Abortion, generalized vaccinia
Poliovirus	Congenital poliomyelitis
Measles virus	Stillbirth, congenital measles
Mumps virus	Abortion, endocardial fibroelastosis
Herpes simplex virus	Abortion, excessive brain damage, hepatoadrenal necrosis
Hepatitis B virus	Neonatal hepatitis, stillbirth, abortion
Echovirus	Hydrocephalus and neurological sequelae, jaundice (most infections are asymptomatic or mild)
Coxsackievirus B	Myocarditis and central nervous system involvement
Arbovirus	Congenital encephalitis
Treponema pallidum (bacterium)	Stillbirth, abortion, saddle nose, notched teeth, central nervous system involvement
Toxoplasma gondii (protozoan)	Stillbirth, hydrocephalus, mental retardation
Perinatal infection	
Herpes simplex virus	Localized infection of oral cavity, skin, eye
Neisseria gonorrhoeae (bacterium)	Infections of the eye (ophthalmia neonatorum)
Chlamydia trachomatis (bacterium)	Inclusion conjunctivitis
Streptococcus group B (bacterium)	Pneumonia, septicemia, meningitis

Transmission to the offspring via the germ line is also possible. Ova and sperm may be infected with microbial agents such as viruses. These agents, provided they do no harm to ova or sperm, could conceivably be transferred to the developing embryo. This type of transmission has been observed in animals. The mouse mammary tumor virus, for example, is transmitted via sperm in some laboratory strains. Viruses, such as the herpes simplex virus, cytomegalovirus, hepatitis virus, Marburg virus, and Ebola virus, have been found in human semen although they have not been found to be involved in germ-line transmission. The established examples of germ-line transmission are the oncoviruses, whose genome becomes part of the host's genome during infection. Human sex cells can transmit the virus to the offspring.

Patterns of Disease in the Community

ENDEMIC, EPIDEMIC, AND SPORADIC DISEASE

Infectious diseases occur in a population with a particular frequency, which may be defined as **endemic, epidemic,** or **sporadic.** To determine which term applies to the disease in question, one must have some idea of the history of the disease in the community. The history of the disease can be evaluated by noting when the disease has occurred and the number of persons involved. **Endemic** disease implies that the disease continues in a specified population without interruption. Cholera, for example, is a disease endemic to Southeast Asia. Diseases become endemic when an equilibrium has been established between the host and the parasite. One characteristic of endemic disease is that many individuals in the community have clinically inapparent disease. An influx of persons, for example, from a geographical area where the disease is not endemic represents a highly susceptible population. Endemic disease may also be associated with animal populations, where it is referred to as **enzootic disease.** An outbreak of two or three cases of diphtheria every 8 to 10 years exemplifies a sporadic disease.

When the number of new cases of disease in a defined period of time rises above its normal endemic level, we speak of the disease as being **epidemic.** The epidemic usually begins with a sudden occurrence of disease in those who are susceptible and who come into contact with an infected source. Epidemics involve specific populations that may vary from a single site such as a hospital, to a city, to large geographic areas that may encompass the globe. The term **pandemic** is used to denote worldwide epidemics.

Sporadic diseases are those that occur in such an irregular pattern that their frequency cannot be calculated. For example, a disease may develop after fracture of a limb.

INCIDENCE AND PREVALENCE

The occurrence of disease in a population may be quantified by determining its incidence and prevalence. **Incidence** refers to the number of new cases in a particular population within a specifically defined time period. For example, the incidence may be expressed as the number of new cases per 10,000 or 100,000 individuals in the population per year. The incidence may also be referred to as **morbidity rate.** The number of individuals who have died as a result of disease in a specific time is referred to as the **mortality rate.** A constant check on morbidity and mortality rates by epidemiologists helps health care officials to ward off future outbreaks and to warn the public of how to avoid disease. **Prevalence** refers to the total number of cases (both new and old) of disease in a defined population within a specified time. It includes patients with newly detected disease as well as those with disease at an earlier time whose symptoms are still clinically apparent. If an individual had a disease that lasted eight weeks, he or she would be counted once in an incidence survey. If two prevalence studies were performed in that eight-week period, the infected patient would be counted both times.

A list of the diseases reported to the Centers for Disease Control for 1992 may be found in Appendix F.

HERD IMMUNITY

The rate at which an epidemic spreads and the number of individuals involved are determined by the factors that affect the communicability of the disease and the immunity of the population. Many diseases are highly communicable because of the manner in which they are spread. Respiratory diseases, for example, often spread rapidly, particularly in confined populations, such as in classrooms, military barracks, hospitals, and institutions for the infirmed. Foodborne and waterborne diseases occur with great rapidity and involve large numbers of individuals because the victims have been exposed to a common source and because the incubation period is often very short. There are instances when exposure to a common source does not reveal itself as an epidemic because the incubation period for the disease is long and variable. Hepatitis B, for example, has an incubation period of several weeks. Thus the number of cases of hepatitis that have been defined are spread out over several weeks. With this type of disease it is difficult to identify the source and thus control the spread of disease.

The number of individuals in whom disease develops during an epidemic is also related to the immunity of the host. An individual who, by either passive or active means, is immune to the disease removes himself or herself as a potential source of infection to others (unless the person is a carrier). When many immune individuals are present in a community, there exists what is called **herd immunity.** The herd immunity concept is based on the relative number of immune and susceptible individuals in a population. Immune individuals act as a barrier to the spread of infectious agents from infected persons to susceptible individuals. Even though a highly communicable disease may cause an epidemic, many nonimmune individuals will be protected because of the unlikelihood of their coming in contact with an infected person. One of the values of vaccine immunization is that enough individuals will be protected from disease to prevent its rapid spread to those in the population who have not received the vaccine.

DESCRIPTIVE EPIDEMIOLOGY

The routine surveillance of disease in a community to show its distribution is called **descriptive epidemiology.** Descriptive epidemiology takes into account (1) host factors that may contribute to susceptibility to disease, (2) the geographical areas where the host came in contact with the infectious agent, and (3) the time of the appearance of disease.

Host Factors

Many host factors, including age, sex, race, underlying disease, and immunization status, contribute to the susceptibility to disease. These variables are discussed in Chapter 14. All of them must be considered in evaluating the development of disease in a community.

Place

Knowing the place where contact between host and infectious agent occurs is very important in evaluating diseases in a community. If one is able to determine the site where contact has been made, measures can be taken to break the chain of transmission. Determining the place of contact between host and infectious agent is usually much easier in a confined environment such as a hospital than in the community, where infected individuals may be spread out.

Time

Time in relationship to the disease process can be viewed from different perspectives. One may observe seasonal trends, month-to-month variations, or long-term trends that span several years. Seasonal patterns are important for determining in which seasons diseases are more likely to occur. Respiratory diseases, for example, are at a considerably higher level in the fall and winter than in the summer months. Foodborne diseases, on the other hand, occur more frequently during the summer months because the ambient temperatures are higher, which permits microorganisms contaminating food to multiply rapidly. Long-term evaluations of epidemiological patterns have been important in determining the periodicity of diseases such as influenza A. Influenza A reaches epidemic proportions every two to three years. One strain of the influenza A virus is able to bring about sufficient immunity in a community after an epidemic, but then the virus spontaneously changes the chemical nature of its surface molecules (antigenic drift). The new strain is not recognized by the immune system of those who developed immunity to the first strain. Thus the entire population becomes susceptible to the new strain of virus (see Chapter 32 for more details on viral surface changes during infection).

An epidemic can be represented graphically by plotting the number of cases of disease against time. The time scale will vary according to the incubation period of the dis-

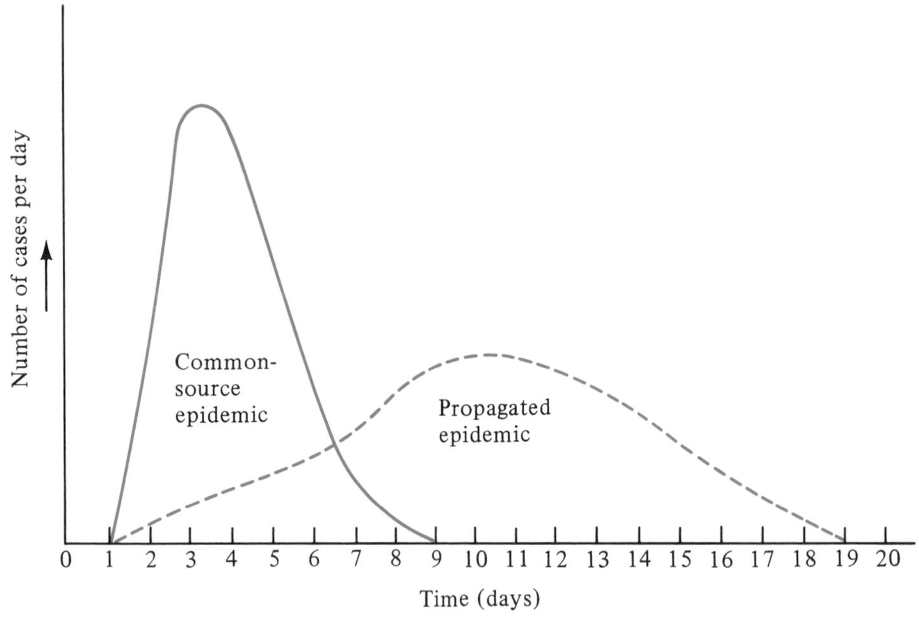

FIGURE 15-2
Comparison of common-source epidemic and a propagated epidemic. Food poisoning resulting from contamination of a food eaten by a group is an example of a common-source epidemic. Influenza, which is spread by contact between individuals, is an example of a propagated epidemic.

ease. The epidemic curve begins with the **index case,** that is, the first case observed in the disease outbreak. The upslope of the curve is influenced by the incubation period, the number of exposed individuals, and the rapidity with which transmission occurs. The downslope of the curve is usually more gradual than the upslope because of the decreasing numbers of individuals susceptible to disease. Epidemics that are the result of contact with a contaminated material such as food or water are called **common-source epidemics.** In a common-source epidemic the epidemic curve rises sharply and then gradually falls off (Fig. 15–2). Epidemics that arise from person-to-person contact are called **propagated** or **contact-spread epidemics.** The epidemic curve in propagated epidemics rises slowly, has a flatter peak than the common-source epidemic, and then falls off gradually.

Laboratory Techniques in Epidemiology

Epidemiological investigations, as we now know, provide us with valuable information that can lead to the breaking of the chain of transmission of disease and reduce its incidence. During an epidemiological investigation the symptoms of disease are often sufficient to establish the cause of disease. The causal agent of disease is also isolated in many epidemics to determine the source of disease. Many strains of an organism may exist in a community—some strains may be involved in the epidemic, but others may be nonepidemic. The problem is to separate the epidemic strains from the nonepidemic ones. *Escherichia coli,* for example, may be involved in an epidemic of urinary tract infections. The *E. coli* strains isolated from the infected patients may be identified by several laboratory procedures. Since *E. coli* is harbored by all humans, we must find a property that is unique to the epidemic strains and not to the strains found in the healthy population. A biochemical, serological, or other type of test may differentiate the two types of strains. These differentiating characteristics are extremely important not only for determining the source of the epidemic; they also have practical value. The bacterium causing pneumonia, *S. pneumoniae,* for example, produces a capsule. Many strains of *S. pneumoniae* exist; these can be separated on the basis of the antigenic characteristics of the capsule. Only a few strains, however, are regularly found during epidemics. To produce an effective vaccine using capsular antigens, it is necessary to know which strains are the most frequently associated with disease in the community.

Several conventional laboratory techniques have been employed in epidemiological investigations. These include **biotyping, serotyping, antibiograms,** and **phage typing.** Some of these techniques can be useful in differentiating species but not strains within a species. Often these techniques are highly variable or too slow to be of practical value. They require the use of a reference laboratory and are not practical for small clinical laboratories. Still, hospital personnel should know which organisms can be typed in case an epidemiological investigation is required. For the larger clinical laboratories, plasmid pattern analysis and restriction endonuclease analysis of plasmid and genomic DNA are simple to perform and highly reproducible. A brief analysis of these techniques is provided.

CONVENTIONAL METHODS

Biotyping

Biotyping is used to differentiate biochemical characteristics. It is useful for differentiating species but additional tests are required to separate epidemic from nonepidemic strains.

Serotyping

Serotyping involves antigenic differentiation between strains of species. This has been useful in differentiating several gram-negative aerobic bacilli such as *Klebsiella* and *Pseudomonas* species and *E. coli.* The antigens differentiated are often capsular.

Antibiograms

Antibiograms are tests used to determine a microorganism's susceptibility to antibiotics or other antimicrobials. They are useful if the trait examined is chromosomal. However, if the antimicrobial trait is plasmid-associated, antibiograms are not reliable. This is because of the rapid exchange of these traits with other microorganisms, particularly among the Enterobacteriaceae.

Phage Typing

Phage typing is based on the susceptibility of specific strains of a species to infection by a standard set of bacterial viruses (Fig. 15-3). Phage typing has been used with some success for differentiating strains of *S. aureus* and *Pseudomonas aeruginosa*. Plasmid transfer of traits, however, could confuse this differentiation process.

Bacteriocin Typing

Bacteriocins are metabolic products released by some microorganisms that inhibit the growth of other microorganisms. Bacteriocins are active against strains of the same or closely related species. Production of the bacteriocin by an epidemic strain or susceptibility of an organism to a bacteriocin produced by other bacteria can be used for typing (Fig. 15-4).

MOLECULAR METHODS

Plasmid Profiles

Sometimes the more routinely used typing systems are not applicable to the identification of some microbial species, or when used, do not provide results suitable for differentiation. Under these circumstances the epidemiologist must use other techniques. One of the newly developed techniques is **plasmid characterization.** Plasmids are infectious and carry many important bacterial determinants, including antibiotic resistance, toxin formation, bacteriocin production, heavy-metal resistance, and metabolic enzyme activity. Techniques involving plasmids fall into two categories, direct and indirect.

Direct plasmid analysis involves hybridization of plasmid DNA from different strains, which allows the quantitative assessment of base sequence homology. **Indirect techniques** include agarose gel electrophoresis and restriction endonuclease analysis. In the agarose gel technique the clinical isolates are cultivated and lysed, and then the supernatant is electrophoresed on agarose gel. The gel is washed and stained by ethidium bromide,

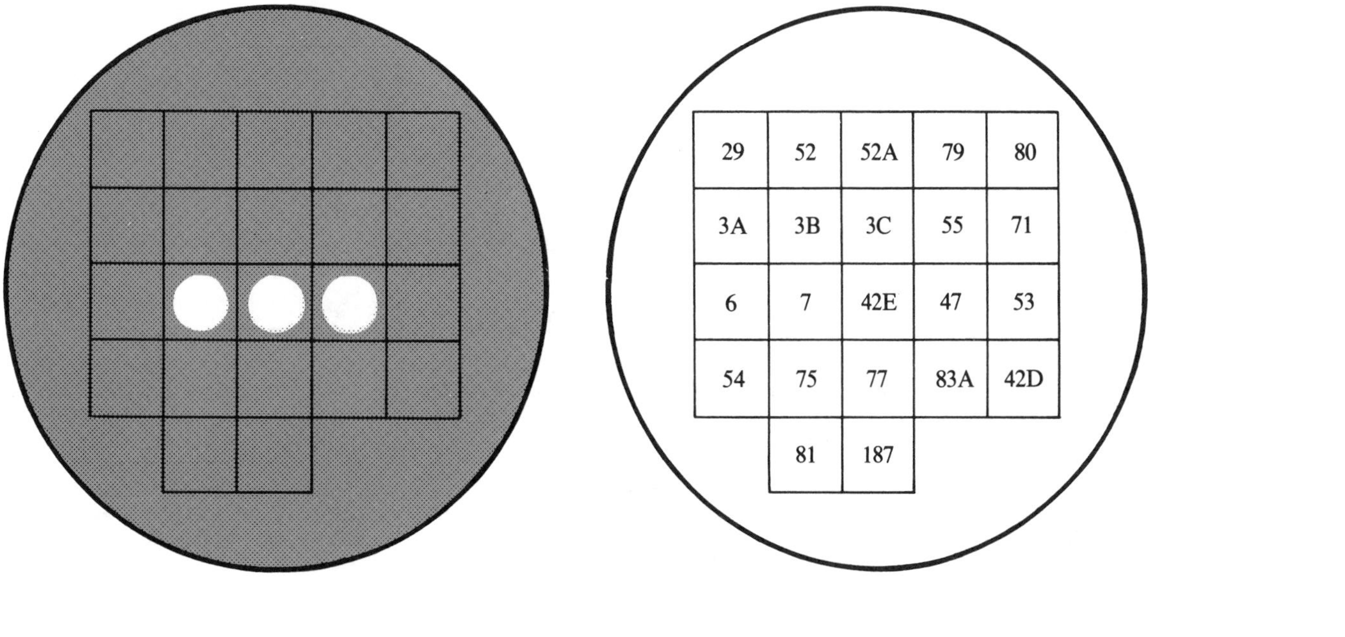

FIGURE 15-3
Phage typing of staphylococci. An agar plate is marked off in squares. The plate is then streaked with *Staphylococcus aureus* and allowed to dry. Specific phage suspensions, corresponding to the strains indicated on the right, are placed in the appropriate squares. After being allowed to dry again, the plate is incubated for 12 to 18 hours. The plate on the left shows confluent growth except where plaques (areas of cell lysis) appear in the squares corresponding to phage preparation 7, 42E, and 47.

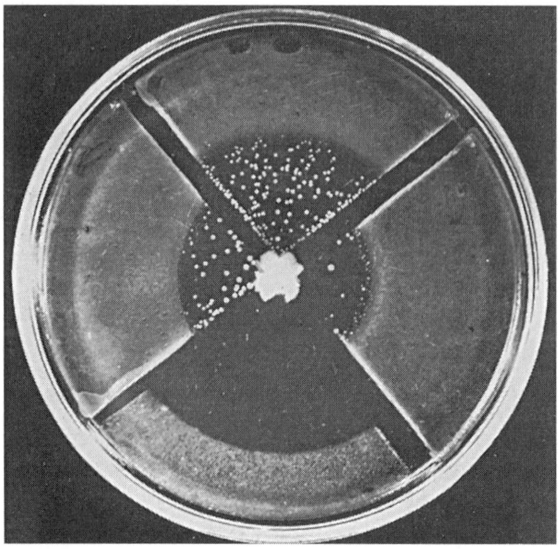

FIGURE 15-4
Bacteriocin typing. Colicin sensitivity of strains of *Escherichia coli*. The macrocolony of *E. coli* in the center of the plate is an active colicin producer. As it is produced, the colicin diffuses out from the colony into the medium. This colony was grown for 24 hours, after which each of the four quarters of the plate was seeded with strains of *E. coli* with various degrees of sensitivity to the colicin. After incubation, zones of inhibition proportional to the sensitivity of the strain developed. Within the zones, growth of colicin-resistant colonies can be seen. (From L. E. Hawker and A. H. Linton, eds., *Microorganisms: Function, Form and Environment*, 2nd ed. London: Edward Arnold, 1979.)

transluminated with ultraviolet light, and photographed. Plasmid size is determined by comparing gel migration distances (Fig. 15-5) of unknown plasmids with those of plasmids of known molecular size. Plasmids of the same size may have entirely different base sequences, and these differences can be detected by using restriction endonucleases. Restriction endonucleases cleave double-stranded DNA at specific recognition sites and produce several plasmid fragments. If two plasmids are of the same size and yield identical patterns of fragments on restriction endonuclease analysis, they are assumed to be identical or nearly so. If the plasmids of equal size have different sequences, then different fragments will be produced from endonuclease digestion.

Restriction endonuclease fingerprinting can also be applied to chromosomal DNA. This technique has been used to differentiate strains of some bacteria such as *Vibrio cholerae* and *Campylobacter* species. Typing of herpes simplex viruses is now performed by using restriction endonuclease fingerprinting.

DNA Probes

DNA probes are specific single-stranded DNA sequences derived from one microorganism **(the probe).** The probe DNA represents a specific microbial feature that distinguishes it from other microorganisms. Once the DNA probe is isolated, it is reproduced in large quantities by cloning it in *E. coli*. DNA probes are discussed in Chapter 6.

Polymerase Chain Reaction

The polymerase chain reaction is being used primarily for diagnostic purposes but it probably will be useful as an epidemiological tool for infectious agents that cannot be cultured by ordinary means. The sensitivity of this technique is unparalleled; however, this sensitivity is also an Achilles' heel. Minuscule quantities of contaminating nucleic acids may give false-positive results. The polymerase chain reaction technique is discussed in Chapter 6.

Summary

1. Epidemiology is the study of determinants, occurrence, and distribution of health and disease in a population.

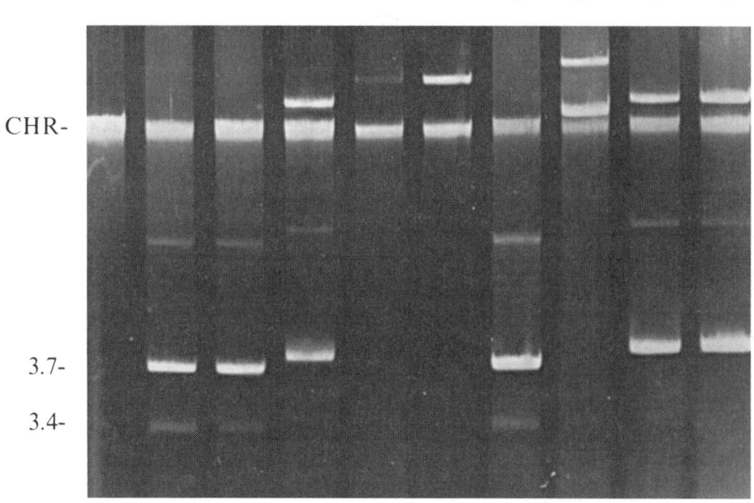

FIGURE 15-5
Agarose gel electrophoresis of *Salmonella newport* from isolated cases in Pennsylvania and New Jersey, June to August 1981. Lanes B, C, and G represent the epidemic strains. CHR = chromosome band. (From L. W. Riley et al., *J. Infect. Dis.* 148:12, 1983.)

2. Humans respond to infectious agents in different ways depending on the traits of the microorganism and the immunological state of the host. Some infections are subclinical or inapparent. Most human infections are acute; that is, the symptoms are intense but quickly subside and the microbe is eliminated.

3. Acute diseases can be divided into stages: (1) incubation period, (2) prodromal period, (3) acute period, and (4) convalescent period. One of the most frequent characteristics of infection is fever. Fever helps to enhance the inflammatory response and prevent microbial multiplication, but fever also has detrimental effects to the host.

4. Another characteristic of many infections is rash formation. Rashes can be divided into four major types: macular, papular, vesicular, and pustular. Other symptoms of disease include cough in respiratory infections and diarrhea or dysentery in intestinal infection.

5. Chronic diseases represent a type of persistent infection in which the microbe avoids the normal immunological responses of the host.

6. In order for microorganisms to survive and gain access to a host, they must have a site for multiplication, that is, a reservoir, and they must have a site for transmission to the host, that is, a source. Sources may be animate or inanimate objects.

7. Reservoirs may be animate and include humans, animals, and insects. Inanimate reservoirs include soil, water, or food. Some human reservoirs act as carriers; that is, they shed infectious microorganisms without showing symptoms. Carriers may be of two types: convalescent and healthy.

8. Diseases that occur primarily in animals but can be transmitted to humans are called zoonoses. Insects behave as vectors in the transmission of infectious agents to humans. Mechanical insect vectors are not involved in the life cycle of the infectious microbe but biological vectors serve as host and reservoir of the infectious agent.

9. Microorganisms can be spread by direct or indirect contact. Direct contact includes handshaking, kissing, sneezing, coughing, and sexual contact. Indirect contact implies transmission of microbes from human to human via objects such as food, water, or fomites (inanimate objects).

10. Waterborne diseases in the United States are frequently associated with community and noncommunity water systems. *Giardia lamblia* is the most frequently recovered pathogen. Most foodborne diseases are associated with restaurants, with *Salmonella* species, *Staphylococcus aureus*, and *Clostridium perfringens* the most frequently implicated microbial agents.

11. Air acts as an avenue for transmission of infectious microorganisms. Spores from the soil are easily disseminated by air and many fungal diseases are spread by this means. Indoors, microorganisms are disseminated in dust or as droplet nuclei. Aerosols generated by humidifiers, for example, also carry infectious microorganisms.

12. Microorganisms can be spread horizontally or vertically. Horizontal transmission implies spread by everyday contact, that is, air, food, water, direct or indirect contact, and vectors. Vertical transmission implies spread from parent to offspring via sperm, ova, and so on. Vertical spread may occur after birth (postnatal), before birth (congenital), or during birth (perinatal).

13. The patterns of disease in a community may be referred to as endemic, epidemic, or sporadic. **Endemic** implies continuous presence of the disease. **Epidemic** refers to levels of disease above the endemic level. Global epidemics are referred to as pandemics. **Sporadic** diseases do not occur with any regularity.

14. Occurrence of disease in a population may be quantified by determining the incidence and prevalence. **Incidence,** or morbidity, refers to the number of new cases of disease in a specific population within a defined time period. **Prevalence** refers to the number of new and existing cases of disease in a certain time frame.

15. The rate at which a disease spreads is to some extent influenced by the number of immune individuals at the time of the epidemic. They represent a barrier to spread of disease, a concept called **herd immunity.**

16. Descriptive epidemiology uses surveillance measures that take into account (1) host factors that affect the spread of disease, (2) the place of contact with the infectious agent, and (3) the time of the appearance of disease.

17. Several laboratory techniques can be used to differentiate epidemic from nonepidemic strains of microbial species: biotyping, serotyping, bacteriophage typing, bacteriocin typing, antibiograms, plasmid profiles, DNA probes, and polymerase chain reactions.

Questions for Study

1. Why is reliance on antibiograms as an epidemiological tool not always appropriate?
2. What are the similarities and differences between chronic and acute disease?
3. What is the distinction between a reservoir and source of disease? Can they be the same? Are there any examples of when they are and are not the same?
4. You are assisting a surgeon in an operation involving the chest cavity. List the various ways in which the patient could become infected.
5. List the three major bacterial foodborne diseases and three bacterial waterborne diseases. What viruses are associated with waterborne disease? Viral foodborne disease?
6. What is meant by herd immunity? Give examples for when it does and does not apply.

PART

V

Bacteria That Cause Infectious Disease

CHAPTER

16 Clinical Microbiology

OBJECTIVES

To outline the precautions that are required when collecting specimens

To outline briefly the steps that are ordinarily taken in the laboratory identification of a bacterial specimen

To list the various types of microscopes used in the clinical laboratory and discuss how each is used

To discuss briefly the importance of the Gram stain

To list the biochemical tests that are routinely used in identification of bacteria and what they measure

To discuss some of the advantages and disadvantages in the use of molecular techniques in laboratory identification

To outline the safety measures that are necessary to prevent infection of the clinical staff as well as the patient

OUTLINE

SPECIMEN COLLECTION
- General Guidelines
- Guidelines for Specific Specimens
  - Blood
  - Urine
  - Feces
  - Cerebrospinal Fluid

LABORATORY IDENTIFICATION
- Microscopy
- Culture
- Biochemical Characteristics
  - Fluorogenic and Chromogenic Substrates
- Serological Characteristics
- Rapid Identification Techniques
- Molecular Techniques
  - Nucleic Acid Analysis
  - Flow Cytometry
  - Gas-Liquid Chromatography

ANTIMICROBIAL SUSCEPTIBILITY TESTING

COMPUTERS IN THE CLINICAL LABORATORY

LABORATORY SAFETY

TERMINOLOGY
- Prefixes
- Suffixes

Clinical microbiology is the science that deals with the isolation, identification, and antimicrobial susceptibility determination of microorganisms. The information collected from these procedures will guide the clinician in the proper care and treatment of the patient. The following discussions are not all-inclusive. Instead, we present some of the guidelines and procedures that are currently incorporated in the clinical laboratory. Many schemes or procedures are discussed elsewhere in the text and they will be pointed out. Unless otherwise stated, our discussion involves bacteria.

Specimen Collection

The precise laboratory information needed by the physician cannot be obtained unless consideration is first given to the proper collection of a specimen. Improperly collected specimens often result in incorrect identification. The consequences of this could be very serious to the patient.

GENERAL GUIDELINES

General guidelines for the collection of various specimens are as follows:

1. Whenever possible, collect specimens before the administration of antimicrobial agents. If antimicrobials have been administered, it may be necessary to obtain several specimens in order to isolate the infectious agent.
2. The specimen must be representative of the infected site. Specimens contaminated by indigenous microorganisms from adjacent body sites (saliva, feces, etc.) are not suitable for processing. Collection of specimens (deep wound) by needle should be performed by a physician specialist.
3. The specimen should be collected in a proper container. A variety of transport containers are available. Most specimens are collected with a swab made of rayon, calcium alginate, or polyester. Since swab specimens may dry out before being submitted to the laboratory, several types of transport media are available. Some commercially manufactured swabs contain a transport medium. A transport medium is not always essential for viruses. Some viruses in urine, cerebrospinal fluid (CSF), or blood can be transported in the specimen itself.

   Strict anaerobes are usually collected by aspirating material with a needle and syringe. The syringe may be capped and transported directly to the laboratory for processing. If processing is to be delayed, the specimen should be injected into specially designed anaerobe transport vials containing specific media.
4. The specimen container should be labeled properly with the patient's name, identification number, date and time of collection, name of the ordering physician, specific specimen source, and examination requested.
5. Specimens should be transported in sturdy containers with lids that do not create aerosols when opened.
6. Specimens should be processed within 1 hour of collection. If this is not possible, the specimens may be refrigerated. Some specimens that are sensitive to refrigeration may require holding at room temperature. All viral specimens should be refrigerated because their decay rate is a function of temperature.

GUIDELINES FOR SPECIFIC SPECIMENS

Blood

The detection of most bacteremias can be accomplished via three sets of separately collected blood samples. A single blood sample often will not be sufficient to detect microorganisms when there is intermittent bacteremia.

Before collection of blood samples, skin decontamination of the venipuncture site is necessary. The site is cleansed with 70% alcohol followed by an iodophor.

Urine

Urine specimens may be obtained by voiding or instrumentation. The external genitalia is cleansed and then rinsed to prevent contamination of the voided urine. The first portion of urine is not collected but passed into a receptacle. The midstream portion of urine is collected in wide-mouth sterile containers.

Catheterization can also be used to collect urine (see Chapter 35 for discussions of catheterization), particularly if clean, voided urine cannot be obtained.

If anaerobic infections are suspected, suprapubic bladder aspiration is required. Urine transport kits are available.

Feces

Intestinal pathogens can be detected from fecal specimens. If fecal specimens cannot be processed within an hour after collection, they should be mixed with a transport medium. Swabs are used to collect fastidious microorganisms such as *Shigella* species, *Neisseria gonorrhoeae*, or human immunodeficiency virus (HIV).

Cerebrospinal Fluid

CSF is usually collected by lumbar puncture and requires a trained physician. CSF is examined when meningitis is suspected.

Laboratory Identification

Identification techniques for specific organisms are discussed in the chapters on specific microbial agents. The following offers an overview of the techniques used in the identification process.

MICROSCOPY

One of the first procedures used in the identification of bacteria is to prepare a slide for microscopic examination (see Appendix A for a discussion of microscopy and staining). The slide may be a wet mount or a stained preparation. For example, the result of a Gram stain is an important differentiating characteristic that aids the microbiologist as well as the physician (see Under the Microscope 54, Appendix A). There are occasions when microscopy can provide a presumptive diagnosis of the infectious agent involved. For example, fluorescent microscopy can be used on sputum samples to identify *Mycobacterium tuberculosis,* the etiological agent of tuberculosis. Dark-field microscopy can be used on specimens from skin lesions to identify the spirochete causing syphilis *(Treponema pallidum).*

Staining may also be used to identify specific structures on the bacterial cell. Structures such as capsules or spores aid in the identification process.

CULTURE

Pure cultures are made when the specimen is streaked or filtered on appropriate media. A particularly important cultural characteristic that can be observed on blood agar is **hemolytic activity.** Certain bacteria cultured on blood agar produce **hemolysins** that affect red blood cells in different ways. Blood agar plate hemolytic activity is of the following types:

1. **Alpha hemolysis.** There is partial destruction of red blood cells with a loss of some hemoglobin. This results in a greenish-brownish discoloration of the medium.
2. **Beta hemolysis.** Red blood cell membranes disappear and a clear, colorless zone surrounds the colony.
3. **No hemolysis.** When there is no apparent hemolytic activity, the bacteria are said to be nonhemolytic (or gamma hemolysis).

The majority of culturing in the clinical laboratory involves bacteria. Less frequently cultured are microorganisms that cannot be cultivated on ordinary media, that is, the viruses. Although cultivation on various types of host cells is the "gold standard" for viruses in the laboratory, serological tests as well as nucleic acid technology are suitable for preliminary identification.

Viral replication in cell cultures is often detected by visual changes in the host cells called **cytopathic effects** (see Chapter 31).

BIOCHEMICAL CHARACTERISTICS

Biochemical testing most often leads to identification of the bacterial species. Species differentiation is feasible because bacterial species often have distinct enzyme profiles.

Biochemical tests are performed on specially designed culture media that contain compounds that are metabolized by the enzymes of specific bacteria. A set of differing media is inoculated from a pure culture, incubated, and examined for a particular metabolic activity. The results of metabolic activity usually are observable immediately by color changes. In other tests, specific reagents must be added to produce an observable change. Some of the more common biochemical tests evaluate the following:

1. **Fermentation reactions.** Fermentation tests are the most frequently used of all biochemical tests. The test medium contains a single carbohydrate, a pH indicator, and a vial to capture gas. A change in the color of the pH indicator signifies acid formation, and the appearance of a bubble in the vial indicates the presence of gas.
2. **Catalase production.** The transfer of hydrogen to oxygen during respiration in some organisms results in the production of hydrogen peroxide (H_2O_2). Most aerobic bacteria produce an enzyme, catalase, that is capable of oxidizing the peroxide to water and oxygen. When colonies on an agar surface are flooded with H_2O_2, bubbles of oxygen will appear if the cells in the colony produce catalase.
3. **Hydrogen sulfide production.** Some microorganisms are capable of reducing sulfur to hydrogen sulfide (H_2S). A medium containing high concentrations of the amino acid cysteine and iron salts is inoculated with the test organisms. After suitable incubation, a black or brown precipitate will appear if the organisms remove sulfur from cysteine and reduce it to H_2S. The precipitate is ferrous sulfide (FeS), formed according to the following reaction:

$$FeSO_4 + H_2S \rightarrow FeS + H_2SO_4$$

Many other biochemical tests are used in the laboratory. They are discussed as they apply to the specific groups of microorganisms.

Fluorogenic and Chromogenic Substrates

New techniques using chromogenic and fluorogenic substrates are available for the detection of activities of specific bacterial enzymes. For example, in one group of reactions a change in fluorescence or absorbance of a pH indicator in a mixture of bacteria and substrate is measured. The change in fluorescence is caused by specific enzyme activity, such as the increase in pH caused by urease activity.

Another type of reaction is brought about by the hydrolysis of a synthetic substrate by bacterial enzymes, causing an increase in the fluorescence and/or absorption of the bacterium-substrate mixture.

These tests are available in some of the automated systems discussed below.

SEROLOGICAL CHARACTERISTICS

Antigen-antibody interactions can be used for the purposes of laboratory identification in two ways:

1. Known microorganisms are injected into animal hosts. Immune sera or antisera for each injected microorganism are prepared and refrigerated (they can also be obtained commercially). If at some time an organism is isolated from a patient, the unknown microorganisms can be tested against one of the known antisera.

2. Known antigen suspensions of whole cells, capsules, flagella, or other structures are prepared in the laboratory. Unknown antisera from infected hosts can be tested against known antigen preparations. A positive reaction with one of the known antigens indicates which microorganisms have infected the host and caused the production of antibodies. Antibody detection is used often, for example, to verify immunity as in preemployment and prenatal screening. In addition, it is also used in the serological test for syphilis (see Chapter 26). Some of the serological tests used in the clinical laboratory are discussed in Appendix B; others are discussed in the chapters on specific infectious agents such as viruses.

RAPID IDENTIFICATION TECHNIQUES

Many of the techniques previously discussed or implied represent multistep procedures that are often time-consuming and not always economical. Recent advances in miniaturization automation, computer programming, and molecular biology have provided techniques for the rapid identification of microorganisms. One of the first rapid identification systems was the **miniaturized kit** called the **API 20E system.** This is a manual biochemical system consisting of a plastic strip with 20 microtubes containing dehydrated substrates that can detect specific biochemical characteristics. The test substrates are inoculated with a standard inoculum. After incubation for 5 hours or overnight, the 20 test results are converted to a seven- or nine-digit profile. The profile number can be used with a computer or a prepared booklet to find the name of the bacterium.

Several automated systems are now available, including the **AutoMicrobic System,** which was originally used to detect and identify pathogens directly from urine specimens of astronauts in space. The **Sensititer** fluorogenic system is a modular system composed of a computer and an automated reader. This system identifies gram-negative bacilli and performs susceptibility tests on both gram-positive and gram-negative bacteria in either 5 or 18 hours. The **Walkaway-96** is a computer-controlled system that incubates microtiter panels and automatically interprets biochemical or susceptibility results with a photometric or a fluorogenic reader. Recently introduced was the **Biolog** system, which has the capacity to identify a broad range of aerobic gram-positive and gram-negative bacteria (Fig. 16-1). The system consists of 96-well dehydrated panels containing tetrazolium violet, a buffered medium, and a different carbon source for each well except the control. The microwells are rehydrated with a cell suspension and read at either 4 hours or overnight for the ability to utilize the carbon source. Tetrazolium is a redox dye that turns purple when the carbon source is

FIGURE 16-1
Automated multitest system. The 96-well MicroPlate *(upper right)* before inoculation contains a dried film of nutrients and reagents. Addition of a bacterial cell suspension activates the identification process. If the cells oxidize the carbon source, a purple-colored dye product forms after 4 to 24 hours of incubation; 95 reactions from the MicroPlate can be read directly from the MicroStation reader into the MicroStation computer, yielding an identification in seconds from a data base of over 300 species or groups of gram-negative aerobes. (Courtesy of Barry Buchner, Biolog, Inc., Hayward, CA.)

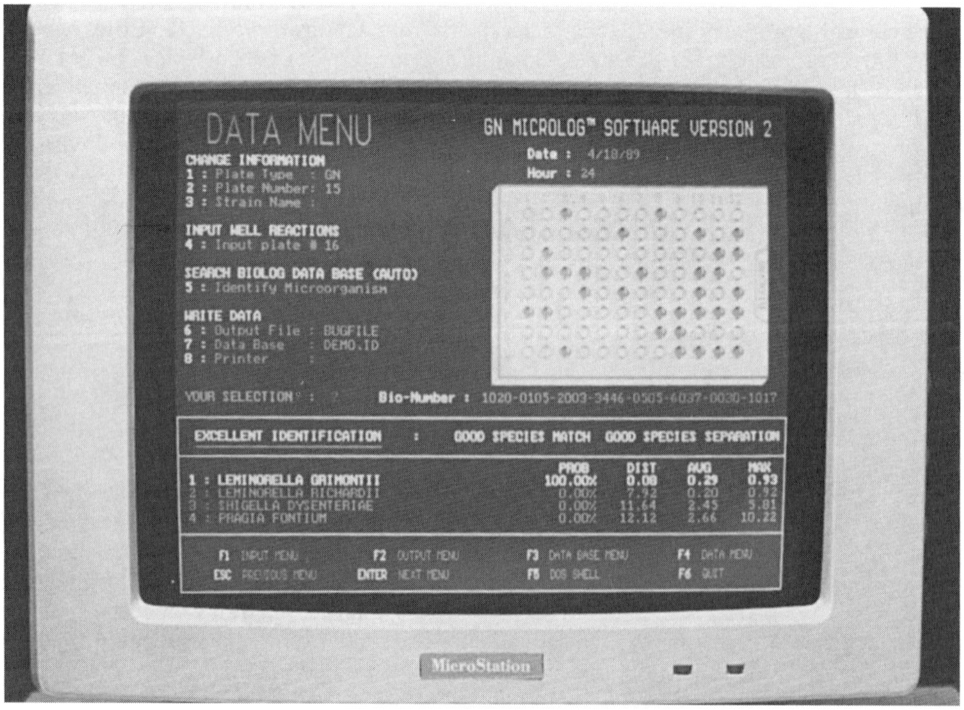

used or remains colorless if the carbon source was not used. The Biolog system data base includes information for identification of 569 species of aerobic gram-negative bacteria and 225 species of gram-positive bacteria.

MOLECULAR TECHNIQUES

Nucleic Acid Analysis

In Chapter 15, we discussed several molecular techniques such as plasmid analysis and DNA probes with respect to epidemiological studies. These as well as the following techniques can also be applied to diagnostics even though most are beyond the scope of smaller clinical laboratories.

Flow Cytometry

Flow cytometry is not a standard tool for the majority of clinical laboratories but it does have some advantages. In flow cytometry, cells or other particles in suspension flow in a single file at uniform speeds through a laser light beam with which they interact individually. For each cell or particle, this produces a light scatter pattern which gives information about cell size, shape, density, and surface morphology. In addition, fluorophore labeling and measurement can give quantitative data on specific target molecules or subcellular constituents and their distribution in a cell population. Flow cytometry can quantitate any cell-associated property for which there is a fluorescent probe. The probes are now commercially available for such components as nucleic acid, immune complexes, viruses, proteins, and a variety of cell organelles. Flow cytometry is a rapid method for determining antibodies to the agent of Lyme disease and may soon become a better serodiagnostic test for this disease.

Gas-Liquid Chromatography

The basis of gas-liquid chromatography is that a chemical mixture carried by liquid or gas is separated into individual components because of processes such as ion exchange and partitioning between different solvent phases. Fatty acids can be extracted from the cells using a solvent such as ether. Gas-liquid chromatography has been especially helpful in the analysis and comparison of whole cell fatty acids of strict anaerobes and other fastidious bacteria. For example, the detection of fatty acids such as butyric, isovaleric, and isobutyric in blood cultures is a reliable indicator of the presence of anaerobic bacteria. Gas-liquid chromatography is beneficial for identifying strains when other methods are not useful. Components separated by the chromatographic process can also be analyzed by mass spectrometry, nuclear magnetic resonance, and other recently advanced techniques. The combination of techniques has been useful in discovering specific chemical markers.

Antimicrobial Susceptibility Testing

Once the infectious microorganism has been identified, the clinical laboratory is assigned the responsibility of providing the physician with information concerning the activity of various drugs against the organism in question. A variety of standardized tests are available for determining antimicrobial susceptibility and these are discussed in Chapter 8.

Computers in the Clinical Laboratory

Transmission of data by handwritten means is inefficient and can lead to incorrect interpretations. The computer is capable of replacing such inefficient routines.

The major functions of the computer in the laboratory are test ordering, test result entries, and printed reports with entries in chronological order. The computer can also act as a management tool. For example, epidemiological data or antimicrobial susceptibility profiles for various hospital sites can be recorded and provided to the appropriate hospital personnel. After a suitable length of time, the data can be retrieved and reviewed for possible changes in hospital or laboratory procedures.

The computer also has diagnostic functions. A wide variety of tests are utilized to identify certain bacteria, such as the Enterobacteriaceae. Before the computer, the utilization of biochemical data was often inefficient and time-consuming in identifying bacteria. Computer manipulation of a large data base can be accomplished efficiently and with far more accuracy than by the older techniques. The newer assay kits also contain tests for determining antimicrobial susceptibility using computer technology.

Laboratory Safety

Clinical microbiologists must be concerned about safety since they are working with potentially contaminated blood and body fluids from patients. In 1987 the Centers for Disease Control (see Additional Readings) provided guidelines for laboratory safety. These are outlined below.

1. All specimens of blood and body fluids should be put in a well constructed container with a secure lid, to prevent leaking during transport. When collecting each specimen, clinicians should be careful to avoid contaminating the outside of the container and the laboratory form accompanying the specimen.
2. All persons processing blood and body fluid specimens (e.g., removing tops from vacuum tubes) should wear gloves. Masks and protective eyewear should be worn if mucous membrane contact with blood or body fluids is anticipated. Gloves should be changed and hands washed after completion of specimen processing.
3. For routine procedures, such as histological and pathological studies or microbiological culturing, a biological safety cabinet is not necessary. However, biological safety cabinets (class I or II) should be used whenever procedures that have a high poten-

tial for generating droplets are conducted. These include activities such as blending, sonicating, and vigorous mixing.
4. Mechanical pipetting devices should be used for manipulating all liquids in the laboratory. **Pipetting by mouth must not be done.**
5. Use of needles and syringes should be limited to situations in which there is no alternative, and the recommendations for preventing injuries with needles should be followed.
6. Laboratory work surfaces should be decontaminated with an appropriate chemical germicide when blood or other body fluids are spilled and when work activities are completed.
7. Contaminated materials used in laboratory tests should be decontaminated before processing or be placed in bags and disposed of in accordance with institutional policies for disposal of infectious waste.
8. Scientific equipment that has been contaminated with blood or other body fluids should be decontaminated and cleaned before being repaired in the laboratory or transported to the manufacturer.
9. All persons should wash their hands after completing laboratory activities and should remove protective clothing before leaving the laboratory.

Terminology

Infectious disease is a pathological condition. Several terms and concepts from pathology are used to describe it. An understanding of the following terms will improve the student's comprehension of the discussion of infectious diseases. It is advisable to review the events of inflammation and the cell types that participate in inflammation, antibody formation, cell-mediated immunity, phagocytosis, and allergic reactions that are described in Part III, Immunology.

Abscess. A circumscribed accumulation of pus.
Edema. The accumulation of fluid portions of the blood in tissues; accounts for or contributes to the swelling, blockage, pain, induration, and blanching of the affected site.
Embolus. A pathological, space occupying aggregate that moves in the vascular system with the constant threat of blocking important vascular channels or spaces, for example, clots.
Exudate. Blood components, both fluid and formed elements, that accumulate in tissues, spaces, and surfaces as one manifestation of an inflammatory response.
Icterus. Jaundice or yellowing of the tissue.
Ischemia. Lack or diminution of blood in a tissue; may be due to blockage, vascular collapse or interruption, pressure, or hemorrhage.
Leukocytosis. Temporary increase in white blood cell count, which may occur in response to injury or disease; may be more specifically termed, depending on which white blood cell type shows an increase (for example, lymphocytosis is an increase in lymphocytes).
Leukopenia. Temporary diminution of white blood cells.
Mucosa. Internal epithelial surface lubricated by mucus.
Pathogenesis. Sequence of events leading to the disease state; the development of the pathological condition.
Purulent. Pus containing.
Pyogenic. Pus inducing, pus eliciting, pus generating.
Pyrogenic. Fever inducing.
Signs. Disease manifestations detectable by an observer.
Symptoms. Disease indications or subjective experiences felt by the patient.
Thrombus. A blood clot attached in the cardiovascular system.
Ulcer. Circumscribed, necrotic, denuded surface area of the skin or mucosa.
Vesicle. A blister; a small circumscribed, elevated area of the skin or mucosa that contains clear fluid.

Several combining terms (prefixes and suffixes) are used repeatedly, and an understanding of these helps to interpret the meaning of many words.

PREFIXES

A(n)-. Negative, lack of, deficient, against, reverse of.
Adeno-. Pertaining to the glands.
Arthro-. Pertaining to joints.
Ecto-. External.
Endo-. Internal.
Entero-. Intestinal.
Hema-, hemato-. Pertaining to the blood.
Hyper-. Above, increased, more than normal; equivalent to *super-*.
Hypo-. Below, decreased, less than the normal; equivalent to *sub-*.
Inter-. Between.
Intra-. Within.
Myo-. Pertaining to muscle.
Oligo-. Few.
Peri-. Around.
Poly-. Many.
Stomato-. Pertaining to the mouth.

SUFFIXES

-Algia. Pain.
-Dynia. Pain.
-Ectomy. Surgical excision.
-Emia. A condition of the blood.
-Genic. Causing, eliciting, generating.
-Itis. Inflammation.
-Lytic. Dissolving, causing to flow.
-Oma. Tumor.
-Ostomy. Surgical opening.
-Rhea. Flowing, discharge.
-Trophic. Nourishing.
-Tropic. Turning toward or attaching to.
-Uria. A condition of the urine.

Summary

1. Specimen collection is the most important first step for the clinical microbiologist if identification is to be accurate. There are specific guidelines for collecting specimens from the various body sites.

2. There are a variety of laboratory techniques, none of which alone can provide an absolute identification. These techniques include microscopy, culture, biochemical characteristics, serological characteristics, rapid identification techniques, and molecular techniques.

3. The once time-consuming biochemical procedures used to identify microorganisms have been supplanted by automated and semiautomated techniques. In some instances, the newer testing procedures are also computerized, thus providing greater proficiency and accuracy.

4. Once the infectious agent has been identified, the clinical laboratory provides the physician with the results of antimicrobial susceptibility.

5. The Centers for Disease Control have provided guidelines for maintaining laboratory safety. Among the most important of these are (1) properly securing all specimens in well constructed containers, (2) wearing gloves when processing blood and body fluid specimens, and (3) using a safety cabinet whenever specimens are processed in such a way as to create aerosols.

6. Knowing the meaning of important suffixes and prefixes aids in the understanding of various medical terms.

Questions for Study

1. Why is the transport of viral specimens considered more difficult than that of bacterial specimens?
2. How should anaerobes be transported to the laboratory? Are there any special laboratory techniques for identifying anaerobes? If so, name them.
3. Are there any serological techniques that could be considered rapid? If so, name them.
4. What are the advantages of computers in laboratory identification? Are there any potential disadvantages?
5. Why is flow cytometry a potentially important tool in microbial identification?
6. List what you consider to be the three most important guidelines for safety in the laboratory.
7. Take the suffixes and prefixes indicated in the section Terminology and give an example of each as it applies to infectious disease.

CHAPTER

17 The Gram-Positive Cocci

OBJECTIVES

To describe the infectious diseases caused by staphylococci

To list the various factors associated with the virulence of *Staphylococcus aureus* and the streptococci

To describe the laboratory tests that differentiate *S. aureus* from *Staphylococcus epidermidis*

To describe briefly the techniques for laboratory diagnosis, treatment, and control of staphylococcal and streptococcal infections

To comment on the increasing importance of coagulase-negative staphylococci as causative agents of disease

To comment on invasive group A streptococcal disease

To describe the laboratory tests used to identify group A streptococci

To list the diseases associated primarily with group B, group C, and group D streptococci and enterococci

To describe *Streptococcus pneumoniae* in terms of virulence factors, disease associations, and laboratory identification

OUTLINE

THE STAPHYLOCOCCI
- General Characteristics

STAPHYLOCOCCUS AUREUS
- Pathogenesis
  - Virulence Factors
    - Coagulase
    - Hemolysins
    - Leukocidin
    - Protein A
  - Infections of the Skin
    - Pyoderma: Abscesses, Furuncles, Sties, Carbuncles, Impetigo
    - Scalded Skin Syndrome
  - Gastrointestinal Disease
    - Staphylococcal Enterocolitis
    - Staphylococcal Food Poisoning
  - Deeper Infections
    - Osteomyelitis
    - Toxic Shock Syndrome
- Laboratory Identification
  - Differentiation Between *S. aureus* and *S. epidermidis*
- Treatment and Prevention
- Coagulase-Negative Staphylococci

THE MICROCOCCI

THE STREPTOCOCCI
- Classification
- Group A Streptococci *(Streptococcus pyogenes)*
  - Streptococcal Antigens and/or Virulence Factors
    - Hyaluronic Acid Capsule
    - Cell Wall Proteins (M, R, and T)
    - Cell Wall Carbohydrate
    - Cell Wall Peptidoglycan
    - Cytoplasmic Membrane
  - Extracellular Streptococcal Products
    - Erythrogenic Toxin
    - Cardiohepatic Toxin and Nephrotoxin
    - Hemolysins
    - Spreading Factors

OUTLINE (*continued*)

Pathogenesis and Epidemiology
Suppurative Diseases
Nonsuppurative Diseases
Laboratory Diagnosis
Treatment and Prevention
Group B Streptococci
Group C Streptococci
Viridans Streptococci
Group D Streptococci and Enterococci
Group F Streptococci and Other Streptococci
Anaerobic Streptococci
Streptococcus pneumoniae (Pneumococci)
General Characteristics
Pathogenesis
Laboratory Diagnosis
Treatment and Prevention

Gram-positive cocci of medical importance are members of the genera *Staphylococcus, Streptococcus,* and *Enterococcus*. They can cause infection in virtually any tissue, organ, tract, or system of the body. Since the majority of infections are acute, the pathogenic cocci (also includes gram-negative cocci, i.e., *Neisseria*) are often referred to as **pyogenic** (pus generating) **cocci.**

The Staphylococci

GENERAL CHARACTERISTICS

Members of the genera *Staphylococcus* and *Micrococcus* belong to the family Micrococcaceae. There are 23 recognized staphylococcal species, 12 of which are part of the normal or occasional microflora of humans. Only three are recognized as being clinically important, namely, *S. aureus, S. epidermidis,* and *S. saprophyticus. S. aureus* is a pathogen. The other two are regarded as opportunistic or nosocomial pathogens.

S. aureus is the only coagulase-positive (see under Laboratory Identification) human species. All other human species collectively are referred to as the coagulase-negative staphylococci (CONS or CNS). *S. hominis, S. haemolyticus,* and *S. simulans* and other species, to an even lesser extent, account for a small percentage of infections.

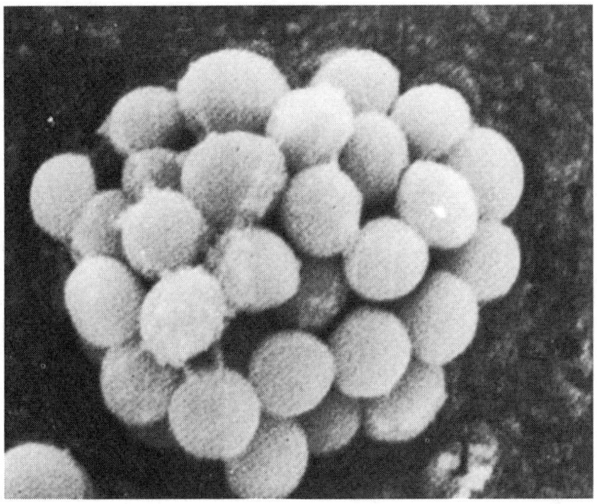

FIGURE 17-1
Scanning electron micrograph of microcolonies of *Staphylococcus aureus*. (× 14,000.) (Courtesy of Z. Yoshii.)

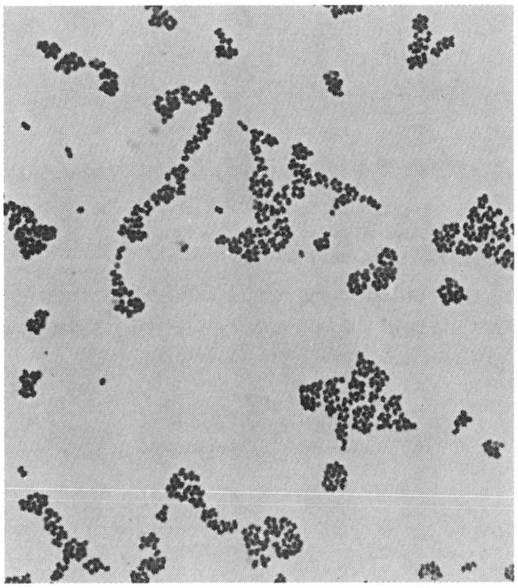

FIGURE 17-2
Light micrograph of smear of *S. aureus* taken from a broth culture. (From A. S. Klainer and I. Geis, *Agents of Bacterial Disease*. New York: Harper & Row, 1973.)

Staphylococci aggregate characteristically in irregular groups like clusters of grapes (Figs. 17-1 and 17-2). They are aerobic to facultatively anaerobic, nonmotile, and nonsporeforming. They are strongly catalase-positive (that is, if one adds hydrogen peroxide to colonial growth, immediate evolution of bubbles of oxygen will be visible). Staphylococci, particularly *S. epidermidis* and *S. hominis*, are among the major natural inhabitants of the skin. Large populations are present in the armpits, anterior nares, and perineum. Staphylococci may also be found in the throat, mouth, vagina, intestinal tract, and mammary glands, but in smaller numbers than on the skin.

Staphylococcus aureus

PATHOGENESIS

S. aureus causes a broad range of serious infections throughout the body. The infections and diseases specifically or primarily associated with *S. aureus* are boils, carbuncles, bullous impetigo, scalded skin syndrome, staphylococcal food poisoning, staphylococcal enterocolitis, staphylococcal osteomyelitis, and toxic shock syndrome (TSS).

Virulence Factors

Staphylococcal disease is multifactorial and is usually due to the production of several pathogenic factors. With some exceptions, the association of a single virulence factor with the clinical symptoms of disease has been lacking. Three toxins are specifically related to disease: **exfoliative toxin** with **scalded skin syndrome, toxic shock syndrome toxin-1 (TSST-1),** and **enterotoxin** associated with **food poisoning.** These toxins are discussed with the specific diseases with which they are associated. Other factors that are primarily associated with pathogenic *S. aureus* include coagulase, alpha and delta hemolysins, leukocidin, and protein A.

Coagulase. Coagulase is a plasma clotting protein produced by pathogenic *S. aureus* and by a few other bacteria. A role for coagulase causing disease has not been discovered. Coagulase, however, does coat staphylococci with fibrin and may prevent phagocytosis. Coagulase formation is the major criterion for laboratory identification (see Laboratory Identification).

Hemolysins. Staphylococci produce several exotoxins or hemolysins but only the alpha and delta toxins are of major significance in human infection. More than 90 percent of the staphylococcal strains that are pathogenic for humans produce a combination of alpha and delta toxins. These toxins, although cytotoxic for red blood cells, can also affect other cell types such as monocytes, platelets, and neutrophils. The importance of these hemolysins in the disease process has not been determined, except to say that erythrocyte hemolysis is not relevant.

Leukocidin. Many *S. aureus* strains produce a leukocidin that differs from the hemolysins in action and composition. Leukocidin increases the permeability of leukocytes to cations and so leads to swelling and rounding up of the cells. The membranes of cytoplasmic granules fuse with the cytoplasmic membrane of the cell, causing release of the cytoplasmic granules and cell disruption.

Protein A. Protein A is a surface component of most *S. aureus* strains. It is linked to the peptidoglycan layer of the cell wall, but some of it is released extracellularly. Protein A has the unusual property that the Fc portion of IgG nonspecifically binds to it.* Protein A, because of this property of binding immunoglobulin, is believed to be antiphagocytic by competing with neutrophils for the Fc portion of specific opsonins. Protein A has other biological effects: It elicits hypersensitivity and inflammation, it injures platelets, and it prevents the absorption of bacterial viruses that are specific for *S. aureus* (staphylophages).

Infections of the Skin

Pyoderma: Abscesses, Furuncles, Sties, Carbuncles, Impetigo. *S. aureus* causes various types of purulent skin infections (pyoderma) and subcutaneous infections. The infection of hair follicles—**folliculitis**—leads to the formation of furuncles (boils) in the skin or sties in the eyelids. **Carbuncles** represent a deeper, more serious condition that results from tunneling, coalescing abscesses (Fig. 17-3). Either *S. aureus* or *Streptococcus pyogenes* alone or the two agents as coinfectors cause **impetigo** (Fig. 17-4), a skin infection found primarily in children. Impetigo often begins in the nasal area and spreads from there over the face. Impetigo is characterized by fragile blisters, which when broken leave erosions covered by honey-colored crusts.

Scalded Skin Syndrome. Scalded skin syndrome is a condition in which there is extensive denuding of the skin. It is most often observed in infants and young children. The syndrome usually begins as erythema around the mouth and nose and spreads rapidly to affect the skin of the neck, the trunk, and sometimes the extremities. This condition is mediated by an exfoliative toxin of types A and B. Scalded skin syndrome is seldom fatal because it is limited largely to the superficial layers of the skin.

Gastrointestinal Disease

Staphylococcal Enterocolitis. The overgrowth of *S. aureus* in the intestinal tract can lead to a condition called **enterocolitis.** Staphylococcal overgrowth, which is due to the

FIGURE 17-3
Carbuncle caused by *S. aureus* in a diabetic patient. (From F. H. Top, Sr., and P. F. Wehrle, eds., *Communicable and Infectious Diseases*, 8th ed. St. Louis: Mosby, 1976.)

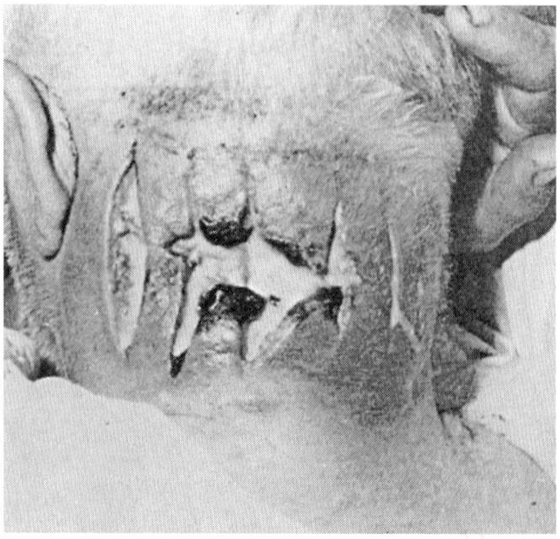

* Coagglutination test: A cleverly designed serological test, the coagglutination test is based on the unusual property of protein A to bind nonspecifically to the Fc portion of IgG. Antibodies that are specific for other bacteria such as streptococci, salmonellae, neisseriae, and Hemophilus are allowed to couple via the Fc portion of the antibody molecule to protein A that is bound to killed staphylococci. This leaves the antigen-specific end of the molecule, the Fab end, free to attach to the bacteria for which the Fab is specific. When bacteria for which the Fab is specific are added, a lattice is formed that is visible as a coagglutinate (clumps of the staphylococci and the test bacteria).

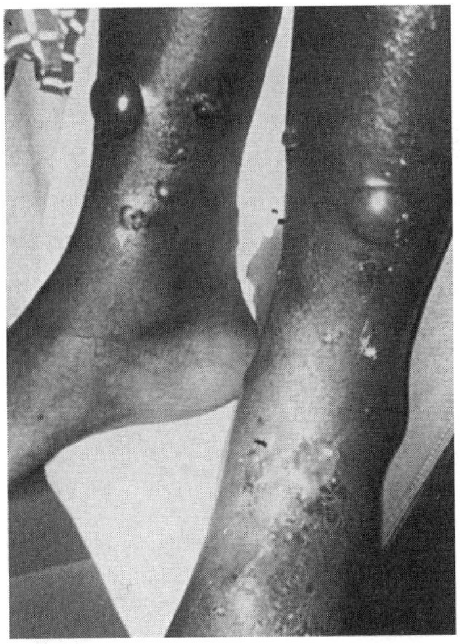

FIGURE 17-4
Bullous impetigo caused by *S. aureus.* (Courtesy of H. Dillon.)

use of oral antibiotics that reduce the normal intestinal microflora, is known as a **superinfection.** The staphylococci are resistant to the antibiotic and are capable of unrestricted growth. Clinical manifestations include diarrhea, fever, abdominal cramps, electrolyte imbalance, and loss of fluids. Most cases of enterocolitis are due to the bacterium *Clostridium difficile* following antibiotic treatment (see Chapter 19).

Staphylococcal Food Poisoning. Approximately one-third of the strains of *S. aureus* excrete into foods a heat-stable exotoxin called **staphylococcal enterotoxin.** There are six chemically and immunologically related enterotoxins. They can withstand 30 minutes of boiling and are not inactivated by digestive enzymes. When ingested with the food, the enterotoxin causes a type of food poisoning that is accompanied by vehement vomiting (projectile vomiting), cramps, diarrhea, and prostration two to eight hours after ingestion. Enterotoxin food poisoning is rarely fatal. The patient is fully recovered in 24 to 48 hours. Many foods support the growth of staphylococci. They usually include those that contain a high amount of protein—ham, poultry, and potato and egg salads.

Outbreaks of food poisoning occur when a contaminated food is held at inappropriate temperatures long enough to allow the bacteria to grow and release toxin. Food preparers and handlers who have staphylococcal lesions of the skin, especially of the hands, and nasopharyngeal carriers are the most likely to contaminate food. Absence of lesions is no guarantee of safety.

Deeper Infections

Deep staphylococcal infections may be primary infections involving a variety of organs and tissues or they may be an infection that has metastasized from a cutaneous infection or from a carrier site. Deep infections are rare in healthy individuals. They occur primarily in those who have a precondition such as diabetes, burn wounds, extensive surgery, cystic fibrosis, or lower respiratory tract viral infection and in those who are immunosuppressed or immunodefective in phagocytic properties (see Chapter 9). *S. aureus* can cause infections in many tissues and organs: endocarditis, meningitis, pneumonia, cystitis, septicemia, infections of postoperative wounds, vascular and valvular infections, and others.

Osteomyelitis. Osteomyelitis (inflammation of the bone) is a condition primarily due to *S. aureus.* The bacteria arrive at the site of infection via a hematogenous (blood) spread from a focus of infection such as a furuncle. They can also enter the site of infection because of surgery or a deep penetrating trauma. In the latter instance, the bones are likely to be those that require surgical pinning after a compound fracture. Symptoms of acute osteomyelitis include fever, chills, pain over bone, and muscle spasms in the affected bone area.

Toxic Shock Syndrome. TSS is a multisystem, febrile illness with abrupt onset and with hypotension (shock). Vomiting, diarrhea, a diffuse macular erythematous rash with resulting palmar and plantar desquamation (peeling of the skin on the palms of the hands and soles of the feet), and hyperemia of mucous membranes regularly occur. Disseminated intravascular clotting is an occasional complication. Death may be caused by profound shock, respiratory failure, and disseminated intravascular coagulation. TSS is caused by a toxin, TSST-1, which is assumed to stimulate the production of interleukin (IL)-1 by macrophages. IL-1 has numerous biological effects, among which are fever induction and the release of acute-phase proteins from the liver. The severity of infection is believed to be associated with the superantigenic behavior of the TSS toxin (see Under the Microscope 12). About 90 percent of healthy individuals have protective antibodies against TSST-1.

TSS was first described in 1978 as a syndrome among a high percentage of menstruating females who used tampons. High-absorbency tampons were promptly identified as a high-risk factor. The number of tampon-associated cases of TSS decreased substantially starting in 1981 when manufacturers lowered the absorbency of tampons. Nonmenstrual high-risk groups are postpartum women, patients with focal staphylococcal and surgical wound infections, and patients with infections associated with nasal surgery and packing. The highest risk is in children and young adults but it can occur in any age group. Approximately 2 to 5 percent of patients with TSS die. TSS requires fluid replacement, drainage of any foci of infection, and chemotherapy.

LABORATORY IDENTIFICATION

The routine clinical laboratory identification of staphylococci poses one of the less difficult bacterial identification problems. It may be necessary first to differentiate among the gram-positive cocci, namely, staphylococci, strepytococci, and micrococci. Differentiation from the strep-

UNDER THE MICROSCOPE 12

Superantigens

The term superantigen refers to a family of microbial proteins that stimulate virtually all T lymphocytes bearing certain V_β elements. Superantigens stimulate a very energetic immune response and induce a variety of pathogenic disorders such as food poisoning and toxic shock syndrome (TSS). Superantigens have also been associated with diseases such as rheumatic fever and glomerulonephritis. The latter conditions are believed to be autoimmune diseases associated with the M protein of group A streptococci. The mechanisms of T cell stimulation by superantigens has only recently been determined and is briefly elucidated here.

Normally the number of T cells that respond to a particular antigen represents no more than 0.0001 to 0.0100 percent of the resting T cell population. This is because the T cell specificity for the protein is determined by the highly variable elements of the T cell receptor. Each superantigen, however, appears to react with relatively invariant sequences within the V_β region. Each superantigen has a characteristic affinity for a set of V_β elements and stimulates virtually all T cells bearing those elements, regardless of their antigenic specificity. Therefore, from 5 to 20 percent of resting T cells can be activated by a single superantigen. This immense immune stimulation causes distress in the immune system and leads to tissue damage.

For further discussion of superantigens, see articles by Johnson et al. and by Schlievert, listed under Additional Readings.

tococci is accomplished by the catalase test, colony characteristics, type of blood agar plate hemolysis, and microscopical characteristics. Differentiation from the micrococci is described later under The Micrococci.

Once it is established that the isolate is a staphylococcus, some clinical laboratories go no further than to differentiate *S. aureus* and *S. epidermidis*. However, there are more and more instances in which coagulase-negative staphylococci are agents of nosocomial infections and should therefore be identified to the species level. The other important clinical laboratory procedure is the testing of the isolate for antimicrobial susceptibility.

Blood agar containing sheep red blood cells is the recommended medium when contamination by other organisms is likely to be minimal (for example, in a specimen from a boil). A selective medium is employed when contamination by other organisms is expected to be heavy, as in a fecal specimen from a patient with a suspected staphylococcal enteritis. Staphylococci tolerate high concentrations of salt (7.5–10%) and they are relatively resistant to polymyxin, phenylethyl alcohol, and tellurite. Thus, selective media that contain these substances are employed in the isolation of staphylococci.

One of the better-known selective media used for staphylococcal isolation and identification is **mannitol salt agar** (MSA). It contains a high concentration of salt, 7.5% (about 0.5% is the usual concentration in other culture media), which is inhibitory to most other bacteria. In addition to being a selective medium, MSA is a differential medium. The carbohydrate mannitol and a pH indicator, phenol red, serve as its differential components. The medium surrounding a mannitol-positive colony turns from the typical red color of the indicator to a yellow color. This reaction is the result of acids produced from the fermentation of mannitol. Mannitol fermentation under anaerobic conditions helps in differentiating *S. aureus* from *S. epidermidis*.

Differentiation Between *S. aureus* and *S. epidermidis*

Coagulase production is considered the definitive test for differentiating *S. aureus* from *S. epidermidis* but there are other differences as well (Table 17-1). Two types of coagulase tests are used: the tube test and the slide test. The slide test is performed by making a heavy suspension of bacteria in distilled water, adding a drop of plasma, and observing for clumping within 10 seconds. False-negative results occur about 17 percent of the time and must be confirmed by the tube test.

The tube test is the more definitive test. The test bacteria are suspended in citrated or oxalated plasma (rabbit plasma is the preferred animal plasma) and the inoculated plasma is incubated. Clotting usually occurs within a range of a few minutes to several hours. The test, however, is observed for 24 hours before the result is declared negative. An alternative to the coagulase test is a commer-

TABLE 17-1
Characteristics Differentiating *Staphylococcus aureus* from *Staphylococcus epidermidis*

Characteristic	*S. aureus*	*S. epidermidis*
Coagulase	+	−
DNase	+	−
Nuclease (thermostable)	+	−
Mannitol fermentation	+	−
Colony pigment (yellow to yellow-orange)	+	−

cially available rapid test. In this test immunoglobulin is bound to latex beads which react with protein A of the *S. aureus* cell wall.

The detection of antibodies to cell wall teichoic acids of *S. aureus* correlates with the presence of staphylococcal infective endocarditis or deep tissue infection.

TREATMENT AND PREVENTION

Superficial infections in an otherwise healthy person require no chemotherapy. Treatment, if required, consists of drainage, application of moist heat, and immobilization. Deep-seated infections require intensive prolonged chemotherapy, often with a multidrug regimen. Recently the antibiotic **mupirocin** was approved for the treatment of impetigo. Its use is restricted to situations for controlling carriage of methicillin-resistant *S. aureus* in the nasal cavity.

Once uniformly susceptible to penicillin, most strains of *S. aureus* are now resistant. This resistance is associated with a plasmid-mediated beta-lactamase gene. Methicillin, introduced in 1959, was thought to solve the resistance problem but methicillin-resistant strains appeared almost immediately. Methicillin resistance is of a heterogeneous type; that is, some strains can be considered to be composed of two types of cells: relatively susceptible cells and highly resistant cells. Resistance is associated with production of a unique penicillin-binding protein (PBP) that is bound and inactivated only at high concentrations of beta-lactam antibiotics. Expression of resistance in the laboratory is subject to considerable variation because of cultural conditions. Resistance can be missed if (1) an inappropriate or improperly stored beta-lactam is tested, (2) a temperature of 37 C is used, (3) the inoculum is too low, or (4) the incubation time is too short. Methicillin resistance results in cross resistance among several classes of beta-lactam antibiotics. No beta-lactam antibiotic can be recommended for therapy if the infection is caused by a methicillin-resistant strain of staphylococci. The majority of methicillin-resistant *S. aureus* strains are also resistant to gentamicin, tobramycin, netilmicin, amikacin, streptomycin, and erythromycin.

Any isolated *S. aureus* should be promptly assayed for susceptibility or resistance to antimicrobials. For penicillin-resistant strains, beta-lactamase–resistant drugs are available and include methicillin, nafcillin, or oxacillin. If the staphylococcal strain is methicillin-resistant, vancomycin is the drug of choice, sometimes in combination with rifampin or gentamicin. The combination trimethoprim-sulfamethoxazole is a second choice.

When antibiotic susceptibility information is not available, a beta-lactamase–resistant synthetic penicillin is usually chosen. If the patient is allergic to penicillin, vancomycin, cephalosporins, or clindamycin may be administered.

In hospitals persons with lesions should not be allowed to come in contact with susceptible patients. Carriers among hospital personnel should be identified when hospital outbreaks occur. The carrier rate among hospital personnel is between 70 and 80 percent (30 percent in the general population). Nursery and surgery patients are especially vulnerable to staphylococcal infections; therefore, personnel in these sections must be particularly diligent about aseptic practices.

It has been impossible to eliminate permanently the principal reservoir of staphylococci, the nasal carrier. Topical applications of neomycin, bacitracin, and gentamicin ointment have been attempted for periods of time, especially for those who repeatedly experience staphylococcal infections.

COAGULASE-NEGATIVE STAPHYLOCOCCI

Of the currently 13 distinct coagulase-negative staphylococci of human origin, only *S. epidermidis* and *S. saprophyticus* are known to cause disease. Coagulase-negative staphylococci (primarily *S. epidermidis*) are implicated in a great proportion of infections associated with synthetic catheters as well as foreign bodies such as heart valves, atrioventricular shunts, and prosthetic hips. The biopolymers of these devices are usually hydrophobic and they act as an adhesive for many bacterial pathogens whose surfaces are also hydrophobic.

The pathogenesis of *S. epidermidis* associated with foreign devices is due to adherence to the device and production of a slime layer. The slime inhibits the polymorphonuclear cell response to chemotactic substances and stimulates these cells to degranulate, thus reducing the uptake and killing of bacteria. Slime layers also act as barriers to the penetration of antimicrobials. *S. epidermidis* is frequently associated with endocarditis, colonization of prostheses, bacteremia, wound infections, and urinary tract infections in elderly hospitalized men.

It has become important to identify the individual species of coagulase-negative staphylococci involved in an infection because of the clinical, economical, and therapeutic implications. Conventional laboratory tests and observations used to differentiate among these staphylococci include novobiocin resistance, colonial pigmentation, hemolysis, nitrate reduction, alkaline phosphatase and urease production, arginine utilization, and fermentation of selected carbohydrates. Several commercially available rapid and miniaturized identification systems are also available.

Many hospital strains of coagulase-negative staphylococci are now resistant to many antimicrobials including the penicillins, gentamicin, erythromycin, and chloramphenicol. Susceptibility tests are required before antimicrobial therapy is started. **Vancomycin** has become the principal drug of choice for treating hospital-associated antibiotic-resistant strains. Teichoplanin also is a valuable antimicrobial for treating coagulase-negative staphylococcal infections in the hospital environment.

S. saprophyticus has a predilection for the urinary tract, especially in young women; it is now recognized as an important cause of urinary tract infections in sexually active females. *S. saprophyticus* is novobiocin-resistant, a major and reliable characteristic in differentiating it from *S. epidermidis*.

The Micrococci

Members of the genus *Micrococcus* bear certain resemblances to staphylococci: gram-positivity, colonial similarity, and transient presence on skin and mucous membranes. Micrococci are widely distributed in soil and fresh water and are commonly recovered from environmental samples. Species include *M. luteus, M. roseus*, and *M. varians*. In rare instances, they cause endocarditis. They may appear in specimens as contaminants and must therefore be differentiated from other gram-positive cocci. Micrococci are distinguished from staphylococci by the following:

1. Micrococci lack susceptibility to lysis by lysostaphin, an endopeptidase that cleaves glycine-glycine interpeptide linkages of the peptidoglycan;
2. Micrococci fail to ferment glucose anaerobically; and
3. Micrococci fail to produce glycerol when they are grown in the presence of erythromycin.

Three commercially available, easily performed disk tests also differentiate micrococci from staphylococci: the furazolidone susceptibility test (micrococci are resistant), the bacitracin susceptibility test (micrococci are susceptible), and the modified oxidase test (micrococci are modified oxidase-positive).

The Streptococci

The streptococci are gram-positive spherical microorganisms that appear in chains or clusters (Fig. 17-5). Most species are facultative anaerobes, although species of *Peptococcus* and *Peptostreptococcus* that inhabit the intestinal tract and female genital tract are strict anaerobes. The genus *Streptococcus* is homofermentative; that is, the end product of glucose fermentation is primarily lactic acid. Streptococci do not produce cytochrome oxidase. This characteristic, along with the Gram stain and cellular morphology, help distinguish them from *Neisseria* species.

Streptococcal disease in humans includes pharyngitis, scarlet fever, impetigo, rheumatic fever, pneumonia, meningitis, and other pathological conditions. Streptococci also cause mastitis in cows and can therefore be found in milk used for human consumption. This again indicates the importance of pasteurization to prevent human disease.

FIGURE 17-5
Scanning electron micrograph of *Streptococcus mutans*. (× 6800.) (Courtesy of S. Hamada.)

CLASSIFICATION

Hemolytic activity (see Chapter 16) has been used as a preliminary criterion for differentiating various species of *Streptococcus*. Most of the alpha-hemolytic species are members of a group referred to as the **viridans** group. The beta-hemolytic streptococci are the most important group because they contain the major human pathogens. Some beta-hemolytic streptococci are, however, not pathogenic. Gamma-hemolytic or nonhemolytic streptococci are a heterogeneous group and are not considered primary pathogens. Many are found as commensals in humans and animals. Although hemolytic activity is a good presumptive criterion for differentiation, it is not suitable for determining pathogenicity, and immunological differences must be used.

Rebecca Lancefield and her co-workers developed a technique for differentiation of the streptococci. They placed them into serological groups A through O on the basis of the antigenic characteristics of a cell wall carbohydrate called the **C substance.** The main pathogenic groups for humans are A, B, C, D, and G, and each group is given a species name. Some groups have but a single species. More than 90 percent of streptococcal disease in humans is caused by group A beta-hemolytic streptococci. This group has been given the species name *S. pyogenes*. Group B streptococci are named *S. agalactiae;* groups C and D are composed of several species to be discussed later. Each group can be further separated into serological types according to the antigenic characteristics of certain cell wall proteins: the M, R, and T proteins.

GROUP A STREPTOCOCCI *(STREPTOCOCCUS PYOGENES)*

Streptococcal Antigens and/or Virulence Factors

Several antigenic components of the streptococci are believed to be important in pathogenesis and classification.

Hyaluronic Acid Capsule. Hyaluronic acid is a capsular material produced primarily by group A and C streptococcal species. Hyaluronic acid is not immunogenic, which appears to be related to the fact it is also a prominent component of mammalian connective tissue. The capsule is an antiphagocytic substance that disappears during the later stages of the streptococcal growth cycle.

Cell Wall Proteins (M, R, and T). The M protein of the streptococcal cell wall is the major virulence factor of group A beta-hemolytic streptococci (Fig. 17-6). It enables the bacterial cell to inhibit phagocytosis. On the basis of differences in their M protein, the members of group A streptococci have been separated into more than 80 different types. Theoretically, one could expect to have 80 different *S. pyogenes* infections in one's lifetime before becoming completely immune to *S. pyogenes.* Antibodies produced in a patient to a type-specific M protein confer long-lasting immunity against infection from the same streptococcal strain.

M protein is now believed to play a major role in the pathogenesis of postinfection sequelae such as rheumatic fever. Less than a dozen M protein serotypes show high association with rheumatic fever (see Nonsuppurative Diseases).

The T protein provides a system of serotyping strains that cannot be typed by their M protein. T protein is often used for identification of streptococcal strains isolated from patients with impetigo.

The R protein has no clinical or pathogenic significance.

FIGURE 17-6
Electron micrograph of cross sections of *Streptococcus pyogenes* with M protein (A) and without M protein (B). M protein appears as a pililike appendage on the bacterial surface. (× 84,000 before 33 percent reduction.) (From E. H. Beachey and G. H. Stollerman. In D. C. Dumonde, ed., *Infection and Immunology in the Rheumatic Diseases.* Oxford, England: Blackwell, 1976.)

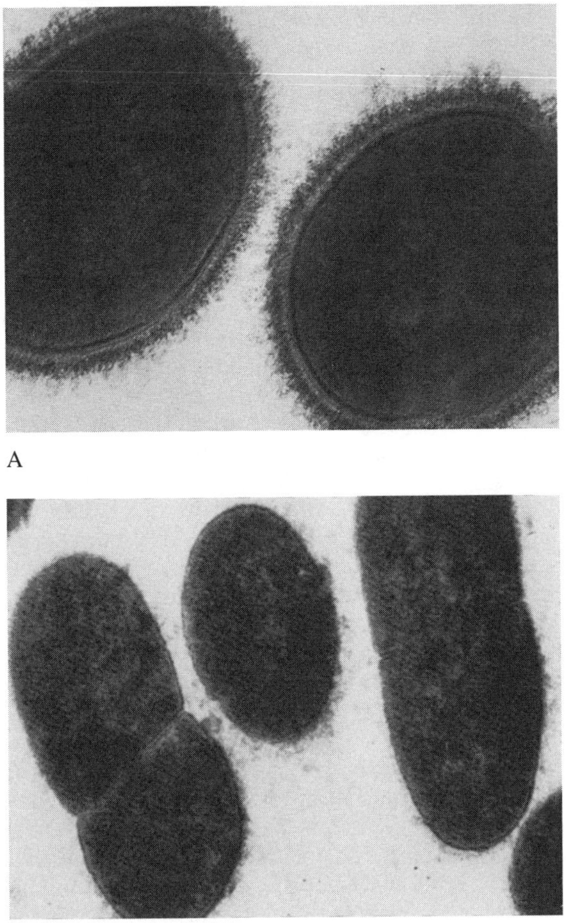

A

B

Cell Wall Carbohydrate. The cell wall carbohydrate, or C substance of group A streptococci is related chemically to the carbohydrate found in heart valves of humans. Patients with rheumatic fever, a complication following streptococcal infection, have high levels of serum antibodies to the C substance. These serum antibodies may contribute to the heart valve damage associated with rheumatic fever.

Cell Wall Peptidoglycan. Peptidoglycan is antigenic. The toxicity of the peptidoglycan is similar to that of endotoxin of gram-negative bacteria.

Cytoplasmic Membrane. Antigenic components in the cell membrane cross-react with heart, kidney, and connective tissues. These components may be involved in postinfection sequelae such as rheumatic fever and glomerulonephritis (see later discussions).

Extracellular Streptococcal Products

The streptococci elaborate extracellular products in vivo and in vitro. Many of them are believed to be important in the pathogenesis of streptococcal infection. Some are used in diagnosing such infections.

Erythrogenic Toxin. In some upper respiratory tract infections the streptococcal strain produces an extracellular toxin called **erythrogenic toxin.** Erythrogenic strains are phage-infected and carry the toxin determinant in the phage genome. The toxin is responsible for the rash associated with scarlet fever (Plate 3). Injection of the antitoxin intradermally causes the rash to disappear. This technique is the basis of the Schultz-Charlton reaction used in the diagnosis of scarlet fever.

Erythrogenic toxin is composed of three potent exotoxins, A, B, and C. Exotoxin A–producing strains are the most virulent. These same strains may also be responsible for septic shock (see later discussion on invasive group A streptococcal disease and toxic shock–like syndrome).

Cardiohepatic Toxin and Nephrotoxin. When injected into animals, these toxins can damage heart, liver, and kidney tissues. The role of these toxins in human disease is not known.

Hemolysins. The hemolytic activity of many streptococcal strains is due to the production of two distinct extracellular hemolysins, called **streptolysin O (SLO)** and **streptolysin S (SLS).** SLO is oxygen-labile, and its activity is dependent on reducing conditions. It is immunogenic, and detection of anti-SLO antibodies is used extensively in the diagnosis of streptococcal infections. SLO can lyse animal red blood cells and leukocytes in vivo. SLO has been implicated as a factor in the pathogenesis of rheumatic fever.

SLS is oxygen-stable and accounts for the zone of beta hemolysis seen around surface colonies of streptococci on blood agar plates. Like SLO, SLS is capable of lysing mammalian red blood cells and leukocytes. The role of SLS in pathogenesis is not known.

Spreading Factors. In primary streptococcal infections the infecting strain is often capable of spreading to surrounding tissue. This capacity is probably due to the formation of extracellular products. These products can dissolve the matrix of connective tissue and clotted material accumulated as a result of the inflammatory process. Spreading factors include

1. Hyaluronidase. Hyaluronic acid, a component of intracellular substance, is the substrate for hyaluronidase.
2. Proteinase. Proteinase digests some peptides and proteins. Proteinase injected into animals can cause heart damage.
3. Streptokinase. Streptokinase is produced by most group A strains. It can interact with the proenzyme plasminogen of human serum, converting it to plasmin. Plasmin can digest fibrin and other serum factors important in the formation of blood clots.
4. Nucleases. Ribonuclease and deoxyribonuclease are produced by virulent streptococci. Accumulated nuclear exudate from dead or injured white blood cells can be digested by these enzymes. The released purine and pyrimidine bases can also be used nutritionally by the streptococci.

Pathogenesis and Epidemiology

As stated previously, more than 90 percent of streptococcal diseases are caused by group A strains of *S. pyogenes.* Transmission from person to person is usually by contact with an asymptomatic carrier. Carriers harbor organisms in the upper respiratory tract, skin, or rectum. Occasionally food contaminated by a carrier may be a source of infection.

Streptococcal disease is divided into two categories: the **suppurative** or primary infections, and the **nonsuppurative** or those infections regarded as complications following primary infection.

Suppurative Diseases. Suppurative diseases are those in which pus is formed. One group of suppurative diseases often begins as acute pharyngitis, which can be complicated by meningitis, otitis media, and pneumonia. The other group includes puerperal fever, as well as such skin infections as impetigo, cellulitis, and erysipelas. In about 25 percent of the patients, a carrier state will develop despite appropriate therapy.

Impetigo is a highly contagious skin disease found primarily in children. The infection begins as small blisters that can spread to adjacent areas. The sores become covered with crusts. If the infecting strain is nephritogenic, a streptococcal complication called acute glomerulonephritis can result (see later).

Cellulitis is an inflammatory condition associated with streptococcal invasion of connective tissue. This type of disease can occasionally result in gangrene with later invasion of the bloodstream. **Puerperal fever** is a uterine infection that frequently accompanies childbirth when aseptic techniques are not followed. **Erysipelas** is an infection of the skin or mucous membrane and is characterized by a spreading inflammation (Plate 4). It is frequently seen on the face.

In suppurative infections the virulence of the streptococcus is directly related to the presence of M protein. In the majority of primary streptococcal infections, the microorganisms are destroyed by the host's immune system. In some instances, however, because of either the particular streptococcal strain involved or the host's immunological state, nonsuppurative complications develop.

Nonsuppurative Diseases. The principal nonsuppurative complications following primary infection are **scarlet fever, rheumatic fever, acute glomerulonephritis,** and **erythema nodosum.** Their exact cause is still in doubt. One theory holds that a toxin or toxic factor directly affects the tissue; another maintains that it is the host's response to the microbe or its products that damages tissue.

Scarlet fever is associated with the formation of erythrogenic toxin and was discussed earlier.

Rheumatic fever is a condition that follows about five weeks after pharyngeal infection by any number of group A streptococcal throat strains. The condition is characterized by heart muscle damage and is often accompanied by tissue destruction of heart valves as well as inflammation of the joints. The highest incidence of rheumatic fever is among those aged 5 to 19 years, especially among the urban poor of all races and ethnic groups. Rheumatic fever is rarely seen in the United States but recent outbreaks have been observed in military facilities and in some large cities.

Rheumatic fever is considered by many to be an autoimmune disease. Autoantibodies and M protein epitopes that are cross-reactive with a variety of host proteins have been found in rheumatic fever patients. The ability of M proteins to elicit autoantibodies suggests that rheumatic fever is a disease of molecular mimicry (see also Chapter 14). Thus, the M protein mimics some of the components of host tissue such as myosin. M protein injected into animals can elicit autoantibodies; however, it does not induce symptoms similar to rheumatic fever. Hence, other factors are probably involved in this disease.

Recent evidence suggests that M proteins act as "superantigens" by stimulating T cells to produce cytotoxic T lymphocytes (see Under the Microscope 12). Cytotoxic T cells have been found infiltrating the heart tissue of rheumatic fever patients. Since only a few M serotypes are associated with rheumatic fever, there is reason to believe that M proteins are the initiator of the disorder. However, other factors such as streptococcal polysaccharides and toxins probably play a role.

Acute glomerulonephritis is a nonsuppurative complication that follows throat or skin infections by a relatively few serological types. Clinical symptoms, which appear one to four weeks after the primary infection, include proteinuria, hematuria, and oliguria. Bacteria cannot be recovered. The pathogenesis is believed to be due to an immune-complex reaction. Antigens from the bacterial cytoplasmic membrane are believed to cross-react with the basement membrane of the glomerulus of the kidney. This results in the precipitation of the immune complex.

UNDER THE MICROSCOPE 13

Changing Streptococcal Epidemiology

The appearance of widespread invasive group A streptococcal disease has also been associated with a shift in the epidemiology of erythrogenic toxins. In the early years of the twentieth century, most group A streptococcal strains produced type B and C erythrogenic toxins. Today there appear to be more strains producing the more potent type A toxin. There is evidence to suggest that type A toxin acts as a "superantigen" eliciting extensive T cell activation and production of tumor necrosis factor. The toxin may work with cytokines to cause capillary leaks and to kill lymphocytes. The toxin may not act alone and some epidemiological studies indicate that certain M protein serotypes may also influence virulence. Streptococcal shock syndrome affects mainly those between the ages of 15 and 45 years and is frequently observed in intravenous drug users.

The epidemiology of invasive group A streptococcal disease has not been clearly resolved. However, it often follows cutaneous infections (cellulitis or wound infections) that do not resolve on their own. These infections progress into bacteremia and shock. Epidemics can be seen among elderly and debilitated patients, and in surgical wards. Recently an epidemic was observed in slaughterhouse workers. Individuals without underlying illness can also be affected by this disease. In many studies 50 percent of affected patients are relatively young and were previously healthy.

Antibiotics are of no use in the treatment; only bed rest and administration of salicylates are of therapeutic value.

Erythema nodosum is a skin condition in which small red nodules appear under the surface of the skin. It exists in a variety of other diseases such as tuberculosis and coccidioidomycosis. Many authorities believe that erythema nodosum is the result of hypersensitivity to the peptidoglycan portion of the streptococcal cell wall.

In recent years there has been a reemergence of life-threatening **invasive group A streptococcal disease.** The spectrum of diseases includes **toxic shock–like syndrome** as well as invasive soft tissue infections (myositis and fascitis), pneumonia, and bacteremia (see Plate 3). Many of these infections are accompanied by rapid development of shock and multiple-organ dysfunction. Mortality rates may vary from 5 to 47 percent. The sudden and unexpected death of Jim Henson, the creator of the Muppets, has created public awareness of the potential virulence of group A streptococci (see Under the Microscope 13).

Laboratory Diagnosis

The clinical symptoms of many streptococcal infections are shared by other bacterial and viral diseases. The clinical symptoms of acute pharyngitis, for example, are similar to those of numerous respiratory virus infections. In a certain percentage of patients with streptococcal disease the typical symptoms of host immunological responses do not appear. Accurate diagnosis requires both clinical and bacteriological support. The most accurate identification of group A, B, and G beta-hemolytic streptococci is made by serological procedures. Physiological tests are used to identify other groups such as group D streptococci (Table 17-2).

TABLE 17-2
Tests Used in the Presumptive Identification of Streptococci

Test	Group A	Group B	Group D	Viridans	Pneumococcus
Susceptibility to bacitracin	+	−	−	+[a]	+
Susceptibility to sulfamethoxazole and trimethoprim	−	−	−[b]	+	?
Hippurate hydrolysis	−	+	−[a]	−[a]	−
PYR hydrolysis	+	−	+	−	−
Growth in 6.5% NaCl	−	+[a]	+[c]	−	−
Optochin susceptibility and bile solubility	−	−	−	−	+
CAMP reaction[d]	−	+	−	−	−

+ = positive or susceptible reaction; − = negative or resistant reaction; PYR = L-pyrrolidonyl-β-naphthylamide.
[a] Occasional exceptions.
[b] Some group D nonenterococci are susceptible.
[c] Group D nonenterococci will not grow in 6.5% NaCl.
[d] A discussion of CAMP test is presented under Group B Streptococci.

Presumptive identification of group A streptococci can be made on throat cultures if the throat swab contains sufficient numbers of microorganisms. The swab can be treated with nitrous acid to produce an extract containing streptococcal antigens. An aliquot of the extracted antigen is added to a coagglutination group A antibody reagent (for example, the Phadebact system). A positive test result is represented by an agglutination reaction. The test can yield results in 30 minutes after taking the swab. Several commercial kits are available for testing swab as well as blood cultures. The kits contain material for extracting streptococcal antigen by enzymatic or nonenzymatic means. The antigen detection system may be a group of agglutination reactions or an enzyme-linked immunosorbent assay.

Two antibody determinations that are useful in evaluating patients with recent streptococcal disease are the anti-SLO (ASO) test and the anti–DNase B (ADN-B) test. The ADN-B test is believed to be the superior one because it is more reliable in confirming infection when rheumatic fever or acute glomerulonephritis is suspected.

Treatment and Prevention

To date, all strains of group A beta-hemolytic streptococci have been shown to be susceptible to penicillin. Penicillin G benzathine is usually prescribed because of its prolonged action. Material for follow-up cultures should be obtained after discontinuation of therapy to determine whether all streptococci have been eliminated. For invasive streptococcal disease, clindamycin is suggested as an alternative for those allergic to penicillin.

The prevention of streptococcal infections also prevents rheumatic fever. Penicillin treatment does not alter the course of rheumatic fever. To minimize the risk of streptococcal infections in rheumatic fever patients, an injection of penicillin G benzathine is usually prescribed each month. This regimen is considered necessary for at least five years after the rheumatic attack. For individuals sensitive to penicillin, erythromycin is a suitable alternative.

GROUP B STREPTOCOCCI

S. agalactiae is the species designation for members of group B streptococci. Group B streptococci are commensals found in the oral cavity, intestinal tract, and vagina. For the past two decades they have been important pathogens in neonates, young infants, and postpartum women. In the United States, group B streptococci are the most frequent cause of life-threatening disease in newborns. Nearly 41 percent of pregnant women have been colonized with group B streptococci, with the gastrointestinal tract the suggested source. The incidence of group B streptococci infection in the United States is 1.1 to 3.7 per 1000 live births. Factors conducive to these infections are premature labor, prolonged rupture of placental membranes, and birth weight less than 3 pounds.

There are two forms of group B streptococcal disease in neonates: **early onset** and **late onset.** Early-onset disease results from the vertical transmission of the microorganism from mother to infant in utero or during passage through the birth canal. Early-onset disease occurs within a few days of delivery and has a high mortality rate as the result of sepsis or pneumonia.

Late-onset disease may be acquired from mothers, hospital personnel, or contacts outside the hospital. Most late-onset disease in infants is believed to occur by contact with the contaminated hands of hospital personnel. Meningitis is the most frequent complication of late-onset disease.

In adults group B infection is seen in those compromised by chemotherapy, diabetes, or pregnancy. Adult diseases include endocarditis, meningitis, pneumonia, and postpartum infection.

There are five distinct group B serotypes, with type III being the most common cause of neonatal infection. The sialic acid capsule is an important virulence factor and inhibits the alternative complement pathway.

Group B infections can be treated with penicillin. These infections, however, are not as susceptible to penicillin as are group A infections. Ampicillin or ampicillin plus gentamicin has been shown to be effective in treatment. Prevention of disease has been approached in two ways. Intravenous intrapartum therapy with ampicillin prevents neonatal colonization with group B streptococci. A second technique is to treat the neonate with penicillin less than two hours after birth.

Group B strains are easily distinguished from other streptococci by the former's ability to hydrolyze hippurate and resistance to the antibiotic bacitracin. The **CAMP** test is also used as a presumptive test for group B streptococci identification. The CAMP test, named from the initials of the investigators who perfected it, is based on the production of a "CAMP factor"—a protein elaborated by group B streptococci. The test is performed by making a single streak of a streptococcal strain perpendicular to but not touching a disk containing betalysin on a sheep blood agar plate. If the streptococcal strain produces CAMP factor, a crescent-shaped clearing appears at the juncture of the betalysin-containing disk and the streptococci. The CAMP factor thus enlarges the zone of lysis produced by betalysin (Fig. 17-7).

Beta-hemolytic group B streptococci produce an orange carotenoid pigment that can be detected on a selective and differential medium (New Granada Medium). The method is very specific but does not detect nonhemolytic and nonpigmented strains that occasionally are implicated in neonatal sepsis.

A chemiluminescent DNA probe has been developed for identification of group B streptococci. The probe is a DNA oligomer having a sequence complementary to a segment of *S. agalactiae* RNA. The probe is labeled with an acridinium ester. Results can be obtained in 40 minutes.

GROUP C STREPTOCOCCI

Group C streptococci are frequent causes of infection in many animal species but are a rare cause of disease in humans. This group of streptococci is composed of four

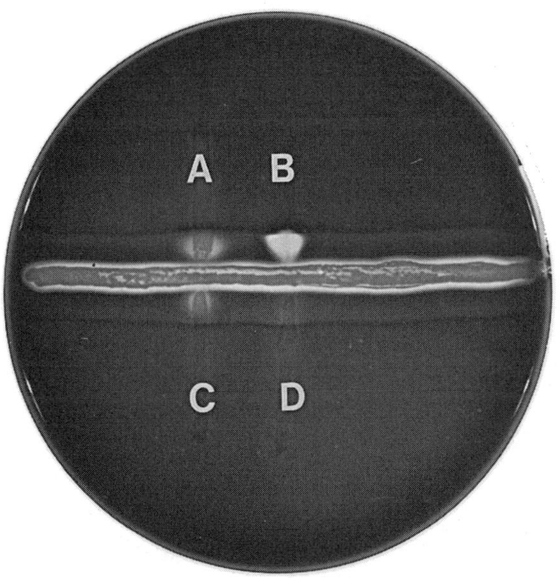

FIGURE 17-7
CAMP test on blood agar. The horizontal streak is *S. aureus*. The perpendicular streaks are *E. coli* (A), *Streptococcus agalactiae* (B), *E. coli* strain (C), and *E. coli* strain (D). (From O. Schneewind, K. Friedrich, and R. Lütticken, *Infect. Immun.* 56:2174, 1989.)

species: *S. equi*, *S. dysgalactiae*, *S. equisimilis*, and *S. zooepidemicus*. Only the latter two species are more commonly associated with human infection. *S. equisimilis* is primarily associated with human illness in the United States. These illnesses include endocarditis, pneumonia, meningitis, epiglottitis, and wound infections. Outbreaks of disease have been associated with unpasteurized milk or cheese made from unpasteurized milk. *S. zooepidemicus* has been associated with outbreaks of pharyngitis and nephritis in Europe and recently with illness in the United States.

VIRIDANS STREPTOCOCCI

Viridans streptococci are commensals and a major component of the oral microflora of humans. This group is for the most part alpha-hemolytic but some are also nonhemolytic. Viridans streptococci do not react with Lancefield grouping sera.

Classification of viridans streptococci has been unsettled for many years. There are seven species, which in the past have been given a variety of names. These species are *S. anginosus*, *S. bovis* variants, *S. mitis*, *S. mutans*, *S. salivarius*, *S. sanguis*, and *S. vestibularis*. These species are not primary pathogens but act as opportunistic challengers to the host. *S. mutans*, for example, is the causative agent of tooth decay.

The major disease associated with viridans streptococci is **subacute bacterial endocarditis (SBE).** SBE is commonly preceded by dental extraction or some type of oral surgery that displaces alpha-hemolytic species from the oral cavity into the bloodstream. The disease occurs most frequently in patients with rheumatic fever or congenital heart disease. Dislodged streptococci are capable of localizing on the affected heart tissue and can bring about further heart valve damage. Left untreated, SBE can lead to heart failure, but the disease can be treated with antibiotics. Penicillin alone is enough for most patients but a second drug such as an aminoglycoside may also be needed.

Treatment failures have been noted, particularly when the endocarditis is caused by **nutritionally deficient streptococci.** These variants have a requirement for pyridoxal. They are the cause of 5 to 6 percent of infections due to viridans streptococci. The poor response of these streptococci to antibiotics appears to be due to a slow rate of metabolism.

A prophylactic regimen for patients with rheumatic fever, heart disease, or prosthetic valves includes the administration of penicillin or other drugs before and after oral surgery.

GROUP D STREPTOCOCCI AND ENTEROCOCCI

Group D streptococci are commensals in the intestinal tract. They had been previously divided into two groups: enterococcal and nonenterococcal. Enterococcal members, such as *S. faecalis*, *S. faecium*, and *S. durans* have now been assigned the genus name *Enterococcus* (*E. faecalis*, *E. faecium*, etc.). Most species of *Enterococcus* possess these characteristics: ability to grow in 6. 5% NaCl and pH 9.6, to grow at 10 C and usually 45 C, and for the most part to survive at 60 C for 30 minutes. Nonenterococcal group D streptococci are *S. bovis* and *S. equinus*.

Enterococci are found in the feces of most healthy adults. The two most commonly encountered species are *E. faecalis* and *E. faecium*. From 80 to 90 percent of all clinical isolates have been *E. faecalis*, with *E. faecium* representing most of the remainder of isolates. Enterococci are now the third most common cause of infective endocarditis, following streptococci and *S. aureus*. The disease is seen most often in older men. The enterococci can infect normal heart valves as well as already damaged valves. The most frequent source of infection is the genitourinary tract.

Enterococci are also a frequent cause of urinary tract infections, particularly in hospitalized patients. Studies by the Centers for Disease Control indicate that enterococci cause 10 to 15 percent of all hospital-associated urinary tract infections.

Currently, the enterococci are the third most reported cause of hospital-associated infections. Enterococci are also recognized as an important cause of neonatal meningitis.

The enterococci show an intrinsic resistance to many beta-lactam antibiotics and quickly develop resistance to other antimicrobials. Treatment of endocarditis can be accomplished through the use of penicillin or vancomycin plus an aminoglycoside. Urinary tract infections are treated with vancomycin or nitrofurantoin. Susceptibility testing should be routinely performed on clinical specimens.

GROUP F STREPTOCOCCI AND OTHER STREPTOCOCCI

Group F streptococci are commensals in the oropharyngeal and bowel areas of humans. They are not frequent causes of human infections. Group F streptococci have a tendency to cause cutaneous abscesses following trauma. Abscesses can also occur in the cervicofacial and intraabdominal areas. Group F streptococci are susceptible to penicillin.

Group G streptococci are known to be associated with clinically asymptomatic pharyngitis. Approximately 20 to 25 percent of humans carry group G strains in the pharynx. Epidemic pharyngitis caused by this group of organisms is usually associated with food contamination but contaminated respiratory secretions may also be a source of infection.

Human infections by other groups of streptococci (E, L, M, etc.) are rare but they are important in veterinary medicine.

ANAEROBIC STREPTOCOCCI

The anaerobic streptococci are classified in the genera *Peptococcus* and *Peptostreptococcus*. Most are nonhemolytic. Anaerobic streptococci are found in the oral cavity, intestinal tract, and vagina. They have been incriminated in such infections as puerperal sepsis, SBE, and deep wound abscesses. Many strains are resistant to penicillin but sensitive to bacitracin and chloramphenicol. Teichoplanin is also active against anaerobic streptococci.

STREPTOCOCCUS PNEUMONIAE (PNEUMOCOCCI)

General Characteristics

The pneumococci are inhabitants of the upper respiratory tract and, depending on seasonal variations, can be found in 30 to 70 percent of the population. They are gram-positive cocci that occur singly, in pairs (diplococci) (Plate 5), or in chains. The typical paired or short-chain forms appear in clinical material. They show a lancet shape and are surrounded by a capsule (Fig. 17-8). Only encapsulated strains are virulent. On repeated subculture in the laboratory the capsule is lost. There are approximately 83 pneumococcal serotypes, differing in composition of their capsular polysaccharide.

The pneumococci are facultative anaerobes that are very fastidious in their cultural requirements. Some strains need an elevated level of carbon dioxide for initial isolation. Meat extracts supplemented with defibrinated blood are one of the foremost cultural media for isolation of pneumococci. The addition of blood to culture media supplies the enzyme catalase, which is not produced by the pneumococci. Under aerobic conditions the pneumococci produce hydrogen peroxide, which can be toxic to them. The enzyme catalase acts to remove the accumulated hydrogen peroxide. On blood agar pneumococcal colonies exhibit alpha hemolysis and closely resemble colonies of alpha-hemolytic streptococci.

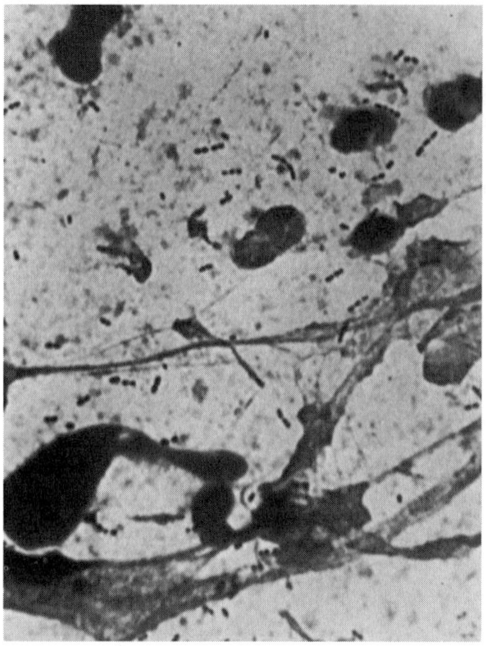

FIGURE 17-8
Sputum sample taken from a patient with pneumococcal pneumonia. The pneumococci appear lancet-shaped in pairs or short chains. (From A. S. Kaliner and I. Geis, *Agents of Bacterial Disease.* New York: Harper & Row, 1973.)

Pathogenesis

The primary virulence factor of the pneumococci is the capsular polysaccharide. The capsule prevents binding of antibody to the cell wall of the pneumococci and thus inhibits phagocytosis. Death from pneumococcal infection is not due to the capsule but is probably due to inflammatory responses to pneumococcal proteins. These proteins may include a hemolysin (pneumolysin) and neuraminidase. For example, both coma and bacteremia occur more significantly when the concentration of N-acetylneuraminic acid in the cerebrospinal fluid is elevated.

S. pneumoniae is the primary cause of community-associated pneumonia. It is also the most frequent cause of otitis media (inflammation of the middle ear) and bacteremia in infants and children. *S. pneumoniae* is the most common cause of bacterial meningitis in adults and the second most common in young children, ranking behind *Hemophilus influenzae.*

Pneumonia and related pneumococcal infections are acquired endogenously through lowered host resistance rather than exogenously by direct contact. In adults and children, infections occur after the recent acquisition of a particular serotype rather than after prolonged carriage. Age, underlying illness, and viral infection are important predisposing factors.

In the healthy individual numerous barriers prevent establishment of infection in the lungs and bronchioles. Mucus-laden pneumococci can be expelled naturally by the combined action of ciliated epithelium and the cough

TABLE 17-3
Physical, Chemical, and Immunological Factors That Predispose to Pneumococcal Pneumonia

Physical and chemical factors
Skull fracture
Eustachian tube obstruction
Edema due to congestive failure
Alcohol intoxication
Narcotic intoxication
Immunological factors
Defects in phagocytic function as in neutropenia or hyposplenia
Hypogammaglobulinemia
Complement deficiency (C2, C3, for example)
Specific antibody deficiency

reflex or through the phagocytic action of macrophages lining the alveoli of the lungs.

If the physical and immunological barriers of the host are impaired, for example, in the debilitated person or chronic alcoholic, the pneumococci can infect the respiratory tree (Table 17-3). Encapsulated pneumococci become trapped in the bronchioles, where they proliferate and eventually infect the alveoli. The inflammatory response of the host leads to the accumulation of an alveolar exudate consisting of large numbers of neutrophils and red blood cells. During this stage the patient's sputum also resembles the alveolar exudate and will appear bloody. During the recovery stage the pneumococci are phagocytized, the alveolar exudate is resorbed, and the lung tissue appears as healthy as before infection. When immediate recovery does not take place, the alveoli can become fibrous and inelastic because of deposition of fibroblasts, and breathing becomes difficult.

In the inflammatory stage of pneumonia, as well as with other diseases in which there is an inflammatory process, a special protein called the **C-reactive protein** is found in the blood. It precipitates a polysaccharide component of the pneumococcal cell wall called the C substance (discussed earlier in this chapter).

Laboratory Diagnosis

Presumptive identification of pneumococcal pneumonia can be made by Gram-staining sputum cultures (or cerebrospinal fluid for meningitis). Sputum specimens must contain areas with at least 15 to 20 white blood cells in a microscopic field under ×1000 magnification. The specimen should also be free of epithelial cells which contain large numbers of viridans streptococci. Identification can also be made by applying an anticapsular serum to the sputum sample and observing capsular swelling (called the **quellung** reaction).

If sputum samples cannot be obtained for examination, swabs of the laryngeal areas of the lung should be examined. Transtracheal aspiration is also widely used for obtaining samples for direct examination.

Latex agglutination and coagglutination tests can be used to detect pneumococcal antigen in respiratory samples. Both tests provide the most reliable diagnostic evidence of pneumococcal etiology when later confirmed by other methods.

Definitive diagnosis of pneumococcal pneumonia can be made if the organisms are isolated directly from clinical specimens. The specimens are plated on blood agar and incubated overnight. Once cultured, the pneumococci can be differentiated from alpha-hemolytic streptococci by the following procedures:

1. Quellung reaction. This reaction is the most accurate and specific test for the identification of pneumococci (Fig. 17-9). The clinical material or culture is spread on a slide and mixed with antiserum against type-specific polysaccharide or the polyvalent antiserum. The polyvalent antiserum contains antibodies to 33 of the most prevalent types in the United States or all 83 pneumococcal types.

FIGURE 17-9
Quellung reaction. A. Control (absence of antiserum). B. Capsular swelling of bacteria after application of antiserum. A capsular halo can be observed around the diplococci. (Courtesy of R. Austrian.)

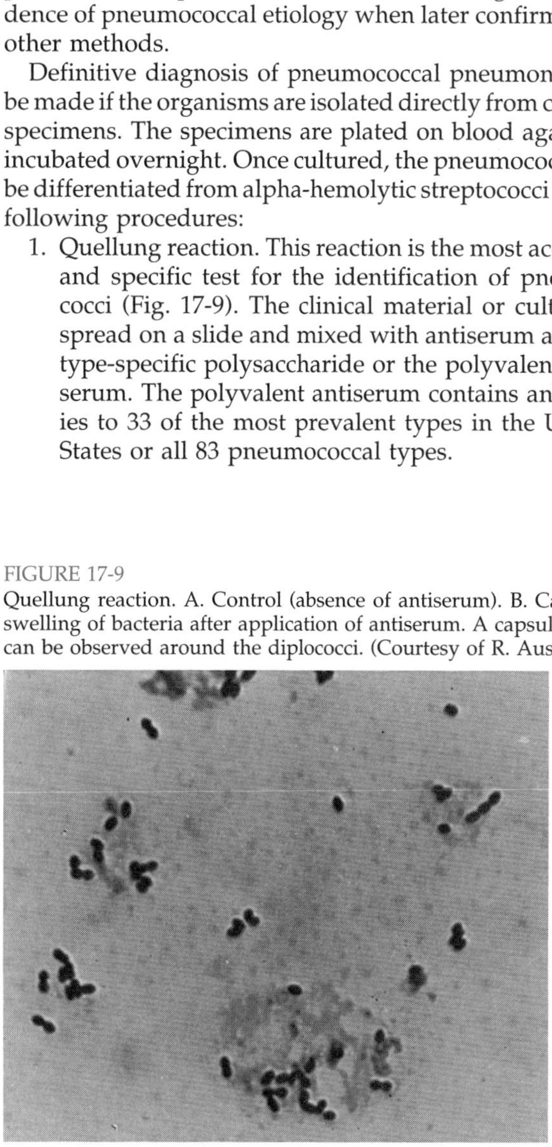
A

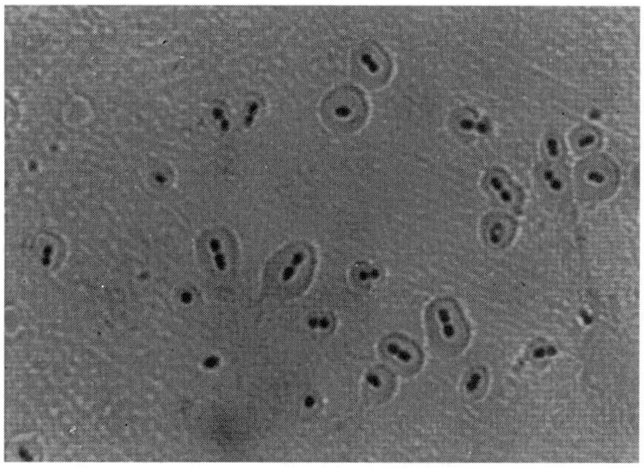
B

2. Optochin susceptibility. Optochin is an antimicrobial drug derived from quinine. When disks containing the drug are placed on blood agar previously seeded with pneumococci, zones of inhibition can be observed around the optochin. Alpha-hemolytic streptococci are resistant to optochin (see Table 17-2).
3. Bile solubility test. The pneumococci produce an enzyme (amidase) that cleaves specific covalent bonds in the peptidoglycan layer. This enzyme is activated by bile or bile salts such as sodium deoxycholate. When a few drops of 10% sodium deoxycholate solution are added to a broth culture of pneumococci, the cells are rapidly lysed. Alpha-hemolytic streptococci are not lysed by bile (see Table 17-2).

In cases of meningitis, the cerebrospinal fluid is examined for capsular antigen if the patient has had prior antibiotic therapy or a Gram stain indicates no organisms. Counterimmunoelectrophoresis, coagglutination, and latex agglutination have been adapted for the rapid and direct detection of soluble bacterial antigens. Blood cultures will be positive for all patients with meningitis if antibiotics have not been administered.

Treatment and Prevention

Penicillin G (IV) procaine is the drug of choice in the treatment of hospitalized patients with pneumococcal infection. Amoxicillin is a good choice for oral administration. *S. pneumoniae* has gradually become more resistant to penicillin and higher concentrations of the drug may be required. Some highly resistant strains have also been observed in the United States and other areas of the world. These strains are resistant to drugs such as ampicillin, erythromycin, penicillin, tetracycline, chloramphenicol, and streptomycin (most laboratories use an oxacillin disk to screen for penicillin-resistant pneumococci). Vancomycin is still effective against these multiantibiotic-resistant strains.

Only 23 of the 83 different pneumococcal types are usually associated with disease. A vaccine containing polysaccharide antigens from these 23 types is available. The vaccine is used for high-risk groups: the aged, those com-

TABLE 17-4
Characteristics of Gram-Positive Staphylococci

Genus/species	Site of commensalism or source of infection	Major disease association	Treatment*
Staphylococcus aureus (coagulase-positive)	Commensal on skin	Abscess, carbuncle, impetigo, sties	None usually required
		Scalded skin syndrome (SSS); exfoliative toxin produced	None usually required
	Intestinal commensal	Enterocolitis often occurs following intensive chemotherapy for other illness	Discontinuation of chemotherapy
	Skin, particularly hands, and nasopharynx	Food poisoning due to heat-stable exotoxin released in high-protein foods	None usually required
	S. aureus skin infection seeding bloodstream	Osteomyelitis	Synthetic penicillin such as methicillin, vancomycin
	Commensal on skin; genitourinary tract	Toxic shock syndrome, associated primarily with highly absorbent tampons but various types of surgeries also important	Fluid replacement, drainage of foci of infection, antimicrobial therapy
S. epidermidis (coagulase-negative)	Commensal in nares and on skin, especially axillae, head, legs, and arms	Endocarditis, colonization of prostheses, bacteremia from indwelling venous catheters	Removal of foreign body or prosthesis, drainage of infection site, antimicrobial therapy such as nafcillin, oxacillin, cephalothin
S. saprophyticus (coagulase-negative)	Occasionally isolated from skin; but has predilection for urinary tract	Major cause of acute, recurrent cystitis in young women	Antimicrobial therapy; organism is susceptible to most common antimicrobials

* Prevention of most *Staphylococcus* infections can be accomplished by frequent handwashing by health care personnel, maintaining aseptic technique in surgery, and proper insertion and management of intravenous and arterial catheters.

promised by underlying illnesses, and persons in epidemic-prone areas such as military bases. The vaccine is less antigenic for children under 2 years old. The vaccine is recommended for children over 2 years old who have chronic illness specifically associated with an increased risk for pneumococcal disease. Vaccination should be repeated at five-year intervals.

Summary

1. The staphylococci are gram-positive spherical cells arranged in grape-like clusters. They are aerobic to facultatively anaerobic. Staphylococci can be found as commensals in various areas of the body, particularly the skin and nares.

2. The staphylococci produce a wide range of infections throughout the body, with *S. aureus* being the most common culprit. *S. epidermidis* is primarily an opportunistic pathogen. Table 17-4 describes the various types of infections caused by staphylococci.

3. Laboratory identification of staphylococci may first require differentiation from micrococci and streptococci. Mannitol salt agar is used as a selective medium for isolation and identification of staphylococci. The coagulase test is considered the most important test for differentiating *S. aureus* from *S. epidermidis.*

4. The staphylococci are frequently resistant to several antimicrobials, particularly penicillin and its derivatives. The resistance is usually due to the formation of enzymes called beta-lactamases.

5. The streptococci are gram-positive, spherical cells that occur in chains of varying length. Most are facultative anaerobes but a few are obligate anaerobes. They are classified primarily by hemolytic behavior and antigenic characteristics associated with a cell wall carbohydrate called C substance.

6. Beta-hemolytic group A streptococci *(S. pyogenes)* are the most important human pathogens. The major antigen associated with pathogenesis is the M protein, which inhibits phagocytosis. Other antigens associated with pathogenesis include various toxins, hemolysins, and spreading factors. The primary virulence factor for *S. pneumoniae* is the capsular polysaccharide that inhibits phagocytosis. The major streptococcal groups and the diseases with which they are associated are outlined in Table 17-5.

7. Serological detection of group-specific antigens of beta-hemolytic streptococci provides the most accurate method of identification but presumptive identification can be made (see Table 17-2). Various kits are available for detecting group A beta-hemolytic streptococcal antigens from throat cultures. Determining the anti–streptolysin O (ASO) titer is the principal diagnostic test for poststrep-

TABLE 17-5
Characteristics of the Pathogenic Streptococci

Species and/or group	Site of commensalism	Major disease associations	Treatment/ prevention
Group A beta-hemolytic (*S. pyogenes*)	Nasopharynx, skin, vagina, rectum	Suppurative: impetigo, cellulitis, puerperal fever, erysipelas; nonsuppurative: rheumatic fever, acute glomerulonephritis, erythema nodosum, scarlet fever, invasive disease	Penicillin
Group B (*S. agalactiae*)	Oral cavity, intestinal tract, vagina	Neonatal disease: early onset (pneumonia, sepsis), late onset (meningitis); adult disease (pneumonia, meningitis, endocarditis) in compromised patient	Penicillin
Group C (*S. equisimilis*, etc.)	Not a commensal in humans but associated with infected animals	Endocarditis, meningitis, pneumonia, pharyngitis	Penicillin
Group D (*E. faecalis*, etc.)*	Intestinal tract	Wound infections, bacteremia, urinary tract infections, endocarditis	Penicillin plus streptomycin
Group F	Oropharynx and bowel	Abscess formation following trauma	Penicillin
Viridans (*S. mitis*, etc.)	Oral cavity	Caries (*S. mutans*) and endocarditis	Penicillin plus aminoglycoside
Anaerobic streptococci	Intestinal tract and vagina	Subacute bacterial endocarditis and wound abscesses	Bacitracin, chloramphenicol
S. pneumoniae	Upper respiratory tract	Otitis media and bacteremia in children; pneumonia and meningitis in all populations	Penicillin; polyvalent vaccine for compromised adults

* *S. faecalis* is now referred to as *Enterococcus faecalis.*

tococcal disease such as rheumatic fever. The quellung reaction is the most definitive test for *S. pneumoniae.* Cultured pneumococci can be differentiated from alpha-hemolytic streptococci by various tests such as optochin susceptibility, bile solubility, and quellung reaction.

8. Nearly all streptococci are susceptible to penicillin (see Table 17-5). A polyvalent vaccine is available for adults and others who have been compromised by some underlying disease or illness. The vaccine is not suitable for children under 2 years old.

Questions for Study

1. Why do some members of the medical community refer to the staphylococci as "the infectious agent for all seasons"?
2. What are the underlying conditions or circumstances that contribute to the following infectious disease states: enterocolitis, toxic shock syndrome, scalded skin syndrome, endocarditis, rheumatic fever, and late-onset meningitis in neonates? What species is responsible for each?
3. Explain why invasive group A streptococcal disease has recently become an important type of streptococcal infection.
4. If you examined a Gram-stained slide and observed large groups of cocci, how could you differentiate between micrococci and staphylococci?
5. Is the treatment for *S. aureus* and *S. epidermidis* infections the same? Explain.
6. Are group B streptococci of importance in the newborn? Explain.
7. Make a list of all the gram-positive cocci and indicate which ones are commensals. Also indicate their site of habitation and the type of infection with which each one is most often associated.

CHAPTER 18

Gram-Negative Diplococci: The *Neisseria* and Related Genera

OBJECTIVES

To describe the properties of the *Neisseria* that distinguish them from other genera of bacteria

To describe the properties that are used to differentiate the species within the genus *Neisseria* and the properties that distinguish the pathogens from nonpathogens

To describe *Neisseria meningitidis* in terms of the diseases it causes, epidemiology, antigens, laboratory diagnostic procedures, chemotherapy, and active immunization

To describe *Neisseria gonorrhoeae* in terms of pathogenic mechanisms, clinical aspects of genital and extragenital infections, diagnostic procedures, and chemotherapy

To understand the importance of pelvic inflammatory disease and how it can be prevented

To list other members of the Neisseriaceae family that are opportunistic pathogens

OUTLINE

NEISSERIA
- General Characteristics

NEISSERIA MENINGITIDIS—THE MENINGOCOCCUS
- Pathogenesis
  - Nasopharyngitis
  - Meningococcal Septicemia
  - Meningococcal Meningitis
- Epidemiology
- Laboratory Diagnosis
  - Rapid Test Methods
  - Serological Tests
- Treatment and Prevention

NEISSERIA GONORRHOEAE—THE GONOCOCCUS
- Epidemiology
- Pathogenesis
  - Genitourinary Tract Infections in the Male
  - Genitourinary Tract Infections in the Female
    - Pelvic Inflammatory Disease
  - Extragenital Infections
    - Local Infections
    - Disseminated Gonococcal Infection
  - Laboratory Diagnosis
  - Treatment and Prevention

OTHER MEMBERS OF THE NEISSERIACEAE
- Nonpathogenic *Neisseria* Species
  - Acinetobacter
  - Branhamella
  - Kingella
  - Moraxella

Neisseria

Neisseria species are pathogens as well as normal flora in humans. *Neisseria* belong to the family Neisseriaceae, which also includes the genera *Acinetobacter, Branhamella, Kingella,* and *Moraxella*. The *Neisseria* are the most important of these genera and are the first to be discussed.

GENERAL CHARACTERISTICS

1. All species are gram-negative diplococci. Where the paired bacteria abut, they are flat-sided, so each member of the pair presents a bean-shaped configuration (Fig. 18-1).
2. All species parasitize the mucous membranes of humans.
3. All species are aerobic or facultatively anaerobic. The pathogens grow better in 5 to 10% carbon dioxide.
4. All species produce the enzyme cytochrome oxidase. Members of the genus are said to be oxidase-positive as determined by the oxidase test.

The major species of the genus *Neisseria* and some of their differentiating properties are outlined in Table 18-1.

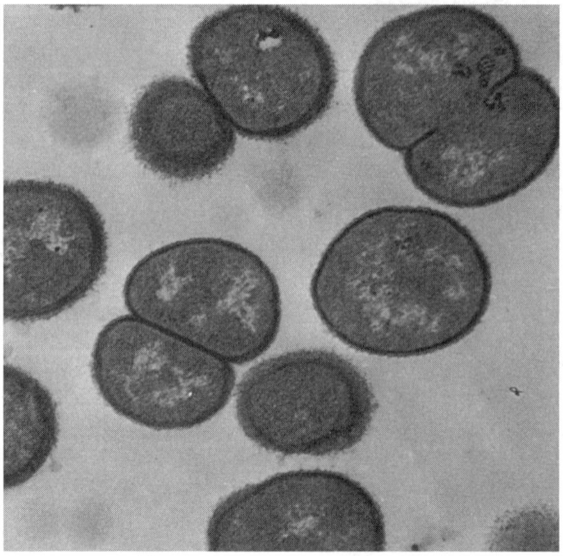

FIGURE 18-1
Electron micrograph of *Neisseria*. (× 27,000.) From A. S. Dajani, *Infect. Immun.* 14:776, 1976.)

Neisseria meningitidis— The Meningococcus

PATHOGENESIS

Meningococcal disease can be divided into three major clinical entities: **nasopharyngitis, meningococcal septicemia,** and **meningococcal meningitis.**

Nasopharyngitis

Infection of the nasopharynx is usually short-lived and frequently symptomless. Meningococci that colonize the nasopharynx can spread from that site into the bloodstream to cause septicemia. They can also spread to adjacent sites and into the bloodstream to cause meningitis.

Meningococcal Septicemia

Infection of the bloodstream can be accompanied by high fever, arthritis, blockages of small vessels, and a rash. The rash commences as **pinpoint hemorrhages (petechiae)** of the skin and mucous membranes. In severe infections the skin lesions become more extensive. Irregularly shaped, **dusky red blotches (purpura),** hemorrhage, and necrosis occur (see Plate 6). A serious development is a **fulminating sepsis,** which produces **hemorrhagic necrosis** in the

TABLE 18-1
Differentiative Properties of *Neisseria*

Species	Acid produced from					Production of IgA protease	Production of pigment	Growth on			Reduction of	
	Glucose	Maltose	Sucrose	Fructose	Lactose			Nutrient agar at 35°C	Chocolate blood agar at 22°C	MTM, ML, or NYC medium	NO_3	NO_2
*N. gonorrhoeae**	+	−	−	−	−	+	−	−	−	+	−	−
N. meningitidis	+	+	−	−	−	+	−	−	−	+	−	d
N. lactamica	+	+	−	−	+		−	−	−	+	−	d
N. cinerea	−	−	−	−	−		−	−	−	−	−	+
N. polysaccharea	+	+	−	−	−		−	+	−	+	−	d
N. flavescens	−	−	−	−	−	−	+	−	−	+	−	−
N. sicca	+	+	+	+	−	−	d	+	+	−		
N. subflava	+	+	d	d	−	−	+	+	+	−	−	+
N. mucosa	+	+	+	+	−		+	+	+	−	+	+

d = some strains positive, some negative; MTM = modified Thayer-Martin; ML = Martin-Lewis; NYC = New York City.
* Superoxol test: Only *N. gonorrhoeae* and *N. kochii* (not listed here) are Superoxol-positive. They give a strong reaction (bubbles of oxygen) when 30% hydrogen peroxide is applied to colonies.

cortex of both adrenal glands (adrenal apoplexy). The profound physiological effects of adrenal insufficiency lead to rapid collapse and death. Probably no other acute bacterial infection is so swiftly fatal as meningococcal septicemia. The complex of changes accompanying the bilateral adrenal cortical hemorrhage is termed **Waterhouse-Friderichsen syndrome,** a syndrome that is most frequently associated with the meningococcus.

Meningococcal Meningitis

Eighty-four percent of reported cases of bacterial (septic) meningitis in patients over one month of age are caused by *Neisseria meningitidis, Streptococcus pneumoniae,* and *Hemophilus influenzae.* All three of these species are indigenous to the nasopharynx. Because the meningococcus is the only microorganism to cause septic meningitis in epidemic form, it is designated the causal agent of **epidemic meningitis.**

Meningococcal meningitis usually begins suddenly with high fever, severe headache, and pain and stiffness of the neck, back, and shoulders. Nausea and vomiting occur frequently. Petechial or purpuric lesions occur in about 50 percent of the patients. Survivors may have major residual effects (sequelae) such as deafness, mental retardation, and behavioral defects.

The exact molecular mechanisms for meningococcal pathogenesis are not totally understood. Meningococci (as well as gonococci) attach only to microvilli of nonciliated columnar epithelial cells (Fig. 18-2). The attachment is apparently mediated by pili on the meningococcal or gonococcal surface but other surface components also may be involved. Multiplication of the meningococci and gonococci is enhanced probably by virtue of their ability to acquire iron from the environment. The bacteria then invade the mucosal surface by a process similar to phagocytosis. Mucosal invasion also may result in access of the bacteria to the bloodstream, leading to dissemination. For the meningococci, additional virulence factors may be involved. These virulence factors include the capsule, which may prevent phagocytosis, and a protease that cleaves IgA antibodies.

Once established, the meningococcus can be devastating. In fact, the mortality of meningococcal meningitis is 85 percent and that figure has not changed even since the discovery of penicillin and other antibiotics. Studies now suggest that endotoxin or lipooligosaccharide (LOS) is the major factor responsible for meningococcal septic shock. Endotoxin may mediate toxicity directly (disseminated intravascular clotting) or may induce the release of tumor necrosis factor (TNF), interleukin (IL)-1, and IL-6 from endotoxin-activated macrophages. Experiments in animals indicate that rapid lysis of bacteria by bactericidal drugs leads to release of endotoxin and probably worsens the outcome of infection.

FIGURE 18-2
Scanning electron micrograph of meningococci attaching to nonciliated columnar epithelial cells but not ciliated cells of human nasopharyngeal organ cultures. The arrows point to elongated microvilli interacting with attaching meningococci. (From D. Stephens, *Clin. Microbiol. Rev.* 2[Suppl.]:104, 1989.)

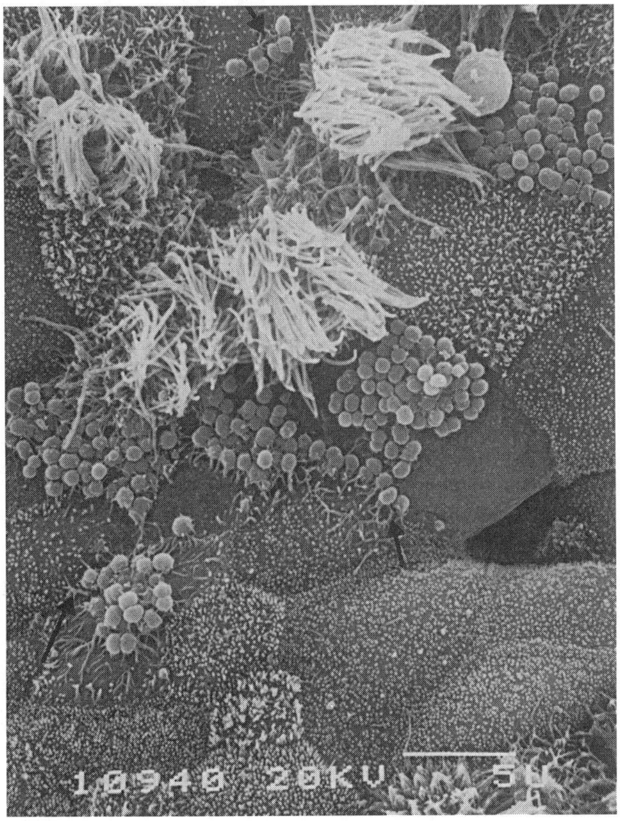

EPIDEMIOLOGY

Humans are the only natural host for *N. meningitidis.* Spread is via respiratory droplets. Rates of endemic disease in the United States are 1 to 3 per 100,000; in parts of the developing world the rates are 10 to 25 per 100,000. In epidemic periods the rates may be as high as 500 per 100,000.

The pathogenicity of *N. meningitidis* is associated with specific serogroups and serotypes. There are 13 serogroups of meningococci. Encapsulated strains belonging to serogroups A, B, C, and W135 have been associated most frequently with epidemics (see Serological Tests). The most common epidemic strains belong to group A while the others cause sporadic epidemics. Meningococci may be carried asymptomatically in the oropharynx and nasopharynx. They also may be isolated from urogenital sites in men and women. Between 3 and 30 percent of healthy persons may be asymptomatic carriers of the meningococci. Carriage rates are highest among school-age children and young adults. In the United States the carriage rate is between 0.6 to 5.7 percent. The rate increases markedly in closed populations such as at military installations that process recruits. During epidemics among military recruits, about 95 percent of them may be carriers but disease will develop in only 1 percent.

Disease is severalfold more likely to develop in close contacts of persons with meningococcal disease than in the general population. Persons at highest risk are household contacts, day-care center contacts, and persons who have had oral contact or who have shared food and beverages with infected persons. Nearly one-third of the contacts who develop meningococcal disease do so within four days after the index (source) patient is hospitalized.

The condition of the pharyngeal mucosa and respiratory epithelium seems to be an important factor in protection from invasive disease. For example, outbreaks in sub-Saharan Africa (meningitis belt) tend to appear at 8- to 12-year intervals in the dry season. This trend is apparently related to constant irritation of the respiratory mucosa during that season. Concurrent viral respiratory tract illness appears to be a predisposing factor, as is poor general health.

LABORATORY DIAGNOSIS

The organism can be isolated from blood, the nasopharynx, skin lesions, cerebrospinal fluid (CSF), and other sites, such as the urethra, the endocervix, and the anal canal of homosexuals. Specimens should be cultured as soon as possible because *Neisseria* pathogens autolyze readily and are somewhat temperature-sensitive. Specimens are cultured on supplemented chocolate agar or **Thayer-Martin, Martin-Lewis,** or **New York medium.** The latter three media are made selective by the addition of combinations of six different antimicrobials. Antimicrobials prevent the growth of nonpathogenic *Neisseria,* as well as yeasts, gram-negative bacilli, and other forms. Growth is augmented by incubation in an environment with elevated carbon dioxide levels.

The examination of clinical materials, especially of CSF, yields important information for diagnosis. The cornerstone of diagnosis of all acute bacterial (septic) meningitis is a lumbar puncture to obtain CSF. The CSF in patients with acute bacterial (septic) meningitis, as opposed to acute aseptic meningitis, is under increased pressure and cloudy. In addition, the white blood cell count is increased, the protein concentration is elevated, and the glucose level is reduced in the CSF. Some of the CSF is Gram-stained for a presumptive diagnosis. In acute infections the meningococci (and the gonococci) characteristically appear in their distinctive morphology and grouping within the cytoplasm of neutrophils (Fig. 18-3).

FIGURE 18-3
Smear of urethral pus containing gonorrhea organisms. In acute infections, the paired, bean-shaped *Neisseria* appear mostly within the cytoplasm of neutrophils *(center).* The large, dark structures are the lobed nuclei of the neutrophils. The circular grouping of the gonococci is due to their confinement within the indistinct cytoplasmic membrane of the neutrophils. (From R. W. Thatcher and T. H. Pettit. Reprinted from the *Journal of the American Medical Association,* March 1, 1971, Volume 215, Copyright © 1971, American Medical Association.)

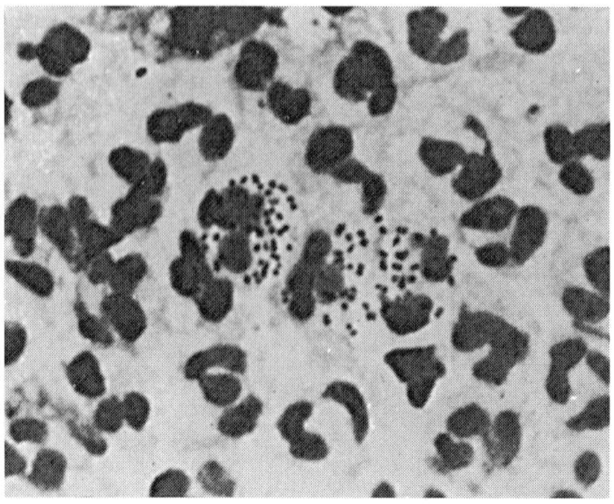

Colony characteristics and Gram-stained smears prepared from colonies are examined. The **cytochrome oxidase test** (simply referred to as the **"oxidase test"**) is performed to identify the isolate as a member of the genus *Neisseria.* The oxidase test is performed by dropping oxidase reagent directly onto colonies or by transferring some of the growth from a colony onto a filter strip moistened with the reagent. In a positive test result, the colony or the filter strip progressively changes color from pink to maroon or black. Carbohydrate utilization tests along with other selected differential tests are used to differentiate *N. meningitidis* from the other *Neisseria* species (see Table 18-1).

Rapid Test Methods

Rapid test methods available for the identification of *Neisseria* include tests to detect acid production from carbohydrates, tests to detect specific enzymes, serological tests, and DNA probe tests.

Serological Tests

There are three ways in which the antigens of serologically and chemically different strains of meningococci are organized: serogroups, serotypes, and subtypes. Serogrouping is based on chemical and structural characteristics of the capsular polysaccharides. Serotyping and subtyping are based on outer membrane proteins of the cell wall. At present, meningococci are referred to primarily on the basis of their serogroup antigens such as A, B, C, D, and so on.

The serological tests that can be performed directly on CSF include the fluorescent antibody staining procedure and counterimmunoelectrophoresis (CIE). Traditional agglutination tests also can be performed on fresh cultures. Latex agglutination tests (using antimeningococcal antibodies attached to latex particles) and coagglutination tests (see Chapter 17, *Staphylococcus aureus,* Protein A) for detecting meningococcal antigens in body fluids are commercially available. Monoclonal antibodies against serogroup B are available, and they can be used to detect the bacterium in CSF, blood, and urine.

TREATMENT AND PREVENTION

The seriousness of meningococcal disease makes it imperative to begin treatment promptly. The use of antimicrobial drugs should not await the completion of laboratory studies. Third-generation cephalosporins such as cefotaxime are the drugs of choice in children with meningitis, or cefotaxime plus ampicillin for infants with infection. Chloramphenicol is an alternative choice when there is penicillin hypersensitivity. A combination of ampicillin and moxalactam is also highly active against the meningococcus.

Since antibiotic therapy apparently has little effect on the fatality rate, a variety of new adjunctive therapeutic approaches are being investigated. Drugs that are known to regulate the inflammatory response are being investigated. In experimental meningitis, dexamethasone, for example, leads to a reduction in intracranial hypertension. Dexamethasone reduces TNF activity and also causes a decrease in the production of leukotrienes. Investigational treatments include use of (1) antibodies directed to the O antigens of the endotoxin, (2) monoclonal antibodies directed at regions of lipid A, and (3) other proteins that neutralize TNF.

Four licensed polysaccharide vaccines are available in the United States for serogroups or combinations of serogroups: A, C, AC, and ACYW135. Infants respond poorly to the polysaccharide antigens, and so the vaccines are less efficacious for the group at highest risk. Furthermore, the antibody level declines rapidly in young children and there is no secondary immune response of note.

Group B meningococci account for about 50 percent of meningococcal illness in the United States. There is only a weak response to the B polysaccharide in humans, so no vaccine is available.

Currently, routine immunization in the industrialized nations is not recommended. The risk of infection is low, vaccines are not very efficacious in infants (the group at highest risk), and there is no vaccine available against group B. A single-dose tetravalent vaccine is recommended for persons with anatomical or functional asplenia and deficiencies of the terminal component of the complement system. Additionally, travelers to areas with hyperendemic or epidemic meningococcal disease (for example, sub-Saharan Africa) should be immunized.

Early use of rifampin is recommended for close contacts of persons with meningococcal disease. An adjunct to chemoprophylaxis is active immunization. In more than 50 percent of the high-risk close contacts who get a meningococcal infection, the infection develops more than five days after contact with the index patient—sufficient time for the active immunization to yield some benefit against disease serogroups A, C, Y, and W135.

Neisseria gonorrhoeae— The Gonococcus

EPIDEMIOLOGY

Of the *Neisseria* species, only *N. gonorrhoeae* strains are always pathogenic. *N. gonorrhoeae* strains infect mucosal surfaces of the cervix, urethra, rectum, and oropharynx and nasopharynx, causing symptomatic or asymptomatic infections. Asymptomatic infections are more prevalent in the oropharynx and nasopharynx.

Except vulvovaginitis in prepubertal (usually institutionalized) girls and conjunctivitis in the newborn, gonococcal infections are usually spread by sexual contact. The number of cases of gonorrhea reported to the Centers for Disease Control each year has been higher than 450,000. This figure exemplifies the extent of infection in the population and the enormity of the control problem. In addition, many of the infected also carry other sexually transmitted infectious agents such as chlamydia.

Among the factors that predispose to the epidemic proportions of gonorrhea are (1) the high degree of transmissibility; (2) short incubation period; (3) high rate of asymptomatic carriers; (4) lack of protective immunity; (5) increasing resistance to antibiotics; and (6) conceivably, changes in sexual mores and practices.

PATHOGENESIS

As with the meningococci, the gonococci invade host cells by a process similar to phagocytosis. Clinical signs of infection are apparently due to migration of leukocytes and activation of complement at the site of infection. Gonococci are known to persist in the infected host. This persistence is probably due to their phagocytosis by epithelial cells, a process that protects them from the phagocytic activities of leukocytes. The gonococci also produce an IgA protease that inactivates secretory IgA. The gonococci may exert direct cytotoxic effects but this has not been unequivocally proved. Characteristics of disease in men and women are described below.

Genitourinary Tract Infections in the Male

Infection in men usually takes the form of acute urethritis. Among the early symptoms are sensations of discomfort and pain. The inflammatory response initially triggers a mucoid discharge followed by a purulent exudate, usually in 2 to 5 days (Fig. 18-4). The infection can progress from the anterior urethra to the posterior urethra in 10 to 14 days. Symptoms include increasing dysuria (difficult urination), polyuria (frequent urination), and occasionally headache and fever. The glands, ducts, and vesicles of the male genitourinary tract may become sites of local complications. Chronic infections of the prostate, seminal

FIGURE 18-4
Purulent discharge typical of gonorrhea in men. Often it is only a drop of pus noticed on arising, but in men with severe disease the discharge is continuous and heavy. (From B. N. Morton, *VD: A Guide for Nurses and Counselors.* Boston: Little, Brown, 1976.)

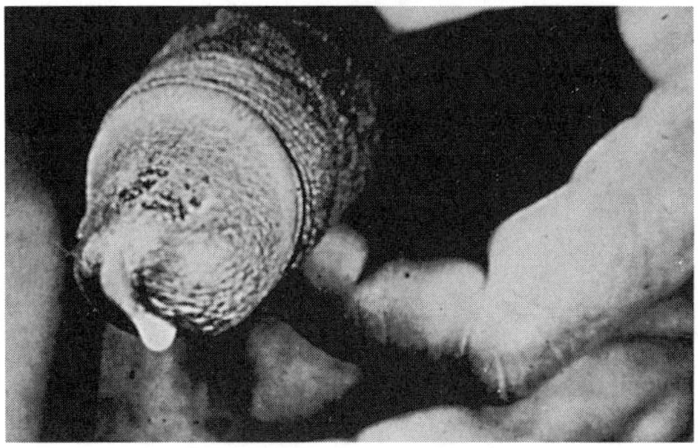

vesicles, and epididymides may ensue. Urethral strictures may occur.

Asymptomatic infections are now known to occur in as many as 40 percent of the infected male population.

Genitourinary Tract Infections in the Female

In females acute gonorrhea may involve the urethra, Skene's and Bartholin's glands, and the endocervix (Fig. 18-5). The endocervix glands are the traditional site of infection, but the rectum is also a common site. Exudate from the endocervix probably contaminates the perineum, and the microorganisms spread to the rectal mucosa. There is no gonococcal vaginitis in the postpubertal female. Symptoms of acute infection of the lower tract are seldom severe. The most prevalent symptoms of acute infection are abdominal or pelvic pain, vaginal discharge (which originates in the endocervix), and dysuria. Chronic infections may be indicated by tenderness of the lower abdomen, backaches, low-grade inflammations of the urethra and genitourinary tract–associated structures, and profuse menstrual flow. Asymptomatic carriers represent a major obstacle in controlling the spread of gonorrhea.

Pelvic Inflammatory Disease. Pelvic inflammatory disease (PID) refers to the syndrome among women resulting from infection involving the uterus, fallopian tubes, ovaries, peritoneal surfaces, or contiguous structures. Symptoms of acute infection include chills, fever to 102 F, severe bilateral lower abdominal pain, and rebound tenderness (pain on release of manual pressure). Most PID results from the ascending spread of microorganisms from the vagina and endocervix to the upper genital sites. Individual cases of PID may be defined by the site of infection, for example, endometritis (endometrium of the uterus) and salpingitis (fallopian tubes). At least four factors can contribute to the ascent of bacteria to the upper genital tract:

FIGURE 18-5
The discharge caused by gonorrhea in women is noticeable on the cervix rather than on the vaginal walls. The test sample is taken from the cervical os, the small opening at the center of the cervix. (From B. N. Morton, *VD: A Guide for Nurses and Counselors*. Boston: Little, Brown, 1976.)

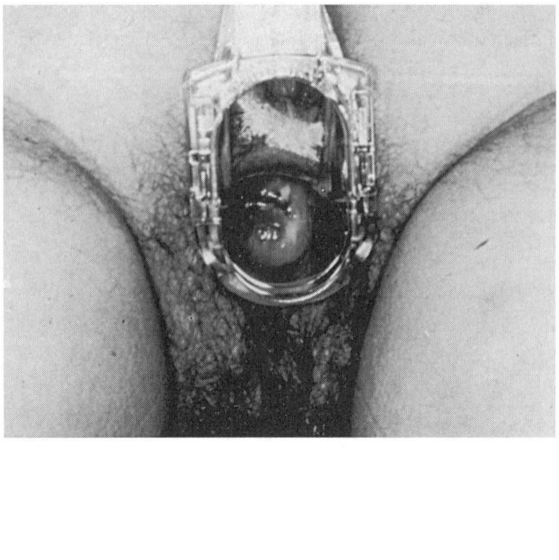

1. Insertion of an intrauterine device (IUD),
2. Hormonal changes during menses in which barriers (mucus, for example) to ascent are broken down,
3. Retrograde menstruation favoring ascent, and
4. Individual virulence factors of the microorganisms associated with pathogenesis.

About 1 million women in the United States experience an episode of PID. These women are at increased risk of ectopic pregnancy and tubal infertility. After one episode of PID a woman's risk of becoming infertile is 12 percent and jumps to 50 percent if she has had three episodes of PID. Many women with PID are asymptomatic and their rates of tubal infertility are very high.

Most cases of PID are associated primarily with the pathogens *N. gonorrhoeae* and *Chlamydia trachomatis* and a wide variety of anaerobic and aerobic bacteria. The most common anaerobic bacteria are *Bacteroides, Peptostreptococcus,* and *Peptococcus* while the most common facultative bacteria are *Gardnerella vaginalis, Streptococcus* species, *Escherichia coli,* and *Hemophilus influenzae.* There is some evidence that the syndrome **bacterial vaginosis** (see Chapter 30) is a precursor to PID.

Preventive measures include (1) limitations on the number of sex partners; (2) avoiding "casual" sex; (3) questioning potential sex partners about sexually transmitted diseases; (4) avoiding sex with infected persons; (5) abstinence from sex if sexually transmitted disease symptoms appear; and (6) use of barriers such as condoms, diaphragms, and/or vaginal spermicides for protection against sexually transmitted diseases.

Extragenital Infections

Local Infections. Local infections occur in various areas of the body, determined usually by the mode of contact: **Pharyngitis, conjunctivitis,** and **proctitis** are examples. Blindness in the newborn **(ophthalmia neonatorum)** can develop from infection of the eyes as the child passes through the birth canal of an infected mother.

Disseminated Gonococcal Infection. Gonococci from primary sites of infection (endocervix, rectum, male urethra, etc.) can spread via the bloodstream to cause most commonly, an **arthritis-dermatitis syndrome** and occasionally, meningitis, endocarditis, and other conditions. Disseminated gonococcal infection (DGI) develops in 1 to 3 percent of individuals with genital infections. Those in whom DGI develops are usually asymptomatic with regard to the primary site of infection. Fever, chills, myalgia, and malaise are nonspecific symptoms of the bacteremic phase of DGI. Between 50 and 70 percent of patients with DGI have dermatitis and more than 90 percent have arthropathy. Active skin lesions are usually found in those who have joint involvement. An average of 5 to 30 lesions appear, mostly on the extremities, and they progress from red papular to pustular, hemorrhagic, or necrotic lesions. The presence of such lesions in various stages of development in sexually active individuals should lead the physician to rule out DGI. The arthritis is usually felt in several joints, with the knees, ankles, and wrists being the most frequently involved. Joint destruction can occur if the infection is left untreated.

LABORATORY DIAGNOSIS

The laboratory characteristics that were cited for the meningococcus apply as well to the gonococcus: the fragility of the bacteria, types of culture media employed for isolation, requirements for elevated carbon dioxide environment for growth (more important for gonococci), typical gram-negative diplococci appearing in the cytoplasm of pus cells, and the availability of rapid identification methods.

The finding of intracellular gram-negative diplococci in smears of urethral pus is viewed as presumptive evidence of gonorrheal infection in men (see Fig. 18-4). Smears of specimens from the female genital tract are much less reliable for diagnostic purposes. Acute infections are not nearly so apparent as in the male, and other organisms that resemble gonococci may appear in such specimens. Smears from the pharynx or rectum have little reliable diagnostic value.

To diagnose a gonorrheal infection reliably, it is necessary to culture the organisms to establish identity. Careful attention must be paid to the collection of appropriate specimens and to the processing of the specimens. Oropharyngeal and anorectal specimens should also be obtained along with the regularly collected urethral and endocervical specimens. This sampling is necessary if there is reason to believe that oral or anal contact has occurred. Colonial and microscopical characteristics, the oxidase test, and carbohydrate utilization tests are the principal observations and tests that are routinely conducted on the isolated organisms. Additional tests are indicated in Table 18-1.

N. gonorrhoeae displays four colony types. Colony types T1 and T2 are small, sticky, and dark (when obliquely lighted); they develop in primary culture from clinical material. T1 and T2 colonies are correlated with virulence.

The **Superoxol test** is an inexpensive, rapid screening test for organisms growing on selective media. The test is similar to the conventional catalase test except the concentration of hydrogen peroxide is 30% rather than 3%. Any organism that grows on these media and is Superoxol-positive is likely to be *N. gonorrhoeae.*

There are two customary serological tests used to identify *N. gonorrhoeae:* the direct fluorescent antibody technique and the staphylococcal coagglutination technique. The latter technique employs a strain of protein A–containing staphylococci that are coated with antigonococcal antibodies (see under Protein A in Chapter 17). A more rapid technique is the urea-based enzyme-linked immunosorbent assay utilizing monoclonal antibodies.

TREATMENT AND PREVENTION

In recent years there has been a high frequency of cotransmitted and coexisting gonococcal and chlamydial infections. There is concern about the complications of these infections because of the increasing resistance of more than 20 percent of the gonococci to penicillin and tetracycline (see Under the Microscope 14). Resistance to an alternative drug, spectinomycin, has also been reported. Susceptibilities to antibiotics vary in parts of the country. State and local health departments are encouraged to determine antimicrobial susceptibilities of isolates from se-

UNDER THE MICROSCOPE 14

Plasmid-Mediated Antimicrobial Resistance in *Neisseria gonorrhoeae*

There has been a steady increase in plasmid-mediated antimicrobial resistance to *N. gonorrhoeae* since 1976. Penicillinase-producing *N. gonorrhoeae* (PPNG) was first isolated in the United States in 1976, and antimicrobial resistance has increased steadily since that time. The main foci of PPNG infections were initially identified in Los Angeles, Miami, and New York City. Spread of PPNG has now encompassed all regions of the country.

PPNG now accounts for 3 to 7 percent of isolated gonococci. The beta-lactamase produced by PPNG strains renders drugs such as penicillin G, ampicillin, and amoxicillin inadequate for treatment. It is believed that these plasmids may have been acquired initially from *Hemophilus ducreyi* (the agent of a sexually transmitted disease called chancroid, see Chapter 24) or possibly other *Hemophilus* species. Spread of PPNG is fostered by the presence of a large plasmid called a **transfer plasmid.** The transfer plasmid permits the transfer of smaller plasmids such as the PPNG plasmid to other gonococci.

A chromosomal mutation encoding for tetracycline resistance in *N. gonorrhoeae* was recognized in 1985. These gonococci contain a large transfer plasmid that includes the tetracycline mutation. The tetracycline resistance plasmid can be self-transmitted to a wide variety of bacteria. The tetracycline transfer plasmid can mobilize the transmission of penicillinase-encoding plasmids. Thus, almost 1 percent of gonococci isolated in sexually transmitted disease clinics in the United States are both PPNG- and tetracycline-resistant.

Despite widespread resistance to the traditional antimicrobial agents, *N. gonorrhoeae* is sensitive to a number of newer drugs, particularly the quinolones and the cephalosporins. Ciprofloxacin and ofloxacin have high levels of activity against the microorganism.

lected patients. In this way any emerging resistance pattern can be detected and therapeutic revisions instigated.

In view of the possibility of cotransmitted chlamydial infection and the increasing number of resistant strains, the recommended regimen for uncomplicated urethral, endocervical, or rectal infections is ceftriaxone, 250 mg intramuscularly (IM) once, plus doxycycline, 100 mg orally twice per day for 7 days. Doxycycline is used to eradicate coexisting *C. trachomatis*. Ceftriaxone is also recommended for virtually all other types of gonococcal infections: pharyngitis, meningitis, endocarditis, adult ophthalmia, DGI, infections during pregnancy, and infections in infants and children. The regimens for these other types vary in respect to dosage, number and spacing of doses, and additional or alternative drugs.

A new drug, **enoxacin** (a fluoroquinolone), is also being evaluated as an alternative for drug-resistant strains. Enoxacin is equally effective against penicillin-susceptible and penicillin-resistant strains. A single oral dose of the drug is effective in treating genital gonorrhea in males. Another drug, **cefixime,** is being recommended by some as an alternative to ceftriaxone. Cefixime can be given orally, is as efficacious as ceftriaxone, and is cost-efficient.

Treatment of PID involves a broad-spectrum approach and includes cefoxitin or other cephalosporins plus doxycycline, and clindamycin plus gentamicin.

Most states have a law that requires the instillation of a prophylactic agent into the eyes of newborn infants immediately post partum to prevent gonococcal ophthalmia neonatorum. Silver nitrate solution 1% (Crede's method) is effective for gonococcal ophthalmia neonatorum but is not effective against chlamydial conjunctivitis. Either erythromycin (0.5%) ophthalmic ointment or tetracycline (1.0%) is effective against both agents.

Long-lasting immunity does not appear to develop as a result of natural infections with *N. gonorrhoeae*. Repeated infections occur in an individual, and an acute infection may be superimposed on a chronic one. Antigonococcal secretory IgA is found, however, in genital secretions. Bactericidal serum antibodies can be demonstrated.

Extensive efforts have been made to develop a vaccine against gonorrhea but so far have been unsuccessful (see Additional Readings for studies on vaccines).

Other Members of the Neisseriaceae

NONPATHOGENIC *NEISSERIA* SPECIES

Members of the genus *Neisseria*, other than *N. gonorrhoeae* and *N. meningitidis*, are not frequently involved in overt disease. Their importance lies in the following facts: (1) They are the second most prevalent microorganisms in the oral cavity and upper respiratory tract, and some are occasionally recovered from genital sites; (2) it is usually necessary to differentiate them from the pathogens; and (3) occasionally they are found as causal agents of infections such as meningitis, endocarditis, pneumonia, osteomyelitis, and septicemia. Some of the important species are *N. lactamica, N. cinerea, N. polysaccharea, N. sicca, N. mucosa, N. subflava*, and *N. flavescens*.

Acinetobacter

Acinetobacter is a genus with many species of gram-negative diplococci or coccobacilli. Its members are widely distributed in nature and often are part of the normal flora of the skin and throat. There is one recognized species, *A. calcoaceticus* (which includes the former *Herellea vaginocola* and *Mima polymorpha*), that is being reported with increasing frequency as an opportunistic pathogen. It causes a variety of infections, especially hospital-associated infections: pneumonia, bacteremia, nongonococcal urethritis, meningitis, and wound infections. *Acinetobacter* is often resistant to cefotaxime but sensitive to gentamicin and penicillins.

Branhamella

Branhamella catarrhalis is a gram-negative diplococcus, formerly known as *Neisseria catarrhalis*. This species recently has come to be recognized as a significant cause of maxillary sinusitis and otitis media in children. The organism is an infrequent but significant cause of pneumonia, bronchitis, endocarditis, meningitis, conjunctivitis, and septicemia, especially in individuals with a compromised health status. Characteristics that help differentiate *B. catarrhalis* from other *Neisseria* are as follows:

1. *Branhamella* does not produce acids from the dissimilation of carbohydrates.
2. *Branhamella* reduces nitrates.
3. *Branhamella* hydrolyzes DNA and tributyrin.
4. *Branhamella* is Superoxol-negative.
5. *Branhamella* colonies are nonpigmented or gray, and growth is variable on selective media.

Beta-lactamase–producing strains are present throughout the world. All strains in the United States are susceptible to alternative drugs such as erythromycin, and rifampin and beta-lactams that are resistant to beta-lactamase.

Kingella

Members of *Kingella* (three recognized species) are gram-negative coccobacilli that occur in pairs and short chains. Members of the genus are occasional indigenous inhabitants of the upper respiratory tract but rarely are significant pathogens. Infections have occurred in normal and immunocompromised hosts. Pathogenically *Kingella* is similar to *N. meningitidis*. *Kingella* species colonize and infect mucous membranes of the nasopharynx, with later invasion of the bloodstream. Bloodstream invasion results in widely disseminated infections involving the heart valves, skin, bones, joints, and disk spaces. The organism is sensitive to penicillin.

Moraxella

Moraxella species can be found as normal inhabitants of the upper respiratory tract and skin of humans and animals. *M. lacunata* and *M. nonliquefaciens* are more frequently associated with otolaryngological or ocular infections while *M. urethralis* is isolated primarily from the urine. Diseases associated with infection include pericarditis, pulmonary abscesses, arthritis, disk infections, conjunctivitis, keratitis, and urogenital disease. Penicillin is the drug of choice.

TABLE 18-2
Characteristics of Pathogenic *Neisseria*

	Disease association	Morphological and physiological characteristics	Virulence factors	Mode of transmission	Treatment and prevention
N. meningitidis	Septicemia: high fever, disseminated intravascular clotting, vascular damage, shock Septic meningitis: high fever, severe headache, nausea, disorientation, sequelae	Gram-negative diplococci, intracellular habitat in smears of pus, Thayer-Martin medium and elevated CO_2 for laboratory growth, cytochrome oxidase–positive	Pili, capsules, IgA protease, ability to remove iron from host transferrin, mechanism to traverse mucosa; endotoxins	Respiratory droplets	Penicillin; chloramphenicol; rifampin prophylactically for close contacts
N. gonorrhoeae	Males: acute urethritis; chronic infection of other genitourinary tract sites; asymptomatic carrier state Females: infection of endocervix, rectum, periurethral glands; pelvic inflammatory disease; asymptomatic carrier state Extragenital infections: local—governed by mode of contact, pharyngitis; proctitis, conjunctivitis; systemic—arthritis-dermatitis, endocarditis, meningitis	Same as above	Pili, IgA, protease, epithelial endocytosis; endotoxins	Venereal	Ceftriaxone; use of penicillin, tetracycline, spectinomycin determined by patient hypersensitivity or regional occurrence of resistant strains; 1% silver nitrate or erythromycin or tetracycline into eyes of newborn

Summary

1. Some of the main features of the major *Neisseria* pathogens are outlined in Table 18-2. Differentiation of species within the genus is based primarily on carbohydrate utilization.

2. Both *N. meningitidis* and *N. gonorrhoeae* are associated with asymptomatic infections and this is a major problem in controlling infection. Of major concern is the coexistence of *Chlamydia* with *N. gonorrhoeae* and the threat of pelvic inflammatory disease in women.

3. The site of localized extragenital infections (pharyngitis, proctitis, conjunctivitis) caused by *N. gonorrhoeae* usually is determined by mode of contact. Disseminated gonococcal infections are spread via the hematogenous route and mostly take the form of an arthritis-dermatitis syndrome.

4. Other members of the family Neisseriaceae include *Acinetobacter, Branhamella, Kingella,* and *Moraxella.* They are found as commensals in the upper respiratory tract and skin and are infrequent but important causes of infection.

Questions for Study

1. How is it possible for the gonococcus to penetrate epithelial cells that are not considered phagocytic?
2. What is the principal method for differentiating the various species within the genus *Neisseria?*
3. What is believed to be responsible for the high rate of mortality associated with meningococcal meningitis? Create a scenario involving the bacterium and the inflammatory process.
4. Assuming a patient had pharyngitis, what laboratory techniques would you use to determine if the offending organism was streptococcal or gonococcal?
5. What factors are conducive to the acquisition of pelvic inflammatory disease? How may it be prevented? (See Additional Readings.)
6. What symptoms might make you suspect a patient had meningococcal meningitis? Describe how you would go about determining whether *N. meningitidis* is involved.

CHAPTER 19

The Gram-Positive Sporeformers: The Bacilli and Clostridia

OBJECTIVES

- To describe the types of disease caused by the genus *Bacillus* and the virulence factors associated with them
- To discuss the techniques used to treat and control disease caused by *Bacillus* species
- To list the major species of *Clostridium* and the diseases they cause in humans
- To explain the various laboratory techniques used to differentiate species of *Clostridium*
- To explain the mechanism of action of the clostridial toxins
- To describe the methods used to treat and prevent clostridial infections

OUTLINE

- *BACILLUS*
  - *Bacillus anthracis*
    - General Characteristics
    - Antigens and Virulence Factors
  - Pathogenesis and Epidemiology
  - Immunity
  - Laboratory Diagnosis
  - Treatment and Prevention
  - *Bacillus cereus* and Other Bacilli
- *CLOSTRIDIUM*
  - General Characteristics
  - Diseases Caused by Clostridia
    - Food Poisoning (Botulism)
      - *Clostridium botulinum* Toxin
      - Pathogenesis
      - Laboratory Diagnosis
      - Treatment and Prevention
    - Gas Gangrene
      - *Clostridium perfringens* Toxins
      - Pathogenesis
      - Laboratory Diagnosis
      - Treatment and Prevention
    - Food Poisoning *(Clostridium perfringens)*
    - Enterotoxin-Associated Diarrhea
    - Tetanus
      - Tetanus Toxins
      - Pathogenesis
      - Laboratory Diagnosis
      - Treatment
      - Prevention
    - Other Clostridial Conditions
      - *Clostridium difficile*–Associated Colitis and Pseudomembranous Colitis
      - Necrotizing Enterocolitis
      - Neutropenic Enterocolitis

The gram-positive sporeformers comprise two major genera of bacteria: *Bacillus* and *Clostridium*. In culture they appear as long rods varying in length between 3 and 8 μm. In the spore state they are relatively resistant to heat and many chemicals. Autoclaving for 15 minutes at 120 C and 15 pounds of pressure is the most effective way to destroy them. Most species exist as saprophytes in soil, water, and vegetation, although some are harbored in the intestinal tract of animals and humans. Only a few species are pathogenic to humans. They are, however, the most virulent.

Bacillus

BACILLUS ANTHRACIS

General Characteristics

The anthrax bacillus is a nonmotile, facultative anaerobe that is 3 to 5 μm in length and 1.0 to 1.5 μm in width. The spore, located in the center of the cell (endospore), is produced only when the cells are cultivated outside animal host tissue. Colonies on blood agar or other laboratory media have a rough texture (ground-glass appearance) and a serrated edge. As the colonies age, the edge gives the appearance of undulating bands and is referred to as "medusa head." When the bacillus is cultivated in the presence of elevated concentrations of carbon dioxide, the colonies become mucoid due to capsule formation. The capsule is a polypeptide (polyglutamic acid) and its formation in the presence of carbon dioxide is characteristic of virulent *Bacillus anthracis*. This trait is not characteristic for other *Bacillus* species.

The vegetative cells of *B. anthracis* in clinical specimens occur as non-sporeforming cells in short chains (Fig. 19-1). In culture, long chains of endospore-forming rods are observed and resemble a jointed rod. Vegetative cells are easily stained with ordinary laboratory dyes. The M'Fadyean stain is used to detect the capsule but the latter can be detected by fluorescent antibody as well.

FIGURE 19-1
Appearance of anthrax bacillus (*arrow*) as observed in tissue. (Courtesy of Armed Forces Institute of Pathology, AFIP 28-59.)

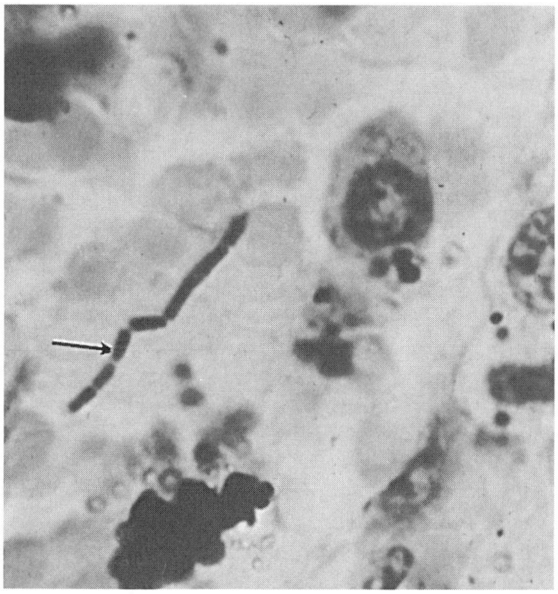

Antigens and Virulence Factors

To be fully virulent, *B. anthracis* must produce a capsule and a protein exotoxin. The polypeptide capsular material enables the microorganism to evade phagocytosis. The capsular material, however, does not stimulate the formation of protective antibodies. The protein exotoxin is a complex of three protein factors: **edema factor (EF), protective antigen (PA),** and **lethal factor (LF).** Separately the toxins are nontoxic but act in combinations of two to produce two distinct toxic responses: edema in skin and lethality. EF is an inactive form of **adenylate cyclase,** whose function is to convert adenosine triphosphate to cyclic adenosine 3',5'-monophosphate (cAMP) (see Under the Microscope 11, Chapter 14). Apparently PA binds to

FIGURE 19-2
Mechanism for internalization of edema factor (EF) and its activation. EF binds to protective antigen (PA) factor, which is inserted into the cytoplasmic membrane of the host cell. PA facilitates the transfer of EF into the cytoplasm, where it interacts with calmodulin (CAD) to become an active adenyl cyclase.

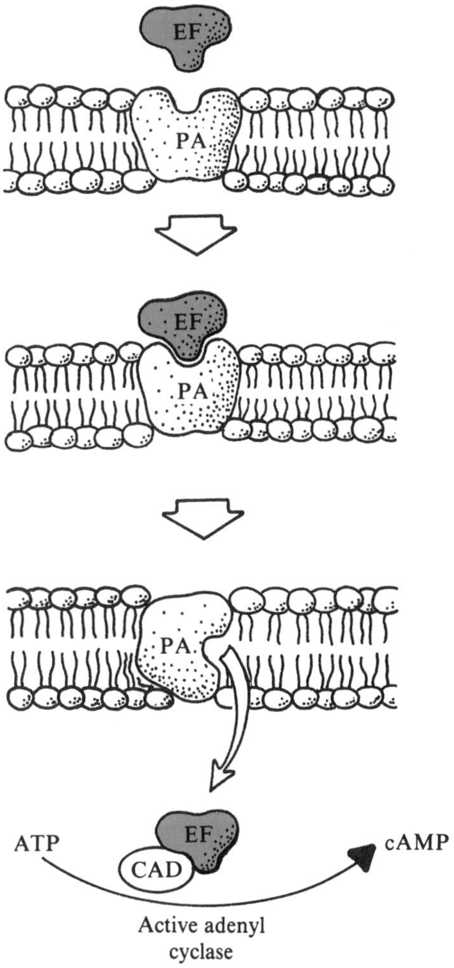

the cytoplasmic membrane of host cells and then interacts with EF. This interaction causes EF to be transported into the cytoplasm of the host cell (Fig. 19-2). In the cytoplasm EF interacts with a cellular molecule called calmodulin to become an active adenyl cyclase. The production of cAMP causes mammalian cells to oversecrete (edema).

PATHOGENESIS AND EPIDEMIOLOGY

Anthrax is primarily a disease of herbivorous animals—sheep, horses, and cattle—that can be acquired by humans. The spores, which are found in the soil and on vegetation, are ingested or inhaled. They gain entrance to the subcutaneous tissue through abraded skin or mucosa. After the spores germinate in the tissue, the vegetative cells produce an exotoxin that, in combination with the capsule, inhibits phagocytosis. If the bacilli reach the lymph and bloodstream, fatal septicemia may develop. The pathophysiology of toxin and infection is not completely understood. Some observers believe the primary site of action is the capillaries, whose altered permeability by toxin results in severe loss of vascular fluid. Others believe the central nervous system to be the primary site of action, with death resulting from respiratory failure.

In humans the disease is considered an occupational hazard for those working in areas where livestock is handled, and in microbiology laboratories. Inhalation of anthrax spores can result in a condition referred to as **woolsorters' disease.** The inhaled spores settle in the respiratory tract, producing local hemorrhaging and edema. Septicemia sometimes occurs, leading to meningitis. The most common form of the disease in humans, however, is called **cutaneous anthrax.** The organisms gain entrance to the body by contact with an abraded portion of the skin (Fig. 19-3). Files and mosquitoes have been implicated as vectors in the transmission from animals to humans in large outbreaks in African communities. The vectors feed on bacteremic animals and then bite humans to produce cutaneous anthrax. The fully developed lesion appears as a dark necrotic area surrounded by a rim of edema. In severe cases the regional lymph nodes may enlarge. Once the blood is invaded, the disease may prove fatal. Another form of the disease called **gastrointestinal anthrax** is uncommon in the United States but occurs more frequently in underdeveloped countries where contaminated meats are sold. The toxin produced in the intestinal tract forms a necrotic lesion in the ileum or cecum. Case-fatality rates for this condition are high.

FIGURE 19-3
Cutaneous anthrax lesion containing a central dark area (eschar) is observed on the forearm. (Courtesy of P. Brachman.)

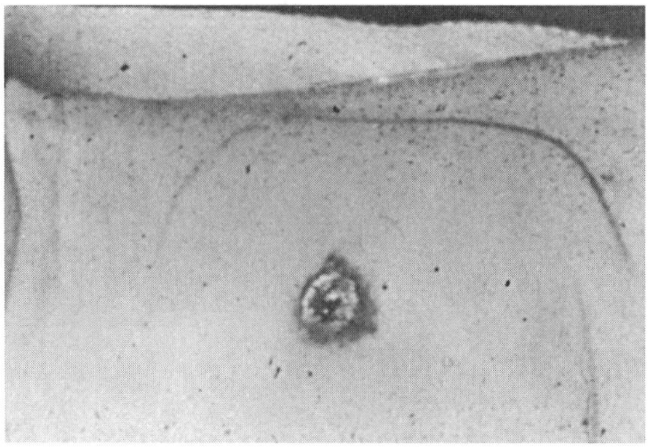

IMMUNITY

Recovery from infection by *B. anthracis* brings permanent immunity for humans and animals. Protective antibodies are produced as a result of the host's response to the exotoxin complex. At present, the only vaccine safe enough for human use is a toxoid prepared from a fraction of the exotoxin.

LABORATORY DIAGNOSIS

The anthrax bacillus can be cultured from the soil, cutaneous lesions, the respiratory tract, or blood (see Fig. 19-1). The appearance of other sporeforming bacilli from some of these sites occasionally makes identification difficult. A motility test is a reliable technique for the screening of *Bacillus* isolates for *B. anthracis.* Any *Bacillus* isolate showing motility is assumed to be a species other than *B. anthracis.* Some of the recommended procedures for identification of the bacillus include the following:

1. Culture the specimen on sheep blood agar or a selective medium when highly contaminated specimens are encountered.
2. Culture isolates from item 1 above in a bicarbonate- and serum-containing medium in the presence of 5% carbon dioxide. Determine the presence of a capsule.
3. Determine the presence of toxin by using antitoxin. Positive reaction confirms *B. anthracis.*
4. Determine the susceptibility to penicillin. *B. anthracis* is susceptible to penicillin; other bacilli are resistant.
5. Determine the susceptibility to gamma phage. *B. anthracis* is sensitive while other *Bacillus* species (except *B. mycoides*) are invariably sensitive.

TREATMENT AND PREVENTION

Penicillin is often the drug of choice, but streptomycin, tetracycline, and erythromycin are also effective against the anthrax bacillus. Treatment before the appearance of bacteremia is important because the antibiotics are not effective against the toxin.

Anthrax is endemic in many areas of the world, especially the underdeveloped ones. Epizootic outbreaks still occur in the United States when unusual climatic conditions such as prolonged and heavy rains prevail. The most effective control program is vaccination of cattle, cremation or burial with quicklime of infected animals, and restricted movement of livestock.

Cutaneous anthrax is infrequently observed in the United States. Many of the cases recorded result from contact with goat hair or with animal hides that have not been decontaminated. Overseas travelers buying articles made of animal products must be made aware of these potential sources of infection.

Control of disease in humans, whose occupation may be a predisposing factor, is provided by immunization with toxoid.

Animals can be immunized with live spore vaccine; the Sterne strain vaccine is prepared from avirulent anthrax spores.

BACILLUS CEREUS AND OTHER BACILLI

B. cereus produces two enterotoxins that are responsible for two clinical entities. One is a typical gastroenteritis, characterized by diarrhea and abdominal pain. The other is characterized by vomiting (emetic type), but not diarrhea. Gastroenteritis occurs 8 to 16 hours after ingestion of contaminated food. The emetic type occurs 1 to 5 hours after ingestion of contaminated food, particularly rice dishes. Both conditions are self-limiting and require no special treatment.

B. cereus is also being recognized as a major cause of ocular disease following trauma from nonsurgical penetrating objects. The organism infects the vitreous humor of the eye and can cause retinal damage with loss of vision. *B. cereus* produces beta-lactamases and is resistant to beta-lactams including third-generation cephalosporins. Therapy for infection includes clindamycin plus an aminoglycoside. Other nongastrointestinal diseases can also be found in the hospital setting when there is contamination of dressings, intravenous catheters, and linens.

In the compromised patient, other species of *Bacillus* such as *B. circulans*, *B. macerans*, *B. brevis*, and *B. coagulans* are occasionally associated with a variety of infections.

Because of ease in cultivation and heat resistance, the spores of some bacilli are routinely used in the laboratory for experimental and testing procedures. *B. subtilis* is employed as a test organism to measure the effectiveness of ethylene oxide sterilization. Spores of *B. stearothermophilus*, because of their unusually high resistance to heat, are employed to test the efficiency of autoclaving. Finally, spores of *B. pumilis* are used to test the efficiency of sterilization by radiation.

Clostridium

The genus *Clostridium* includes many species that inhabit water, soil, and vegetation. They play a major role in animal and plant putrefaction. Some species are commensals in the mammalian intestinal tract. A few species from these habitats are pathogenic. They are the causative agents of **botulism, tetanus, gas gangrene,** and other clinical entities.

GENERAL CHARACTERISTICS

All clostridia are gram-positive sporeforming rods varying from 3 to 8 μm in length and from 0.4 to 1.2 μm in width. In most species the sporangia (vegetative cells with the enclosed spore) appear swollen (Fig. 19-4). Most clostridia are obligate anaerobes and some are aerotolerant. Most species of *Clostridium* are motile by peritrichous flagella, with the notable exception being *C. perfringens* which is nonmotile. With few exceptions the spores of this genus do not germinate unless suitable reducing conditions are available and oxygen is absent. The spores are unusually resistant to heat and can withstand temperatures of 120 C for as long as 10 to 15 minutes.

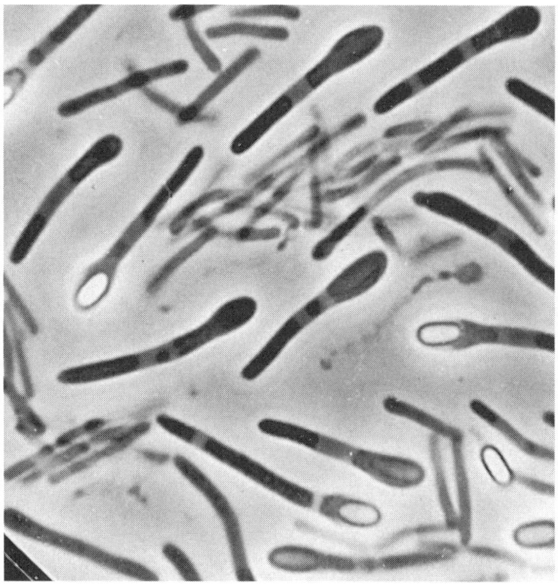

FIGURE 19-4
Phase-contrast micrograph of the endospores of a species of *Clostridium*. Note the refractile body and the swollen appearance of the vegetative cell. (× 3600.) (Courtesy of P. C. Fitz-James.)

The clostridia are easily cultivated in the laboratory when anaerobic conditions prevail. The most commonly used method for isolation of anaerobes is incubating streaked blood agar and egg yolk agar plates anaerobically for 48 to 72 hours. After incubation, the blood agar colonies should be examined for hemolysis, colony structure, and swarming of motile cells. Egg yolk agar should be examined for evidence of lecithinase and lipase activity. Lecithinase activity is indicated by an opaque, whitish precipitate within the agar, while lipase activity is indicated by an iridescent sheen on the surface growth.

Many specimens suspected of containing clostridia are often contaminated with gram-negative species, and primary isolation on plates incubated anaerobically is difficult. Some alternatives to primary isolation are as follows:

1. The specimen is heated to 80 C for 10 to 15 minutes to destroy any vegetative bacteria. It is then incubated at 37 C before being subcultured on laboratory media. This spore selection technique can also be accomplished by treating the specimen with ethyl alcohol.
2. The specimen (except some strains of *C. tetani*) is placed in tubes of thioglycolate broth containing glucose, incubated for 24 to 48 hours, and subcultured. In the thioglycolate broth the clostridial species fer-

TABLE 19-1
Characteristics Distinguishing Some of the Important Species of *Clostridium*

				Fermentation						
Species	Motility	Gelatin hydrolysis	Milk digestion	Glucose	Maltose	Lactose	Sucrose	Mannitol	Indole formation	Spores
*C. botulinum**	Yes	+	+	+	+	−	−	−	−	OS
C. tetani	Yes	+	−	−	−	−	−	−	V	RT
C. perfringens	No	+	+	+	+	+	+	−	−	OS
C. ramosum	Yes	−	−	+	+	+	+	V	−	R/OT
C. innocuum	Yes	−	−	+	−	−	V	+	−	OT
C. difficile	Yes	V	−	+	−	−	−	+	−	OS
C. butyricum	Yes	−	−	+	+	+	+	−	−	OS

+ = positive reaction; − = negative reaction; V = variable reaction; / = either/or; O = oval; R = round; S = subterminal; T = terminal.
* Toxin neutralization test required for identification.

ment glucose, and the acids produced inhibit the growth of gram-negative organisms.

3. The specimen is transferred to chopped meat medium and sealed with petrolatum. The latter procedure is routinely used to isolate anaerobic bacteria, especially when they appear to be in small numbers in the specimen. After suitable incubation at 37 C, a subculture is made on other media.

The fermentation of various sugars is an important characteristic used in separating species of clostridia. Table 19-1 illustrates some fermentative and biochemical properties of the major species. In addition, some clostridia produce a considerable amount of gas during growth, a property that can be used in identifying *C. perfringens*. When milk is inoculated with this organism, the clotted milk is torn apart by the accumulated gas ("stormy fermentation").

An unusually large number of enzymes and toxins have been recovered from the filtrates of cultured clostridial species. They include hemolysins, collagenase, lipase, deoxyribonuclease, hyaluronidase, and the two potent exotoxins that cause tetanus and botulism. Many of these products are helpful in the identification or separation of species within the genus. For example, toxin tests are occasionally necessary for the identification of a few species. Sometimes only a toxin neutralization test will distinguish *C. botulinum* from *C. sporogenes* and *C. novyi*.

DISEASES CAUSED BY CLOSTRIDIA

C. botulinum, *C. perfringens*, and *C. tetani* produce potent exotoxins responsible for potentially fatal diseases: botulism, gas gangrene, and tetanus, respectively. However, the majority of clinical clostridial diseases are caused by other species.

Food Poisoning (Botulism)

Botulism is a noninfectious disease that results from the ingestion of preformed toxin in foods. About 25 percent of the incidence of clostridial food poisoning can be directly attributed to the species *C. botulinum*. *Clostridium perfringens*, the primary causal agent of gas gangrene, is involved in the remainder of clostridial food poisonings. Food botulism is rarely seen in the United States (25 cases in 1992), but when outbreaks occur they are associated primarily with home canning procedures and not with commercial preparations. Most outbreaks are due to improper cooking of low-acid vegetables or to fermentation procedures. Isolated cases have been attributed to improper heating of fish (see Under the Microscope 15).

***Clostridium botulinum* Toxin.** *C. botulinum* produces eight immunologically distinct neurotoxins (A, B, C_1, C_2, D, E, F, and G), permitting its separation into types. Types A, B, E, and F are responsible for human poisonings. The toxins of some nonproteolytic strains are not completely active unless activated by proteolytic enzymes such as trypsin. Proteolytic strains produce their own enzymes to activate the toxin.

Type A toxin, which is responsible for most outbreaks of food poisonings associated with *C. botulinum*, is a complex consisting of the neurotoxin and a hemagglutinin. At least 1000 times more neurotoxin than neurotoxin-hemagglutinin complex is required to cause food poisoning in animals. It is believed that the hemagglutinin protects the neurotoxin from stomach acids and enzymes. Neurotoxin alone is rapidly inactivated by gastric enzymes and lowered pH. The complete toxin is sensitive to heat. To give some idea of the toxicity of *C. botulinum* toxin, less than 1×10^{-9} gm of toxin can kill a mouse. For comparison, the lethal concentration of toxin from *C. perfringens* is 3.6×10^{-6} gm.

Pathogenesis. Botulism resulting from the ingestion of toxin-contaminated food is considered an **intoxication** rather than an infection. Once the active toxin is released in the intestine, it is absorbed and transported into the lymph and then the bloodstream. Clinical symptoms usually appear between 24 and 72 hours after the toxin has been absorbed from the intestinal tract. The toxin acts specifically on the peripheral nervous system, particularly the cranial nerves, and not the central nervous system. Toxin prevents the release of acetylcholine at the

UNDER THE MICROSCOPE 15

Fish Botulism

Three members of a Hawaiian family were treated for fish botulism in 1990. All members had eaten surgeon fish that had been purchased fresh and cleaned at a retail fish market, the day of the meal. After grilling the fish, one member of the family opened the fish and noted remnants of the intestines inside it. The three affected patients ate the fish's intestines and/or meat around it. A fourth family member ate only the back of the fish and had no symptoms.

Fish botulism accounts for approximately 13 percent of foodborne outbreaks of botulism in the United States. In all instances, except the one described above, the fish had been processed and held before consumption.

Clostridium botulinum spores are common in marine sediments and can be detected in fish intestines. Previous outbreaks have been associated with consumption of eviscerated fish soaked in brine and air-dried. In these outbreaks, salt concentrations were considered too low in the intestine to inhibit the growth of *C. botulinum.* Localization of toxin within the fish may be important because the consumption of fish intestines may be common in some ethnic groups.

Because refrigeration had been inadequate at the fish market, the internal temperature of the fish may have been elevated for lengthy periods. The conditions around the retained gut may have facilitated an anaerobic environment, allowing production of toxin. Cooking was apparently insufficient to inactivate the toxin.

From *M.M.W.R.* 40 (24):412, 1991.

neural synapses. Thus, the muscle response to a nerve impulse is blocked because no neurotransmitter (acetylcholine) is released to excite the muscle. Some of the first symptoms to be noticed include double vision (diplopia) and dizziness, often followed by difficulty in swallowing and breathing. Nausea and vomiting may also be present during these manifestations. Death is usually due to respiratory failure from paralysis of the diaphragm. Fatality rates are high for type A poisoning (75 percent) and lower for the other types (20 percent).

Botulism also can be caused by the production of toxin by *C. botulinum* in wounds. **Wound botulism** has been recognized as a clinical entity since 1976, but only four or five cases are reported each year. The symptoms are the same as those in food poisoning caused by *C. botulinum.* Type A is usually implicated, with a case-fatality rate of 25 percent. Although microorganisms are present in the wound, chemotherapy with antibiotics has not proved efficacious, probably because of a lack of blood supply in necrotic areas.

Infant botulism is the most frequently reported form of botulism, with approximately 60 cases being reported each year in the United States. Infant botulism is an infection resulting from the ingestion of spores that germinate in the intestine and release toxin. Ingestion of honey contaminated with botulinal spores has been implicated in several cases of the disease. The Centers for Disease Control recommends that honey not be fed to infants less than 1 year old.

Most of the infants affected by infant botulism are less than 6 months old. The first signs of infection are constipation, followed by weakened sucking and swallowing and a diminished gag reflex. Later there is a loss of head control. The most important aspect in the treatment of infant botulism is supportive care because of the possibility of respiratory insufficiency. The effect of antibiotics and antitoxin has not been established. Infant botulism is being investigated as one of the causes of sudden infant death syndrome.

Laboratory Diagnosis. Initial diagnosis depends on the identification of the toxin in the serum or stools of the affected individual. In infant botulism only stools consistently reveal the presence of toxin. Identification is often followed by intraperitoneal injections of extracts of the patient's serum or liquefied stool samples into laboratory mice. The mice will succumb in one to four days if *C. botulinum* toxin is present in the specimens. If the suspect food is available, it too can be checked for the presence of toxin or anaerobic sporeformers. In wound botulism, anaerobic cultures of wound abscesses can be made, followed by specific toxin typing.

Treatment and Prevention. The earlier botulism is detected, the better the prognosis. Case-fatality rates in the 1950s were near 60 percent but have since declined to less than 15 percent because of advances in acute respiratory intensive care. Even before a bacteriological diagnosis is made, trivalent antitoxin prepared against the toxins of A, B, and E is given intravenously to patients with foodborne or wound botulism. The antitoxin is not given to patients with infant botulism. Because the antitoxin is prepared from horse serum, the patient is normally tested for sensitivity before injection. If the patient has neurological symptoms, he or she should be placed in an intensive care unit, where cardiac and respiratory function can be monitored. Guanidine hydrochloride is sometimes used

UNDER THE MICROSCOPE 16

Botulinal Toxin for Human Treatment

The toxin of *Clostridium botulinum* is one of the most poisonous substances known to humans. Yet in small quantities, this neurotoxin is of benefit in the treatment of certain muscle disorders classified as **dystonias.** Dystonias are caused by involuntary sustained muscle contractions that lead to persistent and sometimes painful movements. Most of the dystonias involve the muscles of the eye. The names of some of these focal dystonias and the symptoms they induce are

1. Strabismus: crossed eyes
2. Blepharospasm: spasmodic eye closure
3. Hemifacial spasm: facial twitching and spasms
4. Eyelid disorders: inward turning of the eyelid

The function of botulinal toxin in treatment is to paralyze the target muscles that are responsible for the sustained muscle contractions. The toxin interferes with the release of acetylcholine. A single injection provides relief from 1 to 2 months but repeated injections are required to maintain relief.

The neurotoxin will not replace conventional surgery but it is considered a useful adjunct. Treatment with neurotoxin, however, is much less costly and less disfiguring than surgery.

Side effects include difficulty in swallowing and other complications associated with weakening of muscles near the target area. Toxin treatment is not considered safe for women during pregnancy or while breast-feeding. The toxin has not been approved for use in children under 12 years old.

during treatment to enhance the release of acetylcholine in the nerve junctions to prevent respiratory failure.

Prevention of botulism is best accomplished in the home by using sterilized containers and pressure cookers. Since the *C. botulinum* toxin is heat-labile, it is suggested that whenever possible, home-canned fruits and vegetables be heated to 100 C for 10 minutes before ingestion.

C. botulinum toxin also has some medical uses (see Under the Microscope 16).

Gas Gangrene

Gas gangrene is a disease in which there are severe muscle necrosis and invasion of the bloodstream by clostridial species such as *C. perfringens.* Other clostridial species that may act in concert with *C. perfringens* are *C. novyi, C. septicum,* and *C. histolyticum. C. perfringens* is a nonmotile aerotolerant organism that does not produce spores in ordinary culture media. All the *Clostridium* species associated with gas gangrene can be found as commensals in the intestinal tract of humans and animals. All of them produce potent toxins.

***Clostridium perfringens* Toxins.** Of the 11 toxins produced by *C. perfringens,* four are used to separate the species into five toxigenic groups (A, B, C, D, and E). Only types A and C produce disease in humans. All five types produce various proportions of four toxins (alpha, beta, epsilon, and iota). The most important is the **alpha toxin,** also called **phospholipase C.** Alpha toxin acts as lecithinase and hydrolyzes lecithin, a component of eukaryotic membranes, and during infection destroys red blood cells and leukocytes. Other toxins released during infection that may take part in pathogenesis are collagenase, hemolysin, proteinase, and deoxyribonuclease. The toxin demonstrating collagenase activity is believed to attack healthy connective tissue in the skin and the connective tissue supporting muscle fibers. It is the probable cause of the extensive muscle destruction observed in gas gangrene. Hemolysin lyses the red blood cells of most mammalian species. Proteinase is thought to be important in degrading necrotic tissue, while deoxyribonuclease may destroy leukocytes by its ability to depolymerize DNA.

Pathogenesis. Gas gangrene is an infection that requires a site for germination of spores and replication of vegetative cells. Such a site is available when tissue has been traumatized by foreign bodies (for example, puncture wounds) and is devitalized, thereby offering an anaerobic environment. Clostridial wound infections can be divided into two major clinical conditions: **anaerobic cellulitis** and **anaerobic myositis** (true gas gangrene). Anaerobic cellulitis is the less severe infection because the organism does not invade healthy tissue. There is seldom toxemia or shock.

True gas gangrene is often a mixed infection involving several *Clostridium* species. Most cases of the disease appear during war or after automobile accidents or surgical procedures such as those involving the uterus. Deep wounds and areas of dead tissue favor germination. Toxins are liberated by vegetative cells, and during infection gases such as hydrogen and carbon dioxide may be released by metabolizing bacteria. The first symptoms of infection are usually observed 72 hours after traumatization of tissue. Severe local pain is felt in the area of the wound. A few hours later there is swelling of the wound, giving it a stretched and reddened appearance. Still later the skin ruptures, revealing a necrotic, foul-smelling wound. The most important symptoms of gas gangrene are the delirium, apathy, and disorientation exhibited by the patient in the early stages of the disease. Death is believed to be due to severe toxemia and to the effect of toxin on vital organs.

Laboratory Diagnosis. A tentative diagnosis of gas gangrene is often made by examination of the wound for gram-positive sporeformers. This is usually difficult because *C. perfringens* does not often sporulate in tissue. In addition, the wound may contain a wide variety of other microorganisms including nonpathogenic clostridia. Presumptive identification of *C. perfringens* can be made by first inoculating a blood (rabbit, sheep, or human) agar plate with the specimen and incubating it anaerobically. Gram-stained cells show a typical "boxcar" shape as opposed to the rounded ends of other clostridial species (Fig. 19-5). Colonies of *C. perfringens* appear surrounded by an inner zone of complete hemolysis and an outer zone of incomplete hemolysis. The isolated colonies also can be subcultured to egg yolk agar plates to demonstrate the production of alpha toxin (lecithinase).

Treatment and Prevention. Successful treatment of gas gangrene should begin with the immediate debridement of the wound to remove all dead tissue. This is followed by the application of antiserum that has been prepared from filtrates of the major clostridial species that produce gas gangrene. Finally, antibiotic therapy should be initiated. Penicillin and tetracyclines have been the antibiotic drugs of choice.

Treatment with high concentrations of oxygen at elevated pressures is also useful. This procedure is called **hyperbaric oxygen therapy.** At one time this type of therapy was used almost exclusively for persons who had carbon monoxide poisoning and decompression sickness. The patient inhales 100% oxygen through an aviator's mask in a chamber initially pressurized to approximately 3 atmospheres of air for 1 hour. Then follows a 30-minute period of 100% oxygen at 2 atmospheres of pressure, and finally comes a 30-minute period of 100% oxygen at 1 atmosphere. The treatment is repeated every 8 hours, the total number of treatments seldom exceeding eight. The principle behind this treatment is that anaerobes in the presence of oxygen produce a strong oxidizing agent, hydrogen peroxide, or superoxide. These oxidizing agents are lethal to the organisms. Oxygen has no effect on the circulating toxin, which must be detoxified in the body. Hyperbaric oxygen treatment is potentially very dangerous and must be administered by qualified personnel.

Gas gangrene is always a possible hazard when surgery is being performed on areas of the body that are easily contaminated by one's intestinal microflora—the lower limbs, thighs, and buttocks. Infections have been greatly reduced when the area to be operated on and surrounding tissue are first swabbed with compresses of iodophors. Best results are obtained when the area is swabbed just 15 minutes before surgery.

FIGURE 19-5
Photomicrograph of *Clostridium perfringens.* Note the boxcar shape of the cells. (Courtesy of P. D. Walker.)

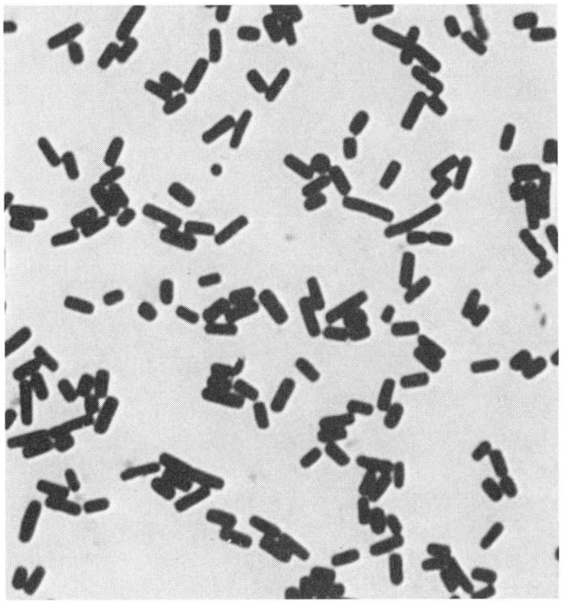

Food Poisoning *(Clostridium perfringens)*

C. perfringens is a common cause of a mild form of food poisoning in humans. The condition is the result of ingestion of numerous viable vegetative cells. Foodborne disease in the United States is due to type A *C. perfringens* and is most frequently associated with a meat product. The organism survives cooking by sporulation and then germinates when food is cooled. If the food is not reheated, many vegetative cells are produced. Ingestion of approximately 10^8 cells will cause food poisoning. The ingested bacteria sporulate in the intestine and produce an enterotoxin that is part of the spore coat. The enterotoxin causes secretion of fluid and electrolytes (sodium and chloride ions).

Foodborne disease by *C. perfringens* type C is associated with a high mortality. The illness is referred to as **enteritis necroticans** and is characterized by hemorrhaging and gangrene of the intestine. The severity of the disease is believed to be due to a beta toxin that is normally inactivated by proteolytic enzymes. The disease is observed primarily in areas outside the United States. Large outbreaks of disease have been observed in New Guinea. Infection is associated with feasts where contaminated and improperly cooked pork is ingested. The disease is called "pig-bel."

C. perfringens type A food poisoning ranks high in number of cases per year in the United States. The vehicles implicated in disease, in order of importance, are beef, Mexican food, turkey, ham, and chicken. Improper storage or holding temperature and inadequate cooking of food are the principal causes of disease. The major symptoms are abdominal pain, diarrhea, nausea, and vomiting. The incubation period is 24 to 30 hours and rarely are fatalities encountered.

Confirmation of foodborne illness can be determined by (1) a count of more than 10^5 organisms per gram of suspected food, (2) a median spore count higher than 10^6 per gram of stool, or (3) isolation of the same serotype from food and stool. Serological tests for enterotoxin detection in feces are now available. Enterotoxin cannot be detected in culture unless sufficient sporulation has taken place.

Treatment of *C. perfringens* food poisoning does not require antibiotics since the disease is mild and self-limiting. It is important that body fluids and electrolytes be replenished. This type of food poisoning can be prevented by properly cooking food and, if food is to be reheated, by ensuring that the internal temperature of the food is higher than 75 C so that vegetative cells are destroyed.

Enterotoxin-Associated Diarrhea

There is accumulating evidence that enterotoxin-induced diarrhea can occur without a food vehicle. The diarrhea is associated with antibiotic treatment and occurs almost exclusively in the hospitalized elderly patient. The number of *C. perfringens* in the stools of these patients ranges from 5×10^7 to 4×10^9 per gram of stool. The diarrhea lasts at least seven days, compared to the 24 hours seen in foodborne diarrhea.

Tetanus

Tetanus, like gas gangrene, is an infection often stemming from a complication of traumatized tissue. The causative agent, *C. tetani,* is found primarily in cultivated soil but also appears in the intestinal tract of about 25 percent of humans. In underdeveloped countries, tetanus is a common cause of neonatal death. In the United States, 48 cases of tetanus were recorded in 1993.

Tetanus Toxins. The complications of tetanus are due to release of a potent neurotoxin called **tetanospasmin.** Tetanospasmin is a heat-labile protein with a toxicity similar to that of *C. botulinum* toxin. Every milligram of toxin-nitrogen is lethal for 2×10^8 laboratory mice. The toxin that is released on lysis of the vegetative cell acts on the central nervous system. Unlike botulinum toxin, which blocks transmission of nerve impulses, tetanus toxin causes the continued excitation of motor neurons in the spinal cord. This occurs because tetanus toxin prevents the release of inhibitory mediators. The effect of tetanus toxin can be observed as a spastic paralysis.

Pathogenesis. *C. tetani* gains entrance to the body through wounds or abrasions. The spores germinate only in the absence of oxygen, and such a condition is encountered when the wound is deep or contains considerable necrotic tissue. Piercing of ears, circumcisions, and abortions are also predisposing factors that can lead to tetanus when hygienic precautions are not taken.

Tetanus neonatorum is a frequent cause of death in developing countries. This type of tetanus is the direct result of cutting the umbilical cord with unsterilized instruments or packing the umbilical stump with mud. Once the organism germinates in the tissue, the toxin acts directly on the motor neurons of the central nervous system. The toxin causes the continued contraction of voluntary muscles, which is referred to as **tetany.**

The symptoms of tetanus appear in four to six days as a rule; however, an appearance in as long as six weeks is not unusual. This wide range in incubation time seems to depend on two factors: the time for anaerobic conditions to develop at the site of infection and the time required for any toxin to reach the central nervous system. The predominant symptoms of tetanus are primarily muscle rigidity and muscle spasm. Rigidity affects the muscles of the jaw (masseter muscles), abdomen, and spine. Muscle spasms are seen most often in the mouth but may occur in any part of the body. The convulsive contraction of the voluntary muscles of the jaw is referred to as **lockjaw (trismus).** Death is often the result of some type of respiratory failure—pneumonia, pulmonary edema, or asphyxia.

Laboratory Diagnosis. Diagnosis can be made on clinical grounds. Patients usually have a wound, exhibit trismus, and have a history of no immunization. Stained smears of the material from a wound are very unreliable for the identification of *C. tetani* because of the presence of other clostridia. Material from the wound can be cultured directly on blood agar or transferred to cooked meat medium heated at 80 C for 10 to 15 minutes. This procedure kills non-sporeformers. After a 24-hour incubation period, the blood agar plate should be examined for motility (swarming of cells). A spore stain reveals characteristic terminal spores, giving the cell the shape of a tennis racket (Fig. 19-6).

Definitive proof that the isolated species is *C. tetani* is obtained by determining neurotoxin production. This is measured by injecting the filtrate from a pure culture of

FIGURE 19-6
Photomicrograph of *Clostridium tetani* demonstrating the characteristic tennis racket–shaped terminal spores. (Courtesy of P. D. Walker.)

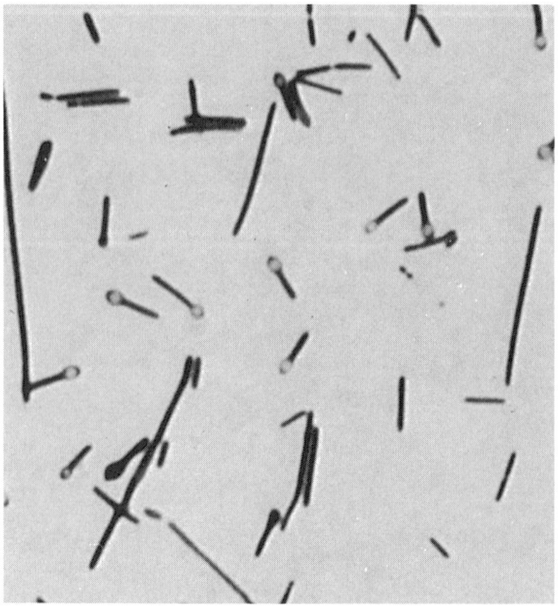

C. tetani into the leg of a mouse; a second mouse receives an injection of the filtrate plus tetanus antitoxin. After a few hours the unprotected mouse displays stiffness and muscular spasms in the injected leg. The protected mouse shows no adverse effects from the toxin.

Treatment. Patients suspected to have tetanus, even before isolation of the microorganism, are first treated by administration of tetanus antitoxin. Antitoxin neutralizes any toxin in the blood. The antitoxin does not neutralize toxin already fixed to nerve cells. Antibiotics such as penicillin are usually given to destroy any clostridial cells and prevent further toxin production. Where there is a foul contaminated wound, it is important to remove surgically the necrotic tissue or debris that is creating the anaerobic environment. Even if all these measures are performed, once the toxin is attached to the nerve cells they will not alter the course of the disease. The basic treatment is symptomatic; that is, the convulsions and spasms must be controlled by drugs. Barbiturates are therefore routinely employed to sedate the patient and to control the spasm.

Tetanus antitoxin (tetanus immune globulin, or TIG) prepared from the gamma globulin fraction of humans is available. If antitoxin from humans is not accessible, horse serum antitoxin can be used. Hypersensitivity reactions to the horse serum are a potential risk and must be considered before administration.

Prevention. The only effective way to control tetanus is through the prophylactic use of the tetanus toxoid. The toxoid is given routinely with diphtheria toxoid and pertussis vaccine (DTP) plus *Hemophilus influenzae* type b vaccine (see Chapter 20 for DTP doses). The booster doses usually provide protection for 10 to 20 years. Thus, additional booster doses are recommended only when an individual has sustained a wound infection.

In developing countries, where health services and delivery teams are limited, neonatal tetanus is a problem that requires special attention. Continuous immunization of pregnant women and of all women of childbearing age is recommended. In addition, the training of midwives has caused a precipitous drop in neonatal tetanus. These strategies are used in addition to the primary immunization in early childhood and at schools.

Other Clostridial Conditions

***Clostridium difficile*–Associated Colitis and Pseudomembranous Colitis.** *C. difficile* can be associated with

TABLE 19-2
Some of the Important Species of *Clostridium* and Their Toxins That Are Associated with Human Disease

Species	Toxin	Activity/disease
C. botulinum	Neurotoxin	Prevents release of acetylcholine from nerve ending/botulism
C. tetani	Neurotoxin	Prevents release of inhibitory mediators of spinal cord motor neurons/tetanus
C. perfringens	Major	
	Alpha	Phospholipase C/gas gangrene (myonecrosis)
	Beta (B and C strains)	Necrotic enteritis (pig-bel)/enterotoxemia
	Epsilon (B and D strains)	Increases permeability of intestine/enterotoxemia
	Iota	ADP-ribosylation/enterotoxemia
	Other	
	Enterotoxin	Altered membrane permeability/foodborne diarrhea
	Delta (B and C strains)	Hemolysin/gas gangrene
	Kappa	Collagenase/gas gangrene
	Lambda (B, D, E strains)	Protease (digests gelatin, hemoglobin)/gas gangrene
	Mu	Hyaluronidase/gas gangrene
	Nu	DNase/gas gangrene
	Neuraminidase	Hydrolysis of neuraminic acid/gas gangrene
C. difficile	Toxin A	Enterotoxin-altered membrane permeability/antibiotic-associated pseudomembranous colitis
	Toxin B	Cytotoxin/antibiotic-associated pseudomembranous colitis
C. sordellii (C. bifermentans)	Alpha	Phospholipase C/acute edematous wound infections
	Beta	Contains lethal and hemorrhagic components that are equivalent to toxins A and B, respectively, of *C. difficile*/acute edematous wound infections
C. novyi	Alpha	Lethal/gas gangrene
	Beta and gamma	Phospholipase C
C. chauvoei (C. septicum)	Alpha	Lethal, necrotizing/gas gangrene, neutropenic enterocolitis
	Beta	DNase
	Gamma	Hyaluronidase
C. histolyticum	Alpha	Lethal, necrotizing/toxemia of gas gangrene
	Beta	Collagenase/gas gangrene

colitis when the patient is being treated with antimicrobials. Colitis means inflammation of the colon while enterocolitis means inflammation of the small intestine or colon. Pseudomembranous colitis is a disease characterized by pseudomembrane formation on the colon wall.

All antimicrobial compounds given orally or parenterally can give rise to enteritis (inflammation of the intestine). The antibiotics most frequently implicated are ampicillin, clindamycin, and the cephalosporins. Antimicrobials inhibit the growth of the normal intestinal flora, allowing the overgrowth of the bacterium *C. difficile* in the colon portion of the intestine. Pseudomembranous colitis is characterized by a pseudomembrane composed of fibrin, mucus, necrotic epithelial cells, and leukocytes. Symptoms of this disease include diarrhea, fever, and nausea and may progress to dehydration, septicemia, shock, and death.

C. difficile is not frequently found in the healthy adult but is found often in the hospital environment. In addition, infants carry high levels of *C. difficile* in the intestine but are refractory to the disease. Hospital personnel are often responsible for transmitting the microorganism to patients. *C. difficile* can persist in the environment for months because of its ability to produce spores.

C. difficile produces two toxins, A and B, both of which are cytotoxic. Toxin A is thought to cause most of the symptoms of disease. Not all strains produce toxin.

Culturing for the organism, latex agglutination for detection of glutamate dehydrogenase, tissue culture assay for detection of toxin B, and enzyme-linked immunosorbent assay for detection of toxins A and B are used in the diagnosis of disease.

Treatment of pseudomembranous colitis can often be achieved by discontinuation of the offending antibiotic.

TABLE 19-3
Characteristics of the Major Species of *Bacillus* and *Clostridium*

Genus and species	Important morphological, physiological, and staining traits	Disease association	Mechanism of transmission	Virulence factors	Treatment and prevention
Bacillus	Gram-positive aerobic sporeformers				
B. anthracis	Capsule produced in culture	Anthrax–cutaneous, respiratory, and gastrointestinal	Contact with contaminated animals or hides	Capsule; protein exotoxin composed of three fractions	Penicillin; vaccination of cattle; toxoid for humans to prevent occupation-associated infections
B. cereus		Food poisoning, ocular disease	Ingestion of contaminated food; ocular disease from penetrating wounds	Two enterotoxins for gastrointestinal disease	None required for food poisoning; clindamycin plus aminoglycoside for ocular disease
Clostridium	Gram-positive anaerobic sporeformers				
C. botulinum	Motile	Food poisoning, wound botulism, infant botulism	Ingestion of contaminated food; soil contamination of wound; ingestion of spore-contaminated foods by infants	Neurotoxin	Trivalent antitoxin for foodborne and wound botulism; supportive care for infant botulism
C. perfringens	Nonmotile	Gas gangrene	Soil contamination of deep wounds	Alpha toxin (lecithinase)	Wound debridement, application of antiserum, and penicillin therapy; hyperbaric oxygen for extreme cases
		Food poisoning	Ingestion of contaminated food	Enterotoxin	Replenishment of body fluids
C. tetani	Motile, terminal spores	Tetanus	Soil contamination of deep wounds	Neurotoxin	Tetanus antitoxin plus penicillin; toxoid as part of DTP immunization
C. difficile		Antibiotic-associated pseudomembranous colitis	Contact with infected hospital personnel or contaminated environment	Enterotoxin and cytotoxin	Vancomycin for treatment and discontinuation of original antibiotic therapy

The most common method is to use an antibiotic, such as vancomycin, to kill *C. difficile*. Metronidazole is used in Europe to treat the disease.

Necrotizing Enterocolitis. Necrotizing enterocolitis is a fulminating, sometimes lethal condition of sick premature babies caused by clostridial species. Symptoms include abdominal distention, blood in stools, shock, and gas in the bowel wall. Breast-fed babies are protected against this disease. It is believed that immunoglobulins or other factors in the mother's milk protect the baby from the overgrowth of clostridial species in the intestinal tract.

Neutropenic Enterocolitis. Neutropenic enterocolitis is an infection associated with congenital neutropenia, or neutropenia associated with cancer chemotherapy, leukemia, and cancer of the colon. The most commonly associated pathogen is *C. septicum* but other indigenous *Clostridium* species also may be involved. Infection results in edema, hemorrhage, and necrosis of cecum and colon. The case-fatality rate is 50 to 100 percent. Surgical intervention is required to prevent fatal outcomes.

There are a wide variety of toxins produced by species of *Clostridium* and keeping track of them is difficult. We have outlined in Table 19-2 some but not all of the clostridial toxins and their known activities in human disease.

Summary

A summary of the characteristics of *Bacillus* and *Clostridium* species is presented in Table 19-3.

Questions for Study

1. Make a list of the major pathogenic clostridial species, indicating the mechanism of action of their toxins or other components associated with infection.
2. Are clindamycin, ampicillin, and cephalosporins the only agents to cause pseudomembranous colitis? Would penicillin or tetracycline also cause the same condition? Explain.
3. What suggestions would you make to someone preparing to preserve fruits, meats, or vegetables? to someone eating canned vegetables, fruits, or meats?
4. What may be some possible medicinal uses for tetanus toxin? (See Additional Readings.)
5. In clostridial food poisonings if toxin cannot be found in the stools, what other diagnostic techniques can be used?
6. Make a list of circumstances in which you might contract anthrax.
7. What are the risk factors for transmission of *C. difficile*–associated pseudomembranous colitis? (See Additional Readings.)

CHAPTER

20 *Corynebacterium diphtheriae* and Related Bacteria

OBJECTIVES

To describe the symptoms associated with diphtheria

To describe the mechanism of action of diphtheria toxin

To describe the in vivo test for determining the toxigenicity of *C. diphtheriae*

To describe the methods used to treat and prevent diphtheria

To outline the schedule for immunization against diphtheria

To describe the factors believed to be responsible for the development of acne

To explain the importance of diphtheroids, *Listeria,* and *Erysipelothrix rhusiopathiae* as agents of disease

OUTLINE

CORYNEBACTERIUM DIPHTHERIAE
- General Characteristics
- Pathogenesis
- Immunity
- Laboratory Diagnosis
- Epidemiology
- Treatment and Prevention

OTHER CORYNEBACTERIA, *LISTERIA,* AND *ERYSIPELOTHRIX RHUSIOPATHIAE*
- *Listeria*
  - General Characteristics
  - Pathogenesis
  - Laboratory Diagnosis
  - Treatment and Prevention
- *Erysipelothrix rhusiopathiae*
  - General Characteristics
  - Pathogenesis
  - Laboratory Diagnosis and Treatment

Corynebacterium is a genus belonging to a group of bacteria called **coryneforms.** Coryneforms include several genera that are plant and animal pathogens. They include both aerobic and anaerobic, nonbranching, gram-positive rods that do not form spores. The most important human pathogen, *Corynebacterium diphtheriae,* is the etiological agent of the disease **diphtheria.** Diphtheria is rarely seen in developed countries because of mass immunization programs but it is still an important disease in developing countries. The effect that the immunization program has had on the incidence and mortality of the disease in the United States is illustrated in Figure 20-1. We first discuss the characteristics of *C. diphtheriae* and then examine related groups of organisms.

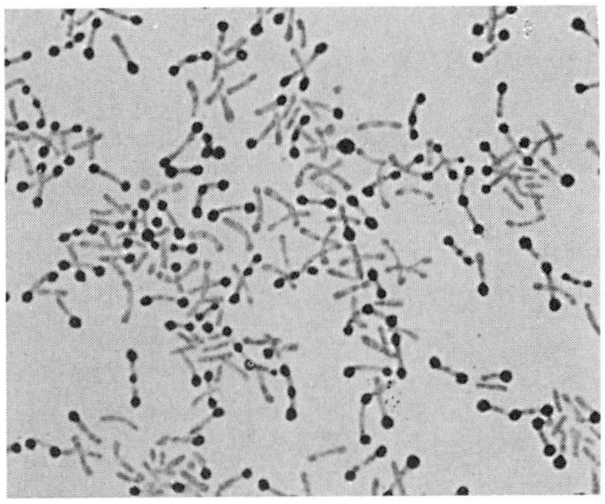

FIGURE 20-2
Stained smear of diphtheria bacilli. The darkly stained areas are polyphosphate or metachromatic granules. (From. R. R. Gillies and T. C. Dodds, *Bacteriology Illustrated.* London: Churchill Livingstone, 1976.)

Corynebacterium diphtheriae

GENERAL CHARACTERISTICS

C. diphtheriae is an obligate aerobe found in the upper respiratory tract of humans. It is a nonmotile bacillus averaging between 2 and 6 μm in length and 0.5 and 1.0 μm in diameter. In older cultures the bacilli appear club-shaped. The bacilli are capable of concentrating phosphate in the form of polymerized metaphosphate granules. When the cell is stained with methylene blue, the granules become apparent and give the bacillus a beaded appearance (Fig. 20-2). These granules are called **metachromatic granules.**

Because of their unusual arrangement after cell division, the bacilli appear in palisades (parallel rows) and resemble Chinese letters. *Corynebacterium* and other coryneforms have a close relationship with the mycobacteria and *Nocardia* organisms because of their cell walls (see Chapters 25 and 29). The cell walls of these groups possess arabinose, galactose, meso-diaminopimelic acid, and mycolic acid.

There are three characteristic biotypes of *C. diphtheriae: gravis, intermedius,* and *mitis.* Their names purportedly correspond to the severity of the disease; however, this is not always the case. The toxigenicity of these strains is directly related to the presence of a temperate (does not lyse the cell) bacteriophage that carries information for toxin production (tox gene). If "cured" of its temperate virus, the bacterium is no longer toxigenic.

PATHOGENESIS

Humans are the only natural host of *C. diphtheriae.* The organism is found in the upper respiratory tract but skin lesions may also be a source of the organism (cutaneous

FIGURE 20-1
Diphtheria: annual incidence and mortality ratios and case-fatality ratios in the United States, 1920 to 1993. (Courtesy of Centers for Disease Control, Atlanta, GA.)

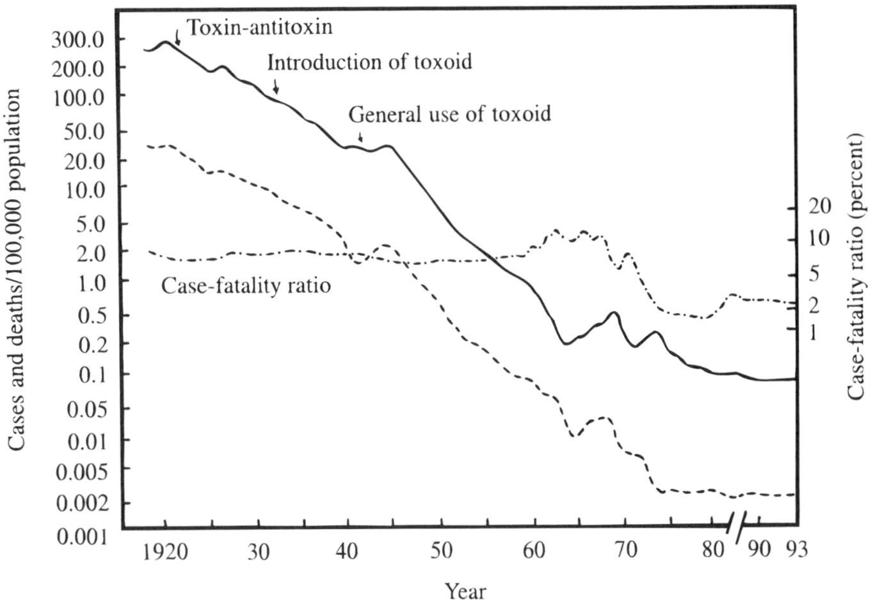

diphtheria). Contact with respiratory or cutaneous discharges is the means of transmission from person to person.

Diphtheria may be divided into two types: **respiratory diphtheria** and **cutaneous diphtheria.** The incubation period for respiratory diphtheria is two to six days. Symptoms include sore throat, slight fever, and malaise. There may also be a serosanguineous discharge and enlarged lymph nodes. The bacilli are harbored in the mucous membranes of the passageways of the oral cavity. The toxin elaborated by the bacilli causes necrosis of the mucosal cells, which aids in bacterial multiplication. The bacilli do not invade any underlying tissue, nor do they enter the bloodstream. The inflammatory response of the infected tissue causes the accumulation of a grayish-white exudate. The exudate clots and attaches to various passageways, forming a pseudomembrane. The pseudomembrane consists of neutrophils, corynebacteria, and desquamated epithelial cells enmeshed in a dense fibrinous network. The membrane can be found over the mucosa of the mouth, pharynx, larynx, or trachea. If the inflammatory response involves the laryngeal or tracheal areas, respiratory obstruction can occur. If not remedied by tracheostomy or intubation, this condition can cause suffocation. In most instances, however, death results from heart failure owing to the effects of the toxin on heart tissue.

Nontoxigenic strains of *gravis, intermedius,* and *mitis* were isolated from patients with clinical symptoms similar to those of diphtheria. In these patients a sufficient level of antitoxin was still present in the serum for protection against toxigenic strains. Presumably other bacteria or viruses may cooperate with the nontoxigenic strains to produce a diphtheria-like illness. In the majority of patients with such infections the clinical symptoms are less severe than those produced by toxigenic biotypes.

Expression of the tox gene is controlled by the level of iron in the cell. Maximum levels of toxin are produced only when iron becomes the growth-limiting nutrient. It is currently believed that *C. diphtheriae* synthesizes an inactive molecule that in the presence of iron becomes activated and represses the synthesis of toxin. Toxin is released by the bacterial cell as a single inactive polypeptide but is later cleaved into two fragments, A and B. Toxin presumably enters eukaryotic cells and inhibits protein synthesis in the following way:

1. The hydrophilic (carboxyl) end of the toxin is positively charged and interacts with specific receptors on the cytoplasmic membrane of the eukaryotic cell.
2. A cellular protease nicks the polypeptide, causing the release of the carboxyl tail (Fig. 20-3), and also affects the amino end of the polypeptide.
3. Release of the carboxyl tail allows the hydrophobic portion of the molecule (fragment B) to enter the lipid bilayer. This action facilitates the transport of fragment A into the cytoplasm.
4. Both fragments A and B are required to halt protein synthesis in living cells, but only fragment A is enzymatically active in inhibiting eukaryotic peptide chain elongation. The toxin accomplishes this by catalyzing the transfer of the ADP-ribose component from NAD^+ to a single amino acid residue of elongation factor. This response results in the inactivation of elongation factor. Once the toxin has entered the cell, antitoxin has no effect on its activity. If the toxin is only absorbed to the cell surface, antitoxin can neutralize it.

Cutaneous diphtheria can be manifested as an impetigo-like lesion on the face or the legs. Both toxigenic and nontoxigenic strains can be found in the lesions. Infections are often the result of insect bites or other skin trauma as well as poor personal hygiene. Cutaneous diphtheria is more common in tropical areas. In the United States most cases occur in southern states. Some studies demonstrated that the strain carried in the cutaneous lesion is also carried in the respiratory tract in more than 50 percent of patients. The cutaneous carrier may be a source of respiratory diphtheria.

IMMUNITY

All members of the community should have access to prophylactic immunization with the diphtheria toxoid. Many

FIGURE 20-3
Proposed action of cellular protease on the polypeptide toxin of *Corynebacterium diphtheriae.*

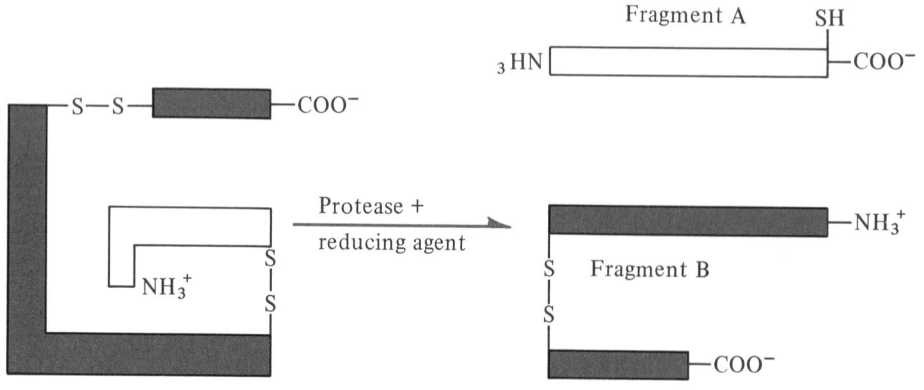

individuals who have an artificially acquired or a natural immunity are hypersensitive to the toxoid and should not be given injections of toxoid. The **Schick test** is a screening device used to separate immune from susceptible individuals. In the test a small amount of dilute toxin is injected intracutaneously in the forearm. A positive test result indicates there is little or no antitoxin in the serum. It is characterized by a localized erythema 24 to 48 hours after injection. A negative test result or no erythema at the site of injection indicates there is sufficient antitoxin in the serum to protect the individual. False-positive results often arise among older children and adults despite high levels of antitoxin in their serum. For this reason a control test is performed on the opposite arm by using toxin detoxified by heating. An allergic response, however, to the detoxified protein can still occur. If the tissue response at the control site parallels that at the test site in size and duration, the result of the Schick test is considered negative.

LABORATORY DIAGNOSIS

The fluorescent antibody technique provides a rapid presumptive test but should be used with other laboratory tests. Swab cultures should be taken from the nares, pharynx, nasopharynx, or cutaneous sites and plated on Loeffler (coagulated serum) medium. The overnight culture can be stained with methylene blue for presumptive diagnosis **(metachromatic granules)** and observed for typical morphology. Growth from the overnight culture should be subcultured to a blood agar and cysteine-tellurite medium. On cysteine-tellurite medium, corynebacterium reduces tellurite and the colonies appear black or gun-metal gray. Each colony type should be Gram-stained. Coryneforms on the cysteine-tellurite plates should be subcultured for biochemical and toxin testing (see Table 20-1 for a list of important biochemical tests). The blood agar plate is used to screen beta-hemolytic streptococci and *Staphylococcus aureus* and any corynebacteria not growing on cysteine-tellurite.

All *C. diphtheriae* isolates are sent to a reference laboratory for toxin testing. The toxin tests may be of the in vitro or in vivo type. In the in vivo test, a small area of the abdomen of two guinea pigs is shaved. One animal is administered diphtheria antitoxin intraperitoneally. After two to four hours both animals are injected intradermally with a dilution of the unknown suspension of bacilli. If toxigenic bacilli are present in the unknown suspension, only the animal unprotected by antitoxin will sustain any ill effects. The animal protected by antitoxin will show no adverse effects. In the in vitro test **(Elek method)** a sterile strip of filter paper impregnated with diphtheria antitoxin is pushed below the surface of a molten enriched agar medium. After the agar hardens, an inoculum of the unknown culture is streaked at right angles to the filter strip. If the unknown bacilli are toxigenic, a precipitate will be formed. The precipitate indicates specific antigen-antibody interaction (Fig. 20-4).

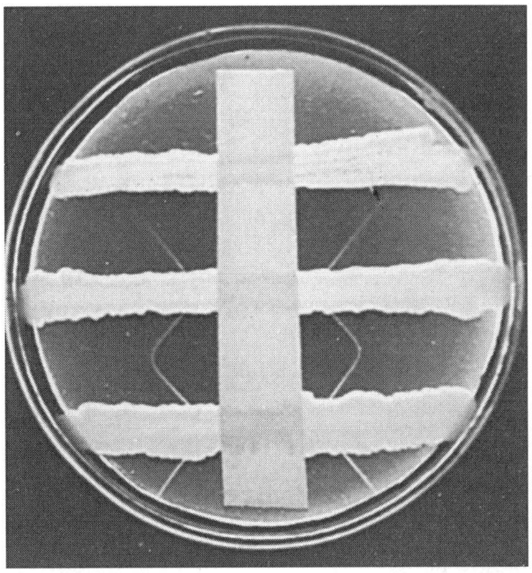

FIGURE 20-4
Gel diffusion plate for demonstrating the toxigenicity of strains of *C. diphtheriae* (Elek method). A filter strip soaked in diphtheria antitoxin is placed in the center and just below the surface of the agar. The plate is inoculated on each side of the strip and incubated for 24 to 48 hours. In the figure, three test strains have been inoculated. A positive test (toxigenic strain) is evidenced by the formation of one or more white lines of toxin-antitoxin precipitate. The two lower test cultures are positive. (From R. J. Olds, *Color Atlas of Microbiology*. London: Wolfe, 1975.)

EPIDEMIOLOGY

Eradication of the diphtheria microorganism in carriers and maintenance of immunization levels in children have resulted in removal of diphtheria from the list of major infectious diseases in the United States. Epidemics do occur periodically, but they are limited to very small geographical areas. Most vulnerable to diphtheria are people of low socioeconomic status with limited access to health care facilities. More than 80 percent of the recorded cases of diphtheria occur in the 1- to 19-year-old age group. The highest incidence of disease occurs among those between 10 and 14 years old. Disease is also frequent in older adults because of low immunization status. Complications after infection are severe in older adults.

TREATMENT AND PREVENTION

In any patients suspected to have diphtheria, the antitoxin should be administered to neutralize preformed toxin. The antitoxin is prepared from horse serum and allergic reactions develop in approximately 10 percent of persons receiving therapy. The physician should therefore determine the patient's sensitivity to the serum before administration of antitoxin. Antibiotics, although not a substitute for antitoxin, will destroy the toxin-producing bacilli. Penicillin and erythromycin are effective antimicrobial agents. Erythromycin is especially useful in the eradication of the carrier state.

For cutaneous diphtheria, compresses soaked in penicillin can be applied to the lesions.

Mass immunization has been a major factor in the control of diphtheria, as well as pertussis, tetanus, and *Hemophilus influenzae* type b (Hib). In 1993 the Food and Drug Administration recommended that all infants receive a primary series of the licensed *H. influenzae* conjugate vaccines beginning at the age of 2 months and a booster dose at the age of 12 to 15 months. Infants should also receive a four-dose primary series of diphtheria and tetanus toxoids and pertussis vaccine at the ages of 2, 4, 6, and 15 to 18 months and a booster dose at 4 to 6 years. For unimmunized persons 7 years and older, a series of three doses of tetanus and diphtheria toxoid (Td) is administered. Pertussis vaccine is not administered because pertussis is infrequent and less severe in this age group.

Diphtheria prophylaxis is recommended for household contacts of patients with respiratory diphtheria, especially those previously unimmunized or inadequately immunized. The contacts should receive diphtheria toxoid as well as an intramuscular injection of penicillin G benzathine. The major problem in diphtheria control is elimination of the carrier state. Present control efforts include (1) isolation and treatment of patients with clinical disease, (2) use of erythromycin and penicillin in the treatment of household and other contacts shown to be carriers of *C. diphtheriae*, and (3) full immunization of all preschool children with diphtheria toxoid and maintenance of diphtheria antitoxin serum levels by booster injections.

Other Corynebacteria, *Listeria*, and *Erysipelothrix rhusiopathiae*

Many species of *Corynebacterium* are found in humans and animals. Some have been implicated in human infections while others are considered nonpathogenic. The nonpathogenic corynebacteria, called **diphtheroids,** reside on the skin and in the mouth, vagina, and urethra. The anaerobic corynebacteria have now been classified in the genus *Propionibacterium*. For example, *C. acnes* is now *P. acnes* (see Under the Microscope 17). The diphtheroids exhibit the same morphology and biochemical characteristics as other coryneforms.

The diphtheroids are considered opportunistic pathogens. They are known to be the cause of endocarditis in patients who have been compromised by cardiac surgery or valvular prostheses. Diphtheroids have also been implicated in meningitis and osteomyelitis. Diphtheroids do not elaborate exotoxin.

Bacteriological diagnosis of diphtheroid infections is difficult because of the confusion with strains of *Streptococcus* and *Listeria monocytogenes*. *Streptococcus* organisms under certain growth conditions appear rod-shaped while *L. monocytogenes* is motile and catalase-positive. Isolation of diphtheroids can be achieved by using a selective medium containing a base of trypticase soy and yeast ex-

UNDER THE MICROSCOPE 17

Acne and *Propionibacterium acnes*

Acne is a common skin disease associated with young adults. Lesions usually encompass the more benign whiteheads or blackheads but also may include deeper inflammatory lesions. If not treated early, the inflammatory lesions can cause scarring.

Three etiological factors are postulated to be involved in the development of acne: increased sebum production, hypercornification of follicle ducts, and altered metabolism of cutaneous microflora such as *Propionibacterium acnes*. Sebum production is regulated by metabolites of testosterone, as well as adrenal and ovarian hormones. Some drugs that reduce sebum production have been shown to be therapeutic. The ducts in sebaceous follicles become blocked with dead cells (hypercornification) and microorganisms that lead to the formation of blackheads. It is believed that *P. acnes* produces lipases that hydrolyze sebum triglycerides to free fatty acids. Apparently the free fatty acids or their oxidation products may be involved in the formation of blackheads. Three genera of microorganisms inhabit sebaceous follicles: propionibacteria, staphylococci, and yeasts. There is no conclusive proof that any of them are involved in the development of acne lesions. It has been suggested that *P. acnes* may produce and release exocellular enzymes, or biologically active substances such as histamine and fatty acids that could play a role in disease.

Treatment of acne is a slow process, often requiring several months of therapy. Mild acne is treated with topical agents such as tetracycline, erythromycin, and clindamycin. For moderate to severe acne, oral and topical treatment is recommended. Oral antibiotics include tetracycline, doxycycline, minocycline, and erythromycin. Combinations of dissimilar drugs for oral and topical treatment should be avoided. Such combinations are likely to promote antibiotic resistance of cutaneous propionibacteria. For severe acne the drug 13-*cis*-retinoic acid is recommended. This drug virtually eradicates acne after a four- to six-month course of treatment. Topical antibiotics and benzoyl peroxide are used as maintenance therapy following retinoic acid treatment.

TABLE 20-1
Characteristics of Some Important Species of *Corynebacterium* That Cause Disease in Humans

Species	Normal habitat	Disease	Important biochemical properties
C. diphtheriae	Normal flora of upper respiratory tract of humans	Respiratory (diphtheria), cutaneous	Ferments glucose and maltose; produces catalase; most strains reduce nitrate; acid without gas is produced from glucose and maltose
C. equi (*Rhodococcus equi* formerly)	Found in soil near livestock	Pulmonary infection in patients with neoplastic disease	Cannot ferment carbohydrates
C. xerosis	Normal flora of skin and nasopharynx of humans	Endocarditis in patients with prosthetic cardiac valves	Can reduce nitrate, ferments several carbohydrates
C. pseudodiphtheriticum (C. hofmanii)	Normal flora of pharynx of humans	Endocarditis	Cannot ferment carbohydrates, produces urease, can reduce nitrate
C. jeikeium (formerly called CDC Group JK)	Indigenous to skin	Blood, tissue, and wound infections in those with indwelling catheters	Cannot produce urease, cannot reduce nitrate, cannot ferment carbohydrates
C. ulcerans	Pharynx of humans	Diphtheria-like illness	Produces urease, does not reduce nitrate
C. pseudotuberculosis (C. ovis)	Respiratory tract of domestic animals	Lymphadenitis, pneumonia	Produces phospholipase D and urease
Arcanobacterium (Corynebacterium haemolyticum)	Occasionally isolated from throat	Pharyngitis, skin lesions	Demonstrates beta hemolysis and is catalase-negative
C. urealyticum (CDC coryneform group D-2)	May be found on healthy skin in 35 percent of hospitalized patients	Urinary tract infections	Produces urease

tract supplemented with (1) polysorbate 80 (Tween 80) to support the growth of lipophilic strains, (2) oil red to distinguish lipophilic from nonlipophilic strains, and (3) furazolidone (Furoxone) to inhibit the growth of gram-negative bacilli and gram-positive cocci. Differentiation of *Corynebacterium* species is routinely performed through biochemical reactions. Characteristics of some of these species are outlined in Table 20-1.

LISTERIA

General Characteristics

The genus *Listeria* is included with *Lactobacillus, Erysipelothrix,* and other genera in a section entitled Regular, Nonsporing Gram-Positive Rods of *Bergey's Manual of Determinative Bacteriology*. The most important species is *L. monocytogenes,* which is a facultative anaerobe that grows between the temperatures −0.4 and 50 C. It is catalase-positive and oxidase-negative and produces a beta hemolysin. The organism is peritrichously flagellated and is widely present in plant, soil, and surface water. It also has been found in sewage, slaughterhouse waste milk of normal and mastitic cows, and human and animal feces.

Pathogenesis

Human disease caused by *Listeria* is called **listeriosis.** Listeriosis is a rare but serious illness in the United States. Infections are more likely to occur in those who are compromised or have a condition that leads to a deficient T cell immunity. Persons at increased risk are pregnant women, the elderly, and those with immunosuppressive conditions. The highest incidence of infection is seen in the neonate. There are two forms of **neonatal listeriosis,** early- and late-onset forms. The early-onset form presumably occurs in infants infected in utero. The disease is called **granulomatosis infantisepticum.** The organism is widely disseminated in the body, with lesions found typically in the liver and other organs. The infected infant displays respiratory distress, cyanosis, apnea, and pneumonia. The mortality rate is between 15 and 50 percent.

In late-onset listeriosis the infant is colonized during passage through the genital tract or from the environment shortly after birth. The predominant manifestation of late-onset disease is meningitis. The mortality rate is between 10 and 20 percent.

The principal vehicle of infection by *L. monocytogenes* is contaminated food. Outbreaks of listeriosis occur sporadically in the United States and throughout the world.

Many of these outbreaks have been due to consumption of non-reheated hot dogs, undercooked chicken, various soft cheeses, and food purchased from store delicatessens. Very seldom do healthy individuals contract disease.

The organism is a facultative intracellular parasite that utilizes parasite-directed endocytosis to enter the host cell. Several virulence factors for *L. monocytogenes* have been proposed but virulence is probably multifactorial. The hemolysin of the organism, called **listerolysin O,** appears to be a major virulence factor. Its secretion is essential for promoting intracellular growth and T cell recognition of the organism.

Laboratory Diagnosis

Early recognition of listeriosis is needed to prevent neonatal infection. Diagnosis is best made by bacterial culture of specimens from sites such as blood or cerebrospinal fluid. Stool cultures are not reliable because enteric colonization is not always associated with disease.

Clinical specimens can be inoculated onto sheep blood agar plates. Colonies of *L. monocytogenes* are surrounded by a narrow zone of beta hemolysis. Isolates of *L. monocytogenes* can be inoculated into semisolid media, one at room temperature (20–25 C) and the other at 35 C, for two to five days. At room temperature the microorganism produces an "umbrella" growth below the surface of the medium. Most other diphtheroids are nonmotile and do not grow below the surface of the motility medium. Motility at 35 C is minimal.

Treatment and Prevention

Penicillin and ampicillin are effective agents in the treatment of listeriosis. Sepsis and meningitis have been treated successfully with trimethoprim-sulfamethoxazole.

Prevention of listeriosis* includes the following:

1. Thoroughly cooking raw food from animal sources
2. Thoroughly washing raw vegetables before eating
3. Avoiding consumption of raw (unpasteurized) milk or foods made from raw milk
4. Washing hands, knives, and cutting boards after handling uncooked foods

* From *M.M.W.R.* 41(No. 15):April 17, 1992.

ERYSIPELOTHRIX RHUSIOPATHIAE

General Characteristics

E. rhusiopathiae is a gram-positive facultative anaerobic, non-sporeforming, rod-shaped bacterium. It is found in nature where nitrogenous materials decompose. The organism has been isolated from several animals and also fish, shellfish, and birds. The major reservoir of *E. rhusiopathiae* is believed to be swine. It is presumed that excretion of the organism by infected and colonized animals leads to contamination of the environment and to acquisition of infection by humans.

Pathogenesis

Most human cases of disease are related to occupational exposure. Individuals at great risk of infection are butchers, fishermen, abattoir workers, veterinarians, and housewives. Most cases in humans occur via scratches or puncture wounds of the skin. *E. rhusiopathiae* is killed by moist heat at 55 C for 15 minutes but it is resistant to salting, pickling, and smoking. Thus, some food processing does not prevent infection.

There are three types of human infection: (1) a mild cutaneous form, usually found on the hands, which is called **erysipeloid,** "whale finger," and "seal finger"; (2) a rare cutaneous form in which the organism can cause systemic disease; and (3) a septic form developing from localized infection. The septic form usually develops into endocarditis.

Laboratory Diagnosis and Treatment

Blood culture media are used to culture the microorganism from specimens. Selective media are required only if the specimen is heavily contaminated. After preliminary identification as a gram-positive rod, the organism is subjected to tests to differentiate it from *Corynebacterium* species, *Lactobacillus* species, and *L. monocytogenes.* Table 20-2 illustrates the results of these tests.

Erysipeloid is a self-limited condition in which the lesions resolve on their own within three weeks. The healing of second attacks can be accelerated by antibiotic therapy. Most strains are susceptible to penicillin, cephalosporins, erythromycin, and clindamycin. Penicillin G is the drug of choice for serious infections.

TABLE 20-2
Tests Used in the Differentiation of *Erysipelothrix rhusiopathiae* from *Corynebacterium* Species, *Lactobacillus** Species, and *Listeria monocytogenes*

Characteristic	*E. rhusiopathiae*	*Corynebacterium*	*Lactobacillus*	*Listeria monocytogenes*
Hemolysis on blood agar	Beta hemolysis	Variable	None	Beta hemolysis
Motility	−	−	−	+
Catalase reaction	−	+/−	−	+
H_2S formation in triple sugar iron agar	−	+	−	−

\+ = positive reaction or characteristic; − = negative reaction or characteristic.
* Lactobacilli are gram-positive, non-sporeforming anaerobic bacilli found as commensals in the oropharynx, intestinal tract, and vagina.

Summary

1. The corynebacteria and related bacteria are gram-positive, aerobic, pleomorphic bacilli. They concentrate phosphate into stainable granules. *Corynebacterium diphtheriae* is the etiological agent of diphtheria. Its virulence is due to a toxin whose genetic determinant is carried on a bacteriophage.

2. Diphtheria toxin is composed of two fragments; one attaches to the host cytoplasmic membrane and affects the transport of the other fragment into the cytoplasm of the cell. Diphtheria toxin acts on respiratory tissue and causes the formation of a pseudomembrane. The toxin penetrates the bloodstream and affects protein synthesis in all tissue, especially the heart.

3. Diphtheria may also be of the cutaneous type, which is found in tropical and semitropical climates. Cutaneous diphtheria is not a fatal disease but it may be a source of microorganisms for respiratory diphtheria. Penicillin can be used in the treatment of both cutaneous and respiratory diphtheria.

4. Diphtheria is practically nonexistent in developed countries because of mass immunization programs with toxoid. The toxoid is part of the complex (DTP) containing pertussis vaccine and tetanus toxoid.

5. *C. diphtheriae* can be detected in the laboratory by cultivation of specimens on appropriate media, staining to observe metachromatic granules and cellular morphology, and observation of colony appearance. All isolates are tested for toxin production by in vivo (guinea pig) and in vitro (gel diffusion) tests.

6. *Corynebacterium* species other than *C. diphtheriae* are found in soil or as part of the normal flora of animals and humans. These species are pathogenic primarily in the compromised host and are not considered major pathogens.

7. Anaerobic corynebacteria are now classified in the genus *Propionibacterium*. One of the important species is *P. acne*. This species is believed to be an important factor in the development of the skin disease acne.

8. Two groups of bacteria that may be confused with *Corynebacterium* are *Listeria* and *Erysipelothrix*. *Listeria monocytogenes* is found in nature and is a cause of disease primarily in compromised patients, especially the neonate. The organism has a predilection for nervous tissue and for this reason, meningitis is a major pathological consequence of infection.

9. *Erysipelothrix rhusiopathiae* is found in nature where nitrogen material decomposes. It causes occupation-associated diseases, particularly for those in contact with infected animals. Cutaneous infections are more common but occasionally they can lead to endocarditis. Penicillin is the drug of choice.

Questions for Study

1. What techniques would you use to differentiate *Listeria monocytogenes* from corynebacteria?
2. Discuss the factors that are potentially conducive to the development of acne.
3. What characteristics differentiate cutaneous diphtheria from respiratory diphtheria?
4. What is meant by a pseudomembrane and of what is it composed?
5. What clinical signs would make you suspect a patient had diphtheria? What tests would you use to confirm your diagnosis?
6. Where is *Erysipelothrix rhusiopathiae* found and what group of people are subject to infection?
7. What group of individuals is susceptible to infection by *Listeria monocytogenes?* Explain why this is so.

CHAPTER

21 Gram-Negative Enteric Bacteria

OBJECTIVES

To list the traits that are common to most members of the Enterobacteriaceae

To outline briefly in a flow chart the laboratory procedures used to isolate and differentiate members of the Enterobacteriaceae

To describe the intestinal and extraintestinal diseases caused by *Escherichia coli*

To describe the virulence factors associated with infections caused by *E. coli, Salmonella* species, *Shigella* species, and *Yersinia* species

To explain the methods of treatment for intestinal and extraintestinal disease caused by the Enterobacteriaceae

To describe the different disease states associated with salmonella infections

To describe the epidemiology of plague

To list the opportunistic Enterobacteriaceae and the types of infections with which they are associated

OUTLINE

CHARACTERISTICS OF THE ENTEROBACTERIACEAE

ISOLATION OF THE ENTEROBACTERIACEAE
- Selective Enrichment Media
- Primary Isolation Media
- Differential Selective Media

SCREENING AND IDENTIFICATION OF THE ENTEROBACTERIACEAE
- Rapid Identification Techniques

ESCHERICHIA COLI
- Pathogenesis
  - Extraintestinal Disease
  - Intestinal Disease
  - Laboratory Diagnosis
  - Treatment and Prevention

SALMONELLA
- Pathogenesis
  - Gastroenteritis
  - Enteric Fever (Typhoid, Paratyphoid, and Nontyphoidal Fevers)
- Bacteremia
- Carrier State
- Epidemiology
- Laboratory Diagnosis
- Treatment
- Prevention and Control

SHIGELLA
- Pathogenesis
- Epidemiology
- Laboratory Diagnosis
- Treatment
- Prevention and Control

YERSINIA
- *Yersinia pestis*
  - Pathogenesis
  - Epidemiology
  - Laboratory Diagnosis
  - Treatment
  - Prevention and Control
- *Yersinia enterocolitica* and *Y. pseudotuberculosis*

OPPORTUNISTIC ENTERIC BACILLI

Many gram-negative, non-sporeforming bacilli are commensals in the intestinal tract of humans and animals. These enteric bacilli for the most part belong to the family Enterobacteriaceae (Table 21-1). Other gram-negative bacilli that either are found as intestinal pathogens or are recovered from infections associated with enteric bacilli belong to the families Vibrionaceae and Pseudomonadaceae. They are discussed in later chapters.

The term **coliform** is sometimes used to denote all the enteric bacilli. It is used more often, however, to describe gram-negative fermentative inhabitants of the intestinal tract: *Escherichia coli*, *Klebsiella pnemoniae*, and *Enterobacter aerogenes*.

The enteric bacilli have replaced the gram-positive organisms, such as staphylococci and streptococci, as the major cause of disease in the hospital. Enterobacteriaceae may account for approximately 50 percent of all clinically significant isolates. They are the major cause of septicemia, urinary tract infections, and intestinal infections in the hospital.

TABLE 21-1
Current Classification of Enterobacteriaceae Based on *Bergey's Manual of Determinative Bacteriology*, 9th ed.*

FAMILY: Enterobacteriaceae
- GENUS: *Escherichia*
  - SPECIES: *E. coli*
- GENUS: *Shigella*
  - SPECIES: *S. dysenteriae*, *S. flexneri*, *S. boydii*, *S. sonnei*
- GENUS: *Edwardsiella*
  - SPECIES: *E. tarda*
- GENUS: *Citrobacter*
  - SPECIES: *C. freundii*, *C. diversus*
- GENUS: *Salmonella*
  - SPECIES: *S. choleraesuis*, *S. typhi*, *S. paratyphi A*, *S. typhimurium*, *S. enteritidis*, *S. arizonae*
- GENUS: *Klebsiella*
  - SPECIES: *K. pneumoniae* subsp. *pneumoniae*, *K. pneumoniae* subsp. *ozaenae*, *K. pneumoniae* subsp. *rhinoscleromatis*, *K. oxytoca*
- GENUS: *Enterobacter*
  - SPECIES: *E. cloacae*, *E. aerogenes*, *E. agglomerans*
- GENUS: *Hafnia*
  - SPECIES: *H. alvei*
- GENUS: *Serratia*
  - SPECIES: *S. marcescens*, *S. liquefaciens*
- GENUS: *Proteus*
  - SPECIES: *P. vulgaris*, *P. mirabilis*
- GENUS: *Providencia*
  - SPECIES: *P. alcalifaciens*, *P. rettgeri*
- GENUS: *Yersinia*
  - SPECIES: *Y. pestis*, *Y. pseudotuberculosis*, *Y. enterocolitica*

* Not all the genera or species are indicated, only those that are major human pathogens.

Characteristics of the Enterobacteriaceae

No single morphological or biochemical characteristic can be used to differentiate all the Enterobacteriaceae. Some generalizations, however, can be made about the majority of them.

1. All members are gram-negative aerobic or facultatively anaerobic rods that vary in length from 1 to 8 μm. They ferment glucose, do not produce oxidase, and reduce nitrates to nitrites.
2. Most can be cultivated on ordinary laboratory media and stained with aniline dyes.
3. Most species are active fermenters of glucose and other carbohydrates. Many of the pathogens can be separated from the nonpathogens on the basis of the former's ability to ferment lactose.
4. Motile as well as nonmotile species are found in the group. The species that are motile are peritrichous (have flagella over the entire surface of the bacterium).
5. Pili are found on the cell surface (Fig. 21-1). The

FIGURE 21-1
Fimbrial adhesins of *Escherichia coli*. (From S. C. M. To, *Infect Immun.* 43:549, 1979.)

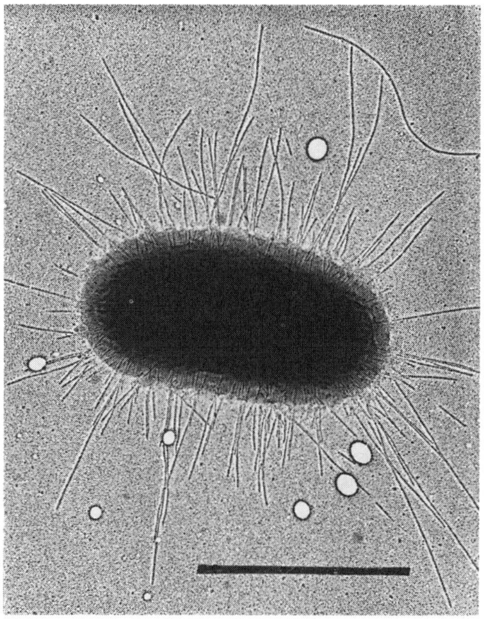

sex pili are important in the transfer of antibiotic resistance factors (R factors) between the same or different family members. Adhesive pili are the most numerous pili found on the surface of the organisms. They are responsible for adherence to epithelial surfaces. Adhesive pili are also called K antigens but they are to be distinguished from the capsular K antigen, which is a polysaccharide.

6. Antibiotic susceptibility testing must be routinely performed on isolates because of rapid transfer of antibiotic resistance plasmid between microorganisms.
7. The lipopolysaccharides (LPS) of the cell wall are toxic and are called **endotoxins.** The biological properties of endotoxins are discussed in Chapter 14. The function of LPS is also discussed in Chapter 2.
8. Many enteric species are capable of producing bacteriocins (see Chapter 15).
9. Many species are classified by their cell envelope-associated antigens, that is, the O, K, and H antigens (Fig. 21-2). The **O** or **somatic antigen** is the O-specific polysaccharide of the LPS component of the cell wall (see Fig. 2-9). The O polysaccharide is responsible for the O antigen specificity of the Enterobacteriaceae. There are at least 164 somatic O antigens. The O-specific polysaccharide protects some species against host resistance factors.

   Lipid A is the toxic component of the LPS complex. It is similar in all of the different Enterobacteriaceae.
10. The capsular polysaccharide of the Enterobacteriaceae is referred to as the **K antigen.** Among the *E. coli* strains there are at least 100 different K antigens. Not all species in the family possess K antigens, but those that do are usually more pathogenic. Some K polysaccharides are poorly immunogenic because of their structural similarity to human tissue. The K polysaccharide also provides a barrier to phagocytosis because of its ability to resist activation of the alternative complement pathway.
11. Flagellar proteins are referred to as **H antigens.** They are responsible for motility. Their identification often represents the last step in the procedure of serotyping various strains within a genus of bacteria. (**Serotypes** are divisions based on antigenic relatedness, for example, similarity of O antigens. **Biotypes** are strains of the same serotype that differ in a biochemical characteristic, for example, sugar fermentation.)
12. Because of the ease of cultivating them, many Enterobacteriaceae have been used in research efforts. They have been used in the elucidation of metabolic pathways, protein synthesis, and genetic mechanisms and in biotechnology. *E. coli,* for example, is the most studied of all bacteria and it is used as a vehicle in recombinant DNA technology (see Chapter 6).

FIGURE 21-2
Antigenic components found on the surface of members of the Enterobacteriaceae.

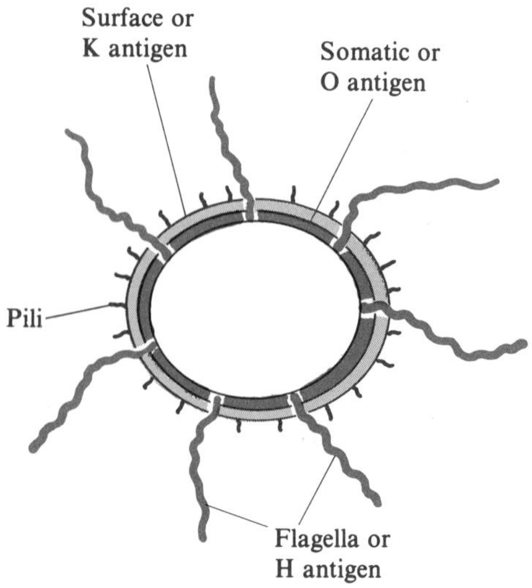

Isolation of Enterobacteriaceae

The enteric laboratory represents the largest division in the clinical microbiology section of a hospital. For this reason we provide more detailed description of laboratory isolation and identification techniques than what is included in other chapters. Enteric bacilli are involved in numerous hospital-associated diseases. They can be isolated from feces, urine, blood, and cerebrospinal fluid. The kind of medium to use for isolation depends on the source of the specimen. If it is from a nonintestinal source such as blood or urine, the organisms may be a practically pure culture. Hence, the specimen may be plated on blood agar and a differential medium. If the specimen is from an intestinal source, the infecting pathogen will be greatly outnumbered by commensal species and will initially require a selective enrichment medium. A variety of selective, differential, and enrichment media are available to resolve these problems.

SELECTIVE ENRICHMENT MEDIA

If the infecting pathogen (for example, *Salmonella* or *Shigella* species) is from an intestinal source, a selective medium is often needed. Selective media such as tetrathionate, Hajna GN broth, and selenite broth inhibit gram-positive bacteria and coliforms, permitting the rapid multiplication of *Salmonella* and *Shigella* species. Once the pathogen has grown to sufficient numbers, it is inoculated into various selective or differential media.

PRIMARY ISOLATION MEDIA

Primary isolation media include eosin–methylene blue (EMB) and MacConkey agar. These media contain chemicals that inhibit gram-positive organisms. They also contain lactose, a disaccharide that permits a presumptive differentiation of lactose fermenters from nonlactose fermenters. Lactose fermenters such as *E. coli* and *E. aerogenes* produce colored colonies. The nonlactose fermenters such as *Salmonella* and *Shigella* organisms exhibit colorless colonies because they do not ferment lactose.

DIFFERENTIAL SELECTIVE MEDIA

Differential selective media such as Salmonella-Shigella (SS), deoxycholate-citrate, bismuth sulfite, and brilliant green agars are used primarily for the isolation of *Salmonella* and *Shigella* species. These media are selective against gram-positive organisms as well as most coliforms.

Screening and Identification of the Enterobacteriaceae

Many biochemical tests can be used to identify a member of the Enterobacteriaceae. A spot test for oxidase, performed immediately on isolates, will separate oxidase-negative Enterobacteriaceae from oxidase-positive, gram-negative organisms such as *Pasteurella*. A battery of 28 biochemical tests will differentiate all of the pathogenic Enterobacteriaceae. A battery of 14 primary tests, however, is sufficient to differentiate most isolates to the genus and some to the species level. The primary tests are outlined in Table 21-2.

Secondary tests are primarily fermentation tests. Several of the primary tests can be determined in a single medium. For example, triple sugar iron (TSI) agar provides results for gas and hydrogen sulfide production and glucose fermentation. Phenylalanine-urease broth provides testing for phenylalanine deaminase and urease while motility-indole-ornithine medium provides results for motility, indole production, and ornithine decarboxylase production. Since TSI is so important, we briefly describe the test.

An isolated colony from the selective or differential media is first stabbed into the butt of a TSI agar slant, then streaked onto the surface of the slant. The TSI agar tube contains glucose (0.1%), sucrose (1%), and lactose (1%), plus phenol red to indicate fermentation and ferrous sulfate to detect hydrogen sulfide production. The small amount of glucose in the TSI slant, compared to the other sugars, enables one to detect the fermentation of this sugar. If glucose is the only carbohydrate fermented, the small amount of acid produced on the slant is oxidized to a neutral product, and the slant remains alkaline (red). Acid produced in the butt is not oxidized and the butt remains yellow. If lactose and sucrose are also fermented, there is so much acid produced that both the slant and the butt become yellow. All inoculated TSI tubes are read after 18 to 24 hours (Table 21-3).

TABLE 21-2
Primary Biochemical Tests (14) Used To Identify Some of the Major Species in the Enterobacteriaceae

Test or substrate	*E. coli*	*Salmonella typhi*	*Shigella dysenteriae*	*Klebsiella pneumoniae*	*Enterobacter sakazakii*	*Serratia marcescens*	*Proteus mirabilis*	*Yersinia pestis*
D-adonitol	∓	–	–	±	–	V	–	–
Voges-Proskauer	–	–	–	±	+	±	∓	–
Citrate utilization	–	–	–	±	+	±	±	–
Arginine dihydrolase	∓	∓	∓	–	+	–	–	–
Motility	±	±	+	–	±	±	±	–
Indole production	+	–	V	–	∓	∓	∓	–
H_2S (on TSI agar)	–	±	–	–	–	–	±	–
Urease production	–	–	–	±	–	∓	±	∓
Phenylalanine deaminase	–	–	–	–	V	–	±	–
Ornithine decarboxylase	V	–	–	–	±	+	+	–
Lysine decarboxylase	±	±	–	±	–	+	–	–
Sucrose	V	–	–	+	+	+	∓	–
DNase	–	–	–	–	–	±	–	–
Gas from glucose	+	–	–	±	±	V	±	–

∓ = over 90 percent of isolates are negative; ± = over 90 percent of isolates are positive; V = variable, that is, as many positive as negative isolates; TSI = triple sugar iron agar.

TABLE 21-3
Key to Identification of the Enterobacteriaceae on Triple Sugar Iron Agar

Reaction	Biochemical interpretation	Organisms most likely to be involved
Acid slant, acid-gas butt, no H_2S produced	Glucose fermented and lactose or sucrose fermented with acid and gas produced	*Escherichia coli, Enterobacter, Klebsiella,* and *Proteus* species
Acid slant, acid-gas butt, H_2S produced	Glucose fermented and lactose or sucrose fermented with acid and gas produced	*Citrobacter* species
Alkaline slant, acid butt, no H_2S produced	Glucose fermented with acid and no gas produced	*Proteus, Shigella,* and *Serratia* species
Alkaline slant, acid-gas butt, no H_2S produced	Glucose fermented with acid and no gas produced	*Proteus, Citrobacter, Salmonella, Providencia,* and *Hafnia* species
Alkaline slant, acid-gas butt, H_2S produced	Glucose fermented with acid and gas produced	*Proteus, Arizona, Salmonella,* and *Edwardsiella* species
Alkaline slant, acid butt, H_2S produced	Glucose fermented with acid and no gas produced	*Salmonella* species
No reaction, but green pigment produced	Peptone only source of carbon and energy	*Pseudomonas* species

RAPID IDENTIFICATION TECHNIQUES

In the past 20 years rapid progress has been made in methods for identifying Enterobacteriaceae. We have gone from the conventional tubed biochemicals to miniaturized biochemical panels and plates to semiautomated systems, all of which yield identification in 18 to 24 hours. In addition, some fully automated systems provide results in two to four hours.

One of the first miniaturized systems was the API 20E identification system. It is still in widespread use and is considered the "gold standard" for evaluating other systems. The API system consists of a strip containing 20 chambers, each consisting of a microtube and a depression called a cupule. Each of the tubes contains dehydrated substrates. The dehydrated substrates are rehydrated by adding a saline suspension. To create anaerobic conditions in some of the tubes, mineral oil is added. The strip is incubated for 18 to 24 hours at 35 to 37 C. The strip is read by noting color changes in the cupules containing the affected substrates. Identification of the unknown bacterium is accomplished by determining a seven-digit **profile index number** and referring to the **API 20E Profile Recognition System** or **API 20E Profile Index Booklet.**

Escherichia coli

PATHOGENESIS

E. coli is a commensal found in the intestinal tract of humans and animals. One gram of feces may contain from 1×10^7 to 1×10^8 organisms.* Despite being commensals, some strains of *E. coli* are pathogenic and cause diarrheal disease and extraintestinal infections. Classification of pathogenic *E. coli* isolates according to serotypes has been difficult since there are over 160 O antigens, over 80 K antigens, and 55 H antigens. The majority of pathogenic as well as nonpathogenic strains possess a common type of pilus, called **type 1.**

Extraintestinal Disease

Extraintestinal disease caused by *E. coli* is usually the result of person-to-person contact. The infections may also be endogenous in which the organism travels from the intestine to the urinary tract. In the community outside the hospital, *E. coli* is the most common cause of urinary tract infections. This preference for the urinary tract is probably due to the close association between the organisms' normal habitat and the urinary tract (especially in women). In addition, some strains contain special adherence mechanisms.

Hospital-associated infections represent another group of extraintestinal infections caused by *E. coli.* Again, the most frequent site of infection is the urinary tract. *E. coli* is implicated in approximately 20 percent of all urinary tract infections in the hospital.

Strains of *E. coli* that are associated with urinary tract infections often possess adhesins called **P pili.** More P pili–containing strains are found, however, in more severe forms of urinary tract disease such as **pyelonephritis** (inflammation of the kidney usually arising from infection ascending from the ureter). In compromised patients the requirement for P pili is decreased, probably because normal host defense mechanisms have been altered. Other virulence factors include the following:

1. Aerobactin: Aerobactin is a siderophore that provides the bacterial cell with iron. After it is secreted by the bacterial cell, aerobactin extracts Fe^{3+} from host iron-binding proteins and transports iron into the bacterial cell.
2. Hemolysin: *E. coli* produces an alpha hemolysin that

* Species of *Bacteroides*, an anaerobe, are the most abundant group of bacteria in the intestinal tract. Some species are also found in the oral cavity and vagina. *Bacteroides* is implicated in diseases such as brain abscesses, respiratory tract disease, diseases of the female genital tract (pelvic inflammatory disease), and bacterial vaginosis (see Chapter 30).

lyses erythrocytes. The hemolysin probably contributes to the inflammation and tissue injury associated with infection.

3. K antigen or capsular polysaccharide: The negative charge and hydrophobicity of the K antigen are antiphagocytic. The polysaccharide also blocks opsonization by interfering with complement deposition. This is due in part to the presence of sialic acid in the capsule (see Chapter 14). Activation of complement by the classic pathway is impaired by K antigen because the latter is a poor immunogen. K1 is a polysaccharide found in patients with severe urinary tract infections. In addition, 80 percent of *E. coli* strains involved in neonatal meningitis produce the K1 capsular polysaccharide.

Intestinal Disease

At present we recognize four distinct groups of *E. coli* that are considered intestinal pathogens and that cause diarrhea (diarrheagenic). These groups are (1) **enterotoxigenic** *E. coli,* (2) **enteroinvasive** *E. coli,* (3) **enteropathogenic** *E. coli,* and (4) **enterohemorrhagic** *E. coli* (EHEC). All of these groups are distinct but they do have some common underlying characteristics:

1. Important virulence traits are encoded on plasmids.
2. They interact with the intestinal mucosa.
3. They produce enterotoxins or cytotoxins.
4. Within each category the strains fall within certain O:H serotypes.

Table 21-4 characterizes the four major groups of diarrheogenic *E. coli.** Here we discuss only the most virulent of the group, the EHEC. All EHEC serotypes produce a **Shiga-like toxin** (also called Vero toxin). They are commonly isolated from cattle, which may explain their epidemiological association with eating undercooked hamburger. EHEC are able to attach to and destroy the intestinal mucosa, resulting in a copious bloody diarrhea. Other clinical manifestations include cramps with an absence of leukocytes in the stool. One-half of the patients have nausea and vomiting.

EHEC is also associated with the clinical entities called **hemolytic-uremic syndrome** and **thrombotic thrombocytopenic purpura.** These two complications of EHEC are the result of vascular lesions and are associated with hemolytic anemia, renal failure, and thrombocytopenia. This triad of clinical manifestations can be fatal, particularly in young children, if treatment is not quickly initiated. The highest incidence of hemolytic-uremic syndrome is in Argentina but many cases are also found in the United States. In the state of Washington during the month of January 1993, 230 persons had bloody diarrhea, and in some hemolytic-uremic syndrome developed. The cases were linked to consumption of hamburger from one fast-food chain. *E. coli* 0157:H7 was found in the same lots of ground beef that had been distributed to three other states where other cases of bloody diarrhea appeared. Antibiotic use does not appear to alter the out-

* A fifth type called **enteroaggregative** has been identified in South and Central America, India, and the United Kingdom but has not been observed in the United States.

TABLE 21-4
Characteristics of the Major Groups of Diarrheogenic *Escherichia coli*

E. coli group	Epidemiology and disease symptoms	Mechanism of transmission and site of action	Virulence factors
Enterotoxigenic	Major cause of infant diarrhea in less developed countries and traveler's diarrhea; diarrhea in the United States rarely caused by this agent; watery diarrhea, abdominal cramps, low-grade fever	Ingestion of contaminated food (raw vegetables, fish, meat) or water; colonizes proximal small intestine	Heat-labile (LT) or heat-stable (ST) enterotoxin; LT resembles cholera toxin in chemistry and action; fimbrial adhesin called colonization factor (CFA)
Enteropathogenic	Not well defined; in some countries it is the most important cause of infant diarrhea; fever, vomiting, diarrhea with large amounts of mucus; distinctive lesions in which microvilli are destroyed	Ingestion of contaminated food or water; proximal intestine	Do not produce toxin and do not invade; adherence factor may be responsible for diarrhea
Enteroinvasive	Diarrhea in adults and infants; resembles shigella in pathogenicity, i.e., causes epithelial cell death; fever, severe abdominal cramps, watery diarrhea followed by gross dysentery with bloody stools and mucus	Ingestion of contaminated food or water; predilection for mucosa of the colon	Several outer membrane proteins, similar to shigella, involved in invasiveness; Shiga-like toxin produced
Enterohemorrhagic	Sporadic and epidemic cases of gastrointestinal illness in United States, Canada, and Great Britain since 1982; affects both adults and children; severe abdominal cramps and copious bloody diarrhea; no fever or fecal leukocytes—which distinguishes it from dysentery due to shigella	Ingestion of contaminated food or water; proximal intestine	Shiga-like toxins that are related to Shiga toxin of *Shigella dysenteriae* type 1

come of infection. Treatment is directed at the symptoms, for example, renal dialysis.

LABORATORY DIAGNOSIS

E. coli is a lactose fermenter and is readily separated from other enteric species by its characteristic colonial appearance on EMB agar and biochemical reactions outlined in Table 20-3.

Detecting specific serotypes of diarrheogenic *E. coli* requires enterotoxin testing and serotyping. These are not routine procedures for most clinical laboratories. DNA probes have been developed to identify toxigenic strains in the clinical laboratory. Detection of EHEC can be accomplished by plating stool specimens on MacConkey sorbitol agar containing rhamnose and cefixime. EHEC isolates do not ferment sorbitol and colonies appear colorless (other *E. coli* strains are pink). Colonies can then be screened for agglutination with EHEC antiserum. An indirect hemagglutination assay consisting of sheep erythrocytes coated with LPS from *E. coli* 0157 can also be used to diagnose infections in children one week after the onset of diarrhea.

TREATMENT AND PREVENTION

Antibiotics are not recommended for gastrointestinal infections. Successful treatment largely depends on the replacement of water and electrolytes. Chloramphenicol, tetracyclines, and nalidixic acid are used to treat urinary tract infections. Antibiotics are not recommended for treatment of EHEC infection. If antibiotics are required, susceptibility testing is mandatory for enteric bacilli since most carry antibiotic resistance plasmids.

Prophylactic drugs are recommended for the prevention of traveler's diarrhea. The drugs are for (1) persons visiting high-risk areas (Mexico, for example) for short periods (2–5 days) and (2) persons with underlying disease that might increase susceptibility to diarrhea during travel in high-risk areas. Chemoprophylaxis is to be avoided if visits to high-risk areas last more than two weeks. Trimethoprim-sulfamethoxazole is an effective chemoprophylactic drug. Bismuth subsalicylate (Pepto-Bismol) is also effective in preventing traveler's diarrhea. Infection by *E. coli* 0157:H7 can be prevented by cooking beef until the pink disappears, pasteurizing milk, and careful handwashing.

Salmonella

Members of the *Salmonella* genus are rod-shaped cells that, with few exceptions, are actively motile. They are capable of causing disease in both animals and humans. Salmonellae are hardy organisms that can survive in moist environments and in the frozen state for several months. Salmonella disease **(salmonellosis)** is customarily acquired by the ingestion of contaminated food or water.

The three recognized species of *Salmonella* are *S. typhi*, *S. choleraesuis*, and *S. enteritidis*. *S. enteritidis* includes all the *Salmonella* organisms except those of *S. typhi* and *S. choleraesuis*. There are more than 1500 serotypes of *S. enteritidis* but most infections are caused by about 10 serotypes. The most common serotype is *S. enteritidis* serotype *typhimurium*. Many investigators still prefer to use the serotypes of *S. enteritidis* as species names; for example, *S. enteritidis* serotype *typhimurium* is called *S. typhimurium*. We will follow this practice.

PATHOGENESIS

The manifestations of disease caused by salmonellae may include gastroenteritis, enteric fever, and bacteremia. Each type may be associated with the carrier state. Most infections in the United States are of the gastrointestinal variety and result from ingestion of contaminated food or water. Enteric fevers (for example, typhoid fever) are seldom observed in the United States but they are quite common in developing countries.

The factors that determine the severity of infection by salmonella are size of inoculum, serotype, and state of health of the host. As few as 17 or as many as 1×10^7 microorganisms may be required to cause disease. Immunocompromised individuals require fewer organisms to cause disease. One of the defense mechanisms of the salmonellae is their ability to tolerate acid pH. They can survive the acid pH of the phagolysosome (pH 5) as well as the stomach (less than pH 4). Salmonellae possess an inducible acid defense system in which the intracellular pH is maintained at one level even while the extracellular pH is decreasing.

Gastroenteritis

Following oral ingestion the bacilli enter the intestinal tract. The bacilli invade the intestinal epithelium by first interacting with microvilli and disrupting the brush border (see Fig. 14-8). On entering the cells the bacteria are enclosed in a membrane-bound vacuole, the phagosome. The bacilli survive and multiply in the phagosome. This internalization process is similar to that for *Shigella* (see *Shigella* for details) and is referred to as receptor-mediated endocytosis. Survival in the phagosome is directly related to the ability of salmonella to inhibit the fusion of lysosome with phagosome. Salmonellae use the epithelium as a route to gain access to the lamina propria where they multiply. The more invasive bacilli can enter mesenteric lymph nodes and finally the bloodstream. Lymphatic barriers (for example, the macrophages in lymph nodes) can prevent the less virulent serotypes from invading the bloodstream, thus keeping the infection intestinal.

Symptoms of gastroenteritis appear four to five days after ingestion of contaminated food or water. Diarrhea is not dependent on the production of an enterotoxin. Instead, diarrhea production is believed to be due to the induction of adenyl cyclase and formation of adenosine 3′,5′-cyclic monophosphate (cAMP). Increased cAMP formation results in hypersecretion of fluid (see Chapter 14).

Diarrhea lasts three to five days and is accompanied by fever and abdominal pain. During acute gastroenteritis, 10^6 to 10^8 salmonellae per gram of feces may be present.

Enteric Fever (Typhoid, Paratyphoid, and Nontyphoidal Fevers)

The ingested bacilli that cause enteric fever are more invasive than those that cause only gastroenteritis. Invasive bacilli are capable of resisting host defenses in lymph nodes and can multiply in the macrophage (Plate 7). Infected macrophages enter the bloodstream and can infect any tissue of the body, including the intestine. The reinfection of lymph tissue in the intestine provides an avenue for shedding of bacilli in the stool. Invasive salmonellae routinely infect the gallbladder, where they multiply and also provide a focal point for shedding of bacilli into the intestinal tract.

The major species or serotypes that cause enteric fevers are *S. typhi* (typhoid fever), *S. paratyphi A* and *S. paratyphi B* (paratyphoid fever), and *S. schottmuelleri* (nontyphoidal enteric fever). The incubation period for enteric fever is approximately one to two weeks. During the first week there is a gradual increase in fever accompanied by anorexia and general headaches and pains. A continual headache is the principal symptom, and more than 60 percent of patients demonstrate a nonproductive cough. During the second week, the fever remains as high as 104 F, and there are symptoms of diarrhea and abdominal discomfort and general weakness. During this period, which corresponds to the chronic bacteremic stage, rose-colored spots may appear on the abdomen. If no complications occur, the disease begins to terminate during the third week. Complications include abscess formation, intestinal perforation (Fig. 21-3), pneumonia, and thrombophlebitis. The death rate for typhoid fever varies from 2 to 10 percent. Paratyphoid fever is similar to typhoid fever but is of shorter duration and milder.

FIGURE 21-3
Typhoid ulceration of ileum. Ulcerations appear as small craters. (Courtesy of Air Force Institute of Pathology, AFIP 2803.)

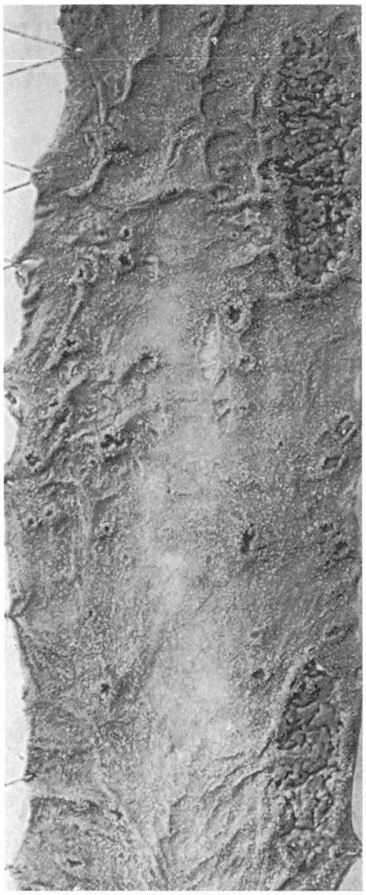

The virulence factors of *S. typhi* and other invasive salmonellae are still a subject of controversy. Adherence is associated with invasion but does not require motility or carriage of pili by the infecting organism. Carriage of these traits, however, does enhance invasion. One of the K antigens of salmonella is called the **Vi antigen.** The Vi antigen is believed to be important in the pathogenesis and immunity to typhoid fever. The Vi antigen appears to act as a protective factor for the O antigen by preventing phagocytosis and the bactericidal action of serum.

The manifestations of typhoid fever are believed to be a result of molecules released from infected macrophages. These molecules include arachidonic acid metabolite and free oxygen radicals. The endotoxin of *S. typhi* appears to contribute to the pathogenesis of typhoid fever by enhancing local inflammatory responses at the tissue site of *S. typhi* multiplication.

Bacteremia

Salmonellae may be transiently present in the bloodstream or may persist for long periods. The more invasive species such as *S. typhimurium*, *S. dublin*, and *S. choleraesuis* are usually involved in bacteremia. The most serious consequence of bacteremia is metastatic infection, which may involve the bones and joints, the cardiovascular system, and the meninges. Fever and chills are the principal symptoms associated with bacteremia.

Carrier State

Shedding of salmonellae normally occurs five to six months after the development of an acute infection. Carriers, however, are classified as those who shed bacilli for one year after infection. The factors that appear to determine whether the carrier state will develop are as follows:

1. The species or serotype involved. *S. typhi*, *S. paratyphi A*, and *S. paratyphi B* are frequently associated with the carrier state.
2. The dose of salmonellae. A dose of salmonellae too small to cause overt disease may induce the carrier state.
3. Disorders of the biliary tract. Diseases of the biliary tract are asymptomatic and severe as sources for the shedding of bacilli.

Chronic carriers are most often elderly people (see Under the Microscope 18).

UNDER THE MICROSCOPE 18

Typhoid Mary

Mary Mallon was a cook in a family for 3 years, and in 1901 she developed typhoid fever. About the same time a visitor to the family had the disease. One month later the laundress in this family was taken ill.

In 1902, Mary obtained a new place, and 2 weeks after her arrival the laundress was taken ill with typhoid fever. In a week, a second case developed, and soon seven members of the household were sick.

In 1904, Mary went to a home on Long Island. There were four in the family, besides seven servants. Within 3 weeks after her arrival, four servants were attacked.

In 1906, Mary went to another family, and 6 of the 11 members of this family were attacked with typhoid between August 27 and September 3. At this time, the cook was first suspected. She entered another family on September 21, and on October 5 the laundress developed typhoid fever.

In 1907, she entered a home in New York City and 2 months after her arrival 2 cases developed, one of which proved fatal. During these 5 years, "Typhoid Mary" is known to have been the cause of 26 cases of typhoid fever.

She was virtually imprisoned by the New York Department of Health in a hospital from March 19, 1907. Cultures taken every few days showed bacilli now and then for 3 years. Sometimes the stools contained enormous numbers of typhoid bacilli and again for days none could be found.

Typhoid Mary then escaped from observation until 1914. In October of that year, she was engaged as cook in the Sloane Hospital for Women in New York. In January and February of 1915, an outbreak of typhoid occurred, principally among the doctors, nurses, and help of the institution, involving 25 cases. The cook was suspected but she left the premises on a few hours' leave, and did not return or leave her address. She was, however, located by the health department under an assumed name, and an investigation established her identity as the famous Typhoid Mary.

A subsequent study of her career showed that she had infected still other individuals beyond those already mentioned, and that she may have given rise to the well-known waterborne outbreak of typhoid in Ithaca, New York, in 1903, involving over 1300 cases. The fact is that a person by the name of Mary Mallon had been employed as a cook in the vicinity of the place where the first case appeared, and from which contamination of the water supply occurred.

From M. J. Rosenau, *Preventive Medicine and Hygiene,* 6th ed. New York: Appleton, 1935.

EPIDEMIOLOGY

Approximately 40,000 cases of salmonellosis are reported each year to the Centers for Disease Control and fewer than 500 are typhoid fever. The actual incidence of infection is believed to be near 1 million cases per year. The estimated incidence of typhoid fever throughout the world, excluding China, is 12.5 million cases per year. The highest incidence of infection is among the very young and elderly. Mortality is highest in children less than 1 year old. The increased susceptibility of this age group may be due to the fact that children less than 2 months old produce little hydrochloric acid, a natural barrier to many microorganisms. Patients who have had a gastrectomy or who are taking antacids are also more susceptible to infection by low numbers of ingested salmonellae.

S. typhi, S. paratyphi A, and *S. paratyphi B,* unlike most other *Salmonella* species, are harbored by humans and not animals. Transmission of these species is from person to person via fecally contaminated food or water. Contamination of food occurs only by secondary contamination during the processing or handling of meat and animal products by human carriers. Often, asymptomatic carriers of *S. typhi* have caused large epidemics. The death rate for typhoid fever in the United States is less than 1 percent. In developing countries both the number of cases and the death rate are high.

Nontyphoidal *Salmonella* species can be found in a wide variety of animal species, which serve as a common source of infection to humans. The main sources are turkeys, chickens, eggs and egg products, swine, and other domestic animals. Since 1979 most of the outbreaks caused by *S. enteritidis* have been associated with Grade A shell eggs. Because of the mass processing of meats and other animal-related products used for human consumption, the number of cases of salmonellosis is rising. *S. typhimurium* is the most frequently reported serotype, followed by *S. enteritidis* (Fig. 21-4).

Nontyphoidal *Salmonella* infections are spread from animal to animal and then to humans either directly or indirectly via animal-processing procedures. Person-to-per-

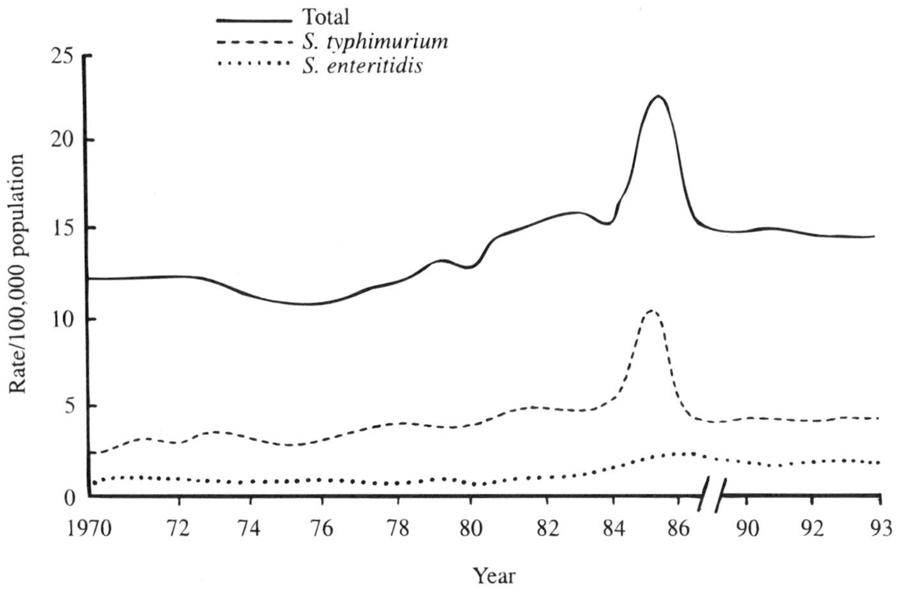

FIGURE 21-4
Salmonella isolation rates by total, and by serotypes *S. typhimurium* and *S. enteritidis* and year, United States, 1970 to 1993. (Courtesy of Centers for Disease Control, Atlanta, GA.)

son transfer seems to be less important than transfer by contaminated foodstuffs. The majority of cases of salmonellosis occur when large groups of people are served dishes that were prepared 24 to 48 hours before and were perhaps left standing for several hours at room temperature.

Cross contamination as well as foodborne spread occur in hospitals and institutions. Cross contamination is mediated by vehicles such as hands of health care workers, wash basins, and ward dust. Morbidity and mortality are highest in these institutions. Most epidemics begin by ingestion of contaminated foodstuffs or medical products of animal origin—pancreatin, vitamins, and gelatin. From these index patients, the organisms can be spread by contact between persons. Nursery epidemics are often related to the presence of an infant "shedder" of the salmonellae.

LABORATORY DIAGNOSIS

Diagnosis of *Salmonella* infection rests on the isolation and identification of the suspected species from feces (gastroenteritis), urine (typhoid fever), blood (typhoid fever), or contaminated food.

Suspected samples, for example, stool specimens, are plated on MacConkey agar and Hektoen enteric agar. Specimens are also introduced into selenite broth and gram-negative broth. The broths can be subcultured on Hektoen enteric agar and MacConkey agar. Suspected colonies on the primary agar or subculture plates can be screened for *Salmonella* species by applying lysis by the O1 *Salmonella* bacteriophage. Serological tests of O, H, or Vi antigens and biochemical tests can also be used.

The O (somatic) antigen has been assigned Arabic numbers from 1 to 67. For convenience, the salmonellae have been placed into serogroups A through Z, each group containing specific O antigens. For example, one serotype in group A might contain O antigens 1, 4, 12, and 27. For identification of the most important salmonellae, a commercial grouping serum is available. Some groups contain common antigens, and single-factor antiserum is available for more specific identification. For example, somatic antigen O:2 is characteristic of *S. paratyphi A*. The Vi antigen surrounds *S. typhi* and can prevent agglutination of O antigens. When negative reactions occur with O grouping sera, the Vi antiserum should be applied.

Serotype identification is based on the characteristics of the H or flagellar antigens. Most salmonellae have two different H antigens. The H antigens are designated by a lowercase letter: a, b, c, and so on. The two different H antigens occur in phases and can be influenced by the age and composition of the culture medium. Speciation of salmonellae requires identification of both phases. Serotyping is usually provided only by special reference laboratories.

TREATMENT

The traditional drugs for treatment of typhoid fever or bacteremia are chloramphenicol, ampicillin, amoxicillin, and trimethoprim-sulfamethoxazole. Trimethoprim-sulfamethoxazole is often administered when the infecting microorganism is resistant to chloramphenicol. There is increasing resistance to all of the mentioned drugs. Newer drugs that were being used include third-generation cephalosporins, cefoperazone, ceftriaxone, and cefotaxime. The 4-fluoroquinolones such as ciprofloxacin are an important addition to therapy. They can be used orally and are effective against multiply-resistant *Salmonella* species. The fluoroquinolones, however, are toxic to bone development and should not be used on children under 18 years old.

Antimicrobial therapy for uncomplicated gastroenteritis is not recommended. Since the disease is self-limiting, there are lack of benefit from antibiotics, prolongation of shedding of the organism, and potential to promote spread of resistant microorganisms.

Chronic carriers (excretion of organisms for more than one year) are treated with ampicillin combined with probenecid. Treatment of convalescent carriers (up to four weeks) with new or older antimicrobials has not been particularly effective.

Immunocompromised patients such as (1) those with acquired immunodeficiency syndrome (AIDS), (2) those on hemodialysis, and (3) renal transplant patients have an increased susceptibility to infection by *Salmonella*. Most of the traditional drugs produce serious side effects in this group of patients. Quinolones, however, are effective agents.

PREVENTION AND CONTROL

Salmonella infections can be controlled or at least reduced by (1) proper sanitation, with special emphasis on sewage disposal and maintenance of unpolluted water supplies; (2) supervision of the preparation of products by the food industries; (3) proper refrigeration of foods, particularly poultry and related products; and (4) detection of asymptomatic carriers and their removal from occupations involved in the handling of food or care of the hospitalized until the carriers are adequately treated.

S. typhi vaccines are seldom administered in the United States; however, they are employed for military personnel and those traveling to areas where typhoid is endemic. In 1990 an oral vaccine was released. Clinical trials indicated that a three- or four-dose regimen provides protection for up to three years for up to 96 percent of the vaccine recipients. A parenteral vaccine utilizing purified Vi antigen is also effective but has not been released in the United States. Live attenuated *Salmonella* species are also being used as vaccine vectors (see Under the Microscope 19).

Shigella

Shigella species are the cause of gastrointestinal disease called **bacillary dysentery.** There are four species of *Shigella: S. dysenteriae, S. flexneri, S. boydii,* and *S. sonnei.* With few exceptions the shigellae are harbored by humans and

UNDER THE MICROSCOPE 19

Salmonella as Vaccine Vectors

If you ever wondered why the study of microbial genetics is so important, you only have to consider some recent experiments on the use of *Salmonella* as carriers of foreign antigens.

Salmonella is one among several human pathogens that infect mucosal surfaces. Respiratory and intestinal infections are the single most important causes of mortality throughout the world. One of the ways to protect against intestinal pathogens, for example, is to stimulate the formation of special mucosal secretory IgA antibodies. Oral immunization involving the gut mucosa can stimulate production of secretory antibodies on gut as well as other mucosal surfaces.

Scientists have genetically altered *Salmonella* species to an avirulent status. Because we have learned so much about virulence traits and their position on the genome, it has been possible to produce strains that do not express the virulence traits. In addition, the strains are genetically stable and will not revert back to a virulent form. After the avirulent strains are developed, genes for various heterologous antigens from other pathogenic organisms can be incorporated into the *Salmonella* genome. For example, epitopes from the following antigens have been tested in this system: cholera toxin subunit B, hepatitis B surface protein, human immunodeficiency virus (HIV) surface glycoprotein, and *Streptococcus pyogenes* M protein. Testing in animals has shown that there is a significant induction of serum antibodies against the epitopes after immunization with the recombinant *Salmonella* strains. When mutant vaccine enters the intestine, the bacteria deliver antigen to the B and T lymphocytes present in gut-associated lymphoid tissue (GALT). Primed B cells migrate to the mesenteric lymph nodes, where they differentiate and enter the circulation via the thoracic duct. These cells eventually populate the gut and other mucosal tissue and differentiate into plasma cells. The end result is the production of serum and mucosal antibodies against *Salmonella* as well as the transported foreign antigen.

It is hoped that someday immunization using a single carrier with multiple heterologous antigens can provide immunity against several pathogens. A number of foreign genes also have been cloned in the vaccinia virus. The vaccinia virus as a vaccine vector presents problems that are discussed in Chapter 12.

transferred by the fecal-oral route. Shigellae are also important historically because they were the first recognized microorganisms isolated from humans that carried multiple antibiotic resistance markers on plasmids.

PATHOGENESIS

Like the salmonellae, the shigellae are transferred from person to person by contaminated food, water, or fomites. The incubation period for shigellosis is 36 to 72 hours. As few as 200 ingested *Shigella* organisms are enough to initiate infection. Shigellae possess virulence determinants like those of *E. coli* (see Under the Microscope 20). The shigellae invade the intestinal epithelium like the invasive *Salmonella* species (see *Salmonella* Species and Fig. 14-8 for discussion of the invasion process). Shigellae remain free in the cytoplasm of epithelial cells and spread laterally to invade adjacent cells. Inflammation in the lamina propria results in abscess formation and ulceration. Up to 10^{10} organisms can be found per gram of stool during disease. Abdominal cramps, fever, and watery diarrhea occur early in the disease. Dysentery occurs during the ulceration process, with high concentrations of neutrophils in the stools.

The symptoms of shigellosis are mild or severe depending on the species causing infection. The most severe forms of shigellosis are caused by *S. dysenteriae* type 1, also called the **Shiga bacillus.** *S. dysenteriae* produces a toxin called the **Shiga toxin.** The Shiga toxin may contribute to the necrotic lesions of the colon (cytotoxic activity) and probably the diarrhea associated with disease (enterotoxic activity). Shiga toxin belongs to the group of toxins (cholera, diphtheria, and pertussis, for example) that possess A and B subunits (see Chapter 14 for discussion of toxins). When released during infection, the Shiga toxin is taken up by mammalian cells (intestinal microvilli, for example). This activity leads to cell death. The primary site of Shiga toxin action is the ribosomal binding site for aminoacyl transfer RNA (tRNA), that is, the 60S ribosomal unit. *Shigella* species other than *S. dysenteriae* produce a milder toxin referred to as **Shiga-like.** The Shiga-like toxin is similar in chemistry and action to toxins produced by *E. coli*, *Campylobacter* species, and others.

EPIDEMIOLOGY

The number of cases of shigellosis reported in the United States averages between 20,000 and 30,000 per year. *S. sonnei* accounts for nearly 80 percent of all *Shigella* isolates while *S. dysenteriae* accounts for approximately 1 percent. The highest rates of shigellosis are in the western states and among children from 1 to 5 years old (Fig. 21-5).

Epidemics of shigellosis occur in crowded communities where human carriers of *Shigella* exist. *Shigella* can be spread by flies, fingers, food, or feces. Many cases of shigellosis are associated with day-care centers, prisons, and institutions for the mentally retarded. Military field groups and travelers to countries with unsanitary conditions are also likely victims.

UNDER THE MICROSCOPE 20

Shigella and the Genetics of Virulence

One of the important discoveries in the past 10 years has been the discovery of the pathogenic mechanisms of shigellosis and the discovery of the *Shigella* invasion plasmid. The virulence of *Shigella* species is associated with chromosomal as well as plasmid-associated genes. The products of these genes directly affect the ability of shigella to invade and retain viability in host tissue.

Chromosomal genes associated with virulence code for products such as aerobactin, superoxide dismutase, and somatic antigens. They affect the ability of shigellae to survive in intestinal tissue. Aerobactin is a siderophore that increases the utilization of iron by the bacterial cell (see Chapter 14). Superoxide dismutase inactivates superoxide radicals produced by the respiratory burst in phagocytes (see Chapter 14). The somatic antigen or lipopolysaccharide of shigellae affects the ability of shigellae to interact with host cells. Chromosomal loci also code for the synthesis of Shiga toxin, which causes damage in the colonic epithelium.

Invasive shigellae possess a **virulence plasmid** whose determinants are primarily associated with invasion of the host cell and intercellular spread. Genetic loci on the plasmid control the synthesis of invasion antigens, which are inserted into the outer membrane. These plasmid genes are believed to have been acquired from invasive *Escherichia coli* strains during evolution. Certain shigellae plasmid virulence genes are remarkably similar to virulence genes in *E. coli*. It should be no surprise that some virulence-associated chromosomal genes in *E. coli* have counterparts in shigellae, for example, the aerobactin gene. In addition, enterohemorrhagic *E. coli* (EHEC) possesses a Shiga-like toxin that is identical to the Shiga toxin of *S. dysenteriae*. What may even be more interesting is that the hemolytic-uremic syndrome associated with EHEC has also been implicated with some Shiga toxin–producing *S. dysenteriae* in areas outside the United States.

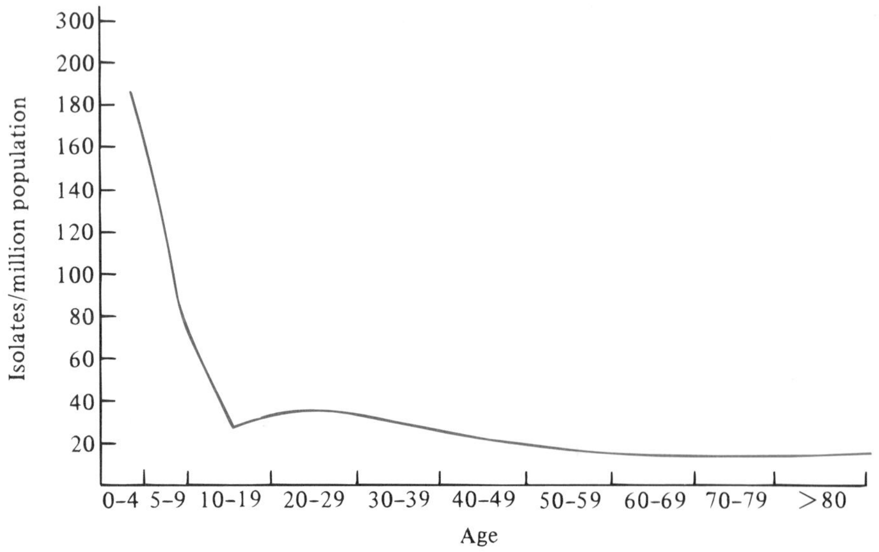

FIGURE 21-5
Rate of reported isolates of *Shigella* by age. (Courtesy of Centers for Disease Control, Atlanta, GA.)

LABORATORY DIAGNOSIS

As a presumptive test for shigellosis, some clinicians examine fecal specimens for the presence of sheets of neutrophils. Confirmatory tests are carried out by plating the specimen on various selective or differential media. Isolated species are then subjected to specific biochemical tests. Species that are nonmotile, do not ferment lactose, produce no gas from carbohydrate fermentation, and fail to produce hydrogen sulfide are possibly *Shigella.* Three biochemical tests are helpful in separating species of *Shigella* (Table 21-5), but serological testing is needed for confirmation. There are four species: Group A *(S. dysenteriae),* Group B *(S. flexneri),* Group C *(S. boydii),* and Group D *(S. sonnei).* Latex agglutination based on agglutination of antibody-coated latex particles in the presence of homologous antigen is available. Agglutination reactions plus biochemical reactions provide species identification.

Several of the "invasive plasmids" in *Shigella* organisms have recently been cloned and used as DNA probes to detect virulence genes in clinical specimens.

TABLE 21-5
Biochemical Tests Used to Differentiate Species of *Shigella*

	Response of			
Test	*S. dysenteriae*	*S. flexneri*	*S. boydii*	*S. sonnei*
Mannitol fermentation	–	+	+	+
ONPG	V	–	V	+
Ornithine decarboxylase	–	–	–	+

– = 9 percent of strains are positive; V = 10 to 89 percent of strains are positive; + = 90 percent of strains are positive; ONPG = ortho-nitrophenyl-beta-D-galactopyranoside.

TREATMENT

Most cases of shigellosis are mild and do not require antibiotics. Antibiotics can shorten the duration of the diarrhea and eliminate the bacillus from the stool. Thus, possible spread to others in the community can be prevented. Patients who experience dehydration should have oral fluid and electrolyte replacement. Oral rehydration, however, is ineffective in changing the course of the disease.

Shigellosis caused by *S. dysenteriae* only should warrant antibiotic administration. The first-choice antibiotic is trimethoprim-sulfamethoxazole or ampicillin. If there is resistance to these drugs, nalidixic acid is the choice for treatment. Newer quinolones may also be used but only for those over 18 years old.

PREVENTION AND CONTROL

Improving sanitation and hygienic practices is the most important factor in the control of shigellosis. Because of overcrowding and sometimes poor hygienic practices or procedures, custodial institutions are a major reservoir of disease. Control measures in institutions should include isolation of the infected patient, restriction of infected personnel from handling food or working with patients, and in-service training for all personnel.

An oral vaccine is available and has been successful in reducing epidemics in custodial institutions. Protective immunity is serotype-dependent.

Yersinia

Diseases caused by *Yersinia* organisms are found primarily among the animal population. In general, humans are only accidental hosts for infection. The genus *Yersinia* has three important pathogenic species: *Y. pestis, Y. pseudotuberculosis,* and *Y. enterocolitica. Y. pestis* is the etiological agent of **bubonic plague** (black death) in humans. *Y. pseudotuberculosis* causes epizootic disease in animals and is a minor gastrointestinal pathogen in humans. *Y. enterocolitica* is recognized as an important agent of gastrointestinal illness in humans.

YERSINIA PESTIS

In the fourteenth century, bubonic plague was responsible for the deaths of more than 25 percent of the population of Europe. The most recent pandemic occurred in Asia in 1904, when more than a million people succumbed. Today the disease is a rarity.

The organism causing plague is harbored by rodents and transmitted to humans by insect vectors such as the rat flea. Infection can also occur by direct contact with infected animal tissue. The widespread use of insecticides and other control measures have controlled the vectors responsible for transmission.

The plague bacillus is a gram-negative, nonmotile, facultative anaerobe that possesses bipolar granules. It produces a capsule in animal tissue. The organism grows optimally on blood agar or media supplemented with blood. Optimal growth temperatures are between 27 and 30 C.

Pathogenesis

The rat flea picks up the bacillus by biting an infected rodent. Bacilli that enter the host, after the bite of the infected flea, lack a protective capsule. From the site of the flea bite, bacilli migrate to regional lymph nodes (femoral and inguinal, for example), causing their enlargement. The enlarged nodes are called **buboes,** hence, the term **bubonic plague.** The bacilli are phagocytosed by mononuclear cells and then acquire antiphagocytic factors. These antiphagocytic factors include the capsule as well as antigens **V** and **W.** The bacilli proliferate freely in the mononuclear cells. If proliferating bacilli in the lymph nodes enter the circulation **(septicemic plague),** they can infect several different organs. On rare occasions the bacilli infect the lungs **(pneumonic plague),** producing massive hemorrhages. From the lungs bacilli can enter the bloodstream. Toxemia caused by the LPS endotoxin of *Y. pestis* is the principal cause of death.

The incubation period for bubonic plague is two to six days. Fever and vomiting are frequent symptoms of infection. Inguinal and femoral nodes are enlarged in about 50 percent of patients. Axillary and cervical nodes are less frequently involved.

The incubation period for pneumonic plague (acquired by inhalation of *Y. pestis* in respiratory secretions from an infected patient or animal), is one to three days. The sputum becomes mucoid and profuse and may even be bloody. Untreated pneumonic plague results in death within 36 to 48 hours.

Epidemiology

Plague is primarily a disease of rodents. It is transmitted from animal to animal or animal to humans by infected fleas (Fig. 21-6). Plague is found in Southeast Asia, Africa, and South America where rats are the primary reservoir, and is a widely spread zoonosis in the western United States. The animal vectors most commonly implicated in the United States are squirrels, chipmunks, deer mice, wood rats, and prairie dogs. Human disease may result from direct exposure to infected rodents, rabbits, or carnivores as well as the bite of an infected flea. Plague among rodents is called **sylvatic plague.** Plague transmitted from person to person is called **demic plague.** Pneumonic plague is contracted from respiratory secretions of persons or animals with plague pneumonia.

Laboratory Diagnosis

Depending on the nature of the plague, blood cultures, sputum samples, or aspirates of buboes should be examined for typical bacilli. Caution should be exhibited in handling specimens in the laboratory. The bacilli grow rapidly both aerobically and anaerobically, especially in the presence of blood or other tissue fluids. Bacilli can be identified by (1) staining with Wayson's technique (methylene blue plus basic fuchsin) to demonstrate bipolar staining (Fig. 21-7), (2) the fluorescent antibody technique using *Y. pestis* antiserum, and (3) biochemical reactions.

Treatment

Because of the severity of the disease, rapid treatment is required even before final laboratory diagnosis. Streptomycin plus tetracycline or chloramphenicol is considered the primary therapy. Trimethoprim-sulfamethoxazole is also an effective drug.

Prevention and Control

It is neither possible nor desirable to eliminate the rodent population. The major avenue of control is directed at eliminating or reducing the flea population. Fumigation of ships traveling to and from various ports has proved effective in controlling the transmission of plague. In the United States, when epidemics occur among the wild rodent population, bait stations are set up in certain tracts of land, particularly wooded areas. These stations contain rodent attractants as well as insecticides such as permethrin, which is lethal to fleas.

Vaccines have had limited success. Dead, whole-organism plague vaccines are still believed to be the most useful for human vaccination. A formalin-killed vaccine is being used for people working in areas where plague is endemic. Vaccination is recommended for laboratory personnel who are working with *Y. pestis* organisms resistant to antimicrobials, persons engaged in aerosol experiments with *Y. pestis,* and persons working in areas with enzootic

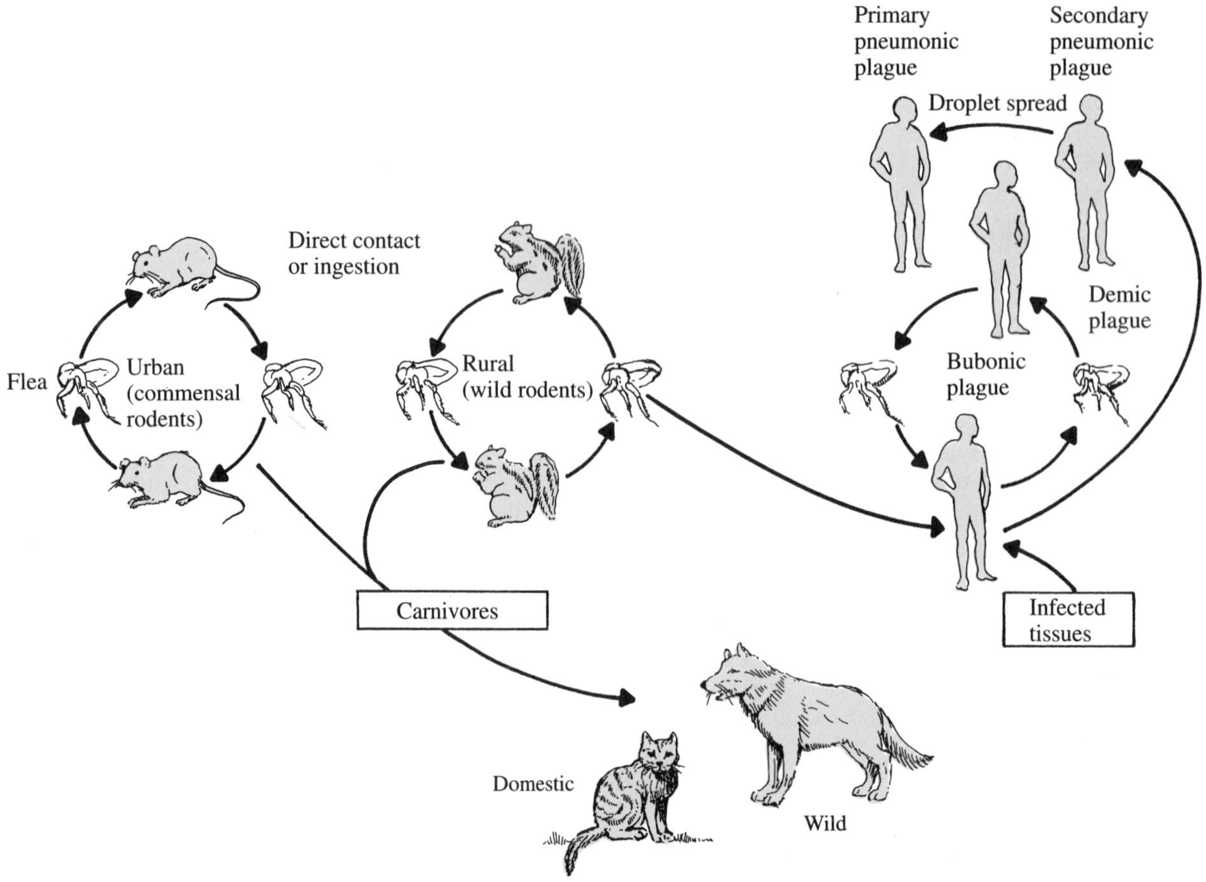

FIGURE 21-6
Epidemiology of infection by *Yersinia pestis.* (Adapted from J. Poland. In P. D. Hoeprich, ed., *Infectious Diseases.* Hagerstown, MD: Harper & Row, 1977.)

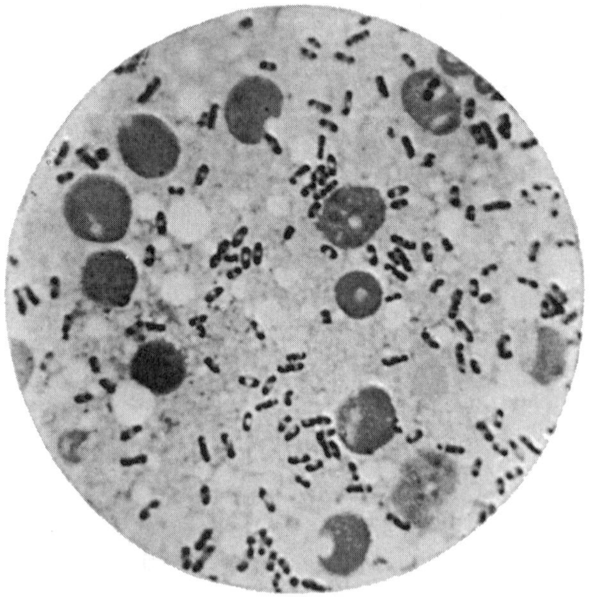

FIGURE 21-7
Smear prepared from lymph gland for demonstration of *Y. pestis.* Note the bipolar staining. (From R. R. Gillies and T. C. Dodds, *Bacteriology Illustrated.* London: Churchill Livingstone, 1976.)

plague. Vaccination should also be considered for laboratory personnel working with plague-infected rodents and those whose occupation or residence brings them into continual contact with wild rodents or rabbits in enzootic areas.

YERSINIA ENTEROCOLITICA AND *Y. PSEUDOTUBERCULOSIS*

Diseases caused by *Yersinia* species other than *Y. pestis* are called **yersinoses.** Two species are associated with yersinosis, *Y. enterocolitica* and *Y. pseudotuberculosis.* Both species are found in many domestic animals. The most important of these two species is *Y. enterocolitica* and most of our discussion centers on it.

Y. enterocolitica is found more often in cool climates. Swine have been implicated as the principal reservoir of human pathogenic strains. Human disease is primarily the result of ingestion of contaminated water, milk, or milk products. Blood transfusion transmission has also been documented. The incubation period may be from 1 to 14 days. The organism may persist in the stools for up to six weeks. Only a few serotypes are associated with disease.

Two genetic loci that confer invasiveness and are necessary for virulence have been identified on the bacterial chromosome. These are the **inv** (invasion) locus of *Y. enterocolitica* and *Y. pseudotuberculosis* and the **ail** (attachment invasion locus) region of *Y. enterocolitica.* A heat-stable enterotoxin is also thought to be involved in virulence. The gene for toxin (*yst*) has been cloned and sequenced.

The manifestations of infection by *Y. enterocolitica* depend on the age and immunological status of the host. The most common clinical manifestation of disease is enterocolitis. The majority of infections occur in children and are similar to shigellosis: diarrhea, fever, abdominal pain, and vomiting. Fecal leukocytes and blood are also demonstrable. The disease is usually self-limiting but complications do occur. Complications include mesenteric lymphadenitis, which mimics appendicitis in children and young adults, as well as reactive arthritis and erythema nodosum with subcutaneous nodules on the legs. *Y. enterocolitica* sepsis was recently associated with transfusion of contaminated erythrocytes. This type of infection has a high mortality rate and has been reported from several countries.

Laboratory identification of *Y. enterocolitica* and *Y. pseudotuberculosis* is complicated because these organisms are not usually sought in the clinical laboratory. *Y. enterocolitica* will grow on routine enteric media. The organism will ferment glucose, is oxidase-negative, and is motile at 25 C and nonmotile at 37 C. Recovery is enhanced by initial incubation in the cold or at 25 C for 48 hours. Some biochemical tests can aid in separating the three major *Yersinia* species (Table 21-6).

Antibiotics are not required for gastrointestinal disease. Replacement of fluids is usually sufficient to control infection. Nongastrointestinal disease should be treated with antimicrobials. Doxycycline and trimethoprim-sulfamethoxazole are the primary drugs. Alternative agents include aminoglycosides, fluoroquinolones, and third-generation cephalosporins.

TABLE 21-6
Biochemical Tests Used in Differentiating Pathogenic *Yersinia* Species

	Response of		
Test	***Y. pestis***	***Y. enterocolitica***	***Y. pseudotuberculosis***
Melibiose fermentation	V	−	V
Ornithine decarboxylase	−	+	−
Raffinose fermentation	−	−	V
Rhamnose fermentation	−	−	V
Sucrose fermentation	−	+	−
Urease formation	−	V	+

− = 9 percent of strains are positive; V = 10 to 89 percent of strains are positive; + = 90 percent of strains are positive.
Tests are performed at 37 C and results may vary if performed at 25 C.

TABLE 21-7
Characteristics of Some Genera of Opportunistic Enteric Bacilli That Occasionally Cause Opportunistic Infections in Humans*

Genus	Clinically important species	Primary site of infection or disease	Treatment
Enterobacter	*E. aerogenes,* *E. cloacae,* *E. agglomerans*	Extraintestinal (pulmonary, bloodstream, central nervous system, etc.)	Aminoglycosides, chloramphenicol, tetracyclines
Providencia	*P. alcalifaciens,* *P. rettgeri,* *P. stuartii*	Urinary tract infections, burn wound infections	Resistant to many antimicrobials in vivo; antimicrobial susceptibility testing critical
Klebsiella	*K. pneumoniae,* *K. ozaenae,* *K. rhinoscleromatis,* *K. oxytoca*	*K. pneumoniae* important cause of septicemia in pediatric wards; pneumonia and other respiratory tract infections in compromised patients *K. ozaenae* may cause middle ear and soft tissue infections	Some aminoglycosides, tetracyclines
Proteus	*P. mirabilis,* *P. penneri,* *P. vulgaris*	Urinary tract infections	Ampicillin, cephalothin, aminoglycosides
Serratia	*S. marcescens*	Extraintestinal (urinary tract, septicemia, central nervous system)	Gentamicin, carbenicillin, kanamycin

* Not all enteric bacilli are represented in this table.

Opportunistic Enteric Bacilli

Several genera of enteric bacilli are seldom encountered in community-associated infections. Instead, these bacilli are causes of a variety of infections in the compromised host, especially those who have been hospitalized. Table 21-7 outlines the characteristics of these opportunistic bacteria.

Summary

1. The Enterobacteriaceae family contains facultative, gram-negative rods that ferment glucose, are oxidase-negative, and reduce nitrates to nitrite. They may be motile or nonmotile.

2. Enterobacteriaceae species are widely distributed on plants, in the soil, and in the intestines of humans and animals. They are associated with many types of infections, some of which are community-associated while others are opportunistic. The lipopolysaccharide of the Enterobacteriaceae is probably responsible for the effects of shock and death in patients with septicemia.

3. The characteristics of the major pathogenic genera in the family Enterobacteriaceae are described in Table 21-8.

4. The pathogenic genera of Enterobacteriaceae can be identified in the laboratory by biochemical testing. Genera such as *Escherichia*, *Shigella*, and *Salmonella* are also identified by the presence of O antigens and sometimes H and K antigens.

5. Enterobacteriaceae species are frequently resistant to many antimicrobials and susceptibility testing is required. Most species are susceptible to some type of aminoglycoside, a tetracycline, or trimethoprim-sulfamethoxazole.

TABLE 21-8
Characteristics of the Major Pathogenic Species in the Family Enterobacteriaceae

Genera	Major pathogenic species	Disease	Virulence factor	Mechanism of transmission	Treatment and prevention
Escherichia	*E. coli*	Extraintestinal; urinary tract in compromised host; neonatal meningitis Intestinal: see Table 21-4	Pili; K1 antigen, aerobactin See Table 21-4	Person to person (extraintestinal); ingestion of contaminated food or water (intestinal)	Chloramphenicol, tetracycline in extraintestinal; replacement of fluids and electrolytes in intestinal infections
Salmonella	*S. typhi, S. paratyphi A, S. paratyphi B*	Enteric fever: gastrointestinal illness followed by bacteremia; complications may occur (e.g., perforated intestine)	Vi antigen to prevent phagocytosis; endotoxin for inflammation (*S. typhi*)	Person to person via fecally contaminated food or water	Chloramphenicol, ampicillin, trimethoprim-sulfamethoxazole; surgery for perforated intestine; killed vaccine for travelers to areas endemic for typhoid
	Many serotypes other than those causing enteric fevers	Gastroenteritis: diarrhea	Enterotoxin similar to cholera toxin	Ingestion of food products contaminated by salmonella indigenous to animals	Replenishment of fluids and electrolytes
Shigella	*S. dysenteriae* type 1, *S. sonnei, S. flexneri, S. sonnei*	Bacillary dysentery: *S. dysenteriae* type 1 produces most severe symptoms	Shiga toxin (*S. dysenteriae*); Shiga-like toxin for other species	Ingestion of fecally contaminated food or water	Replenishment of fluids and electrolytes; trimethoprim-sulfamethoxazole, ampicillin
Yersinia	*Y. pestis*	Bubonic plague: infection of lymph tissue Pneumonic plague: infection of lung	Capsule, W and V antigens	Bite of infected flea (bubonic plague); contact with respiratory secretions or via bacteremia (pneumonic plague)	Streptomycin, chloramphenicol, trimethoprim-sulfamethoxazole; killed vaccine in areas endemic for disease
	Y. enterocolitica, Y. pseudotuberculosis	Gastroenteritis: diarrhea; sometimes complicated by arthritis and erythema nodosum	Invasion loci products; enterotoxin	Ingestion of contaminated food or water; transfusion of contaminated red blood cells	Replenishment of fluids and electrolytes; doxycycline, trimethoprim-sulfamethoxazole

Questions for Study

1. What are the virulence factors for *Salmonella typhi, Shigella dysenteriae,* enterohemorrhagic *Escherichia coli,* and *Yersinia pestis?*
2. An individual is given an attenuated oral vaccine. Describe what host or microbial factors might interfere with the immunogenic potential of the vaccine. Provide a flow diagram showing that you understand the mechanism of antibody production in the intestinal mucosa as well as other mucosal surfaces when the vaccine enters the intestinal tract.
3. You have obtained a stool specimen from a patient who recently returned from Pakistan and has gastroenteritis and a high fever. You suspect the patient has typhoid fever. Using a flow chart, describe what laboratory procedures you would use to confirm your suspicion.
4. Provide explanation(s) as to why some of the enteric bacilli appear to have similar virulence factors.
5. If the lipopolysaccharide of the enteric bacilli is responsible for some of the pathological effects of infection, why aren't all strains virulent?
6. Children who are diagnosed with salmonellosis are often refused admittance back to day-care centers for several weeks after treatment. Why?
7. Of what value is it to identify the genes associated with virulence in microorganisms such as the enteric bacilli?

CHAPTER

22

Pseudomonas and Related Organisms

OBJECTIVES

To describe the virulence factors associated with *Pseudomonas* infections

To explain the techniques used to identify strains of *Pseudomonas aeruginosa*

To describe the relationship between *P. aeruginosa* and cystic fibrosis

To list the drugs most effective in the treatment of *P. aeruginosa* infections and to explain why the organism is so resistant to most antimicrobials

To list some *Pseudomonas* species other than *P. aeruginosa* that are associated with human infection

OUTLINE

PSEUDOMONAS AERUGINOSA
- General Characteristics
- Pathogenesis and Epidemiology
  - In Cystic Fibrosis
  - In Other Conditions
- Virulence Traits
  - Exotoxin A
  - Elastase
  - Mucoid Exopolysaccharide (Alginate)
  - Phospholipase
- Laboratory Diagnosis
- Treatment and Prevention

OTHER *PSEUDOMONAS* SPECIES AND RELATED BACILLI

The genus *Pseudomonas* belongs to a group of bacteria that are characterized as gram-negative, nonfermentative, aerobic bacilli. Members of this group, or pseudomonads, are opportunistic pathogens that cause disease in compromised patients. Other opportunistic bacilli included with the pseudomonads are *Alcaligenes, Achromobacter, Acinetobacter, Moraxella, Flavobacterium, Eikenella,* and *Agrobacterium* species.

Pseudomonads are known for their ability to catabolize a wide variety of carbon sources. They can be found in soil, water, and related habitats. The most important pathogen in this group is *Pseudomonas aeruginosa.*

Pseudomonas aeruginosa

GENERAL CHARACTERISTICS

P. aeruginosa are rod-shaped organisms varying in length from 2 to 4 μm. Most strains are motile and produce a slime layer. The success of *P. aeruginosa* in colonizing and multiplying in a wide variety of environments is due to its biphasic growth patterns. Sometimes the organism exists as a highly motile cell capable of swimming from site to site. Other times the organism produces a slimy layer that enables it to multiply in the form of an adherent microcolony or biofilm (see Under the Microscope 10 in Chapter 14).

Many strains of *P. aeruginosa* produce yellowish water-soluble fluorescent pigments called **pyoverdins.** Only *P. aeruginosa* produces the nonfluorescent water-soluble pigment called **pyocyanin.** Strains that produce pyocyanin and pyoverdin frequently impart a greenish color to culture media. Cultures of *P. aeruginosa* or wounds infected by this organism give off a distinctive grape-like odor due to one of their pigments, **2-aminoacetophenone.**

PATHOGENESIS AND EPIDEMIOLOGY

P. aeruginosa is unable to cross the defense barriers of the healthy individual. However, this organism can cause life-threatening infections in immunocompromised hosts. Burn patients, patients with cystic fibrosis, and patients with respiratory disease are the most likely to be threatened by *P. aeruginosa.*

In Cystic Fibrosis

Cystic fibrosis is a lethal genetic disease that causes abnormal electrolyte transport and mucous secretion from exocrine glands and secretory epithelia. The disease is characterized by chronic pulmonary manifestations with a persistent cough. The secretion of a hyperviscous mucus in the cystic fibrosis–affected lung is believed to increase the incidence of infection by *Staphylococcus aureus, Hemophilus influenzae,* and *P. aeruginosa. P. aeruginosa* is the most highly resistant of the three species to antimicrobial therapy. Consequently, *P. aeruginosa* eventually dominates the microbial flora within the cystic fibrosis–affected lung.

One of the unique characteristics of patients with cystic fibrosis is the recovery of an unusual morphotype of *P. aeruginosa.* This morphotype has been designated **"mucoid."** The mucoid morphotype is rarely seen in patients who do not have cystic fibrosis. Early in the disease, nonmucoid types infect the lung, but as the disease progresses, the mucoid morphotype dominates the microbial flora. The mucoid morphotype is the result of production of large amounts of a polysaccharide called **alginate.** Alginate appears to provide the organism with a selective advantage in the lung by producing a biofilm. The alginate layer appears to prevent antibody coating and thus blocks opsonic phagocytosis. In addition, the alginate layer also appears to act as a barrier against penetration by various antibiotics.

In Other Conditions

Pseudomonas species, particularly *P. aeruginosa,* are the most likely to cause life-threatening infections in burn patients (Fig. 22-1). *Pseudomonas* organisms thrive in an aquatic environment. Since hydrotherapy is used routinely in the care of burn patients, *Pseudomonas* is frequently transmitted by this route. This organism is also one of the leading causes of gram-negative infections of the urinary tract and surgical wounds.

The presence of *Pseudomonas* in various watery habitats has led to infections of an unusual nature. For example, the increasing use of hot tubs and whirlpools in private residences has given rise to cutaneous (folliculitis) infec-

FIGURE 22-1
Generalized invasive *Pseudomonas* burn wound sepsis in a child. (From B. A. Pruitt et al., *Rev. Infect. Dis.* 5[Suppl. 5]:899. © 1983 University of Chicago.)

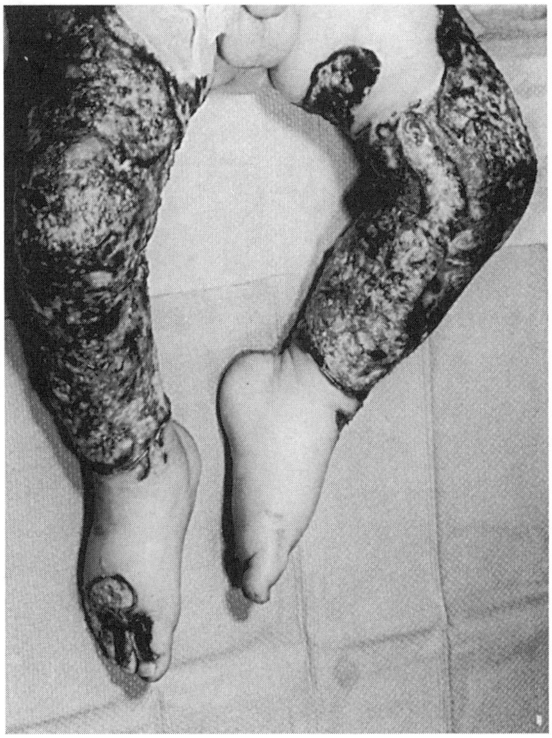

TABLE 22-1
Possible Virulence Determinants of *Pseudomonas aeruginosa*

Determinant	Biological activity
Cellular factors	
Pili	Adherence to epithelial cells
Slime polysaccharide	Adherence to substrates
Mucoid exopolysaccharide	Antiphagocytic, decreased pulmonary clearance
Lipid A	Endotoxic effects, induces protective antibodies
Extracellular factors	
Elastase	Digests proteins (elastin, collagen, IgA, IgG)
Exotoxin A	Cytotoxicity, inhibits protein synthesis
Phospholipase	Degradation of cytoplasmic membrane components

tions. However, when recreational water is maintained at pH 7.2 to 7.8 with residual chlorine, outbreaks of cutaneous infections are prevented.

P. aeruginosa infections have been observed in eyes. This organism is one of the most common pathogens associated with bacterial corneal ulcers. Corneal injury is a major predisposing factor to infection. Keratitis due to *P. aeruginosa* also has been observed in the wearers of extended-wear contact lenses.

VIRULENCE TRAITS

Pseudomonas species are well suited to colonization of the host once the primary defense barriers are no longer intact. They possess several components and elaborate several products that contribute to virulence. We discuss some of the important ones—the others are outlined in Table 22-1.

Exotoxin A

Exotoxin A is the most toxic of the extracellular products released by *P. aeruginosa*. It contains three domains: one for binding to receptors on target cells, one that helps transport the molecule across the cell membrane of target cells (Fig. 22-2), and one that is the toxic component. Once inside the cytoplasm of the target cell, the toxin becomes activated. The toxin behaves like diphtheria toxin. Exotoxin A catalyzes the transfer of the adenosine diphosphate ribosyl moiety from nicotinamide-adenine dinucleotide (NAD) to a covalent linkage with elongation factor 2 (EF-2). This results in the inhibition of protein synthesis. In animals the toxin causes respiratory failure.

Elastase

Elastase is an endopeptidase that can digest several human proteins, including elastin, collagen, fibrin, IgG, IgA, complement components, and transferrin. It is easy to see why release of elastase in host cells could cause devastating effects.

Mucoid Exopolysaccharide (Alginate)

Alginate polysaccharide produced in the lungs of cystic fibrosis patients differs from the slime polysaccharide produced by nonmucoid strains of *P. aeruginosa* (see Under the Microscope 21). The role of alginate in cystic fibrosis was discussed earlier.

Phospholipase

Phospholipase is an extracellular product that liberates phosphorylcholine from lecithin, the component of eukaryotic membranes. This enzyme is capable of causing pulmonary necrosis in laboratory animals.

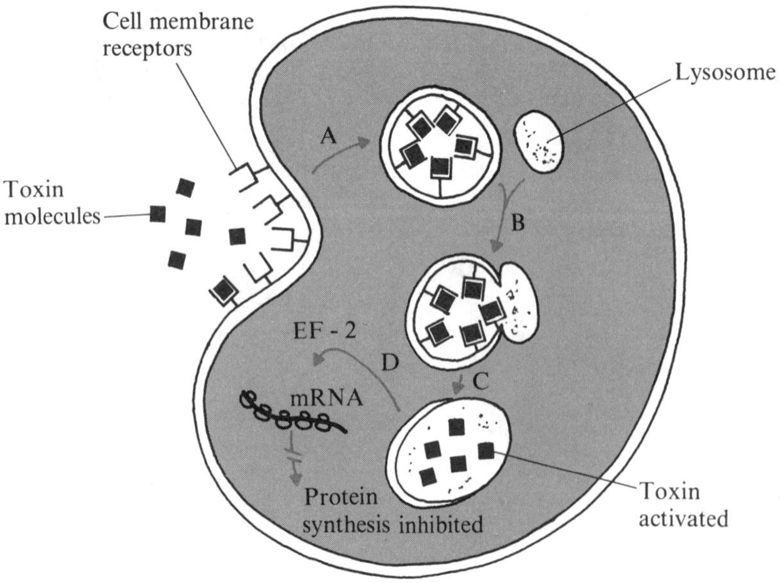

FIGURE 22-2
Mechanism of exotoxin A transport and activation in the cell. A. Toxin binds to cell receptors and is transported into the cytoplasm within a vesicle. B. Lysosome fuses with the toxin-containing vesicle, and lysosomal activity stimulates the toxin. C. Activated toxin is released into the cytoplasm where it inhibits cellular protein synthesis by interfering with elongation factor (EF-2).

UNDER THE MICROSCROPE 21

Slime Exopolysaccharide and Hospital-Associated Infections

The mucoid exopolysaccharide of *P. aeruginosa* is an important virulence factor in patients with cystic fibrosis. The slime material also appears to be indirectly involved in hospital-associated infections.

There have been three instances since 1981 of clusters of *P. aeruginosa* and *P. cepacia* infections in hospitalized patients. In each case it was suspected that povidone-iodine disinfectant solutions had been contaminated by these microorganisms. In one instance the disinfectant had been used to disinfect the tops of blood-culture bottles before inoculation while in another instance the disinfectant was used as a peritoneal catheter disinfectant. Investigators now believe that *Pseudomonas* species, which are commonly found in water, colonize water distribution pipes or filters in plants that manufacture iodine solutions. The exopolysaccharides enable *Pseudomonas* species to adhere to the surface of polyvinylchloride distribution pipes and pipes of other composition. The development of microcolonies with a slime layer could enable individual bacteria to be protected from the bactericidal action of the iodophor solution.

From *M.M.W.R.* 38(No. 8):133, 1989.

LABORATORY DIAGNOSIS

Clinical specimens from blood, burns, and other sources can be cultured on Mueller-Hinton agar. Contaminated specimens can be cultured on certain selective media such as cetrimide agar. Isolates can be examined for pyocin production (blue to blue-green pigment). Isolates should also be Gram-stained and evaluated for oxidase activity and motility. Routine culture of respiratory secretions from patients with cystic fibrosis can be made with MacConkey agar. The culture is incubated for two to three days at 35 to 37 C.

A simple identification procedure involves the use of a disk containing phenanthroline and C-390 (PC disk). The PC disks are placed on cultured Mueller-Hinton agar. Susceptibility to the disks is examined after incubation for 24 hours at 35 C. All isolates of oxidase-positive gram-negative rods, except *P. aeruginosa,* are inhibited by the PC disk. Pigment production also can be observed on the disks. Other tests that are employed for presumptive identification are outlined in Table 22-2.

TABLE 22-2
Minimal Characteristics for Identification of *Pseudomonas aeruginosa* Strains

Characteristic	Sign
Gram-negative rod	+
Motility (polar monotrichous)	+
Oxidative-fermentative glucose medium, open, acid	+
Oxidative-fermentative maltose medium, acid	−
Indophenol oxidase	+
L-lysine decarboxylase	−
L-arginine dihydrolase	+
Black butt (hydrogen sulfide) in triple sugar iron agar	−
Growth at 42 C	+

TREATMENT AND PREVENTION

P. aeruginosa is resistant to most antibiotics. In vitro antibiotic sensitivity tests should be performed before antibiotic therapy is begun. Most strains are susceptible to polymyxin B, colistin, and gentamicin, but these drugs are very toxic and must be used sparingly. Severe infections are usually treated with carbenicillin, carbenicillin plus gentamicin, or tobramycin plus azlocillin.

Antibiotics rarely eradicate *P. aeruginosa* from the lungs of cystic fibrosis patients but early treatment improves lung function and survival time.

For patients with severe burns, antibiotic therapy combined with intravenous infusions of human IgG containing antibodies to lipopolysaccharide antigens of *P. aeruginosa* significantly lowers the mortality better than when antibiotics are used alone.

Vaccines have been evaluated in burn patients. A polyvalent vaccine containing a crude whole-cell extract of *P. aeruginosa* is effective in preventing infection.

Other *Pseudomonas* Species and Related Bacilli

Several other *Pseudomonas* species as well as related bacilli occasionally cause disease in humans. These species play a role in hospital-acquired infections and are outlined in Table 22-3.

Summary

1. *Pseudomonas* is the most important member of a group of bacteria that are gram-negative, nonfermen-

TABLE 22-3
Characteristics of *Pseudomonas* Species Other Than *P. aeruginosa* and Related Bacilli

Species	Disease association	Other characteristics
Pseudomonas fluorescens	Respiratory and urinary tract, wounds, bacteremia	Produces pyoverdins but not pyocyanin, no growth at 42 C, produces lecithinase
P. putida	Same as *P. fluorescens*	Does not produce pyocyanin or lecithinase, no growth at 42 C
P. cepacia	Endocarditis, septicemia, wound infections; recurrent infection in those with chronic granulomatous disease	No growth at 42 C
P. stutzeri	Same as *P. fluorescens*	No growth at 42 C
P. maltophilia	Found normally in oral cavity; urinary tract infections; except for *P. aeruginosa* most frequently isolated *Pseudomonas* species	Growth at 42 C, lavender-green color on blood agar, only oxidase-negative *Pseudomonas* species
P. mallei	Cause of glanders, a disease of horses occasionally transmitted to humans	Nonmotile, no growth at 42 C
P. pseudomallei	Cause of melioidosis, a pneumonia that may progress to fatal septicemia, in humans	Pyocyanin and pyoverdins not produced, growth at 42 C
Acinetobacter species	Part of indigenous flora of humans; respiratory and urinary tract infections, bacteremia	Coccobacillary, confused with *Neisseria* (see Chapter 18)
Alcaligenes species	Recovered from urinary tract and blood	Oxidase-positive, asaccharolytic
Achromobacter species	Isolated from blood, spinal fluid, urine, and respiratory tract	Saccharolytic, oxidase-positive
Moraxella species	Isolated from blood, respiratory tract, and urine	Oxidase-positive, asaccharolytic
Flavobacterium species	Rarely pathogenic but occasionally cause neonatal meningitis	Nonmotile, proteolytic, prefer cool environment
Eikenella corrodens	Isolated from wounds, respiratory tract, blood, and bone	Nonmotile, asaccharolytic, produces craters in agar
Agrobacterium species	Plant pathogens, but one species, *A. radiobacter*, isolated from wounds and spinal fluid in humans	Motile, oxidase-positive

tative, aerobic to facultatively anaerobic bacilli. The most important pathogen is *P. aeruginosa*. This organism is an opportunistic species that causes infections in burn patients, patients with cystic fibrosis, and other hospitalized individuals.

2. Mucoid strains of *P. aeruginosa* produce a polysaccharide that forms a biofilm in the lungs of cystic fibrosis patients. The polysaccharide is a major contributor to persistence of the pathogen in the lungs.

3. *P. aeruginosa* inhabits watery environments and is a significant pathogen in burn patients on hydrotherapy. The organisms can also cause cutaneous lesions in those who use whirlpools and is a cause of keratitis in contact lens wearers.

4. Some of the virulence factors associated with *P. aeruginosa* include (1) exopolysaccharide, (2) exotoxin A, (3) elastase, and (4) phospholipase.

5. Laboratory identification of *P. aeruginosa* includes pyocyanin detection on agar and resistance to PC disks. Other laboratory-determined characteristics are outlined in Table 22-2.

6. Antibiotic susceptibility tests should be performed on clinical isolates. An aminoglycoside plus a penicillin derivative is a frequent treatment regimen. Antibiotic therapy combined with administration of human immunoglobulin is particularly effective. A vaccine is also available.

7. Several genera of *Pseudomonas*-related nonfermentative bacilli are important in hospital-associated infections. They are outlined in Table 22-3.

Questions for Study

1. Explain how the virulence factors of *P. aeruginosa* contribute to the pathogenesis of cystic fibrosis.
2. *Pseudomonas* species are considered to be opportunistic pathogens and not invasive ones. What does this mean?
3. What approach would you use to determine whether *Pseudomonas* species are in a sputum sample?
4. Some references discussing cystic fibrosis refer to the formation of microcolonies in the lungs. What are they talking about and how does this contribute to disease?

CHAPTER 23 Vibrionaceae

OBJECTIVES

To explain the mechanisms by which *Vibrio cholerae* can penetrate the intestinal epithelium and cause diarrhea

To describe the types of diseases associated with *Vibrio cholerae,* non-01, *V. parahaemolyticus, V. vulnificus,* and *V. alginolyticus*

To explain how gastrointestinal disease caused by species of *Vibrio* can be treated and prevented

To describe the habitat and types of diseases caused by *Aeromonas* and *Plesiomonas* species

OUTLINE

VIBRIO
- *Vibrio cholerae*
  - Pathogenesis of *Vibrio cholerae* 01
  - Pathogenesis of *Vibrio cholerae* non-01
  - Epidemiology
  - Laboratory Diagnosis
  - Treatment and Prevention
- Other Pathogenic Vibrios
  - *Vibrio parahaemolyticus*
  - *Vibrio vulnificus*
  - *Vibrio alginolyticus*

AEROMONAS

PLESIOMONAS

Vibrio

Vibrios are straight or curved rods that belong to the family Vibrionaceae. Four genera are included in this family: *Vibrio, Aeromonas, Plesiomonas,* and *Photobacterium. Photobacterium* organisms are not human pathogens. *Vibrio* species are major human pathogens.

Vibrios are gram-negative facultative anaerobes that are motile by a polar flagellum or flagella. They demonstrate both respiration and fermentation. Like the Enterobacteriaceae, vibrios do not have exacting nutritional requirements. They are found in fresh and marine waters and some are the causes of intestinal and extraintestinal disease in humans.

There are several species of *Vibrio,* the most important of which is *V. cholerae,* the etiological agent of **cholera.** Other species include *V. parahaemolyticus, V. vulnificus,* and *V. alginolyticus.*

VIBRIO CHOLERAE

V. cholerae (serotype 01, biotype *cholerae*) is the cause of the classic Asiatic cholera that devastated populations for several centuries (Fig. 23-1). In 1961 the biotype of *V. cholerae,* called El Tor, emerged as an important cause of cholera pandemics. Until recently only 01 strains caused epidemic outbreaks of disease. In 1992 a newly identified strain designated 0139 was found to be responsible for epidemics in India and Bangladesh.

Cholera is still a major cause of gastrointestinal illness in developing countries but is infrequently observed in the United States. In the United States *V. cholerae* non-01 causes more gastroenteritis than does *V. cholerae* 01.

Pathogenesis of *Vibrio cholerae* 01

Cholera caused by *V. cholerae* 01 is spread from person to person by ingestion of contaminated water or uncooked foods, especially fish. The microorganism is very susceptible to gastric secretions. Ingestion of 10^9 vibrios in food or water is required to initiate disease. If the individual's gastric contents have been neutralized by bicarbonate or other antacids, 10^6 vibrios may cause disease. The pathogenesis of strains 01 and 0139 are the same.

The incubation period for cholera is approximately two to three days and is followed by a period of vomiting and diarrhea. Ten to 25 liters of fluid may be lost during infection. Rapid dehydration is accompanied by loss of electrolytes such as potassium and bicarbonate. The loss of electrolytes is due to a microbial enterotoxin. Prostration can occur at any time and is directly related to the amount of fluid lost.

The major causes of death in cholera are shock, metabolic acidosis, and renal failure. *V. cholerae* 01 rarely causes extraintestinal infections. There is apparently no complete immunity to reinfection since reinfection does occur in areas where the disease is endemic.

The relationship between adherence properties and pathogenesis has not been clearly established. It is believed that the flagellum is a prerequisite to attachment to the epithelial surface. The flagellum enables the organism to penetrate the mucous gel covering the intestinal epithelial surface. Adherence to the epithelial surface may also be mediated by other types of surface adhesins.

Once attached to the epithelial surface, the microorganisms can multiply and produce enterotoxin. Enterotoxin is a protein composed of A and B subunits. The entry of toxin into the host cell is depicted in Figure 23-2. Once inside host cells the A subunit is activated by a cellular protease. The A subunit affects the enzyme adenyl cyclase (see Under the Microscope 11 in Chapter 14). The A subunit catalyzes the transfer of the ADP-ribose moiety of nicotinamide-adenine dinucleotide (NAD) to a membrane protein. The ADP-ribosylated membrane protein activates adenyl cyclase and causes the conversion of ATP to adenosine 3′,5′-cyclic monophosphate (cAMP). Increased cAMP alters the ion transport mechanisms associated with the cytoplasmic membrane. Permeability changes involving sodium (Na^+) and chlorine (Cl^-) cause an efflux of water from the mucosal surface and hence cause diarrhea.

FIGURE 23-1
Scanning electron micrograph of *Vibrio cholerae.* Polar flagellum of the organism can be seen adhering to the intestinal epithelium. (× 12,000). (From J. Teppema et al., *Infect. Immun.* 55:2093, 1987.)

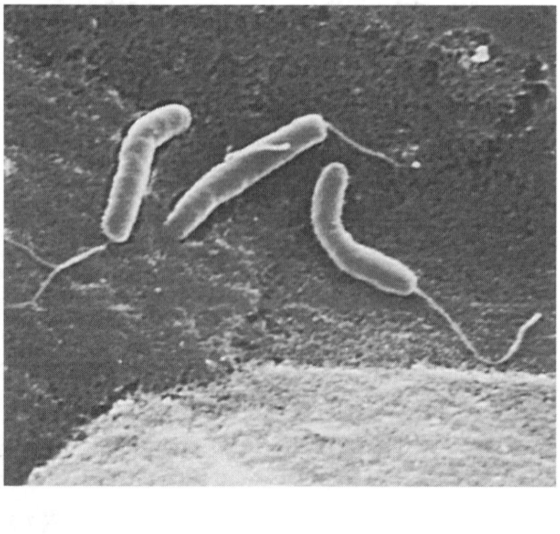

Pathogenesis of *Vibrio cholerae* non-01

Non-01 *V. cholerae* are the strains that are not agglutinated by 01 antiserum. Non-01 *V. cholerae* are found in sewage, estuarine waters (both polluted and nonpolluted), seafoods, and animals. The strains found in estuarine waters appear to be indigenous free-living forms. They are found in greater numbers during the summer than during other seasons.

Non-01 *V. cholerae* has been isolated in outbreaks of gastroenteritis but unlike 01 strains, has also been implicated with extraintestinal disease. Non-01 organisms have been isolated from blood and infected wounds. Over 90 percent of affected patients have some underlying condition (diabetes, abnormalities of gastrointestinal tract, malignancy, etc.).

Non-01 organisms produce a cholera-like toxin that is

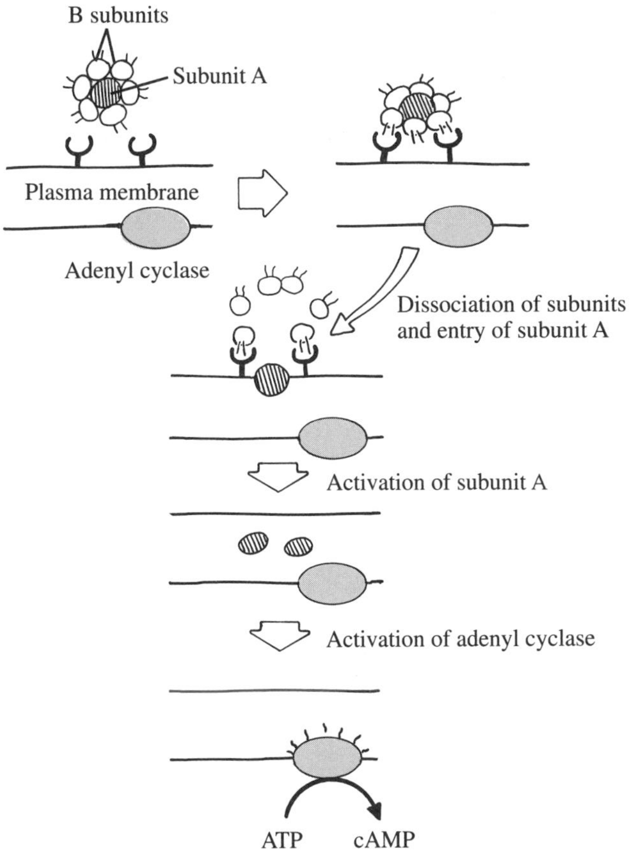

FIGURE 23-2
Mechanism of entry of cholera toxin into intestinal epithelium.

believed to be associated with gastrointestinal symptoms. Most cases are sporadic and not associated with pandemics, as classic cholera is. The symptoms of non-01 disease are similar to those of classic cholera but are less severe. Many outbreaks result from the ingestion of mollusks, especially raw oysters. Most diseases in the United States occur in southern coastal areas.

The reservoir of non-01 strains that cause human disease is not known. Humans may be the reservoir, and occasional carriers have been identified.

Epidemiology

The most recent outbreak of 01 strain cholera began in Peru in January 1991 and spread to most countries in South America. This was the first epidemic in the Western Hemisphere in nearly a century. By March 1992, about 450,000 cases had been reported, and the death toll was more than 4000. The causative agent of this epidemic was *V. cholerae* 01 biotype El Tor. Sporadic cases occurred in the United States but these were associated with travel to countries endemic for cholera. The isolates from this epidemic are different from the 01 strains that have been isolated in the United States. Usually, 20 to 30 cases of cholera are reported to the Centers for Disease Control each year (18 in 1993). As discussed previously, strain 0139 was responsible for over 23,000 cases in late 1992 but little is known of its epidemiology.

Most cases of gastroenteritis or wound infections in the United States are associated with the coastal waters of Louisiana and Texas. Most of these infections involved *V. cholerae* non-01. All types of shellfish products including oysters, mussels, clams, shrimp, and crabs may be the source of infection. Drinking contaminated water is also a means of infection.

Laboratory Diagnosis

Separation of *Vibrio* species from other clinically important bacteria can be carried out by using the following tests:

1. The indolphenol oxidase test differentiates Enterobacteriaceae (oxidase-negative) from *Vibrio* species (oxidase-positive).
2. The oxidative-fermentative test differentiates oxidase-positive *Pseudomonas* (oxidative) from *Vibrio* species (fermentative).
3. The sodium chloride (NaCl) requirement for growth differentiates *Vibrio* (require NaCl) from *Aeromonas* organisms (do not require NaCl).
4. Susceptibility to compound 0/129 differentiates *Vibrio* (susceptible) from *Aeromonas* (resistant) and *Plesiomonas* species (variable).

When vibrios are suspected in a gastrointestinal illness, their isolation from fecal material is fairly easy to carry out. Vibrios are able to tolerate alkaline pH and are motile. It is recommended that one enrichment medium and at least one plating medium be used in the isolation and identification procedures. The enrichment medium is alkaline peptone broth (pH 8.4), which suppresses the growth of other intestinal microorganisms. The most frequently used plating medium is thiosulfate citrate bile salts sucrose (TCBS) agar. TCBS is a selective medium on which *V. cholerae* produces yellow colonies. Typical colonies are then streaked on appropriate media or tested with *V. cholerae* polyvalent 01 or 0139 antiserum. Final identification rests on certain biochemical tests that differentiate *Vibrio* species.

The subtyping of *V. cholerae* 01 to facilitate epidemiological studies has been carried out by phage typing and biotyping. Since the potential to cause epidemics is associated with cholera toxin, genotypic tests are now being used to detect toxin genes. The polymerase chain reaction is being used in this way.

Treatment and Prevention

Cholera is a self-limiting disease when water and electrolytes are replaced. A replacement fluid consisting of NaCl, sodium bicarbonate, and potassium chloride can be given intravenously for patients in severe shock. Oral rehydration therapy for patients with less severe disease includes the use of glucose or sucrose in addition to the salts just mentioned. The addition of sugars permits fluid balance in the gut by preventing the loss of sodium. Precooked rice powder has been used as a substitute for glucose to reduce the rate of purging.

Antibiotics, although not required in treatment, lessen

the duration and volume of diarrhea by 60 percent. Antibiotics also reduce the vibrio population in the intestinal tract, thereby preventing shedding. Tetracycline is used for adults while trimethoprim-sulfamethoxazole and furazolidone are used for children and pregnant women, respectively. 0139 strains are resistant to trimethoprim-sulfamethoxazole but are susceptible to tetracycline.

Cholera can be prevented by adhering to certain sanitary procedures. There must be adequate sewage treatment and purification of water supplies. Travelers to foreign countries, especially Africa and Asia, are advised against eating raw seafood and uncooked vegetables. Thorough cooking of potentially contaminated food and careful storage of food prevent foodborne cholera and related gastrointestinal disease.

V. cholerae 01 can survive in crabs boiled for 8 minutes but not crabs boiled for 10 minutes. Storage of food should be at temperatures too low (less than 4 C) or too high (higher than 60 C) to permit microbial multiplication. Extraintestinal infections can be prevented by avoiding contact with potentially contaminated water. This is especially true for those with skin abrasions or underlying illness.

Trials using oral vaccines consisting of whole cells alone or with addition of the B subunit have been conducted. The vaccines did not give complete immunity and are not effective against 0139 strains. Residual protection declines significantly over a period of three years.

OTHER PATHOGENIC VIBRIOS

Several species of *Vibrio* are infrequently pathogenic for humans. Here we discuss only three of them: *V. parahaemolyticus*, *V. vulnificus*, and *V. alginolyticus*.

Vibrio parahaemolyticus

V. parahaemolyticus is part of the normal flora of estuarine and other coastal waters throughout the world. Most of the organisms are associated with zooplankton. During winter months these microorganisms remain in the sediment, but as the waters warm, the vibrios are released. The released vibrios become attached to crustaceans, where they proliferate. Most infections result from ingestion of improperly cooked crabs.

V. parahaemolyticus is associated with two types of clinical gastrointestinal syndromes. The most common manifestation of disease is watery diarrhea, accompanied by abdominal cramps, nausea, and vomiting. The disease is self-limiting. A more severe syndrome may be manifested by dehydration, dysentery, and acidosis. This syndrome too is usually self-limiting, but occasionally hospitalization is required. No deaths have been recorded in the United States, but some have been recorded in other countries.

The organism may also cause extraintestinal disease. *V. parahaemolyticus* has been isolated from wounds and blood. Trauma to a body site followed by contact with contaminated water is the usual history for these infections. Extraintestinal infections may require antimicrobial therapy (chloramphenicol, tetracyclines, aminoglycosides, etc.).

Few cases of *V. parahaemolyticus* disease have been recorded in the United States. Most are reported from Asia, where the disease is usually transmitted by raw or uncooked seafood. If left at refrigeration temperatures, raw food sustains the growth of vibrios. *V. parahaemolyticus* has a maximum generation time of 9 minutes and grows well at temperatures between 25 and 44 C. The principal reservoirs of these vibrios are seafoods and seawater. Carriers do not appear to be important in disease transmission.

Pathogenic strains of *V. parahaemolyticus* can be differentiated from nonpathogenic strains by the **Kanagawa test.** This test is based on the detection of a heat-stable hemolysin in a special medium (Wagatsum agar) that contains human erythrocytes. Pathogenic strains hemolyze the erythrocytes while nonpathogenic strains do not.

Vibrio vulnificus

V. vulnificus is believed to be part of the normal flora of seawater but can be found in fresh water also. Disease caused by this organism has been reported in the United States as well as Japan and Belgium. The disease may present itself in two ways. Primary cutaneous infection can occur following bathing in seawater. Percutaneous penetration occurs via wounds sustained in seawater or exposure of a preexisting wound while one is gathering shellfish. Patients with underlying problems such as alcoholics are at high risk of infection. Septicemia is also possible when individuals ingest raw or uncooked seafood, especially oysters and clams. In 70 percent of these patients secondary cutaneous lesions are the result of hematogenous seeding.

Primary cutaneous infection is characterized by rapid swelling around the wound. Infection may also involve surrounding tissue. Large vesicles or bullae are common. Primary septicemia is characterized by metastatic lesions. The mortality from septicemia is as high as 60 percent if treatment is not initiated. Surgical procedures—debridement, incision, and drainage of wounds—are often required in those with septicemia. *V. vulnificus* infections can be treated with antimicrobials such as ampicillin, tetracyclines, chloramphenicol, and aminoglycosides.

Vibrio alginolyticus

V. alginolyticus is a normal inhabitant of seawater and has a worldwide distribution. The organism is associated with extraintestinal infections such as wounds or ear infections. Most of these infections occur after swimming or activities at the seashore. Most lesions require debridement or drainage, but no serious complications occur and most patients respond to antibiotic (chloramphenicol, gentamicin, or nalidixic acid) therapy.

Aeromonas

The genus *Aeromonas* has been recognized for years as a pathogen in reptiles, amphibia, and fish. Infections in humans occur infrequently. The habitat of *Aeromonas* species includes various bodies of fresh and brackish waters, sewage, marine life, and soil. The species pathogenic for humans is *A. hydrophila.*

Aeromonas organisms, like *V. vulnificus,* are capable of causing cutaneous and intestinal infections. Most infections involve the intestinal tract, resulting in diarrhea that may last for up to seven days. Ingestion of contaminated water is the mechanism of transmission of *Aeromonas*-associated gastroenteritis. Wound infections are due to lacerations or punctures obtained during activities in water. Inflammation of connective tissue (cellulitis) is characteristic of infection.

Septicemia has been observed following insertion of an intravenous cannula. The infection is characterized by a fatal, rapidly spreading, crepitant myonecrosis of the lower limbs. *Aeromonas* septicemia in patients already compromised by underlying conditions has a high mortality rate (25–75 percent).

A. hydrophila is susceptible to several antibiotics including chloramphenicol, gentamicin, nitrofurantoin, tetracyclines, and trimethoprim-sulfamethoxazole.

Plesiomonas

The species for the genus *Plesiomonas* is *P. shigelloides.* It is found primarily in freshwater or estuarine environments.

TABLE 23-1
Characteristics of *Vibrio, Aeromonas,* and *Plesiomonas* Species

Species	Primary disease associations	Virulence factor	Mechanism of transmission	Treatment/prevention
Vibrio cholerae 01	Cholera—a severe gastroenteritis	Cholera enterotoxin affects adenyl cyclase activity	Ingesting contaminated water or foods (fish)	Replenishment of fluids and electrolytes; oral killed vaccine under trial
V. cholerae non-01	Cholera-like gastroenteritis less severe than with 01; extraintestinal infections involving blood and wounds	Cholera-like toxin	Ingestion of mollusks (e.g., raw oysters) or contact with contaminated water	Replenishment of fluids
V. parahaemolyticus	Gastroenteritis—one type severe with dehydration and dysentery, the other a less severe diarrhea; extraintestinal infections involving blood and wounds	None firmly established as cause of disease	Ingestion of raw seafood; contact of wound with water or object contaminated with water	Gastroenteritis is a self-limiting disease; antimicrobials for extraintestinal disease
V. vulnificus	Wound infections and septicemia	None firmly established as cause of disease	Contact with contaminated water	Surgical debridement, antimicrobials (ampicillin, chloramphenicol, gentamicin)
V. alginolyticus	Wounds, ear infections	None firmly established as cause of disease	Contact with contaminated water (e.g., after swimming)	Debridement or drainage, antibiotics such as chloramphenicol, gentamicin
Aeromonas hydrophila	Gastroenteritis, wounds, septicemia	None firmly established as cause of disease	Ingestion of contaminated water; contact of lacerated skin with contaminated water	None usually required for gastroenteritis; septicemia requires antibiotics (chloramphenicol, aminoglycosides)
Plesiomonas shigelloides	Gastroenteritis	None firmly established as cause of disease	Ingestion of or contact with contaminated water	Antimicrobial therapy (chloramphenicol, tetracyclines, aminoglycosides) required for over 60 percent of patients

Disease may follow ingestion of or contact with contaminated water or consumption of raw shellfish.

Gastroenteritis is the most common form of *Plesiomonas*-associated disease. Gastroenteritis symptoms include fever, abdominal pain, vomiting, headache, and dehydration. Diarrhea may be prolonged, lasting up to three weeks. As many as 30 bowel movements may occur each day. Over 60 percent of patients require hospitalization, antimicrobial therapy, or both. Most patients with *Plesiomonas*-associated diarrhea have an underlying illness (for example, cancer) or risk factor such as consumption of raw seafood.

Extraintestinal infections by *Plesiomonas* are severe but rare. Infections may be characterized, in order of importance, by meningitis, sepsis, cellulitis, and arthritis.

Plesiomonas organisms are susceptible to several antibiotics including chloramphenicol, tetracyclines, trimethoprim-sulfamethoxazole, and aminoglycosides.

Plesiomonas can be differentiated from *Aeromonas* by several biochemical tests. For example, *Plesiomonas* species, in contrast to *Aeromonas*, ferment inositol and do not ferment mannitol or sucrose.

Summary

Vibrio, *Aeromonas*, and *Plesiomonas* organisms are straight or curved, gram-negative, motile rods that are aerobic to facultatively anaerobic. They are found in fresh, marine, or estuarine waters. The major characteristics of these genera and species are outlined in Table 23-1.

Questions for Study

1. Using a flow diagram, describe the isolation of vibrios from a stool sample. How would you differentiate *V. cholerae* 01 from non-01 strains?
2. A patient arrives in the hospital with a severe wound infection. The patient is a shrimp sheller and you suspect a vibrio infection. What laboratory techniques would you use to determine what type of vibrio is involved?
3. What characteristics of the vibrios enable you to differentiate them from other bacterial groups?
4. What is the mechanism of action of cholera toxin? Does it differ from that of any other enterotoxins? Explain.

CHAPTER

24 Gram-Negative Coccobacillary Aerobic Bacteria

OBJECTIVES

To understand the types of infections associated with *Hemophilus influenzae* type b

To describe the various stages in whooping cough and the microbial factors believed to be associated with their appearance

To understand the importance and risks of vaccination against whooping cough

To explain the various ways in which the agents of brucellosis and tularemia may be transmitted to humans

To outline the methods used to treat and prevent *H. influenzae* type b infections, brucellosis, whooping cough, and tularemia

OUTLINE

HEMOPHILUS
- General Characteristics
- Pathogenesis
  - Encapsulated *Hemophilus influenzae*
  - Nonencapsulated *Hemophilus influenzae*
- Laboratory Diagnosis
- Treatment and Prevention
- Pathogenic Species Other Than *H. influenzae*

BORDETELLA
- General Characteristics
- Epidemiology and Pathogenesis
- Laboratory Diagnosis
- Treatment and Prevention

BRUCELLA
- General Characteristics
- Epidemiology and Pathogenesis
- Laboratory Diagnosis
- Treatment and Prevention

FRANCISELLA
- General Characteristics
- Epidemiology and Pathogenesis
- Laboratory Diagnosis
- Treatment and Prevention

The genera *Hemophilus, Bordetella, Brucella,* and *Francisella* belong to a group referred to as gram-negative coccobacillary bacteria. They are the causative agents of meningitis, whooping cough (pertussis), brucellosis (undulant fever), and tularemia, respectively. All organisms of these genera are nonmotile and are aerobic to microaerophilic. Their growth on laboratory media is favored by the addition of blood or serum or elevated concentrations of carbon dioxide (CO_2). Except for species of *Hemophilus,* most are resistant to penicillin.

Hemophilus

GENERAL CHARACTERISTICS

Hemophilus species make up a substantial portion of the indigenous microflora of the upper respiratory tract. Nearly all individuals over the age of 1 year are carriers for one or more species of *Hemophilus.* Species found in the upper respiratory tract include *H. influenzae, H. parainfluenzae, H. haemolyticus,* and *H. parahaemolyticus.* Of these species *H. influenzae* is the most pathogenic.

H. influenzae is fastidious in its growth requirements. It grows best on chocolate agar or enriched media supplemented with two nutritional factors called **X** (hemin) and **V** (nicotinamide-adenine dinucleotide [NAD]). Incubation in a CO_2 environment enhances the growth of most species. Colonies of *H. influenzae* increase in size if they are cultivated in the vicinity of other bacterial colonies, staphylococci, for example. This cooperative effect is called the **satellite phenomenon** and is due to the production of NAD by the staphylococcal colonies (Plate 8).

H. influenzae can be divided into two groups: **encapsulated** and **nonencapsulated.**

PATHOGENESIS

Encapsulated *Hemophilus influenzae*

Infection with *H. influenzae* occurs following inhalation of respiratory droplets from patients or carriers. Most invasive infections in the upper respiratory tract are caused by type b encapsulated strains (HIB). HIB serotypes are associated primarily with systemic infections that are the result of invasion of the bloodstream, for example, meningitis, epiglottitis, cellulitis, septic arthritis, and pneumonia. Type b serotypes are the principal cause of bacterial meningitis in children under 4 years old (Table 24-1). In this group of children, meningitis, even after chemotherapy, can lead to serious sequelae such as mental retardation.

TABLE 24-1
Causative Agents of Meningitis and the Frequency with Which They Are Associated with Disease

Agent	Frequency[a] (percent)
Hemophilus influenzae[b]	40–50
Neisseria meningitidis	20–25
Streptococcus pneumoniae	20–25
Escherichia coli	4–5
Other species	3–5

[a] The values are approximate and vary from year to year as well as from one community to another.
[b] In children under 4 years old, *H. influenzae* accounts for over 65 percent of the cases of meningitis.

HIB infections in adults are rare. Adult infections occur more frequently when the patient is compromised by respiratory problems, diabetes, or alcoholism. Infection is manifested as pneumonia and may be caused by nonencapsulated as well as capsulated strains.

The mechanism of pathogenesis of type b serotypes is not fully understood. Adherence of bacteria to the respiratory tract may be due to delayed mucociliary clearance. For example, smoking or prior viral infection could cause loss of ciliary epithelium. As the epithelial surface becomes damaged, host receptors could be exposed, leading to interaction with bacterial adhesins. Bacteria invade the bloodstream, where they multiply and cross the blood-brain barrier. The capsule of HIB organisms appears to protect them from intravascular clearance mechanisms. Bacterial products as well as cell wall lipopolysaccharide (LPS) and peptidoglycan may play a role in the inflammation and tissue damage associated with meningitis.

H. influenzae is found in the upper respiratory tract of most healthy individuals. HIB serotypes are found in the upper respiratory tract of less than 1 percent of children 6 months or younger. In infants 2 months or younger, maternal antibody provides protection from infection by HIB strains. The majority of HIB meningitis infections occur in children between the ages of 2 and 18 months. From the ages of 2 months to 5 years, HIB serotypes can be found in 5 percent of the children. Most children over the age of 5 years and adults will have naturally acquired immunity to HIB serotypes. Consequently 95 percent of HIB disease is found in children less than 4 years old. Nonencapsulated strains become less prevalent as commensals with increasing age.

Approximately 12,000 cases of HIB infections are reported each year in the United States. The mortality rate is less than 10 percent but 10 to 15 percent of the survivors are left with neurological complications. Several studies indicated that children at day-care centers are at an increased risk of infection. Meningitis caused by *H. influenzae* has a seasonal distribution, with major incidences of the disease occurring in the fall and spring. Higher rates of the disease occur in blacks, American Indians, and Eskimos.

Nonencapsulated *Hemophilus influenzae*

Seventy-five percent of the *H. influenzae* strains in the upper respiratory tract are nonencapsulated. Nonencapsulated strains rarely cause systemic disease. Mucous membrane infections such as otitis media, sinusitis, bronchitis, alveolitis, conjunctivitis, and infections involving the female genital tract during delivery of the baby are, however, common. Pneumonia caused by nonencapsulated strains is more common in the elderly and in patients with chronic bronchitis. These strains (along with *Streptococcus pneumoniae*) are the most frequent cause of **otitis media** in children between the ages of 6 and 24 months. By the age of 3 years, more than two-thirds of children have had one or more episodes of acute otitis media. Meningitis occurs primarily in predisposed patients. Of all meningitis cases in adults, about 50 percent are caused by nonencapsulated strains.

LABORATORY DIAGNOSIS

Specimens (usually blood or cerebrospinal fluid for HIB) can be Gram-stained for identification of coccobacilli. The capsule can be demonstrated by a capsular swelling reaction (quellung; see Chapter 17) after using HIB antiserum. An immunofluorescent technique using fluorescein-conjugated anti-HIB serum is another way to identify the organism in clinical specimens.

Isolation of *H. influenzae* is achieved by culturing specimens on chocolate agar (heated blood agar) or richer media such as Levinthal's medium. Both media contain X factor and V factor. Colonial isolates can be identified by the serological tests discussed above plus others such as counterimmunoelectrophoresis, latex agglutination, and coagglutination using antisera.

All *Hemophilus* species except *H. aphrophilus* and *H. ducreyi* require V factor (Table 24-2). Paper disks containing V factor can be placed on blood agar medium (devoid of V factor) to identify V factor–requiring species. X factor requirements for further differentiation of *Hemophilus* species can be obtained on the basis of the ability of species to utilize gamma-aminolevulinic acid. Differentiation of *Hemophilus* species is also based on the growth response to CO_2, fermentation, hemolysis, and catalase production.

TREATMENT AND PREVENTION

Ampicillin and chloramphenicol were once considered the most effective drugs in treating infections caused by *H. influenzae*, but drug-resistant strains have now become prevalent. Sensitivity tests should be performed on clinical isolates before an antimicrobial regimen is begun. Ampicillin resistance is caused primarily by beta-lactamase production. One treatment regimen includes the combination of a beta-lactamase inhibitor (sulbactam, for example) plus ampicillin. Third-generation cephalosporins such as cefotaxime and ceftazidime in combination with ampicillin have become the drugs of choice in the treatment of any meningitis in infants and children.

Intravenous dexamethasone is also suggested for patients older than 2 months. This drug is known to reduce the duration of fever and the incidence of neurological sequelae. Dexamethasone reduces tumor necrosis factor activity, an important event in the pathophysiology of inflammation (see Under the Microscope 6 in Chapter 11).

Although early treatment of *H. influenzae* infections is almost 100 percent effective, a few patients who recover have residual central nervous system injury.

A conjugate vaccine was licensed in 1987 to provide effective immune responses in infants (over 2 months old) and younger children. Four conjugate vaccines are available. Three of the vaccines consist of the polyribosyl ribitol phosphate (PRP) capsule of HIB conjugated to protein carriers. The protein carriers may be diphtheria toxoid, *Neisseria meningitidis* outer membrane protein complex, or tetanus toxoid (see Additional Readings). HIB conjugate vaccine is now administered with combined diphtheria-tetanus-pertussis vaccines, discussed in Chapter 20.

There is an increased risk of disease in children who come in contact with a person with HIB meningitis, because the organism is transmitted by respiratory droplets. The attack rate is highest in those under 2 years old. The Immunization Practices Advisory Committee (ACIP) recommends that the drug rifampin be considered for all classroom contacts of a child with invasive HIB disease if any exposed classroom contact is under 2 years old. Rifampin should not be used for pregnant women because of the drug's teratogenic (capable of causing congenital malformation) potential.

TABLE 24-2
Characteristics of Species of *Hemophilus* Occasionally Associated with Disease

Species	Disease association	Other characteristics
H. aegyptius	Communicable form of conjunctivitis (pinkeye)*	Requires X and V factors; serologically related to *H. influenzae*
H. hemolyticus	Sinusitis, otitis media, and lower respiratory disease	Found normally in upper respiratory tract; beta-hemolytic; requires X and V factors
H. parainfluenzae	Respiratory tract infection and endocarditis	Found normally in respiratory tract; requires V factor
H. ducreyi	Sexually transmitted disease (chancroid)	Fastidious growth requirements; difficult to isolate from lesions; requires X factor
H. paraphrophilus	Infrequent cause of disease but disease is usually severe—endocarditis, septicemia, and meningitis	Does not require V or X factor

* Bacteremia following recovery from conjunctivitis can lead to a frequently fatal illness (called Brazilian purpuric fever) in young children. This disease has been seen almost exclusively in Brazil.

PATHOGENIC SPECIES OTHER THAN *H. INFLUENZAE*

Several species of *Hemophilus* are occasionally associated with disease (see Table 24-2). One of the more important of these is *H. ducreyi*. This organism is the etiological agent of the sexually transmitted disease called **chancroid.** Chancroid refers to the soft, painful ulcers seen in the genital area. The base of the chancroid ulcer, in contrast to the smooth base of the syphilis ulcer, is irregular and granular in appearance. Little inflammation surrounds the ulcer. In males the distal prepuce is the most common site of involvement while in females most of these lesions are at the entrance of the vagina. Painful tender inguinal lymphadenopathy is a characteristic feature in up to 50 percent of the patients. Involved lymph nodes (buboes) may spontaneously rupture (Plate 9).

Chancroid is prevalent in developing countries but uncommon in the United States. Just over 3470 cases were reported to the Centers for Disease Control in 1991. The disease is probably underreported. Whether asymptomatic carriers play a role in disease transmission is uncertain. Of particular concern in developing countries is the high rate of transmission of human immunodeficiency virus (HIV) between sexual partners in the presence of chancroid.

Definitive diagnosis of chancroid requires the isolation and identification of *H. ducreyi*. Isolation of the organism, however, is difficult and the available media will not support the growth of all strains. Chocolate agar containing hemoglobin, fetal bovine serum, and vancomycin (to inhibit gram-positive organisms) appears to be the most effective isolation medium.

Recommended treatment regimens for chancroid are azithromycin or ceftriaxone or erythromycin. Alternative regimens are amoxicillin plus clavulanic acid or ciprofloxacin.

Bordetella

GENERAL CHARACTERISTICS

Species of *Bordetella* are common inhabitants of the human upper respiratory tract. *B. pertussis* is the causative agent of **whooping cough (pertussis)** and is morphologically indistinguishable from other coccobacillary forms. *B. pertussis* is a strict aerobe and is among the most fastidious pathogenic bacteria. Two other species that share antigens with *B. pertussis* are *B. parapertussis* and *B. bronchiseptica*. *B. parapertussis* can also cause whooping cough while *B. bronchiseptica* may cause respiratory or wound infections. These two species are less fastidious than *B. pertussis* and can be differentiated from the latter in several ways (Table 24-3).

TABLE 24-3
Characteristics Differentiating Species of *Bordetella*

Test	*B. pertussis*	*B. parapertussis*	*B. bronchiseptica*
Pigment production	−	+	−
Urease production	−	+	+
Oxidase production	+	−	+
Nitrate reduction	−	−	+
Motility	−	−	+
Citrate utilization	−	+	+

EPIDEMIOLOGY AND PATHOGENESIS

B. pertussis is pathogenic only for humans. Pertussis is worldwide in distribution, with most instances of disease occurring in the very young. It is highly communicable and is spread by exposure of susceptible individuals to aerosols generated by infected persons.

Pertussis is divided into three symptomatic stages: **catarrhal, paroxysmal,** and **convalescent.** Following exposure to the infectious agent, symptoms of infection may appear from 6 to 20 days later. In the catarrhal stage the symptoms are similar to those of a cold: conjunctivitis, watery eyes, mild cough, and low-grade fever. The catarrhal stage may last from one to two weeks or more with episodes of severe coughing.

The paroxysmal (sudden attacks occurring periodically) stage is characterized by severe coughing, first at night and then during the day as well. As many as 15 to 25 coughing episodes occur within a 24-hour period. The coughing leads to mucous expulsion followed by inspiration of air into the lungs, causing the classic "whooping" associated with the disease. Whooping is not usually observed in adults with pertussis.

The paroxysmal stage is the most contagious phase of the disease, and the bacilli can be seen attached to the epithelium of the bronchi or trachea (Fig. 24-1). As the disease progresses and more respiratory tissue is involved, blockage of the bronchial passages may take place. This blockage often leads to lung infection from pyogenic cocci, convulsions, and sometimes death. The bacteria never invade the bloodstream. The paroxysmal stage may last from one to four weeks.

The convalescent stage follows the paroxysmal stage and is distinguished by fewer and less severe symptoms. During convalescence mild to severe coughing may occur periodically for up to six months after the initial infection.

B. pertussis produces several potential virulence factors. **Filamentous hemagglutinin (FHA)** is a surface protein, similar to pili, that is believed to be associated with adherence to the upper respiratory tract. **Pertussis toxin (PT)** is a protein exotoxin of the A-B subunit type (see Chapter 14). The A subunit catalyzes the transfer of the ADP-ribose moiety from NAD to a cell membrane protein. The cell membrane protein controls the production of adenosine 3′,5′-cyclic monophosphate (cAMP), a characteristic similar to cholera toxin (see Under the Microscope 11 in

FIGURE 24-1
Bordetella pertussis. A. Scanning electron micrograph of mouse tracheal epithelium incubated in sterile medium. (× 3000 before reduction.) B. Scanning electron micrograph of mouse tracheal epithelium infected with *B. pertussis.* (From L. B. Opremcak and M. S. Rheins, *Can. J. Microbiol.* 29:415, 1983.)

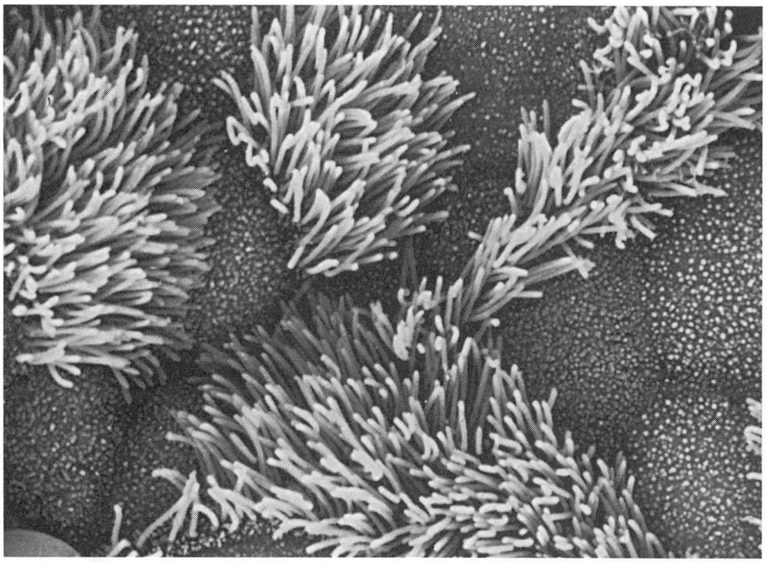

A

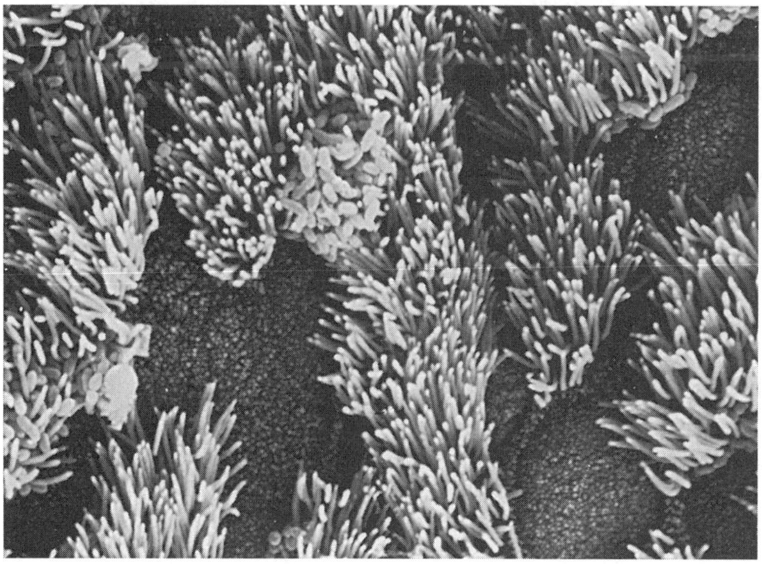

B

Chapter 14). Pertussis toxin has a variety of biological effects, such as histamine sensitization, which may be responsible for maintaining the infection as well as contributing to secondary infections.

Another virulence factor is **adenylate cyclase,** which is found on the surface of *B. pertussis* cells. This enzyme is believed to inhibit phagocytic activity. The enzyme apparently enters phagocytic cells, where it is activated by a mammalian protein called calmodulin (see also *Bacillus anthracis* pathogenesis in Chapter 19). Activation of adenylate cyclase induces high levels of intracellular cAMP, which impairs the bactericidal activity of polymorphonuclear leukocytes and macrophages.

Other potential virulence factors include a hemolysin, fimbriae, tracheal cytotoxin, lipopolysaccharide, and heat-labile dermonecrotic factor. Recent studies showed that **tracheal cytotoxin** is the cause of respiratory epithelial cell destruction. Tracheal cytotoxin induces the cells themselves to produce interleukin (IL)-1. IL-1 triggers the production of nitric oxide by the same respiratory cells. The nitric oxide, which in other systems can kill tumor cells, then destroys the respiratory cells. This is an example of a cytokine causing a negative effect on the host.

LABORATORY DIAGNOSIS

No single laboratory or clinical diagnostic test has been shown to be optimally sensitive and specific for *B. pertussis.* Culture of *B. pertussis* from nasopharyngeal secretions, although specific as a diagnostic test, shows low sensitivity. The tip of a Nichrome wire is covered with cotton. The wire is passed through the nose and allowed to touch the nasopharyngeal wall. The wire is removed and the material on it is streaked on a charcoal–horse blood agar plate. The plates are incubated and examined daily since colonies may not appear before three days. Typical colonies are tiny and glistening and resemble bisected pearls. Colonies should be Gram-stained. If small, gram-negative rods, or coccobacilli are observed, fluorescent antibody tests can be used for serological confirmation. However, some studies have shown direct fluorescent antibody testing to lack sensitivity. Laboratory tests combined with clinical criteria (cough, for example) are suggested for the diagnosis of pertussis. Biochemical tests can be used to differentiate *Bordetella* species (see Table 24-3).

TREATMENT AND PREVENTION

Although whooping cough is often self-limiting, antibiotics such as erythromycin, tetracycline, and chloramphenicol are important in lessening its communicability. These antibiotics are also helpful in reducing the possibility of secondary pneumonia infections. Treatment, if provided after infection has already been established, has little effect on the course of the illness. However, penicillin may be given to reduce secondary infections by pyogenic cocci.

Since the first vaccine for pertussis was administered, the number of cases of whooping cough has decreased from a high of 120,000 per year in 1950 to 4083 cases in 1992. Immunization as of 1993 includes the use of an acellular vaccine combined with diphtheria and tetanus (DTP) vaccines. Vaccination begins in infancy and was discussed in Chapter 20. The acellular pertussis vaccine prevents the severe side effects associated with the previously used whole-cell vaccine.

Brucella

GENERAL CHARACTERISTICS

Members of the genus *Brucella* are facultative intracellular parasites that cause chronic disease in animals and humans. There are three major pathogenic species: *B. abortus*, which infects cattle; *B. melitensis*, which infects goats and sheep; and *B. suis*, which infects swine. Human infection caused by brucellae is referred to as **brucellosis** or **undulant fever.**

The brucellae are gram-negative, nonmotile, and coccobacillary in shape. If present, capsules are small. Brucellae are strict aerobes that require complex media for cultivation.

EPIDEMIOLOGY AND PATHOGENESIS

Brucellosis is primarily a zoonosis. It is transmitted to humans through consumption of raw milk or its products, through contact with products of animal conception, or sometimes through ingestion of meat from infected animals.

Brucellosis is worldwide in distribution and travelers to areas where the disease is endemic in animals are at increased risk. In the United States fewer than 125 cases are reported each year. In areas of Africa, however, the annual incidence of brucellosis per 100,000 population is as high as 128.

Outbreaks of brucellosis in the United States are frequently associated with the ingestion of cheese from unpasteurized goat's milk. Sporadic cases of disease may occur among farmers, veterinary surgeons, and slaughterhouse personnel who come in contact with infected animals. Domestic swine are the major source of infection in the United States.

Brucella organisms gain entrance to the body through abraded skin or mucous membranes of the intestinal or respiratory tract. They do not persist long at the site of entry and are ingested by neutrophils. Infected neutrophils settle in regional lymph nodes. The bacilli reproduce in neutrophils and later lyse them. The released bacteria at this stage may be destroyed by phagocytes, or they may overcome host defenses. If they overcome host defenses, they can be transported within macrophages via the blood to many areas of the body. The bacilli localize in tissue (liver, bone, spleen) where granulomas similar to those found in tuberculosis are produced. Viable bacilli may persist for several months in the granulomas, giving rise to acute or chronic symptoms. For this reason the incubation period in brucellosis may be very long.

The acute stage appears approximately one to two weeks after infection. It is characterized by fever and enlargement of the lymph nodes, spleen, and liver. Body temperature during the acute phase ranges between 101 and 104 F and may continue for several weeks with intermittent remissions (**undulant fever**). About 80 percent of patients recover spontaneously during the acute stage.

The chronic stage is generally associated with a hypersensitivity in which there are swelling of the joints and persistence of a low-grade fever. Inflammation of spinal vertebrae (spondylitis) resulting in severe back pain is a common complication of brucellosis, particularly in older men.

LABORATORY DIAGNOSIS

Diagnosis of brucellosis is difficult because the disease is commonly chronic and is accompanied by fever and few symptoms. The microorganisms are best recovered from the blood during the fever stage. Blood cultures often become negative after the first few weeks of infection because of the serum antibodies.

Culture and isolation of *Brucella* can be made from blood, abscess, and tissue samples. Clinical specimens are cultured on tryptose agar or brucella agar in an atmosphere of 2 to 10% CO_2. Plates should be incubated for 10 days at 35 to 37 C. Colony isolates should be Gram-stained. Nonhemolytic colonies that are gram-negative coccobacilli, do not ferment lactose or glucose, are obligate aerobes, and are oxidase-positive are tested for agglutination in *Brucella* antiserum. These tests define the genus *Brucella*. Other tests are used to differentiate species and biotypes of *Brucella* (Table 24-4). Brucellosis, however, is more commonly diagnosed serologically, either

TABLE 24-4
Characteristics Used in Differentiating the Three Major Species of *Brucella*

Species	H_2S production	Growth in presence of: Basic fuchsin (1:25,000)	Growth in presence of: Thionin (1:25,000)	CO_2 requirement	Urease activity	Reaction to monospecific/serum of: *B. abortus*	Reaction to monospecific/serum of: *B. melitensis*
B. abortus	±	±	−	±	+	+	−
B. melitensis	−	+	+	−	V	−	+
B. suis	∓	V	±	−	+	+	−

± = most biotypes are positive; ∓ = most biotypes are negative; V = variable, as many positive biotypes as negative biotypes.

by a fourfold rise in serum agglutination test titer over several weeks or a single titer of at least 160 : 1 in a person with compatible clinical manifestations.

TREATMENT AND PREVENTION

Mass testing, slaughter of infected cattle, and vaccination of heifers have reduced the infection rate of cattle in the United States to less than 5 percent. Infection in swine, however, remains at a very high level. Brucellosis is highest among personnel at slaughterhouses.

Because of the presence of brucella within host cells, effective treatment is often difficult. Brucellae are susceptible to ampicillin, streptomycin, and tetracycline. Tetracyclines are the first choice in treatment. Successful treatment is best obtained during the acute stage of the disease. During chronic infections antibiotics are unsatisfactory and relapses are common. The antibiotic regimen recommended by the World Health Organization includes a six-week course of doxycycline and rifampin.

Francisella

GENERAL CHARACTERISTICS

The most important species in the genus *Francisella* is *F. tularensis,* the causative agent of **tularemia.** The genus designation honors Dr. Francis, while the species name relates to Tulare County in California, where the disease was first described. Tularemia is a disease of rodents, particularly rabbits, and is transmissible to humans.

F. tularensis is a gram-negative, nonmotile bacillus that can produce a capsule in vivo. Like the *Brucella, Francisella* species are facultative intracellular parasites. The organism is highly pleomorphic in culture and can resemble filamentous, coccal, or bacillary forms. It is fastidious in its cultural requirements. Reducing agents such as cystine or thioglycolate must be supplied in the medium if it is to achieve maximum growth.

EPIDEMIOLOGY AND PATHOGENESIS

Humans can acquire tularemia in the following ways: (1) by direct contact with infected animals, (2) by handling or ingesting contaminated meat, (3) by the bite of infected insect vectors such as ticks or deerflies, or (4) by inhalation of contaminated aerosols. From 200 to 250 cases of tularemia are reported each year in the United States. Rodents or rabbits are the major reservoirs of infection but wild and domestic animals including fox, deer, opossum, dogs, and sheep can become infected.

Most cases of tularemia result from contact with infected animal tissue, for example, skinning rabbits (so-called **rabbit fever**) or eating infected meat. One-third of the cases of tularemia in the United States are the consequence of bites of infected ticks or deerflies. Laboratory personnel caring for animals can contract tularemia through contaminated aerosols generated by sneezing animals.

Two types of *F. tularensis,* each with different characteristics, have been described. Type A strains are more virulent than type B strains. The former cause 5 to 7 percent mortality in untreated patients and are usually associated with rabbits and tick vectors. Type B strains are less virulent and rarely cause death in untreated patients. They are associated primarily with rodents, such as muskrats. Type A strains are found only in North America, where they cause 80 to 90 percent of the reported cases.

The incubation period in tularemia is from 2 to 10 days and is coupled with fever and headache. From the original site of infection, bacilli migrate to regional lymph nodes, causing their enlargement. *F. tularensis* can persist within phagocytes. Carried within the phagocyte, the bacilli can enter the bloodstream and infect several organs, including the spleen, liver, and lungs, where they produce granulomas.

The manifestations of tularemia often depend on how the microorganism was acquired. The most common type is the **ulceroglandular** variety. Ulceroglandular tularemia usually results from contact of abraded skin with infected animal tissue (skinning infected animals, for example). The primary lesion, typically found on the hands and arms, becomes ulcerated in six to eight days (Fig. 24-2). During this period there will be fever and involvement of local lymph nodes. The lesions may take four to seven weeks to heal.

Accidental contamination of the eye can result in **oculoglandular** tularemia, in which there is ulceration of the conjunctiva.

The most severe form of tularemia is the **pneumonic** variety, usually contracted through contaminated aero-

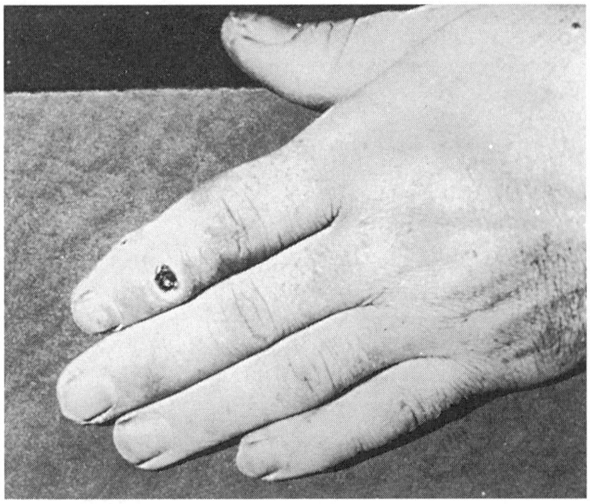

FIGURE 24-2
Typical cutaneous lesion of tularemia. (Courtesy of Armed Forces Institute of Pathology, AFIP 83587-2.)

sols. If left untreated, this clinical type of tularemia can be fatal to 30 percent of the persons infected.

Recovery from all three forms of tularemia confers permanent immunity.

LABORATORY DIAGNOSIS

The risk of infection by *F. tularensis* to laboratory personnel is very high. Consequently, tularemia is diagnosed on the basis of clinical findings, immunoserological methods, and the patient's history of recent animal or tick exposure. In addition, it is very difficult to isolate this very fastidious organism.

Culturing of *F. tularensis* specimens from local lesions, regional lymph nodes, sputum, or conjunctival scrapings can be performed using media rich in cystine or other reducing agents. The most popular medium is blood-cystine-dextrose agar. The colonies appear about three to five days after incubation of the specimen and are minute and transparent.

Biochemical characterization is not necessary or recommended for identification. Direct or indirect fluorescent antibody techniques are considered the best tools for

TABLE 24-5
Characteristics of the Gram-Negative Coccobacillary Bacteria

Genus	Major pathogenic species	Disease	Virulence factors	Mechanism of transmission	Treatment and prevention
Hemophilus	*H. influenzae* type b	Meningitis in children under 4 years old; otitis in children	Capsule (polyribitol phosphate)	Inhalation of respiratory droplets from patients with active disease or carriers	Ampicillin, ampicillin plus a beta-lactamase inhibitor; 3rd-generation cephalosporins; conjugate vaccine available
	H. influenzae nonencapsulated	Otitis media in children; neonatal infections; pneumonia in elderly	Unknown	Inhalation of respiratory droplets; mother to newborn	Same as for *H. influenzae*
Bordetella	*B. pertussis* *B. parapertussis*	Pertussis (whooping cough)	Filamentous hemagglutinin, pertussis toxin, adenylate cyclase	Inhalation of aerosols generated by infected individuals	Erythromycin, tetracycline, chloramphenicol; killed vaccine as part of DTP and/or acellular vaccine
Brucella	*B. abortus* (cattle) *B. melitensis* (goats, sheep) *B. suis* (swine)	Brucellosis (undulant fever)	Unknown	A zoonosis transmitted to humans by consumption of raw milk or its products; contact with products of conception; or ingestion of meat from infected animals	Ampicillin, streptomycin, tetracycline; mass testing, slaughter of infected cattle, and vaccination of heifers
Francisella	*F. tularensis*	Tularemia (rabbit fever)	Unknown	Direct contact with infected animals by handling or ingesting contaminated meat; bite of insect vectors; or inhalation of contaminated aerosols generated by infected animals	Streptomycin; attenuated vaccine for laboratory personnel

rapid and specific identification of bacilli in exudates, tissue sections, and so on. Serodiagnosis can be accomplished by using an agglutination test on the patient's serum. The test result becomes positive about 10 to 14 days after infection. The titer rises significantly at three weeks after infection.

TREATMENT AND PREVENTION

Streptomycin is the most effective drug in the treatment of tularemia. Chloramphenicol and tetracycline also can be used in treatment. Relapses are more common when tetracycline and chloramphenicol are used because they fail to penetrate the phagocyte, where the bacilli may be located. If precautions are taken, laboratory personnel are at minimal risk of incurring infection. An attenuated vaccine is available for use by laboratory personnel who are continually in contact with potentially infected animals.

Summary

The gram-negative coccobacillary bacteria include *Hemophilus, Bordetella, Brucella,* and *Francisella.* They are nonmotile and aerobic to microaerophilic. Their growth on laboratory media is favored by the addition of blood, serum, or elevated concentrations of CO_2. The clinical importance of these groups is outlined in Table 24-5.

Questions for Study

1. Describe the three symptomatic stages in the disease pertussis.
2. Describe the differences, if any, between host and parasite adenyl cyclase in the pathogenesis of certain infectious diseases.
3. What is believed to be responsible for the inflammatory response associated with meningitis caused by organisms such as *Hemophilus influenzae?*
4. Explain why children from the ages of 2 months to 4 years are more susceptible to meningitis caused by *Hemophilus influenzae.*
5. Explain why the disease brucellosis is often difficult to diagnose.
6. How is tularemia transmitted to humans? What group is more likely to become infected by *Francisella tularensis?*

CHAPTER

25 Mycobacteria

OBJECTIVES

To describe the stages from inhalation of the tubercle bacillus to the formation of a tubercle

To outline the drugs used in the treatment and prevention of tuberculosis

To understand the immune response associated with tuberculosis and its relationship to vaccination and resistance to infection

To describe the techniques used to identify mycobacteria in the laboratory

To understand the importance of tuberculosis in patients with acquired immunodeficiency syndrome (AIDS)

To outline the features of nontuberculous mycobacterioses that distinguish them from *Mycobacterium tuberculosis* disease

To describe the clinical features of indeterminate, tuberculous, and tuberculoid leprosy

OUTLINE

MYCOBACTERIUM TUBERCULOSIS
- General Characteristics
- Pathogenesis
  - Human Immunodeficiency Virus Infection and Tuberculosis
- Immunity
  - Tuberculin Tests
- Laboratory Diagnosis
- Epidemiology
- Treatment and Prevention

NONTUBERCULOUS MYCOBACTERIOSES
- Pathogenesis
  - *Mycobacterium avium* Complex
  - *Mycobacterium fortuitum* Complex
- Laboratory Diagnosis, Treatment, and Prevention

MYCOBACTERIUM LEPRAE
- General Characteristics
- Epidemiology
- Pathogenesis
- Laboratory Diagnosis, Treatment, and Prevention

The mycobacteria are ubiquitous microorganisms that can be readily found in animals and humans. Two diseases of medical importance, **tuberculosis (TB)** and **leprosy,** are caused by *Mycobacterium* species. Diseases caused by the mycobacteria are called **mycobacterioses.**

The causative agents of TB in humans are *M. tuberculosis,* the human strain, and *M. bovis,* the strain found in cattle. Just a few years ago there was hope that TB, like smallpox, might be eliminated. Now we are confronted with new problems. First, the acquired immunodeficiency syndrome (AIDS) epidemic has contributed to the rising incidence of TB in individuals between the ages of 25 and 44 years. Second, there has been nosocomial transmission of multidrug-resistant TB, particularly among AIDS patients. In developing countries, as many as 5 million people each year die of TB.

Leprosy is a disfiguring disease that produces lesions of the skin and nerves. It is caused by *M. leprae.* Leprosy is found in Asia, islands of the South Pacific, and other tropical areas. There are approximately 5 million lepers in the world; few deaths, however, are directly related to the disease.

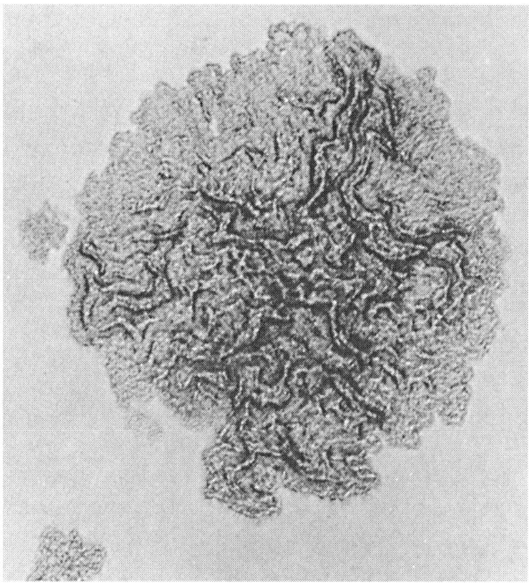

FIGURE 25-1
Serpentine cord colony of *Mycobacterium tuberculosis.* (From E. H. Runyon, A. G. Karlson, G. P. Kubica, and L. G. Wayne. In F. H. Lennette, A. Balows, W. J. Hausler, Jr., and J. P. Truant, eds., *Manual of Clinical Microbiology,* 3rd ed. Washington, D.C.: American Society for Microbiology, 1980.)

Mycobacterium tuberculosis

GENERAL CHARACTERISTICS

There are several characteristics that distinguish *M. tuberculosis,* as well as other mycobacteria, from most gram-positive and gram-negative bacteria. Most of these differences are due to the nature of the cell wall.

1. Mycobacteria possess a peptidoglycan layer that cannot be stained by Gram stain reagents because layers of lipid surround the mycobacterial peptidoglycan. The majority of these lipids are called **mycolic acids.** The lipid content of the mycobacteria may be as high as 60 percent of the cell weight (5–20 percent lipid content in most gram-negative bacteria).
2. Mycobacteria resist the acid-alcohol decolorization step and thus are referred to as **acid-fast bacilli.** Acid-fast stains such as the those in the Ziehl-Nielsen procedure are used to force, by heat, stains into the cell (see Appendix A).
3. Some mycolic acids are called the **cord factor** because they are responsible for the serpentine cords that mycobacteria produce when cultured on certain media (Fig. 25-1).
4. Mycobacterial cells divide every 18 to 24 hours (every 30 minutes for *E. coli*). This lengthy doubling time is reflected in the time it takes for colonies to become visible on laboratory media (2–10 weeks, depending on the species). It is also reflected in the time for symptoms to develop in disease (several weeks to months).
5. Mycobacteria produce pigments that are constitutive (produced under any environmental conditions) and are called **scotochromogens.** Some mycobacteria produce pigments that are produced only in the presence of light and are called **photochromogens.**

PATHOGENESIS

TB is a chronic disease. The TB bacillus can infect any organ of the body but is usually associated with the lungs. *M. bovis* is not a major cause of disease in developed countries of the world. *M. tuberculosis,* however, is still an important pathogen, even in developed countries.

There are two pathogenic sequences in which TB can develop: (1) a direct course due to recent acquisition of the disease, and (2) activation of a previously acquired latent infection. Direct progression is the result of contact with contaminated droplet nuclei, ingestion of contaminated milk, or inhalation of contaminated dust particles. The magnitude of infection is not related to the virulence of the infecting bacilli but to such factors as the **immunity of the host, the hypersensitivity of the host,** and the **infecting dose of bacilli.**

After inhalation of the bacilli, a lesion develops in the alveoli of one lung. This is followed by an inflammatory response in which there is accumulation of neutrophils and macrophages. Bacilli can be transported to regional lymph nodes. Bacilli in lung or lymph tissue lesions are ingested by macrophages and continue to multiply. The **primary lesion** may heal with resorption of the inflammatory-derived exudate and destruction of the bacilli. If bacilli survive, they may reach the thoracic duct and bloodstream, eventually finding their way to other parts of the body.

At 3 to 12 weeks after the initial infection, an immunological response can be detected. T cells and B cells appear at the lesion and respond to the appearance of the mycobacteria. The lesions, whether in the lungs or other organs and tissue, are walled off in up to 85 to 95 percent of individuals infected. These individuals show no symptoms of disease although they do exhibit a delayed hypersensitivity. The walled-off lesions, however, still retain viable bacilli, which can later be reactivated.

In 5 to 15 percent of infected individuals there is a pathological response. The bacilli proliferate and the patient shows evidence of TB that may be respiratory or involve other organs. Microorganisms that persist and multiply at the site of infection are joined by mononuclear cells, tissue macrophages, and other cells. The macrophages arrange themselves in the form of dense elongated epithelioid cells to form **tubercles** (Fig. 25-2). Some of these cells fuse to form **giant cells.** The tubercle appears as a granular nodule (**granuloma**) and represents the host's mechanism for inhibiting bacillary multiplication.

If large numbers of bacilli are produced in the tubercle, the immune response of the host to the tuberculoprotein of the bacillus appears more evident. Neutrophils at the lesion release lysosomal enzymes that destroy not only the bacilli but also the tubercle. This destruction of tissue results in a semisolid coagulated mass of host cells and bacilli referred to as **caseation necrosis** (cheese).

The caseous lesion may heal by calcification and the bacilli within it may remain viable for years. Calcification of the lesion permits its radiographic visualization for the life of the patient. If the infection is not brought under control, the caseous lesion may become liquefied. Release of the liquefied material results in the formation of a **cavity** in the lung. Bacilli released from the lesion can be disseminated by a systemic or pulmonary vessel to other organs. Viable bacilli can be carried to a bronchus, where they can infect healthy tissue. Bacilli can also be aspirated into the lower portions of both lungs (Fig. 25-3) and into the sputum.

Even when the disease has apparently terminated, reinfection may occur by (1) activation of the bacilli that survived the primary infection or (2) inhalation or ingestion of new bacilli from the environment. This manifestation of disease is called **reactivation tuberculosis** and occurs primarily in the elderly. Malnutrition, diabetes mellitus, prolonged corticosteroid therapy, and chronic alcoholism are factors that predispose a patient to reactivation of TB. A strong tuberculin skin sensitivity in an infected individual indicates a greater probability of active disease developing (see Immunity).

FIGURE 25-2
Histology of a tubercle. A tubercle is in the bone marrow of a wild turkey. Central necrosis can be observed with multinucleated giant cells surrounding it. A well defined capsule delineates the tubercle. (× 160 before 35 percent reduction.) (From C. O. Thoen, A. G. Karlson, and E. M. Himes, *Rev. Infect. Dis.* 3:960. © 1981 University of Chicago.)

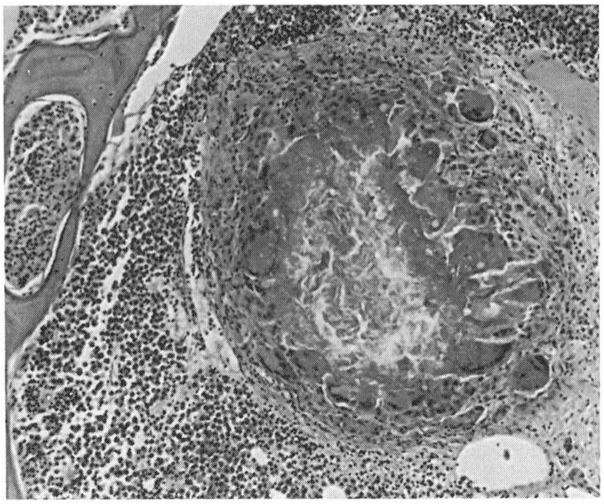

M. tuberculosis is trapped in the phagolysosome during the infection process. However, these microorganisms get out of this prison by a unique escape mechanism. The bacilli bud out of the fused phagolysosome, pulling around them a nonfused membrane. Avirulent strains remain sitting in the nonfused vesicle. The virulent strains escape into the cytoplasm where they can generate a cytotoxic T cell response. Bacteria killed in the macrophage can elicit an immune response. The immune response is expressed by granuloma formation and hypersensitivity to tuberculoprotein. This response leads to caseation. Evidence now suggests that **tumor necrosis factor** plays an important role in both processes. **Cord factor** (Fig. 25-4), a component of the TB bacillus, also appears to be associated with virulence. Cord factor injected into mice causes pulmonary granuloma formation, which is indistinguishable from that caused by injection of *M. bovis* into healthy mice.

Human Immunodeficiency Virus Infection and Tuberculosis

The medical community has become alarmed at the rising incidence of TB in patients infected with the human immunodeficiency virus (HIV). Even more alarming is the fact that much of the TB in this group is caused by multidrug-resistant strains of the bacillus. For HIV-infected persons who have latent TB infection, the risk of developing active TB is 7 to 10 percent per year. Of particular concern to the medical community is the scenario that evolves when persons infected with HIV become newly infected with *M. tuberculosis.* TB develops within one to three months in 40 percent of these HIV-infected patients exposed to infectious TB patients. In addition, the infection in these persons develops so rapidly that many of them are dead within 6 weeks.

The clinical presentation of disseminated TB is the same for patients without underlying HIV infection as it is for patients infected with the HIV. This is not true for pulmonary TB. In most HIV-infected patients radiographs suggest a primary infection. In patients without underlying HIV infection the radiographs suggest reactivation TB. In addition, HIV-infected patients with advanced immunodeficiency do not respond to the purified protein derivative (PPD) that is used to determine infection with the TB bacillus.

TB in patients with advanced HIV infection is often disseminated. Many unusual manifestations of disease have been noted. These include brain abscesses, bone disease, meningitis, gastric tuberculosis, pericarditis, and scrotal TB.

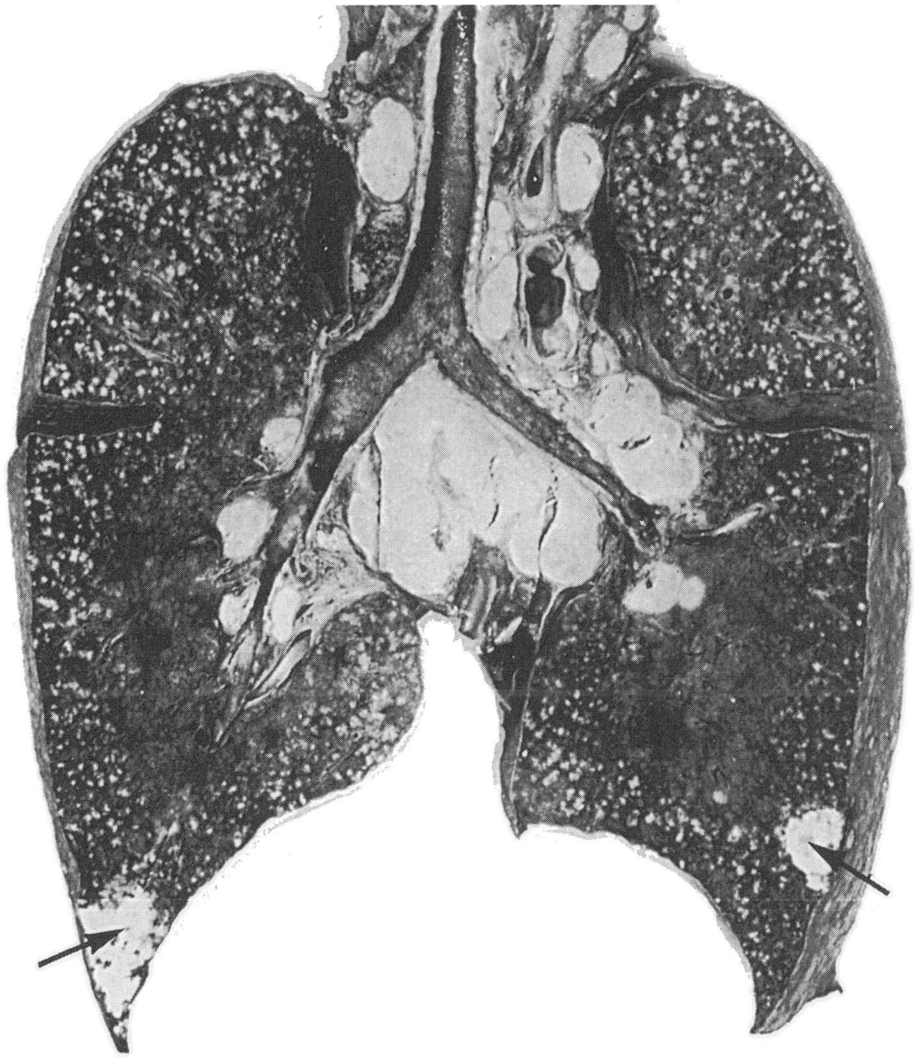

FIGURE 25-3
Bilateral tuberculosis. Caseous necrosis is observed in each lower lobe (*arrows*) as well as in hilar and tracheobronchial nodes. Advanced miliary dissemination can be seen (as white speckled areas) throughout both lungs. (From W. Giese. In E. Kaufmann and M. Staemmler, eds., *Lehrbuch der Speziellen Pathologischen Anatomie.* Vol. 2, Berlin: Walter De Gruyter, 1959–1960.)

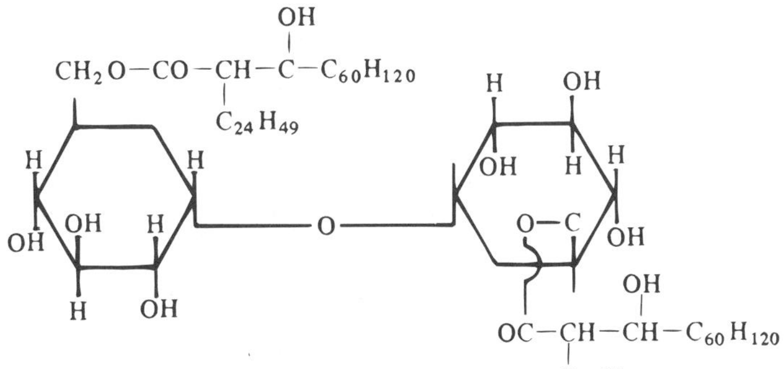

FIGURE 25-4
Structure of the cord factor.

IMMUNITY

Infection by the TB bacillus results in delayed hypersensitivity by the host. The magnitude of the hypersensitivity, however, cannot be correlated with the degree of acquired resistance. The intensity of the hypersensitivity response is directly proportional to the amount of mycobacterial antigen in the infected host. Large numbers of tubercle bacilli in tissue are associated with a highly destructive lesion because of the sensitivity to mycobacterial antigen (**tuberculin**). This hypersensitivity does not prevent bacilli from multiplying in tissue.

Resistance to TB is related to the ability of macrophages to kill the bacilli or to prevent them from multiplying. The immune cells that carry out the killing or inhibition of microbial growth are primarily **activated macrophages.** Activation is brought about by lymphokines released by sensitized T cells. Activated macrophages are rich in lysosomes and other products (see Chapter 9). If macrophages prevent the bacilli from multiplying, an individual can remain infected for years without demonstrating overt disease.

T cell sensitivity to *M. tuberculosis* does not apparently provide lifelong immunity. Studies in nursing homes indicate that immunocompetent elderly persons who were at one time tuberculin-positive may become nonreactive to *M. tuberculosis.* Such nonreactive persons are at risk of contracting an entirely new or primary infection.

Tuberculin Tests

Purified tuberculin protein derivative (PPD) is used in skin sensitivity tests. When injected intracutaneously (**Mantoux test**) into hypersensitive individuals, tuberculin evokes an intense inflammatory reaction (delayed hypersensitivity, see Chapter 13) at the site of injection. The activity of PPD is standardized into tuberculin units from 1 to 100. The standard dose in testing procedures is 5 tuberculin units. The degree of induration at the site of injection is an indication of the individual's present or past association with the TB bacillus. This is not always true in those with immunodeficiency who show some degree of anergy.

An induration of 1 to 5 mm after 48 to 72 hours is considered a negative response. The test is usually repeated with a higher dose strength of PPD for confirmation. If both test results are negative, the individual has presumably not had contact with the TB bacillus. An induration of 5 to 9 mm is called a doubtful reaction, and the test is usually repeated. An induration of 10 to 33 mm reflects a hypersensitivity resulting from either previous or present infection with the TB bacillus. Depending on clinical presentation, appropriate treatment may be necessary for these individuals. The skin test response does not turn positive during the first three to seven weeks after infection. In HIV-infected individuals (who may lack hypersensitivity) an induration of 5 mm or larger can be regarded as indicative of TB infection.

Tuberculin skin testing can also be performed using the **multiple-puncture** method. In this technique tuberculin is introduced into the skin through tuberculin-coated prongs. Since this method gives many false-negative and false-positive results, it is recommended only in large populations with a low prevalence of TB infection.

LABORATORY DIAGNOSIS

The techniques for detecting TB and determining possible communicability to others include the tuberculin skin tests, chest x-ray, and examination of sputum smears and cultures for *M. tuberculosis.*

Because TB is primarily a disease of the lungs, the major source of infecting bacilli for laboratory diagnosis is the sputum or lung secretions. When sputum samples cannot be obtained, gastric contents can be collected and examined. In disseminated TB the clinical material can be cerebrospinal fluid, urine, joint material, or feces.

Confirmation of *M. tuberculosis* infection is established by (1) identification of the bacilli in a stained smear of clinical material (smears are not performed on urine or gastric aspirations), (2) cultivation of the microorganisms from clinical material on suitable laboratory media, and (3) biochemical and other tests.

Presumptive identification of *M. tuberculosis* can be made by demonstration of acid-fast bacteria in sputum samples or other clinical material (Plate 10). When 10^5 bacilli per milliliter are present, the smear is considered positive. An alternative procedure is fluorescence microscopy using auramine-rhodamine as the staining agent. The bacilli appear as bright yellow-green rods (Plate 11). Although direct microscopic examination is the least sensitive of all tests, it does indicate, especially if the clinical material is sputum, that the patient may be highly infectious.

Accurate identification of mycobacteria is obtained by cultural methods. Sputum samples, because of their viscosity and the presence of contaminating microorganisms, are liquefied and decontaminated. This is accomplished by treating samples with sodium hydroxide and N-acetyl-L-cysteine. Traditionally, the sample is centrifuged and neutralized before it is plated on media. The medium used is the egg-based Löwenstein-Jensen medium or the agar-based Middlebrook 7H10 or 7H11 medium.

Broth systems have now been developed for growth of mycobacteria. In these systems, growth is detected by measuring bacterial production of carbon dioxide. The time to detection in these systems is 10 to 13 days compared to 3 to 4 weeks using conventional solid media. Identification of mycobacterial isolates on solid media often relies on rate of growth, pigmentation, and colonial morphology. Once growth is detected, the microorganisms can be identified as *M. tuberculosis* by using specific inhibition by *p*-nitro-α-acetylamino-β-hydroxypropiophenone **(NAP)** (a precursor in the synthesis of chloramphenicol), DNA probes, high-performance liquid chromatography (HPLC), or the standard biochemical tests for the production of niacin, catalase, and nitrate reductase. Identification by pigment production can also be carried out on many mycobacteria but not *M. tuberculosis* and

TABLE 25-1
Characteristics of the Most Frequently Isolated Nontuberculous *Mycobacterium* Species

Runyon group	Species	Source	Most common clinical manifestation	Basis of grouping	Treatment
I	*M. kansasii*	Milk, water; natural reservoir unknown	Pulmonary disease similar to tuberculosis	Pigment produced when exposed to light (photochromogen)	Two or more antituberculous drugs, one of which is rifampin
	M. marinum	Water; found in fish	Cutaneous and disseminated disease		Lesions may resolve spontaneously but drainage or excision of lesion may be required; antituberculous drugs for disseminated disease
	M. simiae	Water; found in monkeys	Chronic pulmonary disease, osteomyelitis		No recommended therapeutic approach, but antituberculous drugs stabilize disease
II	*M. scrofulaceum*	Water, soil, milk and dairy products	Cervical adenitis in children	Pigment produced in dark (scotochromogens)	Resistance to many antimicrobials; rifampin usually suggested
	M. szulgai	Soil, water; natural reservoir unknown	Pulmonary disease, cervical adenitis		Sensitive to antituberculous drugs
	M. xenopi	Soil, water; birds may be reservoir	Pulmonary disease, bone and lymph node involvement		Sensitive to antituberculous drugs
III	*M. avium-intracellulare complex*	Soil, water	Pulmonary disease similar to tuberculosis	Nonpigmented	Antituberculous drugs; but drug resistance is common in AIDS patients
	M. malmoense	Natural reservoir unknown	Chronic pulmonary disease		Sensitive to antituberculous drugs; but treatment usually unsatisfactory
	M. haemophilum	Natural reservoir unknown	Cutaneous lesions; disseminated in immunosuppressed		Rifampin, isoniazid, and ethambutol plus surgical debridement
IV	*M. fortuitum-chelonei* complex	Water, soil	Pulmonary, cutaneous, abscesses; postoperative wound infections	Rapid growth (3–5 days)	Resistance to many antimicrobials; amikacin plus cefoxitin in combination

M. bovis (Table 25-1). Biochemical identification is more definitive but may require several weeks. The **NAP test,** however, requires only three to five days for completion. DNA probes and HPLC can be completed in two to four hours. The DNA probes consist of acridinium ester–labeled single-stranded DNA complementary to ribosomal RNA.

EPIDEMIOLOGY

In the early part of the twentieth century, TB was primarily a disease of infants and young adults. Today, the disease is primarily associated with older men, alcoholics, drug addicts, and others with depressed immune systems. TB was considered on the decline in the early 1980s but since that time there have been steady increases in the incidence of the disease. Many factors have contributed to this rise: an increase in poverty, homelessness, and drug abuse which is conducive to TB spread; active TB developing in infected immigrants; and the increased incidence of AIDS.

In the United States about 10 million individuals are infected with *M. tuberculosis,* with 20,000 additional individuals becoming infected annually. About 25,000 to 28,000 new cases of TB develop each year. Most of these new cases are in individuals with long-term latent infections. When we consider the effect of HIV infection on the disease as well as the emergence of drug-resistant strains, we realize that we have a major public health problem.

TREATMENT AND PREVENTION

Treatment of TB has undergone many revisions over the years. Most of these changes are due to the chronic nature of the disease and the prolonged nature of therapy. At present, a six-month drug regimen is used. For two months isoniazid, rifampin, and pyrazinamide are used, followed by four months of either daily or weekly doses of isoniazid and rifampin. TB in HIV-infected patients is highly responsive to treatment. In communities where drug resistance (see below) is prevalent, the Centers for Disease Control recommends an initial regimen of isoniazid plus rifampin plus pyrazinamide along with two additional drugs to which the organism is likely to be susceptible (for example, ethambutol, streptomycin, ethionamide). Furthermore, the treatment regimen has to be continued for 18 to 24 months if (1) the regimen does not include isoniazid and rifampin, and (2) the regimen is for treatment of multidrug-resistant strains (see below). Antimicrobial susceptibility testing usually is not required for patients with newly diagnosed TB. Susceptibility testing should be performed when the patient has not responded to therapy after three to four months.

Hospitalization is not required for most patients diagnosed with TB. Once the patient is undergoing treatment, any tubercle bacilli that might have been transmitted by the sputum are destroyed. Thus, transmission to healthy persons is no longer considered a factor in the prevention of the disease. A person with active TB can prevent the spread of bacilli by covering the mouth and nose when coughing or sneezing. Adequate ventilation and use of ultraviolet lights help to prevent dissemination of bacilli.

In recent years TB treatment has become more difficult because of the development of drug-resistant strains of *M. tuberculosis*. Throughout the United States nearly 15 percent of patients reported had organisms resistant to at least one antituberculous drug and about 4 percent had organisms resistant to both isoniazid and rifampin. About 7 percent of patients with recurrent TB demonstrate resistance to the two drugs.

A serious new phenomenon is appearing in institutional settings: outbreaks of **multidrug-resistant** TB. In virtually all outbreaks of multidrug-resistant TB, the isolates were resistant to both isoniazid and rifampin. In some instances the isolates were resistant to as many as seven drugs including ethambutol, streptomycin, ethionamide, and kanamycin. The basic problem is compliance with therapy, which is difficult for many individuals, including persons who are born in another country or are homeless, who have substance abuse problems or mental illness, or who have socioeconomic or medical problems such as HIV infection. The increasing incidence of TB in some areas, for example, large cities like New York City, has resulted in more persons with active infectious TB being seen in institutional settings such as nursing homes and correctional facilities.

Solutions to these problems include screening and preventive therapy, patient management, and infection control. Individuals who are infected with the TB bacillus but are not yet sick must be identified. Tuberculin skin testing of workers in settings where there is a risk of TB transmission is important. Once identified, they can be subjected to preventive therapy through the use of **isoniazid.** Isoniazid is recommended when an induration larger than 5 mm is seen after administration of the tuberculin skin test. Isoniazid prophylaxis is also recommended for members of a household with patients with recently diagnosed TB. Isoniazid therapy is usually carried out for six months to one year. Isoniazid can cause liver damage; therefore, patients should be monitored. Patient compliance with therapy should be maintained, particularly in institutions and correctional facilities. Persons caring for and exposed to TB patients must take special precautions (respiratory protective devices, ultraviolet light, proper ventilation, etc.) to prevent acquiring TB themselves.

The bacillus of Calmette and Guérin (BCG), isolated from a strain of *M. bovis,* has been used since 1921 in a live vaccine for the prevention of TB. The vaccine has been used more frequently in other countries than in the United States. The vaccine is not recommended in the United States because it results in the recipient's having a positive response on the tuberculin test; hence, a valuable diagnostic tool is lost.

BCG vaccination is recommended for infants and children with negative tuberculin test results who are exposed for long periods to (1) patients who are untreated or ineffectively treated or (2) patients who have bacilli resistant to isoniazid and rifampin. BCG is also recommended for tuberculin-negative infants and children in groups in which the rate of new infection exceeds 1 percent per year, for example, in groups to whom health care is not regularly accessible.

BCG vaccine should not be given to anyone who is tuberculin-positive or to individuals with impaired immune responses. BCG vaccination has been known to cause death in children with immunological disorders. In the United States isoniazid chemoprophylaxis rather than BCG vaccination is recommended for prevention. In developed countries, where the level of resistance to TB is relatively high, it is much cheaper to treat the disease with drugs than to use preventive methods on a large segment of the population.

Nontuberculous Mycobacterioses

Mycobacteria other than *M. tuberculosis* (MOTT) differ from the latter in several ways. First, person-to-person transmission seldom occurs. Second, MOTT are ubiquitous in nature and can be found as saprophytes in the environment, particularly water. Third, MOTT may colonize an individual without causing disease. The three most common conditions associated with MOTT are **pulmonary disease, lymphadenitis,** and **disseminated disease.** Less frequently encountered conditions are cutaneous and soft tissue infections.

Infections caused by MOTT are not usually invasive unless the patient has some predisposing condition. MOTT are especially troublesome in the hospital because of their resistance to disinfectants such as chlorine and glutaraldehyde. They have been incriminated in infections following such hospital procedures as dialysis, open-heart surgery, and insertion of implant devices (for example, porcine heart valves). In general, MOTT tend to infect young children and immunodepleted adults who come in contact with contaminated food or water. To distinguish MOTT from *M. tuberculosis* and *M. bovis,* Runyon in 1959 proposed a classification scheme in which there were four groups, each group containing several species (see Table 25-1). These groups were differentiated on the basis of colony pigmentation and growth rate.

PATHOGENESIS

Several MOTT are outlined in Table 25-1; however, here we concern ourselves only with some of the more recently documented members.

Mycobacterium avium Complex

The *M. avium* complex includes two important species, *M. avium* and *M. intracellulare*. Infection is more common in patients compromised by chronic pulmonary conditions such as emphysema and bronchitis. Aerosols are a likely source of infection. Symptomatic disease usually progresses and can be fatal unless treated. Symptoms include fever, weight loss, and bone pain. Lymphadenopathy, hepatosplenomegaly, and a variety of skin lesions are also observed.

Recently, disseminated infection by *M. avium* and *M. intracellulare* has become a grave problem in AIDS patients. Approximately 90 percent of the mycobacterioses in AIDS patients involve either *M. avium* or *M. tuberculosis*. Disseminated infection with *M. avium* is the most common systemic bacterial infection complicating AIDS in the United States. Infection contributes to patient morbidity and has adverse effects on survival. In most disseminated cases the *M. avium* complex infection does not lead to extensive inflammation, granulomatous processes, or interference with organ function. This is in contrast to infections caused by *M. tuberculosis* or *M. kansasii*, which do cause these effects in AIDS patients. In about 5 percent of AIDS patients, however, disseminated disease develops and leads to death.

Respiratory or intestinal colonization may precede dissemination. Primary infections of the lung develop in very few AIDS patients. These infections probably occur as a result of colonization of the bronchi by aerosolized waterborne microorganisms. The intestinal tract appears to be the principal portal of entry preceding dissemination. Intestinal colonization can result in massive involvement of Peyer's patch and mesenteric lymph nodes and the development of chronic diarrhea. In a very few AIDS patients there may be other clinical syndromes. Primary rectocolonic mycobacterial lesions develop in some patients. *M. avium* organisms seed the local lymphoid tissue and ultimately infect the spleen and lungs. These infections are invariably fatal. Direct rectal transfer can occur in some homosexual AIDS patients.

The prognosis for *M. avium* complex–infected patients is very poor, due to the resistance of these organisms to some of the available antituberculous drugs and to the high toxicity of the drugs. Most drugs are at best bacteriostatic, and bacterial growth resumes when the drugs are curtailed because of toxicity. In 1993, however, three drugs were approved for prophylaxis and treatment of disseminated *M. avium* complex infection: **rifabutin, charithromycin,** and **azithromycin.** Trials have indicated success, particularly in the prevention of infection.

Mycobacterium fortuitum Complex

This complex includes the species *M. fortuitum* and *M. chelonei*. These rapidly growing species are common environmental saprophytes. *M. fortuitum* is more widely distributed and is a cause of cutaneous infections. *M. chelonei* appears to be more virulent than *M. fortuitum* and is more frequently associated with disseminated disease. In humans, colonization with *M. chelonei* is often transient and its presence in sputum samples is not indicative of infection.

Disseminated disease by *M. chelonei* is most common among immunocompromised patients and often involves the skin and lungs. Renal transplant patients appear to be at greatest risk of serious infection by this organism. Patients receiving steroids and cytotoxic drugs for connective tissue disorders are also at risk of disseminated disease. In immunocompetent patients, cutaneous infection with *M. chelonei* has a 70 percent rate of cure over two to three years, while pulmonary disease runs a chronic relapsing course. Infection in immunocompromised patients follows a more aggressive course. Such infections respond slowly to treatment and may require long-term suppressive therapy.

LABORATORY DIAGNOSIS, TREATMENT, AND PREVENTION

Clinical characteristics may suggest nontuberculous mycobacterioses, but repeated isolation of the organism from specimens such as sputum is required. Identification of the mycobacterial species is required if optimal therapy is to be obtained. Nontuberculous mycobacteria do not always respond to the usual antituberculous drugs (see Table 25-1). Lymphadenitis generally responds to surgery alone. Cutaneous lesions due to *M. marinum* may also require surgery. *M. kansasii* responds well to antituberculous drugs except when the infection is disseminated.

Besides determinations of pigment production and growth rate, several biochemical and cultural tests are used in the identification of nontuberculous mycobacteria (see *Manual of Clinical Microbiology*, 5th ed., listed in Additional Readings). DNA probes are now available for rapid identification of species, for example, differentiation of *M. avium* from *M. intracellulare*.

Mycobacterium leprae

Leprosy (Hansen's disease) is a chronic mycobacterial infection that was recorded about 600 B.C. in India. The causative agent, *M. leprae*, still has not been cultured in vitro. Infected individuals who show maximum resistance to the bacilli demonstrate a disease affecting superficial nerve endings and related skin areas. In persons with minimal resistance to the bacilli, the infection may involve organs such as the eyes, testicles, and bones.

GENERAL CHARACTERISTICS

M. leprae is an intracellular parasite that cannot be cultivated in vitro but can be cultivated in vivo. The bacillus can be cultured on mouse foot pads or armadillos. Like most other mycobacteria, *M. leprae* exhibits slow growth and has a generation time of 12 days.

EPIDEMIOLOGY

Leprosy is a disease found primarily in Asia and Africa. The total number of leprosy patients in the world is estimated to be between 10 and 12 million. In the United States there are an estimated 5000 patients and most of these are immigrants. The annual incidence among native-born Americans in the past 50 years is about 25 to 35 new cases per year.

Transmission of the leprosy bacillus is believed to occur through (1) inhalation of bacilli onto the nasal mucosa, (2) intact skin, or (3) penetrating wounds such as thorns. Inhalation of aerosols is believed to be the most common method of transmission. Leprosy is a natural infection of wild armadillos. Whether these animals are a source of infection to humans is not clear since most leprosy cases occur where armadillos are absent.

PATHOGENESIS

Leprosy exhibits different forms of disease depending on the ability of the host to mount a cell-mediated immune response. People in areas endemic for leprosy become infected without any overt symptoms being manifested. Disease symptoms appear two to four years after infection. In one form of the disease called **indeterminate leprosy,** a few hypopigmented areas of the skin plus a dermatitis may be the first clinical manifestations of disease. Most of these individuals will recover spontaneously but the remainder will progress to one of the established forms of the disease, called **lepromatous leprosy** or **tuberculoid leprosy.**

Lepromatous leprosy is the most disfiguring form of the disease because of the host's lack of immunity to the bacillus (Plate 12). Skin lesions range from diffuse to nodular (the nodules are called **lepromas**). The skin lesions appear in the cooler parts of the body (nasal mucosa, anterior one-third of the eye, and peripheral nerve trunks at specific sites such as the elbow, wrist, and ankle). The patient has few symptoms other than those caused by the nodular masses. Patients with advanced disease have sensory loss due to the involvement of nerve fibers. The lesions are filled with macrophages, which contain large numbers of bacilli.

Tuberculoid leprosy (Plate 13) represents a localized form of the disease in which there are a few well circumscribed skin lesions. The lesions appear flat, are blanched, and contain few bacilli. The clinical picture is due to bacterial proliferation followed by a relatively efficient immune response of the host to the bacilli.

In most leprosy patients there is some degree of irreversible peripheral nerve damage. In patients with advanced disease, widespread destruction of nerve trunks can result in loss of feeling and permanent paralysis involving the face, hands, and feet. The lack of pain sensations allows the patient to suffer self-damage and self-deformation through continued use of an extremity.

The pathogenic mechanisms of *M. leprae* have never been clearly defined. The organism can live intracellularly because it is a poor stimulator of the respiratory burst in monocytes. *M. leprae* possesses a phenolic glycolipid that is released extracellularly. This compound can be released in macrophages, where it acts as an antioxidant and scavenges various oxygen-derived metabolites that are thought to be important in microbial killing. A surface compound of *M. leprae,* called **lipoarabinomannan,** inhibits the proliferation of T cells. These two chemical compounds may represent mechanisms for preventing effective immune responses by the host during infection.

LABORATORY DIAGNOSIS, TREATMENT, AND PREVENTION

The methods available for diagnosing typical leprosy include skin examination, neurological evaluation of extremities, palpation of peripheral nerves, and skin smears for acid-fast bacilli.

It is difficult to diagnose atypical disease or asymptomatic disease. The most recent development in diagnostic techniques is the polymerase chain reaction. This sensitive technique could conceivably detect *M. leprae* in healthy individuals.

At present, four drugs are used in chemotherapy: dapsone, rifampin, clofazimine, and either ethionamide or prothionamide. The latter two exhibit a high degree of hepatotoxicity and are expensive. In the United States current therapy recommendations for tuberculoid or indeterminate leprosy are dapsone plus rifampin for six months followed by dapsone alone for three years. Management of leprosy patients also includes minimizing permanent nerve damage and irreversible eye damage. These goals can be accomplished using corticosteroids plus high doses of antibacterial drugs such as clofazimine. Prophylaxis is considered for family members of leprosy patients.

An antileprosy vaccine is undergoing trials in India. The vaccine consists of ICRC (Indian Cancer Research Center) bacillus, a cultivatable mycobacterium isolated from human lepromata.

Summary

1. The major human pathogenic species of *Mycobacterium* are *M. tuberculosis* and *M. bovis,* the causative agents of tuberculosis (TB), and *M. leprae,* the cause of leprosy. Nontuberculous mycobacteria are found as saprophytes in water and soil. They are the agents of three types of disease: lymphadenitis, cutaneous infections, and pulmonary infections (see Table 25-1). The *M. avium* complex has become an important pathogen in AIDS patients.

2. *Mycobacterium* organisms differ from other bacteria in certain respects: (1) Mycobacteria have a high lipid content, (2) they are acid-fast bacilli, (3) they produce serpentine colonies on specific agar, (4) they divide every 18 to 24 hours, and (5) they produce pigments that may be induced or may be constitutive.

3. TB is primarily a respiratory disease, but any organ can be infected. Apparently only activated macrophages

can kill TB bacilli. The inflammatory response to TB bacilli results in formation of a tubercle. Tubercles can liquefy to produce caseation necrosis.

4. Caseous lesions may heal and retain active bacilli for years or bacilli may spill out into the bloodstream to infect any organ. Some caseous lesions can rupture, allowing bacilli to be carried to healthy lung tissue. Bacilli in healed lesions can be reactivated years later to cause active disease.

5. The virulence of *M. tuberculosis* is associated with its ability to prevent phagosome-lysosome fusion in the macrophage. The cord factor may be the virulence factor.

6. TB is a disease manifested as a hypersensitivity to antigens of the TB bacillus. Once infected by the bacillus, the host is sensitive to antigens such as purified tuberculin protein. This sensitivity is the basis of the tuberculin test, which determines one's present or past contact with the TB bacillus.

7. Laboratory diagnosis of TB relies on detecting bacilli in sputum or other secretions via acid-fast stain or fluorescent antibody. The TB bacillus can be cultured on special agar media but broth culture systems are available for more rapid growth. Colonial and biochemical identification tests are available. DNA probes are also available for rapid identification.

8. Anyone is susceptible to TB, which is spread by contact with infected respiratory secretions. Between 25,000 and 28,000 cases are reported each year in the United States but as many as 10 million people may be infected.

9. Treatment of TB requires a multidrug regimen including isoniazid, rifampin, ethambutol, streptomycin, and pyrazinamide. Multidrug resistance has been on the increase and treatment is now more difficult. Isoniazid is used to prevent infection in the United States. In other countries BCG vaccine is used for prevention.

10. The leprosy bacillus cannot be cultivated in vitro but can be cultured in the armadillo and mouse foot pad. Leprosy is seen primarily in Asia and Africa. Only a few cases of leprosy are observed in the United States.

11. Leprosy is believed to be acquired by inhalation of contaminated aerosols generated by infected patients. Most individuals have a natural resistance to the leprosy bacillus and show only minor symptoms. Individuals who do respond to the bacillus usually demonstrate one of three forms of the disease: indeterminate, tuberculoid, or lepromatous leprosy.

12. Indeterminate leprosy is manifested as only a few hypopigmented areas on the skin plus dermatitis. Most of these patients will recover spontaneously. The remainder progress into tuberculoid or lepromatous leprosy. In tuberculoid leprosy the patient has some immunity and the disease is localized. Immunity is lacking in lepromatous leprosy, which can be the most disfiguring form of the disease.

13. Diagnosis of leprosy is usually based on the appearance of lesions but acid-fast bacilli can be identified in scrapings from skin, nasal secretions, and so on. Four drugs, including dapsone and rifampin, are the principal agents used to treat leprosy. Some form of lifelong treatment may be required for lepromatous leprosy patients.

Questions for Study

1. What characteristics distinguish the mycobacteria from gram-positive and gram-negative bacteria?
2. What host or microbial factors contribute to the lesions observed in tuberculosis?
3. What influence has the AIDS epidemic had on tuberculosis? Why is it difficult to diagnose tuberculosis in AIDS patients?
4. What factors have contributed to the emergence of multidrug resistance among the mycobacteria? What can be done to prevent this type of scenario?
5. What types of infections are associated with nontuberculous mycobacteria? Do any of the species cause disease that cannot be distinguished from that caused by *M. tuberculosis?*
6. What group of nontuberculous mycobacteria are frequently associated with disease in AIDS patients? What clinical syndromes are they associated with?
7. Describe the different manifestations of infection by the leprosy bacillus.

CHAPTER 26

Spirochetes and Spiral and Curved Rods

OBJECTIVES

To outline the various symptoms associated with the different stages of syphilis

To outline the treatment regimen for the different groups of individuals who have syphilis

To describe briefly the most important laboratory tests used to identify the syphilis organism

To list the causative agent, method of transmission, site of infection, and method of treatment for leptospirosis, relapsing fever, Lyme disease, rat-bite fever, and *Campylobacter* and *Helicobacter* infections

OUTLINE

THE SPIROCHETES
- Genus *Treponema (Treponema pallidum)*
  - General Characteristics of *Treponema pallidum*
  - Pathogenesis
    - Primary Syphilis
    - Secondary Syphilis
    - Latent Syphilis
    - Tertiary or Late Syphilis
    - Congenital Syphilis
  - Epidemiology
  - Laboratory Diagnosis
    - Dark-Field Examination
    - Immunofluorescence
    - Serological Tests
    - Biological False-Positives and -Negatives
  - Treatment
  - Prevention and Control
  - Nonvenereal Syphilis
- Genus *Borrelia*
  - General Characteristics
  - Epidemiology and Pathogenesis
    - Relapsing Fever
    - Lyme Disease
  - Laboratory Diagnosis
  - Treatment and Prevention
- Genus *Leptospira*
  - General Characteristics
  - Epidemiology and Pathogenesis
  - Laboratory Diagnosis and Treatment

SPIRAL AND CURVED RODS
- Genus *Spirillum*
- Genus *Campylobacter*
  - Epidemiology and Pathogenesis
  - Laboratory Diagnosis, Treatment, and Prevention
- *Helicobacter pylori*
  - Epidemiology and Pathogenesis
  - Laboratory Diagnosis and Treatment

Several helical and curved bacteria are indigenous to soil and water, and some can be found as commensals in animals. Only a few, however, are human pathogens. The **spirochetes** are a group with a distinct morphology and method of movement that distinguishes them from the **spiral and curved rods.** There are three important genera of human pathogenic spirochetes: *Treponema, Borrelia,* and *Leptospira.* The spiral and curved rods include three important genera: *Spirillum, Campylobacter,* and *Helicobacter.*

The Spirochetes

The spirochetes are long, slender, helically shaped cells that are actively motile by flagellum-like filaments called **axial filaments.** The axial filaments, which originate at each pole of the cell, are located between an outer envelope or sheath and an inner protoplasmic cylinder (see Fig. 2-13). The number of axial filaments varies depending on the genus.

Spirochetes are gram-negative (but the Gram procedure is rarely used to identify them). They are 3 to 500 μm in length and 0.20 to 0.75 μm in diameter. Human pathogens, however, are seldom more than 40 μm long. They all divide by transverse fission. They may be aerobic, facultatively anaerobic, or anaerobic. Routine staining procedures are not ordinarily employed, because the width of many spirochetes is at or just below the resolving power of the light microscope (see Appendix A for a discussion of microscopy). Spirochetes are best recognized by dark-field microscopy. The only reliable method for differentiation among the pathogenic spirochetes is based on the size, number, and spacing of the helical coils (Fig. 26-1).

GENUS *TREPONEMA (TREPONEMA PALLIDUM)*

Treponemal species can be found as commensals in the oral cavity, gastrointestinal tract, and urogenital tract of animals. The pathogenic treponemes are *Treponema pallidum,* the causative agent of venereal syphilis; *T. pertenue,* the agent of **yaws,** a tropical disease; and *T. carateum,* the agent of a chronic skin disease found in Central and South America called **pinta.** Diseases caused by species of *Treponema* are called **treponematoses.**

General Characteristics of *Treponema pallidum*

T. pallidum is 6 to 14 μm in length and 0.1 to 0.2 μm in width. The organism cannot be easily stained by ordinary dyes and is best observed by dark-field microscopy. When observed microscopically, the coils are seen to be evenly spaced 1 μm from each other (Fig. 26-2).

Pathogenic treponemes are not cultivatable with any consistency in artificial laboratory media. They are ordinarily cultivated in rabbit testicular tissue. *T. pallidum* is microaerophilic and sensitive to environmental influences. It is easily inactivated by heat (temperatures above 42 C), desiccation, cold, osmotic changes, and heavy metals. Heavy metals such as arsenic, antimony, and bismuth

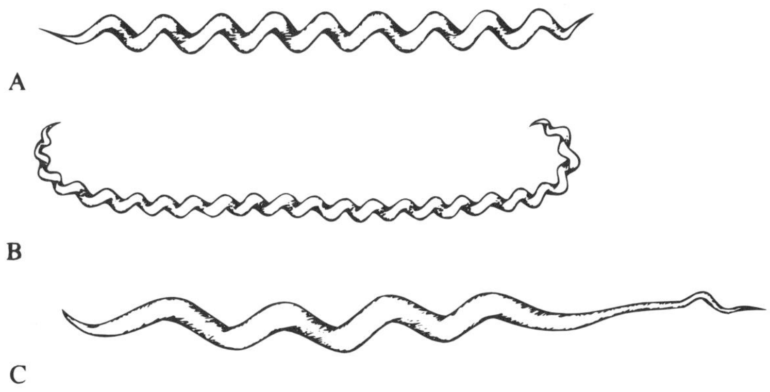

FIGURE 26-1
Relative size and shape of spirochetes. A. Genus *Treponema.* B. Genus *Leptospira.* C. Genus *Borrelia.*

FIGURE 26-2
Electron micrograph of *Treponema pallidum* attached to rabbit testes. (From T. J. Fitzgerald, *J. Bacteriol.* 130: 1333, 1977.)

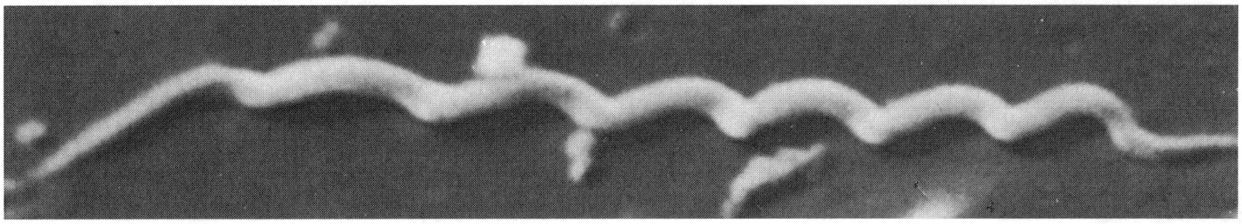

were used to treat syphilis up until the discovery of penicillin. Many deaths were caused by heavy-metal poisoning.

Pathogenesis

Syphilis is almost always contracted by direct transmission. Direct contact takes place by sexual means or by accidental contact with infectious lesions such as those that occur in the mouth. Congenital transfer between mother and fetus also occurs. Almost 90 percent of the cases of syphilis are caused by sexual contact.

Untreated syphilis either progresses through several stages to debilitation and death or terminates spontaneously with no apparent detrimental effects. The symptoms in each stage, if present, are varied and often unpredictable.

Primary Syphilis. In more than 90 percent of affected patients, a single lesion appears on the cervix of the female or the penis of the male. The primary lesion may also be evident on any cutaneous or mucous membrane surface, for example, the scrotum, labia, nipples, rectum, eyelids, fingers, or mouth. At the initial site of infection, a papule, the base of which is hard but painless, develops into an ulcerated sore (Fig. 26-3, Plate 14). This lesion is called a **hard chancre.**

The time required for the appearance of the chancre varies between 10 and 90 days, the average being about 3 weeks. In women a lesion on the cervix may go unnoticed. The chancre will disappear within a week if the patient is treated immediately with antibiotics. Untreated, it may disappear spontaneously within 4 to 12 weeks. Accompanying the primary chancre is the development of enlarged lymph nodes near the initial lesion. Once into the lymph, the organism is capable of reaching the bloodstream and infecting other tissues.

As many as 25 percent of patients with primary syphilis have negative results on serological tests. At this stage the only absolute diagnostic test is dark-field microscopic examination of material from the lesion. Material from the lesion is highly infectious.

Studies in the early part of the twentieth century indicated that in 75 percent of untreated patients, syphilis did not progress beyond the primary stage. This implies that a certain degree of immunity results from primary infection.

Secondary Syphilis. Systemic dispersal of microorganisms from the primary lesion leads to the secondary stage. The chancre produced in the primary stage may still be present during the secondary stage. Symptoms of the secondary stage may appear from six weeks to several months after infection. They are manifested by the development of cutaneous as well as mucous membrane lesions.

In more than 80 percent of persons infected, a macular skin rash appears on the trunk or limbs, but seldom on the face. There may be a papular rash in which the lesion is raised and indurated (Fig. 26-4). The papules usually develop on the trunk and limbs, as well as the palms of the hands (Plate 15) and soles of the feet. They also appear on the face. The papular lesion may break down, resulting in ulceration. Lesions on the scalp can cause temporary loss of hair (alopecia).

Mucous membrane lesions can occur at the mucocutaneous junctions. Sometimes these lesions coalesce to form large masses called **condylomata.** They are more prevalent around the anus and labia (Plate 16). Lesions of the mucous membrane are also common in the mouth and on the tongue and tonsils. Such a lesion is known as a **mucous patch** and is raised and covered with a gray-white membrane.

FIGURE 26-3
Primary stage of syphilis. Chancres on the penis. (Courtesy of Centers for Disease Control, Atlanta, GA.)

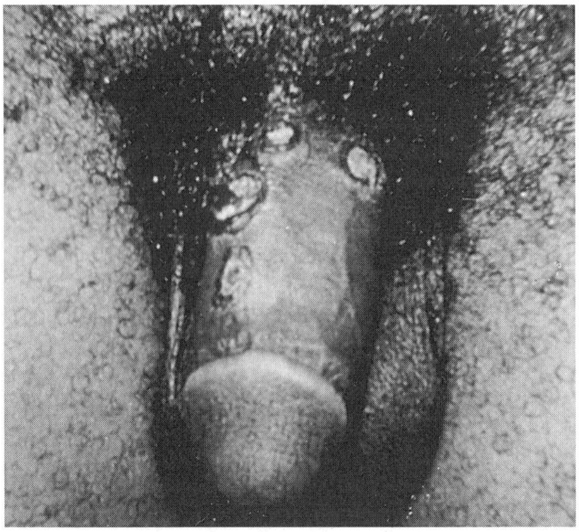

FIGURE 26-4
Secondary cutaneous syphilis. (From A. H. Rudolph. In P. H. Wehrle and F. H. Top, Sr., eds., *Communicable and Infectious Diseases*, 8th ed. St. Louis: Mosby, 1976.)

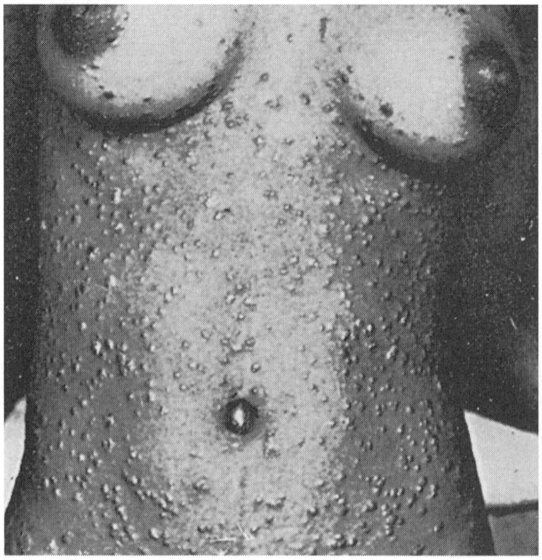

The spirochete can be demonstrated in any of the cutaneous or mucous membrane lesions by dark-field microscopy. Serological examination of patients during this stage reveals high antibody titers that remain relatively high for up to two years after infection—after that the serological findings are often negative. Patients in the primary and secondary stages are highly infectious. The infectious stage usually ends when the lesions of the secondary stage have healed and the treponemes are no longer demonstrable in them. Some treponemes, however, remain viable after the disappearance of the secondary symptoms and give rise to a quiescent period called **latent syphilis.**

Latent Syphilis. In latent syphilis a relatively high serological titer is evident, but clinical symptoms are lacking. This stage is subdivided into early and late latent periods. **Early latent syphilis** is a latent infection of two years or less. During this period the patient may have relapses in which secondary lesions reappear and render the patient potentially infectious. The **late latent period,** considered a noninfectious stage, is a latent infection of more than two years. This stage may last the lifetime of the patient or until certain clinical symptoms are manifested as occurs in the tertiary stage of syphilis.

Tertiary or Late Syphilis. Lesions of the tertiary stage may occur any time after the appearance of the primary and secondary stages, or they may never arise. In this noninfectious stage the tertiary lesions may or may not be debilitating. **Gummas** are the most typical tertiary lesions. Gummas contain no treponemes but rather are due to a hypersensitivity on the part of the host. They are granulomatous lesions of the skin, subcutaneous tissue, mucous membrane, bone, or viscera. Gummas of the skin (Fig. 26-5) are painless, firm, indurated nodules and may show scaling. Gummas of the subcutaneous tissue result in ulceration, with the lesion giving the appearance of being punched out. They may be found on the leg, hand, scalp, or face. Gummas of the mucous membranes can eventually destroy deeper tissue such as bone and cartilage. Gummas of the mouth can lead to perforation of the hard palate as well as deformities of the soft palate and uvula. Glossitis, a superficial inflammation of the tongue, causes an initial swelling that may later result in the formation of deep fissures.

FIGURE 26-5
Gumma of the hand, characteristic of tertiary syphilis. (Courtesy of Centers for Disease Control, Atlanta, GA.)

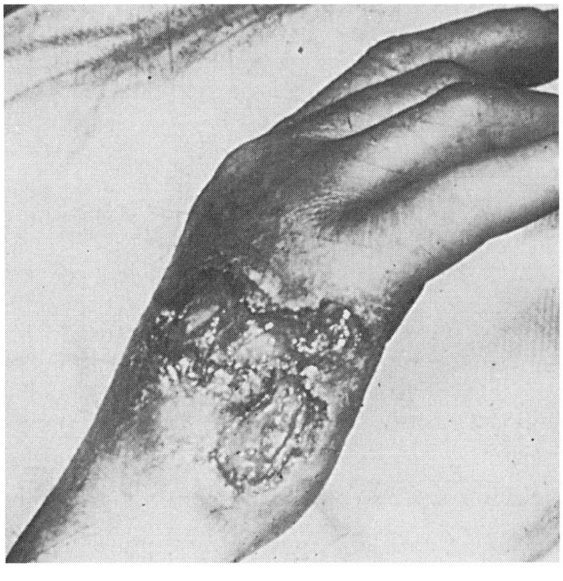

Syphilis of the bone may result in periostitis. This is characterized by proliferation of the bone under the periosteum, or osteitis, in which destructive lesions are produced. Periostitis of the tibia causes a bowing of the front of the bone and is called **saber shin syndrome.** In osteitis, flat bones, particularly those of the skull, as well as the nasal bones and palate, may be severely affected and become deformed. Gummas of the viscera are manifested most frequently in lesions of the liver.

The most destructive and debilitating lesions involve the cardiovascular and central nervous systems. The prognosis for cardiovascular syphilis is death, often as a result of aneurysms in the vessels of the heart. Neurosyphilis can actually be broken down into early and late. Early neurosyphilis is characterized by meningitis and cranial nerve abnormalities. **Early neurosyphilis** was relatively uncommon in the preantibiotic era. It was first observed in patients who were inadequately treated with arsenicals. After the discovery of penicillin, early neurosyphilis was rarely observed but now is appearing more frequently in patients with acquired immunodeficiency syndrome (AIDS). Studies with AIDS patients indicate that about 2 percent have neurosyphilis. The symptoms include meningitis, optic neuritis, or neuroretinitis. One of the major problems is that some of the serological tests used to diagnose syphilis fail to detect infection.

Late neurosyphilis gives rise to the following conditions: (1) In **tabes dorsalis** the spinal cord is affected, resulting in loss of control of the lower extremities; in such cases death is often the result of some other complication. (2) In **paresis,** also called **general paresis of the insane,** there is first a personality change and then the patient becomes demented and bedridden. In the preantibiotic era late neurosyphilis was very common among individuals who were untreated. It is seldom observed today.

Dark-field examination of tertiary lesions is usually negative for spirochetes. Serological tests can disclose the presence of antibodies in more than 70 percent of patients. In others antibodies cannot be detected. To date, no *T. pallidum* antigen has been shown conclusively to be a virulence factor.

Congenital Syphilis. A mother with untreated primary or secondary syphilis is a potential threat to the fetus. After the sixteenth week of pregnancy, the fetus is vulnerable to infection. Treatment of the mother before the sixteenth week almost always prevents infection in the newborn. Treatment after the sixteenth week brings about an in utero cure but may not be in time to prevent bone or joint involvement, deafness, or interstitial keratitis.

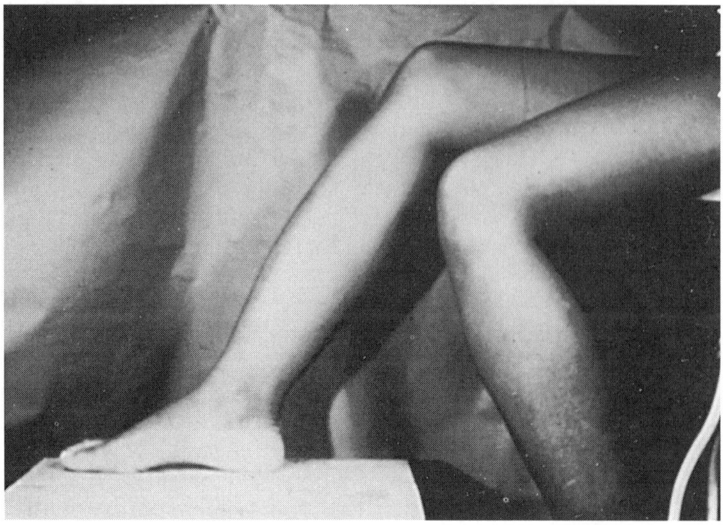

FIGURE 26-6
Saber shin, characteristic of congenital syphilis. (Courtesy of Centers for Disease Control, Atlanta, GA.)

If infected fetuses are left untreated, 20 to 25 percent will die as a result of stillbirth or spontaneous abortion, another 20 to 25 percent will die soon after birth, and 50 percent of the survivors will have severe infection.

Although many infected infants appear healthy at birth, symptoms begin to manifest themselves. The syphilitic is often born with or develops a rash similar to that incurred with secondary syphilis. The rash is papular and may cover the entire body but is particularly evident on the palms, soles, and areas about the mouth. Mucous patches may also appear. In the nose these patches give rise to a nasal discharge called **snuffles.** Snuffles often progresses to inflammation of the bone (osteitis), causing a deformity referred to as **saddle nose.** The liver is often enlarged, causing a distended abdomen. The bones can also be affected, resulting in periostitis of the long bones, a very painful condition.

After the second year of life, noninfectious manifestations of congenital syphilis develop. Gummas can destroy the nasal septum and perforate the soft and hard palates. Periostitis of the tibia leads to bowing of the leg (saber shin, Fig. 26-6). The most common lesion is interstitial keratitis, which can involve both eyes. Each attack leaves some scarring on the cornea, which eventually impairs vision. **Hutchinson's teeth,** a condition in which the central incisors of the permanent teeth are notched and translucent, is also a common late congenital symptom. Failure of the maxilla to develop makes the jaw look prominent, producing a bulldog appearance.

Epidemiology

From 1981 to 1989 the incidence of primary and secondary syphilis increased from 13.7 to 18.4 cases per 100,000 persons in the United States. More cases were reported in 1990 (50,223) than in any year since 1949 (41,942). Syphilis in the United States today is a predominantly heterosexually transmitted disease concentrated in the inner city and among minorities. There is an increasing proportion of infected women, which has manifested as an increase in congenital syphilis. The number of cases of congenital syphilis in 1983 was 158. In 1993 there were 3211 cases of congenital syphilis. The major factors contributing to these increases in recent years are (1) the exchange of nonintravenous drugs, such as crack cocaine, for sex, and (2) decreased resources available for syphilis control programs.

The increase in syphilis can be reversed by (1) removing financial barriers that prevent access to quality care, (2) screening for sexually transmitted diseases in high-risk populations, (3) utilizing interviews for locating and treating sexual partners, and (4) providing the necessary information to educate all age groups about the disease and how it can be avoided.

Recent studies showed an epidemiological link between syphilis and human immunodeficiency virus (HIV) infection. Although it has been difficult to establish which infection came first, individuals with sexually transmitted diseases such as syphilis appear to be at increased risk for HIV infection. Persons with positive syphilis serology, for example, were eight times more likely to be HIV-seropositive than were those with negative syphilis serological findings.

Laboratory Diagnosis

Dark-Field Examination. Examination of exudate from syphilitic lesions or rashes by dark-field microscopy is the only absolute diagnostic test for *T. pallidum* (Plate 17). Such examination cannot be used for all stages of syphilis because suspected lesions may not exist or may be inaccessible. The suspected lesions, if they are from the tertiary stage of syphilis or if the patient has received antibiotic treatment before examination, may also reveal no spirochetes.

Immunofluorescence. The exudate from tissue can be fixed to a slide and stained with a fluorescein-labeled anti-treponeme serum. Identification is made by fluorescence microscopy.

Serological Tests. Two types of antibodies are produced in response to treponemal infections: **reagin,** a nonspecific antitreponemal antibody, and a specific antitreponemal antibody. Several serological tests for syphilis can be used to detect antibodies. None of the tests, however, is absolute because biological false-positives can occur in any of them.

Reagin is produced by all syphilitics, but it is not a protective antibody. It is a mixture of IgG and IgM antibodies produced during several conditions and diseases beside syphilis. Reagin reacts with a cardiolipin extracted from beef heart. The most common tests used to detect the reagin-cardiolipin complex are the agglutination tests.

The **Venereal Disease Research Laboratories (VDRL)** test is an agglutination test. A positive reaction is the appearance of discrete clumps when the cardiolipin antigen is added to the patient's serum. The VDRL test is used primarily as a screening test for routine physical examination, blood bank screening, hospital admissions, prenatal examinations, and venereal disease clinics.

A second agglutination test is the **rapid plasma reagin (RPR)** card test. It also detects reagin but uses charcoal particles so the test can be read microscopically. The nontreponemal VDRL and RPR tests are not ideal because they cannot distinguish between IgG and IgM without previous separation of serum. Detection of IgM is important for the diagnosis of congenital syphilis. IgM does not cross the placenta and IgM in a newborn indicates active syphilis. VDRL and RPR tests are not particularly sensitive in the early stages of primary or late latent syphilis.

Antitreponemal antibody tests are more specific than the nontreponemal antibody tests. They are confirmatory tests that are used to resolve problems that arise from the initial screening procedures. The two major antitreponemal tests are the **fluorescent treponemal antibody (FTA)** and the ***Treponema pallidum*** **hemagglutination (TPHA)** test.

1. The **FTA test** is sensitive in all stages of syphilis (but least sensitive in primary syphilis). The most widely used variant of this test is the **FTA absorbed (FTA-ABS) test.** In the FTA-ABS test nonspecific treponemal antibodies are removed from the test serum by absorption with an extract of Reiter protein. Reiter protein is prepared from a nonpathogenic treponemal strain called the Reiter strain. The FTA-ABS test is performed as follows:
   a. Killed *T. pallidum* is fixed to the slide.
   b. The patient's serum is applied to the slide and incubated for 30 minutes. If antibodies to *T. pallidum* are present in the serum, they will bind to the spirochete.
   c. Goat or rabbit anti–human globulin previously tagged with fluorescein is added to the slide. If the test result is positive, a fluorescein-antibody-spirochete complex will be formed. The immunoglobulin to which the fluorescein dye is conjugated is IgG.

   For the detection of congenital syphilis, human IgG is replaced by IgM in some laboratories. The test has been found to be more specific than any of the serological tests generally used for congenital syphilis. The reason is that total IgM is elevated in the umbilical cord or blood during syphilis infection.
2. **TPHA** tests have become popular in recent years. Red blood cells from certain animal species plus Reiter treponeme components are used. The test detects, by hemagglutination, the presence of treponemal antibodies. The test is very inexpensive and easy to perform. It compares favorably with the FTA-ABS test except in primary syphilis. This test is favored outside the United States as a confirmatory test.

Currently, there is no specific serological test for congenital syphilis, principally due to the problem of transplacental transfer of maternal antitreponemal (and nontreponemal) IgG into the fetal circulation. The presence of *T. pallidum* in amniotic fluid, not conventionally used to establish a diagnosis of congenital infection, has been found useful as a putative marker for congenital infection. Evaluation can be made by dark-field microscopy or by immunofluorescence assays.

Biological False-Positives and -Negatives. In some individuals, results of serological tests for syphilis are positive when in fact the patient does not have and never had syphilis. Such results are called **biological false-positives.** Any serological test for syphilis may give a false-positive. Reagin, which the VDRL test detects, can be produced in several conditions other than syphilis, including immunization, drug addiction, lupus erythematosus, connective tissue diseases, and hepatitis. Most studies have shown that 1 in 4000 nonsyphilitic patients will give a biological false-positive.

In recent years biological false-negatives have become a source of concern (see Under the Microscope 22).

Treatment

Penicillin is the drug of choice for the treatment of all stages of syphilis. Some of the recommendations for treatment of specific groups and some of the problems encountered in these groups are indicated below:

1. Primary, secondary, and latent syphilis of less than one year's duration: Penicillin G benzathine as a single dose may be administered intramuscularly. For nonpregnant penicillin-allergic patients who have primary or secondary syphilis, doxycycline or tetracycline is recommended.
2. Syphilis during pregnancy. Penicillin G benzathine is recommended. Tetracyclines are not recommended because of their toxic effects on the mother and fetus. All infants born to mothers with untreated syphilis require 10 to 14 days of parenteral therapy. There are no proven options to penicillin if the patient is allergic to the drug. Women allergic to penicillin can be treated with the drug after desensitization.

UNDER THE MICROSCOPE 22

Biological False-Negatives and Syphilis

Certain groups of individuals who have syphilis demonstrate negative results on serological tests. False-negatives are more frequently observed in patients with congenital syphilis, in human immunodeficiency virus (HIV)–infected mothers, and in all HIV-infected individuals. The problem resides in the measurement of antibody to cardiolipin in the VDRL or rapid plasma reagent (RPR) test. Cardiolipin is a phospholipid (diphosphatidyl-glycerol) that is a normal constituent of host tissue. Cardiolipin levels are increased in HIV-infected patients, particularly pregnant mothers and patients with congenital syphilis.

In serological agglutination tests one would expect agglutinating activity to decrease with gradual dilution of an antiserum. Some sera, however, give agglutination reactions only when diluted several hundredfold or thousandfold. If the serum sample is undiluted or only slightly diluted, there is excess antibody. Excess antibody hinders agglutination or the formation of clumps. This unreactive condition with excess antibody is called the **prozone phenomenon.**

In several instances, newborn infants with congenital syphilis were born to mothers who were thought to have nonreactive results on VDRL tests using undiluted serum. The titers in their serum were so high that the undiluted sample demonstrated negativity because of prozone. Many laboratories no longer perform dilutions on routine VDRL determinations. Dilutions should be requested to prevent this type of occurrence.

3. Syphilis in HIV-infected patients. Controversy exists as to the proper course of penicillin treatment for HIV-infected patients. Treatment failures have been noted, particularly in those with neurosyphilis. The single dose of penicillin G regimen is being challenged.

In many patients with syphilis, a local or generalized reaction, called the **Jarisch-Herxheimer reaction,** follows the administration of penicillin. The reaction is characterized by headache, fever, and joint pains followed by an intensification of the syphilitic symptoms. Steroid hormones can prevent or diminish the reaction. Herxheimer-like reactions are also detected in patients with other diseases such as borreliosis, brucellosis, and trypanosomiasis.

Prophylactic use of penicillin before intercourse is not recommended because of the danger of masking the usual symptoms of syphilis.

Prevention and Control

To date no active immunizing agent has been produced as a prophylaxis to syphilis infection. Although sexual abstinence would certainly be the ultimate weapon, that proposal would not be met with a great deal of enthusiasm. Control of the disease is difficult because of the high rate of travel, mildness of symptoms, infectiousness in early stages, and ignorance about the transmission, diagnosis, and treatment of syphilis. Prevention should be the ultimate goal, and this can be accomplished by

1. Education. The transmission, diagnosis, and treatment of syphilis among all age groups, especially the young, must be understood.
2. Routine serological testing programs. Screening at pregnancy test sites, and screening and treatment of persons at locations where drugs or sex are sold are two new programs that have proved to be effective forms of intervention. Testing programs are routinely utilized before issuance of marriage licenses, as part of a hospital admission procedure, and during preemployment examinations.
3. Investigation. As rapidly as possible, investigation concerning the treated syphilitic should be conducted so the syphilitic patient's contacts can be found, tested, and if necessary, treated for possible infection.

Nonvenereal Syphilis

Yaws, bejel, and **pinta** are three diseases that resemble syphilis. They are endemic, nonvenereal, and transmitted primarily by contact with eating and drinking utensils in areas lacking hygiene. Yaws is caused by *T. pertenue.* The organism is morphologically and serologically indistinguishable from *T. pallidum.* Yaws is endemic in Africa, India, and parts of South America. The primary lesion, called a **mother yaw,** heals and later develops into a secondary lesion (Fig. 26-7). Tertiary lesions may involve the skin and occasionally the bones. Penicillin is effective treatment.

Pinta, a disease found in Central and South America, is caused by *T. carateum.* This organism, like *T. pertenue,* is morphologically and serologically indistinguishable from *T. pallidum.* Primary lesions do not become necrotic but do become hyperpigmented. As the lesions heal, the affected skin area becomes depigmented. Penicillin is effective treatment.

Bejel is an endemic syphilis occurring primarily in the Middle East. The disease is usually contracted during childhood and is treatable with penicillin.

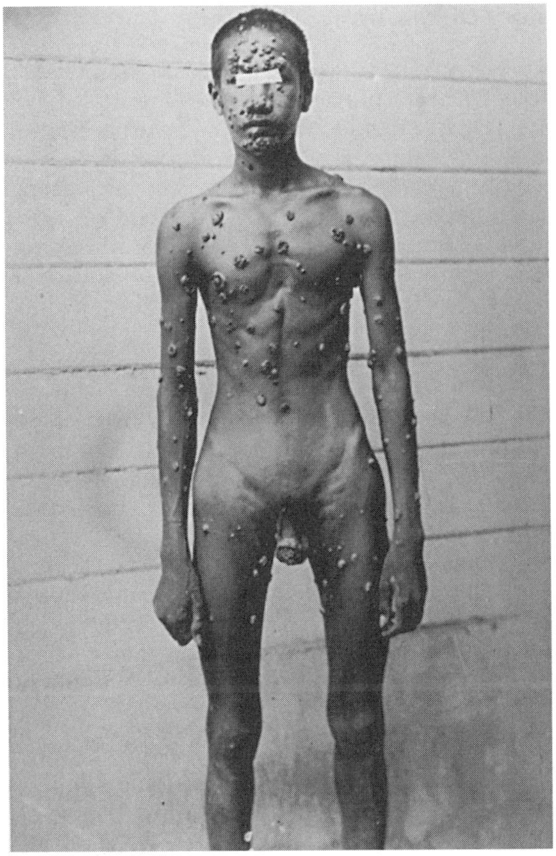

FIGURE 26-7
Characteristic yaws lesions. (Courtesy of Air Force Institute of Pathology, AFIP 39201.)

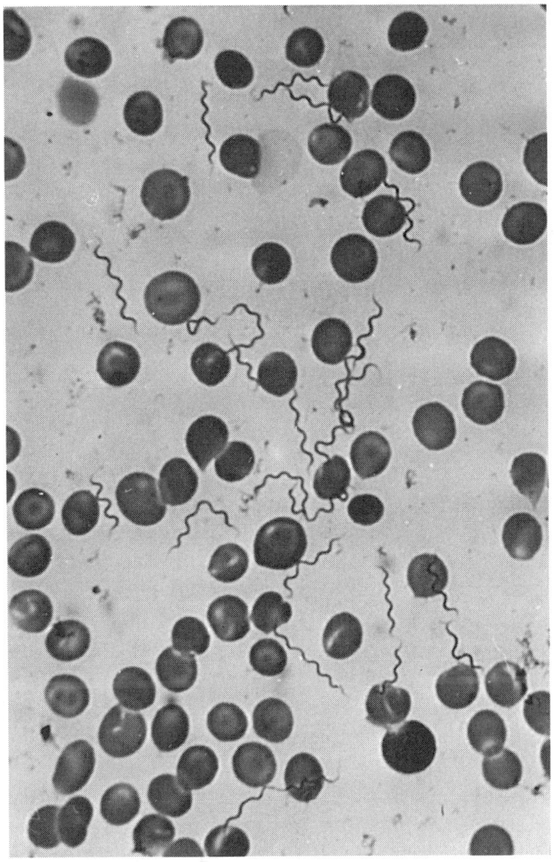

FIGURE 26-8
Borrelia species in rodent blood. (× 1000.) (From W. Burgdorfer. In E. H. Lennette et al., eds., *Manual of Clinical Microbiology*, 3rd ed. Washington, D.C.: American Society for Microbiology, 1980.)

GENUS *BORRELIA*

General Characteristics

The *Borrelia* organisms are the largest of the pathogenic spirochetes, ranging from 10 to 30 μm in length and 0.3 to 0.7 μm in width (Fig. 26-8). They are actively motile, exhibiting a lashing, twisting movement. They have irregularly spaced coils that may range in number from 4 to 30. *Borrelia* species are distinguished from other spirochetes in that they can be stained by ordinary dyes such as crystal violet and carbolfuchsin. When artificial media are supplemented with serum or blood, these organisms can be cultivated in the laboratory.

Epidemiology and Pathogenesis

All Borrelia microorganisms are transmitted to their hosts by arthropod vectors. The hosts infected include rodents, domestic animals, and birds, as well as humans. There are two important human diseases caused by *Borrelia:* **relapsing fever,** which is transmitted by body lice or soft-shelled ticks, and **Lyme disease,** which is transmitted by ixodid ticks.

Relapsing Fever. Louse-borne relapsing fever is caused by *B. recurrentis*. Humans acquire infection by crushing the arthropod and rubbing its infected parts into the bite wound. Humans are the only reservoir. This type of infection is seen predominantly in Africa.

Tick-borne disease occurs sporadically throughout the world. In North America the disease is caused by *B. hermsii, B. turicatae,* and *B. parkeri.* The infectious microorganisms are transferred via tick saliva or body fluids while the tick is feeding on its host. Rodents are the reservoir of tick-borne disease. In the United States approximately 10 to 15 cases are reported each year. Most of the cases occur in western states such as California, Oregon, Colorado, and Texas.

Three to four days after infection there is an onset of chills and fever. This corresponds to high levels of *Borrelia* organisms in the bloodstream. The microorganisms invade several organs and tissues including the spleen, liver, kidneys, eyes, and brain. Tenderness of the liver and spleen, jaundice, and a macular rash are characteristic symptoms during the first episode of fever. The initial attack lasts three to seven days. This is followed by an asymptomatic period and then a relapse with symptoms resembling the first attack. Four or more relapses may occur, each slightly shorter than the previous one and with less severe symptoms.

The recurrent fever is coincidental with the immune response of the host. Relapses are related to antigenic variation of the microorganism. Experimental infections in animals have revealed that as many as four major serotypes can be recovered. Microorganisms disappear from the blood after the initial symptoms of disease have been observed, and this coincides with high levels of antibodies to the infecting serotype. The microorganisms that undergo antigenic variation are resistant to the antibody present and begin to multiply. The multiplication cycle results in the return of clinical symptoms. Once the immune system has responded to the new serotype, the clinical manifestations of disease disappear.

Lyme Disease. Lyme disease is a chronic inflammatory disorder resulting from infection by the tick-borne spirochete *B. burgdorferi.* The disease may also affect dogs and other domestic animals. Lyme disease is the most frequently reported tick-borne disease in the United States. It was first reported in North America in Lyme, Connecticut, in 1977. In 1993, 8257 cases were reported to the Centers for Disease Control. The increasing number of cases seen since the disease was first reported is thought to be due to the increased number of deer and to inadvertent reforestation.

Lyme disease is transmitted by ixodid ticks. Shortly after infection, *B. burgdorferi* disseminates hematogenously to many sites including the skin, central nervous system, and joints. The pathogenesis of this disease is complex and results from the host response to a few microorganisms. The first stage of infection is characterized by an expanding lesion called **erythema chronicum migrans (ECM).** ECM develops at the site of the tick bite sustained 3 to 14 days previously. The patient often complains of headache, low fever, stiff neck, and arthralgia. Skin lesions may also appear on the ear lobes, nipples, scrotum, and extremities. They are often red-to-brown-to-purple in color.

The second stage of Lyme disease appears a few weeks to a few months after the primary stage. This stage is characterized by arthritis and pain in the tendons, bursa, and muscle. Arthritis usually involves a knee or other large joint. Untreated arthritis may become destructive and involve erosion of cartilage and bone. Cardiac involvement may also appear in this stage but is usually a self-limiting condition. In approximately 15 percent of untreated patients, neurological manifestations develop. Meningoencephalitis associated with cranial neuropathy, particularly facial palsy, is the principal feature. These patients complain of constant fatigue and altered mental states. Chronic manifestations of disease appearing many months or years after disease onset comprise the tertiary stage.

There is considerable evidence to suggest that the chronic nature of the disease is an autoimmune response. An immune response to spirochetal determinants shared with host proteins could lead to chronic inflammatory conditions.

Laboratory Diagnosis

The borrelias of relapsing fever are easily observed in stained blood smears, provided the blood is sampled during the fever period and antibiotics have not been used previously. The microorganisms can also be detected in unstained preparations by phase-contrast microscopy. When spirochetes cannot be detected in blood smears, a blood sample or other tissue specimen from the infected patient can be injected intraperitoneally into white mice. After 48 hours borrelia can be perceived in the tail blood of the infected mice.

B. burgdorferi can be detected in stained blood smears during the early stages of infection when fever is present. Later the organism is difficult to find in any tissue. Serological testing is an important addition in confirming Lyme disease. Tests such as the enzyme-linked immunosorbent assay (ELISA) and indirect immunofluorescence assay (IFA) often give false-positives because of cross-reactive antigens that are present on the flagella of *B. burgdorferi* and *T. pallidum.* Other tests that show promise are flow cytometry, which is used to detect antibody that kills *B. burgdorferi,* and the polymerase chain reaction, which can detect as few as five spirochetes in a sample.

Treatment and Prevention

Tetracyclines and chloramphenicol are the drugs of choice for the treatment of relapsing fever. If drugs do not cause an immediate cure, they do reduce the rate of relapse. Tetracycline treatment does incite a Jarisch-Herxheimer–like reaction, but the reaction is not severe.

Doxycycline and amoxicillin are highly effective in early uncomplicated Lyme disease. For late Lyme disease ceftriaxone or cefotaxime is recommended. Ceftriaxone is associated with biliary complications. The drug precipitates out as a calcium salt in the gallbladder. Precipitates disappear after discontinuation of the drug. Penicillin G is an alternative for patients unable to tolerate ceftriaxone. Treatment for late disease is often continued for several months.

No vaccine has proved effective for relapsing fever and none has been developed for Lyme disease. Prevention is centered on control of the insect vectors. In building sites where ticks may be present, sprays containing 1% aldrin or 0.5% malathion can be applied. Persons going to areas that are potential tick habitats should cover as much of their bodies as possible and check their skin periodically for the presence of ticks.

GENUS *LEPTOSPIRA*

The genus *Leptospira* contains several species that are saprophytes and are harmless to humans or animals. Several species, however, are parasitic and cause infections (**leptospiroses**). They are characterized by their effect on the liver, kidneys, lungs, and meninges. The pathogenic leptospires are classified under a single species name, *L. interrogans,* with serogroups such as *canicola, pomona,* and *icterohaemorrhagiae.*

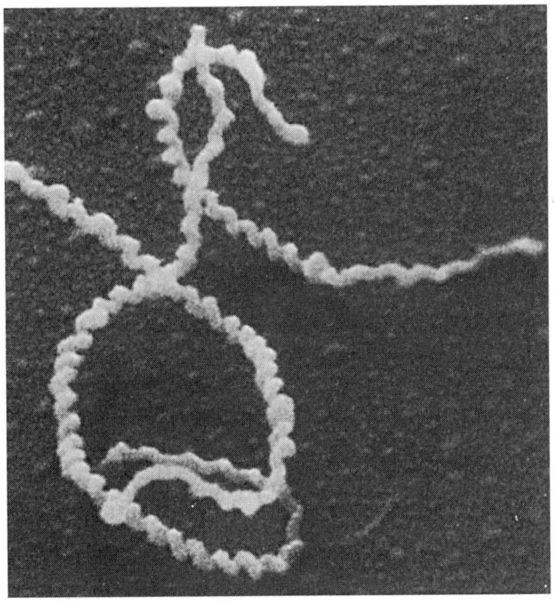

FIGURE 26-9
Scanning electron micrograph of a leptospire. Note the compactness of the coils. (Courtesy of Z. Yoshii.)

General Characteristics

Leptospires are thin and spiral-shaped. They range from 6 to 20 μm in length and are 0.1 μm in width. The spirals have numerous coils and hooked ends (Fig. 26-9). The coils can be observed when a living culture is examined by dark-field microscopy. The leptospires are not readily stained by ordinary dyes but can be perceived in preparations stained by silver impregnation methods. Most species can be cultivated on ordinary media supplemented with animal serum fractions. The leptospires are obligate aerobes.

Epidemiology and Pathogenesis

The pathogenic leptospires are harbored by wild rodents and domestic animals. *L. icterohaemorrhagiae* is the most pathogenic serogroup, although most of the serogroups produce some disease symptoms. In wild rodents, in which the disease is never fatal, the organisms localize in the kidneys and are shed in the urine.

Transmission from animals to humans is usually indirect. Animal urination in soil or water is a frequent mode of transmission. People working in an environment that associates rats or infected livestock with water are especially prone to infection. Leptospirosis is a major public health problem in the tropics but is relatively infrequent in the United States (58 cases in 1991). In the United States recreational exposure (swimming) and household pets are the major sources of infection. In the United Kingdom leptospirosis predominates in agricultural workers.

Organisms enter humans through abrasions of the skin or through mucosal surfaces. Organisms multiply in the blood and can infect other areas of the body such as the liver, kidneys, lungs, and meninges. The incubation period of 8 to 12 days is followed by chills, headache, and severe muscular pain. Muscular pain can be excruciating and occurs most commonly in the thighs, calves, and abdomen. The most serious form of disease is called **infectious jaundice (Weil's disease).** Infectious jaundice is characterized by jaundice, renal dysfunction, hemorrhagic manifestations, and a high mortality rate. Patient survival is dependent on management of renal dysfunction.

After several days of apparent recovery, the disease resumes in some individuals. Symptoms last for two to four days and are characterized by mild fever, myalgias, and gastrointestinal disturbance. Meningitis is the hallmark of this stage.

There is no vaccine for leptospirosis. Doxycycline taken once a week prevents infection in those who might be at high risk for a short time. Surface decontamination, wearing of protective clothing, and rodent control are important preventive methods.

Laboratory Diagnosis and Treatment

The macroscopic slide agglutination test is the only commercially available method but lacks sensitivity and specificity. The microscopic agglutination test is considered the serodiagnostic method of choice but its complexity limits it to reference laboratories. The presence of leptospires in blood or other tissue can be determined by culture but the process can take up to two months. Other diagnostic methods, such as polymerase chain reaction, are being investigated.

Several antibiotics including penicillin, ampicillin, tetracyclines, and some third-generation cephalosporins are effective treatment. Intravenous penicillin decreases the duration of fever and renal dysfunction in patients with severe, late disease.

Spiral and Curved Rods

The motility of spiral and curved rods arises from the presence of polar flagella and not with axial filaments, as in the spirochetes. Three important genera are *Spirillum*, *Campylobacter*, and *Helicobacter*.

GENUS *SPIRILLUM*

S. minor is the only human pathogen in the genus *Spirillum*. It is the cause of a form of **rat-bite fever** (see Table 30-2). The organism has not been cultivated in the laboratory. Identification was originally derived from the experimental inoculation of humans with blood containing the microorganisms.

Rat-bite fever is a disease of rats that is transmissible to humans by the bite of an infected rat or cat. The incubation period lasts 6 to 14 days. It is followed by swelling of the wound site and formation of an ulcer. There is an undulating fever that may continue for several weeks. Local lymph nodes may also be enlarged. During the fever period a maculopapular rash appears on the arms, legs, and trunk. The rash subsides with a decrease in the patient's temperature. The disease is self-limiting unless a secondary infection arises at the site of the bite. Penicillin is the drug of choice when complications do arise.

Diagnosis of disease can be made by microscopic examination of blood or material from the bite. The organisms can be stained by the Giemsa or Wright technique. If this is not possible, animals can be inoculated and their blood examined for the organism.

GENUS *CAMPYLOBACTER*

Campylobacter species are gram-negative, slender, spirally curved rods. They are 0.2 to 0.5 μm in width and 0.5 to 5.0 μm in length and have a single polar flagellum (Fig. 26-10). *Campylobacter* organisms are important pathogens in animals and in the past 10 years have become the most frequent cause of bacterial gastroenteritis in humans in industrialized countries. *C. jejuni*, *C. coli*, and *C. fetus* subspecies *fetus* are the most frequently isolated from humans.

FIGURE 26-10
Electron micrograph of *Campylobacter fetus* subspecies *jejuni*. Note the curved shape of the organisms and the polar flagella. (× 33,740 before reduction.) (From P. J. Mead, *J. Med. Microbiol.* 12:383, 1979.)

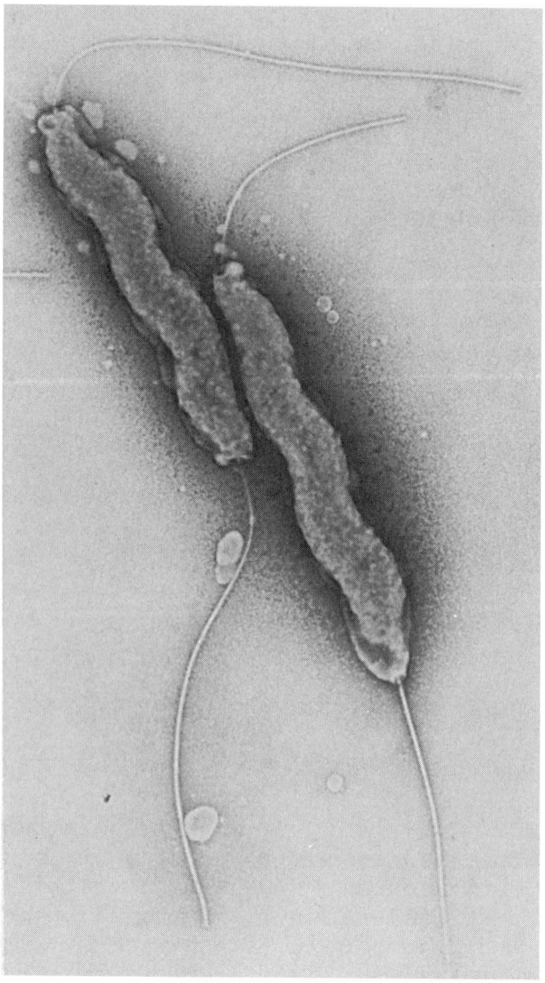

Epidemiology and Pathogenesis

Campylobacteriosis is primarily a foodborne infection in which foods of animal origin play an important role. Most meat, but especially poultry, is contaminated with *Campylobacter* organisms. Barbecues and other related occasions permit easy transfer of bacteria from raw meat to hands and other foods and thence to the mouth. Raw or inadequately treated water has also been incriminated as a source of outbreaks (Table 26-1). Direct transmission is mainly occupational, for example, among butchers, abattoir workers, and poultry processors. Perinatal transmission may be due to exposure in utero or during the first days of life. The infected mother may or may not be symptomatic.

Not all infections are symptomatic. Some patients may become asymptomatic excreters. The incubation period is usually two to five days. Diarrhea may be preceded by fever, myalgia, and abdominal pain. Abdominal pain mimics acute peritonitis. Diarrhea lasts about two to three days but abdominal pain may persist. Stools may contain fresh blood, pus, or mucus, indicating colorectal inflammation. *C. jejuni* causes infectious proctitis in homosexual men. There is also a close association between *C. jejuni* and Guillain-Barré syndrome (see Under the Microscope 23).

In developing countries the disease is confined to young children. In these children, immunity to diseases develops through repeated exposure to infection.

Laboratory Diagnosis, Treatment, and Prevention

Direct examination of fresh feces by dark-field or phase-contrast microscopy can be used in the diagnosis of *Campylobacter* enteritis. The organisms exhibit a darting and spinning motion that distinguishes them from other organisms. Selective media with and without blood have been used to isolate organisms from stools (see Under the Microscope 24). Care must be taken in the organisms'

TABLE 26-1
Reported Outbreaks of *Campylobacter* Infections, by Vehicle of Transmission, United States, 1978–1986

Vehicle	No. of outbreaks	No. of ill persons
All foodborne	45	1308
Raw milk	26	829
Poultry	3	27
Egg	1	26
Other	6	87
Unknown	9	339
All waterborne	11	4983
Community water supply	7	4930
Other	4	53
Travel-associated	1	150
Total	57	6441

SOURCE: CDC Surveillance Summaries, *M.M.W.R.* 37(No. SS-2): June 1988.

UNDER THE MICROSCOPE 23

Guillain-Barré Syndrome and *Campylobacter*

Guillain-Barré syndrome (GBS) is a common cause of acute neuromuscular paralysis in both adults and children. The annual incidence in the industrialized world is between 1 and 2 cases per 100,000 population. Epidemiological studies have revealed that approximately 75 percent of the time GBS is preceded by infection with a variety of agents. These agents have included hepatitis B virus, cytomegalovirus, Epstein-Barr virus, varicella-zoster virus, rubeola virus, and *Mycoplasma pneumoniae*. In most cases of GBS the preceding infection is usually associated with the upper respiratory tract. Recent reports suggested that infections with *Campylobacter jejuni*, a common enteric pathogen, may cause GBS by triggering demyelination of peripheral nerves.

Recent studies of GBS indicated that 10 to 30 percent of cases are preceded by gastrointestinal infections. Because of the extensive axonal damage in GBS, many investigators believe that a neurotoxin may be involved. Unfortunately, the toxic activity of *C. jejuni* has not been demonstrated in vivo. Studies from Japan indicated that nerve damage may be due to an immunological response; they indicated that many patients with GBS possess a particular HLA type. A specific strain of *C. jejuni* appears also to be involved in precipitating GBS. There is some reason to believe that the bacterial strain possesses specific antigens that stimulate the production of antibodies that react with peripheral nerve myelin and cause GBS. For example, one study showed that titers of IgM antibodies to a neutral glycolipid in peripheral nerve myelin were elevated in patients with GBS but were absent in control subjects. Many of these findings, however, have not been duplicated and the exact contribution of these factors to the pathogenesis of *C. jejuni*–associated GBS has not been determined.

UNDER THE MICROSCOPE 24

Laboratory Diagnosis: *Campylobacter*

Most laboratories use selective media for the routine isolation of *Campylobacter* species. Use of antimicrobials in these media demonstrated that some of the newly isolated species of *Campylobacter* are sensitive to these drugs. Many laboratories are now using a **filtration** technique in addition to selective media for isolating less common species associated with infection. The filtration technique is based on the fact that *Campylobacter* organisms can pass through a 0.65-μm cellulose-nitrate filter while other bacteria do not readily pass through the filter. Filtration is performed by placing a 0.65-μm cellulose-acetate filter disk on the surface of a nonselective blood agar medium. Five drops or more of the fecal suspension is placed on the filter, and incubated for 1 hour at room temperature or 37 C.

A test demonstrates positivity when there are 10^5 colony-forming units per gram of stool.

transfer since they are sensitive to oxygen. Some tests that aid in differentiating the major species of *Campylobacter* include (1) growth at 25 C, (2) hippurate hydrolysis, and (3) sensitivity to nalidixic acid and cephalothin.

By the time diagnosis of *Campylobacter* enteritis is made, the patient has already recovered. Chemotherapy is not warranted. Erythromycin may be justified for prolonged illness.

Prevention of *Campylobacter* infection is possible when (1) water supplies are purified properly, (2) milk for human consumption is heat-treated, (3) there is hygienic handling of raw meats, and (4) there is control of infection at all stages of poultry production.

HELICOBACTER PYLORI

H. pylori was first isolated from human gastric mucosa in 1983. The organism colonizes the stomach for years or decades. Studies have demonstrated that this organism is the major etiological agent of chronic active (type B) gastritis and that it may dispose the patient to peptic ulceration.

Epidemiology and Pathogenesis

The organism appears to be spread by close familial contact but the route of transmission is not known. The incidence of infection increases after the age of 7 years.

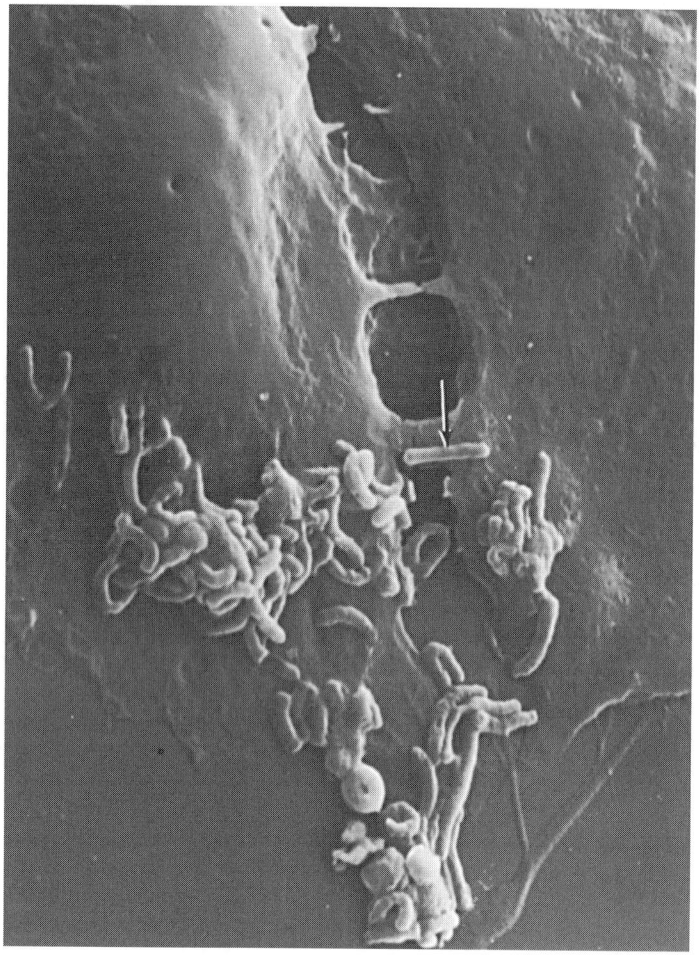

FIGURE 26-11
Scanning electron micrograph of *Helicobacter pylori* adhering to gastric cells. (× 3441.) (From V. Neman-Simha and F. Mégraud, *Infect. Immun.* 56:3329, 1988.)

The pathogenic mechanisms of *H. pylori* infection are as yet poorly defined. The organism colonizes only gastric-type epithelium, apparently by adhesive pili (Fig. 26-11). The organism produces **urease** and it has been postulated that this compound acts as a protective device. Ammonia is a product of urease activity and it could protect the microorganism from stomach acidity. High concentrations of ammonia produced by large numbers of bacteria could also be responsible for the inflammatory condition in the stomach. Chronic inflammation often remains clinically silent.

H. pylori can colonize the duodenum as well as the stomach and may be responsible for peptic ulcer. When individuals with peptic ulcer are treated with acid-reducing therapies, there is temporary cure. Once the treatment is stopped, the ulcers reappear in about 70 percent of patients. If these individuals are later treated with antimicrobials against *H. pylori,* ulcer recurrences are reduced significantly.

Laboratory Diagnosis and Treatment

H. pylori can be diagnosed by culture of gastric biopsy specimens, examination of stained biopsy specimens for the presence of bacteria, or detection of urease activity in biopsy specimens. Cultured organisms are readily identified on the basis of cellular and colonial morphology, oxidase and catalase activity, and urea hydrolysis. ELISA is the most common serological test and can be used to monitor eradication of *H. pylori* after treatment.

The most effective treatment for eradicating *H. pylori* is the combination of a bismuth salt (colloidal bismuth subcitrate or bismuth subsalicylate [Pepto-Bismol]) with metronidazole or tinidazole in conjunction with either amoxicillin or tetracycline.

Summary

1. Spirochetes and curved rods exhibit spiral morphology but differ in certain aspects of motility. Spirochetes possess flagella that originate at the poles and wrap around the body of the microorganism. The flagella of spirochetes do not come into contact with the environment. Curved rods have polar flagella, either single or multiple, that are in contact with the environment.

2. The characteristics of the diseases caused by spirochetes and curved rods are outlined in Table 26-2.

TABLE 26-2
Characteristics of the Diseases Caused by Spirochetes and Spiral and Curved Rods

Group and species	Disease	Mechanism of transmission	Treatment and prevention
Spirochetes			
Treponema pallidum	*Syphilis:* Primary stage: chancre; secondary stage: rash and mucous membrane lesions; tertiary stage: lesions called gummas	Sexual contact, accidental contact with lesions	Penicillin, tetracycline or erythromycin; treatment of contacts to prevent spread
	Congenital: Stillbirth, abortion, or secondary syphilis	Congenital transfer	
T. pertenue	*Yaws:* Primary and secondary skin lesions	Contact with eating and drinking utensils	Penicillin; improve hygiene
T. carateum	*Pinta:* Skin lesions, hyperpigmented	Same as for *T. pertenue*	Penicillin; improve hygiene
Borrelia recurrentis *B. hermsii* *B. turicatae* *B. parkeri*	*Relapsing fever:* Bloodstream infected—followed by invasion of kidneys, liver, eyes, brain; episodes of fever caused by antigenic variation of borrelia	Louse-borne relapsing fever (*B. recurrentis*); tick-borne relapsing fever caused by remaining borrelia	Tetracyclines, chloramphenicol; avoid tick-infested areas
B. burgdorferi	*Lyme disease:* Skin lesions in first stage; second and third stages: arthritis; neurological and cardiac symptoms	Ixodid ticks	Oral phenoxymethyl penicillin or tetracycline for first stage; penicillin G, chloramphenicol, or ceftriaxone for second stage
Leptospira interrogans, serogroup *icterohaemorrhagiae*	*Infectious jaundice:* Bloodstream invaded—followed by liver, kidneys, lungs, and meninges	Ingestion of water contaminated by urinating animals	Penicillin, ampicillin, tetracycline
Spiral and curved rods			
Spirillum minor	*Rat-bite fever:* Formation of ulcer at site of bite plus body rash	Bite of infected animal such as cat	Self-limiting; but penicillin treatment if complications occur
Campylobacter jejuni, C. coli	*Diarrhea* or dysentery-like syndrome	Ingestion of contaminated food or water, unpasteurized milk	Self-limiting; but erythromycin used in prolonged illnesses
Helicobacter pylori	Possible cause of gastritis and stomach or duodenal ulcers	Unknown	Combination of bismuth salt with metronidazole, or tinidazole with amoxicillin or tetracycline

Questions for Study

1. What type of lesions are observed in congenital syphilis? What is the reason for this?
2. List the various stages of syphilis and describe the clinical picture in each. Which stages are infectious?
3. Describe the advantages and disadvantages of the various serological tests for syphilis.
4. What is meant by biological false-positives and biological false-negatives in syphilis serology? What are the conditions in which they occur?
5. What is the reason for the relapses seen in relapsing fever?
6. Lyme disease has spread from areas of the Northeast to areas of the Southeast in a relatively short period. Provide some reasons for why this would occur.
7. Describe how leptospires might contaminate water and how you could contract leptospirosis.
8. What are the major ways in which one could acquire *Campylobacter* enteritis?
9. A recent article stated that Koch's postulates for *Helicobacter pylori* as an agent of disease had not been fulfilled. What was meant by this statement and does it have any relevance?

CHAPTER

27

Mycoplasmas and L-forms

OBJECTIVES

To describe the differences between mycoplasmas and L-forms

To outline the mechanism of transmission, symptoms, and treatment for *Mycoplasma pneumoniae* infection

To describe the relationship between genital mycoplasmas and the diseases they cause in males and females

To understand the importance of *Ureaplasma urealyticum* in pregnancy

OUTLINE

GENERAL CHARACTERISTICS OF THE MYCOPLASMAS

GENERAL CHARACTERISTICS OF L-FORMS

PATHOGENESIS

Mycoplasma pneumoniae

Other Mycoplasmas and L-forms

LABORATORY DIAGNOSIS

TREATMENT AND PREVENTION

The mycoplasmas are a unique group of bacteria because they lack a cell wall and yet are free-living. They can be found in animals, humans, soil, and plants. They are so small (0.2–0.3 μm) that until the late 1930s many investigators referred to them as small bacteria or even viruses. Mycoplasmas can pass through bacterial filters.

The mycoplasmas belong to three families: **Mycoplasmataceae, Acholeplasmataceae,** and **Spiroplasmataceae.** Only the Mycoplasmataceae are human pathogens. The mycoplasmas causing disease in humans are *M. pneumoniae, M. hominis, Ureaplasma urealyticum,* and *M. genitalium.*

Streptobacillus moniliformis produces colonies that resemble the mycoplasmas in structure and appearance (*S. moniliformis* is one of the etiological agents of rat-bite fever, see Chapter 30). These organisms lack cell walls and cannot be stained by the usual methods. These organisms are actually variants of the cell wall–containing parent cell and are now referred to as **L (Lister)-forms.** L-forms differ from mycoplasmas because the former are able to revert to the typical parental form. L-forms have now been found in most species of bacteria.

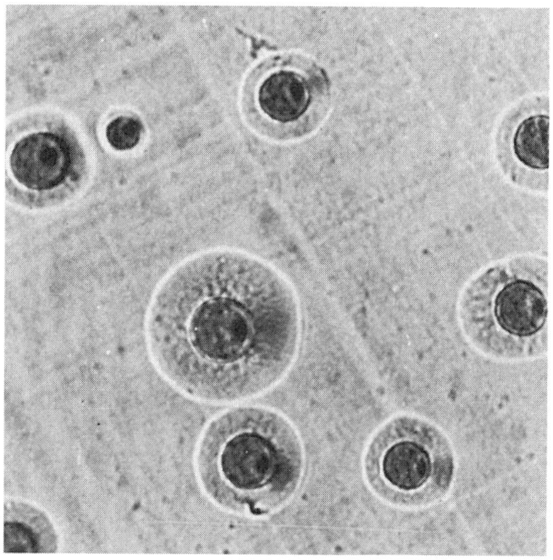

FIGURE 27-2
Colony of *Mycoplasma salivarium* showing typical umbonate (button-like) or fried-egg shape. Colonies are 0.1 mm in diameter. (From P. F. Smith, *The Biology of the Mycoplasmas*. New York: Academic, 1971.)

General Characteristics of the Mycoplasmas

Mycoplasmas can assume a variety of morphological forms, such as coccoid, filamentous, or cocci in chains. This characteristic illustrates the importance of the cell wall to shape. The coccoid units vary from 0.2 to 0.3 μm in diameter. Some of the different morphological forms are illustrated in Figure 27-1. The mycoplasmas are stable in ordinary culture media, apparently because of the presence of sterols in the cytoplasmic membrane. These sterols are not found in any other bacterial cells or their L-forms.

Most *Mycoplasma* species are aerobes or facultative anaerobes. A few species require anaerobic conditions for initial isolation in the laboratory. A basal medium of meat infusion and peptone supplemented with horse serum or ascitic fluid is needed to cultivate them. Serum or ascitic fluid supplies the fatty acids or lipid precursors required by many species. The medium is usually supplemented with penicillin and thallium acetate to inhibit growth of any bacterial contaminants.

FIGURE 27-1
Electron micrograph of a species of *Mycoplasma* showing different morphological forms. (Courtesy of E. S. Boatman.)

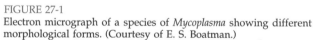

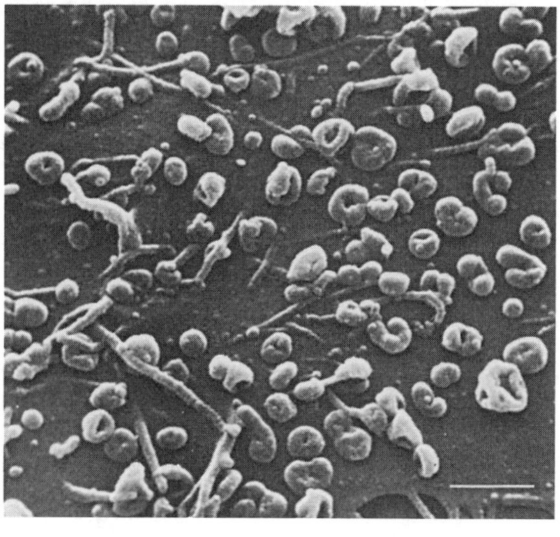

Most mycoplasmas exhibit optimal growth at temperatures between 30 and 36 C in media at alkaline pHs. *Ureaplasma* species exhibit optimal growth at acid pHs and are capable of hydrolyzing urea. This hydrolytic property is important in differentiating them from other mycoplasmas.

Cells from broth culture are best visualized by dark-field or phase-contrast microscopy. Mycoplasmas are recognized by their colony formation on semisolid media. Colonies that are 10 to 300 μm in diameter give the appearance of "fried eggs" and are visible only with the aid of a microscope (Fig. 27-2).

General Characteristics of L-forms

The L-form is a wall-deficient bacterial variant that may occur spontaneously in a bacterial culture. It also may be induced by certain agents such as penicillin or ultraviolet light.

In a population of L-forms, some are stable and fail to revert to the parental type while others are unstable and revert to the parental type. In a few instances, the stable L-form may be maintained on isotonic media. However, most stable L-forms require high concentrations of an osmotic stabilizer. L-forms can produce cell wall intermediates but for some reason the latter cannot be assembled into complete cell walls. L-forms differ from the mycoplasmas in the following ways:

1. L-forms can be cultivated only in a culture medium that has a high concentration of nonmetabolizable solute (sodium chloride [NaCl], for example). These solutes contribute to the high osmotic pressure required to prevent lysis of L-forms. Mycoplasmas do not require these osmotic forces.
2. L-forms can revert to the stable bacterial parental type. Mycoplasmas do not revert to any other bacterial form.
3. L-forms do not have a high lipid content or sterols in the membrane as do the mycoplasmas.
4. Reproduction of L-forms is inhibited in the presence of penicillin. Penicillin has no effect on the mycoplasmas.

Pathogenesis

MYCOPLASMA PNEUMONIAE

M. pneumoniae is a noncommensal that is associated with the human disease called **atypical pneumonia** or **walking pneumonia.** The agent of this disease is a common cause of acute upper and lower respiratory tract infection in children and young adults. Transmission usually requires close contact, and therefore many outbreaks are associated with institutions where confinement and close contact prevail. The organism is transmitted by coughing or sneezing.

Atypical pneumonia is slow to develop, and the incubation period may be as long as three weeks. The disease is usually self-limiting with infrequent complications.

FIGURE 27-3
Electron micrograph of *Mycoplasma genitalium.* The terminal structure is the organelle of attachment and is covered with a nap that extends to the areas indicated by the arrowheads. The nap is apparently the protein called P1 that initiates attachment to respiratory epithelium. (Bar = 0.1 μm.) (From P. C. Hu et al., *Infect. Immun.* 55: 1126, 1987.)

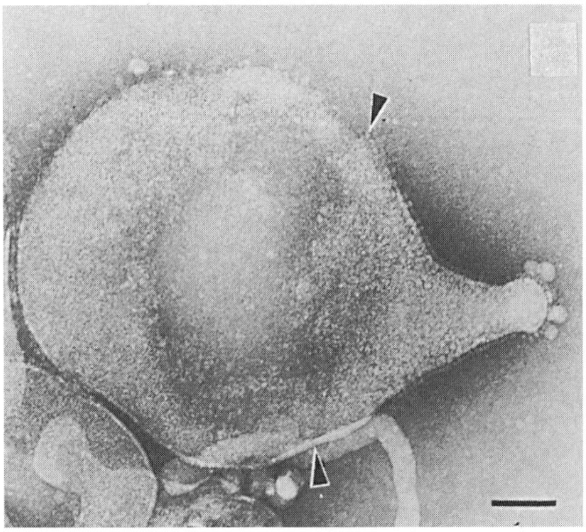

Symptoms include fever, headache, and a persistent nonproductive cough.

M. pneumoniae binds to the surface of respiratory cells by an adherence protein called **P1 protein** (Fig. 27-3). Once mycoplasmas are adsorbed to the respiratory tract, there is epithelial cell injury and loss of cilia.

The level of immunity acquired after infection by *M. pneumoniae* is related to the intensity of the disease. Immunity, however, is usually short-lived and lasts no more than seven to eight years.

OTHER MYCOPLASMAS AND L-FORMS

U. urealyticum and *M. hominis* colonize the genitourinary tracts of sexually active men and women. Both organisms are opportunistic pathogens and can be transmitted by sexual contact. Colonization occurs initially during birth as the infant passes through the birth canal. The number of organisms increases after puberty and increased sexual activity. It declines after menopause.

U. urealyticum has been implicated as one of the causes of nongonococcal urethritis. In women this organism appears to be an opportunistic pathogen during pregnancy. It is a cause of **chorioamnionitis,** which often leads to premature spontaneous labor and delivery. Stillbirths and perinatal deaths have been associated with infection. Congenital and neonatal pneumonia, septicemia, and meningitis also have been associated with infection of the chorioamnion by *U. urealyticum.* These infections are particularly evident in infants born prematurely.

M. hominis has been associated with some cases of pelvic inflammatory disease, postpartum fever, and pyelonephritis. There is mounting evidence that this organism may also be associated with preterm labor. *M. hominis* can also be involved in nongenitourinary tract infections such as bacteremia, wound infections, and joint infections. The source of organisms is the genitourinary tract.

M. genitalium is believed to play a role in genitourinary tract disease and may account for some cases of acute nongonococcal urethritis.

There is only one recorded instance in which an L-form was considered the causal agent of disease. Most information on the pathogenicity of L-forms is circumstantial. It has been suggested that the L-form is a survival mechanism for the bacterial cell. For example, under adverse environmental conditions the cell could maintain its viability by remaining as an L-form until environmental conditions improve. The presence of a cell wall inhibitor such as penicillin could induce this state.

Laboratory Diagnosis

Isolation of mycoplasmas from clinical material is accomplished by swabbing infected areas and inoculating onto a selective agar medium. The medium contains penicillin, thallium acetate, and other inhibitors of bacterial growth. Thallium acetate is not used if *M. genitalium* or *U. urealyticum* is to be isolated. There are broth and agar systems

TABLE 27-1
Pathogenic Characteristics of the Mycoplasmas

Species	Site of infection and pathogenesis	Mechanism of transmission	Treatment and prevention
Mycoplasma pneumoniae	Respiratory tract; self-limiting pneumonia with infrequent complications	Sneezing, coughing in confined areas	Erythromycin, tetracycline; vaccine under investigation
M. hominis	Urogenital tract; several possibilities: pelvic inflammatory disease, postpartum fever, pyelonephritis, and nongenitourinary tract infections	Opportunistic but may be transmitted sexually or congenitally	Erythromycin, tetracycline
M. genitalium	Urogenital tract; possibly associated with nongonococcal urethritis	Opportunistic pathogen; may be transmitted sexually	Erythromycin, tetracycline
Ureaplasma urealyticum	Urogenital tract; nongonococcal urethritis, chorioamnionitis in pregnancy leading to premature delivery and neonatal infections	Opportunistic pathogen	Erythromycin, tetracycline

(A8 agar and arginine-urea–based broth) available for isolation. *U. urealyticum* can be differentiated from all other mycoplasmas by its ability to hydrolyze urea. Culturing of the mycoplasmas, however, is time-consuming (2–3 weeks).

In most cases the diagnosis of *M. pneumoniae* infection is confirmed by serology. The ***M. pneumoniae* complement fixation (MPCF) test** has been the most commonly used serological test. The **cold agglutinin test** is used as a supplement to the MPCF test. A variety of DNA probes, enzyme immunoassays, and polymerase chain reactions are being evaluated for identification of all mycoplasmas.

The isolation and identification of L-forms have never been part of the usual regimen in the clinical laboratory and are more suited to the research laboratory.

Treatment and Prevention

Erythromycin as well as several tetracyclines are effective in the treatment of *Mycoplasma pneumoniae* infection. Erythromycin is preferred for the treatment of children because tetracycline can stain immature teeth. Treatment of other mycoplasma infections is difficult because of the spectrum of disease, particularly *U. urealyticum* infections.

Formalin-killed vaccines of *M. pneumoniae* have been used with some success in the military. Live vaccines are being evaluated.

Nongonococcal urethritis caused by *U. urealyticum* or *M. hominis* infection responds to treatment with tetracyclines. Patients allergic to tetracyclines may take erythromycin. Female sexual partners of men with nongonococcal urethritis should also be treated with tetracycline.

Summary

1. Bacteria without cell walls belong to two groups: the mycoplasmas and L-forms. L-forms are variants of any cell wall–containing species while mycoplasmas are a specific group of bacteria.
2. Mycoplasmas are aerobic to facultative anaerobes that are pleomorphic and about the size of large viruses. Mycoplasmas are unique in that they possess sterols in their cytoplasmic membranes. Sterols provide cellular stability. L-forms, unlike mycoplasmas, can revert to the parental wall-containing types. L-forms can be isolated only on media that create a high osmotic pressure.
3. The pathogenic characteristics of the mycoplasmas are outlined in Table 27-1.

Questions for Study

1. What are the ways in which mycoplasmas differ from L-forms?
2. With what types of infections are the mycoplasmas frequently associated?
3. Why is penicillin used in media for isolating mycoplasmas?
4. What is the relationship of *U. urealyticum* to pregnancy?

CHAPTER

28 Rickettsiae and Chlamydiae

OBJECTIVES

To outline the differences and similarities between the rickettsiae and chlamydiae

To list the causative agent, method of transmission, pathogenesis, symptoms, and treatment of Rocky Mountain spotted fever, epidemic typhus, Q fever, trench fever, ehrlichiosis, bacillary angiomatosis, and cat-scratch disease

To describe the types of disease and groups affected by infection with *Chlamydia trachomatis* and by *Chlamydia psittaci*

To list the methods of treatment and prevention for chlamydial disease

OUTLINE

THE RICKETTSIAE
- General Characteristics
- Epidemiology and Pathogenesis
  - Typhus Group
    - Epidemic or Louse-Borne Typhus
    - Endemic Typhus
  - Spotted Fever Group
    - Rocky Mountain Spotted Fever
    - Boutonneuse Fever
    - Siberian Tick Typhus
    - Rickettsialpox and Queensland Tick Typhus
  - Scrub Typhus
  - Q Fever
  - Trench Fever
  - Ehrlichioses
  - Other *Rochalimaea* Infections
    - Cat-Scratch Disease
    - Bacillary Angiomatosis
- Laboratory Diagnosis
- Treatment, Prevention, and Control

THE CHLAMYDIAE
- General Characteristics
- Epidemiology and Pathogenesis
  - *Chlamydia trachomatis*
    - Ocular Disease
    - Male Genital Tract Disease
    - Female Genital Tract Disease
    - Lymphogranuloma Venereum
    - *Chlamydia psittaci*
    - *Chlamydia pneumoniae*
  - Laboratory Diagnosis
  - Treatment and Prevention

The Rickettsiae

GENERAL CHARACTERISTICS

The rickettsial family of obligate intracellular parasites includes three genera: *Rickettsia, Coxiella,* and *Ehrlichia. Rochalimaea* also belongs to the rickettsial family but it is not an intracellular parasite. The typical rickettsial species is approximately 0.3 to 0.7 μm in diameter and 2.0 μm in length. Rickettsial species are pleomorphic but usually appear as rods. They possess a cell wall that is structurally similar to the gram-negative cell wall (Fig. 28-1). Rickettsiae can be cultivated in the yolk sac of embryonated eggs, in laboratory animals, in certain arthropods, and in some tissue cultures.

As intracellular parasites, *Rickettsia* and *Coxiella* show some differences. When *Rickettsia* species are taken up by host cells, they enter the cytoplasm as part of a vacuole (phagosome) that responds differently to their environment (see Chapter 9 and Fig. 9-8 for discussion of evasion of phagocytosis). *Rickettsia* and *Coxiella* species differ in other ways:

1. *Coxiella* metabolism is activated by acid pH while other rickettsiae are inactivated by acid pH.
2. *Coxiella* species are resistant to desiccation and can survive in water and milk for up to three years. They are also resistant to disinfectants at concentrations that would kill most other bacteria, including other rickettsiae. *Rickettsia* species are very sensitive to environmental conditions.
3. *Coxiella* species possess a special developmental cycle that is not present in other rickettsiae.

EPIDEMIOLOGY AND PATHOGENESIS

The rickettsiae, except *Coxiella burnetii,* are transmitted to humans exclusively by insect vectors: ticks, mites, lice, and fleas. The rickettsiae multiply in the salivary glands of ticks and mice. In fleas and lice, however, the rickettsiae multiply in the gut and are excreted in the feces. Transfer of rickettsiae from fleas and lice to a human host occurs by crushing of the arthropod or by arthropod defecation at the site of the bite.

In general, the pathological features of most rickettsial diseases, except Q fever, differ only in the severity of clinical symptoms. Once the rickettsiae have penetrated the skin, they quickly reach the bloodstream. In the vascular system they have an affinity for the endothelial cells of small blood vessels. They replicate in the infected endothelial cells and become detached from the blood vessels. In the bloodstream, infected endothelial cells can bring about vascular obstruction that eventually leads to tissue necrosis.

Many of the symptoms of rickettsial infection—rash, myocarditis, and neurological changes—are due to rickettsiae in the vascular tissue of such organs as the skin, heart, and brain, respectively. At the site of the arthropod bite, an encrusted ulcer **(eschar)** may appear. Later during the disease, the ulcer develops a black necrotic center. The eschar is not found in all rickettsial diseases, but when it is, it provides a diagnostic clue.

The rickettsial diseases of humans have been historically classified into five major groups: the **typhus group,** the **spotted fever group, scrub typhus, Q fever,** and **trench fever** (Table 28-1). **Ehrlichiosis** is a rare rickettsial disease of humans that is discussed separately. In 1991 *Rochalimaea* species were found to be associated with clinical syndromes other than trench fever. The new *Rochalimaea* infections are discussed separately.

Typhus Group

Epidemic or Louse-Borne Typhus. Louse-borne typhus is caused by *Rickettsia prowazekii.* The organism is transmitted to humans by the body louse. Organisms are passed in the louse feces during biting and enter the wound around the bite. Before the discovery and use of DDT (dichlorodiphenyltrichlorethane) and other insecticides, severe epidemics of louse-borne typhus were common in times of war and famine. The disease persists in mountainous areas of Ethiopia and much of northeastern and central Africa as well as in the highlands of Central and South America.

In the United States most infections caused by *R. prowazekii* are found in the East and Southeast. In several instances flying squirrels or nests of flying squirrels were found in the homes of the patients. Flying squirrels often nest in attics during the winter months, and over 75 percent of the infections occur during winter months. The disease, sometimes referred to as **sylvatic typhus,** is milder than classic louse-borne infection. Transmission of

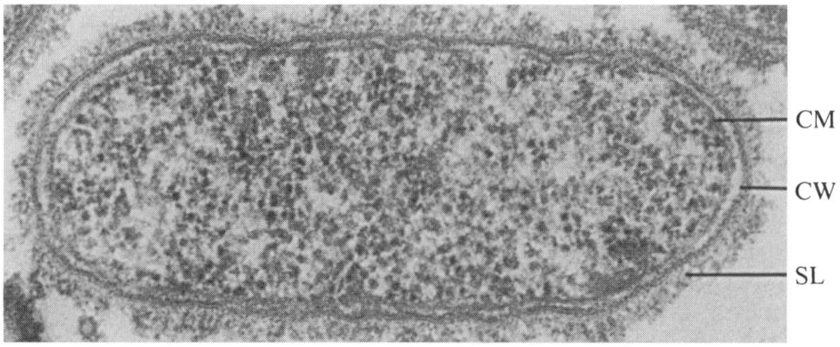

FIGURE 28-1
Electron micrograph of *Rickettsia rickettsii.* The cell wall is typical of gram-negative bacteria. (× 69,500.) CM = cytoplasmic membrane; CW = cell wall; SL = slime layer. (From D. J. Silverman and C. L. Wisseman, Jr., *Infect. Immun.* 21:1020, 1978.)

TABLE 28-1
Human Rickettsial Diseases[a]

Group	Causative agent	Common name	Mode of transmission	Reservoir of rickettsiae	Geographic distribution
Typhus	*Rickettsia prowazekii*	Epidemic typhus[b]	Louse feces rubbed in skin	Humans, flying squirrels	Worldwide
	R. typhi (*R. mooseri*)	Murine typhus	Flea feces rubbed in skin	Rodents	Worldwide
Spotted fever	*R. rickettsii*	Rocky Mountain spotted fever	Ixodid tick bite	Rodents	Western hemisphere
	R. sibirica	Siberian tick typhus	Ixodid tick bite	Rodents	Central Asia, Siberia, Mongolia, Central Europe
	R. conorii	Boutonneuse fever	Ixodid tick bite	Rodents, dogs	Mediterranean, Black Sea, Middle East, India, Africa
	R. australis	Queensland tick typhus	Mite bite	Marsupials, mice	Australia
	R. akari	Rickettsialpox	Mite bite	House mice	North America, former Soviet Union, South Africa, Korea
Scrub typhus	*R. tsutsugamushi*	Scrub typhus	Mite bite	Rodents	Asia, Australia, Pacific Islands
Q fever	*Coxiella burnetii*	Q fever	Inhalation of contaminated aerosol	Cattle, sheep, goats, rodents	Worldwide
Trench fever	*Rochalimaea quintana*	Trench fever	Infected louse feces rubbed into skin	Humans	Europe, Africa, North America

[a] Does not include infections caused by *Ehrlichia* or recently identified *Rochalimaea* species, which are discussed separately.
[b] Epidemic typhus infections may become latent and the infected carrier develops disease in the future (called **Brill-Zinsser disease**).

disease is believed to be caused by the bite of flying squirrel lice or by aerosol transmission of infected squirrel-louse feces.

The incubation period of classic louse-borne typhus lasts from 10 to 14 days and is characterized by a high fever. The fever tends to remain during the course of the illness. On the fourth or fifth day a rash appears on the trunk and spreads to the extremities. The rash is seldom seen on the face, palms, or soles. Death is the result of myocardial or neurological involvement.

In some individuals who have recovered from an initial attack of epidemic typhus, surviving rickettsial organisms may enter a latent state. Disease can develop in the infected carrier in the future but will not demonstrate the characteristic rash. The carrier state has been referred to as **Brill-Zinsser disease.**

Endemic Typhus. Endemic or murine typhus is a mild form of typhus transmitted to humans by the rat flea. The causative agent is *Rickettsia typhi (R. mooseri).* The symptoms of endemic typhus are similar to those of epidemic typhus but are much milder. Immunity to infection by epidemic typhus microorganisms also confers immunity to endemic typhus.

As many as 5000 cases of murine typhus were reported in the United States in the 1940s. In 1992 only 28 cases were reported to the Centers for Disease Control, with most of these reported from Texas.

Spotted Fever Group

Rocky Mountain Spotted Fever. Rocky Mountain spotted fever is the most frequently reported rickettsial disease in the United States. It is primarily a disease of children and young adults. The causative agent is *Rickettsia rickettsii.* Most cases are found east of the Mississippi, particularly in Virginia, North Carolina, and Tennessee (Fig. 28-2). The American dog tick is the primary vector in the

FIGURE 28-2
Rocky Mountain spotted fever, reported cases by county, United States, 1992. (Courtesy of Centers for Disease Control, Atlanta, GA.)

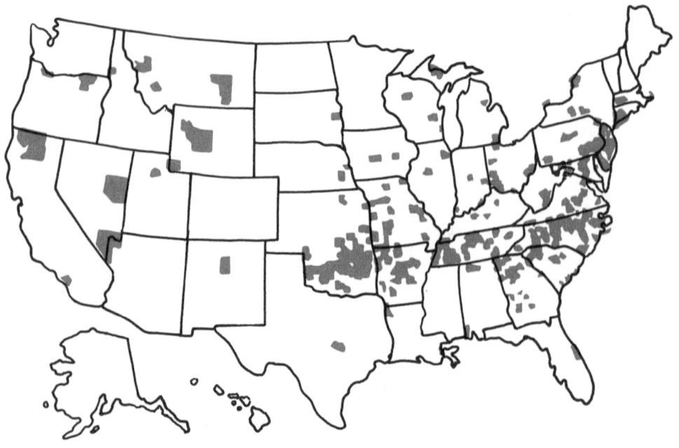

transmission of microorganisms in the eastern United States. The dog tick is harbored by the rabbit, raccoon, fox, woodchuck, and deer. The wood tick is responsible for transmission of Rocky Mountain spotted fever in the western United States.

Clinical symptoms appear on the average two to five days after the tick bite. Symptoms include fever, headache, lymphadenopathy, and rash. Sometimes a rash never appears. The rash, when present, generally starts on the wrists and then spreads to the trunk, face, and extremities. In contrast with other rickettsial infections, an eschar seldom appears at the site of the tick bite. Symptoms are often misdiagnosed as those of measles, encephalitis, meningococcemia, or rubella. Consequently, the case-fatality rate may reach as high as 15 : 1.

Death usually occurs 10 days after the appearance of the first symptoms. Death is due to progressive hypotension culminating in convulsions or cardiac arrest. In some instances death results from intravascular coagulation.

Boutonneuse Fever. The agent of **boutonneuse fever** (also called **Mediterranean spotted fever**) is the tick-borne *Rickettsia conorii.* The clinical symptoms are similar to those of Rocky Mountain spotted fever except that an eschar develops at the site of the tick bite. The disease is seldom fatal.

Siberian Tick Typhus. Like boutonneuse fever, this infection occurs rarely. Clinical symptoms are mild. The causative agent is *Rickettsia sibirica.*

Rickettsialpox and Queensland Tick Typhus. These are the mildest of all rickettsial diseases. They are caused by *Rickettsia akari* and *R. australis,* respectively. Rickettsialpox is found in North America, the former Soviet Union, South Africa, and Korea. Queensland tick typhus is found in Australia. The vector for transmission is the tick.

Scrub Typhus

Scrub typhus is caused by *Rickettsia tsutsugamushi* and is transmitted to humans by mites carried on rodents. The disease is more prevalent in eastern Asia and the islands of the South Pacific. Clinical symptoms include a maculopapular rash that covers most of the body and an eschar at the site of the mite bite. Enlargement of the spleen occurs in more than 50 percent of patients. Treatment with antibiotics brings complete recovery. In untreated patients the disease progresses until there are serious respiratory, neurological, and cardiovascular complications. These complications often lead to death.

Q Fever

Q fever is caused by *C. burnetii.* The designation Q was used to indicate fever of unknown origin, or "query" fever. Q fever has a worldwide distribution but numerous cases are reported from Australia and Great Britain.

The primary reservoirs of *C. burnetii* are sheep, goats, and cattle and ticks. Q fever is a zoonosis transmitted from infected animals to humans who come in contact with the reservoirs. In animals Q fever is a subclinical disease in which rickettsiae are excreted in large numbers in the milk, urine, or feces. Q fever rickettsiae released in the afterbirth, milk, or urine of animals can survive in the environment for periods of time. The survival characteristic is associated with a developmental cycle in which there is believed to be a vegetative and sporeforming state. The spore resembles an endospore and is the resistant form of the organism (Fig. 28-3).

Humans acquire Q fever most often by inhalation of aerosols that have been generated from the dried parturition products of farm animals. *C. burnetii* is highly infectious and a single inhaled organism is sufficient to cause disease.

The incubation period of Q fever is 14 to 39 days. The fever is intermittent, with spikes of 104 to 105 F. Headache, persistent cough, myalgia, and chest pain accompany the fever. Pneumonia is one manifestation of illness, but its incidence may vary from 0 to 90 percent, depending on the particular outbreak of disease. Q fever may also be manifested by liver involvement (hepatitis). Complications from acute disease are rare and are usually self-limiting. A rare but severe and often fatal complication of Q fever is endocarditis. Endocarditis is seldom seen in the United States.

FIGURE 28-3
Electron micrograph of *Coxiella burnetii,* demonstrating the endospore-like component (*arrow*). (From T. F. McCaul and J. C. Williams, *J. Bacteriol.* 147:1963, 1981.)

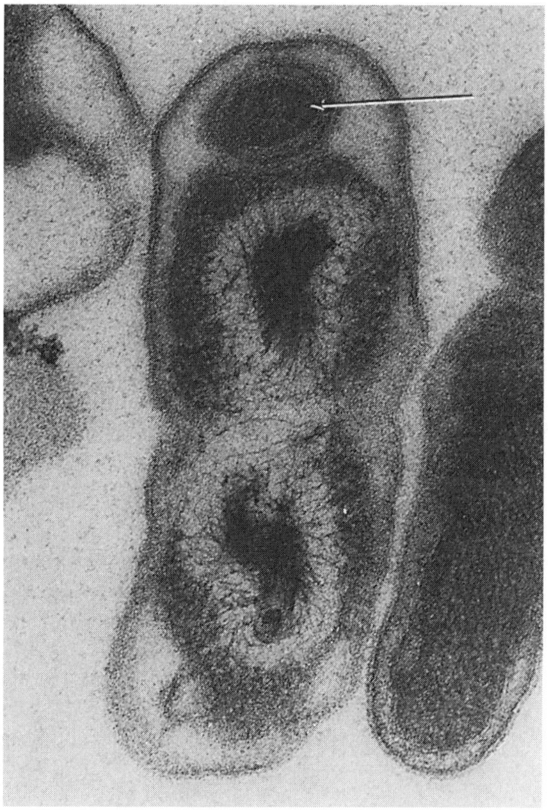

Trench Fever

Rochalimaea quintana is the causative agent of trench fever. Humans are the reservoir of infection. The body louse is the only known vector. Trench fever was an important clinical entity during the two world wars. Because the symptoms are mild, trench fever is not considered a public health problem.

Ehrlichioses

Ehrlichioses are diseases caused by species of *Ehrlichia.* They have been known to cause disease in animals but recently have also been implicated in human disease. Three important human pathogens are *E. sennetsu, E. canis,* and *E. chaffeensis.*

E. sennetsu (*sennetsu* from the Japanese meaning "glandular fever") is the cause of glandular fever in humans. It is observed only in western Japan and Malaysia. It is not known how the infectious agent is transmitted to humans. The incubation period for glandular fever is 14 days. The symptoms of disease resemble those of infectious mononucleosis. There is remittent fever with daily fluctuations accompanied by headache, chills, sore throat, and sleeplessness. About five days after these initial symptoms occur, there is lymph node enlargement about the face and neck. Hepatosplenomegaly is observed in about one-third of patients.

E. canis and *E. chafeensis* are associated with human infection in the United States. The disease is believed to be transmitted by the brown dog tick. The median incubation period is nine days. Often the disease is first diagnosed as Rocky Mountain spotted fever. Over one-half of the patients are hospitalized. Fever, often accompanied by gastrointestinal abnormalities, is present in most patients. Severe illness is characterized by cough, diarrhea, and lymphadenopathy. Severe complications include respiratory insufficiency, renal insufficiency, and central nervous system abnormalities. Hematopoietic cells such as those in the bone marrow are the primary targets of ehrlichiae. It is not known whether ehrlichiae-mediated vascular damage is the major pathogenic event in infection.

Other *Rochalimaea* Infections

Since 1991 *Rochalimaea* species have been associated with three additional human infections: **bacillary angiomatosis, bacillary peliosis hepatitis,** and **cat-scratch disease.** The spectrum of illness associated with these organisms is continuing to expand. Bacillary peliosis hepatitis is a liver condition associated with human immunodeficiency virus (HIV)–infected patients and is not discussed further.

Cat-Scratch Disease. Cat-scratch disease is the most common cause of chronic lymphadenopathy in children. It is also a common cause of lymphadenopathy in adults. Cat-scratch disease begins as a papule or pustule about 3 to 10 days after the scratch occurs. The lesion usually heals without any apparent complications. Regional lymphadenopathy develops about two to three weeks after the time of the scratch. The enlarged nodes are found in the head, neck, or axillary areas. Lymphadenopathy may persist for two to four months. The most unusual complications are Parinaud's oculoglandular syndrome, encephalopathy, and systemic disease involving the liver or spleen.

Diagnosis is usually based on exclusion of other diseases. The principal criteria for diagnosis are

1. History of contact with cats and a regional inoculation lesion or scratch
2. Negative laboratory findings for other diseases
3. Positive response on the cat-scratch skin test
4. Biopsied lymph node or lesion showing small pleomorphic bacilli on sections stained with Warthin-Starry silver stain

The cause of cat-scratch disease has been an enigma for many years. DNA hybridization tests and fatty acid analysis now suggest that it may be caused by two species: *Rochalimaea henselae* (90 percent of patients) or *Afipia felis* (patients in whom serology for *R. henselae* is negative). In most patients the disease resolves on its own in two to four months. Complicated cases can be treated with erythromycin, doxycycline, and rifampin.

Bacillary Angiomatosis. The history of this disease began in 1983 when an atypical subcutaneous bacterial infection was discovered in a patient with acquired immunodeficiency syndrome (AIDS). Several vascular tumors (**angiomas**) that resembled Kaposi's sarcoma were found but they could be differentiated by histopathology. Bacilli isolated from the lesion resembled those that cause cat-scratch disease. By polymerase chain reaction, a 16S RNA molecule from the bacteria was amplified and used to compare isolates from various lesions. The newly identified organism was found to represent a new species of *Rochalimaea* and was called *R. henselae.* This organism has now been repeatedly isolated from the blood of patients with bacillary angiomatosis and bacillary peliosis hepatitis. Consequently, cat-scratch disease and bacillary angiomatosis appear to be manifestations of the same infection.

The most common form of bacillary angiomatosis is dermal and begins as an enlarging red papule with resemblance to a cranberry. Most infections are observed in HIV-infected patients. The lesion enlarges and can become several centimeters in diameter. Lesions may be single or multiple. Bacillary angiomatosis can occur in every organ system, including the brain. It is difficult to differentiate from mycobacterial and fungal infections or malignancy without the use of biopsy. Bacillary angiomatosis responds to erythromycin, rifampin, and doxycycline.

LABORATORY DIAGNOSIS

Rickettsiae are difficult and dangerous to work with in the laboratory. The single most important diagnostic aid in identification of rickettsial disease such as Rocky Mountain spotted fever is the demonstration of a rise in serum antibody during illness. Serodiagnosis is not a rapid accurate test since antibodies to *R. rickettsii* are not detected during the acute stage of illness. Serodiagnosis is therefore retrospective. The highest sensitivities are obtained with the indirect immunofluorescent antibody

(IFA) test and latex agglutination tests. The IFA test, which is accepted as the best serological test, is performed on whole rickettsiae. The organisms are affixed to a microscopical slide and are reacted with serial dilutions of the patient's serum. The IFA test is also the only available test for human ehrlichiosis and is also used in the diagnosis of Q fever.

Diagnosis of Mediterranean spotted fever can be confirmed serologically by the Western immunoblot test. *R. conorii* can also be isolated from blood culture with use of the shell vial cell culture technique.

TREATMENT, PREVENTION, AND CONTROL

Treatment of rickettsial disease with tetracycline or chloramphenicol often results in complete recovery (includes ehrlichioses). Because of the toxic effects of chloramphenicol, tetracycline is the preferred drug. In some rickettsial diseases, such as Rocky Mountain spotted fever, early treatment is absolutely necessary. Treatment should be based on clinical symptoms and not serology since antibodies do not always develop in the early stages of disease.

Many fatalities from rickettsial infections such as Rocky Mountain spotted fever are the result of misdiagnosis and institution of penicillin or ampicillin therapy. Both drugs have no effect on the rickettsiae. Early therapy, particularly in scrub typhus, does not allow enough time for immunity to develop. Relapses are possible unless treatment is extended for several weeks.

Vaccination programs have met with little success. A Q fever vaccine is available for laboratory personnel. No Rocky Mountain spotted fever vaccine is currently available but some vaccines are under investigation.

Chemical control with insecticides can be easily applied against fleas and lice since both are closely associated with humans and rats. Control of woodland ticks and mites is more difficult because of the variety of mammals that harbor the arthropod vector. The most practical protection is the use of repellents and personal cleanliness.

The Chlamydiae

The chlamydiae, which are intracellular parasites, are important pathogens found throughout the animal kingdom. Only a few species are pathogenic for humans but one of them *(Chlamydia trachomatis)* is the leading cause of sexually transmitted disease in the United States. Females of childbearing age are at particular risk of infection which can lead to infertility and ectopic pregnancy.

GENERAL CHARACTERISTICS

Chlamydiae range in size from 0.2 to 1.0 μm. They have no peptidoglycan layer in the cell wall, which distinguishes them from the rickettsiae. The chlamydial cell wall does possess an outer membrane characteristic of that in gram-negative bacteria. Metabolically, chlamydiae are unable to produce their own energy sources such as ATP.

Three species of *Chlamydia* are recognized: *C. trachomatis, C. pneumoniae* (formerly called *Chlamydia* species strain TWAR), and *C. psittaci.* They have an unusual developmental cycle in which two forms of the microorganism exist: the **elementary body,** which is the extracellular and infectious form, and the **reticulate body,** which is the intracellular, noninfectious form of the organism. The developmental cycle can be broken down into the following stages (Fig. 28-4):

1. The infectious elementary body is internalized by host cells and in the process forms a phagosome.
2. Chlamydiae, once internalized, remain within the phagosome and in some as yet unknown way prevent phagosome-lysosome fusion.
3. Elementary bodies undergo a reorganization into another form, the reticulate body.
4. The reticulate bodies multiply by binary fission. During this multiplication process the phagosome enlarges and is referred to as an **inclusion body** (Plate 18).
5. Some of the reticulate bodies, instead of multiplying, undergo reorganization and become elementary bodies.
6. Elementary bodies are released from the inclusion body and the host cell. These elementary bodies are ready to infect adjacent host cells.

EPIDEMIOLOGY AND PATHOGENESIS

Chlamydia trachomatis

Ocular Disease. Trachoma is a chronic ocular disease caused by repeated infections of the conjunctiva and cornea by *C. trachomatis*. Trachoma is endemic in certain areas such as the Punjab region of India, isolated regions of Africa, and a few south central states in the United States. Worldwide, trachoma affects 500 million people and up to 9 million are reported to be blind from this condition.

The agent of trachoma is spread by (1) contaminated fingers; (2) items such as facecloths and clothing; (3) infective discharges on bed linen, pillows, and so on; and (4) direct contact between parents and children. Repeated infections cause a delayed-type hypersensitivity to the chlamydial antigen. Chronic conjunctivitis results in the formation of conjunctival follicles that enlarge. Necrosis of the follicles can cause scarring. Over a period of years the scars contract and turn in the upper eyelid, resulting in abrasions of the cornea by eyelashes. Blindness may be the result of conjunctival scarring or secondary bacterial infections. Any cultural practice that reduces intrafamilial transmission reduces the incidence as well as severity of the disease.

Inclusion conjunctivitis is a general term referring to ocular chlamydial infection in adults and infants that does not result in blindness. Infants become infected during passage through the infected birth canal of mothers. This type of infection, called **ophthalmia neonatorum,** can also

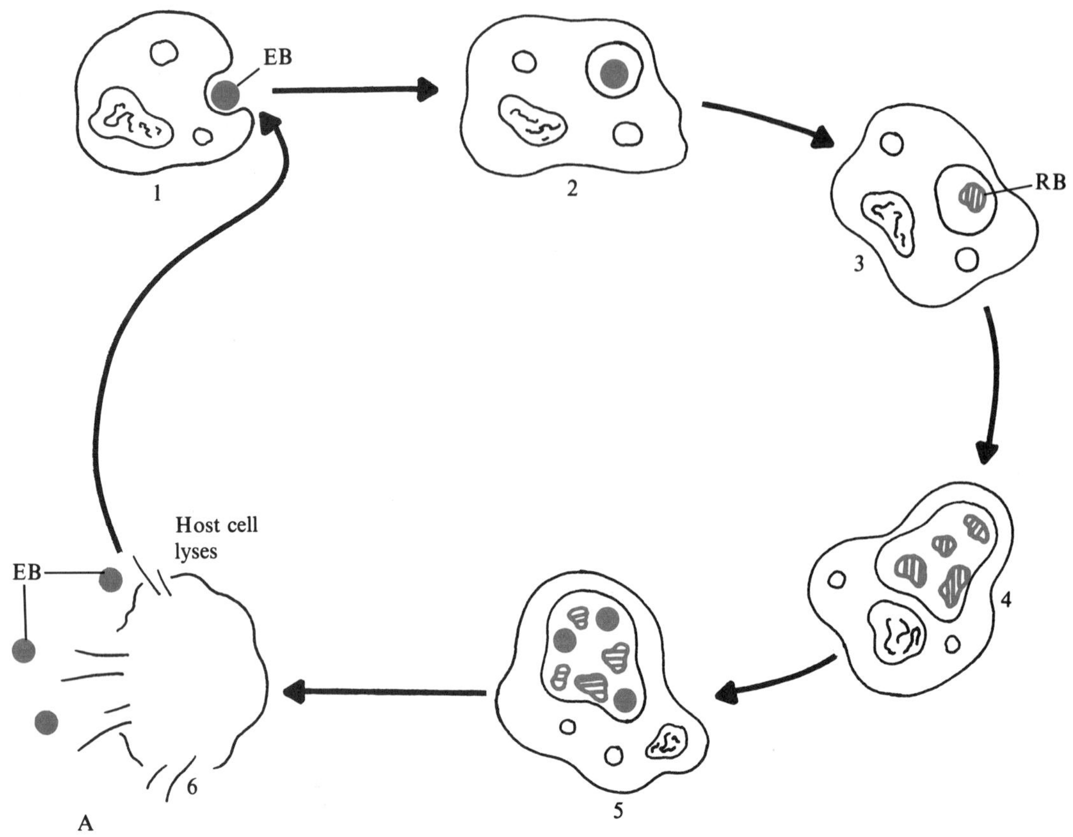

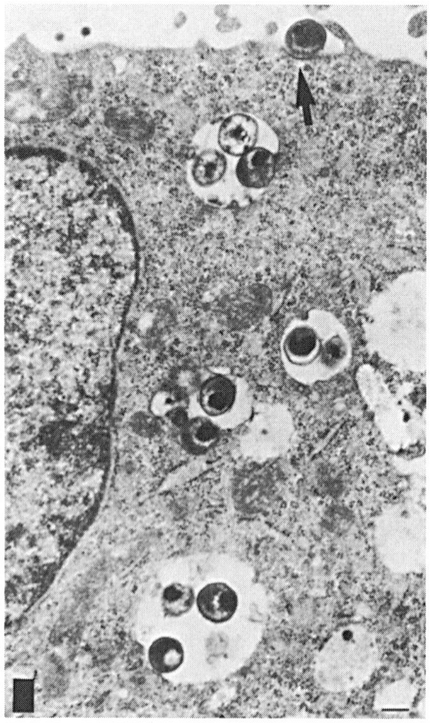

FIGURE 28-4
Developmental cycle of chlamydiae. A. Diagrammatic illustration: *1,* infectious elementary body (EB) is internalized by a host cell; *2,* EB is within the phagosome; *3,* EB reorganizes into a reticulate body (RB); *4,* RB multiplies and phagosome occupies most of the internal content of the cell; *5,* some RB become EB; *6,* infected host cell dies and releases infectious EB, which infects adjacent cells. B. Electron micrograph of EB and phagosome formation: one EB (*arrow*) is internalized, while in the cytoplasm four phagosomes can be observed to contain two or three EB. (From P. Wyrick, *Infect. Immun.* 56:1456, 1988.)

be caused by *Neisseria gonorrhoeae* (see Chapter 18). In the United States about 5 percent of the women having vaginal deliveries are infected with *C. trachomatis*. Inclusion conjunctivitis will develop in about 20 percent of the infants exposed to infected mothers, and **neonatal pneumonia** will develop in another 15 percent.

Inclusion conjunctivitis in adults occurs primarily by contact with microorganisms derived from the genital tract. Many cases of adult ocular disease can be traced to swimming pools contaminated with the microorganisms. Inclusion conjunctivitis in infants and adults is usually a self-limiting disease; however, scarring has been noted in infants in whom treatment was delayed.

Male Genital Tract Disease. *C. trachomatis* is the primary agent of a sexually transmitted disease in men called **nongonococcal urethritis.** Up to one-third of men with nongonococcal urethritis are asymptomatic and many also have gonococcal urethritis. Consequently, treatment of the symptomatic disease with penicillin is not effective against *C. trachomatis*. The symptom, a white discharge, often takes two to three weeks to be manifested (gonococcal urethritis takes 2–7 days).

The highest rate of *C. trachomatis* among men is found in those who are sexually promiscuous. Female sex partners of men with nongonococcal urethritis also carry the organism on the cervix. The disease is self-limiting but sometimes epididymitis is a complication.

Female Genital Tract Disease. Chlamydial infection in women usually involves the cervix. The infection is initially asymptomatic but **pelvic inflammatory disease** (PID) may develop in 2 to 18 percent (see Chapter 18 for discussion). In the United States over 1 million cases of PID are reported each year. Several agents can cause PID (*N. gonohorrhoeae, Mycoplasma hominis, Ureaplasma urealyticum,* and *C. trachomatis*) but *C. trachomatis* is more frequently associated with the complication of infertility. Women with tubal infertility begin sexual activity sooner, have more sex partners, and more often have a history of sexually transmitted disease.

Lymphogranuloma Venereum. Lymphogranuloma venereum is a sexually transmitted disease caused by *C. trachomatis*. Fewer than 400 cases are reported each year in the United States. Following genital inoculation the organisms invade the lymphatic and circulatory systems. After an incubation period of one to four weeks a lesion develops in the inguinal or femoral lymph nodes. The lymph nodes may become necrotic, but they eventually heal (Fig. 28-5). The most severe complications of this disease are the development of perianal abscesses and fistulas that may arise 1 to 10 years after infection.

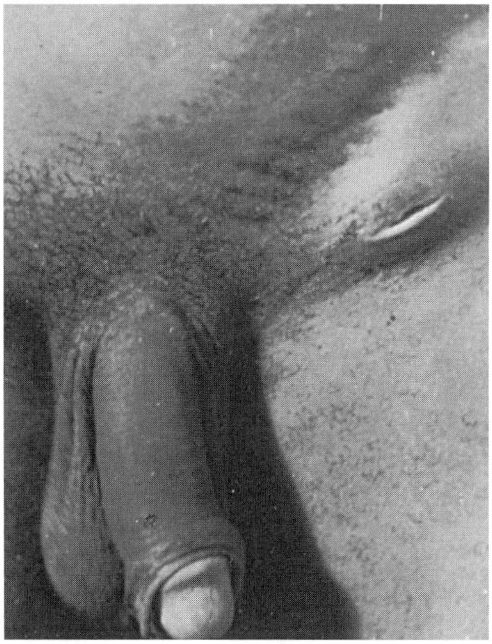

FIGURE 28-5
Lymphogranuloma venereum. Acute bubo, which has been surgically incised. (From E. V. Hamm. In W. A. D. Anderson and J. M. Kissane, eds., *Pathology*, 7th ed. St. Louis: Mosby, 1977.)

Chlamydia psittaci

C. psittaci is the agent of **psittacosis.** *C. psittaci* infections occur more frequently in avian and mammalian populations. Psittacosis is primarily an occupational disease for those working in poultry-processing plants. Pet birds and occasionally wild birds transmit the infectious agent to humans. Infected birds show no clinical signs of disease.

Psittacosis is usually asymptomatic but an atypical pneumonia may develop. About 150 cases of pneumonia are reported each year to the Centers for Disease Control. The incubation period of one to three weeks is followed by chills, fever, headache, and persistent cough. Symptoms subside in less than two weeks.

Chlamydia pneumoniae

C. pneumoniae (formerly called *Chlamydia* species strain **TWAR** or Taiwan-Acute-Respiratory) was first isolated in 1965. Pneumonia and bronchitis are the most recognized symptoms of infection but most infections are actually asymptomatic or go unrecognized. The mode of transmission is from person to person.

Pneumonia due to *C. pneumoniae* is more common among the elderly and less common among persons younger than 20 years. The estimated number of pneumonia cases annually in the United States is 300,000. The first symptoms are sore throat and hoarseness. A cough develops about a week or longer after infection. Most infections are mild but complete recovery is unusually slow, even with appropriate therapy. In young adults about 5 percent of sinusitis is associated with *C. pneumoniae* infection.

LABORATORY DIAGNOSIS

Culture is usually considered the gold standard for most chlamydial disease. The cost and complexity of microbiological diagnosis, however, do not allow for ordinary hospital identification. Diagnosis is usually based on clinical signs and symptoms.

The genital swab is the most frequent specimen for isolation of *C. trachomatis*. Transport media are required for transfer to the laboratory. The specimens can be identified on slides by direct fluorescent antibody staining.

Cell culture systems are commercially available and identification can be based on observations of intracytoplasmic inclusions. Giemsa or iodine staining does not differentiate species, however. Inclusions can be detected by staining with genus-specific immunofluorescence reagent using monoclonal antibodies. Enzyme immunoassays (EIA) are also available for detecting chlamydial antigen. The most sensitive serological test for diagnosing infection by chlamydiae is the **microimmunofluorescence** test.

Physicians who wish to determine if a first-visit patient requires treatment for nongonococcal urethritis can utilize a two-step evaluation procedure. The combination of historical factors (age, sexual partners, etc.) plus a simple test for the presence of infection can be helpful. One test is the **leukocyte esterase** test on voided urine. The test is an indicator of urethritis. The test detects enzymes that are produced by polymorphonuclear cells. These enzymes hydrolyze an indoxylcarbonic acid ester on the dipstick to indoxyl, which reacts with an indicator in the strip to produce a purple color. If the result is positive, the physician can then have a culture made to identify *N. gonorrhoeae* or *C. trachomatis*.

For more details on various laboratory tests, see the 1993 Centers for Disease Control publication listed in Additional Readings.

TREATMENT AND PREVENTION

Individuals who have acquired and recovered from chlamydial infection remain susceptible to reinfection. Reinfection occurs despite development of antibody in both serum and secretions such as genital secretions.

Doxycycline and azithromycin are the drugs of choice for the treatment of most chlamydial disease. Alternative regimens include ofloxacin, erythromycin, or sulfisoxazole. Erythromycin and amoxicillin are recommended for pregnant women.

For PID, the antibiotic regimen may include cefoxitin or other cephalosporins plus doxycycline as well as clindamycin to inhibit anaerobes. Erythromycin syrup administered orally is used to treat established inclusion conjunctivitis in the newborn as well as infant pneumonia.

Vaccines are not currently available for chlamydial dis-

TABLE 28-2
Characteristics That Distinguish Rickettsiae from Chlamydiae

	Group	
Characteristic	**Rickettsiae**	**Chlamydiae**
Size	2.0 μm in length	0.2–1.0 μm in length
Cell wall composition	Contain peptidoglycan	Do not contain peptidoglycan
Developmental cycle	Simple binary fission except for *Coxiella burnetii*, which exists in endospore and vegetative state	Two forms of the agent: the infectious or elementary particle and the noninfectious reticulate body
Energy source	Can produce their own	Cannot produce their own
Method of evasion of phagocytes	Break down membrane of phagosome and survive in cytoplasm: *Coxiella* resistant to acid hydrolases of phagolysosome	Developmental cycle occurs in phagosome and somehow prevents fusion with lysosome
Transmission to humans	Insect vectors (tick, mite, flea, louse); *C. burnetii* transmitted via inhalation of aerosols from dried parturition products	Direct sexual contact (NGU, neonatal inclusion conjunctivitis, neonatal pneumonia, PID, lymphogranuloma venereum); indirect contact (trachoma, psittacosis, pneumonia)
Disease characteristics	Affinity for vascular tissue eventually causes obstruction; rash often characteristic of infection; Q fever (*C. burnetii*) associated with lung tissue and no rash is involved; lymphadenopathy and vascular tumors from *Rochalimaea* infection	Affinity for tissue of eye (trachoma, inclusion conjunctivitis) and genital tract (NGU, PID, lymphogranuloma venereum); affinity for respiratory tissue (psittacosis, pneumonia)
Laboratory diagnosis	Serological tests (IFA, LA) performed during course of illness	Cell culture or detection of antigens in specimens by immunofluorescence or EIA
Antibiotic sensitivity	Sensitive to tetracyclines but *not* sensitive to penicillins	Sensitive to doxycycline, tetracyclines, erythromycin, and amoxicillin

IFA = indirect fluorescent antibody; PID = pelvic inflammatory disease; LA = lutex agglutination; NGU = nongonococcal urethritis; EIA = enzyme immunoassay.

ease. Prevention of psittacosis is dependent on preventing avian infection by prophylaxis. Imported birds are supposed to be treated at quarantine stations.

Antibiotics such as erythromycin or tetracycline are used on the eyes of newborns to prevent chlamydial conjunctivitis. Prevention of trachoma was discussed previously.

Summary

Both rickettsiae and chlamydiae are gram-negative intracellular parasites that cannot be cultivated on ordinary laboratory media. The differences that distinguish most rickettsiae from chlamydiae are outlined in Table 28-2.

Questions for Study

1. Why would *C. trachomatis* rather than *Neisseria gonorrhoeae* be a more frequent cause of pelvic inflammatory disease? Isn't *N. gonorrhoeae* more virulent than *C. trachomatis?*
2. How does the infection process of *Rickettsia* species differ from that of *Coxiella* species?
3. Why do diseases such as Rocky Mountain spotted fever, which are easily treatable, have high fatality rates?
4. What are some of the possible consequences of chlamydial infection in young women?
5. What tissues are the primary target of rickettsiae? Ehrlichiae?
6. What is the relationship between bacillary angiomatosis and cat-scratch disease?
7. Briefly describe the various presentations of infection by *C. trachomatis.*

CHAPTER

29 Actinomycetes

OBJECTIVES

To list the most important species of *Actinomyces* and the types of infections with which they are associated

To describe briefly the association between *Actinomyces* species and caries and periodontal disease

To outline the similarities and differences between *Nocardia* and *Actinomyces*

To describe the types of infections associated with *Nocardia*

To describe the types of treatment required for actinomycoses and nocardioses

OUTLINE

ACTINOMYCOSIS
- Pathogenesis
  - Cervicofacial Actinomycosis
  - Thoracic Actinomycosis
  - Abdominal Actinomycosis
  - Genital Actinomycosis
- Laboratory Diagnosis
- Treatment

NOCARDIOSIS AND ACTINOMYCETOMA
- Pathogenesis
- Laboratory Diagnosis
- Treatment

CARIES, PERIODONTAL DISEASE, AND ACTINOMYCETES

Actinomycetes are a large group of bacteria that have characteristics of bacteria and fungi. Most of the species in this group have the ability to form branches or filaments. The filaments are referred to as **hyphae** (singular, hypha) and are characteristic of all fungi (Fig. 29-1). The diseases caused by actinomycetes also resemble those caused by eukaryotic fungi. Bacterial characteristics of actinomycetes include their prokaryotic cell walls and other structural components and their susceptibility to penicillin. Fungi are uniformly resistant to penicillin.

Many species in the actinomycetes, particularly species of the genus *Streptomyces* (Fig. 29-2), are widely known because of their production of **antibiotics.** Actinomycetes also include genera such as *Corynebacterium* and *Mycobacterium* which have human pathogenic potential. The actinomycetes described in the chapter are less pathogenic. We discuss three types of infections caused by them: **actinomycosis, nocardiosis,** and **actinomycetoma.**

Actinomycosis

Actinomycosis can be caused by several actinomycete species belonging to genera such as *Actinomyces, Rothia, Arachnia, Bifidobacterium, Corynebacterium,* and so on. The most important of these genera is *Actinomyces.*

Actinomyces species are facultative anaerobes that make up the microbial flora of the oral cavity, intestinal tract, and pelvic area. They produce branching filaments during growth but do not produce aerial filaments. The most frequently recovered pathogenic species are *Actinomyces israelii, Actinomyes naeslundii,* and *Arachnia propionica* (formerly *Actinomyces propionica*).

Actinomycosis is a chronic, suppurative infection characterized by abscess formation and draining sinuses. The draining sinuses contain white or yellow granules (called **sulfur granules**) composed of microcolonies of the branching microorganism. The major forms of the disease involve the cervicofacial, abdominal, thoracic, and genital regions.

FIGURE 29-1
Scanning electron micrograph of *Actinomyces israelii* microcolony. Note the branching filaments. (From J. M. Slack and M. A. Gerencser, *Actinomyces, Filamentous Bacteria: Biology and Pathogenicity.* Minneapolis: Burgess, 1975.)

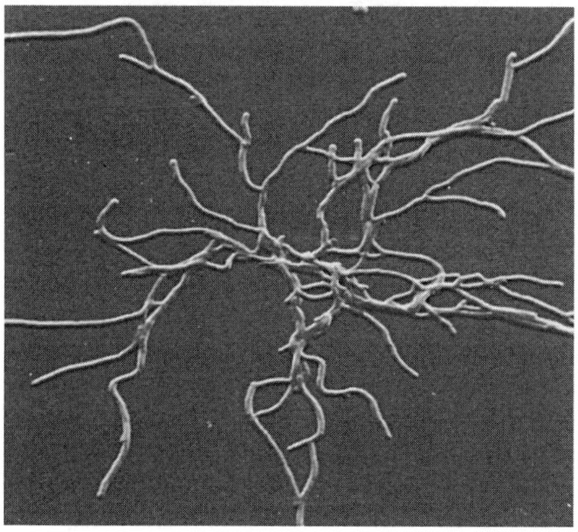

PATHOGENESIS

Cervicofacial Actinomycosis

Cervicofacial actinomycosis is the most common type of actinomycosis and is usually associated with the lower jaw. Individuals predisposed by conditions such as tooth decay, jaw fracture, or tooth extraction are most susceptible to infection. The disease is characterized by abscess formation and development of sinus tracts (Plate 19). The sinus tracts eventually reach the skin, producing nodules that can break and form fistulas. The tissues around the fistula often shrink, leaving an area of depression. In advanced forms the infection may penetrate the orbital cavity, causing blindness.

Thoracic Actinomycosis

Thoracic actinomycosis can be the result of (1) aspiration of microorganisms from the oral cavity, (2) extension of infection from cervicofacial actinomycosis, and (3) hematogenous spreading. Lesions occur in the lung and may involve both lobes. The infection extends to the pleura and eventually penetrates the thoracic wall through multiple draining sinuses. Fistulas and the characteristic depression of the chest are also evident. During the disease there may be chest pain, fever, and cough resembling those of other respiratory diseases, such as tuberculosis.

Abdominal Actinomycosis

Abdominal actinomycosis results most frequently from trauma of the intestinal tract or abdominal wall. Many cases of the disease are a consequence of appendectomies that fail to heal or of perforated appendices. Sinus tracts may develop and penetrate the abdominal wall.

Genital Actinomycosis

Genital actinomycosis is a potential consequence of women wearing intrauterine devices (IUDs). Prevalence of the disease may range from 1 to 36 percent. Infection is believed to be the result of inflammation and breakdown of the endometrium. This is followed by colonization by *Actinomyces* species. In most patients removal of the IUD is sufficient treatment and antibiotics are not required. Invasive disease is rare but when present can be fatal.

LABORATORY DIAGNOSIS

Pus from fistulas and sputum can be examined for the appearance of yellow or white granules; however, they are not always present. When granules are present in the fistulas, the wound should be covered with gauze and examined the next day. Gram-staining the granules permits the identification of gram-positive filamentous or diphtheroid bacilli. Clinical specimens or granules should be inoculated into thioglycolate broth or brain-heart infu-

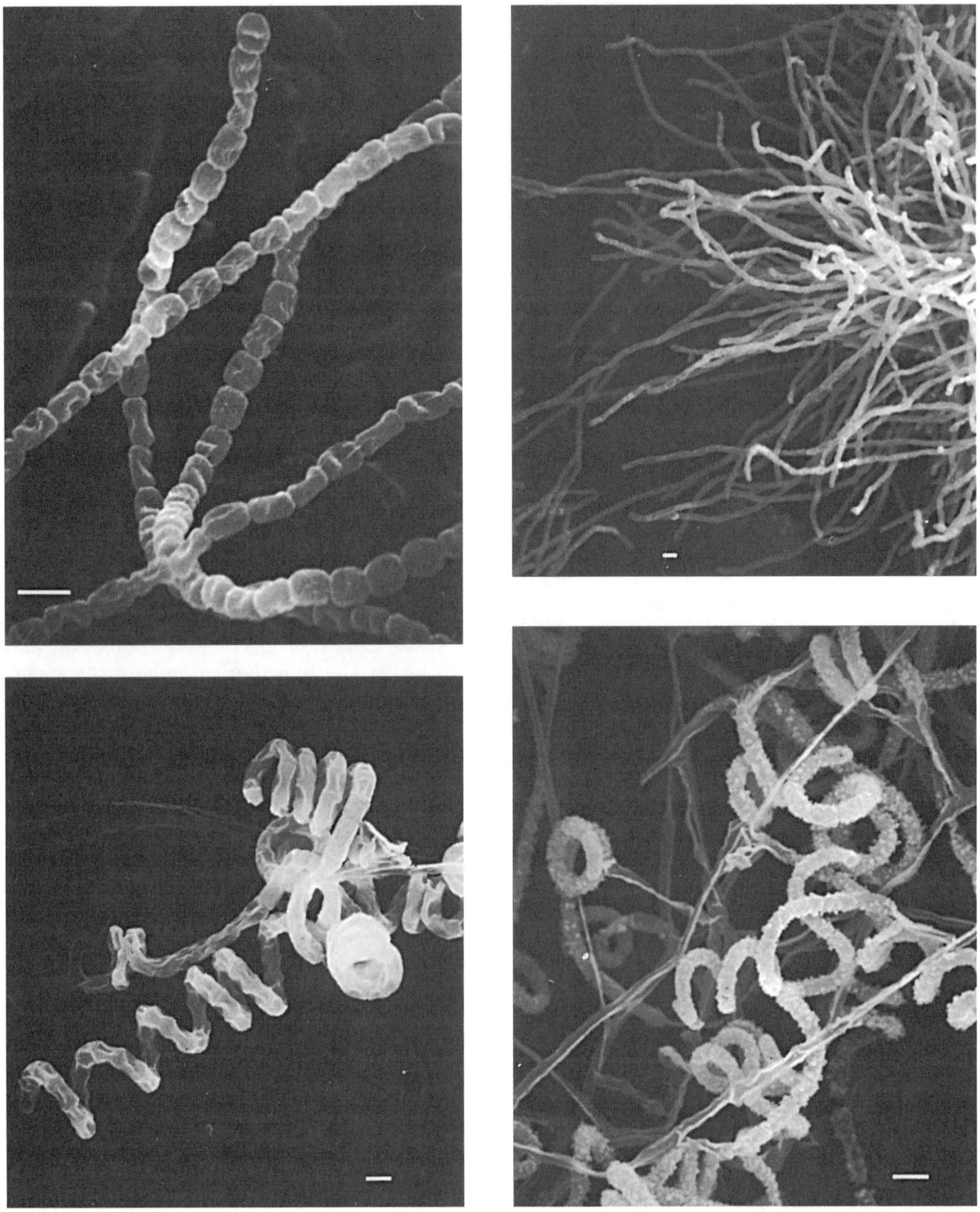

FIGURE 29-2
Types of *Streptomyces* species found in the soil. (Bar = 1 μm.) (From S. Omura, *Microbiol. Rev.* 50:259, 1986.)

sion agar and incubated anaerobically for two to five days. When colonies develop, the growth should be checked for the appearance of gram-positive bacilli. Species of *Actinomyces* can be identified directly in clinical specimens by immunofluorescent techniques.

Available identification kits can determine aerotolerance, Gram reaction, morphology, colonial characteristics, and patterns of fermentation of carbohydrates and products of specific enzyme reactions.

TREATMENT

Surgical debridement of damaged tissue is the prerequisite to antibiotic therapy. Penicillin G administered over a period of three to four weeks remains the treatment of choice. Combinations of trimethoprim and sulfamethoxazole have resulted in more rapid cures, particularly in patients with cervicofacial or abdominal infections.

In women with asymptomatic genital infection, removal of the IUD is sufficient therapy. Patients with pelvic symptoms should receive a full course of antibiotic therapy to prevent systemic dissemination of the infection.

Nocardiosis and Actinomycetoma

Nocardioses are infections caused by species of *Nocardia* that are indigenous to soil and water. *Nocardia* organisms also differ from *Actinomyces* species in that the former are aerobic and produce aerial filaments. The filaments can undergo fragmentation. In order of frequency the most important human pathogens are *N. asteroides, N. brasiliensis,* and *N. otitidiscaviarum.*

PATHOGENESIS

Nocardioses are usually found in compromised patients. The compromising factor may be immunosuppressive therapy for neoplastic disease or transplantation, or underlying chronic pulmonary disease. Corticosteroids adversely affect tissue macrophage activity at sites such as the liver, spleen, and lung. *Nocardia* is more resistant than most other microorganisms to oxidative killing by macrophages. Steroid administration, therefore, makes some patients more susceptible to infection by *Nocardia.*

Most *Nocardia* infections result from the inhalation of the organism, usually *N. asteroides. N. brasiliensis* and *N. otitidiscaviarum* cause infections usually by direct inoculation into traumatized tissue. These latter organisms are more frequently associated with skin and soft tissue infections.

N. asteroides lung infections are accompanied by pleuritic pain and cough, often 8 to 12 weeks after immunosuppressive therapy. Nodular abscesses can be observed on chest radiographs of the lung. Many times no symptoms are evident. The infection can become disseminated if early treatment is not instituted. Metastatic infection can involve the nervous system and kidneys. Fatality rates for disseminated disease can reach 80 percent.

Skin and soft tissue infections caused by species other than *N. asteroides* usually involve the lower extremity following trauma. Infection is localized and is characterized by draining sinuses and the presence of granules. As the infection becomes more chronic, sinus tracts extend more deeply into the body and involve both muscle and bone. These types of infections are called **actinomycetoma** (Fig. 29-3). Actinomycetoma also can be caused by microorganisms such as *Actinomadura madurae, Actinomadura pelletieri, Streptomyces somaliensis,* and *Streptomyces paraguayensis.*

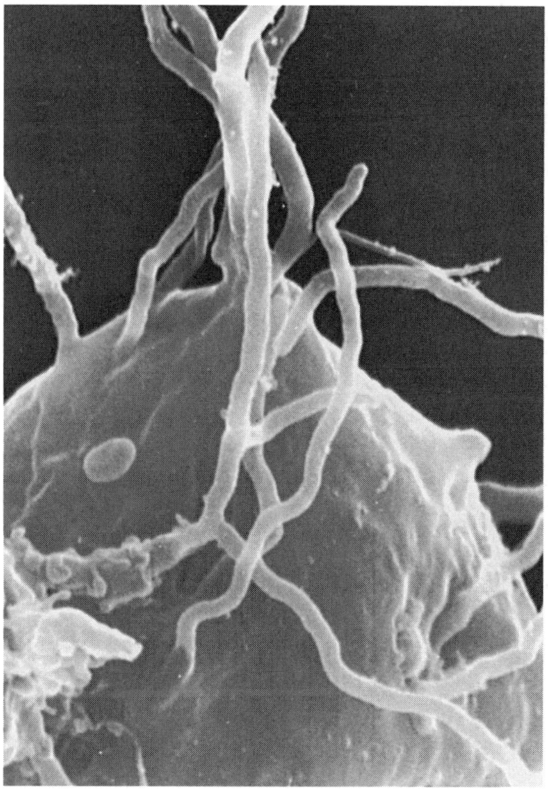

FIGURE 29-3
Mycetoma of the foot caused by *Actinomadura madurae.* (Courtesy of V. V. Pankaja Lakshmi.)

LABORATORY DIAGNOSIS

Diseases caused by *Nocardia* and *Actinomyces* organisms are very similar. Differentiation of these genera is important because successful treatment requires different therapeutics. Exudative material from lesions should be examined microscopically for microcolonies of granules. Sputum, spinal fluid, urine, and exudative material can be examined microscopically for the typical thin, highly branched filaments (Fig. 29-4). Isolates can be inoculated onto Löwenstein-Jensen medium. Growth will appear in about 7 to 10 days. The organism is gram-positive and acid-fast. The organism can also be grown on blood agar plates, with cream-colored colonies appearing after three days at 37 C. A variety of biochemical tests can be used to differentiate *Nocardia* species from other actinomycetes. These tests include casein hydrolysis (+), tyrosine hydrolysis (+), urea hydrolysis (+), and inability to hydrolyze xanthine.

TREATMENT

As in actinomycosis, surgical debridement of damaged tissue should be performed whenever possible before chemotherapy is initiated. *N. asteroides* responds rapidly to treatment. Early diagnosis is important since recovery

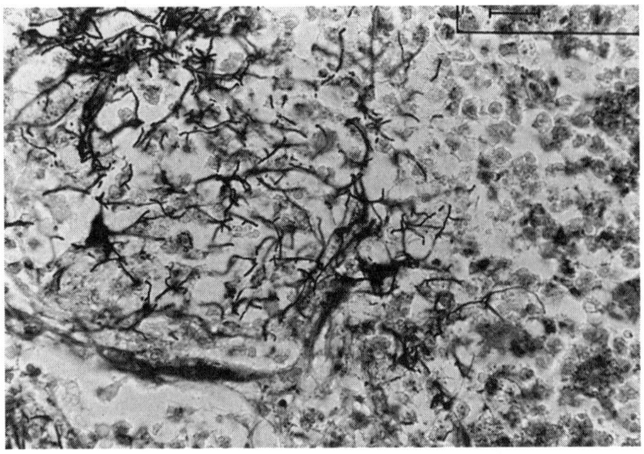

FIGURE 29-4
Nocardia organisms in lung tissue, showing branched filaments. (× 630, bar = 15.9 μm.) (Courtesy of M. M. McNeil, Centers for Disease Control, Atlanta, GA.)

rates after systemic infection are very low. Treatment is with cotrimazole or sulfadiazine. Several months of treatment may be required for respiratory infections.

Caries, Periodontal Disease, and Actinomycetes

A variety of nonbiological and biological factors are associated with diseases of the teeth (**caries,** or tooth decay) and tissues surrounding the teeth **(periodontal disease)**. Microorganisms form only one link in the chain of events that lead to tooth decay and periodontal disease. Actinomycetes represent but one group of bacteria that play a role in these diseases. That role is in the formation of **plaque.** Plaque is a structureless accumulation of bacteria, microbial polysaccharides, and host proteins that is attached to the enamel surrounding the tooth's surface. Plaque formation is invariably a prerequisite to caries and periodontal disease.

Two actinomycetes that appear to be important in plaque formation are *Actinomyces viscosus* and *A. naeslundii.* Both species produce pili and extracellular polysaccharides. Bacterial polysaccharides are sticky enough to enable various bacterial species to aggregate and to attach to the tooth's surface. Plaque represents a thin sticky environment that becomes a structured ecosystem where various bacterial species reside and thrive. When we eat foods high in sucrose, this sugar is metabolized by plaque bacteria such as actinomycetes and others (*Streptococcus mutans,* for example), and acids are produced. High levels of acid cause demineralization of tooth enamel. Thus, a cavity or tooth decay has taken place. If plaque is not removed, it thickens and the bacteria and the products they release cause inflammation of the gums **(gingivitis)**. This inflammatory condition leads to destruction of the bone supporting the teeth and **periodontitis** is the result.

Summary

Actinomycetes are bacteria having the characteristics of bacteria and fungi. They produce hyphae, a fungal characteristic, and the diseases they cause also resemble fungal diseases. The cell wall and other structural components of actinomycetes are bacterial in composition and function. Table 29-1 outlines the characteristics of the two major pathogenic actinomycetes: *Actinomyces* and *Nocardia.*

TABLE 29-1
Characteristics of *Actinomyces* and *Nocardia*

Characteristics	***Actinomyces***	***Nocardia***
Oxygen requirements	Facultative anaerobes	Aerobes
Environmental source of human pathogens	Oral cavity, intestinal tract, and pelvic region	Soil and water
Morphology	Do not produce aerial filaments	Do produce aerial filaments
Disease characteristics in humans	Chronic, suppurative, infections with sinus tracts that may cause dissemination	Same as *Actinomyces*
Site of disease in humans	Cervicofacial, thoracic, abdomen, and genital tract	Lung; subcutaneous tissue, especially of extremities
Mechanism of transmission of infectious agent	Opportunistic because of underlying condition (cervicofacial), aspiration (thoracic), trauma (abdominal), wearing intrauterine devices (genital)	Most infections from inhalation of organisms but some infections from trauma to skin, particularly in extremities
Treatment of infection	Surgical debridement followed by penicillin G therapy	Surgical debridement followed by cotrimazole or sulfonamide therapy

Questions for Study

1. Why is it necessary to differentiate *Nocardia* from *Actinomyces?*
2. *Streptococcus mutans* produces a polysaccharide that is associated with tooth decay. Describe a scenario in which this organism could play a part in that decay process.
3. What are sinus tracts? Do they have anything to do with nasal sinuses?
4. What are the characteristics that distinguish *Nocardia* from *Actinomyces?*

CHAPTER

30 Miscellaneous Pathogens

OBJECTIVES

To describe the method of transmission, sources of disease, site of infection, and treatment for legionnaires' disease

To list the type of infection associated with *Capnocytophaga, Actinobacillus, Calymmatobacterium, Streptobacillus, Chromobacterium, Eikenella, Gardnerella, Bacteroides,* and *Agrobacterium* species

To understand the microbiology of bacterial vaginosis

OUTLINE

LEGIONELLA
- General Characteristics
- Epidemiology
- Pathogenesis
- Laboratory Diagnosis
- Treatment

Legionella is a recently discovered (1976) respiratory pathogen that is becoming more frequently associated with disease. Each year since its discovery, new species have been identified. Approximately 85 percent of the cases of **legionellosis** are due to *L. pneumophila*, with about 50 percent of all disease due to *L. pneumophila* serogroup 1 and 10 percent to serogroup 6. The remainder (40%) of the cases are due to other serogroups of *L. pneumophila, L. micdadei,* and several other species. Some of the more frequently isolated species of *Legionella* are outlined in Table 30-1.

Several bacteria other than *Legionella* are infrequent causes of disease in humans. The classification of many of them is not complete. In *Bergey's Manual,* they are referred to as "other genera" in the various groups that are classified. The list of infrequent pathogens is not complete but represents those for which some clinical information is available. Most of our attention here is to the genus *Legionella,* while the remaining genera are outlined in Table 30-2.

TABLE 30-1
Some of the Isolated Species of *Legionella*

Species	Original source of isolation
L. pneumophila	Human respiratory tissue
L. bozemanii	Human respiratory tissue
L. dumoffii	Human respiratory tissue
L. micdadei	Enzootic in pigs
L. gormanii	Creek bank
L. jordanis	Water and sewage
L. longbeachae	Human respiratory tissue

TABLE 30-2
Characteristics of Miscellaneous Bacterial Species Pathogenic to Humans

Species	Characteristics of disease	Characteristics of organism	Treatment
Calymmatobacterium granulomatis	Granuloma inguinale, an infrequent sexually transmitted disease: lesions in pubic area that may lead to elephantiasis; occasionally found in southern United States	Pleomorphic facultative anaerobe, gram-negative, nonmotile rod that is heavily encapsulated	Streptomycin, tetracycline, or erythromycin
Streptobacillus moniliformis	One type of rat-bite fever acquired by bite of rat or ingestion of contaminated food: fever, rash, and polyarthritis are major symptoms	Pleomorphic, facultatively anaerobic gram-negative rod; normal inhabitant of rat throat and nasopharynx	Penicillin or streptomycin; penicillin induces L-forms
Actinobacillus actinomycetemcomitans	Periodontal disease; soft tissue abscess; systemic (endocarditis)	Nonmotile, gram-negative, facultatively anaerobic coccobacillus; part of human oral flora	Tetracyclines, fluoroquinolones, chloramphenicol
Capnocytophaga species	Juvenile periodontosis and bacteremia in immunosuppressed	Gram-negative gliding bacterium; normal inhabitant of human oral cavity; *C. ochracea* most important pathogen	Penicillin
Cardiobacterium hominis	Recovered in cases of endocarditis	Pleomorphic, gram-negative, nonmotile rod; normal inhabitant of respiratory and intestinal tract of humans	Penicillin, tetracyclines, aminoglycosides
Chromobacterium violaceum	Abscess formation and bacteremia; human infections often fatal; septicemia invariably fatal; most cases in Southeast Asia and southeastern United States; cause of recurrent infections in chronic granulomatous disease	Motile, gram-negative, slightly curved rod; found in soil and water; produces violet pigment in broth and on agar	Aminoglycosides, chloramphenicol, tetracyclines
Eikenella corrodens	Often in mixed infections involving mucous membranes of oral cavity, intestinal tract, and genitourinary tract; infections from trauma such as fist fights or human bites	Inhabitant of oral cavity and upper respiratory tract; gram-negative facultative anaerobic bacillus; pits agar surface	Ampicillin
Gardnerella vaginalis (see Under the Microscope 25)	One of a complex of organisms associated with nonspecific vaginitis (bacterial vaginosis)	Gram-negative facultatively anaerobic bacillus; increases in vagina with decrease in lactobacilli and increase in anaerobes; difficult to cultivate	Metronidazole, if condition does not resolve on its own
Agrobacterium species	Bacteremia in those with indwelling plastic catheters	Gram-negative rod; aerobic plant pathogen	Not defined because of multiple resistance
Bacteroides species	Periodontal disease; preterm delivery; deep tissue abscesses	Gram-negative anaerobic rod	Clindamycin, metronidazole, moxalactam

UNDER THE MICROSCOPE 25

Bacterial Vaginosis

Microbial infections of the vagina are rather common and involve bacterial as well as fungal and protozoal agents. In some instances the infectious agent may be transmitted to the sex partner or the fetus. The fungal agent associated with vaginitis is *Candida albicans* (see Chapter 33), while the protozoal agent is *Trichomonas vaginalis* (see Chapter 34). **Bacterial vaginosis** is a syndrome defined microbiologically by decreased numbers of *Lactobacillus* species and increased numbers of *Gardnerella vaginalis, Mycoplasma hominis,* and *Bacteroides, Prevotella, Mobiluncus,* and *Peptostreptococcus* species. Bacterial vaginosis may be a risk factor for chorioamnionitis, postcesarean endometritis, and prematurity.

The virulence factors associated with bacterial vaginosis are poorly understood. In recent studies **sialidases** (neuraminidases) were linked to virulence. Sialidases are enzymes that cleave alpha-ketosidic linkages between the sugar residues of glycoproteins (only one example) and sialic acid (a sugar). Sialidase is believed to interact with tissues in such a way as to enhance the ability of vaginal anaerobes to adhere and invade them. Two genera that produce sialidases are *Prevotella* and *Bacteroides.* Vaginal colonization by *Prevotella* and *Bacteroides* organisms has been linked to risk of preterm delivery.

The diagnosis of bacterial vaginosis is made when three of the following criteria have been established:

1. Homogeneous vaginal discharge
2. pH of vaginal discharge less than 4.7
3. Release of an amine-like odor when the vaginal discharge is mixed with potassium hydroxide
4. **Clue** cells representing more than 20 percent of the vaginal epithelial cells

Clue cells are vaginal epithelial cells covered by adherent gram-negative rods present in vaginal smears of women with bacterial vaginosis but not in clinically normal women. *G. vaginalis* occurs in higher counts on clue cells than do other bacterial species. The finding of clue cells is vital to the diagnosis of bacterial vaginosis.

The treatment options for bacterial vaginosis are (1) no treatment, since many cases resolve on their own; (2) local treatment with chlorhexidine; and (3) oral therapy with metronidazole or the use of medicated sponges containing metronidazole.

Legionella

More than 200 persons were stricken with a respiratory disease of unknown origin at the American Legion Convention in Philadelphia in 1976 and 34 died. The causal agent of the disease at first resisted isolation. Researchers at the Centers for Disease Control in Atlanta identified the previously unknown bacterium and called it the **legionnaires' disease bacterium.** The organism is now classified as *L. pneumophila.*

GENERAL CHARACTERISTICS

L. pneumophila is a gram-negative aerobic bacillus that is 0.3 to 0.4 μm in diameter and 2.0 to 3.0 μm in length (Fig. 30-1). The organism is a facultative intracellular parasite that lives within the lungs of infected individuals. Legionellae do not grow on the usual bacteriological media. Buffered charcoal yeast extract (BYCE) agar is the preferred medium.

EPIDEMIOLOGY

Legionella organisms are found in fresh water. They have been isolated from rivers, lakes, wet soil, and other environments. They can tolerate temperatures to 55 C and can grow at 35 to 45 C. Consequently, they can flourish in the water systems of buildings. *Legionella* attach to elements of the water system such as pipes, rubber, plastics, and sediments. In addition, they can be engulfed by ameba contained in water systems and multiply within them. This permits the bacteria to remain protected from alterations in their environment, for example, during chlorination procedures.

Outbreaks of disease have been associated with contaminated cooling towers, heat-exchange apparatus, shower water, tap water, and potable water following chlorination. The most important mechanism of transfer is by aerosols. Human-to-human transmission has never been documented.

The incidence of *Legionella* pneumonia in the United States is believed to be somewhere between 25,000 and 30,000 cases per year (only 1280 cases were reported to

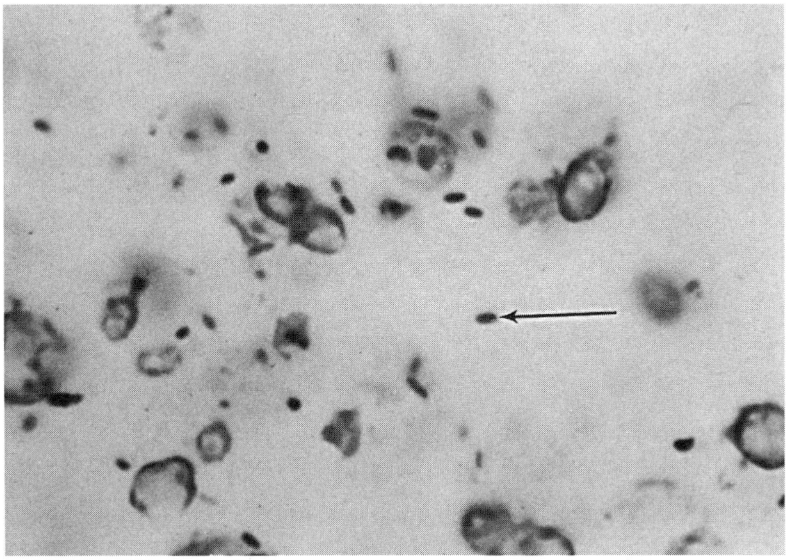

FIGURE 30-1
Photomicrograph of *Legionella pneumophila*. Bacterial cells are observed as plump rods (*arrow*). (Courtesy of Centers for Disease Control, Atlanta, GA.)

the Centers for Disease Control in 1993). *L. pneumophila* may be acquired in the community or in the hospital. About 70 percent of affected patients have some predisposing condition or illness, are older, or are heavy smokers. Outbreaks of disease are more common during the summer due to increased contact with contaminated aerosols from evaporative air-conditioning systems as well as recreational water.

PATHOGENESIS

Legionellae are intracellular parasites that replicate preferentially in the cytoplasm of alveolar macrophages. The bacteria replicate in the phagosome and are able to prevent phagosome-lysosome fusion. Activation of neutrophils and monocytes is impaired and phagocytosis of the bacteria is handicapped.

The development of disease is a multifactorial process. The dose of organisms, presence of virulence factors, and health status of the host play an important role in disease. Replication of legionellae in amebae, for example, could be an important way to present large numbers of bacteria to the susceptible host.

Two virulence factors of legionellae that inhibit phagocyte activation have been described. First, *L. micdadei* possesses a **phosphatase** that blocks superoxide anion production by stimulated neutrophils. The second factor is the *Legionella* **cytotoxin,** which blocks neutrophil oxidative metabolism. Several other *Legionella* proteins have been identified as potential virulence factors but conclusive proof is missing.

Pneumonia caused by *Legionella* is virtually indistinguishable from that caused by other gram-negative bacteria. The incubation period is 2 to 10 days. The first symptoms are fever, headache, and weakness. Diarrhea may appear before or after respiratory symptoms. The fever is unremitting, and about one-third of patients demonstrate lethargy, confusion, disorientation, and other central nervous system symptoms. The major pathological findings are confined to the respiratory tissue. Severe bronchopneumonia with inflammation in the alveoli and respiratory bronchioles is common. Extrapulmonary complications of disease are rare.

L. pneumophila is also the etiological agent of a nonpneumonic influenza-like illness known as **Pontiac fever.** Pontiac fever has a one- or two-day incubation period. It attacks healthy individuals and has a zero fatality rate. Pleuritic pain is associated with infection but the disease is self-limiting.

LABORATORY DIAGNOSIS

Culture from sputum or lung specimens is the most definitive means of diagnosis; however, recovery of the organisms is difficult and time-consuming. Organisms recovered on BYCE agar have a distinctive cut-glass appearance (Fig. 30-2).

Direct fluorescent antibody (DFA) testing can demonstrate organisms in tissue but it is only moderately sensitive when sputum and pulmonary secretions are used. Serological diagnosis by use of indirect fluorescent antibody (IFA) tests requires a fourfold rise in titer (128). In only 75 percent of patients with clinical disease does a fourfold or higher rise in titer develop early in the disease process. Therefore, serological tests are of little value to the clinicians during the early stages of disease. Detection of soluble *L. pneumophila* antigens in urine by a variety of techniques is now being investigated. A commercial radioimmunoassay kit is available to detect antigen in urine and has a more than 86 percent sensitivity for samples obtained during the first week of illness.

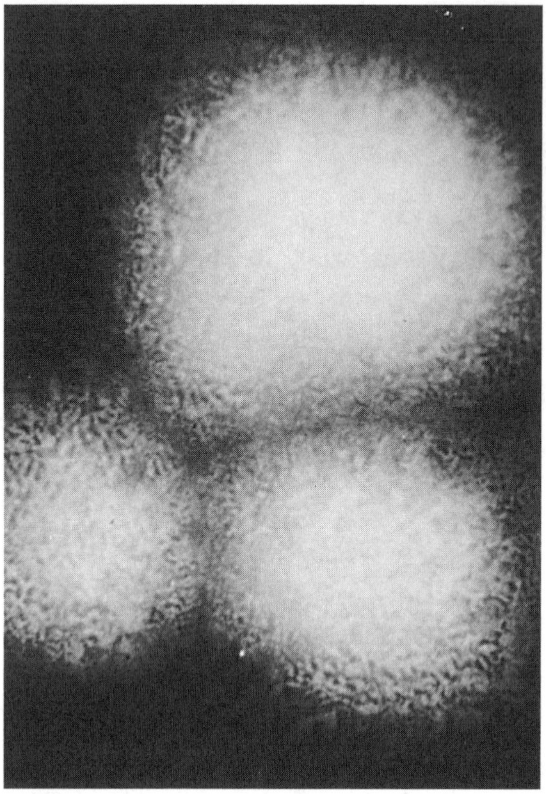

FIGURE 30-2
Colonies of *L. pneumophila* on buffered charcoal yeast extract agar. Colonies resemble cut glass. (From W. C. Winn, Jr., *Clin. Microbiol. Rev.* 1:60, 1988.)

TREATMENT

Eradication of *Legionella* organisms from environmental sources is often difficult. A biocide such as chlorine can be used on cooling towers and evaporative condensers. When potable water sources are implicated, treatment usually involves using super-heated water. The use of chlorine for potable water sources may damage the plumbing.

Erythromycin administered orally is the drug of choice for the treatment of *Legionella* pneumonia. In immunosuppressed patients without therapy the disease is invariably fatal.

Summary

1. *Legionella* is a recently discovered respiratory pathogen. It is a gram-negative aerobic bacillus that is easily recovered from aqueous environments.
2. The most important mechanism of transmission of *Legionella* is via aerosols. The compromised patient is most susceptible to infection. Infections resemble bronchopneumonia and can be fatal if not treated. The organism also causes a self-limiting respiratory infection called Pontiac fever.
3. *Legionella* is an intracellular parasite that can survive in alveolar macrophages by preventing phagosome-lysosome fusion. A phosphatase and a cytotoxin are two virulence factors that prevent activation of phagocytes.
4. Culture is the most definitive method for laboratory diagnosis of *Legionella;* however, other techniques such as direct and indirect fluorescent antibody assays are more frequently used. Serological techniques are not effective in early stages of disease.
5. Erythromycin is the drug of choice for treating *Legionella* pneumonia. Outbreaks of disease can be prevented by proper maintenance of cooling apparatuses and potable water sources.
6. Bacterial vaginosis is a condition resulting from the replacement of lactobacilli by a variety of anaerobes in the vagina. The replacement anaerobes may be associated with preterm delivery and other conditions.
7. Several miscellaneous pathogens that cause disease in humans are outlined in Table 30-2.

Questions for Study

1. What is the mechanism used by *Legionella* to prevent activation of neutrophils and monocytes (utilize the Additional Readings)?
2. How do *Legionella* organisms prevent phagocytosis? How does their mechanism differ from *Coxiella? Rickettsia rickettsii? Mycobacterium tuberculosis?*
3. What is bacterial vaginosis? What microorganisms are involved?
4. If lactobacilli are absent in bacterial vaginosis, what then is the role of lactobacilli in the vaginal flora of healthy individuals?
5. Make a list of the bacterial agents that are associated with sexually transmitted disease. What are the infections or conditions with which the microorganisms are associated? Virulence factors?

PART

VI Virology

CHAPTER

31 Viruses

OBJECTIVES

- To outline the steps and mechanisms involved in the infection of a host cell by animal viruses
- To list the cytopathic effects on host cells following viral infection
- To explain the mechanisms by which viruses transform mammalian cells
- To outline the effects of viral transformation on mammalian cells
- To explain how DNA and RNA viruses are thought to cause cancer in humans
- To outline the techniques used in the cultivation and identification of animal viruses
- To list the principal viral chemotherapeutic agents and the diseases for which they are prescribed
- To describe the component parts of the T series of bacterial viruses and their function in the infection process
- To compare and contrast the infection process by temperate and lytic bacterial viruses
- To describe how temperate bacterial viruses can influence the infectious disease process in humans

OUTLINE

- ANIMAL VIRUSES
  - Structure and Composition
    - Morphology
    - Nucleic Acids
    - Lipids
    - Proteins
  - Epidemiology and Physiology of Animal Virus Infection
    - Adsorption
    - Penetration and Uncoating
    - Genome Expression
      - Expression of DNA Genomes
      - Expression of RNA Genomes
    - Maturation and Assembly
    - Release
  - Effect of Viral Infection on the Host Cell
    - Direct and Indirect Damage
    - Inclusion Body Formation
    - Cell Fusion (Syncytia Formation)
    - Changes in Surface Antigens
    - Interferon Production
    - Persistent Viral Infection
  - Viruses and Cancer
    - Properties of Transformed Cells
    - Oncogenic DNA Viruses
      - Hepatitis B Virus and Hepatitis C Virus
      - Herpesviruses
      - Human Papillomaviruses
    - Oncogenic RNA Viruses
      - General Characteristics
      - Oncogenes and Transformation
  - Diagnostic Virology
    - Cultivation of Virus from Clinical Material
      - Effects of Virus on Cultured Cells
    - Serological Methods
    - Rapid Methods in Diagnostic Virology
      - Electron Microscopy
      - Immunological and Other Methods of Identification
  - Viral Classification
  - Treatment and Control of Viral Infections
    - Chemotherapeutic Agents
    - Vaccines

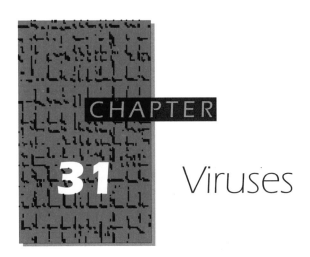

OUTLINE (*continued*)

BACTERIAL VIRUSES
General Characteristics and Replication
Lytic Cycle of Phage
Lysogeny

Until the latter half of the nineteenth century, it was believed that certain submicroscopic infectious agents of mammalian hosts were merely small forms of bacteria. Scientists in these earlier times rationalized that their inability to cultivate these small bacteria only implied they were fastidious in their nutritional requirements. After the turn of the century scientists proposed that these submicroscopic forms of life be called **viruses.** In 1915 even bacteria were discovered to be capable of being infected by viruses. The bacterial invaders were called **bacteriophages** or simply **phages.**

Not until the discovery of the electron microscope and other technological advances were scientists able to discard fact from fiction regarding viruses. A virus is now defined as **a subcellular agent consisting of a core of nucleic acid surrounded by a protein coat that must use the metabolic machinery of a living host to replicate and produce more viral particles.**

We begin with a discussion of animal viruses and then conclude with one on bacterial viruses.

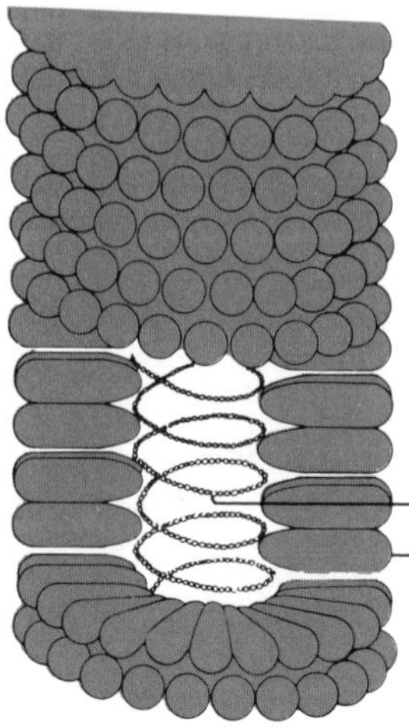

FIGURE 31-1
Tobacco mosaic virus, a helical virus that infects plants.

Animal Viruses

STRUCTURE AND COMPOSITION

Morphology

Animal virus morphology can be divided into two important types based on how the nucleic acid is packaged. Some viruses are **rod-like** or **helical** while others are **spherical** or **isometric.** The nucleic acid of nearly all viruses is surrounded by a **coat** (also called **capsid**) of protein molecules. The individual protein molecules in the capsid are referred to as **capsomeres.** The capsid and the nucleic acid form what is called the **nucleocapsid.**

In helical viruses the capsomeres bind in a periodic way along the nucleic acid molecule. This arrangement usually gives the virus the appearance of a rod containing flexible coils (similar to a mattress spring covered with a cloth). The tobacco mosaic virus (TMV) is a helical plant virus that is similar to many animal viruses (Fig. 31-1). The nucleocapsid of helical viruses is frequently surrounded by other structures that protect the virus (see Lipids).

In spherical viruses the nucleic acid is independent of the organization of protein molecules surrounding it. The capsid surrounding the spherical virus has **icosahedral symmetry.** Most animal viruses, such as the adenoviruses, exhibit icosahedral symmetry (Fig. 31-2). The capsomeres are readily visible on electron micrographs of spherical viruses.

The poxviruses display a combination of both helical and spherical symmetry. This type of symmetry is **complex** and is more characteristic of bacterial viruses.

Animal viruses range in size from 25 to 30 nm for smaller viruses, such as the poliovirus, to 225 to 300 nm for the larger poxviruses.

Nucleic Acids

The nucleic acid of the animal virus is either DNA or RNA and may be single- or double-stranded. Except for the papovavirus, viral nucleic acids are linear molecules. The molecular weight of animal virus nucleic acids ranges from 1.5 to 3 $\times$ 10^6 for picornaviruses to 1 to 2 $\times$ 10^8 for the largest viruses, the poxviruses.

Some viruses have segmented genomes. The **reoviruses** and **rotaviruses** consist of 10 and 11 segments, respectively. The genomes of the influenza viruses, bunyaviruses, and arenaviruses are also segmented. One of the consequences of this segmentation is that genetic recombination can occur more efficiently than in unsegmented genomes. Thus, strains of these viruses may demonstrate considerable antigenic variability. The virus causing acquired immunodeficiency syndrome (AIDS) is a rotavirus and also demonstrates this genetic variability (see Chapter 32).

Lipids

Many nucleocapsids are surrounded by an **envelope** of lipid that mimics the composition of the cytoplasmic membrane of the infected host (Fig. 31-3). The lipid enve-

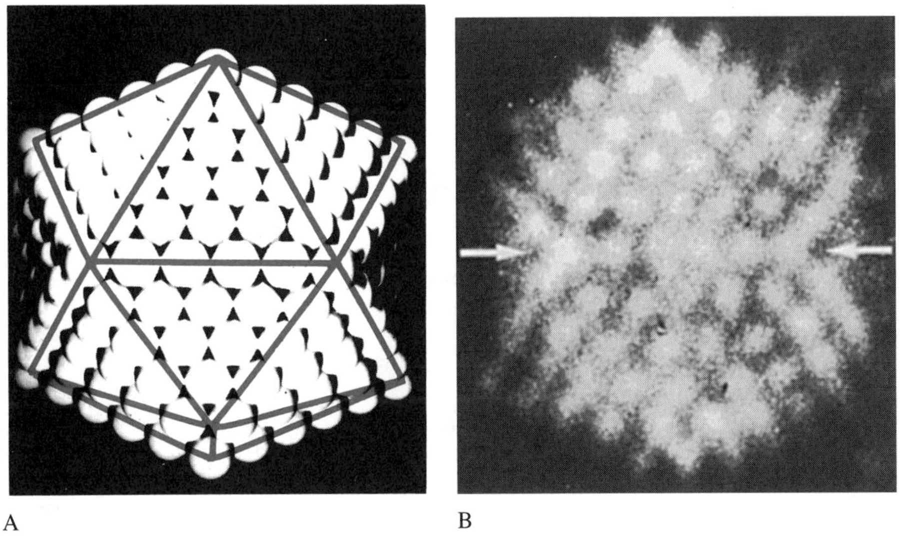

FIGURE 31-2
Icosahedral symmetry. A. Model of a capsid exhibiting icosahedral symmetry. The colored lines outline the various facets or sides of the icosahedron. B. A negatively stained adenovirus particle showing the arrangement of capsomeres. (From R. W. Horne and P. Wildy, *Br. Med. Bull.* 18:199, 1962.)

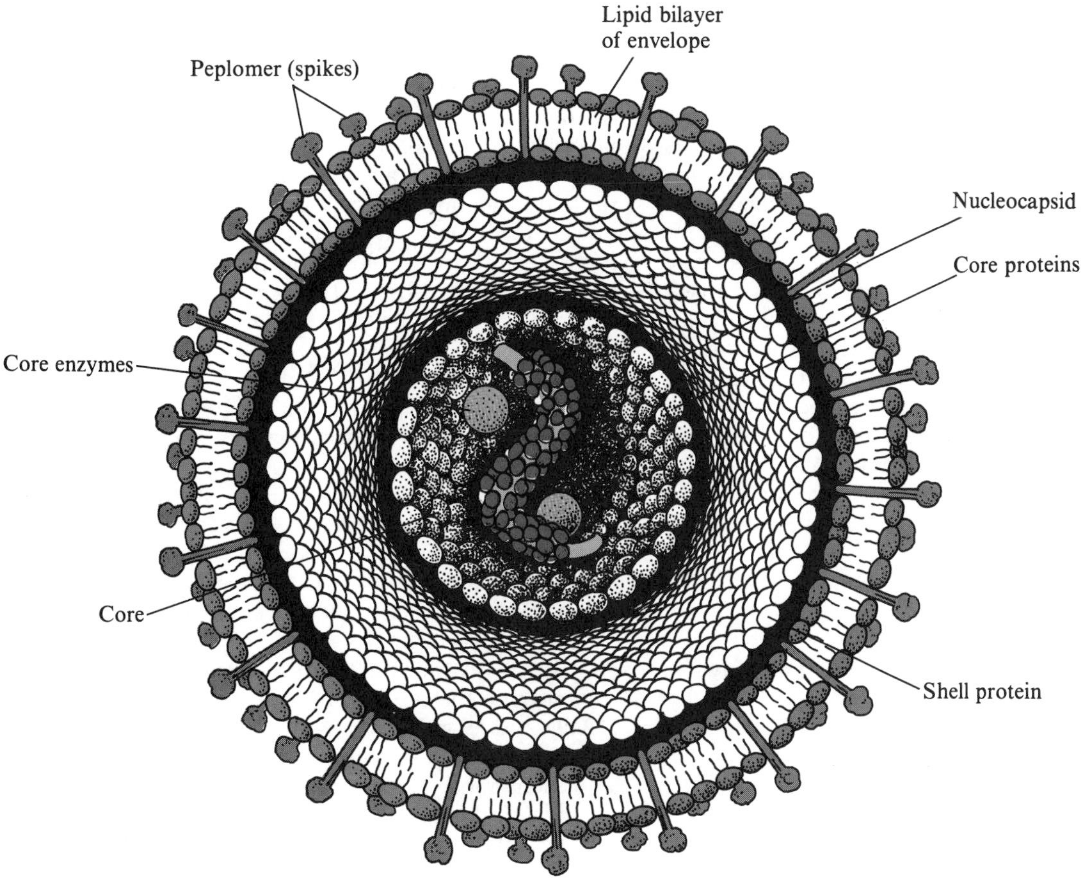

FIGURE 31-3
Idealized structure of an enveloped helical virus as seen in cross section. The nucleocapsid, which is helical, is itself encased in a core of structural proteins. The core may also contain enzymes that are used by the virus to replicate in the infected mammalian cell. The core may in turn be surrounded by an outer shell of structural proteins. Adjacent to the shell is an envelope, or lipid layer, within which are embedded glycoprotein spikes called peplomers.

lope is a bilayered structure that acts as a protective device for the nucleocapsid. If the envelope is removed, the virus loses its infectivity. Various proteins may be associated with the lipid envelope and these are discussed in the next section. The enveloped viruses are outlined in Figures 31-17 and 31-18 at the end of the animal virus section.

Proteins

In addition to the structural proteins that make up the capsid, there are other proteins that have enzymatic as well as structural functions. Some enveloped viruses have nucleocapsids that are tightly enclosed within an assembly of proteins called a **viral core** (see Fig. 31-3). The nucleocapsid or core in enveloped viruses is in turn surrounded by a layer of protein called a **protein shell** (see Fig. 31-3). The proteins surrounding the core or nucleocapsid are protective structural proteins.

Complex proteins, such as glycoproteins, are found on the surface of viral envelopes and are in the form of projections called **spikes** (also called **peplomers**). Glycoprotein spikes are important as antigenic determinants, and some are involved in the binding of virus to host tissue (see Fig. 31-3). One type of glycoprotein spike found on viruses is called **hemagglutinin.** Hemagglutinin is able to agglutinate red blood cells and is found on influenza viruses.

Enzymatic proteins are also found in or on viruses. Some viruses, such as the poxviruses, contain a DNA-dependent RNA polymerase. RNA tumor viruses contain an RNA-dependent DNA polymerase. These enzymes and others are found in the core of the virus. They become active once the virus has invaded the cell and the capsid has been partially degraded. The surface spike of the influenza virus exhibits neuraminidase activity. This spike is used by the virus to dissolve neuraminic acid, a component of the cytoplasmic membrane of mammalian cells. Neuraminidase enables the virus to spread in host tissue.

A completely assembled and infective virus is called a **virion.** Defective or incompletely assembled viruses are usually noninfective; for example, enveloped viruses without their envelope are noninfective. A virus whose infective status is not known is referred to as a **viral particle.**

EPIDEMIOLOGY AND PHYSIOLOGY OF ANIMAL VIRUS INFECTION

Viruses enter the mammalian host primarily via the respiratory tract, gastrointestinal tract, direct inoculation by arthropods into the bloodstream, or breaks in the skin (viral diseases affecting specific tissues and organs are listed in Appendix C). Viral transmission from one individual to another is called **horizontal transmission.** Viruses can also be transferred from parent to offspring, for example, from the blood of an infected mother through the placenta to the fetus. This type of transfer is called **vertical transmission.**

Viruses have specific target cells (tissue tropisms) in which they replicate. Not all viruses are created equal in this type of response. Viruses have an affinity for certain cells based on the chemical composition of the viral surface and the cytoplasmic membrane with which it interacts. Viruses such as the poliovirus and measles virus infect only human tissue and are thus very selective. The rabies virus is relatively nonspecific because it can infect several animal species as well as humans. Occasionally mutation in the viral genome can expand the number of tissues the virus can infect. For example, outbreaks of human influenza have been associated with individuals working with influenza-infected swine. The swine-associated virus apparently underwent a mutation that altered a surface protein. The altered surface protein enabled the virus to infect human cells in addition to its natural host, swine.

Once virus has made contact with a host cell and invaded it, an infectious process develops. The infectious process can be broken down into five stages: **adsorption, penetration and uncoating, genome expression, maturation and assembly,** and **release.**

Adsorption

Dispersed over the surface of the target cell are many **receptors** to which virus can adsorb. The receptors, which are major determinants in susceptibility to infection, number from 10^4 to 10^5 per cell. Most receptors are glycoproteins whose composition varies from one cell type to another. The influenza virus, for example, uses its neuraminidase-containing glycoprotein spikes to adhere to the neuraminic acid–containing glycoprotein receptors on host cell membrane. Sometimes the binding process alters the virus. Binding can cause a rearrangement of capsid proteins and this in turn can affect the release of viral nucleic acid. Once virus has adsorbed to the cell membrane, its infectivity is lost. This period of loss of infectivity is called the **eclipse.** The eclipse is due to partial or total uncoating of the virus (see below).

Penetration and Uncoating

There are three major mechanisms of viral entry into a host cell and a single virus may use more than one of them:

1. **Endocytosis.** Virus binds to specific receptors on the cell membrane surface. Virus-receptor complexes are concentrated in pits, which invaginate to form vesicles (Fig. 31-4A). As these vesicles move deeper into the cytoplasm, they fuse with lysosomes to produce a **lysosomal vesicle.** Lysosomal enzymes digest away the viral layers and release the nucleocapsid into the cytoplasm.
2. **Fusion.** Some enveloped viruses gain access to the cytoplasm of the cell by fusing with the cytoplasmic membrane. Fusion produces an opening through which the nucleocapsid may pass directly into the cytoplasm (Fig. 31-4B).
3. **Direct penetration.** Some nonenveloped viruses may be so small that they are able to pass directly through the cytoplasmic membrane and enter the cytoplasm (Fig. 31-4C). It is possible that the attachment process disrupts the capsid so uncoating takes place.

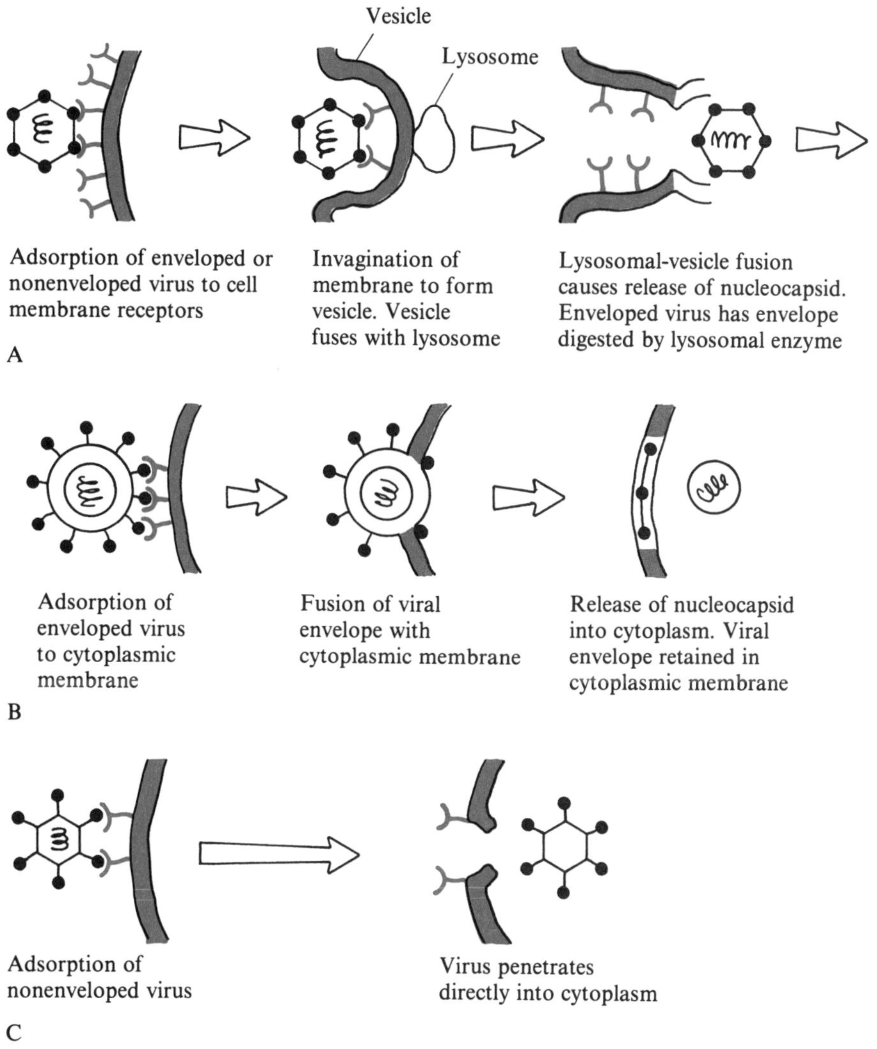
Vesicle
Lysosome
Adsorption of enveloped or nonenveloped virus to cell membrane receptors
Invagination of membrane to form vesicle. Vesicle fuses with lysosome
Lysosomal-vesicle fusion causes release of nucleocapsid. Enveloped virus has envelope digested by lysosomal enzyme
A
Adsorption of enveloped virus to cytoplasmic membrane
Fusion of viral envelope with cytoplasmic membrane
Release of nucleocapsid into cytoplasm. Viral envelope retained in cytoplasmic membrane
B
Adsorption of nonenveloped virus
Virus penetrates directly into cytoplasm
C

FIGURE 31-4
Mechanism of viral penetration of a cell and uncoating of a virus. A. Endocytosis. B. Fusion with the cytoplasmic membrane. C. Direct penetration.

Depending on the site of viral multiplication, viral nucleocapsids may be uncoated in the cytoplasm or enter the nucleus to be uncoated. For most viruses uncoating occurs in the cytoplasm. Once uncoating occurs, the viral nucleic acid is released and primed for expression.

Genome Expression

Viral genomes are diverse; that is, they may be single-stranded or double-stranded. They may contain DNA or RNA, and they may be segmented or nonsegmented. With all of this diversity, describing the mechanisms for transcribing them can be confusing. The pattern of animal virus expression can be divided into six classes (Fig. 31-5). For each class, keep in mind that two functions must be fulfilled. First, a strand of the genome will be utilized in the formation of messenger RNA (mRNA) (expressed as plus [+] polarity). Some of the proteins translated from the mRNA will be used as enzymes in the replication of viral nucleic acid. Other proteins will be used structurally in the assembly of new virus. The second function is to replicate viral nucleic acid so each viral particle assembled in the infected cell will possess a genome.

Expression of DNA Genomes. Except for the poxviruses, replication of DNA viruses occurs in the nucleus. Most DNA viruses contain a double-stranded molecule **(class I)** consisting of a minus and a plus strand. The minus strand is transcribed into mRNA by the enzyme RNA polymerase. Both DNA strands are replicated to produce plus (+) and minus (−) strands that form double-stranded DNA. The double-stranded molecules serve as genomes for new viral particles (see Fig. 31-5).

Single-stranded DNA viruses (family Parvoviridae) belong to **class II.** The viral genome is first converted to a double-stranded **replicative form.** The replicative form can be transcribed into mRNA and can be used as a replica

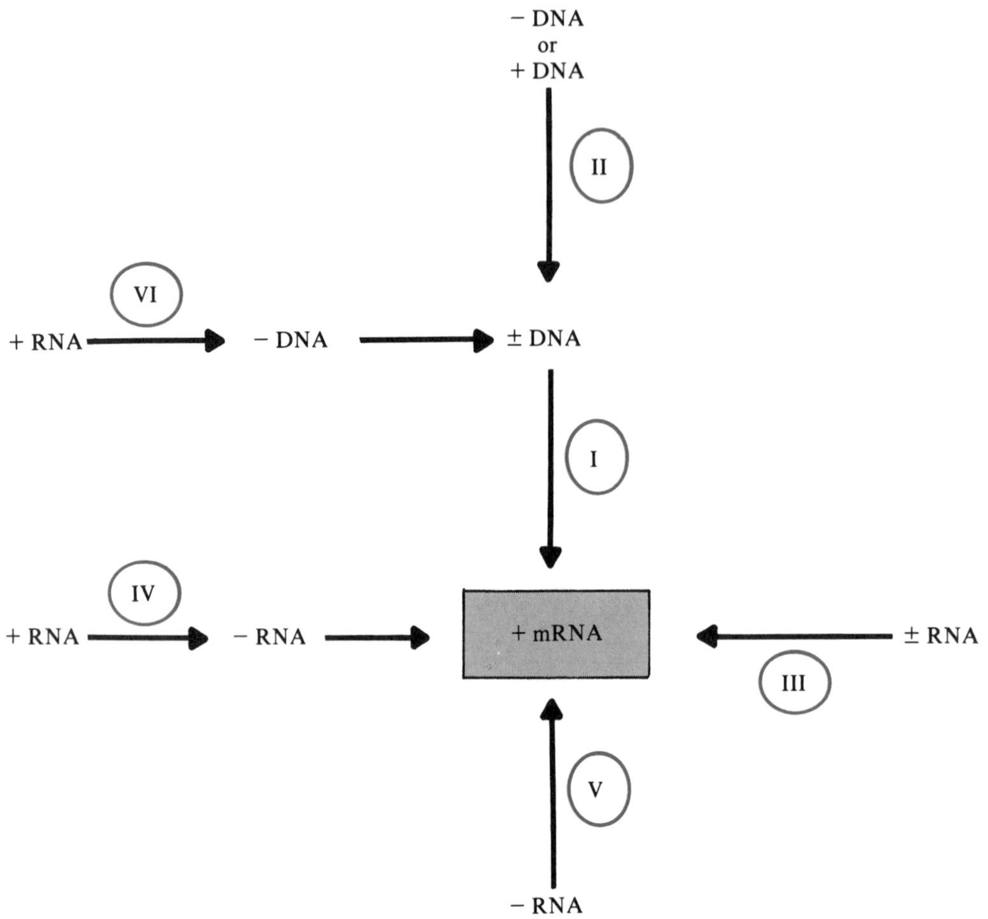

FIGURE 31-5
Virus classes depicting the expression of various virus genomes. Regardless of the polarity of the viral genome, a process is utilized to produce mRNA that has plus (+) polarity. The template for (+) mRNA synthesis in each case is a minus (−) strand of nucleic acid. (From D. Baltimore, *Bacteriol. Rev.* 35:235, 1971.)

for single-stranded DNA. Single-stranded DNAs serve as genomes for new virus particles.

Expression of RNA Genomes. Double-stranded (±) RNA viruses (**class III**) include the reovirus and rotavirus, both of which possess segmented genomes. Each of the double-stranded segments is transcribed into single-stranded mRNA. The mRNA are translated into protein. Each of the double-stranded segments is also replicated to produce progeny RNA (Fig. 31-6A).

Plus (+)-stranded RNA viruses **(class IV)** include the families Picornaviridae and Togaviridae. Since the viral genome has the same polarity as mRNA, the naked RNA can by itself initiate infection in the host. The viral genome is translated into proteins, some of which aid in the transcription of the genome into a **minus-strand replicative complex.** Plus RNA strands can be produced from this complex (Fig. 31-6B) and they become the genomes of new virus particles.

Minus (−)-stranded RNA viruses **(class V)** include Orthomyxoviridae, Paramyxoviridae, and Rhabdoviridae. The viral genome is used as a template for transcription into mRNA (Fig. 31-6C). The mRNA not only is translated into proteins but also is used to produce minus-strand replicas. The minus-strand replicas will become the genomes of new viral particles.

Some RNA viruses have a DNA intermediate **(class VI)**, a characteristic of the family Retroviridae or those viruses that cause tumors (Fig. 31-6D). Retroviruses possess an RNA genome containing two identical plus strands. A minus strand of DNA is produced with the assistance of an unusual enzyme called **reverse transcriptase** (a RNA-dependent DNA polymerase). In other words, the reaction (RNA → DNA) is the reverse to the usual flow of information in the cell (DNA → RNA). The minus DNA strand binds to a plus RNA strand to produce an RNA-DNA hybrid. The RNA in the hybrid is later degraded and the DNA acts as a template for formation of double-stranded DNA. The DNA can be transcribed into mRNA and is also replicated to form plus RNA strands. The plus RNA strands will provide the genetic material for a new generation of virus (see sections on oncogenic viruses for a more detailed discussion of these viruses).

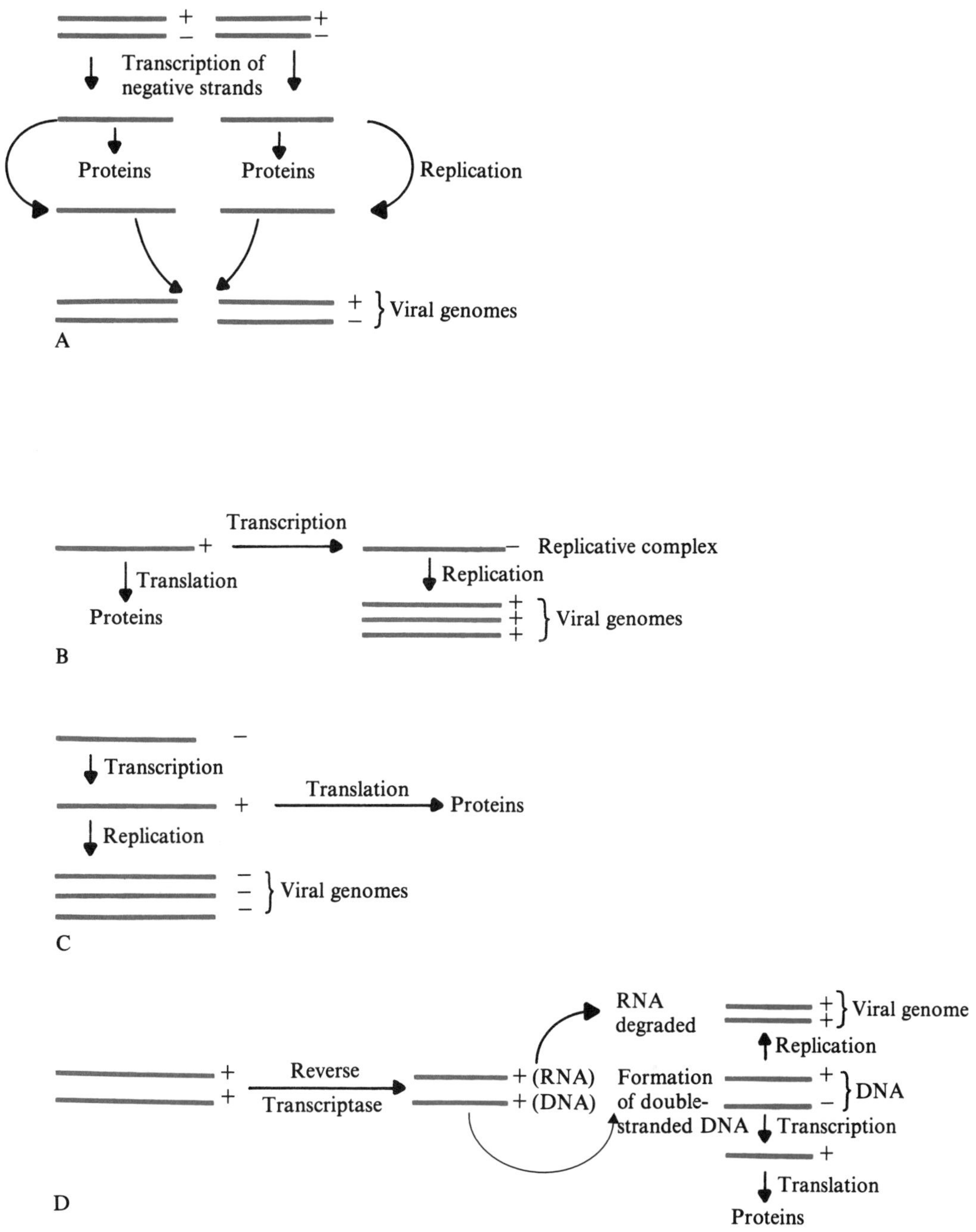

FIGURE 31-6
Replication mechanism for RNA viruses. A. Double-stranded RNA (±) virus. B. Plus (+)-stranded RNA virus. C. Minus (−)-stranded RNA virus. D. Identical plus-stranded RNA virus.

Maturation and Assembly

The maturation of viruses can be viewed as a growth cycle (even though viruses do not grow like other infectious agents) during which viral nucleic acids and proteins are produced. As stated previously, after adsorption there is a period, called **eclipse,** during which no new viral particles can be detected (Fig. 31-7). During this period of growth, **early proteins** are synthesized. Some early proteins are used to inhibit host functions. Many early proteins such as DNA and RNA polymerase are used to produce viral genomes. The synthesis of viral nucleic acids may occur in the cytoplasm or nucleus depending on the final site of viral assembly. Most **late proteins** are used in the assembly or construction of the viral capsid and other structural components.

As the concentration of structural proteins increases, capsid assembly begins and there is formation of nucleo-

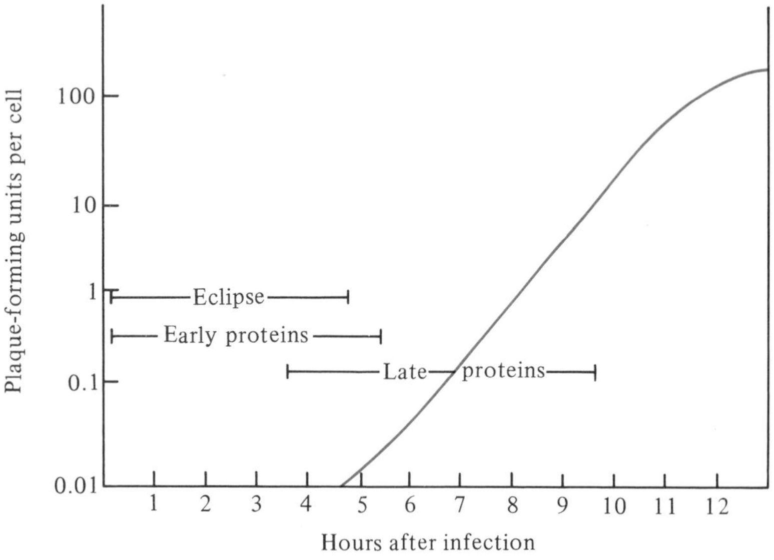

FIGURE 31-7
Growth cycle of animal virus. Mature particles do not make their appearance until nearly 5 hours after infection. The maximum number of virus particles appears about 12 hours after infection. The time periods vary from one virus to another.

capsids. Nucleocapsids of most DNA viruses are assembled in the nucleus while most RNA-containing nucleocapsids are assembled in the cytoplasm. All proteins are synthesized on ribosomes in the cytoplasm. Consequently proteins must pass through the nuclear pores when nucleocapsids are assembled in the nucleus.

The assembly of viruses is an autocatalytic process based primarily on the interaction of capsid polypeptides. During assembly of virus, large quasicrystalline arrays are produced and are microscopically observable in the nucleus or cytoplasm (Fig. 31-8).

Release

Some nonenveloped viruses are released from the cell only after the cell has disintegrated. The release of enveloped virus is more complex because of the addition of the envelope. The lipid bilayer of the viral envelope can be acquired from the host's membrane system. If the virus is assembled in the nucleus, the nuclear membrane is used. If the virus is assembled in the cytoplasm, the cytoplasmic membrane is used.

The viral envelope also contains glycoprotein spikes

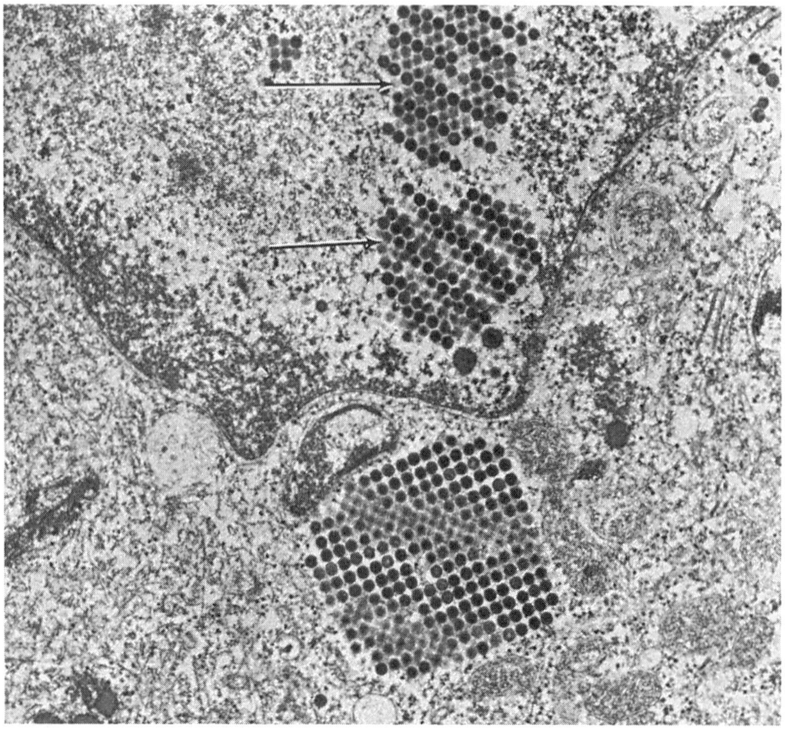

FIGURE 31-8
Electron micrograph of quasicrystalline accumulation of adenovirus. Two accumulations of virus appear in the nucleus (*arrows*) and one is free in the cytoplasm. (× 30,000.) (From R. Wigand, H. Gilderbloo, and H. Brandis, *Arch. Virol.* 64:225, 1980.)

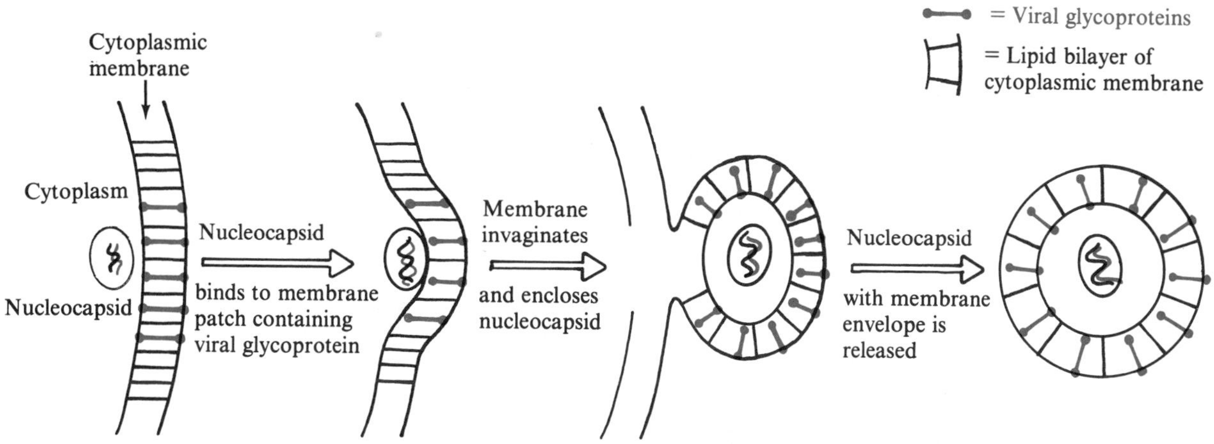
= Viral glycoproteins
= Lipid bilayer of cytoplasmic membrane
Cytoplasmic membrane
Cytoplasm
Nucleocapsid
Nucleocapsid
binds to membrane patch containing viral glycoprotein
Membrane invaginates
and encloses nucleocapsid
Nucleocapsid
with membrane envelope is released

A

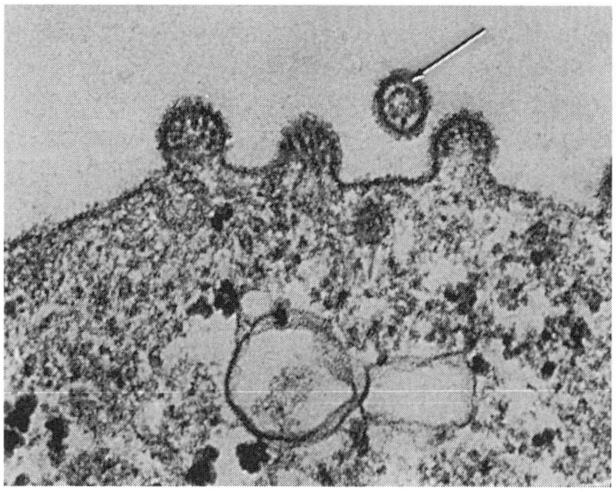

B

FIGURE 31-9
Budding process for enveloped viruses. A. Diagrammatic illustration. B. Electron micrograph showing a budded virus (*arrow*) and three viruses in various stages of budding. (× 86,000.) (From E. Norby, H. Marusky, and L. Orvell, *J. Virol.* 6:237, 1979.)

whose information for synthesis is encoded by the virus. The glycoprotein spikes are synthesized in the cytoplasm and then transported to and inserted into the cell membrane. The envelope is acquired by the virus when the nucleocapsid makes contact with that portion of the cell membrane containing the spikes. Once contact is made, the cell membrane protrudes and literally encloses the nucleocapsid. The enveloped nucleocapsid then pinches off or **buds** from the cell membrane (Fig. 31-9). The cell membrane beneath the bud reforms and the continuity of the cell membrane is retained and a virus is released.

EFFECTS OF VIRAL INFECTION ON THE HOST CELL

It seems logical that if a virus is to survive, it must engage in an association with one or more of its hosts in such a way that the host is not killed. Viruses replicate only in living cells! Some viruses appear to replicate in cells without causing any obvious damage. Other viruses bring about a variety of changes, some of which can be lethal. These alterations or changes are referred to as **cytopathic effects.** Let us examine some of the ways in which viral infection affects host cells.

Direct and Indirect Damage

Some viruses are able to shut down host macromolecule synthesis and thus directly damage host cells. The damaged cells lyse, which is a cytopathic effect that can be detected in the laboratory. Lysis of cultured cells produces observable lesions (see section of cultivation of viruses). Cell lysis may result in temporary or permanent loss of function. For example, during poliovirus infection, lysis of motor neurons can cause loss of function of the corresponding muscles. Yet no viral toxin has been discovered for any viruses. The accumulation of capsid proteins in the cell, however, may be enough to produce cytopathic effects.

Some virus infections indirectly affect the function of tissues or organs in the host. This effect is illustrated during influenza virus infection. The influenza virus damages the respiratory epithelium and ciliary activity is severely affected. This results in the accumulation of bacteria that normally would be eliminated by ciliary action.

Bacteria, such as staphylococci, streptococci, and hemophili, adhere to respiratory tissue, multiply, and cause disease. Thus, death from influenza is often due to pneumonia caused by *Staphylococcus aureus*, *Streptococcus pneumoniae*, or *Hemophilus* species. Another example of the indirect effect of viral infection is the AIDS virus, which affects immune cells. The virus brings about immunological changes that result in the patient's dying from infections caused by other infectious agents (see Chapter 32 for a discussion of AIDS).

Inclusion Body Formation

The replication of virus in the cytoplasm or nucleus of infected cells often results in the accumulation of viral as well as cellular products. These accumulations, which may be nucleic acids, proteins, and so on, can be stained and are referred to as inclusion bodies. For example, the quasicrystalline arrays of virus observed in Figure 31-8 are inclusion bodies. Some inclusion bodies are so distinctive that their presence is diagnostic (referred to as **pathognomonic effect**). Rabies virus inclusions, called **Negri bodies,** are also of diagnostic value (Plate 20).

Cell Fusion (Syncytia Formation)

Enveloped viruses, such as the herpesvirus, paramyxovirus, and AIDS virus, release specific proteins that become incorporated into the cytoplasmic membrane of the infected cell. These proteins act like magnets on the infected cell and attract uninfected cells to their surface. This results in infection of the originally uninfected cell. Repetition of this process results in the aggregation of several infected cells. These aggregated cells eventually fuse, producing a giant multinucleated cell or **syncytium** (Fig. 31-10).

Changes in Surface Antigens

Enveloped as well as nonenveloped viruses insert novel antigens into the cell membrane of infected cells. These novel antigens make the cell a target for immunological destruction by virus-specific antibodies. Some of these virus-specified proteins are discussed later.

Interferon Production

Some cells infected by virus are able to produce a protein called **interferon.** Interferon has the capacity to prevent the infection of healthy cells. Interferon was discussed at length in Chapter 9.

Persistent Viral Infection

Up to now we have discussed the effects of acute viral disease, that is, virus replication accompanied by cell damage. The intracellular location of viruses permits them to remain as cellular occupants for prolonged periods. This phenomenon, referred to as **persistence,** allows virus to remain undetected and safe from immune forces that exist outside the cell. Some of the major mechanisms for immune evasion or viral persistence are as follows:

1. **Virus-produced defective-interfering particles.** During viral infection, some viral particles are defective. The defective particles are able to prevent multiplication of complete virus. For example, the disease subacute sclerosing panencephalitis (SSPE) is a late sequela of measles virus infection. The virus appears to be defective in its ability to bud from infected cells.
2. **Integration of the viral genome into the host genome.** DNA viruses can insert their genome into host DNA. As a consequence, the virus replicates only when the cell divides. For RNA viruses, integration of the viral genome requires the formation of a DNA intermediate (class VI RNA virus, see Expression of RNA Genomes). Integration of the viral genome is the ultimate mechanism of escape from immune forces. The integrated virus can persist for months or several years until it becomes reactivated by release from the host genome. This reactivation can result in active viral production accompanied by disease symptoms. Several viruses that integrate into the host genome can cause the malignant state, a process called **transformation.** Transformation is discussed at length later.

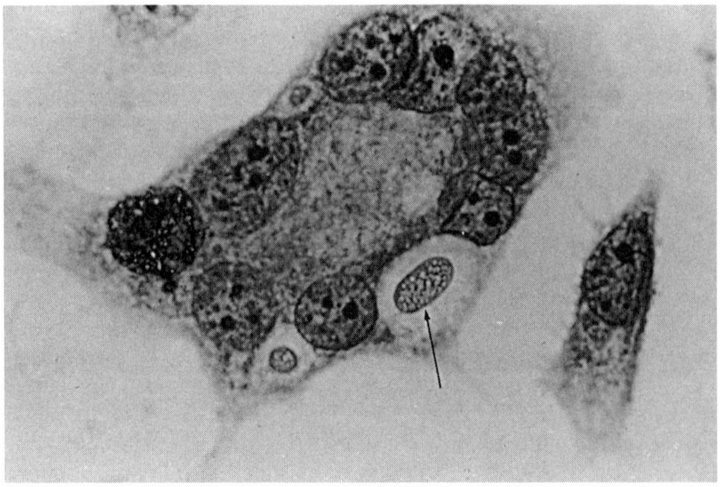

FIGURE 31-10
Syncytium of giant multinucleated cell caused by viral infection. Several cells are enclosed by a single membrane, producing a giant cell. The arrow points to an inclusion body. (Courtesy of H. M. Yamashiroya, Department of Pathology, University of Illinois Medical Center, Chicago, IL.)

3. **Thwarting immune responses.** Some viruses escape immune defenses by interfering with immune responses or by inducing an inadequate response. Some of these strategies are outlined below:
   a. The herpes simplex viruses can reside in neuronal cells that do not express major histocompatibility complex (MHC) antigens and thus avoid recognition.
   b. The herpes simplex viruses express an Fc receptor that is able to bind nonspecifically to IgG. The result of this is an inhibition of the classic complement pathway. These same viruses also encode a complement receptor that binds C3b (see Chapter 12). The result of this is an inhibition of the amplification convertase of the alternative complement pathway.
   c. The human cytomegalovirus can modulate immune recognition structures. The virus produces a protein that binds MHC Class I molecules, which leads to a decreased expression on the cell surface. Certain immune cells (cytotoxic T cells, for example) are unable to recognize and lyse such affected cells.
   d. The human cytomegalovirus also utilizes the strategy of induced immunosuppression to evade the immune system. The virus is known to infect lymphocytes and monocytes. For whatever reason these cells show a marked decrease in natural killer cell activity. In addition, infection by this virus inhibits normal inflammatory cell function.

Persistent infections can be divided into three types: **latent, chronic,** and **slow. Latent** infections are defined as persistent infections in which the viral genome is present, but gene expression is limited and infectious virus is not produced. Clinical symptoms may or may not be present during latency. The herpesviruses are noted for causing latent infections, for example, cold sores (see Chapter 32). **Chronic** infections are those in which the virus causes cytolysis, but symptoms are subclinical and do not impair organ function. Hepatitis caused by hepatitis B virus (HBV) and rubella caused by rubella virus are examples of chronic infections. **Slow** persistent infections are those in which there is a long incubation period (years). The virus continues to multiply, albeit slowly, causing a protracted and continued destruction of tissue. An example of a slow virus disease in humans is **kuru** (see Slow Virus Infections in Chapter 32). Major groups of viruses that cause persistent infections are presented in Table 31-1.

VIRUSES AND CANCER

Cancer can be defined as a malignant growth or neoplasia (Table 31-2), or tumor resulting from the transformation of cells that demonstrate unrestricted growth. Since cancer has never been shown to be contagious, it is hard to see how this disease could be due to an infectious agent. Cancer in humans is usually caused by chemical or physical agents. Early in the twentieth century, investigators Shope, Rous, and Bittner, among others, demonstrated that some animal viruses are responsible for neoplasms (abnormal growth of tissue). However, there was no reason to believe that viruses might be involved in human cancer. In 1951, however, Gross discovered that a mouse leukemia induced by an animal virus was very similar to the leukemia that afflicts humans.

Since Gross's discovery, scientists all over the world have been actively attempting to determine the association between viruses and human cancer. We now know that the **human T lymphotropic viruses (HTLV)** are causes of certain leukemias and lymphomas in humans. One of the HTLV is the cause of AIDS, a disease that predisposes its patients to cancer.

TABLE 31-1
Viruses Causing Persistent Infections in Humans

Viral agent	Disease	Effect on host cell
Rubella virus	Fetal anomalies and panencephalitis	Inhibition of cell division
Measles virus	Subacute sclerosing panencephalitis	Cytolysis
Human papillomavirus	Warts	Transformation
Hepatitis B virus	Hepatitis	Immunopathology
Herpes simplex virus types 1 and 2	Herpes	Cytolysis
Varicella-zoster virus	Zoster (shingles)	Cytolysis
Cytomegalovirus	Mononucleosis	Cytolysis
Epstein-Barr virus	Mononucleosis, Burkitt's lymphoma	Transformation
Kuru virus	Kuru (encephalopathy)	Cytolysis
Creutzfeldt-Jakob virus*	Creutzfeldt-Jakob disease (encephalopathy)	Cytolysis
JC virus	Leukoencephalopathy	Transformation
BK virus	?	None
Adenovirus	?	None

* Creutzfeldt-Jakob disease is caused by an infectious agent (prion) that does not possess a nucleic acid (see Slow Virus Infections, Chapter 32).
SOURCE: Adapted from N. Nathanson and D. Schlessinger, eds., *Microbiology—1977*. Washington, D.C.: American Society for Microbiology, 1977.

TABLE 31-2
Nomenclature of Neoplasms

Neoplasms are classified by cell type or origin. The prefix for a glandular neoplasm is "adeno-." The suffix designation denotes whether the neoplasia is benign or malignant. If the neoplasm is benign, the suffix "-oma" is used. If the neoplasm is malignant and involves epithelial tissue, the suffix "carcinoma" generally is used. Malignant mesenchymal neoplasms ae called **sarcomas.** Examples are listed below.

Tissue	Benign neoplasia	Malignant neoplasia
Epithelium		
Squamous	Squamous cell papilloma	Squamous cell carcinoma
Connective tissue		
Bone	Osteoma	Osteosarcoma
Cartilage	Chondroma	Chondrosarcoma
Endothelium		
Blood vessels	Hemangioma	Hemangiosarcoma
Hematopoietic		
Bone marrow	(Not recognized)	Leukemia
Neural tissue		
Nerve sheath	Neurilemmoma	Neurogenic sarcoma

Viruses classified as tumor viruses may be able to induce tumors when injected into experimental animals, or to transform cells maintained in culture. Tumor-initiating viruses are called **oncogenic viruses.** Some of these viruses can cause cancer in native animal species under natural circumstances while others must be manipulated in the laboratory to produce the desired effect. Before we discuss the various types of tumor viruses, let us first examine what happens to cells to make them malignant, that is, the properties of transformed cells.

Properties of Transformed Cells

Both DNA and RNA viruses are able to induce tumors in experimental animals. In each instance the tumor cell is transformed and acquires properties that make it distinct from uninfected cells, or infected cells in which tumors are not produced. Depending on the virus and the cell type involved, these transformation properties are quite variable. Some important properties of transformed cells are as follows:

1. The viral nucleic acid becomes integrated into or closely associated with the genome of the cell. The cell does not lyse.
2. Transformed cells are rounder than normal cells and show irregular patterns of orientation in cell culture (Fig. 31-11).
3. Transformed cells lose the property of **contact inhibition** (also called **density-dependent growth**) and show a loss of growth-inhibiting ability. Changes in the growth patterns of certain transformed cells cause them to form colonies in soft agar. This property permits the investigator to select transformed from untransformed cells.
4. Some transformed cells can produce tumors when injected into susceptible animals. Whether the tumors are benign or malignant is dependent on the transformed cell used and the type of host being challenged.
5. After transformation, a virus-specific antigen appears on the surface of many tumor cells. It is called **tumor-specific transplantation antigen (TSTA).** Other antigens may also appear on the surface of the cell that make it recognizable by the host's immune system. These surface antigens may be host- or virus-specified.
6. Chromosomal abnormalities, including breakage of some chromosomes and duplication of others, appear after cellular transformation.
7. Several changes occur in the cytoplasmic membrane of transformed cells. One of the earliest changes involves the permeability mechanism. Transformed cells are more permeable to metabolites, such as sugars, than are normal cells. Chemical changes in the membrane involving lipid, carbohydrate, and glycoprotein composition may occur. These changes are not uniform but vary depending on the composition of the growth medium and the growth rate of the cells.
8. The agglutinability of cells by certain glycoproteins called **lectins** or **agglutinins** is altered in transformed cells. The sources of lectins include plant seeds (wheat germ, jack bean), snails, and crabs. Transformed cells are agglutinated readily by lectins because of alteration of the lectin binding sites.

Oncogenic DNA Viruses

There are five families of oncogenic DNA viruses: polyomaviruses, papillomaviruses, adenoviruses, herpesviruses, and HBV. The general scheme of events that occur when a cell is transformed by a DNA virus is illustrated in Figure 31-12. It should be pointed out that it is not necessary for the viral genome to integrate into the host genome to cause transformation. Many transforming DNA genomes remain outside the host chromosome as episomes and in some instances only the transforming genes appear to be integrated into the host genome.

None of the DNA viruses can cause cancer by themselves and other factors are involved. For example, hormonal factors and the genetic constitution of the host also play a role. The role of DNA viruses in cancer is explored below.

Hepatitis B Virus and Hepatitis C Virus. As many as 300 million people, most of them in Asia, are carriers of HBV, the virus that affects the liver. Each carrier's risk of acquiring liver cancer is 100 times greater than that of a noncarrier. Unlike other oncoviruses, HBV does not appear to carry transforming genes. Viral sequences, but not the entire genome, of HBV are inserted into the DNA of liver cells. The mechanism of transformation of liver cells to cancer cells is not known but probably involves disrup-

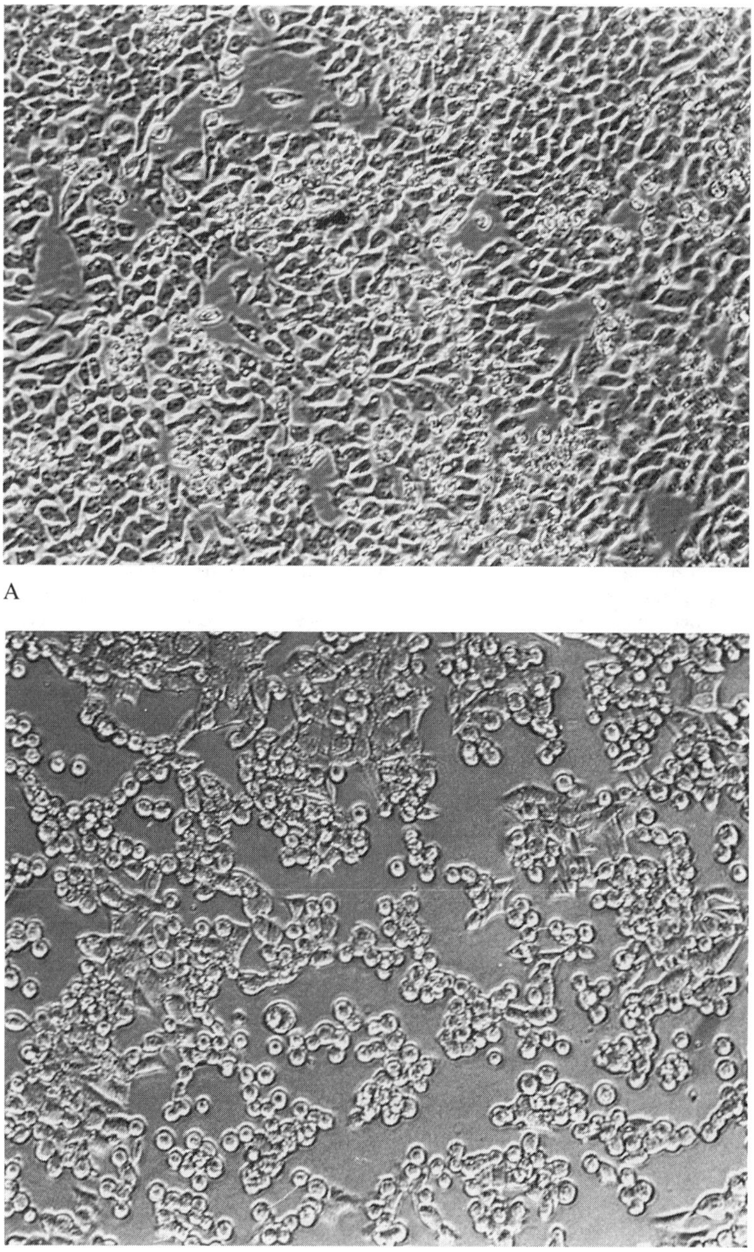

FIGURE 31-11
Transformation of a cell culture by cytomegalovirus. A. Uninfected control. B. Infected culture. (From J. F. Baskar, S. C. Stanat, and E. Huang, *Infect. Immun.* 40:726, 1983.)

tion of the cells' regulatory genes (genes that control growth, metabolism, etc.). An immune attack on virus-infected cells causes liver damage. Liver cells divide to regenerate damaged tissue. The repeated cycles of regeneration may increase the opportunity for abnormal cell growth.

The hepatitis C virus (HCV) recently was recognized as a major cause of chronic hepatitis worldwide. HCV is also a potential candidate for causing liver cancer.

Herpesviruses. The Epstein-Barr virus (EBV) is the only herpesvirus that is currently believed to be associated with certain neoplasms. The EBV has an affinity for lymphocytes and is capable of transforming them from end stage to immortal cells with unlimited life spans. The virus was identified in cultured lymphoid cells from patients afflicted with **Burkitt's lymphoma.** This rare disease is endemic in certain areas of Africa. It is a cancer of the lymphoid system and affects primarily children. There are three steps in the pathogenesis of Burkitt's lymphoma:

1. EBV infection induces nonmalignant polyclonal B cell proliferation.
2. T cell immunodeficiency accompanies B cell proliferation.

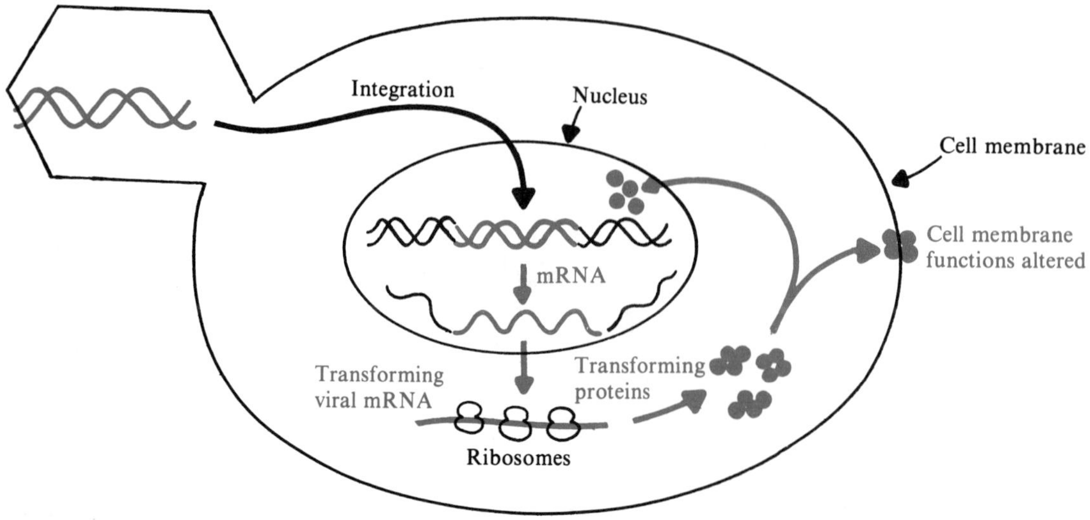

FIGURE 31-12
Events that lead to the transformation of animal cells by oncogenic DNA virus. Virus infects the cell and viral DNA is integrated into the host genome. Viral DNA is transcribed into mRNA, a small portion of which contains transforming genes. Transforming genes code for proteins that affect cell membrane and genome function.

3. Translocations occur in the chromosomes of proliferating infected B cells. B cell differentiation is affected by these translocations. Genetically altered B cells outgrow normal cells because of the enhanced growth and resistance to T cell surveillance.

EBV is also linked to **nasopharnygeal cancer (NPC)** (see Under the Microscope 26). In both Burkitt's lymphoma and NPC, viral-specific antigens and DNA have been detected in the malignant cells.

Human Papillomaviruses. Several types of human papillomaviruses are known to cause warts involving the hands and other body sites and warts and papillomas involving the genitalia. The human papillomavirus is believed to be associated with neoplasias, particularly of the cervix. The mechanism of infection is as follows:

1. Virus enters the female genital tract. If the epithelial surface is disturbed, virus gains access to replicative cells in the basal epithelium.
2. Viral DNA may be in or in proximity to the epithelium for an extended interval of time (latency).
3. As infected basal cells approach the upper layers of the epithelium, the virus replicates and assembles into virions. Local cells affected by the virus become transformed and form genital warts or **condylomata.** There appears to be a strong association between human papillomavirus and cervical tumors. The DNA of human papillomavirus types 16 and 18 have been found in over 60 percent of the cervical tumors examined. Several studies have demonstrated an association between cigarette smoking and cervical cancer.

Cervical cancer is a disease of gene transcription. It appears that infected cells must accumulate damage in several oncogenes and tumor suppressor genes before becoming malignant. Cervical cells strongly resist malignant transformation and for this

UNDER THE MICROSCOPE 26

Epstein-Barr Virus and Nasopharyngeal Carcinoma

In Southeast China, nasopharyngeal carcinoma (NPC) is the most predominant tumor in males, comprising about 20 percent of all cancers. Certain cultural patterns appear to be predisposing factors to this type of cancer. Eating salted fish containing considerable quantities of nitrosodimethylamines appears to be a contributing factor. Another factor is the use of certain medicinal plants in Chinese traditional medicine. Use of extracts of the *Euphorbiaceae* plant appears to induce replication of the Epstein-Barr virus. The active components of these plants are phorbol esters. Chinese immigrants to this country have a lower incidence of NPC in the second generation. Thousands of Chinese are now screened serologically for NPC by measuring antibodies to a EBV antigen called EA-D.

TABLE 31-3
Classification of Human Retroviruses

Retrovirus	Classification	Associated pathology	Endemic area
Human T lymphotropic virus (HTLV) type I	Oncovirus	Adult T cell leukemia/lymphoma	Southeastern United States
HTLV-II	Oncovirus	T cell hairy leukemia	England, New York (IV drug users)
Human immunodeficiency virus (HIV) type 1	Lentivirus	Acquired immunodeficiency syndrome (AIDS); AIDS-related complex (ARC)	Central Africa, Europe, United States
HIV-2	Lentivirus	AIDS	West Africa, Cape Verde
HTLV-V	Not yet classified	Sézary syndrome	Southern Italy

reason most genital cell cancers require 20 or more years to develop. The incidence of genital warts, the incidence of cervical cancer, and the mortality from cervical cancer have increased markedly in recent years. A concerted effort is being made to identify and define individuals who may be at risk of disease.

Oncogenic RNA Viruses

General Characteristics. The oncogenic RNA viruses belong to a group called the **retroviruses** (Table 31-3). Retroviruses are infectious for many mammals and birds. As briefly described previously, retroviruses are a class VI group of viruses in terms of their mode of replication. They produce a double-stranded DNA intermediate with the assistance of the enzyme **reverse transcriptase.** It is the DNA intermediate produced during replication that is integrated into the host genome. This DNA intermediate is called a **provirus.** Once the provirus is integrated, one of the following pathways may be engaged:

1. The provirus may duplicate when cellular DNA duplicates. If the infected cell is a germ cell, the progeny of the host will also carry the provirus. This type of transfer is called **vertical transmission.**
2. Under certain circumstances, the provirus may become activated and released from the host genome. New virus particles that can infect adjacent cells and tissue can be produced. This type of transfer is called **horizontal transmission.**
3. The provirus may carry information that is oncogenic. If the oncogenic information is translated into specific products, the latter may convert the infected cell into a **tumor cell.**

Oncogenic retroviruses, unlike other viruses, carry genes that are closely related to cellular genes (see Under the Microscope 27). These genes are not important for viral replication but they can bring about the transformation of the cells they infect. Viral transforming genes are called **oncogenes (v-onc)**. They are dominant structural genes

UNDER THE MICROSCOPE 27

Human Retrovirus Evolution

Viruses, which require a living cell in which to replicate, very likely evolved along with or from cellular genes. We may not have any cellular fossil records of their existence but we can look at their genetic record. The ideal way to identify microbes is by examining and comparing their nucleic acid sequences. In the case of retroviruses we can find fragments of their DNA in the vertebrate species from which the virus was originally isolated. Investigators have found retrovirus sequences in all vertebrate species. When cell cultures from these species were produced in the laboratory, it was possible, in some cases, to induce the formation of a complete virus particle. Robert Gallo, who was one of the first to isolate the virus causing AIDS (HIV), suspects that retroviral sequences evolved with or from movable genetic elements called **transposons** (see Chapter 5). Transposons are known to influence nearby genes on the chromosome.

Retroviruses may play a role in normal cell biology. Investigators believe that mutation may lead to the formation of an infectious retrovirus. When the retrovirus leaves the cell and enters a new species, it may cause serious pathological results. The origin of some retroviruses has been traced using molecular hybridization techniques. For example, nucleic acid sequences homologous to the feline leukemia retrovirus genome can be found in the chromosomal DNA of normal uninfected cats.

UNDER THE MICROSCOPE 28

The Genetics of Carcinogenesis

Many of the genes encoding **growth factors** and other effector molecules that regulate normal cell growth are designated **proto-oncogenes.** Oncogenes, which are associated with cellular transformation, differ from their proto-oncogenic counterparts by being mutated, overexpressed, or expressed at inappropriate times or locations in the cell. One of the activities of growth factors is to prime cells for cell death. Tumor cells are able to evade programmed cell death. Other proto-oncogenes such as **tumor suppressor genes** (also called **anti-oncogenes**) act in opposition to oncogenes. If a tumor suppressor gene is inactivated, for example, by mutation, the normal controls on cell proliferation are bypassed. Thus, in normal cells there are specific processes that must be overcome to allow cell proliferation. Tumor cells often represent an accumulation of genetic alterations that activate oncogenes and silence tumor suppressor genes, thereby bypassing programmed cell death. For a detailed discussion of these aspects of cancer, please see the following references:

Aaronson, S. A. Molecular themes in oncogenesis. *Science* 254:1146, 1991.
Cross, M., and Dexter, T. M. Growth factors in development, transformation, and tumorigenesis. *Cell* 64:271, 1991.
Rozebgurt, E. Growth factors and cell proliferation. *Curr. Opin. Cell Biol.* 4:161, 1992.
Schmandt, R., and Mills, G. R. Genomic components of carcinogenesis. *Clin. Chem.* 39:2375, 1993.

that encode for proteins capable of transforming the phenotype of the cell. The cellular counterparts of oncogenes are called **proto-oncogenes (c-onc)** (see Under the Microscope 28 before continuing). Each oncogene is given a trivial three-letter name based on the retroviral disease in which its homologues were discovered. For example, *abl* oncogene is the Abelson leukemia virus isolated from a mouse. More than 30 proto-oncogenes have been identified and they encode the following:

1. **Kinases,** which control diverse functions such as cell growth, metabolism, hormone action, nerve signal transmission, fertilization, and gene activity
2. **Growth factors** and **growth factor receptors**
3. **Nuclear regulatory proteins**
4. **Regulatory proteins in signal transduction**

Oncogenes and Transformation. Two of the most widely studied viral oncogenes are v-*src* and v-*ras*. The source of v-*src* is chicken sarcoma while the source of v-*ras* is rat and human sarcoma. To better understand the relationship between viruses and cancer, we need to answer two basic questions: (1) How do retroviruses obtain cellular information? (2) If the cellular proto-oncogenes perform normal functions in the cell, how is transformation induced?

Proto-oncogene activation contributes to the neoplastic process. An activated oncogene is a proto-oncogene that has been altered in such a way that there is inappropriate or overexpression of its products. Activation can occur in several ways but the most common mechanism is called **insertional mutagenesis.** The process begins in the following way (Fig. 31-13):

1. A retrovirus infects a cell and several copies of viral DNA integrate into host DNA. During the integration process a cellular gene becomes inserted into the proviral genome.
2. When the retrovirus replicates and new virus particles are produced, each viral nucleic acid will possess a cellular gene now referred to as viral onc gene.
3. Retrovirus carrying the v-onc gene can infect other cells and several copies of the oncogene can be inserted into the host genome at a site distant from the normal cellular gene site.
4. Retroviral regulatory genes (promoters) then drive transcription of the proto-oncogene. Proto-oncogene activation or enhanced expression could lead to al-

FIGURE 31-13
Insertional mutagenesis. Postulated mechanism for the acquisition of a cellular oncogene by retrovirus. A. Retrovirus integrated into cellular DNA (*black line*) near the cellular oncogene (c-onc). B. Recombinational event between the cellular oncogene and the proviral DNA results in a copy of the gene being inserted into proviral DNA. C. Proviral DNA deintegrated from the cellular genome now carries a viral version of the oncogene (v-onc).

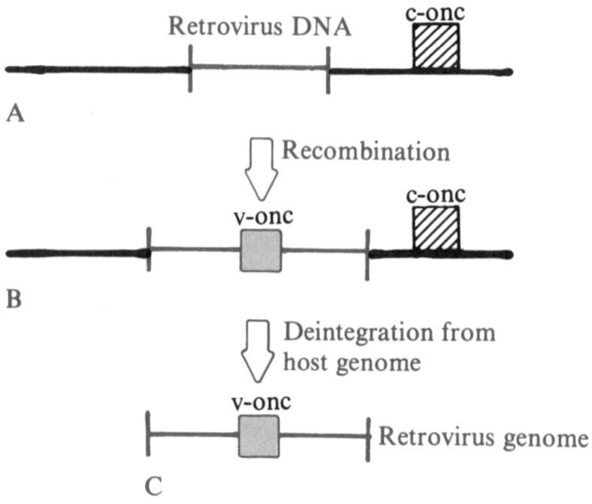

terations of growth and differentiation and thus contribute to neoplasia.

Activation of proto-oncogenes can also occur by mechanisms independent of retroviral involvement. Point mutations and DNA rearrangement can result in proto-oncogene activation by leading to altered levels or expression of a normal protein product or altered levels of expression of abnormal protein (see previous discussions).

The only RNA viruses known to cause cancer in humans are the retroviruses called **HTLV.** HTLV-I and HTLV-II are linked to human leukemia. The virus causing AIDS is related to these viruses. The AIDS virus, however, only predisposes its victims to cancer.

DIAGNOSTIC VIROLOGY

Laboratory diagnosis is often unnecessary for childhood viral infections such as mumps, measles, and chickenpox. Diagnosis becomes important when (1) it is suspected that the virus is one associated with a high mortality and its spread in the community could be devastating (for example, AIDS virus); (2) there is cross infection in the hospitalized patient, resulting in severe illness (for example, influenza, respiratory syncytial virus infections); and (3) a pregnant woman is suspected of carrying viruses that are known to cause abnormalities in the fetus (for example, rubella). At one time even the identification of virus was of little help because antiviral drugs were unavailable for treatment. More antiviral drugs are now becoming available and rapid identification of viral agents is becoming more practical.

Many new and exotic techniques for rapid identification of viruses are available but the mainstays of diagnostic virology are **viral cultivation** and **serology.**

Cultivation of Virus from Clinical Material

Tissue culture is the most widely used technique for virus isolation. There are three major types of tissue culture: **primary cultures, diploid cell lines,** and **continuous cell lines.**

Primary cultures are prepared by removing an organ from a freshly killed animal and then dispersing the cells of the organ by biochemical treatment. The number of cell divisions for primary cultures is relatively small. **Diploid cell lines** have a finite life span consisting of 50 to 60 passages in vitro. Most of the diploid cell lines used in the laboratory are fibroblasts. **Continuous cell lines** are derived from normal or malignant tissue and are immortal in that they can grow indefinitely. Examples of continuous cell lines are **Vero cells** from monkey kidney tissue and **HeLa cells** derived from malignant tumor (see Under the Microscope 29). Which cell line to use depends on its sensitivity to virus.

Cell lines are cultured in glass or plastic vessels containing liquid media. The cells attach to the surface and then begin to divide. Division continues until all available surface has been covered. When the cells reach a state in

---

UNDER THE MICROSCOPE 29

The Legacy of Henrietta Lacks

The term **HeLa** is derived from a woman named Henrietta Lacks who was born in Virginia in 1920. Henrietta began raising a family in Baltimore, Maryland, and was of normal health. She was relatively free of cares until 1951, when she observed a pink discharge in her underclothes. She went to a women's clinic at Johns Hopkins Hospital, where a gynecologist noted an abnormal growth about the cervix. Biopsy of the tissue revealed that it was malignant and that Henrietta Lacks had cervical cancer. A slice of the tumor was given to George and Margaret Gey, who at the time were pioneers in tissue culture. The Geys' greatest hope was that they would be able to establish a continuous culture of a human tumor that could be studied in the test tube. Every day the Geys would see what operations were being performed in the hospital and then retrieve interesting sources of tissue. They would then race to the lab and try to culture the cells for extended periods of time. But no matter how careful their manipulations and culturing techniques, most human cells would shrivel up and die after a few months.

The malignant tissue taken from Henrietta was code-named with the first two letters of the donor's first and last name (HeLa). Cubes of the malignant tissue were cultivated and fed the usual diet of clotted chicken plasma, chopped beef embryo, and blood from human placentas. Within 48 hours a new band of cells could be seen around each cube of tissue. After 4 days the culture tubes became overrun with new cells and, as Mary Gey described it, were "spreading like crabgrass." The tumor cells grew 10 to 20 times faster than normal cervical cells—making them different from any tumor cells previously observed. The tumor within Henrietta Lacks was also different. Most cervical cancers are held in check by radiation, but Henrietta's grew so quickly that it covered the surface of the liver, diaphragm, intestine, appendix, rectum, and heart. In 8 months from the time of discovery of the malignancy Henrietta Lacks was dead; but part of what she had been, escaped and is still surviving.

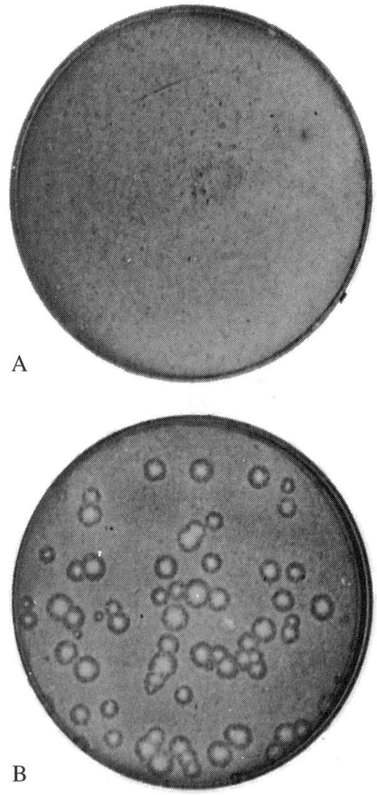

FIGURE 31-14
Viral plaques. Influenza virus grown on human amnion cells. A. Uninfected cells. B. Infected cells after 5 days of incubation. (From A. Sugiura and M. Ueda, *Virology*. 7:499, 1977.)

which their total membrane surface is in contact with adjacent cells, division ceases. This phenomenon, called **contact inhibition,** or **density-dependent growth,** results in the formation of a monolayer of cells in the culture medium. When malignant cells are used to cultivate virus, however, the phenomenon of contact inhibition is lost and the cells pile up.

Sometimes cell cultures are not especially sensitive to virus and other culture systems are required. Two such culture systems are **embryonated eggs** and **suckling mice.** Influenza virus, for example, is cultured in embryonated eggs, while suckling mice are used primarily in the isolation of alphavirus, flaviviruses, and bunyaviruses.

Effects of Virus on Cultured Cells. Regardless of the cell type used for cultivating virus, most viruses will produce a measurable cytopathic effect. These cytopathic effects include the formation of **plaques, pocks, foci,** and **syncytia** (see earlier discussion).

Some virus-infected cells lyse and progeny viruses are released to infect and lyse adjacent cells. After several days a localized area of infection, called a **plaque,** appears (Fig. 31-14). Plaques are similar in appearance to the plaques caused by bacterial viruses on cultured bacteria (see Fig. 31-21).

When some viruses are cultivated on the chorioallantoic membrane of embryonated chicken eggs, lesions called **pocks** are produced. The membrane can be removed and spread out and the pocks counted. Each pock represents the original site of a single virus infection (Fig. 31-15).

Some viruses that infect cells do not cause visible plaques or pocks. Instead, virus infection stimulates cell proliferation and after a time a mass of live cells called a **focus** is formed (Fig. 31-16).

The cytopathic effect produced on host cells offers only a preliminary method of identification of virus. Final identification usually depends on serological tests.

Serological Methods

Serological methods are by far the most important in diagnostic virology. They are based on demonstrating a significant increase in the antibody titer to a given virus antigen

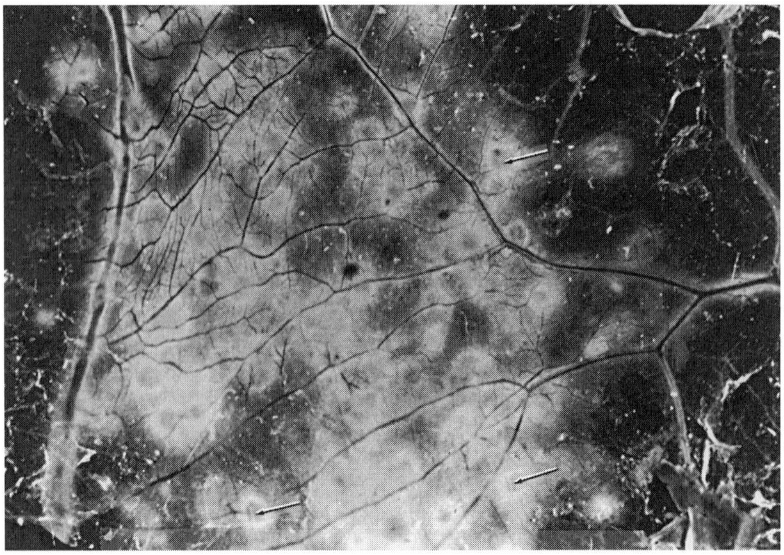

FIGURE 31-15
Viral pocks (*arrows*) produced on the chorioallantoic membrane of an embryonated hen's egg after 5 days' incubation with virus at 35.5 C. (Courtesy of Audio Visual Service, Department of Pathology, University of Illinois Medical Center, Chicago, IL.)

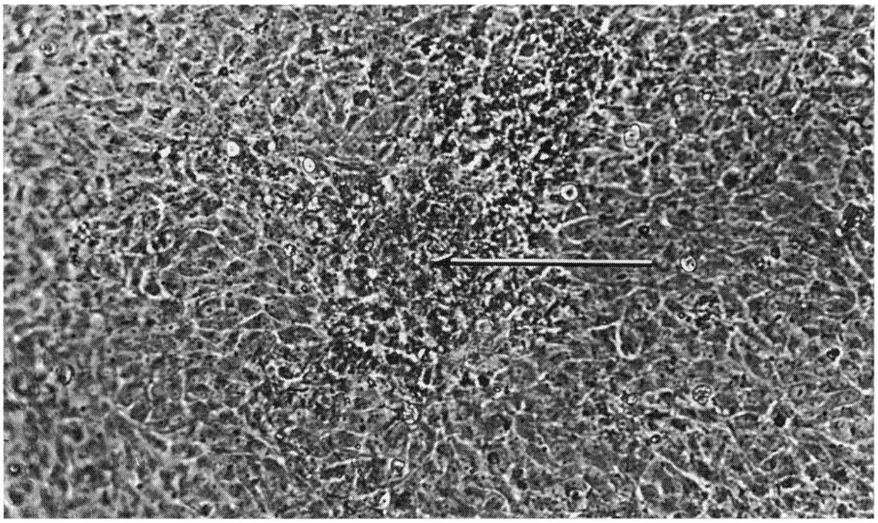

FIGURE 31-16
Cell focus (*arrow*) produced by a virus-infected cell. (From K. Hamada et al., *J. Virol.* 38:327, 1981.)

over the course of the patient's disease; that is, one tests acute- and convalescent-phase serum. The length of time required for testing is a limitation but serological methods are more economical than isolation of virus. In order to prevent the hazards associated with handling infectious antigens, the nucleic acid of viruses can be inactivated before use. A variety of techniques are now available to detect antibody. Some of these techniques are immunoassays and include the following: radioimmunoassay, enzyme immunoassay, immunofluorescence tests, and avidin-biotin immunoassays. These tests are described in more detail in Appendix B. Other immunological tests that measure antibody including complement fixation and neutralization are also described in Appendix B.

Rapid Methods in Diagnostic Virology

The most ideal method for diagnosing viral infection is to detect directly and identify the infectious agent in clinical material. This can be accomplished by examining clinical material directly by electron microscopy or by using immunological or other techniques.

Electron Microscopy. Under most circumstances examination of clinical material is not feasible or practical. Not all laboratories have an electron microscope. The concentration of virus in a sample is often very small and there is considerable tissue debris that hinders identification. In addition, some viruses are so small that their morphology is not discernible enough to permit identification. Skin lesions may contain high concentrations of virus but techniques other than microscopy are more practical for identification.

Electron microscopy can be used for diagnosis if the viral agent, such as the rotavirus, cannot be cultivated by standard procedures. The rotavirus is one of the leading causes of diarrhea. In the case of the rotavirus, extracts of infected epithelial cells of the duodenal mucosa contain high concentrations of virus whose morphology is distinctive enough to permit identification (see Fig. 32-23).

Electron microscopy can be coupled with serology for rapid detection of virus in a technique called **immunoelectron microscopy (IEM)**. In this procedure antiserum containing antibodies specific for the virus is mixed with a large clinical specimen in which virus concentration may be small. The interaction of antibody with virus produces virus-antibody aggregates that are more easily discernible with electron microscopy. The hepatitis A virus was first identified by this procedure.

Immunological and Other Methods of Identification. Virus or viral antigens can be detected in clinical specimens either within cells or outside cells (for example, the blood). Reliable identification is dependent on having sufficient virus or viral antigen in the clinical specimen and having highly specific antisera. The availability of monoclonal antibodies has permitted more precise identification of viral isolates. Monoclonal antibodies can be used in indirect and direct fluorescent antibody tests. One of the major advantages of monoclonal antibody testing is that it provides a technique for identifying not only major antigens but also minor or previously undetected antigenic determinants.

The advent of recombinant DNA technology has permitted investigators to identify virus on the basis of detection of viral genomes or specific viral sequences by **hybridization.** The idea is to select and clone a nucleic acid sequence that is found in only one strain, species, or genus. This DNA should hybridize only with the DNA extracted from specific organisms. This specificity is the basis of what are termed **nucleic acid probes** (see Chapter 6). Probes have been used primarily for epidemiological purposes but they can also have diagnostic advantages. Most probes to date have been used primarily to identify bacterial infectious agents. One of the major advances that has aided the development of hybridization techniques is the **polymerase chain reaction (PCR)**. PCR provides a method for amplification of specific DNA sequences. Detection of virus in body fluids by PCR, for example, is being used as a screening method for congenital infection by cytomegalovirus. PCR was discussed earlier in Chapter 6.

VIRAL CLASSIFICATION

Viral classification has been approached in many ways over the past years. With every major advancement in our understanding of viruses, new classification schemes have evolved. These schemes are based primarily on (1) symptoms of the viral disease, (2) method of transmission of virus, (3) symmetry of the virus capsid, or (4) the tissue or organ affected by the virus. One of the most useful means of separating the viruses is based first on the type of nucleic acid carried by the virus. Further separation is based on capsid symmetry and on the presence or absence of an envelope. These and other properties are summarized in Figures 31-17 and 31-18.

TREATMENT AND CONTROL OF VIRAL INFECTIONS

The most successful approach to the control of viral infection has been the development of vaccines. Unfortunately, vaccines are not available for most viral diseases and in some cases vaccines will never be practical or possible. Therefore, chemotherapy may be the only effective mechanism for controlling viral infections. We begin our discussion with chemotherapeutic agents.

Chemotherapeutic Agents

Many people find it difficult to understand why viruses cannot be treated with the same drugs that are effective against bacteria. The antibiotics used against bacteria for the most part inhibit some process that is peculiar or specific to the bacteria. For instance, the antibiotics that inhibit bacterial cell wall formation are of obvious value in therapy because mammalian cells have no cell walls and thus are not affected. For antibiotics that do inhibit both bacterial and host metabolism, the concentration of drug must be such that the cells of the body are not adversely affected. Viruses are intracellular parasites that use the metabolic machinery of the host. Many systemic antiviral drugs were originally found to be more toxic to the host than the virus. Some of these drugs are now used as topical agents.

Viruses also encode enzymes that are not present in uninfected cells. These enzymes are critical to viral replication but unnecessary for cellular function. It is now possible to find specific inhibitors of viral growth. Other enzymes that might be encoded by both cell and virus can be inhibited by finding variations in their substrate specificity or susceptibility to inhibition by various compounds.

The greatest success in antiviral chemotherapy has been achieved by using inhibitors of nucleic acid synthesis. Many of these antiviral agents are nucleoside analogues, structures that closely resemble the natural nucleosides

FIGURE 31-17
Classification of DNA-containing viruses of vertebrates.

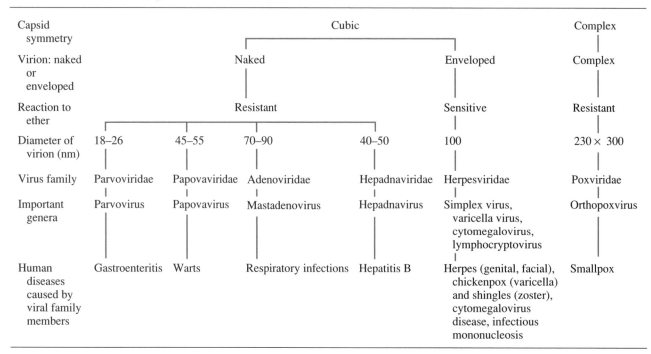

Capsid symmetry	Cubic					Complex
Virion: naked or enveloped	Naked				Enveloped	Complex
Reaction to ether	Resistant				Sensitive	Resistant
Diameter of virion (nm)	18–26	45–55	70–90	40–50	100	230 × 300
Virus family	Parvoviridae	Papovaviridae	Adenoviridae	Hepadnaviridae	Herpesviridae	Poxviridae
Important genera	Parvovirus	Papovavirus	Mastadenovirus	Hepadnavirus	Simplex virus, varicella virus, cytomegalovirus, lymphocryptovirus	Orthopoxvirus
Human diseases caused by viral family members	Gastroenteritis	Warts	Respiratory infections	Hepatitis B	Herpes (genital, facial), chickenpox (varicella) and shingles (zoster), cytomegalovirus disease, infectious mononucleosis	Smallpox

Capsid symmetry	Cubic				Helical		
Virion: naked or enveloped	Naked			Enveloped	Enveloped		
Reaction to ether	Resistant			Sensitive	Sensitive		
Diameter of virion (nm)	24–30	35–39	60–80	40–70	80–120	150–300	60–80
Virus family	Picornaviridae	Caliciviridae	Reoviridae	Togaviridae	Orthomyxoviridae	Paramyxoviridae	Rhabdoviridae
Important genera	Enterovirus, rhinovirus, heparnavirus (enterovirus 72)	Calicivirus, hepevirus	Reovirus, orbivirus, rotavirus	Alphavirus, flavivirus, rubivirus, hepacavirus	Influenza virus	Paramyxovirus, pneumovirus, morbillivirus	Lyssavirus
Human diseases caused by virus family members	Poliomyelitis, gastroenteritis, colds, hepatitis A	Hepatitis E, Norwalk gastroenteritis	Tick fever, gastroenteritis	Yellow fever, encephalitis, rubella, hepatitis C	Influenza	Parainfluenza, mumps, measles	Rabies

Capsid symmetry	Uncertain				
Virion: naked or enveloped	Enveloped				
Reaction to ether	Sensitive				
Diameter of virion (nm)	100	500–300	80	80–130	100
Virus family	Retroviridae	Arenaviridae	Filoviridae	Coronaviridae	Bunyaviridae
Important genera	Type B and C oncovirus	Arenavirus	Filovirus	Coronavirus	Bunyavirus
Human diseases caused by virus family members	Possibly human tumors	Lassa fever, South American hemorrhagic fevers	Marburg and Ebola hemorrhagic fevers	Respiratory infection	Encephalitis

FIGURE 31-18
Classification of RNA-containing viruses of vertebrates.

used as building blocks for DNA synthesis. Still, many of these drugs are toxic to the host and resistance to them is an ever-increasing problem. Investigators are now looking at inhibitors of additional enzymes in the viral replication cycle. Finding such compounds would provide a chemotherapeutic regimen in which more than one compound could be used. Such combination therapy will decrease the chances of toxicity and antiviral resistance. Currently licensed antiviral drugs are outlined in Table 31-4.

Immunoglobulins (see Appendix E) also are used as antiviral agents. They are used primarily, however, as prophylactic agents. Immunoglobulins are made from pooled plasma and contain predominantly IgG. High-titered (hyperimmune) globulins are derived from pooled units of plasma selected for high antibody titers to specific viruses. Immune globulins are used primarily for the prevention of hepatitis A. Hyperimmune globulins are used for postexposure prevention of hepatitis B, chickenpox, and rabies. Intravenous immunoglobulins have also been used for (1) improving survival when used with ganciclovir for the treatment of cytomegalovirus pneumonia in bone marrow recipients, (2) decreasing the frequency of graft-versus-host disease and interstitial pneumonia when given to seropositive bone marrow recipients, and (3) the treatment of chronic enteroviral meningoenphalitis in children with agammaglobulinemia.

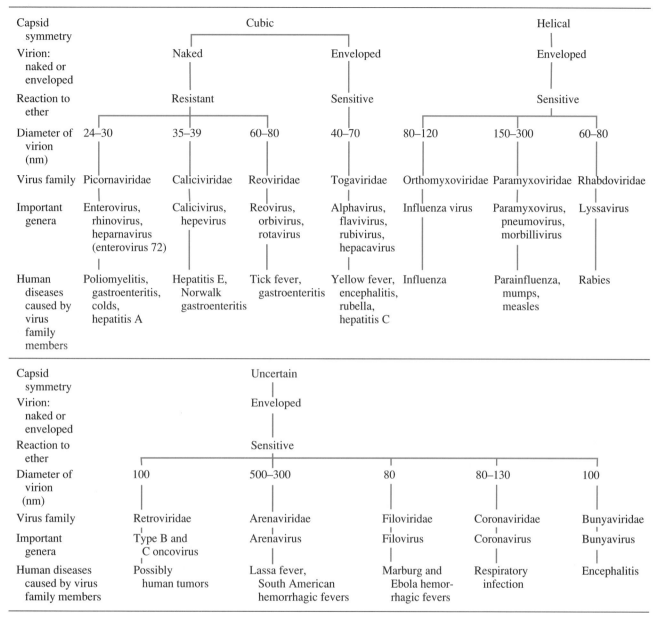

TABLE 31-4
Currently Available Antiviral Agents

Agent	Route of administration	Use
Acyclovir	Oral	Initial and recurrent genital herpes; mucocutaneous herpes in immunocompromised host; zoster (shingles)
	Intravenous	Herpes encephalitis; neonatal herpes; severe genital herpes; mucocutaneous herpes; zoster
	Topical	Initial genital herpes; cutaneous herpes
Ganciclovir	Intravenous	CMV retinitis in AIDS
Zidovudine	Oral	HIV infection
Vidarabine	Intravenous	Herpes encephalitis; neonatal herpes; zoster
	Ophthalmic ointment	Herpes keratitis
Amantadine	Oral	Influenza A
Ribavirin	Aerosol	Severe RSV
	Intravenous	Lassa fever
Interferon	Subcutaneous	Hepatitis B—chronic active liver disease; hepatitis C—chronic liver disease
	Intralesional	Condylomata acuminata (warts)
Foscarnet	Intravenous	CMV retinitis; acyclovir-resistant HSV or VZV
Didanosine	Oral	Zidovudine intolerance or treatment failure in HIV-infected host
Trifluridine	Ophthalmic solution	Herpes keratitis
Idoxuridine	Ophthalmic solution	Herpes keratitis

CMV = cytomegalovirus; AIDS = acquired immunodeficiency syndrome; HIV = human immunodeficiency virus; RSV = respiratory syncytial virus; HSV = herpes simplex virus; VZV = varicella-zoster virus.
SOURCE: Adapted in part from B. Bean, *Clin. Microbiol. Rev.* 5:146, 1992.

Vaccines

The historic epidemics, such as smallpox and yellow fever, that once decimated large populations are no longer a major threat to modern society. In some underdeveloped nations of the world, major epidemics still occur but they are generally curtailed before vast masses of people are affected. One of the primary reasons for a decline in mass epidemics is the vaccine.

Immunizations are particularly important for children. Not only does viral disease have a devastating effect on children but also children rapidly transmit these diseases to other children and adults. Childhood viral diseases are quickly spread in day-care facilities. Childhood immunization is therefore important in reducing morbidity and mortality. The recommended viral immunization schedules for children are outlined in Table 31-5.

Currently licensed viral vaccines are outlined in Table 31-6. A discussion of vaccine preparation, as well as the advantages and disadvantages of them, is presented in Chapter 12.

TABLE 31-5
Recommended Immunization (Viral) Schedule for Children

Age	Immunization child should receive
At birth	Hepatitis B vaccine (first)
2 months	Trivalent oral poliovirus vaccine (first) Hepatitis B vaccine (second)
4 months	Trivalent oral poliovirus vaccine (second) Hepatitis B vaccine (third)
15 months	Measles vaccine Mumps vaccine Rubella vaccine (May be combined as single injection)
18 months	Trivalent oral poliovirus vaccine (third)
4–6 years	Trivalent oral poliovirus vaccine (fourth)

TABLE 31-6
Currently Available Viral Vaccines

Vaccine	Vaccine type	Route of administration
Influenza A	Inactivated	Parenteral
Poliomyelitis	Inactivated and live	Parenteral and oral
Rabies	Inactivated	Parenteral
Hepatitis B	Recombinant subunit	Parenteral
Rubella	Live	Parenteral
Yellow fever	Live	Parenteral
Measles	Live	Parenteral
Adenovirus	Live	Oral
Mumps	Live	Parenteral
Chickenpox (varicella)[a]	Live	Parenteral
Hepatitis A[b]	Inactivated	Parenteral

[a] Still investigational but is very effective when used on immunocompromised individuals. Vaccine is used extensively in Japan.
[b] Currently available in several European countries. Clinical trials are under way in the United States.

Bacterial Viruses

Bacterial viruses (bacteriophage or phage) were discussed previously in regard to two different processes. First, we showed that bacterial viruses could be used to change the genetic constitution of a bacterium. In this process called **transduction,** a piece of bacterial DNA was transferred (transduced) from one bacterium to another by the phage. Second, we showed that phage could be used as an epidemiological tool. Bacteria, for example, could be identified by strain type based on the type of phage that infected them. In the remainder of this chapter we briefly compare and contrast animal viruses with bacterial viruses. More detailed descriptions of bacterial virus composition and structure, physiology, and so on can be found in general microbiology textbooks.

GENERAL CHARACTERISTICS AND REPLICATION

The majority of phages possess double-stranded DNA. Most phages possess a protein coat called the **phage head.** The phage head surrounds the nucleic acid and exhibits **icosahedral symmetry.** Unlike animal viruses the phage head of many phages is attached to a protein **tail.** The tail of viruses that infect *Escherichia coli* also possesses a **base plate** containing **spikes** as well as **tail fibers** (Fig. 31-19). These viruses belong to a group called the T series or **T phage** (for example, T1, T2, T3, etc.).

Lytic Cycle of Phage

The tail fibers of the T phage are used to attach to receptors on the cell wall of the bacterium (Fig. 31-20). There is contraction of the tail and insertion of the tail tube through the cell wall. This is followed by injection of the phage nucleic acid into the cytoplasm of the bacterial cell.

Like animal viruses, phage growth can be divided into early and late periods. Early phage-encoded enzymes are used to

1. Repair the bacterial cell membrane that was damaged during the injection of viral nucleic acid,
2. Alter bacterial RNA polymerase so only viral mRNA can be produced,
3. Degrade bacterial DNA into nucleotides that can be used in the synthesis of viral genomes, and
4. Produce nucleotide triphosphates and subsequently double-stranded DNA.

Late proteins are used to assemble mature phage particles. During late protein synthesis phage-encoded **lysozyme** accumulates. Once assembled, the mature phages are released from the cell by the activity of this enzyme. Lysozyme degrades cell wall peptidoglycan and causes the cell to burst.

We are able to detect the results of phage infection by plating infected bacterial cells on a solid agar surface containing a lawn of bacteria. For example, we may plate 100 infected cells on the agar surface along with uninfected cells. The uninfected cells will produce a lawn of growth.

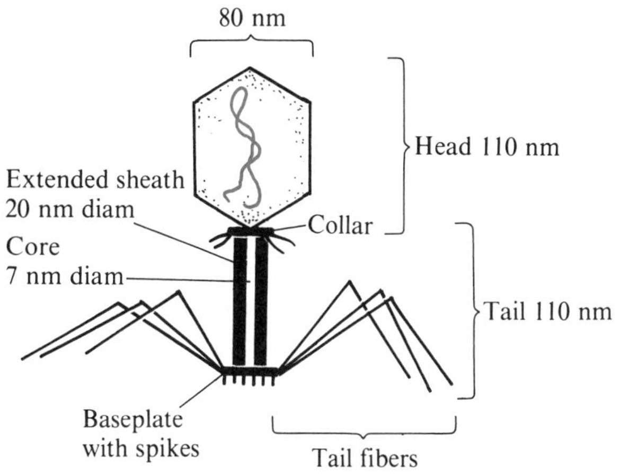

A

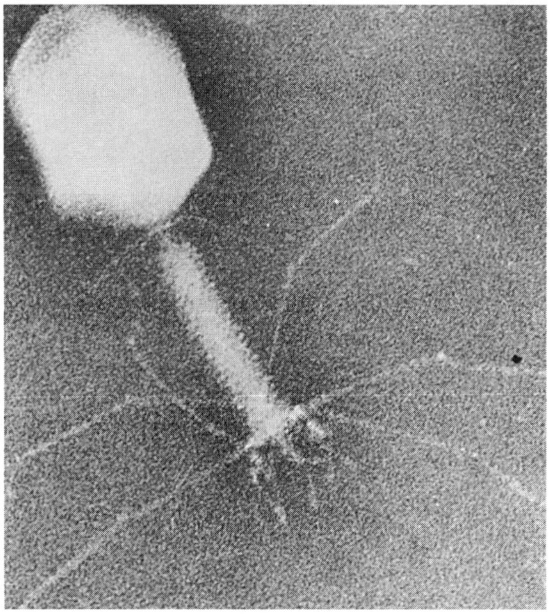

B

FIGURE 31-19
The T4 bacteriophage. A. Diagram. B. Electron micrograph. (From R. C. Williams and H. W. Fisher, *An Electron Micrograph Atlas of Viruses,* 1974. Courtesy of Charles C Thomas, Publisher, Springfield, IL.)

After the first 100 infected cells burst, each one releases a thousand or more phages. These phages in turn infect adjacent cells. Eventually enough bacterial cells are lysed that clear, almost circular areas called **plaques** are produced on the bacterial lawn (Fig. 31-21). Since we plated 100 infected cells, there will be 100 plaques on the bacterial lawn.

Lysogeny

As we showed earlier, some animal viruses can enter into a state of latency. Some bacterial viruses can also enter into a stable relationship with their host without lysing

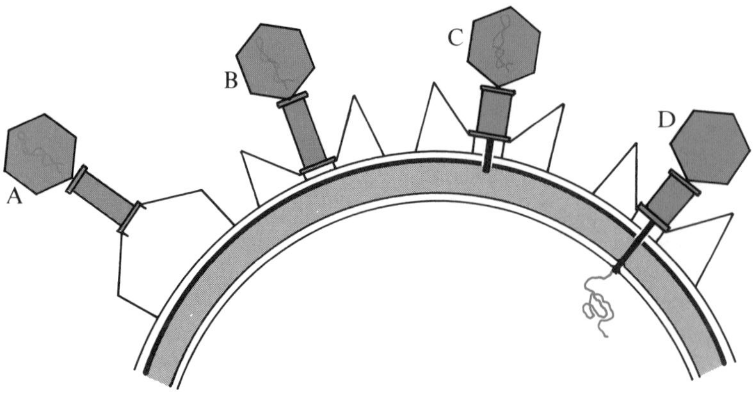

FIGURE 31-20
Bacteriophage infection process. A. Attachment of long tail fibers of the virus to the cell wall. B. Adsorption of viral tail pins to the cell wall. C. Contraction of tail sheath and injection of core into the cell wall. D. DNA injection through the core into the cytoplasm of the bacterial cell.

the cell. This stable phage relationship is called **lysogeny.** The bacterial cell harboring this type of virus is called a **lysogen,** and the virus is called a **temperate virus.** Like their animal counterparts, phage genomes can integrate into the host or they may remain physically independent of the host genome. The viral genome integrated into the bacterial genome is called a **prophage.**

Prophages are capable of changing a bacterial cell's phenotype. This process of change is called **phage conversion** or **lysogenic conversion.** Some examples in which lysogenic conversion has contributed to the infectious disease process in humans are as follows:

FIGURE 31-21
Bacterial plaques. Agar culture medium shows a lawn of *Escherichia coli* growth on which T2 bacteriophages have produced plaques. (From G. S. Stent, *Molecular Biology of Bacterial Viruses.* W. H. Freeman and Company, Copyright © 1963.)

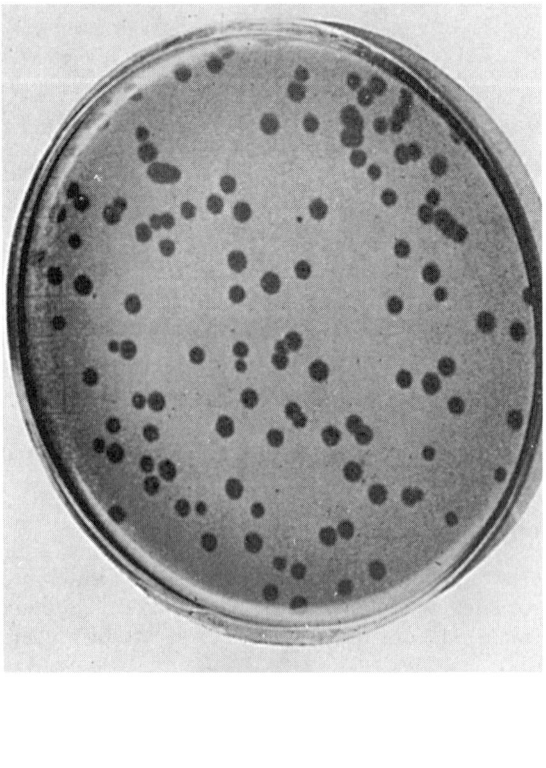

1. *Corynebacterium diphtheriae* is a pathogen whose virulence is related to its ability to produce a toxin. The bacterium is virulent only when it carries a temperate virus. The gene for toxin production apparently resides in the viral genome and not in the host's genome.
2. Only streptococci carrying a temperate phage can produce the erythrogenic toxin associated with scarlet fever.
3. *Clostridium botulinum* type C in the lysogenic state is nontoxigenic.
4. Some lysogenic bacteria can be distinguished from nonlysogenic ones.

Species of *Salmonella,* when infected by a temperate virus, will eventually show changes in their surface components (O antigens). The virus in some way prevents the formation of normal cell surface components. For this reason the antigenic components of the lysogenized cell are different from those of the nonlysogenized cell. This difference can be detected serologically.

Summary

1. Viruses are obligate intracellular agents that possess a single- or double-stranded DNA or RNA surrounded by a coat of protein. Many animal viruses also possess lipid envelopes but the latter are absent from most bacteriophages.

2. The viral protein coat is called a capsid and is made of protein subunits called capsomeres. The capsid may possess either helical or icosahedral symmetry.

3. The lipid bilayer of the viral envelope is derived from the host cell but the glycoproteins are of viral origin and are called spikes or peplomers. Some peplomers help bind virus to the cell but others may possess enzymatic activity that aids in the infectious disease process.

4. The multiplication cycle of animal viruses is divided into five stages: adsorption, penetration and uncoating, genome expression, maturation and assembly, and release. Adsorption of virus is dependent on the chemical nature of viral glycoproteins and host receptors. Viruses may penetrate the cell directly, by fusion with the cyto-

plasmic membrane, or by endocytosis. The viral nucleic acid is released from the nucleocapsid and may remain in the cytoplasm of the cell or it may penetrate the nucleus, depending on the site of viral assembly.

5. Expression of viral genomes in mammalian cells can be divided into six classes. This division is dependent on nucleic acid polarity, type of nucleic acid, and strand number of nucleic acid. All classes transcribe the genome into a messenger RNA (mRNA) molecule and also replicate it to produce many viral genomes.

6. The viral maturation process can be divided into early and late. Early proteins are engaged in synthesis of viral genomes. Late proteins are primarily structural. Nucleocapsids of DNA viruses are assembled primarily in the nucleus while most RNA nucleocapsids are assembled in the cytoplasm.

7. Most nonenveloped viruses are released when the cell lyses. Enveloped viruses must obtain a lipid envelope from either nuclear membrane material or cytoplasmic membrane material. Release of virus through cell membranes is called budding.

8. When animal virus is cultured the infected cells show cytopathic effects which include lysis of cells, inclusion body formation, and syncytia formation. Virus infection also (a) affects the surface antigens of cells, (b) causes the formation of interferon, and (c) may induce persistent infection.

9. Persistent infections can occur in cells if (a) the immune system is somehow evaded, (b) the virus produces defective-interfering particles, or (c) the viral genome integrates into the genome of the host.

10. Cancers are malignant growth resulting from the transformation of cells. Viruses causing cancer are called oncogenic. Viral transformation causes several effects on cells, including changes in morphology and changes in the antigenic characteristics of the cytoplasmic membrane. In addition, the viral genome becomes integrated into or closely associated with the host genome.

11. The oncogenic DNA viruses are the herpesviruses and human papillomaviruses. The Epstein-Barr virus is a herpesvirus associated with Burkitt's lymphoma and nasopharyngeal cancer. Strains of human papillomavirus cause genital warts that may be precursors of cervical cancer.

12. Oncogenic RNA viruses belong to a group called retroviruses. Retroviruses use the enzyme reverse transcriptase to produce a DNA molecule that is inserted into the host genome. Viral oncogenes are not associated with viral replication. They are defective cellular genes. The cellular counterparts of oncogenes are called proto-oncogenes. Proto-oncogenes control cellular processes such as growth and differentiation. The only RNA viruses causing cancer in humans are human T lymphotropic viruses (HTLV).

13. A few viral infections can be diagnosed by their symptomology. The mainstay of diagnostic virology is cultivation and serology. Most virus is cultivated in continuous culture, that is, cells that can be passaged indefinitely. Rapid identification can be made using electron microscopy, immunoidentification using monoclonal antibodies, and hybridization techniques.

14. Infected culture cells can be observed for cytopathic effects such as plaques, pocks, foci, or syncytia. Cytopathic effects permit only presumptive identification and final identification requires serology.

15. Viral classification is based primarily on nucleic acid type, capsid symmetry, and presence or absence of an envelope (see Figs. 31-17 and 31-18).

16. The most frequently used antiviral drugs are analogues of nucleosides. These analogues are primarily inhibitors of nucleic acid synthesis. The currently licensed drugs are outlined in Table 31-4.

17. Viral vaccines are still the most effective way of preventing viral diseases. Immune globulins can also be used as prophylaxis for some viral diseases. Viral vaccines available for humans are outlined in Table 31-6.

18. Bacterial viruses exhibit primarily icosahedral symmetry. The head protein is frequently attached to a tail that also includes a base plate, spikes, and tail fibers.

19. Phage infection can be lytic or the virus may enter into a state of lysogeny. Infection by T series phage is initiated by the binding of tail fibers to the cell wall of the bacterium.

20. Maturation of lytic viruses is similar to that of animal viruses. Virus is released from the cell by the action of lysozyme on the cell wall. Viral infection on a lawn of bacteria is observed as cleared areas called plaques.

21. Lysogeny is a property of temperate phages and resembles latency in animal virus infection. Temperate viruses can change the phenotype of bacterial cells and thus have the potential to influence the infectious disease process in humans.

Questions for Study

1. What are the similarities between animal virus and bacterial virus infection? Differences?
2. What is the difference between a plaque and a pock? A plaque and a focus of infection?
3. What are the advantages to the virus of possessing a lipid envelope? What are the components of the lipid envelope? What is their function and from what are they derived?
4. Describe some of the functions of the early phage proteins.
5. Give some examples of horizontal and vertical viral disease transmission.
6. Describe the ways in which animal virus can penetrate mammalian cells.
7. What is so unusual about the replication cycle of retroviruses?

8. Describe the replication mechanism of a double-stranded RNA virus, a plus-stranded RNA virus, and a minus-stranded RNA virus.
9. List some animal virus cytopathic effects that can be used in identifying viruses.
10. What are the characteristics that distinguish latent, chronic, and slow viral infections? Are there any bacterial infections that might be placed in one of these categories?
11. Describe in some detail the mechanisms by which a virus can establish a persistent infection.
12. What is meant by the viral transformation of a mammalian cell? What changes occur in the mammalian cell following the transformation process?
13. Describe the association between human papillomaviruses and cervical cancer.
14. What is meant by the term provirus? What effect, if any, do proviruses have on the cells they infect?
15. What is the relationship between an oncogene and a proto-oncogene?
16. Describe in some detail how insertional mutagenesis leads to proto-oncogene activation and the development of the neoplastic process.
17. Do any of your chromosomes possess retroviral sequences? If they do, what is the significance of this trait?
18. What are HeLa cells? How were they first discovered?
19. What would be the ideal way to identify a viral agent in clinical material? The most practical? What is the most widely used?
20. Why can't the same drugs used in treating bacterial disease be used for viral infections? Why are so many antiviral drugs toxic to the host? How can this be prevented or at least lessened?
21. What is meant by lysogenic conversion? Does it have any effect on the infectious disease process in humans? Explain.

CHAPTER 32

Viral Diseases

OBJECTIVES

To group the viruses according to the specific tissue or organ they affect

To outline the various types of herpesviruses and describe the types of infections they cause and what group of individuals are most likely to be affected by infection

To outline the viruses that are likely to have devastating effects on the fetus or neonate and how such infections may be recognized and prevented

To describe briefly some of the complications associated with the specific vaccines that are routinely administered in the United States

To list the primary serological tests that are currently used in the laboratory diagnosis of viral disease

To describe some of the rare sequelae of infection by certain viruses

To understand the concepts of antigenic shift and antigenic drift as they apply to the influenza viruses

To differentiate between the viral agents causing sporadic and epidemic encephalitis

To differentiate among hepatitis B, hepatitis A, hepatitis C, hepatitis D, and hepatitis E as to method of transmission, pathogenesis, laboratory diagnosis, treatment, and prevention

To describe what is meant by slow virus infections and the role of prions

To describe in detail the epidemiology, pathogenesis, laboratory diagnosis, treatment, and prevention of human immunodeficiency virus infection

OUTLINE

DNA VIRUSES AND ASSOCIATED DISEASES
- Poxviruses
  - Epidemiology and Pathogenesis
  - Vaccine
- Herpesviruses
  - Cytomegalovirus
    - Pathogenesis
      - Infection in the Newborn
      - Infection in Renal Transplant and Other Immunosuppressed Patients
    - Epidemiology
    - Laboratory Diagnosis
    - Treatment and Prevention
  - Varicella-Zoster Virus (Chickenpox and Shingles)
    - Pathogenesis
      - Varicella
      - Zoster
    - Epidemiology
    - Laboratory Diagnosis
    - Immunity
    - Treatment and Prevention
  - Herpes Simplex Viruses
    - Pathogenesis
      - Type 1 Infections
      - Type 2 Infections
      - Other Manifestations
    - Epidemiology
    - Laboratory Diagnosis
    - Treatment and Prevention
  - Epstein-Barr Virus
  - Human Herpesvirus-6
- The Adenoviruses
  - Pathogenesis
  - Epidemiology
  - Laboratory Diagnosis
  - Treatment and Prevention
- The Papillomaviruses
- The Parvoviruses
  - Parvovirus B19

OUTLINE (*continued*)

RNA VIRUSES AND ASSOCIATED DISEASES
- Measles Virus
  - Pathogenesis
  - Epidemiology
  - Laboratory Diagnosis
  - Immunity
  - Treatment and Prevention
- Mumps Virus
  - Pathogenesis
  - Epidemiology
  - Laboratory Diagnosis
  - Treatment and Prevention
- Rubella Virus
  - Pathogenesis
    - Postnatal Rubella Infection
    - Congenital Rubella Syndrome
  - Epidemiology
  - Laboratory Diagnosis
  - Immunity
  - Treatment and Prevention
- Influenza Viruses
  - Classification
  - Pathogenesis
  - Epidemiology
  - Laboratory Diagnosis
  - Immunity
  - Treatment and Prevention
- Poliovirus (Poliomyelitis)
  - Pathogenesis
  - Epidemiology
  - Laboratory Diagnosis
  - Treatment and Prevention
- Other Enteroviruses
  - Pathogenesis
  - Epidemiology
  - Laboratory Diagnosis
  - Treatment
- Rhinoviruses
- Respiratory Syncytial Virus
- Parainfluenza Viruses
- Rabies Virus
  - Pathogenesis
  - Epidemiology
  - Laboratory Diagnosis
  - Immunity
  - Treatment and Prevention
- Hemorrhagic Fever Viruses
  - Lassa Fever
  - Ebola Hemorrhagic Fever
  - Marburg Hemorrhagic Fever
  - Crimean-Congo Hemorrhagic Fever
  - Hemorrhagic Fever with Renal Syndrome
- The Arboviruses
  - Viral Encephalitis
    - Pathogenesis
    - Diagnosis and Treatment
  - Yellow Fever
    - Pathogenesis
    - Epidemiology
    - Laboratory Diagnosis
    - Treatment and Prevention
  - Dengue Fever and Dengue Hemorrhagic Fever
    - Pathogenesis
    - Epidemiology
    - Laboratory Diagnosis
    - Treatment and Prevention
- Rotaviruses and Other Agents of Gastrointestinal Disease
  - Rotaviruses
    - Pathogenesis
    - Epidemiology
    - Laboratory Diagnosis
    - Treatment and Prevention
  - Other Agents of Gastrointestinal Disease
    - Caliciviruses
    - Astroviruses
- Human Immunodeficiency Virus and Acquired Immunodeficiency Syndrome
  - Pathogenesis
    - Primary or Acute Stage
    - Chronic or Asymptomatic Stage
    - Crisis Stage or AIDS
    - Pediatric AIDS
      - Transmission
      - Clinical Features
  - Epidemiology
  - Laboratory Diagnosis
  - Treatment
  - Prevention
- The Hepatitis Viruses
  - General Characteristics
    - Hepatitis A Virus
    - Hepatitis B Virus
    - Hepatitis C and E Viruses
  - Pathogenesis
  - Epidemiology
    - Hepatitis A
    - Hepatitis B
    - Hepatitis C
    - Hepatitis D
    - Hepatitis E
  - Laboratory Diagnosis
    - Hepatitis A
    - Hepatitis B
    - Hepatitis C
    - Hepatitis D
    - Hepatitis E
  - Immunity
    - Hepatitis A
    - Hepatitis B
    - Hepatitis C and E
  - Treatment and Prevention
    - Hepatitis A
    - Hepatitis B
    - Hepatitis C, D, and E
- Slow Virus Infections
  - Kuru and Creutzfeldt-Jakob Disease
  - Subacute Sclerosing Panencephalitis
  - Progressive Multifocal Leukoencephalopathy

DNA Viruses and Associated Diseases

POXVIRUSES

The poxviruses belong to the family Poxviridae and are divided into subgenera that cause various diseases. The most important genus is called *Orthopoxvirus,* which contains species called **variola virus, monkeypox virus, vaccinia virus,** and **cowpox virus.** Variola virus is the cause of human **smallpox,** a disease that was declared eradicated in 1977. Monkeypox, found only in African and Asian monkeys, is poorly transmitted from person to person.

Vaccinia virus is a laboratory product that was used to vaccinate humans against smallpox. Cowpox, which is found only in Britain and western Europe, is a rare disease. The agent of cowpox is isolated from cattle and farm workers who are in close association with cattle. The cowpox virus is pathogenic for a wide range of animals, such as camels, cats, gerbils, rats, and raccoons.

The poxviruses are the largest of the animal viruses. They range in length from 250 to 300 nm and in width from 200 to 250 nm and are in the shape of a brick (Fig. 32-1). Poxviruses are double-stranded DNA viruses that are assembled in the cytoplasm of the infected cell.

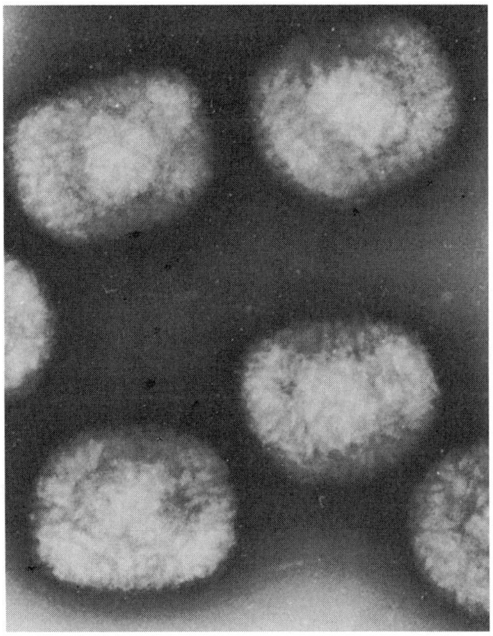

FIGURE 32-1
Electron micrograph of smallpox (vaccinia) virus. (Courtesy of R. C. Williams, Virus Laboratory, University of California, Berkeley, CA.)

Epidemiology and Pathogenesis

Since smallpox is an eradicated disease, clinical descriptions are not provided in any detail here. The student should refer to the readings cited at the end of the chapter to learn more about the disease. To appreciate the significance of the global vaccine procedures that led to eradication of the disease, one should be aware of the virulence of smallpox. Smallpox declined in Europe and North America after the introduction of vaccination in 1796 by Edward Jenner (see Chapter 1). Still in the epidemic years 1930 and 1931, 49,000 cases of smallpox and 173 deaths were recorded in the United States. Fatality rates in developing countries ranged from 15 to 45 percent. In areas endemic for smallpox, such as India, more than 1 million cases and 230,859 deaths were recorded in 1944.

Smallpox is transmitted by inhalation of virus released from lesions in the oropharynx of the infected patient. The incubation period is 10 to 14 days. The virus spreads rapidly from the oropharynx into the bloodstream, finally lodging in various organs and the skin. Virus lodged in the skin produces a rash about the fourth day of infection. The rash becomes pustular (Fig. 32-2) and is more profuse about the face. Those who survive infection are scarred for life.

A poxvirus of mammals—namely, monkeypox—has been associated with disease. Monkeys in Africa and Asia are known to harbor the monkeypox virus and this virus can be transmitted to humans. There is evidence that a person infected with monkeypox virus can transmit the virus to other humans. Human monkeypox, however, is still a rare zoonosis.

The only vestiges of the smallpox virus are currently being held in laboratories in Atlanta and Moscow. The World Health Organization has proposed, since the molecular structure of the virus is known, destruction of the virus. Debate about what to do with the virus continues.

Vaccine

The virus used in vaccines is called the vaccinia virus. Vaccination occasionally causes serious complications, es-

FIGURE 32-2
Smallpox pustules on the sixth day of the rash. (Courtesy of S. O. Foster.)

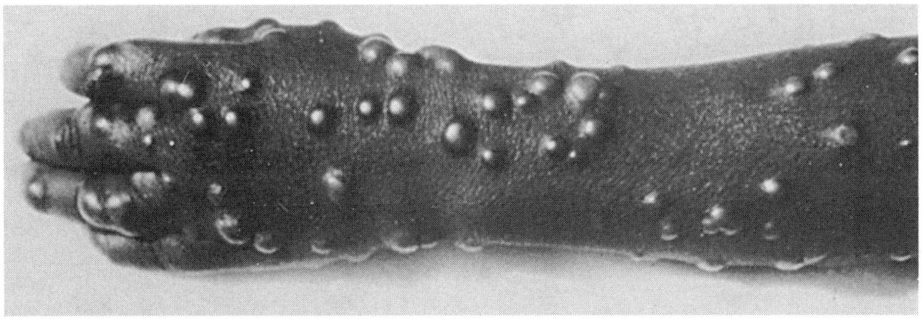

pecially in those with immunological deficiencies. Vaccination is no longer used in the general population but is still recommended for laboratory workers who directly handle cultures or animals contaminated or infected with vaccinia, recombinant vaccinia viruses, or other orthopoxviruses that infect humans (monkeypox, cowpox).

Recombinant vaccinia viruses are being used to carry and express genes coding for other immunizing antigens. Recombinant vaccinia viruses have been created to express the immunizing antigens of herpes, hepatitis B (HBV), rabies, influenza, and human immunodeficiency (HIV) viruses. There are problems, however, that must be addressed. For example, laboratory-acquired infections with vaccinia or recombinant viruses have been reported. This type of infection could be particularly devastating in people with eczema or immunodeficiency.

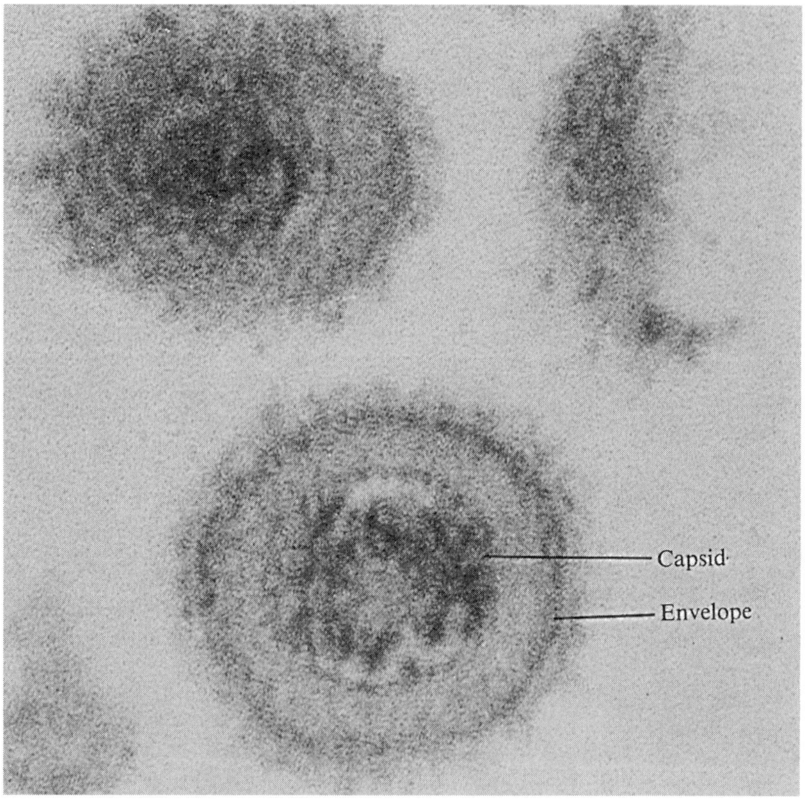

A

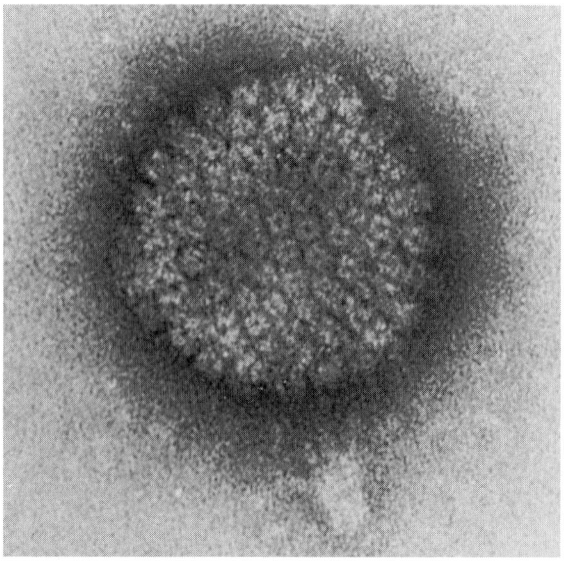

B

FIGURE 32-3
Electron micrographs of herpesvirus. A. Intact herpesvirus particles showing envelope surrounding the capsid. (Courtesy of B. Roizman.) B. Electron micrograph of the herpesvirus capsid. Note the arrangement of the capsomeres. (From R. C. Williams and H. W. Fisher, *An Electron Micrograph Atlas of Viruses*, 1974. Courtesy Charles C Thomas, Publisher, Springfield, IL.)

HERPESVIRUSES

The herpesviruses belong to the family Herpesviridae. They have cubic symmetry, are enveloped (Fig. 32-3), and contain double-stranded DNA. Viral multiplication and assembly take place in the nucleus of the infected cell. The lipid envelope is acquired as the nucleocapsid buds through the nuclear membrane. The important members of this group of viruses are the **cytomegalovirus (CMV), varicella-zoster virus (VZV), Epstein-Barr virus (EBV), herpes simplex viruses (HSV),** and **human herpesvirus-6 (HHV-6).** All herpesviruses are characterized by their ability to cause latent infections in their hosts and are therefore associated with recurrent infections. In their latent state herpesviruses cannot be recovered as infectious particles.

Cytomegalovirus

Pathogenesis. The groups most susceptible to infection by CMV are infants, renal transplant patients, and those compromised by immunosuppressive drugs or conditions, for example, patients with acquired immunodeficiency syndrome (AIDS).

Infection in the Newborn. Congenital CMV disease is the most common serious viral infection among newborn infants in the United States. Pregnant women may acquire CMV by primary infection or by reactivation of a latent infection. Primary infection in the mother results in viremia, and the virus can pass through the placenta and infect the fetus. Nearly every organ of the fetus becomes infected with virus. Unlike rubella virus infection, which has its worst effects during the first trimester, congenital CMV infection has more deleterious effects on the fetus during the second trimester. Symptomatic CMV infection in the newborn is thought to result primarily from a primary maternal infection and not from reinfection or reactivation of a prior infection.

It is estimated that approximately 1 percent of all infants (30,000–35,000 annually in the United States) are born congenitally infected with CMV. Approximately 90 percent of these have subclinical disease that will remain chronic. From 5 to 10 percent of congenitally infected infants manifest symptoms. The symptoms may include retardation of intrauterine growth, hepatosplenomegaly, jaundice, and neurological manifestations including deafness and chorioretinitis. A frequent result of symptomatic infection is permanent mental retardation. Childhood retardation from congenital CMV infection is estimated at 2.5 to 10 per 1000 live births (see Under the Microscope 30).

The most common source of perinatal or postnatal infection is reactivation of latent infections in the mother. Virus may be excreted by the mother from the cervix, in breast milk, and in the urine and throat secretions. The infant becomes infected during passage through the cervix or acquires the virus from the mother's mouth or breast milk. These infections are mild and are marked by respiratory disturbance and some liver malfunction. They are less severe than congenital infections because infants are born with variable levels of maternal antibody. Approximately 2 to 3 percent of all infants are infected perinatally with CMV.

Infection in Renal Transplant and Other Immunosuppressed Patients. CMV infection is common in transplant patients and others receiving immunosuppressive therapy. More than 90 percent of renal transplant recipients become in-

UNDER THE MICROSCOPE 30

Congenital Cytomegalovirus Disease: A Major Health Problem

Congenital cytomegalovirus (CMV) disease has become so serious that in 1990 a registry was initiated by the Centers for Disease Control. The registry was designed for the surveillance of infants with severe symptoms of congenital CMV. Data are being collected on maternal as well as infant clinical characteristics. It is hoped that the information collected will afford a clearer insight into how to identify those at greatest risk of infection and its complications.

Many questions about congenital CMV remain unanswered. Mothers who have never been infected by CMV are at greatest risk of having an infant with congenital CMV disease. For example, mothers with recurrent CMV infections are less likely to give birth to infants with symptomatic disease. It is unclear why 50 percent or fewer mothers with a primary maternal infection pass infection to their fetuses or why symptomatic disease develops in only 10 percent of those infected. It is also unknown how close to conception primary maternal infection must occur to pose an increased risk to the fetus.

Pregnancy termination is one option for women who have primary CMV infection during gestation. The overall risk of delivering an infant with symptomatic congenital infection is about 5 percent.

There is hope that a vaccine may be developed for women of childbearing age. A live attenuated vaccine has been tested in renal transplant patients but has not been tested in women of childbearing age.

fected. The donated kidney is the major source of CMV transmission to seronegative recipients. In contrast, seropositive recipients are believed to undergo reactivation of endogenous CMV or to be infected by exogenous virus from the kidney of the seropositive donor. The requirement for multiple blood transfusions also increases the potential for exposure to CMV. Virus apparently remains in a latent state in donor blood cells.

Factors that determine the degree of symptoms from CMV infection depend on the source of viral infection, intensity of immunosuppressive therapy, and degree of host-graft incompatibility.

A variety of clinical symptoms may be present following CMV infection. Severe pulmonary and hepatic dysfunction is a frequent complication of CMV infection in renal transplant patients. CMV appears to play an important role in AIDS patients (see Under the Microscope 31). In patients receiving massive transfusions, a mononucleosis- or hepatitis-like syndrome may appear. Most CMV mononucleosis patients appear well but a few have irregular fever lasting up to three weeks, myalgia, and leukocytosis. Hepatitis is usually mild. CMV gastrointestinal complications (gastritis, colitis esophagitis, etc.) are frequently observed in heart-lung transplant recipients.

Epidemiology. Close contact is required for the spread of CMV. This contact includes congenital transfer, direct contact with donor organs, blood transfusions, and contact with the body fluids of someone who sheds virus (sexual contact, for example). By the age of 50 years 50 percent of the population in a developed country is seropositive for CMV. If a child is not congenitally or perinatally infected with CMV, he or she may become infected during the preschool years. Children are very likely to acquire CMV in day-care facilities. The infected child represents a risk to a pregnant woman and her fetus.

Intrafamilial transmission is common, particularly in families with young children. Transmission occurs between children and their parents, between siblings, and between parents. Sexual transmission of CMV is also possible. CMV is found more frequently in semen and cervical secretions than in urine. Sexual contact is an important mechanism of CMV transmission in sexually active teenagers and young women with multiple sex partners. In most immunocompetent children and adults who acquire infection, a subclinical form of the disease with few and mild symptoms develops.

Laboratory Diagnosis. Several techniques are available for the diagnosis of infection with CMV. Diagnosis of active infection still relies on viral isolation. Human fibroblasts are infected with washings from the throat or urine. Incubation of the infected culture can take five days to three weeks. Characteristically, infected cells contain a large **intranuclear inclusion,** referred to as "owl's eye" (Fig. 32-4).

An adaptation of cell culture is the **shell vial technique.** In this procedure specimens are inoculated by centrifugation in vials containing a coverslip seeded with fibroblasts. After overnight culture, the coverslip cells are stained by the indirect immunofluorescence technique with a monoclonal antibody to an early CMV antigen.

Another method for detecting viremia is the **antigenemia assay.** Centrifuged preparations of fresh leukocytes are made. The cells are stained with a mixture of monoclonal antibodies to reveal nuclear staining of polymor-

UNDER THE MICROSCOPE 31

Cytomegalovirus and AIDS

Active cytomegalovirus (CMV) infection has been found in 90 percent of AIDS patients. As many as 25 percent of these patients experience sight-threatening or life-threatening infections due to CMV. The statistics provide a frightening story:

1. Retinitis: CMV retinitis is diagnosed in 5 to 10 percent of AIDS patients. The disease is characterized by large white exudates with hemorrhages. Blindness can be the consequence of such infections.
2. Pneumonia: CMV has been documented in 17 to 19 percent of AIDS patients with pneumonitis. CMV was the primary pathogen in 4 percent of AIDS patients.
3. Gastrointestinal infections: CMV infection is associated with gastritis, colitis, esophagitis, and hepatitis.
4. Neurological infection: In about 50 percent of AIDS patients, encephalopathy will develop during the terminal phases of the disease. CMV encephalitis has been implicated in 33 percent of these patients.

There is speculation that co-infection with human immunodeficiency virus (HIV) and CMV may result in more rapid progression of immunosuppression in HIV-infected patients. This is especially true in the case of neurological infections in which co-infection with both viruses was a common finding. The possibility is raised that immunosuppression by one virus enhances the immunosuppressive capabilities of the second virus. Some in vitro studies showed that an early CMV protein can activate HIV transcription.

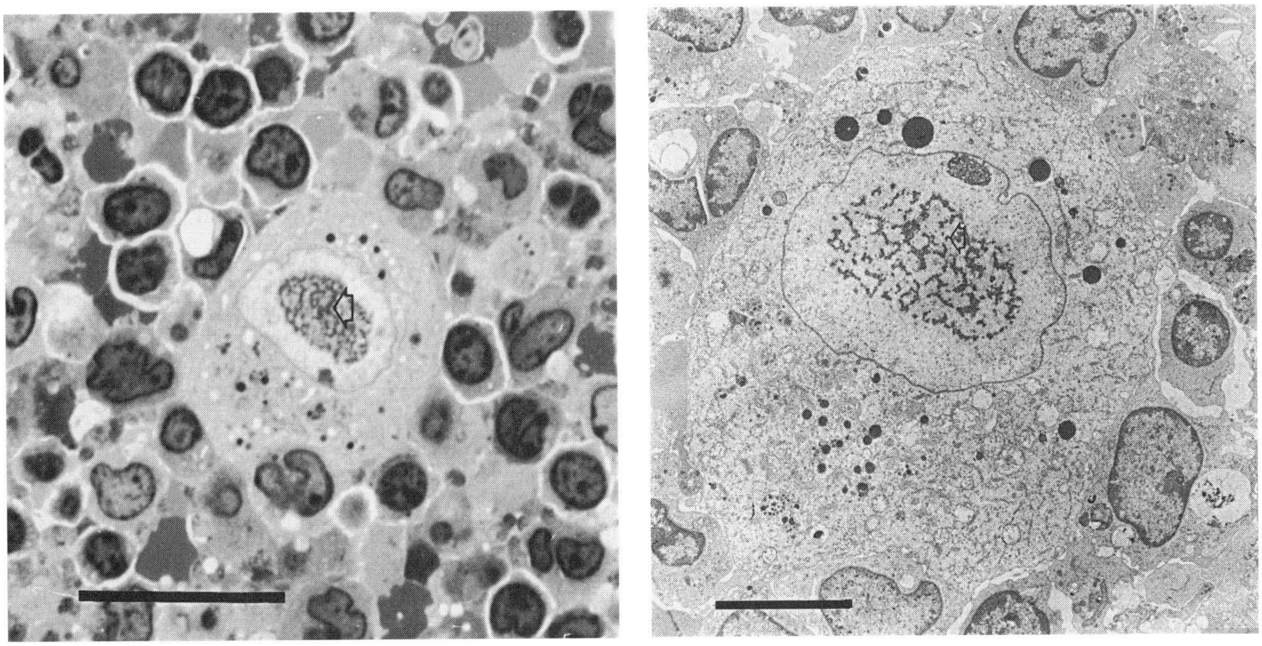

A B

FIGURE 32-4
Cytomegalic inclusion cell in a mononuclear leukocyte from a patient with cytomegalovirus infection. A. Light micrograph B. Electron micrograph. Inclusion (*arrow*) is visible in the nucleus and is surrounded by a translucent halo. (Bars = 20 and 6 μm, respectively.) From A. Grefte, N. Blom, M. van der Giessen, W. van Son, and T. H. The, *J. Infect. Dis.* 168:1110, 1993.)

phonuclear leukocytes and the presence of CMV antigen. The number of cells stained is a reflection of the intensity of viremia and hence the risk of serious disease.

Seroconversion, that is, development of CMV antibody in an individual whose serum was antibody-negative before or early in the course of infection, is usually an excellent marker for primary CMV infection. Probably the best serological assays are indirect hemagglutination and enzyme-linked immunofluorescence antibody assays. Both of these tests have supplanted complement fixation tests. None of the serological tests can be performed with any degree of rapidity.

Recently, a rapid technique for detecting CMV viremia was developed. A specimen of peripheral blood is treated with monoclonal antibody directed against early CMV antigen. The assay can be completed within hours.

Treatment and Prevention. The only promising drug for CMV disease is **ganciclovir,** an analogue of acyclovir. This drug is being evaluated for the treatment of congenital CMV disease as well as pneumonitis associated with organ transplantation. In bone marrow recipients ganciclovir can reduce the severity of CMV disease and terminate viral shedding. Problems with ganciclovir include (1) resumption of viral replication following discontinuation of therapy, (2) emergence of ganciclovir-resistant CMV strains, and (3) drug toxicity (neutropenia, thrombocytopenia).

A **CMV immune globulin** is now commercially available. CMV immune globulin has been administered with ganciclovir, with mixed results. Some studies showed a synergistic effect when the combination was used as therapy for active disease. The results in bone marrow patients revealed no effect.

Acyclovir is still used prophylactically in some transplant centers for bone marrow and kidney recipients. A recently licensed drug for CMV disease is **foscarnet.** In CMV retinitis the drug is as effective as ganciclovir. The issue of foscarnet toxicity, however, must be resolved before more comprehensive uses of this drug can be made.

Whenever possible, the blood or organs to be used in transfusion or transplantation procedures should be from CMV-seronegative donors. Reducing immunosuppressive therapy will also reduce the risk of serious disease.

Attenuated vaccines have been tested in transplant patients but they will not be available soon. There is considerable concern about latency characteristics and the oncogenic potential of the vaccine.

Varicella-Zoster Virus (Chickenpox and Shingles)

Chickenpox and shingles are different clinical manifestations of infection by the same virus. Chickenpox **(varicella)** is a common benign childhood disease. Shingles **(zoster)** is an uncommon disease of later life in which reactivation of the latent varicella infection has occurred.

Pathogenesis

Varicella. Varicella infection begins in the upper respiratory tract. The incubation period is between 15 and 18

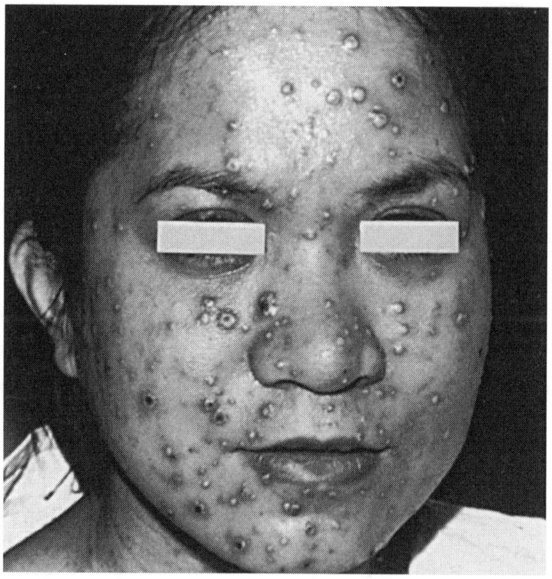

FIGURE 32-5
Chickenpox lesions at various stages of development. (Courtesy of Department of Pathology, University of Illinois Medical Center, Chicago, IL.)

days. Replication of the virus occurs in the respiratory tract and viremia follows. From the blood the virus is taken up by reticuloendothelial cells where it undergoes several replications. The host's immune system becomes overwhelmed and a second viremia develops. During the second viremia the first symptoms of chills and fever become evident.

The virus eventually lodges in capillary endothelial cells and then spreads to epithelial cells of the skin. A rash develops and is followed by vesicle formation (Fig. 32-5). Skin lesions are confined to the thoracic, lumbar, and facial areas. One week after their appearance the vesicles become crusted and fall off, with no visible scarring.

The infectious period of varicella begins one to two days before the appearance of the rash and lasts up to one week after lesions appear. During vesicle development, virus is transported to cranial nerves and dorsal root ganglion cells by movement along sensory nerve fibers.

Chickenpox is regarded as a benign self-limiting disease. The most common cause of morbidity in children is bacterial superinfection. Severe infections caused by either streptococci or staphylococci may occur and may be accompanied by gangrene and deep vein thrombosis. Varicella is more severe in normal adults, and pneumonia has been reported in as many as 16 percent of those infected. In children and adults who have immunodeficiency disease or who are being treated with immunosuppressive drugs, varicella can be life-threatening.

Varicella has the ability to cause congenital abnormalities if the mother is infected during the first trimester of pregnancy. Some of the effects of early fetal infection are low birth weight, bilateral cataracts, an atropic limb, and seizure activity. If the mother is infected during later stages of pregnancy, a rash develops in the infant but there are no congenital abnormalities.

Zoster. Zoster is attributed to the activation of latent varicella virus in posterior root or cranial sensory nerve ganglia. Its incidence and severity increase with age and it seldom occurs in the young. Immunosuppression appears to be the stimulus that consistently induces zoster. Once activated, the virus moves down the sensory nerves until it reaches the skin, where it replicates and produces localized lesions. The lesions are similar to those of chickenpox. Lesions are confined to the same areas as varicella (Plate 21). Before the appearance of the lesions, a generalized rash may arise accompanied by fever and intense pain over the involved nerve. In approximately three to five weeks the lesions heal and the pain subsides.

Postherpetic neuralgia (pain after the vesicles heal) frequently occurs in adults more than 60 years old. It is believed to be due to scarring in the ganglia and afferent portions of the sensory nerve. The symptoms may last as long as six months. Facial nerve paralysis is a common complication of zoster. It is not permanent and resolves two to three months after infection.

Zoster in immunosuppressed patients (AIDS patients, for example) often occurs early in the course of disease. There is severe primary infection with onset of pneumonia. The lesions are frequently disseminated and are of two types: (1) flat pustule lesions that ulcerate and last for months and (2) giant wart-like lesions. AIDS patients are also prone to encephalitis and associated dementia from varicella-zoster–related infection.

Epidemiology. Varicella is a very contagious disease found predominantly in children. The disease is believed to be transmitted by the airborne route. Humans are the only known reservoir of infection. Chickenpox affects approximately 3.5 million people annually in the United States although only about 145,000 cases are reported each year to the Centers for Disease Control.

Zoster is primarily an adult disease resulting from reactivation of virus in those who have had varicella. Herpes zoster is infectious but less so than varicella. Zoster has been known to give rise to varicella, particularly in nonimmune children who come in contact with zoster patients.

Laboratory Diagnosis. Most varicella-zoster infections can be diagnosed by characteristic clinical appearance. In the immunosuppressed and others, the eruptions can resemble those of other viral agents including herpes simplex. A presumptive but rapid test called the **Tzanck test** can be used to determine whether a herpesvirus is involved. In this test, cells at the base of fresh vesicles are smeared on a slide and stained with Giemsa or Wright preparations. Syncytial giant cells can be observed, indicating HSV or VZV.

Differentiation between HSV and VZV can be accomplished using immunofluorescent staining and recently, using monoclonal antibodies and immunoelectron microscopy. Differentiation is important for adequate antiviral therapy. Other rapid virus detection methods include enzyme-linked immunosorbent assay (ELISA) and the polymerase chain reaction (PCR).

Immunity. Natural infection or immunization results in the development of VZV-specific IgG and IgM antibodies in the serum. Antibody that is produced persists for many years, crosses the placenta, and is present before the onset of zoster. Development of serum and nasopharyngeal IgA antibodies occurs with natural infection. Cell-mediated immunity increases immediately after infection and persists for several years. A permanent immunity develops in the majority of varicella patients.

Treatment and Prevention. Treatment is not necessary for uncomplicated varicella or zoster other than relieving the itching of varicella or the pain of zoster. Vidarabine was the first antiviral agent to be used in the treatment of varicella-zoster in immunocompromised patients. This drug has been replaced by acyclovir. Recent studies showed that acyclovir administered to children within 24 hours of developing a rash resulted in fewer skin lesions, less itching, and accelerated healing. Acyclovir has been very effective in decreasing dissemination and other complications of varicella-zoster in immunocompromised patients. In otherwise healthy patients with zoster, acyclovir given intravenously decreases acute pain and accelerates lesion healing. In otherwise healthy adults with chickenpox pneumonia, intravenous acyclovir appears to hasten recovery.

Varicella-zoster immune globulins modify the severity of chickenpox but do not prevent infection. In immunocompromised children less than 15 years old (those who have not had chickenpox) immune globulins are administered as soon as possible after exposure to chickenpox. Immune globulins are expensive and in short supply.

An attenuated varicella-zoster vaccine using an **Oka** strain has been evaluated. The vaccine is useful for preventing chickenpox in high-risk and otherwise healthy individuals. These include patients immunocompromised by disease or therapy, healthy adults susceptible to chickenpox, and healthy children. In addition, the vaccine also prevents congenital varicella.

Herpes Simplex Viruses

HSV is the causal agent of several human infections including cold sores, fever, blisters, keratitis (inflammation of the cornea), and a venereal infection of both men and women. The virus can also be transmitted to the fetus, resulting in a generalized or severe infection. Recurrent HSV infections are common.

There are two serotypes of HSV: type 1 **(HSV-1)**, which is associated primarily with lesions in the oral cavity and facial areas, and type 2 **(HSV-2)**, which is found primarily in the genital area. HSV of either type can cause infection at any site if inoculated at the proper place. A virus called **B virus** is the simian counterpart of HSV (see Under the Microscope 32).

Pathogenesis. HSV infections may be primary (an acute infection that runs its natural course) or recurrent. The cause of recurrent infections is believed to be reactivation of endogenous latent virus. After initial infection at a body site and several rounds of replication, the virus ascends in nerve axons to sensory ganglia. The virus may replicate and cause neuronal damage or the virus may become latent with viral DNA present in the ganglia. After reactivation, virus travels along the axon of peripheral nerves to cause localized infection in the innervated skin. The diversity of clinical illness caused by primary HSV infections is outlined in the following paragraphs.

UNDER THE MICROSCOPE 32

B Viruses: A Simian Counterpart to Herpes Simplex Virus

Only B virus *(Herpesvirus simiae)* of all the nonhuman primate herpesviruses has been shown to cause disease in humans. The pathogenesis, immunology, and epidemiology of B virus in macaques resemble those of herpes simplex viruses in humans. The existence of this agent was first described in 1932. Encephalitis had developed in a monkey handler who had been bitten by the animal. In 1952 the agent of disease was recovered from macaques with a natural infection. Since 1932, 25 well documented cases of human infection have been recorded. Twenty-two patients progressed to various degrees of encephalomyelitis, leading eventually to 16 deaths. Some of the survivors were left with severe neurological impairment and some required institutionalization.

Most cases of B virus infection appear to be the result of direct inoculation with tissue or fluid from a monkey (monkey bites or scratches, for example). Five cases of infection were due to cleaning of a rhesus skull without protective gloves. There is also documentation of person-to-person transfer.

B virus replicates in the skin and is propagated within the peripheral nervous system. Eventually the virus invades the spinal cord and brain. The incubation period from exposure to symptomatic disease varies from less than 2 days to more than 10 years. B virus infections are now treatable with intravenous acyclovir.

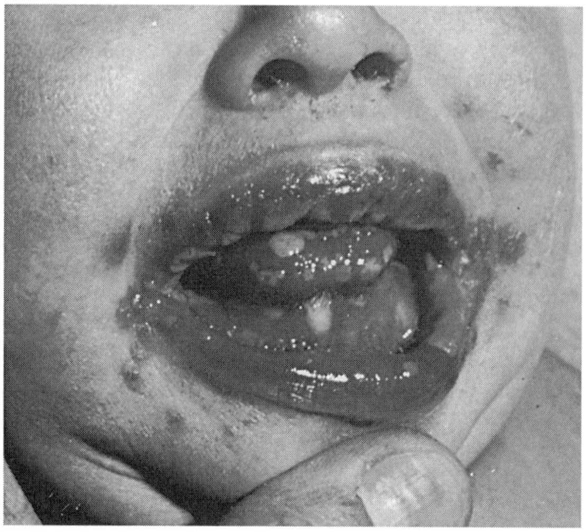

FIGURE 32-6
Gingivostomatitis caused by herpesvirus infection. (From J. C. Overall, Jr. In G. J. Galasso, T. C. Merigan, and R. C. Buchanan, eds., *Antiviral Agents and Viral Diseases in Man*. New York: Raven, 1979.)

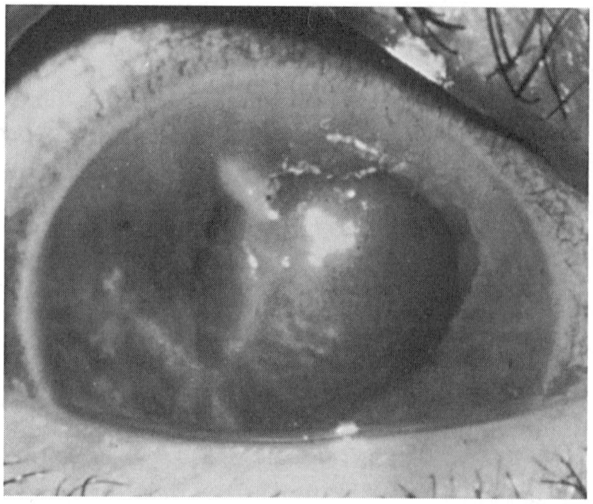

FIGURE 32-7
Herpetic keratoconjunctivitis. Dendritic ulcer stained with fluorescein in the cornea of a patient with recurrent disease. (Courtesy of J. Sugar.)

Type 1 Infections. Type 1 infections include the following:

1. **Acute herpetic gingivostomatitis** is a common HSV-1 infection characterized by ulcerative lesions on the mucous membranes of the oral cavity. The disease may be accompanied by fever and cervical lymphadenopathy. The disease is self-limiting and is resolved in two to three weeks (Fig. 32-6).
2. **Eczema herpeticum** results from accidental inoculation of the virus into the skin lesions associated with eczema. Recurrent attacks are less severe than the initial attack.
3. **Herpetic keratoconjunctivitis** is believed to be the leading cause of loss of vision produced by external eye disease in the United States. Recurrent infections are common and often lead to opacity of the cornea and eventually to impaired vision (Fig. 32-7).
4. **Herpes labialis** is the most prevalent form of HSV-1 infection. Infections involve the mucocutaneous junction of the lips (fever blisters and cold sores) (Fig. 32-8). Recurrent infections are common and are probably due to activation of latent virus by stress, sunlight, hormones, or menstruation. Dental extraction appears also to trigger reactivation of latent HSV. In these instances nerves are traumatized by local anesthetic injection or surgical procedures.
5. **Herpetic encephalitis** acquired after birth is believed to be the most common form of fatal endemic encephalitis in the United States. The virus may enter the host through the nasal cavity and then travel from the olfactory pathway to the base of the brain. Brain infection may also be the result of reactivation of latent virus in the trigeminal ganglion, followed by spread to the brain. Many patients die within three weeks after onset of symptoms. Both HSV-1 and HSV-2 are frequently associated with encephalitis. HSV-2–associated encephalitis in children presents with a higher frequency of brain damage and seizures than does HSV-1–associated infections. This finding is the reverse of that seen in adults with HSV encephalitis.

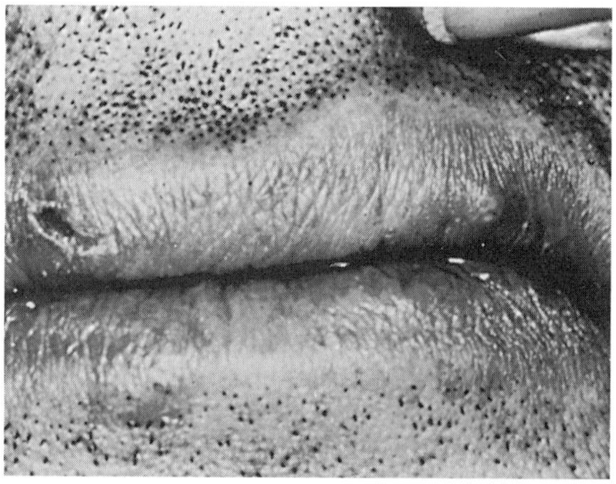

FIGURE 32-8
Cutaneous lesions on lips and skin around the mouth of an individual with recurrent herpes labialis. (Courtesy of L. J. LeBeau.)

Type 2 Infections. HSV-2 infections include primarily genital herpes and neonatal herpes.

1. Primary **genital herpes** infections occur most frequently in adolescents and young adults. Infection in children is often the result of sexual abuse. Most genital herpes is subclinical and often goes unrecognized. Persons with asymptomatic or subclinical infection are the major transmitters of genital herpes to others. In some cases, however, infection can be a serious disease causing severe tissue inflammation. Lesions appear on the vagina, cervix, or vulva. In men the lesions appear primarily on the penis. They

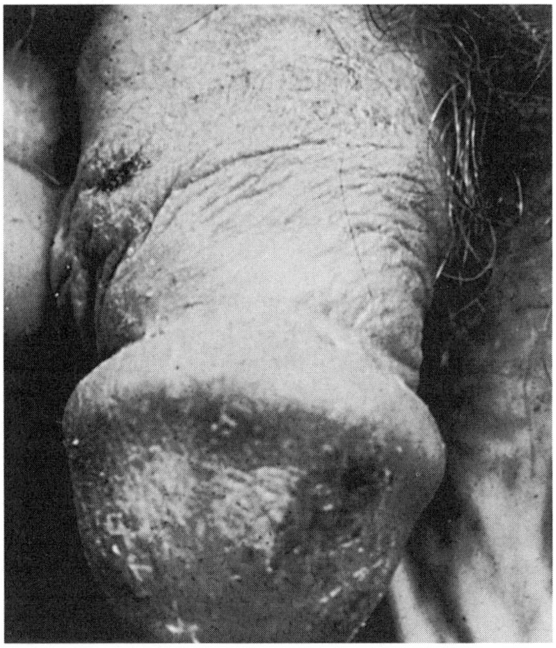

FIGURE 32-9
Genital lesions caused by herpes simplex virus infection. (Courtesy of L. Solomon, Department of Dermatology, University of Illinois Medical Center, Chicago, IL.)

are painful and are associated with a watery discharge (Fig. 32-9).

Previous infection with HSV-1 not only alleviates the clinical course of first-episode genital herpes but also reduces susceptibility to HSV-2.

2. Mothers with genital herpes are the primary source of **neonatal herpes** infections. Adverse outcomes for the neonate are greater when pregnancies are complicated by a first rather than a recurrent episode of genital herpes. Neonatal herpes infection may result in three types of disease: (1) disseminated; (2) central nervous system (i.e., encephalitis); or (3) skin, eye, and mouth infections. Disseminated infections may involve several organs. The mortality from disseminated disease is 80 percent.

   Fewer than 10 percent of the survivors of disseminated or central nervous system disease develop normally. The mortality from central nervous system disease is more than 50 percent. Babies with skin, eye, or mouth infections do not usually die. In about 25 percent of them, however, neurological impairment develops later. In addition about 75 percent of them, if left untreated, will progress to either central nervous system or disseminated disease.

Other Manifestations. Lesions on the fingers or hands of physicians, dentists, and medical personnel have been called **herpetic whitlows.** They can be caused by contact with HSV skin lesions and type 1 or 2 may be involved. Since type 2 is associated with genital herpes, it is suspected that finger contact with genital lesions is one means of transmission to any part of the body, including the eyes. The lesion is characterized as a vesicle with a rim of edema and imparts a stinging sensation to the patient. The lesions begin to heal after three weeks.

Epidemiology. HSV-1 is primarily associated with oral disease and HSV-2 with genital disease but either strain may be involved with genital or oral disease. For example, pharyngitis due to type 2 has been observed in patients who engaged in oral sex. Because genital herpes simplex is a lifelong infection, once patients are infected they are potentially infectious to their sexual partner, one of the major reasons being that they are intermittent asymptomatic shedders.

The prevalence of genital HSV infection in women during pregnancy and at term, when transmission to the neonate occurs, has not been clearly defined. Most studies indicate that approximately 30 percent of the mothers of neonates have a history of genital herpes. It is estimated that upwards of 30 million people in the United States suffer from genital herpes. Condom use could significantly reduce transmission of disease.

Laboratory Diagnosis. The typical herpetic lesion, especially in patients with recurrent infections, can be identified by the physician through patient history and physical examination. This is not true for the lesion in patients with primary infection, which may resemble lesions caused by a variety of other microbial agents. The diagnosis of HSV infection can be confirmed by serological diagnosis, but only for primary infection in the patient who has not been previously infected with HSV-1 or HSV-2.

Tissue culture remains the most sensitive method to detect HSV and this is confirmed by observation of cytopathic effects. This technique requires three days to complete. The importance of early recognition cannot be overemphasized. Rapid identification permits more rapid treatment. In addition, rapid detection of HSV shedding in immunocompromised patients can be important for monitoring the effectiveness of prophylaxis and for identifying the development of acyclovir resistance. Several tests are available for detecting directly HSV antigen in clinical specimens or if need be, in culture fluid as a means of culture confirmation. ELISA and direct and indirect fluorescent antibody assays have been the most widely used for detecting antigen.

In recent years, serological techniques based on antibody reactivity to HSV-specific proteins have been useful for assessing the seroprevalence of HSV-1 and HSV-2. Two assays that have been used with some success are either glycoprotein G (gG)–specific immunoassays or Western blot (immunoblot) assays. Commercial enzyme immunoassays can give inaccurate or misleading results regarding virus type.

Differentiation of HSV-1 from HSV-2 is important if the proper treatment regimen is to be instituted. Differentiation can be performed by nucleic acid hybridization techniques or by immunofluorescence.

Treatment and Prevention. The drugs currently used in the treatment of HSV infections are as follows (see also Table 31-4):

1. **Acyclovir** has become the most important anti-HSV drug and in some cases has supplanted vidarabine. If resistance to acyclovir is a problem, vidarabine or foscarnet can be used as an alternative.
2. **Vidarabine** is used intravenously for herpes encephalitis and neonatal herpes.
3. **Trifluridine** and **idoxuridine** are used as an ophthalmic solution in the treatment of herpes keratitis.

One of the major concerns today is how to prevent neonatal herpes. Diagnosis of the expectant mother was previously performed by examining genital cultures for HSV during the third trimester. The results of such a test would determine whether a vaginal delivery or cesarean section should be performed. Problems with testing, however, brought about abandonment of such analysis. It is currently recommended that vaginal delivery be allowed in the absence of signs or symptoms of genital herpetic infection at delivery.

A subunit glycoprotein vaccine is being evaluated in clinical trials.

Epstein-Barr Virus

The EBV was initially discovered in a Burkitt's lymphoma cell line in 1964 (see Chapter 31). Infection by EBV is usually established early in childhood in most parts of the world and remains silent throughout a person's life. EBV is associated with several clinical entities. Its association with Burkitt's lymphoma and nasopharyngeal cancer was discussed previously (see Chapter 31). We discuss here three other EBV associations: **infectious mononucleosis, chronic mononucleosis syndrome,** and **EBV-induced disorders in immunodeficient patients.**

Infectious mononucleosis develops in about two-thirds of uninfected adolescents and young adults who are exposed to EBV. Symptoms of infection appear about 5 to 10 days after contact with the virus. The disease is characterized by a sore throat, fever, fatigue, enlarged cervical lymph nodes, and often splenomegaly. The major route of transmission of virus is through the saliva and very rarely by blood transfusion.

In the United States about 15 to 20 percent of young adults are shedders of virus. Infected individuals who are immunosuppressed (organ transplant patients, AIDS patients, etc.) are common shedders of virus. EBV inhabits B lymphocytes, where it can remain indefinitely in a latent state. Most adults with EBV-infected B lymphocytes do not demonstrate reactivation disease. Immunosuppression of individuals who have recovered from infectious mononucleosis, however, activates virus.

Infectious mononucleosis customarily resolves on its own within one month after infection but occasionally long-lasting fatigue persists. Complications of disease may include hemolytic anemia, aplastic anemia, and agranulocytosis.

Chronic mononucleosis syndrome is a protracted illness. It is usually preceded by infectious mononucleosis and may last from months to years. The symptoms of disease include (1) either intermittent or persistent fever, (2) lymphadenopathy or hepatosplenomegaly, (3) a tendency for pancytopenia and polyclonal gammopathy, and (4) no apparent manifestation of underlying disease. Rarely, life-threatening complications develop over the course of the disease in some young children and adults. The precise mechanism by which EBV causes the syndrome is not known. There is no available treatment.

EBV-induced disorders in immunodeficient patients are the result of abnormal proliferation of lymphocytes. AIDS patients, organ transplant recipients, and others with genetically acquired immunodeficiency disorders may be subject to life-threatening EBV infections. In AIDS patients EBV-associated disorders include (1) oral hairy leukoplakia, (2) malignant lymphoma, (3) lymphadenopathy, and (4) lymphoid interstitial pneumonitis. Oral hairy leukoplakia can be treated with acyclovir, ganciclovir, or retinoic acid.

Infectious mononucleosis may be presumptively diagnosed on the basis of clinical symptoms plus the finding of elevated lymphocyte levels. The **Paul-Bunnell-Davidson test** detects IgM heterophile (nonspecific) antibodies that agglutinate sheep and horse red blood cells. When patients with infectious mononucleosis are heterophile antibody–negative or when heterophile antibody–positive patients present with atypical manifestations, serodiagnostic tests are required for diagnosis. The interpretation of serological tests is based on the profile of antibody against viral antigens such as capsid, early, and nuclear antigens. Immunofluorescence and ELISA are two serological methods used to detect these antigens.

The diagnosis of lymphoproliferative disorders or malignant lymphoma depends on histological evaluation of tissue biopsy specimens, but distinguishing between benign and malignant disorders is difficult. Nucleic acid hybridization techniques can be used to detect **EBV nuclear antigen,** which is found only in tissues from patients with active EBV infection having neoplastic or other lymphoproliferative disorders (lymphoma or lymphoproliferative lesions).

Human Herpesvirus-6

In 1986 a new herpesvirus was found in the leukocytes of patients with AIDS-associated lymphoma and leukemia. The virus was designated **human lymphotropic virus** or **human herpesvirus-6** (HHV-6).*

HHV-6 appears to be distinct from HSV, CMV, VZV, and EBV. T cells (CD4 lymphocytes) appear to be the primary target of infection. CD4 lymphocytes are also the target of HIV.

HHV-6 is believed to be acquired early in life and to establish a latent infection. It has been linked to an exanthem (eruption) called **roseola infantum.** HHV-6 has also been associated with chronic fatigue syndrome. Some studies showed that 90 percent of patients with chronic fatigue syndrome were seropositive against the antigen for HHV-6.

---

* HHV-7, isolated in 1990, is similar to HHV-6 in structure and epidemiology. The clinical signs and sequelae of primary HHV-7 infection, however, are unknown.

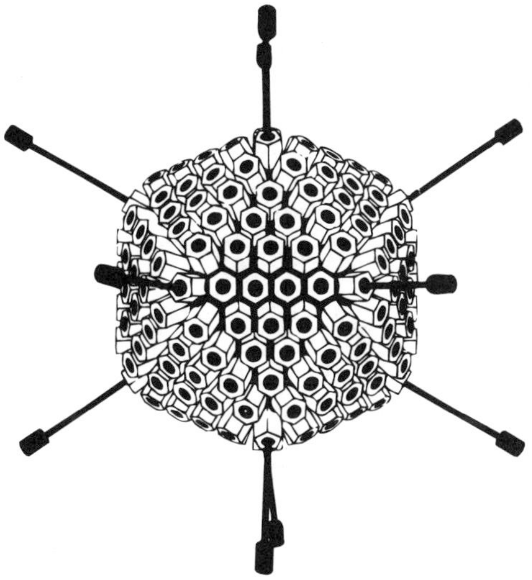

FIGURE 32-10
Model of adenovirus showing capsomeres' arrangement as well as placement of the 12 pentons (only 10 are shown in this figure). Each penton consists of a penton-capsomere, a fiber, and a terminal knob. (From R. W. Horne, I. P. Ronchetti, and J. M. Hobart, *J. Ultrastruct. Res.* 51:233, 1975.)

THE ADENOVIRUSES

The adenoviruses belong to the family Adenoviridae. They can be found in many animal species including humans. Over 40 immunologically distinct adenoviruses of human origin are recognized. The virion is made up of 240 nonvertex hollow capsomeres called **hexons** in an icosahedral pattern of cubic symmetry (Fig. 32-10). In addition there are 12 vertex capsomeres called **pentons.** Each penton has a fiber attached to it and some viruses have a knob attached to the end of the fiber. The complete virion gives the appearance of a laboratory-constructed earth satellite. The penton fibers and terminal knobs can be seen on electron micrographs. The fibers are antigenic and are believed to serve as organs of attachment. Except adenovirus type 18, the fibers are responsible for hemagglutinating activity.

Pathogenesis

Adenoviruses have an affinity for mucocutaneous surfaces and are usually associated with respiratory illness, particularly in infants. Gastrointestinal disease is not an uncommon response to adenovirus infection. Adenoviruses are associated with a variety of clinical syndromes. Except pneumonia, most adenovirus infections are not fatal. Occasionally adenoviruses are the cause of meningoencephalitis, acute hemorrhagic cystitis, and neonatal sepsis. Table 32-1 lists the major clinical syndromes in which adenoviruses have been implicated.

Epidemiology

Adenovirus infections are associated with respiratory and ocular diseases and occasionally gastrointestinal conditions. Serological evidence indicates that every child in the United States should have had at least one adenovirus infection by the age of 5 years.

Respiratory disease is seldom seen in adults except military recruits. Adenoviruses account for nearly 2 percent of all acute respiratory diseases in nonhospitalized children and for 5 to 25 percent of those in hospitalized children. Only 10 to 12 serological types have been routinely associated with disease. Children under 6 years old are most susceptible to infection by adenoviruses. The clinical conditions associated with infection in children include pharyngitis, bronchitis, croup, and pneumonia. Types 3, 7, and 21 have been associated with "swimming

TABLE 32-1
Adenovirus-Associated Syndromes and Viral Type Most Frequently Recovered

Syndrome	Adenovirus types	Symptoms and signs
Acute respiratory disease	Types 4 and 7 in military camps; types 3, 14, and 21 in civilian populations	Sore throat, cervical lymphadenopathy, fever
Pharyngoconjunctival fever	Usually types 3 and 7; types 1, 4, and 14 less frequent; worldwide summer epidemics among infants; acute follicular conjunctivitis more frequent in adults	Pharyngitis, conjunctivitis, sore throat, fever, and cervical lymphadenopathy
Pharyngitis	Types 3, 4, 7, 14, and 21	Pharyngitis and intestinal pain often observed in infants
Pneumonia	Types 3 and 7; mortality highest in this syndrome, which occurs primarily in infants	—
Epidemic keratoconjunctivitis	Types 8 and 19 most frequent cause of this syndrome in the United States	A localized infection in which subepithelial opacities occur in the cornea and may remain for up to 2 years
Gastrointestinal disease	Types 40 and 41	Diarrhea with or without vomiting (second most important cause of infantile gastroenteritis after rotavirus, but milder than rotavirus infections)

pool'' conjunctivitis and lower respiratory tract disease. See Table 32-1 for other adenovirus-associated conditions.

Keratoconjunctivitis, caused by types 8 and 19, is a serious eye disease. Outbreaks of keratoconjunctivitis occur frequently in industrial settings and in the offices of ophthalmologists (because of contaminated ophthalmic solutions or equipment).

Gastroenteritis is caused by types 40 and 41. Adenovirus is the second most commonly identified agent after rotavirus. Infections are common in infants worldwide.

Laboratory Diagnosis

Diagnosis by cell culture takes several days and thus does not make it clinically relevant. More rapid tests include the shell vial technique using monoclonal antibodies (see Cytomegalovirus, Laboratory Diagnosis for a discussion of the shell vial technique) and fluorescent monoclonal antibody systems.

Adenovirus types 40 and 41 can be detected in stool samples using a monoclonal antibody–based ELISA.

Neutralization with type-specific antiserum is the best method for typing adenovirus isolates.

Treatment and Prevention

The frequent outbreaks of respiratory disease caused by type 7 adenovirus in military camps led to the development of a vaccine. Live vaccines of types 4 and 7 have been produced for oral administration. The virus is encased in a capsule, which when released in the intestine causes an asymptomatic response. No chemotherapeutic agent has proved effective in treating any adenovirus-associated condition, including conjunctivitis.

THE PAPILLOMAVIRUSES

The papillomaviruses (Fig. 32-11) are structurally similar to the polyomaviruses, such as SV40 and the BK and JC viruses, discussed in Chapter 31. The papillomaviruses, however, cannot replicate in cultured cells.

FIGURE 32-11
Electron micrograph of human papillomavirus. (From B. Janis. In P. D. Hoeprich, ed., *Infectious Diseases,* 2nd ed. New York: Harper & Row, 1977.)

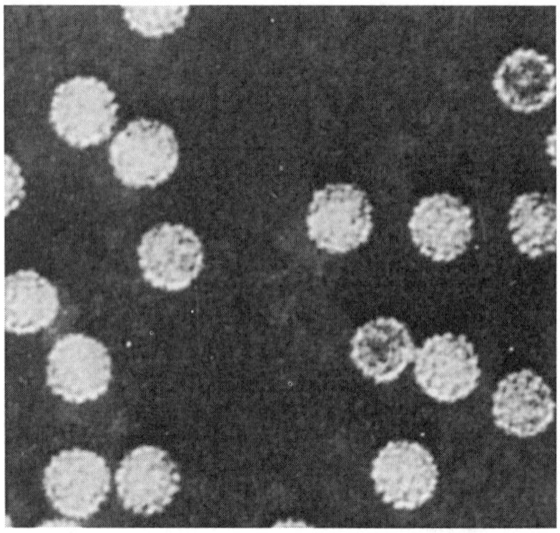

Human papillomaviruses (HPV) are the cause of **warts** and humans are the only hosts. Warts can be transmitted from person to person. The virus infects cells and stimulates them to divide. Papillomas begin as a proliferation of connective tissue followed by an increase of epidermal cells. Six months may pass before the warts become visible.

Warts are divided into four clinical types: (1) **verruca vulgaris** (common wart), (2) **verruca plana** (flat wart), (3) **verucca plantaris** (plantar wart), and (4) **condylomata acuminata** (venereal warts). Each clinical type is distinct and should be distinguished because therapy for each differs. Each type of wart may be caused by more than one virus type. Most warts regress, but if they persist they can be treated by electrosurgery or cryosurgery or by topical application of drugs, such as podophyllotoxin or trichloroacetic acid. Podophyllotoxin is contraindicated in pregnancy.

Venereal warts are soft, pink, cauliflower-like growths that appear singly or in clusters on the external genitalia and rectum. The disease is one of the most common sexually transmitted diseases in the United States. It is estimated that between 12 and 14 million people in the United States are infected with the papillomavirus. Anogenital warts in children have been associated with child abuse but nonvenereal transmission accounts for most cases. Transmission of virus may occur during the birth process or via routine nonsexual family contact (e.g., hand-genital contact).

There is a direct association between venereal warts and other sexually transmitted diseases. Nearly 30 percent of women with venereal warts also have gonorrhea. Most homosexual men with perianal warts also have syphilis or gonorrhea.

Subclinical papillomavirus infections are associated with lesions that are not visible on routine inspection. The lesions show histological changes similar to those found in warts when 3% acetic acid is applied to the lesion and it is examined under magnification. Subclinical infections are difficult to eradicate.

Spontaneous regression of venereal warts occurs, but when they do not regress, serious consequences may take place. Large growths may be responsible for transmission to neonates. Such transmission may give rise to childhood **laryngeal papillomatosis.** There is also some evidence that patients with a history of anogenital warts are predisposed to cervical and perianal neoplasias.

Electrocauterization and cryotherapy appear to be the best methods of treatment. Recurrent warts may be removed by surgery. Other recently tested techniques include (1) podophyllotoxin treatment, (2) interferon alfa, (3) carbon dioxide laser therapy, and (4) idoxuridine cream for vulvar condylomata.

The most sensitive method for diagnosing HPV infection is by DNA hybridization using cloned, type-specific virus probes.

THE PARVOVIRUSES

Parvoviruses belong to the family Parvoviridae. They are nonenveloped single-stranded DNA viruses with icosahedral symmetry. The capsids have a diameter of 20 to 25 nm. Included in this group of viruses pathogenic for humans are the adeno-associated virus (AAV) and parvovirus B19. AAV infection of humans is common but occurs only in association with adenovirus infection. Replication of AAV can occur only with its helper adenovirus. No unique disease has been associated with AAV.

Parvovirus B19

Parvovirus B19 was first discovered in human blood in 1975. Erythroid progenitor cells are the primary target of the virus but in the fetus other cells may be infected.

Parvovirus B19 is the cause of **erythema infectiosum (fifth disease)**, a mild epidemic disease of children. Fifth disease derives its name from a nineteenth-century numbering system given to the exanthems during that period (e.g., measles #1, scarlet fever #2, etc.). In the United States 2 to 15 percent of preschool children are immune to the disease. Transmission of virus is by infected respiratory secretions. Following viremia a rash appears and often resembles rubella. In adults infection is often more severe and arthralgia or arthritis is commonly observed. Adults often complain of fatigue and depression.

Children with hereditary hemolytic anemias are susceptible to infection. B19 virus infection in this group leads to a condition called **transient aplastic crisis (TAC)**. The virus interrupts normal red blood cell proliferation. Patients with TAC have a moderate to severe anemia that may require transfusion and hospitalization. Immunodeficient children are also at high risk of infection by this virus. Infection causes chronic erythroblastopenia and chronic erythrocyte aplasia.

Parvovirus B19 infection during pregnancy is associated with a less than 10 percent risk of fetal loss from spontaneous abortion, stillbirth, or the delivery of a hydropic infant. **Hydrops** (edema) **fetalis** pathogenesis is usually a severe, aplastic anemia but occasionally is a myocarditis. The virus preferentially destroys fetal erythroid progenitors. Virus also can infect liver cells and cause their degeneration. About 40 to 60 percent of women of childbearing age are B19-seronegative, and are thus susceptible to infection when exposed to the virus. Most reported cases of fetal death due to hydrops have occurred in the second trimester. The majority of fetuses infected in utero survive to term and are normal neonates.

Pregnant health care workers should not care for patients with B19-induced aplastic crisis as they are highly contagious. Neonates infected in utero are generally nonviremic and not a hazard in the hospital.

Parvovirus B19 infection is diagnosed by measuring B19 IgM and IgG in serum or detecting viral antigen in blood, secretions, or tissues. The usual test is the IgM antibody capture radioimmunoassay.

RNA Viruses and Associated Diseases

MEASLES VIRUS

Measles as a clinical entity has been recognized for several hundred years. In 1963 an attenuated vaccine was made available to the public and since that time the number of measles cases has dropped precipitously in developed countries. In developing countries measles is still a significant cause of morbidity and mortality. In 1989 there were an estimated 49 million cases of measles in developing countries, resulting in the death of 1.5 million children worldwide.

The measles virus is an enveloped, spherical RNA virus measuring approximately 150 nm in diameter. It belongs to the Paramyxoviridae family. The envelope contains hemagglutinin peplomers but does not carry neuraminidase, as many other paramyxoviruses do. The virus is very labile at 37 C but is stable when stored at sub-zero temperatures.

Pathogenesis

Measles infection is initiated by spread of virus to the respiratory tract, mouth, pharynx, and conjunctiva. The incubation period lasts 7 to 10 days, during which time fever, conjunctivitis, sore throat, photophobia, and headache appear. In the incubation period the virus multiplies in the respiratory mucosa and is then disseminated to the entire body via the bloodstream.

A rash first appears on the face and then spreads to the extremities. The rash, which is made up of reddish elevated macules that tend to coalesce, lasts for only three to four days (Plate 22). Throughout the incubation period and up to two days after the appearance of the rash, the patient is highly contagious. Virus can be shed from the conjunctiva or the respiratory mucosa.

A day or so before the rash is visible, small red macules with a bluish-white center appear on the inside of the cheek in more than 95 percent of persons infected. These lesions are called **Koplik's spots** and are important in measles identification.

Measles is a self-limiting disease; however, secondary infections of the upper respiratory tract such as pneumonia do occur, particularly in patients debilitated by other illnesses. Measles-associated encephalitis occurs in 1 of every 1000 patients. A very small percentage of patients contract a demyelinating encephalitis, which is fatal to one-half of those affected. The remainder of those with encephalitis have varying degrees of central nervous system injury that may result in loss of mental and motor functions.

A rare sequela of measles infection is **subacute sclerosing panencephalitis (SSPE)** (see Slow Virus Infections later in the chapter). It is characterized by changes in personality, motor loss, speech difficulty, and mental retardation. Death is the invariable outcome of SSPE.

Serious complications of measles are associated with pregnancy. Measles during pregnancy is associated with premature labor, spontaneous abortions, and low birth weight infants. For the pregnant woman, measles infection is also identified with pneumonitis and hepatitis.

Epidemiology

Measles is one of the most communicable diseases of humans and is seen everywhere in the world. In unimmunized populations almost every child will get measles early in life. Before 1963, when attenuated measles vaccine was first licensed, more than 400,000 cases occurred annually in the United States. In 1988 there were only 3394 cases reported to the Centers for Disease Control (Fig. 32-12). From 1988 to 1990, the incidence of measles increased eightfold (27,786 cases in 1990). A massive inoculation campaign has resulted in a precipitous drop in measles cases (less than 312 in 1993). Local epidemics are due to low vaccination coverage among the generally highly vaccinated populations. About 3 percent of infections result in complications such as otitis media (5.4 percent) and encephalitis (0.1 percent). Encephalitis can leave the patient with residual brain damage manifested by conditions such as mental retardation, seizure disorders, and nerve deafness.

Vaccine administration has resulted in a reduction of the incidence of disease in school-age children. The highest incidence is now observed in children under 5 years old (Table 32-2). About 40 percent of the cases in the United States are also observed in individuals of reproductive age.

TABLE 32-2
Age Distribution and Estimated Incidence Rates (per 100,000 Population) of Measles—United States, 1990

Age group (years)	Number of cases	Percent	Rate
< 1	4709	16.9	119.3
1–4	8873	31.5	59.3
5–9	2687	9.6	14.9
10–14	2278	8.2	13.4
15–19	3118	11.2	17.4
20–24	2500	9.1	13.3
25	3600	13.1	2.3

SOURCE: Centers for Disease Control, *M.M.W.R.* 41(No. SS-6): November 29, 1992.

Laboratory Diagnosis

Measles is diagnosed on the basis of certain clinical features, for example, Koplik's spots and rash. During measles infection the virus causes the formation of multinucleate giant cells two to six days after the disappearance of the rash. Indirect fluorescent antibody can detect these giant cells in nasopharyngeal cells aspirated from the patient.

Measles diagnosis also may be confirmed serologically by detection of anti–measles virus IgM. This can be accomplished using radioimmunoassay, ELISA, and indirect fluorescent antibody techniques.

Immunity

Infants are protected for up to 12 months after birth because of maternal antibodies. Following acute disease, lifelong immunity is established. Subclinical infections can occur if virus is circulating in the community.

Treatment and Prevention

Vaccination is the best method for controlling measles. An attenuated vaccine, prepared from chick embryo cell culture, has been available since 1968. The vaccine is available in monovalent form and in combinations: measles-rubella (MR) and measles-mumps-rubella (MMR). A rou-

FIGURE 32-12
Number of reported cases of measles in the United States, 1960 to 1993. (Courtesy of Centers for Disease Control, Atlanta, GA.)

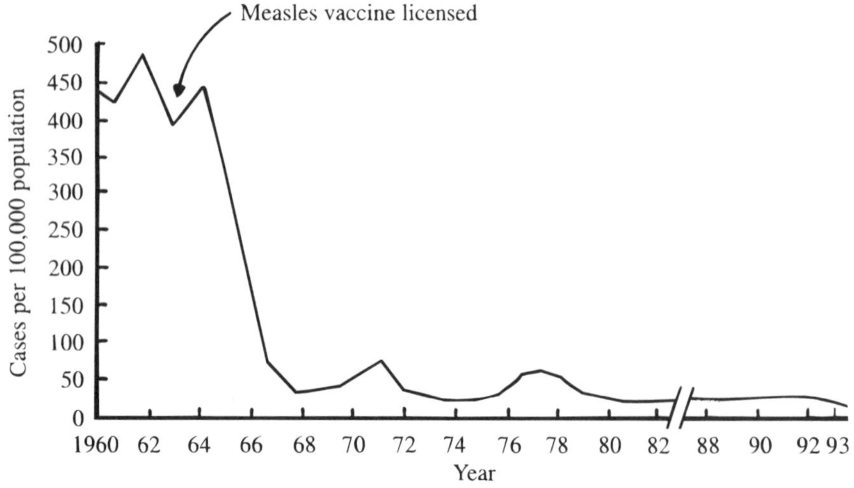

tine two-dose vaccination schedule is now recommended. The first dose is recommended at the age of 15 months for children in most areas of the country, but at the age of 12 months for children in some areas with recurrent measles transmission. The second dose is recommended when a child enters school at kindergarten or first grade. When outbreaks of measles occur, vaccination is also recommended. For example, if measles is occurring in children less than 1 year old, vaccination can be initiated in children as young as 6 months. This is followed by revaccination at the age of 15 months.

Both doses of measles vaccine should be given as a combined MMR vaccine when given on or after the first birthday. Measles vaccine should not be given to women who are pregnant or to anyone with a febrile illness.

Immune serum globulin provides short-term protection if given less than six days before exposure to virus. Immune serum globulin is especially valuable for susceptible household contact of measles patients, particularly those less than 1 year old. Vaccine should not be given at the time of immune serum globulin administration. At least three months should elapse before vaccine is administered. Immune serum globulin does not prevent infections from occurring at a later date.

MUMPS VIRUS

The mumps virus belongs to the Paramyxoviridae family. The virus is a pleomorphic, roughly spherical, enveloped RNA virus whose size may range from 100 to 600 nm. The RNA genome is single-stranded and nonsegmented. The envelope carries glycoprotein peplomers **(hemagglutinins)** as well as the enzyme **neuraminidase.** Neuraminidase can destroy cell receptor sites and thus may interfere with the hemagglutinin reaction. A glycoprotein called **F (fusion)** is also part of the viral envelope. F protein mediates the fusion of the viral envelope with the cytoplasmic membrane of the host cell (Fig. 32-13).

Pathogenesis

The incubation period of mumps (also called epidemic parotitis) is 16 to 21 days. During this period the virus multiplies in the upper respiratory tract. Later the virus enters the blood and infects other organs and tissues including the central nervous system. The salivary (parotid) glands are invariably infected, with swelling and sometimes intense pain. (In the view of some researchers, the virus in the oral cavity goes to Stensen's duct and then the parotid gland, where it multiplies and finally causes a general viremia.)

FIGURE 32-13
Paramyxovirus penetration of the cell and role of HN and F glycoproteins. HN glycoprotein is required for membrane attachment. Once attachment has taken place, the F protein is cleaved by a protease that promotes membrane fusion and infectivity. Cells deficient in protease do not show membrane fusion, and infectivity is lost.

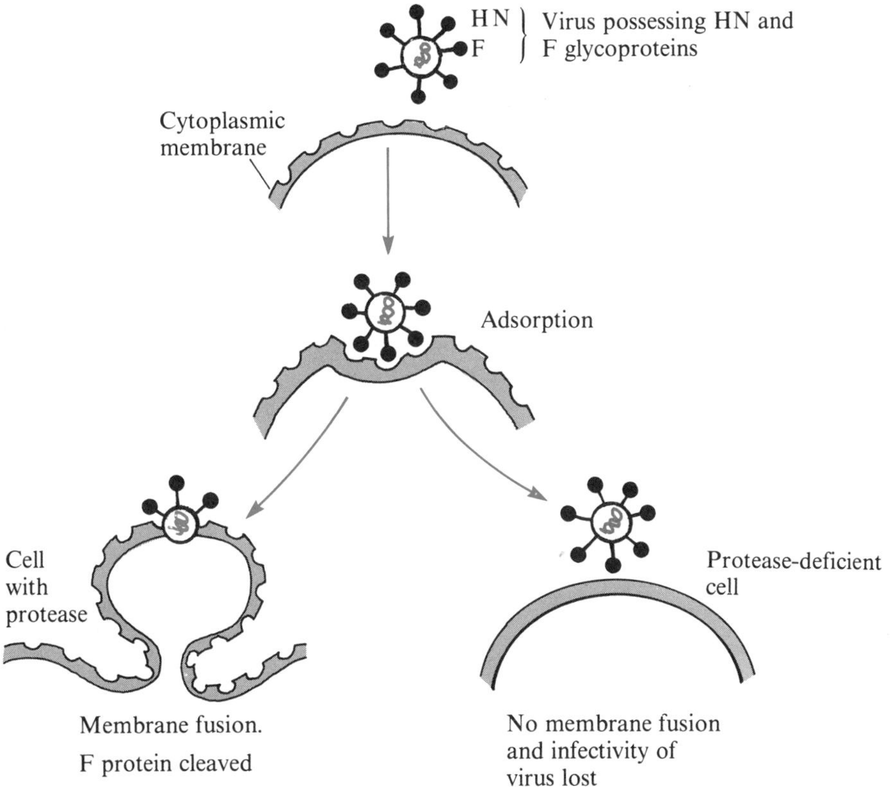

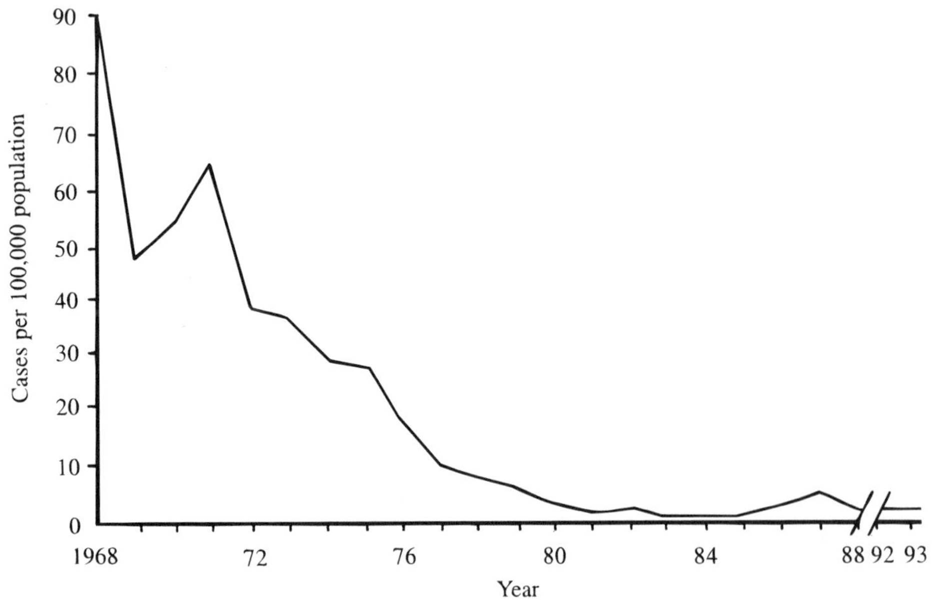

FIGURE 32-14
Reported mumps cases per 100,000 population by year, United States, 1968 to 1993. (Courtesy of Centers for Disease Control, Atlanta, GA.)

Unilateral infection of the testes occurs in approximately 25 percent of men infected. Infections are rare in infants up to 6 months old because of the protective influence of maternal antibody. Early infections of the fetus may cause death or premature onset of labor, but not congenital malformations.

Mumps is a benign disease although complications can occur. These include (1) pancreatitis, which may or may not induce diabetes; (2) thrombocytopenia, a disease characterized by bleeding caused by a decrease in the number of blood platelets; (3) aseptic meningitis,* which may occur in up to 10 percent of those infected; (4) meningoencephalitis, a complication of the central nervous system that may afflict 0.5 to 10 percent of those infected without causing permanent damage; and (5) orchitis (infection of the testes), which may accompany 20 percent of the clinical cases of mumps in postpubertal males (unilateral infection does not usually result in sterility, but bilateral involvement poses a risk). In females the ovaries may be infected but there is no threat of sterility.

Epidemiology

Mumps is a disease endemic throughout the world. Humans are the only known host of the mumps virus. The virus is transmitted by respiratory droplets or fomites contaminated with saliva. Mumps is contagious primarily because as many as 50 percent of persons infected may be asymptomatic. In addition, virus is shed from saliva and urine several days before symptoms appear.

In 1967, the year the mumps vaccine was licensed, 186,691 cases were reported in the United States; in 1993, 1692 cases were reported. This represents a 98 percent decrease (Fig. 32-14). Most cases used to be found in elementary school children but most outbreaks today occur in high schools and on college campuses. The reason for this trend, which is also characteristic of measles and rubella, is that some individuals did not become vaccinated or have the disease at a younger age. Immunity to mumps is usually acquired between the ages of 5 and 14 and is long-lived.

Laboratory Diagnosis

Like measles, laboratory diagnosis is not required for mumps. Virus can be isolated from urine, saliva, or central nervous system specimens within four to five days of onset of illness. Virus can be identified by immunofluorescence. Virus cultivated in cell culture can be identified by hemagglutination inhibition or fluorescent antibody tests.

Treatment and Prevention

A single dose of live mumps vaccine provides protective and long-lasting immunity in 90 percent of recipients or more. If recipients are likely to be susceptible to measles or rubella or both as well as to mumps, MMR is the vaccine of choice. If MMR is used, it should be administered at the age of 15 months to ensure maximum seroconversion for measles (maternal antibody can interfere with maximum seroconversion). Mumps vaccine is also recommended for adolescents and adults who have not encountered mumps during childhood. Vaccine is not recommended for pregnant women, those who are immunocompromised, or adults born before 1957 (they are likely to be naturally immune).

* Aseptic meningitis refers to viral meningitis, in which spinal fluid is clear. In bacterial meningitis spinal fluid is often purulent or cloudy, owing to large numbers of bacteria and leukocytes.

RUBELLA VIRUS

The disease rubella was first described in Germany in the 1800s and was subsequently called **German measles.** The full clinical implications of rubella infection were not realized until the pandemic of 1964, in which more than 30,000 infants were born with congenital anomalies.

Rubella virus belongs to the family Togaviridae. It is a spherical virus that is 60 nm in diameter and consists of a nucleocapsid surrounded by a lipoprotein envelope. The RNA of the rubella virus is single-stranded. The virus is easily isolated from clinical specimens by cell culture.

Pathogenesis

Postnatal Rubella Infection. Postnatal rubella infection is transmitted via the respiratory tract. The incubation period for the disease is 14 to 21 days. The virus multiplies in the respiratory mucosa and spreads to the bloodstream. During the viremic stage the virus is routinely found in the throat, blood, and feces. As the antibody level increases during infection, the amount of circulating virus decreases. A rash appears and virus is found only in the nasopharynx. Maximal shedding of virus occurs one to two days before and three to five days after the onset of rash. In addition to the rash, symptoms include fever, leukopenia, and suboccipital lymphadenopathy. The disease is self-limiting although complications such as arthritis and arthralgia are commonly encountered by young women. Chronic arthritis lasting for a year or more may also be encountered.

Congenital Rubella Syndrome. Congenital rubella syndrome (CRS) results from infection of the fetus during the viremic stage in the pregnant mother. Disease is more prevalent when infection occurs during the first trimester. CRS occurs in 85 percent of those infected during the first trimester. Manifestations of CRS range from mild to severe. Severe infection results in multiple abnormalities including cataracts, glaucoma, pulmonary artery stenosis, meningoencephalitis, and mental retardation. Virus is not lethal to fetal tissue but does cause inhibition of mitosis, which culminates in underdeveloped organs or tissues. The mortality for babies symptomatic at birth is 20 percent.

Epidemiology

Rubella is worldwide in distribution and occurs more frequently during the winter and spring months. Virus is harbored in the upper respiratory tract of infected individuals and is transmitted by person-to-person contact. Both symptomatic and asymptomatic persons can shed virus. In CRS the virus is shed for several months after delivery. This is a particularly important aspect of rubella infection because infant viral carriers are a constant source of infection to unimmunized nurses and other female personnel who come in contact with them.

The incidence of rubella and CRS has steadily declined since 1969, the year the rubella vaccine was first made available to the public (Fig. 32-15). In 1992 there were only 160 cases of rubella and 11 cases of CRS.

FIGURE 32-15
Incidence rates of reported rubella cases and congenital rubella cases, United States, 1967 to 1993.

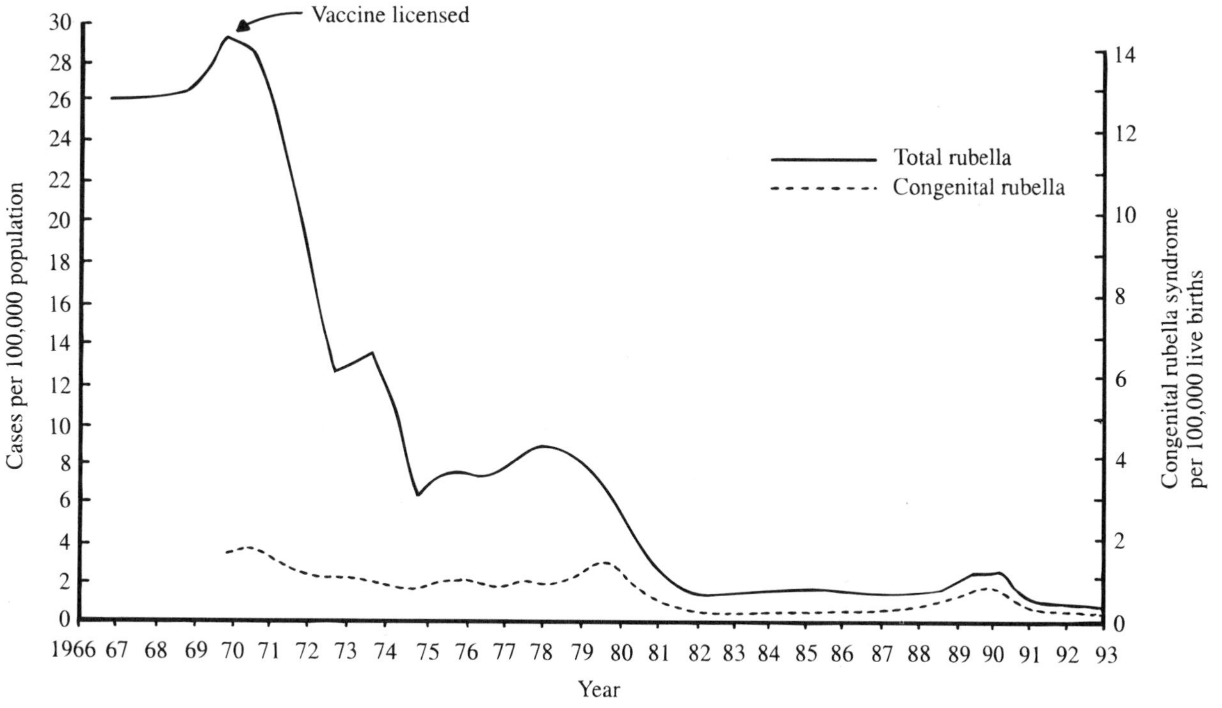

Laboratory Diagnosis

There are relatively few situations in which viral isolation is necessary for laboratory diagnosis. Serological diagnosis is the preferred method for assessing the state of acute and congenital disease. The standard test has been hemagglutination inhibition; however, that test has been supplanted by more rapid tests including ELISA, enzyme immunoassay, latex agglutination, and others.

Immunity

Immunity to rubella infection is apparently lifelong, but not enough years have elapsed since licensure of the vaccine to determine the effect of vaccination. Recent studies showed that low levels of antibody six years after vaccination can be present in about 10 percent of those vaccinated. Vaccinated individuals can present with subclinical infection but the period of virus shedding is short. Susceptible contacts are not believed to be at risk and immune women reinfected are unlikely to infect their fetuses.

Treatment and Prevention

There is no treatment for either congenital or postnatal rubella infection. If infection occurs during the first trimester of pregnancy, therapeutic abortion is recommended by many physicians.

Control of rubella rests primarily on vaccination procedures aimed at protecting women of childbearing age. Immunization in the United States is advised for children between the age of 1 year and puberty, and for adolescent girls and adult women who are seronegative and in whom pregnancy can be avoided for at least three months after vaccination. The current vaccine (live and attenuated) may be given subcutaneously. It is used either in monovalent form or in combination with measles or measles-mumps vaccines (MMR).

Vaccine is not given to women during early pregnancy since fetal infection may occur. Rubella vaccination during pregnancy should not ordinarily be a reason to recommend interruption of pregnancy. The risk of vaccine-associated malformations is so small as to be negligible. Postpartum women who lack evidence of immunity should be vaccinated before discharge from the hospital. Hospital personnel should be screened for immunity to rubella.

Vaccine side effects such as arthritis are more severe in adults, particularly women, than in children. Arthritis symptoms may last a few weeks but chronic effects are not unusual.

INFLUENZA VIRUSES

The influenza viruses belong to the family of RNA viruses called the Orthomyxoviridae. They are usually spherical, although filamentous forms are known, and measure 80 to 100 nm in diameter (Fig. 32-16). Surrounding the internal ribonucleoprotein is a lipid envelope from which project **hemagglutinin (HA)** and **neuraminidase (NA)** peplomers. The role of these peplomers is discussed later under Pathogenesis.

The RNA genome of the influenza viruses is unique among RNA viruses. It consists of eight distinct RNA molecules that may be linked as a complete unit only in the mature virion. The presence of these distinct RNA units during replication in the animal host explains the high rate of genetic recombination observed when cells are infected with different strains of influenza virus. Recombination is the genetic mechanism responsible for the major antigenic differences in pandemics caused by the influenza virus.

Classification

There are three types of influenza viruses: A, B, and C. Types B and C have been isolated only from humans, while type A has been found in horses, swine, and birds as well as humans. **Type specificity** is based on differences in the antigenicity of their ribonucleoprotein and M protein. The latter are part of the lipid layer of the envelope (see Fig. 32-16). **Strain specificity** resides in the HA and NA peplomers. Four types of hemagglutinin (H0, H1, H2, H3) and two types of neuraminidase (N1, N2) are recognized among influenza A strains causing illness in humans. These antigens are the basis for classifying new strains. Classification is based on the following:

1. Antigenic type of nucleocapsid: A, B, or C; for example, influenza A
2. Geographical location or origin of the isolate, for example, A/Taiwan/
3. Year of isolation: A/Taiwan/68
4. Strain number: A/Taiwan/5/68
5. The antigenic identity of hemagglutinin (H) subtype and neuraminidase (N) subtype: A/Taiwan/5/68 (H2N2)

Pathogenesis

Influenza A and B viruses cause the same spectrum of illness. Type C viruses are not associated with severe disease as are types A and B. Influenza is a disease of the upper respiratory tract. Infection is acquired primarily by inhalation of aerosols produced by infected individuals. The HA peplomer allows attachment of virus to host receptor cells and causes fusion of the virion and cell membranes during entry. The fusion process requires the cleavage of HA into two components. The relative ease with which the HA of a given virus is cleaved in a particular host is one of the determinants of pathogenicity. Cleavage of HA is caused by **proteases.** Several studies imply that proteases from various microorganisms (e.g., staphylococcus) present in the respiratory tract are capable of enhancing influenza activity by activation of HA. The exact function of neuraminidase is not known. Since the substrate of neuraminidase is neuraminic acid, a component of the mucosa, the NA peplomer may cause liquefaction of the mucosa. This leaves the underlying epithelial layer unprotected from infection by other microbial agents and promotes spread of virus.

The incubation period for influenza is 24 to 48 hours. It is usually followed by fever, cough, headache, muscular aches, sore throat, and conjunctivitis. Acute symptoms last about three to five days. Otitis media, croup, and pneumonia are more likely to develop in children infected

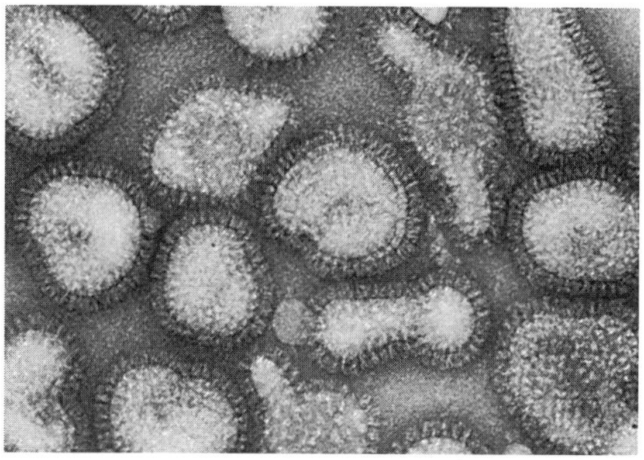

A

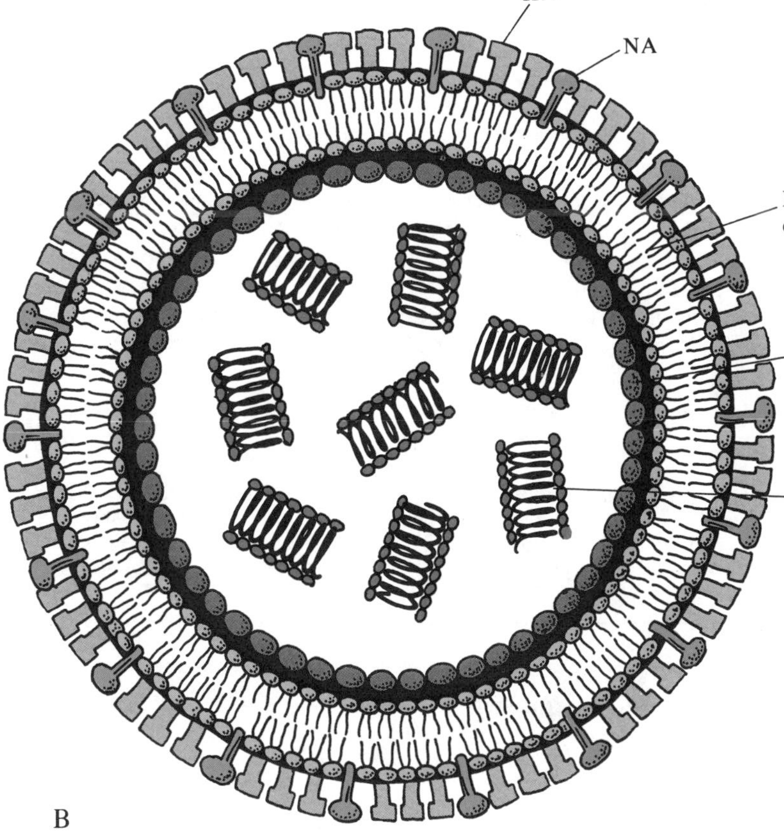

B

FIGURE 32-16
Influenza virus. A. Electron micrograph of human influenza virus. (× 180,000 before 25 percent reduction.) (Courtesy of R. C. Williams.) B. Diagrammatic illustration of influenza virus. HA = hemagglutinin peplomer; NA = neuraminidase peplomer; M = protein shell; NP = ribonucleoprotein. (From R. C. Compans and P. C. Choppin, *Compr. Virol.* 4:179, 1975.)

by virus than in adults. Loss of the mucociliary blanket during infection makes the patient susceptible to infections by bacterial agents such as *Staphylococcus aureus, Streptococcus pneumoniae,* and *Hemophilus influenzae.* These agents plus the influenza virus are capable of causing pneumonia, particularly in the elderly and those with underlying illnesses.

A complication of influenza A and B infections as well as varicella is called **Reye's syndrome.** The syndrome occurs in children between the ages of 6 and 11 years who are recovering from infection by these viruses. Manifestations of the disease include intractable vomiting, lethargy, and delirium. Untreated, the disease may progress to coma and death. Brain damage has been documented in some survivors, but most recover without affliction. Several studies suggested that treatment of respiratory infections with salicylates to reduce fever may be a contributing factor to the syndrome. One of the characteristics of Reye's syndrome is injury to mitochondria, especially in the liver. The risk of Reye's syndrome is highest after influenza B infection, followed by varicella-zoster and influenza A infections.

Epidemiology

Influenza is an endemic disease in which epidemics take place every two to five years. The pandemics that occur approximately every 8 to 10 years are caused by influenza A virus. Influenza A virus was first isolated in 1934, followed by influenza B virus in 1940 and influenza C in 1949.

With influenza A and B viruses there have been different degrees of variation since they were first discovered. Both viruses undergo gradual antigenic variations in the HA and NA peplomers, referred to as **antigenic drift.** Type A viruses also undergo less frequent, major antigenic changes referred to as **antigenic shift.** The major changes result in the emergence of new influenza subtypes and are associated with pandemics of varying severity. The most recent antigenic shifts occurred in 1957 when type A (H2N2) viruses replaced A (H1N1) strains and in 1968 when type A (H3N2) strains replaced the H2N2 viruses. H1N1 viruses reemerged in 1977 and now circulate with H3N2 virus. In the 1957 pandemic, over 80 million cases of influenza were recorded. In the United States alone, an estimated 88,000 deaths were pneumonia- and influenza-related. Most deaths occurred in the elderly and seriously debilitated patients. As the population develops an immunity to the new pandemic strain, there are likely to be periodic small epidemics among those who did not come in contact with the new strain and thus did not develop an immunity against it (Fig. 32-17). Type B and C influenza viruses have not been shown to undergo antigenic shifts probably because they lack the extensive animal reservoir of the type A viruses.

The segmented nature of the influenza genome is responsible for the variations in both genotype and phenotype. When a cell is infected with more than one strain of influenza virus, reassortment of gene segments produces progeny with varied genotypes. New pandemic strains of type A virus are thought to arise from the reassortment of the genes of human and animal strains during dual infection of an intermediate host such as swine (see Under the Microscope 33).

Type C influenza is prevalent throughout the world, and infection occurs early in life. Outbreaks caused by type C virus are rarely reported and are usually discovered retrospectively by serological studies associated with other types of influenza.

Laboratory Diagnosis

Symptoms of influenza resemble many other respiratory pathogens; therefore, influenza cannot be diagnosed on clinical grounds alone. However, during an epidemic, influenza will be responsible for a majority of respiratory illnesses.

Diagnosis can be confirmed only by laboratory tests. Virus can be isolated from swabs or washings from the patient's throat or nasopharynx. A variety of cell culture systems, primarily mammalian kidney, can be used for

FIGURE 32-17
Scheme for occurrence of influenza pandemics and epidemics in relation to the level of immunity in the population. — = incidence of clinically manifest influenza; - - - - = mean level of population antibody against A/HxNx/; - - - · · · = mean level of population antibody against A/HyNy/. (From R. G. Douglas. In G. J. Galasso, T. C. Merigan, and R. C. Buchanan, eds., *Antiviral Agents and Viral Diseases of Man.* New York, Raven, 1979.)

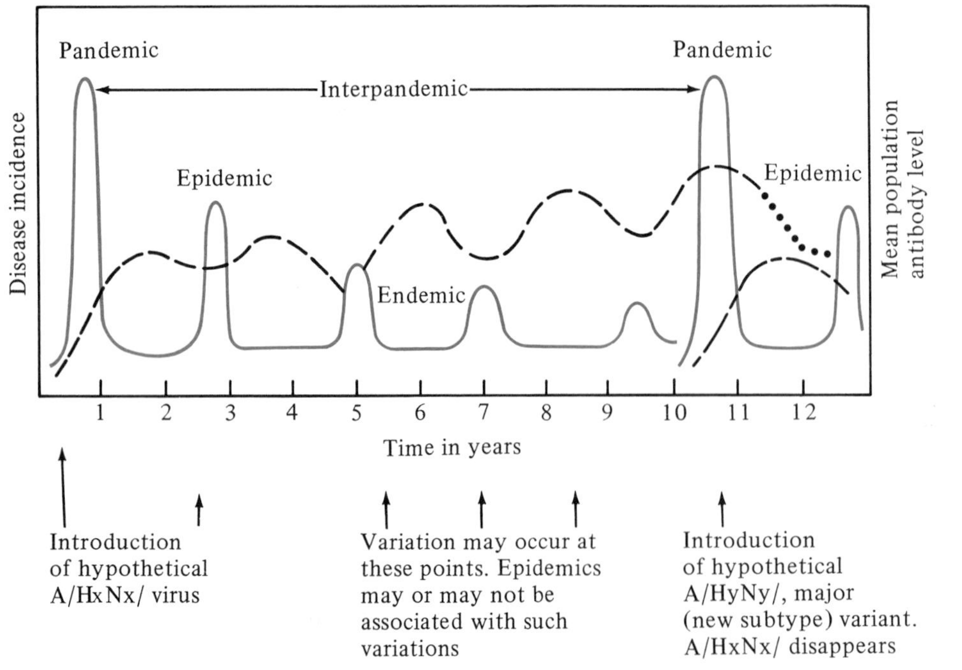

UNDER THE MICROSCOPE 33

Influenza Viruses: Evolution and Variation

Influenza viruses infect a variety of animals including humans, pigs, horses, sea mammals, and birds. Recent phylogenetic studies revealed that the prevalence of interspecies transmission depends on the animal species. It has been hypothesized that all of the influenza A viruses of mammalian sources originated from the avian gene pool. The different virus lineages are predominantly host-specific, but there are periodic exchanges of influenza virus genes or whole viruses between species. These exchanges give rise to pandemics of disease in humans, lower animals, and birds.

The influenza viruses currently circulating in humans and pigs in North America are believed to have originated by transmission of all genes from the avian reservoir prior to the 1918 Spanish influenza pandemic. The influenza virus gene pool in aquatic birds of the world is perpetuated by transmission within that species throughout the year. There is also speculation that pigs may serve as the intermediate host in genetic exchanges between influenza viruses in avians and humans.

See *Microbiol. Rev.* 56:152, 1992.

isolation of virus. Viral antigen can be detected in the specimen by using any one of several techniques, including direct immunofluorescence, solid-phase immunoassay, antigen capture, and staining of cells with monoclonal antibodies.

In all cases, the isolated viruses must be characterized serologically to confirm diagnosis. Serological diagnosis is based on a fourfold rise in antibody titer between the acute and convalescent sera.

Characterization of specific antibody can be accomplished using the following tests: hemagglutination inhibition, virus neutralization, hemadsorption inhibition, enzyme-linked immunoassay, and complement fixation.

Immunity

Infection results in the production of antibodies to several viral proteins including HA and NA peplomers. These antibodies are associated with resistance to infection. After infection, immunity lasts for only one or two years. Reinfection depends on the antigenic characteristics of the infecting virus strain and the patient's prior contact with related strains. Resistance to one strain does not confer resistance to other strains.

A person's serological response to influenza A is dominated throughout life by the type of antibody produced as a result of his or her first experience with the virus. A person challenged with one antigen and then rechallenged with an influenza virus containing related and unrelated antigens will exhibit two immunological responses: First, an anamnestic response is initiated by the related antigen. Second, the unrelated antigen stimulates a primary response. Repeated challenges with related antigen will result in the production of antibodies against the first strain. This has been called the **doctrine of original antigenic sin.**

Treatment and Prevention

Amantadine is currently licensed in the United States for influenza A virus prophylaxis and therapy. It is most beneficial when administered within the first two days of the illness and should be continued as long as there is exposure to virus. The drug is recommended for persons at high risk during epidemics, that is, those with chronic pulmonary, heart, or kidney disease and those older than 65.

Rimantadine is also effective against type A and B influenza viruses. It causes fewer side effects than amantadine and is most often used in aerosolized form. In 1993 the Food and Drug Administration approved the use of rimantadine in oral form for adults but not children with influenza.

Vaccine provides protection during serious epidemics and consists of type A and B virus strains. Because of antigenic instability, the antigenic characteristics of current strains provide the basis for selecting virus strains to be included in the vaccine for a given year. Vaccine should be utilized by high-risk groups, such as the elderly, adults and children with chronic disorders, residents of nursing homes, and individuals who care for these groups. Children and teenagers who are receiving long-term aspirin therapy and may be at risk of Reye's syndrome after influenza infection should also be vaccinated.

Most of the side effects from vaccine administration appear in children. They include fever, allergic response to vaccine components, and the **Guillain-Barré syndrome.** This syndrome is a self-limited paralysis that occurs within eight weeks after vaccination in 10 of every million vaccinations. Roughly 5 to 10 percent of the persons with Guillain-Barré syndrome have residual weakness, and approximately 5 percent die.

POLIOVIRUS (POLIOMYELITIS)

In the early years of the twentieth century, paralytic poliomyelitis was a feared and dreaded disease much like AIDS is today. In the 1950s there was an average of about 20,000 poliomyelitis cases per year, with a peak of 57,879

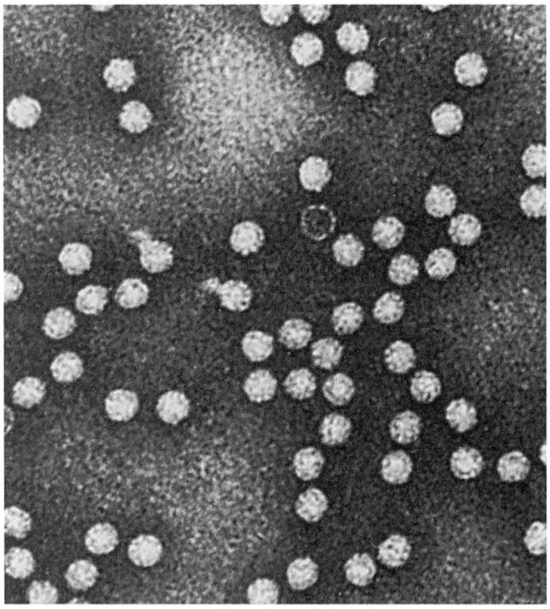

FIGURE 32-18
Electron micrograph of poliovirus. (From J. L. Melnick, *Intervirology* 20:61, 1983.)

cases in 1952. After the introduction of a vaccine in 1955, the average number of cases of poliomyelitis in the 1980s was only 9. Poliomyelitis caused by wild-type virus is virtually nonexistent in the United States. Since 1980 only vaccine-associated paralytic disease has emerged as the predominant form of the disease.

The poliovirus belongs to the family Picornaviridae, whose members also include the human hepatitis A virus, foot-and-mouth disease virus, and rhinoviruses. They are among the smallest viruses, measuring approximately 25 to 30 nm in diameter (Fig. 32-18). They are nonenveloped and their genome is a single-stranded RNA molecule. The poliovirus belongs to the genus *Enterovirus*. The other enteroviruses are discussed later.

Pathogenesis

In more than 99 percent of persons infected with the poliovirus, clinical symptoms are very mild or inapparent. The virus is, under most circumstances, taken into the mouth through contaminated food, water, or milk. It multiplies in the tonsils, lymph nodes of the neck, and intestinal mucosa of the small intestine. From these sites of multiplication the virus is disseminated via the bloodstream. During the incubation period, which lasts 10 to 15 days, virus can be shed in the feces and will continue to be shed despite high titers of humoral antibodies. Virus is also present in the pharynx one to two weeks after infection.

At the onset of illness the patient has fever, headache, and stiffness in the neck. In nonparalytic polio these symptoms subside in a few days and recovery is complete. In about 1 percent of patients paralysis occurs. Paralysis is the result of invasion of the central nervous system by the virus from the bloodstream. Invasion also may occur along the axons of peripheral nerves to the anterior horn cells of the spinal cord. Multiplication of virus in the neurons causes their destruction. Therefore, nerve cells innervating the voluntary muscles are no longer functional and the muscles atrophy. Full or partial restoration of muscle function depends on the number of uninjured neurons that remain to innervate the muscle and the ability of unaffected muscles to hypertrophy and assume motor function.

Epidemiology

Poliomyelitis has been declared the next target disease for global eradication. The eradication program has been successful in South and Central America and developed countries, but epidemics still occur in many developing countries. Disease due to indigenously acquired poliovirus has been nonexistent in the United States since 1980 (Fig. 32-19). Since 1980 poliomyelitis cases have been vaccine-associated (98 cases from 1980–1992), except those that have been imported.

There are three poliovirus serotypes, with type 1 causing most infections in the United States. Permanent immunity is acquired only to the serotype causing infection.

Poliovirus is spread by the fecal-oral route and can infect any age group. Paralytic cases occur primarily in young adults and adolescents. Infection in the very young and infants often produces an asymptomatic disease that brings complete immunity. It is a paradox that before the discovery of polio vaccines, improvement in sanitation practices had actually increased the risk of paralytic polio. Before improvements in sanitation the poliovirus was transmitted to infants through feces-contaminated food, milk, or water. Infection in the infant invariably resulted in asymptomatic disease that provided permanent immunity. In addition, most women of childbearing age had been exposed to the three poliovirus types, and passive immunity was transferred from mother to infant. As sanitation practices improved, many of the unvaccinated were not exposed to the virus until adolescence or adulthood, the period when infection most often causes paralysis or death.

Laboratory Diagnosis

Isolation of virus is the preferred method of diagnosis. Fecal specimens are cultured in monkey kidney or human cells and observed daily for cytopathic effects. Presumptive diagnosis is made from the clinical history and cytopathic effects produced in culture. Since other enteroviruses may have similar effects, identification of poliovirus rests on neutralization of the virus by antipoliomyelitis serum.

Serological diagnosis can be made using paired sera. The microneutralization test or indirect immunofluorescence can be used to determine antibody titer against all three poliovirus types.

Treatment and Prevention

Two vaccines are currently in use in the United States. The inactivated poliovirus vaccine (IPV) and oral poliovirus vaccine (OPV). OPV has been the vaccine of choice since

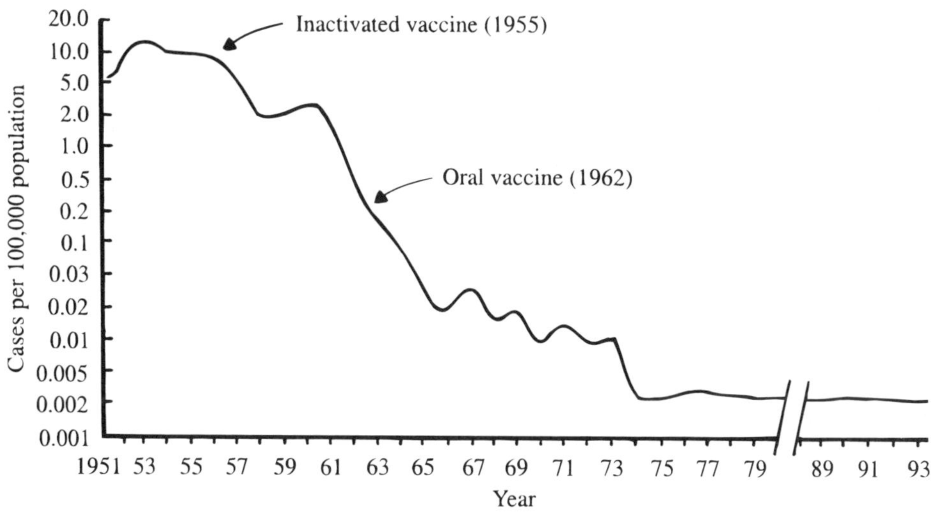

FIGURE 32-19
Reported paralytic poliovirus attack rates by year, United States, 1951 to 1993. (Courtesy of Centers for Disease Control, Atlanta, GA.)

it was first introduced in 1961. The reasons for this are (1) it multiplies in the intestinal tract and establishes intestinal immunity to reinfection, thus breaking the chain of transmission; (2) it is simple to administer; (3) it does not require periodic boosters; (4) it is well accepted by patients; and (5) it has a record of having eliminated disease associated with wild poliovirus. OPV, however, has been associated with vaccine-associated disease. The vaccine contains live virus and can cause disease in those exposed either by active immunization or by contact with a vaccinated person. For every 2.5 million doses of OPV distributed, there is approximately one vaccine-associated case of polio. There have been many who advocate using a more potent IPV called **enhanced-potency inactivated poliovirus vaccine (E-IPV)**. E-IPV is not identified with vaccine-associated disease. E-IPV does produce equivalent or higher seroconversion rates and higher serum antibody levels than OPV. E-IPV, however, is less effective than OPV in preventing and limiting intestinal infection.

Three groups are at risk of vaccine-associated disease: recipients of OPV, usually infants receiving their first dose; persons in contact with OPV recipients (mostly unvaccinated or inadequately vaccinated adults); and immunologically abnormal individuals. E-IPV is preferred for unvaccinated adults who because of foreign travel or health occupation are at a greater risk of exposure than the general population.

Primary vaccination with either OPV or E-IPV produces immunity to all three types of poliovirus in 95 percent of recipients or more. The primary series of OPV consists of three doses: two doses given 6 to 8 weeks apart and a third dose given at least 6 weeks and customarily 12 months after the second. For infants the first OPV dose is often given with the first dose of DTP. The primary E-IPV series also consists of three doses: two doses each given 4 to 8 weeks apart and a third dose given 6 to 12 months after the second.

OTHER ENTEROVIRUSES

The enteroviruses, which include the poliovirus just discussed, inhabit the alimentary tract. Other important members of the genus *Enterovirus* include hepatitis A virus, to be discussed later, as well as group A coxsackieviruses, echoviruses, and human enteroviruses types 68 to 71.

Pathogenesis

The pathogenesis of the enteroviruses is similar to that of the poliovirus except that different target organs are involved. Most infections are mild with symptoms including respiratory tract involvement, fever, and sometimes rash. However, more serious illnesses may occur and include the following:

Aseptic meningitis is caused primarily by echoviruses but coxsackieviruses A and B may also be involved. The symptoms of aseptic meningitis include headache, fever, and vomiting, followed by stiffness of the neck and muscular weakness. The disease is self-limiting.

Herpangina is an infection of the throat caused primarily by group A coxsackieviruses. The disease is characterized by fever and sore throat with ulcerated lesions appearing on the mucous membranes of the oral cavity. Herpangina occurs primarily in children between the ages of 3 and 10 years and is self-limiting.

Myocarditis is caused primarily by group A and B coxsackieviruses. Infection occurs in the newborn as well as in children and adults. Infection in neonates, which is often fatal, results from dissemination of virus to a variety of organs. Rapidly developing cyanosis and circulatory collapse precede death. Most older children and adults recover from myocarditis, but permanent heart injury may occur.

Pleurodynia is a muscular disease caused primarily by group B coxsackieviruses. The illness occurs in children between the ages of 5 and 15 years and in their parents. Pain over the lower rib cage or upper abdomen is the most characteristic symptom. The illness is self-limiting and most patients do not require bed confinement. The average duration of illness is 4 to 7 days.

Respiratory illness includes several coxsackieviruses and echovirus types that are associated with pharyngitis. Illness has been observed among military recruits and unlike other viral respiratory illness, appears during summer months.

Conjunctivitis can be caused by both echoviruses and coxsackieviruses. Very explosive epidemics of disease called **acute hemorrhagic conjunctivitis** occur frequently in tropical coastal cities. Symptoms may last for three to five days. Outbreaks may affect 50 percent or more of persons in the community with a low socioeconomic status within a one- to two-month period. Major outbreaks are associated with enterovirus 70 and group A coxsackievirus type 24.

Neonatal disease may be acquired transplacentally but is usually acquired in the hospital. The infection may result in an asymptomatic response or may cause cardiac or respiratory distress and death. Aseptic meningitis is one of the most frequent clinical syndromes. Coxsackievirus B serotypes and echoviruses are the principal etiological agents of disease.

Epidemiology

Humans are the only reservoir of the human enteroviruses. The enteroviruses can be found in the oropharynx and intestine. Virus can be shed in the stools; thus, fecal contamination of food, water, and utensils is the most frequent source of infection. Some viral isolates, however, can be spread by contamination of fomites from nasal or conjunctival secretions. Nearly 60 percent of the cases of enteroviral disease are found in those under 10 years old. Twenty-five percent are found in those under 1 year old.

Virus is more easily spread in warm weather and isolates are more frequently recovered during the summer months. Enteric viruses are found in wastewater, and in underdeveloped countries this is a frequent source of infection. In the period 1970 to 1983 in the United States, 52 percent of the nonpolio enterovirus isolates were echoviruses, and 5 percent were group A coxsackieviruses. Data from several viral watch studies suggest that 10 to 15 million illnesses due to nonpolio enteroviruses occur each year in the United States.

Laboratory Diagnosis

Presumptive diagnosis of enteroviral disease can be established on the basis of the symptoms of the illness, the time of year the viral isolate was recovered, the type of cell culture system that supports viral growth, and the cytopathic effect in culture. Cell culture is the mainstay of enterovirus diagnosis but it has many limitations. As many as 35 percent of enterovirus isolates do not grow in cell culture. Serological testing has only a limited role in diagnosis. Antigen detection has been limited to coxsackievirus B serotypes. Nucleic acid amplification systems such as PCR seem to be the best chance for *in situ* diagnosis in the future.

Treatment

There are no satisfactory antiviral agents for the treatment of enteroviral disease (excluding poliomyelitis) other than providing supportive care, which includes bed rest. Hospital-associated outbreaks of disease, especially in neonates, necessitate isolation techniques to prevent transmission.

RHINOVIRUSES

Several viruses, both respiratory and nonrespiratory, produce symptoms that resemble the common cold. The rhinoviruses account for approximately 50 percent of these upper respiratory tract infections. About 20 percent of colds are caused by **coronaviruses.** Very little is known about coronavirus pathogenesis; therefore, a discussion of them is not provided. The remaining percentages of colds are caused by respiratory syncytial virus, influenza A and B, and enteroviruses.

The rhinoviruses are a subgroup of the picornaviruses. There are about 89 serotypes of the rhinovirus subgroup, with biophysical and biochemical properties similar to those of the other picornaviruses. The rhinoviruses can be separated from the enteroviruses by determining their acid stability. Rhinoviruses lose their infectivity when they are subjected to pHs between 3 and 5, while enteroviruses are unaffected. The structure of the rhinovirus has been determined and this has provided scientists with very useful information (see Under the Microscope 34).

Rhinovirus infections are spread from person to person by viral-contaminated respiratory secretions. The highest incidence of rhinovirus-associated illness occurs in September and October. The incubation period for rhinovirus infections is one to three days. The most frequent symptoms of infection are coryza, sore throat, and cough. Fever is usually not present. In children rhinovirus infection may cause more severe disease such as bronchitis or otitis media. Infection from one serotype provides protection from challenge with the same serotype for up to two years. Persons with low levels of type-specific antibody are asymptomatic but shed virus on reinfection. Those with high antibody titers are immune to infection.

Diagnosis of the cold is made from observations of clinical symptoms. There are no procedures for direct examination of clinical specimens or for serological diagnosis. Rhinovirus can be isolated from clinical specimens. The latter are made into suspensions, and then inoculated into tubes containing human fetal diploid cells. Cultures are observed daily for cytopathic effects, a rounding up of the cells.

Because of the mildness of colds and the great number of serotypes that may be involved, vaccine prophylaxis is not practical. Preliminary experiments with human volunteers, however, indicate that vaccines prepared from some serotypes are protective for up to six months while others elicit no immunological response.

UNDER THE MICROSCOPE 34

Rhinovirus Structure and Drug Design

In 1986 the x-ray crystallographic structure of the rhinovirus was solved by Rossman and colleagues. The capsid of the virus was shown to be made up of four barrel-shaped proteins that assemble into an icosahedron. So what is the big deal? Shortly after the structure of the virus had been determined, some scientists developed drugs that prevented viruses like the rhinovirus (other picornaviruses) from infecting cells. However, they could not determine how the drugs affected the virus. They asked Rossman and colleagues to find out how the drugs interacted with the virus. What they learned was that the drugs diffused into the barrel cavity of one of the capsid proteins. The drugs stabilized the capsid to such an extent that it could not release the RNA of the virus once the latter had entered the cell. The pH inside the host cell is different from that outside the cell, and this difference is enough to cause the capsid to fall apart once the virus has entered the cell. The drug, however, stabilized the capsid to such a degree that it was unaffected by the change in pH. The data were then sent to scientists working with supercomputers to determine how the drugs were bound within the barrel-shaped capsid protein. The intramolecular interactions were calculated. These data also gave hints as to what portions of the drug are required for most efficient binding and what portions of the molecule might be modified without affecting antiviral activity.

Having the three-dimensional crystal structure of a virus provides the scientist with a shape into which a drug could be designed to fill that space. Computer programs are being designed to match drugs with target shape. A library of drug structures could then be screened quickly by computer to determine what drugs might be the best candidates for clinical trials. This approach will hopefully speed up the search and discovery of clinically useful antiviral agents, which, to date, are few in number.

RESPIRATORY SYNCYTIAL VIRUS

Respiratory syncytial virus (RSV) is the major cause of lower respiratory tract disease in infants and children. Each year RSV is associated with an estimated 90,000 hospitalizations and 4500 deaths from lower respiratory tract disease in infants and young children. RSV is an enveloped, pleomorphic virus that ranges from 150 to 300 nm in diameter. The RNA genome is nonsegmented and single-stranded. RSV is a member of the genus called *Pneumovirus.*

Our knowledge of the mechanism of pathogenesis of RSV infection is incomplete. One pathogenic factor is probably the site of infection, the terminal respiratory airways (bronchioles). In infants, whose airway diameter is very small, inflammation from RSV infection causes the airways to become obstructed, thereby preventing entry of oxygen to the lungs. It is also believed that some segment of the immune system plays a role in the development of illness. One of the prevailing theories is that the relative concentration of IgE at the time of infection influences the outcome. Production of a small amount of IgE at the time of infection appears to have a negative effect on the outcome of illness. This is probably due to the release of mediators such as prostaglandins and leukotrienes by immune cells.

In normal infants RSV infection usually causes only upper respiratory tract symptoms that resolve without incident. Lower respiratory tract disease is frequently associated with high-risk infants (congenital heart disease, preterm birth, immunodeficiency) and children. Common infectious syndromes associated with RSV include bronchiolitis, pneumonia, and croup, with otitis media as a frequent complication. Infection in this latter group often requires prolonged hospitalization and assisted respiratory ventilation. RSV infections in older children and adults tend to be mild.

Antibody passively transferred from mother to fetus is of protective value during the first six weeks after birth but antibody titer declines precipitously. Two months after birth children are especially susceptible to RSV infections. Infection does not confer a permanent immunity although later infections are milder.

Children with RSV infection in the hospital place other hospitalized children and hospital attendants at risk for infection. Studies have shown there is a 15 to 40 percent mortality rate when immunocompromised children who have combined immunodeficiency or who are receiving chemotherapy are infected with RSV. RSV pneumonia frequently develops in HIV-infected children. Hospital staff members acquire infection by self-inoculation with contaminated secretions carried on their hands or on fomites. Strict handwashing and separating infected children can reduce the transmission of RSV.

Rapid diagnosis of RSV infection may be important for the choice of therapy and the use of preventive measures, such as isolation or barrier nursing. Rapid diagnosis can be obtained using a direct immunofluorescence assay or using test kits that utilize an enzyme immunoassay. Tests are performed on nasopharyngeal aspirates.

Bronchiolitis can be managed by providing supplemental oxygen to the patient and by replacing fluids. Mortality from infection is low in immunocompetent individuals. Ribavirin supplied in the form of an aerosol is used only for severe forms of the disease. The drug prevents respiratory failure and shortens the course of hospitalization.

PARAINFLUENZA VIRUSES

Parainfluenza viruses, like RSV, are important respiratory pathogens in infants and children. Parainfluenza viruses are enveloped, pleomorphic viruses whose diameter ranges from 150 to 200 nm. They belong to the Paramyxoviridae family, and share antigens with the mumps virus.

There are four parainfluenza antigen types but only types 1, 2, and 3 cause medically important infections. They are second only to rhinovirus as the most common viral agents infecting humans. At birth, maternally acquired antibody is sufficient to prevent disease in infants by types 1 and 2 but this is not true for type 3. Type 3 is second only to RSV as a cause of pneumonia and bronchiolitis in infants.

Primary infections with types 1, 2, and 3 usually cause coryza (sneezing and watery eyes), pharyngitis, bronchitis, or a combination of them. The temperature of the patient is usually elevated to 100 F for two to three days. Type 1 and 2 infections may extend to the larynx and trachea, causing croup. **Croup** is the most severe manifestation of infection and is characterized by a coarse cough and hoarseness. Croup can lead to fatal pneumonia.

Type 3 virus infection occurs early in life and by the age of 3 years almost all children have been infected. Type 3 virus produces disease that primarily affects the bronchi, producing bronchopneumonia or bronchitis. Reinfections with parainfluenza viruses are common and may occur within three months to a year after primary infection. The symptoms of disease are less severe with reinfection.

Direct examination of respiratory secretions is the preferred method for identification of parainfluenza viruses. Rapid viral diagnostic tests are now used extensively to detect the antigen of parainfluenza viruses 1 and 3. These tests include immunofluorescence and ELISA. The shell vial technique (see Cytomegalovirus, Laboratory Diagnosis) is one method for antigen detection via immunofluorescence.

Therapy for severe infections consists primarily of supportive care. Vaccines are being tested but none has yet proved effective.

RABIES VIRUS

Rabies is an infectious viral disease that affects the central nervous system. Even before the discovery of viruses, Pasteur recognized that the causal agent of rabies was not a bacterium but a submicroscopic microorganism. He prepared the first rabies vaccine by intracerebral passage of the infectious agent in rabbits. The vaccine was first administered to a French peasant boy who was later to become the gatekeeper at the Pasteur Institute in Paris. In 1944 Negri made the first histological diagnosis of rabies when he observed inclusion bodies in the cytoplasm of nervous tissue. These inclusion bodies bear his name: **Negri bodies** (see Plate 20).

The rabies virus is a RNA virus belonging to the family Rhabdoviridae. It is bullet-shaped and measures 180 × 75 mm (Fig. 32-20). A lipoprotein envelope encompasses the nucleocapsid and contains glycoprotein peplomers that constitute the hemagglutinins of the virus.

The rabies virus can infect most warm-blooded animals, including humans. Wild virus isolated from nature is termed **street virus.** Wild virus attenuated in the laboratory is referred to as **fixed virus.** Fixed virus has a higher infectivity titer and shorter incubation period than does street virus.

Pathogenesis

Rabies is usually transmitted to people through the bite of infected animals, although exposure to open wounds or membranes occasionally occurs. A few infections are also caused by aerosols created by infected bats and rabies-infected corneal grafts.

The incubation period for human disease is long and variable. This period may range from 2 to 16 weeks to several years. The incubation period depends on the site of infection, the infectious dose of the virus, and the length of time required for the virus to migrate to the spinal cord or brain. Once the virus leaves the initial site of infection, it travels to the spinal cord. The virus replicates in the spinal ganglia and then migrates up the spinal cord to

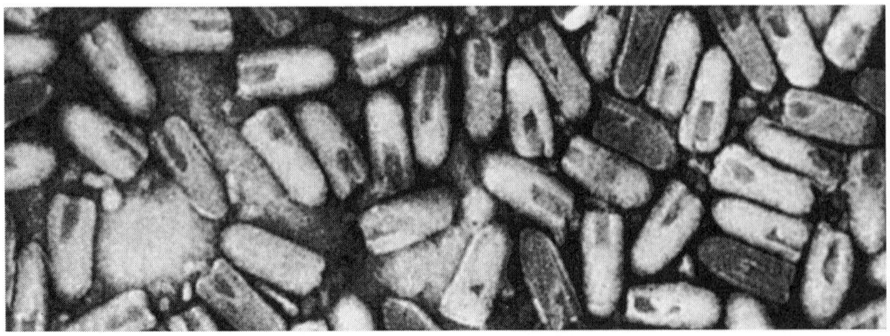

FIGURE 32-20
Electron micrograph of a purified preparation of rhabdovirus particles. Note the bullet shape of the particles. (From R. W. Horne, *Virus Structure.* New York: Academic, 1974.)

reach the medulla and brain. In the brain it causes severe nerve cell damage. Demyelination occurs in the white matter.

Pain at the site of the bite is one of the first prodromal symptoms in 60 percent of affected patients. In about 40 percent, itching occurs at the site of the bite or involves the whole bitten limb. Nonspecific symptoms of infection include fever, changes in temperament, and coryza. Patients may demonstrate the furious (agitated) type or paralytic (dumb) type of rabies when symptoms become evident. **Hydrophobia** (fear of water) is the best-known symptom of furious rabies and is pathognomonic of this condition. Hydrophobia is a violent, jerky contraction of the diaphragm and accessory muscles of inspiration that is triggered by the patient's attempt to swallow liquid. Other features of the infection are terror and excitement and generalized convulsions. During the last stages of disease before death the patient becomes comatose and hydrophobia is replaced by an irregular pattern of respiration.

Epidemiology

Rabies is now rare in industrialized nations of the temperate zones. In many tropical areas, however, rabies is still a familiar and no less frightening disease than it was nearly 2000 years ago. From 1980 to 1992 only 16 cases of human rabies were reported in the United States and about half of these were acquired here. In Latin America the incidence of human rabies varies from 0.3 to 2.8 per 100,000 population. In Brazil as many as 1000 deaths from human rabies are recorded each year.

In nature the virus's permanent host is the skunk, weasel, or mongoose. The virus is maintained in wildlife because of its ability to invade and replicate in various tissues and organs such as kidneys, lungs, and salivary glands without invading neural tissue and causing encephalitis.

Various wild animals are a source of infection for domestic animals such as dogs and cats and even occasionally cattle and horses (Fig. 32-21). The United States continues to have a wild animal rabies problem. Epizootics involving skunks and raccoons are occurring in the United States. The arctic fox transmits rabies in Alaska. Rabid bats, which account for over 13 percent of all animal rabies, have been found in all 48 contiguous states.

Domestic dogs and cats are still the most important source of human disease in areas where domestic rabies has not been controlled by animal vaccination. In areas where domestic animals have been vaccinated, most human cases result from wild animal bites or from imported cases of rabies.

Laboratory Diagnosis

Microscopic examination of brain tissue for rabies virus is the most common laboratory diagnostic technique. The fluorescent antibody test provides a rapid diagnostic procedure and has replaced other tests such as Negri body determination and isolation of virus by mouse inoculation.

In humans diagnosis of rabies is dependent on clinical illness and epidemiological evidence of potential rabies exposure. Serological techniques are of little value since antibody does not appear until the eighth day of the illness. Sometimes viral antigen can be detected in smears prepared from corneal, salivary, or nasal swabs by the direct fluorescent antibody technique. High levels of antibody in the cerebrospinal fluid can be accepted as diagnostic of rabies even after administration of vaccine. Clinical rabies, but not vaccine, can stimulate production of antibodies in the cerebrospinal fluid.

Immunity

The fact that antibody is not present in the infected individual until the eighth day of illness indicates that rabies

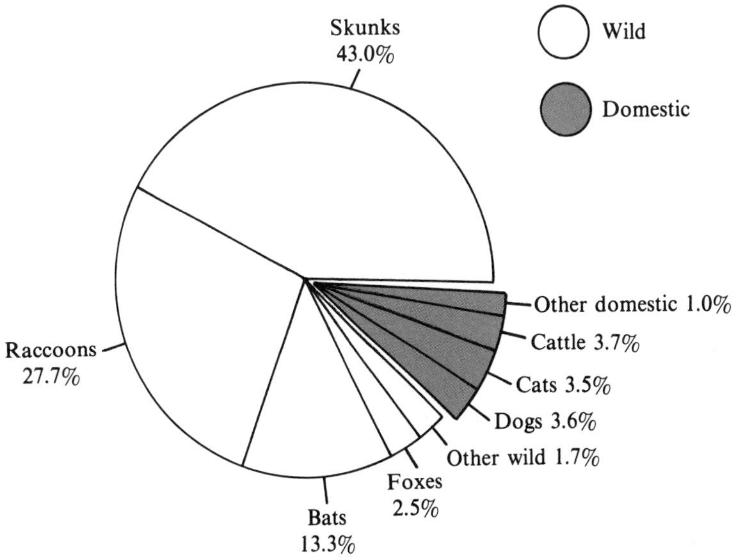

FIGURE 32-21
Animal rabies, United States, 1987. (Courtesy of Centers for Disease Control, Atlanta, GA.)

does not stimulate the host immune system until the virus reaches the brain. A person receiving no therapy within this period will die before his or her own immune system can respond. Only three persons with clinical rabies have ever been known to survive.

Treatment and Prevention

After attack by a rabid animal or one suspected of being rabid, the bite wound should be cleansed by flushing with soap and water. This should be followed by application of 40 to 70% alcohol, tincture of iodine, or 0.1% quaternary ammonium compounds. Vaccine and immune serum are administered according to the schedule indicated later. During hospitalization of the patient, many complications involving vital functions may occur. Pulmonary and cardiovascular problems are common, and these vital systems must be monitored continuously. Sedation of the patient is imperative if seizures are to be controlled. Such procedures protect not only the patient but also the attending hospital personnel from bodily injury and possible infection.

Vaccine and immune serum are available for the prevention and control of rabies in humans. The vaccine currently available for administration is prepared from human fibroblasts, and is called human diploid cell virus **(HDCV)**. A second vaccine called rabies vaccine adsorbed **(RVA)** is available only for residents of Michigan. Immune serum globulin prepared from human volunteers is also available for prevention.

The immune serum and vaccine are used for preexposure and postexposure prophylaxis. Preexposure prophylaxis consists of three injections of vaccine given intramuscularly or intradermally. For individuals receiving postexposure prophylaxis, human rabies immune globulin **(HRIG)** is given in a single dose. This is followed by five doses (intramuscular) of HDCV—one each on days 0, 3, 7, 14, and 28. Persons continually exposed to the risk of rabies should receive booster doses of vaccine at two-year intervals. Postexposure vaccine is administered to over 35,000 individuals per year in the United States.

Prevention of human rabies is best accomplished by the prevention of rabies in domestic animals such as dogs and cats. Wild animal rabies is still a problem. Impressive results have been obtained using oral baits containing live-attenuated virus to control rabies in foxes in Italy and in Canada. Similar studies are being conducted in the United States.

HEMORRHAGIC FEVER VIRUSES

Viral hemorrhagic fevers are a group of illnesses characterized by the common feature of hemorrhage. There are 12 known viral hemorrhagic fevers (Table 32-3) and all are capable of causing life-threatening illnesses. Most

TABLE 32-3
Characteristics of the Hemorrhagic Fever (HF) Viruses

Family and virus	Disease	Distribution	Means of transmission
Arenaviridae			
Lassa	Lassa fever	West Africa	Rodent; human-to-human transmission important in hospital-associated outbreaks
Junín	Argentine HF	Argentina	Rodent; exposure primarily in rural areas
Machupo	Bolivian HF	Bolivia	Rodent; human-to-human transmission occasionally occurs
Bunyaviridae			
Rift Valley fever	Rift Valley fever	Sub-Saharan Africa	Mosquito; human disease most often during epizootics
Crimean-Congo HF	Crimean-Congo HF	Africa, Asia, former U.S.S.R.	Tick or contact with infected animal
Hantaan and related viruses	HF with renal syndrome	Asia, Balkans, former U.S.S.R., Europe	Rodent; highly seasonal—disease found primarily in farmers during grain harvesting
Filoviridae			
Marburg	Marburg HF	Sub-Saharan Africa	Unknown
Ebola	Ebola HF	Sub-Saharan Africa	Unknown
Flaviviridae			
Yellow fever*	Yellow fever	Tropical Americas, sub-Saharan Africa	Mosquito
Dengue*	Dengue fever, dengue HF	Asia, Africa, Pacific, Americas	Mosquito
Kyasanur Forest disease	Kyasanur Forest disease	India	Tick
Omsk	Omsk HF	Former U.S.S.R.	Tick; disease primarily among muskrat trappers and skinners

* Yellow fever and dengue are discussed in more detail later in the chapter.

hemorrhagic fevers are zoonoses, with the major exception of dengue viruses. The majority of these diseases are seldom seen in the United States. Transmission to humans is frequently by the bite of an infected tick or mosquito, or by the aerosolized excreta of infected rodents. Human-to-human transmission is possible and is important in the epidemiology of some illnesses.

Two important hemorrhagic fevers associated with the Americas are yellow fever and dengue. These two viral diseases are discussed separately under The Arboviruses. We discuss only five of the remaining hemorrhagic fevers: (1) Lassa fever, (2) Ebola hemorrhagic fever, (3) Marburg hemorrhagic fever, (4) Crimean-Congo hemorrhagic fever (CCHF), and (5) hemorrhagic fever with renal syndrome (HFRS).

Lassa Fever

Lassa fever was first described in 1969 in northern Nigeria. The virus is morphologically and antigenically related to the lymphocytic choriomeningitis virus and to the viruses causing hemorrhagic fever in Bolivia (Machupo virus) and Argentina (Junín virus). Only the last two are implicated in human hemorrhagic fevers.

The Lassa virus is an enveloped single-stranded RNA virus, classified in the family Arenaviridae (*arena* means "sand" in Latin and electron micrographs of the virus give this appearance; Fig. 32-22).

Lassa fever is the most frequently imported viral hemorrhagic fever in the United States and Europe. The natural host of the virus is the African rat *(Mastomys natalensis)*, which lives near humans in rural areas. Virus is excreted in urine that contaminates the environment around living areas. Human infection occurs by contact with the contaminated environment but also may occur by contact with contaminated blood. Infected humans are contagious and household or hospital outbreaks are a serious threat. As many as 100,000 to 300,000 cases of Lassa fever occur annually in West Africa.

The incubation period is one to three weeks and symptoms appear initially as fever, sore throat, and weakness. Later there are pains in the joints and lower back together with a nonproductive cough, vomiting, and diarrhea. Patients with milder disease may have symptoms for one week and then recover. In those with severe disease edema of the face and neck, conjunctival hemorrhage, cyanosis, encephalopathy, and shock are present. One of the most notable findings in severe disease is platelet dysfunction, which is characterized by the platelets' reduced ability to aggregate in the presence of adenosine diphosphate. The mortality rate for patients hospitalized with Lassa fever is 15 to 20 percent. The prognosis is poor for pregnant women and fetal damage is frequent if infection occurs in the third trimester.

Specific diagnosis is made by (1) isolating the virus from blood, urine, or throat washings; (2) demonstrating the presence of IgM antibody to Lassa virus; and (3) measuring antibody in acute and convalescent sera using the indirect fluorescent antibody technique.

Human-to-human transmission can be prevented by avoiding contact with infected tissue, blood secretions, and excretions. Ribavirin is the drug of choice for treatment. Ribavirin can also be used to prevent infection by administering it to contacts of infected individuals.

Ebola Hemorrhagic Fever

The Ebola virus, named after a small river in Zaire, Africa, is a single-stranded, enveloped RNA virus that is a mem-

FIGURE 32-22
Electron micrograph of arenavirus (*arrow*) cultivated in Vero cells. Note the sand-like electron-dense particles in the virus. (× 90,000.) (Courtesy of R. Graham and P. Jahrling.)

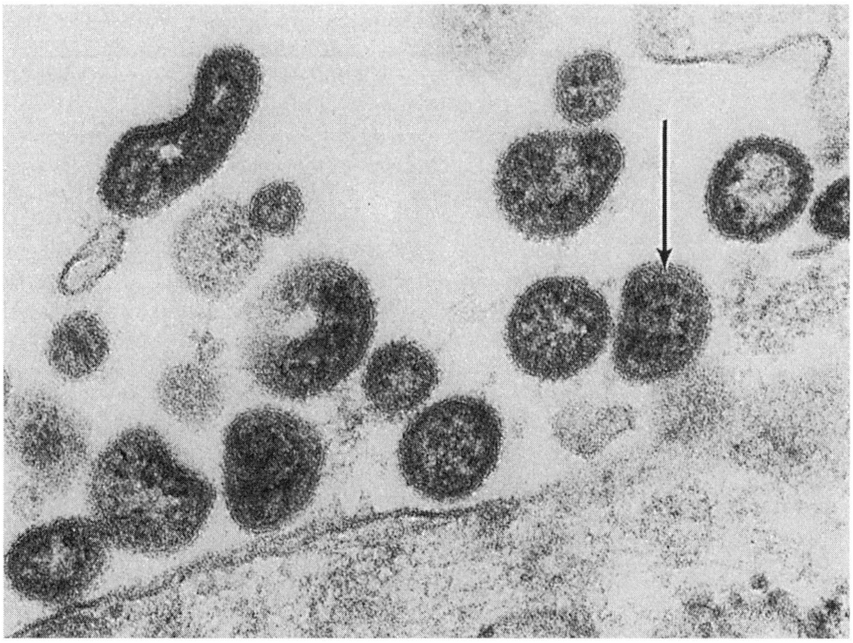

ber of the family Filoviridae. The reservoir of virus in nature is not known.

Ebola hemorrhagic fever was first recognized in 1976. The method of acquiring infection is not known but transmission from human to human can occur through close personal contact. In the first recognized epidemic of the disease, 284 patients acquired infection from the index patient and 53 percent of them died. In 1989 an Ebola-like virus was spread in the United States following importation of macaque monkeys from the Philippines.

The incubation period ranges from 2 to 21 days. Initial symptoms resemble those of influenza, that is, fever, myalgia, joint pain, and sore throat. These symptoms are followed by diarrhea and abdominal pain in most patients. A transient skin rash appears at the end of the first week and is frequently accompanied by an exudative pharyngitis. Hemorrhagic manifestations occur about the third day of illness and include petechiae as well as bleeding from the gastrointestinal tract and from multiple other sites.

Specific diagnosis requires isolation of the virus from blood or demonstrating rising antibodies by indirect fluorescent antibody. Recently an enzyme immunosorbent assay was designed for detection of antigen in tissues.

Treatment is supportive and no specific viral drug has been shown to be effective. No vaccine is available.

Marburg Hemorrhagic Fever

Marburg virus, named after a town in Germany, is a single-stranded, enveloped RNA virus. It is morphologically similar to the Ebola virus but is antigenically distinct from it. Reservoir of the virus is not known.

How infection is acquired naturally is not known. The first outbreak occurred after 25 people had handled infected material of African green monkeys. Secondary spread occurs by close personal contact or contact with blood secretions or excretions. Sexual transmission is also possible. Marburg disease appears to be endemic in Central and East Africa.

The incubation period is 3 to 10 days and the clinical and laboratory features are virtually the same as for Ebola virus infection. The treatment is also the same as that for Ebola virus disease.

Crimean-Congo Hemorrhagic Fever

CCHF virus is a single-stranded RNA virus that belongs to the family Bunyaviridae. The disease has been recognized in Asia since the 1940s. Several domestic animals such as cattle, sheep, goats, and hares are reservoirs for the virus. Ixodid (hard) ticks act as reservoirs and vectors for the virus.

CCHF is endemic in eastern Europe, especially the former Soviet Union, but has also appeared in Africa, India, China, and around the Mediterranean. Humans acquire infection by tick bite or by crushing ticks on abraded skin. Transmission to humans may occur by contact with blood, secretions, or excretions of infected animals or humans.

The incubation period for the disease is two to nine days. Symptoms include fever, headache, myalgia, arthralgia, abdominal pain, and vomiting. A petechial rash is common and frequently precedes abnormal bleeding and hemorrhage from multiple other sites. The case-fatality rate ranges from 15 to 70 percent but mild infections do occur.

Diagnosis requires viral isolation from the blood during the first week of illness or detecting rising antibody titer by indirect fluorescent antibody or other methods, such as ELISA.

Treatment is supportive and no antiviral drug has yet proved effective in vivo.

Hemorrhagic Fever with Renal Syndrome

HFRS is the designation for a group of illnesses caused by viruses belonging to the genus *Hantavirus*. There are four distinct hantaviruses: Hantaan, Seoul, Puumala, and Prospect Hill. A severe form of disease is seen in East Asia but a milder form is found in Europe. Infection by the hantaviruses first attracted attention during World War II and the Korean War. In Korea, 500 to 900 patients have been hospitalized annually since 1951. Recent outbreaks (1993) of diseases in Indian reservations in the United States have brought attention to these viruses (see Under the Microscope 35).

The hantaviruses are maintained in nature by asymptomatic infection in rodent hosts. Although predominantly associated with urban areas, the viruses can be a problem for laboratory personnel working with rodents.

HFRS produces a spectrum of manifestations that include fever, hemorrhage, and renal failure (but respiratory illness in the United States; see Under the Microscope 35). The clinical course of the disease can be separated into five distinct phases: febrile, hypotensive, oliguric, diuretic, and convalescent. Hemorrhage is a result of vascular injury and a deficit of functional platelets. Disseminated intravascular coagulation contributes to hemorrhage in some patients. Tubular necrosis in the kidneys results in renal failure. HFRS is an immune-mediated disease and evidence suggests that patients with a more vigorous immune response are likely to have more severe illness. The mortality rate for severe forms of HFRS is as high as 30 percent. Mild forms of HFRS occur in Europe. For example, in Scandinavia the disease is referred to as **nephropathia epidemica,** which has a lower mortality than the severe form of HFRS.

Sera can be tested by indirect fluorescent antibody with fluorescein-labeled goat anti-human immunoglobulin. Serological diagnosis is confirmed by measuring increasing antibody titers to Hantaan virus.

Treatment includes lessening the severity of hemorrhage. This includes fluid therapy and administration of vasopressors to reduce disseminated intravascular coagulation, platelet dysfunction, and vascular injury. Early dialysis can also reduce the damage from uremia. Results from antimicrobials are inconclusive. Chinese investigators recently produced a formalin-inactivated vaccine and preliminary trials are encouraging.

UNDER THE MICROSCOPE 35

Hantavirus Infection—United States

Hantaviruses were first isolated from field mice in Korea where human infections were first documented. Hantavirus infection has not been considered an important disease in the United States. However, in May 1993, 12 cases of hantavirus infection were confirmed in the Southwest. Nine of the 12 infected persons died. Infection is insidious, with the initial symptoms suggesting a mild cold—fever, muscle ache, and mild respiratory symptoms. Within five to six days of the initial symptoms, 70 percent of the patients are dead.

Collection and testing of rodents in the areas of infection revealed a high prevalence of hantavirus antibodies in deer mice. Transmission of disease to humans is associated with exposure to rodent excreta and saliva. There is no evidence that human-to-human transmission occurs. Most hantavirus infections outside the United States are associated with a renal syndrome. The outbreak in the United States was characterized by fever, myalgias, adult respiratory distress syndrome (ARDS), and only limited renal involvement.

Many researchers now believe that many unexplained cases of ARDS, which claims thousands of lives each year, may in fact be due to hantavirus infection. This scenario may be similar to that for legionnaires' disease, a recently discovered disease. Serum samples that were obtained from army personnel in the 1940s were examined in the 1980s and revealed antibodies to the bacterium. People were dying from infection by the legionnaire bacillus long before the bacterium was isolated.

Prevention of disease can be accomplished by avoiding activities that can result in contact with wild rodents, disruption of rodent burrows, or aerosolization of dried rodent excreta. Although the deer mouse appears to be the primary reservoir of disease, other rodents (voles, moles, etc.) plus small mammals can also carry the virus.

THE ARBOVIRUSES

The term **arbovirus** refers to **ar**thropod-**bo**rne viruses. They are a heterogeneous group belonging to several viral genera. The most important of the arboviruses belong to three major groups: (1) *Alphavirus,* (2) *Flavivirus,* and (3) *Bunyavirus.* The specific viruses in these groups cause several important types of infections, only three of which are discussed here: **viral encephalitis, yellow fever,** and **dengue fever.**

Viral Encephalitis

Encephalitis caused by measles, mumps, or herpes simplex virus is not considered epidemic in nature. Some flaviviruses, however, are responsible for **epidemic encephalitis.** Epidemic encephalitis in humans is not common but some viruses cause a highly fatal disease. The principal causes of epidemic viral encephalitis are **western equine encephalitis (WEE) virus, eastern equine encephalitis (EEE)** virus, St. Louis encephalitis **(SEE) virus,** and **Japanese B encephalitis (JBE) virus. LaCrosse virus** also causes a mild form of the disease that is endemic in the eastern United States. Characteristics of some of the major viral agents causing encephalitis are outlined in Table 32-4.

Pathogenesis. Human viral encephalitis results from the bite of mosquitoes.* The virus multiplies in local tissues and regional lymph nodes following the bite of the mosquito. Virus is carried via the thoracic duct into the bloodstream, from whence virus is seeded into other tissues and further viral replication takes place. How virus reaches neural tissue is still a matter of controversy, but in humans the thalamus and cerebellum are most vulnerable.

Infections by the LaCrosse virus are rarely fatal but infections by the EEE virus often result in 30 percent of the cases being fatal. The mortality rate for JBE virus infections in older age groups may be as high as 80 percent.

Recovery from some viral encephalitides may be prolonged in 30 to 50 percent of patients. Some of the symptoms incurred during convalescence include sleeplessness, depression, memory loss, and headaches lasting up to three years. As many as 20 percent of these patients have symptoms that persist even longer and include speech and gait disturbance.

Diagnosis and Treatment. Isolation of virus is extremely difficult and most laboratory diagnosis is based on serology and examination of acute and convalescent sera. Fluorescent antibody, hemagglutination inhibition, and complement fixation methods can be used to measure serum antibodies.

There is no antiviral treatment for viral encephalitis and only supportive care can be utilized.

Yellow Fever

Yellow fever is transmitted to humans by the bite of a mosquito. The virus belongs to the flaviviruses, which

* Powassan (POW) virus is transmitted by ticks. The vector in North America is fairly localized in Canada and northern United States.

TABLE 32-4
Some of the Major Viral Agents Causing Encephalitis in the United States*

Viral group	Virus	Mosquito vector	Reservoir in nature	Vertebrate host	Distribution	Other characteristics
Alphavirus	Venezuelan encephalitis (VEE) virus	*Aedes* species	Rodent	Horses, humans	Northern South America, Caribbean, Florida	Most infections are inapparent; encephalitis not common
	Eastern equine encephalitis (EEE) virus	*Aedes* species	Bird	Horses, pheasants, humans	Eastern U.S.A., Caribbean, South America	Rare disease in U.S.A.; incidence greater in children; case-fatality ratios between 50 and 80 percent
	Western equine encephalitis (WEE) virus	*Culex tarsalis*	Bird	Horses, sparrow, finches, pheasants, humans	Western U.S.A., Canada, Caribbean, South America	One-third of patients are infants, in whom 50 percent will have brain damage
Flavivirus	St. Louis encephalitis (SEE) virus	*Culex* species	Birds	Birds (e.g., sparrows, finches), humans	Central U.S.A.	Principal cause of endemic encephalitis in U.S.A.; case-fatality rate highest in elderly
Bunyavirus	LaCrosse encephalitis (LEE) virus	*Aedes triseriatus*	Small mammals	Small mammals, humans	U.S.A., endemic in eastern states	Cases primarily in young boys; rarely fatal

* The Japanese B encephalitis virus (JBE) is the principal cause of most cases of epidemic encephalitis. JBE causes annual epidemics among children in Asia. *Culex* species are the mosquito vector for JBE, while birds are the principal reservoir in nature.

are single-stranded, spherical, enveloped RNA viruses. Yellow fever is found primarily in the Americas and sub-Saharan Africa.

Pathogenesis. Yellow fever produces a hemorrhagic fever that is similar to other viral hemorrhagic fevers discussed previously. There are three clinical periods in yellow fever: (1) **infection,** (2) **remission,** and (3) **intoxication.**

The **infection** period follows a three- to six-day incubation period and is characterized by fever, headache, lumbosacral pain, nausea, and vomiting. The infection period lasts about three days and virus is present in the bloodstream. Virus in the bloodstream may be a source of virus for mosquitoes. Symptoms of the infection stage may go into **remission** for as long as 24 hours.

During the **intoxication** phase virus is cleared from the blood and infects various organs, especially the liver, spleen, kidneys, and heart. Symptoms during this period include jaundice, albuminuria, hemorrhagic manifestations (for example, in the liver, heart, and kidneys), and central nervous system symptoms such as stupor, delirium, convulsive seizures, and coma. Death usually occurs between 7 and 10 days after infection. The case-fatality rate is 20 percent. Patients who survive show renal failure and a slow convalescence.

Epidemiology. There are two yellow fever cycles in nature. One cycle involves humans and the *Aedes aegypti* mosquito. This cycle is associated with epidemics in urban areas and is termed **urban yellow fever.** Urban yellow fever has not been observed in the Americas in over 30 years because of vector control measures. The second cycle involves virus infection of monkeys. In this instance the monkey serves as a source of virus for the mosquitoes of the genus *Haemogogus*. This genus of mosquito can transmit virus to other monkeys or to humans. This cycle is referred to as **jungle** or **sylvatic yellow fever.**

Vector control measures that led to the eradication of *A. aegypti* and urban yellow fever are almost impossible to implement in forested areas where yellow fever is endemic. There is great concern that urban yellow fever may reappear because of the reinvasion of countries by *A. aegypti.*

The actual number of cases of yellow fever that occur each year is difficult to evaluate because most epidemics occur in areas where surveillance is not adequate.

Laboratory Diagnosis. Diagnosis on clinical grounds is almost impossible in the infection phase of the disease. Severe forms of yellow fever resemble other hemorrhagic fevers. It is possible to detect yellow fever viral antigens in serum, blood, and liver tissue by enzyme immunoassays in which monoclonal or polyclonal IgM antibodies are used. IgM antibodies can be detected in the patient's serum by using enzyme immunoassays.

Treatment and Prevention. There is no specific treatment for yellow fever other than supportive care. Liver failure and shock can be treated by introducing 10 to 20% glucose intravenously to maintain adequate nutrition and prevent hypoglycemia. Renal changes must be monitored and treated since many patients die of renal tubular necrosis.

Prevention of yellow fever depends on control of the mosquito vector. A live attenuated virus vaccine, 17D, induces an effective antibody level that persists for at least 10 years and is recommended for anyone traveling to areas where yellow fever is endemic. Since the vaccine is produced in chick embryo cell culture, it should not be administered to persons who are hypersensitive to eggs.

Dengue Fever and Dengue Hemorrhagic Fever

Dengue is a disease cause by a flavivirus transmitted to humans primarily by the *A. aegypti* mosquito, but other mosquito vectors can be involved. Four serological types of virus are involved in two types of syndromes: **classic dengue fever** and **dengue hemorrhagic fever (DHF)**.

Pathogenesis. Classic dengue fever produces a self-limiting infection in humans. There is an incubation period of two to seven days following the mosquito bite. The initial symptoms include high fever, headache, and lumbosacral pain. Later there is soreness in the joints, myalgia, nausea, and vomiting. A macular rash may appear on the first or second day and this is followed by a maculopapular rash a few days later. Pinpoint hemorrhages (petechiae) may appear over the dorsum of the feet or on the legs, hands, or fingers. Classic dengue fever is rarely fatal unless complications occur.

Although the four dengue virus serotypes are antigenically related, they are not cross protective. It is believed that dengue may be more severe if an infection with one dengue serotype follows infection with another serotype. DHF is the severe form of disease; it is serious and frequently fatal. Hemorrhages with leakage of plasma and erythrocytes lead to severe necrosis. Major histopathological changes occur in the liver, vascular system, and reticuloendothelial system. Replicating virus is believed to cause the release of vasoactive mediators that cause vascular permeability. In some instances this condition results in a shock syndrome called **dengue shock syndrome (DSS)**. Without physiological treatment, up to 50 percent of patients with DHF/DSS die.

Epidemiology. Dengue fever and DHF/DSS occur wherever the mosquito vector is present. Most cases of dengue virus infection are associated with tropical areas: the Americas and tropical Asia. *A. aegypti* is the most important vector in transmission of the dengue fever virus throughout all tropical areas. *Aedes albopictus* is an important vector in Asia and the Pacific and is now appearing in the Americas. *A. albopictus* breeds in water found in tires stored outside. Infestations of this mosquito in the United States and other areas were the result of shipments of used tires from Asia. The tires contained eggs and larvae of the mosquito vector. Outbreaks of classic disease have also been reported from Somalia.

Outbreaks of dengue continue in the Americas. In 1989 and 1990 during a three-month period 3000 cases of DHF/DSS occurred in a coastal town in Venezuela. DHF/DSS has become an important disease in Asia since the 1960s. Before 1960 only classic dengue fever was the principal manifestation of infection. It now appears that a human gene controls the severity of secondary infections. Blacks are less likely to have severe infections because the gene is inhomogeneously distributed among them.

Laboratory Diagnosis. Specific diagnosis of dengue fever depends on virus isolation and serological tests. The most widely used serological test is the hemagglutination inhibition assay. Development of type-specific virus monoclonal antibodies has aided in the identification and typing of the viruses. The test is time-consuming. PCR is being evaluated.

Treatment and Prevention. Treatment for classic dengue fever is only supportive and includes bed rest and electrolyte replacement in dehydrated patients. Because of platelet dysfunction, aspirin or other salicylates are not recommended. For DHF/DSS, fluid replacement is necessary to replace plasma volume. Oxygen should be administered and if intravascular coagulation occurs, heparin therapy may be necessary. Blood transfusions may be necessary if hemorrhaging is severe.

Prevention of dengue relies on eradication of *A. aegypti* and other species via larvicides and spraying of insecticides. Eradication was begun in the 1920s and 1930s in the Americas but reinfestation seems to be occurring in certain regions. Reinfestation may be due to import of new mosquito vectors, as well as to increased insecticide resistance of some mosquito vectors.

ROTAVIRUSES AND OTHER AGENTS OF GASTROINTESTINAL DISEASE

In developing countries viral gastroenteritis is the second most important clinical entity, second only to viral upper respiratory tract disease. Acute gastroenteritis affects over 500 million children yearly and is a leading cause of death of children in developing countries.

The principal viral agents causing gastroenteritis are RNA viruses. DNA viruses such as adenovirus types 40 and 41 plus Norwalk virus, however, may also be associated with this syndrome. Rotaviruses are the most important viral agents causing morbidity and mortality, and most of our discussion centers on this group.

Rotaviruses

Rotaviruses belong to the family Reoviridae. They infect a wide variety of mammals, including humans and birds. The virus (*rota* means "wheel" in Latin) possesses a double-shelled capsid that encloses a double-stranded RNA composed of 11 segments. The outer capsid gives the appearance of the rim of a wheel (Fig. 32-23).

Pathogenesis. The rotavirus is transmitted by the fecal-oral route. The virus is acid-labile but can survive the pH of the stomach if the latter is buffered or is protected by the contents of the meal. The incubation period for infection is 48 hours. Fever, vomiting, and diarrhea are present at the onset of symptoms. The virus infects the small intestine and confines its activities to the epithelial cells on the tips of villi. During infection there are abnormally low levels of maltase, sucrase, and lactase in children with the disease. Most infected children also have lactose malabsorption and intolerance. If they are fed lactose, diarrhea actually increases; thus a non-lactose-containing formula is given during rotavirus gastroenteritis. Normal lactose tolerance returns 10 to 14 days after the onset of symptoms.

Loss of fluids during gastroenteritis leads to severe dehydration and even death. In developing countries recur-

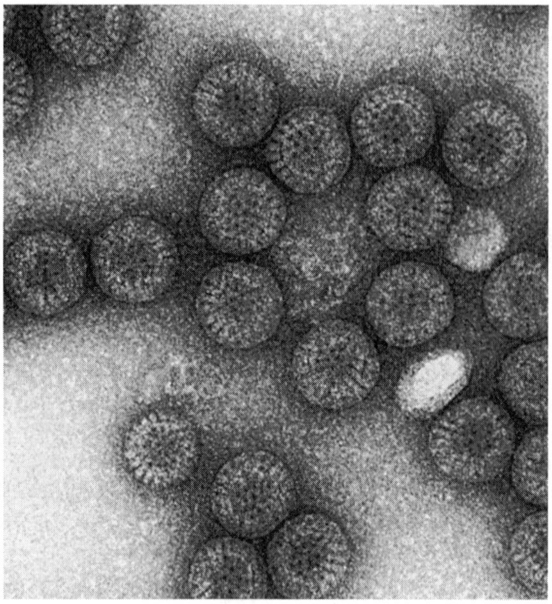

FIGURE 32-23
Electron micrograph of rotavirus. (Courtesy of H. Gelderblom.)

rent bouts of gastroenteritis cause protracted diarrhea, food intolerance, and malnutrition. Dehydrating diarrhea may last five to seven days. In countries where many infants and children are already malnourished, rotavirus infection can be devastating.

Infection in neonates usually results in a mild or asymptomatic disease. Less than one-third of the neonates demonstrate diarrhea. Strains that infect neonates are different from those that infect older children. Neonatal infection appears to incite an immune response that provides protection against severe rotavirus-associated disease but not against symptomatic rotavirus infection later in life.

Epidemiology. There are three serotypes of rotavirus (A, B, and C). Group A is the major cause of endemic severe diarrhea in infants and children worldwide. Rotaviruses infect nearly every child within the first 4 years of life. In the United States the Centers for Disease Control estimates that 16.5 million children under 5 years old have diarrhea each year, resulting in 220,000 hospital admissions and about 375 deaths. Approximately 110,000 of these children are hospitalized with rotavirus infection. The virus can also cause gastroenteritis in adults, particularly the elderly. Rotavirus is now recognized as a cause of diarrhea in adult patients after renal transplantation.

The source of infection for infants is an older sibling or parent with subclinical disease. Rotavirus infection is prevalent in many settings such as day-care centers from whence it can be spread to family contacts. Rotavirus infection in nursing homes can become extensive and involve 50 percent or more of the patients.

Laboratory Diagnosis. Rotavirus cultivation is usually not carried out in clinical laboratories. Stool samples contain from 10^7 to 10^9 rotavirus particles per gram of stool. They can be detected by immunoelectron microscopy or polyacrylamide gel electrophoresis and silver staining of viral nucleic acid. ELISA or radioimmunoassays can also be utilized to detect viral antigen.

Treatment and Prevention. Replacement of fluids and electrolytes lost through dehydration is the most effective treatment. Fluid replacement can be accomplished by either oral or intravenous administration of water and electrolytes. Oral glucose-electrolyte solutions are preferred for routine use while intravenous solutions may be required for severe forms of the disease.

Vaccines are being developed but so far the results from field trials have not been encouraging.

Other Agents of Gastrointestinal Disease

Caliciviruses. Caliciviruses are single-stranded RNA viruses that have a distinctive morphology. They derive their name from the 32 cup-shaped depressions on the surface of the virion. The genome of the virus has been characterized and is related to the Norwalk virus as well as the hepatitis E virus.

Caliciviruses cause gastroenteritis in infants and young children but are not an important cause of sporadic or epidemic gastroenteritis. Caliciviruses can also cause disease in the elderly. Most individuals are infected by these viruses at an early age and infections can occur throughout the year. The symptoms of disease are as severe as those caused by rotaviruses. Diarrhea and vomiting are the most prominent features of infection.

Caliciviruses have not been isolated in routine cell cultures. Virus detection in stools is accomplished by electron microscopy and by radioimmunoassay.

Treatment of calicivirus infection is the same as for rotavirus infection.

No vaccine is available.

The **Norwalk** virus (identified during an epidemic in Norwalk, Ohio) is a prototype for several viruses that cause a mild epidemic form of gastroenteritis. It belongs to the family Caliciviridae. Norwalk viruses cannot be cultivated in cell culture by standard techniques, but they can be identified by immunoelectron microscopy, (see Chapter 31).

Norwalk or Norwalk-like viruses have been implicated in 42 percent of foodborne outbreaks in the United States investigated by the Centers for Disease Control. The virus is a major cause of waterborne gastroenteritis and is also an important cause of shellfish-associated gastroenteritis. The disease is mild and is characterized by vomiting, nausea, diarrhea, and abdominal pain. The disease resolves on its own. The mildness of disease is comparable to infection by astroviruses and caliciviruses.

Norwalk virus is usually acquired by ingestion of contaminated food or water (see Under the Microscope 36). Administration of fluids is suggested to replace the fluids lost through diarrhea. Immunity to reinfection may be short term or long term. Short-term resistance is serotype-specific for 6 to 14 weeks after the initial infection. The reasons for long-term immunity are not known, since most individuals who resist viral challenge have little if

UNDER THE MICROSCOPE 36

Ice and the Norwalk Virus

Within a period of one week in 1987, a cluster of outbreaks of gastrointestinal illness occurred among persons who had attended a fund-raiser in Wilmington, Delaware, and an intercollegiate football game in Philadelphia. Of the 614 people attending these events, 191 became ill. A survey showed that those who consumed ice were 12 times more likely to experience vomiting or diarrhea than those who did not. Ice consumed at the events was traced to a manufacturer in southern Pennsylvania. The manufacturer's wells had been contaminated when flooded by a nearby creek after a torrential rainfall about two weeks before the illnesses occurred. Ice for the fund-raiser was consumed almost exclusively with alcoholic beverages. Forty-eight percent of the band members who consumed ice in beverages became ill. The musicians who did not have ice did not become ill.

One might expect the alcohol or low pH of some of the beverages to have had a disinfectant effect on the virus. Infectivity of the virus was not affected by freezing or short-term exposure to these beverages.

Manufacturers using independent water supplies and not municipal water should adequately treat the water used for ice making.

any antibody to the virus. Studies do indicate that an individual must be exposed to the virus several times before immunity develops.

Astroviruses. Astroviruses are responsible for about 5 percent of the cases of infantile gastroenteritis. The virus is a single-stranded RNA virus that has a star-shaped (astro) configuration. Symptomatic disease with astroviruses is most likely to develop in children from infancy to 5 to 7 years old.

The incubation period is 24 to 36 hours, with symptoms similar to those of gastroenteritis caused by other viruses: vomiting, diarrhea, and fever. Most acute infections, unlike rotavirus infection, do not require hospitalization. There is no treatment for infection other than maintaining fluid and electrolyte balance.

Astroviruses can be detected in stool suspensions by electron microscopy or by an enzyme immunoassay that detects antigen.

HUMAN IMMUNODEFICIENCY VIRUS AND ACQUIRED IMMUNODEFICIENCY SYNDROME

The HIV has become an important challenge to the medical community since the manifestations of infection by the virus were first discovered in 1979. Infection by HIV leads to progressive deterioration of the immune system. This deterioration leads to the final stage of HIV disease called **AIDS**. To date AIDS is an incurable condition and no vaccine is available.

The HIV belongs to a class of retroviruses called human T lymphotropic viruses (HTLV). HTLV-I and HTLV-II are associated with human T cell leukemia and lymphoma while HTLV-III (now called HIV-1) is the cause of AIDS. HIV-1 consists of a central core in which are enclosed two identical strands of RNA and enzymes such as reverse transcriptase, protease, and integrase (Fig. 32-24). Surrounding the core is a bilayered envelope, the inner side of which is adjacent to a protein shell. Embedded in the envelope are glycoprotein spikes that protrude from the surface of the virus. The glycoprotein of the spike that is found on the surface is called **gp 120.** As we shall see later, this protein plays an important role in the disease process.

The HIV-1 genome encodes at least nine genes, the most studied of which are *gag*, *pol*, and *env*. The *gag* gene encodes the internal core proteins. The *pol* gene specifies a reverse transcriptase, a protease, and an integrase. The **integrase** facilitates the integration of the viral genome into the host chromosome. A very interesting aspect of HIV is its inability to repair mutations that occur in the genome, a characteristic unlike other viruses. As many as 28 different HIV variants have been found in a single infected individual. Many of the variants arise following treatment with drugs such as zidovudine (AZT) and some of these mutant strains can be especially virulent.

Pathogenesis

Infection by HIV-1 involves interaction with the $CD4^+$ receptor, which is expressed at greatest concentration on **$CD4^+$ helper T4 cells.** It is also expressed in lower amounts on monocytes and macrophages (Table 32-5). The viral component that interacts with the CD antigen is the **gp 120** glycoprotein. The gp 120 protein is anchored to **gp 41** (see Fig. 32-24). The initial binding of virus results in the uncovering of gp 41. The gp 41 protein embeds itself in the cytoplasmic membrane of the host cell and thus a fusion of viral and cell membrane takes place. During the fusion process the virus core is believed to be injected into the cell (the molecular biology of virus assembly was discussed previously).

HIV-1 can apparently enter both resting and stimulated $CD4^+$ cells. HIV replication only proceeds to completion

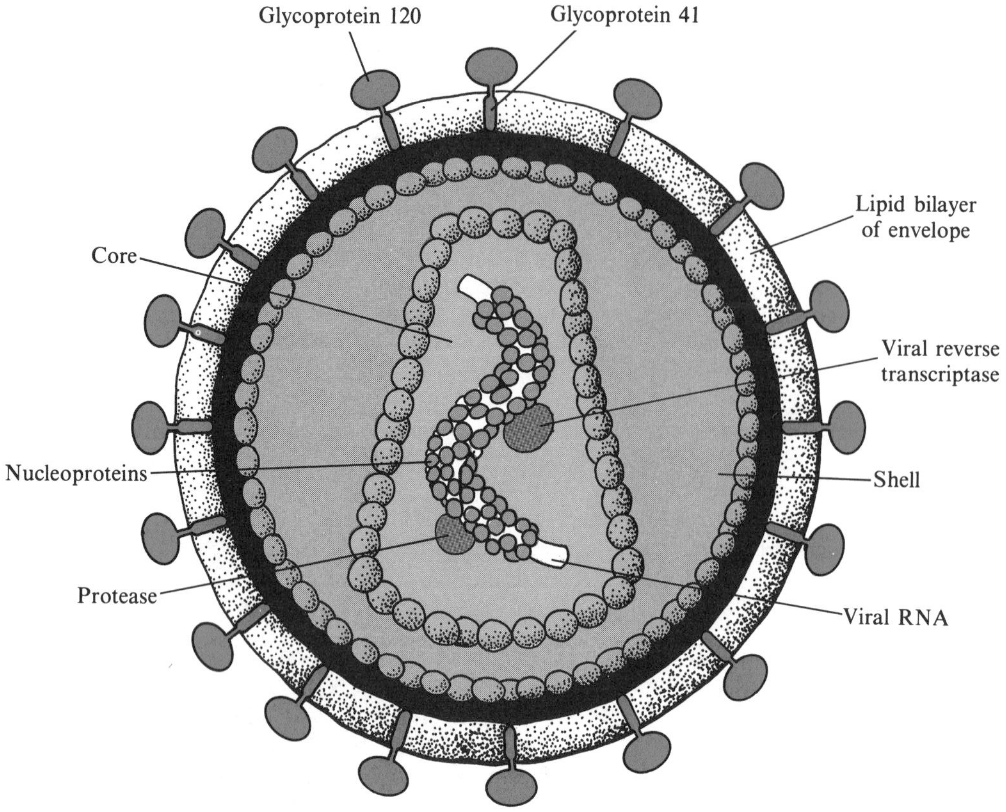

FIGURE 32-24
Basic structure of the human immunodeficiency virus (HIV).

in stimulated CD4$^+$ lymphocytes. The CD4$^+$ or helper T cell and the virus p24 antigen are the surrogate markers that most closely correlate with the particular stage of HIV-1 infection. HIV-1 infection can be broken down into three stages: **primary** or **acute** period, **chronic** or **asymptomatic** period, and **crisis** or **AIDS** period.

Primary or Acute Stage. Prior to the primary stage, an individual may have been infected with virus for six weeks to one year before virus or virus antibodies can be detected. The acute or primary stage is associated with the symptoms of fever, headache, lymphadenopathy, pharyngitis, myalgias, and rash. Viral titers are evident in the plasma and up to 1 percent of the CD4$^+$ lymphocytes in the peripheral bloodstream are infected. It appears that not all of the infected cells are actively replicating virus. This may explain why there is such a long incubation period for HIV infection. During the acute stage there is a rapid production of viral variants. These variants may be cytopathic or noncytopathic. There is a slight and transient decline in the peripheral CD4$^+$ count (Fig. 32-25) during this period (a normal CD4$^+$ count is 800 per microliter of blood). With CD4$^+$ decline there is a concomitant rise in CD8$^+$ (cytotoxic T cells) cells.

About 1 month after the appearance of the acute stage the symptoms subside. The virus titer, as measured by p24 core antigen, declines. In addition, there is an increase in anti-p24 antibodies. Thus, the antiviral humoral immune response has contributed to decreasing viral replication. At the end of this stage the CD4$^+$ count is almost back to normal. The primary stage is considered ended with seroconversion and establishment of a low-level chronic viremia.

Chronic or Asymptomatic Stage. Following the acute stage there is an asymptomatic period lasting from 7 to 11 years. This period, previously described as latency, may in fact represent a smoldering infection in which there is continual and persistent destruction of the immune system (see Under the Microscope 37). During this period the CD4$^+$ count remains almost normal but the

TABLE 32-5
Sites of Cell-Specific Human Immunodeficiency Virus Replication

CD4$^+$ cells	CD4$^-$ cells
T4 lymphocytes	T8 lymphocytes
Monocyte-macrophages	Fibroblasts
Langerhans cells	Neural cells
B lymphocytes	Glial cells
	Endothelial cells

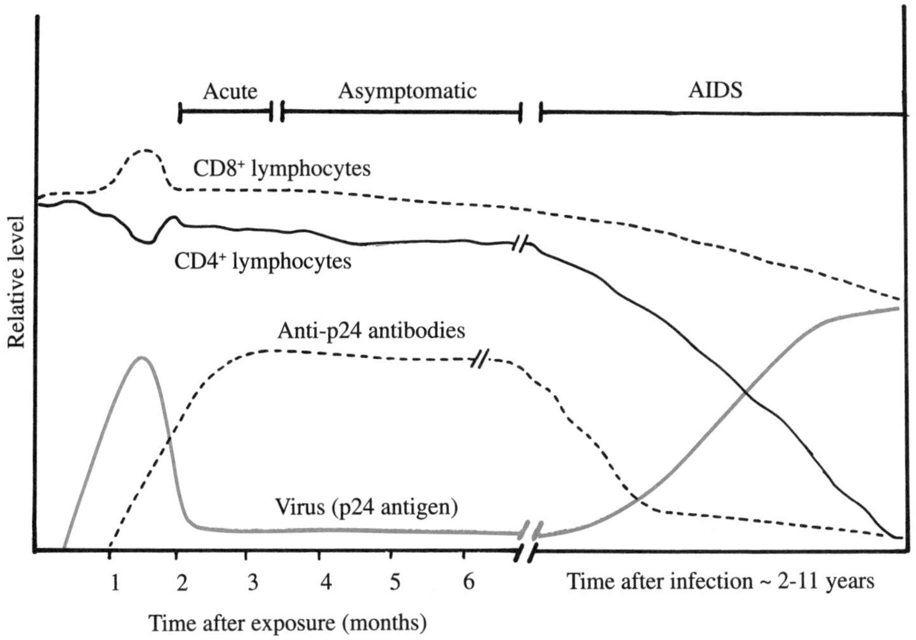

FIGURE 32-25
Stages of HIV infection and levels of associated factors in blood.

UNDER THE MICROSCOPE 37

HIV and Latency: Maybe Not

Conventional dogma about HIV pathogenesis states that virus enters a period of latency before the devastating stage called AIDS occurs. The theory states that at the end of the latent stage, an as yet unknown trigger signals the virus to replicate. This replication is manifested as a precipitous drop in $CD4^+$ T cell count and one or more of the symptoms of AIDS. Critics of this doctrine, such as Anthony Fauci and members of his laboratory, suggest that the virus leaves the bloodstream and moves to the lymph nodes and thymus where it remains active.

Fauci suggests that virus trapped in lymph nodes takes advantage of the presence of B cells. Virus antigen activates B cells, which in turn release IgG as well as cytokines. The cytokines are a prerequisite for activating $CD4^+$ cells. When $CD4^+$ cells migrate through the lymph nodes, they become activated and in this condition are infected and killed by HIV.

A second line of evidence comes from electron micrographs of HIV-infected lymph nodes. Virus apparently is slowly disrupting the architecture of the antigen-trapping follicular dendritic cells (these are found in lymph node and thymus). This renders the dendritic cells incapable of trapping any antigen including HIV. By the time the $CD4^+$ count has reached dangerously low levels (200 cells per microliter or lower), the follicular dendritic cells are swollen and necrotic. Since the lymph nodes are no longer able to handle HIV particles or their antigens, the latter go back into the blood. Fauci believes this is why there is such a tremendous increase in virus as AIDS appears.

A third line of evidence, using human thymic transplants in mice, suggests that thymic HIV infection slowly devastates the progenitor T cell population, the population that would normally replenish the T cells killed through lymph node infection.

See *Science* 245:305, 1989.

number of infected $CD4^+$ lymphocytes increases. The effects of immune system deterioration during this period become more evident.

Cell-mediated immune responses are progressively lost during the asymptomatic stage. The individual is unable to respond to microbial antigens. This is reflected in a loss of **delayed-type hypersensitivity** on skin testing. This immune unresponsiveness (anergy) may be due to defective antigen presenting capacity, or a viral factor that interferes with lymphocyte activation. It should be pointed out that the virus at this stage and during AIDS is not the same virus that initiated the acute stage of infection. The virus in the chronic stage replicates faster, has an enhanced cellular host range, is more destructive to the $CD4^+$ population, and appears to resist neutralization.

The clinical predictors that are associated with an increased likelihood of progression to AIDS include oral manifestations such as oral candidiasis or hairy leukoplakia, and the presence of certain symptoms such as fever and weight loss. Humoral response to the viral p24 core antigen has no prognostic significance during the asymptomatic stage (see Fig. 32-25). An increase in virus population, however, may be a predictor of the development of AIDS.

The major cofactor influencing delay in disease progression is the inherited genetic makeup of the host. This genetic makeup determines the susceptibility of cells to HIV replication and the effectiveness of the antiviral immune response.

Crisis Stage or AIDS. The laboratory predictor of progression to AIDS is the $CD4^+$ lymphocyte count. When the count gets too low, the host is subject to opportunistic infections. The reason for this is that once helper T4 cells are depleted, they cannot carry out their important functions: (1) activation of B lymphocytes that are responsible for antibody production, (2) influence on cytotoxic cells and natural killer cells in the cell-mediated immune response, and (3) influence on macrophages whose products modulate the activity of many cell types.

During the crisis stage there is a progressive drop in $CD4^+$ lymphocyte count. When the count is between 200 and 499 cells per microliter and various clinical manifestations are present, the physician should consider aggressive clinical management. The disease manifestations include the following:

1. Bacillary angiomatosis
2. Candidiasis (thrush)
3. Cervical dysplasia/cervical carcinoma
4. Fever and diarrhea lasting more than one month
5. Hairy leukoplakia
6. Herpes zoster
7. Idiopathic thrombocytopenic purpura
8. Pelvic inflammatory disease
9. Peripheral neuropathy

When the $CD4^+$ lymphocyte count goes below 200 cells per microliter, adolescents and adults are considered in the AIDS indicator category. The conditions included in this category are outlined in Table 32-6. The spectrum of "usual" opportunistic infections includes those caused by *Pneumocystis carinii, Toxoplasma gondii, Cryptococcus neoformans, Candida* species, cytomegalovirus, and the *Mycobacterium avium* complex. In the United States, for example, the most common opportunistic infection among AIDS patients is *P. carinii* pneumonia. Disseminated opportunistic infection indicates an almost total loss of T4 cell function.

In the terminal stages of AIDS, many patients have **AIDS dementia complex,** a syndrome characterized by gradual loss of mental control over thought and motion. The affected individuals are usually unable to communicate effectively or walk.

TABLE 32-6
Some of the Opportunistic Diseases That Are Included in the 1993 AIDS Surveillance Case Definition*

1. Candidiasis of esophagus, trachea, bronchi, or lung (see page 485)
2. Cryptococcosis, disseminated or extrapulmonary (see page 478)
3. Cryptosporidiosis, chronic intestinal, > 1 month's duration (see page 516)
4. Cytomegalovirus disease, other than liver, spleen, or nodes (see page 411)
5. Kaposi's sarcoma (Plate 23)
6. *Mycobacterium avium* complex or *M. kansasii* infection, disseminated or extrapulmonary (see page 337)
7. *Mycobacterium tuberculosis* infection, pulmonary or extrapulmonary (see page 332)
8. *Pneumocystis carinii* pneumonia
9. Wasting syndrome due to HIV
10. Progressive multifocal leukoencephalopathy
11. Herpes simplex: chronic ulcer (> 1 month's duration); or bronchitis, pneumonitis, or esophagitis (see page 415)
12. Histoplasmosis, disseminated or extrapulmonary (see page 474)

* See Centers for Disease Control, *M.M.W.R.* 41(No. RR-17): December 18, 1992 for remaining opportunistic diseases or conditions.

Pediatric AIDS

Transmission. The number of children diagnosed with AIDS is steadily increasing and AIDS will likely become one of the major causes of death in this population. Transmission of HIV to children can occur horizontally or vertically. Horizontal transmission can occur via contact with contaminated blood or blood products (hemophiliacs, for example), illegal drug injection (primarily by adolescents), and sexual intercourse, which also includes the sexual abuse of very young children.

Vertical transmission can occur via the placenta, during delivery, or through breast-feeding. Placental transmission can occur by active transport of the HIV IgG complex via Fc receptors on trophoblastic cells, passive transport of HIV when virus concentration in the blood is high, passage of infected maternal cells, and infection of the placenta itself. The rate of transmission of HIV by breast-feeding is believed to be relatively low. Because of its protective effects, breast-feeding is still recommended for

HIV-infected mothers in developing countries but not in developed countries where other alternatives and safe water to reconstitute infant formula exist.

In the United States the percentage of women with AIDS is about 10 percent but this figure is rising. Worldwide nearly 50 percent of the AIDS cases occur in women. Since over 80 percent of women with AIDS are of child-bearing age, the number of children infected with HIV is increasing at an alarming rate. Vertical transmission from mother to child is therefore becoming more common.

Studies indicate that vertical transmission may occur in utero as early as the beginning of the second trimester. The rate of infection in children ranges from 12 to 30 percent. Transmission from an infected mother may not occur with each pregnancy. This presents problems in terms of counseling a woman who becomes pregnant and who wishes to continue the pregnancy even if she has already given birth to one HIV-infected child.

Clinical Features. HIV-infected infants show similarities to and differences from HIV-infected adults. In children the B cell defect precedes T cell deficiency and there is an increase in immunoglobulins that are dysfunctional. These children are subject to recurrent bacterial infections by encapsulated bacteria (*Hemophilus influenzae* and *Streptococcus pneumoniae,* for example). The symptoms of pediatric infection appear much earlier than in adults. For example, in infants infected perinatally, symptoms appear at about the age of 9 months and about 90 percent of infected children are diagnosed by the age of 3 years. Certain opportunistic infections normally observed in adults (Kaposi's sarcoma, toxoplasmosis, and cryptococcal meningitis) are rarely observed in children. In contrast, lymphocytic interstitial pneumonitis is much more common in children than in adults. One of the most devastating manifestations of HIV infection in children is **encephalopathy,** which is found in 50 to 90 percent of those with AIDS. Encephalopathy results in slow acquisition of motor skills. Other features of perinatal infection include lymphadenopathy, splenomegaly, or hepatomegaly. Most fatalities occur within the first 12 months of life. By the age of 2 years the illness often stabilizes and in some children improves.

Children diagnosed with *P. carinii* pneumonia or encephalopathy have a poor prognosis while those diagnosed with lymphocytic interstitial pneumonia have a more favorable prognosis.

Epidemiology

The HIV strain causing disease in all populations, except those from West Africa, is called HIV-1. The virus causing infection in West Africa is called HIV-2. HIV-2 is similar to a virus called **simian immunodeficiency virus** (SIV), which is found in African green monkeys. HIV-2 appears to be less virulent than HIV-1 since West Africans infected with HIV-2 are at a low risk for development of AIDS compared to individuals infected with HIV-1.

As of 1994 over 17 million individuals worldwide are infected with HIV. It is projected that by the year 2000 as many as 30 million individuals will be infected. Perinatal transmission is increasing at an alarming rate. In Africa alone there are up to 5 million AIDS orphans.

From 1981 to December 1992 a total of 253,448 cases of AIDS was reported in the United States. The cumulative number of deaths in that same time frame was 148,235. Most cases remain prevalent in metropolitan areas of the East and West Coasts. In addition, AIDS is still predominant among homosexual and bisexual men. Still, in recent years there has been a decline of incidence in this group and an increase in infection among injection drug users and their partners. Concomitant with the increase of AIDS among injection drug abusers there has been a rise in heterosexual transmission. Regardless of the source of infection, HIV infection among women of reproductive age has increased considerably over the years (see Pediatric AIDS).

Risk factors for sexual transmission of HIV include the practice of anal intercourse, lack of condom use, and clinical status (T cell count) of the infected partner. Individuals who have genital ulcers or who are not circumcised are at increased risk of becoming infected. In injection drug abusers the risk factors include sharing of needles and intercourse with a high number of sexual partners. The latter is attributed to the practice of exchanging sex for drugs.

There has been considerable concern that transmission of HIV may occur by casual contact or by insect vectors. Although HIV may appear in the saliva, the concentration of virus is much lower than that in the blood. Studies have shown that exposure of the skin or mucous membrane of health care personnel to the saliva of HIV-infected people has not yet resulted in infection. Studies of families in whom one member was infected with HIV have demonstrated that daily household contact with the infected member has as yet not resulted in any reported cases of disease (except for the sexual partners of infected persons and children born to infected mothers).

Laboratory Diagnosis

In children and adults, a screening assay (ELISA) and a confirmatory test (immunoblot or Western blot) have been the most widely used techniques for establishing the presence of HIV infection. On the ELISA, there will be approximately 100 false-positive results per 10,000 individuals tested in the United States. A confirmatory test is therefore necessary.

For the Western blot assay, HIV antigens are dotted onto a strip of nitrocellulose. The strip is then inoculated with the serum from the individual suspected to have HIV infection. The strip is then placed in anti–human IgG alkaline phosphatase conjugate. The strip is washed to remove excess reagents and then developed with a substrate of the enzyme that will react and produce a colored reaction—a dark blue dot with a double rim indicates a positive reaction.

Tests that measure antibody to HIV in adults are not applicable to infants (less than 15 months old). This is because there is no consistent IgM response by the fetus or infant to the virus. IgG-based ELISA and Western blot tests are also not applicable in pediatric patients because of the presence of maternal anti–HIV IgG antibodies. These antibodies may persist in the child for up to 18 months. In addition, some infants who are seropositive at birth will become seronegative even though they are infected. Some who are seronegative will again become seropositive while others will remain seronegative. HIV culture methods are highly specific and have been adapted for pediatric patients. Polymerase chain reaction is as sensitive as culture and results are available within a few days. Although culture and polymerase chain reaction are not commercially available, it is no longer necessary to wait 18 months to make a diagnosis.

Treatment

One of the major problems in the treatment of AIDS patients is that there are a host of opportunistic microbial agents, each with different antimicrobial susceptibilities. The principal treatment for HIV revolves around the use of **azidothymidine (AZT)**, or zidovudine, plus **dideoxyinosine (DDI)**. Both of these drugs prevent the transcription of retroviral RNA and DNA. A host of drugs are also required for the treatment of opportunistic infections. All of these drugs interact in specific ways that lead to adverse reactions. Table 32-7 outlines the various drugs used to treat HIV as well as opportunistic pathogens.

Treatment of the infected infant or child is a delicate balancing act. Many aspects of therapy must be weighed, including the drugs available and their toxicity, route and duration of drug administration, and possible modification of treatment regimen.

AZT has shown considerable benefit in the treatment of pediatric AIDS. Intravenous administration of AZT, for example, is effective in the treatment of HIV-induced encephalopathy. Prolonged treatment (6 to 12 months) with AZT is often associated with the development of drug resistance and treatment failures. Dideoxyinosine has been approved by the Food and Drug Administration for use in symptomatic HIV-infected children who show evidence of disease progression while receiving AZT. Another drug, 2′3′-dideoxycytidine (ddC), is being evaluated for use in combination with AZT. It is hoped that the drug combination will reduce the toxicity of each individual drug given alone. Myelosuppression is associated with AZT and painful peripheral neuropathy is associated with ddC.

Recurrent bacterial infections are a cause of morbidity in HIV-infected children. Intravenous immunoglobulin G (IVIG) reduces the incidence of recurrent bacterial infections in children with CD4 lymphocyte counts of less than 200 cells per microliter.

P. carinii pneumonia is as devastating to infants and children as it is to adults. Prophylaxis is recommended and trimethoprim-sulfamethoxazole is the recommended first-line agent. Patients intolerant to trimethoprim-sulfa-

TABLE 32-7
Drugs Used in the Treatment of HIV Infection and Some Opportunistic Infections Associated with AIDS

Target microbe or infection	Therapy	Adverse reaction
HIV	Zidovudine (AZT)	Neutropenia, anemia
	Dideoxyinosine (DDI)	Pancreatitis, peripheral neuropathy, diarrhea
Candidiasis	Fluconazole	Intestinal disturbances, skin rash, vomiting
	Ketoconazole	Hepatitis, vomiting, adrenal suppression
Cryptococcosis	Fluconazole	See above
Cytomegalovirus disease	Ganciclovir	Neutropenia, thrombocytopenia
	Foscarnet	Nephrotoxic, hypocalcemia, anemia, neurological toxicity, penile ulcerations
P. carinii pneumonia	Trimethoprim-sulfamethoxazole	Neutropenia, thrombocytopenia, rash, nausea and vomiting
	Trimethoprim-dapsone	Rash, nausea and vomiting
	Pentamidine	Nephrotoxicity, pancreatitis, elevated liver enzyme levels
Toxoplasmosis	Pyrimethamine-sulfadiazine	Rash, leukopenia, thrombocytopenia, elevated liver enzyme levels
Mycobacterial disease	Pyrazinamide	Arthralgia, hyperuricemia
	Ciprofloxacin	Nausea, diarrhea
	Clofazimine	Skin discoloration, nausea, retinal degeneration
	Conventional drugs such as rifampin, isoniazid	
Isosporiasis*	Trimethoprim-sulfamethoxazole; pyrimethamine	See above

* Isosporiasis is caused by the animal parasite *Isospora belli. I. belli* infection causes chronic diarrhea in immunocompromised patients, but it also can cause a mild diarrhea in normal hosts (usually in tropical and subtropical areas). See Under the Microscope 49.

methoxazole can be treated with dapsone or aerosolized or intravenous pentamidine.

Prevention

A vaccine is not yet available for preventing HIV-1 infection* and AIDS. Several vaccines are under trial and include killed virus, subunit virus, HIV subunit in a virus vector, and anti-idiotype vaccines.

At present, worldwide prevention of AIDS is best accomplished through education. Various guidelines to minimize the risk of HIV transmission, particularly among the sexually active, include the following:

1. Avoidance of sexual contact with persons suspected of having AIDS or a positive result on an HIV antibody test
2. Avoidance of anal intercourse
3. Avoidance of sexual contacts with multiple partners
4. Avoidance of sexual contact with people who inject drugs
5. The use of condoms during sexual intercourse
6. Avoidance of oral-genital contact and open-mouthed, intimate kissing

In addition, any man having sex with any other man in the past 10 years should not donate blood, organs, or other tissues. Further, seropositive women in developed countries should not breast-feed their babies.

HIV transmission among laboratory personnel can be prevented by utilizing the biosafety procedures used to prevent hepatitis B infection. These procedures include using latex gloves or vinyl gloves, handwashing with soap and water after handling infectious material, and using protective clothing, including face masks and protective eyewear.

THE HEPATITIS VIRUSES

Viral hepatitis is a disease involving the liver. Sporadic hepatitis can result from infection by several viruses including the CMV and yellow fever virus. Acute hepatitis, however, is caused by four viral agents, designated **hepatitis A virus (HAV)**, **hepatitis B virus (HBV)**, **hepatitis C virus (HCV)**, and **hepatitis E virus (HEV)**. Another distinct type of hepatitis, **hepatitis D (HDV)**, is an infection dependent on the presence of HBV and HDV. The worldwide impact of these viruses is enormous. Thousands of cases are reported each year in the United States. Several hundred thousand people each year die from the late manifestations of acute hepatitis.

Although the hepatitis viruses include both DNA and RNA types, they are discussed together because of their similar pathogenicity.

General Characteristics

Hepatitis A Virus. The HAV was first detected in a stool specimen in 1979 by immunoelectron microscopy (Fig. 32-26). HAV possesses a single-stranded RNA genome and belongs to the family Picornaviridae, genus *Heparnavirus* or enterovirus 72. The virus is stable to treatment with acid and heat (60 C for at least one hour). HAV does not cross-react with HBV.

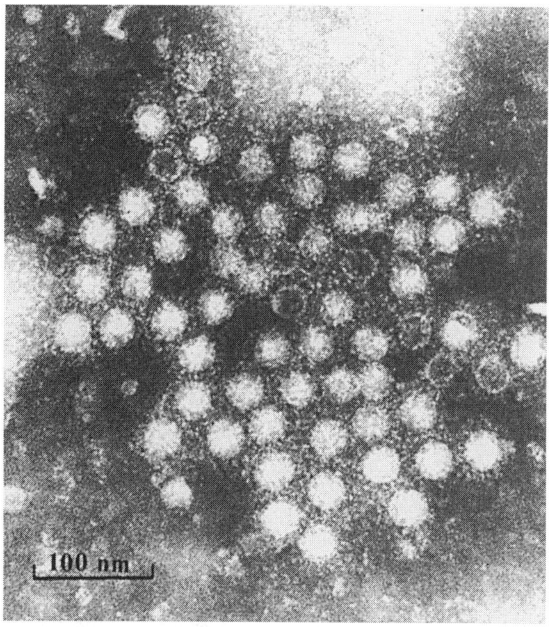

FIGURE 32-26
Immunoelectron microscopy of hepatitis A virus. (From A. MacGregor et al., *J. Clin. Microbiol.* 18:1237, 1983.)

Hepatitis B Virus. The HBV is a DNA virus belonging to the genus *Hepadnavirus*. HBV is a double-shelled virion 40 to 50 nm in diameter (originally called **Dane particles** because of their discovery in 1970 by Dane) with a core 27 nm in diameter. The core contains a double-stranded DNA molecule together with DNA polymerase. Tubular or filamentous forms up to 200 nm in length are also observed; they have a diameter of 22 nm. A third particle form, which is characteristically observed in blood during persistent infection, is 22 nm in diameter (Fig. 32-27). These particles are composed of the same material as the surface antigen of HBV, which is called hepatitis B surface antigen (HBsAg). HBV is resistant to acid (pH 2.4 for 6 hours), heat (60 C for 10 hours), and up to 40 cycles of freezing and thawing.

The surface antigen (HBsAg) manifests a group-specific determinant, *a*, and subtype-specific determinants *d* or *y* and *w* or *r*. With a few exceptions, subtypes *d* and *y* have not been found simultaneously in the same patient, and subtypes *w* and *r* are also mutually exclusive. Of the four possible antigenic combinations—*adw, ayw, adr,* and *ayr*—the first three are epidemiologically predominant.

During hepatitis B infection, several antigens and antibodies will appear. The following is a suggested system of nomenclature:

HBV, a 40- to 50-nm particle with a 27-nm core
HBsAg, found on the surface of the HBV, tubular forms, and the unattached 22-nm particles
Hepatitis B core antigen **(HBcAg)**, closely associated with the nucleocapsid of HBV

* Treatment of pregnant HIV-infected women with AZT reduces the transmission of virus to the fetus.

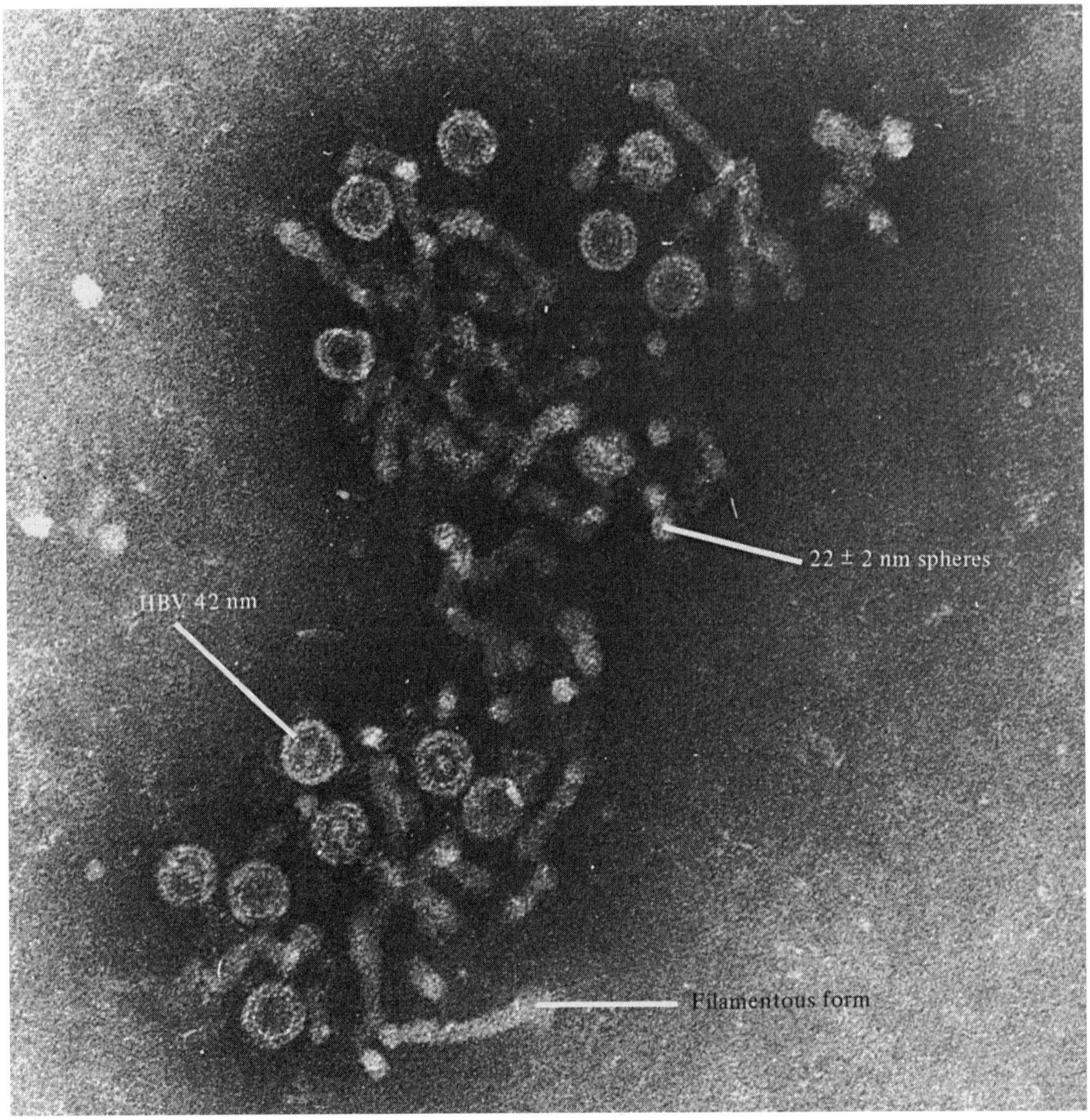

FIGURE 32-27
Electron micrograph of hepatitis B virus (HBV). Three morphological forms are observed: spheres 22 ± 2 nm in diameter, filamentous forms approximately 22 nm in diameter and varying in length, and 42-nm particles. (× 210,000.) (Courtesy of G. A. Cabral and M. Patterson.)

Hepatitis B x antigen **(HBxAg)**, found associated with core particles and important to HBV replication
Antibody to HBsAg (anti-HBs)
Antibody to HBcAg (anti-HBc)
Antibody to HBeAg (anti-HBe)
Antibody to HBxAg (anti-HBx)

Hepatitis C and E Viruses. Negative serological findings for HAV and HBV in certain patients with hepatitis led to the discovery of a hepatitis referred to as **non-A, non-B.** One of the viruses responsible for this type of hepatitis is HCV. HCV is an RNA virus closely related to flavivirus and pestivirus. Its genus name is *Hepacavirus.* HCV is transmitted primarily parenterally and is one of the primary causes of posttransfusion hepatitis.

Another type of non-A, non-B hepatitis is an enterically transmitted type of virus, HEV. HEV outbreaks are seen primarily in developing countries such as those in Asia and Africa. The HEV genome has been characterized. Gene arrangement and physical properties of the particle indicate that HEV is an RNA virus related to calicivirus. Its genus name is *Hepevirus.*

Pathogenesis

It is impossible to differentiate the clinical features of HAV, HBV, HCV, and HEV infection. Hepatitis viruses have an affinity for hepatocytes (liver cells). In HBV infection, core components are apparently synthesized in liver nuclei, whereas the surface antigens are produced in the

TABLE 32-8
Epidemiological and Clinical Features of Hepatitis Virus Infection

Characteristic	Hepatitis A	Hepatitis B	Hepatitis C	Hepatitis D	Hepatitis E
Transmission	Fecal-oral route (close personal contact; water and food as vehicles)	Parenteral (IV drug users); sexual contact (homosexual men primarily)	Parenteral (90 percent of posttransfusion-associated cases); IV drug use	Same as for hepatitis B (virus requires presence of hepatitis B virus)	Fecal-oral route
Incubation period	15–50 days	30–150 days	50–70 days	Same as for hepatitis B	10–40 days
Immunity to reinfection	Solid immunity to homologous agent but not heterologous agents	Reinfection with homologous agent possible but seldom occurs; no immunity to heterologous agents	Reinfection believed to occur	Reinfection shown to be possible in animals	Reinfection possible
Complications	Usually none	10 percent or more become chronic and can lead to liver cancer	Chronic disease may develop	Chronic disease is possible	Chronic disease may develop
Mortality	Less than 1 percent	1 percent	Similar to hepatitis B virus	Similar to hepatitis B virus	1–2 percent in epidemics; 10–20 percent in pregnant women

cytoplasm. The coat antigen (HBsAG) is produced in excess and sometimes is passed into the bloodstream as an unassembled 22-nm particle. The coat antigen is responsible for the antigenemia associated with hepatitis B infection.

The incubation periods for the hepatitis viruses are described in Table 32-8. The first clinical symptoms of infection are usually fever, headache, and vomiting. The illness may be associated with jaundice (icteric) or there may be no jaundice (anicteric). Jaundice is not always associated with illness; for example, jaundice is infrequently observed with HAV infection in children or with HEV infection.

Hepatitic lesions caused by the hepatitis viruses are the same: parenchymal cell degeneration, necrosis, proliferation or reticuloendothelial cells, and inflammation. During the period of necrosis there is increased serum **aminotransferase** activity and elevated **bilirubin** levels. Massive hepatic necrosis can lead to encephalopathy and death. Hepatitis B infection can be either acute or chronic. Infection can range in severity from an asymptomatic infection that resolves completely, to a severe symptomatic infection with progressive and even fatal illness. Patients with persistent HBsAg in the blood for more than six months usually become chronic carriers. Chronic infections can lead to a severe outcome where the mortality is as high as 10 percent.

HAV infection is much less severe than HBV infection and is associated with a self-limiting illness. Persistence is not associated with HAV infections. The immunological and biological events associated with infections by HAV and HBV are outlined in Figures 32-28 and 32-29, respectively.

Chronic disease is associated with HBV and HCV. Both viruses can cause severe liver disease and have the potential to be associated with hepatocellular carcinoma (see Chapter 31). Hepatocellular carcinoma associated with HCV is more predominant in Japan than other parts of the world. There is no indication that HEV is associated with chronic liver disease.

Epidemiology

Hepatitis A. Hepatitis A is usually transmitted by the fecal-oral route. Fecally contaminated food, water, and milk are potential sources of infection. Improperly cooked shellfish obtained from waters contaminated with raw sewage has also been implicated in transmission. Many outbreaks of infection have been traced to food handlers who are actively ill and have contaminated products such as potato salad, doughnuts, and frozen custard. Hepatitis A may also be spread by contaminated blood and blood products, just as hepatitis B; however, this is not the usual means of transmission (see Under the Microscope 38).

The highest incidence of infection occurs in children and adolescents. In developing countries, where hygiene and sanitation are poor, HAV infection occurs at an early age and 90 percent of the population has antibody to the virus. Sporadic outbreaks in the United States are frequently associated with day-care centers. The risk for hepatitis A in day-care centers is highest when (1) the center accepts children less than 2 years old who are not toilet-trained and (2) the day-care center is large and accepts many children. Infected children easily transfer the virus to adults and other children.

Shedding of HAV occurs before the onset of jaundice (if it appears at all) and declines rapidly (see Fig. 32-28). No cases of shedding have been detected after the clinical stages of hepatitis A infection. In the United States 24,238

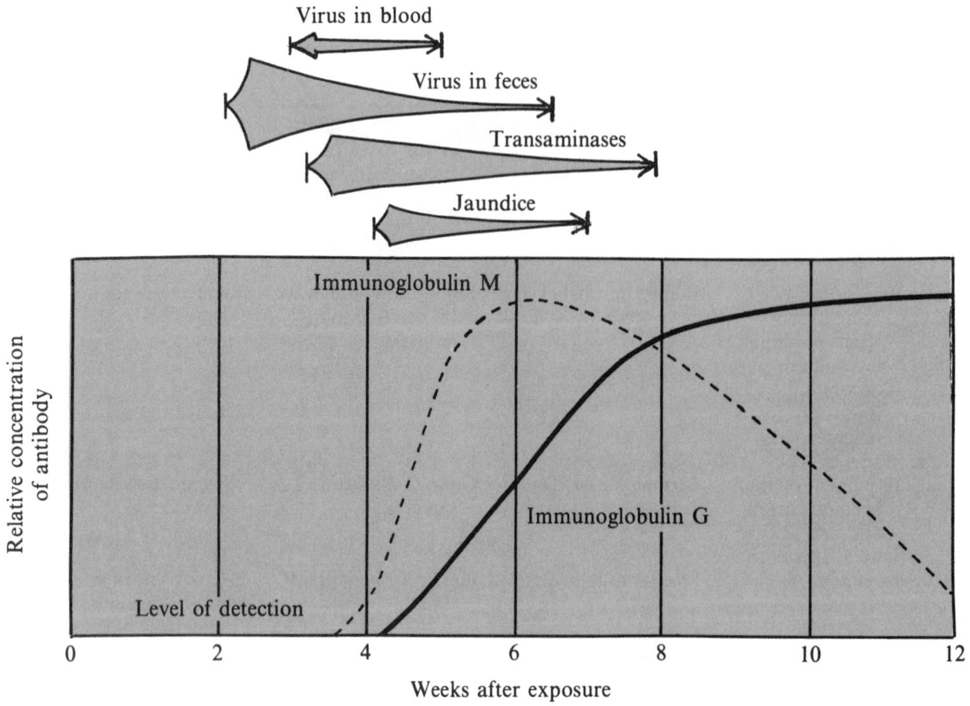

FIGURE 32-28
Immunological and biological events associated with viral hepatitis A. (From F. B. Hollinger and J. L. Dienstag. In E. H. Lennette, ed., *Manual of Clinical Microbiology*, 4th ed. Washington, D.C.: American Society for Microbiology, 1985.)

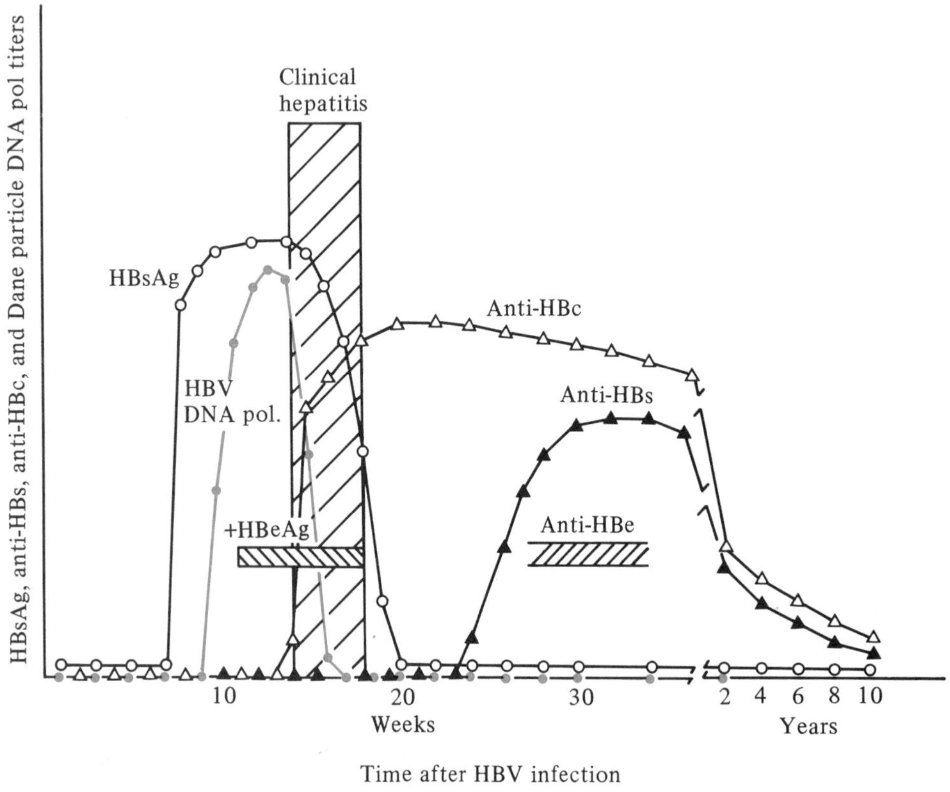

FIGURE 32-29
Hepatitis B viral (HBV) markers in the blood during the course of self-limited HBsAg-positive infection. The antigen levels decline precipitously after a few weeks and the patient seroconverts to corresponding viral antibodies. HBsAg = hepatitis B surface antigen; anti-HBs = antibody to HBsAg; anti-HBc = antibody to hepatitis B core antigen; HBeAg = hepatitis B early antigen; anti-HBe = antibody to HBeAg; DNA pol = DNA polymerase. (From W. S. Robinson. In G. L. Mandell, R. C. Douglas, Jr., and J. E. Bennett, eds., *Principles and Practices of Infectious Diseases*. New York: Wiley, 1979.)

UNDER THE MICROSCOPE 38

Hepatitis A Among Drug Abusers

In the United States transmission of hepatitis A has usually been associated with crowding, poor personal hygiene, improper sanitation, and less commonly, contamination of food or water. Recognized risk factors include intimate or close contact with children in day-care centers. The association of drug use and hepatitis A was recognized only recently, especially in Scandinavian countries.

Two possible explanations for the association between hepatitis A and drug use have been proposed: Hepatitis A virus (HAV) may be transmitted by (1) injection or ingestion* of contaminated drugs (common-source spread) or (2) direct person-to-person contact. Drugs could be contaminated with fecal material containing HAV at the cultivation site (for example, through use of human feces as fertilizer) or during transport, preparation, or distribution (for example, through smuggling in condoms concealed in the rectum or in baby diapers).

Person-to-person transmission of HAV between drug abusers could result from sharing needles, from sexual contact, or from generally poor sanitary and personal hygiene conditions, which have often been observed among drug abusers.

Drug abusers may be candidates for the vaccines against HAV that are currently being developed.

From *M.M.W.R.* 37:297, 1988.
By tasting the drug to assess quality, for example.

cases of hepatitis A were reported to the Centers for Disease Control in 1993.

Hepatitis B. The major risk factors associated with hepatitis B are, in order of importance, injection drug abuse, heterosexual activity, and homosexual activity. In addition, health care professionals, laboratory workers, oral surgeons, and dentists are at high risk for hepatitis B infection. Worldwide there are believed to be 300 million people infected with HBV. In 1993, a total of 13,361 cases of hepatitis B was reported to the Centers for Disease Control. Each year an estimated 300,000 people in the United States are infected with HBV. About 4000 persons die each year from hepatitis-related cirrhosis and more than 800 die from hepatitis-related liver cancer in the United States.

Mosquitoes carry HBsAg after contact with HBV carriers. Transmission by mosquitoes takes place more often in tropical areas than in the United States.

Mother-to-infant transmission can occur in the following ways: (1) transplacentally, by the oral route at delivery from maternal blood or stool or (2) by mother-infant contact immediately after birth. Infants born to mothers positive for HBsAg and HBeAg have a 70 to 90 percent chance of acquiring perinatal HBV infection. About 90 percent of infected infants become chronic carriers. Twenty-five percent of the chronic carriers die from cirrhosis of the liver or liver cancer. In the United States about 3500 infants become chronic carriers each year.

Infectious virus has been recovered from semen and saliva; thus it is clear that venereal contact can lead to infection. The prevalence of HBV among homosexual men ranges from 51 to 76 percent. This is to be compared with 4.4 percent for blood donors, 40 percent of spouses and household members of HBsAg carriers, and 55 to 67 percent of parenteral drug abusers.

The risk of infection among homosexuals is related to the frequency of sexual contact. Passive anal-genital intercourse is most strongly associated with HBV infection, followed by oral-anal intercourse and rectal douching preparation for intercourse. Traumatized rectal tissue may serve as the portal of entry of HBV from infected semen. Oral-oral contact or oral-genital contact is not related to HBV infection.

HBV infection has been associated with liver cancer. In western Europe and the United States about 6000 cases of liver cancer are reported each year. In Africa and Asia, where HBV infection is endemic, liver cancer is one of the most widely recognized carcinomas. In those endemic areas the rate for primary liver cancer in the carrier group is 245 cases per 100,000 population. It is estimated that 500,000 deaths occur annually as the result of liver cancer. When all hepatitis B markers are included, 90 percent of liver cancer patients have evidence of present or past infection with HBV. The latent period from the time of HBV infection to the appearance of the cancer is approximately 30 years. Males are more likely to become and remain carriers. As liver disease progresses, males are more likely to develop liver cancer.

Patients who carry HBsAg for 20 weeks will usually become persistent or chronic carriers of HBV. There are believed to be 750,000 to 1 million chronic carriers in the United States and 175 million chronic carriers worldwide. The most troubling aspect of these figures is that the mortality related to infection is highest in chronic carriers. Persistent carriers have high levels of HBsAg as well as anti-HBc in the serum.

Chronic hepatitis can be divided into two types: **chronic persistent** and **chronic active.** Chronic persistent hepatitis is characterized by little liver damage, and there is no progression to severe liver damage. Chronic active hepatitis is characterized by chronic inflammation and necrosis of liver cells. The most important consequence of chronic active hepatitis is the progression to cirrhosis, which occurs in 50 percent of the affected individuals. Neonatal infection is associated with the highest rate of persistence (up to 90 percent). The rate decreases during childhood, but is still considerably higher than in adults (6–10 percent).

Hepatitis C. Hepatitis C is responsible for nearly 95 percent of transfusion-related hepatitis cases—up to 150,000 each year in the United States. In addition, up to 50 percent of such patients will have chronic hepatitis and may have permanent liver damage. HCV also causes most cases of sporadic or community-acquired non-A, non-B hepatitis not associated with transfusion.

The major risk factor for HCV transmission is injection drug use, followed by transfusion, tattoos, and needlesticks. HCV infection is even more likely to occur in multiply transfused patients, for example, thalassemics, leukemia patients, and hemophiliacs.

Sporadic HCV represents as much as 40 percent of all acute HCV infections. The transmission route for sporadic HCV infection is controversial. Sexual transmission or nonsexual household contact including vertical transmission of HCV has been implicated. Mother-to-infant transmission of HCV appears to occur more frequently when the mother is also infected with HIV.

In some patients infected with HBV, a superimposed HCV infection may play a leading role in causing severe liver disease.

Hepatitis D. Natural infections with HDV are transmitted in the same manner as those caused by HBV. Virus in the blood of an infected individual is spread parenterally. Virus therefore is spread by sexual transmission, use of contaminated needles, or accidental transfusions of contaminated blood or blood products. Worldwide, there are 25 million chronic HDV carriers. When HDV chronicity is coupled with HBV chronicity, there is an increased likelihood of liver damage and development of liver cancer.

Since HDV can replicate only in the presence of HBV, the epidemiology of HDV might be expected to be the same as that of HBV. This is not the case. Many areas of the world have high levels of HBV and little if any HDV. In Italy, for example, nearly 90 percent of those with acute HBsAg hepatitis are also infected with HDV. In Asia where there is a high prevalence of HBsAg, HDV infection is uncommon. In addition, the outcome of HDV infection also varies from one geographical area to another. Infections with HDV can cause severe liver damage and even death but in areas of Greece HDV-associated liver damage is no more than that caused by HBV alone.

Hepatitis E. HEV is an enterically transmitted non-A, non-B hepatitis virus. Virus is transmitted by the fecal-oral route and causes large outbreaks in Asia and Africa, especially in refugee camps. The large outbreaks of disease are typically linked to fecally contaminated water supplies. Symptoms include abdominal pain, arthralgia, and fever. Most patients recover but in pregnant women there is a high fatality rate (20 percent). Hepatitis E is much more common in adults than in children.

Laboratory Diagnosis

The clinical diagnosis of acute hepatitis is based on results from biochemical tests that assess liver damage. Several tests are used to determine the (1) presence and concentration of **bilirubin** in the urine and serum, (2) concentration of serum **alanine** and **aspartate aminotransferase** as indicators of liver cell damage, and (3) **alkaline phosphatase** levels to measure intrahepatic and extrahepatic obstruction.

Hepatitis A. Hepatitis A is diagnosed by specific enzyme immunoassays (ELISA, for example) for total and IgM antibodies to HAV. IgM antibody appears at the onset of illness and remains detectable for six weeks to six months (see Fig. 32-28). The presence of IgM antibodies to HAV in serum is diagnostic of current or recent hepatitis. IgG antibody to HAV appears several weeks after the onset of disease and lasts indefinitely; its presence is diagnostic of past hepatitis.

Hepatitis B. Diagnosis of hepatitis B infection relies on detection of specific hepatitis B seromarkers, that is, HBsAg, HBeAg, and anti-HBc, anti-HBe, and anti-HBs. Enzyme immunoassay kits are commercially available for detecting the following seromarkers:

1. Anti-HBs, which indicates past infection with and immunity to HBV. The antibodies may have also been derived from immune globulin (HBIG) prophylaxis or from vaccination. In carriers, HBsAg persists and anti-HBs does not develop. If the chronic carrier state terminates after many years, the outcome may include seroconversion to anti-HBs. Anti-HBs is a measure of recovery from HBV infection.
2. Anti-HBc, which indicates prior infection with HBV at some undefined time. In acutely infected individuals antibodies to HBcAg appear in serum after the appearance of HBsAg and before the onset of symptoms. IgM anti-HBc can persist at high levels for six months or longer and is a reliable marker of recent infection. Absence of IgM anti-HBc in HBsAg-positive individuals indicates the carrier state.
3. Anti-HBe, which is infrequently observed in patients with chronic infection. Patients with anti-HBe are usually not infectious because they have a low titer of HBV. In addition, they usually have normal liver histology and a good prognosis.
4. HBeAg, which is observed in the serum during the early replicative phase of HBV and is associated with high infectivity. The later low replicative phase of HBV is accompanied by seroconversion to anti-HBe. The HBeAg versus anti-HBe status was at one time used to differentiate active replication from low replication phases. HBV DNA is now the marker for such differentiation.

5. HBsAg and HBcAg. At six weeks to six months after a patient is exposed to HBV, HBsAg becomes detectable in the serum. Any person positive for HBsAg is potentially infectious. HBcAg is found in liver and intact virions but is not found free in the blood. The quantitative amount of HBcAg and HBsAg components in liver tissue, together with histological description of liver cells, may be useful in determining the prognosis of infection. Low levels or no detectable HBcAg in patients seropositive for HBsAg indicates persistent infection with little liver damage. A high level of HBcAg is associated with marked liver damage and doubtful prognosis. Determination of HBsAg only is recommended for universal screening of pregnant women.
6. HBV DNA. HBV DNA in the serum is now considered the major predictor of infectivity. The presence of HBV DNA in anti-HBe–positive patients with chronic HBV infection is associated with severe and progressive liver disease. Occasionally (fewer than 3 percent), patients with chronic hepatitis have HBeAg but not HBV DNA.

Hepatitis C. Detection of acute HCV infection is made by using ELISA and blot immunoassays. They detect IgG and IgM anti-HCV core, respectively. These tests have also been used to determine the prevalence of anti-HCV in blood donors and in recipients of transfusions. HCV transmission is especially marked in multitransfused patients. The rates of posttransfusion hepatitis vary in different parts of the world. In Japan, for example, anti-HCV screening has had a marked effect on reducing posttransfusion hepatitis.

Hepatitis D. The routine laboratory detection of HDV markers is generally carried out by serological assays such as enzyme immunoassays. One of three serological markers is used: HDV antigen (HDAg) for acute infection, anti-HDV antibody (anti-HDV) for past infection and chronic infection, and IgM anti-HDV for indicating chronic HDV infections when at a high titer.

Hepatitis E. Diagnosis of acute icteric hepatitis E usually has been accomplished by exclusion of hepatitis A and B. Recently, Western blot assay has been used for detecting antibody to HEV (anti-HEV).

Immunity

Hepatitis A. Antibodies to HAV can be detected in the serum many years after infection. The appearance of various antibodies during the course of HAV infection was discussed previously (see Fig. 32-28). HAV infection produces a solid immunity and reinfections do not occur; however, infection by HBV or other hepatitis viruses is possible.

Hepatitis B. HBsAg appears in the blood four to eight weeks after infection. Yet, antibodies to the surface antigen do not make their appearance until many months after the illness has terminated (see Fig. 32-29). Antibodies to core antigen (anti-HBc) are produced and can be detected during the clinical manifestations of the disease. These antibodies decline with a decline in anti-HBs but can be detected five to six years after infection. Acute hepatitis B infection is usually of the *a* type specificity, which appears to confer resistance to reinfection by the same or different subtypes. Anti-HBs confers immunity to reinfections, but it has been observed that even when anti-HBs titers are undetectable, resistance to reinfection may still occur. This implies that cell-mediated immune responses are probably involved in resistance.

Hepatitis C and E. Infection with hepatitis C and E viruses does not appear to confer a solid immunity.

Treatment and Prevention

Hepatitis A. There is no treatment for acute hepatitis A infection. Hepatitis A infections can be prevented by improvement of sanitation conditions and through the rapid detection of carriers. Careful handwashing after contact with a person infected with HAV or contact with contaminated objects is important in preventing infections. Food handlers should be screened for hepatitis infection before they are hired.

Human immunoglobulin (IG) administered prior to exposure or early in the incubation period (less than two weeks after exposure) of hepatitis A prevents HAV infection and helps prevent epidemic spread. The duration of protection for IG is less than six months. IG is recommended for preventing the spread of infection in crowded institutions or among people in high-risk occupations (military personnel, missionaries) and those traveling to areas where hepatitis A infection is endemic.

Several live-attenuated and inactivated vaccines are currently under investigation and one should be available in the near future.

Hepatitis B. In most patients, acute hepatitis B resolves on its own with clearance of HBsAg and healing of hepatic injuries. Antiviral agents do not accelerate or improve this process. For the more serious fulminant hepatitis no therapy has proved effective. If survival is unlikely, the current option is for liver transplantation.

Therapies for chronic hepatitis B are being developed. Currently recombinantly cloned interferons are used in treatment. Only a small number of patients respond to therapy, but for those who do respond, disease can be eradicated. Positive response to treatment is indicated when HBV DNA and HBeAg are permanently absent from the serum.

Blood and certain body fluids are considered potentially infectious. The Centers for Disease Control has adopted **universal precautions** that are intended to prevent transmission of HBV (as well as HIV and other blood-borne pathogens). The body fluids included in this recommendation include cerebrospinal fluid, synovial fluid, pleural fluid, peritoneal fluid, pericardial fluid, and amniotic fluid. Protective barriers that reduce the risk of contamination by various body fluids include gloves, gowns, masks, and protective eyewear. These guidelines should be considered a supplement to routine infection control. For example, washing of hands and other body surfaces that are contaminated with blood or potentially contaminated body fluids is considered a routine procedure. The proper use, cleaning, and disposal of needles, scalpels, and other sharp instruments or devices can minimize the risk of hospital-associated infection by hepatitis viruses (for further discussion of precautions for health care workers, see the 1988 Centers for Disease Control publication listed in Additional Readings, The Hepatitis Viruses). Equipment or instruments used in health care settings (syringes, needles, tubing, etc.) should be disposable or sterilized before coming in contact with blood or mucous membranes. Some articles contaminated by blood can be disinfected using sodium hypochlorite (0.5%).

Blood, blood products, and blood donors must be screened for hepatitis B antigen to prevent infection. A reduction in the incidence of posttransfusion hepatitis has resulted from the use of volunteer blood donors. The use of dialysis for known HBsAg carriers has also substantially reduced the risk of cross infections. Routine screening for HBsAg should be done early in pregnancy (to date, this policy has not been fully implemented in the United States). Such testing would identify seropositive women and allow the immediate treatment of infants at birth. These infants should receive HBIG and hepatitis B vaccine within 2 to 12 hours after birth. Such a procedure would prevent about 3500 infants from becoming HBV carriers. Immunization for posttransfusion hepatitis is of little value because most cases are caused by HCV.

Postexposure prophylaxis using **HBIG** is recommended for individuals sustaining needle punctures or mucosal exposure to blood known to contain HBsAg, family members of acute or chronic carriers, and infants of chronically infected mothers. HBIG and hepatitis B vaccine should be given as soon as possible after birth, followed by completion of the hepatitis B vaccine series at the ages of 1 month and 6 months.

HBIG is also given in conjunction with hepatitis B vaccine to health care workers following exposure to blood containing HBsAg and to sexual partners of HBsAg-positive persons.

Two recombinant HBV vaccines are now available. Primary adult vaccination consists of giving three intramuscular doses over a six-month period. The groups for whom vaccine is recommended are outlined in Table 32-9 (see also Under the Microscope 39). Health care workers should still be vigilant even if they have been vaccinated. Studies indicate that less than 90 percent of those vaccinated demonstrate seroconversion. The Centers for Disease Control now recommends routine immunization against hepatitis B for all newborns.

Hepatitis C, D, and E. Interferon is currently approved for the treatment of chronic hepatitis C infection. As with HBV, sustained disease remission occurs only in a small proportion of the patients. It is now recommended that all donations of whole blood and components for transfusion be tested for anti-HCV by enzyme immunoassay. Prevention of HCV infection follows the same guidelines as those proposed for HBV infection (see above). No vaccine is available for preventing HCV infection.

The HDV requires help from HBV. Prevention of HBV infection will therefore serve to prevent HDV infection. No products are available to prevent HDV infection although interferon provides a cure for a few patients who clear HBsAg and seroconvert to anti-HBs.

HEV infection is not recognized as an endemic disease in the United States. The best way to prevent infection, especially when traveling to areas of Asia or Africa, is to avoid potentially contaminated food or water.

TABLE 32-9
Persons for Whom Hepatitis B Vaccine Is Recommended or Should Be Considered

Preexposure

Persons for whom vaccine is recommended:
1. Health care workers having blood or needle-stick exposures
2. Clients and staff of institutions for the developmentally disabled
3. Hemodialysis patients*
4. Homosexually active men
5. Users of illicit injectable drugs
6. Recipients of certain blood products
7. Household members and sexual contacts of HBV carriers
8. Special high-risk populations—e.g., dentists

Persons for whom vaccine should be considered:
1. Inmates of long-term correctional facilities
2. Heterosexually active persons with multiple sexual partners
3. International travelers to HBV-endemic areas

Postexposure

1. Infants born to HBV-positive mothers
2. Health care workers having needle-stick exposures to human blood

* Recombinant vaccine is *not* recommended for hemodialysis patients.
SOURCE: *M.M.W.R.* 36:353, 1987.

SLOW VIRUS INFECTIONS

The history of slow virus diseases had its beginnings nearly 50 years ago in Iceland, where farmers observed pulmonary and neurological conditions in their sheep. These disorders, called **maedi** (an interstitial pneumonia) and **visna** (a paralytic disease), became epidemic and claimed the lives of more than 100,000 animals. Scientists discovered that a filterable agent caused these diseases, whose overt symptoms did not appear until months to years after infection. The term slow infection was used to describe the long incubation period of these diseases. Later studies in the 1950s revealed that a slow infection in sheep called **scrapie** resembled in many ways an exotic neurological condition of the Foré tribe of New Guinea, called **kuru.** Several relatively uncommon neurological conditions such as **Creutzfeldt-Jakob disease, progressive multifocal leukoencephalopathy,** and **subacute sclerosing panencephalitis** (SSPE) are now considered slow infections.

UNDER THE MICROSCOPE 39

Hepatitis B: A Disease Not Taken Seriously Even Among Health Care Workers

A hepatitis B vaccine has been available since 1982. It is one of the safest vaccines ever made, and yet the number of cases of hepatitis B virus (HBV) infection in the United States continues to rise each year. Apathy, ignorance, and hard-to-reach populations are the principal reasons for the continued rise in hepatitis B. Health care workers are one of the high-risk groups for becoming infected with HBV. Yet many health care workers are unaware that in addition to contact with blood or blood products, the virus can be transmitted by sexual contact. The majority of HBV infections (70 percent) occur in "hard-to-reach" populations—that is, injection drug abusers, homosexually active men, and heterosexual persons.

Risk of infection by the human immunodeficiency virus (HIV) has received the most attention among health care workers. In the scientific literature, however, only 26 cases of occupationally acquired HIV infection have been reported. In the United States the Centers for Disease Control estimates that 12,000 health care workers become infected with HBV each year. Of the infected individuals, 250 will die from cirrhosis of the liver or liver cancer. In addition, over 1200 infected individuals will become carriers of the virus.

New strategies have been suggested to control hepatitis B infection. The most important one is the Centers for Disease Control's recommendation that all newborns be vaccinated.

Health care workers should be more aware of the risks associated with HBV infection and utilize all the safety precautions available, which may include vaccination.

UNDER THE MICROSCOPE 40

Prions and Slow Infections

We have become accustomed to the basic tenet of biology that all organisms carry nucleic acids that define their own identity. This tenet is being challenged by the discovery of **prions**—a term that means "proteinaceous infectious particle." Prions are not viruses or bacteria but proteins that are virtually impossible to identify by using any kind of classic technique. Prions were found to be the cause of an animal disease called **scrapie.** Scrapie is a common neurological disorder in sheep. In addition, prions are also the cause of a rare human dementia called Creutzfeldt-Jakob disease. This disease received public attention because it caused the death of the choreographer George Balanchine.

Scientists can transmit scrapie experimentally by taking brain tissue from sick animals and injecting it into healthy animals. Prions in the brains of infected animals form clumps called plaques. The plaques look like those common in the brains of people with Alzheimer's disease, the leading cause of senility. Scientists are now looking for prions in the brains of victims of multiple sclerosis, Lou Gehrig's disease, and Parkinson's disease.

The predominant questions about the prion are how does it replicate and how does it cause disease. One intriguing theory concerning the latter question is that prions are abnormal versions of some normal brain protein. According to this theory, everyone has the genetic potential to manufacture prions. When a prion invades the body, it becomes attached to a cell and somehow turns on a gene that makes a normal protein. In the process, however, the prion alters cell metabolism in such a way that a modified form of the protein—more prions—is produced. The prions accumulate over several years and slowly interfere with neurological function.

In 1989 researchers at the Washington University School of Medicine in St. Louis stumbled on a clue to the possible action of prions. They isolated a protein that stimulates the production of a receptor on chicken muscle fibers. These receptors subsequently become sensitive to chemical signals transmitted by nerves. When the researchers entered into their computer the amino acid sequence of the protein, the computer informed them that about one-third of their protein had amino acid sequences identical to prions. A high degree of sequence similarity indicates a similarity of function, even though the proteins are from different sources. One hypothesis is that prions, which are also found in normal cells, regulate production of neurochemical receptors in the nervous system. Mutant prions could possibly trigger neurodegenerative diseases.

Slow infections in humans may be caused by conventional viral agents—for example, measles virus (SSPE) and polyoma virus (progressive multifocal leukoencephalopathy)—or unconventional agents, which cause kuru and Creutzfeldt-Jakob disease. The unconventional agents differ so radically from viruses that they have now been called **prions** (see Under the Microscope 40). Let us briefly discuss some of the important slow infections.

Kuru and Creutzfeldt-Jakob Disease

Kuru is a chronic degenerative disease discovered in the Foré people of New Guinea. The disease was originally discovered to be transmitted during the ritualistic cannibalistic consumption of their dead relatives as a sign of respect. Women and children, but not men, handled liquefied brain tissue, which was the source of infection. Thus, the infectious agent gained entrance to the body through skin cuts, nasal mucosa, or conjunctiva. Men rarely ate the flesh of dead kuru victims; thus, women and children were more likely to become infected. The latent period for kuru may be as long as two years, but once symptoms appear death occurs within three to nine months. The first symptoms of disease are an unsteadiness in walking and a shivering tremor involving the head, trunk, and legs. Later the patient begins to stammer and there is uncoordinated eye movement. These features worsen until the patient cannot walk and is unable to swallow.

Creutzfeldt-Jakob disease is a degenerative disease of the central nervous system that affects persons between 35 and 65 years old. The disease can be transmitted to nonhuman primates. The infected patient becomes uncoordinated and demented, and death occurs within 9 to 18 months after the onset of symptoms. Accidental transmission of this disease has occurred, although infrequently, during transplantation procedures, which suggests that the infectious agent is not limited to the brain.

There is no treatment for kuru or Creutzfeldt-Jakob disease.

Subacute Sclerosing Panencephalitis

Persistent infection of the central nervous system with measles virus is recognized as the cause of SSPE. The disease occurs most often in children and appears with a frequency of 1 case per million but in the Southeast this ratio is 4 to 5 cases per million. The majority of patients with SSPE had measles at an early age, most before the age of 2 years.

TABLE 32-10
Characteristics of Diseases Caused by DNA Viruses

Viral disease	Viral agent	Epidemiology	Clinical manifestations	Vaccine
Smallpox	Poxvirus	Person to person via direct contact; begins as respiratory infection	Lesions in internal organs and eruptions on skin	No longer available to general public; disease eradicated
Herpesvirus diseases				
Cytomegalovirus disease	Cytomegalovirus	Direct contact	Congenital disease can result in fetal abnormalities; opportunistic for transplant patients (jaundice, hepatosplenomegaly); mononucleosis-like disease from transfusions	Experimental vaccine for renal transplant patients; immune globulin available
Chickenpox	Varicella-zoster virus	Direct contact with respiratory secretions	Viremia followed by rash; usually self-limiting	Yes;* immune globulins also available
Shingles	Varicella-zoster virus	Activation of latent varicella virus	Skin lesions similar to those of chickenpox but more painful	No
Cutaneous herpes	Herpes simplex virus 1	Direct contact; activation of endogenous virus	Lesions on face; encephalitis in neonate	No
	Herpes simplex virus 2	Activation of endogenous virus but can be transferred sexually	Lesions on genitalia; neonatal herpes may be cutaneous or disseminated	No
Infectious mononucleosis	Epstein-Barr virus	Direct contact with respiratory secretions	Fatigue, chills, fever, spleen and liver enlargement	No
Respiratory and ocular disease	Adenoviruses	Direct contact	Bronchitis, croup, pneumonia, conjunctivitis	Yes for military recruits
Epidemic acute gastroenteritis	Some adenovirus types	Fecal-oral	Diarrhea	No
Hepatitis	Hepatitis B virus	Contact with contaminated blood or blood products; sexual transmission	Jaundice, usually self-limiting, but chronic disease very serious	Yes; immunoglobulins also available
Warts	Papillomaviruses	Person to person, including sexual contact	Warts on areas of the body including genitalia	No

* Vaccine has not yet been licensed in the United States.

TABLE 32-11
Characteristics of Diseases Caused by RNA Viruses

Viral disease	Viral agent	Epidemiology	Clinical manifestations	Vaccine
Measles	Measles virus	Direct contact with respiratory secretions	Fever and rash associated with viremia; usually self-limiting; subacute sclerosing panencephalitis a rare sequela of measles	Yes; immune globulin also available
Mumps	Mumps virus	Direct contact with respiratory secretions	Salivary glands enlarged after viremia; usually self-limiting	Yes
Rubella	Rubella virus	Congenital rubella during viremia in mother; postnatal infection via respiratory secretions	Congenital disease can result in death of fetus or deformities at birth; rash in postnatal disease and usually self-limiting	Yes; immune globulin also available
Influenza	Influenza viruses A, B, and C	Contact with respiratory secretions	Cold-like syndrome but in compromised patients can be complicated by pneumonia	Yes
Poliomyelitis	Poliovirus	Fecal-oral	Fever and stiffness of neck; usually self-limiting; 1 percent develop paralytic disease	Yes; oral and parenteral types
Rabies	Rabies virus	Bite of infected animal or inhalation of contaminated aerosols	Fever, difficulty in swallowing, convulsive seizures, coma, and almost invariably death	Yes for animals and humans; immune globulin also available
Yellow fever	Arbovirus	Bite of infected mosquito (*Aedes aegypti*)	Jaundice, extensive liver damage	Yes; immune globulin also available
Encephalitis	Arboviruses (western equine, eastern equine, LaCrosse, and St. Louis encephalitis viruses)	Bite of mosquito	Fever, headache, stiffness of neck; fatalities high in eastern equine encephalitis	No
Colds	Rhinoviruses	Contact with respiratory secretions or contaminated fomites	Coryza, sore throat, and cough	No
Hemorrhagic fever	Lassa fever virus, Ebola virus, Marburg virus, Crimean-Congo hemorrhagic fever virus (CCHF)	Contact with rats (Lassa fever); close personal contact (Ebola); tick bite (CCHF)	Fever, hemorrhaging from multiple sites	No
Hemorrhagic fever with renal syndrome	Hantaviruses	Contact with rodents	Fever, hemorrhage and renal failure	No
Dengue fever and Dengue hemorrhagic fever	Arbovirus	Bite of mosquito (*Aedes aegypti*)	Fever, arthralgia, myalgia (Dengue fever); hemorrhaging and intravascular coagulation (Dengue hemorrhagic fever)	No
Enterovirus disease	Polioviruses, coxsackieviruses A and B, echoviruses, and enterovirus types 68–71	Direct contact with respiratory secretions	Polio; aseptic meningitis, herpangina, myocarditis, and pleurodynia	Yes (polio virus); no (other viruses)
Lower respiratory tract disease	Parainfluenza viruses 1, 2, and 3; respiratory syncytial virus	Direct contact with respiratory secretions	Croup, bronchiolitis, pneumonia	No
Hepatitis	Hepatitis A virus	Fecal-oral	Jaundice; recovery permanent and no persistence	In development; immune globulins available
	Hepatitis C virus	Parenteral transmission	Can cause chronic disease and liver cancer	No
	Hepatitis E virus	Enteric transmission	Fever, abdominal pain, anthralgia, jaundice	No
Epidemic gastroenteritis	Rotavirus	Fecal-oral	Diarrhea accompanied by vomiting and fever	No
	Caliciviruses	Fecal-oral	Diarrhea and vomiting	No
	Astroviruses	Fecal-oral	Diarrhea and vomiting	No
Acquired immunodeficiency syndrome (AIDS)	Retrovirus (human immunodeficiency virus)	Sexual contact; exposure to blood; mother to neonate	Long progression of symptoms terminating in death, usually from opportunistic infections	No

SSPE follows natural measles infection after a latent period of about seven years. The virus apparently remains in the nervous system in a suppressed form and then spreads through the brain without the formation of mature viral particles. SSPE-infected cells can be observed to have nucleocapsids in the nucleus and cytoplasm, but none are aligned at the cytoplasmic membrane for budding. SSPE patients have high titers of measles antibody in the cerebrospinal fluid, a characteristic not associated with natural measles infection. Apparently some nerve cells die and release viral antigens that stimulate antibody production. The suppression of virus formation in nerve cells is believed to be due to the absence of a virus-specific protein or the presence of a suppressive factor. The immune system of the host is unable to neutralize the virus because more virus is hidden intracellularly. The precipitation of disease seven years after measles infection is believed to be due to some hormonal factor associated with puberty, but this is only a hypothesis.

The clinical findings of SSPE can be divided into four stages: stage I, cerebral changes; stage II, convulsive motor signs; stage III, coma and spasms of the head, back, and lower limbs; and stage IV, loss of cerebrocortical function and inability to speak. Most patients live an average of 18 months after diagnosis of SSPE.

Some reports indicate that administration of transfer factor can prevent the progression of symptoms. The drug inosine pranobex (Isoprinosin) has been reported to produce long-term remission. The administration of measles vaccine in the United States has reduced the prevalence of SSPE greatly, but this is not true for developing countries, where measles is still a major cause of morbidity and mortality.

Progressive Multifocal Leukoencephalopathy

Progressive multifocal leukoencephalopathy is a rare demyelinating disease associated with the polyoma viruses, JC virus, and BK virus, discussed earlier.

Summary

Because of the length of this chapter the summary section consists of Tables 32-10 and 32-11, which describe the characteristics of the viral diseases.

Questions for Study

1. What reasons can you give for the relationship between rubella vaccination and chronic arthritis? (You may wish to consult the Additional Readings.)
2. What viral vaccines are available in the United States? Which ones should be administered to children less than 1 year old?
3. Why do influenza vaccines have to be changed almost every year?
4. What is the relationship between bacteria and influenza A virus pathogenicity?
5. If swine are infected by two pathogenic strains of influenza A virus, how is it possible to have progeny that are pathogenic as well as nonpathogenic?
6. What are the benefits and risks associated with the two polio vaccines currently in use?
7. What viruses in particular are associated with upper and lower respiratory tract infections in infants and young children? What is their significance in hospital-associated infections?
8. What are the first things you should do if your child is bitten by a suspected rabid dog?
9. What wild animals are the major sources of rabies virus for domestic animals? What is currently being done to control wild animal rabies?
10. During what stage of pregnancy does primary infection by rubella virus become most devastating to the fetus? Infection by cytomegalovirus?
11. List some of the major reasons why it is so difficult to design and prepare live herpesvirus vaccines.
12. What viruses can be transmitted sexually? By blood transfusion?
13. What is the mechanism of primary infection and reactivation of herpes simplex and varicella-zoster viruses?
14. A patient has a skin eruption that you believe is caused by a herpesvirus. What simple test can be used to determine if a herpesvirus is involved?
15. For what type of infections is acyclovir recommended?
16. What is the potential disease syndrome for neonatal herpes? What techniques are available for preventing neonatal infection?
17. Briefly discuss the clinical entities associated with Epstein-Barr virus infection.
18. Papillomaviruses are associated with what clinical spectrum? What treatment(s) can be utilized?
19. The condition referred to as hydrops fetalis is associated with infection by what virus? What is the outcome of this condition?
20. What surface proteins on the Paramyxoviridae are associated specifically with attachment to cell receptors? With penetration into the cell?
21. With what clinical entities are the coxsackieviruses and echoviruses associated?
22. What is the difference between urban and jungle yellow fever?
23. Are any of the hemorrhagic fever viruses of particular concern to laboratory personnel? Explain.
24. What virus is the single most important cause of diarrhea in neonates? What is the simplest procedure for preventing death in these neonates?
25. List the viruses that are associated with gastroenteritis in children.

26. What evidence indicates that the asymptomatic stage of HIV infection is not a latent stage?
27. What is the major laboratory predictor for patient progression to AIDS?
28. What are the principal opportunistic infections associated with AIDS? Why does this rash of opportunistic infections occur?
29. Describe what serum markers are present during acute HIV infection and progression to AIDS.
30. What are the major precautions for preventing hepatitis B transmission by health care workers?
31. Describe the differences in the epidemiology of the hepatitis viruses.
32. When blood is donated, screening is performed for what infectious agents?
33. What are prions? With what diseases have they been associated?

PART

VII

Medical Mycology

CHAPTER

33 The Pathogenic Fungi

OBJECTIVES

To outline the major differences between fungi and bacteria in terms of size and morphology, reproduction, and laboratory identification

To describe the relationship between dimorphism and pathogenesis

To list briefly the major antifungal drugs and the types of diseases for which they are most frequently used

To make a list of the systemic, cutaneous, subcutaneous, and superficial mycoses and describe briefly the mechanism of transmission for each group, the body tissues affected, and how the diseases are treated

To describe the various types of candidiasis and aspergillosis, particularly regarding the tissue affected, the groups of individuals most likely to be affected, and treatment

To describe briefly the importance of *Pneumocystis carinii* as an opportunistic pathogen

To describe the important mycotoxins and how humans become intoxicated

OUTLINE

- CHARACTERISTICS OF THE FUNGI
  - Size and Morphology
  - Reproduction
    - Sexual Sporulation
    - Asexual Sporulation
  - Cultural Characteristics
  - Pathogenesis
  - Laboratory Diagnosis
  - Resistance to Infection
  - Treatment and Prevention
  - Importance to Humans
  - Classification
- FUNGAL DISEASES
  - Systemic Mycoses
    - Histoplasmosis
      - Epidemiology
      - Pathogenesis
      - Laboratory Diagnosis
      - Treatment
    - Coccidioidomycosis
      - Epidemiology
      - Pathogenesis
      - Laboratory Diagnosis
      - Treatment
    - Blastomycosis
      - Epidemiology
      - Pathogenesis
      - Laboratory Diagnosis
      - Treatment
    - Paracoccidioidomycosis
      - Epidemiology
      - Pathogenesis
      - Laboratory Diagnosis
      - Treatment
    - Cryptococcosis
      - Epidemiology
      - Pathogenesis
      - Laboratory Diagnosis
      - Treatment
  - Subcutaneous Mycoses
    - Sporotrichosis and Other Subcutaneous Mycoses
      - Epidemiology and Pathogenesis

OUTLINE (*continued*)

Laboratory Diagnosis
Treatment
Dermatophytoses (Cutaneous Mycoses)
General Characteristics
Laboratory Diagnosis
Treatment
Tinea Capitis (Ringworm of the Scalp)
Tinea Corporis (Ringworm of the Body)
Tinea Pedis (Ringworm of the Feet)
Tinea Barbae (Ringworm of the Beard Area)
Tinea Favosa (Ringworm of the Scalp)
Tinea Unguium (Ringworm of the Nails)
Tinea Imbricata (Ringworm of the Torso)
Tinea Cruris (Ringworm of the Groin, Jock Itch)
Dermatophytes and Allergy
Superficial Mycoses
Tinea Versicolor
Tinea Nigra Palmaris
Black and White Piedra
Diseases Caused by Opportunistic Fungal Pathogens
Candidiasis
General Characteristics
Pathogenesis
Cutaneous Candidiasis
Systemic Candidiasis
Chronic Mucocutaneous Candidiasis
Laboratory Diagnosis
Treatment
Aspergillosis
Pathogenesis
Laboratory Diagnosis
Treatment
Mucormycosis
Pathogenesis
Laboratory Diagnosis
Treatment
Pneumocystis Pneumonia
Mycotoxins
Mycetismus
Mycotoxicosis

Fungi represent the first of the infectious eukaryotic microorganisms to be discussed. As you remember from Chapter 2, eukaryotes differ in many ways from prokaryotes or bacteria (see Table 2-1). These differences influence the way in which eukaryotes cause disease and the way in which eukaryotic diseases are diagnosed and treated. The purposes of this chapter are (1) to describe briefly how fungal morphology, physiology, growth, and so on influence or affect the disease process, and (2) to outline some of the most important fungal diseases associated with humans.

Characteristics of the Fungi

Fungi are eukaryotes whose members include both macroforms and microforms. Macroforms include the mushrooms while microforms include the single-celled **yeasts.** Most fungi are found as saprophytes in the soil where they engage primarily in the degradation of organic matter.

Soil fungi are important pathogens for plants but relatively few are pathogenic for humans. Fungal diseases in the community are usually the result of occupational contact with the microorganism—for example, farmers, veterinarians, miners, and nursery personnel. Most of the serious fungal infections are found in the immunocompromised, for example, in the hospital setting.

SIZE AND MORPHOLOGY

The fungi are divided into two morphological forms: **yeasts** and **molds.** Yeasts are typically round or oval single cells that measure approximately 4 to 5 μm in diameter (Plate 24). Some yeasts may be as large as 24 μm in diameter. Molds are multicellular and composed of filamentous or tubular structures called **hyphae** (sing., hypha). A single hypha may be 5 to 50 μm in length and 2 to 4 μm in diameter. Some hyphae are partitioned by cross walls called **septa** (Fig. 33-1) that divide them into individual compartments. Each compartment contains cytoplasm and at least one nucleus. Not all hyphae are septate. In hyphae without septa the cytoplasm and nuclei circulate freely. These are referred to as **aseptate** and represent a mass of nucleated protoplasm.

As hyphae branch and grow, they form a mat of intertwined hyphae called a **mycelium.** The mycelium may be divided into two portions: first, a **vegetative** portion, which remains attached to the substrate or penetrates it to obtain nutrients, and second, a **reproductive** portion, which is usually represented by aerial structures. The aerial structures give the mold the appearance of a cottony mass (Plate 25).

Not all fungi grow exclusively as yeasts or molds. Some fungi can exist in either state, depending on chemical and physical factors. These fungi are called **dimorphic.** Dimorphism plays an important role in the pathogenicity of certain fungi, as will be discussed later in the chapter.

Fungi possess cell walls that differ from those of bacteria. The fungal cell wall is relatively rigid and thick, and possesses no peptidoglycan layer. The major constituents of the fungal cell wall are polysaccharides (75 percent) and protein (25 percent). The polysaccharides are primarily **chitin** or **cellulose.** The absence of peptidoglycan enables fungi to resist the action of bacterial cell wall inhibitors such as the penicillins and cephalosporins.

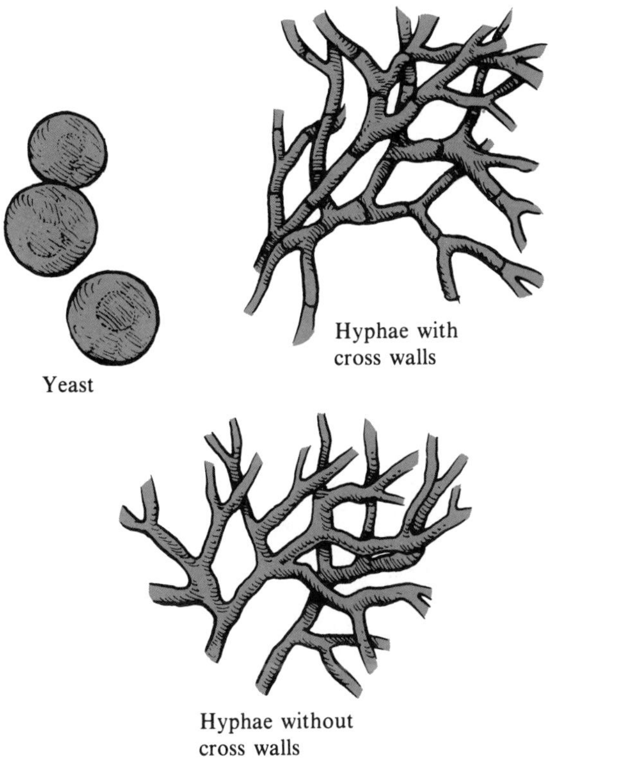

FIGURE 33-1
Characteristic morphology of yeasts and molds. The filamentous molds illustrated are depicted with cross walls called **septa** (sing., septum) but not all molds possess septa.

The cytoplasmic membrane of eukaryotes is similar in structure and composition to that of prokaryotes. The principal difference between them is that eukaryotic cell membranes contain sterols and prokaryotes (except *Mycoplasma*) do not contain them. Sterols are important stabilizing components; therefore antimicrobials that interact with sterols cause permeability changes in the cytoplasmic membrane of the fungal cell. Eukaryotes possess an internal membrane system called the **endoplasmic reticulum** and important organelles, such as **mitochondria,** that are surrounded by a membrane system. These membrane systems also possess sterols and can be adversely affected by antimicrobial agents.

Fungi differ also from bacteria in that (except some aquatic sex cells) they have no structures associated with locomotion. Except *Cryptococcus neoformans,* fungi do not produce capsules. Fungi, therefore, have fewer mechanisms than do bacteria for attachment to host cells.

REPRODUCTION

Reproduction in fungi may be **sexual** or **asexual.** Asexual reproduction is the more important of the two in propagating the organism. Sexual reproduction involves the union of two nuclei, sex cells, or sex organs. Asexual reproduction involves several mechanisms of propagation, including the following:

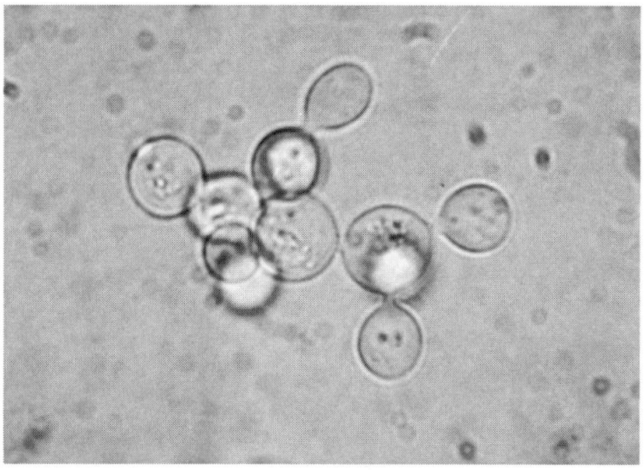

FIGURE 33-2
Photomicrograph of budding yeast cells. The large yeast cell at the lower right shows multiple budding. (× 1666.) (From M. Salazar, A. Restrepo, and D. A. Stevens, *Infect. Immun.* 56:711, 1988.)

1. **Fragmentation** of a hyphal filament, with each fragment growing into a new individual
2. **Fission** of a cell into two daughter cells (similar to binary fission in bacteria)
3. **Budding** of the cells, each bud producing a new individual
4. **Spore** formation, with each spore germinating into hyphae that develop into a mycelium

Yeasts may reproduce asexually by **sporulation, fission,** or budding. Budding is the most common process. During the process of budding, a protuberance, called a **bud,** is formed on the surface of the parent or **mother cell** (Fig. 33-2). As the bud enlarges, it reaches a critical size and separates from the mother cell. Release of the bud leaves a permanent scar, called a **bud scar,** on the surface of the mother cell (Fig. 33-3). If the developing bud does not separate from the mother cell, it (the developing bud)

FIGURE 33-3
Bud scars *(arrows)* on the yeast *Saccharomyces cerevisiae.* (From K. Beran and E. Streiblova, *Adv. Microb. Physiol.* 2:143, 1968. Copyright Academic Press, Inc. [London], Ltd.)

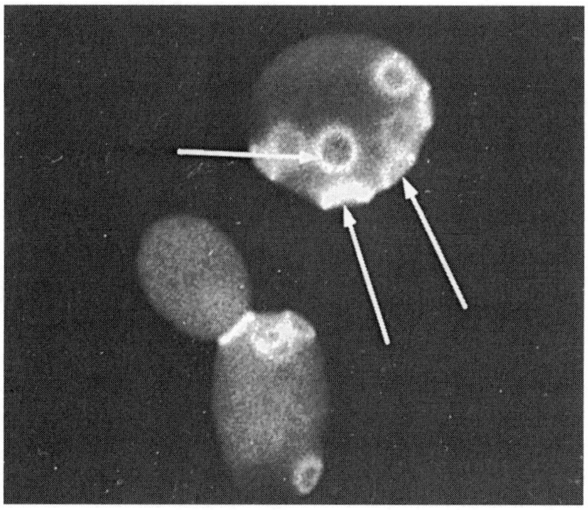

FIGURE 33-4
Edible mushrooms. (Courtesy of Carolina Biological Supply Co.)

may also bud. As the budding process continues, a chain of buds called **pseudohyphae** is formed (Plate 26).

Sporulation, which occurs in both yeasts and molds, may be brought about by sexual or asexual means. Asexual sporulation is the most important mechanism of reproduction and also the most important mechanism for propagating the species. Asexual sporulation produces numerous individuals and occurs repeatedly, as opposed to sexual spore formation, which occurs infrequently.

Sexual Sporulation

Sexual reproduction in fungi rarely occurs in the laboratory or in infected humans. The sexual phase (called the **perfect state**) of several species has not been detected and this is the basis of classification for one group of fungi called **Deuteromycetes (Fungi Imperfecti).** The latter lack a sexual stage of reproduction. Sexual spores may be of various types.

1. **Oospores.** Oospores result from the fertilization of a specialized female structure called an **oogonium** by a male fungal structure called an **antheridium.**
2. **Zygospores.** Zygospores result from the fusion of two hyphae and their nuclear contents to form a single thick-walled spore.

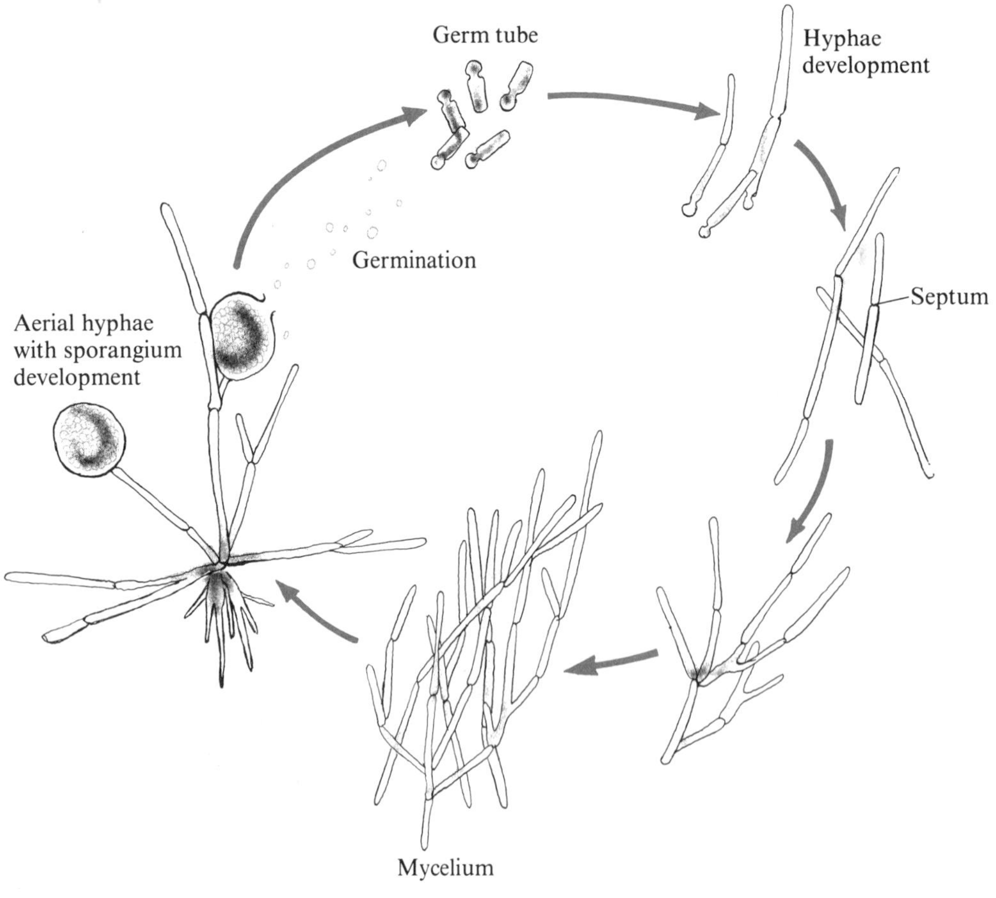

FIGURE 33-5
Stages in the asexual reproduction of a mold. Mycelium develops aerial sporangium in which spores are produced and later are released into the environment. Spores germinate and develop germ tubes, which later multiply and form hyphae.

3. **Ascospores.** Ascospores are formed within a sac called an **ascus.** The ascus is usually enclosed in a fruiting body called an **ascocarp.** Ascocarps vary in size and shape.
4. **Basidiospores.** Basidiospores are formed from the end of a club-shaped structure called a **basidium.** The fungi associated with such structures are mushrooms, puffballs, and other large fungi found in nature (Fig. 33-4).

Asexual Sporulation

Those fungi that form spores only asexually (Fig. 33-5) or not at all are referred to as being in the **imperfect state.** Until recently most human fungal pathogens were characterized as being in the imperfect state, but several species have been induced to produce spores by sexual means.

Asexual spores may be produced in specialized structures that arise from hyphae, or they may be formed by modification of hyphae. **Conidia** are asexual spores produced on specialized stalks called **conidiophores** (Fig. 33-6) from which the spores are pinched and released into the environment. Conidia vary in size, shape, and color (Fig. 33-6), a characteristic that lends itself to classification. Some asexual spores are produced within a specialized sac called a **sporangium** and are called **sporangiospores** (Fig. 33-7). Asexual spores arising directly from hyphae are collectively called **thallospores** and are divided into the following types:

FIGURE 33-6
Conidia. A. Diagram of different morphological forms of conidia (c) and the conidiophores (cp) that bear them. B. Photomicrographs of two types of conidia *(arrows)*. Top, phase-contrast photomicrograph of *Gliomastix mucorum*. (From T. M. Hammill, *Mycologia* 73:229, 1981.) Bottom, differential interference phase-contrast micrograph of *Cladosporium* species. (From M. R. McGinnis, *Laboratory Handbook of Medical Mycology*. New York: Academic, 1980.)

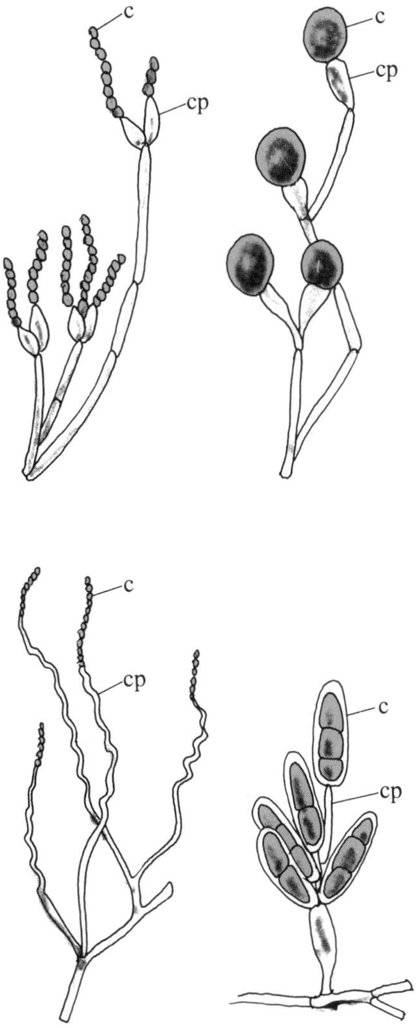

A

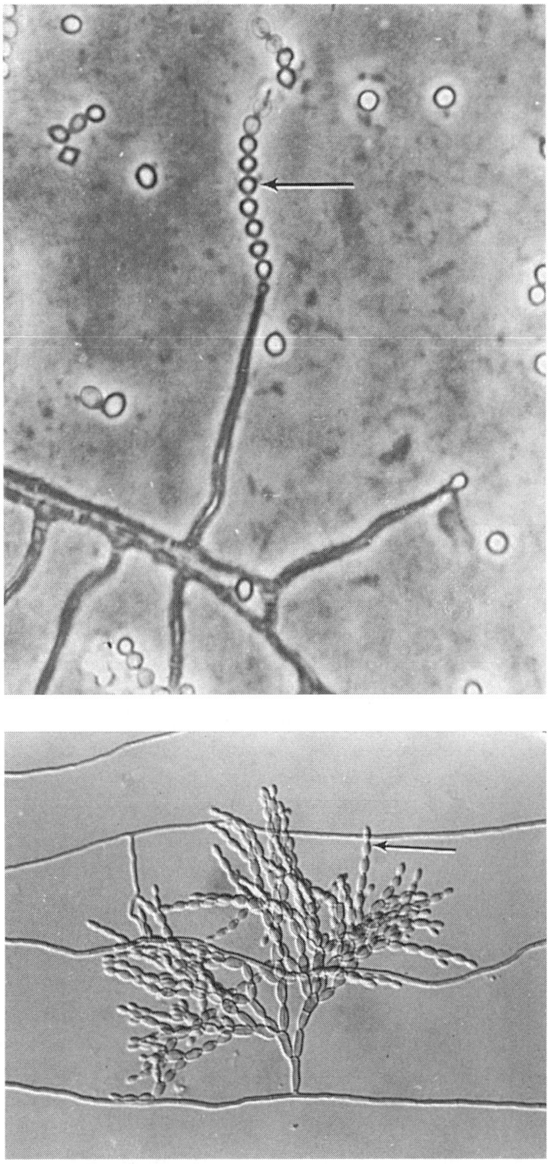

B

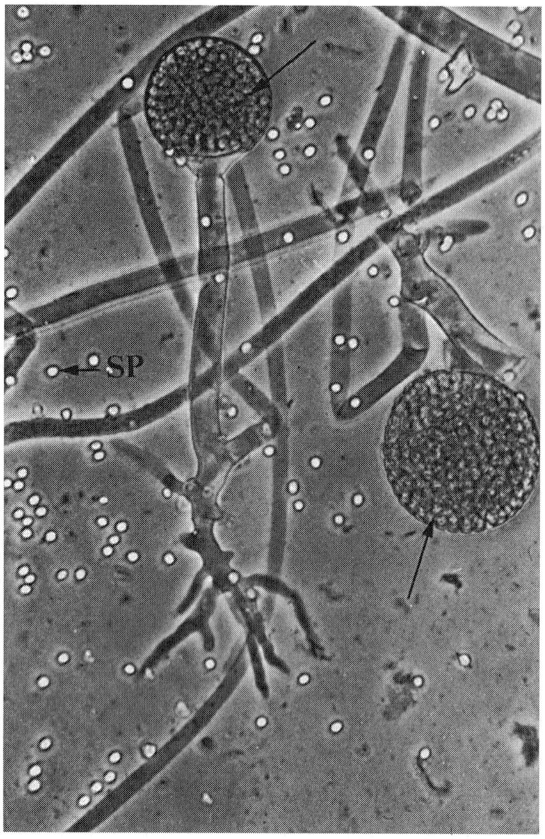

FIGURE 33-7
Photomicrograph of a species of *Rhizopus* demonstrating the sporangium *(arrow)* and its encased sporangiospores (SP). (From E. J. Bottone, *J. Clin. Microbiol.* 9:530, 1979.)

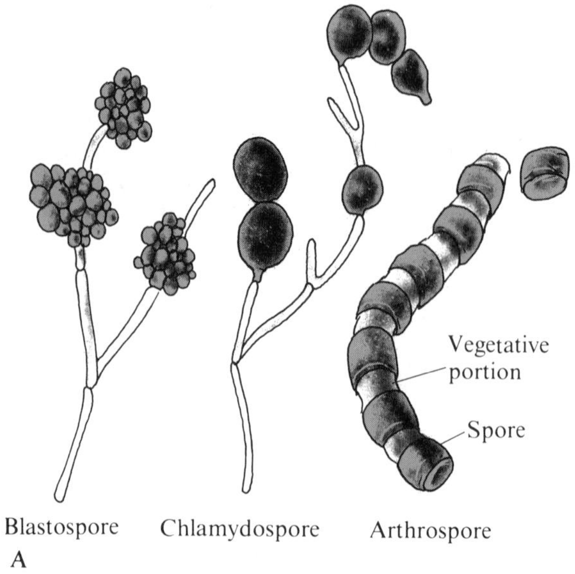

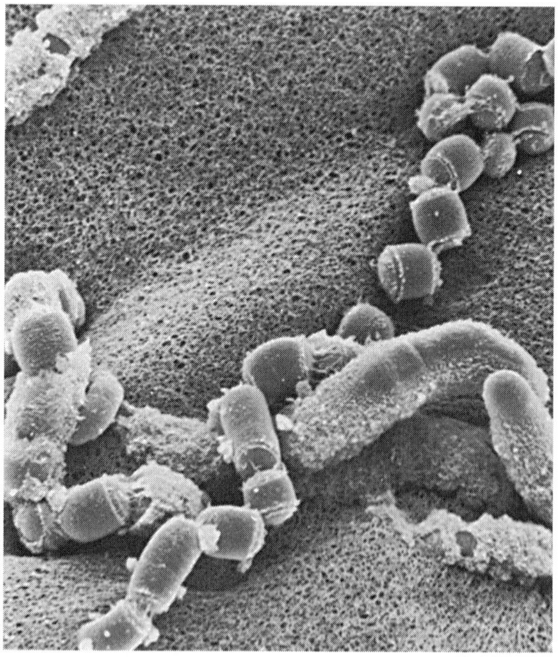

FIGURE 33-8
Types of thallospores. A. Diagram. B. Scanning electron micrograph of arthrospores. (Courtesy of D. J. Bibel.)

1. **Arthrospores.** Arthrospores are barrel-shaped, thick-walled spores produced by the fragmentation of hyphae (Fig. 33-8).
2. **Chlamydospores.** Chlamydospores are sometimes referred to as **resting spores** because they are produced in older, dried-out cultures. They are produced by a swelling of the hyphal fragment and development of a thick wall (Fig. 33-8).
3. **Blastospores.** Blastospores represent a simple budding from the parent cell. They may appear as single daughter cells or as clustered cells, called **pseudohyphae,** that have not been detached (Fig. 33-8).

CULTURAL CHARACTERISTICS

All molds are aerobic, while yeasts are facultative anaerobes. Fungi are endowed with a large arsenal of biosynthetic enzymes that enable them to grow on a variety of substrates. Fungi can tolerate pHs between 2.0 and 9.0, but abundant growth occurs between pH 5.0 and 6.0.

In the laboratory, fungi are cultivated on special media to prevent growth of contaminating bacteria. A widely used isolation media for fungi is called **Sabouraud agar.** This agar contains maltose and peptone as its principal ingredients. It is selective against most bacteria because of its low pH. Antibiotics can be introduced into fungal media to inhibit bacteria selectively.

Fungi can be differentiated into yeasts and molds by their appearance on growth media. Yeasts produce creamy opaque colonies, while mold colonies are fluffy and cottony (see Plate 25). Dimorphic fungi when cultivated at 37 C appear as yeasts, but at 30 C they exist in a mold-like state. Differentiation of some fungal species can be made by demonstrating thermal dimorphism.

PATHOGENESIS

The majority of fungal species that cause disease in humans are soil saprophytes. *Candida* species are one of the few fungi that are part of the microflora of humans. As soil saprophytes, fungi release thousands of spores that are disseminated by air or water into the environment. These spores possess surface components that make them resistant to environmental factors (Fig. 33-9). Spores are ingested or inhaled by humans yet fungal diseases are rare in humans. Some spores are able to infect humans because of physical factors that force them into the host, for example, the lodging of spores in hair follicles. Some spores are present on sharp objects (wood, thorns) that can penetrate subcutaneous tissue. Inhaled spores are sorted out by the respiratory system on the basis of size and density.

Only under unusual circumstances do ingested or inhaled spores cause disease. When the infectious fungal unit makes contact with the host, it must germinate. Depending on the host response, it may or may not cause infection. The diseases caused by fungi are called **mycoses.** Most fungal infections in humans result from occupational hazards. Infection is more likely to occur in those who are constantly in contact with soil or those compromised by underlying disease or some condition that depresses the immune system. Laboratory workers who handle fungal cultures are at an increased risk of infection. Mold cultures must therefore be handled with extreme care. Petri dishes containing mold colonies are handled in special hoods. Fungal infections can occur in the healthy adult only if the fungal infectious units (spores, for example) are in excessive numbers and they make contact with a tissue that supports their growth.

Very little is known about the pathogenic mechanisms of fungi. None appear to produce toxins, which are characteristic of bacteria. Most fungi reaching a mucosal surface are readily attacked by the host's immune system and are walled off. Only *Cryptococcus neoformans* produces a capsule that inhibits phagocytosis. Fungi pathogenic for the skin (dermatophytes) produce **keratinases** that allow them to penetrate the cornified layers. Thus, most fungi that infect humans are opportunistic pathogens.

FIGURE 33-9
Scanning electron micrograph illustrating the surface characteristics of one type of fungal spore. (× 2500 before 25 percent reduction.) (From J. S. Gardner et al., *Mycologia* 75:333, 1983.)

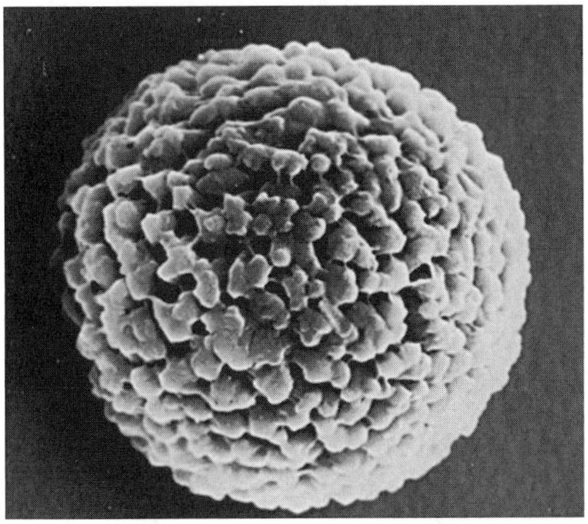

Probably the most important pathogenic device of the fungi is associated with the attribute called **dimorphism.** The major pathogenic dimorphic fungi are *Histoplasma, Coccidioides, Blastomyces, Paracoccidioides,* and *Spororthrix* species. These organisms grow well in the soil at 25 C but by changing their form they can also grow effectively at 37 C in living tissue. They exist in a mycelial state in the soil but in living hosts there is a transition to the yeast state as soon as the temperature reaches 30 C. This transition probably involves genetic modification for adaptation to the new living conditions and for induction of pathogenicity. *Candida* species that are part of the normal microbial flora appear also to use a dimorphic transition to induce pathogenicity. *Candida* is in the yeast state in living tissue but when it becomes pathogenic (the patient is debilitated), the organism produces **pseudohyphae.** Pseudohyphae are apparently required for tissue invasion. Other examples of pathogenic mechanisms are discussed later with the individual organisms.

Fungal diseases can be divided into four types on the basis of the tissue infected: **systemic, subcutaneous, cutaneous,** and **superficial.** In addition, a separate group, **opportunistic** fungal disease, is also discussed.

LABORATORY DIAGNOSIS

The manifestations of many fungal diseases are very similar to those of diseases caused by bacterial agents such as *Actinomyces.* Accurate diagnosis is made by direct microscopic observation, culture technique, and serological tests. The pathogen may also be isolated and identified by exoantigen detection and DNA hybridization techniques. For example, as recently shown, commercially available acridinium ester–labeled DNA probes directed against ribosomal RNA (rRNA) dramatically reduce the time for identification of fungi causing systemic mycoses.

Fungi can be observed directly in clinical specimens such as tissues, sputum, bronchial washings, hair, and skin scrapings. The specimens are usually treated with 10% potassium hydroxide (KOH) and heated to destroy host cellular elements. This process leaves the KOH-resistant cell wall of the fungal agent unaltered. The structures (conidia, conidiophores) of many fungi are distinctive enough in the vegetative phase to permit presumptive diagnosis. Dried and fixed films may be stained with Gram stain, periodic acid–Schiff stain, or Wright stain. The microscopical examination of filamentous molds can be performed by teasing apart a portion of the colony on a microscope slide and adding a drop of lactophenol aniline blue stain. Specimens are also cultured on laboratory media, even when direct examination provides positive results. Sabouraud agar and richer media are used with and without antibiotics to inhibit contaminating bacterial species. Growth at a room temperature of 37 C can be used to distinguish the yeast and mycelial phases of dimorphic fungi. Slide cultures can be made to observe fungal structures in their natural state, but this is not recommended for the agents of systemic mycoses.

Serological tests have value in the diagnosis of mycotic disease, especially if culture or histological results are negative. The results of intradermal injection of skin test antigens of *Aspergillus* species, for example, are important criteria in the diagnosis of disease. Other skin test antigens are sometimes used to assess the prognosis of disease. Serological tests involving antibody determination can also be useful in determining the cause or prognosis of disease. Immunodiffusion, counterimmunoelectrophoresis, and complement fixation are the standard serological tests in the laboratory.

Some fungal pathogens in their mycelial-form cultures produce cell free antigens **(exoantigens)** that are the basis of immunoidentification. The exoantigen test is based on the interaction between antigens released by fungi in culture and homologous antibodies that are specifically generated to precipitate them.

RESISTANCE TO INFECTION

The body's skin and mucous membranes act as barriers to invasion by fungi. This is especially evident in the hospital setting. *Candida* species are indigenous to skin and mucous membranes and will invade tissues only under special circumstances. When the barriers to these organisms are compromised by burn wounds, surgical wounds, and the placement of intravenous catheters, *Candida* can cause serious infections (see Under the Microscope 41).

Antibody is regarded as being less important than cell-mediated immunity as a protective device in response to fungal infections. Patients who have immunoglobulin deficiency, for example, are not usually predisposed to the development of invasive mycoses. Antibodies (and complement) contribute to host defense by opsonizing fungi and facilitating immune recognition.

Phagocytes and neutrophils are of foremost importance in host defenses against mycoses. For example, patients who are neutropenic are particularly predisposed to invasive fungal disease. In patients who have chronic granulomatous disease, a disease in which phagocytes are defective, phagocytes are unable to kill certain fungal species and invasive disease develops. Macrophages such as those in the alveoli are important in destroying inhaled fungal spores. Eosinophils are occasionally involved in allergic fungal diseases since they are part of the inflammatory reaction.

The importance of cell-mediated immunity in resistance to fungal infection is particularly evident in patients with acquired immunodeficiency syndrome (AIDS) and others who are immunosuppressed. Such individuals invariably have a serious fungal disease. Cells that are postulated to function as the effector arm of the cell-mediated immune response include macrophages, natural killer cells, and cytotoxic lymphocytes.

TREATMENT AND PREVENTION

The organelles and membranes of the fungi are similar to those of the host. Therefore, most antifungal drugs are toxic to the host. The number of drugs used to treat fungal infections is considerably smaller than that used to treat bacterial infections.

Even though some of the major antifungal agents were discussed in Chapter 8, we use Table 33-1 to provide a more detailed description of their clinical usefulness.

No vaccines are available to prevent fungal disease. One of the reasons for this is that fungal surfaces are poorly antigenic and second, mycoses are rare in the public. Antimicrobial prophylaxis, however, is being seriously considered because life-threatening fungal infec-

UNDER THE MICROSCOPE 41

Candida Virulence: High-Frequency Switching

Candida albicans and related species possess no single trait that enables them to become a successful pathogen. These fungi are dimorphic and convert to the hyphal stage for dissemination in tissue. Other traits that may contribute to pathogenesis are excretion of phospholipase and acid protease for tissue penetration, selective adhesion to epithelial and plastic surfaces, and responsiveness to female hormones. Recently a potentially new mechanism for virulence, called **high-frequency switching,** was discovered.

High-frequency switching involves the frequent and reversible switching between a number of phenotypes that are distinguishable by colony morphology. High-frequency switching differs from the bud-hypha transition in that bud-hypha transitions are induced and all members of the colony are involved, whereas high-frequency switching occurs spontaneously and only a small number of cells express a different phenotype. Switching is believed to provide the organism with a potential advantage in a different ecological niche represented by different tissues and body locations. Switching has been shown to occur at sites of infection and between episodes of recurrent vaginitis.

TABLE 33-1
Antifungal Agents Currently Available for Clinical Use*

Drug	Formulations	Indications for use
Amphotericin B	Oral, solutions for intravenous (IV) use, creams	Systemic infections caused by *Candida, Cryptococcus, Histoplasma, Blastomyces, Aspergillus, Sporothrix,* and *Mucor*
Nystatin	Oral, cream	*Candida* infections
Flucytosine	Solutions for IV use, oral	Systemic infections caused by *Cryptococcus* and *Candida;* used in combination with amphotericin B
Griseofulvin	Oral	Infections caused by dermatophytes
Clotrimazole	Cream, vaginal tablets, solutions for IV use	Superficial fungal infections, including dermatomycoses, tinea versicolor, and cutaneous and vaginal candidiasis
Miconazole	Cream, vaginal suppositories, solutions for IV use	Systemic infections, including coccidioidomycosis, candidiasis, cryptococcosis, paracoccidioidomycosis, and chronic mucocutaneous candidiasis; tinea versicolor
Econazole	Topical and vaginal creams, sprays and powders	Superficial infections, including dermatomycoses, tinea versicolor, and cutaneous and vaginal candidiasis
Ketoconazole	Oral, creams, and solutions	Systemic infections including blastomycosis, some forms of coccidioidomycosis and histoplasmosis, chronic mucocutaneous candidiasis, chromoblastomycosis, and paracoccidioidomycosis Superficial infections including dermatomycoses and tinea versicolor
Bifonazole	Creams and solutions	Superficial infections including dermatomycoses, tinea versicolor, and cutaneous candidiasis
Croconazole	Creams and gels	Superficial infections including dermatomycoses, tinea versicolor, and cutaneous candidiasis
Fenticonazole	Topical and vaginal creams	Superficial infections including dermatomycoses, tinea versicolor, and cutaneous and vaginal candidiasis
Isoconazole	Topical and vaginal creams	Superficial infections including dermatomycoses, tinea versicolor, and cutaneous and vaginal candidiasis
Sulconazole	Cream	Superficial infections including dermatomycoses, tinea versicolor, and cutaneous candidiasis
Terconazole	Vaginal cream	Vaginal candidiasis
Fluconazole	Oral IV	Cryptococcal meningitis, thrush

* Not all drugs are included; see treatment sections for individual fungal diseases.

tions remain a major complication among immunosuppressed patients. Several antifungal agents in various formulations are now being evaluated in leukemic patients and others with depressed immune systems.

IMPORTANCE TO HUMANS

The fungi play a role in disease but even more important, they are also of value in nature and industry. Fungi, because of highly developed enzymatic systems, can degrade organic material. This property may be of immeasurable value or detriment to humans. Fungi are important in the recycling of carbon and other elements. In addition, they can degrade recalcitrant molecules and have an important role in the disposal of chemical wastes. Their metabolic activities are also responsible for the destruction of many grains, fabrics, and foods. Fungal contamination of grains, peanut crops, and fruits (apples) can lead to the production of **mycotoxins.** Mycotoxins cause serious illness in humans and various domestic animals (mycotoxins are discussed later in the chapter). Fungi play an important role in industry because they are used in the preparation of a variety of products beneficial to humans (Table 33-2). These products include antibiotics, the most well known of which is penicillin, produced by the green mold *Penicillium.* Fungi such as mushrooms, truffles, and morels are also prized food delicacies.

CLASSIFICATION

Modern taxonomists place the fungi in the kingdom Fungi, making it distinct from the animal and plant kingdoms. The kingdom Fungi is separated into two divisions: Myxomycota and Eumycota. The Myxomycota, or slime molds, are nonpathogenic, while the Eumycota are the principal pathogens for humans. The Eumycota can be separated into five subdivisions, four of which are pathogenic to humans:

1. **Zygomycotina.** The Zygomycotina are the most primitive members of the fungi. They are filamentous and lack septa, a characteristic that separates them from other subdivisions. They reproduce sexually and asexually. The asexual spores or sporangiospores are produced in a sac called a **sporangium.** The members of this group are not primary pathogens but are opportunistic in certain predisposed patients.

TABLE 33-2
Industrial Products Obtained Through the Activities of Fungi

Organism	Product
Vitamins	
Eremothecium ashbyi	Riboflavin
Food and beverages	
Saccharomyces cerevisiae	Wine, ale, sake, baker's yeast
Penicillium species	Varieties of cheese
Saccharomyces rouxii	Soy sauce
Saccharomyces carlsbergensis	Lager beer
Organic acids and solvents	
Aspergillus niger	Citric acid and gluconic acid
Saccharomyces cerevisiae	Ethanol from glucose
Single-cell proteins	
Saccharomyces lipolytica	Microbial protein from petroleum alkanes
Candida utilis	Microbial protein from paper pulp waste
Pharmaceuticals	
Penicillium chrysogenum	Penicillins
Cephalosporium acremonium	Cephalosporins
Rhizopus nigricans	Steroid transformation

2. **Ascomycotina.** The Ascomycotina produce asexual and sexual spores. The asexual spores are called **conidia,** and the sexual spores produced by species of medical interest are called **ascospores.** Some members of this group **(dermatophytes)** cause skin infections, while others are pathogenic yeasts.
3. **Basidiomycotina.** The Basidiomycotina produce septate hyphae and sexual spores called **basidiospores.** Mushrooms and puffballs belong to this subdivision.
4. **Deuteromycotina (Fungi Imperfecti).** The Deuteromycotina reproduce asexually. Sexual reproductive structures are unknown. Many species pathogenic to humans belong to this group.

Fungal Diseases

SYSTEMIC MYCOSES

The agents of systemic mycoses are dimorphic fungi found in the soil and are acquired by humans by inhalation of spores. Initially there is a pulmonary infection, which may or may not be symptomatic. Eventually the inhaled organism is disseminated to other organs. The systemic mycoses to be discussed are **histoplasmosis, coccidioidomycosis, blastomycosis, paracoccidioidomycosis,** and **cryptococcosis.**

Histoplasmosis

Histoplasma capsulatum is the causal agent of histoplasmosis, the most common respiratory mycotic infection affecting humans. Histoplasmosis occurs worldwide. In the United States the incidence of infection is highest in the Mississippi Valley. Several million people in the United States are infected by *H. capsulatum,* but fewer than 5 percent are symptomatic.

Epidemiology. *H. capsulatum* is found in soil that is nitrogen-enriched, especially soils containing high levels of avian fecal material. The organism can be easily isolated from excrement in chicken houses and starling roosts and from guano in bat caves. The roosting of several hundred thousand starlings in a midwestern town in the United States was responsible for a large outbreak of histoplasmosis in children. Infections are acquired by inhalation of conidia. Conidia are transmitted through the air when the avian excreta are distributed and aerosolized, but there is no human to human transmission.

Pathogenesis. *H. capsulatum* is an intracellular parasite that preferentially attacks cells of the reticuloendothelial system. The host-parasite relationship in histoplasmosis is poorly understood. Tissue damage by the fungus results in the formation of granulomatous lesions but no toxin has been detected. The virulence of this organism is related to its ability to survive and proliferate within macrophages. Within the macrophage the organism prevents the release of toxic oxygen metabolites (superoxide, hydrogen peroxide, etc.) that normally destroy microbes.

The majority of patients with histoplasmosis are asymptomatic. This is readily evident since 60 to 90 percent of the adults in certain geographical areas show a delayed hypersensitivity to the skin test antigen **histoplasmin.** In patients with acute asymptomatic disease the lung lesion may heal with calcification, a condition that resembles tuberculous lesions.

Pulmonary histoplasmosis sometimes becomes chronic and is almost indistinguishable from tuberculosis. Reactivation of the lesions is more frequent where the disease is endemic. Untreated chronic disease may lead to dissemination of the organism and invasion of the entire reticuloendothelial system. In areas where histoplasmosis is endemic, disseminated histoplasmosis occurs 400 times more often among leukemic patients than the rest of the population. The symptoms include fever with liver, spleen, and lymph node enlargement. The phagocytic cells found in these tissues are gorged with small oval yeasts cells. The infected organs display small granulomas similar to those produced in miliary tuberculosis. In approximately 50 percent of infected individuals, mucocutaneous lesions appear in the oral cavity. The ulcerative oral lesions are often painful and are accompanied by regional lymph node enlargement.

In endemic areas of the United States histoplasmosis is a common opportunistic infection in AIDS patients. The symptoms include a pneumonia that mimics *Pneumocystis carinii* pneumonia. In 10 percent of patients with disseminated infection, there are cutaneous eruptions on the face and extremities.

Laboratory Diagnosis. The mold phase of *H. capsulatum* resembles that of many other fungi. Conventional identification of this organism, therefore, entails examination and culturing of specimens (bone marrow, blood, sputum, urine, etc.) and establishing dimorphism. On Sabouraud agar, mycelial growth reveals the characteristic tuberculate conidia that develop from the hyphae (Fig. 33-10). The yeast phase can be demonstrated by growth on enriched media.

One of the more rapid and accurate procedures has been the **exoantigen** test for immunoidentification of the organism. Still, 7 to 10 days is required to grow sufficient amount of culture and extract the requisite amount of antigens.

Treatment. Histoplasmosis is considered a common benign infection. Treatment of disseminated infection is dependent on early diagnosis. Amphotericin B is effective but must be sustained with weekly infusions to prevent relapse. Itraconazole and fluconazole also appear to be highly effective. Serum or urine polysaccharide *Histoplasma* antigen levels correlate well with response to therapy.

FIGURE 33-10
Histoplasma capsulatum. A. Diagram of tuberculate macroconidia, which appear as round thick-walled spores. Each spore has finger-like projections (tubercles) attached to it. B. Photomicrograph of cultured *H. capsulatum*. (Courtesy of G. Roberts.)

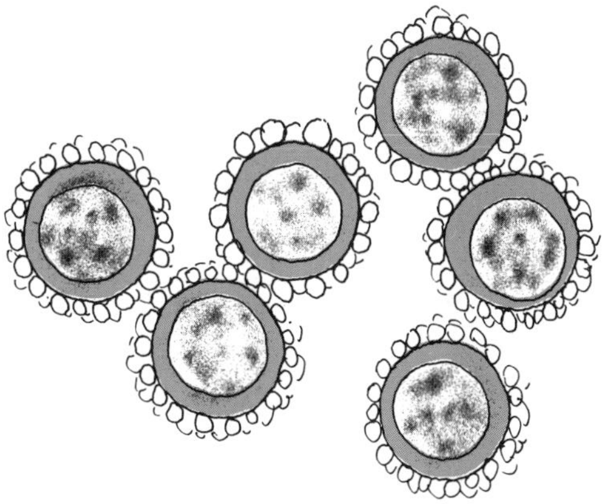

A

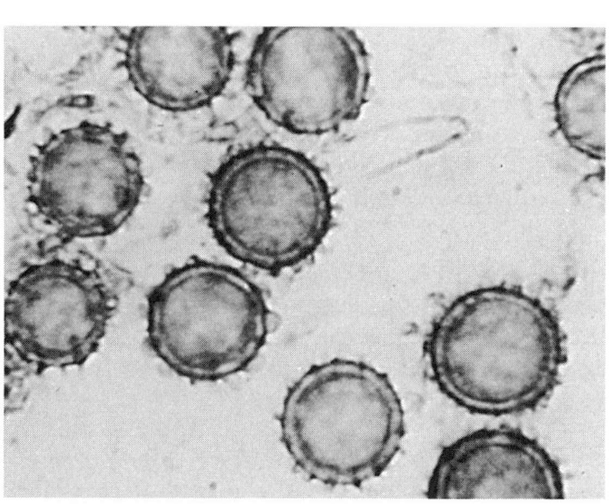

B

Coccidioidomycosis

Coccidioidomycosis is caused by the agent *Coccidioides immitis*. Disease is initiated as an upper respiratory tract infection that usually resolves on its own. Resolution depends on a cell-mediated immune response by the host. In the immunocompromised, disseminated disease often leads to a fatal outcome.

Epidemiology. Coccidioidomycosis is found only in the Western Hemisphere. In the United States it is found in the sandy soils of the lower Sonoran Desert life zone. The fungus lives in the soil in a mycelial form that produces arthroconidia (Fig. 33-11). Arthroconidia released from the mycelium are carried in the air and when inhaled (for example, during dust storms) by an appropriate host, give rise to pulmonary infection.

The disease strikes individuals of all age groups but more serious infections are observed in the very young and elderly. Race plays no part in the incidence of primary pulmonary disease, but dissemination occurs more commonly in Filipinos, African Americans, Hispanics, and Native Americans. Epidemics of disease are associated with construction, archaeological digs, and exploration of oil in sandy soils. The demographics of coccidioidomycosis are changing because of the AIDS epidemic and more life-threatening infections are now being encountered.

Pathogenesis. Nearly 60 percent of patients with coccidioidomycosis are asymptomatic. Others have a respiratory illness characterized by fever, headache, myalgia, and fatigue. These infections are usually very mild and of short duration. All of these infected individuals have a lifetime positive skin reaction to the antigen **coccidioidin.**

In about 25 percent of those with symptomatic disease the manifestations are more severe and include pleuritic chest pain. In the majority of these patients, the disease will also resolve without serious consequences. Only a small minority present with disseminated disease.

Skin manifestations are often present with primary infection in the form of erythema nodosum. Arthritis may also be observed and involves primarily the ankles.

Disseminated disease is observed in less than 1 percent of infected individuals. Practically every organ of the body is affected, except the gastrointestinal tract. Granulomas are present on the skin and abscesses may appear in the subcutaneous areas (Fig. 33-12). Osteomyelitis involving vertebrae, skull, ribs, and long bones is also a frequent result of dissemination. The most severe manifestation of disseminated disease is **meningitis.** Meningitis may progress slowly or it may run its full course, resulting in death in a few weeks.

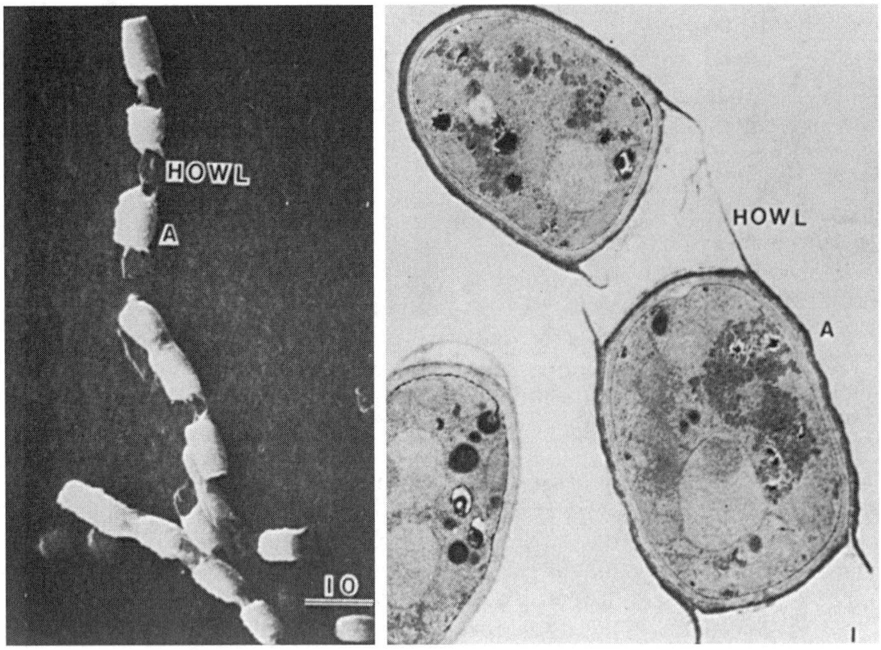

A B

FIGURE 33-11
Coccidioides immitis. A. Scanning electron micrograph of arthroconidia alternating with lysed vegetative components of hypha. HOWL = hyphal outer wall; A = arthroconidium. (Bar = 10 μm.) B. Thin-section electron micrograph of a portion of A. (From M. Hupert et al. In D. Schlesinger, ed., *Microbiology–1983.* Washington, D.C.: American Society for Microbiology, 1983.)

FIGURE 33-12
Coccidioidomycosis. Disseminated disease with granulomatous crusted lesions of the face and nose. (Photograph by A. Gregerson, F.B.P.A. Reproduced with permission from G. M. Lewis, M. E. Hopper, J. W. Wilson, and O. A. Plunkett, *An Introduction to Medical Mycology,* 4th ed. Copyright © 1958 by Year Book Medical Publishers, Inc., Chicago.)

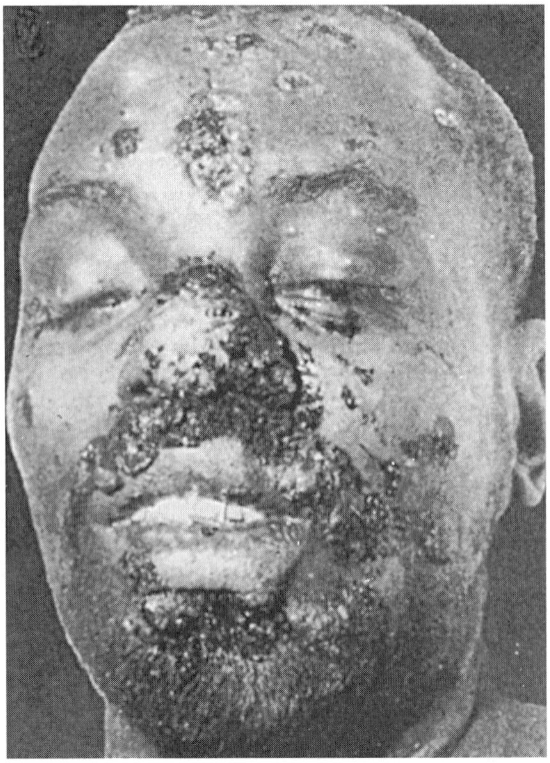

Laboratory Diagnosis. Coccidioidomycosis resembles many other granulomatous diseases. Accurate diagnosis is based on laboratory identification of the fungus in pathological tissue in culture or in serological tests. Clinical specimens of sputum, pus, or tissue can be cultivated on Sabouraud and blood agar to demonstrate the mycelial phase. Inhaled arthrospores are transformed into large spherules in their tissue phase of development. Biopsy material, therefore, will reveal spherules with evidence of endosporulation (Plate 27).

Skin test data using **coccidioidin** are not considered diagnostic, but if the test result is negative, it will help to exclude coccidioidomycosis.

Serological tests are sensitive and many are quite specific. These tests include enzyme immunoassays, tube precipitin tests, and immunodiffusion tests. The most useful test is the complement fixation test for IgG antibodies. This test has the advantage of giving prognostic as well as diagnostic information. Titers of at least 1 : 4 indicate the presence of recent or current infection. Higher titers indicate the disease is active but the prognosis is good. No titer predicts disseminated disease and risk of a poor outcome.

Treatment. For mild to stable disease the drugs ketoconazole and fluconazole are recommended. Both drugs are helpful in preventing disseminated disease. Amphotericin B is recommended for severe or potentially severe disease.

Blastomycosis

Blastomycosis is caused by the dimorphic fungus *Blastomyces dermatitidis.* Disease is initiated primarily by inhalation of spores from the environment. The disease can be chronic and is characterized by granulomatous lesions that may give rise to a disseminated form.

Epidemiology. Blastomycosis in North America is endemic in the southeastern United States (except Florida). The exact ecological niche for the organism is not precisely known. It appears to prefer areas with high acidic pH, high organic content (rotting wood, bird droppings, etc.), and abundant moisture. The fungus is believed to remain dormant in the soil for most of the year and is then stimulated by climatic conditions to reproduce. Outbreaks have occurred among individuals involved in cabin construction and in work near beaver structures and excavation sites.

Pathogenesis. Following inhalation of spores there is an acute pulmonary phase that may be asymptomatic or self-limiting or may result in fulminant infection. Fulminant infection may include respiratory distress or chronic progressive disease. Symptoms suggestive of blastomycosis are cough and fever of 3 days or longer, pleuritic chest pain, night sweats, and weight loss.

Pulmonary lesions may heal but the fungus is usually disseminated with skin involvement (Plate 28). Chronic cutaneous disease is characterized by subcutaneous lesions that ulcerate. The lesions are found primarily on the face, hands, and lower legs, or mucocutaneous areas such as the larynx. Untreated, the disease progresses and involves many unexposed areas of the body. When the lesions heal, they leave deforming scars that cover the face, neck, or other areas. Disseminated disease involves most organs and may also be manifested as cutaneous or osseous (bone) lesions.

Laboratory Diagnosis. *B. dermatitidis* in the yeast phase exists as spherical cell 8 to 15 μm in diameter. When observed in stained sections or preparations, the cytoplasmic membrane of the fungus is seen to shrink and the cell appears double-walled. In addition, the buds of the dividing yeast remain attached to the parent cell, giving the appearance of a figure eight (Fig. 33-13).

Clinical specimens (skin scrapings, sputum, pus, etc.) should be examined for typical thick-walled yeast forms. Yeast as well as mycelial forms can be detected if the organism is cultivated on Sabouraud and enriched media. The results of tissue or exudate identification or culture are sufficient for reliable diagnosis. Serological tests such as immunodiffusion and enzyme-linked immunosorbent assay (ELISA) are not reliable but they have been used as epidemiological tools.

Treatment. Many cases of acute pulmonary blastomycosis are self-limiting. Amphotericin B is effective in severely ill and immunocompromised patients and relapses are rare. Ketoconazole and itraconazole are also effective in the treatment of some forms of blastomycosis. Neither is effective when infections involve the central nervous system or bone.

Paracoccidioidomycosis

Paracoccidioidomycosis, also called **South American blastomycosis,** is a chronic, sometimes fatal disease. It is characterized by lesions of the mucous membranes of the mouth. The disease is caused by *Paracoccidioides brasiliensis* and is seldom observed in the United States.

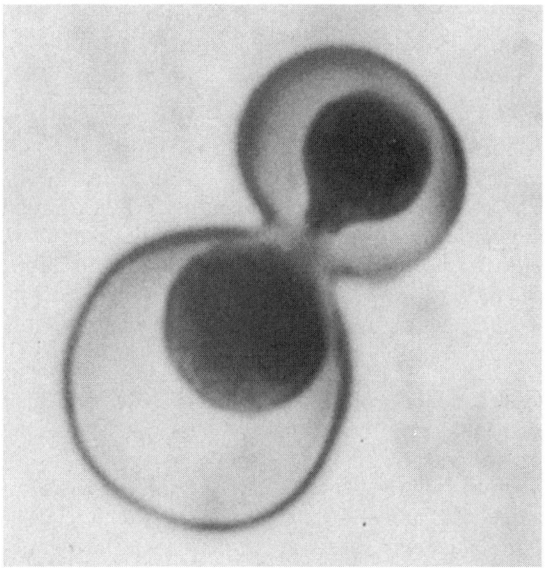

FIGURE 33-13
Stained wet preparation of *Blastomyces dermatitidis*. The membrane shrinks during the staining, giving the appearance of a double wall. The smaller bud remains attached to the mother cell, which gives the appearance of a figure eight. (From H. W. Larsh and N. L. Goodman. In E. H. Lennette, A. Balows, W. J. Hausler, Jr., and J. P. Truant, eds., *Manual of Clinical Microbiology*, 3rd ed. Washington, D.C.: American Society for Microbiology, 1980.)

Epidemiology. It is believed that infection with *P. brasiliensis* occurs by inhalation of airborne mycelial structures. The pathogen is endemic to many regions of Latin America, mainly in Argentina, Brazil, Colombia, and Venezuela. The highest incidence of disease occurs among agricultural workers.

Pathogenesis. Infection by the pathogen is believed to occur first in the respiratory tract. However, oral lesions and enlargement of regional lymph nodes are the earliest signs of disease. The oral lesions are granular but seldom ulcerative. The clinical forms of the disease have been divided into two types. The first, the **acute form,** appears abruptly with intense involvement of the phagocytic mononuclear system. There is also deterioration of the general condition of the host. This form usually involves young individuals of both sexes. The second form is the **chronic form** in which the disease progresses slowly, with lesions restricted to a few organs and preservation of the general condition of the host. The chronic form usually attacks adult men.

Lesions may appear on the skin, in the lymph nodes, and in the lungs. **Granulomas** are the principal pathological response in any infected tissue and they resemble those associated with tuberculosis. In clinical specimens, fungi may be found outside or inside phagocytic cells as oval, multiple budding cells averaging between 25 and

30 μm in diameter. Prognosis for the disseminated form of the disease is very poor, the fatality rate reaching 50 percent.

Laboratory Diagnosis. Clinical diagnosis can be made from the appearance of oral lesions, but confirmation depends on the finding of fungal parasites in clinical specimens. The yeast phase cells show multiple buds, much resembling a ship's wheel, which distinguishes them from *B. dermatitidis.* Serological tests are not totally reliable; however, the immunodiffusion counterimmunoelectrophoresis and complement fixation tests are reasonably specific.

Treatment. Ketoconazole is a particularly effective drug and was considered the drug of choice. Ketoconazole, however, adversely affects erythrocyte enzymes. Itraconazole is now considered the drug of choice because of its higher activity and shorter period of therapy. Licensed alternative drugs include sulfonamides (sulfadiazine and sulfisoxazole) and amphotericin B. Recently the drug saperconazole was shown to act more rapidly than any of the above-mentioned drugs and it eventually may become the drug of choice.

Cryptococcosis

Cryptococcosis is a subacute chronic infection that involves mainly the lungs, brain, and meninges. The causative agent, *Cryptococcus neoformans,* has as its primary reservoir the soil. Pigeon droppings containing organic nitrogen (urea) favor the growth of yeasts. The fungus is not dimorphic, and only the yeast phase exists in the saprophytic and parasitic states.

Epidemiology. Four serotypes of *C. neoformans* are present and two varieties are now recognized (see the 1991 Levitz article listed in Additional Readings). The incidence of disease, which at one time was rarely observed, has increased dramatically in recent years. The reason for this increase has been the AIDS epidemic. Cryptococcosis is the most lethal fungal infection associated with AIDS. Infection is initiated following inhalation of aerosolized fungal particles from the environment.

Pathogenesis. The prevalence of cryptococcosis is markedly increased among immunocompromised patients. At particularly high risk are those with defects in the cell-mediated immune system (AIDS patients, individuals with Hodgkin's disease, transplant recipients, etc.).

Infection first involves the pulmonary system and seldom goes beyond this stage in most immunocompetent individuals. The pulmonary lesions heal without calcification and symptoms go unrecognized. Systemic infection may follow pulmonary involvement. Any organ including the central nervous system may become involved. Central nervous system involvement is characterized by the development of granulomatous lesions of the meninges. Left untreated, these lesions are usually fatal. Cutaneous lesions manifested as papules or abscesses may also be the result of disseminated disease (Fig. 33-14).

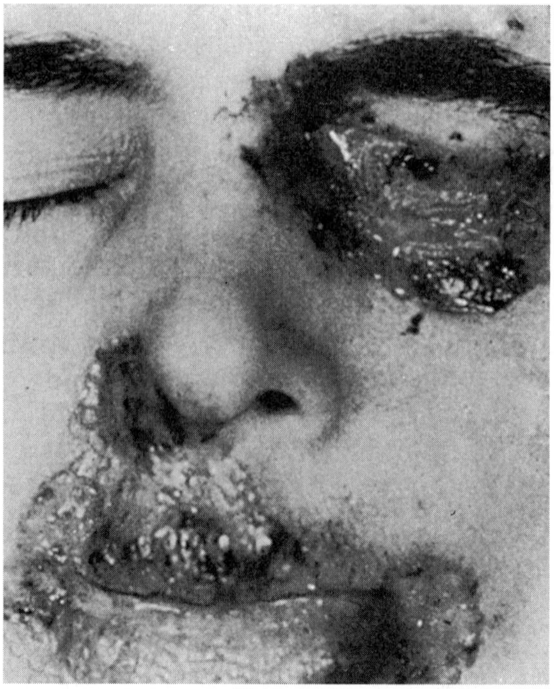

FIGURE 33-14
Cryptococcosis. Extensive cutaneous involvement. The gelatinous material represents fungus in nearly pure culture. (Courtesy of A. C. Curtis, Ann Arbor, MI. Reproduced with permission from G. M. Lewis, M. E. Hopper, J. W. Wilson, and O. A. Plunkett, *An Introduction to Medical Mycology,* 4th ed. Copyright © 1958 by Year Book Medical Publishers, Inc., Chicago.)

The pathogenesis of *C. neoformans* is related to a cell wall antigen and the capsule that surrounds the fungus. The severity of disease is directly related to the concentration of **cryptococcal antigen** in body fluids. The antigen suppresses the delayed-type hypersensitivity response and protective immunity to cryptococci. The capsule inhibits phagocytosis.

Laboratory Diagnosis. India ink or nigrosin preparations of sputum, pus, urine, or infected tissue reveal *C. neoformans* as an oval, thick-walled yeast cell surrounded by a wide clear capsule (Fig. 33-15). Capsule-deficient *C. neoformans* can appear in patients with AIDS. Culture on Sabouraud agar results in slimy, mucoid colonies containing budding cells with large capsules, but no hyphae develop.

The latex agglutination test for the detection of cryptococcal capsular polysaccharide is highly sensitive and specific for the diagnosis of meningeal and disseminated forms of cryptococcosis.

Treatment. Cryptococcal meningitis in all patients including AIDS patients is treated with amphotericin B plus flucytosine. This treatment still results in a failure rate of 20 to 30 percent. Because of toxicity with amphotericin B, other drugs such as fluconazole have been approved for treatment of cryptococcal meningitis.

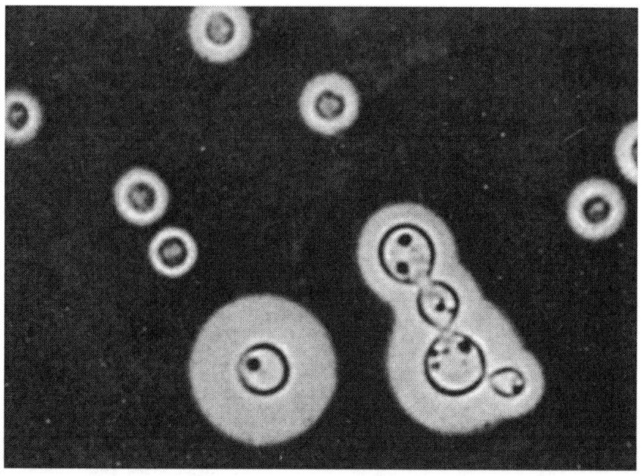

FIGURE 33-15
Cryptococcus neoformans. A nigrosin-stained wet preparation of spinal fluid showing oval fungal cells surrounded by a clear capsule. (From M. Silva-Hunter and B. H. Cooper. In E. Lennette, A. Balows, W. J. Hausler, Jr., and J. P. Truant, eds., *Manual of Clinical Microbiology,* 3rd ed. Washington, D.C.: American Society for Microbiology, 1980.)

SUBCUTANEOUS MYCOSES

Subcutaneous mycotic infections are those that remain localized in subcutaneous tissue. Most infections are the result of puncture wounds by objects contaminated by fungal species found in decaying vegetation and in the soil. Several agents are associated with subcutaneous mycoses. We elaborate on only one, *Sporothrix schenckii,* which is most frequently associated with infection. Subcutaneous diseases caused by other fungal agents are outlined in Table 33-3.

FIGURE 33-16
Chromomycosis involving an arm. (From P. Lavalle et al., *Rev. Infect. Dis.* 9[Suppl. 1]:64, 1987.)

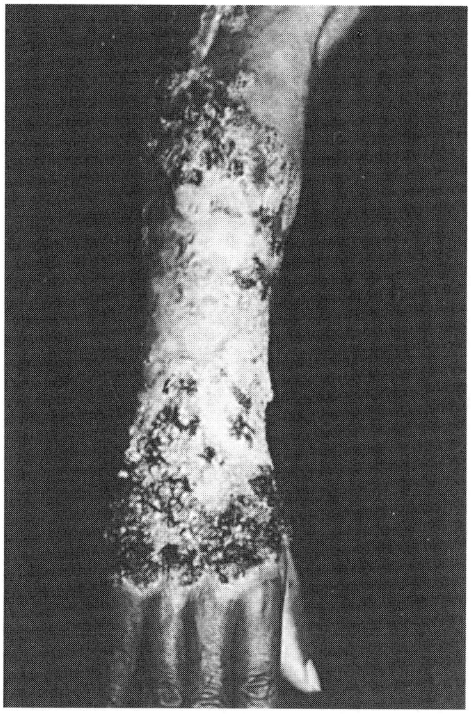

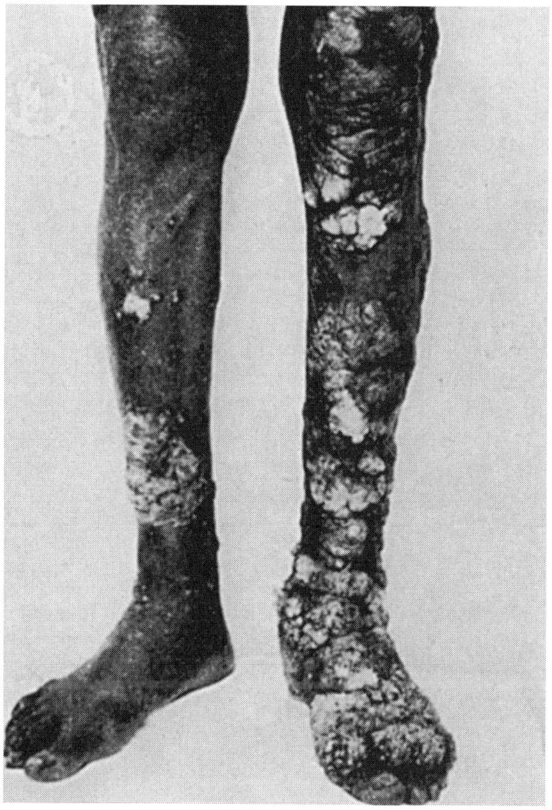

FIGURE 33-17
Lobomycosis. Keloidal lesions of 30 years' duration. (From C. W. Emmons et al., *Medical Mycology,* 3rd ed. Philadelphia: Lea & Febiger, 1977.)

Sporotrichosis and Other Subcutaneous Mycoses

Sporotrichosis is an infection that is seen most often in greenhouse workers, farmers, and others who are constantly exposed to the soil. The causative agent, *S. schenckii,* is found in the soil and vegetation and has worldwide distribution. Sporotrichosis is endemic in parts of Brazil, South Africa, and Zimbabwe. The largest outbreak in the United States was seen in 1988 (see Under the Microscope 42).

Epidemiology and Pathogenesis. Most cases of sporotrichosis result from traumatic implantation of the fungus into the skin, resulting in chronic lesions. The lesions are small, purplish, and ulcerated and soon spread to regional lymph nodes. The lymph nodes become swollen and sometimes necrotic (see Plate 29). The subcutaneous infection remains localized and seldom becomes disseminated. Hematogenous dissemination is usually restricted to the immunocompromised. Disseminated disease often involves the skeletal system and seldom, organ systems (Fig. 33-18).

TABLE 33-3
Characteristics of the Subcutaneous Mycoses and Their Causal Agents

Disease	Agent	Clinical manifestations	Epidemiology	Treatment
Sporotrichosis	*Sporothrix schenckii*	Nodules along lymphatic channels that may ulcerate or superficial lesions not involving lymphatics; extracutaneous infections rare	Infection highest among agricultural workers	Potassium iodide for ulceroglandular and lymphatic forms of disease (itraconazole is also effective); amphotericin B may be required for disseminated joint and pulmonary disease
Chromoblastomycosis (Fig. 33-16)	*Phialophora verrucosa, Cladosporium carrionii, Fonsecaea* species, *Wangiella dermatitidis*	Infections usually on lower extremities with discolored lesions that become raised and cauliflower-like if untreated; systemic invasion rare	Predominant in tropical and subtropical regions among barefoot agriculturalists	Surgery in early disease, flucytosine or itraconazole for advanced cases
Mycetoma	*Petriellidium boydii, Madurella mycetomatis, Madurella grisea, Acremonium kiliense,* and others	Granulomatous lesions with multiple sinus tracts; feet, hands, and other exposed areas usually infected; scar tissue leads to disfigurement of affected area	Found worldwide but most frequently in Africa, Asia, and tropical and subtropical areas	Surgery to remove tissue that prevents drug penetration; nystatin, amphotericin B, and flucytosine
Rhinosporidiosis	*Rhinosporidium seeberi*	Lesions of mucous membranes of nose or soft palate; lesions become enlarged masses that can interfere with breathing	Found primarily in India and Sri Lanka and mostly in males	Surgery
Lobomycosis (Fig. 33-17)	*Loboa loboi*	Lesions localized primarily on feet, legs, or face; lesions spread as enlarged masses	Found primarily in Amazon basin	Surgery and sulfa drugs
Subcutaneous phycomycosis	*Basidiobolus haptosporus*	Nodule formation in subcutaneous tissue; infection usually in abdomen or a limb	Found primarily in Africa among children 5–9 years old	Potassium iodide

UNDER THE MICROSCOPE 42

Multistate Outbreak of Sporotrichosis in Seedling Handlers, 1988

Between April 23 and June 30, 1988, 84 cases of cutaneous sporotrichosis occurred in persons who handled conifer seedlings packed in Pennsylvania with sphagnum moss that had been harvested in Wisconsin. Confirmed cases occurred in 14 states, with the majority occurring in New York (29), Illinois (23), and Pennsylvania (12). Each of the victims handled seedlings from April 4 to May 16; symptoms developed between April 23 and June 30.

Thirty-one cases (37 percent) occurred in state forestry workers and garden club members who participated in annual tree distributions in which seedlings were separated from one another, repacked in moss, and distributed to area residents. In addition, 12 patients had received seedlings through these distributions, 38 had purchased seedlings directly from nurseries, and three were nursery workers. All the patients had contact with seedlings distributed by two Pennsylvania nurseries. *Sporothrix schenckii* was cultured from skin lesions of 38 persons and from five samples of unopened bales of moss obtained from one nursery.

Sphagnum moss harvested in Wisconsin is shipped to nurseries in more than 15 states, and the involved Pennsylvania nurseries ship seedlings and moss to 47 states. Previous outbreaks associated with Wisconsin sphagnum moss have occurred. The largest previously reported U.S. outbreak involved 17 forestry workers in 1976.

From *M.M.W.R.* 37:652, 1988.

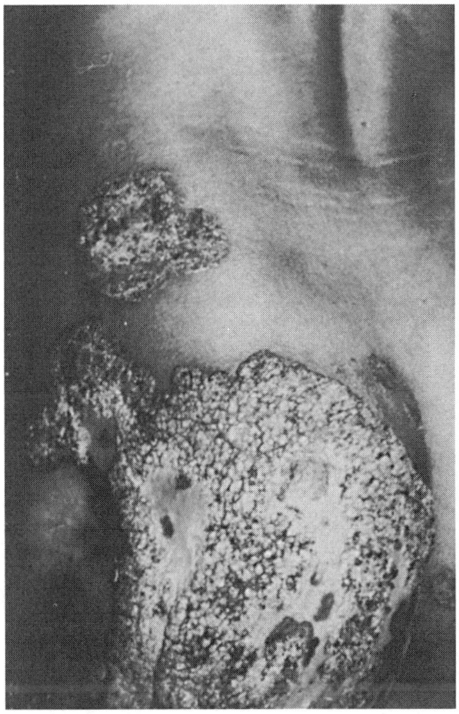

FIGURE 33-18
Disseminated sporotrichosis on buttock. (From P. Lavalle et al., *Rev. Infect. Dis.* 9[Suppl. 1]:64, 1987.)

Less frequently, spores can be inhaled, causing primary pneumonia. Pulmonary infections are observed more frequently in hospitalized patients who inhale spores. Like other systemic mycoses, pulmonary infection by *S. schenckii* mimics tuberculosis.

Laboratory Diagnosis. Aspirated pus from lesions should be cultured on Sabouraud agar or brain-heart infusion agar at 37 C to demonstrate the yeast phase and on Sabouraud agar at room temperature to demonstrate the mycelial phase. Yeast phase cells are oval and sometimes cigar shaped. The mycelial phase is characterized by brown to black colonies in which conidia appear as flower-like clusters on conidiophores (Fig. 33-19).

FIGURE 33-19
Floweret arrangement of conidia on conidiophores of *Sporothrix schenckii*. (Courtesy of G. Roberts.)

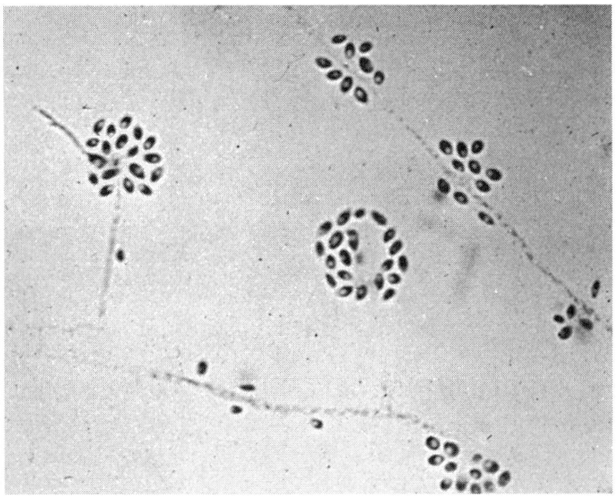

The slide agglutination test is the preferred technique for serological diagnosis.

Treatment. Lymphocutaneous sporotrichosis responds well to saturated solutions of potassium iodide and itraconazole. Amphotericin B is recommended for the treatment of disseminated disease but itraconazole also appears to be effective.

DERMATOPHYTOSES (CUTANEOUS MYCOSES)

General Characteristics

The fungi that invade the keratinized and cutaneous areas of the body (nails, hair, and skin) are called the **dermatophytes.** The dermatophytes are represented by three major genera of pathogenic molds: *Microsporum, Trichophyton,* and *Epidermophyton.* In the United States, *Trichophyton rubrum* is the most frequently encountered causal agent of cutaneous mycoses. The diseases produced by these three genera are referred to as **tineas (ringworms)** of various parts of the body; for example, tinea capitis is ringworm of the scalp. Dermatophytes produce enzymes that enable them to degrade keratinized tissue. These enzymes include keratinase, elastase, and collagenase, which break down keratin, elastin, and collagen, respectively. All of these substrates are components of epithelial and connective tissues. The inability of dermatophytes to invade deep tissue is probably related to the fact that they grow optimally at 25 C. The temperature of outer dead layers of skin is lower than body temperature. In addition, dermatophytes are unable to convert to alternative growth forms as do the dimorphic fungi discussed previously. Other factors such as oxidation-reduction potential and tissue conditions are probably also involved as barriers to dermatophyte infection.

Dermatophytes abound worldwide as saprophytes in the soil, but many of them have evolved to a parasitic existence. Some dermatophytes are strict parasites of humans and are no longer found in the soil. Others no longer found in the soil are parasites of lower-order animals that can also infect humans. Finally, some are found free in nature and accidentally cause infections in humans. The cutaneous mycoses are the only contagious fungal diseases in humans.

Laboratory Diagnosis

Dermatophytic infections of the hair, nails, and skin are sometimes diagnosed from the clinical symptoms—loss of hair, thickened and discolored nails, or generalized scaling. In ringworm of the scalp the patient can be examined directly for skin lesions or areas where there is loss of hair.

In some scalp infections, particularly those caused by *Microsporum,* the infected hair fluoresces a bright yellow-green when exposed to Wood's lamp (ultraviolet). Hair, skin scrapings, or nail clippings can be examined directly by placing the infected material on slides and adding 10% KOH. The preparation is gently heated to free the hyphae from keratinous material. The infected material is examined for the presence of septate hyphae or arthrospores.

Identification of the specific dermatophyte can be accomplished by culturing the infected material on Sabouraud agar and examining the macroscopical colonial characteristics as well as the microscopical morphology of individual species. Sabouraud agar should contain cycloheximide (Acti-Dione), which suppresses the growth of most saprophytic fungi but not dermatophytes. Sabouraud agar should also contain an antibacterial agent such as chlortetracycline hydrochloride (Aureomycin) or chloramphenicol to give the slower-growing dermatophytes a chance to outgrow bacteria.

Treatment

Griseofulvin given orally has proved useful for eliminating scalp infections. For body infections, several antifungal ointments containing the following agents can be applied: 3% salicylic acid, 5% undecylenic acid, 5% benzoic acid, or 5% sodium thiosulfate. For foot infections, potassium permanganate (1 : 4000), 20% zinc undecylenate, 3% salicylic acid, or 5% benzoic acid is helpful in treatment. Drugs such as tolnaftate, miconazole nitrate, and clotrimazole are also available. Recently, fluconazole was shown to be effective for tinea corporis, tinea cruris, and tinea pedis.

Tinea Capitis (Ringworm of the Scalp)

Most species of *Microsporum* and *Trichophyton* can be involved in ringworm of the scalp (Fig. 33-20). *Microsporum canis,* transmitted by infected dogs and cats, is a major causal agent of this disease. The infection is usually acquired during childhood and begins with inflammation and itching of the scalp. The fungi spread on the keratinized areas of the scalp and may even involve the hair shaft, so hair is broken off at the scalp level. If the hyphae are found growing only within the hair shaft, the infection is called **endothrix** infection. If the hyphae are found both within and on the external surface of the hair, the infection is called **ectothrix** infection.

FIGURE 33-20
Tinea capitis. (Courtesy of G. Roberts.)

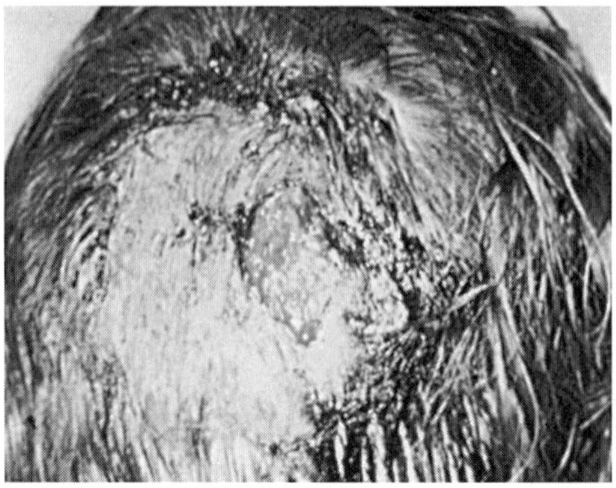

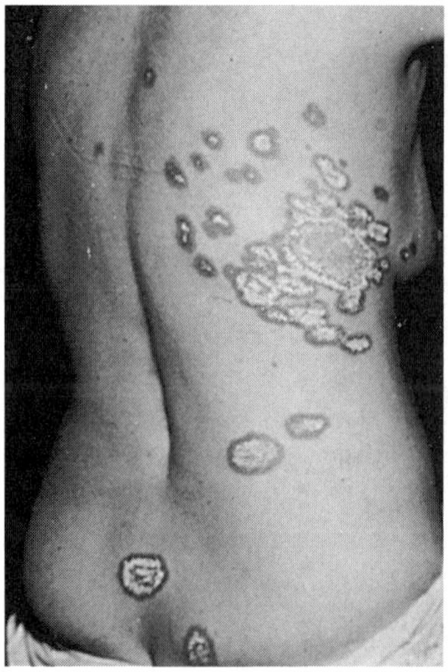

FIGURE 33-21
Tinea corporis. (Courtesy of G. Roberts.)

Tinea Corporis (Ringworm of the Body)

Tinea corporis is a dermatophytosis involving the nonhairy areas of the body (Fig. 33-21). Fungal infections of the face are often misdiagnosed as connective tissue diseases such as lupus erythematosus or disorders caused by overexposure to sunlight. The lesions appear as reddened, scaly, papular eruptions. Pustules are often seen on the periphery of the lesion. Species of *Trichophyton* and *Microsporum* are commonly involved in these infections.

Tinea Pedis (Ringworm of the Feet)

Tinea pedis, usually called **athlete's foot,** is believed by many investigators to be spread primarily through the use of public showers, swimming pools, or other such facilities. The infection is favored by failure to dry one's feet between the toes. Lesions releasing a watery fluid may appear later. Chronic infections show peeling and cracking of the skin, often resembling eczema (Fig. 33-22). The causative agents of athlete's foot may be any number of species of *Microsporum, Trichophyton,* or *Epidermophyton.*

Tinea Barbae (Ringworm of the Beard Area)

Tinea barbae is an infection of the bearded areas of the face. Infection may remain superficial or may become severe and involve deeper tissue. Superficial infection appears as a scaly lesion; the deeper infection is characterized by deep pustules and nodular lesions (Fig. 33-23). Permanent loss of hair is common with severe infection. *Trichophytum rubrum* is the principal agent involved in superficial infections, while *Trichophytum verrucosum* is associated with the more severe form.

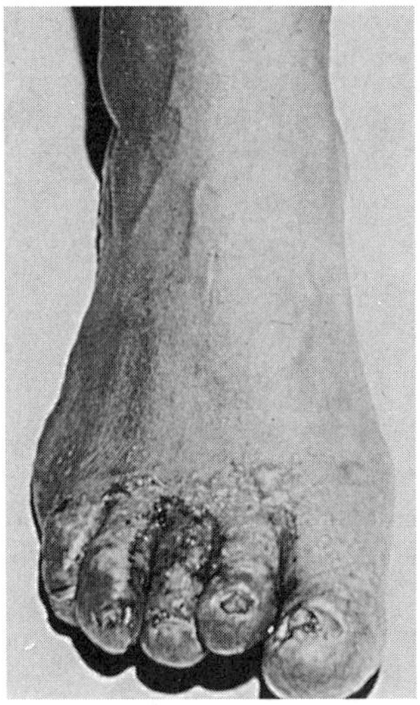

FIGURE 33-22
Tinea pedis. (Courtesy of G. Roberts.)

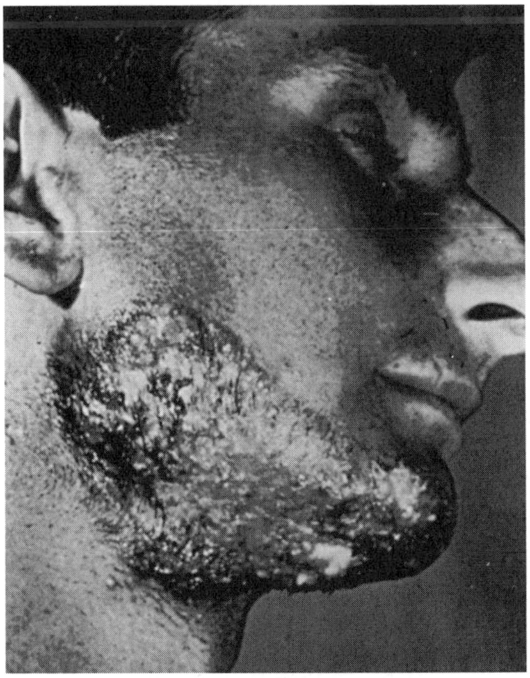

FIGURE 33-23
Tinea barbae. Deep pustular folliculitis in a patient with *Trichophyton verrucosum* infection. (From W. Rippon, *Medical Mycology*, 2nd ed. Philadelphia: Saunders, 1982.)

Tinea Favosa (Ringworm of the Scalp)

Tinea favosa is characterized by the formation of yellow, cup-shaped crusts of matted debris and mycelia on the scalp or torso. The crusts are called **scutula** (Fig. 33-24). The hair follicle is involved, and in more severe cases there is loss of hair. Most cases of disease are caused by *Trichophyton schoenleinii*.

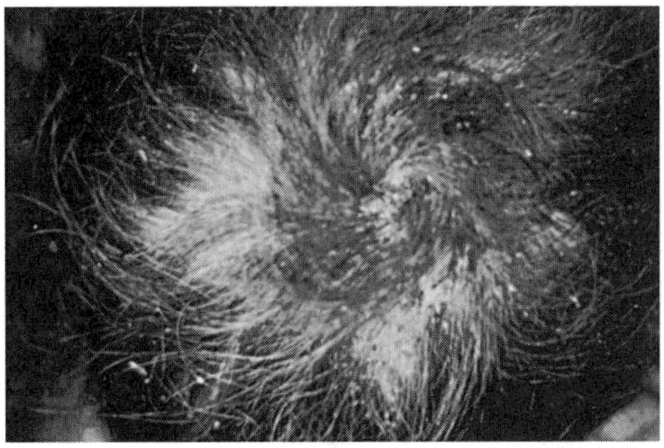

FIGURE 33-24
Tinea favosa. Seborrheic stage of disease showing matted hair and the lesion with an erythematous base. The infected hair is gray, whereas the normal hair is pigmented. (From W. Rippon, *Medical Mycology*, 2nd ed. Philadelphia: Saunders, 1982.)

Tinea Unguium (Ringworm of the Nails)

Invasion of the nail plate is characteristic of tinea unguium. Infection may be of two types: (1) superficial involvement, in which the fungus invades only the pits of the nails, and (2) involvement of the nail surface followed by invasion of the fungus beneath the nail plate (Fig. 33-25). Invasion of hyphae below the nail results in discoloration, keratinization, and distortion of the nail.

FIGURE 33-25
Tinea unguium. A. Initial infection at the distal edge of the nail plate. B. Advanced disease showing grooved nails and dark-brown coloration. (From W. Rippon, *Medical Mycology*, 2nd ed. Philadelphia: Saunders, 1982.]

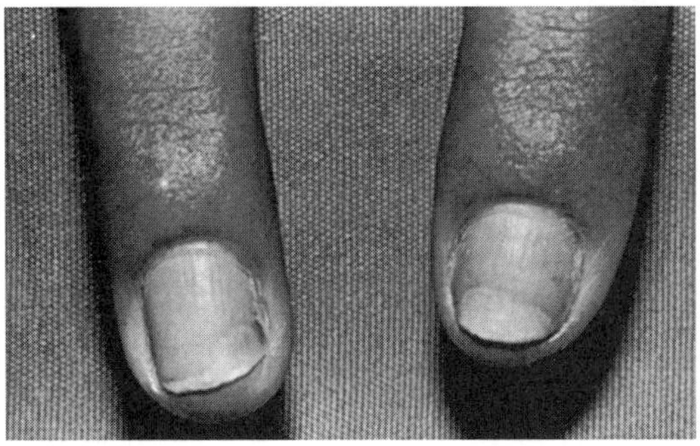

A

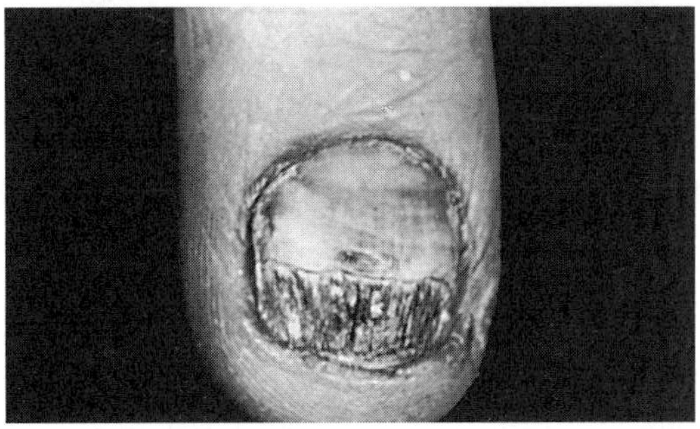

B

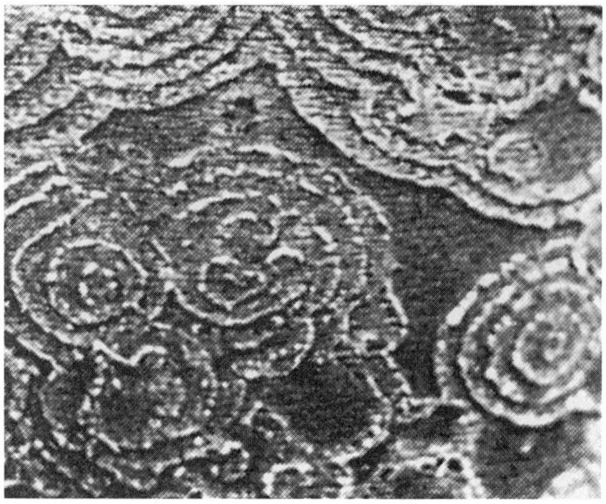

FIGURE 33-26
Tinea imbricata produced by *Trichophyton concentricum* and manifested by concentric rings of scales. (From W. Rippon, *Medical Mycology,* 2nd ed. Philadelphia: Saunders, 1982.)

Tinea Imbricata (Ringworm of the Torso)

Tinea imbricata is restricted to certain areas of the world such as the Pacific Islands, Southeast Asia, and Central and South America. The infection is characterized by the formation of scaly elevated concentric rings that may be scattered over most of the body (Fig. 33-26). The causal agent of disease is *Trichophyton concentricum.* The organism is believed to be transmitted by direct contact from mother to infant.

Tinea Cruris (Ringworm of the Groin, Jock Itch)

Tinea cruris is a common dermatophytic infection that can appear in epidemic form. Careless exchange of clothing or towels may result in transmission of the fungus. The lesions may appear on the groin or perianal areas and are characterized as red, scaly, itchy, and often dry.

Dermatophytes and Allergy

Many fungi act as allergens, causing allergic skin reactions. Allergic manifestations that appear in response to dermatophytosis and candidiasis are often referred to as **ids.** They appear as vesicular lesions at sites distant from the primary site of fungal infection. They give rise to severe itching, especially after antifungal treatment.

SUPERFICIAL MYCOSES

Infections of the most superficial layers of the skin and hair are termed **superficial mycoses.** These infections are generally innocuous and frequently reappear with or without treatment.

Tinea Versicolor

The causal agent of tinea versicolor is *Malassezia furfur* (see also Under the Microscope 43). The lesions, generally on the chest, back, and shoulders, are tan and scaly (Fig. 33-27). Little or no inflammation is associated with them. Irradiation of the infected areas with Wood's light in the dark demonstrates orange-red fluorescing hyphae. Scales also can be removed from the infected areas and examined microscopically for the hyphal elements. A saturated solution of sodium thiosulfate applied two or three times daily is effective in treatment. Tolnaftate 1% in various creams and in polyethylene glycol also provides good results. Other drugs that have proved effective are selenium sulfide (1%) and salicylic acid (10–15%). Miconazole nitrate and other imidazoles are also effective (see Table 33-1).

Tinea Nigra Palmaris

Tinea nigra palmaris is an asymptomatic infection that appears on the hands and fingers as dark-brown or black macular areas. The condition is chronic and may last several years if left untreated. It is seldom seen in the United States. The causal agent is *Exophiala (Cladosporium) wernecki.* Scales removed from the skin should be examined

UNDER THE MICROSCOPE 43

Nonimmune Defense Breakdown and Fungal Infection

A common fungal inhabitant of the skin is a yeast belonging to the genus *Malassezia.* Species of this organism have an absolute requirement for long-chain fatty acids. The keratin layer of the skin possesses fatty acids that are essential to the organism's growth. Most infections caused by this organism are usually limited to the surface of the skin. These infections do not go any deeper because blood and deep tissues lack long-chain fatty acids. These organisms recently were observed to cause invasive disease under specific circumstances. Patients receiving hyperalimentation fluids containing lipid emulsions (primarily low birth weight infants) through intravenous catheters are vulnerable to infection by *Malassezia.* The organism enters superficial tissue via the catheter and the lipid emulsions provide the essential nutrients for systemic growth.

There is some controversy about members of the genus *Malassezia.* Some species have been placed in the genus *Pityrosporum. Pityrosporum* yeasts are members of the normal cutaneous flora and are responsible for **pityriasis versicolor** and **pityrosporum folliculitis.** They also have been associated with seborrheic dermatitis and dandruff.

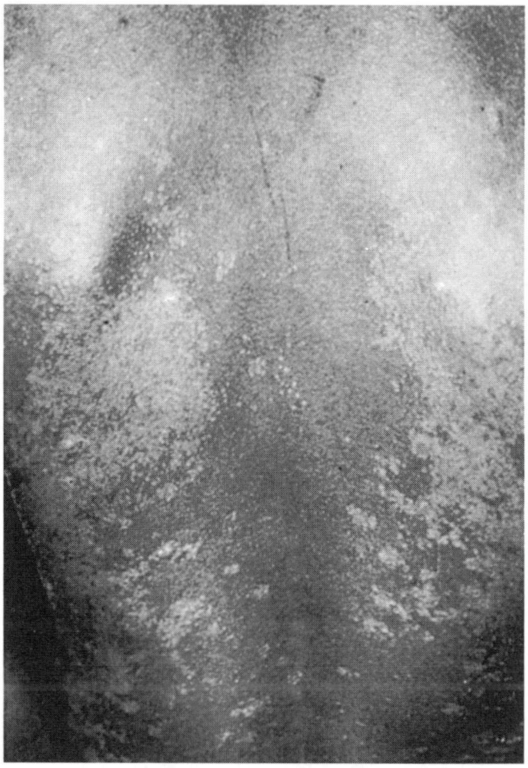

FIGURE 33-27
Tinea versicolor. The pigmented areas represent the infected sites of the skin. (From W. Rippon, *Medical Mycology*, 2nd ed. Philadelphia: Saunders, 1982.)

microscopically on a wet mount containing 10% KOH. The wet mount is gently heated to break up keratinous cells, allowing one to see detached hyphae. The fungus appears in the form of highly branched hyphae. Treatment is the same as for tinea versicolor.

Black and White Piedra

Piedra is a fungus infection of the hair in the form of small nodules. **Black piedra** (caused by *Piedraia hortae*) affects the hair of the scalp, and the nodules produced are very dark. **White piedra** (caused by *Trichosporon beigelii*) affects the hairs of the beard, and the nodules produced are very light. These diseases are rarely seen in the United States. Over the past 15 years, however, sporadic disseminated infections have appeared in immunocompromised patients, especially those with leukemia. Infected hairs with attached nodules can be prepared in wet mounts containing 10% KOH. The nodules contain mycelia and can be examined microscopically. Treatment of black and white piedra is the same as for tinea versicolor, except that amphotericin B is used for disseminated disease.

DISEASES CAUSED BY OPPORTUNISTIC FUNGAL PATHOGENS

In seriously debilitated and traumatized individuals or those under treatment with broad-spectrum antibiotics and immunosuppressive drugs, nonpathogenic fungi can cause grave illness. These opportunistic fungi are found in the environment or are part of the normal flora. They belong to the following groups: *Candida, Aspergillus, Mucor, Rhizopus,* and *Pneumocystis* (*C. neoformans* is also an important opportunistic pathogen and was discussed previously). These groups are the major opportunists, but remember that any of the fungi can also cause disease in the compromised host.

Candidiasis

General Characteristics. *Candida* species are yeasts capable of producing pseudohyphae (see Plate 26). They can be found as commensals in animals and humans, where they inhabit the respiratory tract, intestinal tract, skin, and female genital tract. Most infections are of the **endogenous** type, that is, disease caused by one's own microbial flora. Transmission from mother to fetus and venereal transmission are also possible. The most important *Candida* species is *C. albicans*. Other species, such as *C. tropicalis, C. paropsilosis, C. glabrata, C. lusitaniae,* and *C. krusei* are occasionally involved in disease.

Pathogenesis. The frequency of *Candida* infections has risen dramatically since the advent of antibiotics, the increase in surgical procedures, and the expanded use of immunosuppressive drugs. Infections are either cutaneous or disseminated and usually reflect the type of compromising condition affecting the host.

Cutaneous *Candida* infections are usually naturally occurring and arise because of some condition such as diabetes or other endocrine imbalances, natural immunological deficiencies, or exposure of the skin to moist environments over a long period (for example, in dishwashers). The initial event in cutaneous infection involves the adherence of blastoconidia to epithelial surfaces, fungal proliferation, and invasion of epithelial tissue. An inflammatory response helps to confine the infection to the superficial epidermis.

Disseminated infections are most often **iatrogenic** (produced by physicians; resulting from diagnostic procedures or treatment). The administration of some antibiotics or immunosuppressive drugs encourages the growth of fungal species, such as *C. albicans,* at the expense of bacterial species. The proliferation of *Candida* in the intestinal tract, for example, can lead to the hematogenous spread of the microorganism. The use of catheters, the implantation of prosthetic devices, and various types of surgery also provide an avenue for dissemination of *Candida.*

The virulence of *Candida* is related to several factors, some of which are described in Under the Microscope 41. Another factor is the polysaccharide **mannan,** which is a major component of the cell wall. During disseminated disease mannan is released into the circulation. Mannan has an immunosuppressive effect and interferes with the presentation of candidal antigens to monocytes. The presence of mannan also has diagnostic significance (see Laboratory Diagnosis).

Candida infections can be divided into three clinical types: cutaneous, systemic or deep organ, and mucocutaneous.

Cutaneous Candidiasis. Oral **thrush** is one of the most common cutaneous candidal infections. In thrush the surface of the tongue is covered by white patches of pseudomembranes, which if removed, reveal a raw bleeding undersurface (Fig. 33-28). The pseudomembranes are composed of fungal cells, both yeast and hyphal forms, and epithelial debris. Thrush is most often observed in infants but can occur in any age group. Many infants appear to acquire the disease from mothers who have vaginal candidiasis. Thrush is also a common complication in AIDS patients. Endogenous thrush is a result of the administration of antibiotics, particularly broad-spectrum ones, or various immunosuppressive agents that reduce bacterial flora and permit *Candida* to divide unrestrictedly.

Vaginal candidiasis is frequently associated with diabetes, pregnancy, oral contraceptives, and antibacterial drugs. Lactobacilli in the vaginal tract are known to inhibit the growth of *Candida*. Women undergoing antibiotic therapy with drugs such as penicillin show reduced numbers of lactobacilli in the vagina. The reduction of these bacterial competitors permits the proliferation of *Candida*. The infection is characterized by inflammation of the vagina and the formation of a thick yellow-white discharge. Infection can spread to perianal areas and appear as a diaper rash in infants. Vaginal candidiasis may lead to candidiasis in a sex partner following sexual intercourse. The condition in the male is called **candidal balanitis.** The male infection is characterized by superficial erosions and thin pustules on areas of the penis.

Individuals who have their appendages immersed in water for long periods or whose unexposed body sites are subject to a moist environment are also subject to infection by *Candida*. The condition is called **intertriginous candidiasis**. The feet, hands, groin, axillae, and intergluteal folds are the most commonly affected areas (Fig. 33-29). The lesions resemble eczema and may be scaly, creeping, and erythematous. Intertrigo may also be observed in diabetics, obese individuals, chronic alcoholics, or others with metabolic disorders.

FIGURE 33-28
Thrush. (From E. Drouhet, *Rev. Infect. Dis.* 2:609, 1980.)

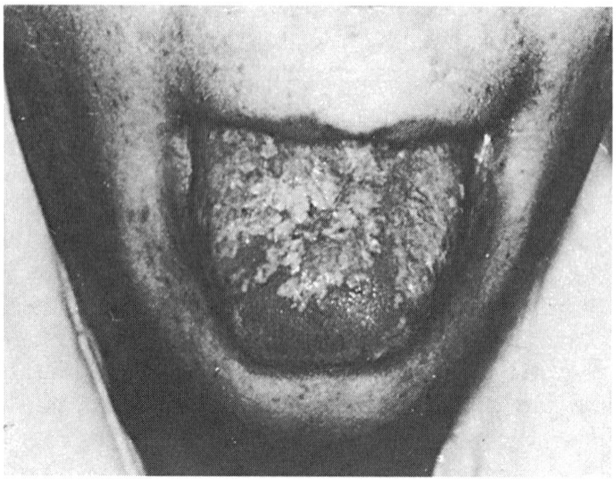

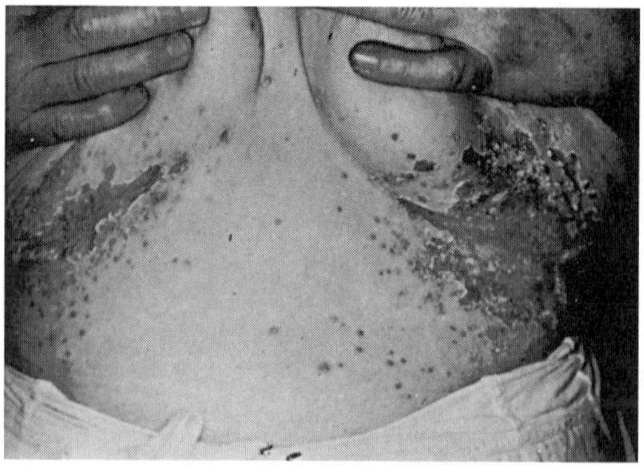

FIGURE 33-29
Intertriginous candidiasis in a diabetic patient. Note the "scalded" skin areas and satellite eruptions. (From W. Rippon, *Medical Mycology*, 2nd ed. Philadelphia: Saunders, 1982.)

Some of the most common cutaneous infections are those involving the nails **(onychia)** or around the nails **(paronychia).** These infections also result from immersion of appendages in water.

Systemic Candidiasis. Systemic candidiasis results from hematogenous spread of the microorganisms and may involve any organ or tissue of the body. The most critical sites of infection are the heart (pericarditis, myocarditis, endocarditis), spinal cord (meningitis), and urethra (urethritis, cystitis). Heart infections may be the result of the use of contaminated needles by heroin addicts (see Under the Microscope 44), surgery involving the implantation of prosthetic valves, and prolonged catheterization with polyethylene catheters. Neonates receiving hyperalimentation and broad-spectrum antibiotics are at an increased risk of candidemia, which often leads to meningitis, arthritis, or osteomyelitis.

Chronic Mucocutaneous Candidiasis. Chronic mucocutaneous candidiasis (CMC) is associated with immunodeficiency. T cell immunodeficiency syndromes with failure in the cell-mediated immune response appear to be the initiating factor. CMC is also frequently observed in patients with other underlying conditions that in some way affect the cell-mediated immune response. Patients are likely to lack delayed hypersensitivity to *Candida* and other skin test antigens. In addition, the lymphocytes of affected patients cannot be transformed in vitro by *Candida* antigen.

CMC infections involve the skin (Plate 30), mucous membranes, or any other epithelial surface including the respiratory tract, gastrointestinal tract, and genital epithelium. Most cases occur in infancy, but the disease may also involve those up to 30 years old. The disease is often refractory to treatment. Fatalities are rare, but when they occur they are usually due to bacterial sepsis.

Laboratory Diagnosis. Presumptive identification of *Candida* species can be made by direct microscopical examination of clinical material for the presence of yeast cells or

UNDER THE MICROSCOPE 44

Heroin, Lemon Juice, and *Candida* Infections

Heroin addicts are at risk for a variety of infectious diseases. Use of contaminated needles and injection of skin microflora are the most frequent methods of transmission. Candidiasis is not the usual microbial complication of drug abuse, but a very unusual circumstance in 1980 contributed to its appearance in this specialized group. Heroin is usually sold as a dry white powder that is relatively soluble in water. In 1980 a brand of heroin that was available was brown in color and poorly soluble in water. This type of heroin required acidification to make it soluble and the preferred method was to use lemon juice. A few drops of lemon juice was added to the heroin and the mixture was heated in a spoon over the flame of a lighter. The heat was removed as soon as the first bubbles appeared and the fluid was drawn into a syringe.

The marked increase of candidiasis in heroin abusers appeared only when the brown heroin appeared on the drug market. The lemon juice was apparently contaminated by the heroin abuser and served as a source of *Candida.* Lemon juice with its low pH is an excellent selective medium that supports the growth of *Candida* but inhibits bacteria such as *Staphylococcus aureus* and *Pseudomonas aeruginosa.*

Disseminated candidiasis in the heroin abuser can be manifested in several ways: cutaneous lesions, particularly on hairy parts of the body such as the scalp; ocular involvement such as chorioretinitis; and bone involvement such as osteoarthritis.

pseudohyphae (see Plate 26.) A valuable presumptive test is the **germ tube test,** in which a suspension of yeast cells from a colony is mixed with serum and incubated for two to four hours at 37 C. The mixture is examined for the presence of germ tubes. Chlamydospore production in nutritionally deficient media such as rice extract agar and trypan blue agar is also used for identification of the fungus.

Disseminated infections can be diagnosed by detection of cell wall mannan. **Mannans** determine the antigenic specificity of *Candida* species and *C. albicans* serotypes. Antimannan antibodies are present in the sera of most healthy individuals and are increased during disseminated disease. Antimannan antibodies allow the detection of antigenemia in sera from patients with systemic *Candida* infection. Enzyme immunoassay or latex agglutination is used to detect mannan.

Tests for detecting specific *Candida* metabolites such as D-arabinitol in the serum are also being evaluated.

Treatment. Most cutaneous infections are treated with creams or powders containing nystatin, gentian violet, or a variety of imidazoles (see Table 33-1).

Disseminated candidiasis is treated using amphotericin B. Amphotericin B should not be administered to persons who have systemic candidiasis after kidney transplantation since the drug is toxic to the kidneys. The addition of flucytosine improves the response rate for infections caused by *C. tropicalis,* which is often resistant to amphotericin B. Fluconazole appears to be effective after initial treatment is begun with amphotericin B, particularly in patients with chronic disseminated candidiasis. In compromised patients with systemic candidiasis, amphotericin B encapsulated in liposomes is especially effective (see Under the Microscope 4).

Intravaginal formulations for the treatment of vaginal candidiasis include butoconazole, clotrimazole, miconazole, ticonazole, and terconazole.

Mucocutaneous candidiasis responds to treatment with ketoconazole, while esophageal candidiasis is effectively treated with amphotericin B. Fluconazole is the drug now recommended for the treatment of thrush.

ASPERGILLOSIS

Aspergillosis represents a spectrum of diseases caused by species of *Aspergillus.* These organisms are ubiquitous and are found in soil, water, decaying vegetation, and any area that contains organic debris. The respiratory tract is the principal portal of entry, and inhaled spores can cause disease in healthy as well as compromised individuals. The species most frequently associated with disease is *A. fumigatus,* but other species such as *A. flavus, A. niger,* and *A. terreus* are occasionally involved.

Pathogenesis. The clinical manifestations of aspergillosis can be divided into three types: allergic, colonizing (aspergilloma), and invasive.

Allergic aspergillosis may be represented in the form of an asthma-like response, an allergic rhinitis or sinusitis, or hypersensitivity pneumonitis. Allergic asthma is a chronic disease following exposure to an allergen, that is, the fungal spore. The spores usually fail to germinate unless the host is severely compromised. This asthma-like illness is characterized by fever, cough, and wheezing induced by the presence of reaginic IgE antibodies. The syndrome may become severe and chronic with bronchial plugging. Occasionally in the chronic form, the spores will germinate and be released from fruiting heads (see Laboratory Diagnosis).

Allergic rhinitis or hay fever may develop in individuals on exposure to mold spores and mycelia. The disease may occur as a seasonal or nonseasonal condition. The disease develops as a result of the interaction of allergens and IgE fixed to specific mast cells in the epithelial surface of the nasal mucosa. Symptoms are similar to those caused by inhalation of pollen or dust.

Hypersensitivity pneumonitis is caused by a number of different organisms including *Aspergillus.* Included in this disease group are farmer's lung, bagassosis, and mushroom worker's lung. These diseases result from exposure to thermophilic actinomycetes in hay, bagasse (the dry residue of sugar cane after the juice has been expressed), and mushroom compost, respectively. Sensitization occurs following exposure to the antigen, and on subsequent exposures symptoms develop usually 4 to 8 hours after inhalation. Symptoms persist for about 12 hours and recovery is spontaneous.

Colonizing aspergillosis, which may develop after allergic aspergillosis, is characterized by the formation of a fungus ball **(aspergilloma).** The aspergilloma is a dense collection of hyphae from which the fungus grows and colonizes the pulmonary surfaces. Symptoms are similar to those of allergic aspergillosis but spitting of blood (hemoptysis) is frequently encountered.

Invasive aspergillosis can develop from the allergic or colonizing forms of the disease, or it can arise independently. **Invasive** implies that *Aspergillus* hyphae have penetrated tissue as either a localized or a disseminated form of the disease. Several factors may dispose the patient to invasive disease: (1) cytotoxic chemotherapy, (2) therapy with broad-spectrum antimicrobial agents, (3) leukopenia, and (4) acute leukemia.

Mortality is very high, especially among renal transplant recipients and leukemia and lymphoma patients. Invasive disease affects primarily the respiratory tract. Usually the fungus colonizes the tracheobronchial tree, and this leads to bronchopneumonia. Hyphae invade the lumina and walls of blood vessels, causing pulmonary hemorrhage. Lung tissue may also be invaded as a direct result of hematogenous spread, for example, after parenteral therapy. Untreated invasive disease results in death within two weeks after the onset of symptoms. Invasive disease may also affect the nose and paranasal sinuses. This type of infection is endemic in the Sudan. Endocarditis caused by aspergilli is associated with prosthetic valve implantation.

Invasive disease can be followed by **disseminated aspergillosis,** which is the most severe form of infection. Either antimicrobial agents or glucocorticosteroids have been implicated as predisposing factors. Occasionally disseminated disease develops in healthy individuals. There is widespread organ involvement, with the lungs as the principal target. Death usually results from bilateral pneumonia or intracerebral hemorrhage with fungal invasion and thrombosis.

It appears that two lines of host defense must be breached before aspergilli can invade tissue. When spores of aspergillus are deposited in lung tissue, they are metabolically inactive and are coated by a thick wall. Resting spores ingested by neutrophils are not killed because the respiratory burst is not sufficient to release oxidative metabolites. In contrast, if the resting spore begins to swell and germinate, it can be killed by neutrophils. Neutrophils are therefore active against hyphal forms. On the other hand, macrophages can ingest resting spores and kill them. This dual defense by the host normally prevents *Aspergillus* (and other fungi) species from causing invasive pulmonary disease. In immunocompromised patients receiving corticosteroids, the host defenses are breached and invasive pulmonary disease is the rule rather than the exception. Corticosteroids impair the ability of macrophages to destroy resting spores. Spore germination leads to mycelial invasion of blood vessels, hemorrhage, and necrosis. When the dosage of corticosteroids in compromised patients (for example, renal transplant patients) is reduced, the frequency of fungal invasive disease also decreases precipitously.

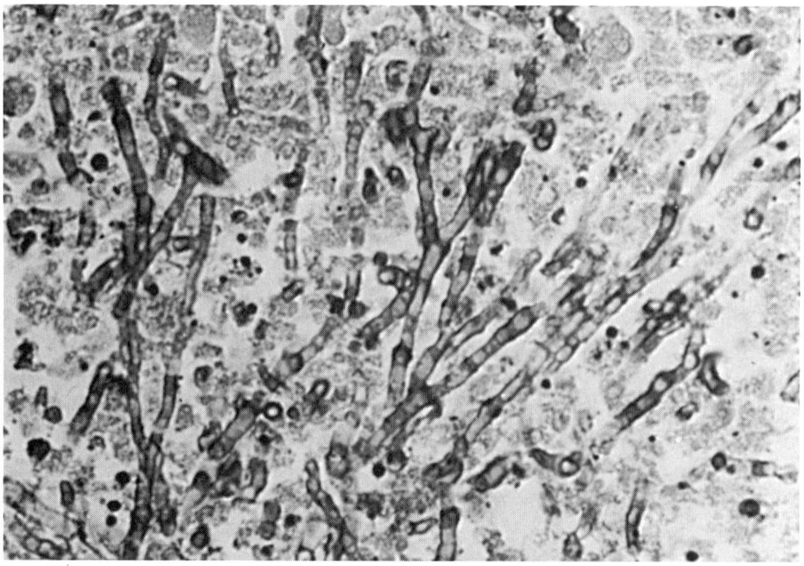

FIGURE 33-30
Aspergillus hyphae in lung tissue. (Courtesy of K. J. Kwon-Chung.)

Laboratory Diagnosis. Diagnosis of aspergillosis is dependent on demonstrating fungal elements in pathological material and repeated isolation of the organism from clinical specimens. Identification in tissue is dependent on (1) finding uniform-sized hyphae 3 to 4 μm in width (Fig. 33-30), (2) finding characteristic dichotomous branching of hyphae at 45-degree angles, (3) the staining of hyphae by special stains, (4) a positive fluorescent antibody response, (5) the presence of characteristic conidiophores (Fig. 33-31), and (6) the presence of septate hyphae. Tissue identification techniques should be backed up by cultural tests.

Invasive disease is difficult to diagnose with biopsy. Therefore, serological techniques play an important role in diagnosis. Still, results of tests for rises in antibody titers are positive in only about one-half of the patients. In addition, in immunosuppressed patients, antibodies are not often demonstrable. Immunodiffusion tests and several enzyme immunoassays are available for diagnosis.

Intradermal injection of *Aspergillus* antigens can produce skin reactions that are important criteria in the diagnosis of allergic pulmonary aspergillosis.

Treatment. Administration of amphotericin B is the only treatment of proven efficacy for invasive disease. In some

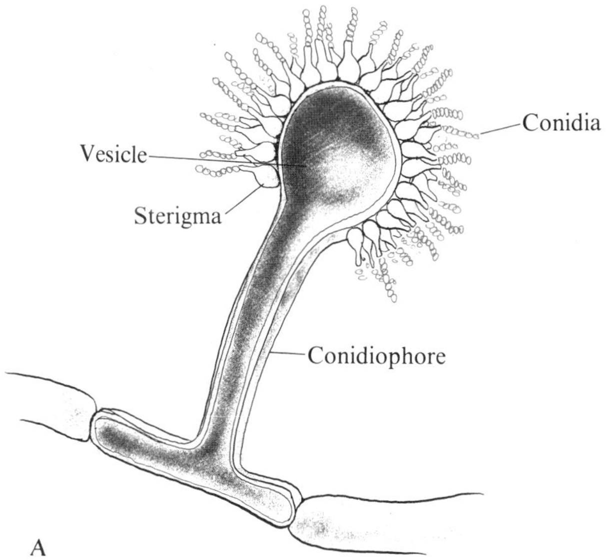

A

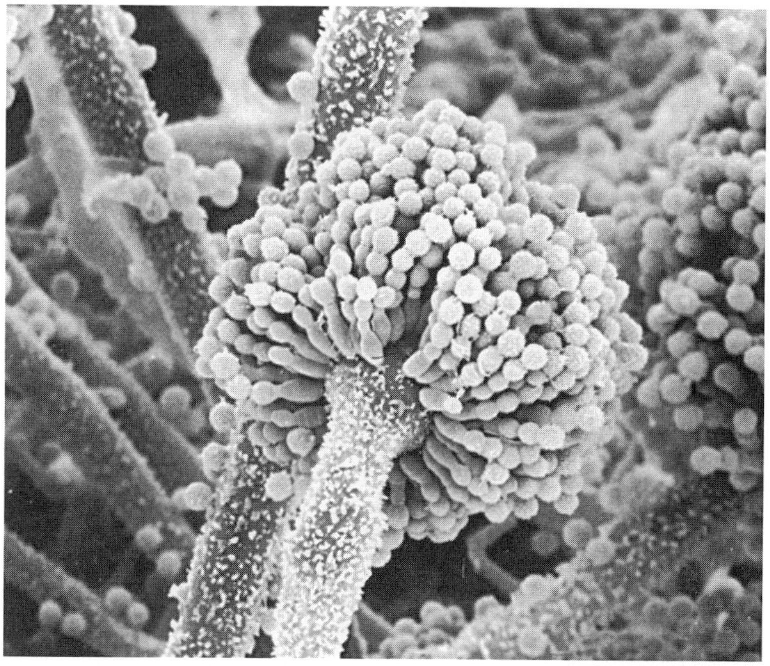

B

FIGURE 33-31
Aspergillus conidiophore. A. Diagram. B. Scanning electron micrograph of the conidiophore, terminal vesicle, sterigma, and conidia of *Aspergillus flavus.* (From E. U. King and M. F. Brown, *Can. J. Microbiol.* 29:653, 1983.)

instances, extirpation of a lung lesion persistently evident on roentgenography has been recommended, especially when a patient is to undergo cytotoxic chemotherapy. An alternative that has been shown to be successful is to treat the patient with amphotericin B before and during the period of cytotoxic chemotherapy.

Allergic forms of the disease can be treated with corticosteroids (but not in immunosuppressed patients). Surgical resection may be necessary for aspergilloma.

Mucormycosis

Mucormycosis (sometimes called **zygomycosis** or **phycomycosis**) refers to diseases caused by members of the order Mucorales. The causal agents of disease include primarily species of *Rhizopus, Rhizomucor,* and *Absidia* and less frequently *Mucor, Cunninghamella, Mortierella, Saksenaea,* and *Apophysomyces.* The members of these genera are inhabitants of the soil and are commonly found on fruits and bread. Infections occur not only in compromised patients such as those with ketoacidosis resulting from diabetes but also in leukemic patients, burn patients, and those undergoing immunosuppressive therapy (for example, during organ transplantation).

Pathogenesis. Infections follow the inhalation of spores, although cutaneous infections also occur. Several clinical manifestations of mucormycosis exist, including rhinocerebral, pulmonary, cutaneous, gastrointestinal, central nervous system, and disseminated ones.

The most severe forms of the disease involve the nasal region (rhinocerebral mucormycosis) and the lung. Sporangiospores are inhaled and germinate either in the nasal surface or in the lung. Nasal invasion takes place with the formation of hyphae that can spread and involve the orbit, face, meninges, and frontal lobes of the brain. The most characteristic feature of mucormycosis is hyphal invasion of blood vessels, resulting in hemorrhage, thrombosis, and necrosis of tissue. Edema and necrotic tissue can be found around the eye and in the nose (Fig. 33-32). Death can occur within a few days after onset. The overall mortality from rhinocerebral mucormycosis is 50 percent. Diabetics have the best survival rate.

FIGURE 33-32
Mucormycosis. (Courtesy of G. Roberts.)

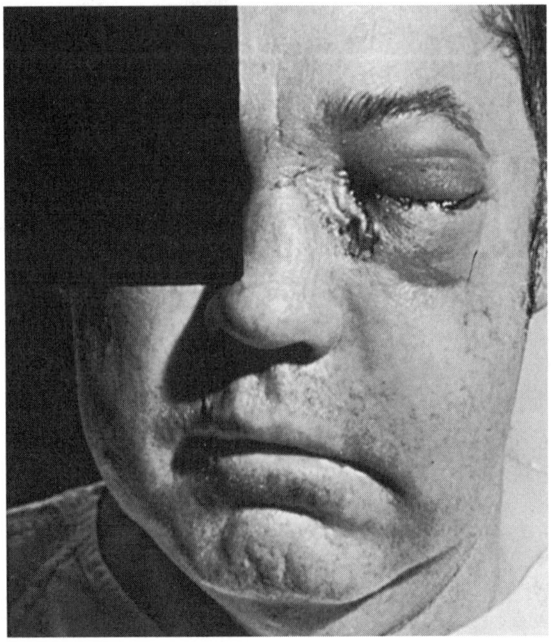

Hyphae that invade the lung cause mass lesions and bronchopneumonia. Hyphae invade the walls of blood vessels and cause thrombosis. Dissemination of disease to the central nervous system is a frequent complication of pulmonary infection. Pulmonary infection occurs in patients with uncontrolled leukemia.

Cutaneous mucormycosis is found in patients who sustain trauma or who have had bandages applied to the skin. Spores on the skin or contaminating bandages can be introduced into wounds where they proliferate and invade cutaneous tissue. Gastrointestinal mucormycosis is seen more often in developing countries where malnutrition is a problem.

Laboratory Diagnosis. Thrombosis and hemorrhage are clues in the differential diagnosis of mucormycosis. However, pulmonary aspects of the disease resemble those of aspergillosis. Culture and examination of biopsy specimens are the only definitive ways to differentiate between the genera.

Definitive diagnosis is made by visualizing the characteristic hyphae. Mucorales appear in tissue as irregularly shaped, broad (10–20 μm in diameter) hyphae with right-angle branching (Fig. 33-33). Hyphae can be stained by the periodic acid–Schiff reaction or by methenamine–silver nitrate stains.

Treatment. Surgical debridement is the most important option for patients with mucormycosis. Debridement may have to be repeated. Amphotericin B treatment is also used as an adjunct to surgery. The duration of therapy and dosage of drug greatly depend on controlling or removing the compromising condition (diabetes, immunosuppressive therapy, etc.).

Pneumocystis Pneumonia

Pneumocystis pneumonia is caused by *P. carinii.* This organism originally was thought to be a protozoan but is now considered a fungus based on rRNA analysis. *P. carinii* has become a pathogen of increasing importance because of the appearance of AIDS.

The organism exists widely in nature as a saprophyte in the lungs of humans and a variety of animals. *P. carinii* causes pneumonia in premature, malnourished infants; patients receiving corticosteroids or other immunosuppressive drugs; and persons with AIDS. *Pneumocystis* pneumonia has been used as an index diagnosis of AIDS. The organism is the cause of pneumonia in over 80 percent of AIDS patients.

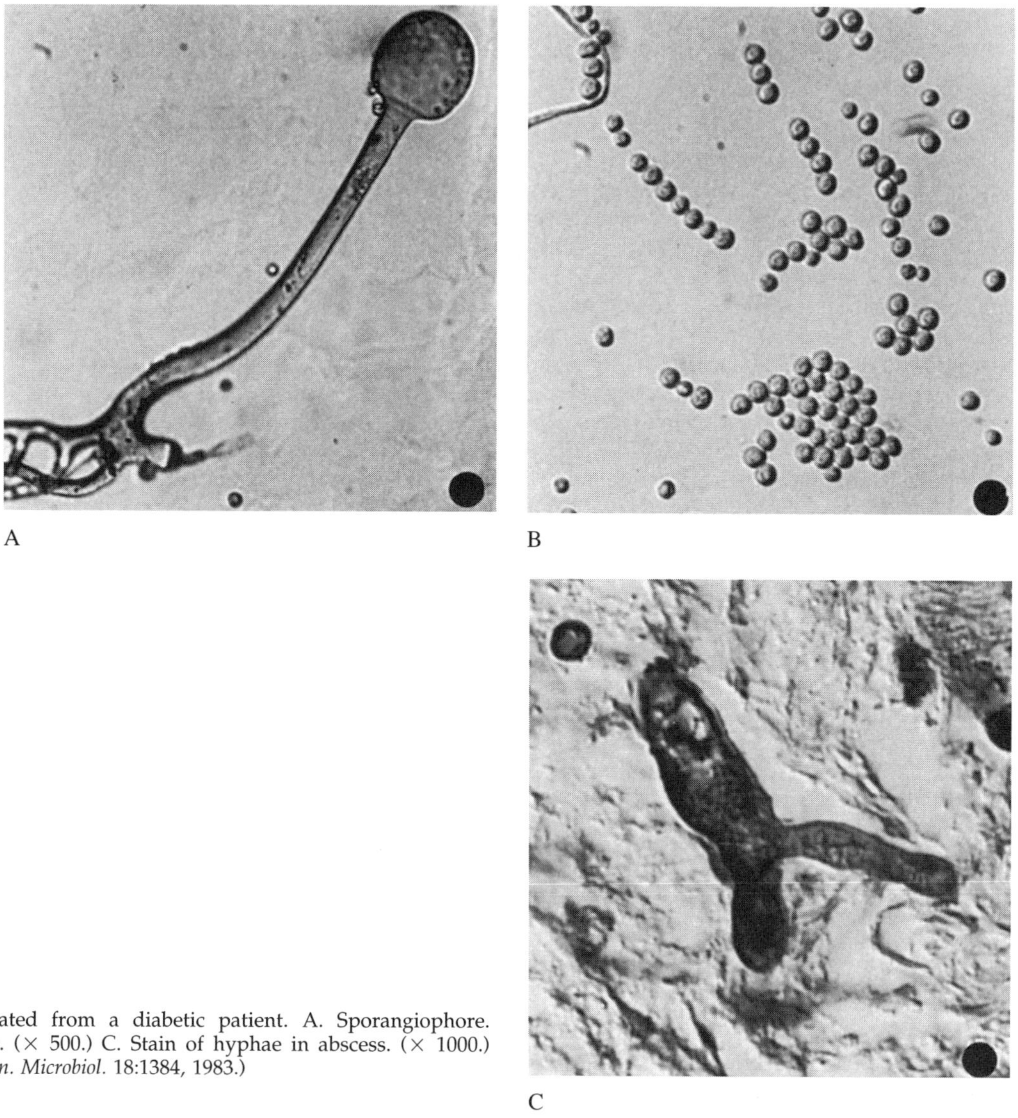

FIGURE 33-33
Rhizopus rhizopodiformis isolated from a diabetic patient. A. Sporangiophore. (× 250.) B. Sporangiospores. (× 500.) C. Stain of hyphae in abscess. (× 1000.) (From B. C. West et al., *J. Clin. Microbiol.* 18:1384, 1983.)

The most frequent symptoms of *Pneumocystis* pneumonia are fever, cough, and shortness of breath. The cough is usually nonproductive. Diagnosis of infection is difficult and may require different sampling options. These options include sputum examination, bronchoalveolar lavage, and transbronchial lung biopsy. Lavage specimens, for example, can be stained with methenamine silver, Gram-Weigert, and Giemsa stains. All these stains are nonspecific and *P. carinii* must be distinguished from other yeasts on the basis of morphology. The polymerase chain reaction appears to be the future choice for routine identification in the laboratory.

Trimethoprim-sulfamethoxazole effectively prevents *Pneumocystis* pneumonia in both children with cancer and HIV-infected adults and is the first-line agent. Alternative drugs for patients intolerant to trimethoprim-sulfamethoxazole are dapsone and aerosolized and intravenous pentamidine. All of these drugs exhibit a great deal of toxicity (see also Chapter 8).

MYCOTOXINS

Mycetismus

Mycetismus, or mushroom poisoning, is caused by the ingestion of certain poisonous fleshy field fungi. Mushroom poisoning is not so common in the United States as it is in areas of eastern Europe where mushroom gathering is a common family practice. The most common symptoms of mushroom poisoning involve the gastrointestinal tract and nervous system. Symptoms, which appear 1 to 2 hours after ingestion, include profuse sweating, violent gastrointestinal involvement, and convulsions. If the dose of toxin is sufficiently high, death may occur within 10 to 12 hours of onset. The most toxic mushrooms are those belonging to the genus *Amanita*.

Mycotoxicosis

Unlike mycetismus, in which the toxic substance is part of the fungal tissue, mycotoxicosis is due to a toxin that is produced as a secondary metabolite. The mycotoxins of interest are produced by species of the genera *Penicillium, Fusarium, Streptomyces,* and *Aspergillus*. These organisms are a common contaminant of grains and food. Mycotoxins are intimately associated with every food or feed and can be produced at every stage of harvesting, production, and storage of food. When certain environmental conditions prevail (moisture content, temperature, and others) the fungal contaminants grow and release toxic secondary metabolites. Some of the more widely recognized mycotoxins are **aflatoxins,** which are produced by *A. flavus* and *Aspergillus parasiticus*. Aflatoxins were first discovered in 1960 when 100,000 turkeys and several thousand other domestic birds died after ingesting contaminated Brazilian peanut meal. Investigations into the cause of death revealed that the bird feed was contaminated by *A. flavus*.

Aflatoxin B_1 is the most potent naturally occurring carcinogen. Studies showed that liver cancers occur with greater frequency in countries or areas where aflatoxin is known to contaminate stored grains. In parts of the Far East and India, maize, corn, rice, and other grains that have high concentrations of aflatoxin are consumed in large amounts. Autopsies on individuals there reveal that many organs contain high levels of aflatoxin. Occasionally in the United States peanut butter has been contaminated with these toxins.

Mycotoxins of current concern are produced by species of *Fusarium*. Two of these toxins are called T-2 and **vomitoxin.** These toxins are produced by growth of the fungal species on various grains and have been implicated in animal disease (see Under the Microscope 45).

Summary

1. Fungi are eukaryotic microorganisms that can be divided into two morphological forms: spherical yeasts and filamentous molds. The filaments of molds are composed of units called hyphae. Hyphae may or may not be compartmentalized. Some fungi can exist in both morphological forms and are called dimorphic.

2. The fungal cell wall is primarily polysaccharide and possesses no peptidoglycan. It is therefore unaffected by penicillin and other bacterial cell wall inhibitors. Cell membranes of fungi possess sterols that distinguish them from bacterial cell membranes.

3. Fungi can reproduce by sexual or asexual means, but asexual processes are the more important. Sporulation is the most effective reproductive technique for propagating the species and may be sexual or asexual.

4. Sexual spores include oospores, zygospores, ascospores, and basidiospores. Conidia and sporangiospores are asexual spores produced on special hyphal structures while arthrospores, chlamydospores, and blastospores are asexual spores arising directly from hyphae.

5. Fungi grow best at pHs between 5 and 6 but they can tolerate and grow at pHs between 2 and 9. Sabouraud agar is the most widely used isolation medium for fungi. Yeasts produce creamy opaque colonies while mold colonies appear cottony on agar media.

6. Most fungal diseases are primarily due to occupational exposure to large numbers of fungal spores. The highest mortality from fungal diseases is found in those compromised by some underlying disease or condition. Most fungi can be observed directly in tissue via staining or by cultivation of specimens in the laboratory. If culture and histological results are negative, serological tests have diagnostic value.

7. Immunity to fungal diseases is primarily by cell-

UNDER THE MICROSCOPE 45

Fusarium: Infectious Agent

Fusarial toxicosis occurs in animals (including humans) and has been implicated in many outbreaks outside the United States. These fusarial toxins are called trichothecenes and were responsible for the large epidemics in Russia in the 1930s. Starvation in rural areas of Russia led to consumption of overwintered grains contaminated by toxin-producing *Fusarium* species. The effects of toxicosis ranged from gastrointestinal illness to suppression of the bone marrow, resulting in aplasia. This severe and often fatal form of toxin poisoning occurred in individuals who continually ingested contaminated grains. The condition is recognized as **alimentary toxic aleukia** in Siberia and **akakabi-byo** in Japan.

Fusarium causes infections in plants (fusarial wilt, for example, of tomatoes and other vegetable plants) and has economic significance. Infections can also occur in humans in whom there may be local, invasive, or disseminated disease. Some localized invasive infections include endophthalmitis, osteomyelitis, peritonitis, septic arthritis, brain abscess, and skin infections. These infections are usually resolved by surgery or by antifungal therapy. Disseminated infections are invariably fatal and are associated with patients having some underlying hematological malignancy (leukemia, lymphoma, etc.).

TABLE 33-4
Characteristics of the Systemic Mycoses

Disease	Etiological agent	Transmission	Primary site of infection	Treatment
Histoplasmosis	*Histoplasma capsulatum*	Inhalation of conidia found associated with bird dung	Lung primary site but can be disseminated to organs via reticuloendothelial system	Amphotericin B; fluconazole
Coccidioidomycosis	*Coccidioides immitis*	Inhalation of arthrospores from semiarid and dusty areas	Lung primary site but if disseminated to meninges is invariably fatal	Amphotericin B for systemic disease; ketoconazole for cutaneous disease and fluconazole for meningitis
Blastomycosis	*Blastomyces dermatitidis*	Inhalation of spores from contaminated soil	Lung primary site with dissemination to skin and organs; chronic cutaneous occasionally encountered	Amphotericin B; ketoconazole
Paracoccidioido-mycosis	*Paracoccidioides brasiliensis*	Inhalation of spores (?)	Lungs primary site but can be disseminated to skin and lymph nodes	Ketoconazole and sulfonamides
Cryptococcosis	*Cryptococcus neoformans*	Inhalation of spores found in pigeon droppings	Lungs; but in compromised patients systemic involvement possible, including central nervous system	Amphotericin B plus flucytosine or ketoconazole; fluconazole

mediated immunity. Antibodies appear to play a minor role in protecting the host; thus, diagnostic serological techniques are difficult to evaluate. Some fungi produce an allergic response mediated by IgE antibodies. Drugs used to treat fungal disease are outlined in Table 33-1.

8. Fungal diseases can be divided into five types: systemic, subcutaneous, cutaneous, superficial, and opportunistic. The systemic diseases are outlined in Table 33-4. The subcutaneous mycoses are outlined in Table 33-3.

9. Cutaneous fungal infections, or dermatophytoses, are caused primarily by three genera: *Microsporum*, *Trichophyton*, and *Epidermophyton*. They invade keratinized areas of the body and are transmitted by contact with clothing or articles contaminated by human dermatophytes or by contact with infected animals. These infections are referred to as tineas or ringworms. Several topical solutions such as potassium permanganate, benzoic acid, and salicylic acid as well as orally administered drugs such as griseofulvin are available for treatment. The allergic manifestations caused by some dermatophytes are called ids.

10. Superficial mycoses involve superficial areas of the skin and usually do not require treatment. Lesions are usually scaly eruptions on the chest, back, and shoulders. Some pathogens can attack the scalp or beard hair. Three important infections are called tinea versicolor, tinea nigra palmaris, and black and white piedra.

11. Opportunistic fungal pathogens cause disease primarily in compromised patients. The opportunistic fungal diseases are outlined in Table 33-5.

12. Fungi can be toxic because of the nature of their own tissue (mycetismus) or because they produce secondary metabolites when growing on various foods or grains (mycotoxicosis). One of the most toxic secondary metabolites is aflatoxin B_1, which is believed to cause liver cancer when contaminated grains are ingested over long periods.

TABLE 33-5
Characteristics of Opportunistic Fungal Pathogens

Disease	Etiological agent(s)	Pathogenesis	Primary compromising situation or condition	Treatment
Candidiasis	*Candida* species (*C. albicans, C. krusei, C. tropicalis,* etc.)	***Cutaneous***		
		A. Thrush	Antibiotic administration; acquired immunodeficiency syndrome	Discontinue drug treatment; nystatin orally; fluconazole
		B. Vaginal	Antibiotic administration, pregnancy, diabetes, oral contraceptives	Discontinue drug treatment; creams and other topical ointments (see Table 33-1)
		C. Intertriginous	Body site exposure to moist environments	Topical creams and ointments (see Table 33-1)
		Systemic	Implantation of prosthetic devices, contaminated needles, prolonged catheterization	Amphotericin B; fluconazole
		Chronic mucocutaneous	T cell immunodeficiency	Usually refractory to treatment
Aspergillosis	*Aspergillus* species (*A. fumigatus, A. flavus, A. niger*)	***Allergic***	Inhalation of spore	Corticosteroids, but not in immunocompromised patients
		Colonizing	Formation of fungus ball in lung	Surgical resection
		Invasive	Can develop from allergic or colonizing and usually found in patients compromised by drugs	Amphotericin B alone or in combination with flucytosine
Mucormycosis	Species of *Mucor, Rhizopus, Absidia,* etc.	Rhinocerebral mucormycosis	Diabetes, burn wounds, immunosuppressive drugs	Surgical debridement; amphotericin B
Pneumocystis pneumonia	*Pneumocystis carinii*	Pneumonia	AIDS patients, premature malnourished infants, patients on immunosuppressive drugs	Trimethoprim-sulfamethoxazole, dapsone, pentamidine
Cryptococcosis	*Cryptococcus neoformans*	Discussed under Systemic Mycoses		

Questions for Study

1. Explain why the drugs used to treat bacterial infections are not suitable for the treatment of fungal diseases.
2. What is meant by the term dimorphism and what groups of fungi exhibit this trait? When is dimorphism exhibited? Does it give the fungus any competitive advantage?
3. Describe the methods used by fungi to reproduce asexually. Which is the most important for propagating the species?
4. What is the simplest method for selectively isolating fungi from a specimen contaminated with bacterial species?
5. Describe the body's barriers to infection by fungi.
6. Make a list of some of the fungi that are indigenous to the human body.

7. What component of the *Candida* cell wall is a virulence factor? Does this component have any other value?
8. What fungal diseases might be misdiagnosed as tuberculosis?
9. What is the exoantigen test?
10. Describe a scenario in which you might be at risk of acquiring coccidioidomycosis.
11. Choose three of the most effective drugs used in the treatment of systemic mycoses.
12. What characteristic of *Blastomyces dermatitidis* makes identification relatively easy?
13. What characteristic of *Cryptococcus neoformans* makes identification relatively simple?
14. What type of mycosis might you be at risk of acquiring if you worked in an area containing substantial peat moss?
15. Describe the activity that might place you at risk of acquiring the following: ringworm of the scalp, ringworm of the body, ringworm of the feet, intertriginous candidiasis.
16. What areas of the body contain indigenous *Candida* species? What circumstances induce them to cause infections in these areas? What are the clinical conditions called?
17. Are any fungi responsible for sexually transmitted diseases? Explain.
18. What circumstances permit *Malassezia furfur* to cause neonatal sepsis when the organism is usually associated with superficial infections?
19. Explain the host's normal immune response to the presence of *Aspergillus* spores. How can these barriers be overwhelmed and lead to disease?
20. Several outbreaks of *Aspergillus* infection have been associated with hospital construction. Explain how this is possible and what can be done to prevent these infections from occurring.
21. What is the distinction between mycetismus and mycotoxicosis?
22. What is the most characteristic feature of mucormycosis? Does it have any significance in diagnosis?

PART

VIII Medical Parasitology

CHAPTER

34 Protozoa, Helminths, and Arthropods

OBJECTIVES

To discuss parasitism and parasitic disease in terms of types of life cycles and hosts, adaptations, modes of transmission, factors that affect the geographical distribution and incidence, laboratory identification procedures, and control and treatment measures

To give the names of the parasite, the principal clinical manifestations, identification procedures, mode of transmission, and treatment and control measures

To associate the following with specific parasites: primary amebic meningoencephalitis, opportunistic pathogens in the immunosuppressed, visceral and larval migrans, pinworm or seatworm, muscle worm, swimmer's itch, improperly cooked pork, cats, beavers, and female *Anopheles* mosquito

To comment on the importance of the changing of surface antigens by trypanosomes

To summarize the disease-related involvements of invertebrate arthropods

OUTLINE

GENERAL CHARACTERISTICS OF PARASITES AND PARASITIC INFECTIONS
- Incidence of Parasitic Infection
- Factors That Influence the Incidence of Parasitic Infection
- Infective Forms and Life Cycles
- The Nature of Parasitic Disease
- Laboratory Diagnosis
  - Diagnosis of Intestinal and Biliary Parasites
  - Diagnosis of Blood and Tissue Parasites
  - Serological Techniques
- Treatment and Control

THE PROTOZOA
- Sarcodina—The Amebae
  - Amebiasis and Amebic Dysentery
    - Pathogenesis
    - Laboratory Diagnosis
    - Epidemiology
    - Treatment and Control
  - Primary Amebic Meningoencephalitis
  - Acanthamoebiasis
- Mastigophora—The Flagellated Protozoa
  - Giardiasis
    - Pathogenesis
    - Laboratory Diagnosis
    - Epidemiology
    - Treatment and Control
  - Trichomoniasis
    - Pathogenesis
    - Laboratory Diagnosis
    - Treatment and Control
  - Trypanosomiasis (*Trypanosoma* and *Leishmania*)
    - African Trypanosomiasis (African Sleeping Sickness)
      - Pathogenesis
      - Laboratory Diagnosis
      - Epidemiology
      - Treatment and Control
    - American Trypanosomiasis (Chagas' Disease)
      - Pathogenesis
      - Laboratory Diagnosis

OUTLINE (*continued*)

Epidemiology
Treatment and Control
Leishmaniasis
Cutaneous Leishmaniasis
Mucocutaneous Leishmaniasis
Visceral Leishmaniasis (Kala-azar)
Diagnosis and Treatment
Ciliata—The Ciliated Protozoa
Balantidiasis (Ciliary Dysentery)
Sporozoa—The Sporozoite-Forming Protozoa
Malaria—Plasmodiasis
Life Cycle
Pathogenesis
Laboratory Diagnosis
Epidemiology
Treatment and Control
Toxoplasmosis
Life Cycle
Pathogenesis
Laboratory Diagnosis
Epidemiology
Treatment and Control
Babesiosis (Nantucket Fever)
Cryptosporidiosis
Pathogenesis
Laboratory Diagnosis
Epidemiology
Treatment and Control

THE NEMATHELMINTHES
Ascariasis (Roundworm Infection)
Pathogenesis
Laboratory Diagnosis
Epidemiology
Treatment and Control
Visceral Larva Migrans
Hookworm Infection
Pathogenesis
Laboratory Diagnosis
Epidemiology
Treatment and Control
Cutaneous Larva Migrans
Strongyloidiasis
Life Cycle
Pathogenesis
Laboratory Diagnosis
Epidemiology
Treatment
Enterobiasis (Pinworm or Seatworm Infection)
Pathogenesis
Laboratory Diagnosis
Epidemiology
Treatment and Control
Trichinosis (Muscle Worm Infection)
Life Cycle
Pathogenesis
Laboratory Diagnosis
Epidemiology
Treatment and Control
Filariasis
Pathogenesis
Wuchereria bancrofti and *Brugia malayi*
Onchocerca volvulus (Onchocerciasis)
Loa loa (Loaiasis)
Laboratory Diagnosis
Treatment

THE PLATYHELMINTHES
Trematoda (Flukes)
Schistosomiasis (Bilharziasis)
Life Cycle
Pathogenesis
Laboratory Diagnosis
Epidemiology
Treatment and Control
Schistosome Dermatitis
Cestoidea (Tapeworms)
Taeniasis
Pork Tapeworm (*Taenia solium*)
Echinococcosis

THE ARTHROPODA

General Characteristics of Parasites and Parasitic Infections

The term **parasite** is often used as a general term referring to an organism (either prokaryote or eukaryote) that survives on or at the expense of a living host. In the field of medical parasitology the term **parasite** refers specifically to organisms from the animal kingdom. **Animal parasites** have life cycles in which they take up temporary or permanent residence in animals (including humans). It is during this residence that animal parasites can cause disease.

Parasites are found in four divisions of the animal kingdom: the Protozoa, or single-celled animal parasites; the Nemathelminthes or **roundworms;** the Platyhelminthes or **flatworms;** and the Arthropoda or invertebrate animals with jointed appendages. Many of the members of these divisions can be seen without the use of a microscope. For example, large tapeworms can reach the length of 25 to 30 feet. However, the microscope is still an important tool in the identification of the eggs and larvae of these macroscopic organisms.

INCIDENCE OF PARASITIC INFECTION

Medical parasitology frequently draws little attention in developed countries of the world. This is primarily due to the fact that many animal parasite diseases are confined to areas of high population density such as the tropics and subtropics. In addition, poor hygiene and lack of health services in these areas contribute to their problems. In developing countries parasitic diseases take an exacting toll in human suffering: disfigurement, blindness, and

TABLE 34-1
Deaths due to Parasitic Diseases in the Developing World (1990 WHO Figures)

Diseases	Deaths
Malaria	1–2 million
Schistosomiasis	200,000
Amebiasis	40,000–110,000
African trypanosomiasis (sleeping sickness)	20,000
Hookworm	50,000–60,000
Ascariasis	20,000

death (Table 34-1). Consider these statistics: One in four people in the world has malaria or is exposed to it, one in five people has hookworm infection, 50 million Africans harbor a protozoa that may cause sleeping sickness, and one of every four inhabitants of the earth carries roundworms in the intestinal tract.

In the United States the major parasitic infections are caused by the protozoa. Epidemics of disease occur when hygienic conditions break down and there is a lack of sanitary facilities or the facilities are in disrepair. Sporadic cases of parasitic disease can also occur after transfusions in which parasites are present in donor blood or when there is an influx of immigrants. Many more cases of parasitic infections are now observed in the immunocompromised host, for example, in patients with acquired immunodeficiency syndrome (AIDS).

FACTORS THAT INFLUENCE THE INCIDENCE OF PARASITIC INFECTION

The incidence of infection is related to such factors as climate, the availability of suitable intermediate and definitive hosts and vectors, eating and sanitary habits of the human population, mode of dress, occupation, and nutritional status.

The eating habits of various population groups have a bearing on the incidence and persistence of certain parasitic diseases. The consumption of uncooked vegetables, particularly leafy vegetables, where human excrement ("night soil") has been used as a fertilizer is a mode of transmission. Protozoal infections such as amebiasis and giardiasis and helminthic infections such as ascariasis and trichuriasis are transmitted in this way. The ingestion of raw fish may lead to anemia caused by infection with the fish tapeworm or to liver and gastrointestinal pathology caused by flukes.

INFECTIVE FORMS AND LIFE CYCLES

The developmental stages that take place throughout the life history of the parasite are referred to as **life cycles.** During the life cycle the parasite may exist in different forms. For example, in the soil the protozoa are found in a quiescent, resistant form called the **cyst** or **sporozoite.** When ingested by a suitable host, the cyst undergoes transformation from an infective form to a replicative form that causes disease. Some worms produce **eggs** from which **larval forms** develop. Other worms directly produce larvae that are infective forms. It is usually the adult worm, however, that is the direct cause of disease.

The number of hosts and the developmental stages that occur in a host vary from one group to another. The host in which a parasite reaches maturity or the most important host is called a **definitive host.** Humans and other vertebrates are definitive hosts to most parasites. An **intermediate host** is one in which some development of the parasite occurs but it does not reach maturity. For example, in malaria, mosquitoes are definitive hosts while humans or other vertebrates are the intermediate host. Arthropods may be intermediate hosts for some parasites and definitive hosts for others (Fig. 34-1).

More than one intermediate host may be involved in parasite development. For example, in the fish tapeworm life cycle, eggs may leave a definitive host such as humans and enter water. In the water, ciliated embryos develop and are ingested by crustaceans. In the crustacean the embryos develop into parasitic larvae that are eventually eaten by fish, the second intermediate host. Consumption of raw fish by humans or other species completes the cycle.

THE NATURE OF PARASITIC DISEASE

A common warning to travelers in Third World countries is don't drink the water. Yet when travelers arrive at these countries, they see that the local inhabitants drink the water with no apparent effects on their health. Animal parasites often become well adjusted to their hosts and an apparently healthy individual may be host to hundreds of parasitic worms or protozoa. Many parasites cause minimal tissue damage and the host's repair mechanisms are sufficient to keep pace with the damage. In a different host the parasite may become pathogenic, causing severe damage or even death.

Parasites may cause physical trauma, nutrition robbing, or cell destruction by chemical or mechanical means. Worms may become so numerous or damaging that they are able to occlude vessels or cause distension of tissues or organs. In the disease elephantiasis, for example, the parasite causes an inflammatory response in the lymphatics that leads to pools of lymph collecting in tissues. Parasites such as the fish tapeworm have an affinity for vitamin B_{12} and absorb large amounts of it from the intestinal tract of its host. Since the vitamin is necessary for erythrocyte development, a severe anemia can be the result of infection. The malaria parasite spends part of its life cycle in the erythrocyte and eventually ruptures it. Erythrocyte rupture releases parasite waste products that are responsible for many of the symptoms of disease.

Despite the potential for severe tissue damage, many parasites have achieved a tolerant accommodation with their hosts. Individuals can harbor tapeworms several feet in length and show no signs of disease. The evolution of this tolerance could be due to the fact that over many generations the important antigenic determinants of the parasite become more like the hosts they infect. A second possibility is that the parasite may be able to mask itself

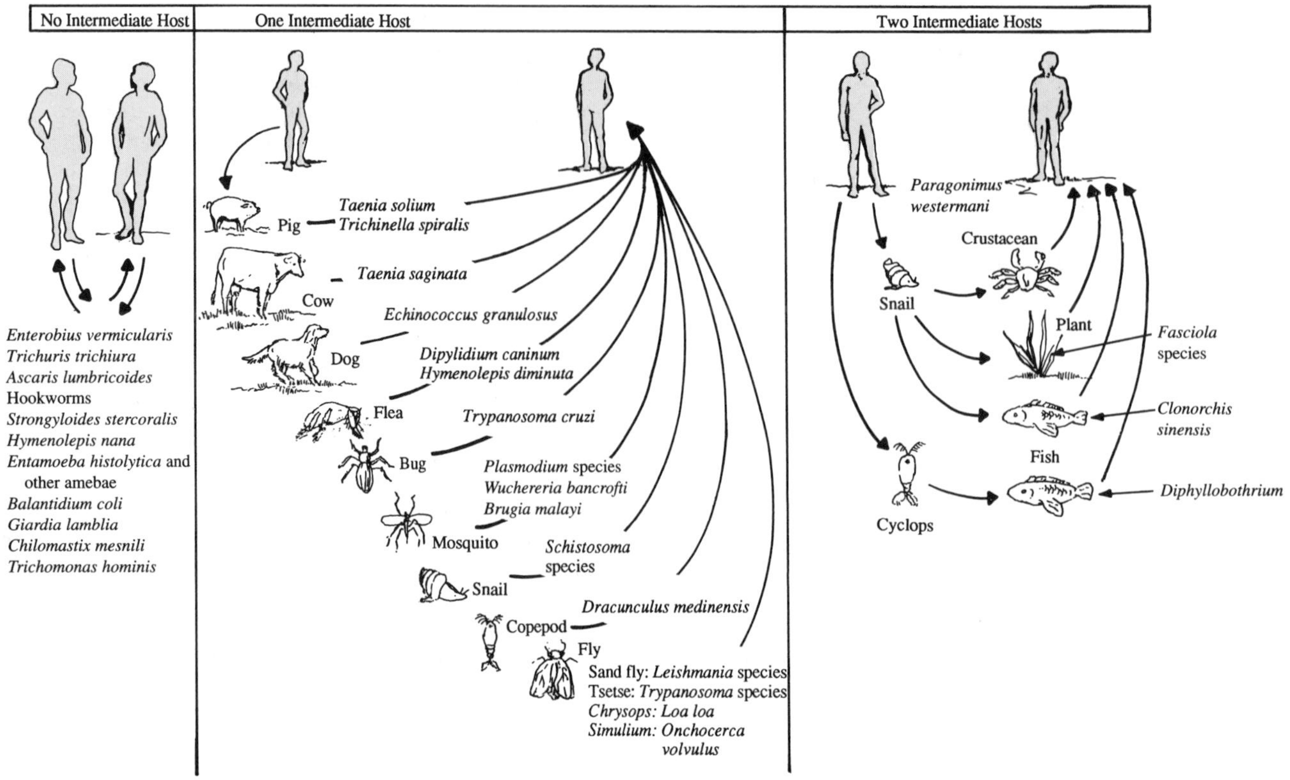

FIGURE 34-1
Overview of the life cycles of parasites of importance to humans. Copepods are crustaceans. Cyclops is a type of copepod. (Adapted from E. W. Koneman et al., *Color Atlas and Textbook of Diagnostic Microbiology*. Philadelphia: Lippincott, 1979.)

with host components. In this way the host does not recognize the parasite as foreign. As you learned earlier in Chapter 14, some parasites are capable of changing the nature of their surface components repeatedly during the infectious disease process.

LABORATORY DIAGNOSIS

Many parasitic diseases, particularly in areas where the disease is not endemic, often go unrecognized. The diagnosis of most parasitic diseases is dependent on the laboratory. Most intestinal and blood parasites are identified by their morphology at various stages in their life cycles. For example, the microscopic cysts and trophozoites of the protozoa or the distinctive eggs and larvae of the helminths can be identified this way. Tissue parasites are identified primarily by immunodiagnostic techniques.

Diagnosis of Intestinal and Biliary Parasites

Most intestinal and biliary pathogens are diagnosed by identifying stages in the feces or other intestinal material. The laboratory usually examines at least three fecal specimens serially collected at 24- to 48-hour intervals. Fecal specimens, collected in dry, clean containers, are first grossly inspected for blood, mucus, adult forms of worms, and consistency. Duodenal contents can be sampled by using the **Entero-Test method.** In this technique the patient swallows a gelatin capsule that is packed with a nylon thread 140 cm long. The free end of the thread is fastened to the patient's face. After the capsule dissolves, the thread is carried by peristaltic action to the duodenum. The thread is gently retrieved after 4 hours. The droplets of duodenal contents on the distal end of the thread are then examined for parasites. Examination of fecal or duodenal material may be performed using a **wet mount.** The wet mount is useful for detecting motile trophozoites, motile larvae, and protozoan cysts and helminth eggs.

After parasites are separated from the fecal material, the specimen can be stained. Permanent stains are useful for identification of protozoan trophozoites and cysts. Sometimes the eggs are counted to assess the intensity of infection.

Diagnosis of Blood and Tissue Parasites

Blood films are prepared to detect parasites that invade the bloodstream, for example, the parasite causing malaria. Blood films can be prepared as thick or thin films on glass microscope slides. The films are then stained with Giemsa or Wright stains. For the diagnosis of filarial infections, blood specimens can be concentrated by a variety of techniques such as membrane filtration or saponin lysis of erythrocytes.

Tissues may be examined in histology sections or impression smears. Bone marrow aspirates or fluids such as those from bronchial washings and cerebrospinal fluid can also be examined directly by staining. For parasites that circulate in the skin and not the blood, skin snips can be taken with needle and knife. The snip is then placed in a saline solution and examined.

Serological Techniques

Serological techniques are used primarily in the diagnosis of infections caused by parasites that invade the tissues. Tissue parasites evoke a stronger immune response than do parasites that remain in the lumen of the intestine. The use of serological tests in parasitic disease is especially helpful when the infecting organism is relatively scarce in the bloodstream. All of these serological tests employ material derived from parasites grown in culture as target antigens. The tests usually lack sensitivity and specificity. In addition, the materials often are not available commercially.

TREATMENT AND CONTROL

Relatively few drugs are effective in eradicating animal parasites. The drugs for schistosomiasis and onchocerciasis recently were improved but the drugs for other parasitic infections either are toxic or carcinogenic or allow reinfection to occur. For Chagas' disease there is no adequate drug. Some of the drugs that are used on a broad-spectrum basis are **mebendazole, metronidazole, thiabendazole,** and **niclosamide.**

The eradication of many parasitic diseases would entail the expensive and formidable task of totally regulating intermediate hosts (insects, mollusks) and strictly managing environmental conditions (breeding places of insects, soil contamination with excreta, etc.). Insecticides, molluscicides, and other agents can be used to control or destroy intermediate hosts and vectors. For example, malaria has been eradicated from many areas of the world including the United States by destroying the mosquito vector.

Travelers to tropical and subtropical areas must be knowledgeable about the potential for acquiring parasitic infections. Immunization or prophylactic drugs should be given consideration before embarking on travel to areas endemic for parasitic diseases. The Centers for Disease Control (CDC) in Atlanta, Georgia, annually publishes *Health Information for International Travel.*

Vaccine development is under way, particularly for malaria. Vaccine development is hampered by several factors associated with parasites. Complex antigens are present on animal parasites and different antigens present at various stages of infection. In addition, some parasites are able to change their antigenic character during the infection process. Currently, important antigens are defined by the development of monoclonal antibodies against antigens that appear at various stages of the parasite life cycle. In some instances, the antibodies provide partial passive immunity and indicate candidate antigens for vaccine development.

The Protozoa

The parasitic protozoa are customarily divided into four groups, variously termed subphyla, classes, or subdivisions: **Sarcodina, Mastigophora, Ciliata** or **Ciliophora,** and **Sporozoa.** A summary of the protozoal diseases described in this chapter is presented in Table 34-2.

SARCODINA—THE AMEBAE

Amebae that regularly parasitize humans (Fig. 34-2), *Endolimax nana, Iodamoeba buetschlii, Entamoeba coli,* and *Dientamoeba fragilis,* are commensals that colonize the intestinal tract. They are important because they must be differentiated from the one intestinal pathogen, *Entamoeba histolytica.*

Entamoeba gingivalis is found in the oral cavity and is generally regarded as nonpathogenic. Its numbers increase only when unhygienic conditions exist in the oral cavity.

There are two genera of free-living amebae, *Naegleria* and *Acanthamoeba.* They do not require an animal host but occasionally cause serious infections in humans.

Amebiasis and Amebic Dysentery

Amebiasis or amebic dysentery is caused by *E. histolytica.* Strains of the organism exhibit major differences in virulence. Amebiasis is primarily a disease of the tropics.

Pathogenesis. *E. histolytica* is unusual among intestinal amebae because of its ability to invade tissue. The organism colonizes the intestinal tract as a trophozoite; however, the mechanisms of colonization and pathogenicity are not understood. More virulent strains stimulate mucin secretion, making epithelial surfaces more vulnerable to invasion. There also appears to be a direct relationship between proteinase activity by the organism and pathogenicity. Proteinases can degrade matrix proteins such as collagen, laminin, and fibronectin. Evidence now supports the view that there are two morphologically identical forms of *E. histolytica,* one nonpathogenic and the other pathogenic (see Under the Microscope 46).

Most human infections are asymptomatic, with the organism behaving as a commensal in over 90 percent of those infected. These individuals seldom become symptomatic and excrete cysts in the stool for only a short time. In addition, the amebae present in these patients may be pathogenic or nonpathogenic.

The patient with symptomatic infection may exhibit **intestinal** or **extraintestinal** pathology. The patient with **intestinal** disease exhibits abdominal pain and increased frequency of bowel movements. The symptoms associated with invasive amebiasis are gradual and include abdominal pain, diarrhea, dysentery, and weight loss.

Invasion of the colon results in inflammation and formation of ulcers. Initially the ulcer has a pinhead center composed of debris and *E. histolytica* trophozoites. As the ulcer enlarges and deepens, it forms the classic **flask-shaped ulcer** of amebiasis. When ulcers coalesce, the mucosa undergoes necrosis and sloughs, resulting in violent dysentery and stools with blood-stained mucus. The ulcers often become secondarily infected with bacteria. This form of amebiasis has a high mortality. Chronic ulceration, particularly in the cecum, sigmoid colon, and rectum, produces lesions filled with granulation tissue. These lesions are called **amebomas** and are often mis-

TABLE 34-2
Characteristics of Protozoal Diseases

Disease name and agent	Clinical condition	Infective form; mode of transmission	Specimen examined; diagnostic form	Comments	Treatment
Amebiasis *Entamoeba histolytica*	Intestinal: diarrhea, dysentery Extraintestinal: related to abscess formation in liver, brain, lung	*Cyst* Food (night soil), water; anal intercourse	*Stool, serum* Cysts or trophozoites; antibodies		Metronidazole plus iodoquinol (intestinal); metronidazole and dehydroemetine with chloroquine (extraintestinal)
Primary amebic meningoencephalitis *Naegleria fowleri*	Fever, severe headache, nausea, disorientation, coma	*Cysts and trophozoites* Warm stagnant water entering nares	*CNS fluid* Trophozoites	Soil-water ameboflagellate; swimmers in warm stagnant water	Amphotericin B, miconazole, and rifampin
Acanthamebiasis *Acanthamoeba* species	Keratitis (eye) may lead to blindness Chronic granulomatous amebic encephalitis	*Trophozoites* Eye: improper cleaning of contact lens Other: soil, water, sewage	*Specimen from infected tissue* Cysts or trophozoites	Free-living ameba	Topical miconazole for eye infections
Giardiasis, lambliasis *Giardia lamblia*	Protracted diarrhea, malabsorption syndrome	*Cyst* Person to person (day-care centers, gays) contact; food, water	*Stool, duodenal contents* Cyst or trophozoite	Animal reservoirs: beavers, muskrats Entero-Test	Quinacrine HCl; metronidazole, furazolidone
Trichomoniasis (vaginal) *Trichomonas vaginalis*	Vaginitis with itching, burning, inflammation, discharge	*Trophozoite* Venereal	*Vaginal discharge/ scrapings* Trophozoite	Sometimes found in Pap smear; males usually asymptomatic No cyst form	Metronidazole
African trypanosomiasis (sleeping sickness) *Trypanosoma brucei gambiense* *Trypanosoma brucei rhodesiense*	Skin lesion at site of bite; fever, lymph node enlargement CNS involvement: progressive mental deterioration, coma; death due to pneumonia, starvation, sepsis	*Metatrypanosomes* Bite of tsetse fly	*Blood, cerebrospinal fluid, aspirates of lymph nodes* Trypanosomes	Winterbottom's sign; variation of surface antigens	Eflornithine (Gambian), suramin (Rhodesian); melarsoprol B for Rhodesian encephalitis
American trypanosomiasis *Trypanosoma cruzi*	Chagas' disease; acute disease (especially in children) in visceral organs and heart; chronic disease in adults, megacolon, megaesophagus, enlarged heart	*Trypomastigotes* Feces of reduviid bugs	*Blood* Trypomastigotes	Romaña's sign: xenodiagnosis; domestic and wild animals as hosts and reservoirs	Nifurtimox; benznidazole
Leishmaniasis *Leishmania donovani*	Visceral (kala-azar) leishmaniasis; destruction of macrophages; liver, spleen enlargement; protracted fever	*Promastigotes* Bite of sandfly	*Bone marrow aspirate* Leishmania in macrophages	Dogs and foxes, important reservoirs; thatched roofs as breeding places for sandflies	Antimony compounds

TABLE 34-2 (Continued)

Disease name and agent	Clinical condition	Infective form; mode of transmission	Specimen examined; diagnostic form	Comments	Treatment
Leishmania tropica *Leishmania mexicana*	Cutaneous leishmaniasis; ulcerating lesions at site of insect bite	*Promastigotes* Bite of sandfly	*Biopsy or scrapings of ulcer* Leishmania	Dogs, forest rodents, anteaters important reservoirs; thatched roofs as breeding places for sandflies	Antimony compounds
Leishmania braziliensis	Mucocutaneous leishmaniasis; cutaneous lesions followed by multiple lesions, usually at border of mouth, nose; may be disfiguring	*Promastigotes* Bite of sandfly	*Culture of ulcer or biopsy* Leishmania	Dogs, forest rodents, sloths important reservoirs	Antimony compounds
Balantidiasis					
Balantidium coli	Diarrhea, dysentery	*Cysts* Food, water contaminated by pigs	*Stool* Cyst	Largest protozoal parasite	Iodoquinol
Plasmodiasis (malaria)					
Plasmodium vivax, malariae, falciparum, ovale	Periodic fever, chills, sweats; enlargement of spleen, liver; anemia	*Sporozoites* Bite of female *Anopheles* mosquito	*Blood* Cyclical plasmodial forms in red blood cells	Drug resistance is a major problem in falciparum malaria	Chloroquine phosphate; primaquine phosphate, quinine for falciparum malaria
Toxoplasmosis					
Toxoplasma gondii	Primary infection usually asymptomatic or mild; in immuno-compromised, a disseminated infection often involving CNS; congenital infections—anomalies of CNS, eye	*Oocysts or tissue cysts* Ingestion of oocysts or meat containing tissue cysts	*Serum and tissues* Organism not readily observed or cultured from humans	Members of cat family only definitive hosts	Pyramethamine plus sulfadiazine
Babesiosis					
Babesia microti	Nantucket fever; resembles malaria	Bite by nymph of hard ticks	*Blood* Organism in red blood cells	Long recognized as an important infection of domestic and wild animals; deer, mice, and field mice important reservoirs	Clindamycin plus quinine
Cryptosporidiosis					
Cryptosporidium species	Profuse, watery diarrhea	*Oocysts* Feces of animals; feces and respiratory secretions of humans	*Stool, gut tissue* Oocysts observed via phase-contrast microscopy or in acid-fast–stained material	Fatal intractable diarrhea in immuno-compromised; dehydration and parenteral nutrition as supportive therapy	Passive oral transfer of hyperimmune bovine colostrum

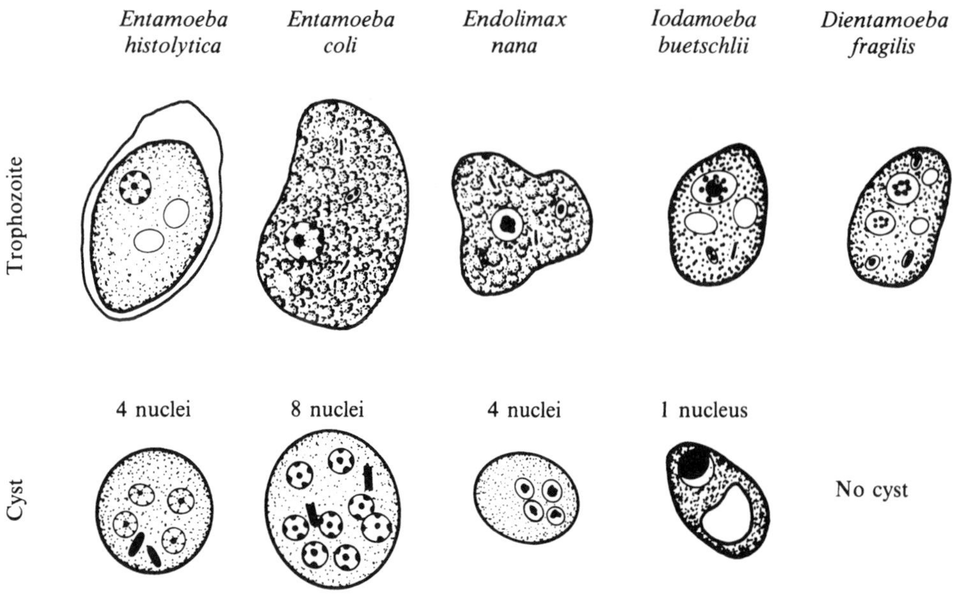

FIGURE 34-2
Amebae found in human stool specimens.

UNDER THE MICROSCOPE 46

Pathogenic vs. Nonpathogenic *Entamoeba histolytica*

There is a very high rate of asymptomatic carriage of *Entamoeba histolytica*. For example, clinical symptoms will develop in only 10 percent of those infected and of this group only 2 to 20 percent will have invasive disease. It has been postulated that the large number of asymptomatic patients are infected with the nonpathogenic strain. Given the toxicity of drugs used in treatment, it is important to differentiate pathogenic from nonpathogenic strains. Recently the differentiation has been based on isoenzyme (zymodeme) analysis, monoclonal antibodies, and molecular probes.

Isoenzymes are enzymes that perform the same function in all strains but differ in the phenotypic expression of that enzyme. The term **zymodeme** is defined as a population of amebae in which the electrophoretic mobilities of specific enzymes differ from those in similar populations. There is still controversy concerning the use of zymodeme analysis because of isoenzyme stability. Through the use of recombinant DNA technology, however, two genetically distinct forms of *E. histolytica* have been found to exist.

taken for tumors. Perforation of the colon by amebic ulcers occurs in about 20 percent of the patients with acute amebic colitis and may result in peritonitis and liver abscess.

Extraintestinal disease is the result of intestinal invasion by trophozoites. Trophozoites enter the circulation and are carried to the liver. Abscesses are formed in the liver but seldom become secondarily infected by bacteria. Amebae are not responsible for liver cell destruction. Tissue destruction is due to lysis of leukocytes and macrophages by the amebae. Other organs associated with disseminated disease include the lungs, pericardium, brain, and skin.

Laboratory Diagnosis. Stool samples, sigmoidoscopy smears, tissue biopsy specimens, and so on can be examined for parasites. Stool samples are concentrated and stained for detection and identification of cysts or parasites. Serological techniques such as indirect fluorescent antibody and immunodiffusion tests are used for extraintestinal amebiasis.

Epidemiology. It has been estimated that approximately 480 million people, or 12 percent of the world's population, are infected with *E. histolytica*. The number of people who die each year from amebiasis is 40,000 to 110,000. About 10 percent of those infected present with clinical symptoms and about 90 percent of them demonstrate intestinal symptoms.

Humans are the major reservoir of infection. Ingestion of food and drink contaminated with *E. histolytica* cysts from human feces, and direct fecal-oral contact are the most common means of infection. Use of untreated water for drinking or human feces as fertilizer is common in Third World countries and represents important sources of disease. In the United States most epidemics are the result of fecal contamination of a faulty water supply. Cysts may remain viable for as long as three months but can be destroyed in water by hyperchlorination or iodination.

High-risk groups include travelers, immigrants, migrant workers, immunocompromised individuals, and sexually active male homosexuals. Invasive disease in homosexuals, however, is rare.

Treatment and Control. For symptomatic intestinal disease, metronidazole plus iodoquinol or metronidazole plus diloxanide furoate is recommended. For extraintestinal disease several combinations are used, including metronidazole and dehydroemetine with chloroquine. Chloroquine is useful for treating liver abscess. Extraintestinal therapy should be followed with a luminal amebicide such as iodoquinol.

Asymptomatic patients who are cyst passers may be treated with diloxanide furoate, iodoquinol, or paromomycin.

Control of *E. histolytica* infection depends on improved hygiene, sanitation, and water treatment; isolation of patients; and education about the risks of anal-oral contact.

Primary Amebic Meningoencephalitis

Primary amebic meningoencephalitis is caused by an ameboflagellate (an ameba that can transform into a flagellate) called *Naegleria fowleri*. This organism is **thermophilic** with an optimal growth temperature of 22 to 35 C. Sources for *Naegleria* include soil, water, cooling towers, nasal and throat swabs, sewage sludge, hospital hydrothermal pools, and swimming pools. Most human infections with *N. fowleri* have been associated with swimming in warm fresh waters. Most recorded cases have been fatal.

The parasite enters the nasal cavity by inhalation of dust or aspiration of water contaminated with trophozoites. The incubation period is 3 to 15 days. The olfactory neuroepithelium is the site of lesion formation. The parasite is phagocytosed and migrates to the central nervous system. The parasite travels along nerve pathways into the olfactory bulbs and thence into other areas of the central nervous system. There is hemorrhagic necrosis in the cerebral gray and white matter. If treatment is not initiated, the patient dies within 7 to 10 days after the time of exposure.

The symptoms of infection include severe bifrontal or bitemporal headache, fever, nausea, and vomiting. This is quickly followed by meningeal irritation and encephalitis leading to coma and seizures. The vast majority of patients die about 1 week after the appearance of symptoms.

Diagnosis of infection cannot be made on clinical grounds, but is usually based on isolation and culture of free-living amebae from central spinal fluid or the presence of trophozoites in biopsied brain tissue. No satisfactory treatment for primary amebic meningoencephalitis exists. One patient, an 8-year-old girl from California became infected following swimming in a hot-springs pool. She was diagnosed early and was successfully treated with amphotericin B, miconazole, and rifampin.

Acanthamoebiasis

Acanthamoeba are free-living, soil or water facultative parasites. Well water, dust, and soil have been identified as sources of infection in some patients. In most cases, however, contaminated air, water, and contact lenses have been the sources of infection (see Under the Microscope 47).

The primary site of infection is the skin or respiratory tract. Infection may spread from these sites to other tissues. Spread to the central nervous system results in a chronic granulomatous encephalitis **(chronic amoebic encephalitis** or **GAE).** GAE is usually found in chronically ill and debilitated or immunologically impaired individuals (AIDS patients, for example). Associated disorders of GAE include skin ulcers, liver disease, pneumonitis, renal failure, and pharyngitis. The incubation period of GAE is not known. Some of the clinical manifestations of disease include fever, headache, stiff neck, altered mental status, paresis, lethargy, and coma. The usual cause of death is bronchopneumonia.

Acanthamoeba **keratitis** is discussed in Under the Microscope 47.

Any specimen indicating GAE caused by *Acanthamoeba* is best confirmed by smear preparations and cultures. This procedure applies to central nervous system infection as well as keratitis.

MASTIGOPHORA—THE FLAGELLATED PROTOZOA

At some time in their life cycle the Mastigophora possess whip-like flagella as locomotory organelles. Some possess undulating membranes. Parasitic flagellates appear in the oral cavity *(Trichomonas tenax)*, in the intestine *(Giardia lamblia, Trichomonas hominis, Retortamonas intestinalis)*, in the genitourinary tract *(Trichomonas vaginalis)*, and in the circulation and tissues (the hemoflagellates and tissue flagellates of the genera *Trypanosoma* and *Leishmania*).

Giardiasis

G. lamblia is a flagellated intestinal protozoan that is now recognized as a cause of disease in travelers worldwide. In the United States *G. lamblia* causes intestinal disease in persons drinking contaminated water, in children in daycare centers, and in homosexual males.

The trophozoite, when viewed from the ventral side, is a pear-shaped organism 9 to 16 μm in length, 9 to 12 μm in width, and 2 to 5 μm in thickness (Fig. 34-3). The organism possesses a ventral concave sucking disk that is used to attach to the epithelial surface (Fig. 34-4). The trophozoites exhibit an erratic tumbling motion described as "falling leaf" motility.

Pathogenesis. Cysts are ingested in contaminated food or water and pass through the stomach unharmed. In the duodenum excystation takes place and two trophozoites

UNDER THE MICROSCOPE 47

Acanthamoeba Keratitis in Soft Contact Lens Wearers

Within a nine-month period, from mid-1985 to February 1986, the Centers for Disease Control received reports of 24 cases of *Acanthamoeba* keratitis, a much higher number than previously reported during similar time periods.

Acanthamoeba keratitis is a serious infection of the cornea caused by amebae of the genus *Acanthamoeba*. The mechanism by which *Acanthamoeba* infects the human cornea is unknown. Historically, the infection has been associated with penetrating corneal trauma. More recently, an association with contact lens wear has become apparent.

The risk factors identified in this study suggest deviations from contact lens wear and care procedures recommended by lens manufacturers and health care professionals. Current U.S. Food and Drug Administration licensure of commercial salt tablets (used to make homemade saline solution) applies only to using the saline solutions before and during thermal disinfection of lenses, not as a postdisinfection rinse or wetting agent. Thermal disinfection of soft contact lenses is effective in killing *Acanthamoeba* trophozoites and cysts, suggesting that use of homemade saline solutions before and during the thermal disinfection phase is safe.

Persons wearing contact lenses should be reminded to adhere closely to recommended contact lens wear and care procedures. These include using sterile solutions after disinfecting lenses, using solutions and disinfection methods appropriate for the specific lens type, cleaning and disinfecting lenses each time they are removed, and handwashing before handling lenses. Contact lens wearers who do not comply with these recommendations may be increasing their risk for infection with *Acanthamoeba* and other organisms. As a result, they could develop partial or total loss of vision.

From *M.M.W.R.* 36:397, 1987.

emerge from each mature cyst. The alkaline pH of the duodenum and upper jejunum favors trophozoite growth. Trophozoites seldom invade tissue.

The mechanisms associated with pathogenesis are not understood. In addition, it is not understood why some infected individuals are symptomatic while others are asymptomatic. Symptoms appear 9 to 15 days after infection. The clinical features of acute infection include nausea and low-grade fever, followed by explosive, watery, and foul-smelling diarrhea. These symptoms may last about 3 to 4 days before the infection clears. Sometimes a chronic infection develops in which patients have intermittent diarrhea for two or more years. The chronic stage is characterized by headache and myalgia with continued weight loss, anorexia, and **malabsorption syndrome.** Malabsorption syndrome is associated with an interference with the absorption of fats, carbohydrates, and steatorrhea (high fat content of feces).

The trophozoites must encyst in order to survive. Encystation is favored by alkaline pH, the presence of bile, and lactic acid.

FIGURE 34-3
Giardia lamblia.

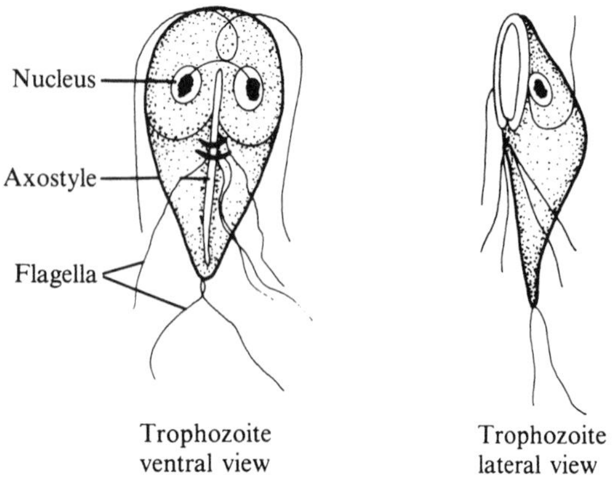

Laboratory Diagnosis. Diagnosis is made by finding trophozoites or cysts in feces, intestinal aspirates, or material retrieved via the Entero-test method described earlier. A long incubation period should also alert the physician to the possibility of giardiasis. Stools may not always reveal the trophozoites since they are very delicate and can be destroyed before defecation. Cysts can be identified based on size, shape, and internal structures.

Since *G. lamblia* is so common in the United States, especially in day-care centers, commercial enzyme-linked immunosorbent assays (ELISA) have become widely used to detect *Giardia* antigen.

Epidemiology. Giardiasis is the most commonly reported pathogenic protozoal disease in the United States. Infection is spread from person to person primarily by the fecal-oral route. Water is the most common vehicle for the transmission of cysts.

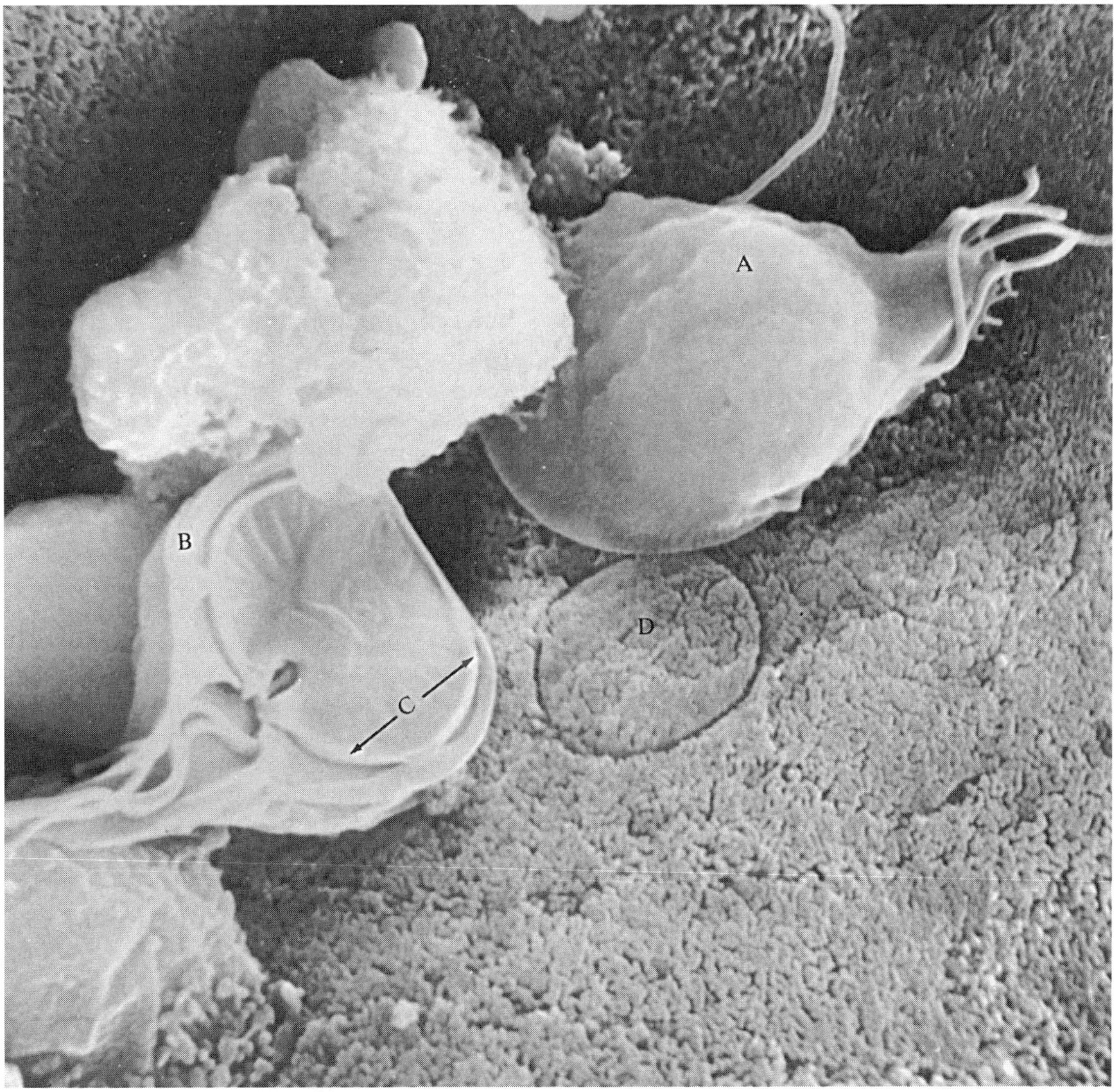

FIGURE 34-4
Scanning electron micrograph of *Giardia muris* trophozoites in mouse intestine. A. Dorsal view. B. Ventral view. C. Adhesive disk on ventral surface. D. Circular mark left by the adhesive disk on the columnar cell microvilli of intestine. (× 8026.) (From R. L. Owen, P. C. Nemanic, and D. P. Stevens, *Gastroenterology* 76: 757, 1979.)

In the United States most infections are the result of drinking untreated stream water by campers, for example, and using water that has been fecally contaminated. Infections occur in day-care centers and other institutional settings as well as among homosexuals engaging in oral-anal sex.

Humans are the main reservoir of the parasite but a variety of animals carry *Giardia* species similar to those infecting humans. The parasite has been found in beavers, muskrats, and water moles. These animal sources may explain why backpackers and mountain climbers acquire infection after drinking from mountain streams.

Treatment and Control. The drugs available for treatment include metronidazole, quinacrine, and furazolidone. Nitroimidazole compounds are available for treatment in countries outside the United States.

Water purification breakdown is often the reason for many waterborne outbreaks. The cysts can survive standard concentrations of chlorine used in water purification systems. Several outbreaks have been associated with unfiltered surface water systems in which chlorination was the only treatment. Cyst destruction often requires longer contact times and higher concentrations of chlorine. This is especially true if the water being treated is very cold. Cysts can survive one to three months in cold water.

For individual protection, one minute of boiling destroys *Giardia* cysts. If boiling is not possible, household bleach (2–4 drops) or 0.5 ml of 2% tincture of iodine can be added to each liter of water and held for one hour before drinking. Hot, cooked food also prevents ingestion of viable cysts.

Trichomoniasis

Trichomonads are globular protozoa possessing three to five anterior flagella (Fig. 34-5) and a prominent oval nucleus. An internal stiff, rod-like structure called an axostyle runs the length of the organism and emerges posteriorly as a caudal spine. An undulating membrane extends along the longitudinal axis. Trichomonads appear only in the trophozoite form, the transmissible form. Three morphologically similar *Trichomonas* species are found in humans: *T. tenax, T. hominis,* and *T. vaginalis.* Each has a specific habitat in humans.

T. tenax, like *E. gingivalis,* is an inhabitant of the oral cavity. It is seldom observed in healthy mouths but increases in number when the periodontium (supporting soft tissue of the teeth) is adversely affected. Transmission is believed to occur via saliva-soiled fomites (for example, tableware) and through kissing.

T. hominis, found in the human intestinal tract, is clinically unimportant.

T. vaginalis is regarded as a pathogen and causes an estimated two to three million cases of symptomatic infection per year among sexually active women in the United States. It is one of the three main causes of vaginitis, the other two being the fungus *Candida albicans* and the bacterium *Gardnerella vaginalis.*

T. vaginalis infection is associated with vaginitis in women, urethritis or prostatitis in men, and asymptomatic infection in both sexes. Although considered to be sexually transmitted, the infection can be transmitted from infected mothers to their infants. The presence of the organism in prepubertal girls strongly suggests sexual abuse. Recent studies suggested that trichomoniasis enhances susceptibility to human immunodeficiency virus (HIV) infection because of genital inflammation. In addition, infection is believed to be associated with delivery of low birth weight infants.

Vaginitis is associated with a thick, yellow, blood-tinged discharge accompanied by burning, itching, or chafing. In men the symptoms are often absent but painful urination may be present.

Laboratory Diagnosis. Diagnosis is usually made by direct microscopical examination of **saline wet mounts** from genitourinary tract specimens. Stained trichomonads are not uncommonly discovered in routine **Papanicolaou** (Pap) **smears** prepared for cancer detection.

DNA probes are being utilized because of their ability to detect infection in asymptomatic patients.

Treatment and Control. Metronidazole is taken orally, and sometimes a metronidazole-containing vaginal suppository is prescribed simultaneously. Regular sex partners of women with vaginal trichomoniasis should also be treated with metronidazole.

Trypanosomiasis *(Trypanosoma* and *Leishmania)*

Blood and tissue flagellate protozoa are collectively referred to as **hemoflagellates.** They appear in two genera: *Trypanosoma* and *Leishmania.* These parasites live alternatively in vertebrate hosts and in bloodsucking insects where they undergo cyclic development. There are four distinct cyclic morphological types: the **amastigote** (leishmanial form), the **promastigote** (leptomonad form), the **epimastigote** (crithidial form), and the **trypomastigote** (trypanosomal form) (Fig. 34-6).

African Trypanosomiasis (African Sleeping Sickness). The *Trypanosoma* species that is medically and economically important is *T. brucei.* It contains three subspecies: *T. brucei gambiense* (chronic sleeping sickness in humans), *T. brucei rhodesiense* (acute sleeping sickness in humans), and *T. brucei brucei* (nagana in cattle).

Pathogenesis. The parasite first lodges in the local tissue where it was introduced by the bite of a **tsetse fly.** After 2 to 3 days there is local inflammation and itching, followed

FIGURE 34-5
Trichomonad.

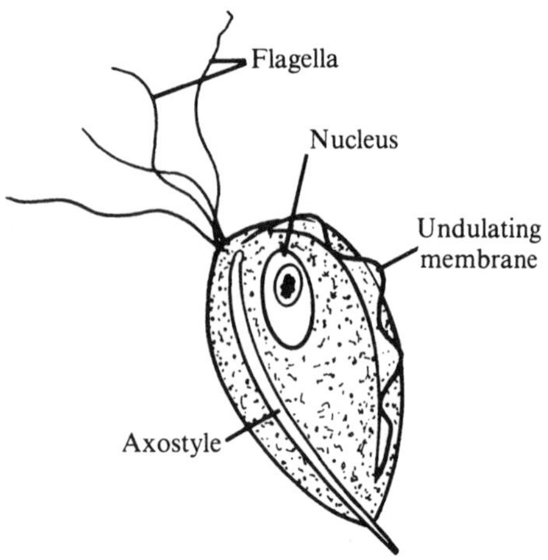

FIGURE 34-6
The body forms of members of the genera *Trypanosoma* and *Leishmania.*

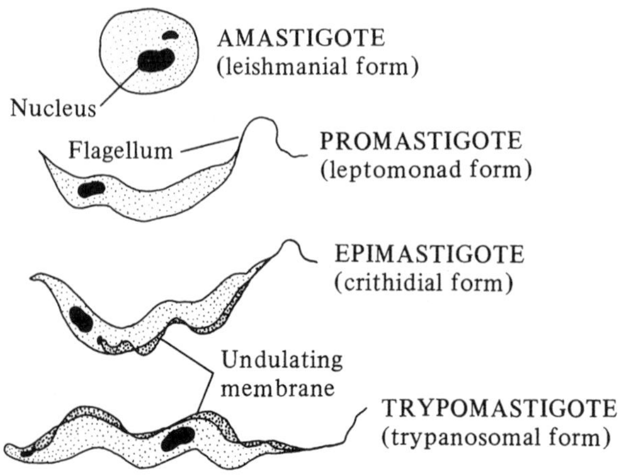

about 4 days later by the development of a chancre. Approximately a week or two after infection the parasite is detectable in the blood. Episodes of parasitemia that last 2 to 3 days follow at intervals of 2 to 10 days. Headaches, joint pain, malaise, and enlarged lymph nodes and spleen accompany the recurring episodes of parasitemia. The second stage of the disease—**sleeping sickness phase**—involves the central nervous system. Insomnia, irritability, personality changes, and decreasing mental acuity precede a gradual loss of central nervous system function. In the advanced stages the patient has convulsions and becomes somnolent and comatose, and eventually dies from malnutrition and secondary infection. Untreated *T. brucei rhodesiense* infections run a course from weeks to months; *T. brucei gambiense* infections, from months to years.

The relapsing parasitemia occurs even though the patient has an elevated IgM response. The parasite is able to evade host defenses by continual variation of its coat of glycoprotein. This variation is brought about by gene arrangement, just as occurs for antibody diversity (see Chapter 10).

Laboratory Diagnosis. A presumptive diagnosis is made on the basis of geographical history and clinical signs and symptoms. A clinical sign, named **Winterbottom's sign,** is enlarged lymph nodes of the posterior cervical triangle. In the laboratory, stained preparations of blood, spinal fluid, and lymph node and bone marrow aspirates are examined for the typical spindle-shaped parasites. If the smears do not demonstrate the parasites, 1 ml of the patient's blood is injected intraperitoneally into rats. The rat's blood is examined in two weeks for the parasites. A variety of serological tests can be used to determine IgM levels. Indirect fluorescent antibody testing is the most commonly used technique.

Epidemiology. **Tsetse flies** transmit *T. brucei rhodesiense* and *gambiense* to humans. A wide range of wild game animals and domestic animals serve as reservoir hosts for *T. brucei rhodesiense. T. brucei gambiense* supposedly is not maintained in nature by animal reservoir hosts, so its cycle involves only humans and tsetse flies.

Treatment and Control. Gambian sleeping sickness is now treated with difluoromethylornithine (eflornithine), a drug that is an irreversible inhibitor of ornithine decarboxylase. Patients with hemolymphatic disease as well as those with encephalitis respond to the drug. Because of the many lives this new drug has saved, it has been called the "resurrection drug." In the Rhodesian form of disease, the very toxic drugs suramin and pentamidine are still used in treatment. Neither drug is effective in reaching the central nervous system. The drug melarsoprol B, an arsenical, is used to treat Rhodesian encephalitis. The drug, however, causes a frequently fatal encephalitis in about 5 percent of those being treated.

Control is achieved primarily through the use of insecticides and modification of the tsetse fly's principal habitat, namely, the dense vegetation along rivers and in forests.

American Trypanosomiasis (Chagas' Disease)

Pathogenesis. Two clinical forms of the disease are recognized: **acute** and **chronic.** In acute disease an inflammatory lesion called a **chagoma** develops at the site of parasite entry. The lesion spreads regionally, producing lymphadenopathy. Cycles of parasite multiplication, cell destruction, and reinfection occur within cells of the reticuloendothelial system. Biochemical changes in cells precede morphological changes. Most persons with acute disease have only mild symptoms. Severe symptoms appear primarily in children and include unilateral painless periorbital edema **(Romaña's sign)** and conjunctivitis. Severe myocarditis develops in a small number of patients. Only a small percentage of patients with acute disease die from complications associated with acute myocarditis or meningoencephalitis. Most patients with acute disease recover within three to four months and most are unaware of having acute illness.

Chronic disease often occurs years after acute infection and is associated with cardiomyopathy. Apical aneurysm is usually found in the left ventricle. Chronic disease is typically characterized by heart enlargement and congestive heart failure. It may also involve the gastrointestinal tract. The colon is frequently dilated and enlarged, as may be the esophagus and gallbladder.

Laboratory Diagnosis. Diagnosis is usually made by the detection of parasites during the acute stages of infection. Active trypomastigotes can be observed in anticoagulated blood or in Giemsa-stained blood smears. If these procedures are not successful, a blood specimen can be inoculated into mice. Blood specimens from the mice are observed microscopically for parasites over a period of a few weeks.

A last-resort identification for acute disease called **xenodiagnosis** can be used. Several dozen laboratory-reared reduviid bugs that transmit disease are fed blood from the person suspected of having acute disease. Thirty to 40 days later the bug's intestinal contents are examined microscopically for parasites. This approach, however, is not totally sensitive for chronic disease.

Diagnosis of chronic Chagas' disease is based on detecting specific antibodies that bind to *T. cruzi* antigens. The assays used include complement fixation, indirect immunofluorescence, and ELISA.

Epidemiology. T. cruzi is an important cause of heart disease in Latin America. Approximately 10 to 20 million people are infected with this parasite and 50,000 deaths annually are associated with the infection. Natural transmission of *T. cruzi* is associated with the bite of the **reduviid bug.** The bug is called the assassin bug or kissing bug in the United States, barbieros in Brazil, and vinchucas in Spanish-speaking South America. Humans, domesticated animals, and wild animals are the most important vertebrate hosts. Cats and dogs serve as the main reservoirs for humans. The reduviid bug deposits excreta containing infectious trypomastigotes that contaminate the bite site.

Transmission via blood transfusion is common in areas

of endemicity and has been reported in the United States and Canada. Chronic symptomatic disease is observed in the United States among the many immigrants from South and Central America. Congenital disease associated with premature birth and abortion has been reported from South America.

Treatment and Control. Nifurtimox and benznidazole are the two drugs used to treat *T. cruzi* infection. The drugs reduce the severity of acute infection but have no effect on chronic disease. Both drugs are toxic with major side effects. Education, construction of reduviid-proof housing, and spraying for insect control are among the preventive measures being pursued.

Leishmaniasis

Leishmaniasis is a worldwide disease whose distribution is limited by the distribution of the vector in warm climates. The disease is transmitted by **sandflies.** The parasite is an intracellular one that survives and multiplies within the phagolysosomes of macrophages. Intracellular parasitism may remain local or spread to mucocutaneous tissues or visceral organs. Several species of *Leishmania* are associated with three clinically different manifestations of disease: **cutaneous, mucocutaneous,** and **visceral.**

Cutaneous Leishmaniasis. In cutaneous leishmaniasis (also called **Oriental sore**), an ulcerating lesion develops at the site of each inoculating insect bite (Fig. 34-7, panel

FIGURE 34-7
Manifestations of leishmaniasis. Panel 1: American cutaneous lesion on the wrist before therapy. Panel 2: Same lesion after 20 days of antimony sodium gluconate (Pentostam) therapy. Panel 3: Same lesion 5 weeks after the end of therapy. Panel 4: Mucosal lesion of the pharynx. Panel 5: Visceral lesion before therapy. Hepatosplenomegaly is outlined. (From J. Berman, *Rev. Infect. Dis.* 10:560, 1988.)

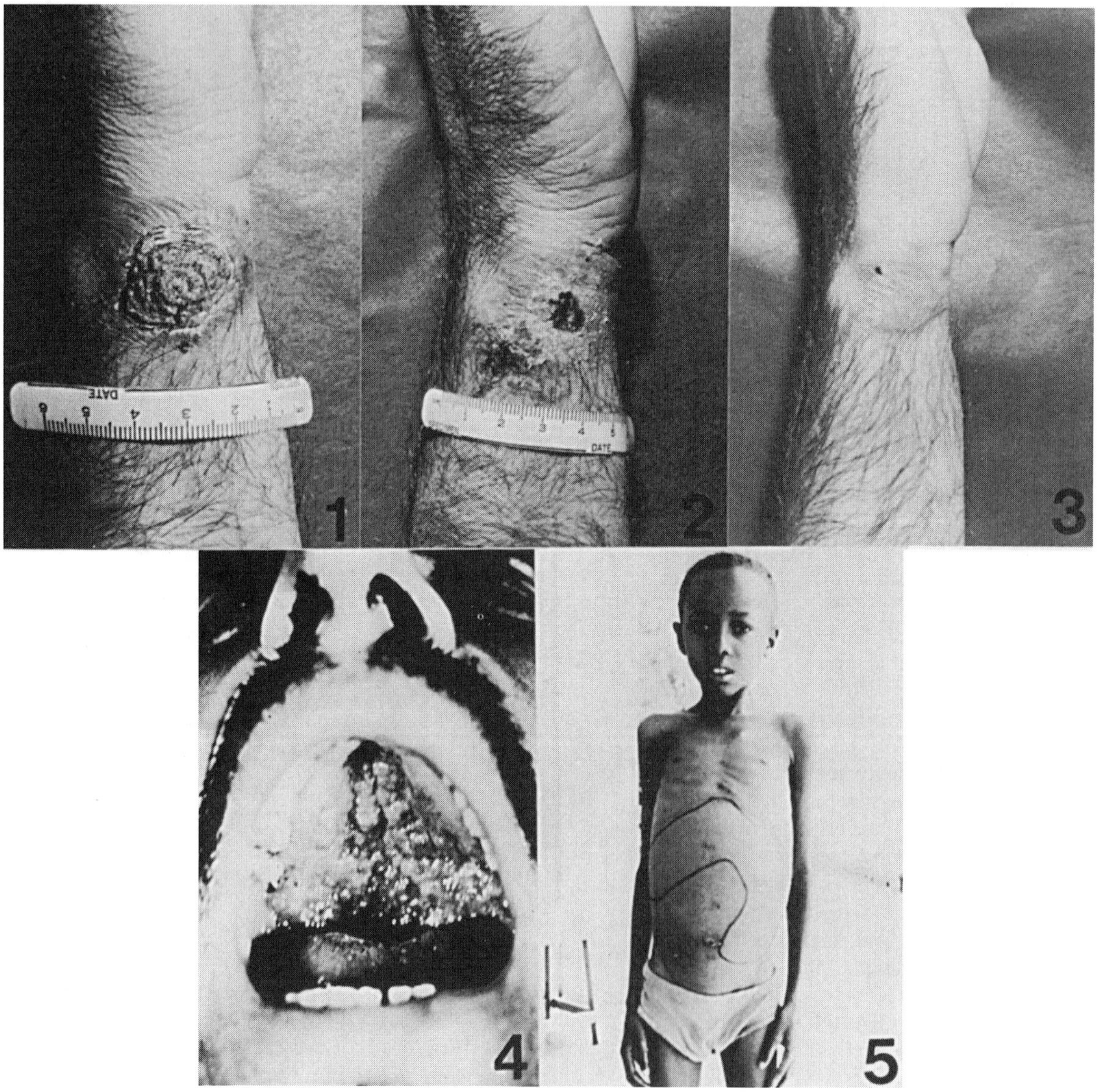

1). The ulcer may become secondarily infected. A permanent depigmented scar develops 9 to 12 months later in untreated patients. The species most often associated with cutaneous disease are *Leishmania major, L. aethiopica, L. tropica, L. braziliensis* subspecies, and *L. mexicana* subspecies.

Mucocutaneous Leishmaniasis. The primary lesion of mucocutaneous leishmaniasis (also called **espundia** and **chiclero ulcer**) resembles the lesion of cutaneous leishmaniasis. The parasite may metastasize to secondary foci, particularly to mucocutaneous junctions, for example, in the vicinity of the nares. Lesions of the oronasal mucosa also occur (Fig. 34-7, panel 4). The lesions that develop at secondary foci are often extensive, erosive, and disfiguring. *L. braziliensis* is responsible for mucocutaneous disease.

Visceral Leishmaniasis (Kala-azar). Visceral leishmaniasis is caused by *L. donovani, L. chagasi,* and *L. infantum.* Phagocytes are stuffed with the amastigote parasites, resulting in enlargement of the spleen, lymph nodes, and other infected organs. There is an accompanying reduction of neutrophils (granulocytopenia), rendering the patient subject to intercurrent infections of the lungs and digestive tract that may be fatal.

Diagnosis and Treatment. Leishmaniasis is diagnosed by demonstrating the organisms in stained smears from lesions or in biopsy tissue. Antimonial compounds (antimony sodium gluconate [Pentostam] or N-methylglucamine [Glucantime]) have been used to treat all forms of leishmaniasis but these drugs are very toxic. In addition, many patients do not respond to them. Alternative drugs that are being used include pentamidine, amphotericin B, allopurinol, and ketoconazole. Lipid-encapsulated amphotericin B is particularly effective in the treatment of visceral leishmaniasis. The lipid-encapsulated drug has a high therapeutic index for visceral leishmaniasis because reticuloendothelial cells (the site where *Leishmania* are found) phagocytize and concentrate the complex. The drug interacts with ergosterol or episterol, which are major membrane sterols in *Leishmania.*

CILIATA—THE CILIATED PROTOZOA

Balantidiasis (Ciliary Dysentery)

Balantidium coli is the only ciliated protozoan that is pathogenic to humans. It is the largest protozoan to infect humans. *B. coli* is a common parasite of swine and of several lower primates. From 60 to 90 percent of hogs harbor *B. coli* or *Balantidium suis.* The latter is more common in hogs. *B. coli* infection in humans is rare. The chief symptom is diarrhea in varying severity. Occasionally a dysentery, termed balantidial dysentery or ciliary dysentery, develops. Diagnosis is based on the identification of the characteristic trophozoites and cysts in diarrheic or formed stools. Iodoquinol and oxytetracycline are used for treatment.

SPOROZOA—THE SPOROZOITE-FORMING PROTOZOA

Sporozoa have no special organelles of locomotion. They have a complex life cycle that includes sexual and asexual generations. The most important sporozoite (animal spore)-forming genera are *Plasmodium,* which contains species that cause malaria, and *Toxoplasma.*

Malaria—Plasmodiasis

Four species of *Plasmodium* are responsible for malaria: *P. falciparum* (**malignant tertian** or **falciparum malaria**), *P. vivax* (**benign tertian** or **vivax malaria**), *P. malariae* (**quartan malaria**), and *P. ovale* (**ovale malaria**).

Life Cycle. A knowledge of the malaria life cycle (Fig. 34-8) aids in understanding the clinical events, treatment, and control measures. The two phases in the life cycle of the malarial parasite are sporogony and schizogony.

FIGURE 34-8
Malaria life cycle. Sporozoites are injected by a female *Anopheles* mosquito as it takes a blood meal. Sporozoites enter liver hepatocytes and form schizonts. Schizonts release merozoites into the blood. Merozoites invade red blood cells (RBC) where they develop sequentially into ring forms and gametocytes (sexual parasites). Male and female gametocytes are taken up in the blood meal of the mosquito and transform into male and female gametes. Fertilization occurs and the zygotes develop into ookinetes, which invade the gut of the mosquito where sporozoites form within oocysts. Sporozoites migrate to the salivary glands of the mosquito to infect humans during the next blood meal. (From T. J. Hadley, F. W. Klotz, and L. H. Miller, *Annu. Rev. Microbiol.* 40:451, 1986.)

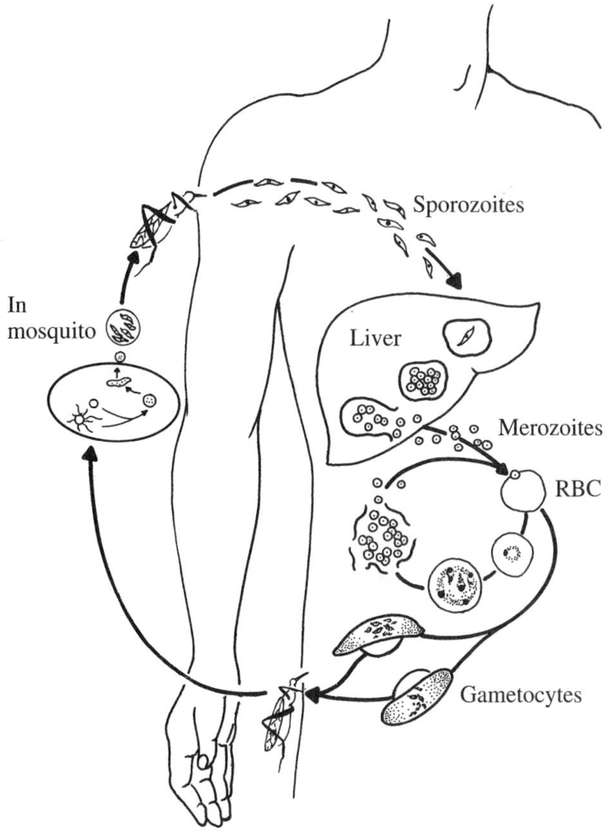

Sporogony is the sexual phase that occurs in the female *Anopheles* mosquito. This cycle is initiated when the mosquito, while consuming a "blood meal" from an infected individual, takes in red blood cells that contain both male and female gametocytes of the malaria parasite (Fig. 34-8). The sexual phase results in the formation of **sporozoites,** which ultimately reach the salivary glands. The mosquito injects the sporozoites into its next victim and within minutes liver cells become infected by them.

The second stage of the life cycle or **schizogony** takes place in the primate or human host. Schizogony (nuclear division and increase in cytoplasmic volume) occurs twice in the host. The first schizogony occurs in the cells of the liver. On reaching maturity the mature schizont ruptures and releases **merozoites** into the bloodstream where they invade erythrocytes. The second schizogony occurs in the erythrocytes. The clinical manifestations of chills and fever are associated with the release of succeeding generations of merozoites from erythrocytes. Male and female gametocytes are produced after two or more cycles and they are taken up by the mosquito. In the mosquito the gametocytes develop into gametes and fertilization occurs. The resulting zygotes develop into ookinetes, which migrate through the stomach wall of the mosquito to form oocysts on the outside of the midgut. Each oocyst matures with nuclei dividing repeatedly and then bursts releasing thousands of motile sporozoites. Sporozoites then travel to the salivary glands, awaiting transfer to another human host.

Pathogenesis. The infected individual experiences the outbursts of malaria in conjunction with the synchronous release of the merozoites. In vivax malaria, synchronous showers of merozoites are released every 48 hours. Vivax malaria is therefore called **tertian malaria** because the interval spans three days. **Falciparum malaria** is also a tertian malaria, although the interval may be less than 48 hours, giving rise to the term **subtertian malaria.** Malaria caused by *P. malariae* is called **quartan malaria** because the episodes occur every 72 hours. *P. falciparum* causes the most severe form of the disease.

In a malarial attack the patient initially experiences chills for 15 to 60 minutes. These symptoms are associated with the release of a progeny of merozoites. This is usually accompanied by headache, nausea, and vomiting. Succeeding the chills is a febrile stage of several hours' duration. Temperatures sometimes spike to 105 F or higher. Profuse sweating concludes the attack. The exhausting episode induces sleep, from which the patient awakens with a feeling of comparative well-being.

The infections may be asymptomatic, severely enfeebling, or fatal. When the red blood cell ruptures, malarial pigments, hemoglobin, and metabolites of the parasite are also released. These products are taken up, especially by the reticuloendothelial system. They account for the marked pigmentation and enlargement seen in the spleen, liver, lymph nodes, and bone marrow. The parasitized red blood cells become sticky and plug up the smaller vessels, especially in patients with falciparum malaria. The obstructive action of the "sludge blood" has a variety of effects: tissue anoxia and necrosis, bursting of vessels, electrolyte imbalance, and other vessel-associated pathology. Many organs including the brain (cerebral malaria) and kidneys may be affected.

Severe malaria (blood vessel occlusion) occurs exclusively in nonimmune persons, that is, children or visitors to areas where *P. falciparum* is endemic. There is evidence that **tumor necrosis factor (TNF)** plays an important role in the pathophysiology of severe malaria. Acquired immunity to malaria develops in persons exposed to high levels of parasite transmission. At least three to five years of exposure to heavy transmission is required to endow one with partial immunity.

Laboratory Diagnosis. The definitive diagnosis of malaria rests on finding the typical parasite forms in stained blood smears. The experienced malariologist is able to differentiate the plasmodial species because of differences in trophozoite forms, malarial pigment, numbers of merozoites, character of the infected red blood cells, and other differences.

Epidemiology. Three billion persons live in areas that are endemic for malaria. Acute disease develops in 3 million persons every year and 3.5 million die from this disease. Most deaths are associated with Africa. For example, the World Health Organization (WHO) estimates that 1 million African children below the age of 5 years die from malaria each year.

The number of cases in the United States in 1992 was 1087. Most civilian cases are imported through travelers and immigrants. Malaria transmitted by drug addict practices falls into the category of **transfusion malaria.** Such an infection incidentally occurs only in the erythrocytic cycle; that is, there is no liver stage to the infection.

Treatment and Control. Chemotherapy may be applied for prophylaxis, for suppression or prevention of an attack in an infected person, or for cure. The two mainstays of chemotherapy are **chloroquine** (used for the erythrocytic stage) and **primaquine phosphate** (used for the liver or exerythrocytic stage). It is necessary to eliminate the tissue phase in order to prevent relapses (see Under the Microscope 48). Unfortunately, *P. falciparum* acquires resistance to the action of all antimalarial drugs. Quinine (from the cinchona bark), which was used for centuries for the treatment of malaria, is now used only to treat *P. falciparum* malaria, particularly severe forms of the disease. It is particularly effective for sensitive infections.

Mefloquine is an alternative to quinine when *P. falciparum* resistance to chloroquine is likely. Mefloquine is recommended for all travelers at risk of infection with chloroquine-resistant *P. falciparum.* Halofantrine is a drug, unlicensed in the United States, that is available in France and in many countries of Asia and Africa.

Many research centers are engaged in the development of a malaria vaccine. There has not been much success because of the variability of the parasites' antigens. Most investigators believe that an effective vaccine will be multivalent and will induce immunity against several stages of the life cycle at once.

UNDER THE MICROSCOPE 48

Malaria Relapse and the Hypnozoite

One of the aspects of infection by *Plasmodium* species is the appearance of relapses. Relapse of malaria refers to the reappearance of parasites in the blood of a patient with sporozoite-induced infection, following adequate therapy to destroy schizonts. A true malaria relapse is associated with a **tissue phase** and not an erythrocytic phase.

For many years a variety of theories were proposed to explain relapses of malaria. These theories included (1) parthenogenesis of macrogametocytes—that is, a modification of sexual reproduction in which an organism develops from an unfertilized egg; (2) persistence of schizonts in the blood where their multiplication is inhibited by immunity and this immunity disappears; and (3) reactivation of an encysted body in the blood. These theories have now been discounted.

Relapse is now believed to be due to the presence of a **uninucleate** stage of the parasite, called the **hypnozoite (sleeping animal).** The hypnozoite can be detected in liver cells by immunofluorescence and is present from 3 to 229 days after sporozoite inoculation. Hypnozoites are present in all *Plasmodium* species that cause relapsing malaria (*P. vivax* and *P. ovale*) and absent in those that do not cause relapsing fever (*P. falciparum* and *P. malariae*). Therefore, hypnozoites represent a latent tissue stage that may be induced to undergo development and produce the symptoms of malaria.

Mosquito control measures include the destruction of mosquito larval forms, the elimination of mosquito breeding places, and the use of netting and repellents.

Toxoplasmosis

Toxoplasma gondii is the causative agent of the disease called toxoplasmosis. The disease can be acquired by immunocompetent as well as immunocompromised individuals such as AIDS patients.

Life Cycle. Members of the cat family serve as the **definitive host** in the life cycle of *Toxoplasma* organisms. Reproduction takes place in the intestinal epithelium of the cat by schizogony, which leads ultimately to the formation of **oocysts.** Oocysts are passed in the feces. Under suitable conditions, four sporozoites develop within the oocyst. The oocyst is highly resistant to environmental conditions and can remain viable in nature for up to 18 months (Fig. 34-9).

Millions of oocysts can be shed by a single cat. Oocysts can be ingested by humans and various animals. From the oocysts ingested by animals develop extraintestinal forms of the organism referred to as trophozoites (tachyzoites) and bradyzoites. These forms remain in the body

FIGURE 34-9
Toxoplasma gondii cycle in the definitive host. Felidae = cat family.

Infection of Felidae	Ingestion of Tachyzoites in flesh of warm-blooded animals or Bradyzoites in flesh of warm-blooded animals or Sporozoites from cat feces
	↓
Oocyst formation in Felidae	After schizogony and gametogony, zygotes are formed in oocysts that are found in gut epithelium of cats
	↓
Shedding of oocysts	After a 3- to 24-day prepatent period (from initial infection to shedding), oocysts are shed in feces
	↓
Sporozoite formation in oocysts	After several days in soil, mature, infective sporozoites are formed in oocysts and remain infective for months under proper conditions of moisture and temperature

tissue and humans can acquire them via ingestion of the infected flesh of warm-blooded animals.

Pathogenesis. Most human infections by *T. gondii* are asymptomatic. In a small percentage of infected individuals the major symptoms are **lymphadenopathy** and **hepatosplenomegaly.** The symptoms often resemble mononucleosis or the flu. Trophozoites first invade the intestinal mucosa and may invade any organ of the body. **Tissue cysts** develop in various organs after primary infection and are accompanied by immunity. These dormant cysts can be reactivated in patients who become immunosuppressed, in AIDS patients, or in those with cancer of the lymphatic system.

Reactivation often leads to disseminated disease. In AIDS patients, the primary site of infection by *T. gondii* is the central nervous system, followed by the lungs. In approximately one-third of patients with positive anti-*Toxoplasma* IgG antibodies, toxoplasmic encephalitis will develop. Infection in both of these sites (central nervous system and lungs) is often fatal, particularly infection of the central nervous system.

Transplacentally acquired (congenital) infections can occur when a woman has a primary infection during pregnancy. The mother rarely is symptomatic. However, in the period when she has parasitemia, *Toxoplasma*-containing cysts may form in the placenta. In the placenta the parasite causes a generalized infection of the fetus. Infection occurs in about 50 percent of fetuses in mothers who have a primary infection during pregnancy. Less than 1 percent of the infected infants have disease sequelae. The infants who do show symptoms have a wide range of illnesses, including chorioretinitis, cerebral calcifications, hydrocephalus, severe thrombocytopenia, and convulsions. Mental retardation and grave visual handicaps are among the outcomes of these conditions. Some congenitally infected children who are normal at birth are latently infected and progressively develop retinal scarring around the age of 3 to 4 years.

Laboratory Diagnosis. In acute infection parasites are in the blood and body tissues. Diagnosis can be based on cell culture, infecting mice with material from appropriate specimens, or gene amplification. Serological diagnosis is preferred to having patients undergo a biopsy. The most frequently used serological test is called the **Sabin-Feldman dye test.** In this test the anti-*Toxoplasma* antibodies in the patient's serum prevent the uptake of methylene blue dye by live trophozoites. The trophozoites are stained by the dye without specific antibodies.

Serological tests alone are not useful for diagnosis in patients with AIDS. Current diagnosis in AIDS patients relies on a compatible clinical presentation, serological evidence of exposure to *T. gondii*, and the discovery of cerebral lesions through computed tomography. Diagnosis is only confirmed if clinical and tomographic responses with specific treatment are observed within 20 days. Rapid diagnosis is needed and several tests are being evaluated, including polymerase chain reaction and DNA probes for detecting infection of cerebrospinal fluid.

Epidemiology. Approximately 50 percent of the world's population is believed to be infected with *T. gondii*. Sandboxes, flower beds, and other places where feces are deposited serve as sources of infection for humans. Besides fecal contamination of water and food, inadequately cooked meat can be an important source of infection. As indicated earlier, transplacental infection can occur in humans (as well as other animals).

Treatment and Control. The combination of pyrimethamine and sulfadiazine is the standard therapy for acute toxoplasmosis. The drugs are effective against trophozoites but not cyst forms. For individuals sensitive to sulfa drugs, clindamycin is an alternative to sulfadiazine.

Practical recommendations that can reduce the incidence of acquisition by as much as 90 percent are especially pertinent to pregnant women. The recommendations include careful handling of raw meat and heating of meat to 150 F throughout, daily cleaning of cat litter boxes, disinfection of litter pans with boiling water, covering of sandboxes when they are not in use, wearing of gloves for gardening, and thorough washing of homegrown vegetables if they are to be eaten raw.

Babesiosis (Nantucket Fever)

Babesiosis is a malaria-like illness that is caused by *Babesia microti*. The organism infects red blood cells and is transmitted by the same ticks that are the primary vector of Lyme disease. *Babesia* infections can also be acquired by transfusions from infected donors.

The first North American case of human babesiosis was recognized in 1966. Endemic foci of infections are now recognized in Massachusetts (Nantucket Island, Martha's Vineyard, and Cape Cod), Rhode Island, and New York. The tick life cycle involves the white-footed mouse, the preferred host for the larval form. The nymph stage is the stage that most commonly transmits the disease to humans. The nymph becomes an adult whose preferred host is the white-tailed deer. At this point the cycle is completed with the deposition of eggs and death of the adult tick.

Human babesiosis is characterized by prolonged symptoms of fever and anemia. Infection varies from inapparent, subclinical infection to fatal disease. Advanced age and history of splenectomy or immunosuppression appear to be important risk factors for the development of severe disease. Diagnosis is based on the patient's history and Wright-Giemsa staining of peripheral blood for the appearance of intraerythrocytic parasites. Treatment relies on the use of clindamycin and quinine.

Cryptosporidiosis

Cryptosporidium organisms are coccidian (see Under the Microscope 49) parasites that are recognized worldwide as gastrointestinal pathogens involved in waterborne epidemics, day-care center outbreaks, traveler's diarrhea, and severe disease in immunocompromised patients (AIDS patients, for example). *Cryptosporidium* species are important causes of gastroenteritis in animals (Fig. 34-10).

UNDER THE MICROSCOPE 49

Coccidia and *Isospora belli*

The coccidia are a subclass of Sporozoa and include the parasites *Cryptosporidium, Toxoplasma gondii,* and *Isospora belli. I. belli* causes diarrhea in immunocompetent and immunocompromised hosts. The parasite is associated with enteric disease in Haiti, Africa, and Latin America. In the United States, infections are observed more often in immunocompromised hosts such as AIDS patients. Unlike most protozoan infections, these infections may be associated with **eosinophilia.** Like *Cryptosporidium, I. belli* is identified by acid-fast staining of stool specimens. Unlike *Cryptosporidium,* acute infections with *I. belli* can be effectively treated with trimethoprim-sulfamethoxazole. Relapses occur in up to one-half of the treated patients. Chronic maintenance regimens are therefore required in immunocompromised patients.

Pathogenesis. Cryptosporidiosis in immunocompetent and immunocompromised hosts results in a watery diarrhea. In immunocompetent hosts the infection resolves in less than one month but in immunocompromised patients the diarrhea becomes unrelenting. Other symptoms include fatigue, nausea, and vomiting. In immunocompromised patients the loss of fluids may reach 3 to 6 liters per day. Untreated, this condition can lead to malnutrition and dehydration.

Laboratory Diagnosis. The mainstay of diagnosis of *Cryptosporidium* infection has been modified acid-fast staining of feces. Acid-fast oocysts stain red and fecal debris, blue or green depending on the counterstain.

Epidemiology. Cryptosporidiosis is transmitted to humans by oocysts that are present in the feces of farm animals, mice, birds, and other animals. The disease is known to be endemic in many cattle herds. Human disease is frequently associated with the ingestion of contaminated water, particularly in developing countries. Disease in day-care centers usually involves children less than 3 years old, in diapers, and not toilet trained. Transmission of disease may also be through contact with infected individuals.

FIGURE 34-10
Scanning electron micrograph of two fused atrophied villi from the ileum of a *Cryptosporidium*-infected calf. (From J. Heine, J. Pohlenz, H. Moon, and G. Woode, *J. Infect. Dis.* 150:768, 1984.)

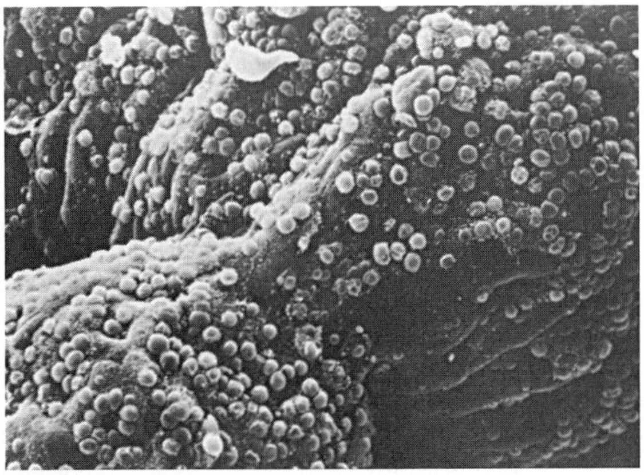

Treatment and Control. Nonspecific treatment relies on the use of antidiarrheal agents, nutritional management, and administration of fluids. Specific chemotherapy has not been shown to be efficacious. The most promising treatment for patients with severe disease is the passive oral transfer of protective antibody in hyperimmune bovine colostrum.

Prevention revolves about maintaining hygienic conditions. Campers, for example, should use boiled or bottled water. In the hospital, health care workers should maintain enteric precautions to prevent transmission from infected patients.

The Nemathelminthes

Members of the animal phylum Nemathelminthes are referred to as **roundworms** because they are oval in cross section. Their body form is elongated and cylindrical, tapering at both ends. Unlike the earthworm, they are nonsegmented. They have a well developed digestive tract. The sexes are separate. A summary of the helminth diseases described in this chapter is presented in Table 34-3.

ASCARIASIS (ROUNDWORM INFECTION)

Ascaris lumbricoides is the largest intestinal nematode to infect humans. The adult worms are 8 to 12 inches long. They resemble the earthworms in size and overall configuration. The males are smaller than the females and have an incurved tail.

Pathogenesis

The larvae in ingested eggs hatch in the duodenum. They then penetrate the mucosa and enter the blood and lymph systems. The larvae are transported to the lungs where they can cause hemorrhage and inflammation. If the infec-

TABLE 34-3
Characteristics of Helminth Diseases

Disease name and agent	Clinical condition	Infective form; mode of transmission	Specimen examined; diagnostic form	Comments	Treatment
Ascariasis *Ascaris lumbricoides*	Most comon in children; abdominal pain; occasionally symptomatology due to obstruction or worm migration	*Eggs* Feces-contaminated food or soil	*Stool* Eggs		Mebendazole or pyrantel pamoate
Hookworm *Necator americanus* *Ancylostoma duodenale*	Epigastric pain, anemia	*Larvae* Larvae in soil or on vegetation penetrate skin	*Stool* Eggs	Sanitary disposal of most human feces is most effective control measure	Mebendazole or pyrantel pamoate
Strongyloidiasis *Strongyloides stercoralis*	Watery, mucous diarrhea	*Larvae* Larvae in soil or on vegetation penetrate skin	*Stool* Eggs	Only nematode worm that can reproduce in host; free-living phase and parasitic phase	Thiobendazole
Enterobiasis *Enterobius vermicularis*	Anal pruritus	*Eggs* Ingestion of eggs	*Anal contact specimen* Eggs	Called *pinworm* or *seatworm infection*	Mebendazole or pyrantel pamoate
Trichinelliasis *Trichinella spiralis*	Fever, myalgia, periorbital edema	*Larvae* Ingestion of meat from pigs, bear, walrus	*Muscle biopsy, serum* Curled-up larvae in muscle; antibodies	Called *muscle worm infection*	Steroids for severe symptoms; thiabendazole for adult stage
Schistosomiasis *Schistosoma mansoni, haematobium*	Fever, lymph node and liver enlargement; obstruction of venous vessels of urinary bladder, liver, intestines	*Larvae (cercariae)* Larvae in snail-infested waters penetrate skin	*Stool, rectal biopsy* Eggs		Praziquantel
Taeniasis *Taenia saginata* (beef) *Taenia solium* (pork)	Tapeworm infection; adult worm infection usually asymptomatic; symptoms (beef); epigastric fullness, nausea	*Larvae (cysticercus)* Ingestion of raw or undercooked beef or pork	*Stool* Eggs or worm segments	Cysticercus larvae of *T. solium* (bladderworm) may cause serious CNS infection (cysticercosis)	Praziquantel, albendazole alternative for neurocysticerocsis
Diphyllobothriasis *Diphyllobothrium latum*	Fish tapeworm; usually asymptomatic; abdominal discomfort, diarrhea, anemia	*Larvae (plerocercoid)* Ingestion of raw or undercooked fish	*Stool* Eggs or worm segments		Niclosamide

tion is severe enough, a pneumonitis or asthma-like response can be generated.

Larvae move from the lungs up the respiratory tree to the esophagus where they are swallowed. Adult worms develop in the intestine, where they may cause minor intestinal symptoms. Because of their tendency to probe and wander, they may obstruct the excretory ducts of the pancreas or the biliary tract or they may appear in other parts of the body. The majority of people are rarely symptomatic. Heavy infections are found more often in children and tend to produce toxic symptoms or intestinal obstruction. Combinations of *Ascaris, Trichuris,* and hookworm in the same individual are not uncommon in areas of hyperendemism. These vitality-sapping parasitic infec-

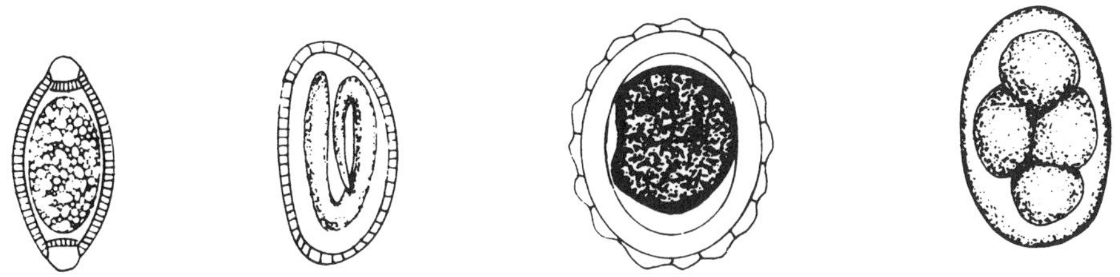

Trichuris trichiura *Enterobius vermicularis* *Ascaris lumbricoides* Hookworm

FIGURE 34-11
Nematode eggs.

tions, compounded by malnutrition that is ever present in economically depressed areas, may produce physical and mental retardation.

Laboratory Diagnosis

The identification of the typical fertilized or unfertilized eggs in the feces is diagnostic (Fig. 34-11).

Epidemiology

A. lumbricoides is found worldwide. It is thought to infect some one billion people. Virtually all members of the population in some areas of the world harbor the parasite. Fecal contamination and the use of human excreta as fertilizer are mainly responsible for the maintenance of the parasite in regions where ascariasis is endemic. Each female worm produces 200,000 eggs per day. Infective larvae develop in about two to four weeks in fertilized eggs that have been deposited in the soil. The eggs remain viable for months, possibly as long as 10 years. Immigrants from areas where ascariasis is highly endemic do not pose a threat because adequate sewage disposal prevents exposure of the public to the infective eggs.

Treatment and Control

Mebendazole or pyrantel pamoate is the drug of choice. If there is a heavy *Ascaris* worm burden, the compacted worms may cause intestinal obstruction. This condition requires surgical intervention. There is no specific anthelmintic (antiworm) drug for the larvae during the period of migration. The control of ascariasis, as with other helminthic infections, depends on education and chemotherapy.

Visceral Larva Migrans

Larvae of nematodes that infect other mammalian species sometimes infect humans, but they are unable to develop into adult worms. They survive for a time to migrate through organs of the body (**visceral larva migrans**) or to tunnel through the skin (**cutaneous larva migrans**); see Hookworm Infection. In visceral larva migrans there may be fever, infiltration of the lungs, hepatomegaly, hyperglobulinemia, and granuloma formation in the brain, eye, lungs, and other organs. Visceral larva migrans is most likely to occur in children between the ages of 1 and 5 years who are in contact with pets or who have **pica** (an unnatural craving for bizarre food such as dirt). Most often implicated are dog and cat ascarids (close relatives of *A. lumbricoides*) in the genus *Toxocara*. *Toxocara canis* is found in at least 20 percent of the 30 million dogs in the United States.

HOOKWORM INFECTION

Human hookworm infection is usually caused by one of two nematodes, *Necator americanus* (New World hookworm) or *Ancylostoma duodenale* (Old World hookworm). Infection is acquired when filariform larvae (larval forms of certain nematodes) that have developed from eggs deposited in the soil penetrate the skin. The larvae find their way to the tops of grass blades, rocks, and so on, increasing their chances to contact skin. They enter the venous circulation, sojourn through the lung, migrate up the respiratory tract over the epiglottis, and are swallowed. It is in the jejunum where the larvae develop into adults.

Pathogenesis

Classically, individuals who carry a heavy hookworm burden are markedly anemic and have low serum iron. Loss of proteins of the blood in already malnourished people adds to the debility. Severe, protracted, or repetitive infections, of children especially, may lead to stunting of physical growth and mental retardation.

Laboratory Diagnosis

Routine diagnosis is based on identification of the eggs in feces (see Fig. 34-11).

Epidemiology

Hookworm is prevalent in tropical and temperate climates. In the United States it is found primarily along the Atlantic seaboard. Hookworm infection in the United States has declined so that it is no longer a public health problem.

Treatment and Control

Mebendazole is the drug of choice, as it is for most non-tissue-invasive, lumen-dwelling parasites. Pyrantel pamoate likewise is effective. It is necessary to remedy the malnutrition and the loss of iron in the severely diseased. Control is difficult where hookworm is hyperendemic be-

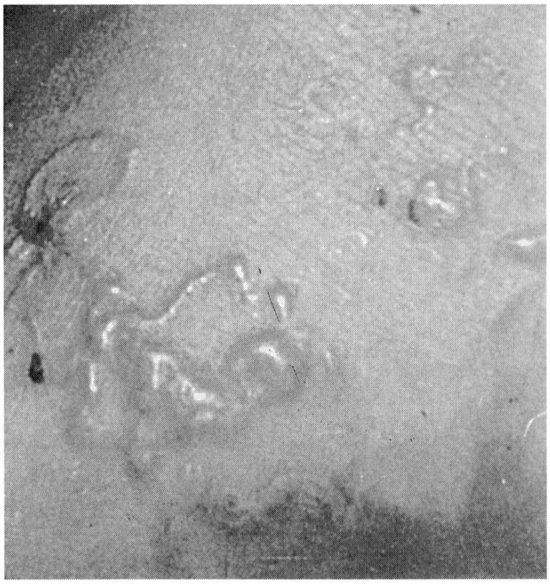

FIGURE 34-12
Creeping eruption in a human being. This dermatosis is caused by larval hookworms of the species *Ancylostoma braziliense, Unicinaria stenocephala,* and perhaps *Ancylostoma caninum,* all of which are natural parasites of dogs and cats. The infective larvae apparently penetrate the skin but are unable to pierce through the dermis. (From W. Orris. In A. A. Fisher, ed., *Atlas of Aquatic Dermatology.* New York: Grune & Stratton, 1978. Copyright 1978 American Cyanamid Company, Lederle Laboratories Division.)

cause the soil in areas of human habitation is constantly being contaminated with human excreta and the wearing of footwear is not customary. Chemotherapy is, therefore, only temporarily effective and will probably remain so until the population is educated to dispose of human excreta properly.

Cutaneous Larva Migrans

Filariform larvae of dogs and cat hookworm species *(Ancylostoma braziliense* and *Ancylostoma caninum)* and a larvae of nonhuman species of *Strongyloides* penetrate the skin. Those most affected are children, farmers, craftsmen, and others who have contacted warm, moist, sandy soil, especially where dogs and cats have defecated. The larvae burrow into the subcutaneous tissues and produce linear, pruritic, papulovesicular lesions (Fig. 34-12). The condition is referred to as **serpiginous dermatitis, creeping eruption,** or **ground itch.** Secondary bacterial infections may occur as a consequence of the scratching that is done in response to the intense itching. Thiabendazole applied topically is the drug of choice.

STRONGYLOIDIASIS

Strongyloides stercoralis is an intestinal parasite of humans that is associated with a wide range of manifestations.

Life Cycle

The life cycle begins with larvae penetrating the intact skin of a susceptible host. Larvae migrate to a venous or lymphatic channel and are transported to the lungs. In the lungs the larvae break out of the capillaries into the alveoli and migrate upward into the trachea as they mature. Eventually they are swallowed into the stomach. Female parasites lodge themselves in the duodenum and jejunum where they lay eggs daily. Larvae (rhabditiform larvae) emerge from the hatching eggs and are passed in the feces. Depending on environmental conditions, the larvae may molt into infective forms (filariform larvae) that are able to penetrate a host or they may switch to a free-living cycle. In this latter form, the parasite goes through several molts to develop into adult male and female worms. These mate and produce a generation of offspring that can reenter parasitic life.

Some of the intestinal larvae (rhabditiform) can also molt and develop into infective forms (filariform). These infective forms can penetrate the colon, complete their internal cycle, and establish themselves as mature adults in the intestine. This process is referred to as **autoinfection.** Autoinfection enables the parasite to persist indefinitely in the host.

The rate of autoinfection is believed to be regulated by the host's cell-mediated immunity. In an immunocompetent person the parasitic life cycle would remain but the patient would remain asymptomatic. When the cell-mediated immunity regulatory function is compromised (during corticosteroid therapy, for example), increasing numbers of autoinfective larvae complete the cycle and the population of parasitic worms increases. Eventually, the large numbers of migrating larvae disseminate to organs other than the lungs and intestine. Liver, kidneys, brain, lymph nodes, and cutaneous and subcutaneous tissues may become invaded. Hemorrhages occur in these organs and tissues, followed by inflammatory processes. This disseminated form of the disease is often fatal.

Pathogenesis

Most infections are asymptomatic but heavy infections can cause anorexia, diarrhea, ulceration of the mucosa, and anemia. The effects of autoinfection were discussed previously. Bacterial infections that accompany strongyloidiasis frequently cause death in the immunocompromised.

Laboratory Diagnosis

Diagnosis is made by microscopical examinations of stool, duodenal fluid (obtained by the Entero-Test technique), the mucosal biopsy specimens. Immunological tests are based on the ELISA technique.

Epidemiology

S. stercoralis is found especially in warm, moist, tropical climates. The number of infected people in the world is estimated to be 100,000 to 200,000. In the United States it is most common in the rural Southeast.

Treatment

Uncomplicated strongyloidiasis is effectively treated with thiabendazole. Use of antibiotics and intravenous fluid and other supportive measures are also required for the disseminated syndrome.

ENTEROBIASIS (PINWORM OR SEATWORM INFECTION)

Infections caused by *Enterobius vermicularis* are called **enterobiasis** or **oxyuriasis** and in the vernacular **pinworm** or **seatworm** infections. The worms are yellowish-white. Males are 2 to 5 mm long; females, 8 to 13 mm long, with pointed tails.

Pathogenesis

Infections caused by *Enterobius* species are comparatively innocuous. The adult worms inhabit the cecum, ileum, and appendix, where they may cause a mild inflammatory reaction. The chief complaint of seatworm infection is anal pruritus. Restless sleep is another common symptom. Discomfort in the perianal area occurs when the egg-laden female migrates out of the anus, usually during the night, to deposit eggs in the perianal region. The intense itching encourages scratching, which in turn may abrade the area sufficiently to introduce secondary bacterial infection. Furthermore, scratching collects eggs under the fingernails and on the fingers. This can lead to autoinfections or to the contamination of articles that will spread the infection to others. The eggs are found on clothing, bedding, windowsills, floors, and elsewhere in the environment of an infected individual.

Laboratory Diagnosis

The **transparent tape swab method** or digital rectal examination is used to obtain specimens. For the swab method, parents frequently are asked to obtain the specimen when the child first awakens in the morning. The sticky side of the tape is applied several times to the anal area. The tape is then fastened, adhesive side down, to a glass slide. The contact areas are examined under the microscope for the presence of the typical conspicuously flat-sided eggs (see Fig. 34-11). The same technique is sometimes used for tapeworm infections.

Epidemiology

Distribution is worldwide. Humans are the only natural hosts. Enterobiasis is the most common worm infection in temperate climates. The greatest incidence is in children between the ages of 5 and 9 years.

Treatment and Control

Several highly effective and relatively nontoxic drugs can produce a 90 to 100 percent cure rate. Mebendazole and pyrantel paomate are the drugs of choice. The life span of the worm is about one month. Reinfection is not uncommon, so retreatment may be necessary. Scrupulous hygienic practices such as boiling bed linens and disinfecting toilet seats were recommended at one time to rid a family of the pinworms. How effective and how necessary these practices are is questionable, especially in view of the physiological trauma such admonitions may initiate in embarrassed parents. Rather, parents should be told of the commonness of pinworm infection, its relative innocuousness, and the effectiveness of drug treatment.

TRICHINOSIS (MUSCLE WORM INFECTION)

Life Cycle

Several animals serve as hosts for *Trichinella spiralis*, the causative agent of trichinosis. The adult and larval forms appear in the same animal. When flesh that contains live encysted larvae is ingested, the larvae emerge in the duodenum and mature into adults. Impregnated females penetrate the wall of the intestine and start to produce live larvae after about one week. Each female produces about 500 larvae over a two-week period. The larvae enter the capillaries and lymphatics and migrate through the lungs into the heart and the systemic circulation. No tissues are immune to invasion. The heaviest infections are in the striated muscles, but the heart, the central nervous system, and the serous cavities are also favored sites of localization. The larvae coil up in muscle fibers, and the body surrounds the area with a calcified wall in six months to two years (Plate 31). The encysted larvae may remain viable for as long as 10 years. They are at a dead end here unless the flesh is ingested by another host.

Pathogenesis

The symptoms of trichinosis are related to the clinical phase of the infection. During establishment of the adult worms in the intestine, the symptoms—diarrhea, abdominal discomfort, and vomiting—suggest food intoxication or infectious diarrhea. Beginning about the tenth day and reaching a peak in the second to third week, when the larvae are migrating and being filtered out in the muscles, symptoms appear. They include periorbital swelling (occurs in about 80 percent of symptomatic patients), fever (in 90 percent), myalgia (in 80 percent), and rash (in nearly 100 percent). It is estimated that at least 100 larvae are required to initiate symptoms. In the third clinical phase, when the larvae are encysted and the body responds with repair measures, the patient experiences muscle pain, weakness, and cachexia (wasting). The symptoms just described are related primarily to muscle invasion, but no tissue or organ is immune.

Laboratory Diagnosis

Trichinosis should be suspected in patients who have periorbital edema, fever, and myalgia. The likelihood of trichinosis is increased if others who shared the same diet have the typical signs and symptoms. A definitive diagnosis can be made only by detection of the larvae in a muscle biopsy specimen. The biopsy material is taken from a tender swollen muscle. Biopsy is not always necessary if the clinical signs and symptoms are fortified with a positive dietary history, high eosinophil count, and positive serology findings. There is a skin test, but it does not differentiate between past and recent infections.

Epidemiology

Trichinosis formerly was one of the more prevalent worm infections in the United States. Autopsies conducted in the 1930s and early 1940s revealed an incidence of about 16 percent. From 1980 to 1985 the reported morbidity averaged 89 cases each year and mortality averaged fewer than two deaths per year. Rodents are largely responsible for maintaining the infection in nature. A wide variety of carnivores are infected. Humans contract the infection by eating meat that contains viable encysted larvae. During the period 1975 to 1985, pork was implicated in 78.7 percent of reported cases; ground beef, in 6 to 7 percent; and wild animals (wild boar, bear, walrus, etc.), in 13.8 percent.

Treatment and Control

There is no satisfactory treatment for trichinosis. Thiabendazole is useful in the very early intestinal phase of the infection, but the infection is rarely diagnosed at this juncture. Treatment is largely for symptomatic relief: salicylates as a mainstay for pain and corticosteroids for inflammation. Human muscle worm infection has declined in the United States because of education of the public, use of deep freezers, and a decrease in the prevalence of infection in swine. The public is repeatedly urged to cook pork thoroughly, to the point at which none of the meat is pink. An internal temperature of at least 137 F kills trichinae. Deepfreezing of pork at the temperature of the average home freezer (5 F or −15 C) for 20 days destroys the trichina larvae in cuts of meat that are less than 6 inches thick. The enactment in 1952 of a law that required garbage fed to hogs to be cooked reduced the incidence of *Trichinella* infections from between 5 and 10 percent to 0.3 percent in garbage-fed hogs. The incidence in grain-fed swine has decreased from the former 1 percent to 0.1 percent.

About 70 percent of the pork products are processed through federally inspected meat-processing firms. The meat, however, is inspected only macroscopically, since microscopical examination is impractical in the automated American abattoirs. Some infections are traceable to homemade sausages, to small, local meat firms, and to the culinary preferences for raw pork by some ethnic groups. Infected pork may adulterate other types of meats if it is mixed with them, as in hamburger or through the use of a common meat grinder. Smoking, heavy spicing, salting, pickling, and drying of meats do not reliably destroy trichinae.

FILARIASIS

Filariasis is a group of infectious diseases caused by arthropod-borne nematodes. Infections are common in the tropics and constitute a major health problem, particularly in the Indian subcontinent and the South Pacific. Some of the clinically important species are outlined in Table 34-4. As you can see from the table, the adult worms inhabit specific body sites.

Infection of the human host is initiated by the deposition of immature larvae in the skin following the bite of an infected arthropod (mosquito, fly, etc.). Over a period of months to one year, these larvae mature and develop into adult worms that inhabit the lymphatics or subcutaneous tissues. After fertilization by male worms, female worms produce and release live larvae called **microfilariae.** The microfilariae enter the bloodstream or the skin where they can be available for uptake by the intermediate arthropod host.

TABLE 34-4
Characteristics of the Agents of Filariasis

Organism	Geographical distribution	Pathogenicity	Sites of infection	Vector
Wuchereria bancrofti	Asia, South Pacific, Africa, parts of South America	Lymphangitis, fever, elephantiasis	Lymphatics of extremities and genitalia	Mosquito
Brugia malayi	South and East Asia	Lymphangitis, fever, elephantiasis	Lymphatics of extremities	Mosquito
Onchocerca volvulus	Africa, Central and South America	Subcutaneous nodules, ocular complications (river blindness), depigmentation, dermatitis	Subcutaneous tissues	Black fly
Loa loa	Equatorial and West Africa	Skin swellings and allergic reactions	Subcutaneous tissues	Deerfly
Mansonella perstans	Africa and South America	No definite pathogenicity	Subcutaneous tissues, peritoneal cavity	Biting midge
Mansonella ozzardi	Central and South America	No definite pathogencity	Peritoneal cavity	Biting midge
Dipetalonema streptocerca	Africa	Cutaneous edema, elephantiasis	Subcutaneous tissues	Biting midge

SOURCE: J. Nanduri and J. W. Kazura, *Clin. Microbiol. Rev.* 2:39, 1989.

Unlike bacterial, viral, and protozoan pathogens, inoculation of the host with a small number of helminths does not generally result in overt disease. Repeated or acute heavy exposure is required, in large part because adult-stage organisms do not multiply within the host. Filariae are not directly pathogenic but elicit host immune responses that not only may mediate resistance but also may result in disease manifestations. The filariases are debilitating diseases that cause little direct mortality but provoke a spectrum of clinical symptoms. We discuss the pathogenesis of some of the more important species.

Pathogenesis

***Wuchereria bancrofti* and *Brugia malayi*.** These two species are responsible for **lymphatic filariasis.** Some patients may be asymptomatic but others exhibit a range of symptoms including fever, lymphangitis, lymphadenitis, and inflammation of lymphatics of male genitalia (epididymitis, testicular swelling, etc.). The accumulation of fluid in lymph tissue due to obstruction leads to gross enlargement of limbs or genitalia and is referred to as **elephantiasis.** Teenagers and young adults may experience these syndromes, which may last several days and may recur five to eight times per year. Lymphatic filariasis is linked to a rare allergic syndrome called **tropical pulmonary eosinophilia.** Tropical pulmonary eosinophilia is seen more frequently in southern India and is characterized by extreme elevations of serum IgE, high antimicrofilarial antibody titers, nocturnal asthmatic symptoms, and eosinophilia.

***Onchocerca volvulus* (Onchocerciasis).** Onchocerciasis is a disease affecting subcutaneous tissue. The major clinical signs of disease include dermatitis, subcutaneous nodules, lymph node enlargement, and eye disease. Skin disease is manifested as pruritus. Hypopigmentation and hyperpigmentation of the skin are especially common in individuals living in the rain forests of Africa. The subcutaneous nodules or **onchocercomata** contain adult worms. The nodules are painless and several centimeters in diameter. They tend to be localized near the pelvis in Africans and the upper torso and head in Central Americans. Lymphatic disease is less common than filariasis and tends to occur in the femoral or inguinal area. A severe form of lymphatic disease is called "hanging groin." Ocular disease is the most devastating manifestation of infection and is referred to as **river blindness.** It is one of the leading preventable causes of blindness worldwide. Keratitis appears to be a result of an inflammatory response to the microfilariae dying in the cornea.

***Loa loa* (Loaiasis).** Infection with *Loa loa* causes distinct syndromes in lifetime residents of endemic areas and uninfected visitors to endemic areas. For most longtime residents, infections are asymptomatic or migratory lesions or swellings called **Calabar swellings** occasionally develop. These lesions are up to 10 cm in diameter, erythematous, and last from one day to several days. The lesions also may be recurrent. In subcutaneous tissues of residents, parasites can be calcified and observed by radiographic means or worms can be directly visualized passing through the conjunctiva. Visitors to areas endemic for disease show greater sensitivity to the parasites. Calabar swellings are more painful, larger, and more frequent.

Laboratory Diagnosis

The only unequivocal means of determining active filarial infection is by demonstrating parasites in host tissue. For lymphatic filariasis and loaiasis, this is most commonly achieved by detection of microfilariae in the bloodstream. Adult *L. loa* may occasionally be observed passing through the conjunctiva. Blood samples are usually obtained between 10 PM and 2 AM, the period when parasites are at their highest levels in the blood. If the human host reverses its routine sleep and wake cycle, the periodicity of microfilariae is also reversed. Apparently periodicity is due to differences in oxygen tension between the arterial and venous blood in the lungs. Microfilariae of *Onchocerca volvulus* are usually detected in the skin and eye. To examine skin, blood-free biopsy specimens are obtained from the interscapular area and gluteal area of Africans and the deltoids of Central Americans. The specimen is incubated in a medium for several hours. Microfilariae emerge from the skin and can be counted under a dissecting microscope. Direct examination of the eye can be performed with an ophthalmoscope or slit lamp.

Treatment

Diethylcarbamazine citrate is the drug of choice for the treatment of infections caused by the microfilariae of all species discussed. Ivermectin is an alternative drug that is still in the trial stage.

The Platyhelminthes

Members of the animal phylum Platyhelminthes collectively are termed the **flatworms.** They are characteristically flat when viewed in dorsoventral section and are bilaterally symmetrical. Nearly all are hermaphroditic. The medically important flatworms appear in two classes, the **Trematoda** or **flukes,** and the **Cestoidea** or **tapeworms.**

TREMATODA (FLUKES)

Discussion of medically important flukes is generally organized on the basis of the habitat of the adult worm in the host. Thus, *Fasciola hepatica, Clonorchis sinensis, Opisthorchis felineus,* and *Opisthorchis viverrini* are the liver flukes; *Fasciolopsis buski* is the intestinal fluke; *Paragonimus westermani* is the lung fluke; and species of the genus *Schistosoma* are the blood flukes.

The liver, intestinal, and lung flukes are leaf-shaped, hermaphroditic worms that attach to the host by means of ventral suckers. Their life cycles are among the most complex found in animal species. Specific species of snails (always) and crustacea (sometimes) serve as intermediate hosts for the flukes' several larval forms such as **miracidia, cercariae,** and **metacercariae.** *F. hepatica,* which infects ruminants primarily, is cosmopolitan. It is the only one of the flukes that is enzootic in the United States. The other hermaphroditic flukes are found mainly in the Orient, where millions of persons are infected.

Infections are transmitted to humans largely through the ingestion of raw or poorly cooked fish, crabs, crayfish, and aquatic plants. The symptoms are related to the site of infection. Clinical diagnosis is guided by the anatomical location of the symptoms and by the dietary and geographical history of the patient. Definitive laboratory diagnosis is made through the identification of the typical operculated (having a lid) eggs.

The blood flukes are an exception in that they are not hermaphroditic and the body configuration of the adults is not leaf-like. They produce a major parasitic disease of humans, **schistosomiasis** or **bilharziasis.**

Schistosomiasis (Bilharziasis)

Life Cycle. Humans are infected when they are exposed to cercariae in infested fresh water. A single infected snail may release 500 to 2000 cercariae each day. After penetration of the skin, the cercaria loses its tail and develops into a **schistosomulum,** which migrates through the lungs and develops in the liver into an adult over a period of one to four weeks. During its migration through the lung, the schistosomulum appears to acquire human antigens on its surface. This characteristic makes the parasite nonantigenic and protects it from immunological recognition during the remainder of its intravascular life. Adult male and female schistosomes mate in the liver and then migrate as pairs against blood flow to the inferior mesenteric plexus (the destination of *Schistosoma mansoni*) or the venous plexus of the bladder (the destination of *Schistosoma haematobium*). The average life span of adult worms is three to seven years.

Four to six weeks after the initial penetration of the skin by cercariae, the adult females begin laying eggs. About 50 percent of the eggs enter the bloodstream and become lodged in the liver and other organs. The remaining 50 percent of the eggs penetrate the wall of the vascular bed and after about a week many of the eggs reach the lumen of the bladder or intestine where they are excreted. Eggs trapped in the bladder or intestine incite a granulomatous reaction, and the eggs die and calcify.

Pathogenesis. The response of the host to schistosomes or their eggs results in different pathologies. **Dermatitis** occurs when the cercariae penetrate the skin of the host. Patients experience itching within one hour after contact. The rash, which appears as erythematous papules, may persist for several days. In the United States exposure to duck schistosomes can result in a dermatitis referred to as **"swimmer's itch."** After penetration, the schistosomes die in the skin of their unnatural host. Swimmer's itch is transient and mild (Fig. 34-13).

Acute schistosomiasis is a clinical syndrome often seen in nonimmune individuals (tourists, immigrants, or the indigenous population) who have been exposed in an endemic area to a primary infection. The syndrome is sometimes called **Katayama fever** in Japan following infection with *Schistosoma japonicum* worms. Acute manifestations rarely appear among reinfected individuals. Symptoms of acute infection appear 4 to 10 weeks after heavy exposure to cercariae. Fever, malaise, hepatosplenomegaly, eosinophilia, and diarrhea are the most predominant symptoms. These symptoms are transient and spontaneously disappear with the transition to the chronic stage. Complications involving the central nervous system, lungs, liver, or intestine may occur, sometimes with fatal consequences. The clinical symptoms of acute disease are induced by schistosomal adult worms and egg antigens.

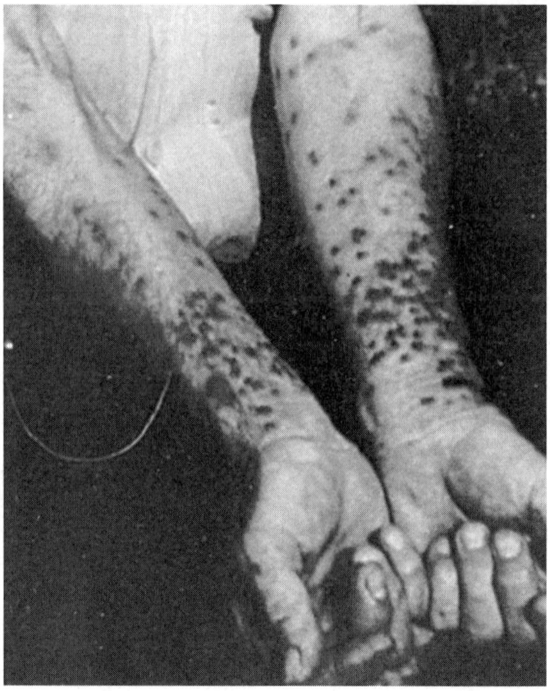

FIGURE 34-13
Cercarial (schistosome) dermatitis (swimmer's itch). The eruption appeared on the arms of a patient exposed to avian schistosome cercariae while he was sitting on a dock jutting out over a lake. (From H. D. Blankespoor. In A. A. Fisher, ed., *Atlas of Aquatic Dermatology*. New York: Grune & Stratton, 1978. Copyright 1978 American Cyanamid Company, Lederle Laboratories Division.)

Chronic schistosomiasis is associated with granulomatous reactions involving many organs and tissues. Manifestations such as liver and spleen enlargement and esophageal varices (enlarged and tortuous vessels) do not become apparent until several years after infection. Early manifestations of chronic infection include chronic mild intermittent diarrhea and polyps in the colon. Renal pathology in which there are glomerular lesions also may be evident. This condition is believed to be due to circulating immune complexes. The major contributor to the pathology of chronic disease is the granulomatous host response around disseminated parasite eggs. This response is aggravated by fibrosis. Granuloma formation is initiated by antigens secreted by the miracidium through pores in the eggshell. Eggs deposited in the circulation reach the intestinal tract and liver, where each one evokes a granulomatous response. As granulomas grow, they displace and damage tissue. As the granulomas resolve, fibrosis ensues. Fibrous tissue consists of a complex array of connective matrix material and collagen. Fibrous tissue formation is accumulative, mostly irreversible, and a primary contributor to the systemic manifestations of disease.

Laboratory Diagnosis. Diagnosis can be accomplished by examination of stool (for ova of *S. mansoni*) or urine (for ova of *S. haematobium*). Although serological tests are available, documentation of ova remains the most important diagnostic tool.

Epidemiology. Schistosomiasis is a debilitating illness that affects 250 million people throughout the world. It is estimated that 600 million people are in constant threat of acquiring the disease. It is also estimated that 400,000 infected persons, many of them Puerto Ricans, live in the United States. No risk in transmission, however, is involved since appropriate snail hosts are lacking and sanitation is good.

S. mansoni and *S. haematobium* coexist in Africa. *S. haematobium* is also found in the Near East while *S. mansoni* can be found in the Western Hemisphere—Brazil, Venezuela, the West Indies, and extension to Puerto Rico. In the Far East *S. japonicum* is the primary cause of disease.

Treatment and Control. Praziquantel is the drug of choice for treating schistosomiasis. For cerebral disease, the concomitant use of corticosteroids is also recommended to decrease inflammatory reactions. Corticosteroids should also be used in addition to praziquantel for life-threatening schistosomiasis.

The most important preventive measure is to avoid snail-infested fresh water. Additional control measures include the use of molluscides such as niclosamide.

Schistosome Dermatitis. In a schistosomal disease entity that occurs commonly in the United States, humans serve as the accidental hosts to the cercariae of blood flukes of birds and mammals. The condition is called *schistosome dermatitis, swimmer's itch, clam digger's itch,* or *sea bather's itch.* When infected birds (especially migratory fowl) and mammals pollute lakes, ponds, and streams, the miracidia that emerge from the schistosome eggs infect snails. The free-swimming furcocercous (fork-tailed) cercariae that emerge from the snails penetrate the skin of humans, lose their tails, and become schistosomulae (juvenile worms). The parasite is at a dead end because maturation of animal schistosomes does not occur in humans. The larval infestation of skin rarely leads to a serious condition. The erythematous pustular lesions (accompanied by intense itching) appear within hours of exposure and subside gradually after the second or third day. Antihistamines and antipruritics may alleviate discomfort.

CESTOIDEA (TAPEWORMS)

Members of the other class of flatworms that include parasites of medical importance are the **Cestoidea.** They are dorsoventrally flat, ribbon-like worms collectively referred to as **tapeworms.** Tapeworms are primarily intestinal parasites but a few invade the tissues of the body in larval stages.

The tapeworm is not a single individual but a collection of individuals linked in a chain. The chain can be divided into regions. The **head** or **scolex** is a pinhead-size structure that anchors in the mucosa by means of a holdfast organ. The holdfast structure contains either four suction cups or two elongated sucking grooves. The scolex tapers into a neck region from which segments called **proglottids** proliferate. The series of proglottids progresses from immature proglottids immediately behind the neck region through sexually mature proglottids to the gravid (egg-laden) proglottids at the distal end of the worm.

Some tapeworms consist of only several segments; others, such as the fish tapeworm, may reach extraordinary lengths of 3000 to 4000 segments. As long as the head region with the proliferative neck region remains attached, new segments will continue to be formed. The tapeworm possesses no digestive system and is therefore dependent on the absorption of simple nutrients from its host. **Niclosamide** is the drug of choice for treatment of all adult tapeworm infections.

Several tapeworms cause disease in humans and these are outlined in Table 34-5. Here we discuss in more detail only two of them: taeniasis caused by the pork tapeworm, and echinococcosis. Figure 34-14 shows the important stages of the major tapeworms and their characteristics.

FIGURE 34-14
Important stages and diagnostic characteristics of the major tapeworms that parasitize humans.

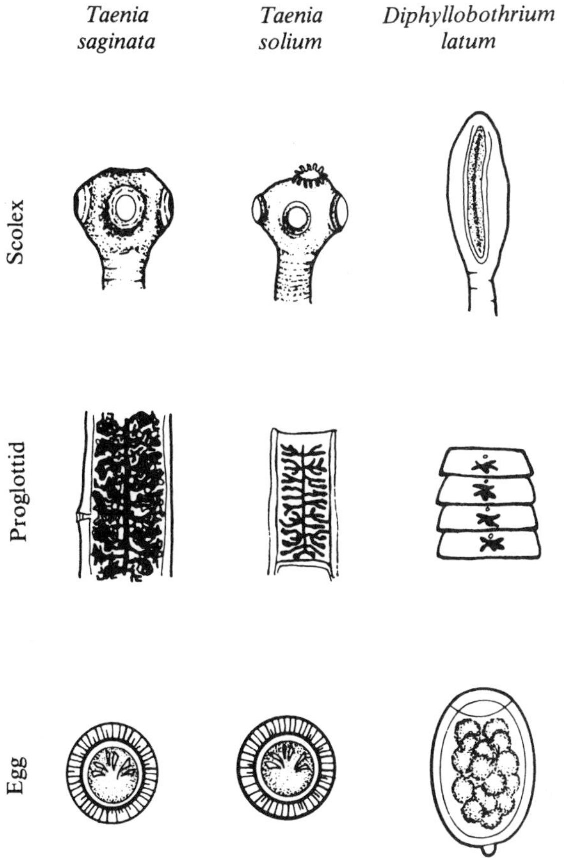

TABLE 34-5
Characteristics of Major Tapeworm Diseases

Disease name and agent	Clinical condition	Infective form; mode of transmission	Specimen examined; diagnostic form	Comments	Treatment
Taeniasis (see Table 34-3)					
Diphyllobothriasis (see Table 34-3)					
Hymenolepis diminuta	Rat tapeworm; mild symptoms, spontaneous loss of worm	*Larvae (cysticercus)* Ingestion of cereals contaminated by infected grain beetles	*Eggs in feces*		Niclosamide
Hymenolepis nana	Dwarf tapeworm; abdominal pain, nausea, and vomiting in heavy infections	*Larvae (cysticercus)* Hand-to-mouth contact and ingestion of mouse feces	*Eggs in feces*	Most common tapeworm in southeastern United States, children affected	Niclosamide
Dipylidium caninum	Dog and cat tapeworm; abdominal pain, diarrhea	*Proglottids* Accidental ingestion of flea	*Proglottids*	Primarily in infants	Usually not necessary; niclosamide
Echinococcosis *Echinococcus granulosa*	Tapeworm of dogs and similar animals; cysts in liver may cause damage and impaired function; dissemination to other organs	*Eggs* Ingestion of eggs	ELISA, indirect hemagglutination	Infection heaviest in cattle- and sheep-raising areas	Surgical resection; mebendazole

Taeniasis

Taeniasis refers to infection by species of *Taenia. Taenia solium* is the pork tapeworm and *Taenia saginata* is the beef tapeworm. Infections with both *adult* tapeworms are seldom serious. Symptoms, if present, usually take the form of epigastric pain or vague abdominal discomfort. However, problems arise from infection of the **larval form** of the pork tapeworm, which we discuss in more detail.

Pork Tapeworm (*Taenia solium*). The adult tapeworm usually infects the human as its definitive host. It sheds proglottids, which are then passed in human feces. Pigs are infected by eating material contaminated by human feces. The protein coats of ova ingested by the pig are digested, releasing embryos called **oncospheres.** The latter invade the gut mucosa, enter the bloodstream, and disseminate throughout the pig's body. Oncospheres lodge in skeletal muscle and produce larval cysts *(Cysticercus cellulosae)*. Humans are infected by eating cyst-bearing pork and mature tapeworms are formed in the small bowel.

If humans ingest *T. solium* ova from food, drink, or fingers contaminated with ova-bearing human feces, the oncospheres are released in the gut. They migrate throughout the body and produce human **cysticercosis.** Cysticercosis is considered as infection by a **somatic tapeworm.** The larval cysts in human cysticercosis can develop in any organ but have a predilection for the central nervous system, eye, and skeletal muscle.

After the cysts form in the brain **(neurocysticercosis)** or another organ, an inflammatory response ensues. The cysticerci usually die after several months to two years. The cyst wall collapses and calcifies.

Cysticercosis is the most common parasitic disease of the central nervous system and is endemic not only in developing countries but also in industrialized nations with high rates of immigration from endemic areas. In Mexico 3 percent of autopsies show the presence of larvae.

Clinical manifestations of neurocysticercosis are varied and nonspecific. Epilepsy, the most frequent clinical sign, is present in only 50 percent of the patients. Other signs of disease include increased intracranial pressure, mental disturbances, and diminution of visual acuity. Twenty-five percent of the patients are normal. Diagnosis of disease is based on ultrasonography, computed tomography, and cerebrospinal fluid studies. Serological diagnosis may be based on ELISA results. Praziquantel is the drug of choice for the treatment of all forms of active cysticercosis. Albendazole is an alternative drug for neurocysticercosis. Surgical intervention is still a choice in the treatment of neurocysticercosis.

Echinococcosis

Echinococcus species are the smallest tapeworms of medical significance. Most human infections are caused by *Echinococcus granulosus. E. granulosus* is parasitic in dogs and similar animals. The disease is common in sheep- and cattle-raising countries. Adult worms live in dogs while sheep are typically intermediate hosts. In an intermediate host the larval stage infects internal organs and is called **hydatid disease** or **hydatidosis.** In the definitive host the disease is called **echinococcosis.** Humans are an accidental host in the organism's life cycle.

In the dog the tapeworm resides in the jejunum where eggs are eventually released into the feces. Sheep ingest the eggs and liberated embryos gain access to the bloodstream. Cystic lesions (called **hydatid cysts**) develop in various organs of sheep. Humans often become intermediate hosts because of association with dogs and fecal-oral exposure to eggs.

Echinococcosis in humans often involves the liver and less often the lungs, but almost every bodily organ can be infected. The cysts may be asymptomatic for several years. In the liver the cysts can enlarge to nearly 10 cm before they induce symptoms. The liver itself can be enlarged and there is abdominal pain, nausea, and vomiting. If a cyst ruptures, the contents can spill into a major blood vessel and cause severe consequences. Slow leakage causes allergic symptoms, edema, and asthma. Sudden spillage can cause anaphylactic shock and death. A cyst can rupture in the bile duct or gallbladder and mimic a gallbladder attack. A cyst also can be invaded by bacteria, resulting in the formation of abscesses.

Antibodies to echinococcal antigens can be detected by ELISA, complement fixation, or indirect hemagglutination. Surgical resection can be used for the treatment of a single symptomatic cyst. Patients with multiple cysts are usually treated with mebendazole.

The Arthropoda

Arthropods are the most highly organized of the invertebrate animals. Sometime during their life cycle they have paired, jointed appendages, a chitinized (horny polysaccharide) exoskeleton, and a hemocele (body cavity through which a blood-like fluid circulates). The majority of the medically important arthropods are found in the classes Insecta and Arachnida. Flies, fleas, lice, bees, and wasps are members of the class Insecta (arthropods with three pairs of walking legs).

Arthropods periodically shed (molt) the entire exoskeleton. The stages between moltings are called **instars.** Immature instar forms that resemble adults are called **nymphs;** those that are morphologically quite distinct from the adult form are called **larvae.** Larvae are worm-like in character. In some arthropods there is a non-feeding form, the **pupa,** that appears between the larval form and the adult form.

Only the medical importance of arthropods is noted here. The larvae and adults may affect humans in several ways: as **ectoparasites,** as **intermediate** or **definitive hosts** of other animal parasites, as **venom-producing agents,** or as **vectors** of infectious disease.

As ectoparasites, they cause disease while feeding or taking up abode on the skin and underlying tissues. That association is an **infestation.** Examples of arthropods that cause infestations of humans are the itch mite (which causes **scabies,** see Under the Microscope 50) and the lar-

UNDER THE MICROSCOPE 50

Scabies

Scabies is observed among nursing home residents and the immunosuppressed. For example, scabietic infestation is a common cause of pruritus in the HIV-infected patient. The quantity of mites carried by infested patients expedites transmission. Transmission can occur directly via contact between patients or indirectly through contact with hospital staff.

Skin scraping is the only consistent means of detecting mites, assessing the degree of transmissibility, and evaluating treatment when skin lesions persist or reappear. Any red, raised, pruritic skin lesions (especially on the upper back) that are not obviously due to other causes are suspect and should be scraped to detect mites. **Lindane** has been the drug of choice in treatment; however, it has potential neurotoxicity. Today **permethrin** cream is the drug of choice. The cream can be left on overnight and then washed off the following morning. The treatment protocol should also include administration of drugs to close relatives and staff who come in contact with the infested patient. Treatment should include the entire body from the neck down, with special attention to the underside of well trimmed fingernails.

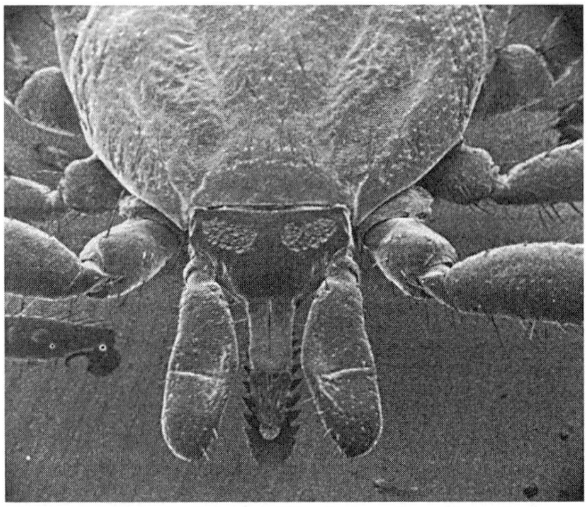

FIGURE 34-15
Forepart of the tick. When biting, the tick thrusts the serrated biting organ (center) through the skin into deeper-lying tissue. It is the serrations that make dislodgement so difficult. (From P. B. Armstrong, D. W. Deamer, and J. J. Mais, *J. Natl. Hist.* June/July 1972.)

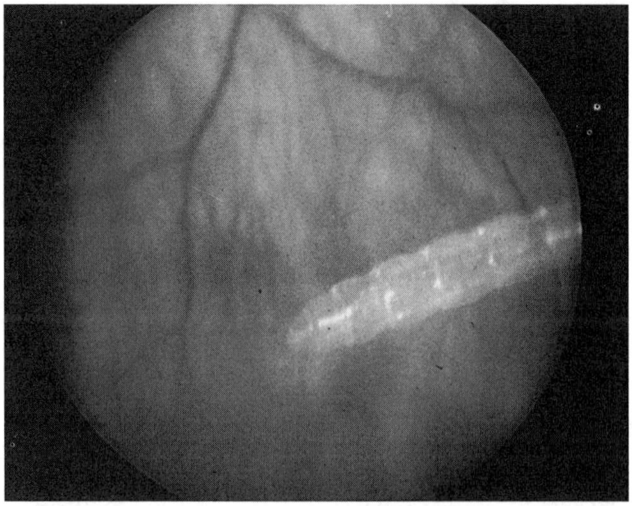

FIGURE 34-17
Myiasis. Larvae *(Cochliomyia hominivorax)* within vitreous humor of the eye. (From J. Chodosh and J. Clarridge, *Clin. Infect. Dis.* 14:444, 1992.)

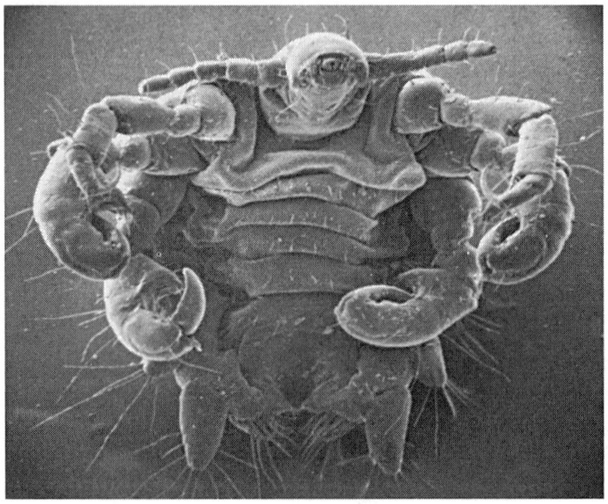

FIGURE 34-16
A human crab louse from underneath. The thick legs and large claws are used to grasp hair shafts of the host. (From P. B. Armstrong, D. W. Deamer, and J. J. Mais, *J. Natl. Hist.* June/July 1972.)

val mites known as chiggers; fleas (which have backward-projecting bristles and spines that enable them to proceed through hair and fur without becoming entangled), often from infested pets; ticks (Fig. 34-15), bedbugs, and kissing bugs; the body louse (Fig. 34-16); and larval forms of flies (maggots) that infest the body (myiasis, Fig. 34-17).

The role of arthropods as intermediate and definitive hosts should have been apparent in the preceding descriptions of the parasitic diseases. As venom producers, arthropods such as bees, wasps, spiders, and tarantulas produce substances that are toxic or that induce allergic reactions (see Chapter 13 under Type I Hypersensitivities). The importance of arthropods as mechanical and biological vectors of bacterial, viral, rickettsial, and mycotic disease agents is evident in the descriptions of those diseases. In summary, arthropods directly cause medical problems as ectoparasites and as venenators, or they do so by fulfilling a role in the development or transmission of other disease agents.

Summary

1. Traditionally the term parasites is applied to the infectious disease agents that are found in four divisions of the animal kingdom: the Protozoa, the Nemathelminthes (roundworms), the Platyhelminthes (flatworms), and the Arthropoda.
2. The distribution and incidence of parasitic disease are governed by such factors as availability of suitable definitive and intermediate hosts and appropriate vectors, climate, socioeconomic conditions, sanitary practices, and ethnic eating habits.
3. The infective forms that are involved in the transmission of parasites are the trophozoites, cysts, and sporozoites of protozoa and eggs and larvae of worms.
4. The major mode of laboratory diagnosis is identification by microscope of the various morphological forms of trophozoites, cysts, eggs, and larvae.
5. Control of parasitic disease includes the destruction of vectors and intermediate hosts and management of their breeding places, education of the populace, proper sanitation, and the use of appropriate drugs.
6. For summaries of the parasitic diseases described in this chapter, see Tables 34-2 to 34-5.

Questions for Study

1. What procedures are used for the identification of intestinal parasites? Blood parasites?
2. How does one distinguish between a definitive and intermediate host?
3. What is responsible for the liver abscesses associated with disseminated amebiasis? What bacterial infection causes a similar pathology?
4. How does the source of most *Naegleria* infections differ from those of *Acanthamoeba?*
5. Why is serological diagnosis of *Naegleria* infection not utilized?
6. What parasite must contact lens wearers be concerned about? What are the preventive measures?
7. What groups of individuals are susceptible to infection by *Giardia lamblia?*
8. What is meant by the term malabsorption syndrome? With what parasite is this syndrome associated?
9. What are the three major causes of vaginitis? What tests does one use to differentiate among them?
10. Describe the disease that is transmitted to humans by the reduviid or kissing bug? What are the most severe forms of this disease?
11. What chemotherapeutic agent has been called the "resurrection drug"? Why has it been so named?
12. Name the vector involved in the transmission of each of the following diseases: malaria, leishmaniasis, sleeping sickness, Chagas' disease, and Nantucket fever.
13. What is meant by the term xenodiagnosis? With what parasitic disease is this diagnostic procedure identified?
14. What parasitic diseases can be transmitted by blood transfusion?
15. Describe and differentiate the life cycle phases of sporogony and schizogony that occur in the disease malaria.
16. What is the hypnozoite and with what aspect of malaria is it associated?
17. What aspect of the *Strongyloides* life cycle distinguishes it from other nematodes?
18. What diagnostic technique is used for pinworm? Describe it.
19. Under what conditions would you be considered a source of infection by *Trichinella spiralis?*
20. List some of the major arthropods and briefly describe what animal parasite they transmit.
21. What is meant by parasite periodicity? What factors affect it?
22. Which fluke is enzootic in the United States? How is it transmitted?
23. Describe the life cycle of *Schistosoma* from the time of infection of the human host until the release of eggs in the feces. What makes this organism capable of evading the host's immune system?
24. What precautions would you take to prevent parasite disease, assuming you were going to Pakistan for several months?
25. What is the relationship of taeniasis to cysticercosis?
26. What is the most common parasitic disease of the central nervous system? Describe its clinical manifestations.
27. What is the smallest tapeworm of medical significance? How is it acquired by humans? What is the pathophysiology of disease?
28. Describe some disease manifestations caused by ectoparasitic arthropods.

PART

IX Hospital Infections

CHAPTER

35 Hospital-Acquired Diseases

OBJECTIVES

To outline the various ways in which hospital-associated diseases can be acquired

To list the major causes of hospital-acquired diseases at all sites

To list the predisposing factors that contribute to hospital-associated infections

To understand the relationship of antibiotic use and hospital-associated infections

To list the hospital procedures that contribute to hospital-associated infections

To describe urinary and vascular indwelling catheterization with respect to the specific source of infection, organisms involved, and method of prevention and treatment

To outline the techniques and practices that help to prevent hospital-associated infections

OUTLINE

EPIDEMIOLOGY
- Transmission
  - Direct Contact
  - Contaminated Fomites and Fluids
  - Airborne Spread
- Nosocomial Infection Rates and Agents Involved

FACTORS IMPORTANT IN NOSOCOMIAL INFECTIONS
- Microbial Factors
- Immunological State of the Host
  - Age
  - Metabolic Disorders
  - Immunosuppressive Drugs
  - Trauma
- Hospital Procedures
  - Surgery
  - Catheterization
    - Urinary Catheterization
      - Pathogenesis
      - Prevention and Control
    - Vascular Indwelling Catheters
      - Diagnosis
      - Pathogenesis
      - Prevention
      - Treatment and Management
  - Antibiotic Chemotherapy
  - Hypodermic Injections
  - Diagnostic Procedures

PREVENTION AND CONTROL OF NOSOCOMIAL INFECTIONS
- Environmental Surveillance
- Hygienic Practices
- Hospital Personnel Surveillance
- Patient Surveillance

Infections acquired in the hospital are referred to as **nosocomial** (Greek *noso* meaning "disease" and *komeion* meaning "to take care of"). One of the reasons why we have a separate chapter on hospital-associated diseases is that their epidemiology differs dramatically from that of community-associated diseases, discussed in Chapter 15. Ironically, hospital-associated diseases have become a major health problem because of our advances in medicine. The services now provided by hospitals are complex and involve such practices as organ transplantation, implantation of foreign devices, and replacement and repair of defective tissues. In addition, a variety of invasive devices for therapeutic and diagnostic purposes provide vehicles for the transmission of infectious agents.

The purpose of this chapter is to outline briefly the factors that contribute to hospital-associated diseases and how they may be prevented and controlled. A knowledge of these factors is an important aspect of the health professional's education.

Epidemiology

TRANSMISSION

The percentage of nosocomial infections acquired from community sources is not easily established in the hospital setting. Infectious microorganisms may reach the patient by direct contact with other patients and with hospital personnel, contact with contaminated fomites, or contact with contaminated air.

Direct Contact

On entry into the hospital, individuals who are considered infectious require some type of isolation. *Handwashing is the single most important isolation precaution because it removes organisms acquired from infected patients.* If the patient can transmit microorganisms by air, it may be necessary to place him or her in a private room to prevent cross infection between patients. Direct contact between hospital personnel and the patient, however, remains a major avenue of infection. Transmission by hands is the most important route for transfer of the infectious agent under these circumstances. For example, a physician removing a dressing from a bacterially contaminated wound could accidentally contaminate his or her hands with infectious microorganisms and transfer them to other patients.

Infections may also be caused by microorganisms of low virulence that are members of one's own microbial flora (endogenous microorganisms). In **endogenous infections** the virulence of the pathogen is not as important as the number of microorganisms present in the host and the physiological state of the host. For example, *Escherichia coli* is considered a nonpathogen or an opportunistic pathogen. It exists in equilibrium with other residents in the gut as well as the host tissue. There is no dramatic increase in the numbers of *E. coli* and no pathological response of the host to its presence. *E. coli* displaced into the genitourinary tract, however, finds itself in a new environment where ecological and physiological pressures may not be exerted on it. Depending on the site of infection and the immunological response of the host, *E. coli* can become highly pathogenic.

Endogenous infections are often the result of surgical manipulation, chemotherapeutic treatment, and diagnostic or therapeutic procedures (**iatrogenic infections**). Frequently during these procedures microorganisms are accidentally displaced from their normal habitat into other areas of the host.

Contaminated Fomites and Fluids

The contact of any instrument with open wounds, mucous membranes, or internal organs of the body represents a mechanism of transmission of infectious agents to the patient. Various solutions or fluids such as intravenous fluids, drugs, blood, or blood products may also be contaminated either by the distributor (see Under the Microscope 51) or by the hospital pharmacy. In other

---

UNDER THE MICROSCOPE 51

Povidone-Iodine Solution Contamination

Povidone-iodine and poloxamer-iodine are the iodine solutions most commonly used in hospitals as antiseptics and disinfectants. Before 1980 intrinsic bacterial contamination of povidone-iodine solutions was thought to be impossible. However, three outbreaks of *Pseudomonas* infections have since been attributed to intrinsic contamination.

Pseudomonas organisms (*P. aeruginosa, P. cepacia,* for example) are commonly found in water. Laboratory studies have shown that these organisms are able to attach to polyvinylchloride or other materials used in water distribution pipes in iodophor solution manufacturing plants. Once attached, the organisms produce a biofilm (glycocalyx) that is believed to be responsible for their resistance to iodine.

Free iodine is the major chemical and microbicidal agent in iodophor solutions. If there are low levels of free iodine in certain lots of the iodophor solution, bacterial contamination can occur. The level of free iodine determines whether the germicide is used as an antiseptic or disinfectant. Improper formulation of iodine solutions by manufacturers can lead to contamination and subsequent hospital-associated infections.

---

words, a common vehicle may be the source of disease and can result in hospital epidemics. Most infections caused by contact with inanimate objects are incurred during various hospital procedures such as surgery, catheterization, hypodermic injection, and diagnostic tests.

Many inanimate objects within the hospital environment can act as sources of infection to hospitalized patients. These include potted flowers, bed linen, fruits and vegetables, carpeting, and walls and floors and other smooth surfaces. These objects, however, are not the most frequent sources of infection.

Airborne Spread

Air is a major vehicle for the dissemination of microorganisms. Usually the airborne microbes are derived from nasal carriers or from the desquamated epithelium of patients and personnel. Individuals with upper respiratory tract infections or asymptomatic carriers can infect others by discharging air droplets that carry potentially pathogenic microorganisms. These contaminated mucous discharges can make direct contact with the patient, or they may settle on various surfaces to remain infectious for anyone coming in contact with them.

Aerosolized bacteria can also be generated by inanimate disseminators. Many cases of pneumonia, for example, have been traced to the use of inhalation equipment. Such instruments are used to generate aerosols of medication for patients with respiratory problems. If equipment or medication becomes contaminated, the nebulizer in the unit will generate bacterial aerosols that are inhaled by the patient. *Pseudomonas* species such as *P. cepacia* and *P. aeruginosa* can proliferate in relatively pure water. *P. cepacia*, for example, can multiply to levels of 10^7 per milliliter and remain at those levels for weeks in distilled water (see also Under the Microscope 51). Outbreaks of legionnaires' disease have been traced to the aerosolization of potable water, for example, in shower heads.

Microorganisms on the skin have been found on desquamated epithelium, which is readily shed onto bedclothes and thus dispersed into the air while the bed is being made. Individuals with skin diseases such as eczema are prolific disseminators of skin microorganisms because they have more skin scales and because the smaller size of the scales facilitates their transmission. In addition, humans normally liberate 3×10^8 scales per day and most *Staphylococcus aureus* organisms are carried on these flakes. Outbreaks of *S. aureus* surgical wound infections have been linked to airborne spread from human dispensers in the operating room.

Microorganisms dispersed into the air from any source can be acquired by the patient through inhalation, by deposition on the skin, or indirectly by contaminated fomites. In the hospital, airborne infections are therefore related to the kind of disseminator in operation, the type of filtration system, and the velocity and patterns of airflow in the hospital.

Laboratory techniques used to trace hospital-associated infections are discussed in Chapter 15.

Nosocomial Infection Rates and Agents Involved

Data have been collected from hospitals in the United States to determine the rates of infection for hospital services as well as the agents implicated in the infection. The microbial groups, in order of importance, are bacteria, fungi, viruses, and animal parasites. Over 80 percent of nosocomial infections are caused by bacteria while very few are ever caused by animal parasites such as protozoa.

The relative frequency of the 10 most commonly isolated pathogens for each of the major sites of infection is provided in Table 35-1. This table clearly illustrates the importance of gram-negative species in nosocomial disease. *E. coli*, for example, is the most frequently isolated pathogen from all sites. The dominance of gram-negative species is due to the abundant number of currently available antibiotics that affect gram-negative species. Increased use of these antimicrobial agents has encouraged the selection of antibiotic-resistant strains of the offending species.

Even though Table 35-1 indicates the importance of bacteria in nosocomial disease, fungi and viruses also play an important role, particularly in the past few years. The emergence of acquired immunodeficiency syndrome (AIDS) and the increased use of corticosteroids for specialized groups of patients are the principal reasons for these increases. Each one affects cell-mediated immunity, the major host defense mechanisms against fungi and viruses.

Candida and *Aspergillus* species are the most frequently

TABLE 35-1
Distribution (Percent) of the 10 Major Nosocomial Pathogens Isolated from Major Infection Sites, 1990 Through 1992, Hospital-wide

Pathogen	All sites	UT	SS	BS	Lungs	Other
Escherichia coli	12	25	8	5	4	4
Staphylococcus aureus	12	2	19	16	20	17
Coagulase-negative staphylococci	11	4	14	31	2	14
Enterococcus species	10	16	12	9	2	5
Pseudomonas aeruginosa	9	11	8	3	16	6
Enterobacter species	6	5	7	4	11	4
Candida albicans	5	8	3	5	5	5
Klebsiella pneumoniae	5	7	3	4	7	3
Gram-positive anaerobes	4	0	1	1	0	19
Proteus mirabilis	3	5	3	1	2	2

UT = urinary tract; SS = surgical site; BS = bloodstream (primary infection).
SOURCE: National Nosocomial Infections Surveillance (NNIS) System, Centers for Disease Control, Atlanta, GA.

TABLE 35-2
Most Frequently Isolated Fungal Pathogens in the Hospital

Mycoses or fungal groups	Clinical manifestation; type of individuals affected	Treatment
Candidiasis (*Candida albicans, C. tropicalis, C. torulopsis, C. glabrata, C. parapsilosis*)	Onychomycosis; HIV-infected patients	Ketoconazole
	Chronic mucocutaneous; acquired T lymphocyte deficiency	Ketoconazole
	Thrush; HIV-infected and other T lymphocyte deficiency states	Oral nystatin, oral ketoconazole
	Gastrointestinal—acute leukemia	Amphotericin B
	Genitourinary tract—indwelling catheter	Amphotericin B with or without flucytosine
	Disseminated—leukemia patients, intravascular catheterization	Amphotericin B with or without flucytosine
Aspergillosis (*Aspergillus fumigatus, A. flavus, A. niger, A. terreus*)	Pulmonary—patients with acute leukemia, those undergoing bone marrow transplantation	Surgical debridement, amphotericin B
Zygomycosis (species of *Mucor, Rhizopus, Absidia, Cunninghamella, Saksenaea*)	Pulmonary—uncontrolled leukemia, organ transplantation	Amphotericin B
	Rhinocerebral—uncontrolled diabetes, organ transplantation	Debridement and amphotericin B
Cryptococcosis (*Cryptococcus neoformans*)	Meningitis—those receiving high doses of corticosteroids	Amphotericin B
Trichosporonosis (*Trichosporon* species)	Disseminated (lesions in skin, kidney, liver, eyes, lung) hematological malignancies	Amphotericin B, ketoconazole, miconazole
Pseudallescheriasis (*Pseudallescheria boydii*)	Pulmonary; disseminated involving kidney, thyroid, brain, and heart; local lesions in paranasal sinuses	Surgical debridement, amphotericin B
Fusarium infection (*Fusarium solani, F. moniliforme, F. proliferatum*)	Disseminated skin lesions—patients with leukemia	Amphotericin B

encountered fungal pathogens in the hospital but others may also be involved (Table 35-2). *Candida albicans* is the *Candida* species most frequently isolated from the hospital. This organism is indigenous to the skin and gastrointestinal tract. Patients exposed to antimicrobials that suppress the bacterial flora of the gastrointestinal tract are subject to overcolonization by *C. albicans.* The yeast may become invasive if the patient is undergoing surgery or is receiving cytotoxic chemotherapy. Intravenous catheterization may permit cutaneous colonization and subcutaneous invasion by *Candida. Aspergillus* species are ubiquitous in the environment. In the hospital, air is the principal route of transmission of *Aspergillus* and the respiratory tract, the most common portal of entry. The conidia of *Aspergillus* are so small that they easily reach the lungs.

Contamination of air ventilation systems is usually involved in nosocomial aspergillosis. Hospital construction is occasionally another source of airborne transmission of *Aspergillus.* In 1974 and 1975 there were eight cases of aspergillosis at the National Cancer Institute in Baltimore, Maryland, during the process of relocating to a new facility. All the cases were due to *Aspergillus flavus,* which had colonized the fireproofing material used to coat the steel and cement superstructure.

Viruses are not included in nosocomial statistical studies but their importance in nosocomial diseases cannot be overlooked. Most viruses can cause nosocomial disease, but the ones that either are highly transmissible or have devastating effects in the host are

1. Rubella virus
2. Respiratory syncytial virus
3. Varicella-zoster virus
4. Herpes simplex virus
5. Hepatitis A virus

Endogenous viruses such as cytomegalovirus, Epstein-Barr virus, and herpes simplex virus are activated in the host by physical and chemical factors. These factors include trauma, immunosuppression, and hormonal imbalance. Latent viruses, when activated, replicate and are shed by the host.

Factors Important in Nosocomial Infections

MICROBIAL FACTORS

Most nosocomial infections are associated with microorganisms previously described as opportunistic, for example, *E. coli, Staphylococcus epidermidis,* and *Serratia marcescens.* In the compromised host all microorganisms must be considered potentially pathogenic, partly because changes in medical procedures have brought about changes in the microorganism, its environment, and its disease manifestations. New or unusual microorganisms now appear as permanent residents in the hospital environment, and each must be treated as a potential pathogen. Most microbial changes have been the result of the increased use, both medical and nonmedical, of antibiotics.

Microorganisms that inhabit human bodies are in various ecological niches (respiratory tract, intestinal tract, and other sites), where they are in equilibrium with other microorganisms as well as the host. Under normal healthy conditions this relationship does not allow for the indiscriminate increase in numbers of one species over another. For example, there is an independent mutual antagonism between gram-positive cocci and gram-negative bacilli in the human respiratory tract. The two groups of bacteria are antagonistic to the fungi.

A microbial imbalance is evident in the host when broad-spectrum antibiotics are administered over a long period. In this situation the numbers of gram-negative and gram-positive bacteria are greatly reduced, and secondary fungal infections tend to occur. The virtual absence of bacteria allows uninhibited multiplication of fungal species. Since the advent of antibiotics and other drugs, the intermicrobial environment of the microorganisms in the host has been constantly challenged. Drugs are now a part of people's food, drink, and cosmetics, and because of their antimicrobial activities they encourage the growth of infrequent low-grade pathogens.

The increasing use of new procedures and instruments has also changed the pattern of microorganisms in the hospital. Some microorganisms are equipped to survive in and around these new instruments. Together these factors can lead to the replacement of normal microbial inhabitants in the host with infrequently encountered microorganisms. Such altered relationships are likely to lead to serious infection.

Organisms causing nosocomial infections are frequently resistant to antimicrobial agents. This resistance involves not only microorganisms of low virulence but also the more frequently isolated pathogens such as *S. aureus.* As many as 75 percent of hospital personnel can be described as carriers of antimicrobial-resistant *S. aureus.* For many years the resistance of this organism was confined to the antibiotic penicillin G, but the organism is now resistant to several aminoglycosides as well as methicillin.

Gram-negative organisms such as *Serratia, Klebsiella,* and *Pseudomonas* species are resistant to a variety of antimicrobials including many of the important aminoglycosides. Still there are some microbial species that have remained uniformly susceptible to specific antimicrobials. These include group A streptococci, meningococcus, and *Treponema pallidum,* all of which are susceptible to penicillin. In addition, the resistant organisms that inhabit the host do not usually persist when the antimicrobial is no longer part of the treatment. The resistant species are usually unable to compete with the normal microbial flora. Despite these positive signs, antimicrobial resistance does affect the outcome of infection in the patient.

Two factors leading to an increasing prevalence of antimicrobial resistance as a cause of nosocomial infections are the frequent use of antimicrobials and the mechanisms of resistance transfer in microorganisms. Chromosome-mediated resistance is a problem, but most of our concern today is with resistance mediated by **plasmid transfer factors** and **transposons.** Resistance transfer occurs not only between members of the same genus and species but also between species and within genera.

Microorganisms regarded as nonpathogenic can be the source of **resistance factors.** The most common sites of resistance transfer are the gastrointestinal tract and the skin. Resistance transfer in the bowel does not depend on the affected individual receiving antimicrobial agents at the time of transfer. Transfer on the skin, however, appears to occur more frequently in the presence of topically applied antimicrobial agents. Because plasmids can carry multiple resistance markers, selection of resistance to one drug used in treatment may be accompanied by resistance to unrelated drugs.

Within the hospital environment, the selective pressures for survival of the multiply resistant strains are related to the frequency of use of each of the drugs. Even when antimicrobial usage is decreased, resistant microorganisms are capable of persisting. The fact that hospital-associated strains are also transferred to those in the community (and vice versa) is of great concern to the medical community. Many examples now exist in which some microorganisms have developed resistance to antimicrobials outside the hospital: *Hemophilus influenzae* to ampicillin, *Salmonella typhimurium* to ampicillin, *S. aureus* to methicillin, pneumococcus to penicillin and tetracyclines, and *Shigella* species to sulfonamides and tetracycline. The hospitalized patient undergoing drug therapy, therefore, represents a source of multiply resistant microorganisms not only to other hospitalized personnel but also to the community.

IMMUNOLOGICAL STATE OF THE HOST

The most important factor influencing susceptibility to infection is the relative immunological state of the host at the time of infection. The immunological state can be depressed under certain conditions.

Age

During the few months after birth, the infant, especially the premature one, is very susceptible to bacterial infection. It is well known that the serum of the newborn does not exert the bactericidal activity that the maternal serum does. The infant serum shows little opsonic activity against such gram-negative bacteria as *E. coli* and *S. marcescens.* Diarrhea caused by enteropathogenic *E. coli* is a major affliction of infants in the hospital nursery. Neonatal sepsis occurs more frequently in premature infants, and the fatality rate is as high as 50 percent. *E. coli* is the most frequent cause of neonatal sepsis. Pediatric patients up to the age of 6 years remain highly susceptible to infection with *H. influenzae*. In consequence, the number of infants with fatal meningitis has risen.

Older patients with cardiovascular disease, urinary tract abnormalities, or respiratory conditions are especially prone to infections while in the hospital. So are older patients kept alive with immunosuppressive drugs and immunosuppressive procedures. When catheterization, positive pressure apparatus, or anesthesiology equipment is applied to these compromised patients, they are often unable to withstand the challenge of the microbe.

Metabolic Disorders

Patients with leukemia or any hematological disorder that involves the immune system must be considered likely candidates for hospital-acquired infections. In leukemic patients the problem is often compounded because the need for radiation or drug therapy to reduce the number of leukocytes leads to immunological deficiencies.

Diabetics are also highly susceptible to nosocomial infections. Their susceptibility is related to secondary effects of the disease such as renal insufficiency, acidosis, and vascular insufficiency, particularly of the lower extremities. Insulin-dependent patients with diabetes mellitus have more frequent and severe staphylococcal infections than do nondiabetics.

Immunosuppressive Drugs

Immunosuppressive drugs are used therapeutically for immunological diseases in which there is a need to reduce the level of leukocytes in the host. They are also used prophylactically to prevent the rejection of transplant tissues in the immunologically sensitive recipient. The three classes of immunosuppressive agents are (1) the lymphocytolytic agents such as the **corticosteroids;** (2) the metabolic analogues, such as **azathioprine,** which interferes with DNA synthesis of lymphoid tissue; and (3) the alkylating agents, such as **nitrogen mustard,** which depurinates nucleic acids. The function of these agents is to suppress the cellular or humoral immune systems of the host. Corticosteroids, for example, generally depress the formation of antibodies and suppress the delayed hypersensitivity reaction that is believed to be responsible for transplantation immunity. **Cyclosporine** is a selective immunosuppressive drug that has reduced the incidence of infection as well as decreased the incidence of graft loss.

In the immunosuppressed state the patient is literally at the mercy of any opportunistic pathogen. In renal transplant recipients, for instance, pneumonia is the most common cause of death, with bacteria causing about 60 percent of the infections, followed by viruses (25 percent) and fungi (15 percent). Most fatalities of fungal origin in immunocompromised patients are associated with species of *Candida* and *Aspergillus*. Fatal septicemias of bacterial origin are attributed to the gram-negative bacilli, particularly species of *Pseudomonas*. Hepatitis is often the most serious viral complication. Cytomegalovirus infection is also a frequent complication in renal transplant recipients but is seldom fatal.

Trauma

Individuals in accidents that cause trauma are susceptible to infection. Traumatic wounds produced by crushing and tearing contain large amounts of dead fat with poor vascularity. In addition, burn wounds appear to depress numerous immune resistance factors such as neutrophil function. This type of condition lends itself to microbial contamination and sepsis by microorganisms usually considered to be noninvasive. Microorganisms associated with burn wound infections are *P. aeruginosa, S. aureus,* and enterococci. *P. aeruginosa* and other *Pseudomonas* species thrive in moist environments, and in the hospital they are frequent contaminants of humidifiers and nebulizers. *Pseudomonas* species also are resistant to many antimicrobial agents and disinfectants. The mortality from *Pseudomonas* septicemia in burn wound patients can be greatly reduced with the administration of a polyvalent vaccine in conjunction with an immunoglobulin prepared from the serum of vaccinated healthy volunteers.

HOSPITAL PROCEDURES

Surgery

Unsterilized instruments, sutures, sponges, and irrigating solutions as well as the surgical team itself are the main sources of infection related to surgery. Only sterile equipment and solutions are used during surgical activities. In addition, the surgical team members wear sterile gowns, masks, and gloves. The patient has many nonspecific mechanisms for resisting infection. Surgery and related procedures can interfere with these natural resistance factors and may be responsible for severe and sometimes fatal infections. Since tissue is being cut, the normal host defense mechanisms are breached, and the reduction in host resistance is worsened by anesthesia. The number of microorganisms that gain entrance to the traumatized tissue and the site of the surgical operation influence the rate of infection. Wounds can be divided into four types: clean, clean-contaminated, contaminated, and dirty (Table 35-3).

1. **Clean wounds** are those in which no hollow muscular organ (gastrointestinal or respiratory tract) was opened and no break in aseptic technique occurred.

TABLE 35-3
Surgical Wound Infection (SWI) Rates among 84,691 Operations (1987–1990) by Traditional Wound Classification

Type of wound	Percent of wounds	SWI rate
Clean	58	2.1
Clean-contaminated	36	3.3
Contaminated	4	6.4
Dirty	2	7.1

SOURCE: Hospital Infections Program, Centers for Disease Control, Atlanta, GA.

2. **Clean-contaminated wounds** refers to the opening of a hollow muscular organ with minimal spillage of contents.
3. **Contaminated wounds** refers to the opening of hollow organs with gross spillage of contents and acute inflammation without pus formation.
4. **Dirty wounds** refers to the presence of pus or perforated viscera.

The probability of infection increases further if the patient has been compromised by immunosuppressive drugs, malnutrition, or an underlying illness. Studies with animals show that within the first three hours of bacterial contamination of tissue, the host's antimicrobial defenses are at their peak. This three-hour peak of activity can be strengthened through the use of antibiotics. If the peak antimicrobial activity of the antibiotic can be coordinated with the host's, there is a better chance of resisting infection. For most operations, **cefazolin** is currently the drug of choice for prophylaxis against *S. aureus* infections.

Most postoperative infections occur after surgery has been performed on the alimentary, respiratory, or genitourinary tract. In recent years the number of postoperative infections caused by gram-negative species, especially species of *Pseudomonas, Klebsiella, Proteus,* and *Serratia,* has increased. Much of this increase is directly correlated with the prophylactic use of antibiotics. The major problems result from the extended use of antibiotics after surgery. When antibiotics are continued longer than one week after surgery, the incidence of infection rises dramatically.

Catheterization

Catheterization is a process in which a tubular device (catheter) is inserted into the urinary tract or into a blood vessel. Since the catheter is the single most important predisposing factor in nosocomial infections, we devote extensive coverage to this device and its implications in nosocomial disease.

Urinary Catheterization. Urinary catheterization accounts for 80 percent of urinary tract infections or bacteriuria. Bacteriuria refers to the asymptomatic colonization of the urinary tract without invasion of tissue. Infection of the urinary tract implies there is inflammation of the urethra, kidneys, or bladder. Approximately 10 percent of all hospitalized patients undergo urethral catheterization; therefore, the use and care of urinary catheters continue to be of utmost importance.

Ten to 20 percent of patients who do not have bacteria in the urine at the time of catheterization will become bacteriuric in 24 to 48 hours. Each day of catheterization increases the incidence of colonization. At the end of one month the prevalence of infection in catheterized patients is virtually 100 percent.

Pathogenesis. Colonization of the area around the urinary meatus by gram-negative bacteria such as *E. coli* predisposes patients to urinary tract infections (Fig. 35-1). Female patients, the elderly, and patients taking antibiotics are prone to microbial colonization of the meatus. Bacteria also may colonize the periurethral area and they can be pulled into the bladder when the catheter is inserted. In addition, bacteria in the mucous sheath on the outside of the catheter can also gain entry into the bladder.

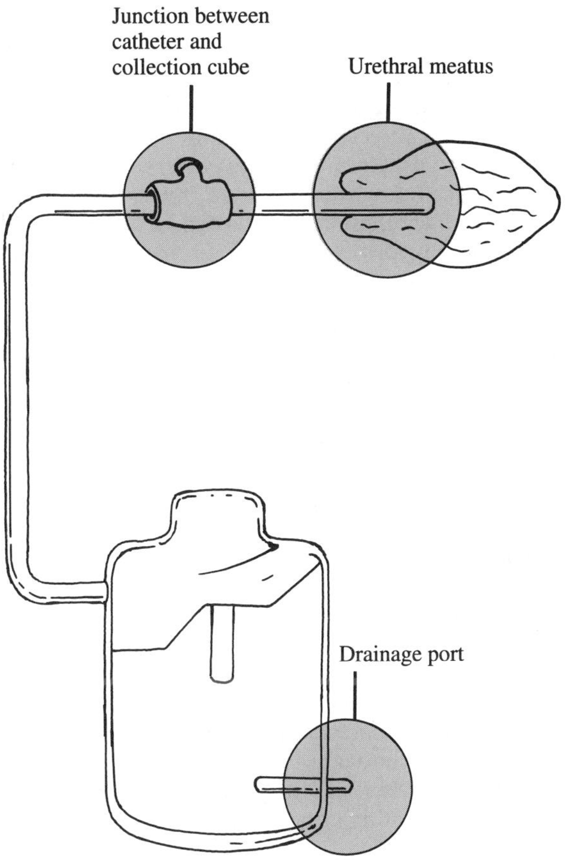

FIGURE 35-1
Sites of contamination during catheterization.

Women, because they have a short urethra, are especially prone to infection by bacteria in the mucous sheath. In men most urinary tract infections are caused by contamination of the catheter or the drainage bag by bacteria carried on the hands of hospital personnel. Even closed drainage techniques are not strictly maintained and contamination of urine occurs. Urine can become contaminated when catheter junctions are broken or the drainage bag is handled improperly. Bacteria, such as *S. marcescens* and *P. aeruginosa,* are frequently permanent members of the hospital environment. They are regularly associated with cross contamination and are responsible for clusters of urinary tract infections.

Bacteria possess adhesins that permit attachment to bladder epithelial cells and to catheter materials. Bacteria also secrete sticky compounds that promote the attachment of other bacteria as well as debris to the site of colonization. Eventually obstructions are formed and interfere with the normal flow or urine. In addition, the catheter causes mechanical injury that impairs normal host defenses and increases the likelihood of infection.

Approximately 70 percent of patients who become bacteriuric at catheterization will become culture negative without treatment. Of the remaining 30 percent, only 2 to 5 percent will have urinary tract involvement. Pyelonephritis and renal abscesses are complications for some of these individuals. Gram-negative bacteremia is a very serious complication of urinary tract involvement. The case-fatality rate for these infections can be as high as 30 percent depending on the patient's underlying disease before catheterization.

Prevention and Control. Indwelling catheters should be avoided when possible and removed as soon as circumstances permit. Early removal of catheters may prevent as many as 40 percent of urinary tract infections. Alternative drainage methods, such as intermittent catheterization and suprapubic catheters, do not reduce substantially the risk of infection. Preventing infection by eradicating organisms that colonize the perineum or urinary meatus or by removing bacteria that colonize bladder urine is not always successful. These approaches often predispose the patient to colonization by drug-resistant microorganisms. Exogenous contamination of the drainage system can be reduced by using closed, sterile bladder drainage. However, the use of presealed catheters and antireflux valves and instillation of antibacterial solutions into the drainage bag have not been shown to be effective.

The Centers for Disease Control (CDC) has developed guidelines for preventing urinary tract infections: (1) catheterize only when necessary; (2) educate personnel about the proper technique of catheter insertion; (3) use an aseptic technique when inserting the catheter; (4) emphasize handwashing; (5) secure the catheter properly; (6) maintain closed sterile drainage; (7) when irrigation of the catheter is necessary, use an intermittent method; (8) obtain urine samples aseptically; and (9) maintain unobstructed urine flow.

Effective surveillance in high-risk areas of the hospital to identify increased rates of infection is important. When a cluster of cases is identified, an investigation should be conducted to identify the source of infection. Antiseptics placed in drainage bag reservoirs may be effective in decreasing contamination and reducing the cross transmission of infection. In some instances it may be necessary to treat colonized patients with antibiotics or urinary suppressants.

Vascular Indwelling Catheters. It is estimated that vascular catheters are inserted into 20 million patients each year in the United States. Short-term noncuffed central venous catheters (CVC) are associated with the highest rate of septicemia (4–14 percent). It is estimated that there are, at a minimum, 120,000 cases of CVC-related septicemia each year. Most of these infections can be resolved with proper diagnosis and treatment.

Diagnosis. Catheter-associated infections may be local or systemic. Local infections are characterized by purulence

FIGURE 35-2
Sources of intravascular cannula-related infection. The major sources are the skin flora, contaminated catheter hub, contaminated infusate, and hematogenous colonization of the intravascular device and its fibronectin-fibrin sheath. (From D. G. Maki. In J. V. Bennett and P. S. Brachman, eds., *Hospital Infections*, 3rd ed. Boston: Little, Brown, 1992.)

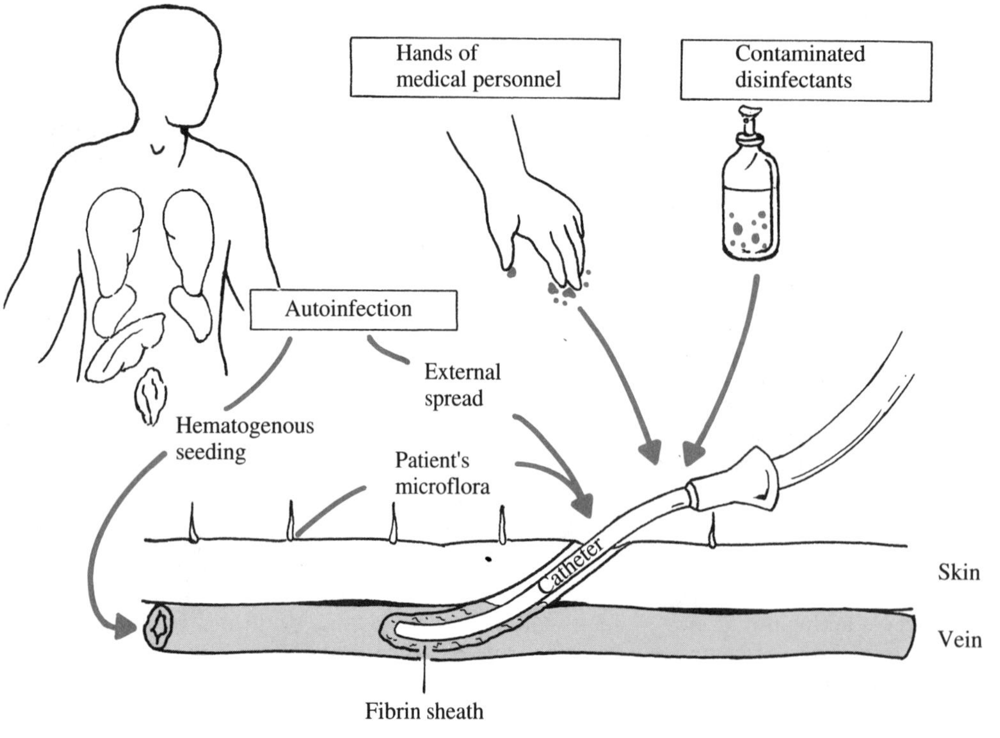

around the catheter insertion site without a bloodstream infection. Systemic catheter-related septicemia is brought about by organisms from the skin of the patient (*S. aureus, S. epidermidis,* and *Candida*). The latter diagnosis is based on exclusion of other sources of infection such as pneumonia, wound, or urinary tract infection.

Implication of the catheter as the source of infection is confirmed by the results of either quantitative catheter cultures or quantitative blood cultures. One of the limitations of the catheter culture technique is that the clinician has to remove or exchange the catheter to obtain specimens for culture. For quantitative blood cultures, simultaneous blood samples are drawn through the catheter and a peripheral vein without removal or exchange of the catheter. When the number of organisms obtained through the CVC is severalfold greater than that quantitated from a peripheral blood culture, catheter-related sepsis is diagnosed.

Pathogenesis. The sources for catheter colonization and catheter-related sepsis include (1) the skin insertion site, (2) the catheter hub, (3) hematogenous seeding of the catheter, and (4) infusate contamination (Fig. 35-2). The first two sources are the most important. The skin of the patient is the most common source of short-term catheter colonization and infection. The catheter hub is the most frequent site of contamination by medical personnel. Contaminating organisms can migrate along the internal surface of the catheter and eventually invade the bloodstream. Hematogenous seeding implies that microorganisms from a distant site (for example, a lung) colonize the catheter. Infusion-related bacteremia, for example, from contaminated parenteral nutrition solutions, is due primarily to gram-negative bacilli, such as *Enterobacter, Pseudomonas, Serratia,* and *Citrobacter* species.

The body responds to the presence of a catheter by forming a layer of fibrin and fibronectin around the sleeve. This film of material is strongly adhered to by species such as *S. aureus* and *Candida* (Fig. 35-3). Microbial adherence can be enhanced by slime-producing organisms such as *S. epidermidis.* The biofilm of host and microbial components acts as a barrier to antimicrobials, phagocytes, and antibodies. In addition to host and microbial factors, the catheter material plays an important role in the adherence process. For example, *S. aureus* and *Candida* species (*C. albicans, C. parapsilosis*) adhere better to polyvinylchloride than to Teflon catheters.

Prevention. Recognition of the risk factors is the first most important step in the prevention of catheter-associated infections. These risk factors are summarized in Table 35-4.

A very successful technique for preventing catheter-associated infections is the establishment of an expert infusion-therapy team. Such a team can be especially cost-effective in institutions where there is a high rate of catheter-related infections. The second most effective technique is to use topical disinfectants and antibiotics at the skin insertion site. Povidone-iodine ointment does not appear

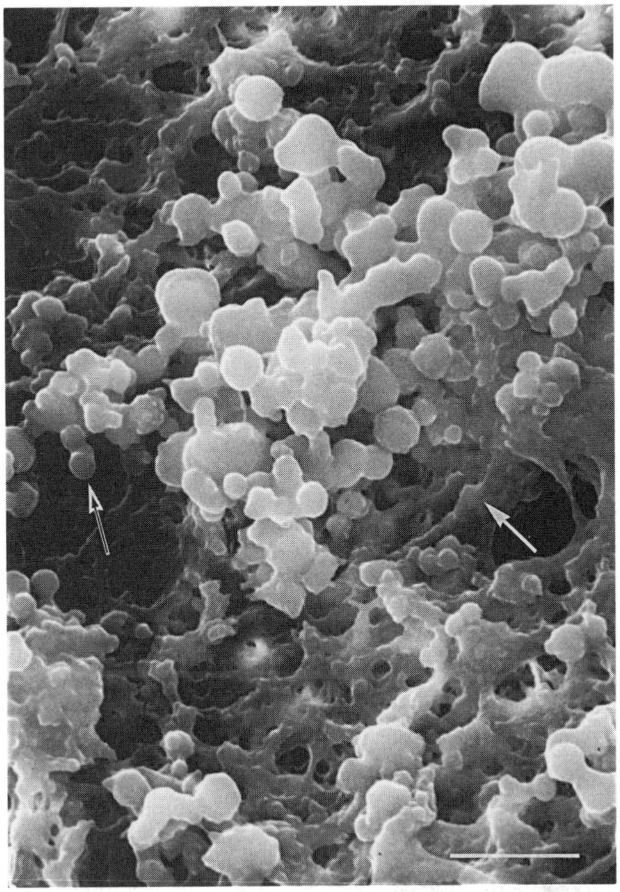

FIGURE 35-3
Scanning electron micrograph of a *Staphylococcus aureus*–infected central venous silicone catheter. The white arrow points to the biofilm and the black arrow points to coccal forms. (× 5000, bar = 5 μm.) (From I. I. Raad and G. P. Bodey, *Clin. Infect. Dis.* 15:197, 1992.)

to reduce the rate of catheter-related infections. Chlorhexidine gluconate, however, is effective in reducing the rate of catheter-related bacteremia. Topical antibiotics (polymyxin in combination with bacitracin and neomycin) dramatically reduce the incidence of bacterial infections. Unfortunately, they also increase the risk of infections by *Candida* species that are resistant to the antibiotics. A technique that is effective in reducing infection is the coating of CVC with antibiotics or antiseptics. For example, coatings of silver sulfadiazine and chlorhexidine can bring about a fourfold reduction in the rate of catheter-related bacteremias compared to noncoated CVC.

The attachable silver-impregnated cuff can reduce the incidence of catheter-related infections in patients using CVC short-term (mean in-place duration of 5.6–9.1 days). Patients using CVC long-term (mean duration of 20 days) are not protected by the silver cuff.

Treatment and Management. Treatment of catheter-related infections depends on the condition of the patient, the type of infection, the catheter material, and the microbial species involved.

TABLE 35-4
Risk Factors Associated with Catheter-Related Infection

Factor	Comments
Prolonged catheterization	CVC risk of infection increases 3.3%/day.
Transparent plastic dressings at insertion site	Dressings provide warm moist area for microbial growth.
Frequent manipulation of catheter	
Catheter material	Flexible silicone and polyurethane are less thrombogenic than polyvinylchloride. Teflon is better than polyvinylchloride in preventing adherence of microorganisms.
Number of catheter lumina	Single-lumen CVC are associated with lower risk of infection than are triple-lumen CVC.
Catheter location	The infection rate is higher for CVC than for arterial or short peripheral catheters.
Improper aseptic techniques	Improper insertion and maintenance techniques and use of cutdowns for the insertion of catheters.
Contaminated skin solutions	Contaminated skin solutions used at site of catheter insertion.

CVC = central venous catheter.

Local infections may be treated without removal of the tunneled catheter. Tunnel infections* are more serious and require catheter removal and intravenous administration of antibiotics.

Septicemia may be uncomplicated or may be complicated by septic thrombosis. Uncomplicated septicemia may be managed by intravenous antibiotic therapy for up to one week. Septic thrombosis should be treated with parenteral antibiotics for at least four weeks.

Treatment and management of specific microbial species include the following:

1. Coagulase-negative staphylococci (e.g., *S. epidermidis*). Since 50 to 80 percent of coagulase-negative staphylococci are resistant to the antistaphylococcal penicillins, intravenous vancomycin is the treatment of choice. Treatment can proceed without catheter removal; however, without catheter removal there is a greater risk of recurrent bacteremia.
2. *S. aureus.* Bacteremia involving this microorganism may be uncomplicated or complicated. Complicated bacteremia is frequent in high-risk patients such as cancer patients and may consist of septic emboli, endocarditis, osteomyelitis, and abscesses. Uncomplicated bacteremia can be treated intravenously with semisynthetic penicillins or vancomycin for 10 to 14 days. Complicated cases should be treated for at least four weeks. Catheter removal is suggested for *S. aureus* bacteremia.
3. Yeasts. Catheter-related infections caused by *Candida* can be treated with amphotericin B. Catheter removal is suggested only if the patient does not respond to therapy after 96 hours.
4. Gram-negative bacilli. Enteric bacilli are rarely involved in catheter-related infections. *Acinetobacter, Achromobacter, Xanthomonas maltophilia,* and non-*aeruginosa Pseudomonas* species have occasionally been involved in catheter-related infections. *X. maltophilia* infection is treated with trimethoprim-sulfamethoxazole while other gram-negative infections can be successfully treated with third-generation cephalosporins, carbapenems, aminoglycosides, and quinolones. The duration of therapy should not exceed two weeks and catheter removal is not necessary. However, catheter removal is recommended for infections caused by *Pseudomonas* species.
5. Gram-positive bacilli and mycobacteria. Catheter-related infections caused by *Bacillus* species can be treated with vancomycin. *Corynebacterium* species can cause endocarditis and their management requires removal of the catheter during therapy. Atypical mycobacteria such as *Mycobacterium chelonae* and *Mycobacterium fortuitum* can cause catheter-related infections. They are best treated by catheter removal and parenteral administration of cefoxitin and amikacin.

* This condition is characterized by a spreading cellulitis around the subcutaneous tunnel tract of tunneled long-term catheters such as Hickman-Broviac catheters.

Antibiotic Chemotherapy

The areas within the hospital having the highest usage of antimicrobials are the intensive care units, burn units, and special surgery care areas. These areas also have the highest prevalence of antimicrobial-resistant bacteria. Colonization with these resistant bacteria will occur even in those who are not being treated with antimicrobial agents. This is related to the individual's time of exposure to patients who are being treated with antimicrobials.

There has been considerable debate concerning the prophylactic use of antimicrobials for surgical techniques. Antimicrobial-resistant microorganisms can arise endogenously if the antimicrobials are improperly used. For surgical operations in which there is no contamination, the administration of antimicrobials is not recommended. Antimicrobial prophylaxis is currently considered acceptable for the following procedures:

1. Cardiovascular—valve and open heart, coronary artery bypass
2. Orthopedic—prosthetic joint replacement
3. Biliary tract—patient over 70 years old, acute cholecystitis, obstructive jaundice, or stones in common bile duct
4. Intestinal—colonic
5. Gynecological—vaginal hysterectomy, cesarean section
6. Urological—patients bacteriuric before urological procedures

The antimicrobial agent should be administered 1 to 2 hours before surgery, and the last dose (the number of doses should not exceed six) should be administered less than 24 hours after surgery.

Some techniques that have supplanted surgery may also require antibiotic prophylaxis (see Under the Microscope 52).

Hypodermic Injections

Hypodermic injections can be a source of infection in three ways: (1) use of contaminated needles or syringes, (2) displacement of an infectious agent from the surface of the skin into the bloodstream or underlying tissue in the injection process, and (3) use of contaminated solutions for injection. Of the three, injection of contaminated solutions is the principal source of infection. Any kind of injectable fluid such as blood, vitamins, and vaccines may be contaminated before injection and thereby transmit infectious microorganisms to the patient. In the United States, 20,000 to 30,000 cases of viral hepatitis arising from transfused blood acquired from donors infected with the hepatitis virus are reported each year. Blood donors are now being screened for hepatitis viruses (hepatitis B, hepatitis C). Whenever possible, washed packed red blood cells should be used for transfusions. These procedures alone have begun to reduce the incidence of transfusion-related hepatitis.

Diagnostic Procedures

Diagnostic procedures or equipment used on patients by physicians or other medical personnel have been implicated as sources of nosocomial infection. These devices or instruments often are not decontaminated before use on the next patient. In addition, endogenous microorganisms may be displaced into abraded tissue, thereby giving rise to infection. Among the instruments implicated are cystoscopes, urometers, cannulas of urinary catheters, gastrointestinal fiberoptic endoscopes, and pressure monitoring devices such as venous and arterial pressure transducers.

Prevention and Control of Nosocomial Infections

ENVIRONMENTAL SURVEILLANCE

One of the keys to the management and control of hospital-acquired infections is surveillance. It has become evident that antibiotics have not reduced the risk of hospital-associated infections. The only important change brought about by the use of these drugs is a shift in the type of infectious agent involved in infections. Today, the gram-negative bacilli have replaced the gram-positive cocci in terms of the number of hospital-acquired infections. Many hospitals now have resident epidemiologists or infection-control nurses whose duty is to determine the frequency and kind of nosocomial infections. Attempts to reduce infection by surveillance and control of environmental factors, however, have been only moderately successful. Culturing of the entire hospital environment is not practical and in many instances is of little value. Procedures that are believed to be of maximum benefit should be performed in all hospitals:

1. Environmental culturing only as part of an investigation of a disease outbreak or other problems of patient infection.

UNDER THE MICROSCOPE 52

A New Hospital Technique—Lithotripsy

Lithotripsy is a new technique that has become the preferred method for the treatment of urinary stones or calculi. The treatment, which involves the use of shock waves, has almost completely supplanted open surgery and, to a lesser extent, endourological approaches. When the stones are broken up, thousands of minute fragments are released and can remain in the collecting system of the patient for weeks to months. Many of these stones are infected with urea-splitting microorganisms that may cause urinary tract infections, obstructive pyelonephritis, and septicemia.

Recent studies demonstrated that there may be a need for antibiotic prophylaxis in a select group of patients: those with staghorn or struvite calculi, a large stone burden, infected urine, or a documented history of recurrent urinary tract infections. In the absence of complicating factors there is no indication for antibiotic prophylaxis. Characterization of organisms and their antibiotic sensitivities, before lithotripsy is initiated, is necessary should infection occur in those with complications.

These studies once again demonstrate that with each new hospital procedure the risk of hospital-associated infection increases.

---

2. Testing the effectiveness of steam and ethylene oxide sterilizers.
3. Testing the sterility of products prepared in the hospital that have been shown to present risk of contamination. These products include infant formula, hyperalimentation fluids prepared in the hospital, and breast milk collected for group use.
4. Testing the effectiveness of decontamination and disinfection of instruments such as endoscopes, inhalation therapy equipment, and physical therapy equipment.

Environmental surveillance is but one of the roles of the infection-control nurse, who must also become involved in control, teaching, and implementation policy.

HYGIENIC PRACTICES

It is important that housekeeping practices as well as patient-related medical procedures be evaluated. The maintenance of a satisfactory standard of hygienic practices is the duty of all hospital personnel, from physician to kitchen cook. Disinfectants and antiseptics are used in the hospital to maintain a standard of hygiene (Table 35-5). The use of a particular disinfectant or antiseptic depends on several factors (see Chapter 7).

Hygienic practices are extremely important in controlling and preventing nosocomial infections. It is necessary to maintain aseptic technique while handling instruments, catheters, intravenous therapy equipment, and any other type of device that may come in contact with the hospitalized patient. The one practice that probably reduces the incidence of nosocomial infections more than any other, and yet is often overlooked, is **handwashing.** It is estimated that at least 50 percent of hospital infections could be prevented by handwashing. Although cross contamination by hand transmission occurs frequently in the hospitalized patient, handwashing is not consistently performed. The microflora of the skin harbors an indigenous population of microorganisms such as *S. epidermidis* and *Propionibacterium* species, both of which are considered relatively nonvirulent. Because of constant contact with patients and the perpetuation of certain species in the hospital, large numbers of more virulent microorganisms are also carried on the skin, for example, *S. aureus* and gram-negative species.

The human immunodeficiency virus (HIV) epidemic has affected the practice of surgery as well as other hospital personnel and patient interactions with HIV-infected patients (see Under the Microscope 53). To reduce the risk of HIV transmission and other blood-borne viruses in the health care setting, the CDC has recommended **universal precautions.** These precautions are based on the premise that blood is a toxic substance. Universal precautions were described in the discussion of hepatitis viruses in Chapter 32 (see also the 1988 Centers for Disease Control publication listed in Additional Readings).

During the handling of patients it is very important to remove contaminating microorganisms from the skin.

TABLE 35-5
Useful Disinfectants and Antiseptics Employed in the Hospital

	Activity against				
Compound*	Vegetative bacteria and fungi	TB bacillus	Hepatitis virus	Spores	Uses (and limitations)
Alcohols					
Ethyl	+	+	−	−	Skin antiseptic
Isopropyl	+	+	−	−	Skin antiseptic
Iodine					
Tincture of iodine	+	?	−	−	Skin antiseptic
Iodophors	+	+	−	−	Unstable, skin antiseptic
Phenols and cresols					
1–2% Phenols	+	+	−	−	Disinfectant, stable in solution
Chlorophenol	+	+	−	−	More active than phenol but more toxic
Hexachlorophene	+	−	−	−	Antiseptic, good surgical scrub
Chlorhexidine	+	−	−	−	Skin antiseptic
Chlorine					
Chloramine	+	−	−	−	1–2% solution for wounds
Sodium hypochlorite	+	+	+	?	Disinfectant, unstable in solution
Formaldehyde	+	+	+	+	Disinfectant, noxious fumes
Glutaraldehyde	+	+	+	+	Disinfectant, unstable, toxic
Ethylene oxide	+	+	+	+	Disinfectant, toxic, absorbed by porous material
Quaternary ammonium compounds	+	−	−	−	Antiseptic, ineffective against gram-negatives

* 0.2% Sodium nitrite added to alcohols, formalin, quaternary ammonium compounds, and iodophors prevents corrosive actions of these agents; 0.5% sodium bicarbonate added to phenolic compounds reduces the corrosive action of those compounds.

UNDER THE MICROSCOPE 53

HIV Infection in Health Care Workers

There have been at least 65 case reports of health care workers whose HIV infection is associated with occupational exposure. Included below are some descriptions of the conditions in which some of these infections took place.

1. A hospital worker accidentally self-injected several milliliters of blood while collecting blood in a vacuum collection tube from an AIDS patient.
2. A phlebotomist reported that blood splattered on her face and in her mouth when the top of a vacuum blood collection tube flew off while she was collecting blood from an HIV-infected patient. The worker was wearing gloves and glasses and reported that no blood got into her eyes. She did not have any open wounds but did have acne on her face.
3. A health care worker was accidentally stuck with a 21-gauge needle while attempting to resuscitate an AIDS patient.
4. A medical technologist was exposed to a blood spill that covered most of her hands and forearms while she was manipulating an apheresis machine, which is a machine that separates blood components, retains some, and returns the remainder to the donor. Although she was not wearing gloves, she did not recall having any open wounds on her hands. However, she had dermatitis on her ear and may have touched that ear.
5. A health care worker applied pressure to an HIV-infected patient's arterial catheter insertion site to stop bleeding. During the procedure, she may have had a small amount of blood on her index finger for 20 minutes before washing her hands. She did not wear gloves during the procedure, and her hands were chapped.
6. A 33-year-old U.S. Navy hospital corpsman punctured his fingertip while disposing of a phlebotomy needle used to draw blood from an AIDS patient.

Washing one's hands with soap and water is sufficient to reduce the microbial populations of the skin. Because of the drying effect of soap and the failure of soap to remain bacteriostatic for any length of time, other antiseptic agents are more suitable. Iodophors and 3% hexachlorophene are two agents that are extensively used. In 1976 the Food and Drug Administration approved the use of chlorhexidine gluconate with 4% isopropyl alcohol in a sudsing base (Hibiclens) as a surgical scrub, patient-care handwashing agent, and superficial wound cleanser. This preparation appears to achieve a more immediate reduction in the amount of skin flora than do the other agents and has a more sustained antimicrobial effect.

HOSPITAL PERSONNEL SURVEILLANCE

The immunization records of all hospital personnel should be checked and vaccinations given or recommended if they have not been done. Certain personnel should be vaccinated for tuberculosis and offered immunization against poliomyelitis, tetanus, diphtheria, hepatitis B, and rubella. The rubella vaccination is especially important for members of hospital staff who come in contact with nurses, physicians, patients, and pregnant women (see Chapter 32).

PATIENT SURVEILLANCE

When patients are admitted to the hospital, their medical files should include an infection "report card." During their stay, data regarding disease treatment should be recorded. This information should include

1. The type of infection, if any, the patient has on admission to the hospital
2. The kind and site of any hospital-acquired infection
3. The organism isolated from the infection site
4. Any surgical procedure or chemotherapy that preceded the development of infection
5. The antibiotic regimen employed to combat infection
6. The length of time required to control the infection

The information gathered from the report card can be compiled each week and a monthly report distributed to the infection-control committee. The data would thus include statistics on infections as to site, causative agents isolated, and antibiotic regimen employed. An increase in the rate of infection can then be investigated and the source of infection uncovered.

If an infectious disease is detected in the patient on admission to the hospital, he or she may require isolation. Isolation is necessary for persons who have such diseases as meningococcal meningitis, staphylococcal pneumonia, tuberculosis, diphtheria, whooping cough, measles (rubella and rubeola), chickenpox, mumps, influenza, or pneumonic plague. Patients who have been compromised by hospital procedures should also be isolated from other patients. This group would include patients recovering from open-heart surgery or transplantation, burn patients, and those requiring renal dialysis. It is very important to protect these individuals from airborne microbes that are easily transferred in an open ward. Isolation can be accomplished by means of plastic tents and laminar airflow, in which a positive current of filtered air is directed at the patient. The positive pressure of this airflow prevents access of contaminated air from other sources.

Summary

1. The term nosocomial disease is a synonym for hospital-associated disease. Nosocomial diseases differ from community-acquired diseases primarily in their epidemiology.

2. The microbial agents responsible for nosocomial diseases can be transmitted from patient to patient indirectly via hospital personnel, directly by contact with contaminated fomites or solutions, and by air. However, most nosocomial infections are caused by species that are part of the victim's own microbial flora.

3. The most prevalent microbial groups causing infection are the gram-negative bacilli, which include *Escherichia coli, Pseudomonas aeruginosa,* and species of *Klebsiella, Serratia,* and others. *Staphylococcus aureus* is one of the most frequently isolated species, primarily because most hospital personnel are carriers of the microbial species.

4. *Candida* and *Aspergillus* are the two most frequently isolated genera of fungi causing disease, while viruses such as rubella, respiratory syncytial virus, varicella-zoster virus, herpes simplex virus, and hepatitis A virus are the most frequent causes of nosocomial disease. Some viruses such as herpes simplex and cytomegalovirus are endogenous viruses that may be activated by hospital procedures or conditions of the host.

5. Microbial factors contributing to nosocomial disease have been brought about by the frequent use of antimicrobial agents, whose presence encourages the selection of resistant strains of a microbial species. Many of these resistant strains can readily transfer their resistance factors, via plasmids, to other species.

6. The immunological state of the host is the single most important factor determining an individual's susceptibility to infection. Age, metabolic disorders, use of immunosuppressive drugs, and burn wounds reduce one's resistance to infection, particularly infection by opportunistic microorganisms.

7. Hospital procedures including surgery, antibiotic chemotherapy, hypodermic injection, and diagnostic and therapeutic procedures lead to the introduction of microorganisms into host tissue. Most of the time the organisms are part of the host's flora that were displaced by surgery or diagnostic procedures.

8. Catheterization, which is performed on many patients, is the single most important procedure causing predisposition to infection. The Centers for Disease Control has specific recommendations for the prevention of catheter-associated infections.

9. Antibiotic prophylaxis is necessary for surgical procedures during which microbial contamination is certain and infection could be catastrophic.

10. Hypodermic injections can be a source of infection in three ways: (1) by use of contaminated needles, (2) by displacement of infectious agents from the skin, and (3) by use of contaminated solutions. Blood transfusions, for example, can cause hepatitis.

11. Diagnostic procedures that utilize devices such as cystoscopes and fiberoptic endoscopes can be causes of nosocomial disease. The infections may arise because of contamination of the instrument or displacement of endogenous microorganisms.

12. Studies have demonstrated that hospital infection-control programs headed by an infection-control nurse and/or physician can bring about significant reductions in the number of nosocomial diseases. These programs include techniques for environmental surveillance, maintenance of hygienic practices, and surveillance of patient and hospital personnel.

Questions for Study

1. Discuss the reasons why there appears to be an increase in hospital-associated infections during the past 15 years.
2. What microorganism is most frequently associated with nosocomial infections? What is the reason for this?
3. Describe the situations in the hospital where handwashing is an absolute must in preventing infection.
4. Make a list of the six most frequently isolated microorganisms from nosocomial infection sites. Also describe the body site most frequently associated with infection by each of the six species or genera.
5. Discuss the microbial factors that are responsible for differences in community- versus hospital-associated infections.
6. Describe some of the advantages and disadvantages of immunosuppressive drugs.
7. Describe the procedures that help reduce the incidence of infection in patients undergoing surgery.
8. When is the prophylactic use of antibiotics indicated in the hospital? Under what conditions can their use be harmful?
9. What guidelines should a nurse follow while attempting to prevent catheter-associated infections? What genera or species of microbes are most frequently associated with infections following urinary catheterization?
10. Why are *Candida* and *Aspergillus* species often associated with nosocomial infections? What factors contribute to their association with infection?

Appendices

APPENDIX

A Observation of Microorganisms: Microscopy and Staining

Probably one of the more exciting aspects of microbiology for the beginning student is the realization that individual microorganisms, as small as they are, have shape and are composed of structures that can be identified. Visualization of microorganisms is impossible with the naked eye because they are so small (Fig. A-1). Microbial images can be magnified with the aid of a microscope. Most of the time, because of their transparency, microorganisms must be stained to enhance their visualization.

The purpose of this appendix is to discuss the various types of microscopes that are used in the research and clinical laboratory to identify and characterize microorganisms and viruses. In addition, we discuss the primary staining techniques used in the clinical laboratory.

Microscopy

RESOLVING POWER

One of the purposes of a microscope is to enlarge or magnify the image, but magnification is of no value if the image is blurred. It is therefore important that the microorganism is clearly defined when observed. The property of definition is called the **resolving power,** and it is this property that determines the quality of the microscope. The resolving power of a microscope refers to the smallest detectable separation of two points or objects. In other words, how close can two objects be brought together and still be seen as two clearly defined objects? The resolving power of a microscope is dependent on the **wavelength** of light used in the optical system as well as a characteristic of the objective lens, called the **numerical aperture.** The formula for resolving power (RP) is

$$RP = \frac{\text{Wavelength}}{2 \times \text{Numerical aperture}}$$

Since both the wavelength and the numerical aperture have narrow limits, the resolving power of the microscope using conventional light sources is very limited. Only with the advent of the electron microscope has it been possible to increase greatly the magnification and, more important, the resolving power of optical instruments.

TYPES OF MICROSCOPES

Compound Bright-Field

The compound bright-field microscope (Fig. A-2) is called **compound** because the total magnification is due to the contribution of two magnifying lenses: an objective lens and an ocular lens. It is called **bright-field** because the light passing through it produces a brightly illuminated field around the object being viewed. The source of illumination is visible light, usually from an incandescent light bulb. The proper manipulation of the condenser and iris diaphragm is essential to achieve optimum contrast, depth of field, and resolution. The **condenser** contains lenses that bring the light rays into focus on the specimen, while the **iris diaphragm**, located between the condenser and the light source, controls the amount of light entering the condenser. The background surrounding the specimen will therefore appear very bright by using the conventional bright-field condenser.

Magnification in the compound bright-field microscope is equal to the product of the objective lens and ocular lens magnifications. The standard microscope has at least three objective lenses, with magnifications of 10×, 44×, and 100×. The **ocular lens** has a magnification of 10×. Thus, the maximum magnification that can be obtained is 1000×. The 100× **objective lens** is called the **oil immersion lens,** and when it is used oil is placed between the coverslip covering the specimen and the lens. By using the oil immersion lens with the 100× objective, the mathematical expression for the numerical aperture can be increased, thereby increasing the resolving power of the

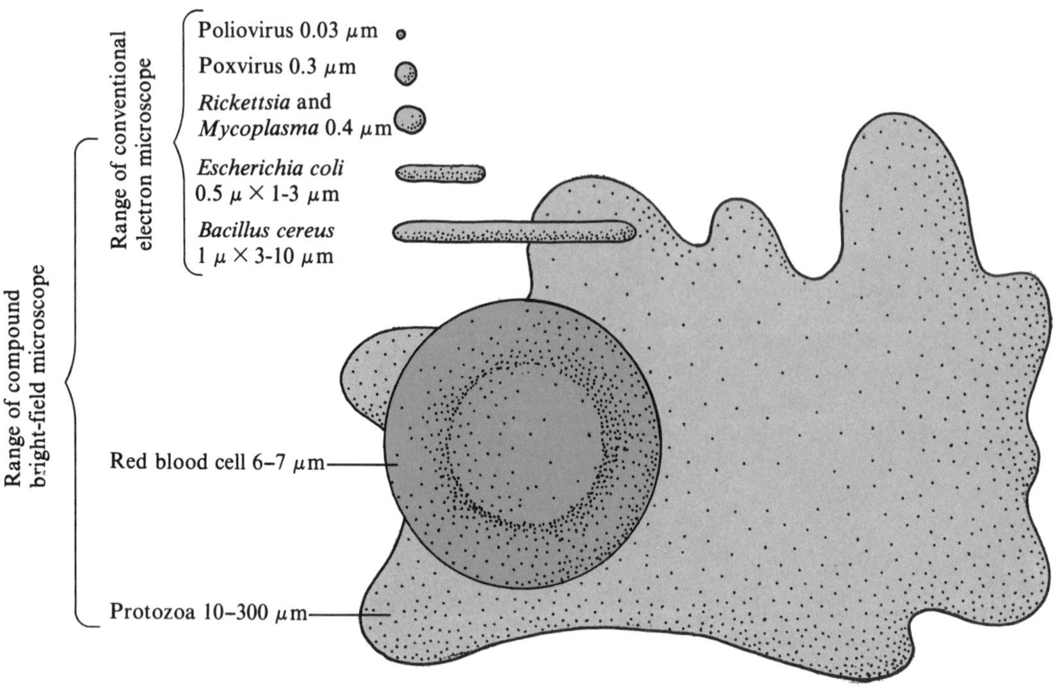

FIGURE A-1
Comparative size of microorganisms.

microscope. Immersion oil has the same refractive index* as the glass slide, and therefore light rays are not further refracted, as they would be in air. The resolving power of the compound bright-field microscope is approximately 0.2 μm; that is, if two bacterial cells 0.2 μm or more apart are examined, each can be clearly distinguished. If they are closer than 0.2 μm, they will appear as a blurred single cell.

Conventional bright-field illumination will not reveal brightness differences between the structural details of the specimen and its surroundings. In other words, the bacteria appear transparent. The transparency problem can be rectified by staining the cells or by using other microscopical techniques that take advantage of differences in optical density and refractive index produced in the specimen.

One of the advantages of bright-field microscopy is that living specimens can be examined. For example, it is relatively easy to determine the motility of bacteria.

Dark-Field

The dark-field microscope is frequently used to observe viable microorganisms that are very small or thin and whose morphology is best observed without staining. The condensers are the key to dark-field microscopy. A special light condenser is substituted for the customary bright-field condenser. Dark-field condensers channel the light rays at such an oblique angle that undiffracted rays are not collected by the objective lens. Only the rays diffracted by the specimen on the slide enter the objective. The background surrounding the specimen appears dark or black (Fig. A-3). Organisms or structures whose diameter is less than the resolving power of the compound microscope can be observed by this technique. Bacterial flagella, which are only 0.02 μm in diameter, can be observed because they scatter enough light for their profile to be seen. Spirochetes, for example, are bacteria whose width is between 0.15 and 0.2 μm and they can be easily observed using dark-field microscopy (see Plate 17).

Phase-Contrast

The phase-contrast microscope has special condensers and objectives that are capable of altering light as it passes through and around the specimen. Light can be diffracted not only by the cell wall but also by any large structures in the cytoplasm whose density is greater than that of the surrounding medium. Every object observed by this technique is surrounded by a halo of light (Fig. A-4A), which does not represent a real structure. The internal structure of the cell can be revealed by this technique. For example, nuclear bodies and endospores (Fig. A-5) are easily observed.

Nomarski Interference

Nomarski interference microscopy is similar in many respects to phase-contrast microscopy. This technique requires specimens that are thicker than bacteria, for example, vegetative (growing) cells and spores of fungi. The

* Refractive index (RI) is a measure of the extent to which light is slowed down by a medium. Oil has the same RI as glass, but air has a lower RI than glass.

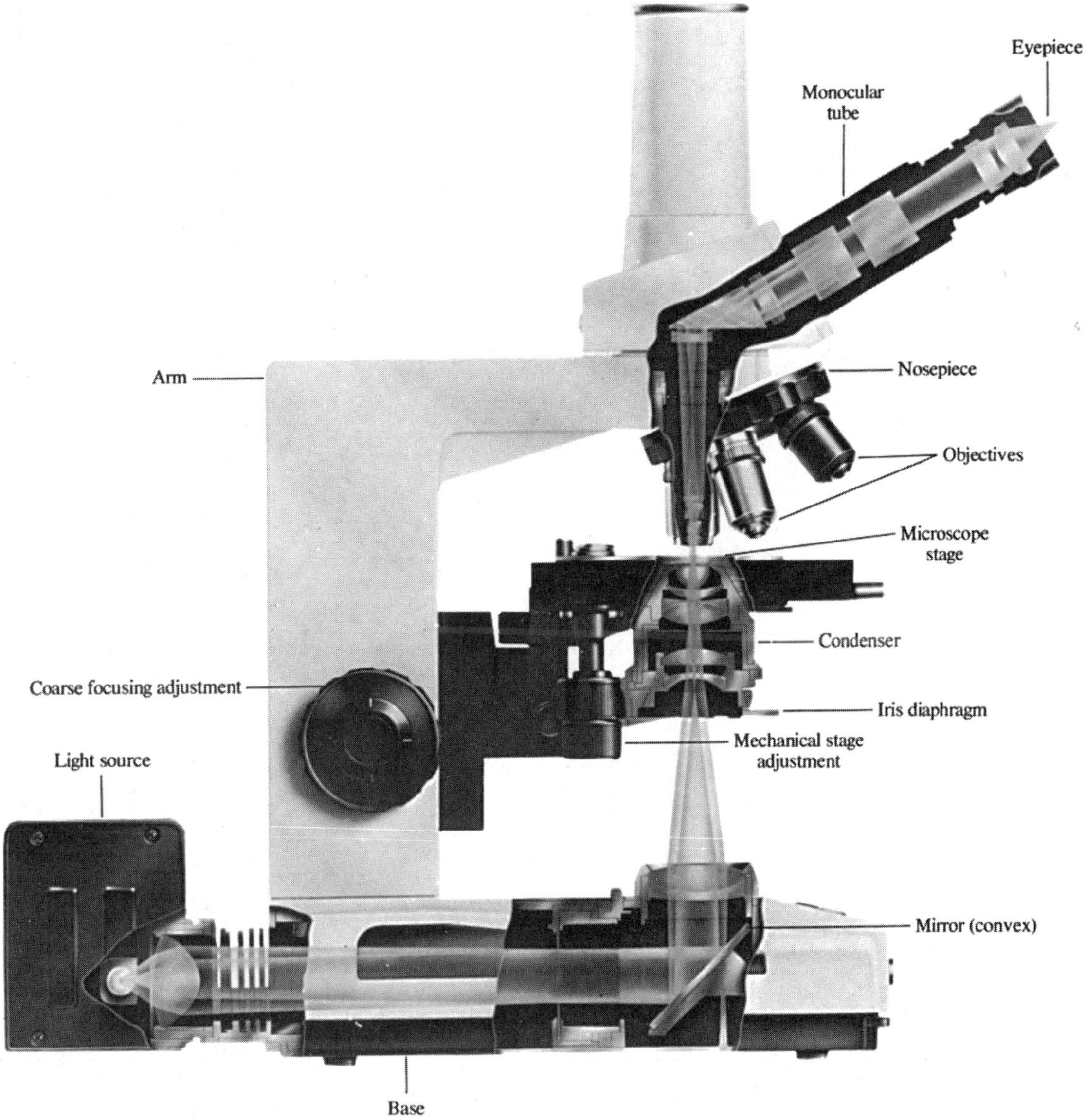

FIGURE A-2
Compound bright-field microscope. (Courtesy of Nikon, Inc., Rochester, NY.)

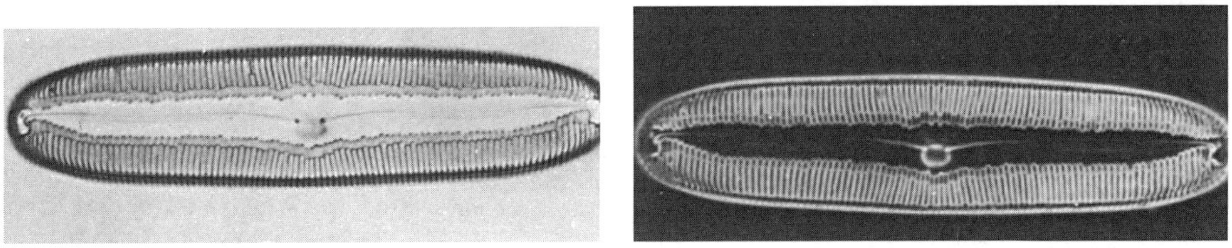

A B

FIGURE A-3
Comparison of the images produced by (A) compound bright-field microscopy and (B) dark-field microscopy. (From R. F. Smith, *Microscopy and Photomicrography.* New York: Appleton-Century-Crofts, 1982.)

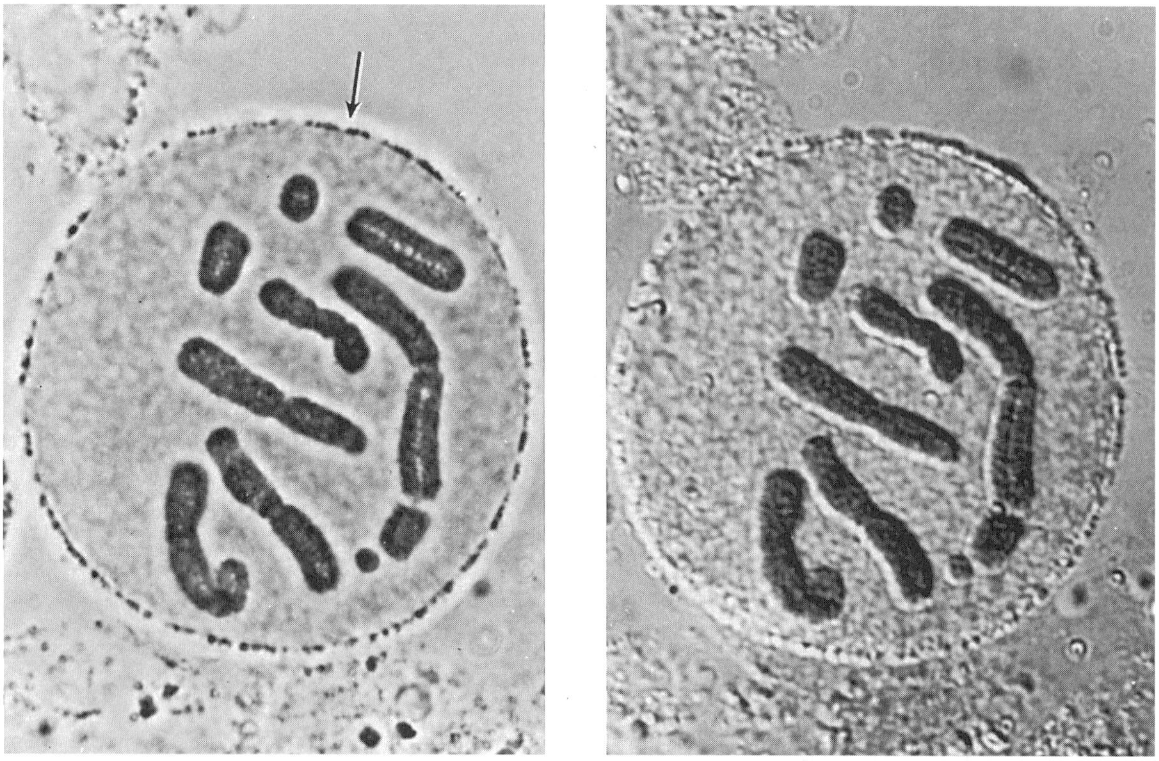

A B

FIGURE A-4

A. Phase-contrast microscopy. Note the halo *(arrow)* around the spherical nucleus. B. Nomarski interference microscopy. Note that Nomarski microscopy appears to provide greater definition or clarity than does phase-contrast microscopy. (From R. F. Smith, *Microscopy and Photomicrography.* New York: Appleton-Century-Crofts, 1982.)

FIGURE A-5

Phase-contrast micrograph of bacterial cells in which endospores *(arrow)* have been produced. (× 3600.) (Courtesy of P. C. Fitz-James.)

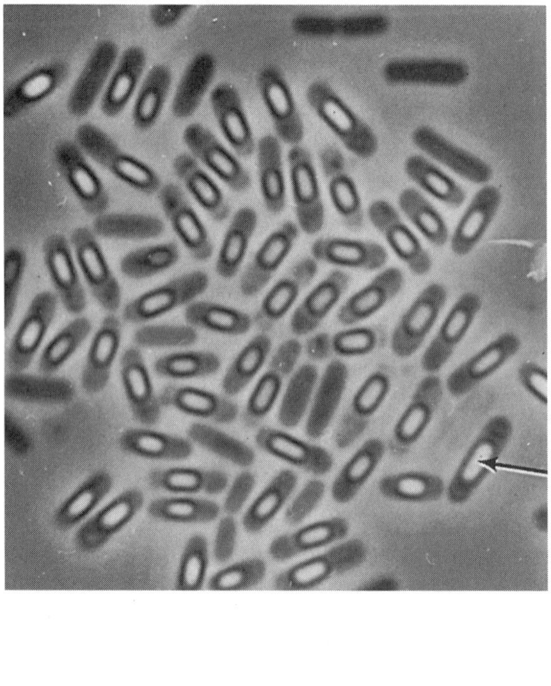

presence of a polarizer and special prisms in the condenser results in the formation of an image clearer than that obtained with phase contrast. The object being examined, for example, has no halo and there is a three-dimensional appearance to the specimen (Fig. A-4B). The resolving power in Nomarski interference microscopy is about twice that of the bright-field microscope, which is 0.1 μm.

Fluorescent

Many materials are luminescent; that is, they absorb energy and release light. If the material absorbs a quantity of light and, after a delay of less than one-millionth of a second, re-emits a quantity of light of a larger wavelength, the material is called **fluorescent.** A few compounds fluoresce when illuminated with ultraviolet light or other short wavelengths of light and they are called **fluorochromes.** One of the most frequently used fluorochromes is called **fluorescein.** Microbiological material can be studied by coating it with fluorochromes. An important type of fluorescent microscopy is called **immunofluorescent microscopy.** In this technique fluorochromes may be conjugated (complexed) to specific antibodies to identify unknown specimens or structures, or conversely, they may be conjugated to specific antigens to detect antibod-

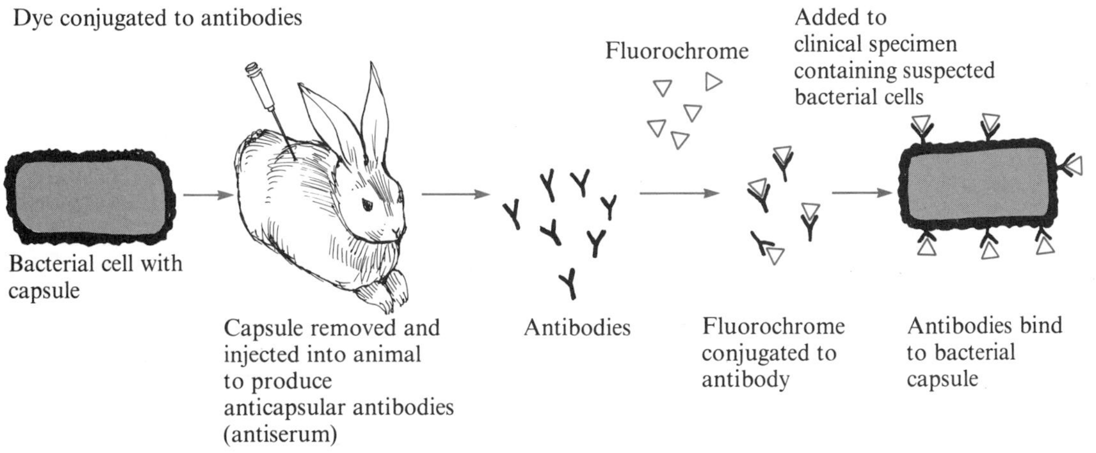
Dye conjugated to antibodies
Fluorochrome
Added to clinical specimen containing suspected bacterial cells
Bacterial cell with capsule
Capsule removed and injected into animal to produce anticapsular antibodies (antiserum)
Antibodies
Fluorochrome conjugated to antibody
Antibodies bind to bacterial capsule

FIGURE A-6
Technique for producing fluorescent antibodies. The bacterial capsule (composed of a polysaccharide that appears here as a ring surrounding the cell wall) is removed and injected into a rabbit. Antibodies to the capsule are produced in the rabbit and then removed. A fluorochrome is conjugated to the antibodies, which will bind to organisms possessing the specific capsule. Organisms will be seen to glow when observed microscopically.

ies. **Antibodies** are proteins induced in mammalian systems in response to foreign molecules called **antigens.** For example, a bacterium could be the foreign agent and when injected into an animal will induce the animal to produce antibodies. These antibodies are specific for the bacterium (usually a protein or carbohydrate on the surface of the bacterium) and aid the host in destroying the infectious agent. Figure A-6 illustrates how the technique is utilized in the clinical laboratory. Commercially prepared conjugated antibodies are readily available for detecting specific antigens of microbial species. If antibody is specific for the antigen in the clinical specimen, a complex of antigen, fluorochrome, and antibody is formed. The complex is then exposed to wavelengths of 350 nm produced by a high-pressure mercury vapor lamp or halogen lamp. The ultraviolet wavelengths (350 nm) strike the complex and visible wavelengths of light are released to produce an image seen by the observer (Fig. A-7 and see Plate 11).

Electron

One of the most important developments that advanced our knowledge concerning cell structure and function was the electron microscope (Fig. A-8). By utilizing wavelengths of radiation from electrons instead of light, resolving power is increased several thousand times (0.0005 μm, compared to 0.2 μm in light microscopy). In transmission electron microscopy (TEM) the electrons penetrate the specimen, while in scanning electron microscopy (SEM), a more recent development, the electrons do not penetrate the specimen. We discuss SEM later.

An electrically heated tungsten filament is the source of radiation in both light and electron microscopy. In contrast to light microscopy, in which light is focused on the specimen, electron microscopy utilizes electrons to focus on the specimen (Fig. A-9). Both light and electron microscopy use condensers to focus light and electrons, respectively, on the specimen. The condenser in the light microscope consists of glass lenses, but in the electron microscope large electromagnetic coils are used. In the light microscope the image is viewed through an ocular lens. The image in an electron microscope can be seen in two different ways: (1) the image can be viewed after projecting it on a movable zinc sulfide screen, so that when electrons hit the screen the zinc sulfide is excited and visible light is emitted, or (2) the image can be captured on photographic film in a camera mounted below the zinc sulfide screen. Magnifications in large electron microscopes are in the range of 500,000× and larger.

In TEM the electrons have to pass through the specimen; therefore, the specimen must be very thin. Electrons can reach the specimen only because the microscope is in a vacuum. The vacuum causes the specimen to dry out, and this prevents the investigator from observing cells in the living state as in light microscopy. There are basically three ways to prepare biological material for electron microscopy: **whole mount, ultrathin sectioning,** and **replication.**

Whole Mount. Whole mount preparations are usually objects that are thin enough for electrons to penetrate, for example, viruses. The specimen is placed on a copper grid and then stained with heavy metals such as lead or uranium salts. When electrons strike heavy metals, they are deflected and this creates contrast. Specimen staining may involve three different techniques:

1. **Positive staining.** The object itself is stained with heavy metals such as osmium tetroxide.
2. **Negative staining.** The background around the object is stained with compounds of uranium or tung-

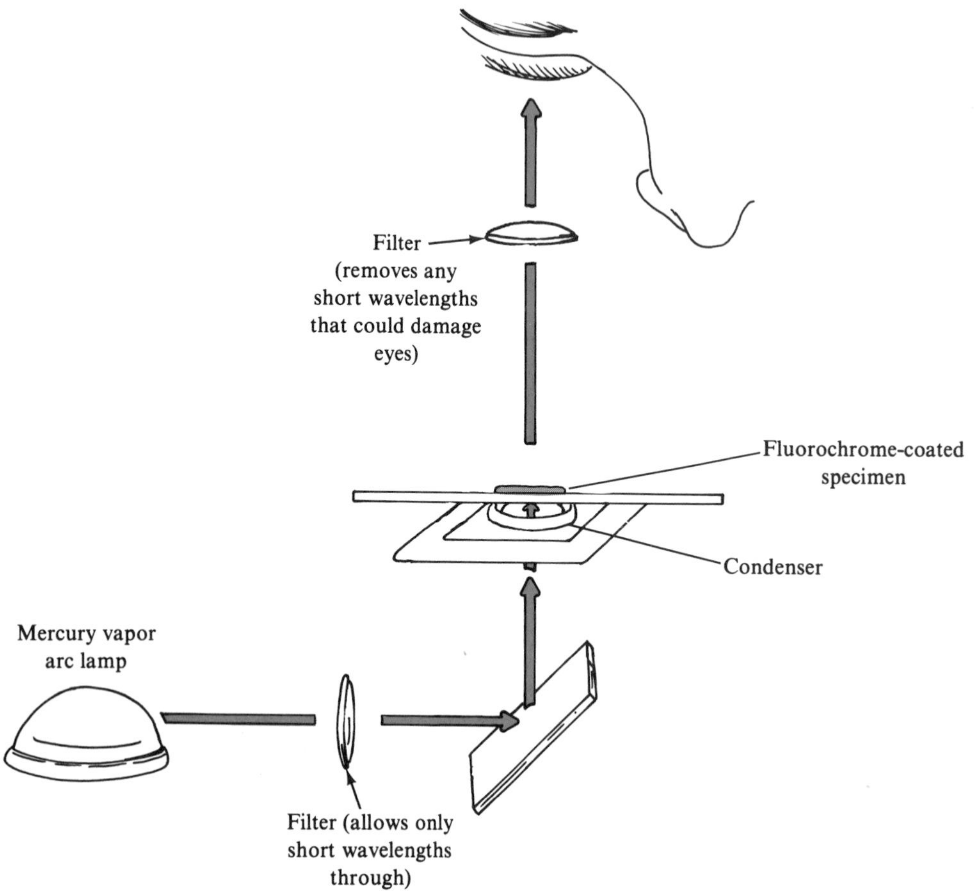

FIGURE A-7
Schematic of fluorescent microscopy.

sten. The object appears bright against the dark background.

3. Evaporation of heavy metal. A thin layer of heavy-metal atoms (platinum, for example) is deposited on a specimen at a precise angle so that the metal piles up on one side of the object in the specimen and leaves a clear area behind it. When photomicrographs are printed, shadows are cast, and this gives the observer an idea of the general size and shape of the object being viewed. This technique is referred to as **shadow casting.**

Ultrathin Sectioning. The biological material is fixed chemically (osmium tetroxide), stained with heavy metals, and embedded in epoxy resin. Ultrathin sections (less than 0.050 μm) are cut with an instrument called a microtome that uses diamond or glass knives.

Replication. Sometimes the object to be viewed cannot be brought into the electron microscope. Under these circumstances a thin replica is made by evaporating a layer of heavy metal on the specimen (see item 3 above). The replica is liberated from the object by digesting away any adhering organic material. The replication technique is used in a process called **freeze fracturing,** which utilizes three steps. First, the specimen is frozen to -150 C in liquid freon. Second, the frozen object is transferred to an evacuated chamber containing a microtome. The microtome produces a fracture plane that follows the topographical peculiarities of the specimen. Freeze-fractured cells are three-dimensional because sometimes an entire organelle or object may be plucked out or left projecting while at other times the organelle may be cross-fractured, exposing its outer membrane and contents (Fig. A-10). Third, a replica is made and depressions and protrusions receive a one-sided coating of the heavy metal that gives the image-shadowing effect. Freeze fracturing has been an important technique for observing organelles and membranes in both prokaryotic and eukaryotic cells.

In SEM, electrons do not penetrate the specimen but merely scan the surface topography. The resolution of the SEM is approximately 0.002 to 0.010 μm with direct magnifications up to 100,000 to 200,000$\times$, but the most effective range of magnifications is between 15,000 and 50,000$\times$. When the electrons hit the surface of the object, secondary electrons are released and directed to a scintillator. The scintillator converts the electrons into impulses

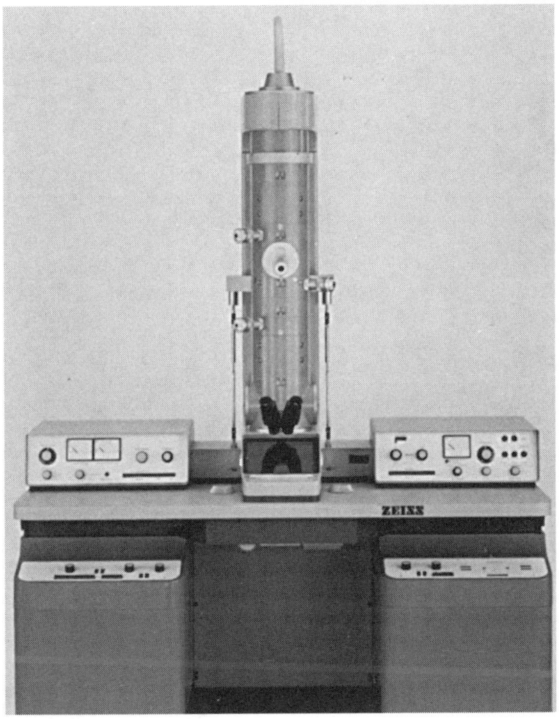

FIGURE A-8
Transmission electron microscope. (Courtesy of Carl Zeiss, Inc., New York, NY.)

that are relayed to a cathode ray tube. The result is an image similar to that produced in a television picture.

Samples examined by SEM are usually first coated with a metal such as gold-palladium alloy. The metal-coated sample is then affixed to a supporting disk that is placed in the path of the electron beam. The specimen can be rotated and thus different views of the object can be obtained from various angles. The image produced is three-dimensional and may be either observed directly or photographically recorded (Fig. A-11).

Table A-1 outlines the characteristics of the various types of microscopes.

PREPARATION OF LIVE SPECIMENS: THE HANGING DROP TECHNIQUE

Another technique, in addition to phase-contrast and dark-field microscopy, for the microscopical examination of bacteria in the living state is called the **hanging drop preparation.** This technique is performed in the following way:

1. Petrolatum is placed on the periphery of a glass coverslip.
2. A drop of a bacterial suspension is transferred with an inoculating loop to the center of the coverslip.
3. A slide with a central depression is placed over the coverslip, and the preparation is inverted. The bacterial suspension will hang in the depression (Fig. A-12) and can be observed under high power of the compound microscope.

FIGURE A-9
Comparison of bright-field and electron microscopes.

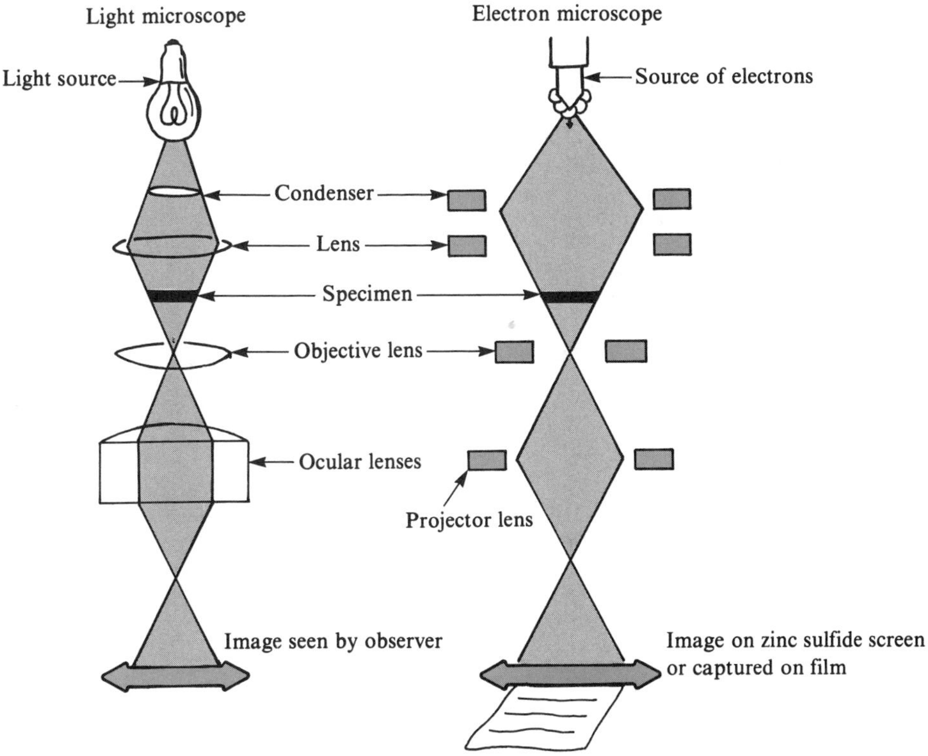

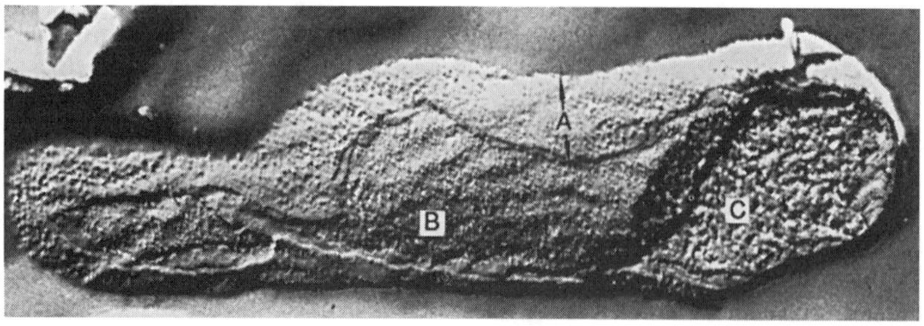

FIGURE A-10
Transmission electron micrograph of a replica of a freeze-fractured preparation of the bacterium *Escherichia coli.* The cell wall (A) is the outermost fraction, followed by the underlying cytoplasmic membrane (B), and last, the cytoplasm (C) of the bacterial cell. (Reproduced, with permission, from the *Annual Review of Microbiology* 33:459, © 1979 by Annual Reviews Inc.)

TABLE A-1
Characteristics of the Microscopes Used in Microbiology

Type	Resolving power	Useful magnification	Advantages	Disadvantages
Bright-field	0.2 μm	1000×	Microorganisms can be observed in living (unstained) state, for example, in hanging drop; morphology of stained organisms can also be observed	Organisms less than 0.2 μm in diameter cannot be resolved
Dark-field	0.2 μm	1000×	Unstained organisms such as spirochetes whose diameter is at or just below resolving power of bright-field microscope can be observed	Manipulation of special condensers makes operation of instrument slightly more difficult than operation of bright-field microscope
Phase-contrast	0.2 μm	1000×	Intensifies contrast between dense structures and transparent cytoplasm of live eukaryotic and prokaryotic microbes	Operation of instrument more difficult than bright-field microscope
Nomarski interference	0.1 μm	1000×	Produces clearer image than phase contrast and has resolving power twice that of phase contrast; can be used on live specimens	Difficult to operate
Fluorescent	0.2 μm	1000×	Important diagnostic tool in clinical laboratory (immunofluorescence); microorganisms can be detected in various types of specimens	Personnel require training in its operation and evaluation of results
Transmission electron	0.0005 μm	200,000× and above	High resolving power; molecular architecture of cells, microorganisms, and organelles can be identified; objects can be viewed on screen or on film	Specimens in living state cannot be examined; image produced is two-dimensional
Scanning electron	0.02 μm*	15,000–50,000 ×	Three-dimensional appearance to specimen; useful for evaluating surface of cells	Low resolving power; specimen must be in nonliving state

* Some instruments may have a resolving power of 0.007 μm.

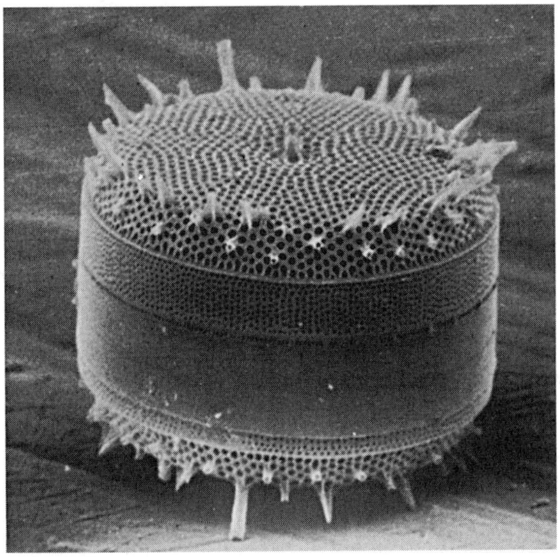

FIGURE A-11
Scanning electron micrograph of a freshwater diatom. (Courtesy of F. E. Round.)

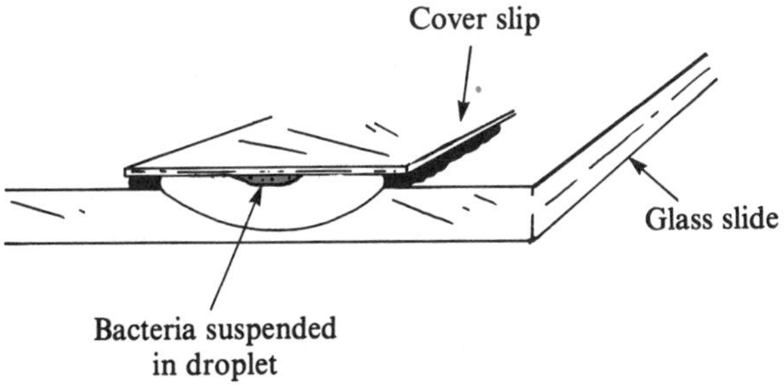

FIGURE A-12
The hanging drop preparation. The bacteria suspended in the concavity of the slide are free to move. Motility can be determined by observing bacterial movement with the high power of the compound microscope.

The hanging drop technique is useful in determining the motility of bacteria and also gives an undistorted view of the morphology and arrangement of bacterial cells.

Staining in Light Microscopy

Bacteria are difficult to observe because of their transparency. Staining is therefore an important consideration in the observation and identification of microorganisms. The microbial surface is negatively charged because of the presence of phosphate and carboxyl groups; therefore, the types of dyes used to stain bacteria are limited. Basic dyes (those that ionize and become positively charged) are used to stain bacteria because they are attracted to the negatively charged bacterial surface. The basic dye will also stain internal components such as proteins and nucleic acids because they also contain many negative charges. Some of the preferred basic dyes used in the laboratory for staining bacteria are **crystal violet, safranin,** and **methylene blue.** In preparation for staining procedures, a bacterial suspension is first smeared with an inoculating loop onto the surface of a slide. The smear is air-dried and then heat-fixed to the slide. The slide is then ready for staining.

SIMPLE STAIN

In simple staining a suitable basic dye is applied to a heat-fixed smear for a few seconds to a few minutes, depending on which dye is used. The excess dye is washed off and the stained preparation is observed microscopically.

DIFFERENTIAL STAINS

The chemical composition of many bacterial components is variable enough so that certain structural distinctions can be made between bacterial species or groups of bacteria. One way this objective can be accomplished is through the use of differential staining procedures, in which two stains and other reagents are applied sequentially to a heat-fixed bacterial smear. The two most widely used differential staining procedures are the **Gram-staining** procedure and the **acid-fast staining** procedure.

Gram Stain

Some years ago Dr. Christian Gram discovered that bacteria could be divided into two groups on the basis of the ability or inability of stained cells to resist decolorization by solvents such as alcohol and acetone. The sequence and function of each component in the Gram stain are as follows (Fig. A-13):

1. Primary stain. The heat-fixed smear is stained with crystal violet, the primary stain. The excess stain is washed off the slide. The cells at this stage appear dark blue or purple.
2. Iodine. The crystal violet can be further fixed to the cell by the addition of a dilute solution of iodine. This produces a crystal violet–iodine complex.
3. Decolorization. A solution of 95% alcohol (or alcohol and acetone) is applied to the stained smear. The alcohol dehydrates carbohydrates, which are present in large amounts in cell walls of gram-positive organisms. Gram-positive organisms retain the stain (or stain-iodine complex). Walls of gram-negative bacteria contain a high concentration of lipids, for which alcohol is a solvent. Pore sizes are presumably enlarged and the dye complex escapes. Gram-negative organisms will therefore appear unstained after decolorization.
4. Counterstain. Safranin, a red dye, is the secondary stain applied to the fixed preparations. If the bacteria are decolorized with alcohol, they will take up the safranin and appear red (gram-negative). If the cells are not decolorized, the safranin will have no effect on the already stained preparation, and the bacteria will remain blue or purple (gram-positive) (see Plates 32 and 33).

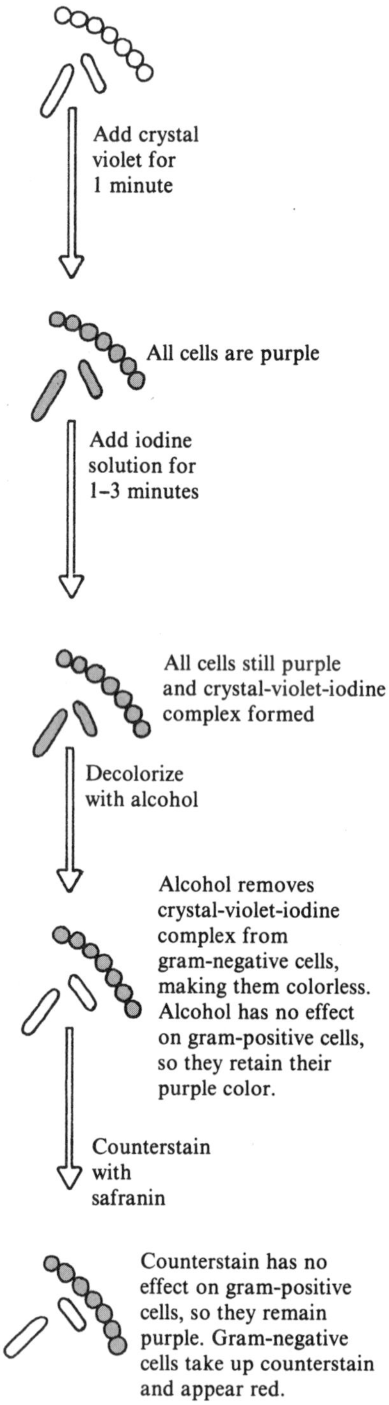
Add crystal violet for 1 minute
All cells are purple
Add iodine solution for 1–3 minutes
All cells still purple and crystal-violet-iodine complex formed
Decolorize with alcohol
Alcohol removes crystal-violet-iodine complex from gram-negative cells, making them colorless. Alcohol has no effect on gram-positive cells, so they retain their purple color.
Counterstain with safranin
Counterstain has no effect on gram-positive cells, so they remain purple. Gram-negative cells take up counterstain and appear red.

FIGURE A-13
Steps in the Gram-staining procedure.

Gram stain is one of the first important identification procedures after the isolation of bacteria (see Under the Microscope 54). This procedure allows one to divide the bacterial world into at least four categories: gram-positive cocci, gram-positive bacilli, gram-negative cocci, and gram-negative bacilli. When the Gram-staining characteristics of the cell have been determined, it is also possible to assign other general properties that apply to the group. They are outlined in Table A-2.

The molecular basis of the Gram stain is not clear. Scientists originally suspected that the concentration of lipid in the cell wall determined the outcome of the Gram stain. Gram-negative cells possess more lipid in their cell walls than do gram-positive cells, and therefore alcohol produces pores in the gram-negative cell that result in loss of the primary stain. Other investigators propose that the shrinking, by alcohol, of the thicker peptidoglycan of the gram-positive cell wall retards the loss of the crystal violet–iodine complex.

Acid-Fast Stain

The cell surface components of some bacteria, such as species of *Mycobacterium* and *Nocardia,* contain waxes and phospholipids that other bacteria do not possess. *Mycobacterium* and *Nocardia* are basically gram-positive if their waxes are removed, but in their natural state ordinary dyes cannot penetrate the waxy surface. These bacteria can be stained by the acid-fast technique. There are two major acid-fast staining techniques: **Kinyoun** and **Ziehl-Neelsen.**

In the Kinyoun method carbolfuchsin, a red dye, is applied to a smear of the bacteria for 3 minutes and then the smear is gently washed in water to remove excess stain. The smear is treated with acid alcohol until no more color appears in the washing and is then washed in water. The smear is counterstained with malachite green and then washed in water. Bacteria that are acid-fast retain the carbolfuchsin, while non-acid-fast bacteria do not retain carbolfuchsin and appear green.

In the Ziehl-Neelsen method there are two major differences. First, the smear is flooded with carbolfuchsin and the slide is gently heated in a flame. Second, the counter-

FIGURE A-14
Capsule-producing rod-shaped bacteria suspended in India ink and observed under oil immersion. Capsules appear as white halos around the rod-shaped bacterial cells. (From D. J. Politis and R. Goodman, *Appl. Environ. Microbiol.* 40:596, 1980.)

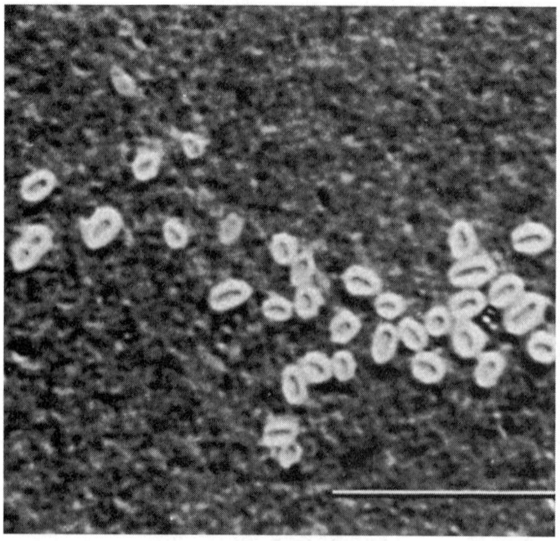

UNDER THE MICROSCOPE 54

The Gram Stain: Important to the Microbiologist and the Physician

One of the important aspects of the Gram stain is that it has helped microbiologists classify bacteria. The most widely accepted classification scheme for bacteria is called *Bergey's Manual of Determinative Bacteriology.* On examining this book one can immediately recognize the importance of the Gram stain, which is used to separate most of the major divisions of bacteria, for example, gram-negative rods, gram-positive rods, gram-negative cocci, gram-positive cocci, and gram-negative helical bacteria.

Identification of bacteria is greatly enhanced by first employing the Gram stain. The results of the Gram stain can also be a valuable piece of information to the physician. There are situations in which individuals with a bacterial infection are so in need of immediate treatment that the time for identification of the bacterium, based on biochemical tests as well as antibiotic sensitivity, is not realistic. The physician is faced with the decision as to which antibiotic to use in treatment. The microbiologist can help by providing the physician with the results of the Gram stain. The reason for this is that antibiotics, which are used to treat most bacterial infections, have different effects on the bacterial cell depending on cell wall composition. For example, many gram-negative bacteria are more resistant to certain antibiotics than are gram-positive bacteria. A knowledge of the Gram stain results could save a life.

TABLE A-2
Some General Properties of Gram-Positive and Gram-Negative Bacteria Based on Cell Wall and Other Characteristics

Characteristic	Gram-positive	Gram-negative
Cell wall composition	Less complex; contains primarily peptidoglycan and very little lipid	Most complex; little peptidoglycan but has outer membrane with considerable lipid, polysaccharide, and protein
Penicillin sensitivity	More sensitive	Less sensitive
Resistance to sonic disruption and other physical measures	More resistant	Less resistant
Resistance to cell wall lytic enzyme, i.e., lysozyme	Less resistant	More resistant
Dye inhibition	Inhibited by crystal violet	Not inhibited by crystal violet
Spore formation	Some bacilli are sporeformers	No bacilli are sporeformers
Toxin production	Toxins are not part of cell wall but are produced in the cytoplasm, i.e., **exotoxins**	One type of toxin in part of the cell wall and is called **endotoxin**

stain, following the acid alcohol step, is methylene blue and non-acid-fast organisms will appear blue (see Plate 10).

NEGATIVE STAIN

Negative staining refers to the use of dyes that have no affinity for the microbial cell but will "stain" the background of a bacterial specimen. Two dyes that are used in negative staining are India ink and nigrosin. They can be added to the bacterial suspension, which is then spread on a microscopical slide and dried. A basic dye can be used to stain the bacterial cell proper if one so desires. Negative staining is valuable in determining the presence of sticky envelopes of carbohydrates, called **capsules,** that surround the cell wall of some bacteria (Fig. A-14).

SPECIAL STAINS

Other staining techniques are available to the technician but are not so routinely used in the clinical laboratory as those previously discussed. They include the following:

1. Flagella stain. The flagella stain is used to stain the organ of motility in bacteria, called the **flagellum.** Flagella staining requires some skill and is sometimes used to classify some bacteria.
2. Spore stain. The spore is a specialized dormant form of the bacterium that is resistant to ordinary staining procedures. Spore location in the bacterial cell is of value in differentiating some *Clostridium* species.
3. Metachromatic granule stain. Metachromatic granules are deposits of phosphates that accumulate in some bacteria. These phosphate deposits can be selectively stained to contrast with the cytoplasm.

APPENDIX

B

Immunological Tests

An important application of immune system products (antibiotics and effector T cells) is their use in identification, diagnosis, and monitoring. The fact that the interactions between antigens and immune system products are essentially highly specific and that these interactions produce detectable reactions make possible a great variety of valuable in vitro and in vivo tests. The subdiscipline of immunology that uses these interactions is variously entitled **serology** or **immunodiagnosis.** The term **serology** implies the use of serum or components thereof in the tests. Serum is commonly used as a test ingredient because the most frequently used immune product—antibodies—is most accessible in serum. It should not be concluded, however, that every immunodiagnostic test involves serum.

The Value of Serological Tests in Medical Microbiology

The information obtained from serological tests is valuable for the following reasons:

1. Sometimes the only way, or the only practical way, to identify the causal agent of an infection is via serological testing. This is the situation with diseases in which the isolation of the causative agent is not feasible or is impractical because of cost-benefit considerations.
2. Serological tests are frequently used to confirm a diagnosis that was made on clinical grounds or by other laboratory findings.
3. It may be important to know the immune status of a person or of a population. A dentist may wish to know if he or she has antibodies to the hepatitis B virus. A woman of childbearing age may wish to know if she is immune to the rubella (German measles) virus.
4. The course or severity of a disease can be followed and the treatment or prognosis or both indicated by such determinations.
5. Sometimes it is important to know the serogroup or serotype of a causal agent. Most species of microorganisms through mutation and selection develop strains that differ in antigenic composition. These strains also frequently differ in immunogenicity and drug susceptibility. Their identification may affect patient therapy and appropriate immunization of a population at risk.

There are many applications of serological tests outside the realm of medical microbiology: cancer detection, diagnosis of allergies, identification and localization of tissue components (immunohistochemistry), immunodetection in forensic pathology, and assessment of the compatibility of donor-recipient transplant tissues and organs.

The General Principles of Immunodiagnosis

Most routinely employed immunodiagnostic tests involve antibodies, and so the descriptions and the tests to follow pertain almost entirely to antibodies.

How can antibodies be detected? How is it determined that an individual has antibodies to a given antigen as a result of immunization or in consequence of infection? Such determinations are valuable for diagnosis.

One of the components, either the antigen or the antibody, in a serological test is known. Thus, if the identity of an infectious agent (an antigen) recovered from a patient is unknown or is to be confirmed, or if its serotype is to be determined, it is tested against an antiserum that has a known antibody content. Conversely, the antibody content of a patient's serum may be the unknown component of the test, in which case the serum is tested against known antigens. A patient with an infection, for example, after a suitable induction period has usually produced antibodies against the infecting microorganism. Blood is drawn, the serum is collected after the blood is allowed to clot, and the serum is tested against known antigen. The antigens and antisera that are used as the known component of a serological test are usually commercially available. They are stable preparations that can be kept in the refrigerator for long periods of time.

Serological tests have a qualitative aspect, and most tests also have a quantitative aspect. The qualitative aspect is to answer one of the following questions: Are there antibodies in this serum for this known antigen? Or: Does this unidentified microorganism react with this serum, which has a known antibody content? Since the antigen-antibody relationship is specific, a positive reaction usually identifies the antigen or antibody—the qualitative aspect. Not only can it be determined that the antigen and antibody interact, however, but the relative quantities of one or the other can be established; that is, a **titer** can be determined. This is the quantitative aspect of serological tests. To determine a titer, either the antigen preparation or the serum is serially diluted in uniform increments. In a typical titration a series of tubes containing doubling dilutions of the test serum is set up. A constant amount of antigen is added to each tube (Fig. B-1). The reciprocal of the highest dilution (i.e., of the last tube of the series) to give a detectable reaction in the form of a precipitation, agglutination, or other reaction is the titer. In the course of an illness it is frequently meaningful to discover that a change in titer has occurred between an early, acute-phase serum specimen and a convalescent or recovery-phase specimen.

The Traditional Serological Tests

For many years, six kinds of antibodies have been designated: **agglutinins, precipitins, antitoxins, cytolysins, opsonins,** and **virus-neutralizing antibodies.** These terms were chosen because they are descriptive of what happens when an antigen interacts with its homologous antibody under the conditions of the test system. The earlier serological test procedures were rather straightforward and uncomplicated, compared with today's refinements. In the earlier procedures straight serum was used without fractionation or conjugation. The tests were conducted primarily in tubes and on slides. This is not to say that such an approach is no longer used or useful. These still are basic serological tests in clinical serodiagnosis. Refinements, however, have increased the sensitivity and the applications of serological tests, especially as investigative tools.

Before antigen-antibody interactions are described, it is important to know the difference between **particulate test antigens** and **soluble test antigens.** Antigens may be particulate, that is, particle-sized, as are intact bacterial cells, red blood cells, white blood cells, and particles and cells artificially coated with soluble antigens. Antigens may also be soluble, consisting of molecules in solution.

PRECIPITATION

Precipitation occurs when a soluble antigen reacts with its homologous antibody in appropriate relative propor-

FIGURE B-1
Titration series (agglutination).

Procedure:

1. Add 1.0 ml of saline (diluent) to each tube.
2. Starting with a 1:4 dilution of the antiserum, serially transfer 1.0 ml of each succeeding dilution to each tube except the control tube.
3. Add 1.0 ml of antigen suspension (no serial dilution) to each tube including the control tube.

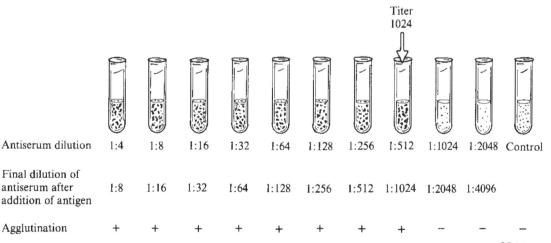

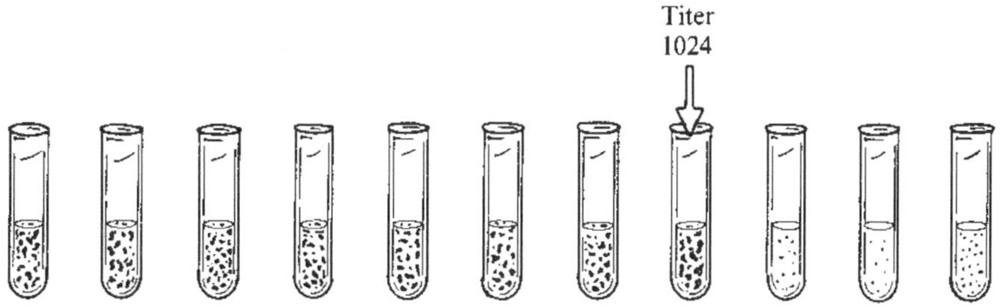

Antiserum dilution	1:4	1:8	1:16	1:32	1:64	1:128	1:256	1:512	1:1024	1:2048	Control
Final dilution of antiserum after addition of antigen	1:8	1:16	1:32	1:64	1:128	1:256	1:512	1:1024	1:2048	1:4096	
Agglutination	+	+	+	+	+	+	+	+	–	–	–

tions. The immunodiffusion technique represents a precipitation reaction.

Immunodiffusion

Immunodiffusion is a form of precipitation test that makes use of agar gel and other support media. Completed reactions are "fixed" in the support medium. In agar gel immunodiffusion, wells are formed in agar gel according to a predetermined pattern (Fig. B-2). Solutions of antigen and antiserum are placed in the respective wells. Antigens and antibodies diffuse toward each other in a radial pattern. Where homologous antibody reacts in proper proportions with antigen, lines of precipitate form within the agar. This **double-diffusion method** is named the **Ouchterlony technique.**

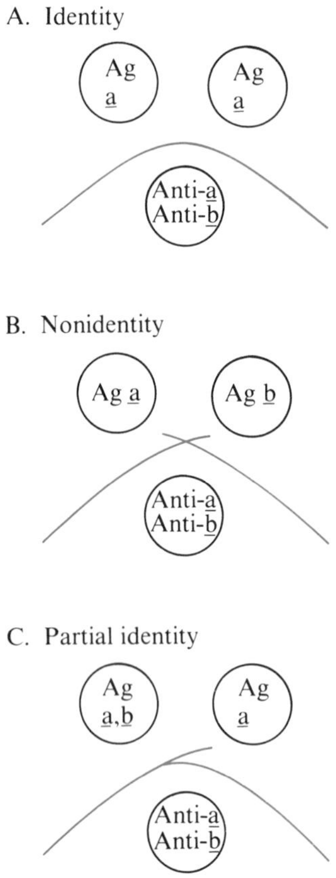

FIGURE B-2
Immunodiffusion in agar gel. Antigen-antibody recognition results in a readily visible opaque band of precipitate in the zone of equivalence of antibody and antigen (Ag). A. Reaction of identity. The continuous precipitation band is termed a **line of identity** and indicates that the antigen in both wells contains the identical antigenic determinant a. B. Reaction of **nonidentity.** The crossed lines of precipitation indicate that the antigen in one well does not possess common antigenic determinants with the antigen in the other well. C. Reaction of **partial identity.** The continuous precipitation band, as in A, indicates that the antigens in both wells contain a common antigenic determinant, a. The spur-like projection in the direction opposite the Ag a,b well indicates that the antigen in that well possesses an antigenic determinant (b) that is not present on the antigen of the other well.

This method has many good features. One is the stability of the precipitate; that is, once the precipitate is formed, it will remain fixed in that position in the agar over a long period of time. In addition, more than one antigen or antibody can be tested because the different antigenic molecules in the solution diffuse and aggregate separately on the basis of their size, configuration, and other properties. And, further, unknown antigens can be identified when known control antigens in a neighboring well form continuous lines of precipitate with the unknown. A continuous line (fusion) indicates identity; crossed lines indicate nonidentity. The major disadvantage of the immunodiffusion procedure is the length of time (days to weeks) it takes for the lines of precipitate to develop.

AGGLUTINATION

The antigen in agglutination reactions is particulate. In the presence of homologous antibody, antigens (such as intact bacterial cells or red blood cells) or uniform particles (as of latex or bentonite onto which soluble antigens have been absorbed or conjugated) clump together to form visible aggregates. Agglutination reactions are widely used for the diagnosis of certain bacterial diseases and in human blood grouping and typing. The reaction can be carried out on a slide by mixing serum with a suspension of the antigen. Most bacterial agglutination tests are serial tube tests in which a titer is determined (see Fig. B-1).

Agglutination of red blood cells is called **hemagglutination.** Tests employing red blood cells that are coated with a soluble antigen are called **passive hemagglutination tests.**

Viral Hemagglutination-Inhibition

Viral Hemagglutination. Influenza, mumps, rubella, and other viruses naturally bind to red blood cells of various animal species. Each virus particle is multivalent and so it can simultaneously attach to more than one blood cell. Binding is between protein spikes (called viral hemagglutinins) on the surface of the virus and receptors on the red blood cell membrane. If enough virus is present, crosslinking takes place and lattice-like aggregates form. Viral hemagglutination is a rapid, accurate method of quantitating viruses. A hemagglutinating titer (HA titer) is obtained by serially diluting the virus and finding the highest virus dilution that will just agglutinate a standardized suspension of red blood cells that is added to each tube of the test. The test is referred to as the HA test.

Viral Hemagglutination-Inhibition. The HA test is used not only to quantitate viruses but also as the basis for identifying viruses in the hemagglutination-inhibition test (HAI test) (Fig. B-3). A standardized suspension of virus, as determined in an HA test, is incubated with the antiserum, followed by the addition of red blood cells. In a positive reaction antibodies in the antiserum are specific

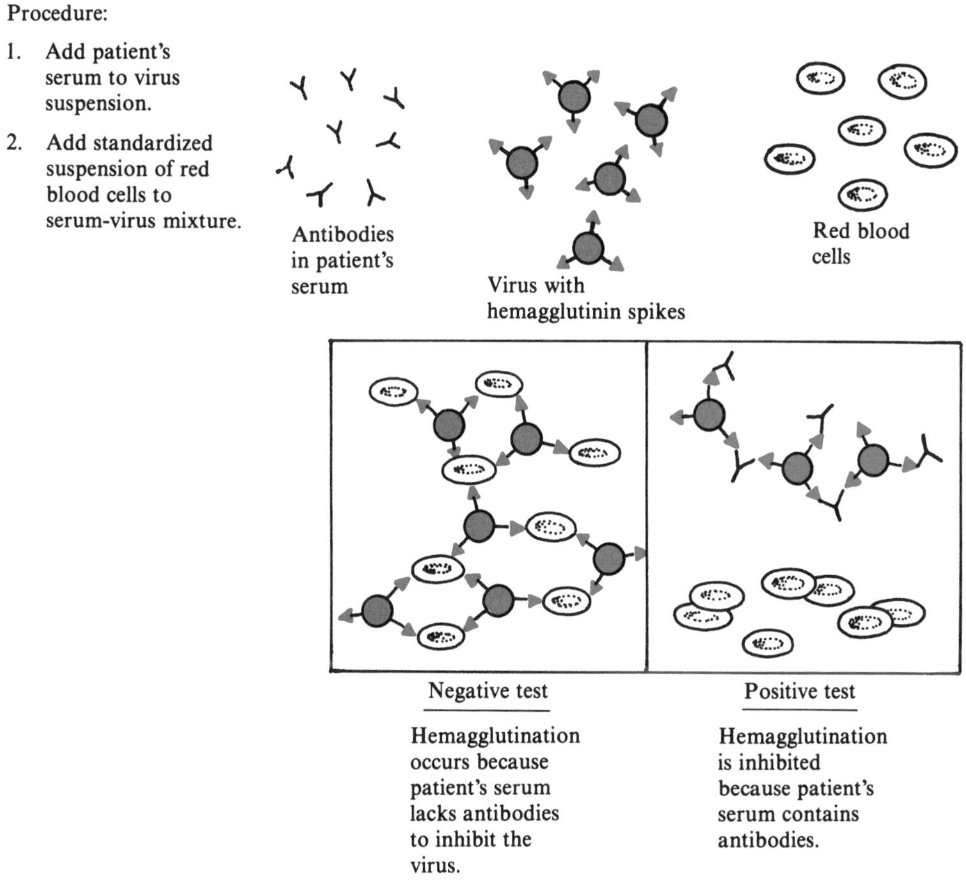
Procedure:
1. Add patient's serum to virus suspension.
2. Add standardized suspension of red blood cells to serum-virus mixture.
Antibodies in patient's serum
Virus with hemagglutinin spikes
Red blood cells
Negative test
Hemagglutination occurs because patient's serum lacks antibodies to inhibit the virus.
Positive test
Hemagglutination is inhibited because patient's serum contains antibodies.

FIGURE B-3
Viral hemagglutination-inhibition test (HAI test).

for the virus and hemagglutination is prevented. The test setup usually is such that a titer can be determined.

VIRUS NEUTRALIZATION

Because of their small size, viruses generally do not give readily visible reactions with their homologous antibodies. Viruses with known effects in animals or on tissue culture are mixed with serum to determine the neutralizing effect of the serum. If specific antiviral antibodies are present in the serum, the effect of the virus on the test animal or the tissue culture cells is neutralized.

IMMUNE CYTOLYSIS

The combination of cell-associated antigen, specific IgG or IgM antibodies, and complement can effect the lysis of cells on which the antigens are located. Lesions created in the cell membrane by the late-acting complement components (membrane attack complex) bring about lysis of the cell. The antigens involved in the reaction may be part of the affected cell itself, such as those on bacterial cells, or the antigens may be soluble antigens that have combined with the cell membrane, for example, of red blood cells.

COMPLEMENT FIXATION

The phenomenon of immune cytolysis involving complement serves as the basis of the complement fixation (CF) test (Fig. B-4). The test has two distinct components, the indicator system and the test system. The systems vie for complement, which is one of the ingredients of the test.

Indicator System

The indicator system consists of sheep red blood cells (SRBC) as the antigen and an antiserum (commercially available) that contains antibodies against SRBC. The SRBC of the indicator system lyse when exposed to the antiserum of the indicator system in the presence of complement. Lysis is a visible reaction because the hemoglobin released from lysed red blood cells produces a pink-to-red color in the otherwise clear, uncolored supernatant fluid.

Test System

In the other component, the test system, either the antigen is unknown or, as is most often the case, the patient's serum is being tested for unknown antibody content. The combination of the antigen with antibody must be able

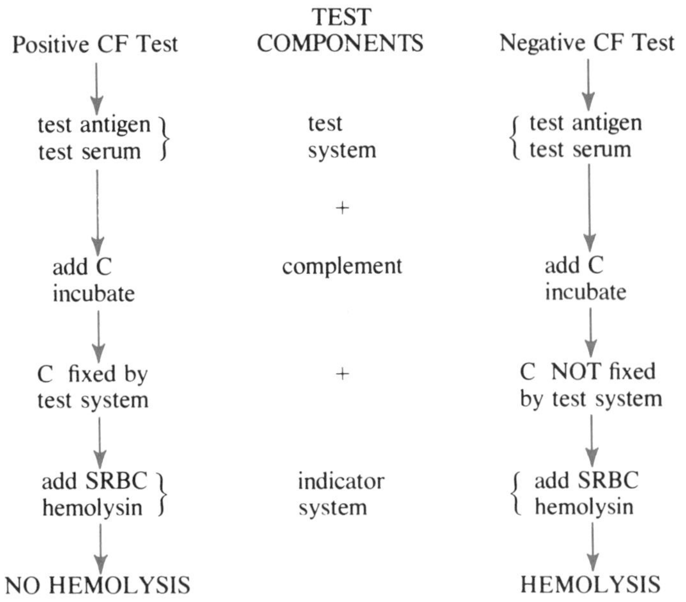

FIGURE B-4
Complement fixation (CF) test. SRBC = sheep red blood cells; C = complement.

to fix complement. Not all antigen-antibody combinations bind complement.

Test Procedure

The first step in the CF test is to inactivate any residual complement in the test serum by heating the test serum for 30 minutes at 56 C. The order of the test procedure is as follows: The test antigen and the inactivated test serum are mixed. A measured amount of complement is added. The complement source is fresh guinea pig serum, which is available commercially in the lyophilized form. After the mixture of the test antigen, test serum, and complement has been incubated, the indicator system is added to the test system tube. If there is antibody in the test system that is specific for the test antigen, complement is fixed or bound to the antigen-antibody combination. In a positive CF test the complement that is fixed by this combination is not available to the indicator system when it is added. Lysis of SRBC therefore does not occur. In a negative CF test, in which the test antibody is not specific for the test antigen, complement is not bound by the test system and remains available to the indicator system. Lysis occurs. The test not only is qualitative, as described, but also can be quantitative; that is, a titer can be determined.

Applications of Complement Fixation

The CF test is especially useful when the test antigen and antibody combination alone does not give a visible reaction. Lysis of SRBC serves as the visible, detectable reaction. The diagnosis of many viral and fungal diseases and of immunological disorders is made or confirmed by this means.

More Recent Immunodiagnostic Techniques

Refinements in testing have led to giving serological tests names that reflect the nature of the testing technique. The same kinds of antibodies are involved, but the reactions are not those typical of precipitation, agglutination, cytolysis, and neutralization.

The more recent techniques are of three major types:

1. There are techniques **for separating out the different antigens** that may be present in the antigen material and techniques **for separating out the different components of serum.** The separations are performed in or on support media such as agar gel and polymeric membranes. Separations take place under the influence of diffusion, osmosis, electrical charge, or combinations of these modalities. The separated components are then detected or identified by additional steps that may include additional diffusion and attachment of marker chemicals to antibodies.
2. Techniques for **attaching soluble antigens or antibodies to cells** (e.g., red blood cells) **or to particles** (e.g., latex, bentonite, beads) allow a visible reaction such as lysis or agglutination to occur when antigen and antibody unite.
3. In some techniques **marker chemicals** (also called **labels) are conjugated to immunoglobulins** (usually) **or to antigens.** Marker chemicals include dyes that fluoresce on ultraviolet irradiation, radioactive materials that are detected by radioactivity-sensing devices, and enzymes whose presence is detected when appropriate substrate is added to the preparation.

Most of these techniques have numerous modifications. Gel precipitation, for example, may take the form of simple diffusion, double diffusion, single radial diffusion, immunoelectrophoresis, or rocket immunoelectrophoresis. The immunodiffusion procedure was discussed in the previous section.

FIGURE B-5
Immunoelectrophoresis. One method of separating molecules or particles in a solution is to apply a current to the support medium. The charged molecules or particles move toward the oppositely charged electrode.

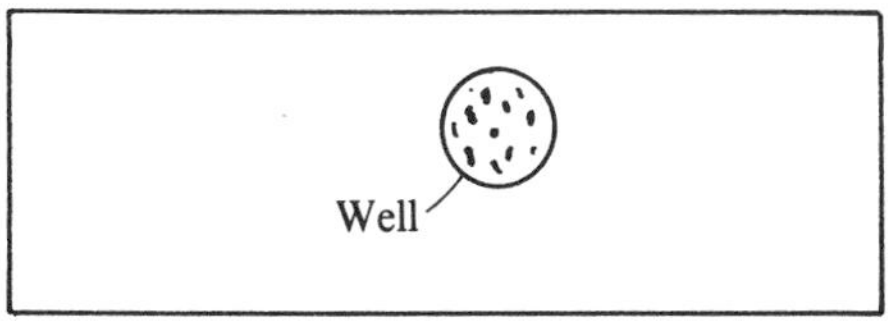

1. Antigen preparation containing four different antigens is placed in well. The well was cut in an agar film that covers the slide.

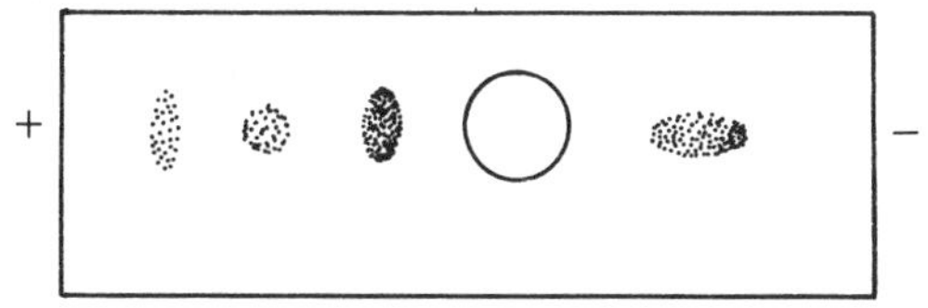

2. The agar is electrophoresed and the four antigens separate.

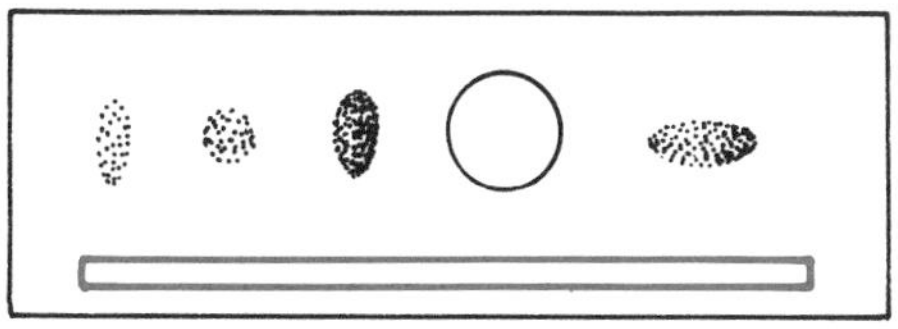

3. Electrodes are removed. A trough is cut in the agar and antiserum is placed in the trough.

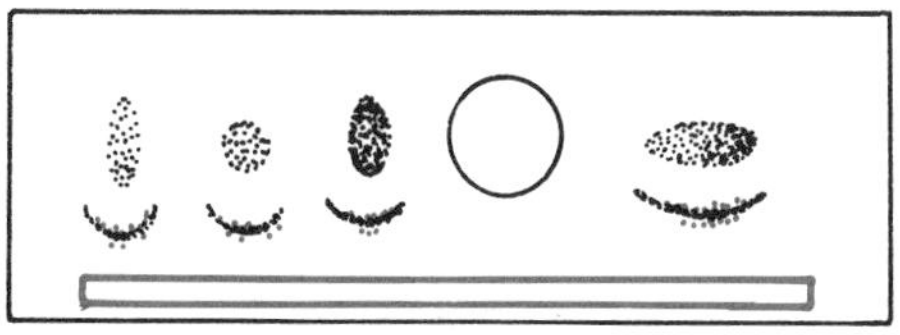

4. The four antigens and their homologous antibodies diffuse toward each other and arcs of precipitate develop where they meet.

IMMUNOELECTROPHORESIS

The separation of different antigens in a solution and their identification can be refined by first **subjecting the solutions within a support medium to electrical current** (electrophoresis) (Fig. B-5). On the basis of their charges, molecular size, and other properties, the various antigens in a solution or proteins of a serum are separated in or on a support medium such as thin layers of agar gel, cellulose acetate, or starch. Electrophoresis is combined with immunodiffusion in immunoelectrophoresis. After electrophoretic separation, troughs for antiserum (or other means of application) are placed parallel to the lines of migration of the electrophoresed solution. Arcs of antigen-antibody precipitate form. Human serum, as antigen, has been extensively investigated by this technique. As many as 37 zones of precipitate, representing different proteins or subgroups of a protein class of the serum, have been distinguished (Fig. B-6).

FIGURE B-6
Crossed immunoelectrophoresis of human serum. A strip of agarose that contains electrophoretically resolved human serum proteins is placed along the bottom edge, and molten agarose that contains goat antiserum is poured over the plate. When the plate has gelled, the antigens in the human serum are forced into the antibody-containing gel layer by electrophoresis. Thirty-seven precipitation zones can be seen. Some of the antigens identified in the human serum are albumin (A), ceruloplasmin (D), hemopexin (H), and gamma globulin (L). (From H. Michin Clarke. In C. Z. Williams and M. W. Chase, eds., *Methods in Immunology and Immunochemistry*. Vol. 3. San Diego: Academic, 1971.)

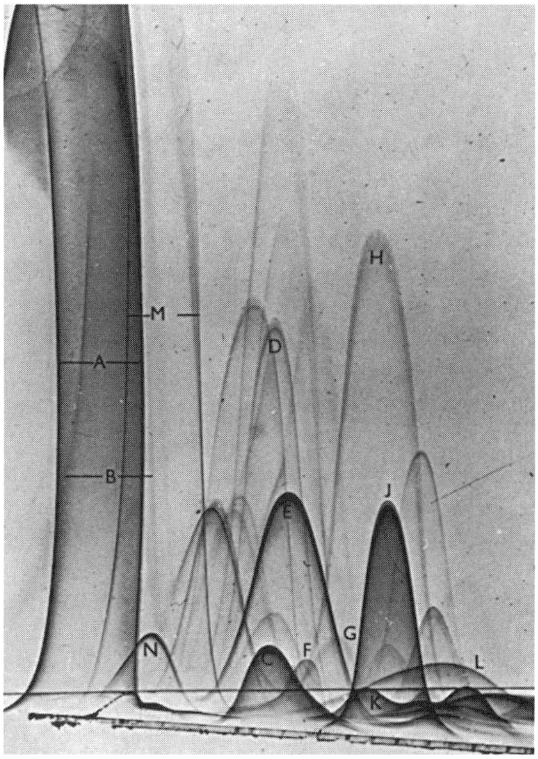

COUNTERIMMUNOELECTROPHORESIS

Counterimmunoelectrophoresis (CIE) is so named because **the antigen and antibody are made to flow toward each other in opposite directions.** The antiserum is placed in a well on the anode side with the antigen in a well on the cathode side. Antibodies move toward the cathode swept there by positively charged buffer ions due to a phenomenon called **electroendosmosis.** Negatively charged antigens move toward the anode. A precipitin line appears after as little as 30 minutes of electrophoresis.

FLUORESCENT ANTIBODY TECHNIQUE

Fluorescent antibody (FA) and its microscopical detection were discussed briefly in Appendix A under Types of Microscopes. Described here are the two ways the FA technique can be utilized: the direct method and the indirect (sandwich) method.

Direct Method

In the direct method the fluorescent dye is conjugated with the antibody that is specific for the antigen (Fig. B-7). Example: A throat specimen suspected of containing group A streptococci is affixed to a slide. An antiserum containing fluorescent anti-group A antibody is applied to the smear for a brief incubation period. After being rinsed, the slide is placed on the microscope stage, irradiated, and viewed. Foci of fluorescence where antibodies have united with bacterial cells indicate the presence of group A streptococci.

Immunofluorescence tests can be used to identify cells in a suspension that possess different surface antigens and have been stained with different fluorescent antibodies. When a suspension of live stained cells is put through a **fluorescent activated cell sorter,** the machine is able to measure the intensity of the dye on the cell surface. The cells can be separated into individual populations based on their specific fluorescent brightness.

Indirect Method

In the indirect method an additional step is required (see Fig. B-7). Antisera can be produced against globulins of another species. If human gamma globulin is injected into a goat, the animal produces antibodies to it. The goat antibody formed against human gamma globulin will interact with human immunoglobulin (antibodies).

The major application of the indirect FA technique is in the situation in which the antibody is the unknown component of the serological test. Example: Does the patient have antibodies to the syphilis organism? The patient's serum cannot be specifically labeled for syphilis antibody because it is not practically possible to separate the syphilis antibody immunoglobulins from the other globulins of the serum. Instead, the patient's unlabeled serum is reacted with the syphilis antigen on the slide. If there are antibodies to the antigen, the reaction is not visible at this time. The patient's serum is rinsed off and the labeled goat antihuman globulin is added. It will attach to bound human globulin (syphilis antibody) and on irradiation there will be foci of fluorescence wherever there is antibody from the patient attached to the syphilis antigen on the slide.

FIGURE B-7
Fluorescent antibody technique.

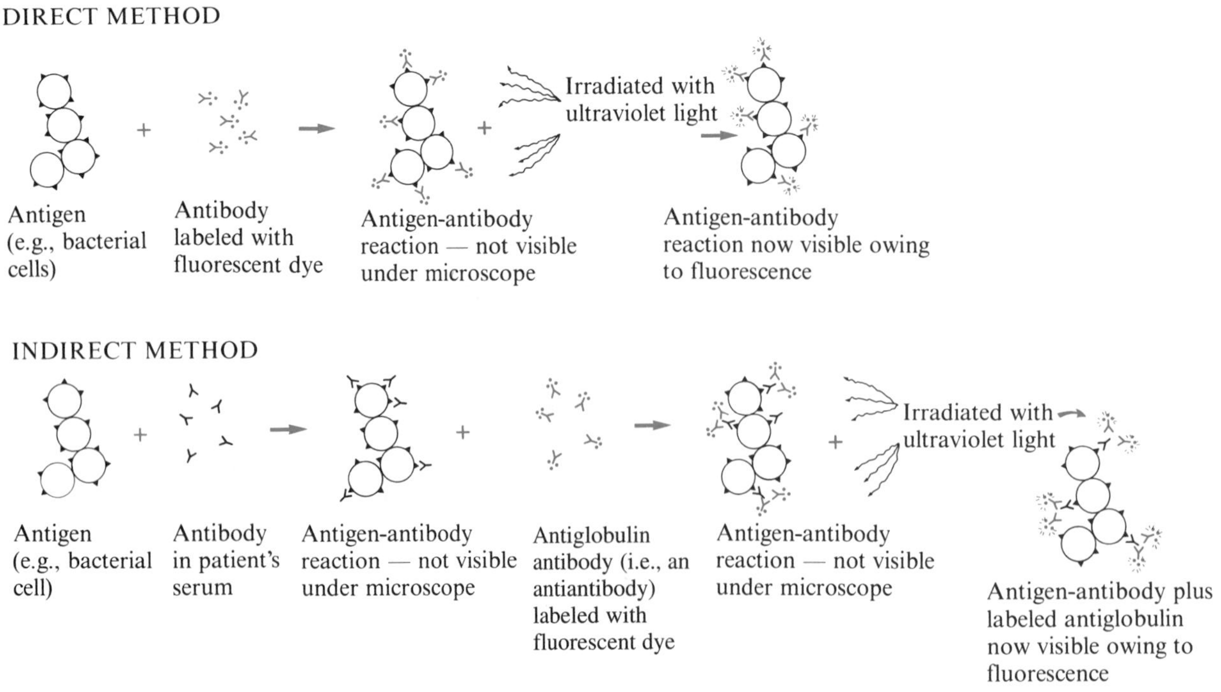

ENZYME IMMUNOASSAY

A popular type of label employs enzymes that have been conjugated with antibody. Enzyme immunoassay (EIA) tests are highly specific, versatile, accurate, reproducible, and relatively inexpensive. When the antibody with the attached enzyme reacts with its specific antigen, the antigen or the antigen location can be detected by adding the substrate that the enzyme attacks. In a positive immunoperoxidase test, for example, a colored reaction is produced when peroxidase substrates, such as benzidine, alphanaphthol, 3,3-diaminobenzidine, or 3-amino-9-ethylcarbazole, are added.

EIA tests have replaced some of the time-honored but nonspecific histological staining methods and as such are referred to as immunohistochemical or immunostaining methods.

A very popular EIA test is the **enzyme-linked immunosorbent assay (ELISA)** (Fig. B-8). In ELISA tests, the antigen (or antibody) is passively or chemically attached to a solid support such as plastic microtiter plates (plates with series of small wells) or to small beads. When the test serum is added, any specific antibody present will attach to the antigen anchored to the solid support. Next added is antiglobulin that has been labeled with an enzyme. The antiglobulin will attach to the antibody of the test serum that has bound to the antigen. Thorough washing with buffer follows each of these steps. Finally, substrate specific for the enzyme is added. The enzyme-labeled antiglobulin adheres if there is specific antibody in the test serum and so hydrolysis of the enzyme substrate with the accompanying color change occurs. Color development is either detected visually or spectrophotometrically measured.

RADIOIMMUNOASSAY

Radioimmunoassay (RIA) is a highly sensitive microtechnique that detects trace amounts of antigens such as drugs, hormones, and biologically active molecules in a patient's serum. This very complex assay can be performed in several ways. A common form of RIA is a **competition test,** in which stock radiolabeled antigen and unlabeled antigen from the patient's serum vie for specific antibody. The test components are a measured amount of known, purified labeled antigen, a measured amount of antibody that is specific for the labeled antigen, and a serum sample from the patient that may or may not contain the same antigen as the known labeled antigen. The patient antigen is unlabeled.

There are two reaction mixtures. Reaction mixture 1, which provides a baseline, contains labeled antigen and only enough antibody to complex with about 70 percent of the labeled antigen. The labeled antigen-antibody complex is separated out from reaction mixture 1 by one of several techniques. The radioactivity remaining in the supernatant fluid (or alternatively, the radioactivity in the antigen-antibody complex) is determined. This now provides a measure of the unbound known antigen. Reaction mixture 2 contains the patient's serum with the unlabeled antigen, plus the same components in the same measured amounts as used in mixture 1. If the unlabeled antigen in the patient's serum is the same antigen as the unlabeled

FIGURE B-8
Positive enzyme-linked immunosorbent assay.

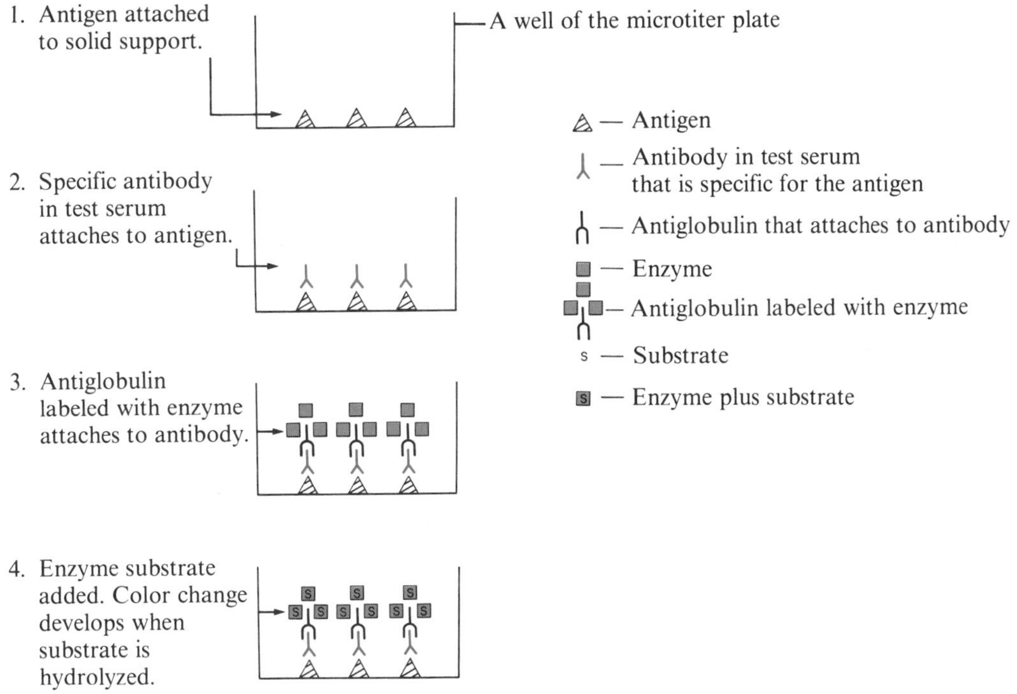
1. Antigen attached to solid support.
A well of the microtiter plate
2. Specific antibody in test serum attaches to antigen.
3. Antiglobulin labeled with enzyme attaches to antibody.
4. Enzyme substrate added. Color change develops when substrate is hydrolyzed.
— Antigen
— Antibody in test serum that is specific for the antigen
— Antiglobulin that attaches to antibody
— Enzyme
— Antiglobulin labeled with enzyme
s — Substrate
— Enzyme plus substrate

antigen, there will be less labeled antigen bound in mixture 2 because the unlabeled antigen of the patient's serum has competed for, and has been bound by, the antibody. Consequently there is more labeled antigen in the supernatant fluid than in mixture 1. A standard curve is constructed by using known amounts of unlabeled antigen in reaction mixture 2. The amount of antigen in the patient's serum can now be determined by referring to the standard curve.

Radioallergosorbent Test (RAST)

This is a widely employed RIA that tests for antibody rather than for antigen. The test is most frequently used to detect IgE antibodies in the serum of patients who suffer common clinical allergies such as hay fever, asthma, and insect sting allergies. The antigen that is suspected to be causing the allergy—for example, pollen extract or bee venom—is impregnated into a cellulose (paper-like) disk. The patient's serum is applied to the disk. After the disk has been washed, radioactively labeled antiglobulin that is specific for human IgE is applied to the disk. After several washings the antibody activity of the patient's serum is determined by counting the radioactivity associated with the disk.

WESTERN BLOT OR IMMUNOBLOT

Analysis of the many proteins in a complex mixture can be accomplished by the technique called Western blotting or immunoblotting. Proteins are transferred from a gel matrix to a membrane surface. Protein detection in the gel is limited because probes (identifying markers) do not easily penetrate the gel matrix. There are three steps to the procedure.

Step 1 The protein mixture is placed in a polyacrylamide gel slab and electrophoresed. This separates the proteins into invisible bands in the gel.

Step 2 The bands from the gel are transferred to an immobilizing paper (a nitrocellulose membrane) by means of a blotting technique. The nitrocellulose sheet is placed onto the agar and the two are sandwiched between buffer-saturated sponges. The sandwich is held together by plastic sheets, immersed in a buffer-filled chamber, and electrophoresed to effect the transfer of the bands from the gel to the nitrocellulose sheet.

Step 3 Enzyme-labeled or isotope-labeled antibodies (as described under the ELISA and RIA techniques) with known specificities are applied to the nitrocellulose sheets and identification of the protein bands is made.

One of the most important Western blot applications is in finding antibodies to HIV (human immunodeficiency virus, or AIDS virus) antigens. This is a multistep indirect ELISA.

AVIDIN-BIOTIN TECHNIQUE

This technique is regarded as four or five times more sensitive than the other labeling procedures. The biotin-avidin complex may be conjugated to antibodies and other labels. Since only one conjugate preparation is required for many different assays, the biotin-avidin system is very attractive for use in immunological procedures. It can also be used in the absence of antibody, as is described next.

Biotin is a small protein molecule that binds readily to other proteins without changing the biological activities of the other proteins. Avidin, obtained from egg white, binds avidly and specifically to biotin. The avidin may be conjugated to an enzyme, for example, horseradish peroxidase. The "sandwich" involved in identifying an unknown protein may consist of

1. The protein that is being identified
2. Biotin bound to the protein
3. Avidin, which specifically and strongly binds to the biotin
4. Horseradish peroxidase, which is conjugated to the biotin

One important application of the avidin-biotin system is in the detection and identification, or in the classification, of bacteria and viruses. The technique involves **nucleic acid hydridization** and **nucleic acid probes.** A nucleic acid probe is an extracted strand of nucleic acid that has a sequence unique to the organism sought. The biotin-avidin–labeled enzyme becomes attached to the probe through biotin, which readily binds to free amino groups of the nucleic acid cytosine bases. If the labeled probe hybridizes (by complementary base pairing) with the extracted DNA of the unknown bacterium or virus, identification is made. The enzyme-labeled avidin substitutes for enzyme-labeled antibodies in this application of the avidin-biotin technique.

MONOCLONAL ANTIBODIES PRODUCED BY HYBRIDOMAS (FUSED CELLS)

An immensely important technique that lends a high degree of specificity, uniformity, and rapidity to immunodiagnosis involves applications of monoclonal antibodies. Monoclonal antibodies initially are produced in vitro by a hybrid cell. **The hybrid cell results from the fusion of a cancerous plasma cell** (called a myeloma cell) **and an antibody-producing lymphocyte** obtained from the spleen.

C. Milstein and G. Kohler fused myeloma cells and spleen cells and the resulting hybridoma produced the first monoclonal antibody of predefined specificity. This monumental biotechnical advance, for which Milstein and Kohler were awarded the Nobel Prize, has launched a multitude of actual and anticipated applications, not only for **immunodiagnosis and immunoidentification,** which is our interest here, but also for **immunotherapy.**

Hybridomas—The Source of Monoclonal Antibodies

Myeloma Cells as the Source of Vast Quantities of Immunoglobulins and "Immortality." The hybridoma consists of two cell types that are experimentally fused. One of the cell types is a malignant plasma cell whose clones produce vast quantities of whole immunoglobulin molecules, or fractions of immunoglobulin molecules that are all of the same kind and type. Plasma cell cancer is called **myeloma** or **plasmacytoma** and the condition it produces is termed **monoclonal gammopathy.** Either the immunoglobulins that are formed are nonspecific, that is, they have no defined antibody function, or their function is against specific antigens, only a few of which have been identified. The study of monoclonal gammopathies has contributed much to the fundamental knowledge about the immune system. The monostructural immunoglobulins produced by myeloma cell strains have been especially important in the determination of the basic structure of the immunoglobulin molecule and in distinguishing the five immunoglobulin classes.

The contribution of the myeloma cell to the hybrid resides in its vigorous, continuous growth both in vitro and in vivo and in the virtually endless supply of immunoglobulins it is capable of producing. The permanent and robust growth has caused some to say that the myeloma half of the hybrid imparts "immortality."

Spleen-Derived Lymphocytes as the Source of Specific Antibodies. The other half of the hybridoma cell is an antibody-producing lymphocyte usually obtained from the spleen of an animal that has been deliberately immunized with a given antigen.

Technique of Creating Hybridomas. Since only a small proportion of the total spleen cell lymphocyte population is responding to the antigen, it is necessary to bring together a large number of spleen (1 to 3 $\times$ 10^8) and myeloma (1 to 10 $\times$ 10^7) cells to increase the likelihood of contact between antibody-producing cells and myeloma cells. Fusion occurs slowly and spontaneously, but it can be enhanced by the addition of polyethylene glycol or by electrofusion (Fig. B-9). Fusion takes place between spleen cell and spleen cell, myeloma cell and myeloma cell, and

FIGURE B-9
Hybridoma technique.

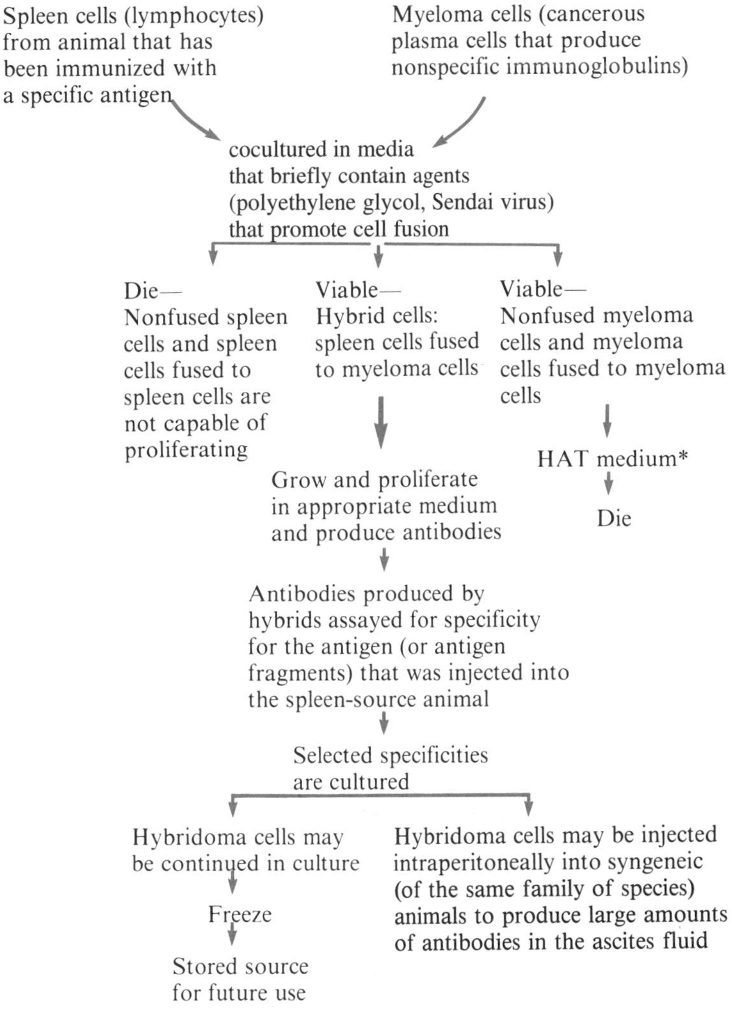

*Unfused myeloma cells and myeloma-myeloma hybrids cannot survive in HAT (hypoxanthine, aminopterin, thymidine) medium because myeloma cells that lack the enzyme HPRT (hypoxanthine phosphoribosyl transferase) are selected.

spleen cell and myeloma cell. It therefore becomes essential to be able to select out the spleen cell–myeloma cell hybrid. Spleen cells that are unfused or that are fused to each other are no problem because they soon die in culture. Unfused and fused myeloma cells are eliminated when they are transferred to a growth medium that contains hypoxanthine, aminopterin, and thymidine (HAT medium). Myeloma cells are deficient in hypoxanthine phosphoribosyltransferase (HRPT). Spleen cells provide HRPT. A mixture of spleen cell–myeloma cell hybrids remains and produces antibodies and grows well in vitro.

Selection of the Hybrids to Be Cloned

The number of hybrids that remain after two to six weeks in the HAT medium may be in the range of 150 to 500 cells. The hybridoma cell mixture is diluted so that individual clones can be grown and sorted to find and identify the cells that are producing antibody for specific antigenic determinants. Transient antibody secretion by the spleen cells becomes a stable and permanent property of an established cell line, the **hybridoma.**

Advantages of Monoclonal Antibodies Over Conventionally Obtained Antibodies

Over the years the conventional method of obtaining antibodies for immunodiagnostic and immunotherapeutic applications consisted of immunizing an animal and harvesting the antibody-containing serum (an antiserum). By comparison with monoclonal antibodies, animal antisera are not very "clean" preparations. To begin with, antigen preparations that are used to immunize the animal usually contain many antigens. The antiserum from the animal therefore is a very heterogeneous mixture of antibody specificities. Even though each B cell makes only one specific antibody, there are hundreds of B cells making different antibodies and their products are mixed in the serum. The "specificity" of a given antiserum, for the most part, is determined by the antibodies that are present in highest concentration; those of lower activity are usually masked.

Monoclonal antibodies, by contrast, have precisely defined characteristics. They are specific for a single antigenic determinant. The hybridomas can be grown continuously in culture, where they yield 10 to 100 μg of antibody per milliliter. The yield can be increased by inoculating the hybridoma cells into the peritoneal cavity of a syngeneic (genetically identical to the hybrid cell) animal.

Applications of Monoclonal Antibodies

The list of already prepared monoclonal antibodies of differing specificities, many of which are commercially available, is long and will continue to expand because of the many actual and anticipated applications in diagnosis, investigation, and therapy (Table B-1). A major advantage that derives from the high degree of specificity of monoclonal antibodies is that the time interval for the identification of infectious disease agents is shortened to 15 to 20 minutes, a great improvement over the conventional time-consuming methods of cultivation, staining, and biochemical testing. Therapeutically, monoclonal antibodies hold great promise for treating cancers through such means as immunotoxins. Being investigated are immunotoxins that are composed of a monoclonal antibody that is specific for antigens of the patient's cancer cells and toxins that are covalently bound to the antibody. The antibody specifically attaches to the cancer cell, and the attached toxin enters the cancer cell and poisons it.

TABLE B-1
Actual and Anticipated Applications of Monoclonal Antibodies

Diagnostic Applications

In vitro diagnosis of infectious disease agents

In vivo diagnosis or localization with labeled (e.g., radioactive) antibodies; specific imaging of tumor metastases, organs, infectious agents, hormone receptors, neuron receptors, etc.

As standardized diagnostic antibodies available in limitless quantities for worldwide distribution

As standardized antibodies for tissue typing or organ transplants

Investigative Applications

Analyses of single antigenic determinants of a complex antigen

Discernment of cell subtypes, e.g., T lymphocyte subtypes

Therapeutic Applications

Highly specific passive immunization against infectious agents, toxic drugs, cancers

As carriers of covalently bound drugs against pathogens

As carriers of toxic substances (immunotoxins) that can be precisely focused on cancer cells

As toxin or virus captors for the extracorporeally circulated blood of patients

Special Serological Tests

C-Reactive Protein. An antibody test for a protein that appears in the serum as a consequence of acute inflammation.

Opsonophagocytic Index. A test that measures the increased ability of phagocytes to ingest encapsulated bacteria in the presence of antibody that is specific for the capsule.

TIP Test. A test for antibodies that immobilize live *Treponema pallidum* (syphilis) bacteria.

Quellung (Capsular Swelling) Test. A test in which the capsule of bacteria enlarges in the presence of specific antibody.

Immunoferritin Technique. An electron microscopy technique in which ferritin molecules that are attached to antibody appear as uniform-shaped spheres that indicate the location of antigens.

In Vivo Immunodiagnostic Tests

In vivo tests are generally not called serological tests unless they are neutralization tests. Instead, in vivo tests are variously named after the mode of application of the test antigen, the disease in question, or the person who devised the test: skin test, histoplasmin test, tuberculin Mantoux test, Schick test, and Frei test, to name a few. Most in vivo tests are qualitative tests, with only one dilution of antigen being used. The size and intensity of the reaction do, however, lend a quantitative aspect.

Radiolabeled antibodies are now being developed as in vivo diagnostic aids to help uncover otherwise undetected sites of infection and cancer metastases in patients.

Immunology of Red Blood Cells

Immunology of the blood, **immunohematology,** is a broad, complex subject. There are hundreds of antigens associated with the human red blood cell alone. The antigens of the red blood cells are grouped into antigenic systems or factors: ABO, Rh, MNSs, Duffy, Kell, Kidd, Lewis, and Lutheran. These antigens can have a bearing on transfusion, but fortunately most of them, except the ABO and Rh antigens, are weak and do not incite a major antibody response or are of limited occurrence. The ABO system is described here because of its importance in the type of transplantation known as blood transfusion, and the Rh system is described because of its role in hemolytic disease of the fetus and newborn.

THE ABO SYSTEM

Two major antigens are involved in the ABO system: A and B. There are **four major blood groups,** A, B, AB, and O, in which humans are placed according to the presence or absence of A or B antigen or combinations of those antigens on their red blood cells. The antigens are termed hemagglutinogens. The antibodies are referred to as hemagglutinins. More specifically, they are called **isohemagglutinogens** and **isohemagglutinins.** Actually it is more correct to use the prefix **allo-** in place of **iso-** but the term **isohemagglutinin** has retained general acceptance (see Transplantation Terminology in Chapter 13 and Table 13-5).

ABO System Genetics

The antigens A and B are genetically determined co-dominants. Transmission follows mendelian inheritance patterns. The blood group that a person belongs to represents the phenotype. The genotypes of groups O and AB are automatically known when the phenotype is known. The genotype of a group O person is OO; of group AB, it is AB. Group AB individuals can transmit the A or the B gene to offspring; group O transmits neither. Group A and group B individuals may be genotypically homozygous (AA, BB) or genotypically heterozygous (AO, BO). Table B-2 shows selected parental phenotypes and genotypes and possible offspring types. There are subgroups to the A and B antigens, of which antigenic variants A_1 and A_2 are the most frequently encountered.

ABO Antibodies

Antibodies (isohemagglutinins or allohemagglutinins) to the A and B antigens are "naturally" occurring. The antibodies belong predominantly to class IgM. They develop spontaneously without a known specific stimulus. Thus, an individual who belongs to blood group A automatically has anti-B antibodies, one in group B has anti-A antibodies, one in group AB has no antibodies to the A and B antigens, and one in group O has anti-A and anti-B antibodies.

ABO Blood Group Typing

Commercially prepared antisera are used in a slide or tube agglutination procedure to determine the ABO phenotype of the patient's red blood cells.

ABO System and Transfusion

The major consideration in blood transfusion is based on the recipient's antibodies versus the donor's cells. Incorrectly matched cells are destroyed by the recipient's antibodies and complement. The donor's antibodies, unless

TABLE B-2
ABO Blood Group System

ABO phenotypes	Serum antibodies	Percent of population	Possible genotypes	Possible phenotypes when mated with					
				AA	AO	BB	BO	OO	AB
A	Anti-B	42	AA	A	A	AB	A, AB	A	A, AB
			AO	A	A, O	B, AB	A, B, AB, O	A, O	A, B, AB
B	Anti-A	10	BB	AB	B, AB	B	B	B	B, AB
			BO	A, AB	A, B, AB, O	B	B, O	B, O	A, B, AB
O	Anti-A, anti-B	44	OO	A	A, O	B	B, O	O	A, B
AB	None	4	AB	A, AB	AB, A, B	B, AB	AB, A, B	A, B	AB, A, B

a large amount of whole blood is being transfused, are diluted by the recipient's volume of blood. Blood group O individuals are termed **universal donors** because their red cells do not have the A and B antigens and so, even if the recipient has antibodies, no reaction normally occurs in respect to the ABO system. AB individuals, who do not have anti-A and anti-B antibodies, are termed **universal recipients.** In routine practice people receive transfusions as much as possible with blood of their own ABO groups and Rh compatibility. It is not safe to transfuse blood solely on the basis of information obtained in the routine ABO and Rh typing procedures. Those are merely preliminary tests to identify the blood group of the cells. Additional testing is explained later.

The ABO System and Disputed Parentage

The ABO blood group system may be of value in determining disputed parentage. It is sometimes possible to exclude an individual accused of fathering a child on the basis of the ABO blood group testing. Thus, an O male could not father an AB child. This technique does not, however, prove that a male is the father just because the blood group of the child is compatible with the blood group of the putative father.

THE RH SYSTEM

The Rh system is particularly crucial in the situation of an Rh-positive fetus borne by an Rh-negative mother. Notable differences from the ABO system are that the Rh antibodies involved in hemolytic disease of the newborn belong to immunoglobulin class IgG (they cross the placenta) and that Rh antibodies are not naturally occurring. For Rh antibodies to develop, there has to be an opportunity for stimulation by the Rh factor or factors.

Determination of Rh Type

In preliminary general testing, individuals are designated Rh-positive if there red blood cells have Rh factor D. They are Rh-negative if they do not have that factor, symbolized by the lowercase letter d. An individual can also be Rh-positive on the basis of other Rh factors, C and E, but these are of much lower incidence. About 85 percent of the population is Rh-positive. Persons who are Rh-positive are homozygous (D/D) or heterozygous (D/d) for the major factor. Thus, a prospective father who phenotypically is Rh-positive may be heterozygous (D/d), and in that case there is a 50 percent chance that the child will be Rh-negative if the mother is Rh-negative.

Rh Isoimmunization (Alloimmunization)

Transfusion to an Rh-negative individual with Rh-positive blood leads to the production of anti-Rh antibodies. If these are formed in sufficient amounts, a subsequent transfusion with red blood cells with the corresponding Rh antigen will cause a transfusion reaction.

Rh incompatibility problems, however, develop primarily because of isoimmunization during pregnancy. An Rh-negative mother carrying an Rh-positive fetus produces anti-Rh antibodies when the fetus's Rh-positive cells enter the mother's circulation (Fig. B-10). The best opportunity for the fetus's cells to enter the mother is during the perinatal period, when "major bleeds" occur. Late in pregnancy the epithelium that covers the placental villi atrophies, rendering the villi more fractious and therefore more vulnerable to penetration by the fetal cells.

FIGURE B-10
Development of Rh hemolytic disease of the newborn. RBC's = red blood cells.

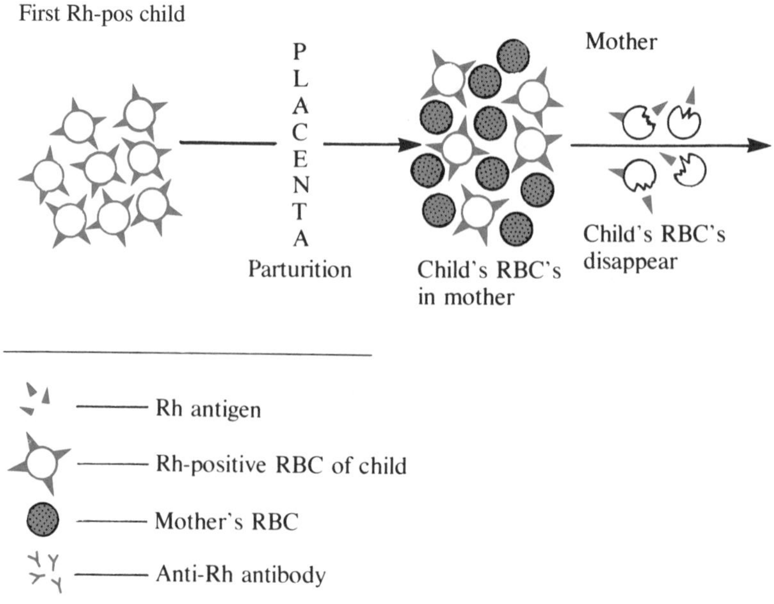

The antigenization by the fetal red blood cells stimulates the production of anti-Rh antibodies by the mother.

Hemolytic Disease of the Newborn

The titer of anti-Rh antibodies generally does not reach a level high enough to be damaging to fetal red blood cells until about the third Rh-incompatible pregnancy. The disease results when the mother's antibodies cause the lysis of the child's red blood cells. The degree of lysis is governed by the titer of the mother's antibodies. In hemolytic disease of the fetus and newborn (erythroblastosis fetalis and erythroblastosis neonatorum) the maternal antibodies destroy red blood cells of the child late in fetal life or in the neonatal period (Fig. B-10). Immature, nucleated red blood cells (erythroblasts) increase in number to replace the lysed red blood cells. Three clinical conditions (listed in order of decreasing severity) can follow: **hydrops fetalis** (extensive pouring out of blood fluid into the tissues), **icterus gravis neonatorum** (jaundice), and **congenital anemia.**

Management of Rh Disease

1. The anti-Rh antibody level of women can be monitored during pregnancy if an Rh incompatibility exists between the mother and the father, or when there has been previous hemolytic disease in offspring of multiparous women. Serious fetal disease is not likely to occur if the mother's titer is less than 1 : 8. A good indication of impending disease is discerned by Coombs' test (see the following section), carried out on cord blood. Serum bilirubin levels in the child reflect the severity of the child's condition.

2. If an exchange transfusion of blood, which is a slow-dilution procedure, is required for the newborn child, the Rh-positive child is transfused with Rh-negative blood. The mother's anti-Rh antibodies in the child's system would destroy transfused Rh-positive red blood cells.

3. It is possible to prevent or to minimize the isoimmunization of a mother who does not already have Rh antibodies by injecting anti-Rh antibodies into the mother within 72 hours after the birth of an Rh-positive child. The anti-Rh antibodies are in the form of a gamma globulin preparation called RhIG. Passive immunization suppresses the antigenization by the fetal cells in the postpartum period. Preventing antibody formation at this juncture forestalls the development of an Rh incompatibility problem in the next pregnancy.

TECHNIQUES FOR DETERMINING ANTI–RED BLOOD CELL ANTIBODIES

It is important to be able to detect incompatibilities in vitro for monitoring purposes and to prevent transfusion reactions. The antibodies, either the naturally occurring ones or those that result from isoimmunization or idiosyncrasies (self-peculiarities), are not all of the same type. Several techniques therefore are employed so as not to overlook the presence of incompatible antibodies. Positive reactions are in the form of hemagglutination or hemolysis.

Crossmatching

After routine ABO and Rh slide and tube tests are carried out with commercial antisera, crossmatches are performed before transfusion. Crossmatching detects incompatibilities that are not discovered in the routine typing and picks up typing procedure errors. In the major crossmatch the donor's cells are tested against the recipient's serum. In the minor crossmatch the donor's serum is tested against the recipient's cells.

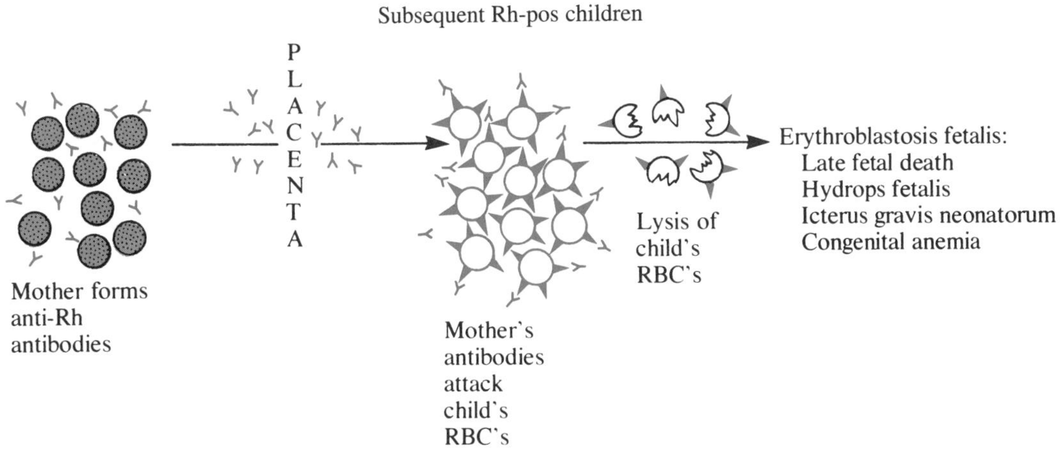

Coombs' Test

Antibodies do not always give a detectable reaction in the crossmatching procedure. Certain particulate antigens such as red blood cells have a net negative charge on their surfaces. When such charged particles are suspended in saline solution, an electrical potential called the **zeta potential** is created between the particles. The potential prevents the cells from getting close to each other. While one antigen-binding site of an antibody molecule is attached to one red blood cell, the other antigen-binding site cannot extend far enough to bind to another red blood cell because of the zeta potential, and so hemagglutination does not occur. The principle of Coombs' test lies in providing a divalent immunoglobulin bridge between the functionally monovalent antibody molecules. The immunoglobulin bridge is an antibody against human immunoglobulin. It is produced by injecting human gamma globulin into goats or rabbits. The animal forms antibodies to the human gamma globulin. When the animal serum is added to antibody-coated cells, the divalent animal molecule joins two human immunoglobulin molecules together, leading to the visible reaction.

Some antibodies are not particularly effective in agglutinating red blood cells; however, they can be detected indirectly. This is accomplished by adding a second antibody that will bind to the antibody on the red blood cell. By binding different antigens on the red blood cell surface, the test can detect antibodies to antigens other than those present on the red blood cell surface.

Serological Typing of Human Leukocyte Antigen

Two customary procedures are used to enhance the survival of allografts: (1) utilizing immunosuppressive techniques and (2) selecting donors with few major histocompatibility complex (MHC) mismatches by utilizing serological techniques. In serological assays a small volume of human antiserum to human leukocyte antigen (HLA), normal guinea pig or rabbit serum as a source of complement, and approximately 2000 lymphocytes from the prospective donor or recipient are incubated. Donor cells carrying HLA antigens recognized by the antiserum undergo cell membrane damage. The damaged cells can be stained with eosin or trypan blue.

APPENDIX C

Tables of Infectious Disease Based on Body Site

The following tables bring together all the different infectious agents that can affect one body site. It is important to note that many diseases that are acquired through various body sites can cause major pathological responses at other body sites. For example, several helminths penetrate the skin but affect internal organs. In some diseases more than one body site may be involved, and for this reason you may see a microbial agent listed more than once. For example, the organism causing plague affects the lymph and cardiovascular systems but pneumonic plague may also be a result of infection. Thus plague can be considered to affect the respiratory tract as well as the lymph and cardiovascular systems. For your convenience the text page where the specific disease is discussed in detail is also included in the tables.

TABLE C-1
Diseases Affecting the Skin and Eyes

	Microbial agent	Mode of transmission	Treatment and/or prevention	Discussion page
Bacterial				
Skin				
Impetigo	*Staphylococcus aureus, Streptococcus pyogenes*	Contact with infected person	None usually required	248
Folliculitis, boils	*Staphylococcus aureus*	Infection of hair follicles by commensals	Methicillin, oxacillin, cephalosporins	248
Scalded skin syndrome	*Staphylococcus aureus*	Infection of infant skin by certain commensal strains	None	248
Erysipelas	Group A beta-hemolytic streptococci	Infection of skin by toxin-producing species	Penicillin	254
Leprosy	*Mycobacterium leprae*	Repeated exposure to infected person	Dapsone, clofazimine	338
Invasive streptococcus	Group A streptococci	Follows cutaneous infection	Penicillin	255
Eye				
Pink eye (conjunctivitis)	*Hemophilus aegyptius*	Person to person contact with infected secretions	None usually required	323
Trachoma	*Chlamydia trachomatis*	Person to person via contaminated fingers or objects	Erythromycin, tetracycline	363
Ophthalmia neonatorum	*Neisseria gonorrhoeae*	From mother to fetus	Tetracycline, erythromycin, silver nitrate	267

(continued)

TABLE C-1 (Continued)

	Microbial agent	Mode of transmission	Treatment and/or prevention	Discussion page
Viral				
Skin				
Smallpox	Smallpox (variola) virus	Contact with pustules or contaminated objects	Disease eradicated in 1977	409
Chickenpox-shingles	Varicella-zoster virus	Contact with skin lesions or respiratory secretions	Acyclovir in complicated cases	413–414
Measles	Measles (rubeola) virus	Contact with oral secretions	None; vaccine available	421
German measles (rubella)	Rubella virus	Contact with respiratory secretions	Vaccine available	425
Warts	Papilloma viruses	Contact with infected person	Podophyllum, surgery	420
Cold sores	Herpes simplex virus type 1	Contact with eye secretions?	Acyclovir	416
Eye				
Herpetic keratoconjunctivitis	Herpes simplex virus type 1	Contact with eye secretions	Vidarabine	416
Epidemic keratoconjunctivitis	Adenoviruses	Contact with eye secretions	None required	420
Acute hemorrhagic conjunctivitis	Echoviruses and coxsackieviruses	Contact with eye secretions	None required	432
Fungal				
Skin				
Superficial mycoses	*Malassezia furfur, Exophiala (Cladosporium) wernecki, Trichosporon beigelii, Piedraia hortae*	Person to person via direct or indirect means	Tolnaftate	484
Subcutaneous mycoses	(See Table 33-3, page 479)	Puncturing of skin by soil-contaminated objects		
Cutaneous mycoses (tineas)	*Trichophyton, Microsporum, Epidermophyton* species	Contact with infected animals; human to human transmission via direct or indirect means	Griseofulvin, tolnaftate, miconazole, clotrimazole	482
Candidiasis	*Candida albicans*	Allergic response to organism (dermatophytid); appendages in water or moist environment; debilitated patients subject to infection	Nystatin, miconazole, clotrimazole	485
Protozoal				
Skin				
Leishmaniasis	*Leishmania tropica, L. braziliensis*	Bite of sandfly	Antimonial compounds, pentamidine	512
Helminth				
Eye				
Loiasis (eye worm)	*Loa loa*	Bite of tabanid fly	Diethylcarbamazine	523
Onchocerciasis (river blindness)	*Onchocerca volvulus*	Bite of black fly		

TABLE C-2
Diseases Affecting the Respiratory Tract

	Microbial agent	Mode of transmission	Treatment and/or prevention	Discussion page
Bacterial				
Tuberculosis	*Mycobacterium tuberculosis*	Contact with respiratory secretions, ingestion of contaminated milk	Isoniazid, pyrazinamide, rifampin; vaccine available	331
Pneumonia	*Streptococcus pneumoniae*	Primarily a complication following respiratory distress	Penicillin; polyvalent vaccine available	258
	Klebsiella pneumoniae	Primarily in those with upper respiratory complications (alcoholics)	Cephalosporins	307
	Mycoplasma pneumoniae	Contact with respiratory secretions	Erythromycin, tetracycline; vaccine available	356
	Legionella pneumophila	Inhalation of contaminated aerosols	Erythromycin	377
	Francisella tularensis	Inhalation of contaminated aerosols generated by animals	Streptomycin; vaccine for lab personnel	327
	Staphylococcus aureus	Primarily a secondary infection following viral infection	Methicillin, cloxacillin, cephalosporins	249
	Hemophilus influenzae	Primarily a secondary infection following viral infection	Ampicillin, beta-lactamase inhibitor; vaccine available	322
	Yersinia pestis	A complication of bubonic plague caused by bite of infected rat flea	Streptomycin, chloramphenicol, tetracycline; vaccine available in areas endemic for disease	305
	Coxiella burnetii	Ingestion of contaminated milk, inhalation of contaminated aerosols from barnyard animals	None usually required	361
	Chlamydia psittaci (see also *C. pneumoniae*, p. 365)	Inhalation of aerosols from infected birds	None usually required	365
Whooping cough	*Bordetella pertussis*	Contact with respiratory secretions	Erythromycin; vaccine available in DPT	324
Diphtheria	*Corynebacterium diphtheriae*	Contact with respiratory secretions	Penicillin; vaccine available in DPT	285
Pharyngitis	*Streptococcus pyogenes*	Contact with respiratory secretions	Penicillin, erythromycin	254
Scarlet fever	Toxin-producing strain of *S. pyogenes*	Contact with respiratory secretions	Penicillin, erythromycin	254
Viral				
Common cold	Rhinovirus	Contact with respiratory secretions	None specific	432
	Parainfluenza virus	Contact with respiratory secretions	None specific	434
	Coronavirus	Contact with respiratory secretions	None specific	432
Pneumonia	Influenza viruses	Contact with respiratory secretions	Amantadine, rimantidine; vaccine available	426
	Respiratory syncytial virus	Contact with respiratory secretions	None specific	433

(continued)

TABLE C-2 (Continued)

	Microbial agent	Mode of transmission	Treatment and/or prevention	Discussion page
Fungal				
Histoplasmosis	*Histoplasma capsulatum*	Inhalation of aerosols from contaminated bird feces	Amphotericin B, itraconazole	474
Cryptococcosis	*Cryptococcus neoformans*	Inhalation of aerosols from contaminated pigeon droppings	Amphotericin B plus flucytosine, fluconazole	478
Coccidioidomycosis	*Coccidioides immitis*	Inhalation of spores from soil	Amphotericin B, ketoconazole	475
Paracoccidioidomycosis	*Paracoccidioides brasiliensis*	Inhalation of spores from soil	Ketoconazole	477
Blastomycosis	*Blastomyces dermatitidis*	Inhalation of spores from soil	Amphotericin B, ketoconazole	477
Aspergillosis	*Aspergillus* species	Inhalation of spores from soil	Amphotericin B	487
Mucormycosis (zygomycosis)	*Rhizopus, Mucor, Absidia* species	Inhalation of spores from soil	Surgical debridement, amphotericin B, flucytosine	490
Pneumocystis pneumonia	*Pneumocystis carinii*	Opportunistic (in AIDS patients, for example)	Trimethoprim-sulfamethoxazole, pentamidine, dapsone	490
Protozoal				
African sleeping sickness	*Trypanosoma* species	A complication following initial nervous system involvement	Eflornithine (Gambian), pentamidine (Rhodesian)	510
Helminth				
Paragonimiasis	*Paragonimus westermani*	Ingestion of raw contaminated crustaceans	Dichlorophenol	523

TABLE C-3
Diseases Affecting the Internal Organs and Digestive System

	Microbial agent	Mode of transmission	Treatment and/or prevention	Discussion page
Bacterial				
Caries (tooth decay)	*Streptococcus mutans*	Indigenous species initiates plaque formation on sucrose diet	Flossing, brushing, fluoridation to prevent plaque, reduction of dietary intake of sucrose	257
Periodontal disease	Many species, including those of *Bacteroides* and *Actinomyces*	Presence of plaque inflames gingiva, which become infected	Flossing, brushing, fluoridation to prevent plaque; antimicrobials in mouthwashes	372
Actinomycosis (lumpy jaw)	*Actinomyces* species	Opportunistic infection resulting from compromising condition such as jaw fracture, pulled tooth	Penicillin, trimethoprim-sulfamethoxazole	369

(continued)

TABLE C-3 (Continued)

	Microbial agent	Mode of transmission	Treatment and/or prevention	Discussion page
Gastroenteritis	*Escherichia coli* strains	Ingestion of contaminated food or water	Fluid and electrolyte replacement	297
	Salmonella species	Ingestion of contaminated food or water	Fluid and electrolyte replacement	298
	Staphylococcus aureus	Ingestion of toxin-contaminated food	Fluid and electrolyte replacement	248
	Vibrio parahaemolyticus	Ingestion of contaminated shellfish	Fluid and electrolyte replacement	318
	Shigella species	Ingestion of contaminated food or water	Fluid and electrolyte replacement	303
	Clostridium perfringens	Ingestion of contaminated food	Fluid and electrolyte replacement	276
	Campylobacter jejuni	Ingestion of contaminated food	Fluid and electrolyte replacement	350
	Yersinia enterocolitica	Ingestion of contaminated food	Fluid and electrolyte replacement	306–307
	Bacillus cereus	Ingestion of contaminated food	Fluid and electrolyte replacement	275
	Vibrio cholerae (see Cholera)			
	Aeromonas hydrophila	Ingestion of contaminated water	Fluid and electrolyte replacement	319
	Plesiomonas shigelloides	Ingestion of contaminated food or water	Many cases require antibiotic therapy (chloramphenicol, tetracycline)	320
Pseudomembranous colitis	*Clostridium difficile*	Associated with antimicrobial therapy	Vancomycin	281
Gastritis and duodenal ulcer	*Helicobacter pylori*	Not known	Bismuth salt and metronidazole plus amoxicillin	351
Typhoid fever	*Salmonella typhi*	Ingestion of contaminated food or water	Chloramphenicol, ampicillin, amoxicillin; vaccine available	299
Cholera	*Vibrio cholerae*	Ingestion of contaminated food or water	Fluid and electrolyte replacement	316
Brucellosis (liver, spleen, bone)	*Brucella* species	Ingestion of contaminated food or water	Tetracycline, ampicillin, streptomycin	326
Rheumatic fever (heart)	*Streptococcus pyogenes*	Complication following pharyngitis	Penicillin	254
Viral				
Infectious hepatitis	Hepatitis A virus (HAV)	Ingestion of contaminated food or water	Immune globulin, vaccine in trials	450
Serum hepatitis	Hepatitis B virus (HBV)	Hypodermic injection (drug addicts), sexual contact	Interferon for chronic; vaccine available	450
Mumps (parotid glands)	Mumps virus	Contact with oral secretions	None; vaccine available	423
Cytomegalovirus inclusion disease (kidney, spleen, liver)	Cytomegalovirus (CMV)	Congenital transfer, transplantation	Ganciclovir, foscarnet; immune globulin	411

(continued)

TABLE C-3 (Continued)

	Microbial agent	Mode of transmission	Treatment and/or prevention	Discussion page
Gastroenteritis	Astroviruses	Fecal-oral or ingestion of contaminated food or water	Fluid and electrolyte replacement	443
	Adenovirus types 40 and 41	Fecal-oral or ingestion of contaminated food or water	Fluid and electrolyte replacement	420
	Caliciviruses	Fecal-oral or ingestion of contaminated food or water	Fluid and electrolyte replacement	442
	Rotavirus	Fecal-oral or ingestion of contaminated food or water	Fluid and electrolyte replacement	441
	Norwalk virus	Ingestion of contaminated food or water	Fluid and electrolyte replacement	442
Yellow fever (liver, spleen, kidney)	Yellow fever virus	Bite of infected *Aedes aegypti* mosquito	None; vaccine available	440
Infectious mononucleosis	Epstein-Barr virus (EBV)	Contact with oral secretions (kissing)	None	418
Fungal				
Mycotoxicosis	Species of *Penicillium, Fusarium, Streptomyces, Aspergillus*	Ingestion of toxin-contaminated foods	None	492
Protozoal				
Giardiasis	*Giardia lamblia*	Ingestion of contaminated food or water	Metronidazole, quinacrine	507
Amoebic dysentery	*Entamoeba histolytica*	Ingestion of contaminated food or water	Metronidazole, iodoquinol	503
Cryptosporidiosis	*Cryptosporidium* species	Animals to humans	None suitable	516–517
Balantidial dysentery	*Balantidium coli*	Ingestion of contaminated food or water	Oxytetracyclines, iodoquinol	513
Chagas' disease	*Trypanosoma cruzi*	Abraded skin contaminated with feces of reduviid bug	Nifurtimox, benznidazole	511
Malaria (kidney, spleen, liver)	*Plasmodium* species	Bite of infected female *Anopheles* mosquito	Chloroquine, primaquine phosphate	514
Visceral leishmaniasis	*Leishmania donovani*	Bite of sandfly	Antimony sodium stibogluconate	513
Helminth				
Tapeworm	*Taenia saginata* (beef) *Taenia solium* (pork) *Diphyllobothrium latum* (fish)	Ingestion of larvae-contaminated fish	Praziquantel	526
Trichinosis	*Trichinella spiralis*	Ingestion of larvae-contaminated meat	Thiabendazole	521
Pinworm	*Enterobius vermicularis*	Person to person via fecal-oral route	Mebendazole and pyrantel pamoate	521
Fascioliasis	*Fasciolopsis buski*	Ingestion of aquatic plants contaminated with larvae	Hexylresorcinol	523
Clonorchiasis	*Clonorchis sinensis*	Ingestion of larvae-infected fish	Chloroquine phosphate	523
Schistosomiasis (liver)	*Schistosoma mansoni, S. haematobium, S. japonicum*	Larvae penetrate skin	Praziquantel	524
Whipworm	*Trichuris trichiura*	Ingestion of eggs from contaminated soil	Mebendazole	—
Ascariasis	*Ascaris lumbricoides*	Ingestion of eggs from contaminated soil or water	Mebendazole	517
Strongyloidiasis	*Strongyloides stercoralis*	Larvae in soil penetrate skin	Thiabendazole	520

TABLE C-4
Diseases Affecting the Lymph and Cardiovascular Systems

	Microbial agent	Mode of transmission	Treatment and/or prevention	Discussion page
Bacterial				
Subacute bacterial endocarditis	Alpha-hemolytic streptococci	Follows bacteremia resulting from displacement of microbes from oral cavity	Penicillin, erythromycin	257
Acute bacterial endocarditis	*Streptococcus pneumoniae, Staphylococcus aureus*	Bacteremia following primary infection	Penicillin (*S. pneumoniae*), methicillin, oxacillin (*S. aureus*)	249
Rheumatic fever	*Streptococcus pyogenes*	Complication of heart following primary infection (pharyngitis)	Penicillin for primary infection	254
Anthrax	*Bacillis anthracis*	Inhalation of spores, contact of abraded skin with spores	Penicillin, streptomycin, tetracycline	274
Gas gangrene	*Clostridium perfringens* and other clostridia	Spore contamination of open wounds	Wound debridement, antiserum, penicillin therapy	278
Plague	*Yersinia pestis*	Bite of infected rat flea	Streptomycin, chloramphenicol, tetracycline; vaccine for endemic areas of plague	305
Brucellosis	*Brucella* species	Contact of abraded skin with infected animal carcasses, ingestion of contaminated milk	Ampicillin, streptomycin, tetracyclines	326
Tularemia	*Francisella tularensis*	Contact of abraded skin with contaminated animal carcasses, bite of infected ticks or deerflies	Streptomycin; vaccine for lab personnel	327
Rat bite fever	*Spirillum minor*	Bite of infected rat	Penicillin, tetracycline	349
Lyme disease	*Borrelia* species	Bite of infected tick	Doxycycline	348
Relapsing fever	*Borrelia* species	Bite of infected body louse	Tetracycline, chloramphenicol	347
Rickettsial disease				
Epidemic typhus	*Rickettsia prowazekii*	Contamination of wound with louse feces	Tetracycline, chloramphenicol	359
Endemic typhus	*R. typhi*	Bite of infected flea	Tetracycline, chloramphenicol	360
Rocky Mountain spotted fever*	*R. rickettsii*	Bite of infected tick	Tetracycline, chloramphenicol	360
Scrub typhus	*R. tsutsugamushi*	Bite of infected mite	Tetracycline, chloramphenicol	361
Viral				
Myocarditis	Coxsackieviruses	Ingestion of contaminated food or water	None	431
Yellow fever	Yellow fever virus	Bite of *Aedes aegypti* mosquito	None; vaccine available	440
Dengue fever	Dengue fever virus	Bite of *Aedes aegypti* mosquito	Only supportive therapy	441
Marburg and Ebola virus disease	Marburg and Ebola viruses	Contact with infected humans (but may be transmitted from African green monkey)	Only supportive therapy	437–438
Infectious mononucleosis	Epstein-Barr virus	Contact with oral secretions	Only supportive therapy	418

(continued)

TABLE C-4 (Continued)

	Microbial agent	Mode of transmission	Treatment and/or prevention	Discussion page
Protozoal				
Malaria	*Plasmodium* species	Bite of female *Anopheles* mosquito	Chloroquine, primaquine, or mefloquine for resistant strains	514
Chagas' disease	*Trypanosoma cruzi*	Contamination of wound with feces of reduviid bug	Nifurtimox, benznidazole	511
Nantucket fever	*Babesia microti*	Bite of infected tick	Clindamycin, quinine	516
Helminth				
Filariasis	*Brugia malayi, Wuchereria bancrofti*	Bite of infected mosquito	Diethylcarbamazine	523
Schistosomiasis	*Schistosoma* species	Contact of skin with contaminated water	Mebendazole, metronidazole	524

* Other spotted fevers of minor interest are outlined in Table 28-1, page 360.

TABLE C-5
Diseases Affecting the Nervous System

	Microbial agent	Mode of transmission	Treatment and/or prevention	Discussion page
Bacterial				
Meningitis	*Neisseria meningitidis*	Contact with respiratory secretions	Cefotaxime or cefotaxime plus ampicillin; vaccine available	265
	Hemophilus influenzae	Contact with respiratory secretions	Cefotaxime plus sulbactam, cefotaxime plus ampicillin	322
	Listeria monocytogenes	To fetus from infected mother	Penicillin, ampicillin	289
	Streptococcus agalactiae	To fetus from infected mother	Penicillin	256
Botulism	*Clostridium botulinum*	Ingestion of toxin-contaminated food	Antitoxins; prevention of respiratory failure	276
Tetanus	*Clostridium tetani*	Contamination of deep wound with spores	Antitoxin followed by penicillin; vaccine (DPT) available	280
Leprosy	*Mycobacterium leprae*	Contact with nasal secretions	Dapsone, rifampin	338
Viral				
Encephalitis	Western equine encephalitis (WEE) virus	Bite of infected mosquito	Supportive therapy	439
	Eastern equine encephalitis (EEE) virus	Bite of infected mosquito	None	439
	St. Louis encephalitis virus	Bite of infected mosquito	None	439
	Venezuela encephalitis virus	Bite of infected mosquito	None	440
	California encephalitis virus	Bite of infected mosquito	None	440
Rabies	Rabies virus	Bite of infected animal or contact with contaminated saliva	Antirabies serum and vaccination	434
Aseptic meningitis	Echoviruses and coxsackieviruses	Ingestion of contaminated food or water	None	431

(continued)

TABLE C-5 (Continued)

	Microbial agent	Mode of transmission	Treatment and/or prevention	Discussion page
Poliomyelitis	Poliovirus	Ingestion of contaminated water	None; vaccine available	430
Creutzfeldt-Jakob disease	Prion	Ingestion of contaminated meat, transplantation procedures	Supportive therapy	458
Kuru	Prion?	Contact with infected tissues	Supportive therapy	458
Nervous system complications of acute viral disease				
Subacute sclerosing panencephalitis (SSPE)	Measles virus	Reactivation of latent measles virus	Remissions with inosine pranobex (Isoprinosine)	458
Progressive multifocal encephalopathy	Papovaviruses	Reactivation of virus in immunocompromised adults		460
Zoster	Varicella virus	Reactivation of latent virus	Acyclovir in compromised patients	414
Guillain-Barré syndrome	Influenza and varicella viruses	Disease follows influenza vaccination or varicella infection		429
Reye's syndrome	Influenza viruses (A and B) and varicella	Disease occurs in children recovering from varicella or influenza infection		427
Fungal				
Cryptococcosis	*Cryptococcus neoformans*	Inhalation of spore-contaminated pigeon droppings	Amphotericin B, flucytosine, fluconazole	478
Protozoal				
Primary amebic meningoencephalitis	*Naegleria fowleri*	Inhalation of contaminated water	Amphotericin B, miconazole	507
African sleeping sickness	*Trypanosoma* species	Bite of tsetse fly	Eflornithine (Gambian), suramin and pentamidine isethionate (Rhodesian)	510
Toxoplasmosis	*Toxoplasma gondii*	Congenital infection	Sulfadiazine, pyrimethamine	516

TABLE C-6
Diseases Affecting the Genitourinary Tract

	Microbial agent	Mode of transmission	Treatment and/or prevention	Discussion page
Bacterial				
Gonorrhea	*Neisseria gonorrhoeae*	Sexual contact	Ceftriaxone plus doxycycline	267
Syphilis	*Treponema pallidum*	Sexual contact	Penicillin	342
Lymphogranuloma venereum	*Chlamydia trachomatis*	Sexual contact	Doxycycline, tetracycline	365
Soft chancre	*Hemophilus ducreyi*	Sexual contact	Erythromycin	324
Granuloma inguinale	*Calymmatobacterium granulomatis*	Sexual contact	Streptomycin, tetracycline	375
Gardnerella vaginitis	*Gardnerella vaginalis*	Opportunistic commensal	Metronidazole	375
Acute glomerulonephritis	*Streptococcus pyogenes* (immune reaction to microbial antigen)	Complication following infection at another body site (cutaneous, respiratory)	Penicillin or erythromycin for eradicating microbe	254
Nongonococcal urethritis	*Chlamydia trachomatis*	Sexual contact	Doxycycline or tetracycline	365
Pelvic inflammatory disease (PID)	*Neisseria gonorrhoeae* and *Chlamydia trachomatis* most important	Sexual contact—complication of primary infection by microbe	Cefoxitin plus doxycycline	267
Leptospirosis	*Leptospira interrogans*	Ingestion of contaminated water or direct contact with infected animals	Penicillin	349
Viral				
Genital warts	Human papilloma virus	Sexual contact	Electrocauterization, podophyllotoxin, trichloroacetic acid	420
Genital herpes	Herpes simplex virus type 2	Sexual contact	Acyclovir	416
Fungal				
Vaginal candidiasis	*Candida albicans*	Opportunistic commensal but can be sexually transmitted	Miconazole, clotrimazole	486
Protozoal				
Trichomoniasis	*Trichomonas vaginalis*	Sexual contact	Metronidazole	510

APPENDIX D

Tables of Human Microflora

TABLE D-1
Microorganisms Found on the Skin, Ear, and Eye

Organism	Diseases with which microorganism may be implicated
Bacteria	
Acinetobacter calcoaceticus	Skin; postoperative wound infections
Bacillus spp.	Skin; panophthalmitis, meningitis
Corynebacterium spp.	Skin, eye, ear; bacterial endocarditis, skin lesions
Hemophilus aegyptius	Eye infections
Micrococcus spp.	Skin; pneumonia, meningitis
Moraxella spp.	Eye infections
Mycobacterium spp.	Skin; mycobacteriosis (see page 337)
Neisseria spp.	Eye; none
Propionibacterium acnes	Skin; pimples, acne, bacterial endocarditis
Staphylococcus aureus	Skin, ear; boils, furuncles, impetigo, mastitis, toxic shock syndrome (see page 248)
Staphylococcus epidermidis	Skin, ear, eye; pimples, acne, endocarditis (see page 251)
Fungi	
Candida albicans and other yeasts	Skin; candidiasis (see page 485)
Trichophyton spp.	Skin; dermatophytoses (see page 481)
Pityrosporum spp.	Skin; tinea versicolor and other cutaneous lesions, including folliculitis (see page 484)
Epidermophyton floccosum	Skin; skin infections such as athlete's foot (see page 482)

TABLE D-2
Microorganisms Found in the Respiratory Tract

Organism	Diseases with which microorganism may be implicated
Bacteria	
Acinetobacter spp.	Meningitis, pneumonia
Actinomyces spp.	Actinomycosis (see page 369)
Arachnia propionica	Actinomycosis (see page 369)
Bacteroides spp.	Lung abscess
Bifidobacterium spp.	Actinomycosis (see page 369)
Corynebacterium spp.	Subacute bacterial endocarditis
Enterococcus spp.	Meningitis, pneumonia, bacterial endocarditis
Fusobacterium spp.	Lung abscess
Hemophilus spp.	Laryngotracheobronchitis, meningitis
Lactobacillus spp.	Bacterial endocarditis
Leptotrichia buccalis	No definitive implications
Micrococcus spp.	No definitive implications

(continued)

TABLE D-2 (Continued)

Organism	Diseases with which microorganism may be implicated
Moraxella spp.	Conjunctivitis
Mycoplasma spp.	Primary atypical pneumonia (see page 356)
Neisseria spp.	Meningitis (see page 265)
Peptococcus spp.	Lung abscess
Peptostreptococcus spp.	Lung abscess
Propionibacterium acnes	Pimples, acne
Rothia dentocariosa	Abscess
Selenomonas sputigena	No definitive implications
Staphylococcus aureus	Pneumonia, otitis (see page 249)
Staphylococcus epidermidis	Subacute bacterial endocarditis (see page 251)
Streptococcus pneumoniae	Pneumonia, meninigitis, otitis media (see page 258)
Treponema denticola	No definitive implications
Veillonella spp.	Bacterial endocarditis
Vibrio sputorum	No definitive implications
Viridans streptococci	Subacute bacterial endocarditis
Fungi	
Candida albicans and other yeasts	Thrush (see page 486)
Torulopsis glabrata	No definitive implications
Animal Parasites	
Entamoeba gingivalis	No definitive implications
Trichomonas tenax	No definitive implications

TABLE D-3
Microorganisms Found in the Genitourinary Tract

Organism	Diseases with which microorganism may be implicated
Bacteria	
Acinetobacter spp.	Urethritis
Bacteroides spp.	Complication of surgery
Bifidobacterium spp.	None
Chlamydia spp.	Urethritis, cervicitis, neonatal disease (see page 365)
Clostridium spp.	Complications of surgery
Corynebacterium spp.	No definitive implication
Enterobacteriaceae	Pyelonephritis, cystitis
Enterococcus spp.	Pyelonephritis, cystitis
Fusobacterium spp.	No definitive implications
Gardnerella vaginalis	Vaginitis (see page 375)
Lactobacillus spp.	None
Moraxella spp.	Postoperative complications
Mycobacterium spp.	None
Mycoplasma spp.	Nonspecific urethritis (see page 356)
Neisseria spp.	None
Peptococcus spp.	Postoperative complications
Peptostreptococcus spp.	Puerperal fever
Prevotella melaninogenica (formerly *Bacteroides melaninogenicus*)	Bacterial vaginosis
Sarcina spp.	Postoperative complications
Staphylococcus aureus	Urethritis, furunculosis (see page 248)
Staphylococcus saprophyticus	Urinary tract infection in women
Streptococcus agalactiae	Neonatal disease, meningitis, endocarditis, osteomyelitis, myocarditis (see page 256)
Viridans streptococci	None
Fungi	
Candida albicans and other yeasts	Candidiasis (see page 486)
Animal Parasites	
Trichomonas vaginalis	Vaginitis

TABLE D-4
Microorganisms Found in the Gastrointestinal Tract

Organism	Diseases with which microorganism may be implicated
Bacteria	
Achromobacter spp.	Postoperative wound infections
Acidaminococcus fermentans	No definitive implications
Acinetobacter calcoaceticus	Postoperative complications
Aeromonas spp.	Osteomyelitis, postoperative complications
Alcaligenes faecalis	No definitive implications
Bacillus spp.	Wound infections
Bacteroides spp.	Peritonitis, abscess, cholecystitis
Bifidobacterium spp.	Peritonitis
Campylobacter spp.	Diarrhea
Clostridium spp.	Pseudomembranous colitis, cholecystitis
Corynebacterium spp.	No definitive implications
Enterobacteriaceae	Peritonitis, diarrhea, postoperative complications, typhoid fever, meningitis, endocarditis
Enterococcus spp.	Peritonitis, postoperative complications
Eubacterium spp.	Peritonitis
Flavobacterium spp.	Meningitis
Fusobacterium spp.	Abscess
Lactobacillus spp.	No definitive implications
Mycobacterium spp.	None
Mycoplasma spp.	No definitive complications
Peptococcus spp.	Peritonitis, abscess
Peptostreptococcus spp.	Cholecystitis, abscess
Propionibacterium spp.	Endocarditis
Pseudomonas aeruginosa	Meningitis, postoperative complications
Ruminococcus bromii	No definitive implications
Sarcina spp.	No definitive implications
Staphylococcus aureus	Pancreatic abscess, enteritis
Veillonella spp.	No definitive implications
Viridans streptococci	No definitive implications
Vibrio spp.	None
Fungi	
Candida albicans and other yeasts	Postoperative complications

APPENDIX

E Vaccines, Toxoids, and Immune Globulins

TABLE E-1
Licensed Vaccines and Toxoids Available in the United States

Vaccine	Type	Route
Adenovirus	Live virus	O
Anthrax	Inactivated bacterium	S
Bacillus of Calmette and Guérin (BCG)	Live bacteria	ID/PC
Cholera	Inactivated bacteria	S or ID
Diphtheria-tetanus-pertussis (DTP)	Toxoids and inactivated whole bacteria	IM
DTP–*Hemophilus influenzae* type b conjugated (DTP-Hib)	Toxoids, inactivated whole bacteria, and bacterial polysaccharide conjugated to protein	IM
Diphtheria-tetanus-acellular pertussis (DTaP)	Toxoids and inactivated bacterial components	IM
Hepatitis B	Inactivated viral antigen	IM
Hemophilus influenzae type b conjugated (Hib)	Bacterial polysaccharide conjugated to protein	IM
Influenza	Inactivated virus or viral components	IM
Japanese encephalitis	Inactivated virus	S
Measles	Live virus	S
Measles-mumps-rubella (MMR)	Live virus	S
Meningococcal	Bacterial polysaccharides of serotypes A/C/Y/W-135	S
Mumps	Live virus	S
Pertussis	Inactivated whole bacteria	IM
Plague	Inactivated bacteria	IM
Pneumococcal	Bacterial polysaccharides of 23 pneumococcal types	IM or S
Poliovirus vaccine, inactivated (IPV)	Inactivated virus of all 3 serotypes	S
Poliovirus vaccine, oral (OPV)	Live virus of all 3 serotypes	O
Rabies	Inactivated virus	IM or ID
Rubella	Inactivated virus	S
Tetanus	Inactivated toxin (toxoid)	IM
Tetanus-diphtheria (Td or DT)	Inactivated toxins (toxoid)	IM
Typhoid (parenteral; Ty21a, oral)	Inactivated bacteria	S
Varicella	Live virus	S
Yellow fever	Live virus	S

O = oral; S = subcutaneous; IM = intramuscular; ID = intradermal.
SOURCE: Centers for Disease Control. General recommendations on immunization. *M.M.W.R.* 43(No. RR-1): 1994.

TABLE E-2
Immune Globulins and Antitoxins[a] Available in the United States

Immunobiological	Type	Indication
Botulinum antitoxin	Specific equine Abs	Treatment of botulism
Cytomegalovirus immune globulin, intravenous (CMV-IGIV)	Specific human Abs	Prophylaxis for bone marrow transfusion and kidney transplantation
Diphtheria antitoxin	Specific equine Abs	Treatment of respiratory diphtheria
Immune globulin (IG)	Pooled human Abs	Hepatitis A preexposure and postexposure prophylaxis; measles postexposure prophylaxis
Immune globulin intravenous (IGIV)	Pooled human Abs	Replacement therapy for Ab deficiency disorder; immune thrombocytopenia purpura (ITP); hypogammaglobulinemia in chronic lymphocytic leukemia; Kawasaki disease
Hepatitis B immune globulin (HBIG)	Specific human Abs	Hepatitis B postexposure prophylaxis
Rabies immune globulin[b] (HRIG)	Specific human Abs	Rabies postexposure management of persons not adequately immunized with tetanus toxoid
Tetanus immune globulin (TIG)	Specific human Abs	Tetanus treatment; postexposure prophylaxis of persons not adequately immunized with tetanus toxoid
Vaccinia immune globulin	Specific human Abs	Treatment of eczema vaccinatum, vaccinia necrosum, and ocular vaccinia
Varicella-zoster immune globulin (VZIG)		Postexposure prophylaxis of susceptible immunocompromised persons, certain susceptible pregnant women, and perinatally exposed newborns

Abs = antibodies.
[a] Immune globulin preparations and antitoxins are administered intramuscularly unless otherwise indicated.
[b] HRIG is administered around the wounds in addition to intramuscularly.

APPENDIX F

Table of Infectious Diseases Reportable to the Centers for Disease Control

TABLE F-1
Summary of Reported Cases, United States, 1993

Disease	Cases	Etiological agent(s)
AIDS	103,691	Human immunodeficiency virus (HIV)
Amebiasis	2,970	*Entamoeba histolytica*
Anthrax	—	*Bacillus anthracis*
Aseptic meningitis	12,848	Number of viral agents
Botulism, all types	97	*Clostridium botulinum*
Brucellosis	120	*Brucella* species
Chancroid	1,399	*Haemophilus ducreyi*
Cholera	18	*Vibrio cholerae*
Diphtheria	—	*Corynebacterium diphtheriae*
Encephalitis, primary and post-infections	1,089	Arboviruses
Gonorrhoea	439,673	*Neisseria gonorrhoeae*
Granuloma inguinale	19	*Calymmatobacterium granulomatis*
Haemophilus influenzae	1,419	—
Hansen's disease (leprosy)	187	*Mycobacterium leprae*
Hepatitis A	24,238	Hepatitis A virus
Hepatitis B	13,361	Hepatitis B virus
Hepatitis, non-A, non-B	4,876	Hepatitis C virus
Hepatitis unspecified	627	—
Legionellosis	1,280	*Legionella pneumophila*
Leptospirosis	51	*Leptospira interrogans*
Lyme disease	8,257	*Borrelia burgdorferi*
Lymphogranuloma venereum	285	*Chlamydia trachomatis*
Malaria	1,411	*Plasmodium* species
Measles (rubeola)	312	Measles virus
Meningococcal infections	2,637	*Neisseria meningitidis*
Mumps	1,692	Mumps virus
Murine typhus fever	25	*Rickettsia typhi*
Pertussis (whooping cough)	6,586	*Bordetella pertussis*
Plague	10	*Yersinia pestis*
Poliomyelitis (paralytic)	3	Poliovirus
Psittacosis	60	*Chlamydia psittaci*
Rabies, animal	9,377	Rabies virus
Rabies, human	3	Rabies virus
Rheumatic fever, acute	112	*Streptococcus pyogenes*
Rocky Mountain spotted fever	456	*Rickettsia rickettsii*

(continued)

TABLE F-1 (Continued)

Disease	Cases	Etiological agent(s)
Rubella (German measles)	192	
Rubella, congenital	5	Rubella virus
Salmonellosis	41,641	*Salmonella* species
Shigellosis	32,198	*Shigella* species
Syphilis		*Treponema pallidum*
Total all stages	101,259	
Primary and secondary	26,498	
Congenital <1	3,211	
Tetanus	48	*Clostridium tetani*
Toxic shock syndrome	212	*Staphylococcus* species
Trichinosis	16	*Trichinella spiralis*
Tuberculosis	25,313	*Mycobacterium tuberculosis*
Tularemia	132	*Francisella tularensis*
Typhoid fever	440	*Salmonella typhi*
Varicella (chickenpox)	134,722	Varicella virus

Glossary

A

Abattoir slaughterhouse

Abscess a localized collection of pus

Accessory cells macrophages and other antigen-presenting cells that express, along with Class II MHC glycoproteins, antigen on their surfaces in a form recognizable by lymphocytes

Acquired pellicle the thin, structureless film of salivary glycoproteins that forms on the tooth surface

Active immunity the acquired immune status that develops as a consequence of an infection or of immunization with vaccines

Acute having a short and relatively severe course

Adaptive immunity antigen-specific protection resulting from the formation of antibodies and effector T cells

ADCC antibody-determined cell-mediated cytotoxicity; the destruction of IgG-coated cells by K cells

Adhesins components on the microbial surface that are used for attachment to host cells or tissue

Adjuvant a substance administered with an antigen (especially with a vaccine) to enhance the immune response to the antigen

Aerobic requiring oxygen for growth

Aerosol a solution delivered as a fine mist

Aerotolerant referring to the ability of obligate anaerobes to tolerate the presence of oxygen

Aflatoxin a fungal toxin produced by certain species of *Aspergillus*

Agglutination a reaction in which cells are clumped, as occurs in the interaction of a particulate antigen with antibody

Agglutinin antibody that can cause agglutination

AIDS acquired immunodeficiency syndrome, an often fatal disease that especially strikes multicontact male homosexuals; probably a defect in cell-mediated immunity in which there is a preponderance of suppressor T cells over helper T cells; opportunistic infections often cause the fatality

Allergen an antigen that elicits allergic reactions

Allergy commonly refers to harmful/unpleasant reactions of immunological or seemingly immunological origin; in the strict sense, a type I reactivity (atopy, anaphylaxis)

Allograft (homograft) a tissue or organ graft between members of the same species who are not identical

Allosteric enzyme an enzyme whose reactivity with another molecule such as its substrate is altered because of interaction of the enzyme with other molecules

Alopecia loss of hair due to disease

Alpha hemolysis a type of blood agar plate hemolysis in which there is partial destruction of the red blood cells and some leakage of hemoglobin resulting in a greenish discoloration of the medium surrounding the microbial colony

Alternative (alternate) complement pathway the complement pathway that is activated at the C3 level; does not require immune products for activation and is therefore important for nonspecific host resistance

Alveolar pertaining to the small sac-like structures in the lung

Alveolar bone the type of bone supporting the teeth

Amphitrichous having one flagellum at each pole of the cell

Amylopectin intracellular storage polysaccharide synthesized by bacteria in dental plaque

Anabolism metabolic process involved in the synthesis of cell material

Anaerobic growing only in the absence of molecular oxygen

Anaerobiosis life in the absence of oxygen

Analogues closely similar compounds that can sometimes replace an essential metabolite

Anamnestic response a rapid increase of antibodies or effector T cells due to immune memory cells following subsequent exposures (e.g., booster doses) to the same antigen

Anaphylatoxin complement fragments C3a or C5a that

mediate intense inflammatory reactions by causing the degranulation of mast cells
Anaphylaxis a type I reactivity in which a hypersensitive individual is sensitized against a specific antigen; reaction primarily involves vasodilation and smooth muscle contraction
Aneurysm a sac formed from the dilation of the walls of an artery or vein and filled with blood
Anhemolytic having no hemolytic activity on blood agar media
Anorexia a condition in which the person has no appetite
Antibiogram pattern of results obtained from tests used to determine a microorganism's susceptibility to antimicrobials
Antibiotic a chemical compound produced by microorganisms that can inhibit or kill other microorganisms
Antibody a glycoprotein produced by mammalian hosts in response to a foreign body called the antigen; the antibody reacts specifically with the antigen that induced it
Anticodon the triplet of nucleotides in a transfer DNA molecule that complements a specific codon on the messenger RNA
Antigen a substance that induces an immune response and that reacts with the products of the immune response
Antigen binding site the variable region of the Fab portion of the immunoglobulin molecule that binds a specific or closely related antigenic determinant
Antigenic determinants small, discrete chemical groups on the antigen surface that combine with the antigen binding site on an immunoglobulin molecule or on a lymphocyte receptor
Antigen presenting cell (APC) (See **Accessory cells**.)
Anti-idiotype an immune product that reacts with the antigenic determinants of the antigen binding site
Antimetabolite a molecule that bears a strong resemblance to one required in a normal physiological reaction
Antiseptic a chemical compound that can be used on the surface of living tissue and that inhibits bacterial growth
Antiserum a serum containing specific antibodies
Antitoxin a specific antibody capable of neutralizing the exotoxin that stimulated its production
ANUG acute necrotizing ulcerative gingivitis
Arthralgia painful swollen joints
Arthropathy disease of joints
Arthropod invertebrate with jointed limbs
Arthrospore an asexually produced fungal spore that is thick-walled and barrel-shaped
Arthus reaction a type III hypersensitivity that is produced when antigen-antibody complexes activate complement; it leads to hemorrhage and inflammation resulting in necrosis
Ascospore a sexual spore of the Ascomycetes
Aseptic free of living microorganisms
Aspergilloma a ball of hyphae of the genus *Aspergillus* that accumulates at the site of infection
Asphyxia suffocation
Aspiration a process in which fluids are removed from body cavities
Assimilation transformation of nutrients into biologically useful compounds or structures
Asthma a respiratory condition causing difficulty in breathing
Atopic allergies common clinical allergies involving IgE
Atrophy the wasting away of a tissue, organ, or limb
Attenuation lessening; reduction of the virulence of microorganisms as in a vaccine
Australia antigen hepatitis B surface antigen associated with serum hepatitis (hepatitis B); originally discovered in an Australian aborigine (hence the name)
Autocatalysis a process in which the product of a reaction acts as a catalyst to accelerate the reaction
Autoclave sealed chamber used for sterilizing
Autograft tissue graft from one site to another in the same person
Autoimmune disease disease in which the host's immune system destroys its own tissue
Autolysis digestion of a cell by enzymes produced by that cell at time of death
Autotroph an organism that obtains energy by the oxidation of inorganic compounds
Auxotroph a mutant microorganism that will grow only on minimal media supplemented with growth factors not required by the normal parent
Axenic a culture of organisms containing but one strain; also called pure culture

B

Bacillus an organism of the genus *Bacillus*; also used to designate rod-shaped bacteria
Bacteremia presence of bacteria in the bloodstream
Bactericide an agent that kills bacteria
Bacteriocin antimicrobial substance produced by bacteria that kills sensitive members of related strains
Bacteriophage a bacterial virus, sometimes referred to as phage
Bacteriostatic agent an agent that inhibits the growth of bacteria
Bacteriuria presence of bacteria in the urine
Bactogen see **Chemostat**
Basidiospore a sexually produced fungal spore of the subdivision Basidiomycotina
BCDF B cell differentiation factor, a lymphokine secreted by antigen-activated T_H cells that stimulates the conversion of activated B cells into plasma cells; also called interleukin-6
BCGF B cell growth factor, a lymphokine secreted by antigen-activated T_H cells that stimulates B cell proliferation
B cells the lymphocyte population involved in the production of antibodies (humoral immunity)
Benign not malignant; subject to recovery
Beta hemolysis complete hemolysis of red blood cells resulting in a clear zone around the microbial colony
Beta oxidation a degradation process of lipids resulting in the release of two carbon fragments

Biological monitors preparations of bacterial spores of a known resistance (to heat and ethylene oxide) that are used as sterilization indicators

Biosynthesis the building up of chemical compounds

Biotransformation a process of detoxification of drugs, primarily by the liver

Biotype a strain of a species differing from other strains in a biochemical property

Biovar a strain within a species having one or more biochemical characteristics that differ from other strains within the species

Blastospore a spore formed by budding, as occurs in yeast cells

Blocking antibody an antibody that interferes with the binding of other antibodies or immune cells to antigen

Boil a localized abscess resulting from infection of a hair follicle; also called a furuncle

Booster dose an amount of immunogen given some time after primary immunization to sustain the immune response at a high level

Bronchiectasis chronic dilatation of the bronchi marked by repeated coughing spells

Brownian movement dancing motion of particles in a liquid caused by thermal agitation

Buboes swollen, inflamed lymph nodes

Buccal pertaining to the cheek

Budding in virology, release of virus through cellular membranes and acquisition of cell envelope components; asexual division in prokaryotes

Bulla a blister or vesicle filled with fluid

Bursa of Fabricius lymphoid organ in avian cloaca from which B cells are derived

C

Cachexia physical wasting due to ill health and/or malnutrition

Calculus a mineralized form of plaque on the surface of teeth in which organic components have been replaced by inorganic ones

Capneic requiring elevated concentrations of CO_2 for growth

Capsid the protein coat of a virus

Capsomere an aggregate of polypeptides forming a unit of the viral capsid

Capsule a slimy envelope that surrounds the cell wall of certain microorganisms

Carbuncle a circumscribed infection of the skin or subcutaneous tissue containing multiple draining sinuses

Caries a disease of the calcified tissue of teeth; tooth decay

Carrier a host that harbors infectious microorganisms and can transmit them to others but shows no disease symptoms

Caseation a type of necrosis in which the tissue resembles an amorphous mass of cheese

Catabolism a metabolic process in which foodstuffs are broken down to release energy

Catalyst a substance that increases the rate of a chemical reaction without being consumed in the reaction

Catarrhal a stage during infection in which there is a discharge from inflamed mucous membranes

Catheter a tubular device used to withdraw fluids from or introduce them into the body cavities

Cell-mediated immunity (CMI) an acquired immunity in which the T lymphocytes play a major role; responsible for resistance to infectious disease, some autoimmune diseases, and certain allergies

Cellulitis diffuse inflammation of connective tissue

Chancre the primary lesion of syphilis

Chemiosmosis a process in which energy is harnessed to produce an electrochemical gradient across cell membranes

Chemoprophylaxis preexposure administration of drugs to prevent disease

Chemostat an apparatus used to maintain bacterial cultures in a state of continuous division

Chemotaxin a leukoattractant such as an antibody or C3a and C5a

Chemotaxis the attraction of microorganisms or phagocytes to chemicals released in the environment or in tissues

Chemotherapy treatment of disease through the administration of drugs

Chorioretinitis inflammation of the choroid and retina of the eye

Chromatin body a network of DNA fibers giving the appearance of a distinct body in the cell

Chromosome a rod-shaped mass of DNA that carries hereditary characteristics

Chronic lasting a long period of time

Cirrhosis a disease of the liver

Class I major histocompatibility (MHC) antigens genetically determined cell membrane proteins that (1) provoke the immune response in graft rejection; (2) are self-markers that must be complexed with foreign antigens on target cell surfaces before effector T cells can destroy the target cells

Class II major histocompatibility (MHC) antigens genetically determined cell membrane proteins that (1) provoke the immune response in graft rejection; (2) are self-markers that must be complexed with antigens on antigen presenting cells before immunocompetent B and T cells can recognize and respond to antigen

Classic complement pathway the complement pathway that is activated at the C1 level, usually by the reaction of an IgG or IgM antibody with antigen

Clonal selection the theory that for each antigenic determinant there is a specific, genetically predetermined receptor on the surface of an immunocompetent lymphocyte; the combination of the determinant with the receptor activates the formation of a clone of cells, each of which forms immune products of the same antigen-binding specificity.

Clone a group of identical organisms or cells derived from a single cell or organism

Coccobacillus an oval bacterial cell resembling both coccus and rod shapes

Coccus spherical bacterium

Codon a nucleotide triplet in messenger RNA that specifies a particular amino acid
Coenzyme an organic molecule that is loosely bound to the enzyme and necessary for the activity of the enzyme
Cofactor in enzymology, an organic or inorganic molecule that is required by an enzyme to become totally active
Colicin a protein secreted by certain strains of *Escherichia coli* and lethal to other strains of the same species
Coliform a gram-negative non-sporeforming, facultative rod that ferments lactose with gas formation within 48 hours at 35 C
Colitis inflammation of the colon
Colony a uniform mass of cells derived from a single cell growing on a solid surface
Commensalism a symbiotic relationship between different species of organisms in which neither is harmed
Complement a series of complex thermolabile plasma proteins; also, the lyophilized preparation of fresh serum that is used in the complement fixation test
Complement system a system of plasma proteins that upon activation proceeds in a serial (cascade) fashion to generate biologically active fragments including opsonins, chemotaxins, anaphylatoxin, and membrane attack units
Condylomata acuminata warts on the genitalia
Condylomata lata moist syphilitic papules
Conidia asexual fungal spores produced on specialized mycelial branches called conidiophores
Conidiophore a hyphal filament on which spores, called conidia, are borne
Conjugation the act of joining together; in bacteria a process in which genetic information is transferred from one cell to another
Conjunctivitis inflammation of the membrane that lines the eyelids and the exposed surfaces of the sclera of the eye
Constant region the relatively unchanging portion of H or L chains that is identical for each immunoglobulin class or the alpha, beta, gamma, and delta chains of the T cell receptor
Constitutive enzyme an enzyme produced by a cell under any environmental conditions
Convalescence period of recovery
Copepod fresh-water or marine crustacean
Coproantibodies antibodies occurring in the intestinal tract, consisting primarily of the IgA class
Coryza inflammation of the nasal mucosa characterized by nasal discharge and watery eyes
Counterimmunoelectrophoresis (CIE) serological procedure in which antigen and antibody are made to migrate toward each other, under the influence of charged buffer ions, to facilitate precipitation
C-reactive protein a plasma protein that appears in response to inflammation in the body
Cristae the inner folded membrane found in the mitochondrion
Cross-reactive antigens antigens that share antigenic determinants or have similarly structured determinants
Croup a condition of children in which there is coughing and hoarseness
Cryosurgery use of extreme cold to destroy tissue
Culture a population of microorganisms growing in a nutrient medium
Cutaneous pertaining to the skin
Cyanosis bluish tinge to the skin due to excessive amounts of reduced hemoglobin (lack of oxygenated hemoglobin)
Cyclosporine drug used to suppress graft rejection
Cyst (of parasites) the resistant quiescent form of some parasites that serves as the vehicle of transmission
Cystitis inflammation of the urinary bladder
Cytochrome a respiratory pigment involved in oxidation-reduction reactions
Cytokines soluble molecules such as lymphokines and monokines that mediate interactions between cells
Cytopathic characterized by pathological change in a cell
Cytopathic effect (CPE) morphological alteration of host cells that usually results in cell death
Cytopenia decrease of cellular elements in the blood
Cytophilic antibody antibody that binds to receptors on cells (macrophages, neutrophils, mast cells) via the Fc portion of the antibody molecule
Cytotoxic T lymphocytes (T_{CTL}) effector (sensitized) T cells that specifically destroy target cells that bear antigens complexed with Class I MHC markers

D

Deamination removal of amino groups
Debilitated characterized by loss of strength or health
Debilitation loss of normal function
Debride remove devitalized tissue
Decarboxylation removal of carboxyl groups
Decubitus ulcers bedsores
Definitive (final) host the host in which the sexually mature or adult stage of parasites occurs; or the most important host
Degenerate in genetics, a code in which more than one code word specifies an amino acid
Degranulation the extracellular release of granules that contain physiologically active or antimicrobial substances
Dehydrogenation a process in which hydrogens are removed from a compound
Delayed-type hypersensitivity (DTH) inflammatory reaction mediated by T_{DTH} cells; skin test reaction develops fully 24 to 72 hours after challenge dose in a sensitized person
Deletion in genetics, loss of genetic material
Dementia mental deterioration
Demyelination removal of the myelin sheath around nerve fibers
Denaturation a process in which a macromolecule loses its configuration and often its biological activity
Dermatophyte fungi that invade keratinized tissue
Desensitization the process of reducing an individual's sensitivity
Desiccate to dry

Desquamation shedding of the superficial layers of skin
Detergent a synthetic cleansing agent
Determinant group (epitope) the chemical grouping of the antigen molecule that binds specifically with the antibody combining site or to the receptor on T cells
Dextro- to the right
Diarrhea abnormal fluidity of fecal discharge
Dimorphic in mycology the ability of the fungus to exist in the yeast or mold state
Diphtheroid resembling the diphtheria bacillus
Diplopia double vision
Disease an abnormal condition of the body having characteristic symptoms
Disinfectant an antimicrobial agent applied to inanimate objects that destroys harmful microorganisms except spores
DTP a vaccine consisting of toxoids of diphtheria and tetanus plus a pertussis bacterial antigen
Dysuria painful urination

E

Ectatic distended
Ectopic not in the normal place
Ectothrix fungal infection in which hyphae remain on external surface of the hair shaft
Eczema an inflammatory skin disease characterized by scales, crusts, and watery lesions
Edema a swelling due to accumulation of fluids in tissues
Effector cell a lymphocyte that has a direct (e.g., killer T cell) or a mediated (e.g., via lymphokines) effect on an antigen (compare **Regulator cell**)
Electrophoresis the separation of differently charged molecules in an electric field
ELISA enzyme-linked immunosorbent assay, a serological test in which enzyme-linked antibodies allow antigen-antibody reactions to become visible upon addition of a color-producing enzyme substrate
Emetic an agent causing vomiting
Empyema pus accumulation in a body cavity
Endemic continually present in a community
Endocarditis inflammation of the endocardium of the heart
Endocytosis the phase of phagocytosis when the extracellular material is entering the phagocyte
Endoenzyme an enzyme produced by a cell whose activity is associated with intracellular processes or an enzyme that attacks the interior of macromolecules
Endogenous produced within the cell; coming from within
Endometritis inflammation of the endometrium of the uterus
Endonuclease an enzyme that attacks the interior of nucleic acid molecules
Endoplasmic reticulum a protoplasmic network in eukaryotic cells consisting of a continuous double membrane system that courses throughout the cytoplasm
Endospore a spore occurring within the cell
Endothelium epithelial lining of heart, blood vessels, and lymph vessels
Endothrix fungal infection resulting from hyphal invasion of the hair shaft
Endotoxin a toxin derived from the cell wall of gram-negative bacteria
Enteric occurring in the gastrointestinal tract
Enterocolitis inflammation of small intestine and colon
Enterotoxin a toxin that gives rise to gastrointestinal symptoms when ingested or formed in the intestine
Envelope a host cell–derived membrane, containing virus-specific antigens, which is acquired during virus maturation
Eosinophil a granular leukocyte readily stained red by eosin; prominent in atopic allergies and parasitic infections
Epidemic an outbreak of a disease affecting a large number of individuals in a community
Epidemiology the science that deals with the incidence, transmission, and prevention of disease
Epididymitis inflammation of the epididymis, which is part of the seminal duct lying posterior to the testes
Epinephrine (Adrenalin) a drug that is a vasoconstrictor and smooth muscle relaxant
Episome a piece of DNA that may be an autonomous unit in the cell or may be integrated into the chromosome
Epithelioid cells macrophage cells in granulomas that resemble epithelial cells
Epitope antigenic determinant
Epizootic an outbreak of disease affecting a large number of animals
Erysipelas a contagious disease of the skin resulting from infection by *Streptococcus pyogenes*
Erythematous having red eruptions on the skin
Erythrogenic able to produce redness
Eschar a dry mass of necrotic (dead) tissue
Etiology study of the causation of a disease
ETO ethylene oxide, a gas used for sterilization
Eukaryotic a cell type in which the nuclear material is bounded by a membrane
Exanthem eruptive disease or fever characterized by nodular eruptions on mucous membrane
Exfoliatin a staphylococcal toxin that causes necrosis of epidermis
Exfoliation shedding of layers of the skin
Exoenzyme an enzyme secreted by the cell and associated in activity with the extracellular process
Exon in eukaryotic genetics, a messenger RNA sequence that codes for information
Exotoxin toxin produced in the cell and released into the environment
Exudate material (fluids, cells, etc.) that has escaped from blood vessels

F

Fab the fraction of the immunoglobulin molecule that contains the antigen binding site
Facultative anaerobes organisms that grow best under aerobic conditions but can grow anaerobically
Faucial pertaining to the upper part of the throat

Fc the crystallizable fragment of the immunoglobulin molecule, composed of the constant regions of the H chains; roles include binding of complement, attachment of immunoglobulin to phagocytes and other cell types, and transplacental passage

Fc receptors receptors on the surface of various cells that bind the Fc portion of antibody molecules

Febrile pertaining to or characterized by fever

Fermentation an anaerobic metabolic process that uses an organic compound as the final electron acceptor

F factor a fertility factor that determines the sex of a bacterium

Fibronectin glycoprotein receptors on cells; believed to be important in binding microorganisms

Fibrosis formation of fibrous tissue

Filamentous composed of long thread-like structures

Fimbria fringe; in microbial genetics, a small protein projection on the surface of bacteria

Fission the act of splitting, a form of asexual reproduction

Fistula an abnormal passageway providing organisms with communication between tissues during infection

Fixed virus an attenuated variant of the virulent "street" rabies virus

Flagella hair-like projections on the cell that aid in locomotion

Flatulence presence of air or gases in the stomach or intestine

Flatworms worms that are flat when viewed in cross section

Flocculation a phenomenon in which suspended components form visible discrete particles

Flora the resident organisms in a particular area

Fluorescence the emission of light while being exposed to light of shorter wavelength than the emitted light

Fluorescent antibody an antibody conjugated with a dye that fluoresces on ultraviolet irradiation; used in serological techniques to detect antigens

Focus in virology, an accumulation of transformed cells

Folliculitis inflammation of follicles (for example, hair follicles)

Fomite an inanimate object that may be involved in disease transmission

Framework regions the less variable regions of the antigen binding site of the antibody molecule that flank the hypervariable subregions where antigen contact actually occurs

Fulminating occurring very suddenly and with intensity

Fungicide an agent capable of destroying fungi

Furuncle a boil

G

Gamete sex cell

Gamma globulin a blood protein fraction with which antibodies are associated

Genetic engineering type of recombinant DNA technology in which foreign genes can be inserted into the DNA of related and unrelated organisms

Genetic restriction (see **MHC restriction**.)

Genome the complete set of hereditary factors

Genotype the genetic constitution of an organism

Genus a taxonomic category

Germicide an agent that destroys pathogenic microorganisms

Germination the sprouting of a spore and the formation of a vegetative cell

Germ tube in fungal reproduction a hyphal element arising from a germinating spore

Gingivae (gums) soft tissue surrounding the teeth

Globulins a class of proteins found in the blood

Glomerulonephritis renal (kidney) disease affecting primarily glomeruli

Glossitis inflammation of the tongue

Glucan extracellular glucose polymers (dextran, mutan)

Glycolysis the anaerobic process in which carbohydrates such as glucose are oxidized to pyruvic or lactic acid

Gnotobiotic animals animals originally germ free, harboring one or more known microorganisms

Golgi membranous complex found in eukaryotes that packages proteins and lipids for transfer to selected sites in the cell

Graft-versus-host reaction (GVHR) a reaction in which the immunocompetent cells of a graft tissue attack the tissues of the graft recipient

Granuloma a tumor-like mass of granulation tissue containing macrophages and fibroblasts and caused by chronic inflammation

Guarnieri's bodies acidophilic intracytoplasmic inclusion bodies in epidermal cells infected with smallpox virus

Gumma granuloma found in tertiary stage of syphilis

H

Halophilic (of bacteria) requiring high concentrations of salt to maintain the integrity of the cell

Hapten a partial or incomplete antigen that alone does not induce antibody formation but can react with certain antibodies

H chain heavy chain, one of the pair of identical polypeptides that represent two of the four polypeptide chains of the basic immunoglobulin molecule; differences in H chain composition are the basis for classification of immunoglobulins into five classes

Helper T cells (T_H) a regulator T cell that initiates most immune responses by specifically recognizing the antigen fragment–Class II MHC complex on the surface of an antigen presenting cell and then promotes the proliferation and differentiation of antigen-specific B and T cell clones

Helminth worm

Hemagglutination clumping of red blood cells

Hemagglutinin (viral hemagglutinin) a nonantibody protein on the outer surface of some viruses (e.g., orthomyxoviruses) that reacts with surface determinant(s) on red cells to cause agglutination of the red cells (hemagglutination)

Hematogenous derived from the bloodstream

Hematuria presence of blood in the urine

Hemolysin any agent that can cause the lysis of red blood cells
Hepatoma tumor involving the liver
Heterophile antigen an antigen common to more than one species such as lens protein antigen
Heterotroph an organism requiring organic material for energy and biosynthesis
Hexon a capsomere surrounded by six capsomeres
Hinge region a flexible H chain region between the Fc and Fab portions of the immunoglobulin molecule that allows the two antigen-binding sites to attach to identical antigenic determinants located at different sites
Histamine a physiologically active substance released by certain cell types, especially mast cells, that affects capillary permeability and smooth muscle contraction
Histocompatible said of cells or tissues that share or have like transplantation antigens
Histone a protein containing many basic amino acids and associated with the DNA of eukaryotic cells
HLA human leukocyte antigens; human transplantation antigens—first discovered on leukocytes
Homograft see **Allograft**
Humoral immunity antibody-mediated immunity
Hybridoma a cell that results from the fusion of two cells; usually refers to a cell fused from a cancerous (myeloma) cell and an antibody-producing cell and that is a source of monoclonal antibodies
Hydrolase an enzyme that catalyzes the hydrolysis of compounds
Hydrolyze to split a compound by the addition of water
Hydrophilic attracted to water
Hydrophobic repelled by water
Hydrops accumulation of fluid; edema
Hyperchromic highly stained
Hyperplasia increase in the number of cells in a tissue
Hypertonic a solution in which the concentration of solutes is higher outside the cell than inside the cell
Hypervariable regions extremely variable regions of the variable H and L regions of immunoglobulins; the "hot spots" where antibodies bind antigenic determinants
Hypha (pl. hyphae) one of the filaments that make up a fungal mycelium
Hyposensitization a process in which an allergen is injected to reduce the allergic state
Hypotonic a solution in which the concentration of solute is lower outside the cell than in the cell

I

Icosahedral 20 sided
Icterus (jaundice) a condition characterized by excess of bile pigments in the blood and tissues that leads to a yellow color of the surface integuments
Id an allergic skin reaction to fungi or fungal products
Idiotope a single determinant of the idiotype
Idiotype the set of antigenic determinants that are part of the antigen binding site of the immunoglobulin molecule
Immediate hypersensitivity a hypersensitivity in which there is a response within seconds to minutes when a sensitized individual is again exposed to the corresponding antigen
Immune complex aggregate of soluble antigen and antibody
Immune globulin a preparation of purified antibody used to confer passive immunity
Immune surveillance a postulated function of the immune system: that it constantly destroys newly formed cancer cells
Immunity state of being protected, especially to microorganisms or their products
Immunodiffusion a serological technique in which antibodies and antigens form lines of precipitate as they diffuse toward each other in an agar gel support medium
Immunofluorescence fluorescence resulting from the conjugation of an immunoglobulin to a fluorescent dye
Immunogen an antigen or a substance that induces an immunity
Immunogenicity that property of an antigen that makes it capable of stimulating an immune response
Immunoglobulins a class of blood proteins with which antibodies are associated
Immunosuppressive inhibiting the normal immunological response of an organism
Immunotoxin in cancer immunotherapy, a toxin (e.g., ricin A) attached to a monoclonal antibody that poisons the cell against which the antibody is specific
Impetigo a streptococcal or staphylococcal infection of the skin
Inclusion bodies in virus infection, the highly stainable components, usually virus, found in the cytoplasm or nucleus of the infected cell
Indigenous native to a particular place
Inducer a molecule capable of stimulating the formation of compounds such as enzymes involved in cellular metabolism
Inducible enzyme an enzyme synthesized only in response to an inducer
Induration a hardened area or lesion
Infant a child usually up to 2 years
Infectious able to cause disease
Infectious dose (ID_{50}; $TCID_{50}$) that amount of virus required to cause a demonstrable infection in 50 percent of the inoculated animals or tissue culture cells, respectively
Inflammation nonspecific response to irritants (chemical, physical, microbial, antigenic) characterized by pain, heat, redness, and swelling
Infusion a preparation in which important components of a substance have been extracted with water
Innate immunity state of protection or resistance to infection due to factors other than immune system products
Inoculum a substance (microorganisms, serum, etc.) introduced into the tissues or culture media
Insertion in genetics, the addition of nucleotides or genes to the chromosome
Insertion sequence small nucleotide sequences that are capable of movement on the DNA

Inspissate to dry by evaporation
Interferon a class of proteins produced by vertebrate cells in response to viruses, endotoxins, and certain chemicals; associated primarily with antiviral activity
Interleukin-1 (IL-1) protein secreted by macrophages that signals the activation of T_H cells in an immune response; also, the endogenous inducer of fever
Interleukin-2 (IL-2) a protein derived from activated T_H cells that promotes the proliferation of other activated T cells and B cells
Interleukin-6 (IL-6) same as BCDF
Intermediate host a host that is required in the life cycle of some parasites in which the asexual or larval stage occurs
Intoxication state of being poisoned by some chemical
Intradermal within the skin
Intraperitoneal within the peritoneum, which is the membrane lining the abdominal cavity
Intron in eukaryotic genetics, a messenger RNA sequence that does not code for information
Intubation insertion of a tube
In utero within the uterus
Invasive able to invade or penetrate the body
In vitro outside the body or performed in artificial environments
In vivo within the body or within a living organism
Iodophors disinfectants consisting of iodine combined with a carrier molecule
Ischemia blood deficiency in a body part
Isoagglutinins antibodies specific for antigenic sites on red blood cells of the same species and causing their agglutination; also called alloagglutinins
Isoantibody an antibody that reacts with alternate forms of an intraspecies antigen (e.g., A and B blood group antigens)
Isoantigen an intraspecies antigen that appears in alternate forms
Isomer a molecule having the same atoms or groups of atoms as another molecule, but with different arrangement

J

Jaundice see **Icterus**
J chain a polypeptide chain that joins basic monomer immunoglobulin units of the same immunoglobulin class to form polymers, as in secreted IgM and secretory IgA

K

Kaposi's sarcoma a relatively benign skin cancer that often takes a more aggressive fatal form in AIDS victims
Karyotype chromosomal makeup of a cell
K cell a lymphocyte with Fc receptors that binds to and kills antibody-coated target cells
Keratitis inflammation of the cornea
Kernicterus a condition associated with high levels of bilirubin in the blood that affects the nervous system
Kinins inflammatory vasoactive peptides produced following tissue injury
Koplik's spots small bluish spots surrounded by a reddened area in the mucous membrane of the mouth and characteristic of measles
Kupffer's cells macrophages lining the hepatic sinusoids
Kuru a chronic, progressive, degenerative disorder of the central nervous system caused by a virus, found among certain natives of New Guinea

L

Labile unstable or susceptible to various chemical or physical agents
Labium a lip; for example, labia in females are two folds of skin of the genitalia
Larva worm-like immature form of arthropods and helminths (worms)
Latency a state of inactivity
L chains (light chains) the two smaller identical polypeptide chains of the four-chain immunoglobulin molecule
LD_{50} lethal dose 50; the dose lethal to 50 percent of the subjects
Lectin glycoprotein found on the surface of plant cells
Leukemia a blood disease characterized by high levels of leukocytes
Leukocidin a substance produced by some pathogenic bacteria and toxic to white blood cells
Leukocyte white blood cell
Leukopenia a smaller than normal number of circulating leukocytes
Leukotrienes secondary or lipoid mediators that arise from changes in cell membrane phospholipids (arachidonic acid), especially when antigen combines with IgE on mast cell surfaces; leukotrienes increase vascular permeability, contract smooth muscles, and attract neutrophils
Levo- to the left
L-forms bacteria with deficient cell walls
Ligase an enzyme that catalyzes the joining together of two molecules coupled with the breakdown of adenosine triphosphate to adenosine diphosphate
Limulus lysate an extract from the amoebocytes of horseshoe crabs that gels with minute quantities of endotoxin
Liposome synthetic phospholipid sac having properties and biological membranes
Local (topical) immunity mucous surface immunity primarily owing to secretory IgA
Lochia vaginal discharge that appears after childbirth
Logarithmic growth the uniform doubling of a population of cells per unit time
Lophotrichous having a tuft of flagella at one end of the cell
Lumbar region lower region of the back, where cerebrospinal fluid usually is drawn ("spinal tap")
Lymphadenopathy infection of a lymph node
Lymphangitis inflammation of lymph vessel
Lymphocyte a white blood cell devoid of cytoplasmic granules, associated with immune response and chronic inflammation

Lymphokines soluble products, especially of sensitized T cells, that are released upon antigen contact and that have among their varied actions the mobilization of uncommitted macrophages, neutrophils, lymphocytes, and other cells

Lymphoma any neoplasia (abnormal growth) associated with the lymph system

Lyophilization process of freeze-drying

Lysin an agent (bacterial, chemical, antibody) capable of causing the destruction of cells

Lysis dissolution (as in cell destruction)

Lysogenic conversion a change in characteristics of an organism due to carriage of a prophage

Lysogeny a state in which a bacteriophage genome is integrated or firmly associated with the host genome

Lysosome a cell organelle derived from the Golgi apparatus containing hydrolytic enzymes collectively termed acid hydrolases

Lysozyme an enzyme that degrades peptidoglycan, a compound of the cell wall

M

Macrophage a versatile cell of the mononuclear phagocyte system (MPS) whose two major functions are (1) processing and presentation of antigens and (2) phagocytosis and destruction of antigens

Macrophage activation factor (MAF) a general term that signifies several lymphokines, including interferon gamma, that enhance the phagocytic and cytotoxic activities of macrophages

Macula a spot; often associated with a type of rash (macular) in which the lesion is not elevated

Major histocompatibility complex the genes of a specific chromosome region that code for the majority of cell membrane surface glycoproteins that serve as transplantation antigens and that guide antigen recognition and cell interactions, especially by T cells

Maladsorption faulty absorption of nutrients through the intestine

Malaise a general feeling of "not being well"

Mast cell a connective tissue cell that is a major source of vasoactive and muscle-contracting compounds, for example, histamine; has Fc receptors for IgE and is the principal intermediate in anaphylactic reactions

Medium a substance that provides nutrients for the growth of microorganisms

Membrane attack complex (MAC) the complex of C5–9 factors of complement that inserts into and destroys cell membranes

Membrane filters paper-thin filters composed of cellulose esters and other materials

Memory cells a reserve of antigen-sensitive immune cells developed in the primary immune response that respond swiftly and to higher levels in the secondary immune response

Meninges membranes that cover the brain and spinal cord

Meningitis inflammation of the membranes (meninges) of brain or spinal cord

Mesophile a microorganism that grows best at temperatures between 20 and 45 C

Mesosome involuted membrane of the bacterial cell

Metabolism the sum total of physical and chemical changes that take place in a cell and maintain the cell's integrity

Metabolite a product of metabolic processes

Metachromatic granules cytoplasmic inclusions that are polymetaphosphates; also called Babès-Ernst bodies or volutin

Metastasis transfer of disease from primary site of infection

MHC antigens genetically determined major histocompatibility antigens that are markers of self and provoke the immune response to foreign grafts

MHC (genetic) restriction the requirement that antigens be complexed with MHC proteins in order to be recognized and responded to by cells of the immune system

Microaerophile an organism requiring less than 1 atmosphere of oxygen

Microtubule cylindrical hollow protein tubes found in eukaryotic cells and associated with motility as well as spindle organization during cell division

Migration inhibiting factor (MIF) a lymphokine that prevents macrophages from leaving the site of cell-mediated immunological reaction

Miliary resembling millet seeds; said of lesions

Missense refers to a mutation that results in a codon being translated into a different amino acid

Mitochondrion rod-shaped organelle found in eukaryotic cells and involved in energy production

Mold another name for fungi that exhibit branching

Monoclonal antibody antibody obtained from an isolated clone of cells (e.g., hybridoma); preparations containing monoclonal antibodies have a highly precise specificity for a given antigenic determinant and are therefore valuable in diagnosis and therapy

Monocyte a macrophage of the circulating blood

Monokines soluble molecules produced by macrophages that mediate interactions between cells (see **interleukin-1**)

Monomer a basic molecule that is repeated in polymers

Monotrichous having one flagellum

Morbidity sickness; the ratio of sick to well individuals of a community

Mordant a chemical that binds dyes to cells or tissues

Morphological related to shape or structure

Mortality fatality; the ratio of the number of deaths to a given population in a defined situation

Mucolytic capable of dissolving mucus

Mucous secreting mucus; for example, mucous gland

Mucus the viscous liquid secreted by mucous glands

Multinucleated giant cell a large cell containing the nuclei of fused macrophages and found in chronic inflammatory lesions

Mutagen a substance that increases the mutation rate of an organism

Mutation a process in which a gene undergoes structural changes

Myalgia pain in the muscles

Mycelium a mat of intertwined hyphae of fungi
Mycetismus mushroom poisoning
Mycetoma a chronic infection, usually involving the foot; but other parts of the body may be involved
Mycotoxin toxic secondary metabolite resulting from the growth of fungi on grains
Myeloma proteins homogenous immunoglobulin molecules or parts of immunoglobulin molecules produced by malignant plasma cells
Myocarditis a condition involving the heart muscle (myocardium)
Myometrium the uterine muscular structure
Myositis inflammation of muscle

N

Natural killer (NK) cells probably a subclass of lymphocytes that occur without antigen stimulation and that serve as effectors of nonspecific immunity (e.g., against malignant cells)
Necrosis death of tissue or cells
Negri bodies inclusion bodies found in brain cells infected with the rabies virus
Nematode roundworm
Neonatal pertaining to the first 4 weeks after birth
Neonatorum pertaining to the newborn
Neoplasia formation of tumors
Nephrotoxic toxic to the kidney
Neurotoxin toxin that affects the nervous system
Neutrophil a leukocyte in which granules do not stain with basic or acid dyes
Nitrogen fixation the union of nitrogen gas with other elements to form chemical compounds
NK cells natural killer cells
Nonsense a mutation that results in a codon not being translated into an amino acid
Nosocomial pertaining to the hospital
Nucleocapsid a unit of viral structure consisting of a protein coat (capsid) and the nucleic acid it encloses
Nucleoid area of DNA concentration in the bacterial cell
Nucleolus a small body within the nucleus rich in ribonucleic acid
Nucleosides a class of compounds consisting of a carbohydrate and a purine or pyrimidine base
Nucleotides a class of compounds consisting of a purine or pyrimidine base, phosphoric acid, and carbohydrate
Nutrient a substance removed from the environment by cells and used in various metabolic processes

O

Obligate necessary or required
Occlusal surface area of the tooth associated with grinding
Okazaki fragment short pieces of DNA synthesized during replication
Oliguria secretion of a diminished amount of urine
Oncogenic able to cause tumors
Onychia infection involving the nails
Operator gene a chromosomal region that is capable of controlling adjacent structural genes
Operon a unit on the chromosome consisting of adjacent genes controlled by an operator
Ophthalmia inflammation of the eye
Opportunistic pathogen a nonpathogen capable of infection only under the most favorable conditions
Opsonin an antibody or complement fragment C3b that attaches antigens to phagocytes, thereby facilitating endocytosis
Orchitis inflammation of the testes
Ornithosis a bird disease, transmissible to humans
Osmosis passage of fluids through a semipermeable membrane
Osteitis inflammation of a bone
Osteoclast a bone-resorbing cell
Osteomyelitis inflammation of the marrow of the bone
Otitis media inflammation of the middle ear
Oxidation loss of electrons by a compound
Oxidative phosphorylation enzymatic addition of phosphate to adenosine diphosphate to form adenosine triphosphate, which is coupled to the electron transport system
Ozena chronic inflammation of the nose

P

Palindromic in genetics, nucleotide sequences that are repeated but inverted on the opposite ends of a double-stranded nucleic acid molecule
Pandemic a worldwide epidemic
Papilloma a benign tumor derived from the epithelium
Papule a small, firm, circumscribed, raised lesion of the skin
Parasite an organism that survives on or at the expense of a living host
Parenteral outside the intestine; subcutaneous or intravenous injection
Paresis a slight paralysis
Paronychia infection involving areas around nails
Paroxysm a state of intensified symptoms
Parturition the process of birth
Passive immunity the temporary acquired immune status that results from the transfer of antibodies from an outside source
Pasteurization a process in which fluids are heated at temperatures below boiling to kill pathogenic microorganisms in the vegetative state
Pathogen an organism capable of habitually causing disease in a percentage of healthy persons
Pathogenesis the progression of tissue, biochemical, and functional alterations that occur during the development of a disease
Pathognomonic refers to a sign or symptom that is so characteristic of a disease that a diagnosis can be made from it
Penton a capsomere surrounded by five capsomeres
Peplomer a projection (spike) extending from the outer surface of a virus envelope

Peptide bond a bond that unites two amino acids
Peptidoglycan the relatively rigid structural component of most bacterial cell walls that consists of layers of polysaccharide made up of N-acetylglucosamine and N-acetylmuramic acid
Percutaneous performed through the skin
Perinatal pertaining to a period of time shortly before and just after birth
Periodontitis inflammation of the periodontium or tissue surrounding and supporting the teeth
Periostitis inflammation of the periosteum, the specialized connective tissue covering all bones
Periplasm contents of a space (periplasmic) that lies between the cell wall outer membrane and cytoplasmic membrane of gram-negative bacteria
Peritrichous having flagella that cover the entire bacterial surface
Permease an enzyme found in cell membranes that transports compounds into the cell cytoplasm
Petechial pinpoint hemorrhages in skin and mucous membranes
Phagocytosis the process of ingestion of foreign particles
Phagolysosome intracytoplasmic vesicle in phagocytic cells formed by the fusion of lysosome and phagosome membranes
Phagosome a cell vacuole resulting from phagocytosis of particulate materials
Phenotype the genetic makeup of an organism; its observable properties
Phlebitis inflammation of a vein
Phosphorylation joining of phosphoric acid to a compound
Photophobia literally, fear of light; painful sensitivity to light
Photosynthetic able to convert light to chemical energy
Phototroph an organism that uses light for energy
Phylogenetic pertaining to the evolutionary history of an organism
Pilus small protein projection on the bacterial cell involved in conjugation or adherence
Pinocytosis the engulfment of liquid droplets by a cell
Plaque a clear area produced by the lytic action of viruses on an opaque lawn of bacteria or on a monolayer of tissue culture cells
Plaque (dental) the structureless accumulation of bacteria, extracellular polysaccharides (e.g., glucans), and host proteins found on the surface of teeth
Plasma the fluid portion of the blood containing elements necessary for clot formation
Plasma cell a fully differentiated B lymphocyte that produces antibodies
Plasmid an extrachromosomal piece of DNA
Plasmolysis shrinkage of the cell caused by osmotic removal of water
Plasmoptysis swelling or bursting of a cell caused by osmotic inflow of water
Platelets (thrombocytes) small non-nucleated cytoplasmic elements in blood responsible for activating blood coagulation, and a source of vasoactive agents
Pleomorphism the state of having more than one form or shape
PMN polymorphonuclear leukocyte (neutrophil)
Pock a pit, spot, or pustule
Polygenic a messenger RNA coding for more than one gene
Polymerization formation of a polymer from monomeric molecules
Polypeptide a polymer made up of amino acids linked by peptide bonds
Polysaccharide a carbohydrate, for example, starch produced from the polymerization of many monosaccharides
Polysome (polyribosome) several ribosomes bound to a single messenger RNA strand
Polyuria frequent urination
Porins channels in the cell wall for solute transport
Postpartum referring to the period after birth
Potable suitable to drink
Precipitin an antibody that causes precipitation
Predisposing conferring a tendency
Proctitis inflammation of the rectum
Prodromal pertaining to early manifestation of disease before specific symptoms appear
Prokaryotic characterized by lack of nuclear membrane and organelles (e.g., bacteria)
Promoter a site on DNA that initiates the transcription of an operon
Properdin a bactericidal protein component of the blood
Prophage state of a virus in which the viral genome is integrated into the host genome
Prophylaxis protection, for example, against disease
Prostatitis inflammation of the prostate gland
Proteolytic able to break down proteins
Proto-oncogene a normal cellular gene capable of conversion to an oncogene and development of neoplasia
Protoplast a viable bacterial cell without its cell wall
Prototroph an organism capable of synthesizing cell material from inorganic compounds
Provirus virus integrated into host chromosome and transmitted from one generation to another
Pruritus itching
Psittacosis a bird disease, transmissible to humans
Psychrophile a microorganism that grows best at temperatures between 0 and 20 C
Puerperal related to the period after childbirth
Purine an organic base found in nucleic acids
Purpura dusky, blotchy hemorrhages in the skin or mucous membrane
Purulent associated with the formation of pus
Pus creamy yellow fluid that is a product of inflammation and consists primarily of leukocytes and serum
Pustule an elevated lesion filled with pus
Putrefaction decomposition of proteins resulting in foul odors
Pyocin bacteriocin produced by *Pseudomonas aeruginosa*

Pyoderma pus-containing lesion in the skin
Pyogenic pus forming
Pyrimidine an organic base found in nucleic acids
Pyrogen an agent that induces fever

Q

Quarantine to detain or isolate individuals because of suspicion of infection
Quellung reaction a test in which the bacterial capsule swells as a result of combining with specific antibody

R

Radioallergosorbent test (RAST) a radioimmunoassay test used for detecting IgE antibodies against a specific allergen
Reagin the nonprotective antibody found in the blood and produced in response to a number of different diseases; also, the antibody of immunoglobulin class IgE, involved in anaphylaxis and atopic allergies
Recalcitrant resistant to change
Recombination in genetics, a process in which genetic information is exchanged
Recrudescence recurrence of symptoms after their abatement
Reduction gain of electrons or hydrogen
Regulator cell a helper or suppressor T cell that regulates an immune response
Regulator gene a genetic unit on the chromosome that controls the synthesis of the repressor protein
Replication a duplication process requiring a template
Replicon any genetic unit capable of autonomous replication
Repressible enzyme an enzyme whose synthesis can be decreased by certain metabolites
Repressor protein a protein whose function is to control the operator gene; the regulator gene controls the synthesis of the repressor protein
Resolving power the ability of a lens (or the eye) to distinguish two closely associated objects as distinct structures
Respiration an oxidative process in which energy is released from foodstuffs
Respiratory burst the generation of toxic oxygen products by activated phagocytes
Reticuloendothelial system (RES) a network of phagocytic cells produced and residing in the bone marrow, spleen, lymph nodes, and liver of vertebrates
Rheumatoid factor a distinctive gamma globulin found in the serum of patients with rheumatoid arthritis
Rhinitis inflammation of the nose
Rhizoid filamentous appendage used by organisms such as fungi to attach to the soil
Ribosome a ribonucleoprotein particle found in the cell cytoplasm and involved in protein synthesis
Ringworm a common name for ring-shaped patches appearing anywhere on the body surface and caused by a group of fungi called dermatophytes; tinea
Roundworms worms that are found or oval in cross section
Rubella German measles
Rubeola measles

S

Saccharolytic capable of breaking down sugars
Salpingitis inflammation of the uterine (fallopian) tube
Sanitize to reduce the number of bacteria to a nonhazardous level
Saprobe an organism that derives its nourishment from dead or decaying material
Sarcoma a solid tumor growing from derivatives of embryonal mesoderm such as connective tissue, bone, muscle, and fat
Sclerosing undergoing a hardening
Scrapie an infectious, usually fatal, disease of sheep
Scrofula tuberculosis of the lymph glands
Secretory IgA polymerized IgA with a secretory piece that appears on mucous membranes where it provides local immunity
Sepsis a toxic condition resulting from the presence of microbes or microbial products in the body
Septicemia a systemic disease in which microorganisms multiply in the bloodstream
Septum a dividing wall or partition
Sequela a morbid (abnormal) condition that develops as a consequence of a disease
Seroconversion the induction of specific antibodies in the serum after their apparent absence from the serum
Serology the study of antigen-antibody reactions in vitro
Serotype a taxonomic subdivision of microorganisms based on the kinds of antigens present
Serum the clear portion of the blood minus the factors necessary for clotting
Serum sickness a type III hypersensitivity in which there are fever, rash, and painful joints due to immune complex formation and the activation of complement following the injection of large amounts of soluble antigen such as an antiserum
Simian pertaining to apes or monkeys
Skin-sensitizing antibody IgE antibody that attaches to mast cells in the skin
Slow-reacting substance of anaphylaxis (SRA) leukotrienes derived from mast cells during anaphylaxis that induce protracted contraction of smooth muscles
Slow virus a virus that causes subacute or chronic disease with an incubation period that lasts several weeks to years before the onset of clinical symptoms
Smear a film of material such as a bacterial suspension spread on a glass slide
Snuffles the nasal discharge from mucous patches associated with congenital syphilis
Specificity that property of a relationship that restricts an agent or a reactant to combine with or to affect a particular group, subject, substance, cell, or molecule
Spectrophotometer an instrument used to measure the absorption of light in test liquids

Spheroplast in bacteriology, a gram-negative cell in which the cell wall has been removed but some cell wall components remain
Spikes surface projections of various lengths spaced at regular intervals on the virus envelope
Spirochete a corkscrew-shaped bacterium
Splenomegaly enlargement of the spleen
Spondylitis inflammation of one vertebra or more
Sporangiospores asexual fungal spores produced in a sac called a sporangium
Sporangium a structure that holds asexual spores
Spore the resistant form of a bacterium derived from the vegetative cell; the reproductive cell of certain organisms
Sporicide an agent that destroys spores
Sporogenesis production of spores
SSS scalded skin syndrome, caused by *Staphylococcus aureus*
Staphylococcal protein A a protein linked to the cell wall of *Staphylococcus aureus* strains; basis for coagglutination test
Steatorrhea excessive loss of fats in the feces
Stem cell a pluripotential precursor cell that can develop into functionally and morphologically different cell types
Sterilization the process that destroys or removes all living microorganisms
Stomatitis inflammation of the oral mucosa
Street virus the virulent type of rabies virus isolated in nature from domestic or wild animals; see **Fixed virus**
Streptolysin a hemolysin produced by streptococci
Stricture narrowing of lumen of a canal or hollow organ
Subacute between acute (short course) and chronic (persisting over a long period)
Subclinical without clinical manifestations of the disease
Substrate a specific compound acted on by an enzyme
Subunit vaccine a vaccine containing purified antigenic components of a microorganisms, for example, capsular polysaccharides
Superinfection an infection superimposed on an already existing infection, for example, a bacterial infection on top of a viral infection
Suppressor T cells (T_S) a regulatory T lymphocyte that suppresses the responses of immune cells
Suppurative pus forming
Surfactant agent that reduces surface tension; a wetting agent
Svedberg the relative sedimentation constant of a component being centrifuged at high speed
Syncytium a mass of cytoplasm with many nuclei and resulting from the fusion of many cells
Syndrome a group of symptoms that characterize a disease
Synergism a phenomenon in which the action of two components together is more than the sum of the two alone
Synovial fluid a thick transparent fluid found in the joints of bones
Synthesize to build up a chemical compound from its individual parts
Systemic relating to the entire organism and not any individual organ

T

Tautomerism existing in a state of equilibrium between two isomeric forms
Taxonomy the orderly classification into distinct categories based on some suitable relationship between groups or individual organisms
T cells thymus-dependent lymphocytes involved in cell-mediated immunity
T (thymus)-dependent antigen an antigen that requires recognition by T_H cells before B cells can produce antibody to the antigen
Temperate phage a nonvirulent bacteriophage
Template a mold for the synthesis of new material
Teratogenic capable of inducing abnormal development and congenital malformations
Thermolabile sensitive to heat
Thermophiles microorganisms growing best at temperatures between 45 and 70 C
Thrombocytopenia a decreased number of blood platelets
Thrombophlebitis inflammation of a vein associated with thrombosis
Thrombosis formation of a clot within a blood vessel
Thrush fungal infection involving the oral mucous membrane
Thymocyte a lymphocyte in the thymus
Thymus the central lymphoid organ, where T cells differentiate and mature
Tincture an alcoholic solution of a particular substance, for example, tincture of iodine
T (thymus)-independent antigen an antigen that can directly elicit antibody formation by B cells without antigen recognition by T_H cells
Tinea a name applied to fungal infections of the skin; ringworm
Titer the concentration of animate or inanimate agents in a medium
Tolerance (immunological) the lack of response to a specific antigen, thereby allowing the antigen to persist
Toxemia a condition in which toxins are in the blood
Toxin an organic (usually) poisonous substance produced by living organisms
Toxoid a modified exotoxin that has been treated to destroy its toxicity and retain immunogenicity
Trachoma ocular disease caused by *Chlamydia trachomatis*
Transamination a chemical reaction in which an amino group is transferred to a keto group
Transcription the formation of messenger RNA from a DNA template
Transduction the transfer of bacterial genetic information from one cell to another by a virus
Transferase an enzyme that catalyzes the exchange of functional groups between compounds
Transformation in genetics, a process in which the genetic constitution of a cell is altered through the uptake of free DNA from the environment

Transition a mutation caused by substitution of one purine for another or one pyrimidine for another
Transplantation antigens major histocompatibility antigens
Transposition in genetics, the ability to be transferred to different sites on the nucleic acid molecule
Transposon an element of DNA containing insertion sequences as well as genetic information
Triplet code a code in which a set of three nucleotides specifies one amino acid
Trismus spasm of the masticatory muscles resulting in difficulty in opening the mouth (lockjaw)
Trophozoite the active vegetative stage of a protozoan
Tropism the involuntary movement of an organism toward or away from a stimulus
TSS toxic shock syndrome, caused by *Staphylococcus aureus*
Tubercle a nodule
Tuberculoprotein (tuberculin) protein extract derived from *Mycobacterium tuberculosis*
Tumor a new growth of tissue in which the multiplication of cells is uncontrolled; a swelling
Type I reactions local and systemic anaphylactic reactions
Type II reactions cytotoxic reactions
Type III reactions immune complex reactions
Type IV reactions delayed hypersensitivity reactions

U

Ulcer a circumscribed area of inflammation characterized by necrosis and found in the epithelial lining
Urticaria hives—a vascular reaction of the skin characterized by elevated patches (wheals)

V

Vaccine a suspension of organisms, usually killed or attenuated, used for immunization
Varicella chickenpox
Variola smallpox
Vascular containing blood vessels
Vasoactive affecting vessels, especially blood vessels
Vector a carrier of pathogenic microorganisms
Vegetative concerned with the growing stage of a microorganism as opposed to the spore state
Venereal transmitted by sexual contact
Venom poisonous substance produced and injected, for example, by arachnids, insects, and snakes
Vesicle a blister; also a membranous unit derived from Golgi and involved in transport
Viremia presence of virus in the bloodstream
Virion a complete virus particle consisting of a core of nucleic acid and a protein capsid
Virogene a viral gene incorporated in the host genome
Viroid an infectious subviral particle consisting of nucleic acid without a protein capsid
Virulence the relative ability of an organism to cause disease
Visceral larva migrans a condition in which larvae that are unable to develop into adult worms invade and migrate through organs of the body
Volutin see **Metachromatic granules**
Vulva the external female genitalia

W

Wheal a flat elevated area of skin caused by edema of underlying tissue
Wild type in microorganisms the most frequently observed phenotype and often referred to as normal (as opposed to mutant) phenotype

X

Xenograft a graft between members of a different species

Y

Yaw a lesion associated with the disease yaws
Yaws an infectious nonvenereal disease occurring in the tropics
Yeast a unicellular fungus

Z

Zoonosis a disease of animals that can be transmitted to humans
Zoster (shingles) an inflammatory response due to activation of the varicella-zoster virus

Additional Readings

Chapter 1. Scope and History of Microbiology

Bibel, D. J. William Bullock's pioneer women of microbiology. *ASM News* 51(7):328, 1985.

Brock, T. D. *Milestones in Microbiology*. Washington, D.C.: American Society for Microbiology, 1975.

Bulloch, W. *The History of Microbiology*. New York: Dover, 1979.

Dixon, C., ed. *Magnificent Microbes*. New York: Atheneum, 1976.

Gest, H. *The World of Microbes*. Menlo Park, CA: Benjamin/Cummings, 1987.

Lechevalier, H. A., and Solotorovsky, M. *Three Centuries of Microbiology*. New York: McGraw-Hill, 1965.

Chapter 2. Characteristics of Bacteria

Beveridge, T. J. The structure of bacteria. In J. S. Poindexter and L. R. Leadbetter, eds. *Bacteria in Nature*. Vol. 3. New York: Plenum, 1991.

Brock, T. D. The bacterial nucleus: A history. *Microbiol. Rev.* 52:397, 1988.

Doetsch, R. N., and Sjoblad, R. D. Flagellar structure and function in eubacteria. *Annu. Rev. Microbiol.* 34:69, 1980.

Ferris, F. G., and Beveridge, T. J. Functions of bacterial cell surface structures. *Bioscience* 35(3):172, 1985.

Hancock, R. E. W. Bacterial outer membranes: Evolving concepts. *ASM News* 57(4):175, 1991.

Rogers, H. J. *Bacterial Cell Structure*. Aspects of Microbiology. Washington, D.C.: American Society for Microbiology, 1983.

Sharon, N. The bacterial cell wall. *Sci. Am.* 221(5):92, 1969.

Silverman, M., and Simon, M. I. Bacterial flagella. *Annu. Rev. Microbiol.* 31:397, 1977.

Stanier, R. Y., Rogers, H. J., and Ward, J. B., eds. *Relation Between Structure and Function in the Prokaryotic Cell*. Twenty-eighth Symposium of the Society for General Microbiology. New York: Cambridge University Press, 1978.

Chapter 3. Microbial Metabolism

Gottschalk, G. *Bacterial Metabolism*, 2nd ed. New York: Springer, 1986.

Hinkle, R. C., and MCarty, R. E. How cells make ATP. *Sci. Am.* 238(1): 104, 1978.

Mandelstam, J., McQuillen, K., and Dawes, I. *Biochemistry of Bacterial Growth*, 3rd ed. London: Blackwell Scientific, 1982.

Mathews, C. K., and van Holde, K. E. *Biochemistry*. Redwood City, CA: Benjamin Cummings, 1990.

Moat, A. G., and Foster, J. W. *Microbial Physiology*, 2nd ed. New York: Wiley, 1988.

Neidhardt, F. C., Ingraham, J. L., and Schaechter, M. *Physiology of the Bacterial Cell: A Molecular Approach*. Sunderland, MA: Sinauer Associates, 1990.

Saier, M. H., Jr. Protein phosphorylation and allosteric control of inducer exclusion and catabolite repression by the bacterial phosphoenolpyruvate sugar phosphotransferase system. *Microbiol. Rev.* 53:109, 1989.

Stryer, L. *Biochemistry*, 3rd ed. New York: Freeman, 1988.

Voet, D., and Voet, J. G. *Biochemistry*. New York: Wiley, 1990.

Chapter 4. Microbial Growth

Cooper, S. Synthesis of the cell surface during the division cycle of rod-shaped gram-negative bacteria. *Microbiol. Rev.* 55:649, 1991.

Edwards, C. *The Microbial Cell Cycle*. Aspects of Microbiology. Washington, D.C.: American Society for Microbiology, 1981.

Ingraham, J. L., Maaløe, O., and Neidhardt, F. C. *Growth of the Bacterial Cell*. Sunderland, ME: Sinauer Associates, 1983.

Koch, A. L. Growth and form of the bacterial cell wall. *Am. Sci.* 78: 327, 1990.

Koch, A. L. Effective growth by the simplest means: The bacterial way. *ASM News* 57(12):633, 1991.

Moat, A. G., and Foster, J. W. *Microbial Physiology*, 2nd ed. New York: Wiley, 1988.

Chapter 5. Microbial Genetics

Bainbridge, B. W. *Genetics of Microbes,* 2nd ed. New York: Chapman and Hall and Methuen, 1987.

Cohen, S. N., and Shapiro, J. A. Transposable genetic elements. *Sci. Am.* 242(2):40, 1980.

Darnell, J. E., Jr. RNA. *Sci. Am.* 253(4):68, 1985.

Freifelder, D. *Molecular Biology,* 2nd ed. New York: Van Nostrand Reinhold, 1987.

Hardy, K. *Bacterial Plasmids,* 2nd ed. Washington, D.C.: American Society for Microbiology, 1986.

Lewin, B. *Genes,* 4th ed. New York: Oxford University Press, 1990.

Maniatis, T., and Ptashne, M. A DNA operator-repressor system. *Sci. Am.* 234(1):64, 1976.

Mayer, L. W. Use of plasmid profiles in epidemiologic surveillance of disease outbreaks and in tracing the transmission of antibiotic resistance. *Clin. Microbiol. Rev.* 1:228, 1988.

Novick, R. P. Plasmids. *Sci. Am.* 243(6):103, 1980.

Ptashne, M., and Gilbert, W. Genetic repressors. *Sci. Am.* 222(6):36, 1970.

Radman, M., and Walker, R. The high fidelity of DNA duplication. *Sci. Am.* 259(2):40, 1988.

Stahl, F. W. Genetic recombination. *Sci. Am.* 256(2):91, 1987.

Stewart, G. J., and Carlson, C. A. The biology of natural transformation. *Annu. Rev. Microbiol.* 40:211, 1986.

Watson, J. D., Hopkins, N. H., Roberts, J. W., Steitz, J. A., and Weiner, A. M. *Molecular Biology of the Gene,* 4th ed. Menlo Park, CA: Benjamin/Cummings, 1987.

Chapter 6. Biotechnology and Medicine

Anderson, W. F., and Diacumakos, E. G. Genetic engineering in mammalian cells. *Sci. Am.* 245(1):106, 1981.

Guyer, R. L., and Koshland, D. E., Jr. The molecule of the year. *Science* 246:153, 1989.

Hopwood, D. A. The genetic programming of industrial microorganisms. *Sci. Am.* 245(3):91, 1981.

Mullis, K. B. The unusual origin of the polymerase chain reaction. *Sci. Am.* 262(4):56, 1990.

Peska, S. The purification and manufacture of human interferon. *Sci. Am.* 249(2):37, 1983.

Peters, P. *Biotechnology: A Guide to Genetic Engineering.* Dubuque, IA: Brown, 1993.

Tenover, F. C. Diagnostic deoxyribonucleic acid probes for infectious disease. *Clin. Microbiol. Rev.* 1:82, 1988.

Watson, J. D., Gilman, M., Witkowski, J., and Zoller, M. *Recombinant DNA,* 2nd ed. San Francisco: Freeman, 1992.

Watson, J. D., Hopkins, N. H., Roberts, J. W., Steitz, J. A., and Weiner, A. M. *Molecular Biology of the Gene,* 4th ed. Vol. 1. Menlo Park, CA: Benjamin/Cummings, 1987.

Wolcott, M. J. Advances in nucleic acid detection methods. *Clin. Microbiol. Rev.* 5:370, 1992.

Chapter 7. Sterilization and Disinfection

Favero, M. S., and Bond, W. W. Chemical disinfection of medical and surgical materials. In Block, S. S. (ed.). *Disinfection, Sterilization and Preservation,* 4th ed. Philadelphia: Lea & Febiger, 1991.

Maki, D. G., Ringer, M., and Alvarado, C. J. Prospective randomized trial of povidone-iodine, alcohol and chlorhexidine for prevention of infection with central venous and arterial catheters. *Lancet* 338: 339, 1991.

Nyström, B. New technology for sterilization and disinfection. *Am. J. Med.* 91:264S, 1991.

Russell, A. D. Bacterial spores and chemical sporicidal agents. *Clin. Microbiol. Rev.* 3:99, 1990.

Rutala, W. A. APIC guidelines for selection and use of disinfectants. *Am. J. Infect. Control* 18:99, 1990.

Rutala, W. A., Clontz, E. P., Weber, D. J., and Hoffmann, K. K. Disinfection practices for endoscopes and other semicritical items. *Infect. Control Hosp. Epidemiol.* 12:282, 1991.

Salzman, M. B., Isenberg, H. D., and Rubin, L. G. Use of disinfectants to reduce microbial contamination of hubs of vascular catheters. *J. Clin. Microbiol.* 31:475, 1993.

Chapter 8. Chemotherapy

Baker, C. N., Stocker, S. A., Culver, D. H., and Thornsberry, C. Comparison of the E test to agar dilution, broth microdilution, and agar diffusion susceptibility testing techniques by using a special challenge set of bacteria. *J. Clin. Microbiol.* 29:533, 1991.

Bean, B. Antiviral therapy: Current concepts and practices. *Clin. Microbiol. Rev.* 5:146, 1992.

Bryan, J. P. New macrolides. *Curr. Opin. Infect. Dis.* 4:722, 1991.

Classen, D. C., Avans, R. S., Pestotnik, S. L., et al. The timing of prophylactic administration of antibiotics and risk of surgical wound infection. *N. Engl. J. Med.* 326:281, 1992.

Evaluation of new oral antimicrobial agents and the experience with cefprozil—A broad-spectrum oral cephalosporin. *Clin. Infect. Dis.* 14(Suppl. 2), 1992.

Davis, B. D. Mechanism of bactericidal action of aminoglycosides. *Microbiol. Rev.* 51:341, 1987.

Dismukes, W. E. Azole antifungal drugs: Old and new. *Ann. Intern. Med.* 109:177, 1988.

Eliopoulos, G. M., and Eliopoulos, C. T. Antibiotic combinations: Should they be tested? *Clin. Microbiol. Rev.* 1:139, 1988.

Graybill, J. R. Future directions of antifungal therapy. *Clin. Infect. Dis.* 14(Suppl. 1):S170, 1992.

Hurley, J. C. Antibiotic-induced release of endotoxin: A reappraisal. *Clin. Infect. Dis.* 15:840, 1992.

Karlowsky, J. A., and Zhanbel, G. G. Concepts on the use of liposomal antimicrobial agents: Applications for aminoglycosides. *Clin. Infect. Dis.* 15:654, 1992.

Lupski, J. R. Molecular mechanisms for transposition of drug resistance genes and other movable genetic elements. *Rev. Infect. Dis.* 9:357, 1988.

Moellering, R., Eliopoulos, G., and Sentochink, D. The carbapenems: New broad spectrum beta-lactam antibiotics. *J. Antimicrob. Chemother.* 24(Suppl. A):1, 1989.

Neu, H. C. Quinolone antimicrobial agents. *Annu. Rev. Med.* 43:465, 1992.

Sanders, C. C. β-Lactamases of gram-negative bacteria: New challenges for new drugs. *Clin. Infect. Dis.* 14:1089, 1992.

Stratton, C. W. Serum bactericidal test. *Clin. Microbiol. Rev.* 1:19, 1988.

Wenzel, R. P. Preoperative antibiotic prophylaxis. *N. Engl. J. Med.* 326:337, 1992.

Chapter 9. Nonspecific Host Resistance

Clark, R. A. The human neutrophil respiratory burst oxidase. *J. Infect. Dis.* 161:1140, 1990.

Gallin, J. I. Interferon-γ in the management of chronic granulomatous disease. *Rev. Infect. Dis.* 13:973, 1991.

Henderson, W. R., Jr. The role of platelet in the pathogenesis of infectious disease. *Curr. Opin. Infect. Dis.* 5:375, 1992.

Kuby, J. *Immunology.* New York: Freeman, 1992.

Ofek, I., Rest, R. F., and Sharon, N. Nonopsonic phagocytosis of microorganisms. *ASM News* 58:429, 1992.

Sawyer, D. W., Donowitz, G. R., and Mandell, G. L. Polymorphonuclear neutrophils: An effective antimicrobial force. *Rev. Infect. Dis.* 11(Suppl. 7):S1532, 1989.

Thomas, E. L., Lehrer, R. I., and Rest, R. F. Human neutrophil antimicrobial activity. *Rev. Infect. Dis.* 10(Suppl. 2):450, 1988.
Tizard, I. R. *Immunology: An Introduction*, 2nd ed. Philadelphia: Saunders, 1988.
Tonegawa, S. The molecules of the immune system. *Sci. Am.* 252(3): 41, 1985.

Chapter 10. Antigens and Antibodies

Coleman, R. M., Lombard, M. F., and Sicard, R. E. *Fundamental Immunology*, 2nd ed. Dubuque, IA: Brown, 1992.
Kennedy, R. C., Melnick, J. L., and Dreesman, G. R. Anti-idiotypes and immunity. *Sci. Am.* 255(5):48, 1986.
Milstein, C. From antibody structure to immunological diversification of immune response. *Science* 231:1261, 1986.
Paul, W. E. *Fundamental Immunology*, 3rd ed. New York: Raven, 1993.
Roitt, I. M., Brostoff, J., and Male, D. K. *Essential Immunology*, 7th ed. Boston: Blackwell Scientific, 1991.

Chapter 11. Cells and Tissues of the Immune System

Grey, H., Allesandro, S., and Buss, S. How T cells see antigen. *Sci. Am.* 261(5):56, 1988.
Marrack, P., and Kappler, J. The T cell and its receptor. *Sci. Am.* 246(3):36, 1986.
Nossal, J. V. Life, death and the immune system. *Sci. Am.* 269(3):53, 1993.
Old, L. J. Tumor necrosis factor. *Sci. Am.* 258(3):59, 1988.
Rennie, J. The body against itself. *Sci. Am.* 263(6):106, 1990.
Roilides, E., and Pizzo, P. Modulation of host defenses by cytokines: Evolving adjuncts in prevention and treatment of serious infections in immunocompromised hosts. *Clin. Infect. Dis.* 15:508, 1992.
Smith, R. A. Interleukin-2. *Sci. Am.* 262(3):50, 1990.
von Boehmer, H., and Kisielow, P. How the immune system learns about self. *Sci. Am.* 265(4):74, 1991.
Weissman, I. L., and Cooper, M. D. How the immune system develops. *Sci. Am.* 269(3):65, 1993.
Young, J. D-E., and Cohn, Z. A. How killer cells kill. *Sci. Am.* 258(1): 38, 1988.

Chapter 12. The Immune Response (Humoral vs. Cell-Mediated Immunity)

Alt, F. W., Blackwell, T. K., and Yancopoulos, G. D. Development of the primary antibody response. *Sci. Am.* 257(5):62, 1987.
Berkman, S. A., Lee, M. L., and Gale, R. P. Clinical uses of intravenous immunoglobulins. *Ann. Intern. Med.* 112:278, 1990.
Coleman, R. J., Lombard, M. F., and Sicard, R. E. *Fundamental Immunology*, 2nd ed. Dubuque, IA: Brown, 1992.
Evolving use of biologicals in the treatment and prevention of infectious diseases. *Rev. Infect. Dis.* 13(5):971, 1991.
Figueroa, J. E., and Densen, P. Infectious diseases associated with complement deficiencies. *Clin. Microbiol. Rev.* 4:359, 1991.
Greene, W. C. AIDS and the immune system. *Sci. Am.* 269(3):99, 1993.
Janeway, C. A., Jr. How the immune system recognizes invaders. *Sci. Am.* 269(3):73, 1993.
Joiner, K. A. Complement evasion by bacteria and parasites. *Annu. Rev. Microbiol.* 42:201, 1988.
Kuby, J. *Immunology*. New York: Freeman, 1992.
Mayer, M. The complement system. *Sci. Am.* 229(5):54, 1973.
Neonatal sepsis and the role of immunotherapy. *Rev. Infect. Dis.* 12(Suppl. 4), 1990.
Paul, W. E. *Fundamental Immunology*, 3rd ed. New York: Raven, 1993.
Paul, W. E. Infectious diseases and the immune system. *Sci. Am.* 269(3):91, 1993.
Roitt, I. M. *Essential Immunology*, 7th ed. Boston: Blackwell Scientific, 1991.
Vildé J-L., and Gerard, L. Immunodeficiency and immunotherapy. *Curr. Opin. Infect. Dis.* 4:386, 1991.

Chapter 13. Immunological Disorders

Bochner, B. S., and Lichtenstein, L. M. Anaphylaxis. *N. Engl. J. Med.* 324:1785, 1991.
Buckley, R. Immunodeficiency diseases. *J.A.M.A.* 258:2841, 1987.
Buisseret, P. D. Allergy. *Sci. Am.* 247(1):86, 1982.
Cohen, I. R. The self, the world, and autoimmunity. *Sci. Am.* 258(4): 52, 1988.
Condemi, J. The autoimmune diseases. *J.A.M.A.* 258:1920, 1987.
Lichtenstein, L. M. Allergy and the immune system. *Sci. Am.* 269(3): 117, 1993.
Old, L. J. Tumor necrosis factor. *Sci. Am.* 258(3):59, 1988.
Ramsdell, F., and Fowlkes, B. Clonal deletion versus clonal anergy. *Science* 248:342, 1990.
Rennie, J. The body against itself. *Sci. Am.* 263(6):106, 1990.
Rosenberg, S. A. Adoptive immunotherapy for cancer. *Sci. Am.* 262(5):62, 1990.
Salvin, R. G., and Ducomb, D. F. Allergic contact dermatitis. *Hosp. Pract.* 24:39, 1989.
Serafin, W. E., and Austin, K. F. Mediators of immediate hypersensitivity reactions. *N. Engl. J. Med.* 317:30, 1987.
Steinman, L. Autoimmune disease. *Sci. Am.* 269(3):107, 1993.
Wigzell, H. The immune system as a therapeutic agent. *Sci. Am.* 269(3):127, 1993.

Chapter 14. Microorganisms as Commensals and Parasites

Ayoub, E. M., ed. *Microbial Determinants of Virulence and Host Response.* Washington, D.C.: American Society for Microbiology, 1990.
Botsford, J. L., and Harman, J. G. Cyclic AMP in prokaryotes. *Microbiol. Rev.* 56:100, 1992.
Dinarello, C. A., Canon, J. G., and Wolff, S. M. New concepts on the pathogenesis of fever. *Rev. Infect. Dis.* 10:168, 1988.
Edelson, R. L., and Fink, J. M. The immunologic function of the skin. *Sci. Am.* 256(1):46, 1985.
Finlay, B. B., and Falkow, S. Common themes in microbial pathogenicity. *Microbiol. Rev.* 53:210, 1989.
Mackowiak, P. A. Mechanisms of fever. *Curr. Opin. Infect. Dis.* 5:348, 1992.
Mackowiak, P. A., ed. *Fever: Basic Mechanisms and Management*. New York: Raven, 1991.
Perspectives on bacterial pathogenesis and host defense. *Rev. Infect. Dis.* 9(Suppl. 5), 1987.
Roth, J. A. *Virulence Mechanisms of Bacterial Pathogens*. Washington, D.C.: American Society for Microbiology, 1988.
Roth, R. R., and James, W. D. Microbial ecology of the skin. *Annu. Rev. Microbiol.* 42:441, 1988.
Weinberg, E. D. The iron-withholding defense system. *ASM News* 59:559, 1993.

Chapter 15. Epidemiology

Ampel, N. M. Plagues—What's past is present: Thoughts on the origin and history of new infectious diseases. *Rev. Infect. Dis.* 13: 658, 1991.

Archer, D. L., and Young, F. E. Contemporary issues: Diseases with a food vector. *Clin. Microbiol. Rev.* 1:377, 1988.
Bennett, J. V., and Brachman, P. S., eds. *Hospital Infections,* 3rd ed. Boston: Little, Brown, 1992.
Eisenstein, B. I. The polymerase chain reaction. A new method of using molecular genetics for medical diagnosis. *N. Engl. J. Med.* 322:178, 1990.
Eisenstein, B. I. New molecular techniques for microbial epidemiology and the diagnosis of infectious diseases. *J. Infect. Dis.* 161:595, 1990.
Mayer, L. W. Use of plasmid profiles in epidemiologic surveillance of disease outbreaks and tracing the transmission of antibiotic resistance. *Clin. Microbiol. Rev.* 1:228, 1988.
Rothman, K. J. *Modern Epidemiology.* Boston: Little, Brown, 1986.
Roueche, B. *The Medical Detectives.* 2 vols. New York: Truman Talley Books, 1984.
Schuchat, A., Swaminathan, B., and Broome, C. V. Epidemiology of human listeriosis. *Clin. Microbiol. Rev.* 4:169, 1991.
Wolcott, M. J. Advances in nucleic acid-based detection methods. *Clin. Microbiol. Rev.* 5:370, 1992.
Zinsser, H. *Rats, Lice, and History.* Boston: Bantam Books, 1935.

Chapter 16. Clinical Microbiology

Baron, E. J., and Finegold, S. M. *Bailey and Scott's Diagnostic Microbiology,* 8th ed. St. Louis: Mosby, 1990.
Centers for Disease Control. Recommendations for prevention of HIV transmission in health-care settings. *M.M.W.R.* 36(Suppl. 2S), 1987.
James, K. Immunoserology of infectious disease. *Clin. Microbiol. Rev.* 3:132, 1990.
Johnson, F. B. Transport of viral specimens. *Clin. Microbiol. Rev.* 3: 120, 1990.
Koneman, E. W., Allen, S. D., Dowell, V. R., Jr., Janda, W. M., Sommers, H. M., and Winn, W. C., Jr. *Color Atlas and Textbook of Diagnostic Microbiology,* 3rd ed. Philadelphia: Lippincott, 1988.
Manafi, M., Kneifel, W., and Bascomb, S. Fluorogenic and chromogenic substrates used in bacterial diagnostics. *Microbiol. Rev.* 55: 335, 1991.
Miller, J. M. Evaluating biochemical identification systems. *J. Clin. Microbiol.* 29:1559, 1991.
Ormerod, M. G. *Flow Cytometry: A Practical Approach.* Oxford, England: IRL Press, 1990.
Stager, E., and Davis, J. R. Automated systems for identification of microorganisms. *Clin. Microbiol. Rev.* 5:302, 1992.

Chapter 17. The Gram-Positive Cocci

Anhalt, J. P., Heiter, B. J., Naumovitz, D. W., and Bourbeau, P. B. Comparison of three methods for detection of group A streptococci in throat swabs. *J. Clin. Microbiol.* 30:2135, 1992.
Antimicrobial resistance in *Streptococcus pneumoniae. Clin. Infect. Dis.* 15:77, 1992.
Bhakdi, S., and Tranum-Jensen, J. Alpha-toxin of *Staphylococcus aureus. Microbiol. Rev.* 55:733, 1991.
Bisno, A. L. The resurgence of acute rheumatic fever in the United States. *Annu. Rev. Med.* 41:319, 1990.
Bisno, A. L. Group A streptococcal infections and acute rheumatic fever. *N. Engl. J. Med.* 325:783, 1991.
Bohach, G. A., Fast, D. J., Nelson, R. D., and Schlievert, P. M. Staphylococcal and streptococcal pyrogenic toxins involved in toxic shock syndrome and related illnesses. *Crit. Rev. Microbiol.* 17:251, 1990.
Centers for Disease Control. Surveillance summaries. Group B streptococcal disease in the United States, 1990: Report from a multistate active surveillance system. *M.M.W.R.* 41(No. ss-6): November 20, 1992.
Demers, B., Simor, A. E., Vellend, H., et al. Severe invasive group A streptococcal infections in Ontario, Canada: 1987–1991. *Clin. Infect. Dis.* 16:792, 1993.
Fidalgo, S., Vázquez, F., Mendoza, M. C., Pérez, F., and Méndez, F. J. Bacteremia due to *Staphylococcus epidermidis:* Microbiologic, epidemiologic, clinical and prognostic features. *Rev. Infect. Dis.* 12: 520, 1990.
Fischetti, V. A. Streptococcal M protein. *Sci. Am.* 264(6):58, 1991.
Johnson, H., Russel, J., and Pontzer, C. Superantigens in human disease. *Sci. Am.* 266(1):92, 1992.
Johnston, R. B., Jr., Pathogenesis of pneumococcal pneumonia. *Rev. Infect. Dis.* 13(Suppl. 6):S509, 1991.
Joklik, W. K., Willett, H. P., Amos, D. B., and Wilfert, C. M. *Zinsser Microbiology,* 20th ed. E. Norwalk, CT: Appleton & Lange, 1992.
Kloos, W. E., and Bannerman, T. L. Update on clinical significance of coagulase-negative staphylococci. *Clin. Microbiol. Rev.* 7:117, 1994.
Mandell, G. L., Douglas, R. G., Jr., and Bennett, J. E. *Principles and Practices of Infectious Diseases,* 3rd ed. New York: Wiley, 1990.
Marrack, P., and Kappler, J. The staphylococcal enterotoxins and their relatives. *Science* 248:705, 1990.
Megran, D. W. Enterococcal endocarditis. *Clin. Infect. Dis.* 15:63, 1992.
Miller, J. M., Jr. Strategies to prevent group B streptococcal neonatal sepsis. *Infect. Med.* 48:30, 1990.
Moellering, R. C., Jr. Emergence of enterococcus as a significant pathogen. *Clin. Infect. Dis.* 14:1173, 1992.
Musher, D. M. Infections caused by *Streptococcus pneumoniae:* Clinical spectrum, pathogenesis, immunity, and treatment. *Clin. Infect. Dis.* 14:801, 1992.
Pfaller, M. A., and Herwaldt, L. A. Laboratory, clinical and epidemiological aspects of coagulase-negative staphylococci. *Clin. Microbiol. Rev.* 3:46, 1990.
Schlievert, P. M. Role of superantigens in human disease. *J. Infect. Dis.* 167:997, 1993.
Shulman, S. T., Phair, J. P., and Sommers, H. M. *The Biologic and Clinical Basis of Infectious Disease,* 4th ed. Philadelphia: Saunders, 1992.
Stevens, D. L. Invasive group A streptococcus infections. *Clin. Infect. Dis.* 14:2, 1992.
Stollerman, G. H. Rheumatogenic group A streptococci and the return of rheumatic fever. *Adv. Intern. Med.* 35:1, 1990.
Todd, J. K. Toxic shock syndrome. *Clin. Microbiol. Rev.* 1:432, 1988.
Wickboldt, L. G., and Fenske, N. A. Streptococcal and staphylococcal infections of the skin. *Hosp. Pract.* 21:41, 1986.

Chapter 18. Gram-Negative Diplococci: The *Neisseria* and Related Genera

Catlin, B. W. *Branhamella catarrhalis:* An organism gaining respect as a pathogen. *Clin. Microbiol. Rev.* 3:293, 1990.
Centers for Disease Control. Plasmid-mediated antimicrobial resistance in *Neisseria gonorrhoeae:* United States, 1988–1989. *M.M.W.R.* 39:284, 1990.
Elliott, B., Brunham, R. C., Laga, M., et al. Maternal gonococcal infection as a preventable risk factor for low birth weight. *J. Infect. Dis.* 161:531, 1990.
Knapp, J. S. Historic perspectives and identification of *Neisseria* and related species. *Clin. Microbiol. Rev.* 1:415, 1988.
Moore, P. S. Meningococcal meningitis in sub-Saharan Africa: A model for the epidemic process. *Clin. Infect. Dis.* 14:515, 1992.
Pelvic inflammatory disease. Recommendations and reports. *M.M.W.R.* 40(No. RR-5): April 26, 1991.
Perspectives on pathogenic *Neisseria. Clin. Microbiol. Rev.* 2(Suppl.), 1989.
Rein, M. F. Gonorrhea. *Curr. Opin. Infect. Dis.* 4:12, 1991.
Shafer, W. M., and Rest, R. F. Interactions of gonococci with phagocytic cells. *Annu. Rev. Microbiol.* 43:121, 1989.
Stephens, D. S., and Farley, M. Pathogenic events during infection of the human nasopharynx with *Neisseria meningitidis* and *Haemophilus influenzae. Rev. Infect. Dis.* 13:22, 1991.
Tramont, E. Gonococcal vaccines. *Clin. Microbiol. Rev.* 2(Suppl.):S74, 1989.

Waage, A., Halstensen, A., Shalaby, R., Brandtzaeg, P., Kierulf, P., and Espevik, T. Local production of tumor necrosis factor-α, interleukin-1, and interleukin-6 in meningococcal meningitis. *J. Exp. Med.* 170:1859, 1990.

Chapter 19. The Gram-Positive Sporeformers: The Bacilli and Clostridia

Archer, D. L., and Young, F. E. Contemporary issues: Diseases with a food vector. *Clin. Microbiol. Rev.* 1:377, 1988.
Arnon, S. S. Infant botulism. *Annu. Rev. Med.* 31:541, 1980.
Centers for Disease Control. Tetanus surveillance—United States, 1989–1991. *M.M.W.R.* 41(No. SS-8): December 11, 1992.
Doern, G. V., Coughlin, R. T., and Wu, L. Laboratory diagnosis of *Clostridium difficile*-associated gastrointestinal disease. *J. Clin. Microbiol.* 30:2042, 1992.
Drobniewski, F. A. *Bacillus cereus* and related species. *Clin. Microbiol. Rev.* 6:324, 1993.
Guerrant, R., and Bobak, D. Bacterial and protozoal gastroenteritis. *N. Engl. J. Med.* 325:327, 1991.
Hatheway, C. L. Toxigenic clostridia. *Clin. Microbiol. Rev.* 3:66, 1990.
Lyerly, D. M., Krivan, H. C., and Wilkins, T. *Clostridium difficile:* Its diseases and toxins. *Clin. Microbiol. Rev.* 1:1, 1988.
McFarland, L. V., Surawicz, C. M., and Stam, W. E. Risk factors for *Clostridium difficile* carriage and *C. difficile*-associated diarrhea in a cohort of hospitalized patients. *J. Infect. Dis.* 162:678, 1990.
Schantz, E. J., and Johnson, E. A. Properties and use of botulinum toxin and other microbial neurotoxins in medicine. *Microbiol. Rev.* 56:80, 1992.
Simpson, L. L., ed. *Botulinum Neurotoxin and Tetanus Toxin.* San Diego: Academic, 1989.
Sugiyama, H. *Clostridium botulinum* neurotoxin. *Microbiol. Rev.* 44: 419, 1980.

Chapter 20. *Corynebacterium diphtheriae* and Related Bacteria

Coyle, M. B., and Lipsky, B. A. Coryneform bacteria in infectious diseases: Clinical and laboratory aspects. *Clin. Microbiol. Rev.* 3: 227, 1990.
Cunliffe, W. J., and Eady, E. A. A reappraisal and update on the pathogenesis and treatment of acne. *Curr. Opin. Infect. Dis.* 5:703, 1992.
Farber, J. M., and Peterkin, P. I. *Listeria monocytogenes,* a food-borne pathogen. *Microbiol. Rev.* 55:476, 1991.
Gorby, G. L., and Peacock, J. R., Jr. *Erysipelothrix rhusiopathiae* endocarditis: Microbiologic, epidemiologic, and clinical features of an occupational disease. *Rev. Infect. Dis.* 10:317, 1988.
Pinner, R., Schuchat, A., Swaminathan, B., et al. Role of foods in sporadic listeriosis: II. Microbiologic and epidemiologic investigation. *J.A.M.A.* 267:2046, 1992.
Reboli, A. C., and Farrar, W. E. *Erysipelothrix rhusiopathiae:* An occupational pathogen. *Clin. Microbiol. Rev.* 2:354, 1989.
Schuchat, A., Swaminathan, B., and Broome, C. V. Epidemiology of human listeriosis. *Clin. Microbiol. Rev.* 4:169, 1991.

Chapter 21. Gram-Negative Enteric Bacteria

Braden, C., and Keusch, G. T. Recent advances in the study of diarrheogenic bacteria. *Curr. Opin. Infect. Dis.* 4:56, 1991.
Cárdenas, L., and Clements, J. D. Oral immunization using live attenuated *Salmonella* species as carriers of foreign antigens. *Clin. Microbiol. Rev.* 5:328, 1992.
Fang, G. Intestinal *Escherichia coli* infections. *Curr. Opin. Infect. Dis.* 6:48, 1993.
Finlay, B. B., Leung, K. Y., Rosenshine, I., and Garcia-Del Portillo, F. *Salmonella* interactions with the epithelial cell. *ASM News* 58: 486, 1992.
Foster, J. W. Beyond pH homeostasis: The acid tolerance response of salmonellae. *ASM News* 58:266, 1992.
Guerrant, R. L., and Bobak, D. A. Bacterial and protozoal gastroenteritis. *N. Engl. J. Med.* 325:327, 1991.
Hale, T. L. Genetic basis of virulence in *Shigella* species. *Microbiol. Rev.* 55:206, 1991.
Hill, D. R. Salmonellosis and typhoid fever. *Curr. Opin. Infect. Dis.* 6:54, 1993.
Hill, S. M., Phillips, A. D., and Walker-Smith, J. A. Enteropathogenic *Escherichia coli* and life threatening chronic diarrhea. *Gut* 32:154, 1991.
Johnson, J. R. Virulence factors in *Escherichia coli* urinary tract infection. *Clin. Microbiol. Rev.* 4:80, 1991.
Johnson, R. H. Yersinia infections. *Curr. Opin. Infect. Dis.* 5:654, 1992.
Krogfelt, K. A. Bacterial adhesion: Genetics, biogenesis, and role in pathogenesis of fimbrial adhesins of *Escherichia coli. Rev. Infect. Dis.* 13:721, 1991.
Levine, O. S., and Levine, M. M. Houseflies (*Musca domestica*) as mechanical vectors of shigellosis. *J. Infect. Dis.* 13:688, 1991.
McEvedy, C. The bubonic plague. *Sci. Am.* 258(2):118, 1988.
Miller, V. L. *Yersinia* invasion genes and their products. *ASM News* 58:26, 1992.
Saito, H., Elting, L., Bodey, G., and Berkey, P. Serratia bacteremia: Review of 118 cases. *Rev. Infect. Dis.* 11:912, 1989.
Sansonetti, P. J. *Escherichia coli, Shigella,* antibiotic-associated diarrhea, and prevention and treatment of gastroenteritis. *Curr. Opin. Infect. Dis.* 5:66, 1992.
Siegler, R. L., Milligan, M. K., Burningham, T. H., et al. Long term outcome and prognostic indicators of the hemolytic uremic syndrome. *J. Pediatr.* 118:195, 1991.
Spangler, B. D. Structure and function of cholera toxin and the related *Escherichia coli* heat-labile enterotoxin. *Microbiol. Rev.* 56:622, 1992.
Warren, J. W. *Providencia stuartii:* A common cause of antibiotic resistant bacteriuria in patients with long term indwelling catheters. *Rev. Infect. Dis.* 8:61, 1986.
Workshop on invasive diarrheas, shigellosis, and dysentery. *Rev. Infect. Dis.* 13(Suppl. 4), 1991.

Chapter 22. *Pseudomonas* and Related Organisms

Cefai, C., Richards, J., Gould, F. K., and McPeake, P. An outbreak of *Acinetobacter* respiratory tract infection from incomplete disinfection of ventilatory equipment. *J. Hospit. Infect.* 15:177, 1990.
Dance, D. A. B. Melioidosis: The tip of the iceberg. *Clin. Microbiol. Rev.* 4:52, 1991.
Fick, R. B., Jr. Pathogenesis of *Pseudomonas aeruginosa* lung lesion in cystic fibrosis. *Chest* 96:158, 1989.
Gilligan, P. H. Microbiology of airway disease in patients with cystic fibrosis. *Clin. Microbiol. Rev.* 4:35, 1991.
Goldmann, D. A., and Klinger, J. D. *Pseudomonas cepacia:* Biology, mechanism of virulence, epidemiology. *J. Pediatr.* 108:806, 1986.
Graham, D. R., Band, J. D., Thornsberry, C., Hollis, D. G., and Weaver, R. E. Infections caused by *Moraxella, Moraxella urethralis, Moraxella*-like groups M-5 and M-6, and *Kingella kingae* in the United States, 1953, 1980. *Rev. Infect. Dis.* 12:423, 1990.
Insler, M. S., and Gore, H. *Pseudomonas* keratitis and folliculitis from whirlpool exposure. *Am. J. Ophthalmol.* 101:41, 1986.
Joshi, N., O'Bryan, T., and Appelbaum, P. C. Pleuropulmonary infections caused by *Eikenella corrodens. Rev. Infect. Dis.* 13:1207, 1991.
Khardori, N., Elting, L., Wong, E., Schable, B., and Bodey, G. P. Nosocomial infections due to *Xanthomonas maltophilia (Pseudomonas maltophilia)* in patients with cancer. *Rev. Infect. Dis.* 12:997, 1990.

Kielhofner, M., Atmar, R. L., Hamill, R. J., and Musher, D. M. Life-threatening *Pseudomonas aeruginosa* infections in patients with human immunodeficiency virus infection. *Clin. Infect. Dis.* 14:403, 1992.
May, T. B., Shinabarger, D., Maharaj, R., et al. Alginate synthesis by *Pseudomonas aeruginosa:* A key pathogenic factor in chronic pulmonary infections of cystic fibrosis patients. *Clin. Microbiol. Rev.* 4: 191, 1991.
Price, D., and Ahearn, D. G. Incidence and persistence of *Pseudomonas aeruginosa* in whirlpools. *J. Clin. Microbiol.* 26:1650, 1988.
Taylor, G. D., Kibsey, P., Kirkland, T., Burroughs, E., and Tredget, E. E. Site, bacteriology, and risk factors for infections occurring in burns intensive care unit. *Burns* 18:332, 1992.
Tredget, E. E., Shankowsky, H. A., Joffe, A. M., et al. Epidemiology of infections with *Pseudomonas aeruginosa* in burn patients: The role of hydrotherapy. *Clin. Infect. Dis.* 15:941, 1992.

Chapter 23. Vibrionaceae

Brenden, R. A., Miller, M. A., and Janda, J. M. Clinical disease spectrum and pathogenic factors associated with *Plesiomonas shigelloides* infection in humans. *Rev. Infect. Dis.* 10:303, 1988.
Carpenter, C. C. J. The treatment of cholera: Clinical science at the bedside. *J. Infect. Dis.* 166:2, 1992.
Centers for Disease Control. Importation of cholera from Peru. *M.M.W.R.* 40:258, 1991.
Gold, W. L., and Salit, I. E. *Aeromonas hydrophila* infections of skin and soft tissue. *Clin. Infect. Dis.* 16:69, 1993.
Hoge, C. W., Watsky, D., Peeler, R. N., et al. Epidemiology and spectrum of vibrio infections in a Chesapeake Bay community. *J. Infect. Dis.* 160:985, 1989.
Janda, J. M., and Duffey, P. S. Mesophilis aeromonads in human disease: Current taxonomy, laboratory identification, and infectious disease spectrum. *Rev. Infect. Dis.* 10:980, 1988.
Janda, J. M., Powers, C., Bryant, R. G., and Abbott, S. L. Current perspectives on the epidemiology and pathogenesis of clinically significant *Vibrio* spp. *Clin. Microbiol. Rev.* 1:245, 1988.
Khardori, N., and Fainstein, V. *Aeromonas* and *Plesiomonas* as etiological agents. *Annu. Rev. Microbiol.* 42:395, 1988.
Park, S. D., Shon, H. S., and Joh, N. J. *Vibrio vulnificus* septicemia in Korea: Clinical and epidemiologic findings in seventy patients. *J. Am. Acad. Dermatol.* 24:397, 1991.
Siddiqui, M. N., Ahmed, I., Faroqui, B. J., and Mushtaq, A. Myonecrosis due to *Aeromonas hydrophila* following insertion of an intravenous cannula: Case report and review. *Clin. Infect. Dis.* 14: 619, 1992.
West, P. A. The human pathogenic vibrios: A public health update with environmental perspectives. *Epidemiol. Infect.* 103:1, 1989.

Chapter 24. Gram-Negative Coccobacillary Aerobic Bacteria

Albritton, W. L. Biology of *Haemophilus ducreyi. Microbiol. Rev.* 53: 377, 1989.
Bonadio, W. A., Mannebach, M., and Krippendorf, R. Bacterial meningitis in older children. *Am. J. Dis. Child.* 144:463, 1990.
Diphtheria, tetanus, and pertussis: Recommendations for vaccine use and other preventive measures. *M.M.W.R.* 40(No. RR-10): August 8, 1991.
Epidemiology, pathogenesis, and prevention of *Haemophilus influenzae* disease. *J. Infect. Dis.* 165(Suppl. 1), 1992.
Haemophilus b conjugate vaccines for prevention of *Haemophilus influenzae* type b disease among infants and children two months of age and older. *M.M.W.R.* 40(No. RR-1): January 11, 1991.
Harrison, L. H., Silva, G. A., Pittman, M., et al. Epidemiology and clinical spectrum of Brazilian purpuric fever. *J. Clin. Microbiol.* 27: 599, 1989.
Morse, S. A. Chancroid and *Haemophilus ducreyi. Clin. Microbiol. Rev.* 2:137, 1989.
Mortimer, E. A. Pertussis and its prevention: A family affair. *J. Infect. Dis.* 161:473, 1990.
Moxon, E. R., and Wilson, R. The role of *Haemophilus influenzae* in the pathogenesis of pneumonia. *Rev. Infect. Dis.* 13(Suppl. 6):S518, 1991.
Pertussis vaccination: Acellular pertussis vaccine for the fourth and fifth doses of the DTP series. *M.M.W.R.* 41(No. RR-15): October 9, 1992.
Recommendations for use of *Haemophilus* b conjugate vaccines and a combined diphtheria, tetanus, pertussis, and *Haemophilus* b vaccine. *M.M.W.R.* 42(No. RR-13): September 17, 1993.
Saez-Llorens, X., and McCracken, G. H., Jr. Bacterial meningitis in neonates and children. *Infect. Dis. Clin. North Am.* 4:623, 1990.
Tärnvik, A. Nature of protective immunity to *Francisella tularensis. Rev. Infect. Dis.* 11:440, 1989.
Wilfert, C. M. Epidemiology of *Haemophilus influenzae* type b infections. *Pediatrics* 85(Suppl.):631, 1990.

Chapter 25. Mycobacteria

Balows, A. ed. *Manual of Clinical Microbiology,* 5th ed. Washington, D.C.: American Society for Microbiology, 1991.
Brisson-Noel, A., Aznar, C., Chureau, C., et al. Diagnosis of tuberculosis by DNA amplification in clinical practice evaluation. *Lancet* 338:364, 1991.
Centers for Disease Control. Nosocomial transmission of multidrug-resistant tuberculosis among HIV-infected patients. *M.M.W.R.* 40: 585, 1991.
Centers for Disease Control. National action plan to combat multidrug-resistant tuberculosis. *M.M.W.R.* 41(No. RR-11): June 19, 1992.
Collins, F. M. Mycobacterial disease, immunosuppression, and acquired immune deficiency syndrome. *Clin. Microbiol. Rev.* 2:360, 1989.
Comstock, G. W. Epidemiology of tuberculosis. *Am. Rev. Respir. Dis.* 125:8, 1982.
Ellner, J. J., Goldberg, M. J., and Parenti, D. M. *Mycobacterium avium* infection and AIDS: A therapeutic dilemma in rapid evolution. *J. Infect. Dis.* 163:1326, 1991.
Fox, J. Coalition reacts to surge of drug-resistant TB. *ASM News* 58: 135, 1992.
Hastings, R. C., Gillis, T. P., Krahenbuhl, J. L., and Franzblau, S. G. Leprosy. *Clin. Microbiol. Rev.* 1:330, 1988.
Hill, A. R., Premkumar, S., Brustein, S., et al. Disseminated tuberculosis in the acquired immune deficiency syndrome era. *Am. Rev. Respir. Dis.* 144:1164, 1991.
Hopwell, P. C. Impact of human immunodeficiency virus infection on the epidemiology, clinical features, management, and control of tuberculosis. *Clin. Infect. Dis.* 15:540, 1992.
Huebner, R. E., Schein, M. F., and Bass, J. B., Jr. The tuberculin skin test. *Clin. Infect. Dis.* 17:968, 1993.
Huebner, R. E., Villarino, M. E., and Snider, D. E. Tuberculin skin testing and the HIV epidemic. *J.A.M.A.* 267:409, 1992.
Sadhana, S., and Sarai, A. Mycobacterial infections. *Curr. Opin. Infect. Dis.* 5:176, 1992.
Small, P. M., Schecter, G. F., Goodman, P. C., et al. Treatment of tuberculosis in patients with advanced human immunodeficiency virus infection. *N. Engl. J. Med.* 324:289, 1991.
Wolinsky, E. Mycobacterial disease other than tuberculosis. *Clin. Infect. Dis.* 15:1, 1992.
Yoder, L. J. Leprosy. *Curr. Opin. Infect. Dis.* 4:302, 1991.
Young, L. S., Inderlied, O. G., Berlin, O. G., and Gottlieb, M. S. Mycobacterial infections in AIDS patients, with an emphasis on the *Mycobacterium avium* complex. *Rev. Infect. Dis.* 8:1024, 1986.
Zanvil, A., and Kaplan, G. Hansen's disease, cell-mediated immunity, and recombinant lymphokines. *J. Infect. Dis.* 163:1195, 1991.

Chapter 26. Spirochetes and Spiral and Curved Rods

Barbour, A. G., and Hayes, S. F. Biology of borrelia species. *Microbiol. Rev.* 50:381, 1986.

Berg, D., Abson, K. G., and Prose, N. S. The laboratory diagnosis of Lyme disease. *Arch. Dermatol.* 127:866, 1991.

Blaser, M. J. *Helicobacter pylori:* Its role in disease. *Clin. Infect. Dis.* 15:386, 1992.

Blaser, M. J., Pérez-Pérez, G. I., Lindebaum, J., et al. Association of infection due to *Helicobacter pylori* with specific upper gastrointestinal pathology. *Rev. Infect. Dis.* 13(Suppl. 8):S704, 1991.

Butzler, J-P., Glupczynski, Y., and Goosens, H. Campylobacter and helicobacter infections. *Curr. Opin. Infect. Dis.* 5:80, 1992.

Centers for Disease Control. Primary and secondary syphilis—United States, 1981–1990. *M.M.W.R.* 40:314, 1991.

Centers for Disease Control. Sexually transmitted disease treatment guidelines. Recommendations and reports. *M.M.W.R.* 42(No. RR-14): September 24, 1993.

Dorfman, D. H., and Glaser, J. H. Congenital syphilis presenting in infants after the newborn period. *N. Engl. J. Med.* 323:1299, 1990.

Dunn, R. A., and Rolfs, R. T. The resurgence of syphilis in the United States. *Curr. Opin. Infect. Dis.* 49:3, 1991.

Engelstein, L. Syphilis, historical and actual: Cultural geography of a disease. *Rev. Infect. Dis.* 8:1036, 1986.

Goldstein, J. C. Household pets and human infections. *Infect. Dis. Clin. North Am.* 5:117, 1991.

Hook, E. W. Syphilis and HIV infection. *J. Infect. Dis.* 160:530, 1989.

Logigian, E. L., Kaplan, R. F., and Steere, A. C. Chronic neurologic manifestations of Lyme disease. *N. Engl. J. Med.* 323:1438, 1990.

Musher, D. M. Syphilis, neurosyphilis, penicillin, and AIDS. *J. Infect. Dis.* 163:1201, 1991.

O'Neil, K. M., Rickman, L. S., and Lazarus, A. A. Pulmonary manifestations of leptospirosis. *Rev. Infect. Dis.* 13:705, 1991.

Penner, J. L. The genus *Campylobacter:* A decade of progress. *Clin. Microbiol. Rev.* 1:157, 1988.

Rahn, D. W., and Malawista, S. E. Clinical judgement in Lyme disease. *Hosp. Pract.* 25:39, 1990.

Rolfs, R. T., Goldberg, M., and Sharrar, R. G. Risk factors for syphilis: Cocaine use and prostitution. *Am. J. Public Health* 80:853, 1990.

Schoen, R. T. Lyme disease. *Curr. Opin. Infect. Dis.* 4:609, 1991.

Szcepanski, A., and Benach, J. L. Lyme borreliosis: Host response to *Borrelia burgdorferi. Microbiol. Rev.* 55:21, 1991.

Walker, R. J., Caldwell, M. B., Lee, E. C., et al. Pathophysiology of campylobacter enteritis. *Microbiol. Rev.* 50:81, 1986.

Watt, G. Leptospirosis. *Curr. Opin. Infect. Dis.* 5:659, 1992.

Zenker, P. N., and Rolfs, R. T. Treatment of syphilis 1989. *Rev. Infect. Dis.* 12(Suppl. 6):S590, 1990.

Chapter 27. Mycoplasmas and L-forms

Cassell, G. H., and Cole, B. C. Mycoplasmas as agents of disease. *N. Engl. J. Med.* 304:80, 1981.

Cassell, G. H., Waites, K. B., Watson, H. L., Crouse, D. T., and Harasawa, R. *Ureaplasma urealyticum* intrauterine infection: Role in prematurity and disease in newborns. *Clin. Microbiol. Rev.* 6:69, 1993.

Denny, F. W., Clyde, W. A., Jr., and Glezen, W. P. *Mycoplasma pneumoniae* disease: Clinical spectrum, pathophysiology, epidemiology, and control. *J. Infect. Dis.* 123:74, 1971.

Grayston, J. T., Alexander, E. R., Kenny, G. E., et al. *Mycoplasma pneumoniae* infections. Clinical and epidemiologic studies. *J.A.M.A.* 191:369, 1965.

Lamont, R. F., Taylor-Robinson, D., Wigglesworth, J. S., et al. The role of mycoplasmas, ureaplasmas, and chlamydiae in the genital tract of women presenting with spontaneous early preterm labor. *J. Med. Microbiol.* 24:253, 1987.

Lin, J. L. Human mycoplasmal infections: Serologic observations. *Rev. Infect. Dis.* 7:216, 1985.

Madoff, S., and Hooper, D. C. Nongenitourinary infections caused by *Mycoplasma hominis* in adults. *Rev. Infect. Dis.* 10:602, 1988.

McMahon, D. K., Dummer, J. S., Pasculle, A. W., and Cassell, G. Extragenital *Mycoplasma hominis* infections in adults. *Am. J. Med.* 89:275, 1990.

Chapter 28. Rickettsiae and Chlamydiae

Barnes, R. C. Laboratory diagnosis of human chlamydial infections. *Clin. Microbiol. Rev.* 2:119, 1989.

Brunham, R. C., et al. Etiology and outcome of acute inflammatory disease. *J. Infect. Dis.* 158:510, 1988.

Cates, W., Jr., and Hinman, A. R. Sexually transmitted diseases in the 1990s. *N. Engl. J. Med.* 325:1368, 1991.

Centers for Disease Control. Epidemic typhus associated with flying squirrels—United States. *M.M.W.R.* 31:555, 1982.

Centers for Disease Control. Human ehrlichiosis—United States. *M.M.W.R.* 37:270, 1988.

Centers for Disease Control. Recommendations for the prevention and management of *Chlamydia trachomatis* infections, 1993. *M.M.W.R.* 42(No. RR-12): August 6, 1993.

Dumler, J. S., and Walker, D. H. Human ehrlichiosis. *Curr. Opin. Infect. Dis.* 4:597, 1991.

Grayston, J. T. Infections caused by *Chlamydia pneumoniae* strain TWAR. *Clin. Infect. Dis.* 15:757, 1992.

Hadfield, T. L. Cat-scratch disease and bacillary angiomatosis. *Curr. Opin. Infect. Dis.* 4:628, 1991.

Hammerschlag, M. R., Chirgwin, K., Roblin, P. M., et al. *Chlamydia pneumoniae* following acute respiratory illness. *Clin. Infect. Dis.* 14: 178, 1992.

Koehler, J. E., and Tappero, J. W. Bacillary angiomatosis in patients infected with human immunodeficiency virus. *Clin. Infect. Dis.* 17: 612, 1993.

Mårdh, P. A. Natural history of genital and chlamydial infections. *Curr. Opin. Infect. Dis.* 5:12, 1992.

Moulder, J. W. Interaction of chlamydiae and host cells in vitro. *Microbiol. Rev.* 55:143, 1991.

Perine, P. L. Chandler, B. P., Krause, D. K., et al. A clinicoepidemiological study of epidemic typhus in Africa. *Clin. Infect. Dis.* 14: 1149, 1992.

Rikihisa, Y. The tribe *Ehrlichieae* and ehrlichial diseases. *Clin. Microbiol. Rev.* 4:286, 1991.

Schwartzman, W. A. Infections due to *Rochalimaea:* The expanding clinical spectrum. *Clin. Infect. Dis.* 15:893, 1992.

Walker, D. H. Rocky Mountain spotted fever: A disease in need of microbiological concern. *Clin. Microbiol. Rev.* 2:227, 1989.

Chapter 29. Actinomycetes

Finegold, S. M. General aspects of anaerobic infection. In S. M. Finegold and W. L. George, eds. *Anaerobic Infections in Humans.* San Diego: Academic, 1989.

Hager, W. D., Douglas, B., Majmudar, B., et al. Pelvic colonization with actinomyces in women using intrauterine contraceptive devices. *Am. J. Obstet. Gynecol.* 140:880, 1981.

Hellyar, A. G. Experience with *Nocardia asteroides* in renal transplant recipients. *J. Hosp. Infect.* 12:13, 1988.

Hiller, S., and Moncla, B. J. Anaerobic gram-positive nonsporeforming bacilli and cocci. In A. Balows, W. J. Hausler, Jr., K. L. Herrmann, H. D. Isenberg, and H. J. Shadomy, eds. *Manual of Clinical Microbiology*, 5th ed. Washington, D.C.: American Society for Microbiology, 1991.

Reiner, S., et al. Primary actinomycosis of an extremity: A case report and review. *Rev. Infect. Dis.* 9:581, 1987.

Schaffner, A., and Schaffner, T. Glucocorticoid-induced impairment of macrophage antimicrobial activity: Mechanisms and dependence on the state of activation. *Rev. Infect. Dis.* 9(Suppl. 5):620, 1987.

Simpson, G. L., Stinson, E. B., Egger, M. J., and Remington, J. S. Nocardial infections in the compromised host: A detailed study in a defined population. *Rev. Infect. Dis.* 3:492, 1981.
Smego, R. A., Jr. Actinomycosis of the central nervous system. *Rev. Infect. Dis.* 9:855, 1987.
Tight, R. R., and Bartlett, M. S. Actinomycetoma in the United States. *Rev. Infect. Dis.* 3:1139, 1981.

Chapter 30. Miscellaneous Pathogens

Alary M., and Joly, J. R. Risk factors for contamination of domestic hot water systems by legionellae. *Appl. Environ. Microbiol.* 57:2360, 1991.
Brieman, R. F., Fields, B. S., Sanden, G. N., Volmer, L., Meier, A., and Spika, J. S. Association of shower use with legionnaires' disease: Possible role of amoebae. *J.A.M.A.* 263:2924, 1990.
Briselden, A. M., Moncla, B. J., Stevens, C. E., and Hillier, S. L. Sialidases (neuraminidases) in bacterial vaginosis and bacterial vaginosis-associated microflora. *J. Clin. Microbiol.* 30:663, 1992.
Catlin, B. W. *Gardnerella vaginalis:* Characteristics, clinical considerations, and controversies. *Clin. Microbiol. Rev.* 5:213, 1992.
Dowling, J. N., Saha, A., and Glew, R. H. Virulence factors of the family Legionellaceae. *Microbiol. Rev.* 56:32, 1992.
Edelstein, P. H. Legionnaires' disease. *Clin. Infect. Dis.* 16:741, 1993.
Hulse, M., Johnson, S., and Ferrieri, P. *Agrobacterium* infections in humans: Experience at one hospital and review. *Clin. Infect. Dis.* 16:112, 1993.
Joshi, N., O'Bryan, T., and Appelbaum, P. C. Pleuropulmonary infections caused by *Eikenella corrodens. Rev. Infect. Dis.* 13:1207, 1991.
Kaplan, A. H., Weber, D. J., Oddone, E. Z., and Perfect, J. R. Infection due to *Actinobacillus actinomycetemcomitans:* 15 cases and review. *Rev. Infect. Dis.* 11:46, 1989.
Klebanoff, S. J., Hillier, S. L., Eschenback, D. A., and Waltersdorph, A. M. Control of the microbial flora of the vagina by H_2O_2-generating lactobacilli. *J. Infect. Dis.* 164:94, 1991.
Krohn, M. A., Hillier, S. L., Lee, M. L., Rabe, L. K., and Eschenbach, D. A. Vaginal *Bacteroides* species are associated with an increased rate of preterm delivery among women in preterm labor. *J. Infect. Dis.* 164:88, 1991.
Latham, R. H., and Schaffner, W. Nosocomial legionnaire's disease. *Curr. Opin. Infect. Dis.* 5:512, 1992.
Parenti, D. M., and Syndam, D. R. *Capnocytophaga* species: Infection in nonimmunocompromised and immunocompromised hosts. *J. Infect. Dis.* 151:140, 1985.
Spiegel, C. A. Bacterial vaginosis. *Clin. Microbiol. Rev.* 4:397, 1991.
Stoloff, A. L., and Gillies, M. L. Infections with *Eikenella corrodens* in a general hospital: A report of 33 cases. *Rev. Infect. Dis.* 8:50, 1986.
Winn, W. C., Jr. Legionnaires' disease: Historic perspective. *Clin. Microbiol. Rev.* 11:60, 1988.

Chapter 31. Viruses

Banks, T. A., and Rouse, B. T. Herpesviruses-immune escape artists. *Clin. Infect. Dis.* 14:932, 1992.
Bean, B. Antiviral therapy: Current concepts and practices. *Clin. Microbiol. Rev.* 5:146, 1992.
Bishop, J. M. The molecular genetics of cancer. *Science* 235:305, 1987.
Bradley, D. E. A Comparative Study of the Structure and Biological Properties of Bacteriophages. In K. Maramorosch and E. Kurstak, eds. *Comparative Virology.* New York: Academic, 1971.
Crum, C. P., Barber, S., and Roche, J. K. Pathobiology of papillomavirus-related cervical diseases: Prospects for immunodiagnosis. *Clin. Microbiol. Rev.* 4:270, 1991.
Fields, B. N., Knipe, D. M., Chanock, R. M., Hirsch, M. S., Melnick, J. L., Monath, T. P., and Roizman, B., eds. *Fields Virology,* 2nd ed. Englewood Cliffs, NJ: Prentice-Hall, 1990.
Franco, E. Viral etiology of cervical cancer: A critique of evidence. *Rev. Infect. Dis.* 13:1195, 1991.
Gallo, R. C. Human retroviruses: A decade of discovery and link with human disease. *J. Infect. Dis.* 164:235, 1991.
Gibbs, J. B., and Marshall, M. S. The *ras* oncogene—An important regulatory element in lower eucaryotic organisms. *Microbiol. Rev.* 53:171, 1989.
Goldberg, D. M., and Diamandis, E. P. Models of neoplasia and their diagnostic implications. *Clin. Chem.* 39(11B):2360, 1993.
Henshaw, N. G. Identification of viruses by methods other than electron microscopy. *ASM News* 54:482, 1988.
Joklik, W. K., Willet, H. P., Amos, D. B., and Wilfert, C. M. *Zinsser Microbiology,* 20th ed. Norwalk, CT: Appleton & Lange, 1992.
Marsh, M., and Helenius, A. Virus entry into animal cells. *Adv. Virus Res.* 36:107, 1989.
Matthews, C. K., Kutter, E. M., Mosig, M., and Berget, P. B., ed. *Bacteriophage T4.* Washington, D.C.: American Society for Microbiology, 1983.
Miller, S. E. Diagnostic virology by electron microscopy. *ASM News* 54:475, 1988.
Nuovo, G. J., and Pedemonte, B. M. Human papillomavirus types and recurrent cervical warts. *J.A.M.A.* 263:1223, 1990.
Okano, M., Thiele, G. M., Davis, J. R., Grierson, H. L., and Purtilo, D. T. Epstein-Barr virus and human diseases: Recent advances in diagnosis. *Clin. Microbiol. Rev.* 1:300, 1988.
Oldstone, M. B. A. Viruses can cause disease in the absence of morphological evidence of cell injury: Implications for uncovering new diseases in the future. *J. Infect. Dis.* 159:384, 1989.
Shah, K. H., Lewis, M. G., Jenson, A. B., Kurman, R. J., and Lancaster, W. D. Papilloma viruses and cervical neoplasia. *Lancet* 2:1190, 1980.
Sherker, A. H., and Marion, P. L. Hepadnaviruses and hepatocellular carcinoma. *Annu. Rev. Microbiol.* 45:475, 1991.
Simons, K., Garoff, H., and Helenius, A. How an animal virus gets into and out of its host cell. *Sci. Am.* 246(2):58, 1982.
Stevens, J. G. Human herpesviruses: A consideration of the latent state. *Microbiol. Rev.* 53:318, 1989.
Varmus, H. Retroviruses. *Science* 240:1427, 1988.
Weinberg, R. A. Molecular basis of cancer. *Sci. Am.* 249(5):126, 1983.
Young, R. Bacteriophage lysis: Mechanism and regulation. *Microbiol. Rev.* 56:430, 1992.
Ziegler, J. L. Burkitt's lymphoma. *N. Engl. J. Med.* 305:735, 1981.

Chapter 32. Viral Diseases

SMALLPOX

Mackett, M. Vaccinia virus as a vector for delivering foreign antigens. *Semin. Virol.* 1:39, 1990.

HERPESVIRUSES

Neyts, J., Snoeck, R., and Clercq, E. Therapy for herpesvirus infections. *Curr. Opin. Infect. Dis.* 5:816, 1992.
Stevens, J. G. Human herpesviruses: A consideration of the latent state. *Microbiol. Rev.* 53:318, 1989.
Weigler, B. J. Biology of B virus in macaque and human hosts: A review. *Clin. Infect. Dis.* 14:555, 1992.

Cytomegalovirus

Alford, C. A., Stagno, S., Pass, R. F., and Britt, W. J. Congenital and perinatal cytomegalovirus infections. *Rev. Infect. Dis.* 12(Suppl. 7): S745, 1990.
Centers for Disease Control. Surveillance of congenital cytomegalovirus disease. *CDC Surveillance Summaries,* M.M.W.R. 41:April 24, 1992.
Chou, S. Cytomegalovirus infection. *Curr. Opin. Infect. Dis.* 5:427, 1992.
Cytomegalovirus infections: Epidemiology, diagnosis, and treatment strategies. *Rev. Infect. Dis.* 12(Suppl. 7), 1990.
Demmler, G. J. Summary of a workshop on surveillance for congenital cytomegalovirus disease. *Rev. Infect. Dis.* 13:315, 1991.

Dres, W. L. Nonpulmonary manifestations of cytomegalovirus infection in immunocompromised patients. *Clin. Microbiol. Rev.* 5:204, 1992.

Smyth, R. L., Scott, J. P., Borysiewicz, L. K., et al. Cytomegalovirus infection in heart-lung transplant recipients: Risk factors, clinical association, and response to treatment. *J. Infect. Dis.* 164:1045, 1991.

Varicella-Zoster

Croen, K. D., and Straus, S. E. Varicella-zoster virus latency. *Annu. Rev. Microbiol.* 45:265, 1991.

The first international conference on the varicella-zoster virus. *J. Infect. Dis.* 166(Suppl. 1), 1992.

Herpes Simplex

Herpes simplex virus vaccine workshop. *Rev. Infect. Dis.* 13(Suppl. 11), 1991.

Libman, M. D., Dascal, A., Kramer, M. S., and Mendelson, J. Strategies for the prevention of neonatal infection with herpes simplex virus: A decision analysis. *Rev. Infect. Dis.* 13:1093, 1991.

Schwarcz, S. K., and Whittington, W. L. Sexual assault and sexually transmitted diseases: Detection and management. *Rev. Infect. Dis.* 12(Suppl. 6):S682, 1990.

Epstein-Barr Virus

Miller, G. The switch between latency and replication of Epstein-Barr virus. *J. Infect. Dis.* 161:833, 1990.

Okano, M., Matsumoto, S., Osato, T., et al. Severe chronic active Epstein-Barr virus infection syndrome. *Clin. Microbiol. Rev.* 4:129, 1991.

Okano, M., Thiele, G. M., Davis, J. R., Grierson, H. L., and Purtilo, D. T. Epstein-Barr virus and human disease: Recent advances in diagnosis. *Clin. Microbiol. Rev.* 1:300, 1988.

ADENOVIRUSES

Cruz, J. R., Caceres, P., Cano, F., Flores, J., Bartlett, A., and Torun, B. Adenovirus types 40 and 41 and rotaviruses associated with diarrhea in children from Guatemala. *J. Clin. Microbiol.* 28:1780, 1990.

Kotloff, K. L., Losonsky, G. A., et al. Enteric adenovirus infection and childhood diarrhea: An epidemiologic study in three clinical settings. *Pediatrics* 84:219, 1989.

PAPILLOMAVIRUSES

Brown, D. R., and Fife, K. H. Human papillomavirus infections of the genital tract. *Med. Clin. North Am.* 74:1455, 1990.

Cohen, B. A., Honig, P., and Androphy, E. Anogenital warts in children. *Arch. Dermatol.* 126:1575, 1990.

Cripe, T. P. Human papillomaviruses: Pediatric perspectives on a family of multi-faceted tumorigenic pathogens. *Pediatr. Infect. Dis. J.* 9:836, 1990.

Oriel, J. D. Clinical features and management of genital human papillomavirus infection. *Curr. Opin. Infect. Dis.* 5:18, 1992.

Roman, A., and Fife, K. Human papillomaviruses: Are we ready to type? *Clin. Microbiol. Rev.* 2:166, 1989.

PARVOVIRUSES

American Academy of Pediatrics, Committee on Infectious Disease. Parvovirus, erythema infectiosum and pregnancy. *Pediatrics* 85: 131, 1990.

Anand, A., Gray, E. S., Brown, T., Clewley, J. P., and Cohen, B. J. Human parvovirus infection and hydrops fetalis. *N. Engl. J. Med.* 316:183, 1987.

Anderson, L. J. Human parvoviruses. *J. Infect. Dis.* 161:603, 1990.

Centers for Disease Control. Risks associated with human parvovirus B19 infection. *M.M.W.R.* 38:81, 1989.

Gray, E. S. Parvovirus B19 infection in the fetus, newborn, and child. *Curr. Opin. Infect. Dis.* 4:485, 1991.

NORWALK VIRUS

Cukor, G., and Blackow, N. R. Human gastroenteritis. *Microbiol. Rev.* 54:157, 1984.

Kaplan, J. E., Gary, G. W., Baron, R. C., et al. Epidemiology of Norwalk gastroenteritis and the role of Norwalk virus in outbreaks of acute nonbacterial gastroenteritis. *Ann. Intern. Med.* 96:756, 1982.

Lieb, S., Gunn, R. A., Medina, R., et al. Norwalk virus gastroenteritis: An outbreak associated with a cafeteria at a college. *Am. J. Epidemiol.* 121:259, 1985.

MEASLES VIRUS

Atmar, R. L., Englund, J. A., and Hammill, H. Complications of measles during pregnancy. *Clin. Infect. Dis.* 14:217, 1992.

Centers for Disease Control. Measles at an international gymnastics competition—Indiana, 1991. *M.M.W.R.* 41(No. 7):109, 1992.

Centers for Disease Control. Measles prevention: Recommendations of the Immunization Practices Advisory Committee (ACIP). *M.M.W.R.* 38(No. S-9), 1989.

Markowitz, L. E., Preblud, S. R., Ornstein, W. A., et al. Patterns of transmission in measles outbreaks in the United States, 1985–1986. *N. Engl. J. Med.* 320:75, 1989.

Schlenker, T. L., Bain, C., Baughman, A. L., and Hadler, S. C. Measles herd immunity: The association of attack rates with immunization rates in preschool children. *Pediatr. Infect. Dis. J.* 10:883, 1991.

RUBELLA VIRUS

Centers for Disease Control. Congenital rubella syndrome among the Amish—Pennsylvania, 1991–1992. *M.M.W.R.* 41(No. 26):468, 1992.

Howson, C. P., Katz, M., Johnston, R. B., Jr., and Fineberg, H. V. Chronic arthritis after rubella vaccination. *Clin. Infect. Dis.* 15:307, 1992.

Lindegren, M. L., Fehrs, L. J., Hadler, S. C., and Hinman, A. R. Update: Rubella and congenital rubella syndrome, 1989–1990. *Epidemiol. Rev.* 13:341, 1991.

INFLUENZA VIRUSES

Ada, G. L., and Jones, P. D. The immune response to influenza infection. *Curr. Top. Microbiol. Immunol.* 128:1, 1986.

Couch, R. B., Kasel, J. A., Glezen, W. P., et al. Influenza: Its control in persons and populations. *J. Infect. Dis.* 153:431, 1986.

Douglas, R. G., Jr. Prophylaxis and treatment of influenza. *N. Engl. J. Med.* 322:443, 1990.

Henderson, I. M., Penny, D., and Hendy, M. D. Influenza viruses, comets, and the science of evolutionary trees. *J. Theor. Biol.* 140: 289, 1989.

Kilbourne, E. D. *Influenza.* New York: Plenum, 1987.

Scheiblauer, H., Reinacher, M., Tashiro, M., and Rott, R. Interactions between bacteria and influenza A virus in the development of influenza pneumonia. *J. Infect. Dis.* 166:783, 1992.

Shaw, M. W., Arden, N. H., and Maassab, H. F. New aspects of influenza viruses. *Clin. Microbiol. Rev.* 5:74, 1992.

Webster, R. G., Bean, W. J., Gorman, O. T., Chambers, T. M., and Kawaoka, Y. Evolution and ecology of influenza viruses. *Microbiol. Rev.* 56:152, 1992.

Webster, R. G., and Rott, R. Influenza A virus pathogenesis: The pivotal role of hemagglutinin. *Cell* 50:665, 1987.

POLIOVIRUS

Beale, A. J. Polio vaccines: Time for a change in immunization policy? *Lancet* 335:839, 1990.

Centers for Disease Control. Update: Progress toward eradicating poliomyelitis from the Americas. *M.M.W.R.* 39:557, 1990.

de Quadros, C. A., Andrus, J. K., et al. The eradication of poliomyelitis: Progress in the Americas. *Pediatr. Infect. Dis. J.* 10:222, 1991.

Hinman, A. R., Koplan, J. P., Orenstein, W. A., Brink, E. W., and Nkowane, B. M. Live or inactivated poliomyelitis vaccine: An analysis of benefits and risks. *Am. J. Public Health* 78:291, 1988.

Racaniello, V. R. Poliovirus neurovirulence. *Adv. Virus Res.* 34:217, 1988.

Sabin, A. B. Pathogenesis of poliomyelitis: Reappraisal in light of new data. *Science* 123:1151, 1956.

Strebel, P. M., Sutter, R. W., Cochi, S. L., et al. Epidemiology of poliomyelitis in the United States one decade after the last reported case of indigenous wild virus-associated disease. *Clin. Infect. Dis.* 14:568, 1992.

NONPOLIO ENTEROVIRUSES

Bowles, N. E., Sewry, C. A., Dubowitz, V., and Archard, L. C. Dermatomyositis, polymyositis, and coxsackie-B virus infection. *Lancet* 1:1004, 1987.

Kaplan, M. H., Klein, S. W., McPhee, J., and Harper, R. G. Group B coxsackievirus infections in infants younger than three months of age: A serious childhood illness. *Rev. Infect. Dis.* 5:1019, 1983.

Leslie, K. R., Blay, K. R., Haisch, C., Lodge, A., Weller, A., and Huber, S. Clinical and experimental aspects of viral myocarditis. *Clin. Microbiol. Rev.* 2:191, 1989.

Melnick, J. L. Enteroviruses: Polioviruses, coxsackieviruses, echoviruses, and newer enteroviruses. In B. N. Fields and D. M. Knipe, eds. *Virology.* New York: Raven, 1990.

Moore, M. Enteroviral disease in the United States, 1970–1979. *J. Infect. Dis.* 146:103, 1982.

Wilfert, C. M., Lehrman, S. N., and Katz, S. L. Enteroviruses and meningitis. *Pediatr. Infect. Dis. J.* 2:333, 1983.

RHINOVIRUSES

Couch, R. B. Rhinoviruses. In B. N. Fields, D. M. Knipe, R. M. Chanock, M. S. Hirsch, J. L. Melnick, T. P. Monath, and B. Roizman, eds. *Fields Virology.* New York: Raven, 1990.

Hendley, J. O., and Gwaltney, J. M., Jr. Mechanisms of transmission of rhinovirus infections. *Epidemiol. Rev.* 10:242, 1988.

Krilov, L. L., Pierik, E., et al. The association of rhinoviruses with lower respiratory tract diseases in hospitalized patients. *J. Med. Virol.* 19:345, 1986.

Tyrell, D. A. Therapy for rhinovirus. *Curr. Opin. Infect. Dis.* 4:809, 1991.

PARAINFLUENZA VIRUSES

Chanock, R. M., and McIntosh, K. Parainfluenzaviruses. In B. N. Fields, D. M. Knipe, R. M. Chanock, M. S. Hirsch, J. L. Melnick, T. P. Monath, and B. Roizman, eds. *Fields Virology.* New York: Raven, 1990.

Hall, C. B., Geiman, J. M., Breese, B. B., and Douglas, R. G., Jr. Parainfluenza viral infections in children: Correlation of shedding with clinical manifestations. *J. Pediatr.* 91:194, 1977.

Heilman, C. A. Respiratory syncytial and parainfluenza viruses. *J. Infect. Dis.* 161:402, 1990.

Hotez, P. J., Goldstein, B., Ziegler, J., Doveikis, S. A., and Pasternak, M. Adult respiratory distress syndrome associated with parainfluenza virus type 1 in children. *Pediatr. Infect. Dis. J.* 9:751, 1990.

Jackson, B. M., Smith, H. D., and Sikes, R. K. Parainfluenza outbreak in a retardation facility. *Am. J. Infect. Control* 18:128, 1990.

Morrison-Smith, J. Parainfluenza infections in the elderly 1976–1982. *B.M.J.* 287:1619, 1983.

Singh-Naz, N. M., Willy, M., and Riggs, N. Outbreak of parainfluenzavirus type 3 in a neonatal nursery. *Pediatr. Infect. Dis. J.* 9:31, 1990.

Welliver, R., Wong, D. T., Choi, T. S., and Ogra, P. L. Natural history of parainfluenza virus infection in childhood. *J. Pediatr.* 101:180, 1982.

RESPIRATORY SYNCYTIAL VIRUS

Abzug, M. J., Beam, A. C., Gyorkos, E. A., and Levin, M. J. Viral pneumonia in the first month of life. *Pediatr. Infect. Dis. J.* 9:881, 1990.

Anderson, L. J., Parker, R. A., and Strikas, R. L. Association between respiratory syncytial virus outbreaks and lower respiratory tract deaths of infants and young children. *J. Infect. Dis.* 161:640, 1991.

Chandwani, S., Borkowsky, W., Krasinski, K., and Welliver, R. Respiratory syncytial virus infection in human immunodeficiency virus-infected children. *J. Pediatr.* 117:251, 1990.

Englund, J. A., Anderson, L. J., and Rhame, R. S. Nosocomial transmission of respiratory syncytial virus in immunocompromised adults. *J. Clin. Microbiol.* 29:115, 1991.

Hall, C. B., Powell, K. R., et al. Respiratory syncytial virus infection in children with compromised immune function. *N. Engl. J. Med.* 315:77, 1986.

McKenzie, S. A. Respiratory tract infections in children. *Curr. Opin. Infect. Dis.* 4:500, 1991.

Welliver, R. C. Detection, pathogenesis, and therapy of respiratory syncytial virus infections. *Clin. Microbiol. Rev.* 1:27, 1989.

RABIES VIRUS

Centers for Disease Control. Human rabies—California, 1992. *M.M.W.R.* 41(No. 26):461, 1992.

Halstead, S. B. Rabies and viral hemorrhagic fevers. *Curr. Opin. Infect. Dis.* 4:296, 1991.

Research towards rabies prevention. *Rev. Infect. Dis.* 10(Suppl. 4), 1988.

Smith, J. S., Fishbein, D. B., Rupprecht, C. F., and Clark, K. Unexplained rabies in three immigrants in the United States: A virologic investigation. *N. Engl. J. Med.* 324:205, 1991.

HEMORRHAGIC FEVER VIRUSES

Bruno, P., Hassel, L. H., Brown, J., Tanner, W., and Lau, A. The protein manifestations of hemorrhagic fever with renal syndrome—A retrospective review of 26 cases from Korea. *Ann. Intern. Med.* 113:385, 1990.

Centers for Disease Control. Outbreak of acute illness—Southwestern United States, 1993. *M.M.W.R.* 42:421, 1993.

Centers for Disease Control. Ebola virus infection in imported primates—Virginia. *M.M.W.R.* 38:831, 1989.

Cosgriff, T. M. Mechanism of disease in hantavirus infection: Pathophysiology of hemorrhagic fever with renal syndrome. *Rev. Infect. Dis.* 13:97, 1991.

Gear, J. H. S. Clinical aspects of African viral hemorrhagic fevers. *Rev. Infect. Dis.* 11(Suppl. 4):S777, 1989.

Henchal, E. A., and Putnak, J. R. The dengue viruses. *Clin. Microbiol. Rev.* 3:376, 1990.

Holmes, G. P., McCormick, J. B., Trock, S. C., et al. Lassa fever in the United States: Investigation of a case and new guidelines for management. *N. Engl. J. Med.* 323:1120, 1990.

Johnson, K. M., and Monath, T. P. Imported Lassa fever: Reexamining the algorithms. *N. Engl. J. Med.* 323:1139, 1990.

LeDuc, J. W. Epidemiology of hemorrhagic fever viruses. *Rev. Infect. Dis.* 11(Suppl. 4):S730, 1989.

Peters, C. J., Liu, C-T., Anderson, G. W., Morrill, J. C., and Jahrling, P. B. Pathogenesis of viral hemorrhagic fevers: Rift Valley fever and Lassa fever contrasted. *Rev. Infect. Dis.* 11(Suppl. 4):S743, 1989.

Poland, J. D., Cropp, C. B., Craven, R. B., and Monath, T. P. Evaluation of the potency and safety of inactivated Japanese encephalitis vaccine in U.S. inhabitants. *J. Infect. Dis.* 161:878, 1990.

Swanepoel, R., Gill, D. E., Sheperd, A. J., et al. The clinical pathology of Crimean-Congo hemorrhagic fever. *Rev. Infect. Dis.* 11(Suppl. 4):S794, 1989.

Yanagihara, R. Hantavirus infection in the United States: Epizootiology and epidemiology. *Rev. Infect. Dis.* 12:449, 1990.

ARBOVIRUSES

Centers for Disease Control. Arboviral disease—United States, 1991. *M.M.W.R.* 41:543, 1992.

Centers for Disease Control. Dengue epidemic: Peru, 1990. *M.M.W.R.* 40:145, 1990.

Centers for Disease Control. St. Louis encephalitis outbreak—Arkansas, 1991. *M.M.W.R.* 40:605, 1991.

Centers for Disease Control. Imported dengue—United States. *M.M.W.R.* 40:519, 1991.

Centers for Disease Control. Update: Filovirus infection among persons with occupational exposure to nonhuman primates. *M.M.W.R.* 39:266, 1990.

Guzman, M. G., Kouri, G. P., Bravo, J., et al. Dengue hemorrhagic fever in Cuba, 1981: A retrospective seroepidemiologic study. *Am. J. Trop. Med. Hyg.* 42:179, 1990.

Henchal, E. A., and Putnak, J. R. The dengue viruses. *Clin. Microbiol. Rev.* 3:376, 1990.

Monath, T. P., ed. *The Arboviruses: Epidemiology and Ecology.* Boca Raton, FL: CRC Press, 1989.

Porterfield, J. S. Yellow fever in West Africa: A retrospective glance. *B.M.J.* 299:23, 1989.

Tsai, T. F. Arboviral infections in the United States. *Infect. Dis. Clin. North Am.* 5:73, 1991.

ROTAVIRUSES AND OTHER AGENTS OF GASTROINTESTINAL DISEASE

Blacklow, N., and Greenberg, H. Viral gastroenteritis. *N. Engl. J. Med.* 325:252, 1991.

Esahli, H. K., Breback, R., Bennet, A., Ehrnst, M., Eriksson, M., and Hedlund, K. Astroviruses as a cause of nosocomial outbreaks of infant diarrhea. *Pediatr. Infect. Dis. J.* 10:511, 1991.

Glass, R. I., Lew, J. F., Gangarosa, R. E., LeBaron, C. W., and Ho, M-S. Estimates of morbidity and mortality rates for diarrheal disease in American children. *J. Pediatr.* 118:S27, 1991.

Haffejee, I. E. Neonatal rotavirus infections. *Rev. Infect. Dis.* 13:957, 1991.

Herrmann, J. E., Taylor, D. N., Echeverría, P., and Blacklow, N. R. Astroviruses as a cause of gastroenteritis in children. *N. Engl. J. Med.* 324:1757, 1991.

LeBaron, C. W., Lew, J., Glass, R. I., et al. Annual rotavirus epidemic patterns in North America. *J.A.M.A.* 264:983, 1990.

Matson, D. O., and Estes, M. K. Impact of rotavirus infection at a large pediatric hospital. *J. Infect. Dis.* 162:598, 1990.

Matson, D. O., Estes, M. K., Glass, R. I., et al. Human calicivirus-associated diarrhea in children attending day care centers. *J. Infect. Dis.* 159:71, 1989.

Matson, D. O., Estes, M. K., Tanaka, T., Bartlett, A. V., and Pickering, L. K. Asymptomatic human calicivirus infection in a day care center. *Pediatr. Infect. Dis. J.* 9:190, 1990.

HUMAN IMMUNODEFICIENCY VIRUS AND AIDS

In addition to the publications listed below, there are journals that deal only with HIV and AIDS: *AIDS* and *Journal of Acquired Immune Deficiency Syndromes.*

Aral, S. O., and Holmes, K. K. Sexually transmitted diseases in the AIDS era. *Sci. Am.* 264(1):62, 1991.

Brennan, T. A. Transmission of the human immunodeficiency virus in the health care setting: Time for action (editorial). *N. Engl. J. Med.* 324:1504, 1991.

Centers for Disease Control. Reports and recommendations. Guidelines for prophylaxis against *Pneumocystis carinii* pneumonia infected with human immunodeficiency virus. *M.M.W.R.* 41(No. RR-4):1, 1992.

Centers for Disease Control. Recommendations and reports. 1993 revised classification system for HIV infection and expanded surveillance case definition for AIDS among adolescents and adults. *M.M.W.R.* 41(No. RR-17):December 18, 1992.

Clark, S. J., Saag, M. S., et al. High titers of cytopathic virus in plasma of patients with symptomatic primary HIV-1 infection. *N. Engl. J. Med.* 324:954, 1991.

Farizo, K. M., Buehler, J. W., Chamberland, M. E., et al. Spectrum of disease in persons with human immunodeficiency virus infection in the United States. *J.A.M.A.* 267:1798, 1992.

Fauci, A. S. The human immunodeficiency virus: Infectivity and mechanisms of pathogenesis. *Science* 239:617, 1988.

Green, W. C. The molecular biology of human immunodeficiency virus type 1 infection. *N. Engl. J. Med.* 324:308, 1991.

Hamilton, J. D., Hartigan, P. M., Simberkoff, M. S., et al. A controlled trial of early versus late treatment with zidovudine in symptomatic human immunodeficiency virus infection. *N. Engl. J. Med.* 326: 437, 1992.

Lee, B. L., and Safrin, S. Drug interactions and toxicities in patients with AIDS. *Curr. Opin. Infect. Dis.* 5:231, 1992.

Levy, J. A. Pathogenesis of human immunodeficiency virus infection. *Microbiol. Rev.* 57:183, 1993.

Levy, J. A. Human immunodeficiency viruses and the pathogenesis of AIDS. *J.A.M.A.* 261:2997, 1989.

Lifson, A. R., Hessol, N. A., and Rutherford, G. W. Progression and clinical outcome of infection due to human immunodeficiency virus. *Clin. Infect. Dis.* 14:966, 1992.

Merigan, T. C., and Katzenstein, D. A. Relation of the pathogenesis of human immunodeficiency virus infection to various strategies for its control. *Rev. Infect. Dis.* 13:292, 1991.

Pantaelo, G., Graziosi, C., Butini, L., Pizzo, P. A., Schnitman, S. M., Kotler, D. P., and Fauci, A. S. Lymphoid organs function as major reservoirs for human immunodeficiency virus. *Proc. Natl. Acad. Sci. U.S.A.* 88:9838, 1991.

Phair, J. P., and Wolinsky, S. Diagnosis of infection with the human immunodeficiency virus. *Clin. Infect. Dis.* 15:13, 1992.

Scott, G. B. HIV infection in children: Clinical features and management. *J. Acquir. Immun. Defic. Syndr.* 4:109, 1991.

Sheppard, H. W., and Ascher, M. S. The natural history and pathogenesis of HIV infection. *Annu. Rev. Microbiol.* 46:533, 1992.

Stein, D. S., Korvick, J. A., and Vermund, S. H. $CD4^+$ lymphocyte cell enumeration for prediction of clinical course of human immunodeficiency virus disease: A review. *J. Infect. Dis.* 165:352, 1992.

Tsoukas, C. M., and Bernard, N. F. Markers predicting progression of human immunodeficiency virus-related disease. *Clin. Microbiol. Rev.* 7:14, 1994.

Walker, C. K., and Sweet, R. L. Pregnancy and pediatric HIV infection. *Curr. Opin. Infect. Dis.* 5:201, 1992.

THE HEPATITIS VIRUSES

Aach, R. D., Stevens, C. E., Hollinger, F. B., et al. Hepatitis C virus infection in post-transfusion hepatitis. *N. Engl. J. Med.* 325:1329, 1992.

Alter, M. J. Hepatitis-C: A sleeping giant. *Am. J. Med.* 91(Suppl. 3B): S112, 1991.

Alter, M. J., Hadler, S. C., Judson, F. N., et al. Risk factors for acute non-A non-B hepatitis in the United States and association with heptatis C virus infection. *J.A.M.A.* 264:2231, 1990.

Barbara, J. A. J. Hepatitis C and blood transfusion. *Curr. Opin. Infect. Dis.* 5:536, 1992.

Centers for Disease Control. Universal precautions for prevention of transmission of human immunodeficiency virus, hepatitis B virus, and other bloodborne pathogens in health-care settings. *M.M.W.R.* 37:377, 1988.

Centers for Disease Control. Enterically transmitted non-A, non-B hepatitis—East Africa. *M.M.W.R.* 36:241, 1987.

Centers for Disease Control. Protection against viral hepatitis. Recommendations of the Immunization Practices Advisory Committee (ACIP). *M.M.W.R.* 39(No. RR-2):February 9, 1990.

Centers for Disease Control. Public health service inter-agency guidelines for screening donors of blood, plasma, organs, tissues, and semen for evidence of hepatitis B and hepatitis C. *M.M.W.R.* 40(No. RR-4):April 19, 1991.

Centers for Disease Control. Recommendations for preventing transmission of human immunodeficiency virus and hepatitis B virus to patients during exposure-prone invasive procedures. *M.M.W.R.* 40(No. RR-8):July 12, 1991.

Eddleston, A. Hepatitis. *Lancet* 335:982, 1990.

Kiyosawa, K., Sodeyama, T., Tanaka, E., et al. Hepatitis-C in hospital employees with needlestick injuries. *Ann. Intern. Med.* 115:367, 1991.

Mbithi, J. N., Springthorpe, V. S., Boulet, J. R., and Sattar, S. A. Survival of hepatitis A virus on human hands and its transfer on contact with animate and inanimate surfaces. *J. Clin. Microbiol.* 30: 757, 1992.

Periera, B. J. G., Milford, E. L., Kirkman, R. I., and Levy, A. S. Transmission of hepatitis C virus by organ transplantation. *N. Engl. J. Med.* 325:454, 1991.

Shapiro, C. N., McCaig, L. F., Gensheimer, K. F., et al. Hepatitis B virus transmission between children in day care. *Pediatr. Infect. Dis. J.* 8:870, 1989.

Sherker, A. H., and Marion, P. L. Hepadnaviruses and hepatocellular carcinoma. *Annu. Rev. Microbiol.* 45:475, 1991.

Sherlock, S. Hepatitis B—The disease. *Vaccine* 8(Suppl.):S69, 1989.

Stevens, C. E., Taylor, P. E., Pindyck, J., et al. Epidemiology of hepatitis C virus. *J.A.M.A.* 263:49, 1990.

Taylor, J. M. The structure and replication of hepatitis delta virus. *Annu. Rev. Microbiol.* 46:253, 1992.

Chapter 33. The Pathogenic Fungi

Armstrong, D. Treatment of opportunistic fungal infections. *Clin. Infect. Dis.* 16:1, 1993.

Bartlett, M. S., and Smith, J. W. *Pneumocystis carinii,* an opportunist in immunocompromised patients. *Clin. Microbiol. Rev.* 4:137, 1991.

Bradsher, R. W. Blastomycosis. *Clin. Infect. Dis.* 14(Suppl. 1):S82, 1992.

Brummer, E., Castaneda, E., and Restrepo, A. Paracoccidioidomycosis: An update. *Clin. Microbiol. Rev.* 6:89, 1993.

Centers for Disease Control. Coccidioidomycosis—United States, 1991–1992. *M.M.W.R.* 42:21, 1993.

Connor, E., Bagarazzi, M., Mcerry, G., et al. Clinical and laboratory correlates of *Pneumocystis carinii* pneumonia in children infected with HIV. *J.A.M.A.* 265:1693, 1991.

Couroux, P., Schieven, B. C., and Hussain, Z. *Pneumocystis carinii. ASM News* 59:179, 1993.

de Repentigny, L. Serodiagnosis of candidiasis, aspergillosis, and cryptococcosis. *Clin. Infect. Dis.* 14(Suppl. 1):S11, 1992.

Diamond, R. D. The growing problems of mycoses in patients infected with the human immunodeficiency virus. *Rev. Infect. Dis.* 13:480, 1991.

Einstein, H. E., and Johnson, R. H. Coccidioidomycosis: New aspects of epidemiology and therapy. *Clin. Infect. Dis.* 16:349, 1993.

Focus on fungal infections: An update on diagnosis and treatment. *Clin. Infect. Dis.* 14(Suppl. 1), 1992.

Galgiani, J. N. Coccidioidomycosis: Changes in clinical expression, serologic diagnosis, and therapeutic options. *Clin. Infect. Dis.* 14(Suppl 1):S100, 1992.

Gamis, A. S., Gudnason, T., Giebink, G. S., and Ramsay, N. K. C. Disseminated infection with *Fusarium* in recipients of bone marrow transplants. *Rev. Infect. Dis.* 13:1077, 1991.

Girard, P-M., and Saimot, A. G. Prophylaxis of *Pneumocystis carinii* pneumonia in human immunodeficiency virus-infected adults. *Curr. Opin. Infect. Dis.* 5:827, 1992.

Ingram, C. W., Sennesh, J., Cooper, J. N., and Perfect, J. R. Disseminated zygomycosis: Report of four cases and review. *Rev. Infect. Dis.* 11:741, 1989.

Kurup, V. P., and Kumar, A. Immunodiagnosis of aspergillosis. *Clin. Microbiol. Rev.* 4:439, 1991.

Leen, C. L. S., and Brettle, R. P. Fungal infections in drug users. *J. Antimicrob. Chemother.* 28:83, 1991.

Levitz, S. M. Overview of host defenses in fungal infections. *Clin. Infect. Dis.* 14(Suppl. 1):S37, 1992.

Levitz, S. M. The ecology of *Cryptococcus neoformans* and the epidemiology of cryptococcosis. *Rev. Infect. Dis.* 13:1163, 1991.

Marcon, M. J. Human infections due to *Malassezia* spp. *Clin. Microbiol. Rev.* 5:101, 1992.

Maresca, B., and Kobayashi, G. S. Dimorphism in *Histoplasma capsulatum:* A model for study of cell differentiation in pathogenic fungi. *Microbiol. Rev.* 53:186, 1989.

Murphy, J. W. Mechanisms of natural resistance to human pathogenic fungi. *Annu. Rev. Microbiol.* 45:509, 1991.

Paparella, S. F., Parry, R. L., MacGillivray, D. C., et al. Hospital-acquired mucormycosis. *Clin. Infect. Dis.* 14:350, 1992.

Richardson, S. E., Bannatyne, R. M., Summerbell, R. C., et al. Disseminated fusarial infection in the immunocompromised host. *Rev. Infect. Dis.* 10:1171, 1988.

Rinaldi, M. G. Problems in the diagnosis of invasive fungal diseases. *Rev. Infect. Dis.* 13:439, 1991.

Rippon, J. W., ed. *Medical Mycology: The Pathogenic Fungi and the Pathogenic Actinomycetes.* Philadelphia: Saunders, 1988.

Saral, R. *Candida* and *Aspergillus* infections in immunocompromised patients: An overview. *Rev. Infect. Dis.* 13:487, 1991.

Soll, D. R. High-frequency switching in *Candida albicans. Clin. Microbiol. Rev.* 5:183, 1992.

Sugar, A. M. Mucormycosis. *Clin. Infect. Dis.* 14(Suppl. 1):S126, 1992.

Vartivarian, S. E. Virulence properties and nonimmune pathogenic mechanisms of fungi. *Clin. Infect. Dis.* 14(Suppl 1):S30, 1992.

Vincent, T., Galgiani, J. N., Huppert, M., and Salkin, D. The natural history of coccidioidal meningitis: VA-armed forces cooperative studies, 1955–1958. *Clin. Infect. Dis.* 16:247, 1993.

Wheat, L. J. Histoplasmosis in Indianapolis. *Clin. Infect. Dis.* 14(Suppl. 1):S91, 1992.

White, M., Cirrincione, C., Blevins, A., and Armstrong, D. Cryptococcal meningitis outcome in patients with neoplastic disease. *J. Infect. Dis.* 165:960, 1992.

Chapter 34. Protozoa, Helminths, and Arthropods

Adam, R. D. The biology of *Giardia* spp. *Microbiol. Rev.* 55:706, 1991.

Ahmed, M, McAdam, K. P. W. J., Sturm, A. W., and Hussain, R. Systemic manifestations of invasive amebiasis. *Clin. Infect. Dis.* 15: 974, 1992.

Bailey, T. M., and Schantz, P. M. Trends in the incidence and transmission patterns of trichinosis in humans in the United States: Comparisons of the periods 1975–1981 and 1982–1986. *Rev. Infect. Dis.* 12:5, 1990.

Berman, J. D. Chemotherapy for leishmaniasis: Biochemical mechanisms, clinical efficacy, and future strategies. *Rev. Infect. Dis.* 10: 560, 1988.

Boros, D. L. Immunopathology of *Schistosoma mansoni* infections. *Clin. Microbiol. Rev.* 2:250, 1989.

Bruckner, D. A. Amebiasis. *Clin. Microbiol. Rev.* 5:356, 1992.

Centers for Disease Control. Locally acquired neurocysticercosis: North Carolina, Massachusetts, and South Carolina, 1989–1991. *M.M.W.R.* 41:1, 1992.

Chang, K-P., and Chaudhuri, G. Molecular determinants of *Leishmania* virulence. *Annu. Rev. Microbiol.* 44:499, 1990.

Cogswell, F. B. The hypnozoite and relapse in primate malaria. *Clin. Microbiol. Rev.* 5:26, 1992.

Craun, G. Waterborne giardiasis in the United States, 1965–1984. *Lancet* 2:513, 1986.

Current, W. L. The biology of *Cryptosporidium. ASM News* 54:605, 1988.

Del Brutto, O. H., and Sotelo, J. Neurocysticercosis: An update. *Rev. Infect. Dis.* 10:1075, 1988.

DeVault, G. A., King, J. W., Rohr, M. S., et al. Opportunistic infections with *Strongyloides stercoralis* in renal transplantation. *Rev. Infect. Dis.* 12:653, 1990.
Earnst, M. P., Reller, L. B., Filley, C. M., and Grek, A. J. Neurocysticercosis in the United States: 35 cases and a review. *Rev. Infect. Dis.* 9:961, 1987.
Ellis, C. J. Prevention and treatment of malaria. *Curr. Opin. Infect. Dis.* 4:834, 1991.
Fayer, R., and Ungar, B. L. P. *Cryptosporidium* spp. and cryptosporidiosis. *Microbiol. Rev.* 50:458, 1986.
Gadbaw, J. J., Anderson, J. F., Carter, M. L., and Hadler, J. L. Babesiosis—Connecticut. *M.M.W.R.* 38:649, 1989.
Genta, R. M. The global epidemiology of strongyloidiasis: Critical review with epidemiologic insights into the prevention of disseminated disease. *Rev. Infect. Dis.* 11:757, 1989.
Hagar, J. M., and Rahimtoola, S. H. Chagas' disease in the United States. *N. Engl. J. Med.* 325:763, 1991.
Haque, R., Hall, A., and Tzipori, S. Zymodemes of *Entamoeba histolytica* in Dhaka, Bangladesh. *Ann. Trop. Med. Parasitol.* 84:629, 1990.
Herwaldt, B. L., Arana, B. A., and Navin, T. R. The natural history of cutaneous leishmaniasis in Guatemala. *J. Infect. Dis.* 165:518, 1992.
Hillyer, G. V., and Rajan, T. V. Schistosomiasis, filariasis, and onchocerciasis. *Curr. Opin. Infect. Dis.* 5:326, 1992.
Jascobs, F., Depierreux, M., Goldman, M., et al. Role of bronchoalveolar lavage in the diagnosis of disseminated toxoplasmosis. *Rev. Infect. Dis.* 13:637, 1991.
Jones, T. R., and Hoffman, S. L. Immunology and pathogenic mechanisms of malaria. *Curr. Opin. Infect. Dis.* 5:310, 1992.
Kain, K. C. Antimalarial chemotherapy in the age of drug resistance. *Curr. Opin. Infect. Dis.* 6:803, 1993.
Lossick, J. G. Treatment of sexually transmitted vaginosis/vaginitis. *Rev. Infect. Dis.* 12(Suppl.):S665, 1990.
Luft, B. J., and Remington, J. S. Toxoplasmic encephalitis in AIDS. *Clin. Infect. Dis.* 15:211, 1992.
Ma, P., Govinda, S., Visvesvara, S., et al. *Naegleria* and *Acanthamoeba* infections: Review. *Rev. Infect. Dis.* 12:490, 1990.
Marciano-Cabral, F. Biology of *Naegleria*. *Microbiol. Rev.* 52:114, 1988.
McAuley, J. B., Michelson, M. K., and Schantz, P. M. Trichinella infection in travelers. *J. Infect. Dis.* 164:1013, 1991.
McCabe, R. E., Brooks, R. G., Dorfman, R. F., and Remington, J. S. Clinical spectrum in 107 cases of toxoplasmic lymphadenopathy. *Rev. Infect. Dis.* 9:754, 1987.
Meldrum, S. C., Birkhead, G. S., White, D. J., Benach, J. L., and Morse, D. L. Human babesiosis in New York State: An epidemiological description of 136 cases. *Clin. Infect. Dis.* 15:1019, 1992.
Nanduri, J., and Kazura, J. W. Clinical and laboratory aspects of filariasis. *Clin. Microbiol. Rev.* 2:39, 1989.
Navin, T. R., and Juranek, D. D. Cryptosporidiosis: Clinical, epidemiologic, and parasitologic review. *Rev. Infect. Dis.* 6:313, 1984.
Nutman, T. B. Experimental infection of humans with filariae. *Rev. Infect. Dis.* 13:1018, 1991.
Orrozco, E. Pathogenesis in amebiasis. *Infect. Agents Dis.* 1:19, 1992.
Petersen, C. Cryptosporidiosis in patients infected with the human immunodeficiency virus. *Clin. Infect. Dis.* 15:903, 1992.
Philipp, M., Davis, T. B., Storey, N., and Carlow, C. K. S. Immunity in filariasis: Perspectives for vaccine development. *Annu. Rev. Microbiol.* 42:685, 1988.
Pomeroy, C., and Filce, G. A. Pulmonary toxoplasmosis: A review. *Clin. Infect. Dis.* 14:863, 1992.
Reed, S. L. Amebiasis: An update. *Clin. Infect. Dis.* 14:385, 1992.
Reed, S. L., Wessel, D. W., and Davis, C. E. *Entamoeba histolytica* infection and AIDS. *Am. J. Med.* 90:269, 1991.
Schaefer, J. W., and Khan, M. Y. Echinococcosis (hydatid disease): Lessons from experience with 59 patients. *Rev. Infect. Dis.* 13:243, 1991.
Schieven, B. C., Brennan, M., and Hussain, Z. *Echinococcus granulosus* hydatid disease. *ASM News* 57:407, 1991.
Shaffer, N., Grau, G. E., Hedberg, K., et al. Tumor necrosis factor and severe malaria. *J. Infect. Dis.* 163:96, 1991.
Soave, R., and Johnson, W. D., Jr. *Cryptosporidium* and *Isospora belli* infections. *J. Infect. Dis.* 133:471, 1988.
Tanowitz, H. B., Kirchhoff, L. V., Simon, D., Morris, S. A., Weiss, L. M., and Wittner, M. Chagas' disease. *Clin. Microbiol. Rev.* 5:400, 1992.
Wiley, C. A. Safrin, R. E., Davis, C. E., et al. *Acanthamoeba* meningoencephalitis in a patient with AIDS. *J. Infect. Dis.* 155:130, 1987.
Wolfe, M. S. Giardiasis. *Clin. Microbiol. Rev.* 5:93, 1992.
Wolner-Hanssen, P., Krieger, J. N., Stevens, C. E., et al. Clinical manifestations of vaginal trichomoniasis. *J.A.M.A.* 261:571, 1989.
Wyler, D. J. Malaria: Overview and update. *Clin. Infect. Dis.* 16:449, 1993.

Chapter 35. Hospital-Acquired Diseases

Bennett, J. V., and Brachman, P. S., ed. *Hospital Infections*, 3rd ed. Boston: Little, Brown, 1992.
Bisno, A. L., and Waldvogel, F. A., ed. *Infections Associated with Indwelling Medical Devices.* Washington, D.C.: American Society for Microbiology, 1989.
Centers for Disease Control. Update: Universal precautions for prevention of transmission of human immunodeficiency virus, hepatitis virus and other blood-borne pathogens in health care settings. *M.M.W.R.* 37:377, 1988.
Centers for Disease Control. Nosocomial infection and pseudoinfection from contaminated endoscopes and bronchoscopes: Wisconsin and Missouri. *M.M.W.R.* 40:675, 1991.
Emori, T. G., and Gaynes, R. P. An overview of nosocomial infections, including the role of the microbiology laboratory. *Clin. Microbiol. Rev.* 6:428, 1993.
Glenister, H., Taylor, L., Bartlett, C., Cooke, M., Sedgwick, J., and Leigh, D. An assessment of selective surveillance methods for detecting hospital-acquired infection. *Am. J. Med.* 91(Suppl. 3B):121S, 1991.
Goldmann, D. A., and Pier, G. B. Pathogenesis of infections related to intravascular catheterization. *Clin. Microbiol. Rev.* 6:176, 1993.
Jarvis, W. R. Nosocomial outbreaks: The Centers for Disease Control's Hospital Infections Program experience, 1980–1990. *Am. J. Med.* 91(Suppl. B):101S–106S, 1991.
Jarvis, W. R., and Martone, W. J. Predominant pathogens in hospital infections. *J. Antimicrob. Chemother.* 29(Suppl A):19, 1992.
Maki, D. G., Ringer, M., and Alvarado, C. J. Prospective randomized trial of povidone-iodine, alcohol and chlorhexidine for prevention of infection with central venous and arterial catheters. *Lancet* 338: 339, 1991.
Raad, I. I., and Bodey, G. P. Infectious complications of indwelling vascular catheters. *Clin. Infect. Dis.* 15:197, 1992.
Rutala, W. A. APIC guideline for selection and use of disinfectants. *Am. J. Infect. Control* 18:99, 1990.
Schaberg, D. R., Culver, D. H., and Gaynes, R. P. Major trends in the microbial etiology of nosocomial infection. *Am. J. Med.* 91(Suppl. B):72, 1991.
Stamm, W. E. Catheter-associated urinary tract infections: Epidemiology, pathogenicity and prevention. *Am. J. Med.* 91(Suppl. B): 865, 1991.
Wenzel, R. P., and Pfaller, M. A. Handwashing: Efficacy versus acceptance; a brief essay. *J. Hosp. Infect.* 18(Suppl. B):65, 1991.

Index

ABO system, 571–572
  antibodies, 571
  blood group typing, 571
  disputed parentage and, 572
  genetics, 571
  transfusion and, 571
Abscess, defined, 244
Acanthamoeba
  acanthamoebiasis caused by, 507
  keratitis caused by, 508
Acanthamoebiasis, 507
N-acetylglucosamine, 19, 20
N-acetylmuramic acid, 19, 20
Achromobacter, pathogenesis, 314
Acid-fast bacilli, 331
Acid-fast stain, 558
Acid hydrolase
  Coxiella resistance to, 138
  phagocytosis and, 136
Acinetobacter
  characteristics of, 270
  pathogenesis, 314
Acquired human immunodeficiency syndrome (AIDS). *See also* Human immunodeficiency virus
  bacillary angiomatosis and, 362
  case definition, 446
  chronic or asymptomatic stage, 444–446
  crisis stage, 446
  dementia complex, 446
  epidemiology, 447
  Epstein-Barr virus and, 418
  laboratory diagnosis, 447–448
  pediatric, 446–447
  prevention, 449
  primary or acute stage, 444
  treatment, 448–449
  tuberculosis and, 337
Acquired immunodeficiency(ies), 185
Acquired immunodeficiency syndrome, *Pneumocystis* pneumonia and, 490–491
Acremonium kiliense, mycetoma caused by, 480
Acridines, mutation caused by, 72
Actinobacillus actinomycetemcomitans, pathogenesis, 375
Actinomyces, characteristics of, 372
Actinomyces israelii, 369
Actinomyces naeslundii, caries and, 372
Actinomyces viscosus, caries and, 372
Actinomycetes, 368–373
Actinomycosis
  characteristics, 369
  laboratory diagnosis, 369–370
  pathogenesis, 369
  treatment, 370–371
Active site, enzyme, 30
Active transport, defined, 17
Acute glomerulonephritis, *Streptococcus pyogenes*, 254–255
Acute disease, 221–222
Acyclovir
  activity of, 114
  cytomegalovirus treatment and, 413
Acyl carrier protein, 42
Adenosine deaminase deficiency disease, 184
  treatment for, 185
Adenosine triphosphate. *See* ATP
Adenovirus
  epidemiology, 419
  laboratory diagnosis, 420
  morphology, 419
  pathogenesis, 419
  syndromes associated with, 419
  treatment and prevention, 420
Adenylate cyclase
  Bacillus anthracis, 273
  bacterial virulence and, 216
  Bordetella pertussis infection and, 325
  cholera infection and, 316
  in disease process, 214
Adherence, capsule and slime layer function in, 22
Adhesins
  biofilms and, 213
  in disease process, 211–212
Adjuvant, defined, 144
Aedes aegypti
  dengue fever and, 441
  yellow fever and, 440
Aedes albopictus, dengue fever and, 441
Aerobactin, *Escherichia coli*, 296
Aerobes
  obligate
    glucose metabolism in, 36
    oxygen requirement of, 50
Aerobic respiration, 38–40
Aeromonas
  characteristics, 319
  differentiation from *Vibrio*, 317
  pathogenesis, 318–319
Aerotaxis, defined, 22
Aerotolerance, bacterial, 50
Aflatoxin, *Aspergillus* species and, 492
African trypanosomiasis
  epidemiology, 511
  laboratory diagnosis, 511
  pathogenesis, 510–511
  treatment and control, 511
Agar, in culture media, 52
Agar-agar, discovery, 6
Agar dilution method, 120–121
Agrobacterium, pathogenesis, 314, 375
Akakabi-byo, *Fusarium* species and, 492
Alcohol, as disinfectant, 100, 544
Alginate, *Pseudomonas aeruginosa*, 311
Alimentary toxic aleukia, *Fusarium* species and, 492
Alkylating agents, as disinfectants, 101–102
Allergic contact dermatitis, 180
  allergens of, 192

Allergies. *See* Hypersensitivities
Allosteric enzymes, metabolic control by, 42–43
Allograft, techniques for survival of, 574
Alpha-ketoglutaric acid, formation of, 38
Alpha toxin, *Clostridium perfringens*, 278, 279
Alphavirus encephalitis, 440
Amantadine, activity of, 113
Amastigote, 510
Amebiasis. *See* Amebic dysentery
Amebic dysentery
  epidemiology, 506–507
  laboratory diagnosis, 506
  pathogenesis, 503–506
  treatment and control, 507
American trypanosomiasis
  epidemiology, 511–512
  pathogenesis, 511
  treatment and control, 512
Ames test, mutant detection by, 74
Amikacin, activity of, 111
2-aminoacetophenone, *Pseudomonas aeruginosa*, 311
Amino acid activation, protein synthesis and, 66–67
Aminoglycosides
  activity of, 111–112
  modifying enzymes of, 119
Amphitrichous flagella, 23
Amphotericin B
  activity of, 110
  liposomes and, 110
Ampicillin, structure, 106
Anabolism, defined, 30
Anaerobes
  cultivation of, 53–54
  facultative, oxygen requirement of, 50
  obligate
    glucose metabolism in, 37
    oxygen requirement of, 50
  specimen collection of, 240
Anaerobic cellulitis, *Clostridium perfringens*, 278
Anaerobic glove box, bacterial cultivation and, 53–54
Anaerobic jar method, bacterial cultivation and, 53
Anaerobic myositis, *Clostridium perfringens*, 278–279
Anaerobic respiration, 40–41
Analogues, defined, 72
Anaphylatoxin, in complement system, 170, 171
Anaphylaxis
  defined, 185
  fire ant and, 187
  systemic, 186–187
Ancylostoma braziliense, as cause of cutaneous larva migrans, 520
Ancylostoma caninum, as cause of cutaneous larva migrans, 520
Ancylostoma duodenale, as cause of hookworm infection, 519–520
Anemia, congenital, 573
Animal parasites
  classification of, 500
  defined, 500
  infection. *See* Parasitic infection
  specific defenses against, 175–176.
Animal virus
  classification, 400
  enveloped, budding of, 389
  identification of
    electron microscopy in, 399
    hybridization methods in, 399–400
    immunological methods in, 399
    serological techniques, 398–399
    tissue culture and, 397–398
  infection
    adsorption process in, 384
    cancer and, 391–397. *See also* Oncogenic viruses
    chronic, 391
    cytopathic effects of, 389–391, 398
    diagnosis of, *See* Animal virus, identification of
    epidemiology and physiology of, 384–391
    genome expression during, 385–386
    host genome integration during, 390
    immune system escape during, 391
    latent, 391
    maturation and assembly during, 387–388
    penetration and uncoating in, 384–385
    persistent, 390–391
    release during, 388
    slow, 391
    treatment and control of, 400–402
  lipids of, 382–383
  morphology, 382
  nucleic acids of, 382
  proteins of, 384
  structure and composition, 382–384
  vaccines, 402
Animals, as disease vectors, 223
Annealing, recombinant DNA, 83
Anopheles mosquito, malaria transmitted by, 514
Antheridium, fungal, 468
Anthrax. *See also Bacillus anthracis*
  cutaneous, 274
  gastrointestinal, 274
Antibiograms, 232, 233
Antibiotic(s)
  activity
    qualitative determination of, 121–124
    quantitative determination of, 120–121
  concentration, serum, 124
  natural peptide, 132
  prophylaxis, hospital procedures requiring, 543
Antibody(ies). *See also* Immunoglobulin(s)
  ABO system, 571
  anti-idiotypic, vaccines containing, 178
  anti-red blood cell, determining, 573–574
  defined, 130
  diversity, 150–152
  fluorescent, technique for producing, 553
  in immunodiagnosis. *See* Immunological test(s)
  monoclonal
    advantages of, 570
    applications of, 570
    cloning, 570
    creating, 569–570
    formation of, 152
    immunotherapy using, 198
    source of, 568–569
  variation
    allotypic, 153
    idiotypic, 153
    isotypic, 153
Antibody-dependent cell-mediated cytotoxicity, 165
Antibody-dependent cytotoxicity, animal parasites and, 176
Anticodon, 67
Antigen(s)
  antibody binding to, 147–148
  antigenic determinants of, 144–145
  capsules and slime layers as, 22
  characteristics of, 144–145
  cluster designation, 161
  defined, 22, 130
  H
    Enterobacteriaceae, 294
    Salmonella identification by, 301
  human leukocyte, 194
  in immunodiagnosis. *See* Immunological test(s)
  immunogenicity, 144
  K
    Enterobacteriaceae, 294
    Escherichia coli, 297
  major histocompatibility, 157–158
  O
    Enterobacteriaceae, 294
    Salmonella identification by, 301
    serum resistance and, 218
  presentation, phagocytosis and, 132–134
  specificity, 144–145
  surface, virus effect on, 390
  T cell receptor protein recognition of, 161
  V, *Yersinia pestis*, 305
  variations, microbial defense and, 218
  Vi, *Salmonella*, 299
  W, *Yersinia pestis*, 305
Antigen-antibody reactions, in laboratory identification, 241–242

Antigenemia assay, cytomegalovirus identification by, 412
Antigenic determinants, 144–145
Antigenic drift, influenza virus, 428
Antigenic shift, influenza virus, 428
Antigen presenting cells, location of, 132
Antimetabolites, activity of, 114–117
Antimicrobial(s). *See also* Antibiotic(s); Chemotherapeutic agent(s)
  activity, measurement of, 105
  defense, cellular mechanism of, 130
    noncellular mechanisms of, 139–141
  genetically engineered, 89
  hospital-associated resistance to, 537
Antimicrobial susceptibility testing. *See also* Antibiotic(s), activity
  laboratory identification and, 243
Antiseptics, hospital utilized, 544
Antitoxins, licensed, 589
API 20E system, 242
  Enterobacteriaceae, 296
Arboviruses, pathogenesis of, 439
Archea, 12
Arenaviridae, hemorrhagic fevers, 436
Arthropoda
  characteristics of, 527
  as ectoparasites, 527–528
Arthroscope, disinfection of, 102
Arthrospores, fungal, 470
Arthus reaction, serum sickness and, 190
Ascariasis
  epidemiology, 519
  laboratory diagnosis, 519
  pathogenesis, 517–519
  treatment and control, 519
Ascaris lumbricoides, ascariasis caused by, 517–519
Ascomycotina, characteristics of, 474
Ascospores, fungal, 469
Aseptic meningitis
  defined, 424
  enterovirus, 432
Aseptic technique, Joseph Lister and, 6
Aspergillosis
  allergic, 487–488
  colonizing, 488
  disseminated, 488
  hospital-associated, 536
  invasive, 488
  laboratory diagnosis of, 489
  pathogenesis, 487–489
  treatment of, 489–490
Aspergillus flavus, aflatoxin production by, 492
Aspergillus parasiticus, aflatoxin production by, 492
Aspergillus species
  aspergillosis caused by, 487–490
  conidiophore, 489
  hospital-associated, 536
Assassin bug, American trypanosomiasis and, 511
Asthma, bronchial, 188
Astrovirus, pathogenesis, 443
Ataxia telangiectasia, 184
Atopic dermatitis, 188
Atopy, type I hypersensitivities and, 187–189
ATP, as energy molecule, 35
Attenuation, 205
  vaccine, 177
Atypical pneumonia. *See Mycoplasma pneumoniae*
Autoclave, sterilization using, 96
Autoimmune disease
  mechanisms for, 193
  types of, 193–194
Automation, laboratory identification and, 242–243
Auxotroph, defined, 74
Avidin-biotin technique, 568
Axial filaments, spirochete, 22, 341
Azidothymidine. *See* AZT
Azoles, activity of, 111
AZT
  activity of, 114
  AIDS treatment with, 448

Babesia microti, babesiosis caused by, 516
Babesiosis, 516
Bacillary angiomatosis, 362
Bacillary peliosis hepatitis, 362
Bacillus, 275
  characteristics of species of, 282
  commercial use of species of, 275
  defined, 14
Bacillus anthracis
  adenylate cyclase 216, 273–274
  antigens of, 273–274
  epidemiology, 274
  general characteristics of, 273
  immunity to, 274
  laboratory diagnosis, 274
  pathogenesis, 274
  prevention, 274–275
  treatment, 274–275
  virulence factors, 273–274
Bacillus of Calmette and Guérin, 336
Bacillus cereus, pathogenesis of, 275
Bacillus pumilis, 275
Bacillus stearothermophilus, 275
Bacillus subtilis, 275
Bacitracin, activity of, 110
Bacteremia, defined, 206
Bacteria
  capsules of, 22
  cell wall of, 18–21
  characteristics of, 11–28
  characteristics of, 328
  classification of, 12–13
  cultivation of, 52–54
  cytoplasmic membrane of, 16–17
  cytoplasmic structures in, 24–27
  endospores of, 26–27
  flagella of, 22
  gram-negative coccobacillary, 321–329
  growth of, 47–59. *See also* Growth, bacterial
  inclusion bodies of, 25–26
  isolation of, 54–56
  morphology of, 14
  nomenclature, 13
  nonspecific defenses against, 172
  nucleoids of, 24–25
  osmosis in, 21
  periplasmic space, 19–21
  pili of, 23–24
  pleomorphism of, 15
  preservation of, 56
  reproduction of, 47
  ribosomes in, 25
  size of, 14
  slime layers of, 22
  specific defenses against, 173–175
  square, 14
  staining of, history of, 8. *See also* Stains
  structure of, 14–27
  wall-less, osmosis and, 21
Bacterial vaginosis, characteristics of, 376
Bacteriocin typing, 233
Bacteriophage
  lysogenic conversion, 404
  lysogeny, 403–404
  lytic cycle, 403
  morphology, 403
  temperate, 403
  transduction by, 77–78
Bacteroides
  intestinal, 296
  pathogenesis, 375
Base pair arrangement, 63
Basidiobolus haptosporus, subcutaneous phycomycosis caused by, 480
Basidiomycotina, characteristics of, 474
Basidiospores, fungal, 469
Basidium, fungal, 469
Basophils, characteristics of, 130–131
B cell(s)
  activation
    T-dependent, 163
    T-independent, 163
  clonal selection, 164–165
  disorders, 184–185
  immunity associated with, 130
  location of, 156
  response to animal parasite infections
  response to bacterial infections, 173
  structure and characteristics of, 163–165
Bees, systemic anaphylaxis and, 186–187
Bejel, 346
Benzethonium chloride, 101
Benzylalkonium chloride, 101
Beta-galactosidase, induction and repression of, 67–68

Beta-lactamase, penicillin resistance and, 108
Beta lactams, 107. *See also* Penicillin; Cephalosporin
  inhibitors of, 108
Beta oxidation, as electron source, 41
Bile solubility test, in *Streptococcus pneumoniae* identification, 260
Bilharziasis. *See* Schistosomiasis
Binary fission, defined, 47
Bio-Bag, bacterial cultivation and, 53
Biofilms, adhesion and, 213
Biolog system, 242
Biosynthesis
  defined, 30
  energy utilization in, 41–42
  reducing power needs for, 42
Brownian movement, defined, 22
Biotechnology, medicine and, 83–89
Biotyping, 232, 233
Blastomycosis
  epidemiology, 476–477
  laboratory diagnosis, 477
  pathogenesis, 477
  treatment, 477
Blastospores, fungal, 470
Blood, specimen collection of, 240
Blood agar, bacterial isolation using, 55–56
Blood clotting factor, medical use of, 89
Blood group typing, 571
Boiling, sterilization using, 96
Bone marrow, immune function of, 156
Bordetella
  characteristics, 324, 328
  species differentiation, 324
Bordetella bronchiseptica, characteristics, 324
Bordetella parapertussis, characteristics, 324
Bordetella pertussis
  adenyl cyclase activity and, 216
  cytotoxin, 325
  epidemiology, 324
  laboratory diagnosis, 325–326
  pathogenesis, 324–325
  prevention, 326
  treatment, 326
Borrelia
  antigenic variation of, 218
  characteristics, 347
Borrelia burgdorferi
  laboratory diagnosis, 348
  pathogenesis, 348
  treatment and prevention, 348
Borrelia hermsii, 347
Borrelia parkeri, 347
Borrelia recurrentis
  epidemiology, 347–348
  pathogenesis, 347–348
Borrelia turicatae, 347
Botulism. *See also Clostridium botulinum*
  fish, 277
  food, 276–277
  infant, 277
  pathogenesis, 276–277
  wound, 277
Boutonneuse fever. *See Rickettsia conorii*
Branhamella, characteristics of, 270
Brill-Zinsser disease, epidemic typhus and, 360
5-bromouracil, mutation caused by, 72
Broth dilution test, 120
Broth
  defined, 52
  nutrient, 52
Brucella
  characteristics, 326, 328
  epidemiology, 326
  laboratory diagnosis, 326–327
  pathogenesis, 326
Brucella abortus, characteristics, 327
Brugia malayi, filariasis caused by, 523
Brucella melitensis, characteristics, 327
Brucella suis, characteristics, 327
Buboes, plague, 305
Bubonic plague. *See Yersinia pestis*
Bud scar, fungal, 467
Budding, fungal, 467
Buffers, growth media, 49
Bunyaviridae, hemorrhagic fevers, 436
Bunyavirus encephalitis, 440
Burkitt's lymphoma, 393–394
Bursa of fabricus, 163
B virus, pathogenesis, 415

C3 convertase, 170
C5 convertase, 170, 171
Calabar swellings, *Loa loa*, 523
Calcium dipicolinate, spore, 26
Calcium, growth requirement for, 50
Calicivirus, pathogenesis, 442
Calmodulin
  adenyl cyclase activity and, 216
  edema factor and, 273
Calymmatobacterium, pathogenesis, 375
CAMP test, in Group B streptococcal identification, 255, 256
Campylobacter
  characteristics, 350
  epidemiology and pathogenesis, 350
  laboratory diagnosis, treatment, and prevention, 350–351
Campylobacter jejuni, 350
  Guillain-Barré syndrome and, 351
Cancer
  DNA viruses causing, 392–395
  RNA viruses causing, 395–397
Candida albicans
  candidiasis caused by, 485–487
  hospital infections caused by, 535
Candida species, hospital-associated, 536
Candida tropicalis, treatment of infections caused by, 487
Candidal balanitis, 486
Candidiasis
  AIDS and treatment of, 448
  chronic mucocutaneous, 486
  cutaneous, 486
  general characteristics of, 485
  hospital-associated, 536
  intertriginous, 486
  IV drug use and, 487
  laboratory diagnosis of, 486–487
  systemic, 486
  treatment of, 487
  vaginal, 486
  virulence factors associated with, 485
Capnocytophaga, pathogenesis, 375
Capsid, animal virus, 382
Capsomere, animal virus, 382
Capsule
  bacterial, structure and function of, 22
  staining of, 559. *See also* Extracellular polymeric substances
  Streptococcus pneumoniae, 258
  Streptococcus pyogenes, 252
Carbapenems, activity of, 109
Carbenicillin, structure, 106
Carbon, bacterial requirement for, 49
Carbuncles, *Staphylococcus aureus*, 248–249
Carcinogen, defined, 74
Carcinogenesis, genetics of, 396
Cardiobacterium hominis, pathogenesis, 375
Cardiohepatic toxin, *Streptococcus pyogenes*, 253
Cardiolipin, syphilis and, 346
Cardiovascular system, microbial agents causing diseases of, 581–582
Caries, actinomycetes and, 372
Carriers, 205
  convalescent, 223
  cytoplasmic membrane, 17
  healthy, 223
  Salmonella, 299–300
Caseation necrosis, tuberculosis and, 332
Catabolism, defined, 30
Catalase production
  in clinical microbiology, 241
  infectious disease implications of, 34
  in oxygen metabolism, 50
Catheter
  cardiac, disinfection of, 102
  central venous, hospital-associated infections and, 540–541
  urinary, hospital-associated infections and, 539–540
  vascular indwelling, hospital-associated infections and, 540–542
Catheter-associated infections
  urinary
    pathogenesis of, 539
    prevention and control of, 540

vascular indwelling
diagnosis of, 540–541
pathogenesis of, 541
prevention of, 541
treatment and management of, 541–542
Cat-scratch disease, 362
Cefamandole, 108
Cefazolin, 108
in prophylaxis, 117
Cefoperazone, 108
Cefotaxime, 108
Cefoxitin, 108
in prophylaxis, 117
Cell(s)
antigen-driven, 152
antigen presenting, location of, 132
B. *See* B cell(s)
dust, 132
effector, clonal selection and, 164
Kupffer, 132
lymphoid, 160–165. *See also specific cell types*
lymphokine-activated, 165
memory, clonal selection and, 164
natural killer, characteristics of, 165
stem, 156
T. *See* T cell(s)
Cell count, 57
Cell density, 57
Cell-mediated immunity, defined, 130
Cell wall
bacterial, 18–21
gram-negative, 19–21
gram-positive, 19
lipopolysaccharide, 19, 21
porins in, 19
synthesis, inhibitors of, 107–110
Cellulitis, *Streptococcus pyogenes*, 254
Cellulose, fungal, 466
Cephalosporin
activity of, 108–109
structure, 109
Cephalothin, 108
Cercaria, larva, 523
Cerebrospinal fluid, specimen collection, 240
Cestoidea. *See* Tapeworm
Cetylpyridinium chloride, 101
Chaga's disease. *See* American trypanosomiasis
Chagoma, defined, 511
Chain, penicillin purification by, 9
Chancre, syphilis, 342
Chédiak-Higashi syndrome, 139
Chemosterilizer, defined, 98
Chemotaxins
complement, 171
cytokines as, 158
Chemotaxis
defined, 22
disorders, phagocytosis and, 139
inflammation and, 134
Chemotherapeutic agent(s). *See also* Antimicrobial(s); Antibiotic(s)
additive effects of, 117
antagonistic effects of, 117
characteristics of, summary of, 123
combinations of, 117
dosage, 117
factors in selecting a, 117–119
indifferent effects of, 117
minimal inhibitory concentration of, 117
in prophylaxis, 117–118
resistance to, 119–120
route of administration of, 117
selective toxicity of, 106
synergistic effects of, 117
therapeutic index of, 106
toxicity of, 118
transport of, drug resistance and, 119
zone size interpretative standards for, 122
Chemotherapy, 104–124
animal virus, 400–401
history of, 8–9
Chickenpox. *See* Varicella virus
Chitin, fungal, 466
Chlamydia pneumoniae, pathogenesis, 365
Chlamydia psittaci, pathogenesis, 365
Chlamydia trachomatis
epidemiology and pathogenesis, 363–365
inclusion conjunctivitis caused by, 363–364
lymphogranuloma venereum caused by, 365
Neisseria gonorrhoeae treatment and, 270
neonatal pneumonia caused by, 365
nongonococcal urethritis caused by, 365
trachoma caused by, 363
Chlamydiae, 363–367. *See also Chlamydia species*
characteristics, 363
developmental cycle, 364
laboratory diagnosis, 365
rickettsia differentiation from, 366
treatment and prevention, 366
Chlamydospores, fungal, 470
Chloramphenicol, activity of, 112
Chlorhexidine, as disinfectant, 102
Chlorhexidine gluconate, catheter-related infections and, 541
Chlorine, as disinfectant, 100, 544
Chloroquine, malaria treatment with, 514
Chocolate blood agar, 56
Cholera. *See Vibrio cholerae*
Chorioamnionitis, *Ureaplasma urealyticum* as cause of, 356
Chromatography, gas-liquid, laboratory identification using, 243
Chromobacterium violaceum, pathogenesis, 375
Chromoblastomycosis, characteristics of, 480
Chromosome, defined, 62
Chronic disease, 222
Chronic granulomatous disease, phagocytosis and, 139
Chronic mononucleosis syndrome, 418
Cilia, as antimicrobial defense factor, 208
Ciliata, infections caused by, 513
Ciprofloxacin, activity of, 113
Citric acid, formation of, 38
Citric acid cycle
aerobic respiration and, 38–40
as source of carbons in biosynthesis, 42
Cladosporium carrionii, chromoblastomycosis caused by, 480
Classification
animal parasite, 500
animal virus, 400
bacterial, 12
enzyme, 33–34
fungal, 473
phylogenetic, 13
protozoa, 503
streptococcal, 252
Clavulanic acid, 108
Clindamycin, activity of, 112
Clonal selection theory, 164–165
Cloning, 83
recombinant DNA, 84–86
Clonorchis sinensis, 523
Clostridium
cultivation of, 275
diseases caused by, 276–283. *See also Clostridium species*
general characteristics of, 275–276, 281, 282
Clostridium botulinum
food poisoning, 276–277
laboratory diagnosis, 277
lysogenic conversion in, 404
pathogenesis, 276–277
prevention, 277–278
toxins, 276, commercial uses of, 277
treatment, 277–278
Clostridium difficile, colitis caused by, 281–283
Clostridium perfringens
alpha toxin, 278
anaerobic cellulitis caused by, 278
anaerobic myositis caused by, 278–279
enterotoxin-associated diarrhea caused by, 280
food poisoning caused by, 279–280
gas gangrene caused by, 278–279
laboratory diagnosis, 279, 280
pathogenesis, 278–280
plasmid determinants of, 79
prevention, 279
toxins, 278
treatment, 279

Clostridium tetani
toxins, 280
pathogenesis, 280
laboratory diagnosis, 280–281
treatment, 281
prevention, 281
Clue cells, bacterial vaginosis and, 376
Coagglutination test, *Staphylococcus aureus* identification using, 248
Coagulase
infectious disease implications of, 34
as invasive factor, 213
as *Staphylococcus aureus* virulence factor, 248
Coagulase test, identification of *Staphylococcus aureus* using, 250
Cobalt, growth requirement for, 50
Cocci, gram-positive. *See* Gram-positive cocci
Coccidia, *Isospora belli* and, 517
Coccidioides immitis, coccidioidomycosis caused by, 475–476
Coccidioidin, 476
Coccidioidomycosis
epidemiology, 475
laboratory diagnosis, 476
pathogenesis, 475
treatment, 476
Coccus
arrangement of, 14
defined, 14
Codon
defined, 66
nonsense, 66
sense, 66
Coenzyme, defined, 30
Coenzyme A, aerobic respiration and, 38
Cofactor, enzyme, 30
Cold agglutinin test, *Mycoplasma* and, 357
Colds. *See* Rhinovirus
Coliform, defined, 293
Collagenase, as invasive factor, 213
Colonization, commensal, 204
Commensals
activities of, 204
intestinal, antimicrobial activity of, 208
Competence, DNA transformation and, 76
Competitive inhibition, enzyme, 33
Complement
in bacterial infections, 173
biological effects of, 181
deficiencies and disease , 171–172
evasion by parasites, 172
functions, 171
pathway
alternative, 170–171
classic, 169–170
phagocytosis role of, 134–135
regulation, 171
type III hypersensitivities and, 190
in virus infections, 174
Complement fixation, 171
Complement fixation test, 563–564
Compound bright-field microscope, 549–550
Condenser, microscope, 549
Condylomata
human papillomavirus, 394, 420
secondary syphilis and, 342
Congenital rubella syndrome, 425
Conidia, morphology of fungal, 469
Conidiophore, fungal, 469
Conjugation
DNA, 76–77
drug resistance and microbial, 119
Conjunctivitis
acute hemorrhagic, enterovirus and, 432
epidemic kerato-, adenovirus and, 419, 420
inclusion, chlamydial, 363–364
kerato-, herpesvirus, 416
microbial agents causing, summary of, 575–576
Contact inhibition, cell transformation and, 392, 398
Convalescence, defined, 222
Coombs' test, 574
Cord factor, *Mycobacteria*, 331, 332
Coronavirus, 432
Cortex, spore, 26
Corticosteroids, aspergillosis and use of, 488
Corynebacterium
differentiation tests, 290
disease causing species of, characteristics of, 289
Corynebacterium diphtheriae
epidemiology, 287
immunity to, 286–287
immunization against, 288
laboratory diagnosis, 287
lysogenic conversion in, 404
pathogenesis, 285–286
prevention, 288
toxin, activity of, 286
treatment, 287
Coryneforms, 285
Counterimmunoelectrophoresis test, 566
Cowpox virus, 409
Coxiella, differentiation from rickettsia, 359
Coxiella burnetii, pathogenesis, 361
C-reactive protein
serological test, 570
Streptococcus pneumoniae, 259
Credé's method, gonococcal ophthalmia neonatorum and, 270
Creeping eruption, 520
Creutzfeldt-Jakob disease, 458
Crimean-Congo hemorrhagic fever, 438
Crossmatching, transfusion, 573–574
Croup, parainfluenza virus as cause of, 434
Cryptococcosis
AIDS and treatment of, 448
epidemiology, 478
hospital-associated, 536
laboratory diagnosis, 478
pathogenesis, 478
treatment, 478
Cryptococcus neoformans
cryptococcosis caused by, 478
hospital-associated, 536
Cryptosporidiosis
epidemiology, 517
laboratory diagnosis, 517
pathogenesis, 517
treatment and control, 517
Cryptosporidium species, cryptosporidiosis caused by, 516–517
C substance, streptococcal, 252
Cultivation, bacteria. *See* Bacteria, cultivation of
Culture
in clinical microbiology, 241
defined, 47
Culture media
all-purpose, 53
for bacterial isolation, 55–56
classification, 52–53
complex, 52
defined, 47, 52
differential, 53
enriched, 53
selective, 53
synthetic, 52
transport, 53
Cunninghamella, as cause of mucormycosis, 490
Cyclic adenosine monophosphate
Bacillus anthracis and, 274
Bordetella pertussis infection and, 325
cholera infection and, 316
as factor in disease process, 214
Salmonella gastroenteritis and, 298
Cycloserine, cloning and, 85
Cyst, animal parasite, 501
Cysteine, enzyme activity and, 32
Cystic fibrosis, *Pseudomonas aeruginosa* in, 311
Cysticercosis, taeniasis and, 526
Cytochrome oxidase, infectious disease implications of, 34
Cytochrome oxidase test, in isolation of *Neisseria meningitidis*, 266
Cytochromes, aerobic respiration and, 39–40
Cytokines
characteristics of, 158–160
defined, 137
Cytomegalovirus
acquired immune deficiency syndrome and, 412, 448
congenital, 411
epidemiology, 412
intranuclear inclusions, 412

laboratory diagnosis, 412–413
as major health problem, 411
neonatal infections caused by, 411
pathogenesis, 411
renal transplant infections by, 411–412
treatment and prevention, 413
Cytopathic effect, virus, 389–391, 398
Cytoplasmic membrane
bacterial, 16–17
function, inhibitors of, 110–111
fungal, 467
model, 18
proteins, function of, 17–18
Cytotoxic T cells, characteristics of, 162
effect on virus, 162
Cytotoxin
cytokines as, 158
Legionella pneumophila, 377

Dane particle, 449
Dapsone
activity of, 116
Dark-field microscopy, 550
syphilis diagnosis and, 344
Death and decline phase, bacterial, 48
Decimal reduction time, sterilization and, 95
Defensins, 132
Definitive host, animal parasite infection and, 501
Degermination, defined, 94
Degranulation
defined, 131
process of lysosome, 136
Dehydrogenation, energy production and, 35
Delayed type hypersensitivity
allergic contact dermatitis as, 192
characteristics of, 162–163
generation of, 163
human immunodeficiency virus syndrome and, 446
mechanism, 191–192
tuberculin hypersensitivity as, 192
Denaturation, enzyme, 31
Dengue fever
epidemiology, 441
laboratory diagnosis, 441
pathogenesis, 441
treatment and prevention, 441
Dengue hemorrhagic fever, 441
Density-dependent growth, cell transformation and, 392, 398
Dermatophytes, major genera of, 481
Dermatophytoses
allergy and, 484
characteristics of, 481
infections caused by, 482–484. *See also* Tinea
laboratory diagnosis of, 481–482
treatment of, 482
Desquamation, in infectious disease process, 206
Detergents, as disinfectant, 100–101
Deuteromycetes, sporulation in, 468
Deuteromycotina, characteristics of, 474
Dexamethasone
Hemophilus influenzae infection and, 323
Neisseria meningitidis treatment, 267
Dideoxyinosine, AIDS treatment with, 448
Digestive system, microbial agents causing diseases of, 578–580
Dihydroxyacetone phosphate, formation, 35
Dimer, DNA, mutation and, 72
Dimorphism, fungal, 466, 471
Dipetalonema streptocerca, filariasis caused by, 522
Diphtheria. *See Corynebacterium diphtheriae*
Diphtheroids, characteristics of, 288
Diphyllobothriasis, characteristics of, 518
Diphyllobothrium latum, stages and diagnostic characteristics of, 525
Diplococcus, defined, 14
Diploid cell lines, virus cultivation and, 397
Dipylidium caninum, tapeworm infestation caused by, 526
Disease(s)
acute, 221–222
autoimmune, 193–194
cardiovascular system, microbial agents causing, 581–582
CDC reportable, 590
chronic, 222
clinical stages of, 221–222
defined, 205
digestive system, microbial agents causing, 578–580
endemic, 230
enzootic, 230
epidemic, 230
eye, microbial agent causing, 575–576
genitourinary tract, microbial agents causing, 584
hospital-associated. *See* Hospital-associated infection(s)
host resistance to, factors influencing, 209–211
host factors affecting, 206–209
immunodeficiency, 184–185
incidence of, 230–231
index case in, 232
internal organ, microbial agents causing, 578–580
lymph system, microbial agents causing, 581–582
microbial factor affecting, 211–218
adherence as, 211–212
invasion of host as, 212–213
toxins as, 214–218
nervous system, microbial agents causing, 582–583
pandemic, 230
pathology, terminology used to describe, 244
persistent, 222
prevalence of, 230–231
reservoirs of, 222–225. *See also* Reservoir(s)
respiratory tract, microbial agents causing, 577–578
sexually transmitted, characteristics of, 227
skin, microbial agents causing, 575–576
sources of, 222
sporadic, 230
surveillance, 231–232
terminology associated with, 205–206
transmission of, 225–230
air in, 229
congenital, 229
direct contact in, 225–226
food in, 227–228
horizontal, 229–230
indirect contact in, 226–230
perinatal, 229
postnatal, 229
vertical, 229–230
water in, 226–227
vector-borne, 224
Disinfectants
alcohols as, 100
alkylating agents as, 101–102
chlorhexidine as, 102
chlorine as, 100
classes of, 99–102
detergents as, 100
heavy metals as, 102
hexachlorophene as, 100
hospital utilized, 544
iodine as, 100
phenols as, 99–100
qualities of universal, 98–99
soaps as, 100
surfactants as, 100–101
Disinfection
critical instrument, 102
methods of, 98–103
noncritical item, 102
practical recommendations for, 103
semicritical instrument, 102
terminology, 94
Disk diffusion test, 121–124
DNA
cell functions of, 62
classification using, 13
complementary, formation of, 87
donor, genetic engineering and, 83
genetic code and, 66
hot spots, mutation and, 70
hybridization
plasmid detection using, 85–86
mutation in, 69–74. *See also* Mutation
nucleoids as, 24–25
plasmid, 78–79

DNA—*Continued*
recombination, 74
replicating forks of, 65
replication, mechanism of, 63–66
structure of, 62–63
transcription, 66
transfer
infectious disease and, 79–80
methods of, 74–80
translation of, 66–67
vector, genetic engineering and, 83
DNA gyrase, 113
DNA ligase, DNA replication and, 66
DNA polymerase
DNA replication and, 65
infectious disease implications of, 34
DNA probes, in epidemiology, 234
DNase, medical use of, 89
DNA virus
diseases associated with, 409–421. *See also specific viral agent*
diseases caused by, summary of, 458
genome expression by, 385–386
Domagk, Gerhard, sulfanilamide discovery by, 9
Doubling time. *See* Generation time, defined
Droplet nucleic, disease transmission by, 229
Drug(s). *See also* Antibiotic(s); Chemotherapeutic agent(s)
antimicrobial *See* Antimicrobial(s)
broad spectrum, 105
narrow spectrum, 105
Drug resistance
genetics of, 119
mechanisms of, 119–120
Dystonia, defined, 278

Ear, microbial flora of, 585
Eastern equine encephalitis, 439, 440
Ebola hemorrhagic fever, 437–438
Echinococcosis, characteristics of, 526, 527
Echinococcus granulosa, tapeworm infestation caused by, 526, 527
Eclipse, virus, 384
Edema
defined, 244
inflammation and, 139
Edema factor, *Bacillus anthracis*, 273
Eflornithine, African trypanosomiasis treatment with, 511
Egg, animal parasite, 501
Ehrlich, Paul, chemotherapy development by, 8–9
Ehrlichia sennetsu, pathogenesis, 362
Ehrlichioses, 362
Eikenella corrodens, pathogenesis, 314, 375
Elastase, *Pseudomonas aeruginosa*, 311
Electron donors, energy metabolism and, 35
Electron microscope, 553–555
Electron transport chain
aerobic respiration and, 39–40
defined, 35
phosphorylation, 35
Elek method, *Corynebacterium diphtheriae* identification using, 287
Elephantiasis, filarial agents of, 523
Embden-Meyerhoff-Parnas pathway. *See* Glycolysis
Embolus, defined, 244
Encephalitis, viral, 439–440
Endemic disease, 230
Endocytosis
phagocyte, 134
virus penetration and, 384
Shigella, 214
Endoenzyme, defined, 34
Endoplasmic reticulum, fungal, 467
Endoscope, disinfection of, 102
Endospore
formation, bacterial, 26
germination, bacterial, 26–27
in sterilization, 95
Endotoxin(s)
exotoxin differentiation from, 215
as factors affecting disease process, 214–218
gram-negative septicemia and, 160, 215–218
structure, 21, 217
Energy of activation, enzymes and, 30
Energy formation
electron sources in, 38, 41
electrons, oxidation and, 34–35
fermentation and, 35–38
glycolysis and, 35–37
respiration and, 38–41
Energy utilization, biosynthesis and, 41–42
Entamoeba histolytica
amebic dysentery caused by, 503–507
pathogenic vs nonpathogenic, 506
Enteric bacilli, 293–308
Enteritis necroticans, *Clostridium perfringens* as cause of, 279
Entero-Test method, animal parasite diagnosis by, 502
Enterobacter species
characteristics of, 307
hospital infections caused by, 535
Enterobacteriaceae
antigen
H, 294
K, 294
O, 294
characteristics, 293
classification of, 293
identification, 295–296
isolation of, 294–295
opportunistic, characteristics of, 307, 308
pathogenic, characteristics of, 308
rapid identification techniques, 296
Enterobiasis
epidemiology, 521
laboratory diagnosis, 521
pathogenesis, 521
treatment and control, 521
Enterobius species, enterobiasis caused by, 521
Enterococcus faecalis 257
Enterococcus faecium, 257
Enterococcus species
hospital infections caused by, 535
pathogenesis of, 257
Enterocolitis, *Staphylococcus aureus*, 248–249
Enterotoxin
Clostridium perfringens, 279
Staphylococcus aureus, 249
Enteroviruses
epidemiology, 432
laboratory diagnosis, 432
pathogenesis, 431–432
treatment, 432
Entner-Doudoroff pathway, 38
Envelope, animal virus, 382–383
Enzootic disease, 230
Enzyme
active site of, 30
allosteric, 42
characteristics of, 30–31
classification, 33–34
constitutive, 68
denaturation, 31
factors affecting, 30–33
inactivation, drug resistance and, 119–120
inducible, 67
infectious disease implications of, 34
inhibitors, 32–33
metabolism controlled by, 42–43
structure of, 30
substrate concentration effect on, 32
Enzyme immunoassay technique, 567
Enzyme-linked immunosorbent assay, 567
Eosin-methylene blue agar, 53
as isolation medium, 56
enterobacteriaceae identification using, 294–295
Eosinophil chemotactic factor of anaphylaxis, 187
Eosinophilic cationic protein, 131
Eosinophils
animal parasite infection and, 176
characteristics of, 131
Epidemic disease, 230
common-source, 232
propagated, 232
Epidemic keratoconjunctivitis, adenovirus and, 419, 420
Epidemic typhus. *See Rickettsia prowazekii*
Epidemiology, 220–235. *See also* Disease(s), transmission of
defined, 221
descriptive, 231–232

laboratory techniques in
conventional, 233
molecular, 233–234
Epidermophyton, infections caused by, 481–485
Epimastigote, 510
Epinephrine, systemic anaphylaxis and, 187
5-Episisomicin, activity of, 111
Epitope, defined, 144–145
Epstein-Barr virus
acquired immune deficiency syndrome and, 418
cancer caused by, 393–394
disorders induced by, 418
pathogenesis, 418
Erysipelas, *Streptococcus pyogenes*, 254
Erysipeloid. *See Erysipelothrix rhusiopathiae*
Erysipelothrix rhusiopathiae
differentiation tests for, 290
general characteristics, 290
laboratory diagnosis, 290
pathogenesis, 290
treatment, 290
Erythema, defined, 186
Erythema chronicum migrans, Lyme disease and, 348
Erythema infectiosum, parvovirus and, 421
Erythema nodosum, *Streptococcus pyogenes* and, 255
Erythroblastosis fetalis, 573
Erythrogenic toxin
Streptococcus pyogenes, 253
as superantigen, 255
Erythromycin, activity of, 112
Eschar, rickettsial, 359
Escherichia, characteristics of pathogenic, 308
Escherichia coli
0157:H7, 297
enteroaggregative, 297
enterohemorrhagic, 297
enteroinvasive, 297
enteropathogenic, 297
enterotoxigenic, 297
extraintestinal disease caused by, 296–297
hospital infections caused by, 535
intestinal disease, 297–298
laboratory diagnosis, 298
pathogenesis, 296–298
plasmid determinants of, 79
prevention, 298
Shiga-like toxin, 297
treatment, 298
virulence factors, 296–297
E test, antimicrobial, 124
Ethambutol, activity of, 116
Ethylene oxide
as disinfectant, 101–102, 544
as sterilization indicator, 97
Eucarya, 12
Eukaryotes, characteristics of, 12
Excision repair, mutation and, 73
Exoantigen
defined, 472
histoplasmosis identified by, 475
Exocytosis, 137
Exoenzyme, defined, 34
Exophiala wernecki, tinea nigris palmaris and, 484
Exotoxin(s)
endotoxin differentiation from, 215
as factors affecting disease process, 214
Exotoxin A, *Pseudomonas aeruginosa*, 311
Extracellular polymeric substances. *See also* Capsule; Slime layer
bacterial, 22
as invasive factors, 213
Exudate, defined, 244
Eye
microbial agents causing diseases of, 575–576
microbial flora of, 585

Facilitated diffusion, defined, 17
Facultative anaerobes
glucose metabolism in, 36
oxygen requirement of, 50
FAD dehydrogenase, citric acid cycle and, 39
Fasciola hepatica, 523
Fasciolopsis buski, 523
Feces, specimen collection, 240
Feedback inhibition, allosteric enzymes and, 42–43
Fermentation
in clinical microbiology, 241
glycolysis and, 35–37
Ferritin, as factor influencing host resistance, 210
Fever
in gram-negative septicemia, 215
induction of, 217
puerperal, 254
rheumatic, 254
scarlet, 253
F factor, conjugation and, 76–77
F glycoprotein, mumps virus, 423
Fibrin, formation of, inflammation and, 134
Fibroblast, inflammation and, 134
Fibroblast activating factor, inflammation and, 134
Fibronectin
as antimicrobial defense factor, 208
in hospital-associated infections,541
as lipoteichoic acid receptor, 211
as opsonins, 134
Filariasis
characteristics of the agents of, 522
laboratory diagnosis, 523
pathogenesis, 522–523
treatment, 523
Filoviridae, hemorrhagic fevers, 436
Fimbriae. *See* Pili
Fission, fungal, 467
Flagella, bacterial, 22–23
Flagella stain, 559
Flaviviridae, hemorrhagic fevers, 436
Flavivirus encephalitis, 440
Flavobacterium, pathogenesis, 314
Flavoproteins, citric acid cycle and, 39
Flea, as disease vector, 224
Fleming, Alexander, penicillin discovery by, 9
Florey, penicillin purification by, 9
Flow cytometry, laboratory identification using, 243
Flucytosine
activity of, 113
amphotericin B administration with, 110
Flukes. *See also* Trematoda
blood, 523
intestinal, 523
liver, 523
lung, 523
Fluorescein, 552
Fluorescent antibody technique, 566
Fluorescent microscope, 552–553
Fluorescent treponemal antibody test, 345
Fluorochrome, defined, 552
Fluoroquinolones, activity of, 113
Fly, as disease vector, 224
Focal disease, defined, 206
Focus, viral, 398
Folliculitis, *Staphylococcus aureus*, 248
Fomites
in disease transmission, 226, 229
hospital-associated infections from contaminated, 534–535
Fonsecaea species, chromoblastomycosis caused by, 480
Food
in disease transmission, 227–229
infection, defined, 229
poisoning, defined, 229
as reservoir of disease, 225
Food-borne disease, reportable, 228
Food poisoning
Clostridium perfringens, 279
Staphylococcus aureus, 249
Foot-and-mouth disease, discovery of, 8
Forespore, bacterial, 26
Formaldehyde, as disinfectant, 101, 544
Formalin, 101
Fortimicin A, activity of, 111
Foscarnet, cytomegalovirus treatment and, 413
Fracastorius, disease concept, 4
Fragmentation, fungal, 467
Frameshift mutation, 72
Francisella tularensis
characteristics, 327, 328
epidemiology, 327
laboratory diagnosis, 328–329
pathogenesis, 327
prevention, 329
treatment, 329

Freeze-drying, preservation of microorganisms by, 56
Freeze fracturing, electron microscopy and, 554
Freezing, preservation of microorganisms by, 56
Frosch, virus discovery by, 8
Fumaric acid, formation of, 39
Fungal disease
  cutaneous, 481–485
  opportunistic species in, 485–491
    characteristics of, 494
  subcutaneous, 479–481
  superficial, 484–485
  systemic, 474–478
    characteristics of, 493
Fungi
  classification of, 473
  cultural characteristics of, 470
  dimorphism in, 466
  importance to humans, 473
  laboratory diagnosis of, 471–472
  mycotoxins of, 491–492
  pathogenesis of, 471. *See also* Fungal disease
  reproduction in, 467–470
  resistance to infection by, 472
  size and morphology of, 466–467
  specific defenses against, 175–176
  treatment and prevention of diseases caused by, 472–473
Fungi Imperfecti, characteristics of, 474
Fusarium
  as cause of mycotoxicosis, 492
  hospital-associated, 536

Gamma globulin, as defense mechanism, 139
Gammopathies, monoclonal, 185
Ganciclovir, cytomegalovirus treatment and, 413
Gardnerella vaginalis, pathogenesis, 375
Gas gangrene. *See Clostridium perfringens*
GasPak, bacterial cultivation and, 53
Gastrointestinal tract, microbial flora of, 587
Gas vacuoles, bacterial, 25
Gene(s)
  beta-galactosidase, 68
  defined, 62
  immunoglobulin, 150–152
  major histocompatibility, 157–158
  permease, 68
  regulator, operon, 68
  structural, operon, 68
  transacetylase, 68
Gene probe, medical uses for, 87
Gene therapy, application of, 89
Generation time, defined, 47
Genetic code, 66, 67
  mutation effects on, 72
Genetic constitution, as factor influencing host resistance, 210
Genetic engineering
  medical applications of, 89
  in modern microbiology, 9
  proteins produced by, 89
  recombinant DNA and, 83. *See also* Recombinant DNA
Genitourinary tract
  as antimicrobial defense factor, 208
  microbial agents causing diseases of, 582–583
  microbial flora of, 586
Genotype, defined, 62
Gentamicin, activity of, 111
Genus, defined, 13
Germ theory, 5–6
  scope of, 4
Germ tube test, candidiasis diagnosis by, 487
German measles. *See* Rubella virus
Germicidal lamps, sterilization using, 98
Germicide. *See* Disinfectants
Germination, bacterial spore, 26–27
Giardia lamblia, giardiasis caused by, 507–510
Giardiasis
  epidemiology, 508–509
  laboratory diagnosis, 508
  pathogenesis, 507–508
  treatment and control, 509–510
Glucose
  oxidation, 34–38
    Entner-Doudoroff pathway in, 38
    pentose phosphate pathway in, 37–38
Glutaraldehyde, as disinfectant, 101, 544
Glyceraldehyde 3-phosphate, formation of, 35
Glycogen, as inclusion body, 26
Glycolysis
  energy formation and, 35–37
  as source of carbons in biosynthesis, 41
Gonococcus. *See Neisseria gonorrhoeae*
Gonorrhoea. *See also Neisseria gonorrhoeae*
  female, 268
  male, 267–268
Graft rejection, 194–196
  preventing, 195–196
Grafts, types of, 194
Gram-negative bacilli, hospital-associated treatment of, 542
Gram-negative bacteria
  cell wall of, 19–21
  general properties of, 559
  outer membrane of, 19
Gram-positive bacilli, hospital-associated treatment of, 542
Gram-positive bacteria
  cell wall of, 19
  general properties of, 559
Gram-positive cocci
  micrococci as, 252
  staphylococci, general characteristics of, 247. *See also Staphylococcus aureus*
  streptococci as. *See* Streptococci
Gram-stain
  importance to microbiologist and physician, 559
  technique, 557–558
Granulocyte colony-stimulating factor, source and function of, 159
Granulocyte-macrophage colony-stimulating factor, source and function of, 159
Granuloma(s)
  coccidioidomycosis, 475
  inflammation and, 134
Granuloma inguinale, 375
Granulomatosis infantisepticum, 289
Group translocation, defined, 18
Growth
  bacterial, 47–59
    chemical requirements for, 48–50
    graphing, 47
    laboratory measurement of, 56–57
    physical requirements for, 51–52
Growth curve, bacterial, 48
Growth factors, bacterial, 49
Growth hormone, medical use of, 89
Guillain-Barré syndrome, influenza virus and, 429
Gumma, tertiary syphilis and, 343

Handwashing, infection prevention using, 534, 544
Hanging drop technique, 555
Hansen's disease. *See Mycobacterium leprae*
Hantavirus, hemorrhagic fever and, 438
H antigen
  enterobacteriaceae, 294
  Salmonella identification by, 301
Haptens, immunogenicity and, 144
Hashimoto's thyroiditis, as autoimmune disease, 193
Heat
  moist, sterilization using, 95
  steam, sterilization using, 96
Heavy chain
  diversity in, 151
  structure, 145
  switch, immunoglobulin function and, 151–152
HeLa cells, origin of, 397
Helical symmetry, animal virus, 382
Helicobacter pylori, epidemiology and pathogenesis, 351–352
Helminth diseases, characteristics of, 518
Helper T cells, characteristics of, 162
Hemagglutination test, viral, 562–563
Hemagglutinin
  animal virus, 384
  Bordetella pertussis, 324

influenza virus, 426, 428
mumps virus, 423
Hematopoietic growth factors, immunotherapy with, 180
Hemodialyzer, disinfection of, 102
Hemoflagellates, morphological types of, 510
Hemolysin(s)
Escherichia coli, 296–297
as invasive factors, 213
Listeria monocytogenes, 290
as *Staphylococcus aureus* virulence factors, 248
Streptococcus pyogenes, 253
Hemolysis
alpha
defined, 56
in laboratory identification, 241
beta
defined, 56
in laboratory identification, 241
gamma
defined, 56
in laboratory identification, 241
Hemolytic-uremic syndrome, *Escherichia coli*, 297
Hemophilus, characteristics of, 322, 323, 328
Hemophilus aegyptius, characteristics of, 323
Hemophilus ducreyi
characteristics of, 323
pathogenesis and treatment, 324
Hemophilus hemolyticus, characteristics of, 323
Hemophilus influenzae
encapsulated, characteristics of, 322
laboratory diagnosis, 323
nonencapsulated, characteristics of, 322–323
PPNG transfer plasmid and, 269
prevention, 323
treatment, 323
Hemophilus parainfluenzae, characteristics of, 323
Hemophilus paraphrophilus, characteristics of, 323
Hemorrhagic fever
Crimean-Congo, 438
Ebola, 437–438
Marburg, 438
with renal syndrome, 438
Hemorrhagic fever viruses, characteristics of, 436–438
Heparin, 187
Hepatitis A
drug abusers and, 453
epidemiology, 451–453
general characteristics, 449
immunity to, 455
immunological and biological events associated with, 452
laboratory diagnosis, 454
pathogenesis, 450–451
treatment and prevention, 455
Hepatitis B
blood markers for, 452
cancer caused by, 392–393
disinfection, 95
epidemiology, 453–454
general characteristics, 449–450
health care workers and, 457
immunity to, 455
laboratory diagnosis, 454–455
pathogenesis, 450–451
treatment and prevention, 455–456
vaccines, 456
Hepatitis C
cancer caused by, 392–393
disinfection, 95
epidemiology, 454
general characteristics, 450
immunity to, 455
laboratory diagnosis, 455
pathogenesis, 450–451
treatment and prevention, 456
Hepatitis D
characteristics, 449
epidemiology, 454
laboratory diagnosis, 455
treatment and prevention, 456
Hepatitis E
epidemiology, 454
general characteristics, 450
immunity to, 455
laboratory diagnosis, 455
pathogenesis, 450–451
treatment and prevention, 456
Hepatitis viruses, 449–456
epidemiology, 451
pathogenesis, 450–451
universal precautions for, 455–456
Herd immunity, 231
Herpangina, enterovirus, 432
Herpes
genital, 416–417
gingivostomatitis, 416
keratoconjunctivitis, 416,
labialis, 416
neonatal, 417
Herpes simplex virus
epidemiology, 417
laboratory diagnosis, 417
serotypes, 415
treatment and prevention, 417–418
type 1 pathogenesis, 416
type 2 pathogenesis, 416–417
Herpesvirus
cancer caused by, 393–394
encephalitis, 416
general characteristics of, 411
Herpetic whitlow, 417
Hesse, Frau, agar-agar discovery of, 6
Heterotrophs, defined, 49
Hfr, conjugation and, 77
High efficiency particulate air filters, sterilization using, 97
High frequency of recombination. *See* Hfr
High-frequency switching, *Candida* virulence and, 472
Histamine, 187
immune cell, 131
in inflammation, 133–134
Histocompatibility testing, 195
Histoplasma capsulatum, as agent of histoplasmosis, 474–475
Histoplasmosis
epidemiology of, 474
laboratory diagnosis, 475
pathogenesis of, 474
treatment, 475
Hn glycoprotein, mumps virus, 423
Holmes, Oliver Wendell, germ theory and, 5
Hookworm infection
epidemiology, 519
laboratory diagnosis, 519
pathogenesis, 519
treatment and control, 519–520
Horizontal disease transmission, 229–230, 384, 395
Hospital-associated infection(s)
epidemiology of, 534–536
factor(s) contributing to
antibiotic chemotherapy as, 542–543
catheterization as. *See* Catheter-associated infections
diagnostic procedures as, 543
hospital procedures as, 538–543
host, 537–538
hypodermic injections as, 543
immunosuppressive drugs as, 538
metabolic disorders as, 538
microbial, 536–537
surgery as, 538–539
trauma as, 538
hygienic practices and, 544–555
microbes involved in, 535–536
patient surveillance and, 545–546
personnel surveillance and, 545
prevention and control of, 543–546
rates, 535–536
transmission of
airborne spread in, 535
contaminated fomites and fluids in, 534–535
direct contact in, 534
universal precautions for, 544
Host, animal parasite, 501
Human herpesvirus-6, pathogenesis, 418
Human immunodeficiency virus. *See also* Acquired immunodeficiency syndrome
characteristics of, 443
latency and, 445
pathogenesis, 443–447
proteins, 443
replication sites, 444
stages of infection, 445
Human leukocyte antigen, 194
serological typing of, 574
Human leukocyte-associated antigen gene cluster, 157
Human neutrophil protein, 132

Human papillomavirus, cancer caused by, 394–395
Human T lymphotropic viruses, 391
Humoral immunity, defined, 130
Hutchinson's teeth, congenital syphilis and, 344
Hyaluronic acid, *Streptococcus pyogenes*, 252
Hyaluronidase
  as invasive factor, 213
  Streptococcus pyogenes, 254
Hybridoma formation, 568–570
Hydatid cysts, echinococcosis and, 527
Hydatidosis, 527
Hydrogen ion
  bacterial growth and, 51
  effect on enzyme activity, 31
Hydrogen peroxide, in oxygen metabolism, 50
Hydrogen sulfide production, in clinical microbiology, 241
Hydrolase, defined, 33
Hydrophobia, rabies virus infection and, 435
Hydrops fetalis
  hemolytic disease of newborn and, 573
  parvovirus and, 421
Hymenolepis diminuta, tapeworm infestation caused by, 526
Hymenolepis nana, tapeworm infestation caused by, 526
Hyperbaric oxygen therapy, gas gangrene treatment using, 279
Hypersensitivity(ies)
  defined, 185
  gastrointestinal, 188
  respiratory, 188
  skin, 188
  testing, 188
  type I
    atopy and, 187–189
    defined, 185
    mechanism of, 186
    systemic anaphylaxis and, 186–187
  type II, 189–190
  type III, 190
  type IV, 190–192. *See also* Delayed-type hypersensitivity
Hypertonic medium, defined, 21
Hypha(e), types of, 466
Hypnozoite, malaria relapse and, 515
Hypochlorites, as disinfectants, 100
Hypochlorous acid, phagocytosis and, 137
Hypogammaglobulinemia, 180, 184
Hyposensitization, 188
Hypotonic medium, defined, 21

Icosahedral symmetry
  animal virus, 382
  bacteriophage, 403
Icterus, defined, 244
Icterus gravis neonatorum, hemolytic disease of newborn and, 573
Idiotopes, defined, 153
Idiotype, defined, 153
Idoxuridine, activity of, 113
Imipenem, 109
Immune complex disease
  characteristics of, 190
  Streptococcus pyogenes and, 254–255
Immune cytolysis test, 563
Immune globulins, licensed, 589
Immune response
  anamnestic, 175
  chemical regulators of, 169–172
  primary, 174
  secondary, 174
Immune serum globulin, immunization with, 180
Immune system
  cancer and, 196–198
  as factor influencing host resistance, 209–210
Immunity
  acquired. *See* Immunity, specific
  cell-mediated, defined, 130
  cell types involved in, 131
  herd, 231
  humoral, defined, 130
  nonphagocytic cells in, 130–132
  nonspecific vs. specific, 130
  phagocytic cells in, 130–132
  specific, characteristics of, 144
  through vaccination, 177–181
Immunization. *See also* Vaccine(s)
  active, 177–180
  child, 402
  passive, 180
  prematriculation, 179
Immunoblotting. *See* Western blot test technique
Immunoelectron microscopy, virus identification by, 399
Immunoelectrophoresis tests, 565
Immunoferritin technique, 570
Immunofluorescence, syphilis diagnosis and, 344
Immunofluorescent microscopy, 552
Immunogen, defined, 144
Immunogenicity
  antigen, 144
  defined, 144
Immunoglobulin(s). *See also specific types*
  antigen binding fragment of, 146
  antigen binding to, 147–148
  as antigens, 152–153
  B cell surface, 163
  classes
    biological properties of, 148–150
    structure of, 147
  constant regions of, 146
  crystallizable fragment of, 146
  as defense mechanisms, 139
  digestion fragments, 145–146
  domains, 146
  genes
    heavy chain switch and function of, 151–152
    heavy chain variable chain reorganization of, 151
    light chain reorganization of, 150–151
  immunotherapy with, 180
  polymers, 146–147
  structure of, 145–146
  variable regions of, 146
Immunoglobulin A
  biological properties of, 149–150
  physicochemical properties of, 149
  secretory
    antimicrobial activity of, 207, 208
    biological properties of, 150
    formation of, 150
    in nonspecific resistance, 172–173
Immunoglobulin D
  biological properties of, 150
  physicochemical properties of, 149
Immunoglobulin E
  in animal parasite infections, 175–176
  biological properties of, 150
  physicochemical properties of, 149
  type I hypersensitivity and, 186
Immunoglobulin G
  biological properties of, 148
  in fetus, 148
  physicochemical properties of, 149
Immunoglobulin M
  biological properties of, 148
  physicochemical properties of, 149
Immunological test(s), 560–574
  agglutination as, 562–563
  avidin-biotin technique as, 568
  complement fixation test, 563–564
  counterimmunoelectrophoresis test, 566
  enzyme immunoassay as, 567
  enzyme-linked immunosorbent assay as, 567
  fluorescent antibody technique as, 566
  immune cytolysis as, 563
  immunodiffusion as, 562
  immunoelectrophoresis as, 565
  in vivo, 571
  monoclonal antibodies in, 568–570. *See also* Antibodies, monoclonal
  precipitation as, 561–562
  principles underlying, 560
  radioallergosorbent test as, 568
  radioimmunoassay as, 567
  recent, 564–570
  special, 570
  traditional, 561–564
  value of, 560
  virus neutralization as, 563
  western blot test as, 568
Immunology
  history of, 8
  red blood cell, 571–573
  transplantation, 194
  tumor, 196–198

Immunosuppression, graft rejection prevention and, 195
Immunosuppressive drugs, hospital-associated infections and, 538
Immunotherapy
  active, 197
  passive, 197–198
  passive immunization and, 180
  tumor, 197–198
Immunotoxins, immunotherapy with, 180
Imperfect state, fungal, 468
Impetigo
  Staphylococcus aureus, 248
  Streptococcus pyogenes, 254
Inapparent disease, defined, 206
Incidence, disease, 230–231
Incineration, sterilization using, 97
Inclusion conjunctivitis, chlamydial, 363–364
Inclusion body
  bacterial, 25–26
  virus formation of, 390
Incubation period, in disease, 221
Index case, 232
India ink, negative stain, 559
Induction, mechanism of enzyme, 67–68
Infant botulism, 277
Infection. *See* Disease(s)
Infectious disease, plasmids associated with, 79–80
Infectious jaundice. *See Leptospira icterohaemorrhagiae*
Infectious mononucleosis, 418
Inflammation
  acute, 133–134
  chemotaxis during, 134
  chronic, 134
  defects in, 138–139
  phagocytosis and, 133–134
Influenza. *See also* Influenza virus
  in disease surveillance, 231
Influenza virus
  antigenic drift, 428
  antigenic shift, 428
  classification, 426
  epidemiology, 428
  evolution and variation, 429
  Guillain-Barré syndrome and, 429
  immunity to, 429
  laboratory diagnosis, 428–429
  morphology, 426
  pathogenesis, 426–427
  treatment and prevention, 429
Insects, as disease vectors, 223–224
Insertion sequences, spontaneous mutations and, 70
Insertional mutagenesis, retroviruses and, 396
Instar, arthropod, 527
Insulin, medical use of genetically engineered, 89
Interferon
  antitumor activity of, 197
  characteristics of, 160
  classification, 140
  mechanism of action of, 140–141
  medical uses of, 89
  virus stimulation of, 390
Interferon alpha
  immunotherapy with, 180
  source and function of, 159
Interferon gamma
  effects of, 160
  immunotherapy with, 180
  macrophage activation and, 137
  source and function of, 159
Interleukin-1
  in bacterial infections, 173
  characteristics of, 158–159
  as endogenous pyrogen, 216
Interleukin-2
  in bacterial infections, 173
  characteristics of, 159
Interleukin-3, characteristics of, 159
Interleukin-4
  in bacterial infections, 173
  characteristics of, 159
Interleukin-5, characteristics of, 159
Interleukin-6
  in bacterial infections, 173
  characteristics of, 159
Interleukin-7, characteristics of, 159
Interleukin-8, characteristics of, 159
Interleukins. *See also specific types*
  as chemotherapeutic agents, 160
  medical uses of, 89
Intermediate host, animal parasite infections and, 501
Internal organs, microbial agents causing diseases of, 578–580
Intestinal tract, as antimicrobial defense factor, 208
Intranuclear inclusions, cytomegalovirus, 412
Intron, defined, 150
Invasiveness
  defined, 205
  microbial products associated with, 212, 213
Iodine
  as disinfectant, 100, 544
  gram-stain, 557
  tincture of, 100
Iodophors, as disinfectants, 100
Ionizing radiation, sterilization using, 98
Iris diaphragm, microscope, 549
Iron
  as factor influencing host resistance, 210, 211
  growth requirement for, 50
Ischemia, defined, 244
Isomerase, defined, 34
Isoniazid
  activity of, 116
  Mycobacterium tuberculosis therapy with, 336
Isospora belli, pathogenesis of, 517
Isosporiasis, AIDS and treatment of, 448
Itraconazole, activity of, 111
Iwanowsky, virus discovery by, 8

Japanese B encephalitis, 439, 440
Jarisch-Herxheimer reaction, syphilis and, 346
J chain, immunoglobulin, 146

Kala-azar. *See* Leishmaniasis, visceral
Kanagawa test, *Vibrio parahaemolyticus*, 318
Kanamycin, activity of, 111
K antigen
  enterobacteriaceae, 294
  Escherichia coli, 297
Kaposi's sarcoma, AIDS and, 446, 447
Katayama fever, schistosomiasis and, 524
Keratinase, fungal, 471
Ketoconazole, activity of, 111
Kingella, characteristics of, 270
Kininogenase, 187
Kinyoun acid-fast stain, 558
Kirby-Bauer method, 121–124
Kissing bug, American trypanosomiasis and, 511
Klebsiella, characteristics of, 307
Klebsiella pneumoniae, hospital infections caused by, 535
Koch, Robert
  germ theory and, 6
  postulates of, 6
Koplik's spots, measles virus and, 421
Krebs cycle. *See* Citric acid cycle
Kuru, 458
Kyasanur forest disease, 436

Laboratory identification, 240–244
  antimicrobial susceptibility testing in, 243
  biochemical characteristics in, 241
  computers in, 243
  culture in, 241
  flow cytometry in, 243
  fluorogenic and chromogenic substrates in, 241
  gas-liquid chromatography, 243
  microscopy in, 240
  molecular techniques in 243
  rapid techniques in, 242–243
  serological characteristics in, 241–242
Laboratory safety, 243–244
Laboratory techniques, epidemiological, 232–234
LaCrosse virus encephalitis, 439, 440
Lactic acid, glycolysis formation of, 35–36
Lactobacillus
  biofilm, protective effect of, 213
  differentiation tests, 290
Lactoferrin
  as antimicrobial defense factor, 207
  as factor influencing host resistance, 210, 211
  phagocytosis and, 137

Lactose operon, 68
Lag phase, bacterial, 48
Lancefield, Rebecca, streptococcal classification, 252
Laparoscope, disinfection of, 102
Larva
 animal parasite, 501
 arthropod, 527
 fluke, 523
Laryngeal papillomatosis, 420
Lassa fever, 437
Latency
 defined, 206
 virus, 391
Lecithinase, as invasive factor, 213
Lectins
 cell agglutinability and, 392
 as mitogens, 158
Legionella pneumophila
 characteristics, 376
 epidemiology, 376–377
 laboratory diagnosis, 377
 pathogenesis, 377
 treatment, 378
Legionella species, 375
Legionnaires disease. *See Legionella pneumophila*
Leishmania braziliensis, mucocutaneous leishmaniasis caused by, 513
Leishmania donovani, visceral leishmaniasis caused by, 513
Leishmania major, cutaneous leishmaniasis caused by, 513
Leishmaniasis
 cutaneous, 512–513
 diagnosis and treatment of, 513
 mucocutaneous, 513
 visceral, 513
Leishmania species, leishmaniasis caused by, 512–513
Lens, oil immersion, 549
Leproma, defined, 338
Leprosy. See also *Mycobacterium leprae*
 indeterminate, 338
 lepromatous, 338
 tuberculoid, 338
Leptospira icterohaemorrhagiae
 characteristics, 349
 epidemiology and pathogenesis, 349
 laboratory diagnosis and treatment, 349
Leptospiroses, defined, 348
Lethal factor, *Bacillus anthracis*, 273
Leukemia, defined, 185
Leukocidin, as *Staphylococcus aureus* virulence factor, 248
Leukocyte esterase test, nongonococcal urethritis and, 366
Leukocytes, nonspecific immunity involvement of, 142
Leukocytosis, defined, 244
Leukopenia, defined, 244
L-forms
 characteristics, 355–356
 pathogenesis, 356
Lice, as disease vector, 224
Ligase, defined, 34
Light chain
 diversity of, 150–151
 structure, 145
Lincomycin, activity of, 112
Lipase, function of, 41
Lipid
 animal virus, 382–383
 as inclusion body, 26
Lipid A
 as factor in disease process, 214–218
 Pseudomonas aeruginosa, 311
Lipooligosaccharide, as cause of septic shock, 265
Lipopolysaccharide, cell wall, 19, 21. *See also* Endotoxin(s)
 in complement evasion, 172
Liposomes
 amphotericin B activity and, 110
 leishmaniasis treatment using, 513
Lipoteichoic acid, as adhesin, 211
Lister, Joseph, aseptic technique and, 6
Listeria monocytogenes
 in food-borne disease, 229
 general characteristics, 289
 laboratory diagnosis, 290
 pathogenesis, 289–290
 prevention, 290
 treatment, 290
Listeriosis, 289
 neonatal, 289
Listerolysin O, 290
Lithotripsy, hospital-associated infections from, 543
Loa loa, loaiasis caused by, 523
Loaiasis, pathogenesis, 523
Loboa loboi, lobomycosis caused by, 480
Lobomycosis, characteristics of, 480
Local disease, defined, 206
Lockjaw, defined, 280
Loeffler
 staining by, 8
 virus discovery by, 8
Logarithmic phase, bacterial, 48
Louse, micrograph of, 528
Louse-borne typhus. *See Rickettsia prowazekii*
Lupus. *See* Systemic lupus erythematosus, as autoimmune disease
Lyase, defined, 34
Lyme disease. *See Borrelia burgdorferi*
Lymphatic system, microbial agents causing diseases of, 581–582
Lymph nodes, location of, 157
Lymphocytes. *See also* T cell(s); B cell(s)
 non-T, non-B, characteristics of, 165
 tumor infiltrating, 198
Lymphogranuloma venereum, 365
Lymphoid cells, characteristics of, 160–165. *See also specific cell types*
Lymphoid system, structure of, 156–157
Lymphokine-activated cells, 165
Lymphokines. *See also* Cytokines
 defined, 158
 helper T cells and, 162
Lymphoma, defined, 185
Lyophilization, preservation of microorganisms by, 56
Lysogen, defined, 404
Lysogeny, bacteriophage, 403–404
Lysosome, phagocytosis and, 136
Lysozyme
 as antimicrobial defense factor, 207
 cell wall removal using, 21
 lysosome, 137

MacConkey agar, as isolation medium, 56
Macrophage
 activation, 137–138
  cytokines and, 158
  Mycobacterium tuberculosis and, 334
 characteristics of, 131–132
 immune system involvement of, 165
 nonspecific functions of, 133
 specific functions of, 133
Macrophage colony-stimulating factor, source and function of, 159
Macule, defined, 222
Madurella grisea, mycetoma caused by, 480
Madurella mycetomatis, mycetoma caused by, 480
Maedi, 456
Magnesium, growth requirement for, 50
Major basic protein, 131
Major histocompatibility complex protein
 graft rejection and, 194–196
 restriction, 158
 structure and function of, 157–158
 T cell recognition, 161
Malabsorption syndrome, giardiasis and, 508
Malaria
 epidemiology, 514
 falciparum, 514
 laboratory diagnosis, 514
 life cycle, 513–514
 pathogenesis, 514
 quartan, 514
 relapse, hypnozoite and, 515
 subtertian, 514
 tertian, 514
 transfusion, 514
 treatment and control, 514
Malassezia furfur, tinea versicolor and, 484
Malic acid, formation of, 39
Manganese, growth requirement for, 50
Mannan, *Candidia* virulence and, 485

Mannitol salt agar, identification of *Staphylococcus aureus* using, 250
Mansonella ozzardi, filariasis caused by, 522
Mansonella perstans, filariasis caused by, 522
Mantoux test, 334
Marburg hemorrhagic fever, 438
Mast cells
  animal parasite infection and, 176
  characteristics of, 130–131
  mediators released by, 187
  type I hypersensitivity and, 186
Mastigophora, infections caused by, 507–513
Measles. *See* Measles virus
Measles virus
  epidemiology, 422
  immunity, 422
  laboratory diagnosis, 422
  morphology, 421
  pathogenesis, 421–422
  treatment and prevention, 422–423
  vaccine, 422–423
Media. *See also* Culture media
  differential selective, Enterobacteriaceae, 294
  primary isolation, Enterobacteriaceae, 294
  selective enrichment, Enterobacteriaceae, 294
Membrane attack complex, 170
Membrane filter, bacterial isolation using, 55
Memory cells, formation of, 163, 164
Meningitis. *See also* Nervous system
  causative bacterial agents of, 322
  Neisseria meningitidis, 265
Meningococcus. *See Neisseria meningitidis*
  SEM of, 265
Mercury, as disinfectant, 102
Merozoites, malaria, 514
Mesophile, defined, 51
Mesosomes, 18
Metabolism
  defined, 30
  energy generation in, 34–41. *See also* Energy formation
  energy utilization in, 41–42
  enzymatic control of, 42–43
  enzymes in, 30–34. *See also* Enzyme
  vitamin function in, 31
Metacercaria, larva, 523
Metachromatic granules, as inclusion bodies, 26
Metachromatic granule stain, 559
Metals
  disinfection using, 102
  resistance to, 79
Methicillin, structure, 106
Microaerophiles, oxygen requirement of, 50
Microbial genetics, 62–80
Microbial metabolism, 29–43. *See also* Metabolism
Microbiology
  clinical
    computers in, 243
    laboratory identification in, 240–244. *See also* Laboratory identification
    laboratory safety in, 243–244
    specimen collection in, 240
  Golden Age of, 6–9
    bacteria discovered during, 7
  history of, 4–9
    disease concepts in, 4
    germ theory and, 5–6
    spontaneous generation in, 4–5
  modern, history of, 9
Micrococci, characteristics of, 252
Microflora
  as antimicrobial defense factor, 207
  ear, 585
  eye, 585
  gastrointestinal tract, 587
  genitourinary tract, 586
  indigenous, activities of, 204
  respiratory tract, 585–586
  skin, 585
Microorganisms
  comparative size of, 550
  laboratory identification of, 240–244. *See also specific microorganisms*
Microscope(s)
  characteristics of, 556
  compound bright-field, 549–550
  dark-field, 550
  electron, 553–555
  fluorescent, 552–553
  Nomarski interference, 550–552
  phase-contrast, 550
  resolving power of, 549
  van Leeuwenhoek's, 4
Microscopy, 549–557. *See also* Microscope(s)
  in clinical microbiology, 240–241
Microsporum, infections caused by, 481–485
Minerals, bacterial requirement for, 50
Minimal bactericidal concentration, 120
Minimal inhibitor concentration, antimicrobial, 117
Miracidia, larva, 523
Missense mutation, 72
Mite, as disease vector, 224
Mixed disease, defined, 206
Mixed leukocyte reaction, graft rejection prevention and, 195
Mold
  asexual reproduction in, 468
  characteristics of, 466
  colony morphology, 470
Molybdenum, growth requirement for, 50
Monkeypoxvirus, 409
Monoclonal antibodies. *See* Antibody(ies), monoclonal
Monoclonal gammopathies, 185
Monocytes
  characteristics of, 131–132
  types of, 131–132
Monokines, defined, 158
Monotrichous flagella, 23
Moraxella
  characteristics of, 270
  pathogenesis, 314
Morbidity rate, 231
Mortality rate, 231
Mosquito, as disease vector, 224
Motility, disorders in, phagocytosis and, 139
M protein
  as antiphagocytic factor, 218
  complement evasion and, 172
  in rheumatic fever, 254
  as *Streptococcus pyogenes* virulence factor, 253
Mucins, as antimicrobial defense factor, 207
Mucor, as cause of mucormycosis, 490
Mucormycosis
  laboratory diagnosis of, 490
  pathogenesis of, 490
  treatment of, 490
Mucosa
  as antimicrobial defense factor, 207
  defined, 244
Mucosal-associated lymphoid tissue, 157
Mucous patch, secondary syphilis and, 342
Multinucleated giant cells, inflammation and, 134
Mumps virus
  epidemiology, 424
  laboratory diagnosis, 424
  morphology, 423
  pathogenesis, 423–424
  treatment and prevention, 424
  vaccine, 424
Muscle worm infection. *See* Trichinosis
Mutagen, defined, 69
Mutagenesis, defined, 69
Mutation
  chemical agents causing, 72
  defined, 69
  drug resistance and microbial, 119
  frameshift, 72
  genetic code changes from, 72
  induced, 70
  missense, 72
  nonsense, 72
  physical agents causing, 72
  rate, 70
  repair of, 72–73
  spontaneous, 70–72
Mutant
  auxotrophic, 74
  detection of, 74
  isolation of, 74
Myasthenia gravis, as autoimmune disease, 193

Mycelium, defined, 466
Mycetismus, 491–492
Mycetoma, characteristics of, 480
Mycobacteria, 330–339
  characteristics, 331
  disinfection of, 95
  nontuberculous, characteristics of, 335
Mycobacterial disease, AIDS and treatment of, 448
Mycobacterium avium-intracellulare complex
  characteristics, 335
  pathogenesis, 337
Mycobacterium bovis, 331, 336
Mycobacterium fortuitum-chelonae complex
  characteristics, 335
  pathogenesis, 337
Mycobacterium haemophilum, characteristics, 335
Mycobacterium kansasii, characteristics, 335
Mycobacterium leprae
  characteristics, 337
  epidemiology, 338
  laboratory diagnosis, treatment, and prevention, 338
  pathogenesis, 338
Mycobacterium malmoense, characteristics, 335
Mycobacterium marinum, characteristics, 335
Mycobacterium scrofulaceum, characteristics, 335
Mycobacterium simiae, characteristics, 335
Mycobacterium szulgai, characteristics, 335
Mycobacterium tuberculosis
  characteristics, 331
  epidemiology, 335
  human immunodeficiency virus and, 332
  immunity, 334
  laboratory diagnosis, 334
  multidrug-resistant, 336
  pathogenesis, 331–332
  prevention, 335–336
  treatment, 335–336
  tuberculin hypersensitivity association with, 192
Mycobacterium xenopi, characteristics, 335
Mycolic acid, *Mycobacteria*, 331
Mycoplasma genitalium, pathogenesis, 356, 357
Mycoplasma hominis, pathogenesis, 356, 357
Mycoplasma
  characteristics, 354–355
  pathogenic, characteristics of, 357
  as wall-less bacteria, 21,
Mycoplasma pneumoniae
  laboratory diagnosis, 356–357
  pathogenesis, 356
  treatment and prevention, 357
Mycoses
  cutaneous, 481–485
  defined, 471
  opportunistic, 485–491
  subcutaneous, 479–481
  superficial, 484–485
  systemic, 474–478
Mycotoxicosis, 492
Mycotoxins, 473, 491–492
Myeloma
  defined, 185
  monoclonal antibody source, 568–569
Myeloperoxidase, phagocytosis and, 136
Myiasis, 527–528
Myocarditis, enterovirus, 432

NAD
  electron transport by, 35
  glycolysis role of, 35
NAD dehydrogenase, citric acid cycle and, 39
NADPH oxidase, phagocytosis and, 137
Naegleria fowleri, primary amebic meningoencephalitis caused by, 507
Nalidixic acid
  activity of, 113
  structure of, 113
Nantucket fever, 516
Nasopharyngeal cancer, Epstein-Barr virus as cause of, 394
Nasopharyngitis
  Neisseria meningitidis as cause of, 264
Natural killer cells, characteristics of, 165
Necator americanus, as cause of hookworm infection, 519–520
Necrotizing enterocolitis, 283
Negative stain, 559
Negri body, as rabies virus inclusion body, 390, 434
Neisseria. See also specific species
  differentiative properties of, 264
  general characteristics, 264
  nonpathogenic, 270
  pathogenic, characteristics of, 271
Neisseria gonorrhoeae
  antigenic variation of, 218
  disseminated infection by, 268
  epidemiology, 267
  extragenital infections, 268
  laboratory diagnosis, 269
  pathogenesis, 267–268
  pelvic inflammatory disease and, 268
  plasmid-mediated antimicrobial resistance in, 269
  prevention, 269–270
  treatment, 269–270
Neisseria meningitidis
  epidemiology, 266
  laboratory diagnosis, 266
  pathogenesis, 264–265
  prevention, 266–267
  rapid tests in identification of, 266
  serological tests in identification of, 266
  treatment, 266–267
  vaccines, 267
Nemathelminthes, diseases caused by, 517–523
Neomycin, activity of, 111
Neonatal pneumonia, chlamydial, 365
Nephropathia epidemica, hantavirus and, 438
Nephrotoxin, *Streptococcus pyogenes*, 253
Nervous system, microbial agents causing diseases of, 582–583
Netilmicin, activity of, 111
Neuraminidase
  influenza virus, 426, 428
  mumps virus, 423
Neurocysticercosis, taeniasis and, 527
Neurosyphilis, 343
Neutropenia, phagocytosis and, 139
Neutropenic enterocolitis, 283
Neutrophil activating factor, 187
Neutrophils, characteristics of, 130
Newborn, hemolytic disease of, 573
Nicotinamide adenine dinucleotide. *See* NAD
Nigrosin, negative stain, 559
Nitric oxide, *Bordetella pertussis* infection and, 325
Nitrofurans, activity of, 116
Nitrofurantoin, activity of, 116–117
Nitrogen
  bacterial requirement for, 49
  gas, as source of nitrogen, 49
Nitrogen fixation, 49
Nitrous acid, mutation caused by, 72
Nocardia, characteristics, 372
Nocardia asteroides, 371
Nocardia brasiliensis, 371
Nocardiosis
  laboratory diagnosis, 371
  pathogenesis, 371
  treatment, 371–372
Nomarski interference, 550–552
Nomenclature, in classification of microorganisms, 13
Noncompetitive inhibition, enzyme, 33
Nongonococcal urethritis
  chlaymdial, 365
  Ureaplasma urealyticum and, 356, 357
Nonsense mutation, 72
Norfloxacin, activity of, 113
Norwalk virus, pathogenesis, 442, 443
Nuclease
  interferons and, 11
  Streptococcus pyogenes, 254
Nucleic acid(s). *See also* DNA; RNA
  animal virus, 382
  hybridization, animal virus identification by, 399

probes, animal virus identification by, 399–400
structure of, 62–63
synthesis, inhibitors of, 112–114
Nucleocapsid, animal virus, 382
Nucleoid, bacterial, 24–25
Nucleotide, defined, 63
Numerical aperture, 549
Nutrient, defined, 48
Nutrition, as factor influencing host resistance, 210
Nystatin, activity of, 110

O antigen
enterobacteriaceae, 294
Salmonella identification by, 301
Obligate aerobes
glucose metabolism in, 36
oxygen requirement of, 50
Obligate anaerobes, glucose metabolism in, 37
Occupation, as factor influencing host resistance, 210
Ofloxacin, activity of, 113
Oil immersion lens, 549
Oleoresin, 192
Omsk hemorrhagic fever, 436
Onchocerca volvulus, onchocerciasis caused by, 523
Onchocerciasis, pathogenesis, 523
Onchocercomata, 523
Onchospheres, taeniasis and, 526
Oncogenes, transformation and, 396–397
Oncogenic viruses
defined, 392
DNA, 392–395
RNA, 395–397
Onychia, 486
Oocyst, toxoplasmosis and, 515
Oogonium, fungal, 468
Oospores, fungal, 468
Operator, in operon model, 68
Operon
inducible, 68
lactose, 68
model of, 68–69
repressible, 69
Opisthorchis viverrini, 523
Opisthorchis felineus, 523
Opportunistic disease
AIDS and, 446
Opsonization
immunoglobulins used in, 148
phagocytosis and, 134–135
Opsonophagocytic index, serological test, 570
Optical density, bacterial growth and, 57
Optochin, in *Streptococcus pneumoniae* identification, 260
Oriental sore. *See* Leishmaniasis, cutaneous
Oropharynx, as antimicrobial defense factor, 208
Osmosis, wall-less bacteria and, 21
Osmotic pressure, bacterial growth and, 52
Osteomyelitis, *Staphylococcus aureus*, 249
Outer membrane, functions of, 19
Oxacillin, structure, 106
Oxaloacetate, formation of, 38
Oxidase test. *See* Cytochrome oxidase test
Oxidation, defined, 35
Oxidative phosphorylation, 35
Oxidoreductase, defined, 33
Oxygen
bacterial requirement for, 49–50
metabolism, products of, 50

P1 protein, *Mycoplasma*, 356
Pandemic disease, 230
Papanicolaou(Pap) smear, trichomoniasis and, 510
Papillomavirus
laboratory diagnosis, 420
pathogenesis, 420
treatment, 420
Papule, defined, 222
Para-aminobenzoic acid, structure of, 115
Para-aminosalicylic acid
activity of, 116
structure of, 115
Paracoccidioides brasiliensis, paracoccidioidomycosis caused by, 477–478
Paracoccidioidomycosis
epidemiology, 477
laboratory diagnosis, 478
pathogenesis, 477
treatment, 478
Paragonimus westermani, 523
Parainfluenza virus
laboratory diagnosis, 434
pathogenesis, 434
treatment, 434
Paramyxovirus, cell penetration by, 423
Parasites
animal
defined, 500
diseases caused by. *See* Parasitic infections
extracellular, characteristics of, 204
intracellular, characteristics of, 204–205
Parasitic infection
incidence of, 500–501
infective forms and life cycles in, 501
laboratory diagnosis of, 502–503
nature of, 501–502
nemathelminthes, 517–523
platyhelminthes, 523–527
protozoan. *See* Protozoan infection
treatment and control, 503
Parasitism, defined, 204
Paratyphoid fever. *See Salmonella*, enteric fever caused by
Paratope, defined, 145
Paresis, syphilis and, 343
Paronychia, 486
Parvovirus, morphology, 421
Parvovirus B19, pathogenesis, 421
Passive diffusion, defined, 17
Pasteur, Louis
germ theory of, 5–6
spontaneous generation experiments of, 4–5
vaccine development by, 8
Pathogenesis, defined, 244
Pathogenicity, defined, 205
Paul-Bunnell-Davidson test, infectious mononucleosis and, 418
Pelvic inflammatory disease
chlamydial, 365
Neisseria gonorrhoeae as cause of, 268
Penicillin-binding proteins, function of, 107
Penicillin
mechanism of action, 107–108
structure 106
Penicillium, as cause of mycotoxicosis, 492
Pentose phosphate pathway
glucose oxidation and, 37–38
as source of carbons in biosynthesis, 42
Peplomer, animal virus, 384
Peptide bond, formation of, 67
Peptidoglycan, cell wall, 19–20
Peptococcus, 252, 258
Peptone, in growth media, 49
Peptostreptococcus, 252, 258
Perennial allergic rhinitis, 188
Perforins, cytotoxic T cells and, 162
Periodontal disease, actinomycetes and, 372
Periplasmic space, bacterial, 19–21
Peritrichous flagella, 23
Permethrin, scabies treatment with, 527
Peroxidase, as antimicrobial defense factor, 207–208
Persistent infection
chronic disease as, 222
types of, 391
Pertussis. *See also Bordetella pertussis*
toxin, 324
Petri dish, discovery of, 6–7
Petriellidium boydii, mycetoma caused by, 480
Petroff-Hauser counter, growth measurement by, 57
Phage conversion, 404
Phage typing, 232, 233
Phagocyte(s)
disorders, 185
mononuclear, 130, 131–132
immune function of, 165–166
polymorphonuclear, immune function of, 165–166
types of, 130

Phagocytosis
capsule and slime layer function in, 22
defects in, 138–139
deleterious effects of, 138–139
dynamics of, 132–137
intracellular survival during, 138
microbicidal disorders and, 139
nonoxidative killing in, 137
oxidative killing in, 137
recognition step in, 134
tissue destruction due to, 138
vacuole formation in, 134
Phagolysosome, formation of, 136
Phagosome, formation of, 134
Phase-contrast microscope, 550
Phenol, as disinfectant, 99–100, 544
Phenotype, defined, 62
Phenylethyl alcohol agar, bacterial isolation using, 55–56
Phialophora verrucosa, chromoblastomycosis caused by, 480
Phosphatase, *Legionella pneumophila*, 377
Phospholipase
Pseudomonas aeruginosa, 311
rickettsial production of, 138
Phospholipase C. *See* Alpha toxin
Phospholipid, structure, 17
Phosphorus, bacterial requirement for, 49
Phosphorylation
defined, 35
electron transport, 35
oxidative, 35
substrate, 35
Photochromogens, *Mycobacteria*, 331
Phototaxis, defined, 22
Piedra, black and white, 485
Piedraia hortae, black piedra caused by, 485
Pig-bel, *Clostridium perfringens* as cause of, 279
Pili
as adhesins in disease process, 211–212
Enterobacteriaceae, 293–294
sex, conjugation and, 77
type 1, 211
types of, 23–24
Pinta, 346
Pinworm infection. *See* Enterobiasis
Pityriasis versicolor, 484
Plague. *See also Yersinia pestis*
bubonic, 305
control, 305–306
demic, 305
epidemiology, 305
laboratory diagnosis, 305
pneumonic, 305
prevention, 305–306
sylvatic, 305
treatment, 305
Plaque
bacteriophage, 403
dental, defined, 22
viral, 398
Plasma, as defense mechanism, 139
Plasma cells, formation of, 163, 164
Plasma membrane. *See* Cytoplasmic membrane
Plasmid(s)
characteristics associated with, 79
clone, detection of, 84–86
conjugative, 78–79
defined, 62
nonconjugative, 79
pBR322, 83
PPNG transfer, 269
as recombinant DNA vector, 83
resistance, 79
virulence, *Shigella*, 303
virulence determinants, 79
Plasmid profiles, in epidemiology, 233–234
Plasmodium species, malaria caused by, 513–514
Plasmodium vivax, as intracellular parasite, 205
Plasmodiasis. *See* Malaria
Plate count, growth measurement by, 57
Platelet, in host defense, 141
Platelet activating factor, 141, 187
Platyhelminthes, infections caused by, 523–527. *See also* Tapeworm; Trematoda
Pleomorphism, bacterial, 15
Plesiomonas
characteristics, 319
differentiation from *Vibrio*, 317
pathogenesis, 319–320
Pleurodynia, enterovirus, 432
Pneumococci. *See Streptococcus pneumoniae*
Pneumocystis carinii
AIDS and treatment of, 448
pneumonia caused by, 490–491
Pneumonia. *See also* Respiratory tract
Chlaymdia pneumoniae, 365
neonatal, chlaymdial, 365
pneumococcal, 258, factors predisposing to, 259
Pock, viral, 398
Poliomyelitis. *See* Poliovirus
Poliovirus
characteristics, 429–430
epidemiology, 430
laboratory diagnosis, 430
morphology, 430
pathogenesis, 430
treatment and prevention, 430–431
vaccines, 431
Pollinosis, 188
Polyene, activity of, 110–111
Polyhedral bodies, bacterial, 25
Polymerase chain reaction
animal virus identification by, 400
in epidemiology, 234
gene amplification using, 86–89
Polymorphonuclear granulocytes, types of, 130–131
Polymyxins, activity of, 111
Polyphosphate, as inclusion body, 26
Pontiac fever, 377
Potassium, growth requirement for, 50
Pour plate, bacterial isolation using, 55
Povidone-iodine, contamination of, hospital infections and, 534
Poxvirus
epidemiology and pathogenesis, 409
morphology, 409
vaccine, 409–410
Predisposing conditions, as factor influencing host resistance, 210–211
Prevalence, disease, 231
Primaquine phosphate, malaria treatment with, 514
Primary disease, defined, 206
Primary amebic meningoencephalitis, 507
Procaine, 107
Prodromal period, in disease, 221
Proglottid, tapeworm, 525
Progressive multifocal leukoencephalopathy, 460
Prokaryote, characteristics of, 12, 28
Promastigote, 510
Promoter, in operon model, 68
Prontosil, 9
Properdin, 170
Prophage, defined, 404
Prophylaxis, antimicrobial, 117–118
Propionibacterium, antimicrobial effect of, 206–207
Propionibacterium acnes, acne and, 288
Prostaglandins
fever and, 215–217
in inflammation, 133–134
Protease, influenza virus infection and, 426
Protective factor, *Bacillus anthracis*, 273
Protein(s)
cytoplasmic membrane, 17–18
genetically engineered, 89
heat destabilizing, DNA replication and, 65
repressor, operon and, 68–69
as sources of nitrogen, 49
synthesis
control of, 67–69
DNA translation and, 66–67
inhibitors of, 111–112
unwinding, DNA replication and, 64–65
Protein A, as *Staphylococcus aureus* virulence factor, 248
Proteinase, *Streptococcus pyogenes*, 254
Protein kinase, interferons and, 141
Proteus, characteristics of, 307
Proteus mirabilis, hospital infections caused by, 535
Protista, characteristics of, 12

Proto-oncogenes, cancer and, 396
Protoplast, preparation of, 21
Prototroph, defined, 74
Protozoa, classification of, 503
Protozoan infection
  characteristics of, 504
  Ciliata in, 513
  Mastigophora in, 507–513
  Sarcodina in, 503–507
  Sporozoa in, 513–517
Providencia, characteristics of, 307
Prozone phenomenon, syphilis diagnosis and, 346
Pruritus, defined, 186
Pseudallescheria boydii, hospital-associated, 536
Pseudallescheriasis, hospital-associated, 536
Pseudohyphae, fungal, 468, 470
Pseudomembranous colitis, *Clostridium difficile* as cause of, 281–283
Pseudomonas
  povidone-iodine solution contamination with, 534
  in sterilization, 95
Pseudomonas aeruginosa
  epidemiology, 311
  general characteristics, 311
  hospital infections caused by, 535
  identification, minimal characteristics for, 313
  laboratory diagnosis, 313
  pathogenesis, 311
  prevention, 313
  treatment, 313
  virulence factors, 312
Pseudomonas cepacia, pathogenesis, 314
Pseudomonas maltophila, pathogenesis, 314
Pseudomonas pseudomallei, pathogenesis, 314
Pseudomonas putida, pathogenesis, 314
Pseudomonas stutzeri, pathogenesis, 314
Psittacosis, 365
Psychrophile, defined, 51
Puerperal fever, *Streptococcus pyogenes*, 254
Pure culture, isolation of, 54–56
Purified protein derivative, 192
Purified tuberculin protein derivative, 334
Purine, atom origination for, 42
Pustule, defined, 222
Pyelonephritis, *Escherichia coli*, 296
Pyemia, defined, 206
Pyocyanins, *Pseudomonas aeruginosa*, 311
Pyoderma, *Staphylococcus aureus*, 248
Pyogenic, defined, 244
Pyoverdins, *Pseudomonas aeruginosa*, 311
Pyrimidine, atom origination for, 42
Pyrogenic, defined, 244
Pyrogens, endogenous, fever and, 215–217
Pyruvic acid
  formation of, 35
  metabolism, products of, 36, 37

Q fever. *See Coxiella burnetii*
Quaternary ammonium compounds, as disinfectant, 544
Queensland tick typhus, 360, 361
Quellung reaction, 22
  Streptococcus pneumoniae and, 259
Quinolones, activity of, 113
Quinone, citric acid cycle and, 39

Rabbit fever. *See Francisella tularensis*
Rabies. *See* Rabies virus
Rabies virus
  epidemiology, 435
  immunity to, 435–436
  laboratory diagnosis, 435
  morphology, 434
  pathogenesis, 434–435
  treatment and prevention, 436
  vaccines, 436
Race, as factor influencing host resistance, 210
Radiation
  graft rejection prevention using, 196
  ionizing, sterilization using, 98
  ultraviolet, sterilization using, 98
Radioallergosorbent test, 188, 568
Radioimmunoassay technique, 567–568
Rapid plasma reagin, syphilis diagnosis and, 345
Rat-bite fever
  Spirillum minor as cause of, 349–350
  Streptobacillus moniliformis as cause of, 375
Reagin, syphilis and, 345
Recombinant DNA, 74
  annealing, 83
  donors for, 83
  genetic engineering and, 83
  immunotherapy using, 198
  mechanisms for producing, 83–86
  vectors in, 83
Recombination, switching sequence, immunoglobulins and, 152
Red blood cells, immunology of, 571–573
Red man syndrome, 110
Redi, Francisco, spontaneous generation , 4
Reduction, defined, 35
Reduviid bug, American trypanosomiasis and, 511
Relapsing fever. *See Borrelia recurrentis*
Replica plating, mutant isolation by, 74
Replication
  DNA
    bacterial, 63–66
    viral, 385–386
  electron microscopy, 554
  RNA, viral, 386
Repression, mechanism of enzyme, 69
Repressor protein, 68
Reproduction, fungal, 467–470. *See also* Replication
Reservoir(s)
  animal, 223
  food as, 225
  human, 222–223
  inanimate, 223, 224–225
  insect, 223–224
  soil as, 225
  water as, 225
Residual body, phagocytosis and, 137
Resistance
  antimicrobial, 79
  heavy metal, 79
  host
    chemical factors associated with, 139–141
    complement system in, 141
    noncellular mechanisms of, 139–141
    platelet function in, 141
  nonspecific, 172–173
  serum, microbial defense and, 218
Respiration
  aerobic, 38–40
  anaerobic, 40–41
Resistance transfer factor, plasmid, 79
Resolving power, 549
Respiratory burst, phagocytosis and, 137
Respiratory syncytial virus
  epidemiology, 433
  laboratory diagnosis, 433–444
  pathogenesis, 433
  treatment, 444
Respiratory tract
  as antimicrobial defense factor, 208
  microbial agents causing diseases of, 577–578
  microbial flora of, 585–586
Restriction endonuclease, fingerprinting, epidemiology and, 234
Restriction enzymes
  function of, 83
  recognition sites for, 83
Retrovirus(es)
  classification of human, 395
  evolution, 395
  in gene therapy, 89
  oncogenic, 395–397
Reverse transcriptase
  complementary DNA formation using, 87
  RNA virus, 386, 395
Reye's syndrome, influenza virus and, 426
Rh system
  disease, management of, 573
  hemolytic disease of newborn and, 573
  isoimmunization, 572–573
  Rh type determination in, 572

Rhabditiform larvae, strongyloidiasis and, 520
Rheumatic fever, 254
Rheumatoid arthritis, as autoimmune disease, 194
Rhinosporidiosis, characteristics of, 480
Rhinosporidium seeberi, rhinosporidiosis caused by, 480
Rhinovirus
  characteristics, 432
  epidemiology, 432
  laboratory diagnosis, 432
  pathogenesis, 432
  structure and drug design, 433
Rhizopus, as cause of mucormycosis, 490
Ribavirin, activity of, 113
Ribosomes, bacterial, 25
Ricin, as immunotoxin, 180–181
Rickettsia australis, pathogenesis, 361
Rickettsia conorii, pathogenesis, 361
Rickettsia prowazekii, pathogenesis, 359
Rickettsia ricketsii, pathogenesis, 360
Rickettsia sibirica, pathogenesis, 361
Rickettsia tsutsugamushi, pathogenesis, 361
Rickettsiae, 359–363
  characteristics, 359
  Chlamydia differentiation from, 366
  Coxiella differentiation from, 359
  diseases caused by, 360
  epidemiology and pathogenesis, 359
  laboratory diagnosis, 362–363
  treatment, prevention, and control, 363
Rickettsialpox, 360, 361
Rifampin, activity of, 113
Rimantadine, activity of, 113
Ringworm, defined, 481. *See also* Dermatophytoses; Tinea
River blindness, 523
RNA
  messenger, DNA transcription and, 66
  ribosomal, structure and function of, 66–67
  transfer, protein synthesis and, 66–67
RNA polymerase, DNA transcription and, 66
RNA virus
  diseases, 421–461. *See also specific virus agents*
    summary of, 459
  genome expression by, 386
Rochalimaea, infections caused by, 362
Rochalimaea henselae, pathogenesis, 362
Rochalimaea quintana, pathogenesis, 362
Rocky Mountain spotted fever. *See Rickettsia ricketsii*
Romaña's sign, American trypanosomiasis and, 511
Roseola infantum, 418
Rotavirus
  epidemiology, 442
  laboratory diagnosis, 442
  pathogenesis, 441–442
  treatment and prevention, 442
Roundworm infection. *See* Ascariasis
Rubella virus
  epidemiology, 424
  immunity to, 426
  laboratory diagnosis, 426
  morphology, 425
  pathogenesis, 425
  treatment and prevention, 426
Runyon classification, mycobacteria and, 336

Saber shin syndrome, syphilis and, 343
Sabin-Feldman dye test, toxoplasmosis diagnosis using, 516
Sabouraud agar, fungal cultivation in, 470, 471–472
Saddle nose, congenital syphilis and, 344
Safety, laboratory, 243–244
Safranin, gram-stain, 557
Saliva, antimicrobial activity of, 208
Salmonella
  bacteremia caused by, 299
  carrier state, 299–300
  characteristics of pathogenic, 308
  control of, 302
  in disease transmission, 229
  eggs and, 300
  enteric fever caused by, 299
  epidemiology, 300–301
  gastroenteritis caused by, 298–299
  laboratory diagnosis, 301
  lysogenic conversion in, 404
  pathogenesis, 298
  prevention, 302
  treatment, 301–302
  vaccines, 302
  as vaccine vectors, 302
Salmonella cholerasuis, 298
Salmonella enteritidis, 298
Salmonella paratyphi, 299
Salmonella schottmüelleri, 299
Salmonella typhi, 298, 299
  virulence factors, 299
Salmonellosis, 298. *See also Salmonella*
Salvarsan, 8–9
Sandfly, leishmaniasis transmitted by, 512
Sanitization, defined, 94
Saperconazole
  paracoccidioidomycosis treatment with, 478
Sarcodina, infections caused by, 503–507
Satellite phenomenon, *Hemophilus influenzae* and, 322
Scabies, 527
Scalded skin syndrome, *Staphylococcus aureus*, 248
Scanning electron microscopy, 553–555
Scarlet fever, 253
Schick test, *Corynebacterium diphtheriae* susceptibility and, 287
Schistosoma species, schistosomiasis caused by, 524–525
Schistosome dermatitis, 525
Schistosomiasis
  acute, 524
  chronic, 524–525
  laboratory diagnosis, 525
  pathogenesis, 524–525
  treatment and control, 525
Schistosomulum, 523
Schizogony, malaria, 514
Schultz-Charlton reaction, 253
Scolex, tapeworm, 525
Scotochromogens, *Mycobacteria*, 331
Scrapie, 456, 457
Scratch test, hypersensitivity, 188
Scrub typhus. *See Rickettsia tsutsugamushi*
Seatworm infection. *See* Enterobiasis
Secondary disease, defined, 206
Secretory immunoglobulin A. *See* Immunoglobulin A, secretory
Semiconservative replication, 63–66
Semmelweis, germ theory and, 5
Sepsis, defined, 94
Septa, hyphal, 466
Septicemia
  defined, 206
  endotoxin and, 215–218
  Neisseria meningitidis as cause of, 264
Septum, bacterial, 18
Serological tests. *See* Immunological test(s)
Serotyping, 232, 233
Serpinous dermatitis, 520
Serratia, characteristics of, 307
Serum sickness, arthus reaction and, 190
Severe combined immunodeficiency disease, 184
  treatment for, 185
Sex factor. *See* F factor
Sexually transmitted disease, reportable, 227
Shadow casting, electron microscopy and, 554
Shell vial technique, cytomegalovirus identification and, 412
Shiga bacillus, 303
Shiga toxin, 303
Shiga-like toxin
  Escherichia coli, 297
  Shigella, 303
Shigella
  characteristics of pathogenic, 308
  control, 304
  differentiation of species of, 304
  epidemiology, 303
  epithelium invasion by, 214
  laboratory diagnosis, 304

pathogenesis, 303
prevention, 304
treatment, 304
virulence of, 303
Shigella boydii, 304
Shigella dysenteriae, 303, 304
Shigella flexneri, 304
Shigella sonnei, 304
Shigellosis. *See Shigella*
Shingles. *See* Zoster virus
Sialic acid
complement evasion using, 172
complement regulation and, 171
Sialidase, bacterial vaginosis and, 376
Sialomucin, immunotherapy and, 197
Siberian tick typhus. *See Rickettsia sibirica*
Siderophores, iron binding by, 210
Silver nitrate, as disinfectant, 102
Simian immunodeficiency virus, 447
Sisomicin, activity of, 111
Skin
cross section of, 207
in infectious disease process, 206–207
microbial agents causing diseases of, 575–576
microbial flora of, 585
Staphylococcus aureus infections of, 248
Skin tests, hypersensitivity, 188
Sleeping sickness. *See* African trypanosomiasis
Slime layer
bacterial, structure and function of, 22
Pseudomonas aeruginosa, 311, 313
Slow virus infections, 456–458
prions and, 457
Snuffles, congenital syphilis and, 344
Sodium, growth requirement for, 50
Sodium hypochlorite, as disinfectant, 100
Soil, as reservoir of disease, 225
Somatostatin
genetic engineering of, 86
medical use of, 89
South American blastomycosis. *See* Paracoccidioidomycosis
Spallanzani, spontaneous generation, 4
Species, defined, 13
Specimen collection, in laboratory identification, 240
Spectinomycin, activity of, 112
Spectrophotometer, growth measurement by, 57
Spheroplast, preparation of, 21
Spikes, animal virus, 384
Spiral and curved rods, 349–353
Spirillum, 349
Spirillum minor, rat-bite fever and, 349
Spirochetes, 340–349. *See also Borrelia; Leptospira icterohaemorrhagiae; Treponema species*
characteristics of, 341
diseases caused by, characteristics of, 353
Spleen, immune function of, 157
Spontaneous generation, 4–5
Sporadic disease, 230
Sporangiospore, fungal, 469
Sporangium, fungal, 469, 473
Spore. *See also* Endospore
bacteria forming, 26
formation, bacterial, 26
resistance of, 26
as sterilization indicator, 97
Spore stain, 559
Sporogony, malaria, 514
Sporothrix schenckii, sporotrichosis caused by, 479–481
Sporotrichosis
epidemiology and pathogenesis, 479–481
laboratory diagnosis, 481
treatment, 481
Sporozoa, infections caused by, 513–517
Sporozoites
animal parasite, 501
malaria, 513–514
Sporulation, 467
asexual, fungal, 469–470
sexual, fungal, 468–469
Stain(s)
differential, 557–559
acid-fast as, 558
gram-stain as, 557–558
flagella, 559
metachromatic granule, 559
negative, 559
electron microscope, 553
positive, electron microscope, 553
simple, 557
spore, 559
Staphylococci
characteristics of, 260
coagulase-negative, pathogenesis of, 251
hospital-associated, 535, 542
defined, 14
phage typing of, 233
Staphylococcus aureus
hospital-associated, 542
laboratory identification of, 249–251
pathogenesis, 247–249
plasmid determinants of, 79
prevention of, 251
SEM of, 247
Staphylococcus epidermidis differentiation from, 250–251
superantigens, 250
treatment of, 251
virulence factors, 248
Staphylococcus epidermidis
pathogenesis of, 251
Staphylococcus aureus differentiation from, 250–251
Staphylococcus saprophyticus, 251
Stationary phase, bacterial, 48
Steers inoculating device, 120, 122
Stem cell
disorders, 184–185
immune, 156
Sterility, defined, 94
Sterilization
exposure periods, 96
indicators, 96
interfering matter in, 95
membrane filters in, 97
modes of achieving, 95
physical methods of, 95–98
problem organisms encountered in, 95
radiation and, 98
terminology, 94
ultrasonic cleaners in, 97–98
St. Louis encephalitis, 439, 440
Streak plate, bacterial isolation using, 55
Streptobacillus moniliformis, pathogenesis, 375
Streptococci, characteristics of, 252. *See also Streptococcus species*
Streptococcus
anaerobic, 258
C substance of, 252
classification of, 252
group A. *See Streptococcus pyogenes*
group B. *See Streptococcus agalactiae*
group C, characteristics of, 256
group D, pathogenesis of, 257. *See also Enterococcus species*
group F, pathogenesis of, 258
nutritionally deficient, 257
plasmid determinants of, 79
presumptive identification of, 255
viridans, 252, 257
Streptococcus agalactiae, 252
identification, 256
pathogenesis, 256
Streptococcus equisimilis, 257
Streptococcus pneumoniae
general characteristics, 258
laboratory diagnosis, 259–260
pathogenesis, 258–259
prevention, 260–261
treatment, 260–261
Streptococcus pyogenes
cardiohepatic toxin, 253
cell wall components, 253
epidemiology, 254–255
erythrogenic toxin, 253
hemolysins, 253
invasive, 255
laboratory diagnosis of, 255–256
nephrotoxin, 253
nonsuppurative diseases of, 254–255
pathogenesis, 254–255
prevention of, 256
spreading factors, 254
suppurative diseases of, 254
treatment of, 256
virulence factors, 252–254

Streptococcus zooepidemicus, 257
Streptokinase
infectious disease implications of, 34
as invasive factor, 213
medical use of, 89
Streptococcus pyogenes, 254
Streptolysin O, 253–254
Streptolysin S, 253–254
Streptomyces, colonial appearance, 389
Streptomycin, activity of, 111
Strongyloidiasis
epidemiology, 520
laboratory diagnosis, 520
life cycle, 520
pathogenesis, 520
treatment, 520–521
Subacute sclerosing panencephalitis, 421, 458, 460
Subcutaneous phycomycosis, characteristics of, 480
Subepithelium, as antimicrobial defense factor, 208–209
Substrate, defined, 30
Substrate phosphorylation, 35
Succinyl-CoA, formation of, 39
Sulbactam, 108
Sulfanilamide
discovery of, 9
structure of, 115
Sulfonamides, activity of, 114–115
Sulfones, activity of, 116
Sulfur
bacterial requirement for, 49
enzyme activity affected by, 31
Sulfur granules
actinomyces and, 369
bacterial, 25
Superinfection, *Staphylococcus aureus*, 249
Superoxide dismutase, in oxygen metabolism, 50
Superoxol test, identification of *Neisseria gonorrhoeae* using, 269
Suppressor T cells, characteristics of, 162
Surgery, hospital-associated infections relating to, 538–539
Svedberg unit, defined, 66
Swimmers itch, 524
Sylvatic typhus, 359
Symptoms, defined, 244
Syncytia formation, viral, 390
Syphilis. *See also Treponema pallidum*
biological false-positive and-negatives, 345
congenital, 343
latent, 343
nonvenereal, 346
primary, 342
secondary, 342–343
tertiary, 343
Systemic disease, defined, 206
Systemic lupus erythematosus, as autoimmune disease, 194
Taenia saginata
stages and diagnostic characteristics of, 525
taeniasis caused by, 526–527
Taeniasis, characteristics of, 526–527
Taenia solium
stages and diagnostic characteristics of, 525
taeniasis caused by, 526–527
Tapeworm
beef, characteristics of disease caused by, 526–527
infections caused by, 526–527
morphology of, 525
pork, characteristics of disease caused by, 526–527
Taxa, defined, 12
Taxis, defined, 22
Taxonomy
defined, 12
methods in, 13
numerical, 13
Tazobactam, 108
T cell(s)
$CD4^+$ helper, human immunodeficiency virus and, 443, 445
$CD8^+$, human immunodeficiency virus and, 444
clonal selection, 164–165
cytotoxic
characteristics of, 162
effect on virus, 162
delayed-type hypersensitivity, 162–163
disorders, 184–185
helper, characteristics of, 162
immunity associated with, 130
location of, 156
receptors, 161
response to animal parasite infections, 176
response to bacterial infections, 173
subsets, 161–163
characteristics of, 166
suppressor, characteristics of, 162
surface markers, 161
T-dependent activation, B cell, 163
Temperature
bacterial growth and, 51–52
control, practical aspects of, 52
effect on enzyme activity, 31
Tetanospasmin, 280
Tetanus. *See also Clostridium tetani*
toxoid, 281
Tetanus neonatorum, 280
Tetany, defined, 280
Tetracyclines, activity of, 112
Tetrad, defined, 14
Thallospores, types of, 469–470
Thayer-Martin medium, *Neisseria meningitidis* isolation using, 266
Therapeutic index, 106
Thermal death time, determination of, 95
Thermophile, defined, 51
Thioglycolate media
bacterial isolation using, 55–56
clostridia cultivation using, 275–276
Thrombocytopenic purpura, *Escherichia coli*, 297
Thromboxanes, 187
Thrombus, defined, 244
Thrush, *Candida albicans* as cause of, 486
Thymus, immune function of, 156
Tick
as disease vector, 224
micrograph of, 528
T-independent activation, B cell, 163
Tinea
barbae, 482
capitis, 482
corporis, 482
cruris, 484
defined, 481
favosa, 483
imbricata, 484
nigra palmaris, 484
pedis, 482
unguium, 483
versicolor, 484
Tissue typing, graft rejection prevention and, 195
Tobacco mosaic virus, structure, 382
Tobramycin, activity of, 111
Toxemia, defined, 206
Toxic shock-like syndrome, *Streptococcus pyogenes* and, 255
Toxic shock syndrome, *Staphylococcus aureus*, 249
Toxicity, selective, 106
Toxin(s)
cardiohepatic, *Streptococcus pyogenes*, 253
clostridial, 281
Clostridium botulinum, 276
commercial uses of, 278
Clostridium perfringens, 278
Clostridium tetani, 280
endo-, 214
erythrogenic, *Streptococcus pyogenes*, 253
exo-, 214
as factor affecting disease process, 214–218
Toxocara canis, ascariasis caused by, 519
Toxoids
immunization with, 177
licensed, 588
Toxoplasma gondii, toxoplasmosis caused by, 515–516
Toxoplasmosis
AIDS and treatment of, 448
congenital, 516
epidemiology, 516
laboratory diagnosis, 516
life cycle, 515–516
pathogenesis, 516
treatment and control, 516
T protein, *Streptococcus pyogenes*, 253

Trachoma. *See Chlamydia trachomatis*
Transcription, DNA, 66
Transduction
  DNA transfer by, 77–78
  drug resistance and microbial, 119
  generalized, 78
Transferase, defined, 33
Transferrin, as factor influencing host resistance, 210, 211
Transformation
  cloning and, 84
  DNA transfer by, 74–76
  drug resistance and bacterial, 119
  oncogenes and cell, 396–397
  virus as cause of cell, 390–391
Transformed cells, properties of, 391
Transfusion
  ABO system and, 571
  crossmatching, 573–574
  Rh system and, 572–573
Transient aplastic crisis, parvovirus and, 421
Transmission, disease. *See* Disease(s), transmission of
Transparent tape swab method, enterobiasis diagnosis using, 521
Transpeptidase, cell wall synthesis and, 107
Transplantation
  antigens, 194
  rejection mechanisms in, 194–195
  terminology, 194
Transport
  medium, 53
  nutrient, 19
Transposon
  drug resistance and, 119
  transfer of, 79
Trematoda, infections caused by, 523–525
Trench fever. *See Rochalimaea quintana*
Treponema carateum, pinta and, 346
Treponema pallidum. *See also* Syphilis
  characteristics, 341–342
  epidemiology, 344
  hemagglutination test, 345
  laboratory diagnosis, 344–345
  pathogenesis, 342–343
  prevention and control, 346
  treatment, 345–346
Treponema pertenue, yaws and, 346
Treponematoses, 341
Trichinella spiralis, trichinosis caused by, 521–522
Trichinosis
  epidemiology, 522
  laboratory diagnosis, 521
  life cycle, 521
  pathogenesis, 521
  treatment and control, 522
Trichomonas hominis, 510
Trichomonas tenax, periodontal disease and, 510
Trichomonas vaginalis, vaginitis associated with, 510
Trichomoniasis
  laboratory diagnosis, 510
  pathogenesis, 510
  treatment and control, 510
Trichophyton, infections caused by, 481–485
Trichophyton concentricum, ringworm of the torso and, 484
Trichophyton schoenleini, ringworm of the scalp and, 483
Trichophyton verrucosum, ringworm of the beard and, 482
Trichosporon beigelii, white piedra caused by, 485
Trichosporon species, hospital-associated, 536
Trichosporonosis, hospital-associated, 536
Trimethoprim, activity of, 116
Triple sugar iron agar, Enterobacteriaceae identification using, 295
Tropical pulmonary eosinophilia, lymphatic filariasis, 523
True bugs, as disease vectors, 224
Trypanosoma brucei, as cause of African trypanosomiasis, 510–511
Trypanosoma cruzi, American trypanosomiasis and, 511
Trypanosomiasis
  African, 510–511
  American, 511–512
Trypomastigote, 510
Tryptase, 187
Tsetse fly, African trypanosomiasis caused by, 510–511
Tubercle, *Mycobacterium tuberculosis*, 332
Tuberculin, 334
Tuberculin test, 192, 334
Tuberculosis. *See also Mycobacterium tuberculosis*
  delayed-type hypersensitivity in, 162
  reactivation, 332
Tularemia. *See also Francisella tularensis*
  oculoglandular, 327
  pneumonic, 327
Tumor, 395. *See also* Cancer
  immunology, 196–198
  immunotherapy, 197–198
  T cell response to, 196
Tumor-associated antigen, 198
Tumor infiltrating lymphocytes, 198
Tumor necrosis factor, 89
  malaria pathogenesis and, 514
  Mycobacterium tuberculosis and, 332
  septicemia and, 160
  source and function of, 159
Tumor-specific transplantation antigen, virus transformed cells and, 392
Tumor suppressor gene, cancer and, 396
Typhoid fever. *See Salmonella*, enteric fever caused by
Typhoid Mary, 300
Typhus
  epidemic. *See Rickettsia prowazekii*
  louse-borne. *See Rickettsia prowazekii*
  Queensland tick. *See Rickettsia australis*
  scrub. *See Rickettsia tsutsugamushi*
  Siberian tick. *See Rickettsia sibirica*
  sylvatic, 359
Tzanck test, varicella virus identification and, 414

Ulcers
  defined, 244
  Helicobacter pylori and, 351–352
Ultrasonic cleaners, in sterilization, 97–98
Undulant fever. *See Brucella*
Universal precautions, blood-borne pathogens and, 455–456
Ureaplasma urealyticum, pathogenesis, 356, 357
Urease, *Helicobacter pylori* and, 352
Urinary tract infections
  hospital associated
    catheterization and, 539–540
    guidelines for preventing, 540
Urine, specimen collection, 240
Urticaria, defined

Vaccination, memory cell participation in, 164
Vaccine(s). *See also specific microbial agent*
  animal virus, 402
  anti-idiotypic antibody, 178
  attenuated, 177
  licensed, 588
  medical use of, 89
  polyvalent, 177
  prematriculation, 179
  Pseudomonas aeruginosa, 313
  purified antigen, 177
  recombinant, 89, 177–178
  smallpox, complications associated with, 409
  subunit, 177
  synthesized immunogens as, 179
  toxoids as, 177
  whole cells as, 177
Vaccinia virus, 409
Vacuole, formation, phagocytosis and, 134
Vaginosis, bacterial, 268, 376
Vancomycin, activity, 110
van Leeuwenhoek, Anton, 4
V antigen, *Yersinia pestis*, 305
Varicella virus
  epidemiology, 414
  immunity to, 415
  laboratory diagnosis, 414–415
  pathogenesis, 413–414
  treatment and prevention, 415
Variola virus, 409

Vector(s)
arthropods as, 527–528
biological, 224
DNA, genetic engineering and, 83
insect, 223–224
mechanical, 223–224
Venereal Disease Research Laboratories, syphilis diagnosis and, 345
Venereal warts, 420
Venezuelan encephalitis, 440
Vero cells, 397
Vero toxin. *See* Shiga-like toxin
Verruca plana, 420
Verruca plantaris, 420
Verruca vulgaris, 420
Vertical disease transmission, 229–230
Vertical transmission, viral, 384, 395
Vesicle, defined, 222, 244
V factor, *Hemophilus influenzae* and, 322, 323
Vi antigen, *Salmonella*, 299
Vibrio, characteristics of, 316, 319
Vibrio alginolyticus
characteristics, 319
pathogenesis, 318
Vibrio cholerae
01
enterotoxin, 316, 317
epidemiology, 317
laboratory diagnosis, 317
pathogenesis, 316
prevention, 318
treatment, 317–318
adhesins of, 211
non-01, pathogenesis, 316–317
Vibrio parahaemolyticus, pathogenesis, 318
Vibrio vulnificus, pathogenesis, 318
characteristics, 319
Vibrionaceae, 315–320. *See also Aeromonas; Plesiomonas; Vibrio*
Vidarabine, activity of, 113
Viral encephalitis
characteristics of, 439
diagnosis and treatment, 439
pathogenesis, 439
Viral hemagglutination-inhibition test, 562–563
Viral hemagglutination test, 562
Viral particle, defined, 384
Viridans streptococci, 255
characteristics of, 257
Virion, defined, 384
Virology, history of, 8
Virulence
defined, 205
genetics of, *Shigella* and, 303
plasmids associated with, 79
Virus. *See also* Animal virus; Bacteriophage
animal. *See* Animal virus
bacterial. *See* Bacteriophage
cultivation, 397–398
defective particles of, 390
definition, 382
DNA. *See* DNA virus
interferon action on, 140–141
nonspecific defenses against, 172–173
persistent infections caused by, 391
replicative form, 385
RNA. *See* RNA virus
specific defenses against, 175
Virus neutralization test, 563
Visceral larva migrans, 519
Visna, 456
Vitamins, as growth factors, 49
Vomitoxin, as mycotoxin, 492

Walkaway-96 system, 242
Wangiella dermatitidis, chromoblastomycosis caused by, 480
W antigen, *Yersinia pestis*, 305
Warts, clinical types, 420
Water
bacterial requirement for, 48
in disease transmission, 226–227
as reservoir of disease, 225
Waterhouse-Friderichsen syndrome, *Neisseria meningitidis* as cause of, 265
Water-borne disease, reportable, 228
Weigert, staining by, 8
Weil's disease. *See Leptospira icterohaemorrhagiae*
Western blot test technique, 568
Western equine encephalitis, 439, 440
Wet mount, animal parasite diagnosis by, 502
White blood cells. *See* Leukocytes; *See specific cell types*
Whooping cough. *See Bordetella pertussis*
Winterbottom's sign, African trypanosomiasis diagnosis using, 511
Wiskott-Aldrich syndrome, 184
Wood's lamp, 481
Woolsorter's disease, *Bacillus anthracis* and, 274
Wuchereria bancrofti, filariasis caused by, 523

Xenodiagnosis, American trypanosomiasis and, 511
X factor, *Hemophilus influenzae* and, 322, 323

Yaws, 346
Yeast
characteristics of, 466
colony morphology, 470
infections, hospital-associated treatment of, 542
Yellow fever
characteristics, 439–440
epidemiology, 440
laboratory diagnosis, 440
pathogenesis, 440
treatment and prevention, 440
Yersinia
biochemical differentiation of, 307
characteristics of pathogenic, 308
Yersinia enterocolitica
biochemical differentiation, 307
pathogenesis, 306–307
virulence factors, 307
Yersinia pestis. See also Plague
biochemical differentiation, 307
pathogenesis, 305
Yersinia pseudotuberculosis, pathogenesis, 306–307
Yersinoses, defined, 306

Zidovudine. *See* AZT
Ziehl-Neelsen acid fast stain, 558–559
Zinc, growth requirement for, 50
Zoonoses, transmission to humans, 223
Zoster virus
epidemiology, 414
pathogenesis, 414
postherpetic neuralgia caused by, 414
Zygomycosis, hospital-associated, 536
Zygomycotina, characteristics of, 473
Zygospore, fungal, 468
Zymodeme, amebae, 506